# 1 MONTH OF
# FREE
# READING

## at

## www.ForgottenBooks.com

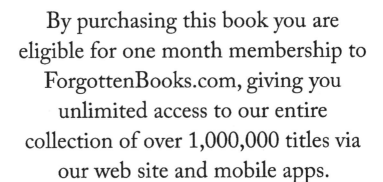

By purchasing this book you are eligible for one month membership to ForgottenBooks.com, giving you unlimited access to our entire collection of over 1,000,000 titles via our web site and mobile apps.

To claim your free month visit:

www.forgottenbooks.com/free1113061

ISBN 978-0-331-36995-3
PIBN 11113061

Forgotten Books is a registered trademark of FB &c Ltd.
Copyright © 2018 FB &c Ltd.
FB &c Ltd, Dalton House, 60 Windsor Avenue, London, SW19 2RR.
Company number 08720141. Registered in England and Wales.

For support please visit www.forgottenbooks.com

# YEAR BOOK

*of the*

# STATE OF COLORADO

## 1932

Detailed information regarding the State, its resources, opportunities and attractions, compiled from official and semi-official sources and published under the authority vested by the State Legislature in the State Board of Immigration.

Compiled and Edited by Tolbert R. Ingram.

STATE BOARD OF IMMIGRATION

THE GOVERNOR, President

THOMAS LYTLE, Montrose      NEIL W. KIMBALL, Golden

FRED M. BETZ, Lamar

---

EDWARD D. FOSTER, Commissioner of Immigration

TOLBERT R. INGRAM, Deputy and Statistician

HELEN M. SAXTON      AGNES F. BARKLEY

FRANKA B. MERZ

THE BRADFORD-ROBINSON PTG. CO., DENVER

# Foreword

THIS edition marks the fourteenth year in which the State Board of Immigration has published the Colorado Year Book, a work which constitutes the year-to-year record of the development of the state and its varied industries. The first number was published in 1918, and since that time publication has been continued without interruption except that the data for 1928 and 1929 were combined in a single volume because of a lack of finances.

For the convenience of those using the book regularly, the material is arranged as nearly as possible in uniform sequence from year to year, and wherever possible changes of figures in text material are made without altering the text, so that readers accustomed to one year's volume may find comparable data for succeeding years in approximately the same location in subsequent issues.

In most instances the information is obtained from official sources, including county and state officials and bureaus of the federal government. Crop and livestock statistics are based largely upon the reports of the county assessors, as edited and revised by the Colorado Co-operative Crop Reporting Service, and most of the other data are gathered from municipal, county, state and federal officials. Where official figures cannot be secured, the best semi-official and private sources are resorted to, the effort always being to adhere to the conservative. In no event are local pride and optimism permitted to color the data concerning a community or an industry.

For those who desire a discussion of the individual counties in text form, the department publishes large editions of district booklets, seven in number, in which counties are grouped with a view to similarity of geography and conditions, and are discussed separately. These booklets may be secured on request. The department also publishes a detailed discussion of the mineral development and possibilities of the state, including both metals and non-metals, and a complete record of oil and gas development.

The Immigration department acknowledges with thanks the continued co-operation of public officials and commercial club executives, whose willingness to aid has made possible the continued improvement of this undertaking.

THE COLORADO STATE BOARD OF IMMIGRATION

State Office Building, Denver, Colorado

November, 1932

# Colorado—General Description

COLORADO lies almost in the center of that part of the United States west of the Mississippi River basin and in the east-central part of the Rocky Mountain region. The center of the state is approximately 1,500 miles west of the Atlantic seaboard, 800 miles east of the Pacific, 650 miles south of the Canadian border and 475 miles north of the Mexican border, measured by air lines due east and west and north and south. The state is bounded on the west by Utah, on the north by Wyoming and Nebraska, on the east by Kansas and Nebraska, and on the south by New Mexico and a small strip of the Oklahoma panhandle.

The state contains the most elevated portions of the Rocky mountains in the United States. Both the United States geological survey and the coast and geodetic survey assign to two peaks in Lake county the honor of being the highest points in the state. These are Mount Elbert and Mount Massive, each with an altitude of 14,402 feet. The highest point in the United States is Mount Whitney, California, 14,501 feet. Colorado has the highest mean altitude of any state, only about one-fourth of its area being below 5,000 feet, while approximately two-thirds of it ranges from 6,000 feet to 14,000 feet. The United States geological survey lists 43 peaks that tower more than 14,000 feet above sea level; three that are rated at 14,000 feet, and approximately 1,000 having altitudes of more than 10,000 feet. The eastern two-fifths of the state lies in the Great Plains, and is a level or broken prairie, crossed by the valleys of the Arkansas and South Platte rivers and their numerous tributaries, and rising gradually from the state line westward to the foothills of the Rockies. The main range of the Rocky mountains passes north and south through the central part of the state, with numerous secondary ranges and spurs running in all directions, giving Colorado the greatest extent and widest variety of mountain scenery found in any state. The western part lies in the Pacific watershed and contains the largest streams in the state. Its surface is much more broken than that of the eastern part, embracing numerous high mesas and fertile, narrow agricultural valleys, and rising to the rugged and wonderfully picturesque San Juan mountains

in the southwest. In outline the state is almost a perfect rectangle, having the most regular form of any state in the Union. It ranks seventh in size, with a land area of 66,341,120 acres or 103,658 square miles. Its water area is 290 square miles, making the total area 103,948 square miles. It is more than twelve times as large as the state of Massachusetts, nearly twice as large as Iowa, and about the same size as New York, Ohio, Connecticut and New Hampshire combined. Its extreme length east and west is about 387 miles, or 37 miles more than the distance from New York City to Portland, Maine, and its width approximately 276 miles, about the same as the distance from Chicago to St. Louis.

**Natural Divisions**—As a result of its large size and the extreme irregularity of its surface, the state is divided into a number of districts that show considerable variation in topography, soil, climatic conditions, industries and products. The most important of these are the following: The non-irrigated prairie section in the eastern part of the state, popularly referred to as Eastern Colorado; the South Platte valley, in the north and northeast; the Arkansas valley, extending through the southern part of the eastern half of the state; the San Luis valley, a vast basin, the bed of an ancient lake, lying in the south-central part of the state, almost wholly surrounded by mountain ranges; the San Juan basin in the southwest; the valleys of the Colorado river and numerous tributary streams in the central-western part; the rugged plateau districts drained by the White and Yampa (Bear) rivers, in the northwest; the mountainous, mineral-bearing districts, extending in a broad, irregular belt across the central part of the state from the Wyoming to the New Mexico line; and the mountain park districts, chief of which are North park, in Jackson county; Middle park, in Grand county; and South park, in Park county. These last are very similar to the San Luis valley, but all have higher average altitudes and consequently have less intensive agricultural development. In topography and climatic conditions the South Platte and Arkansas valleys are very similar to the non-irrigated sections of eastern Colorado, but by reason of the fact that a large supply of water is available in these valleys for irrigation, they enjoy the most extensive agricultural development found in the state and produce a wider range and greater yield of crops than the non-irrigated districts. The San Luis valley has very light rainfall, but an abundant water supply for irrigation is derived from the Rio Grande del Norte and its tributaries. The average altitude is more than 7,500 feet, which limits the range of crops grown; but the fertile soil, abundant water supply and good climate make this valley one of the finest general farming and stock-raising districts in the state. The San Juan basin is a region of from moderate to heavy rainfall, having a considerable area of irrigated land in the river valleys and much good non-irrigated agricultural land on the higher mesas. This is also an excellent stock-raising district. The valleys of the Colorado, Gunnison, Uncompahgre and other rivers and smaller streams of the Colorado river basin contain the principal fruit growing areas of the state, as well as a large amount of the fine general agricultural land. The rainfall in this area is generally inadequate for farming without irrigation, but the water supply is adequate for all land that can be irrigated, and recently farming without irrigation has been undertaken successfully on some of the higher mesa lands, where rainfall is somewhat heavier than in the valleys. The northwest part of the state is less developed than any other district, chiefly because of lack of transportation facilities, but it contains some of the best agricultural and grazing land in Colorado. The mineral area is very extensive, but the principal producing areas are somewhat restricted.

Early History—That part of Colorado lying east of the Rocky mountains was included in the territory acquired by purchase from France in 1803, usually referred to as the Louisiana Purchase. All the southeastern part of the state, lying south of the Arkansas river, and a narrow strip extending north through the mountain district into Wyoming, was claimed by the state of Texas and became a part of the United States when Texas was annexed in 1845. This included a considerable amount of the territory belonging to the Louisiana Purchase, but the controversy regarding the northern boundary of Texas was settled long before Colorado became a state. The western part of what is now Colorado and an additional strip lying west and south of the Rio Grande del Norte was ceded to the United States by Mexico in 1848, following the war with Mexico. The actual settlement of Colorado began with the discovery of gold in the summer of 1858, at which time most of the eastern half of the state was included in Kansas territory under the name of Arapahoe county. The boundaries of this county were very imperfectly defined, and the settlers in the new gold camps, moreover, objected to being governed by a set of territorial officials 400 miles away. They appealed to the federal government for the organization of a new state or territorial government, and finally, in February, 1861, the territory of Colorado was organized, about a month after statehood had been conferred upon the territory of Kansas. The boundaries of the territory were substantially the same as are those of the state at present. In 1876 Colorado was admitted to the Union as the thirty-eighth state.

Population—The population of Colorado has increased steadily and rapidly since its actual settlement began, immediately following the discovery of gold in 1858. The first census of what is now the state was taken in 1860 and showed a population of 34,277. The census bureau gives the population as of April 1, 1930, at 1,035,791, or more than 30 times greater than it was 70 years ago. The state ranks thirty-third in population among the states of the Union.

The following table shows its growth from 1860 to the present time, compared with the growth for the entire country, all figures being taken from census reports:

| Year | Population | Pct. of Increase Over Previous Census | Pct. of Increase for United States |
|---|---|---|---|
| 1860 | 34,277 | .... | .... |
| 1870 | 39,864 | 16.3 | 22.6 |
| 1880 | 194,327 | 387.5 | 30.1 |
| 1890 | 413,249 | 112.7 | 25.5 |
| 1900 | 539,700 | 30.6 | 20.7 |
| 1910 | 799,024 | 48.0 | 21.0 |
| 1920 | 939,629 | 17.6 | 14.9 |
| 1930 | 1,035,791 | 10.2 | 16.1 |

More detailed figures on the population of the state and its subdivisions will be found elsewhere in this volume.

During the two decades following 1860 the population was confined largely to the mining districts and to the city of Denver. The cities of Pueblo, Colorado Springs and Trinidad did not make their appearance in the census population statistics until 1880, when the three had a combined

population of less than 10,000. During
the early 80's the period of agricultural development began, and the
decade ending with 1890 was in many
ways the most important in the history of the state. During that period
24 new counties were organized and
scores of new towns were laid out
in the agricultural districts. In 1910
the density of population for the state
was 7.7 per square mile, as compared
with 30.9 for the United States. Denver county ranked first in this respect,
with 3,679, and Dolores and Jackson
counties were tied for last place, with
0.6. The 1930 census showed the density of population for the state to be
10.0 per square mile. Denver still
holds first place in this respect, with
4,963.2, and Hinsdale county ranks last
with 0.5.

Of Colorado's total population of
1,035,791 on April 1, 1930, 519,882, including 1,789 persons living on farms
within the limits of cities and villages
of 2,500 or more, comprised the urban
population, or persons residing in the
cities and towns. The rural population amounted to 515,909, comprising
281,038 persons living on farms in rural
territory and 234,871 persons not living
on farms. The urban population
formed 50.2 per cent of the total, as
compared with 48.2 per cent in 1920
and 50.7 per cent in 1910. The census
shows that there are but three cities
of more than 25,000 population in the
state, five with population of from
10,000 to 25,000, 10 from 5,000 to 10,000,
nine from 2,500 to 5,000, 42 from 1,000
to 2,500, 47 from 500 to 1,000 and 124
towns of less than 500 population. In
the last classification are 22 towns of
less than 100 population each.

The foreign-born population of Colorado in 1930 amounted to 8.2 per cent
of the total, compared with 12.4 per
cent in 1920 and 15.9 per cent in 1910.

**Land Classification**—A table published elsewhere in this volume gives
a classification of the 66,341,120 acres
of land in the state as far as is prac-
ticable from available records. It is
divided into 63 counties, of which Denver county is the smallest, with an
area of 37,120 acres, and Las Animas
county is the largest, with 3,077,760
acres.

In the land classification table published elsewhere in this volume, eight
counties—Archuleta, Clear Creek, Conejos, Costilla, Gilpin, Hinsdale, Lake
and Mineral—show areas in the various
classifications larger than the total
areas of the respective counties. The
discrepancy probably is due to inaccu-

racies in government surveys and to
the large areas of land which have
never been surveyed.

The area of patented land in the
state has been increasing steadily, due
to the proving up of entries on government land and the issuance of patents on state land sold. The area of
patented land returned for assessment
in recent years was as follows:

| Year | Acres |
|------|-------|
| 1920 | 29,462,459 |
| 1921 | 30,867,235 |
| 1922 | 32,105,994 |
| 1923 | 33,347,491 |
| 1924 | 34,122,665 |
| 1925 | 35,195,619 |
| 1926 | 35,807,193 |
| 1927 | 36,323,737 |
| 1928 | 36,583,930 |
| 1929 | 36,974,946 |
| 1930 | 37,163,043 |
| 1931 | 37,174,876 |

Of the area in private ownership in
1931, the tax commission classifies 35,-
194,697 acres as agricultural land. This
is equal to 53.5 per cent of the entire
land area of the state. The area classified as agricultural land is divided as
follows:

|  | Acres |
|------|-------|
| Fruit land | 20,793 |
| Irrigated land | 2,102,843 |
| Natural hay land | 391,427 |
| Dry farming land | 11,478,779 |
| Grazing land | 21,200,855 |
| Total | 35,194,697 |

These classifications contain some
waste and desert areas of no real value
for agricultural purposes. The term
"dry farming" applies to tillable land
that is non-irrigated. Some of the
grazing land eventually will be placed
under cultivation. The remaining
privately owned area consists mostly
of patented mineral land, railroad
rights of way and town and city lots.

**Drainage and Water Supply**—Containing, as it does, the most elevated
portions of the Rocky mountains,
Colorado is quite naturally the source
of many of the important streams in
the West. The Continental Divide
crosses the west-central part of the
state, and the streams in the western
part flow to the Pacific, while those
in the east find their way to the Gulf
of Mexico. The streams of the western slope are all tributaries of the
Colorado river, from which this state
derives its name. The Colorado
(Grand) river, the largest stream in
the state, has its source in Grand
county. The Green river, which was
regarded as one of the two streams
forming the Colorado when the upper
course of the Colorado was called the
Grand river, flows through the northwestern corner of Moffat county. The
northwestern corner of the state is

drained by tributaries of the Green river, chief of which are the Yampa (Bear) and White rivers. The principal tributary of the Colorado river is the Gunnison, which has its source in Gunnison county and enters the Colorado at the city of Grand Junction. The southwestern corner of the state is drained by the San Juan and Dolores rivers, both tributaries of the Colorado. The south-central part of the state, including the San Luis valley, is drained by the Rio Grande del Norte. The southeastern part is drained by the Arkansas river and its tributaries, and the northeastern part by the South Platte river. The North Platte river has its headwaters in Jackson county and unites with the South Platte in Nebraska to form the Platte river. The Republican river, a tributary of the Kansas, drains a considerable area in the eastern part of the state. These streams have hundreds of small tributaries, most of which have their sources in the mountains where the snowfall is heavy. They furnish the principal water supply for irrigation and for the development of hydro-electric power. Water for domestic purposes is obtained principally from these streams, but in most agricultural sections wells are utilized as a secondary source of domestic water supply. Most of these wells are pumped, but there is a well defined artesian belt in the San Luis valley, and artesian water is found in numerous other places. There are more than 5,000 artesian wells in the state, fully two-thirds of which are in the San Luis valley.

**National Forests**—Fourteen national forests located wholly within the state and one lying partially within its boundaries comprise about 20 per cent of the state's area. These forests embrace 13,323,566 acres, mostly in Colorado, and are administered by the department of agriculture of the federal government. A detailed description of these forests and their operations is given elsewhere in this volume.

**National Parks and Monuments**— Two national parks and five national monuments are located within the boundaries of Colorado and one national monument on the boundary between Colorado and Utah. All of these parks and monuments are administered by the national park service of the department of the interior, with the exception of the Holy Cross and Wheeler national monuments, which are under the jurisdiction of the department of agriculture. Their names, locations and areas are as follows:

Rocky Mountain national park, located in the north middle part of the state, in Larimer, Boulder and Grand counties, and embracing an area of 400.52 square miles, or 256,336 acres. Of the total, 8,768.87 acres is private or state-owned land.

Mesa Verde national park, located in southwestern Colorado in Montezuma county, and embracing about 80 square miles, or 51,273 acres. Total alien land in the park is 790 acres.

Holy Cross national monument, located in Eagle county, and embracing 1,392 acres.

Great Sand Dunes national monument, located in Saguache and Alamosa counties in the San Luis valley, and embracing approximately 46,000 acres.

Colorado national monument, located in Mesa county near Grand Junction and embracing 13,749 acres.

Yucca House national monument, located in the southwestern part of the state in Montezuma county, and embracing 9.6 acres.

Wheeler national monument, located in Mineral county, and embracing 300 acres.

Hovenweep national monument, located on the Colorado-Utah boundary in Montezuma county, and embracing 285.8 acres.

Rocky Mountain national park was created by an act of congress approved January 26, 1915. It lies in the heart of the Rockies and includes some of the most picturesque portions of the range. Its highest point is Longs peak, rising 14,255 feet above sea level. There are within its boundaries 13 other peaks with an altitude of more than 13,000 feet. It is one of the most accessible of the national parks and one of the most popular. It contains remarkable records of the glacial period. On July 17, 1930, President Hoover, by proclamation, added 22.1 square miles to the area of the park, the Never Summer range district on the west side. Annual winter outings in the park are regular features, these usually taking place in February under the auspices of the Colorado Mountain club. Skijoring parties are features of these outings. The favorite summer vacation sport in the park is horseback riding, more than 1,500 horses being used in the park. The government has constructed 200 miles of trail in the park, connecting points of interest.

Total government appropriations made for the Rocky Mountain national park from 1917 to 1932, inclusive, aggregated $1,104,711, of which $973,669 had been expended up to June 30, 1932. In addition, small revenues are received by the service from various operations. The appropriations and expenditures by years are as follows:

| | Appropriated | Expended |
|---|---|---|
| 1917 | $10,000 | $ 9,964.24 |
| 1918 | 10,000 | 9,922.10 |
| 1919 | 10,000 | 9,993.94 |
| 1920 | 10,000 | 9,924.85 |
| 1921 | 40,000 | 39,945.40 |
| 1922 | 65,000 | 64,923.10 |
| 1923 | 73,900 | 73,153.99 |
| 1924 | 74,280 | 74,000.03 |
| 1924 | *26,171 | .......... |
| 1925 | 93,000 | 122,888.53 |
| 1925 | *4,450 | |
| 1926 | 84,660 | 82,259.56 |
| 1927 | 87,000 | 86,100.00 |
| 1928 | 97,620 | 95,612.07 |
| 1929 | 97,880 | 95,230.00 |
| 1930 | 96,000 | 94,871.34 |
| 1931 | 105,950 | 104,880.57 |
| 1932 | 118,800 | ........ |

*Deficiency appropriation.

Visitors and automobiles entering Rocky Mountain national park during the travel season for the years named, as estimated by the park service, were as follows:

| Year | Visitors | Autos |
|---|---|---|
| 1915 | 31,000 | (a) |
| 1916 | 51,000 | (a) |
| 1917 | 117,186 | (a) |
| 1918 | 101,497 | (a) |
| 1919 | 169,942 | (a) |
| 1920 | 240,966 | (a) |
| 1921 | 273,737 | 57,438 |
| 1922 | 219,164 | 52,112 |
| 1923 | 218,000 | 51,800 |
| 1924 | 224,211 | 53,696 |
| 1925 | 233,912 | 58,057 |
| 1926 | 225,027 | 50,407 |
| 1927 | 229,862 | 54,109 |
| 1928 | 235,057 | 57,381 |
| 1929 | 274,408 | 67,682 |
| 1930 | 255,874 | 73,101 |
| 1931 | 265,663 | 75,429 |

(a) No record.

Mesa Verde national park is especially noted for the ruins of homes and villages of the ancient Cliff Dwellers, supposed to have been the earliest inhabitants of this part of the country. It was established by an act of congress approved June 29, 1906. The ruins are found in canons which intersect a high plateau that once is supposed to have supported a population of at least 70,000 people. The numerous ruins are connected by excellent highways and trails, and the government furnishes guides for all visitors. Roads to the park have been greatly improved in recent years. The government maintains a camp for the accommodation of autoists. A museum in the park contains many interesting relics of the ancient people.

Research work conducted in the park in 1930 by Dr. A. E. Douglas, leader of the National Geographic tree-ring expeditions of the last decade, finally succeeded in erecting an unbroken tree-ring chronology extending from shortly before the year 700 A. D. to the present time by means of timbers found in the ruins.

Governmental appropriations for the maintenance and improvement of the park and for archaeological work aggregated $665,895, of which $590,220.76 had been expended up to June 30, 1931. Appropriations and expenditures by years are as follows:

| | Appropriated | Expended |
|---|---|---|
| 1917 | $10,000 | $ 9,999.00 |
| 1918 | 10,000 | 9,913.05 |
| 1919 | 18,000 | 17,022.44 |
| 1920 | 11,000 | 10,959.69 |
| 1921 | 14,000 | 13,929.71 |
| 1922 | 16,400 | 16,339.30 |
| 1923 | 43,000 | 42,812.62 |
| 1924 | 35,000 | 36,685.21 |
| 1924 | *3,000 | ........ |
| 1925 | 42,500 | 43,183.46 |
| 1925 | *1,895 | ........ |
| 1926 | 42,835 | 42,596.97 |
| 1927 | 72,300 | 70,591.36 |
| 1928 | 50,750 | 48,343.59 |
| 1929 | 83,000 | 78,134.00 |
| 1929 | *1,115 | ........ |
| 1930 | 57,000 | 53,910.66 |
| 1931 | 96,800 | 95,799.70 |
| 1932 | 57,300 | ........ |

*Deficiency appropriation.

Visitors and private automobiles entering the park during the travel season for the years named were as follows:

| Year | Visitors | Autos |
|---|---|---|
| 1921 | 3,003 | 651 |
| 1922 | 4,251 | 969 |
| 1923 | 5,236 | 1,255 |
| 1924 | 7,109 | 1,803 |
| 1925 | 9,043 | 2,197 |
| 1926 | 11,356 | 3,054 |
| 1927 | 11,915 | 3,315 |
| 1928 | 16,760 | 4,803 |
| 1929 | *14,517 | 4,224 |
| 1930 | 16,656 | 5,023 |
| 1931 | 18,003 | 5,334 |

*Decrease due to disastrous storms and washouts during July and August.

Great Sand Dunes national monument was created by President Hoover in a proclamation signed on March 17, 1932. It lies on the western slope of the Sangre de Cristo mountain range in the central-southern part of the state mostly in Saguache county and extending over into Alamosa county. The area is noted for its peculiar and colorful formations arising out of wind-shifted sands in past ages.

Holy Cross national monument was created by a proclamation issued by President Hoover on May 20, 1929. The monument received its name from Holy Cross mountain, a peak rising to an elevation of 13,978 feet above sea level, upon the side of which is a figure in the form of a Greek cross formed by snow-filled ravines, which is an object of much public interest.

Colorado national monument is in a picturesque canon which has long been a popular scenic feature of that part of Colorado. The formation is similar to that of the Garden of the Gods at Colorado Springs, but it is generally conceded to be much more picturesque.

Estimated number of visitors to the Colorado monument, by years, is as follows:

| Year | Visitors |
|------|----------|
| 1925 | 9,000 |
| 1926 | 9,000 |
| 1927 | 9,500 |
| 1928 | 10,000 |
| 1929 | 12,000 |
| 1930 | 13,000 |
| 1931 | 16,000 |

Wheeler national monument is especially noted for its weird and very picturesque rock formation, unlike anything found elsewhere in Colorado, due to eccentric erosion and volcanic action.

Yucca House monument is located on the eastern slope of Sleeping Ute mountain and contains ruins of great archaeological value and relics of prehistoric inhabitants.

The estimated number of visitors to Yucca House, by years, is as follows:

| Year | Visitors |
|------|----------|
| 1925 | 100 |
| 1926 | 150 |
| 1927 | 196 |
| 1928 | 174 |
| 1929 | 250 |
| 1930 | 240 |
| 1931 | 264 |

Hovenweep national monument contains four groups of prehistoric towers, pueblos and cliff dwellings.

The estimated number of visitors to the Hovenweep monument, by years, is as follows:

| Year | Visitors |
|------|----------|
| 1925 | 250 |
| 1926 | 250 |
| 1927 | 263 |
| 1928 | 240 |
| 1929 | 450 |
| 1930 | 400 |
| 1931 | 440 |

Industries—The principal industries of the state are agriculture, stock-raising in its various branches, dairying, bee-keeping, manufacturing, mining, quarrying, lumbering, oil and gas production and commerce. These are treated in detail elsewhere.

Climatological Data—As a result of its great size and the extreme irregularity of its surface, the climate of Colorado is wonderfully varied and cannot be described in detail here. Various tables contained in this publication show the most important climatic data for different sections of the state. The mean annual temperature for the entire state is 44.3 degrees, but it varies from about 31 degrees in some of the higher mountain districts to 54 degrees in parts of the Arkansas valley. The average annual precipitation for the state is 17.54 inches, but there is also a very wide range here in the different sections of the state. The lowest average precipitation is about 6.5 inches, in the San Luis valley, and the highest above 40 inches, in the San Juan mountains and a few other mountain districts of restricted areas. The delightful and wonderfully healthful qualities of Colorado's climate are well known throughout the country. More detailed data on this subject are contained in the chapter on Climatological Data on page 64.

High and Low Points—The level of the sea is the basis upon which all geometrical altitudes are reckoned. The fifteenth step from the top leading to the main floor of the state capitol at Denver, at the west entrance, is exactly one mile, or 5,280 feet above sea level. Mount Elbert and Mount Massive, altitude 14,402 feet, or 2.72 miles above sea level, are the highest points in the state. The lowest point is the bed of the Arkansas river near the town of Holly, about three miles west of the Kansas line, in Prowers county, in the southeastern part of the state. Its altitude is 3,385 feet, or 0.64 of a mile above sea level.

The highest incorporated town is Kokomo, in Summit county, which has an altitude of 10,618 feet. The lowest incorporated town is Holly, in Prowers county, 3,387 feet above sea level.

Summit lake, near the top of Mount Evans in Clear Creek county, has the highest elevation of the numerous lakes of the state, being 12,740 feet, or almost 2½ miles above the level of the sea. It was formed in the cone of an extinct volcano and its depth has never been determined, ordinary sounding methods failing to reach bottom. In 1931 a scientific expedition headed by J. C. Stearns, of the University of Denver, and Dr. Arthur Compton, of the University of Chicago, conducted important cosmic rays research on the lake.

The deepest hole ever bored into the earth in Colorado, as far as records disclose, is a test well drilled for oil near Longmont. Boulder county, by the A. A. Rollestone company, which reached a depth of 7,300 feet before it was finally abandoned. The bottom of this hole is about one-third of a mile below the level of the sea.

The highest automobile road in Colorado, as well as in the United States, is the Mount Evans highway in Clear Creek county, which rises to an altitude of 14,260 feet.

The deepest mine in the state is the Portland, in the Cripple Creek district, Teller county, which has been opened to a depth of 3,000 feet.

The approximate mean altitude of Colorado is 6,800 feet, or 700 feet higher than Utah and 100 feet higher than Wyoming.

**Railroads, Telegraph and Telephone Facilities**—There are 28 railroad and terminal companies operating in Colorado, operating an aggregate of 4,973 miles of main line track. Every county in the state has some railroad mileage, though the railroad facilities of some of the counties, particularly in the northwestern and southwestern parts of the state, are inadequate. The total value of railroad property in the state, as returned by the state tax commission for the year 1931 was $170,411,240.

The following table shows the main line tracks owned by the several railroad companies:

| Road | Mileage |
|---|---|
| Atchison, Topeka & Santa Fe Railway Company | 528.88 |
| Chicago, Burlington & Quincy Railroad Company | 395.41 |
| Chicago, Rock Island & Pacific Railroad Company | 165.85 |
| Colorado-Kansas Railroad Co. | 22.20 |
| Colorado & Southern Railroad Co. | 767.83 |
| Colorado & Southeastern Railroad Company | 6.27 |
| Colorado & Wyoming Railroad Company | 40.14 |
| Crystal River Railroad Company. | 20.66 |
| Crystal River & San Juan Co. | 7.32 |
| Denver & Inter-Mountain Railroad Company | 11.57 |
| Denver & Rio Grande Western Railroad Company | 1,444.53 |
| Denver & Salt Lake Railroad Co. | 252.00 |
| Great Western Railway Company | 86.58 |
| Greeley Terminal Railway Co. | 1.60 |
| Laramie, North Park & Western Railroad Company | 43.88 |
| Manitou & Pikes Peak Railway Company | 8.90 |
| Midland Terminal Railroad Co. | 56.15 |
| Missouri Pacific Railroad Co. | 152.04 |
| NorthWestern Terminal Railway Company | 3.18 |
| Rio Grande Junction Railroad Co. | 62.08 |
| Rio Grande Southern Railroad Company | 171.16 |
| San Luis Central Railroad Co. | 12.21 |
| San Luis Southern Railway Co. | 31.53 |
| Silverton, Gladstone & Northerly Railroad Company | 7.17 |
| Silverton Northern Railroad Co. | 8.45 |
| Treasury Mountain Railroad Co. | 4.00 |
| Uintah Railway Company | 50.80 |
| Union Pacific Railroad Company. | 602.02 |

Ninety-eight telephone companies operate in the state, owning an aggregate of 504,190 miles of wire in 1931. The valuation of all telephone property owned by these companies as determined by the state tax commission for taxation purposes was $17,279,370 in 1931. Most of these companies are small and operate in one or two counties only. One company owns and operates more than 97 per cent of the total mileage. All counties in the state have telephone service. Four telegraph companies operate 28,217 miles of wire. Tables published elsewhere in this volume give valuations, mileage, etc., of all companies by counties.

# Colorado—Brief Land History

THE territory now included in the state of Colorado did not all become the property of the United States at the same time, nor was it all conveyed in the same manner or by the same nation. Parts of it have at times belonged to the territories of Kansas, Nebraska, New Mexico and Utah, and a very considerable section of it was claimed by the Republic of Texas when that enterprising little nation won its freedom from Mexico.

The Louisiana Purchase, a vast tract of land acquired by the United States from France in 1803, extended, in a general way, westward from the Mississippi river to the Rocky mountains. About half of the land now comprising the state of Colorado was included in this purchase, the entire cost of which was about $27,250,000.

The area south of the Arkansas river and west of the Rocky mountains was first claimed by Spain and later by Mexico. When Texas, after winning its independence from Mexico, was admitted to the Union in 1845, it claimed that part of what is now Colorado lying south of the Arkansas river, and in addition a rectangular strip extending north through the mountains into Wyoming, lying between the 106th and the 108th meridians. By reference to the map it will be seen that a considerable part of this territory claimed by Texas was included in the Louisiana Purchase, but the controversy over the northern boundary of Texas was amicably settled before Colorado territory was organized.

The western part of Colorado and the territory in the south lying west and south of the Rio Grande del Norte was included in the immense tract of land ceded to the United States by Mexico in 1848, following the war with that country. The eastern boundary of this ceded land was at about the 108th meridian, except on the south, where its boundary, as before stated, was the Rio Grande del Norte.

The territory of Utah was organized in 1850. It extended east to the main range of the Rocky mountains, including nearly one-half of what is now Colorado. In 1854 the territories of Kansas and Nebraska were created by the famous Kansas-Nebraska act. Kansas territory then extended west to the territory of Utah, the southern boundary being the territory of New Mexico, which at that time extended north to the Arkansas river, and the northern boundary being at the 40th parallel, which passes near the present site of the city of Brighton. That part of what is now Colorado, lying north of this parallel and extending west to the boundary of Utah territory, was included in Nebraska territory.

In 1855 that part of Colorado then included in Kansas territory was organized into Arapahoe county, and Allen P. Tibbitts, Levi Mitchell and Jonathan Atwood were named as commissioners to locate the county seat of the new county, which was to be called Mountain City. They were likewise to act as commissioners for the new county, but there is no record available showing that they ever assumed their duties. In 1856 an election was held in Arapahoe county, K. T., and Benjamin F. Simmons was chosen as the first representative from this county in the Kansas territorial legislature.

But the people in the new towns and mining camps, dissatisfied with a government the seat of which was several hundred miles away, and could be reached only after a week's hard travel, soon started a movement for the organization of a new territory, to include that part of Kansas territory known as Arapahoe county. This movement gained strength rapidly, and some of the more ambitious conceived the idea that the creation of a new state was the proper procedure. They spent some months working on the plan and finally agreed that the new state should be called Jefferson and should extend north far into what is now Wyoming. An election held late in 1859 showed that a majority of the voters were in favor of trying a territorial government before attempting statehood, and Robert W.

Steele was elected as the first governor of "Jefferson Territory." The following counties were provided for in the organization of the so-called "Jefferson Territory": Arapahoe, Cheyenne, El Paso, Fountain, Jackson, Jefferson, Mountain, North Park, Saratoga, Steele and St. Vrain.

In the meantime, however, steps were being taken at Washington to bring about the organization of a territory through the regularly constituted legislative channels. In February, 1861, Colorado Territory was regularly organized, its boundaries being substantially the same as those of the state today. On June 6, 1861, Mr. Steele formally abdicated as governor of "Jefferson Territory," and that unique political subdivision passed into history.

Within the vast area formerly claimed by the state of Texas, as well as that ceded by Mexico, there were numerous land grants, made by the Spanish and Mexican governments, all of which were confirmed by the United States when this area became a part of the Union. A special land court was created for the examination and adjudication of these titles, and in all cases where the records showed that the grants were properly made they were formally approved by this court. In addition to these old grants there were large tracts of land which had been set apart for Indian tribes who claimed this territory as their own. In 1861 the federal government entered into a treaty with the Cheyenne and Arapahoe Indians, under which the Indians ceded to the government their lands in eastern Colorado. The Indians did not abide by this treaty, however, and they waged vigorous warfare against the white settlers for several years with a view to driving them from the plains of eastern Colorado. On October 28, 1867, they signed another treaty with the United States, ceding all their lands between the Platte and Arkansas rivers, and agreeing to their removal to Indian Territory.

In the western part of the state settlers came in contact with the Ute Indians. In 1868 a treaty had been made between these Indians and the government by which the government confirmed their title to a large tract of land in the southern and western parts of the state. After the discovery of rich metal deposits in the San Juan district, white settlers began to come in rapidly, and steps were taken to recover the land that had been confirmed by the government as the property of the Utes. The Indians were strongly opposed to giving it up, but in 1873, largely through the influence of Chief Ouray, one of the most illustrious leaders of the red men in Colorado, a treaty was signed by which the Utes ceded to the government the mineral lands in the San Juan district.

They still retained, however, more than 15,500,000 acres of land on the western slope. Numerous encounters occurred between these Indians and the white men during the early settlement of the agricultural lands in this territory, and it was not until 1881 that the Indians in this region, usually known as the Uncompahgre Utes, were removed to the Uintah reservation, in eastern Utah.

An Indian reservation also was established in southwestern Colorado and northwestern New Mexico, to which most of the Southern Utes were removed. This is the only Indian reservation in Colorado at present, though there is some Indian land in La Plata county belonging to Ute Indians.

Colorado Territory as at first organized contained 17 counties, the list including Arapahoe, Boulder, Clear Creek, Conejos (then known as Guadaloupe), Costilla, Douglas, El Paso, Fremont, Gilpin, Huerfano, Jefferson, Lake, Larimer, Park, Pueblo, Summit and Weld. Since that time the number has been increased until there are now 63. New counties were created at various times, but in 1883 a general division of the western slope was made, the counties of Delta, Eagle, Garfield, Mesa, Montrose, Ouray and San Miguel being created from the larger counties of earlier days. The second general division of great areas into smaller counties occurred in 1889, when the gradual settlement of the eastern Colorado plains gave rise to the creation of 11 new subdivisions,

the counties then created being Baca, Cheyenne, Kiowa, Kit Carson, Lincoln, Morgan, Otero, Phillips, Prowers, Sedgwick and Yuma. Montezuma and Rio Blanco, western Colorado counties, also were created in that year. Since that time only eight new counties have been created by the legislature, the later list including Mineral, Teller, Jackson, Crowley, Moffat, Denver, Adams and Alamosa. In 1902 Denver and Adams counties were taken out of Arapahoe county and established as separate entities. No new counties have been established since 1913, when Alamosa county was made up from parts of Conejos and Costilla counties.

## ESTABLISHMENT OF COLORADO COUNTIES

The following table shows the dates of organization of the 63 counties now existing in Colorado. The 17 counties in existence under territorial law and recognized when statehood was achieved are indicated by a star (*).

For the purpose of preserving the earlier record the following changes are noted in the statutes creating counties: Greenwood county was established in 1870 and abolished in 1874, its area being allotted to Elbert and Bent counties; Conejos county originally was known as Guadaloupe county; Carbonate county was established from a part of Lake county in 1879, but at the same legislative session the name of Lake was changed to Chaffee and Carbonate was changed to Lake; Uncompahgre county was established in 1883, but later in the same year the name was changed to Ouray, and what was then Ouray county was changed to San Miguel county.

The names of the present counties and the dates of organization follow:

| County | Year | County | Year | County | Year |
|---|---|---|---|---|---|
| Adams | 1901 | Garfield | 1883 | Otero | 1889 |
| Alamosa | 1913 | Gilpin* | 1861 | Ouray | 1877 |
| Arapahoe* | 1861 | Grand | 1874 | Park* | 1861 |
| Archuleta | 1885 | Gunnison | 1877 | Phillips | 1889 |
| Baca | 1889 | Hinsdale | 1874 | Pitkin | 1881 |
| Bent | 1870 | Huerfano* | 1861 | Prowers | 1889 |
| Boulder* | 1861 | Jackson | 1909 | Pueblo* | 1861 |
| Chaffee | 1879 | Jefferson* | 1861 | Rio Blanco | 1889 |
| Cheyenne | 1889 | Kiowa | 1889 | Rio Grande | 1874 |
| Clear Creek* | 1861 | Kit Carson | 1889 | Routt | 1877 |
| Conejos* | 1861 | Lake* | 1861 | Saguache | 1867 |
| Costilla* | 1861 | La Plata | 1874 | San Juan | 1876 |
| Crowley | 1911 | Larimer* | 1861 | San Miguel | 1883 |
| Custer | 1877 | Las Animas | 1866 | Sedgwick | 1889 |
| Delta | 1883 | Lincoln | 1889 | Summit* | 1861 |
| Denver | 1901 | Logan | 1887 | Teller | 1899 |
| Dolores | 1881 | Mesa | 1883 | Washington | 1887 |
| Douglas* | 1861 | Mineral | 1893 | Weld* | 1861 |
| Eagle | 1883 | Moffat | 1911 | Yuma | 1889 |
| Elbert | 1874 | Montezuma | 1889 | | |
| El Paso* | 1861 | Montrose | 1883 | | |
| Fremont* | 1861 | Morgan | 1889 | | |

# Colorado Land Classification by Counties

## COLORADO'S PLACE AMONG THE STATES OF THE UNION

NOTE—Figures for Colorado of a later date than those given in this table on some items mentioned may be found elsewhere in this volume. Those used in this table are of dates for which comparative data are available.

| DESCRIPTION | Colorado | United States | Colo % of U. S. | Rank Among States |
|---|---|---|---|---|
| Land area (square miles) | 103,658 | 2,973,776 | 3.49 | 7 |
| Water surface (acres) | 185,609 | 33,854,080 | 0.55 | 42 |
| Population (1930) | 1,035,791 | 122,775,046 | 0.84 | 33 |
| Population per square mile (1930) | 10.0 | 41.3 | --- | 39 |
| Population (1920) | 939,629 | 105,710,620 | 0.89 | 33 |
| Population per square mile (1920) | 9.1 | 35.5 | --- | 42 |
| Population increase 1920-1930 (%) | 10.2 | 16.1 | --- | -- |
| Vacant public land July 1, 1931 (acres) | 7,657,140 | 177,101,551 | 4.32 | 9 |
| Area in national forests 1931 (acres) | 13,323,566 | 160,787,687 | 8.29 | 4 |
| Area in national parks and monuments 1929 (acres) | 156,600 | 4,341,220 | 3.61 | 5 |
| Visitors to national parks (1931) | 283,666 | †3,152.845 | 8.99 | -- |
| Value all property (1922) | $3,229,412,000 | $320,803,862,000 | 1.01 | 29 |
| Value manufactured products (1929) | $306,071,051 | $70,434,863,443 | 0.43 | 34 |
| Value all farm property (1930) | $795,387,096 | $57,245,514,269 | 1.39 | 23 |
| Gasoline taxes (1930) | $6,144,626 | $494,683,410 | 1.24 | 32 |
| Developed water power Jan. 1, 1929, (horsepower) | 98,000 | 13,808,000 | 0.71 | 27 |
| Water power, potential h. p. available 50% of the time (Jan. 1, 1928) | 1,609,000 | 59,166,000 | 2.72 | 8 |
| Church membership (1926) | 352,863 | 54,576,346 | 0.65 | 35 |
| Beets produced for sugar, farm value 1921-1929 | $150,966,000 | $476,675,000 | 31.67 | 1 |
| Tons of beet sugar manufactured (1921-1929) | 2,885,000 | 8,659,000 | 33.32 | 1 |
| Livestock on farms, value (1930) | $116,920,000 | $5,864,969,000 | 1.99 | 18 |
| Farm value 75 crops (1930) | $121,430,000 | $6,274,427,000 | 1.94 | 22 |
| Gold produced, value (1929) | $4,553,700 | *$45,651,400 | 9.97 | 5* |
| Silver produced, value (1929) | $2,353,642 | *$32,687,754 | 7.20 | 6 |
| Lead, mine production in short tons (1928) | 26,751 | 627,153 | 4.27 | 5* |
| Zinc, mine production, short tons (1927) | 35,865 | 718,541 | 4.99 | 6* |
| Copper produced, pounds (1929) | 10,519,784 | *2,002,863,135 | 0.53 | 10* |
| Volume wholesale business in 1929 (1930 census) | $540,398,295 | $69,628,448,061 | .78 | 26 |
| Railroads and equipment, value of (1922) | $364,963,000 | $19,950,800,000 | 1.83 | 20 |
| Railway mileage, Dec. 31, 1930 | 4,972 | 249,052 | 2.00 | 23 |
| Motor vehicles registered (1930) | 308,509 | 26,523,779 | 1.16 | 27 |
| State net governmental costs (1928) | $17,412,123 | $1,877,184,189 | 0.93 | 36 |
| Highway mileage, all types (1928) | 68,305 | 3,016,281 | 2.26 | 21 |
| Prohibition convictions in federal courts (1929) | 131 | 47,100 | 0.28 | 44 |
| U. S. Internal revenue receipts (1930) | $12,468,450 | †$3,040,145,733 | 0.41 | 29 |
| Individual income taxes (1930) | $4,212,449 | †$1,146,844,763 | 0.37 | 26 |
| Corporation income taxes (1930) | $7,835,965 | †$1,263,411,466 | 0.62 | 24 |
| Troops in world war | 42,898 | 4,727,988 | 0.93 | 33 |
| Telephones, number (1927) | 183,250 | 18,522,767 | 0.99 | 25 |
| National guard strength (June 30, 1929) | 1,725 | 176,988 | 0.97 | 33 |
| Bread and other bakery products, value of products (1929) | $11,773,612 | $1,526,110,811 | 0.77 | 22 |
| Butter, value manufactured products (1929) | $9,854,633 | $1,066,172,052 | 0.92 | 20 |
| Cheese value (1929) | $846,964 | $110,644,732 | 0.77 | 14 |
| Condensed and evaporated milk, value of output (1927) | $2,499,374 | $200,086,091 | 1.25 | 14 |
| Canning and preserving, fruits, vegetables, etc., value (1927) | $3,487,252 | $572,428,049 | 0.61 | 22 |
| Slaughtering and packing, value of products (1927) | $30,538,016 | $3,057,215,718 | 1.00 | 20 |
| Mining machinery, value of manufactures (1927) | $3,329,797 | $35,259,263 | 9.44 | 3 |
| Flour and other grain mill products, value (1927) | $13,267,581 | $1,148,760,360 | 1.15 | 23 |
| Est. barrels of oil recoverable from Tertiary shale | 47,625,598,000 | 75,335,721,000 | 63.22 | 1 |
| Coal produced, tons, (1929) | 9,920,741 | 608,816,788 | 1.63 | 9 |
| Petroleum output, barrels, bureau of mines figures (1929) | 2,358,000 | 1,007,323,000 | 0.23 | 16 |
| Coke produced, tons (1929) | 570,000 | 53,476,000 | 1.07 | 14 |
| Clay products, value (1925) | $4,351,749 | $333,730,417 | 1.30 | 18 |
| Fluorspar produced, value (1925) | $153,707 | $2,052,342 | 7.49 | 3 |
| Public school property, value (1925-26) | $54,643,686 | $4,676,603,539 | 1.13 | 24 |
| Probable number millionaires (1923) | 44 | 8,600 | 0.51 | 21 |
| Coal, reserve tonnage bituminous, geological survey estimate, figures in millions of tons | 213,071 | 1,441,395 | 14.78 | 1 |
| Lodgepole pine cut, in board feet (1930) | 15,426,000 | 30,401,000 | 50.74 | 1 |

*Includes Alaska.    †Includes Alaska and possessions.

## LAND CLASSIFICATION BY PERCENTAGES

| COUNTY | Area Acres | Patented Land % | Homestead Land % | National Forests % | State Land % | Non-Patented Land % |
|---|---|---|---|---|---|---|
| Adams ........... | 807,680 | 93.58 | .... | .... | 3.62 | 3.62 |
| Alamosa ......... | 465,280 | 64.77 | 10.06 | 6.24 | 10.01 | 26.31 |
| Arapahoe ........ | 538,880 | 95.81 | .... | .... | 2.72 | 2.72 |
| Archuleta ........ | 780,800 | 33.13 | 13.15 | 51.86 | 2.32 | 67.33 |
| Baca ............ | 1,633,280 | 93.92 | 0.05 | .... | 1.88 | 1.93 |
| Bent ........... | 975,360 | 80.87 | 0.36 | .... | 14.18 | 14.54 |
| Boulder ......... | 488,960 | 59.73 | 0 69 | 25.63 | 1.44 | 27.76 |
| Chaffee ......... | 693,120 | 17.15 | 13.10 | 61.27 | 2.60 | 76.97 |
| Cheyenne ........ | 1,137,280 | 94.71 | 0.02 | .... | 4.74 | 4.76 |
| Clear Creek...... | 249,600 | 24.31 | 6.75 | 68.64 | 0.82 | 76.21 |
| Conejos .......... | 801,280 | 32.58 | 31.17 | 34.47 | 7.69 | 73.33 |
| Costilla ......... | 758,400 | 103.25 | .... | .... | .... | .... |
| Crowley ......... | 517,120 | 82.80 | 0.18 | .... | 11.74 | 11.92 |
| Custer .......... | 478,080 | 55.75 | 2.56 | 35.27 | 2.74 | 40.57 |
| Delta ........... | 768,640 | 35.41 | 17.24 | 24.71 | .... | 41.95 |
| Denver .......... | 37,120 | 94.30 | .... | .... | 1.55 | 1.55 |
| Dolores ......... | 667,520 | 31.14 | 7.46 | 49.20 | 1.28 | 57.94 |
| Douglas ......... | 540,800 | 70.91 | 0.01 | 25.21 | 1.63 | 26.85 |
| Eagle ........... | 1,036,800 | 15.21 | 12.05 | 57.32 | 1.70 | 71.07 |
| Elbert .......... | 1,188,480 | 91.28 | 0.02 | .... | 6.45 | 6.47 |
| El Paso.......... | 1,357,440 | 75.06 | 0.14 | 7.41 | 14.09 | 21.64 |
| Fremont ......... | 996,480 | 38.37 | 33.96 | 7.02 | 5.78 | 46.76 |
| Garfield ........ | 1,988,480 | 17.64 | 27.66 | 26.20 | .... | 53.86 |
| Gilpin .......... | 84,480 | 56.67 | 4.12 | 68.01 | 1.47 | 73.60 |
| Grand .......... | 1,194,240 | 25.90 | 5.37 | 44.40 | 5.43 | 55.20 |
| Gunnison ........ | 2,034,560 | 18.39 | 17.06 | 55.55 | 0.94 | 73.55 |
| Hinsdale ........ | 621,440 | 4.33 | 17.42 | 73.73 | 1.33 | 92.48 |
| Huerfano ........ | 960,000 | 70.39 | 5.49 | 14.54 | 4.68 | 24.71 |
| Jackson ......... | 1,044,480 | 30.76 | 16.35 | 38.67 | 4.91 | 59.93 |
| Jefferson ........ | 517,120 | 70.54 | 0.17 | 18.58 | 2.57 | 21.32 |
| Kiowa .......... | 1,150,720 | 90.55 | 0.05 | .... | 5.41 | 5.46 |
| Kit Carson....... | 1,381,760 | 94.73 | 0.02 | .... | 4.15 | 4.17 |
| Lake ........... | 237,440 | 27.13 | 10.09 | 67.04 | 0.73 | 77.86 |
| La Plata......... | 1,184,640 | 37.73 | 12.85 | 32.08 | 1.32 | 46.25 |
| Larimer ......... | 1,682,560 | 46.00 | 1.34 | 35.59 | 4.21 | 41.14 |
| Las Animas....... | 3,077,760 | 89.64 | 1.23 | 0.99 | 5.05 | 7.27 |
| Lincoln ......... | 1,644,800 | 90.66 | 0.08 | .... | 7.62 | 7.70 |
| Logan .......... | 1,166,080 | 85.38 | 0.11 | .... | 12.30 | 12.41 |
| Mesa ........... | 2,024,320 | 24.41 | 37.70 | 2.84 | .... | 40.54 |
| Mineral ......... | 554,240 | 5.60 | .... | 95.27 | 0.12 | 95.39 |
| Moffat .......... | 2,981,120 | 33.79 | 47.23 | 1.41 | 6.94 | 55.58 |
| Montezuma ...... | 1,312,640 | 24.44 | 16.87 | 17.74 | 2.69 | 37.30 |
| Montrose ........ | 1,448,960 | 28.54 | 35.52 | 21.60 | 0.01 | 57.13 |
| Morgan ......... | 823,040 | 90.99 | 0.08 | .... | 7.20 | 7.28 |
| Otero ........... | 805,760 | 78.85 | 0.16 | .... | 14.93 | 15.09 |
| Ouray .......... | 332,160 | 50.55 | 7.59 | 38.09 | 0.95 | 46.63 |
| Park ........... | 1,434,880 | 34.02 | 4.75 | 43.74 | 6.11 | 54.60 |
| Phillips ......... | 440,320 | 93.06 | .... | .... | 3.99 | 3.99 |
| Pitkin .......... | 652,160 | 13.64 | 1.99 | 75.01 | 0.20 | 77.20 |
| Prowers ......... | 1,043,200 | 93.08 | 0.08 | .... | 4.34 | 4.42 |
| Pueblo .......... | 1,557,120 | 77.16 | 0.84 | 1.86 | 14.97 | 17.67 |
| Rio Blanco....... | 2,062,720 | 17.50 | 51.40 | 17.54 | .... | 68.94 |
| Rio Grande....... | 574,720 | 39.46 | 13.26 | 40.55 | 2.55 | 56.36 |
| Routt .......... | 1,477,760 | 42.92 | 3.69 | 37.83 | 4.76 | 46.28 |
| Saguache ........ | 2,005,120 | 28.11 | 16.01 | 43.61 | 4.84 | 64.46 |
| San Juan......... | 289,920 | 8.83 | 15.87 | 64.71 | 2.56 | 83.14 |
| San Miguel....... | 824,320 | 29.43 | 37.65 | 21.45 | 2.62 | 61.72 |
| Sedgwick ........ | 339,840 | 90.52 | .... | .... | 6.48 | 6.48 |
| Summit ......... | 415,360 | 17.40 | 3.28 | 66.31 | 0.23 | 69.82 |
| Teller .......... | 350,080 | 53.47 | 8.06 | 30.45 | 3.03 | 41.54 |
| Washington ...... | 1,613,440 | 91.99 | 0.06 | .... | 5.81 | 5.87 |
| Weld .......... | 2,574,080 | 89.38 | 0.09 | .... | 6.85 | 6.94 |
| Yuma .......... | 1,514,880 | 95.27 | 0.04 | .... | 3.62 | 3.66 |
| State ......... | 66,341,120 | 56.04 | 11.54 | 20.10 | 4.64 | 36.28 |

Note.—Owing to inaccuracies in surveys and other causes, the figures for some counties do not always equal 100 per cent, sometimes going over that total.
In addition to lands shown here there are in most counties areas not accounted for as to title, these areas not being included in this table.

## RANK OF COUNTIES IN THE STATE

| COUNTY | Area | Population (1930) | Bank Deposits (Dec. 31, 1931) | Agricultural Values (¶1) | Dairy Values (1931) | Range Values (¶1) | Value (1931) | Value Swine (1931) | Metal Mining (1930) | Coal Mining (1931) | Manufacturing (¶19) | Miles Railroad (¶1) | Other Values (¶1) | Miles Highways (1932) | Assessed Valuation (1931) |
|---|---|---|---|---|---|---|---|---|---|---|---|---|---|---|---|
| Adams | 35 | 12 | 30 | 6 | 4 | 45 | 50 | 6 | 20 | -- | 9 | 18 | 12 | 15 | 14 |
| Alamosa | 53 | 30 | 22 | 38 | 36 | 42 | 26 | 30 | -- | -- | 28 | 42 | 29 | 40 | 42 |
| Arapahoe | 48 | 10 | 19 | 25 | 10 | 48 | 39 | 26 | 22 | -- | 23 | 34 | 8 | 36 | 19 |
| Archuleta | 38 | 48 | 56 | 50 | 40 | 38 | 16 | 44 | -- | 24 | 29 | 33 | 54 | 42 | 39 |
| Baca | 11 | 22 | 35 | 5 | 34 | 12 | 40 | 9 | -- | -- | 48 | 44 | 22 | 17 | 35 |
| Bent | 31 | 29 | 31 | 18 | 31 | 28 | 29 | 24 | -- | -- | 33 | 26 | 27 | 28 | 22 |
| Boulder | 51 | 7 | 5 | 12 | 8 | 46 | 48 | 25 | 16 | 5 | 5 | 14 | 6 | 33 | 6 |
| Chaffee | 41 | 31 | 21 | 49 | 44 | 49 | 43 | 37 | 19 | -- | 13 | 27 | 32 | 50 | 28 |
| Cheyenne | 26 | 46 | 54 | 34 | 46 | 22 | 37 | 21 | -- | -- | 59 | 32 | 43 | 32 | 29 |
| Clear Creek | 60 | 51 | 52 | 61 | 60 | 61 | 57 | -- | 13 | -- | 45 | 57 | 51 | 55 | 47 |
| Conejos | 37 | 25 | 41 | 21 | 29 | 37 | 3 | 18 | -- | -- | 20 | 38 | 37 | 35 | 44 |
| Costilla | 40 | 38 | 58 | 30 | 56 | 56 | 23 | 32 | -- | -- | 39 | 31 | 47 | 53 | 51 |
| Crowley | 50 | 36 | 40 | 27 | 38 | 41 | 42 | 28 | -- | -- | 19 | 55 | 36 | 27 | 48 |
| Custer | 52 | 52 | 53 | 42 | 42 | 44 | 47 | 45 | -- | -- | 57 | 60 | 52 | 30 | 57 |
| Delta | 39 | 18 | 17 | 11 | 12 | 21 | 10 | 27 | -- | 11 | 30 | 30 | 18 | 37 | 32 |
| Denver | 63 | 1 | 1 | -- | 52 | -- | -- | -- | -- | -- | 1 | 37 | 1 | -- | 1 |
| Dolores | 42 | 58 | -- | 57 | 58 | 53 | 21 | 52 | 7 | -- | 61 | 59 | 61 | 54 | 63 |
| Douglas | 47 | 47 | 39 | 47 | 7 | 23 | 44 | 38 | -- | -- | 18 | 16 | 41 | 34 | 18 |
| Eagle | 29 | 44 | 45 | 40 | 37 | 20 | 17 | 42 | 2 | -- | 53 | 24 | 44 | 45 | 31 |
| Elbert | 22 | 34 | 32 | 28 | 16 | 15 | 32 | 13 | -- | 19 | 59 | 23 | 34 | 5 | 23 |
| El Paso | 19 | 4 | 3 | 31 | 2 | 13 | 41 | 15 | -- | 8 | 10 | 4 | 3 | 9 | 5 |
| Fremont | 30 | 14 | 8 | 33 | 30 | 40 | 51 | 34 | -- | 7 | 7 | 12 | 15 | 49 | 11 |
| Garfield | 8 | 23 | 10 | 19 | 15 | 8 | 1 | 20 | -- | 14 | 32 | 10 | 26 | 16 | 15 |
| Gilpin | 62 | 60 | 51 | 60 | 63 | 59 | 62 | -- | 10 | -- | 51 | 52 | 57 | 62 | 50 |
| Grand | 21 | 53 | 47 | 44 | 41 | 30 | 30 | 51 | -- | -- | 21 | 28 | 49 | 47 | 33 |
| Gunnison | 5 | 40 | 24 | 41 | 35 | 7 | 11 | 49 | 15 | 6 | 40 | 5 | 38 | 43 | 9 |
| Hinsdale | 44 | 63 | -- | 58 | 61 | 57 | 46 | -- | -- | -- | 62 | 61 | 63 | 59 | 60 |
| Huerfano | 32 | 16 | 13 | 46 | 32 | 33 | 24 | 43 | -- | 3 | 34 | 8 | 19 | 41 | 10 |
| Jackson | 27 | 59 | -- | 29 | 48 | 5 | 20 | 53 | -- | 12 | 46 | 46 | 53 | 46 | 61 |
| Jefferson | 49 | 11 | 23 | 20 | 9 | 35 | 56 | 39 | -- | 9 | 22 | 13 | 7 | 18 | 13 |
| Kiowa | 25 | 45 | 49 | 39 | 50 | 29 | 45 | 33 | -- | -- | 56 | 22 | 42 | 29 | 27 |
| Kit Carson | 18 | 26 | 42 | 14 | 13 | 19 | 49 | 2 | -- | -- | 42 | 36 | 20 | 11 | 36 |
| Lake | 61 | 41 | 27 | 56 | 57 | 60 | 59 | -- | 4 | -- | 11 | 39 | 46 | 13 | 34 |
| La Plata | 23 | 20 | 12 | 35 | 24 | 31 | 18 | 31 | 17 | 13 | 15 | 9 | 21 | 59 | 21 |
| Larimer | 9 | 6 | 7 | 2 | 3 | 16 | 27 | 19 | -- | 20 | 3 | 6 | 5 | 19 | 8 |
| Las Animas | 1 | 5 | 6 | 24 | 25 | 1 | 5 | 35 | -- | 2 | 12 | 2 | 10 | 2 | 4 |
| Lincoln | 10 | 33 | 33 | 26 | 23 | 10 | 34 | 11 | -- | -- | 27 | 29 | 30 | 20 | 26 |
| Logan | 24 | 13 | 15 | 3 | 6 | 18 | 54 | 3 | -- | -- | 17 | 7 | 13 | 3 | 7 |
| Mesa | 6 | 8 | 9 | 7 | 5 | 2 | 9 | 16 | -- | 10 | 16 | 11 | 9 | 7 | 17 |
| Mineral | 46 | 62 | -- | 59 | 59 | 58 | 31 | -- | 11 | -- | 63 | 58 | 62 | 61 | 56 |
| Moffat | 2 | 42 | 37 | 45 | 39 | 26 | 2 | 41 | 21 | 18 | 50 | 63 | 40 | 25 | 59 |
| Montezuma | 20 | 32 | 29 | 37 | 26 | 36 | 14 | 40 | -- | 17 | 38 | 35 | 35 | 22 | 58 |
| Montrose | 16 | 21 | 16 | 15 | 20 | 24 | 7 | 22 | 23 | 23 | 24 | 41 | 23 | 23 | 41 |
| Morgan | 34 | 15 | 11 | 4 | 11 | 32 | 53 | 8 | -- | -- | 8 | 20 | 14 | 26 | 16 |
| Otero | 36 | 9 | 14 | 9 | 22 | 34 | 19 | 14 | -- | -- | 6 | 17 | 11 | 14 | 12 |
| Ouray | 58 | 56 | 50 | 51 | 53 | 43 | 28 | 48 | 8 | 21 | 49 | 51 | 55 | 52 | 52 |
| Park | 17 | 54 | 55 | 48 | 45 | 27 | 12 | 55 | 5 | 25 | 44 | 15 | 50 | 31 | 24 |
| Phillips | 54 | 37 | 28 | 22 | 27 | 54 | 61 | 7 | -- | -- | 31 | 53 | 31 | 24 | 43 |
| Pitkin | 43 | 57 | 44 | 52 | 54 | 50 | 33 | 47 | 14 | 15 | 52 | 50 | 58 | 56 | 54 |
| Prowers | 28 | 17 | 20 | 16 | 18 | 25 | 38 | 12 | -- | -- | 14 | 25 | 16 | 12 | 20 |
| Pueblo | 13 | 2 | 2 | 10 | 14 | 17 | 36 | 23 | -- | -- | 2 | 3 | 4 | 4 | 3 |
| Rio Blanco | 4 | 49 | 46 | 43 | 43 | 6 | 8 | 46 | -- | 16 | 43 | 62 | 48 | 44 | 62 |
| Rio Grande | 45 | 24 | 26 | 17 | 33 | 39 | 13 | 17 | 18 | -- | 25 | 40 | 24 | 39 | 46 |
| Routt | 15 | 28 | 48 | 32 | 21 | 4 | 4 | 29 | -- | 4 | 26 | 19 | 28 | 8 | 25 |
| Saguache | 7 | 35 | 34 | 36 | 49 | 11 | 6 | 36 | 6 | -- | 36 | 21 | 39 | 21 | 30 |
| San Juan | 59 | 55 | 38 | -- | 62 | 62 | 35 | -- | 1 | -- | 55 | 56 | 60 | 58 | 55 |
| San Miguel | 33 | 50 | -- | 54 | 47 | 51 | 15 | 50 | 9 | 22 | 41 | 43 | 56 | 51 | 53 |
| Sedgwick | 57 | 39 | 43 | 23 | 28 | 47 | 58 | 10 | -- | -- | 54 | 54 | 33 | 38 | 45 |
| Summit | 55 | 61 | 57 | 55 | 55 | 55 | 52 | 56 | 12 | -- | 61 | 45 | 59 | 60 | 40 |
| Teller | 56 | 43 | 18 | 53 | 51 | 52 | 60 | 54 | 3 | -- | 37 | 49 | 45 | 48 | 49 |
| Washington | 12 | 27 | 36 | 13 | 17 | 14 | 25 | 5 | -- | -- | 47 | 47 | 25 | 6 | 37 |
| Weld | 3 | 3 | 4 | 1 | 1 | 9 | 22 | 4 | -- | 1 | 4 | 1 | 2 | 1 | 2 |
| Yuma | 14 | 19 | 25 | 8 | 19 | 3 | 55 | 1 | -- | -- | 35 | 48 | 17 | 10 | 38 |

## COMPOSITION AND CHARACTERISTICS OF POPULATION BY COUNTIES
(Census 1930)

| COUNTY | Total Population | Native White | Foreign Born White | Negro | Indian | Chinese | Japanese | Mexican |
|---|---|---|---|---|---|---|---|---|
| Adams_____ | 20,245 | 16,349 | 2,133 | 107 | 4 | ---- | 437 | 1,191 |
| Alamosa_____ | 8,602 | 7,810 | 213 | 49 | ---- | ---- | 21 | 507 |
| Arapahoe_____ | 22,647 | 20,588 | 1,652 | 104 | 10 | 1 | 53 | 224 |
| Archuleta____ | 3,204 | 1,582 | 47 | ---- | 5 | ---- | 12 | 1,558 |
| Baca_____ | 10,570 | 10,436 | 80 | 2 | 4 | ---- | ---- | 48 |
| Bent_____ | 9,134 | 7,825 | 239 | 15 | 2 | 20 | 163 | 866 |
| Boulder_____ | 32,456 | 27,792 | 2,702 | 128 | 7 | 7 | 133 | 1,675 |
| Chaffee_____ | 8,126 | 6,416 | 770 | 23 | 1 | ---- | 31 | 884 |
| Cheyenne_____ | 3,723 | 3,491 | 184 | 1 | 1 | ---- | ---- | 46 |
| Clear Creek___ | 2,155 | 1,866 | 269 | 11 | ---- | 2 | ---- | 7 |
| Conejos_____ | 9,803 | 9,614 | 86 | 4 | 13 | ---- | 41 | 26 |
| Costilla_____ | 5,779 | 5,339 | 63 | 1 | 3 | ---- | 171 | 190 |
| Crowley_____ | 5,934 | 4,282 | 292 | 17 | 8 | ---- | 92 | 1,243 |
| Custer_____ | 2,124 | 1,831 | 167 | 36 | ---- | ---- | ---- | 90 |
| Delta_____ | 14,204 | 12,616 | 548 | 1 | 5 | ---- | 49 | 982 |
| Denver_____ | 287,861 | 241,742 | 31,235 | 7,204 | 243 | 154 | 349 | 6,837 |
| Dolores_____ | 1,412 | 1,287 | 91 | ---- | ---- | ---- | 6 | 25 |
| Douglas_____ | 3,498 | 3,163 | 220 | 2 | ---- | ---- | ---- | 112 |
| Eagle_____ | 3,924 | 3,233 | 293 | 1 | ---- | ---- | 1 | 389 |
| Elbert_____ | 6,580 | 6,152 | 357 | 13 | 3 | ---- | 11 | 44 |
| El Paso_____ | 49,570 | 44,424 | 3,247 | 1,096 | 20 | 5 | 10 | 759 |
| Fremont_____ | 18,896 | 15,988 | 1,752 | 216 | 12 | ---- | 4 | 923 |
| Garfield_____ | 9,975 | 8,870 | 752 | 11 | 2 | ---- | ---- | 340 |
| Gilpin_____ | 1,212 | 1,029 | 174 | ---- | ---- | ---- | ---- | 9 |
| Grand_____ | 2,168 | 1,897 | 176 | ---- | ---- | ---- | 7 | 28 |
| Gunnison_____ | 5,527 | 4,544 | 715 | 13 | 3 | ---- | ---- | 252 |
| Hinsdale_____ | 449 | 402 | 29 | 3 | ---- | ---- | ---- | 15 |
| Huerfano____ | 17,062 | 12,555 | 1,786 | 254 | ---- | ---- | 26 | 2,425 |
| Jackson_____ | 1,386 | 1,244 | 113 | ---- | ---- | ---- | ---- | 29 |
| Jefferson_____ | 21,810 | 19,462 | 2,120 | 64 | 14 | 1 | 56 | 92 |
| Kiowa_____ | 3,786 | 3,607 | 87 | 30 | 1 | ---- | ---- | 61 |
| Kit Carson___ | 9,725 | 9,375 | 338 | ---- | ---- | ---- | ---- | 12 |
| Lake_____ | 4,899 | 3,613 | 986 | 17 | 1 | ---- | ---- | 282 |
| La Plata_____ | 12,975 | 9,954 | 752 | 35 | 430 | 14 | 7 | 1,753 |
| Larimer_____ | 33,137 | 28,242 | 2,814 | 13 | 11 | ---- | 3 | 2,054 |
| Las Animas__ | 36,008 | 27,487 | 3,426 | 286 | 51 | 4 | 5 | 4,748 |
| Lincoln_____ | 7,850 | 7,490 | 275 | 1 | 1 | ---- | ---- | 83 |
| Logan_____ | 19,946 | 17,294 | 1,698 | 39 | 3 | ---- | 97 | 815 |
| Mesa_____ | 25,908 | 23,548 | 1,263 | 72 | 10 | 7 | 35 | 973 |
| Mineral_____ | 640 | 566 | 42 | 1 | ---- | ---- | ---- | 31 |
| Moffat_____ | 4,861 | 4,596 | 228 | 1 | ---- | ---- | ---- | 36 |
| Montezuma___ | 7,798 | 6,316 | 199 | 3 | 413 | ---- | ---- | 867 |
| Montrose_____ | 11,742 | 9,927 | 551 | 8 | 8 | ---- | 56 | 1,191 |
| Morgan_____ | 18,284 | 15,109 | 1,721 | 35 | ---- | ---- | 21 | 1,398 |
| Otero_____ | 24,390 | 19,078 | 766 | 222 | 12 | ---- | 332 | 3,941 |
| Ouray_____ | 1,784 | 1,552 | 228 | 3 | ---- | 1 | ---- | ---- |
| Park_____ | 2,052 | 1,864 | 120 | ---- | ---- | ---- | ---- | 68 |
| Phillips_____ | 5,797 | 5,526 | 262 | ---- | 9 | ---- | 1 | ---- |
| Pitkin_____ | 1,770 | 1,374 | 391 | 3 | 1 | ---- | 1 | ---- |
| Prowers_____ | 14,762 | 12,883 | 374 | 46 | 15 | 3 | 5 | 1,436 |
| Pueblo_____ | 66,038 | 52,865 | 6,328 | 1,333 | 26 | 13 | 91 | 5,356 |
| Rio Blanco___ | 2,980 | 2,827 | 103 | 16 | ---- | ---- | ---- | 34 |
| Rio Grande___ | 9,953 | 9,284 | 232 | 4 | 1 | ---- | 2 | 430 |
| Routt_____ | 9,352 | 8,081 | 841 | 125 | 19 | ---- | 65 | 220 |
| Saguache_____ | 6,230 | 5,555 | 187 | 2 | ---- | ---- | 1 | 505 |
| San Juan_____ | 1,935 | 1,314 | 460 | 4 | 4 | ---- | ---- | 157 |
| San Miguel___ | 2,184 | 1,872 | 235 | 2 | 2 | ---- | ---- | 73 |
| Sedgwick_____ | 5,580 | 4,733 | 368 | 4 | ---- | ---- | 91 | 384 |
| Summit_____ | 987 | 856 | 124 | ---- | ---- | ---- | ---- | 7 |
| Teller_____ | 4,141 | 3,695 | 428 | 7 | ---- | ---- | ---- | 11 |
| Washington__ | 9,591 | 8,988 | 453 | 27 | ---- | ---- | 16 | 107 |
| Weld_____ | 65,097 | 49,221 | 6,204 | 111 | 19 | 1 | 712 | 8,792 |
| Yuma_____ | 13,613 | 13,190 | 387 | 2 | 2 | ---- | ---- | 32 |
| State_____ | 1,035,791 | 875,711 | 85,406 | 11,828 | 1,395 | 233 | 3,213 | 57,676 |

Note—To reach the total shown in the first column the following non-classified races, not shown in the table, must be added: Adams, 24; Alamosa, 2; Arapahoe, 15; Bent, 4; Boulder, 12; Chaffee, 1; Conejos, 19; Costilla, 12; Delta, 3; Denver, 97; Douglas, 1; Eagle, 7; El Paso, 9; Fremont, 1; Huerfano, 16; Jefferson, 1; Las Animas, 1; Montrose, 1; Otero, 39; Pueblo, 26; Routt, 1; Weld, 37; total, 329.

## COLORADO POPULATION STATISTICS, BY YEARS AND CLASSIFICATION
(Compiled from Federal Census Reports)

|  | 1930 | 1920 | 1910 | 1900 |
|---|---|---|---|---|
| Total Population................ | 1,035,791 | 939,629 | 799,024 | 539,700 |
| Number per square mile......... | 10.0 | 9.1 | 7.7 | 5.2 |
| Increase over preceding census: |  |  |  |  |
| Number ...................... | 96,162 | 140,605 | 259,324 | 126,451 |
| Per cent increase............. | 10.2 | 17.6 | 48.0 | 30.6 |
| Males ....................... | 530,752 | 492,731 | 430,697 | 368,327 |
| Females ..................... | 505,039 | 446,898 | 368,327 | 244,368 |
| Males to 100 females......... | 105.1 | 110.3 | 116.9 | 120.9 |
| Urban ....................... | 519,882 | 453,259 | 404,840 | 260,651 |
| Males ..................... | 254,319 | 229,374 | 206,805 | 134,267 |
| Females ................... | 265,563 | 223,885 | 198,035 | 126,384 |
| Rural ....................... | 515,909 | 486,370 | 394,184 | 279,049 |
| Males ..................... | 276,433 | 263,357 | 223,892 | 161,065 |
| Females ................... | 239,476 | 223,013 | 170,292 | 117,984 |
| Number illiterate (10 years, or more, age)................. | 23,141 | 24,208 | 23,780 | 17,779 |
| Per cent illiterate.............. | 2.8 | 3.2 | 3.7 | 4.2 |
| **Color and nativity:** |  |  |  |  |
| Native white.................. | 875,711 | 807,149 | 656,564 | 438,571 |
| Foreign-born White............ | 85,406 | *116,954 | 126,851 | 90,475 |
| Negro ....................... | 11,828 | 11,318 | 11,453 | 8,570 |
| Mexicans ................... | 57,676 | * | * | * |
| Indians .................... | 1,395 | 1,383 | 1,482 | 1,437 |
| Chinese .................... | 233 | 291 | 373 | 509 |
| Japanese ................... | 3,213 | 2,464 | 2,300 | 48 |
| All others.................. | 329 | 70 | 1 | 90 |
| **Population by age:** |  |  |  |  |
| Under 5 years................ | 95,670 | 97,058 | 82,562 | 56,999 |
| 5 to 9....................... | 104,780 | 95,086 | 75,616 | 57,277 |
| 10 to 14.................... | 98,940 | 89,214 | 69,688 | 48,871 |
| 15 to 19.................... | 95,132 | 78,632 | 71,045 | 45,014 |
| 20 to 24.................... | 86,913 | 78,338 | 79,050 | 49,600 |
| 25 to 29.................... | 77,310 | 78,905 | 78,885 | 51,335 |
| 30 to 34.................... | 74,191 | 74,825 | 69,313 | 49,938 |
| 35 to 44.................... | 146,667 | 134,428 | 116,508 | 85,691 |
| 45 to 54.................... | 115,665 | 100,424 | 83,259 | 50,889 |
| 55 to 64.................... | 78,035 | 64,002 | 44,022 | 25,890 |
| 65 to 74.................... | 45,073 | 30,049 | 20,158 | 10,621 |
| 75 and over................. | 16,714 | 11,014 | 6,569 | 3,025 |
| Unknown .................... | 701 | 7,654 | 2,349 | 4,550 |
| **Persons 10 years old and over engaged in gainful occupations:** |  |  |  |  |
| Number engaged.............. | 402,867 | 366,457 | 338,724 | 218,263 |
| Per cent of total population... | 28.9 | 39.0 | 42.4 | 40.4 |
| Males ...................... | 321,874 | 303,870 | 285,083 | 190,297 |
| Females ................... | 80,993 | 62,587 | 53,641 | 27,966 |
| **Families in Colorado:** |  |  |  |  |
| Number ..................... | 267,324 | 230,843 | 194,467 | 127,459 |
| Median size ................ | 3.17 | 4.1 | 4.1 | 4.2 |
| Urban ...................... | 141,338 | 112,380 | 97,456 | ...... |
| Rural ...................... | 125,986 | 118,463 | 97,011 | ...... |
| Number of dwellings........... | 242,548 | 211,103 | 183,874 | ...... |
| Homes owned ................ | 131,571 | 116,781 | 96,728 | 56,247 |
| Homes rented ............... | 127,979 | 109,501 | 90,929 | 64,529 |
| Tenure unknown ............. | 7,774 | 4,561 | 6,810 | 6,681 |
| Families having radio sets........ | 100,959 | ...... | ...... | ...... |
| Number of farms............. | 59,956 | 59,934 | 46,170 | 24,700 |
| **Marital conditions (persons 15 years or over):** |  |  |  |  |
| Males, number................ | 379,165 | 350,813 | 315,422 | 213,157 |
| Single ................... | 125,015 | 123,473 | 129,828 | 93,891 |
| Married .................. | 227,494 | 200,800 | 167,799 | 105,902 |
| Widowed ................. | 18,895 | 17,592 | 13,457 | 8,903 |
| Divorced ................. | 6,938 | 4,378 | 2,782 | 1,178 |
| Unknown ................. | 823 | 4,570 | 1,556 | 3,283 |
| Females, number.............. | 357,236 | 307,458 | 255,736 | 163,396 |
| Single ................... | 83,456 | 73,098 | 65,931 | 42,738 |
| Married .................. | 226,078 | 195,193 | 160,546 | 102,388 |
| Widowed ................. | 40,337 | 34,186 | 25,752 | 16,210 |
| Divorced ................. | 7,013 | 4,058 | 3,043 | 1,281 |
| Unknown ................. | 352 | 923 | 464 | 779 |

*Mexicans were not segregated in 1920. 1910 and 1900 and are included in the foreign-born white.

## POPULATION·OF·COLORADO BY COUNTIES

(Compiled from the Census Reports)

| COUNTY | Population | | | | Increase, 1920-1930* | |
|---|---|---|---|---|---|---|
| | 1930 | 1920 | 1910 | 1900 | Number | Per Cent |
| Adams[a][b][c]_____ | 20,245 | 14,430 | 8,892 | _____ | 5,815 | 40.3 |
| Alamosa[d]_____ | 8,602 | 5,148 | _____ | _____ | 3,454 | 67.1 |
| Arapahoe[a][b]_____ | 22,647 | 13,766 | 10,263 | 153,017 | 8,881 | 64.5 |
| Archuleta_____ | 3,204 | 3,590 | 3,302 | 2,117 | —386 | 10.8 |
| Baca_____ | 10,570 | 8,721 | 2,516 | 759 | 1,849 | 21.2 |
| Bent_____ | 9,134 | 9,705 | 5,043 | 3,049 | —571 | 5.9 |
| Boulder_____ | 32,456 | 31,861 | 30,330 | 21,544 | 595 | 1.9 |
| Chaffee_____ | 8,126 | 7,753 | 7,622 | 7,085 | 373 | 4.8 |
| Cheyenne_____ | 3,723 | 3,746 | 3,687 | 501 | —23 | —0.6 |
| Clear Creek_____ | 2,155 | 2,891 | 5,001 | 7,082 | —736 | —25.5 |
| Conejos[d]_____ | 9,803 | 8,416 | 11,285 | 8,794 | 1,387 | 16.5 |
| Costilla[d]_____ | 5,779 | 5,032 | 5,498 | 4,632 | 747 | 14.8 |
| Crowley[e]_____ | 5,934 | 6,383 | _____ | _____ | —449 | —7.0 |
| Custer_____ | 2,124 | 2,172 | 1,947 | 2,937 | —48 | —2.2 |
| Delta_____ | 14,204 | 13,668 | 13,688 | 5,487 | 536 | 3.9 |
| Denver[a][c]_____ | 287,861 | 256,491 | 213,381 | _____ | 31,370 | 12.2 |
| Dolores_____ | 1,412 | 1,243 | 642 | 1,134 | 169 | 13.6 |
| Douglas_____ | 3,498 | 3,517 | 3,192 | 3,120 | —19 | —0.5 |
| Eagle_____ | 3,924 | 3,385 | 2,985 | 3,008 | 539 | 15.9 |
| Elbert_____ | 6,580 | 6,980 | 5,331 | 3,101 | —400 | —5.7 |
| El Paso_____ | 49,570 | 44,027 | 43,321 | 31,602 | 5,543 | 12.6 |
| Fremont_____ | 18,896 | 17,883 | 18,181 | 15,636 | 1,013 | 5.7 |
| Garfield_____ | 9,975 | 9,304 | 10,144 | 5,835 | 671 | 7.2 |
| Gilpin_____ | 1,212 | 1,364 | 4,131 | 6,690 | —152 | —11.1 |
| Grand_____ | 2,108 | 2,659 | 1,862 | 741 | —551 | —20.7 |
| Gunnison_____ | 5,527 | 5,590 | 5,897 | 5,331 | —63 | —1.1 |
| Hinsdale_____ | 449 | 538 | 646 | 1,609 | —89 | —16.5 |
| Huerfano_____ | 17,062 | 16,879 | 13,320 | 8,395 | 183 | 1.1 |
| Jackson[f]_____ | 1,386 | 1,340 | 1,013 | _____ | 46 | 3.4 |
| Jefferson[g]_____ | 21,810 | 14,400 | 14,231 | 9,306 | 7,410 | 51.5 |
| Kiowa_____ | 3,786 | 3,755 | 2,899 | 701 | 31 | 0.8 |
| Kit Carson_____ | 9,725 | 8,915 | 7,483 | 1,580 | 810 | 9.1 |
| Lake_____ | 4,899 | 6,630 | 10,600 | 18,054 | —1,731 | —26.1 |
| La Plata_____ | 12,975 | 11,218 | 10,812 | 7,016 | 1,757 | 15.7 |
| Larimer[f]_____ | 33,137 | 27,872 | 25,270 | 12,168 | 5,265 | 18.9 |
| Las Animas_____ | 36,008 | 38,975 | 33,643 | 21,841 | —2,967 | —7.6 |
| Lincoln_____ | 7,850 | 8,273 | 5,917 | 926 | —423 | —5.1 |
| Logan_____ | 19,946 | 18,427 | 9,549 | 3,292 | 1,519 | 8.2 |
| Mesa_____ | 25,908 | 22,281 | 22,197 | 9,267 | 3,627 | 16.3 |
| Mineral_____ | 640 | 779 | 1,239 | 1,913 | —139 | —17.8 |
| Moffat[h]_____ | 4,861 | 5,129 | _____ | _____ | —268 | —5.2 |
| Montezuma_____ | 7,798 | 6,260 | 5,029 | 3,058 | 1,538 | 24.6 |
| Montrose_____ | 11,742 | 11,852 | 10,291 | 4,535 | —110 | —0.9 |
| Morgan_____ | 18,284 | 16,124 | 9,577 | 3,268 | 2,160 | 13.4 |
| Otero_____ | 24,390 | 22,623 | 20,201 | 11,522 | 1,767 | 7.8 |
| Ouray[j]_____ | 1,784 | 2,620 | 3,514 | 4,731 | —836 | —31.9 |
| Park[g]_____ | 2,052 | 1,977 | 2,492 | 2,998 | 75 | 3.8 |
| Phillips_____ | 5,797 | 5,499 | 3,179 | 1,583 | 298 | 5.4 |
| Pitkin_____ | 1,770 | 2,707 | 4,566 | 7,020 | —937 | —34.6 |
| Prowers_____ | 14,762 | 13,845 | 9,520 | 3,766 | 917 | 6.6 |
| Pueblo_____ | 66,038 | 57,638 | 52,223 | 34,448 | 8,400 | 14.6 |
| Rio Blanco_____ | 2,980 | 3,135 | 2,332 | 1,690 | —155 | —4.9 |
| Rio Grande_____ | 9,953 | 7,855 | 6,563 | 4,080 | 2,098 | 26.7 |
| Routt[h]_____ | 9,352 | 8,948 | 7,561 | 3,661 | 404 | 4.5 |
| Saguache_____ | 6,250 | 4,638 | 4,160 | 3,853 | 1,612 | 34.8 |
| San Juan_____ | 1,935 | 1,700 | 3,063 | 2,343 | 235 | 13.8 |
| San Miguel[j]_____ | 2,184 | 5,281 | 4,700 | 5,379 | —3,097 | —58.6 |
| Sedgwick_____ | 5,580 | 4,207 | 3,061 | 971 | 1,373 | 32.4 |
| Summit_____ | 987 | 1,724 | 2,003 | 2,744 | —737 | —42.7 |
| Teller_____ | 4,141 | 6,696 | 14,351 | 29,002 | —2,555 | —38.2 |
| Washington[b]_____ | 9,591 | 11,208 | 6,002 | 1,241 | —1,617 | —14.4 |
| Weld_____ | 65,097 | 54,059 | 39,177 | 16,808 | 11,038 | 20.4 |
| Yuma[b]_____ | 13,613 | 13,897 | 8,499 | 1,729 | —284 | —2.0 |
| State_____ | 1,035,791 | 939,629 | 799,024 | 539,700 | 96,162 | 10.2 |

*Minus sign (—) denotes decrease.
[a]Adams and Denver counties were organized from parts of Arapahoe county in 1902. Prior thereto Denver was in Arapahoe county.
[b]Parts of Adams and Arapahoe counties were annexed to Washington and Yuma counties in 1903.
[c]Part of Denver county was annexed to Adams county in 1909.
[d]Alamosa county was organized from parts of Conejos and Costilla counties in 1913.
[e]Crowley county was organized from part of Otero county in 1911.
[f]Jackson county was organized from part of Larimer county in 1909.
[g]Part of Jefferson county was annexed to Park county in 1908.
[h]Moffat county was organized from part of Routt county in 1911.
[j]Part of San Miguel county was annexed to Ouray county in 1917.

## DISTRIBUTION OF POPULATION AND PER CAPITA STATISTICS
(Based on the U. S. Census Bureau Population Report for 1930)

| COUNTY | Population | Area Square Miles | Population per Square Mile | Assessed Valuation per Capita, 1930 | Taxes Assessed per Capita, 1930 | Bank Deposits per Capita, 1930 |
|---|---|---|---|---|---|---|
| Adams .......... | 20,245 | 1,262 | 16.0 | $1,588.89 | $39.06 | $ 63.70 |
| Alamosa ........ | 8,602 | 727 | 11.8 | 1,162.20 | 42.40 | 21.72 |
| Arapahoe ....... | 22,647 | 842 | 26.9 | 1,038.40 | 32.65 | 90.93 |
| Archuleta ...... | 3,204 | 1,220 | 2.6 | 1,459.42 | 37.98 | 63.03 |
| Baca .......... | 10,570 | 2,552 | 4.1 | 1,266.77 | 35.57 | 69.24 |
| Bent ........... | 9,134 | 1,524 | 6.0 | 1,504.44 | 37.19 | 116.04 |
| Boulder ........ | 32,456 | 764 | 42.5 | 1,443.89 | 44.02 | 229.98 |
| Chaffee ........ | 8,126 | 1,083 | 7.5 | 1,179.26 | 40.28 | 228.69 |
| Cheyenne ....... | 3,723 | 1,777 | 2.1 | 3,703.83 | 68.25 | 71.92 |
| Clear Creek...... | 2,155 | 390 | 5.5 | 2,514.86 | 72.30 | 207.87 |
| Conejos ........ | 9,803 | 1,252 | 7.8 | 947.81 | 33.33 | 673.95 |
| Costilla ........ | 5,779 | 1,185 | 4.9 | 919.31 | 34.37 | 34.56 |
| Crowley ........ | 5,934 | 808 | 7.3 | 1,713.82 | 47.78 | 109.51 |
| Custer .......... | 2,124 | 747 | 2.8 | 1,438.72 | 40.43 | 110.07 |
| Delta .......... | 14,204 | 1,201 | 11.8 | 1,061.62 | 42.72 | 134.25 |
| Denver ......... | 287,861 | 58 | 4,963.2 | 1,592.05 | 51.60 | 237.32 |
| Dolores ........ | 1,412 | 1,030 | 1.4 | 1,292.57 | 50.00 | ..... |
| Douglas ........ | 3,498 | 845 | 4.1 | 3,282.21 | 63.40 | 154.61 |
| Eagle .......... | 3,924 | 1,620 | 2.4 | 1,828.90 | 55.26 | 116.88 |
| Elbert ......... | 6,580 | 1,857 | 3.5 | 2,691.27 | 56.74 | 140.40 |
| El Paso......... | 49,570 | 2,121 | 23.4 | 1,524.78 | 53.21 | 397.92 |
| Fremont ....... | 18,896 | 1,557 | 12.1 | 1,237.20 | 39.97 | 225.36 |
| Garfield......... | 9,975 | 3,107 | 3.2 | 1,811.38 | 68.52 | 273.38 |
| Gilpin ......... | 1,212 | 132 | 9.2 | 2,374.39 | 71.77 | 208.92 |
| Grand ......... | 2,108 | 1,866 | 1.1 | 2,759.18 | 64.60 | 209.10 |
| Gunnison ...... | 5,527 | 3,179 | 1.7 | 2,879.90 | 71.94 | 298.28 |
| Hinsdale ....... | 449 | 971 | 0.5 | 2,240.22 | 105.08 | ..... |
| Huerfano ....... | 17,062 | 1,500 | 11.4 | 973.27 | 34.69 | 149.64 |
| Jackson ........ | 1,386 | 1,632 | 0.8 | 2,816.56 | 45.74 | ..... |
| Jefferson ....... | 21,810 | 808 | 27.0 | 1,274.50 | 36.65 | 62.92 |
| Kiowa ......... | 3,786 | 1,798 | 2.1 | 3,491.83 | 59.79 | 100.04 |
| Kit Carson....... | 9,725 | 2,159 | 4.5 | 2,189.81 | 57.17 | 93.67 |
| Lake .......... | 4,899 | 371 | 13.2 | 1,552.12 | 57.19 | 239.60 |
| La Plata........ | 12,975 | 1,851 | 7.0 | 1,194.70 | 41.23 | 199.33 |
| Larimer ........ | 33,137 | 2,629 | 12.6 | 1,614.06 | 50.15 | 187.57 |
| Las Animas...... | 36,008 | 4,809 | 7.5 | 1,165.17 | 39.30 | 212.00 |
| Lincoln ........ | 7,850 | 2,570 | 3.1 | 2,599.49 | 64.17 | 102.02 |
| Logan ......... | 19,946 | 1,822 | 10.9 | 1,850.79 | 53.96 | 116.50 |
| Mesa .......... | 25,908 | 3,163 | 8.2 | 1,166.65 | 39.70 | 158.66 |
| Mineral ........ | 640 | 866 | 0.7 | 2,446.31 | 54.84 | ..... |
| Moffat ......... | 4,861 | 4,658 | 1.0 | 1,515.11 | 51.49 | 128.58 |
| Montezuma ...... | 7,798 | 2,051 | 3.8 | 841.78 | 31.76 | 161.84 |
| Montrose ....... | 11,742 | 2,264 | 5.2 | 1,048.75 | 41.25 | 180.71 |
| Morgan ......... | 18,284 | 1,286 | 14.2 | 1,591.62 | 45.33 | 163.79 |
| Otero ......... | 24,390 | 1,259 | 19.4 | 1,324.34 | 38.86 | 113.07 |
| Ouray ......... | 1,784 | 519 | 3.4 | 2,290.38 | 74.77 | 171.41 |
| Park .......... | 2,052 | 2,242 | 0.9 | 4,339.42 | 71.65 | 109.70 |
| Phillips ........ | 5,797 | 688 | 8.4 | 2,662.74 | 54.74 | 215.82 |
| Pitkin ........ | 1,770 | 1,019 | 1.7 | 2,224.95 | 78.27 | 210.58 |
| Prowers ........ | 14,762 | 1,630 | 9.1 | 1,487.75 | 44.60 | 120.69 |
| Pueblo ......... | 66,038 | 2,433 | 27.1 | 1,233.38 | 47.25 | 398.04 |
| Rio Blanco....... | 2,980 | 3,223 | 0.9 | 1,999.39 | 54.31 | 239.08 |
| Rio Grande...... | 9,953 | 898 | 11.1 | 1,099.36 | 44.72 | 189.47 |
| Routt .......... | 9,352 | 2,309 | 4.1 | 1,701.02 | 50.30 | 105.86 |
| Saguache ....... | 6,250 | 3,133 | 2.0 | 1,836.46 | 48.48 | 129.25 |
| San Juan........ | 1,935 | 453 | 4.3 | 1,777.81 | 50.51 | 266.22 |
| San Miguel...... | 2,184 | 1,301 | 1.7 | 2,490.53 | 88.95 | ..... |
| Sedgwick ....... | 5,580 | 531 | 10.5 | 2,379.51 | 70.76 | 115.76 |
| Summit ......... | 987 | 649 | 1.5 | 4,700.25 | 120.27 | 115.19 |
| Teller ......... | 4,141 | 547 | 7.6 | 1,370.34 | 56.74 | 449.32 |
| Washington ..... | 9,591 | 2,521 | 3.8 | 1,798.05 | 48.02 | 56.26 |
| Weld .......... | 65,097 | 4,022 | 16.2 | 1,616.09 | 49.82 | 151.20 |
| Yuma .......... | 13,613 | 2,367 | 5.8 | 1,840.80 | 48.83 | 135.44 |
| State........ | 1,035,791 | 103,658 | 10.0 | $1,538.34 | $47.95 | $202.74 |

## COLORADO COUNTIES AND COUNTY SEATS

| COUNTY | County Seat | Railway Dist'ce from Denver, Miles | Population of County Seat | | |
|---|---|---|---|---|---|
| | | | Census 1930 | Census 1920 | Census 1910 |
| Adams......... | Brighton ........... | 19 | 3,394 | 2,715 | 850 |
| Alamosa........ | Alamosa ........... | 251 | 5,107 | 3,171 | 3,013 |
| Arapahoe....... | Littleton .......... | 10 | 2,019 | 1,636 | 1,373 |
| Archuleta...... | Pagosa Springs...... | 421 | 804 | 1,032 | 669 |
| Baca........... | Springfield‡ ........ | 285 | 1,393 | 295 | ...... |
| Bent.......... | Las Animas......... | 202 | 2,517 | 2,252 | 2,008 |
| Boulder........ | Boulder ........... | 30 | 11,223 | 11,006 | 9,539 |
| Chaffee........ | Salida ............ | 215 | 5,065 | 4,689 | 4,425 |
| Cheyenne...... | Cheyenne Wells...... | 177 | 595 | 508 | 270 |
| Clear Creek..... | Georgetown ........ | 50 | 303 | 703 | 950 |
| Conejos....... | Conejos ........... | 281 | £ | 350 | ...... |
| Costilla........ | San Luis£.......... | 248 | £ | 550 | ...... |
| Crowley....... | Ordway ........... | 169 | 1,139 | 1,186 | 705 |
| Custer........ | Silver Cliff.......... | 209 | 201 | 241 | 250 |
| Delta.......... | Delta ............. | 372 | 2,938 | 2,623 | 2,388 |
| Denver........ | Denver ............ | ... | 287,861 | 256,491 | 213,381 |
| Dolores....... | Rico ............. | 443 | 447 | 326 | 368 |
| Douglas........ | Castle Rock........ | 32 | 478 | 461 | 365 |
| Eagle......... | Eagle ............. | 329 | 341 | 358 | 186 |
| Elbert........ | Kiowa* ............ | 46 | 185 | 148 | ...... |
| El Paso........ | Colorado Springs..... | 75 | 33,237 | 30,105 | 29,078 |
| Fremont....... | Canon City.......... | 160 | 5,938 | †6,386 | 5,162 |
| Garfield........ | Glenwood Springs.... | 360 | 1,825 | 2,073 | 2,019 |
| Gilpin........ | Central City........ | 45 | 572 | 552 | 1,782 |
| Grand......... | Hot Sulphur Springs.. | 86° | 142 | 123 | 182 |
| Gunnison...... | Gunnison .......... | 288 | 1,415 | 1,329 | 1,026 |
| Hinsdale....... | Lake City.......... | 351 | 259 | 317 | 405 |
| Huerfano....... | Walsenburg ........ | 171 | 5,503 | 3,565 | 2,323 |
| Jackson........ | Walden ........... | 256 | 284 | 260 | 162 |
| Jefferson....... | Golden ............ | 16 | 2,426 | 2,135 | 2,477 |
| Kiowa......... | Eads ............. | 230 | 518 | 406 | ...... |
| Kit Carson..... | Burlington ......... | 167 | 1,280 | 991 | 368 |
| Lake.......... | Leadville .......... | 276 | 3,771 | 4,959 | 1,508 |
| La Plata....... | Durango ........... | 451 | 5,400 | 4,116 | 4,686 |
| Larimer........ | Fort Collins........ | 68 | 11,489 | 8,755 | 8,210 |
| Las Animas..... | Trinidad ........... | 212 | 11,732 | 10,906 | 10,204 |
| Lincoln........ | Hugo ............. | 104 | 712 | 838 | 343 |
| Logan......... | Sterling ........... | 123 | 7,195 | 6,415 | 3,044 |
| Mesa.......... | Grand Junction....... | 424 | 10,247 | 8,665 | 7,754 |
| Mineral........ | Creede ............ | 321 | 384 | 500 | 741 |
| Moffat........ | Craig ............. | 232° | 1,418 | 1,297 | 392 |
| Montezuma..... | Cortez ............ | 506 | 921 | 541 | 565 |
| Montrose....... | Montrose .......... | 351 | 3,566 | 3,581 | 3,254 |
| Morgan........ | Fort Morgan........ | 78 | 4,423 | 3,818 | 2,800 |
| Otero......... | La Junta........... | 183 | 7,193 | 4,964 | 4,154 |
| Ouray......... | Ouray ............ | 387 | 707 | 1,165 | 1,644 |
| Park.......... | Fairplay ........... | 115 | 221 | 183 | 265 |
| Phillips........ | Holyoke ........... | 173 | 1,226 | 1,205 | 659 |
| Pitkin........ | Aspen ............ | 401 | 705 | 1,265 | 1,834 |
| Prowers....... | Lamar ............ | 235 | 4,233 | 2,512 | 2,977 |
| Pueblo........ | Pueblo ............ | 119 | 50,096 | 43,050 | 44,395 |
| Rio Blanco..... | Meeker* ........... | 295 | 1,069 | 935 | 807 |
| Rio Grande..... | Del Norte........... | 283 | 1,410 | 1,007 | 840 |
| Routt......... | Steamboat Springs.... | 177° | 1,198 | 1,249 | 1,227 |
| Saguache....... | Saguache* .......... | 265 | 1,010 | 948 | 620 |
| San Juan....... | Silverton .......... | 497 | 1,301 | 1,150 | 2,153 |
| San Miguel..... | Telluride .......... | 422 | 512 | 1,618 | 1,756 |
| Sedgwick....... | Julesburg .......... | 197 | 1,467 | 1,320 | 962 |
| Summit........ | Breckenridge ....... | 110 | 436 | 796 | 834 |
| Teller......... | Cripple Creek........ | 132 | 1,427 | 2,325 | 6,206 |
| Washington.... | Akron ............ | 112 | 1,135 | 1,401 | 647 |
| Weld.......... | Greeley ........... | 52 | 12,203 | 10,958 | 8,179 |
| Yuma......... | Wray ............. | 165 | 1,785 | 1,538 | 1,000 |

* Not directly on railroad.   † Greater Canon City.   ‡ Via Lamar.   Does not have direct rail communication with Denver.   ° Via Moffat tunnel.   £ Not incorporated.

# Persons Engaged in Gainful Occupations

THERE were 402,867 persons 10 years old or more engaged in gainful occupations in Colorado in 1930 as reported by the United States bureau of the census. The term "gainful workers," in census usage, includes all persons who usually follow a gainful occupation, although they may not have been employed when the census was taken. It does not include women doing housework in their own homes, without wages, and having no other employment, or children working at home, merely on general household work, on chores, or at odd times on other work.

The number reported above comprises 38.9 per cent of the total population of 1,035,791 and 48.2 per cent of the 835,341 persons 10 years old and over in 1930. In the seven census years from 1870 to 1930, inclusive, the percentage of persons gainfully occupied has shown a decrease. In 1870, 44.1 per cent of the total population was gainfully employed as against 38.9 per cent in 1930. The percentage in 1930 was the lowest of any in the seven census years. The highest was in 1880 when 52.1 per cent of the total population was gainfully occupied. Relatively the same fluctuations took place in the seven census years in percentages of population 10 years old or over gainfully occupied.

Contrary to the general trend of occupation statistics of both males and females in the seven census years, the percentages of females gainfully occupied have shown increases. There were 505,039 females in Colorado in 1930, of whom 405,843 were 10 years old or over. There were 80,993 of the latter gainfully occupied in 1930. This was equal to 16.0 per cent of the total female population and 20.0 per cent of the female population 10 years old or over. In 1870 only 2.9 per cent of the total female population was gainfully occupied as against 16.0 per cent in 1930 and 4.2 per cent of those 10 years old or over against 20.0 per cent. In 1870, the percentage of the male population 10 years old or over gainfully occupied was 86.0. The general trend in each census year was downward until the lowest per cent, 74.9, was reached in 1930. A chart presented herewith shows the trend of percentages in the census years for male, female and total population. A table also gives the number and per-

centages by census years. Another chart shows the distribution of workers by occupations.

Colorado Springs is the only one of the three cities in the state with a population of 25,000 or more which showed an increase in 1930 over 1920 in the per cent of persons 10 years old or over gainfully occupied. Its percentage was 47.7 as against 45.8 per cent in 1920. Denver reported 53.2 per cent gainfully occupied in 1930 as against 54.0 per cent in 1920, and Pueblo showed 46.9 per cent in 1930 as compared with 50.7 per cent in 1920. All three cities showed increases in the percentage of females gainfully occupied and decreases in the percentage of males.

Agriculture, with 106,068 persons, or 26.3 per cent of the number in the state 10 years old or more gainfully occupied, ranked first among the occupations. The manufacturing and mechanical industries ranked second with 76,-734, or 19.0 per cent, and trade ranked third with 54,757, or 13.6 per cent. Domestic and personal service, in which 41,250, or 10.2 per cent of all gainfully occupied were engaged, ranked fourth. Professional service, including lawyers, doctors, actors, artists, writers, etc., ranked sixth with 33,492, or 8.3 per cent, and just below transportation and communication, which ranked fifth in the number gainfully occupied.

The classification of gainful workers is distributed by the census bureau among 534 occupations. These reports are too elaborate for reproduction here, but are available for all interested in the details and may be found in public libraries. A summary of the number of gainful workers in general divisions of occupations in the state and the three largest cities is published herewith. A further distribution of gainful workers in various occupations will be found in separate chapters in this volume in connection with discussions of different industries.

Of 402,867 persons 10 years old or more gainfully occupied in 1930, 330,-813, or 82.1 per cent, were native white; 46,501, or 11.5 per cent, were foreign-born white; 6,220, or 1.5 per cent, were negroes; and 19,333, or 4.8 per cent, were of other races. The largest number, or 13.3 per cent of those gainfully occupied, were 20 to 24 years old and the second largest number, or 11.7 per cent, were 25 to 29 years old. There were 16,714 persons 75 years old or more gainfully occupied.

Of 80,617 women 15 years old or over gainfully occupied in 1930, there were 54,716, or 67.9 per cent, single, widowed, divorced or unknown, and 25,901, or 32.1 per cent, married. Compared with 1920, when 76 per cent of the women gainfully employed were single, widowed, divorced, or unknown, and 23.3 per cent were married, the percentage of married female gainful workers showed an increase and the percentage of the other classification showed a decrease.

Only 3.1 per cent of the children 10 to 15 years old were gainfully occupied in 1930, which compares with 4.3 per cent in 1920, 7.1 per cent in 1910 and 6.0 per cent in 1900.

## STATE CONSTITUTIONAL CONVENTION

The enabling act, an act of congress authorizing the inhabitants of the territory of Colorado to form for themselves out of the territory a state government which should be admitted to the Union on an equal footing with the original thirteen states, became a law on March 3, 1875. The constitutional convention elected by the people under the provisions of that act, composed of 38 members, held its first meeting in Denver on December 20, 1875. J. C. Wilson was elected president of the convention, and W. W. Coulson, secretary. The constitution was approved and signed by the convention on Tuesday, March 14, 1876, and ratified by the voters on July 1, 1876. The proclamation admitting Colorado into the Union was signed by President U. S. Grant on August 1, 1876.

A measure providing for the calling of a constitutional convention to prepare a new constitution to be submitted to the electorate was voted upon at the general election on November 4, 1930, and was defeated by a vote of 93,879 for and 97,826 against the proposal.

**PERSONS GAINFULLY OCCUPIED, NUMBER, PROPORTION AND SEX, FOR COLORADO BY YEARS**

(From Reports of U. S. Bureau of the Census)

| Census Year | Total Population | Population 10 Years Old and Over | PERSONS 10 YEARS OLD AND OVER GAINFULLY OCCUPIED | | |
|---|---|---|---|---|---|
| | | | Number | Per Cent of Total Population | Per Cent of Population 10 Years Old and Over |
| **Male:** | | | | | |
| 1870 .............. | 24,820 | 19,931 | 17,147 | 69.1 | 86.0 |
| 1880 .............. | 129,131 | 110,896 | 96,472 | 74.7 | 87.0 |
| 1890 .............. | 245,247 | 202,719 | 173,291 | 70.7 | 85.5 |
| 1900 .............. | 295,332 | 237,665 | 190,297 | 64.4 | 80.1 |
| 1910 .............. | 430,697 | 350,684 | 285,083 | 66.2 | 81.3 |
| 1920 .............. | 492,731 | 395,632 | 303,870 | 61.7 | 76.8 |
| 1930 .............. | 530,752 | 429,498 | 321,874 | 60.6 | 74.9 |
| **Female:** | | | | | |
| 1870 .............. | 15,044 | 10,418 | 436 | 2.9 | 4.2 |
| 1880 .............. | 65,196 | 47,324 | 4,779 | 7.3 | 10.1 |
| 1890 .............. | 166,951 | 125,177 | 19,147 | 11.5 | 15.3 |
| 1900 .............. | 244,368 | 187,759 | 27,966 | 11.4 | 14.9 |
| 1910 .............. | 368,327 | 290,162 | 53,641 | 14.6 | 18.5 |
| 1920 .............. | 446,898 | 351,853 | 62,587 | 14.0 | 17.8 |
| 1930 .............. | 505,039 | 405,843 | 80,993 | 16.0 | 20.0 |
| **Total:** | | | | | |
| 1870 .............. | 39,864 | 30,349 | 17,583 | 44.1 | 57.9 |
| 1880 .............. | 194,327 | 158,220 | 101,251 | 52.1 | 64.0 |
| 1890 .............. | 412,198 | 327,896 | 192,438 | 46.7 | 58.7 |
| 1900 .............. | 539,700 | 425,424 | 218,263 | 40.4 | 51.3 |
| 1910 .............. | 799,024 | 640,846 | 338,724 | 42.4 | 52.9 |
| 1920 .............. | 939,629 | 747,485 | 366,457 | 39.0 | 49.0 |
| 1930 .............. | 1,035,791 | 835,341 | 402,867 | 38.9 | 48.2 |

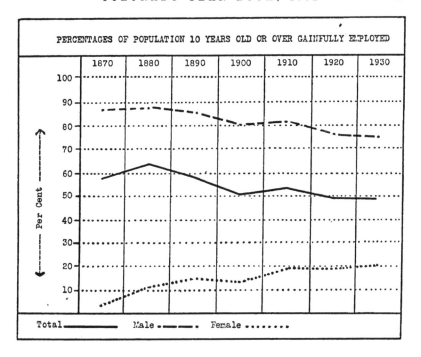

PERCENTAGES OF POPULATION 10 YEARS OLD OR OVER GAINFULLY EMPLOYED

Total———— Male —— Female ........

### GAINFUL WORKERS 10 YEARS OLD AND OVER, BY GENERAL DIVISIONS OF OCCUPATION, FOR DENVER, COLORADO SPRINGS, PUEBLO AND FOR THE STATE, 1930

(Compiled from Census Reports)

| OCCUPATIONS | Denver | Colorado Springs | Pueblo | All Other | Total State |
|---|---|---|---|---|---|
| Agriculture .................. | 2,633 | 385 | 352 | 102,698 | 106,068 |
| Forestry and fishing.......... | 83 | 30 | 3 | 1,134 | 1,250 |
| Extraction of minerals ........ | 1,070 | 319 | 90 | 16,009 | 17,488 |
| Manufacturing and mechanical industries ................ | 33,558 | 3,049 | 7,082 | 33,045 | 76,734 |
| Transportation and communication ...................... | 12,164 | 1,247 | 2,354 | 19,109 | 34,874 |
| Trade ..................... | 26,533 | 2,739 | 3,231 | 22,254 | 54,757 |
| Public service (not elsewhere classified) ................ | 2,483 | 241 | 353 | 3,621 | 6,698 |
| Professional service .......... | 13,115 | 1,766 | 1,822 | 16,789 | 33,492 |
| Domestic and personal service. | 19,551 | 2,572 | 2,280 | 16,847 | 41,250 |
| Clerical occupations .......... | 19,195 | 1,322 | 1,790 | 7,949 | 30,256 |
| Totals ................. | 130,385 | 13,670 | 19,357 | 239,455 | 402,867 |

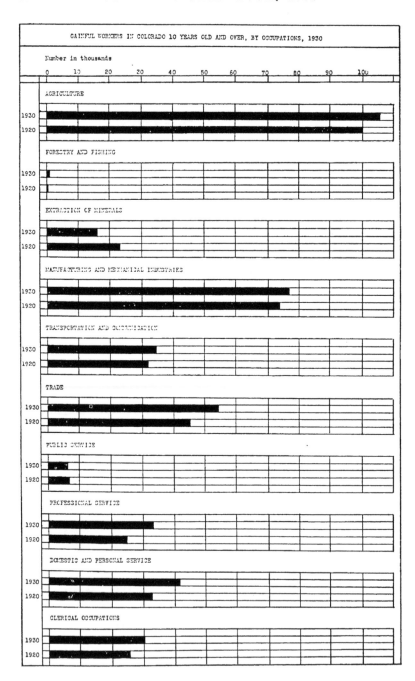

GAINFUL WORKERS IN COLORADO 10 YEARS OLD AND OVER, BY OCCUPATIONS, 1930

## PERSONS ENGAGED IN PROFESSIONAL SERVICES IN COLORADO AND DENVER, 1930

(Compiled from Census Reports on Occupational Statistics of Gainful Workers)

| OCCUPATION | State | | | Denver | | |
|---|---|---|---|---|---|---|
| | Male | Female | Total | Male | Female | Total |
| Actors and showmen....... | 375 | 115 | 490 | 178 | 89 | 267 |
| Architects ............... | 118 | 5 | 123 | 91 | 4 | 95 |
| Artists, sculptors and teachers of art............. | 212 | 219 | 431 | 148 | 144 | 292 |
| Authors, editors and reporters ............... | 413 | 243 | 656 | 181 | 102 | 283 |
| Authors ................ | 62 | 93 | 155 | 38 | 63 | 101 |
| Editors and reporters.... | 351 | 150 | 501 | 143 | 39 | 182 |
| Chemists, assayers and metallurgists ........... | 418 | 12 | 430 | 161 | 8 | 169 |
| Clergymen ............... | 1,290 | 52 | 1,342 | 374 | 14 | 388 |
| College presidents and professors ............... | 511 | 223 | 734 | 119 | 62 | 181 |
| Dentists ................. | 753 | 7 | 760 | 398 | 7 | 405 |
| Designers, draftsmen and inventors ............ | 434 | 31 | 465 | 328 | 22 | 350 |
| Designers ............. | 30 | 20 | 50 | 23 | 16 | 39 |
| Draftsmen ............. | 377 | 11 | 388 | 286 | 6 | 292 |
| Inventors .............. | 27 | .. | 27 | 19 | .. | 19 |
| Lawyers, judges and justices ................ | 1,542 | 21 | 1,563 | 881 | 16 | 897 |
| Musicians and teachers of music ................ | 750 | 1,023 | 1,773 | 447 | 448 | 895 |
| Osteopaths ............... | 77 | 28 | 105 | 32 | 7 | 39 |
| Photographers ............ | 290 | 176 | 466 | 132 | 89 | 221 |
| Physicians and surgeons... | 1,610 | 92 | 1,702 | 750 | 61 | 811 |
| Teachers ................ | 2,022 | 9,535 | 11,557 | 386 | 2,402 | 2,788 |
| Teachers (athletic, dancing, etc.)............ | 112 | 105 | 217 | 51 | 83 | 134 |
| Teachers (school) ....... | 1,910 | 9,430 | 11,340 | 335 | 2,319 | 2,654 |
| Technical engineers ...... | 2,190 | 1 | 2,191 | 1,263 | .. | 1,263 |
| Civil engineers and surveyors ............... | 968 | 1 | 969 | 520 | .. | 520 |
| Electrical engineers ..... | 478 | .. | 478 | 311 | .. | 311 |
| Mechanical engineers.... | 325 | .. | 325 | 220 | .. | 220 |
| Mining engineers ........ | 419 | .. | 419 | 212 | .. | 212 |
| Trained nurses ........... | 43 | 2,885 | 2,928 | 14 | 1,357 | 1,371 |
| Veterinary surgeons ....... | 132 | .. | 132 | 33 | .. | 33 |
| Totals ............... | 18,239 | 24,478 | 42,717 | 8,074 | 7,358 | 15,432 |

## PERSONS ENGAGED IN PROFESSIONAL SERVICES IN COLORADO SPRINGS AND PUEBLO, 1930

(Compiled from Census Reports on Occupational Statistics of Gainful Workers)

| OCCUPATION | Colorado Springs | | | Pueblo | | |
|---|---|---|---|---|---|---|
| | Male | Female | Total | Male | Female | Total |
| Actors and showmen ...... | 18 | 3 | 21 | 31 | 3 | 34 |
| Architects ............... | 8 | .. | 8 | 3 | .. | 3 |
| Artists, sculptors and teachers of art............. | 20 | 17 | 37 | 5 | 4 | 9 |
| Authors, editors and reporters ............... | 19 | 9 | 28 | 23 | 5 | 28 |
| Chemists, assayers and metallurgists ............ | 9 | 1 | 10 | 34 | .. | 34 |
| Clergymen ............... | 74 | 3 | 77 | 70 | 4 | 74 |
| College presidents and professors ............... | 39 | 18 | 57 | 1 | 3 | 4 |
| Dentists ................. | 34 | .. | 34 | 41 | .. | 41 |
| Designers, draftsmen and inventors ............ | 12 | 3 | 15 | 25 | 3 | 28 |
| Lawyers, judges and justices ................ | 64 | .. | 64 | 68 | 1 | 69 |
| Musicians and teachers of music ................ | 45 | 66 | 111 | 52 | 58 | 110 |
| Osteopaths ............... | 6 | 3 | 9 | 4 | 1 | 5 |
| Photographers ............ | 21 | 10 | 31 | 13 | 15 | 28 |
| Physicians and surgeons... | 87 | 1 | 88 | 78 | 3 | 81 |
| Teachers ................. | 93 | 397 | 490 | 69 | 498 | 567 |
| Technical engineers........ | 75 | .. | 75 | 109 | .. | 109 |
| Trained nurses ........... | 4 | 281 | 285 | 4 | 134 | 138 |
| Veterinary surgeons....... | 1 | .. | 1 | 5 | .. | 5 |
| Totals ............... | 629 | 812 | 1,441 | 635 | 732 | 1,367 |

## Movement of Population from and to Farm and City

INFORMATION relative to the movement of population as affecting the farm population was sought for the first time at the census of 1930, through two questions which appeared on the general farm schedule, as follows:

1. How many persons make their home on this farm who have moved here from a city, village or other incorporated place during the last twelve months?

2. How many persons who now make their home in a city, village or other incorporated place have moved there from this farm during the last twelve months?

Movements of students, persons on a visit and laborers staying on the farm only a short time were omitted in the replies.

There were 4,089 farms reporting movement of persons from the city to the farm between April 1, 1929, and March 31, 1930, in Colorado, the number of persons being 12,188. For the same period 2,585 farms reported 7,317 persons moving from the farm to the city.

### CHURCH POPULATION

Colorado has 77 religious bodies, or congregations, with 1,688 organizations, or churches, reporting 352,863 members according to the last church census taken by the United States bureau of the census, in 1926. This compares with 69 religious bodies with 1,455 organizations and 257,977 members in 1916. In 1926 there were 1,383 churches reporting church edifices with a value of $22,713,155, which compares with 1,144 church edifices valued at $10,010,432 in 1916.

The Roman Catholic church, the largest congregation in the United States, as well as in the world, also leads in Colorado with a membership of 125,757 reported in 1926. This was equal to 35.6 per cent of the membership of all congregations. The Methodists were second with a membership of 52,398 for all bodies of that denomination, or 14.8 per cent of the total, and Presbyterians were third with a membership of 29,833 for all branches, or 8.5 per cent of the total.

The church population of the state in 1926 was distributed as follows:

| Denomination | Churches | Members |
|---|---|---|
| Adventists, Seventh Day.. | 63 | 3,169 |
| Assembly of God......... | 11 | 817 |
| Baptists: | | |
|   Northern Baptists...... | 122 | 24,166 |
|   Negro Baptists......... | 15 | 2,298 |
| Brethren: | | |
|   Church of the Brethren. | 12 | 1,427 |
|   Plymouth Brethren II.. | 6 | 152 |
| Church of Christ Scientists | 41 | 2,948 |
| Church of God........... | 18 | 599 |
| Church of God in Christ.. | 14 | 394 |
| Church of the Nazarene... | 39 | 1,728 |
| Church of Christ......... | 26 | 1,477 |
| Congregational Church.... | 91 | 13,561 |
| Disciples of Christ........ | 75 | 17,759 |
| Russian Orthodox Church. | 3 | 531 |
| Evangelical Church....... | 28 | 2,306 |
| Evangelical Synod of N. A. | 15 | 2,305 |
| Pillar of Fire............ | 7 | 474 |
| Free Church of God in Christ ................. | 6 | 184 |
| Friends, Society of....... | 18 | 1,031 |
| Independent Churches .... | 6 | 231 |
| Jewish Congregations..... | 22 | 18,950 |
| Church of Jesus Christ of Latter Day Saints...... | 24 | 5,807 |
| Reorganized Church of Jesus Christ of Latter Day Saints............. | 14 | 1,373 |
| Lutherans (seven branches) | 131 | 17,133 |
| Mennonites .............. | 5 | 400 |
| Methodists: | | |
|   M. E. Episcopal......... | 217 | 46,974 |
|   M. E. Episcopal, South.. | 30 | 2,787 |
|   Free Methodist of N. A.. | 19 | 442 |
|   African M. E......... | 13 | 2,195 |
| Pilgrims Holiness ........ | 18 | 384 |
| Presbyterian: | | |
|   Presbyterian Church in U. S. of A............ | 132 | 27,090 |
|   United Presbyterian of N. A................. | 10 | 2,467 |
|   Reformed Presbyterian. | 3 | 276 |
| Protestant Episcopal..... | 82 | 13,663 |
| Reformed Christian....... | 3 | 994 |
| Roman Catholic .......... | 253 | 125,757 |
| Salvation Army .......... | 17 | 1,197 |
| Scandinavian Evangelical (two branches)......... | 8 | 737 |
| Spiritualists: | | |
|   National Spiritual Ass'n | 8 | 418 |
| American Theosophical Society .............. | 3 | 86 |
| Unitarians .............. | 3 | 450 |
| United Brethren, Church of | 18 | 2,446 |
| All other denominations.. | 39 | 3,280 |
| Totals ................ | 1,688 | 352,863 |

An accompanying table gives a summary of items as reported by the census bureau for the two years. In this table the value of church edifices represents the value of the buildings together with the land on which they stand and all furniture, organs, bells and furnishings owned by the churches and actually used in connection with church services.

Under expenditures are included running expenses, improvements, the pastor's salary, payments on debt and money actually paid for new buildings. It also includes the amount expended for benevolences, home and foreign missions, for denominational support, and all other purposes.

The data shown for Sunday schools represent Sunday schools conducted by the churches of the different denominations and do not include undenominational or union Sunday schools. These data relate entirely to what is known as the Sunday school and do not cover parochial schools, week-day religious schools, or other schools which supplement or sometimes take the place of the Sunday school.

The report for 1916 included statistics for 69 denominations, 13 of which are not shown in the 1926 census. Some have joined other denominations and their statistics are included with them, others are out of existence, etc. There are 21 denominations shown in the 1926 census not reported in 1916. All of them are not new, however, as a number were created by divisions in denominations which were shown as units in 1916.

### SUMMARY OF CHURCH STATISTICS FOR COLORADO

| Item | 1926 | 1916 |
|---|---|---|
| Churches (local organizations)................... | 1,688 | 1,455 |
| Members ........................................ | 352,863 | 257,977 |
| Male ...................................... | 140,868 | 97,650 |
| Female .................................... | 179,263 | 126,943 |
| Sex not reported............................ | 32,732 | 33,384 |
| Church edifices: | | |
| Number ................................... | 1,383 | 1,162 |
| Value: | | |
| Churches reporting ...................... | 1,326 | 1,144 |
| Amount reported ........................ | $22,713,155 | $10,010,432 |
| Debt: | | |
| Churches reporting ...................... | 448 | 386 |
| Amount reported ........................ | $3,248,309 | $1,166,917 |
| Parsonages: | | |
| Value: | | |
| Churches reporting ...................... | 706 | 510 |
| Amount reported ........................ | $2,957,404 | $1,289,528 |
| Expenditures during year: | | |
| Churches reporting ......................... | 1,563 | 1,281 |
| Amount reported ........................... | $5,837,497 | $2,427,365 |
| Sunday schools: | | |
| Churches reporting ......................... | 1,295 | 1,216 |
| Officers and teachers....................... | 17,325 | 14,181 |
| Pupils .................................... | 163,692 | 139,406 |

## INDIAN POPULATION

The territory embraced in what is now the state of Colorado was at one time inhabited by numerous tribes of Indians, but at the present time the Indian population is comparatively small and is confined mostly to the Ute Mountain Utes and Southern Utes reservations in the southwestern corner of the state. The two reservations are directed as a single unit known as the Consolidated Ute agency, with headquarters at Ignacio.

On April 1, 1931, including only those persons of Indian blood who through wardship, treaty or inheritance have acquired certain rights, the Indian population consisted of 807, of which 421 were males and 386 were females, or less than one-half of one per cent of the Indian population of the United States. The population changes slightly and the figures for 1931 represent an increase of only 17 compared with the number on June 30, 1926. The

census bureau defines an Indian as a person having Indian blood to such an extent as to be recognized in his community as an Indian. The Indian population of the state in 1930, as reported by the census under this definition, was 1,395, of which 843 were in La Plata and Montezuma counties, the others being scattered among 37 counties.

The government conducts two schools for the Indians in the agency, one of which is at Ute Mountain and the other at Ignacio. These schools have accommodations for 275 students and the highest grade taught is the sixth.

The total value of the Indian property as of June 30, 1927, was $3,247,917, of which $679,091 was individual property of the Indians and $2,568,826 was tribal property. Funds in bank or in the hands of superintendents for individuals totaled $155,091 and the tribal property included $868,826 in the treasury.

## OUTSTANDING COUNTY, SCHOOL DISTRICT AND MUNICIPAL BONDS, BY COUNTIES, JANUARY 1, 1932

| COUNTY | County General | County School | School District | Municipal General | Municipal Special | Total Municipal | County Total |
|---|---|---|---|---|---|---|---|
| Adams | ------- | ------ | $ 552,800 | $ 441,500 | $ 192,500 | $ 634,000 | $1,186,800 |
| Alamosa | $ 43,000 | ------ | 316,800 | 209,000 | 198,800 | 407,800 | 767,600 |
| Arapahoe | ------- | ------ | 594,600 | 181,000 | 710,000 | 891,000 | 1,485,600 |
| Archuleta | ------ | ------ | 88,200 | 17,500 | -------- | 17,500 | 105,700 |
| Baca | 18,000 | ------ | 258,650 | 140,000 | 67,000 | 207,000 | 483,650 |
| Bent | ------- | 6,000 | 100,100 | -------- | 86,250 | 86,250 | 192,350 |
| Boulder | ------- | ------ | 525,100 | 763,000 | 524,100 | 1,287,100 | 1,812,200 |
| Chaffee | 105,000 | ------- | 106,750 | 145,000 | 5,100 | 150,100 | 361,850 |
| Cheyenne | ------ | 98,000 | 156,000 | 82,000 | -------- | 82,000 | 336,000 |
| Clear Creek | ---- | ------ | 1,000 | 42,500 | -------- | 42,500 | 43,500 |
| Conejos | 13,200 | ------ | 259,300 | 123,600 | 5,400 | 129,000 | 401,500 |
| Costilla | ------- | ------ | 99,300 | -------- | -------- | -------- | 99,300 |
| Crowley | ------- | ------ | 423,000 | 79,500 | 2,400 | 81,900 | 504,900 |
| Custer | ------- | 21,000 | 8,500 | -------- | -------- | -------- | 29,500 |
| Delta | 7,500 | ------ | 320,500 | 409,500 | 40,600 | 450,100 | 778,100 |
| Denver | ------- | ------ | 9,574,500 | 23,282,100 | 9,330,400 | 32,612,500 | 42,187,000 |
| Dolores | 80,000 | ------ | 19,000 | -------- | -------- | -------- | 99,000 |
| Douglas | ------- | ------ | 31,500 | 67,500 | 27,000 | 94,500 | 126,000 |
| Eagle | ------- | ------ | 29,500 | 55,500 | -------- | 55,500 | 85,000 |
| Elbert | ------- | ------ | 137,800 | 44,800 | -------- | 44,800 | 182,600 |
| El Paso | ------- | ------ | 1,601,000 | 3,383,000 | 325,300 | 3,708,300 | 5,309,300 |
| Fremont | ------- | ------ | 605,000 | 693,000 | 328,600 | 1,021,600 | 1,627,500 |
| Garfield | 181,000 | 16,000 | 410,750 | 411,500 | 67,000 | 478,500 | 1,086,250 |
| Gilpin | ------- | ------ | -------- | 75,500 | -------- | 75,500 | 75,500 |
| Grand | ------- | ------ | 35,500 | 36,500 | -------- | 36,500 | 72,000 |
| Gunnison | 132,000 | 150,000 | 236,000 | 147,500 | 29,500 | 177,000 | 695,000 |
| Hinsdale | 105,500 | ------ | -------- | 11,500 | -------- | 11,500 | 117,000 |
| Huerfano | ------- | 32,000 | 71,000 | 441,000 | 258,500 | 699,500 | 802,500 |
| Jackson | 6,000 | 20,000 | -------- | 27,500 | -------- | 27,500 | 53,500 |
| Jefferson | ------- | ------ | 499,100 | 344,000 | 264,200 | 608,200 | 1,107,300 |
| Kiowa | ------- | ------ | 153,800 | 69,000 | -------- | 69,000 | 222,800 |
| Kit Carson | ------- | ------ | 348,400 | 304,500 | 81,300 | 385,800 | 734,200 |
| Lake | ------- | ------ | -------- | 28,000 | -------- | 28,000 | 28,000 |
| La Plata | 52,000 | ------ | 239,000 | 536,400 | 165,200 | 701,600 | 993,500 |
| Larimer | 175,000 | ------ | 997,500 | 2,137,500 | 595,650 | 2,733,150 | 3,905,650 |
| Las Animas | ------ | ------ | 407,500 | 1,201,900 | 692,000 | 1,893,900 | 2,301,400 |
| Lincoln | 90,000 | ------ | 241,400 | 82,000 | 25,600 | 107,600 | 439,000 |
| Logan | 10,000 | 55,000 | 529,200 | 919,000 | 278,000 | 1,197,000 | 1,791,200 |
| Mesa | 150,000 | ------ | 734,850 | 870,900 | 486,200 | 1,357,100 | 2,241,950 |
| Mineral | ------- | ------ | -------- | 11,000 | -------- | 11,000 | 11,000 |
| Moffat | 24,000 | ------ | 74,800 | 47,000 | -------- | 47,000 | 145,800 |
| Montezuma | ------ | ------ | 104,900 | 107,000 | 41,000 | 148,000 | 252,900 |
| Montrose | 116,000 | 35,000 | 164,900 | 260,000 | 18,300 | 278,300 | 594,200 |
| Morgan | ------- | ------ | 735,000 | 366,000 | 279,000 | 645,000 | 1,380,000 |
| Otero | ------- | ------ | 585,900 | 977,800 | 65,500 | 1,043,300 | 1,629,200 |
| Ouray | 48,000 | ------ | 21,200 | 20,000 | -------- | 20,000 | 89,200 |
| Park | ------- | ------ | 23,500 | -------- | -------- | -------- | 23,500 |
| Phillips | 26,000 | 60,000 | 211,400 | 225,000 | 73,500 | 298,500 | 595,900 |
| Pitkin | 105,000 | ------ | -------- | 75,500 | -------- | 75,500 | 180,500 |
| Prowers | ------- | ------ | 461,900 | 906,300 | 235,000 | 1,141,300 | 1,603,200 |
| Pueblo | ------- | ------ | 1,826,300 | 470,000 | 3,216,300 | 3,686,300 | 5,512,600 |
| Rio Blanco | ----- | 75,000 | 45,600 | 152,000 | -------- | 152,000 | 272,600 |
| Rio Grande | ----- | 80,400 | 316,200 | 92,800 | 25,000 | 117,800 | 514,400 |
| Routt | 94,000 | ------ | 230,500 | 190,750 | 39,000 | 229,750 | 554,250 |
| Saguache | ------- | ------ | 176,500 | 51,000 | 7,100 | 58,100 | 234,600 |
| San Juan | 40,000 | ------ | 40,000 | -------- | -------- | -------- | 80,000 |
| San Miguel | 45,000 | ------ | 49,800 | -------- | -------- | -------- | 94,800 |
| Sedgwick | ------- | 213,000 | 232,700 | 210,000 | 17,200 | 227,200 | 672,900 |
| Summit | ------- | ------ | 35,000 | 32,000 | -------- | 32,000 | 67,000 |
| Teller | ------- | ------ | -------- | 306,700 | -------- | 306,700 | 306,700 |
| Washington | ---- | ------ | 215,500 | 140,000 | 37,500 | 177,500 | 393,000 |
| Weld | ------- | ------ | 2,539,600 | 1,024,000 | 269,750 | 1,293,750 | 3,833,350 |
| Yuma | ------- | ------ | 341,900 | 251,000 | 78,300 | 329,300 | 671,200 |
| State | $1,666,200 | $861,400 | $29,147,800 | $43,720,050 | $19,189,050 | $62,909,100 | $94,584,500 |

NOTE—In addition to the above total, state bonds outstanding on January 1, 1932, totaled $7,474,100, compared with $8,864,700 on January 1, 1931. There is also outstanding against counties in the Moffat Tunnel District a total of $15,470,000. No allowance is made in these figures for sinking fund accumulations, the totals shown here being the actual amounts outstanding. In many cases these are offset to a considerable extent by sinking funds.

The municipal bond totals include the following issues requiring explanation: Cheyenne Wells, $41,500 assumed by the Inland Utilities Company; Eads, $69,000 assumed by the Highland Utilities Company; Brush, $96,800 assumed by the Public Service Company; and Holly, $22,000 assumed by the Inland Utilities Company. Also bonds payable from revenues as follows: Colorado Springs, $478,000 gas and electric; Loveland, $100,000 electric; Lamar, $140,000 electric; and Steamboat Springs, $24,000 waterworks. The above total compares with $95,028,600 on January 1, 1931.

## SHORTEST RAILROAD MILEAGE BETWEEN COLORADO TOWNS

NOTE—Where the columns opposite names cross will be found the shortest railroad distance in miles between these cities.

| | Alamosa | Boulder | Burlington | Canon City | Colorado Springs | Craig | Cripple Creek | Delta | Denver | Durango | Fort Collins | Fort Morgan | Glenwood Springs | Grand Junction | Greeley | Holly | Holyoke | Hot Sulphur Springs | Julesburg | La Junta | Las Animas | Leadville | Montrose | Pagosa Springs | Pueblo | Salida | Steamboat Springs | Sterling | Trinidad | Walden | Wray |
|---|---|---|---|---|---|---|---|---|---|---|---|---|---|---|---|---|---|---|---|---|---|---|---|---|---|---|---|---|---|---|---|
| Alamosa | — | 280 | 332 | 149 | 175 | 483 | 233 | 385 | 251 | 200 | 313 | 329 | 373 | 437 | 303 | 275 | 424 | 337 | 448 | 196 | 215 | 289 | 388 | 170 | 132 | 228 | 428 | 374 | 117 | 507 | 416 |
| Boulder | 280 | — | 197 | 190 | 105 | 262 | 162 | 402 | 30 | 481 | 45 | 108 | 390 | 454 | 69 | 293 | 116 | 86 | 206 | 213 | 232 | 306 | 381 | 451 | 205 | 245 | 207 | 149 | 242 | 265 | 195 |
| Burlington | 332 | 197 | — | 327 | 156 | 399 | 299 | 539 | 167 | 613 | 235 | 245 | 527 | 591 | 219 | 344 | 253 | 357 | 364 | 481 | 369 | 443 | 518 | 588 | 201 | 382 | 344 | 300 | 293 | 423 | 332 |
| Canon City | 149 | 190 | 327 | — | 86 | 307 | 143 | 213 | 167 | 373 | 238 | 238 | 285 | 264 | 184 | 333 | 245 | 253 | 357 | 108 | 127 | 116 | 333 | 343 | 41 | 65 | 344 | 246 | 126 | 416 | 335 |
| Colorado Springs | 175 | 105 | 156 | 86 | — | 307 | 57 | 297 | 75 | 376 | 143 | 153 | 285 | 349 | 127 | 200 | 108 | 191 | 272 | 45 | 127 | 201 | 276 | 346 | 45 | 140 | 252 | 198 | 137 | 331 | 240 |
| Craig | 483 | 262 | 399 | 307 | 307 | — | 364 | 604 | 232 | 683 | 364 | 355 | 89 | 212 | 203 | 483 | 370 | 19 | 380 | 370 | 375 | 240 | 296 | 459 | 292 | 388 | 32 | 306 | 399 | 94 | 397 |
| Cripple Creek | 233 | 162 | 299 | 143 | 57 | 364 | — | 354 | 132 | 433 | 209 | 210 | 406 | 305 | 188 | 305 | 268 | 329 | 433 | 184 | 258 | 333 | 403 | 301 | 102 | 197 | 358 | 255 | 135 | 388 | 297 |
| Delta | 385 | 402 | 539 | 213 | 297 | 604 | 354 | — | 372 | 209 | 440 | 450 | 78 | 85 | 424 | 495 | 375 | 301 | 537 | 396 | 434 | 174 | 21 | 301 | 316 | 179 | 350 | 306 | 444 | 628 | 537 |
| Denver | 251 | 30 | 167 | 167 | 75 | 232 | 132 | 372 | — | 451 | 68 | 78 | 360 | 424 | 52 | 245 | 80 | 197 | 183 | 165 | 184 | 258 | 197 | 403 | 102 | 197 | 177 | 123 | 212 | 266 | 165 |
| Durango | 200 | 481 | 613 | 373 | 376 | 683 | 433 | 209 | 451 | — | 519 | 529 | 350 | 261 | 503 | 245 | 375 | 459 | 648 | 183 | 260 | 435 | 188 | 92 | 332 | 428 | 549 | 574 | 280 | 707 | 616 |
| Fort Collins | 313 | 45 | 235 | 238 | 143 | 364 | 209 | 440 | 68 | 519 | — | 85 | 428 | 492 | 68 | 396 | 61 | 183 | 183 | 270 | 344 | 419 | 489 | 197 | 283 | 126 | 242 | 123 | 280 | 261 | 233 |
| Fort Morgan | 329 | 108 | 245 | 238 | 153 | 355 | 210 | 450 | 78 | 529 | 85 | — | 438 | 502 | 41 | 91 | 98 | 240 | 91 | 280 | 354 | 499 | 499 | 442 | 197 | 241 | 245 | 57 | 290 | 261 | 87 |
| Glenwood Springs | 373 | 390 | 527 | 285 | 285 | 89 | 406 | 78 | 360 | 350 | 428 | 438 | — | 89 | 433 | 495 | 375 | 85 | 557 | 537 | 507 | 162 | 89 | 442 | 350 | 335 | 89 | 305 | 335 | 89 | 525 |
| Grand Junction | 437 | 454 | 591 | 264 | 349 | 212 | 305 | 85 | 424 | 261 | 492 | 502 | 89 | — | 476 | 656 | 597 | 283 | 621 | 369 | 507 | 221 | 73 | 353 | 316 | 412 | 229 | 197 | 547 | 342 | 589 |
| Greeley | 303 | 69 | 219 | 184 | 127 | 203 | 188 | 424 | 52 | 503 | 68 | 41 | 433 | 476 | — | 315 | 143 | 155 | 148 | 254 | 325 | 403 | 473 | 473 | 143 | 179 | 229 | 61 | 386 | 204 | 144 |
| Holly | 275 | 293 | 344 | 333 | 200 | 483 | 305 | 495 | 245 | 245 | 396 | 91 | 495 | 656 | 315 | — | 349 | 460 | 349 | 80 | 61 | 375 | 445 | 459 | 143 | 239 | 350 | 306 | 162 | 519 | 428 |
| Holyoke | 424 | 116 | 253 | 245 | 108 | 370 | 268 | 375 | 80 | 375 | 61 | 98 | 375 | 597 | 143 | 349 | — | 259 | 107 | 375 | 385 | 221 | 296 | 385 | 292 | 388 | 350 | 50 | 389 | 342 | 178 |
| Hot Sulphur Springs | 337 | 86 | 360 | 253 | 191 | 19 | 329 | 301 | 197 | 459 | 183 | 240 | 85 | 283 | 155 | 460 | 259 | — | 283 | 473 | 437 | 197 | 197 | 459 | 301 | 453 | 61 | 203 | 398 | 94 | 251 |
| Julesburg | 448 | 206 | 364 | 357 | 272 | 380 | 433 | 537 | 183 | 648 | 183 | 91 | 557 | 621 | 148 | 349 | 107 | 283 | — | 399 | 548 | 473 | 548 | 618 | 316 | 412 | 374 | 57 | 409 | 439 | 185 |
| La Junta | 196 | 213 | 481 | 108 | 45 | 370 | 184 | 396 | 165 | 183 | 270 | 280 | 537 | 369 | 254 | 80 | 375 | 473 | 399 | — | 19 | 221 | 296 | 366 | 83 | 160 | 306 | 326 | 82 | 458 | 348 |
| Las Animas | 215 | 232 | 369 | 127 | 127 | 375 | 258 | 434 | 184 | 260 | 344 | 354 | 507 | 507 | 325 | 61 | 385 | 437 | 548 | 19 | — | 240 | 315 | 385 | 83 | 179 | 325 | 82 | 101 | 532 | 367 |
| Leadville | 289 | 306 | 443 | 116 | 201 | 240 | 333 | 174 | 258 | 435 | 419 | 499 | 162 | 221 | 403 | 375 | 221 | 197 | 459 | 221 | 240 | — | 240 | 459 | 157 | 61 | 197 | 251 | 326 | 82 | 441 |
| Montrose | 388 | 381 | 518 | 333 | 276 | 296 | 403 | 21 | 197 | 188 | 489 | 499 | 89 | 73 | 473 | 445 | 296 | 197 | 618 | 296 | 315 | 240 | — | 280 | 232 | 135 | 474 | 474 | 607 | 677 | 516 |
| Pagosa Springs | 170 | 451 | 588 | 343 | 346 | 459 | 301 | 301 | 403 | 92 | 197 | 442 | 442 | 353 | 473 | 459 | 385 | 459 | 316 | 366 | 385 | 459 | 280 | — | 302 | 398 | 598 | 544 | 396 | 375 | 586 |
| Pueblo | 132 | 205 | 201 | 41 | 45 | 292 | 102 | 316 | 102 | 332 | 283 | 197 | 350 | 316 | 143 | 143 | 292 | 301 | 316 | 83 | 83 | 157 | 232 | 302 | — | 96 | 392 | 338 | 96 | 242 | 284 |
| Salida | 228 | 245 | 382 | 65 | 140 | 388 | 255 | 179 | 197 | 428 | 126 | 241 | 335 | 412 | 179 | 239 | 388 | 453 | 412 | 160 | 179 | 61 | 135 | 398 | 96 | — | 338 | 392 | 338 | 471 | 380 |
| Steamboat Springs | 428 | 207 | 344 | 344 | 252 | 32 | 399 | 350 | 177 | 549 | 242 | 245 | 89 | 229 | 229 | 350 | 350 | 61 | 374 | 306 | 325 | 197 | 474 | 598 | 392 | 338 | — | 300 | 389 | 433 | 342 |
| Sterling | 374 | 149 | 300 | 246 | 198 | 306 | 388 | 306 | 123 | 574 | 123 | 57 | 305 | 197 | 61 | 306 | 50 | 203 | 57 | 326 | 82 | 251 | 474 | 544 | 338 | 392 | 300 | — | 335 | 302 | 128 |
| Trinidad | 117 | 242 | 293 | 126 | 137 | 399 | 297 | 444 | 212 | 280 | 280 | 290 | 335 | 547 | 386 | 162 | 389 | 398 | 409 | 82 | 101 | 326 | 607 | 396 | 96 | 338 | 389 | 335 | — | 468 | 377 |
| Walden | 507 | 265 | 423 | 416 | 331 | 94 | 388 | 628 | 266 | 707 | 261 | 261 | 89 | 342 | 204 | 519 | 342 | 94 | 439 | 458 | 532 | 82 | 677 | 375 | 242 | 471 | 433 | 302 | 468 | — | 348 |
| Wray | 416 | 195 | 332 | 335 | 240 | 397 | 297 | 537 | 165 | 616 | 233 | 87 | 525 | 589 | 144 | 428 | 178 | 251 | 185 | 348 | 367 | 441 | 516 | 586 | 284 | 380 | 342 | 128 | 377 | 348 | — |

# Location and Altitudes of Colorado Mountains

| Name | County | Elevation, Feet |
|------|--------|-----------------|
| Achonee Mountain | Grand | 12.656 |
| Adams Mountain | Grand | 12.115 |
| Aetna Mountain | Chaffee | 13.800 |
| Albion Mountain | Boulder | 12.596 |
| Alpine Peak | Clear Creek | 11.525 |
| Alps Mountain | Clear Creek | 10.508 |
| Anchor Mountain | Dolores | 12.325 |
| Andrews Peak | Grand | 12.564 |
| Antero, Mount | Chaffee | 14.245 |
| Apache Peak | Boulder-Grand | 12.873 |
| Apiatan Mountain | Grand | 10.888 |
| Arapahoe Peak | Boulder-Grand | 13.506 |
| Arkansas Mountain | Lake | 13.797 |
| Arrow Peak | San Juan | 13.803 |
| Arthur Mountain | El Paso | 10.805 |
| Audubon Mountain | Boulder | 13.223 |
| Augusta Mountain | Gunnison | 12.615 |
| Avery Peak | Gunnison | 12.652 |
| Axtel Mountain | Gunnison | 12.013 |
| Baker Mountain | Grand | 12.406 |
| Bald Mountain | Boulder | 11.470 |
| Bald Mountain | Summit | 13.964 |
| Bald Mountain | Teller | 12.365 |
| Baldy Mountain | Gunnison | 12.809 |
| Baldy Peak | Ouray | 10.615 |
| Banded Peak | Archuleta | 12.376 |
| Baxter Mountain | Costilla | 10.629 |
| Bear Mountain | San Juan | 12.950 |
| Beautiful Mountain | Mineral | 12.746 |
| Beckwith Mountain | Gunnison | 12.371 |
| Belleview | Rio Grande | 12.727 |
| Bierstadt Mountain | Clear Creek | 14.046 |
| Big Bull Mountain | Teller | 10.826 |
| Big Chief Mountain | Teller | 11.220 |
| Bison Peak | Park | 12.400 |
| Blackhawk Peak | Gilpin | 10.323 |
| Blackhawk Peak | Dolores | 12.687 |
| Blanca Peak | Costilla-Huerfano-Alamosa | 14.390 |
| Bowen Mountain | Grand | 12.541 |
| Bross Mountain | Park | 14.163 |
| Buck Mountain | Routt-Jackson | 11.375 |
| Buckeye Peak | Lake | 12.863 |
| Buckskin Mountain | Costilla | 10.512 |
| Buffalo Peak | Summit | 13.541 |
| Calico Peak | Dolores | 12.035 |
| Cameron Cone | El Paso | 10.705 |
| Cameron Mountain | Park | 14.233 |
| Capitol Mountain | Pitkin | 13.997 |
| Cascade Mountain | Gunnison | 11.707 |
| Cascade Mountain | Grand | 12.320 |
| Castle Peak | Gunnison-Pitkin | 14.259 |
| Cement Mountain | Gunnison | 12.212 |
| Chama Peak | Archuleta | 12.027 |
| Chapin Mountain | Larimer | 13.052 |
| Chicago Peak | Huerfano-Costilla | 10.960 |
| Chief Mountain | Clear Creek | 11.710 |
| Chimney Peak | Hinsdale-Ouray | 11.785 |
| Chiquita Mountain | Larimer | 12.458 |
| Cinnamon Mountain | Gunnison | 12.270 |
| Cirrus Mountain | Grand | 12.804 |
| Clarence King Mountain | Boulder | 13.176 |
| Clover Mountain | Chaffee | 13.000 |
| Colorado Mountain | Gilpin | 10.884 |
| Columbia Peak | Clear Creek | 14.030 |
| Comanche Peak | Boulder | 13.491 |
| Cone Mountain | Clear Creek | 12.230 |
| Conejos Peak | Conejos | 13.180 |
| Copper Mountain | Summit | 12.475 |
| Copper Mountain | Teller | 10.226 |
| Courthouse Mountain | Hinsdale-Ouray | 12.165 |
| Cover Mountain | Park | 10.165 |
| Coxcomb Peak | Hinsdale-Ouray | 13.663 |
| Craig Mountain | Grand | 12.005 |
| Crested Butte | Gunnison | 12.172 |
| Crestone Needle | Custer-Saguache | 14.130 |
| Crestone Peak | Saguache | 14.233 |

| Name | County | Elevation, Feet |
|------|--------|-----------------|
| Crystal Peak | Hinsdale | 12.927 |
| Culebra Peak | Costilla-Las Animas | 14.069 |
| Cumulus Mountain | Grand | 12.724 |
| Dakota Hill | Gilpin | 10.930 |
| Del Norte Peak | Rio Grande | 12.378 |
| Democrat Mountain | Park-Lake | 14.000 |
| Dickenson Mountain | Larimer | 11.874 |
| Double Top Mountain | Gunnison | 12.192 / 12.178 |
| Dump Mountain | Costilla | 10.310 |
| Dunraven Mountain | Larimer | 12.548 |
| Eagle Peak | Dolores | 12.105 |
| Echo Mountain | La Plata | 13.305 |
| Elbert Mountain* | Lake | 14.402 |
| Electric Peak | Grand | 11.943 |
| Elephant Mountain | Rio Grande | 11.790 |
| Elk Mountain | Mineral | 11.030 |
| Elk Mountain | Eagle-Summit | 12.718 |
| Elliott Mountain | Dolores | 12.337 |
| Emerson Mountain | La Plata | 13.147 |
| Emmons Mountain | Gunnison | 12.414 |
| Engineer Mountain | Hinsdale-Ouray-San Juan | 13.190 |
| Engineer Mountain | San Juan | 12.972 |
| Eolus Mountain | La Plata | 14.079 |
| Estes Cone | Larimer | 11.017 |
| Ethel Mountain | Routt-Jackson | 11.940 |
| Evans Mountain | Park-Lake | 13.580 |
| Evans Mountain | Clear Creek | 14.260 |
| Expectation Mountain | Dolores | 12.071 |
| Fairchild Mountain | Larimer | 13.502 |
| Fisher Mountain | Mineral | 12.855 |
| Fisher Mountain | Grand | 12.280 |
| Fletcher Mountain | Summit | 13.917 |
| Flora Mountain | Clear Creek-Grand | 13.122 |
| Florida Mountain | La Plata | 13.076 |
| Fox Mountain | Mineral | 11.520 |
| Freeman Peak | Jefferson | 11.627 |
| Garfield Mountain | El Paso | 10.925 |
| Garfield Mountain | San Juan | 13.065 |
| Garfield Peak | Gunnison | 12.136 |
| Gilpin Peak | Ouray-San Miguel | 13.682 |
| Glacier Peak | Summit | 12.654 |
| Gothic Mountain | Gunnison | 12.646 |
| Grant Peak | San Juan-San Miguel | 13.692 |
| Gray Head | San Miguel | 10.994 |
| Grayback Mountain | Costilla | 10.575 |
| Grayrock Peak | San Juan | 12.488 |
| Grays Peak | Clear Creek-Summit | 14.274 |
| Graystone Peak | San Juan | 13.489 |
| Greenhorn Mountain | Huerfano-Pueblo | 12.334 |
| Green Mountain | Jefferson | 10.530 |
| Greylock Mountain | La Plata | 13.571 |
| Grizzly Mountain | Pitkin-Chaffee | 14.130 |
| Grizzly Peak | La Plata | 13.695 |
| Grizzly Peak | Dolores-San Juan | 13.738 |
| Hague Peak | Larimer | 13.562 |
| Hale Mountain | Grand | 11.747 |
| Hallet Peak | Grand-Larimer | 12.723 |
| Handies Peak | Hinsdale | 14.008 |
| Harvard, Mount | Chaffee | 14.375 |
| Helmet Peak | Montezuma | 11.976 |
| Hermosa Mountain | Dolores-San Juan | 12.574 |
| Hesperus Peak | Montezuma | 13.225 |
| Holy Cross Mountain | Eagle | 13.978 |
| Homestake Peak | Eagle | 13.217 |

\* Previous figure of **14,420 revised by the U. S. Geological Survey.**

| Name | County | Elevation, Feet |
|---|---|---|
| Hope Mountain | Mineral | 12,841 |
| Horseshoe Mountain | Park-Lake | 13,902 |
| Howard Mountain | Grand | 12,814 |
| Humboldt Peak | Custer-Saguache | 14,044 |
| Hunchback Mountain | San Juan | 13,133 |
| Ida Mountain | Grand-Larimer | 12,868 |
| Irving Peak | La Plata | 13,210 |
| Jacque Mountain | Summit | 13,235 |
| Jacque Peak | Summit | 13,205 |
| Jugged Mountain | San Juan | 13,829 |
| James Peak | Clear Creek-Grand-Gilpin | 13,260 |
| Johnny Bull Mountain | Dolores | 12,018 |
| Jura Knob | San Juan | 12,617 |
| Kendall | San Juan | 13,480 |
| Kingston Peak | Clear Creek-Gilpin | 12,137 |
| Kit Carson Peak | Saguache-Custer | 14,100 |
| Klondike Mountain | Boulder | 10,802 |
| La Garita | Mineral-Saguache | 13,725 |
| La Plata Peak | Chaffee | 14,332 |
| Lead Mountain | Grand | 12,532 |
| Leviathan Peak | San Juan | 13,528 |
| Lillie | Larimer | 11,384 |
| Lincoln Mountain | Park | 14,287 |
| Lizard Head | Dolores-San Miguel | 13,156 |
| London Mountain | Park | 13,161 |
| Lone Cone | San Miguel-Dolores | 12,761 |
| Lonesome Peak | Grand | 10,588 |
| Longs Peak | Boulder | 14,255 |
| Lookout Mountain | Grand | 10,155 |
| Lookout Mountain | Larimer | 10,633 |
| Lookout Peak | San Juan-San Miguel | 13,674 |
| Lulu Mountain | Grand | 11,720 |
| McCauley Peak | La Plata | 13,551 |
| McGregor Mountain | Larimer | 10,482 |
| Madden Peak | Montezuma-La Plata | 11,980 |
| Mahana Peak | Boulder | 12,629 |
| Marcellina Mountain | Gunnison | 11,349 |
| Maroon Peak | Pitkin | 14,126 |
| Martha Washington Mtn. | Larimer | 13,269 |
| Massive, Mount* | Lake | 14,402 |
| Matterhorn Peak | Hinsdale | 13,589 |
| McClellan, Mount | Clear Creek-Summit | 13,423 |
| Meaden Mountain | Routt | |
| Meadow Mountain | Boulder | 11,634 |
| Meeker Mountain | Boulder | 13,911 |
| Metroz Mountain | Mineral | 11,900 |
| Mineral Hill | Summit | 10,885 |
| Mineral Point | Gunnison | 12,541 |
| Missouri Hill | Chaffee | 12,700 |
| Monitor Peak | La Plata | 13,703 |
| Monument Hill | La Plata | 10,830 |
| Monument Peak | Mineral | 10,641 |
| Mosquito Peak | Park-Lake | 13,784 |
| Mummy Mountain | Larimer | 13,413 |
| Naki Peak | Grand | 12,221 |
| Navajo Peak | Boulder-Grand | 13,406 |
| Nebo Mountain | San Juan | 13,192 |
| Nebraska Hill | Gilpin | 11,548 |
| Nigger Hill | Summit | 10,171 |
| Nimbus Mountain | Grand | 12,730 |
| Nipple Mountain | Fremont | 10,068 |
| North Italian Mtn. | Gunnison | 13,225 |
| North Maroon | Pitkin | 14,000 |
| Ohio Peak | Gunnison | 12,251 |
| Old Baldy | Costilla-Huerfano | 14,176 |
| Old Baldy Mountain | Rio Grande | 12,602 |
| Oregon Hill | Gilpin | 10,884 |
| Orton Mountain | Boulder | 11,662 |
| Oso Mountain | La Plata | 13,706 |
| Otis Peak | Grand-Larimer | 12,478 |
| Ouray, Mount | Chaffee | 13,956 |

| Name | County | Elevation, Feet |
|---|---|---|
| Overlook Point | La Plata | 12,995 |
| Owen Mountain | Gunnison | 13,102 |
| Park Mountain | Costilla | 10,396 |
| Parrot Peak | La Plata | 11,876 |
| Parry Peak | Clear Creek-Grand | 13,345 |
| Pearl Mountain | Gunnison | 13,484 |
| Peeler Peak | Gunnison | 12,219 |
| Pigeon Peak | La Plata | 13,961 |
| Pikes Peak | El Paso | 14,109 |
| Pilot Knob | San Juan-San Miguel | 13,750 |
| Pisgah Mountain | Clear Creek-Gilpin | 10,085 |
| Pole Creek Mountain | Hinsdale | 13,740 |
| Pool Table Mountain | Mineral | 12,142 |
| Porphyry Peaks | Grand | { 11,155 / 11,355 } |
| Potato Hill | San Juan | 11,876 |
| Potosi Peak | Ouray | 13,763 |
| Princeton, Mount | Chaffee | 14,196 |
| Prospect Mountain | Lake | 12,608 |
| Ptarmigan Hill | Eagle | 12,174 |
| Ptarmigan Peak | Park-Lake | 13,736 |
| Purple Peak | Gunnison | 12,989 |
| Pyramid Peak | Pitkin | 14,000 |
| Quandary Peak | Summit | 14,256 |
| Red Cloud Peak | Hinsdale | 14,050 |
| Red Hill | La Plata | 10,670 |
| Red Mountain | Grand | 11,505 |
| Republican Mountain | Clear Creek | 12,393 |
| Rhyolite Mountain | Teller | 10,771 |
| Richmond Mountain | Gunnison | 12,543 |
| Richtofen Mountain | Grand | 12,953 |
| Rio Grande Pyramid | Hinsdale | 13,830 |
| Rolling Mountain | San Juan | 13,694 |
| Rosalie Peak | Park | 13,575 |
| Rosa Mountain | Teller | 11,495 |
| Ruby Peak | Gunnison | 12,749 |
| Rudolph Hill | Gunnison | 10,130 |
| Saddle Mountain | Park | 10,815 |
| Saddle Mountain | Mineral | 12,033 |
| St. Vrain Mountain | Boulder | 12,162 |
| San Bernardo Mountain | San Miguel | 11,845 |
| San Luis Mountain | Teller | 10,490 |
| San Luis Mountain | Saguache | 14,149 |
| Satanta Peak | Grand | 11,885 |
| Sawtooth Mountain | Mineral | 12,590 |
| Sawtooth Mountain | Boulder-Grand | 12,304 |
| Saxon Mountain | Clear Creek | 11,535 |
| Schuylkill Mountain | Gunnison | 12,188 |
| Shavano Peak | Chaffee | 14,239 |
| Sheep Mountain | Gunnison | 13,180 |
| Sheep Mountain | Mineral | 12,374 |
| Sheep Mountain | Eagle-Summit | 12,380 |
| Sheep Mountain, North | Eagle-Summit | 12,429 |
| Sheridan Mountain | La Plata | 12,785 |
| Sherman Mountain | Park | 14,037 |
| Shoshone Peak | Boulder | 13,579 |
| Silex Mountain | San Juan | 13,627 |
| Silverheels Mountain | Park | 13,825 |
| Sioux Mountain | Boulder-Grand | 13,310 |
| Sneffels, Mount | Ouray | 14,158 |
| Snowdon Peak | San Juan | 13,070 |
| Snowmass Mountain | Pitkin-Gunnison | 13,970 |
| Sopris, Mount | Pitkin | 12,823 |
| Spanish Peak, West | Huerfano-Las Animas | 13,623 |
| Spanish Peak, East | Huerfano-Las Animas | 12,708 |
| Specimen Mountain | Grand-Larimer | 12,482 |
| Star Peak | Gunnison | 13,562 |
| Stearns Mountain | Huerfano-Costilla | 11,409 |
| Stewart Peak | Saguache | 14,032 |
| Stoll Mountain | Park | 10,915 |
| Stones Peak | Larimer | 12,928 |
| Stony Mountain | Ouray | 12,677 |
| Storm King Peak | San Juan | 13,742 |
| Storm Peak | Larimer | 13,336 |
| Storm Ridge | Gunnison | 11,859 |
| Stormy Peak | Park | 11,748 |

| Name | County | Elevation, Feet |
|---|---|---|
| Sugarloaf | Eagle-Summit | 12,556 |
| Sugarloaf Peak | Clear Creek | 12,513 |
| Sugarloaf Rock | Hinsdale | 10,831 |
| Sultan Mountain | San Juan | 13,336 |
| Summit Peak | Archuleta | 13,272 |
| Sunlight Peak | La Plata | 14,084 |
| Sunshine Mountain | San Miguel | 12,945 |
| Sunshine Peak | Hinsdale | 14,018 |
| Tanima Peak | Boulder-Grand | 12,417 |
| Tarryall Peak | Park | 11,300 |
| Taylor Mountain | Chaffee | 13,600 |
| Taylor Peak | Gunnison | 13,419 |
| Taylor Peak | Grand-Larimer | 13,150 |
| Telescope Mountain | Dolores | 12,210 |
| Teocalli Mountain | Gunnison | 13,220 |
| Terra Tomah Peak | Larimer | 12,686 |
| The Guardian | San Juan | 13,617 |
| Tilton Mountain | Gunnison | 12,633 |
| Torrey Peak | Clear Creek-Summit | 14,264 |
| Trachyte Mountain | Teller | 10,863 |
| Trinchera Mountain | Costilla-Huerfano | 13,546 |
| Trinity Peak | San Juan | { 13,752 / 13,804 / 13,745 } |
| Turret Peak | La Plata | 13,819 |
| Twilight Peak | San Juan | 13,153 |
| Twin Sisters | Larimer | 11,435 |
| Twin Sisters | San Juan | 13,438 |

| Name | County | Elevation, Feet |
|---|---|---|
| Uncompahgre Peak | Hinsdale | 14,306 |
| Union Mountain | Summit | 12,336 |
| Vermillion Peak | San Juan-San Miguel | 13,870 |
| Vestal Peak | San Juan | 13,846 |
| Vigil Peak | El Paso | 10,075 |
| Wasatch Mountain | San Miguel | 13,551 |
| West Needle Mountain | San Juan | 13,050 |
| Wetterhorn Peak | Hinsdale-Ouray | 14,020 |
| Wheatstone Mountain | Gunnison | 12,543 |
| Whitecross Mountain | Hinsdale | 13,550 |
| White Dome | San Juan | 13,607 |
| Whitehouse Mountain | Ouray | 13,496 |
| White Pine Mountain | Larimer | 10,250 |
| White Rock Mountain | Gunnison | 13,532 |
| Wildhorse Peak | Ouray | 13,271 |
| Wilson Mountain | Dolores | 14,250 |
| Wilson Peak | San Miguel | 14,026 |
| Windom Mountain | La Plata | 14,084 |
| Witter Peak | Clear Creek | 12,856 |
| Yale, Mount | Chaffee | 14,187 |
| Ypsilon Mountain | Larimer | 13,507 |
| Zirkel Mountain | Jackson-Routt | 11,815 |

# Lakes and Reservoirs

| Name | County | Altitude |
|---|---|---|
| Arapahoe | Gilpin | 11,165 |
| Antero Res. | Park | 8,934 |
| Adams Res. | Adams | |
| Adobe Creek Res. | Bent-Kiowa | 4,150 |
| Bradford | Huerfano | 5,850 |
| Black Hollow Res. | Weld | 5,065 |
| Bee | Larimer | 5,175 |
| Bolles | Boulder | 5,040 |
| Boedecker | Larimer | 5,075 |
| Bison Res. | Teller | 10,400 |
| Blue | Conejos | 11,937 |
| Burch's | Boulder | 5,145 |
| Beasley Res. | Boulder | 5,195 |
| Boulder | Boulder | 5,228 |
| Boyd Lakes | Larimer | 4,960 |
| Bent County Res. | Bent | 4,300 |
| Barr | Adams | |
| Badger Res. | Morgan | |
| Big Creek Lakes | Jackson | 9,010 |
| Boetcher | Jackson | 8,160 |
| Breman | Gunnison | 10,325 |
| Balsam | San Juan | 11,435 |
| Big Nile | Adams | |
| Clear | Clear Creek | 9,870 |
| Chicago | Clear Creek | 11,350 |
| Crater | Jefferson | 8,877 |
| Chinn | Clear Creek | 11,020 |
| Chasm | Boulder | 11,800 |
| Caroline | Clear Creek | 11,853 |
| Castlewood Res. | Douglas | 6,475 |
| Calkins | Weld | 4,975 |
| Curtis | Larimer | 5,080 |
| Cheesman | Jefferson | 6,856 |
| Clear Lake | San Juan | 11,875 |
| Devils | Hinsdale | 11,968 |
| Duck | Clear Creek | 11,070 |
| Diamond | Boulder | 10,960 |
| Dorothy | Boulder | 12,050 |
| Douglas | Larimer | 5,200 |
| Demmel | Larimer | 5,250 |
| Dead | Teller | 10,900 |
| Dye Res. | Otero | 4,150 |

| Name | County | Altitude |
|---|---|---|
| Echo | Clear Creek | 10,605 |
| Emerald | Hinsdale | 10,020 |
| Eldora | Boulder | 9,245 |
| Edith | Clear Creek | 10,117 |
| Eileen | La Plata | 8,924 |
| Erdman | Pueblo | 4,610 |
| Empire Res. | Morgan-Weld | |
| Fossil Creek Res. | Larimer | 4,890 |
| Fountain Valley Res. | El Paso | 5,800 |
| Grand | Grand | 8,369 |
| Gold | Boulder | 8,600 |
| Gerard Res. | Prowers | 4,050 |
| George | Park | 6,915 |
| Hoffman | Boulder | 5,120 |
| Hazel | San Juan | 11,420 |
| Hazel | La Plata | 12,420 |
| Head | Alamosa | 7,527 |
| Hermit Lakes | Hinsdale | 9,975 |
| Horse Creek Res. | Bent-Otero | 4,950 |
| Hungerford | Pueblo | 4,520 |
| Huerfano | Pueblo | 4,725 |
| Hayden Res. | Pueblo | |
| Ice | Clear Creek | 12,188 |
| Ignacio Res. | La Plata | 8,375 |
| Isabelle | Boulder | 10,852 |
| Irish | Larimer-Boulder | 5,090 |
| Jasper | Boulder | 10,733 |
| Julesburg Res. | Sedgwick-Logan | |
| Jackson | Morgan | |
| Jim Crowe Res. | Weld | |
| King Res. | Kiowa-Prowers | 3,860 |
| Lost | Boulder | 9,980 |
| Lower Crater | Gilpin | 10,580 |
| Los Lagos | Boulder-Gilpin | 8,930 |
| Loch Lomond | Clear Creek | 11,140 |
| Lena | Routt | 9,980 |
| Lorland | Larimer | 5,022 |
| Loch Ivanho | Pitkin | 10,930 |
| Long | Boulder | 10,499 |

| Name | County | Altitude | Name | County | Altitude |
|------|--------|----------|------|--------|----------|
| Marvine | Rio Blanco | 10,500 | Shaw | Mineral | 9,830 |
| McIntosh | Boulder | 5,060 | Spruce Lakes | Mineral | 11,263 |
| Moraine | El Paso | 10,215 | Silver | San Juan | 11,675 |
| Monarch | Grand | 8,340 | Seeley | Weld | 4,175 |
| Mills | Larimer | 11,496 | San Cristobal | Hinsdale | 8,997 |
| Maroon | Pitkin | 9,700 | Santa Maria | Mineral | 9,475 |
| Molas | San Juan | 10,488 | San Luis | Alamosa | 7,525 |
| Margareta | Routt | 10,450 | Strawberry | Grand | 8,340 |
| Milton | Weld | .... | Summit | Clear Creek | 12,740 |
| Middle Plum Res. | Prowers | 4,100 | Slater | Clear Creek | 11,385 |
| Meredith | Crowley | 4,308 | Silver | Boulder | 10,190 |
| Minnequa | Pueblo | 4,740 | Swedes | Boulder | 5,095 |
|  |  |  | Snowden | Otero | 4,820 |
| Naylor | Clear Creek | 11,348 | Seven Lakes | Teller | 10,900 |
| New Windsor Res. | Weld | 4,920 | Sanchez Res. | Costilla | 8,500 |
| North Plum Res. | Prowers | 4,100 | Stanley Res. | Jefferson | .... |
| North Butte Res. | Prowers | 4,200 |  |  |  |
| Nee Noshee Res. No. 3 | Kiowa | 3,870 | Twin Lakes | Lake | 9,012 |
| Nee Sopa Res. No. 5 | Kiowa | 3,860 | Trappers | Rio Blanco | 10,500 |
| Nee Gronda Res. No. 4 | Kiowa | 3,840 | Trout | San Miguel | 9,750 |
| Nee Skah Res. | Kiowa | 3,885 | Terry | Larimer | 5,095 |
|  |  |  | Timnath | Weld | 4,900 |
| Owens | Boulder | 5,220 | Two Buttes Res. | Baca-Prowers | 4,230 |
| Otanawanda | Ouray | 8,900 | Turkey Creek Res. | Pueblo | 5,580 |
|  |  |  | Thatcher | Pueblo-El Paso | 5,395 |
| Palmer | Douglas | 9,210 |  |  |  |
| Peterson | Boulder | 9,245 | Upper Crater | Gilpin | 10,997 |
| Point of Rocks Res. | Logan | 3,800 | Upper Nile | Adams | .... |
| Price Res. | Prowers | 3,850 |  |  |  |
| Prewitt Res. | Logan | 3,900 | Wellington | Jefferson | 9,863 |
| Pisgah | Gilpin | 9,656 | Warren | Larimer | 4,985 |
| Powderhorn | Hinsdale | 11,830 | Woods | Weld | 4,860 |
|  |  |  | Woods | Eagle | 9,405 |
| Res. No. 2 | El Paso | 11,270 | Webster Park Res. | Fremont | 5,950 |
| Res. No. 4 | Teller | 10,900 | Williams-McCreery | Morgan | .... |
| Res. No. 7 | Teller | 10,900 |  |  |  |
| Res. No. 7 | El Paso | 12,080 |  |  |  |
| Res. No. 8 | El Paso-Teller | 11,675 |  |  |  |
| Riverside Res. | Weld | .... |  |  |  |
| Res. No. 1, No. 2 | Kiowa | 3,770 |  |  |  |
| Res. No. 4 | Kiowa | 4,025 |  |  |  |
| Res. No. 1 | Otero | 4,750 |  |  |  |
| Res. No. 4 | Otero | 4,750 |  |  |  |
| Res. No. 5 | Otero | 4,750 |  |  |  |

This list includes only some of the more important lakes and reservoirs in the state. There are hundreds of small lakes in the mountains, many of which have no names. On Battlement mesa and Grand mesa, in Delta and Mesa counties, there are more than a hundred comparatively small lakes lying at an altitude above 8,000 feet, all well stocked with trout.

# Colorado's Mountain Passes

THREE terms — "summit," "divide" and "pass"—are used in Colorado to designate the highest elevations reached by routes which cross the various mountain ranges of the state. More particularly, the terms refer to that portion of the carry from one drainage basin to another whenever the mountain range forming the watershed is one of formidable character. Such a divide is likely to present obstacles to early crossings and the later construction of roads or railroads, even when advantage is taken of natural valleys and natural depressions found within the mountains. In appreciation of this difficulty, the proper one of the three terms, together with a descriptive prefix, is applied, e. g., Kenosha Summit, Dallas Divide, Cochetopa Pass.

"Summit" and "divide" are not as widely employed in this state as is "pass" because, although the terms are broadly similar, their meanings are in many respects quite distinct. For example, "summit" and "divide" are not used at the crossing places of stream divides of the first magnitude, i. e., the Continental Divide, nor in the loftier mountain ranges such as the Sangre de Cristo, the Medicine Bows and the Elk mountains, which separate major streams of the eastern and western slopes. Moreover, these terms are largely employed at the places where railroads, rather than roads, at some time or other have crossed high divides.

The passes are, therefore, at considerable elevations and are confined generally to the more formidable mountain ranges which comprise the vast mountain empire of Colorado. Passes are identified by having a lower elevation than the crests of the ranges with which they are associated, and represent the easiest or most feasible ways over mountain ranges. Very important in this connection is the character of the valley approaches to the mountain depression from either side. Low elevations in the mountains may be of little or no service for routes if the gradient of the mountain slopes defies the economical construction of road-beds up to them. It is for this reason that the passes of Colorado are found at the headwaters of tributary streams, whose valleys provided reasonably easy gradients to the summit.

As a result of this association, the majority of the passes bear the name of either one of the approaching streams; other names of passes are derived from surrounding physical features, such as mountains, and still others bear the name of some prominent figure in Colorado history. There are a large number of depressions in the mountain ranges which have never become passes because it has never been found feasible or necessary to construct routes over them.

There are 136 passes in Colorado, a number bearing eloquent testimony to the barrier-like effect of the Rockies, most of whose numerous mountain members have a north-south alignment —athwart the main lines of travel in western United States. Fifty-one of these passes have the distinction of being Continental Divide passes, but of this number only fourteen have any considerable present-day use, even during the summer season. In the winter time only Tennessee and Cochetopa passes are serviceable for automotive traffic. Berthoud pass is by all odds the most intensively used automobile highway, although it closes in December. Tennessee pass, with its transcontinental railway (the Denver and Rio Grande Western) as well as year-round automobile traffic, also deserves a high position among the state's renowned passes. Argentine pass is the state's highest pass, but Independence pass is the highest automobile highway pass in use today. Fall River pass is also an important pass at a high elevation, but this pass is not on the Continental Divide, though frequently confused with Milner pass, near it on the Divide. The lowest Continental Divide pass is Muddy pass in the Rabbit Ears range.

The tables published herewith present in summary form the more significant information relating to the passes of Colorado. Although probably not complete and perhaps incorrect in some details, the list represents the results of field, map and documentary study extending over a considerable period of time. In the accompanying tables, the passes are arranged in alphabetical order to aid the reader in finding any desired pass.

NOTE—This section has been prepared for the Year Book by Dr. Ralph H. Brown, Geographer, formerly of the University of Colorado but now on the staff of the Department of Geography of the University of Minnesota. Valuable aid has been given on many points by Dr. L. R. Hafen, Curator and Historian of the Colorado Historical society, and by the United States forest service. This material may be found in more comprehensive form in the November, 1929, issue of Colorado Magazine and in the University of Colorado Studies for 1930.

## MOUNTAIN PASS HIGHWAYS

The rapid development of mountain highways in Colorado has made a large number of the passes well known to hundreds of thousands of travelers, there being 30 or more which are traveled regularly during the summer months. Practically all except the lowest are closed during the winter months, as they lie at altitudes where snowfall is heavy and the problem of keeping them open is a financial, if not a physical impossibility. The Colorado highways department spends thousands of dollars annually in an effort to keep the more important passes open as late as possible and to clear them of snow as early as possible in the spring. Likewise considerable money is being spent each year to develop adequate drainage, so that melting snows and the rains of early spring will do the least possible damage to the highways.

The following table lists, in the order of elevation, the passes most commonly known to visitors and to Colorado people who have occasion to cross the mountain ranges frequently:

| Pass | Elevation |
|---|---|
| Independence | 12,095 |
| Fall River | 11,797 |
| Monarch | 11,650 |
| Hoosier | 11,542 |
| Hagerman | 11,495 |
| Fremont | 11,320 |
| Berthoud | 11,315 |
| Red Mountain | 11,018 |
| Wolf Creek | 10,850 |
| Milner | 10,759 |
| Los Pinos | 10,500 |
| Tennessee | 10,424 |
| Cameron | 10,285 |
| Cochetopa | 10,032 |
| Cumbres | 10,003 |
| La Manga | 10,000 |
| Molas Lake | 10,000 |
| Lizard Head | 10,000 |
| Squaw | 9,807 |
| Willow Creek | 9,683 |
| Rabbit Ears | 9,680 |
| La Veta | 9,378 |
| Trout Creek | 9,346 |
| Gore | 9,000 |
| Poncha | 8,945 |
| Muddy | 8,772 |
| Raton | 8,560 |

## ALTITUDE AND LOCATION OF MOUNTAIN PASSES

(Compiled by Dr. Ralph H. Brown, University of Minnesota)

| | | Range | Elevation in Feet | Earliest Known Use | Character of Present Use |
|---|---|---|---|---|---|
| tman or Alpine Tunnel | Chaffee-Gunnison | Sawatch Mountains | 11,606 | 1888 | Abandoned Railroad Tunnel |
| ntelope | Gilpin | Front | 8,050 | 1900 | Railroad |
| nthracite | Gunnison | Elk-West Elk | 9,100* | 1916 | Trail |
| rapahoe | Jackson-Grand | Park-Rabbit Ears | | 1870 | Trail |
| rapahoe | Boulder-Grand | Front | 11,905 | 1900 | Trail |
| rgentine | Clear Creek-Summit | Front | 13,132 | 1872 | Trail |
| valanche | Pitkin | Elk-West Elk | 10,000* | 1926 | Trail |
| ker | Jackson-Grand | Park-Rabbit Ears | 11,300* | 1905 | Trail |
| xter | Garfield | | 9,500* | | Trail |
| ckwith | Gunnison | Elk-West Elk | 9,890 | 1900 | Trail |
| erthoud | Clear Creek-Grand | Front | 11,315 | 1861 | Highway |
| ig Horn | Mineral | San Juan Group | 12,000* | | Trail |
| lue Lake | Ouray | San Juan Group | 11,000* | 1917 | Trail |
| onita | Rio Grande-Mineral | San Juan Group | 12,000* | | Trail |
| oreas | Park-Summit | Front | 11,489 | 1888 | Railroad and Abandoned Road |
| ottle | Grand | Front | 9,800* | 1880 | Trail |
| uchanan | Boulder-Grand | Front | 12,304 | 1902 | Trail |
| uffalo | Routt-Jackson | Park-Rabbit Ears | 10,180 | 1865 | Trail |
| uffalo | Park-Lake | Park-Mosquito | 11,500* | 1870 | Trail |
| ameron | Larimer-Jackson | Medicine Bow | 10,285 | 1878 | Highway |
| ebolla | Hinsdale | San Juan Group | 10,934 | | Trail |
| innamon | Hinsdale-San Juan | San Juan Group | 12,300 | 1878 | Abandoned Road |
| ochetopa (South) | Saguache | Cochetopa Hills | 10,032 | 1820 | Highway |
| ochetopa (North) | Saguache | Cochetopa Hills | 10,000* | 1880 | Trail |
| olumbine | La Plata | San Juan Group | 12,600* | 1902 | Trail |
| olumbine | Montrose | | 8,500* | | Trail |
| omanche | Custer-Saguache | Sangre de Cristo-Culebra | 10,500* | | Trail |
| ottonwood | Chaffee-Gunnison | Sawatch Mountains | 12,000* | 1887 | Trail |
| ucharas | Las Animas-Huerfano | Sangre de Cristo-Culebra | 8,500* | 1877 | Road |
| umbres | Conejos | San Juan Group | 10,003 | 1881 | Highway |
| urecanti | Gunnison | Elk-West Elk | 10,000* | | Trail |
| urrant Creek | Park | | 8,000* | 1877 | Road |
| aisy | Gunnison | Elk-West Elk | 11,200* | 1910 | Trail |
| evil's Thumb | Boulder-Grand | Front | 11,900 | | Trail |
| agle | La Plata | San Juan Group | 10,750 | 1900 | Trail |
| ast Maroon | Gunnison-Pitkin | Elk-West Elk | 12,200* | | Trail |
| ast River | Gunnison | Elk-West Elk | 11,163 | 1880 | Road |
| lwood | Rio Grande | San Juan Group | 12,000* | | Trail |
| all River | Larimer | Front | 11,797 | | Highway |
| awn Creek | Grand | Front | 9,430 | | Railroad |
| remont | Lake-Summit | Front | 11,320 | 1888 | R. R. and Highway |
| eorgia | Park-Summit | Front | 11,476 | 1860 | Abandoned Road |
| ore | Grand | Park-Rabbit Ears | 9,000* | | Highway |
| unshot | Grand | Park-Rabbit Ears | 9,500* | | Trail |
| agerman | Lake-Pitkin | Sawatch Mountains | 11,495 | 1878 | Highway in old R. R. Tunnel |
| alfmoon | Saguache | Cochetopa Hills | 12,712 | | Trail |
| ancock | Chaffee-Gunnison | Sawatch Mountains | 12,263 | 1888 | Trail |
| ayden | Fremont-Saguache | Sangre de Cristo-Culebra | 10,780 | 1878 | Trail |
| oosier | Park-Summit | Park-Rabbit Ears | 11,542 | 1860 | Highway |
| unchback | San Juan | San Juan Group | 12,487 | 1880 | Trail |
| llinois | Jackson-Grand | Park-Rabbit Ears | 10,000* | | Trail |
| mogene | Ouray-San Miguel | San Juan Group | 13,116 | | Trail |
| ndependence | Lake-Pitkin | Sawatch Mountains | 12,095 | 1879 | Highway |
| ndian Camp | Garfield | | 9,000* | | Trail |
| ones | Clear Creek-Grand | Front | 12,453 | 1860 | Trail |
| ebler | Gunnison | Elk-West Elk | 10,000* | | Road |
| ake Creek | Chaffee-Gunnison | Sawatch Mountains | 12,226 | 1872 | Trail |
| a Manga | Conejos | San Juan Group | 10,000* | | Highway |
| a Poudre | Grand-Larimer | Front | 10,193 | 1900 | Trail and Irrigation Ditch |
| a Veta | Costilla | Sangre de Cristo-Culebra | 9,378 | 1877 | Highway |
| izard Head | Dolores-San Miguel | San Juan Group | 10,000* | | R. R. and Highway |
| os Pinos | Saguache | Cochetopa Hills | 10,500* | | Highway |
| ou Creek | Gunnison-Ouray | San Juan Group | 11,260 | 1912 | Trail |
| oveland | Clear Creek-Summit | Front | 11,992 | 1888 | Projected Highway |
| ulu | Jackson-Grand | Park-Rabbit Ears | 11,400* | 1905 | Trail |
| Manzanares Creek | Huerfano-Costilla | Sangre de Cristo-Culebra | 9,000* | 1880 | { Trail North Side<br>{ Road South Side |
| Marcellina | Gunnison | Elk-West Elk | 10,400* | | Road |
| Marshall | Saguache | Sawatch Mountains | 10,950 | 1877 | Railroad |

* Approximate elevation in feet.

### ALTITUDE AND LOCATION OF MOUNTAIN PASSES—Continued

| Name of Pass | Counties | Name of Range | Elevation in Feet | Earliest Known Use | Character of Present Use |
|---|---|---|---|---|---|
| McClure | Gunnison-Pitkin | Elk | 9,500* | ---- | T: |
| Meadows | Rio Grande | San Juan Group | 10,300 | ---- | T: |
| Medano | Huerfano-Saguache | Sangre de Cristo-Culebra | 10,150 | 1850 | T: |
| Milner | Grand-Larimer | Front | 10,759 | 1900 | Highv |
| Minnesota | Gunnison | Elk-West Elk | 10,000* | ---- | T: |
| Molas Lake | San Juan | San Juan Group | 10,000* | ---- | Highv |
| Monarch | Chaffee-Gunnison | Sawatch Mountains | 11,650 | 1880 | Highv |
| Monument | Gunnison | San Juan Group | 11,000* | ---- | T: |
| Mosca | Huerfano-Saguache | Sangre de Cristo-Culebra | 9,713 | 1850 | { Road East S: { Trail West S |
| Mosquito | Park-Lake | Park-Mosquito | 13,188 | 1875 | Abandoned R: |
| Muddy | Jackson-Grand | Park-Rabbit Ears | 8,772 | 1875 | Highv |
| Mummy | Larimer | Front | 11,700* | ---- | T: |
| Music | Huerfano-Saguache | Sangre de Cristo-Culebra | 11,800 | 1878 | T: |
| North Cochetopa | Saguache | Cochetopa Hills | 10,000* | 1880 | T: |
| Ohio | Gunnison | Elk-West Elk | 10,033 | 1900 | T: |
| Ophir | San Juan-San Miguel | San Juan Group | 11,350 | 1888 | T: |
| Owl Creek | Gunnison-Ouray | San Juan Group | 11,120 | 1919 | T: |
| Pass Creek | Huerfano | Sangre de Cristo-Culebra | 9,200* | 1850 | R: |
| Pearl | Gunnison-Pitkin | Elk-West Elk | 12,715* | 1890 | T: |
| Poncha | Chaffee-Saguache | Sangre de Cristo-Culebra | 8,945 | Before 1800 | Highv |
| Ptarmigan | Grand | Park-Rabbit Ears | 11,000* | ---- | T: |
| Rabbit Ears | Jackson-Routt-Grand | Park-Rabbit Ears | 9,680 | 1895 | Highv |
| Railroad | Mineral | San Juan Group | 12,000* | ---- | T: |
| Raton | Las Animas | | 8,560 | 1846 | Highway and R. |
| Red Mountain | Ouray-San Juan | San Juan Group | 11,018 | 1881 | Highv |
| Rogers | Gilpin-Grand | Front | 11,900* | 1902 | T: |
| Rollins | Boulder-Grand | Front | 11,680 | 1860 | Trail and Railr: |
| Sand Creek | Larimer | Medicine Bow | 9,000* | ---- | Passable R: |
| San Francisco | Las Animas | | 8,600* | ---- | T: |
| San Francisco | Las Animas | Sangre de Cristo-Culebra | 8,560 | ---- | T: |
| Sangre de Cristo | Costilla | Sangre de Cristo-Culebra | 9,459 | Before 1800 | Abandoned R: |
| Schofield | Gunnison | Elk-West Elk | 10,000* | 1885 | R: |
| Scotch Creek | Dolores-San Miguel | San Juan Group | 10,500* | ---- | Abandoned R: |
| Silver | Mineral | San Juan Group | 12,000* | ---- | T: |
| Skull Creek | Moffat | | 8,700* | ---- | R: |
| Spring Creek | Hinsdale | San Juan Group | 11,025 | 1878 | R: |
| Squaw | Clear Creek | Front | 9,807 | ---- | High: |
| Stillwater | Grand | Park-Rabbit Ears | 10,000* | ---- | T: |
| St. Louis | Grand | Front | 11,500* | ---- | T: |
| Stony | San Juan | San Juan Group | 12,594 | 1878 | T: |
| Summit | Rio Grande | San Juan Group | 12,000* | ---- | T: |
| Swampy | Gunnison | Elk-West Elk | 10,365 | 1900 | T: |
| Tarryall | Park | Front | 12,456 | ---- | P: |
| Taylor | Gunnison | Elk-West Elk | 12,500* | ---- | |
| Taylor | Gunnison-Pitkin | Elk-West Elk | 12,400* | 1882 | |
| Tennessee | Lake-Eagle | Front | 10,424 | 1873 | R. R. and Hig: |
| Tincup | Chaffee-Gunnison | Sawatch Mountains | 12,000* | 1880 | |
| Trimble | La Plata | San Juan Group | 13,076 | 1902 | |
| Troublesome | Jackson-Grand | Park-Rabbit Ears | 10,000* | ---- | |
| Trout Creek | Park-Chaffee | Park-Mosquito | 9,346 | 1875 | Hig: |
| Twin Creek | Teller | | 8,200* | ---- | |
| Ute | Teller | | 7,600 | Before 1800 | |
| Ute | Routt-Jackson | Park-Rabbit Ears | 11,100* | 1875 | |
| Ute | Grand | Front | 9,800* | 1880 | |
| Ute | Larimer-Jackson | Medicine Bow | 10,500* | 1878 | |
| Vasquez | Clear Creek-Grand | Front | 11,850* | 1862 | |
| Venable | Custer-Saguache | Sangre de Cristo-Culebra | 10,500* | ---- | |
| Veta | Costilla | Sangre de Cristo-Culebra | 9,100* | 1880 | Rai: |
| Victor | Teller | | 10,202 | ---- | Rai: |
| Warmspring | Park | Park-Mosquito | ----- | 1910 | |
| Webster | Park-Summit | Front | 12,102 | 1900 | |
| Weminuche | Hinsdale | San Juan Group | 10,622 | ---- | |
| West Maroon | Gunnison-Pitkin | Elk-West Elk | 12,400* | ---- | |
| Weston | Park-Lake | Park-Mosquito | 12,109 | 1875 | Abandoned |
| Willow Creek | Jackson-Grand | Park-Rabbit Ears | 9,683 | 1878 | Hig: |
| Wolf Creek | Mineral-Archuleta | San Juan Group | 10,850 | 1888 | Hig: |
| Yellowjacket | La Plata | | 8,000* | 1915 | |
| Yellowjacket | Rio Blanco | | 7,400* | 1877 | |
| Yellowjacket | Routt | | 7,500* | ---- | |

* Approximate elevation in feet.

# Homestead Lands

THE United States government had 7,657,140 acres of unappropriated and unreserved land within the boundaries of Colorado on July 1, 1931, subject to entry under homestead and other public land laws. Of that area, 6,536,475 acres was surveyed and 1,120,665 acres unsurveyed. The total area of unreserved public land was 370,328 acres smaller than on the same date in 1930, and 561.735 acres less than in 1929, the decreases being due to increases in the area embraced in original entries during the fiscal years and a smaller number of cancellations through relinquishments and expiration of the statutory periods. The increase in areas appropriated is not confined to Colorado, nor to any particular section of the country and to no one law, but has been general throughout the public land states since 1926.

Exclusive of this vacant land, there was 2,131,471 acres upon which entries had been made, but upon which final proof of compliance with the law had not been presented. Such of these entries as may from time to time be cancelled for failure to submit final proof or for failure to comply with the law will be open to entry by the first qualified applicant, if not withdrawn or reserved, but until there is a forfeiture of the land upon which final proof has not been made, it is not subject to entry by any other than the pending applicant.

The unappropriated and unreserved land is open for entry under various classes of filings, including homestead, soldiers' and sailors' homestead rights, desert entry, timber and stone and other classifications. All of this land is administered by the general land office of the department of the interior, and contact with the public is through the district land offices, to which all applications should be made. The district land offices furnish general information to the public upon application.

There are several classes of entries by which public lands may be taken, but those most generally used are the ordinary 160-acre agricultural homestead entry; the enlarged homestead entry; the desert land entry; the stock-growing, or 640-acre entry, and timber and stone entries. These various classes of public land filings are described in detail in a series of pamphlets published by the Interior Department under direction of the General Land Office, and can be secured from the register of the nearest public land office. The pamphlet most frequently used by those in search of public lands is known as Circular No. 541, entitled "Suggestions to Homesteaders and Persons Desiring to Make Homestead Entries."

Entrymen on public lands must remember that not in all cases does the subsurface title pass to the entryman with the surface title. Under various reservations, withdrawals and classifications coal, oil, gas and other nonmetal deposits frequently are reserved to the government and the entryman secures only surface title. This is particularly true of oil and gas, which are governed largely by the mineral leasing acts of 1914 and 1920. It is practically impossible at present to secure title to such deposits by taking advantage of the public land entries provided by law, such deposits being subject to special leasing acts. Entrymen desirous of securing such mineral titles should consult officials of the Land Office or others who are in a position to advise them.

Some of the unappropriated land is classed as agricultural, but most of it is chiefly valuable for grazing and mineral purposes, and includes large areas in the mountainous districts that lie at elevations of 7,000 feet or more above sea level. Small tracts suitable for farming may be found in the mountain counties, but practically all the land of value for this purpose that lies within a reasonable distance of a railroad has been filed upon. The land that lies in the counties east of the mountains is mostly in small tracts, below the size of a government homestead, or remote from a railroad. The rainfall in some sections is too light for practical farming without irrigation.

It should be borne in mind by prospective settlers who are looking to the government domain as a possible location that the land has been combed by homeseekers for many years and that in most cases that most suited to farming has been filed upon long since. It must also be recognized that the task of subduing raw land and making it productive is one which seldom can be accomplished without some money and some acquaintance with the locality and its farming problems. Newcomers in the state are urged to use care and judgment in selecting homestead land and are advised that it is far better to spend time in investigating the various tracts still open to settlement than to jump to conclusions and select a tract which later may be found to be unfit for farming or to be too remote from railroads and markets to make farming a financial success.

Entries upon the public domain have been decreasing steadily in recent years, due to the prior acquisition of the more desirable tracts by settlers, until the last two years, in which increases have been reported. Public and Indian lands entered in the fiscal year ending June 30, for the past ten years, in acres, were as follows:

| Year | Acres |
|---|---|
| 1922 | 1,258,989 |
| 1923 | 892,124 |
| 1924 | 605,390 |
| 1925 | 417,225 |
| 1926 | 357,464 |
| 1927 | 426,780 |
| 1928 | 345,925 |
| 1929 | 421,000 |
| 1930 | 520,705 |
| 1931 | 463,538 |

There are two district land offices in Colorado, located at Denver and Pueblo, both of which are in the government postoffice buildings. Unappropriated and unreserved land open to entry on July 1, 1930, classified by counties under the two district offices, is shown in an accompanying table. The surveyed land only is open to entry. The quantity of unsurveyed land in any county may be determined by subtracting the surveyed from the total.

| Land District and County | Area in Acres Surveyed | Total |
|---|---|---|
| **Denver Land District:** | | |
| Boulder | 3,360 | 3,360 |
| Chaffee | 89,650 | 89,650 |
| Clear Creek | 5,242 | 16,842 |
| Delta | 130,900 | 132,500 |
| Dolores | 26,511 | 26,511 |
| Douglas | 80 | 80 |
| Eagle | 122,960 | 124,960 |
| Elbert | 80 | 80 |
| Fremont | 25,000 | 25,000 |
| Garfield | 414,559 | 550,088 |
| Gilpin | ...... | 3,480 |

| Land District and County | Area in Acres Surveyed | Total |
|---|---|---|
| Grand | 64,090 | 64,090 |
| Gunnison | 273,250 | 347,150 |
| Hinsdale | 64,880 | 98,330 |
| Jackson | 170,760 | 170,760 |
| Jefferson | 880 | 880 |
| Lake | 11,160 | 23,960 |
| Larimer | 22,600 | 22,600 |
| Logan | 1,240 | 1,240 |
| Mesa | 608,848 | 763,138 |
| Moffat | 1,211,851 | 1,408,081 |
| Montrose | 454,110 | 514,710 |
| Morgan | 640 | 640 |
| Ouray | 25,220 | 25,220 |
| Park | 57,120 | 68,120 |
| Pitkin | 13,007 | 13,007 |
| Rio Blanco | 824,514 | 1,060,214 |
| Routt | 52,788 | 54,488 |
| Saguache | 90,190 | 90,190 |
| San Miguel | 264,600 | 310,340 |
| Summit | 13,680 | 13,680 |
| Teller | 1,520 | 1,520 |
| Washington | 1,040 | 1,040 |
| Weld | 2,440 | 2,440 |
| Yuma | 560 | 560 |
| Total | 5,049,330 | 6,028,949 |
| **Pueblo Land District:** | | |
| Alamosa | 46,824 | 46,824 |
| Archuleta | 93,533 | 102,661 |
| Baca | 799 | 799 |
| Bent | 3,486 | 3,486 |
| Chaffee | 1,121 | 1,121 |
| Cheyenne | 222 | 222 |
| Conejos | 249,756 | 249,756 |
| Crowley | 930 | 930 |
| Custer | 12,220 | 12,220 |
| Dolores | 16,860 | 23,260 |
| Elbert | 120 | 120 |
| El Paso | 1,926 | 1,926 |
| Fremont | 289,113 | 313,403 |
| Hinsdale | ...... | 9,900 |
| Huerfano | 52,705 | 52,705 |
| Kiowa | 571 | 571 |
| Kit Carson | 343 | 343 |
| La Plata | 138,163 | 152,203 |
| Las Animas | 38,003 | 38,003 |
| Lincoln | 1,316 | 1,316 |
| Montezuma | 190,237 | 221,502 |
| Otero | 1,261 | 1,261 |
| Prowers | 873 | 873 |
| Pueblo | 13,069 | 13,069 |
| Rio Grande | 76,187 | 76,187 |
| Saguache | 230,820 | 230,820 |
| San Juan | ...... | 46,023 |
| Teller | 26,687 | 26,687 |
| Total | 1,487,145 | 1,628,191 |
| State total | 6,536,475 | 7,657,140 |

Earnings of the two Colorado land offices, and sources, for the year ending June 30, 1931, are as follows:

| | |
|---|---|
| Fees and commissions | $ 36,152.92 |
| Sale of public lands | 15,637.81 |
| Royalties (leasing act) | 83,581.14 |
| Sale of Indian lands | 33,828.24 |
| Total | $169,200.11 |

Expenses of the two offices for the fiscal year amounted to $22,949.08.

# State or School Lands*

WHAT is popularly known as state land in Colorado and other western public land states comprises the various areas turned over by the federal government to the state governments under general acts of congress and sundry special statutory grants, to be administered for the particular state interests in those states for which the grants were made. The most important of these grants were made under an act of congress passed in 1875, the year before Colorado became a state, by which the United States gave to each of the public land states an amount of land equal to one-eighteenth of the area of the state, for the benefit of the public schools. This is known as school land and quite generally in public land states all state land is referred to as school land, though various grants were made to the states for purposes in no way connected with the schools.

The original school land grant gave to the state sections 16 and 36 in every township. As there were large Indian reservations and extensive private land holdings in Colorado at the time the grant was made, the state was permitted to select other public lands in lieu of those within these reservations and public holdings. As a result, the state acquired large blocks of land in various localities, sometimes almost entire townships. When the national forests were created the state also exchanged considerable areas of state land within the forest boundaries for government land in other localities. The area of state or school lands in each county is shown in the table between pages 12 and 13 in this volume.

After these exchanges and adjustments had been made, the status of state land on November 30, 1930, including all classes of grants, was as follows:

|  | Acres |
|---|---|
| Original grants | 4,500,686 |
| Land sold | 1,424,116 |
| Net remaining | 3,076,570 |
| Land leased† | 2,544,544 |
| Vacant land | 532,026 |
| Total | 3,076,570 |

State land sold from the time of the transfer from the federal government down to December 1, 1930, aggregated 1,678,490 acres, of which 254,374 acres reverted to the state through the cancellation of purchase certificates, leaving a net of 1,424,116 acres. The record period was in the two years ending December 1, 1910, when a total of 287,341 acres was sold. A decline followed until the period of the world war, when again there was a heavy demand for agricultural land. In 1917-1918 the sales increased to 224,006 acres and then declined in the following biennial period to 156,502 acres. The general depression throughout the country in 1921 and 1922 was reflected in a drop in sales to 35,754 acres in those years. The adverse conditions continued during 1923 and 1924, when the minimum was reached. Since then there has been a gradual improvement as reflected in the following table of sales in biennial periods:

|  | Acres |
|---|---|
| 1923-1924 | 10,346 |
| 1925-1926 | 21,384 |
| 1927-1928 | 25,513 |
| 1929-1930 | 99,136 |

The average price per acre of land sold in 1929-1930 was $10.96, which compares with $15.33 in 1927-1928, $13.28 in 1925-1926 and $12.62 in 1923-1924. The maximum average per acre was $21.38 in 1919-1920, and the minimum was $4.35 in 1899-1900.

An accompanying table shows the acreage in the original grants after adjustments and exchanges were made, the purposes for which the grants were made, the acreage sold out of each, the net acreage remaining, and the acreage under lease for agricultural and grazing purposes on November 30, 1930.

A summary of the acreage under lease at the end of the last fiscal year is as follows:

|  | Acres |
|---|---|
| Agriculture and grazing | 2,544,544 |
| Mineral | 1,222 |
| Clays, limestone, etc. | 2,774 |
| Oil and gas | 516,711 |
| Coal | 15,774 |

The state reserves the mineral rights under all land sold and leases for coal, oil, gas and minerals listed above are in part upon land reported sold for agricultural purposes.

Acres of state land under lease for

---

*Owing to a change of policy, whereby compilations of the State Board of Land Commissioners are made biennially instead of annually, tables in this chapter do not contain data for 1931.

†For agricultural and grazing purposes.

oil and gas at the end of biennial periods on November 30 of the years named and rentals and royalties paid were as follows:

| Year | Acres | Rentals and Royalties |
|---|---|---|
| 1924 | 506,386 | $ 52.653 |
| 1926 | 219,398 | 38,756 |
| 1928 | 207,854 | 38,607 |
| 1930 | 516,710 | 103,294 |

Acres leased for coal at the end of biennial periods and income received therefrom during the period were as follows:

| Year | Acres | Income |
|---|---|---|
| 1918 | 13,469 | $190,663 |
| 1920 | 13,634 | 174,113 |
| 1922 | 17,114 | 141,306 |
| 1924 | 13,948 | 171,112 |
| 1926 | 14,034 | 215,231 |
| 1928 | 17,814 | 188,723 |
| 1930 | 15,774 | 197,916 |

Receipts of the land board from all sources, including sales of land, rentals and royalties, interest, etc., for biennial periods ending November 30 of the years named, were as follows:

| Year | Amount |
|---|---|
| 1914 | $1,364,764 |
| 1916 | 1,788,430 |
| 1918 | 2,509,238 |
| 1920 | 3,160,643 |
| 1922 | 2,053,990 |
| 1924 | 1,908,170 |
| 1926 | 2,275,575 |
| 1928 | 1,912,417 |
| 1930 | 1,895,065 |

The terms of the grants from the government provide that funds derived from the sale of land shall go into permanent funds and only the interest and the revenues derived from the administration of the unsold land shall be used for the benefit of the schools or special interests for which the grants were made. These permanent funds are mostly invested in interest-bearing securities. The amounts in the various funds on November 30, 1930, were as follows:

| | |
|---|---|
| Public school | $10,284,787 |
| Internal improvement | 78 |
| Agricultural college | 445,598 |
| University | 88,692 |
| Penitentiary | 1,499 |
| Public building | 812 |
| Saline | 961 |
| Total | $10,822,427 |

The income from these funds is deposited with the state treasurer and on the first of January and July of each year the amount is apportioned to the various counties of the state according to the law. For the biennial period ending November 30, 1930, these transactions were as follows:

| | |
|---|---|
| Reported by treasurer | $1,631,566 |
| Deducted for teachers' minimum salaries | 283,205 |
| Total apportionment | 1,348,361 |
| Deducted for blanks | 20,399 |
| Withheld acct. high school tuition | 38,112 |
| Distribution to counties | 1,289,850 |

On November 30, 1930, the amounts in the income funds were as follows:

| | |
|---|---|
| Public school | $385,118 |
| Internal improvement | 95 |
| Agricultural college | 22,476 |
| University | 1,969 |
| Public building | 1,246 |
| Saline | 15,172 |
| Penitentiary | 1,785 |
| Total | $427,861 |

State land, which is administered by the state board of land commissioners, is leased and sold under regulations made by the board, which may be obtained from that body upon application. Leases are made for grazing purposes, for agriculture and for exploration for oil, gas, minerals, coal, clay, etc. Before any state land can be sold it must be appraised by representatives of the board and the applicant must agree to pay the price fixed by the appraiser. The land is then sold at public auction, selling at or above the appraised price, the minimum legal price being $3.50 per acre. The terms upon which state land may be purchased are very liberal. Ten per cent of the purchase price is payable in cash and the remainder is payable in installments extending over a period of 33 years. Leases are made in much the same way, minimum prices being fixed at which state land may be leased for various purposes.

Of the 3,076,570 acres of state land in Colorado, approximately 473,692 acres is coal land, according to estimates made by the mineral superintendent of the state land board. This is the most valuable asset owned by the state, practically all of which was granted to Colorado by the federal government for the benefit of the public school system. The value of this land is estimated at approximately $100,000,000. It is distributed through nearly every coal-bearing district in the state as follows:

| Canon City District | Acres |
|---|---|
| Fremont county | 1,960 |

| Northern Coal Fields | |
|---|---|
| Adams county | 9,600 |
| Arapahoe county | 9,080 |
| Boulder county | 760 |
| Denver county | 1,920 |
| Douglas county | 13,180 |
| Elbert county | 30,020 |
| El Paso county | 44,700 |
| Jefferson county | 1,820 |
| Weld county | 75,560 |

**Southern Coal Fields**

Huerfano county................ 11,400
Las Animas county............. 33,360

**Yampa Coal Fields**

Moffat county.................120,400
Routt county.................. 69,720

**Miscellaneous**

Archuleta county................ 732
Grand county................... 2,960
Gunnison county................ 3,440
Jackson county................ 25,080
La Plata county................ 9,960
Montezuma county.............. 4,160
Park county.................... 3,880

Total coal area...............473,692

The estimates of the acreage and distribution of state coal lands are based on the reports of the United States geological survey. It is assumed that a very large percentage of the coal acreage will not be found to contain workable coal, and the estimates of value are based on this assumption. Government appraisers have placed the value of public coal land in Colorado at from $100 to $400 per acre, depending on the character of the deposits and their accessibility. The value of state coal land has been estimated at a little more than $200 per acre, which is generally conceded to be very conservative.

### STATUS OF VARIOUS LAND GRANTS, 1930

(From Records of State Board of Land Commissioners)

| GRANT | Acres original grant | Acres sold | Net acres remaining | Acres under lease* |
|---|---|---|---|---|
| School | 3,753,813 | 928,326 | 2,825,487 | 2,338,981 |
| Agricultural college | 90,000 | 57,049 | 32,951 | 29,307 |
| Internal improvement | 499,790 | 341,605 | 158,185 | 134,500 |
| Penitentiary | 31,985 | 22,688 | 9,297 | 7,239 |
| Public building | 31,905 | 27,191 | 4,713 | 3,878 |
| Saline | 18,830 | 5,371 | 13,459 | 13,459 |
| Reformatory | 520 | ------ | 520 | ------ |
| University | 45,843 | 36,793 | 9,051 | 3,263 |
| General fund | 28,000 | 5,093 | 22,907 | 13,917 |
| Total | 4,500,686 | 1,424,116 | 3,076,570 | 2,544,544 |

*Includes some duplication, where surface and mineral leases exist on same areas.

## National Forests

### (By the United States Forest Service)

A LARGE portion of the mountainous area of Colorado is valuable primarily as forest land. Most of this rugged country, along both slopes of the Continental Divide, and extending irregularly along spurs east and west therefrom, is in national forests, which are under the supervision of the United States forest service. These forests are administrative units which have been established for ease in handling, based mainly upon topographic and watershed features. There are 14 forests wholly in the state, and one other, the La Sal, which lies partially within its boundaries. The San Isabel, with 613,652 acres, is the smallest national forest in the state, while the San Juan, with 1,249,121 acres, is the largest. The forests average a little less than 1,000,000 acres each in area, or in all, 13,323,566 acres.

These forests, together with four east of the Continental Divide in Wyoming, those in South Dakota, Nebraska, and Oklahoma, 22 in all, make up the Rocky Mountain Region of the forest service. Colonel Allen S. Peck is regional forester, with headquarters in the Postoffice building, Denver. Assistant regional foresters are in charge of branches of operation, including fire protection, forest management, range management, lands and public relations. A regional engineer and a fiscal agent complete the organization immediately under the regional forester. There are about 150 forest officers in the state, including those in the regional office in Denver.

As far as possible, these timber lands are handled as local enterprises. Although they are a part of an extensive system comprising 150 national forests scattered through 29 states, Porto Rico and Alaska, and although the forest service, as a part of the United States department of agriculture, has its headquarters in Washington, its organization is decentralized to such an extent that local officials handle most of the business with users and purchasers on the ground.

The forests in Colorado comprise a

little more than 8 per cent in area of the 160,787,687 acres of national forest land in the United States. The first "reserve" was created by President Harrison in 1891 in Wyoming, and was known as the Yellowstone Park timberland reserve. The White River reserve was the first forest to be set aside in Colorado, the proclamation of President Harrison having been made October 16, 1891. These and all others set aside until 1907 were known as "reserves." Beginning in that year, however, they were all designated officially as national forests, in which timber was to be grown and utilized instead of reserved. This was an important step in the development of the present system. The accompanying table gives the names of each national forest wholly or partly in this state, and the headquarters of the supervisor.

| National Forest | Headquarters |
|---|---|
| Arapaho | Hot Sulphur Springs |
| Cochetopa | Salida |
| Grand Mesa | Grand Junction |
| Gunnison | Gunnison |
| Holy Cross | Glenwood Springs |
| *La Sal | Moab, Utah |
| Montezuma | Mancos |
| Pike | Colorado Springs |
| Rio Grande | Monte Vista |
| †Roosevelt | Fort Collins |
| Routt | Steamboat Springs |
| San Isabel | Pueblo |
| San Juan | Durango |
| Uncompahgre | Delta |
| White River | Glenwood Springs |

*Lies principally in Utah.
†Name changed from "Colorado" to "Roosevelt" by executive order dated March 28, 1932.

The boundaries of these mountainous tracts are very irregular. Most of the forests lie in two or more counties, while some of them are made up of two or more separated tracts. The location of the various national forests wholly or partly in the state by counties is as follows:

| Forest | Counties |
|---|---|
| Arapaho: | Eagle, Grand, Jackson, Summit. |
| Cochetopa: | Chaffee, Gunnison, Lake, Park, Saguache. |
| Grand Mesa: | Delta, Garfield, Gunnison, Mesa. |
| Gunnison: | Delta, Gunnison, Hinsdale, Montrose, Saguache. |
| Holy Cross: | Eagle, Garfield, Gunnison, Pitkin. |
| Montezuma: | Dolores, La Plata, Montezuma, San Miguel. |
| Pike: | Clear Creek, Douglas, El Paso, Jefferson, Park, Teller. |
| Rio Grande: | Archuleta, Conejos, Hinsdale, La Plata, Mineral, Rio Grande, Saguache, San Juan. |
| Roosevelt: | Boulder, Gilpin, Jefferson, Larimer. |

| Forest | Counties |
|---|---|
| Routt: | Grand, Jackson, Routt, Moffat. |
| San Isabel: | Alamosa, Chaffee, Custer, Fremont, Huerfano, Las Animas, Pueblo, Saguache. |
| San Juan: | Archuleta, Conejos, Hinsdale, La Plata, Mineral, Rio Grande, San Juan. |
| Uncompahgre: | Gunnison, Hinsdale, Mesa, Montrose, Ouray, San Juan, San Miguel. |
| White River: | Eagle, Garfield, Moffat, Rio Blanco, Routt. |
| La Sal: | Mesa, Montrose. |

The national forests were created primarily for the production of timber and the protection of the watersheds which supply municipalities and irrigation enterprises with their liquid gold. There are other important uses, such as grazing and recreation, which must be co-ordinated with the growing of timber in such a way that each will occupy its proper place.

Timber—The total amount of standing merchantable timber within the national forests of Colorado is estimated to be 31,918,969,000 board feet. The annual growth which these forests are capable of producing is approximately 500,000,000 board feet, or more than the timber demand of Colorado's present population.

The annual cut of timber from these national forests varies from 50 to 70 million board feet. In 1931 it amounted to 43,727,000. The size of the sales through which this timber is disposed of varies from a few thousand board feet to over 200,000,000, most of them involving less than $500 worth of timber. The average price paid in 1931 was $2.38 per thousand feet, which in that year produced a revenue of $104,003.83.

Sawtimber makes up about half of the annual cut. Other products, in the order of their importance, are railroad ties, mine props and timbers, telephone poles, posts and cordwood.

In addition to the timber disposed of through sales, 10,894,000 feet was cut by ranchers, settlers and farmers for use on their lands located on or near the national forests. This timber was disposed of without charge to the users under government regulations, which involved the issuance of over four thousand individual permits.

Additional products of the forest, which cannot be reduced to board feet, are sold by the forest service. Among these are Christmas trees and evergreen boughs, which result from thinnings in over-crowded stands of Douglas fir; ornamental seedlings and pine cones. The revenue received from these products in 1931 amounted to $1,373.

The average annual cut of timber in the national forests of Colorado is less than one-sixth of what it could be without exceeding the potential annual replacement through natural growth. During the past several years, with the exception of 1931, however, the yearly cut has increased slightly. Within recent years lodgepole pine has attracted attention as a species suitable for use in the form of telephone and telegraph poles. Plants have been established at Salida and Denver for the preservative treatment of poles, railroad ties, and fence posts produced from nearby forests.

In 1930 pulp-wood species (Engelmann and blue spruce, alpine, corkbark and white fir), of which there are nearly 23,000,000,000 board feet of timber of sawlog size in the national forests of Colorado, received considerable attention from paper manufacturers. It is anticipated that there will be a renewed interest in pulp-wood in the state when economic conditions improve.

With the exception of Christmas tree thinnings, all timber is sold on the stump and is cut and removed by the purchaser under the close supervision of forest officers. Only mature trees are designated for cutting or such trees as it is advisable to remove to secure proper spacing for those which remain. The aim of the methods employed is not only to maintain the forest in a perpetually productive condition, but to increase the productive capacity of the stands as time goes on.

**Reforestation**—Approximately 10 per cent of the timberland within the national forests of Colorado has been denuded by fire or is covered with brush which is of no value except as it prevents erosion and rapid run-off from rain and melting snow. These areas can be restored to productiveness as forest land only through artificial reforestation.

Most of the destruction by fire occurred before 1905. During the past twenty-four years for which records have been kept the total area burned over is equal to about one-fourth of one per cent of the total, or 33,049 acres. The Mt. Herman burn, which was swept by fire in the 80's, covers an area of 10,000 acres, which is approximately 15 times as large as any single fire in the Pike forest which has occurred since 1908. The planting of this area, which is located between Palmer Lake and Woodland Park, will be completed in 1931. The project was started in 1924.

Colorado's forests have a value in protecting watersheds for the large irrigation interests and municipalities of the state, which it is difficult to appraise. Forests retard the melting of snow in the mountains during the spring season and thus tend to equalize the flow of the streams. Three million acres of land in this state, valued at approximately $300,000,000, depend upon such sources for irrigation water. Forests also retard the flow of water in times of flood.

During the calendar year 1931, 1,741 acres of denuded land were planted in the national forests of Colorado. The area planted annually is now being increased. In 1932, it is estimated, a total of 2,200 acres will be planted. A plantation of 500 acres will be established on Cedar mountain above Cheesman dam and 1,500 acres will be planted on denuded lands on the headwaters of the South Platte river above South park. The production of the Monument nursery has recently been increased to produce trees for this increased acreage. A total of 1,606,000 trees was shipped from the Monument nursery during the spring of 1931, and 1,804,000 will be distributed from this nursery in 1932. Of all the area planted to date in Colorado, about 85 per cent supports a stand of 250 trees or more per acre, which is considered the minimum stocking of a successful plantation. During ordinary seasons large survivals are obtained in planting trees and the work can be done quite effectively in the rockiest country at a cost which is not unreasonable in view of the difficulties encountered.

Most of the reforestation in the national forests has been on burned-over watersheds of municipalities, such as those of Colorado Springs, Denver, Trinidad, Salida, and Fruita.

**Recreation**—As the national forests are made more accessible by a good system of roads, people come to them in larger numbers for recreation. The national forests are the only large areas where hunting and fishing may be enjoyed by the ordinary citizen who does not have the money to purchase a privately owned fishing stream or to join a hunting or fishing club. Streams which have always been open to fishing are gradually being posted. As a result, most of the public must go to the national forests if they wish to enjoy this sport.

In 1931, 2,265,070 people used the

national forests of the state for recreation. Of these, 139,600 were hotel, resort, and summer home guests; 247,950 were campers, and 436,550 were picnickers who drove out from the towns and cities for one-day outings. The remainder were transients passing through the forests over the main highways enroute to distant points or driving over one of the numerous scenic routes for which the Colorado mountains are noted.

Although there was a decrease in the number of transient visitors to the forest during 1931, there was a much greater use by picnickers and campers, 132,700 more in 1931 than during the previous year. This class of users is represented mostly by people from the towns adjacent to the forests, and those who come from the rural districts of Colorado and neighboring states for their vacations.

Plans have been prepared for the development of the most desirable and largely used recreational areas in the national forests. In these plans recreation is co-ordinated with other forest activities and one form of recreation with another. Public needs, such as campgrounds, are first provided for, after which sites are selected for hotels, resorts, organization uses, and summer homes. The latter is the lowest in order of priority because it is a restricted use, but after providing for the public there is ample space for all summer home applicants.

There are 80 hotels and resorts and 525 summer homes under permit in the forests of Colorado. Many attractive lots for summer homes have been surveyed and are available for people who wish to build cabins in the national forests. These lots are a half to an acre in size and can be leased from the local supervisors, the annual fee being $10 or $15.

Exchange—There are 1,428,094 acres of private and state-owned land within the exterior boundaries of the national forests in Colorado. Of this area 107,-598 acres is state school land. The state land board and the United States forest service are now negotiating an exchange whereby these scattered holdings will be turned over to the forest service for an equal area of government land in one tract. When this exchange is completed Colorado will have its first state forest. This will be located on the east side of North Park on the west slope of the Medicine Bow range.

Much of the private land is permanently adapted to the production of timber and is no longer desired by the owner. In some cases it was taken up for the merchantable timber, which has now been removed, and in other cases it was taken up in the hope of making a successful farm and proved to be worthless. In still other cases it is mineral ground which has been worked out or proved to be valueless. Some of it is used for grazing and some not at all. Often a single owner has acquired a number of widely separated tracts. On March 20, 1922, the president approved the land exchange act, which authorizes in general language the exchange of private lands for government lands in the national forests, or the exchange of private lands for timber of equivalent value. This makes it possible for private owners to consolidate their holdings and to exchange timber producing land for land of greater value for grazing, and at the same time permits the government to consolidate its holdings in more compact bodies of timber land which will be easier of administration and less expensive to protect. Since 1922, 75,074 acres of privately-owned timber producing lands have been acquired in the national forests of the state in exchange for 25,592 acres and 59,099,000 feet of timber selected by private land owners with whom the exchanges were consummated.

Grazing in National Forests—Intermixed with the stands of timber on the forests are many parks or open places covered with good forage. There is also much grass and other forage plant growth in the timber where the tree growth is not too heavy. Most of this forage, by conservative uses, can be grazed by stock without injury to the timber. Some areas are closed to grazing in order to protect the slopes of streams which furnish municipal water supplies, and other areas, rock slides, etc., are barren of any forage growth. About 9,207,000 acres of the 13,323,566 net acreage in the national forests of Colorado is used for summer pasturage by about 25 to 30 per cent of the cattle and 50 to 60 per cent of the sheep owned in the state. During 1931, 290,221 cattle and horses were grazed by 2,868 permittees, and 1,050,322 sheep and goats by 898 permittees, in the national forests of the state.

Sheep are grazed in the extremely high portions of the forests, where the snow stays until the latter part of June and begins to fall again in September. They are on the ranges from two and one-half to three months. The lower altitudes are set apart for cattle and horses as a rule. The average grazing season for cattle and horses is about five months.

The grazing season of 1931 was the driest known in the memory of old settlers. This was followed by the most severe winter conditions recorded for many years over all the country west of the Continental Divide. But the livestock on the national forest summer ranges in 1931 did well and in only a very few instances was it necessary to remove stock before the close of the regular grazing season on account of feed shortage. This was due to the policy that has been built up through the years of conservatively stocking the ranges during normal seasons and thus building up reserve strength in the forage plants which enables them better to withstand the tests of the abnormal seasons.

**Grazing Fees**—A certain fee per head per month, or a per capita charge, is made for grazing permits. Up to and including 1927 the fees were based on a flat annual rate, regardless of variations in character of individual ranges. An intensive appraisal was conducted, which resulted in the revision of fees based upon the worth of the various individual ranges rather than upon a flat rate for all ranges. In 1927 the secretary of agriculture approved that the established increases in fees be applied in installments of 25 per cent each during the years 1928, 1929, 1930, and 1931. In 1931 the average fee for cattle in Colorado was about 17 cents per head per month and for sheep five and one-half cents per head per month. No charge is made for the natural increase, stock under six months of age, which goes in with the parent stock.

Due to the abnormal conditions during the summer and winter of 1931, on February 24, 1932, the secretary of agriculture, with the recommendation and concurrence of the forest service, reduced the above fees by one-half for the season of 1932. Moreover, payments will not be required until December, thus giving the stockman time to market their 1932 product.

**Larkspur Eradication** — C e r t a i n poisonous plants on the range kill stock, but it has been found that about 90 per cent of this loss in cattle can be prevented by digging or grubbing the principal poisonous plant, which is larkspur. Sheep are not affected by this plant and cattle losses are sometimes controlled in part by "sheeping"

bad patches of the plant early in the season. During the latter part of 1915 definite grubbing of larkspur was begun in Colorado. The progress of this work at the close of 1931 is indicated in the following figures:

Area now infested with poisonous plants ......................334,162
Area poisonous plants treated to close of 1931.................. 14,664
Total cost of treatment to close of 1931 ......................$40,991

Experiments were conducted in the summer of 1930 in the mountains of Colorado on the effectiveness and costs of administering solutions of commercial calcium chlorate to larkspur. Seven strengths were tested, but the costs, which are dependent upon many factors, appear to make this method of eradication prohibitive.

**Range Improvements** — Constructed range improvements that are at present in use on the national forests of Colorado consisted of the following at the close of the fiscal year 1931:

| | Mi. or No. | Value |
|---|---|---|
| Fences ............... | 678 | $112,007 |
| Corrals ............... | 49 | 3,885 |
| Stock driveways....... | 1,263 | 49,346 |
| Stock bridges.......... | 8 | 1,814 |
| Water developments.... | 306 | 13,278 |
| (including springs) | | |

**Game**—Game animals are always interesting and the forest service game census for 1931 shows there are in the national forests of the state approximately 12,200 elk, 3,500 mountain sheep, 112 antelope, 41,150 mule deer, 2,670 black or brown bear and 17 silvertip bear.

Approximately 6,558,800 fish fry were planted by the forest officers in the state in 1931.

State game refuges have been established within the national forests of the state. The forest service cooperates with the state authorities in the protection of these areas, comprising a total acreage of 3,551,970, of which 2,666,484 acres are within the boundaries of the national forests. In addition to these state game refuges, game areas have been established by administrative restrictions embracing 315,858 acres.

**Fire Control**—During 1931 a total of 206 fires occurred on or threatened the national forests in the state. One hundred fifty-one of these covered only one-fourth of an acre or less, 40 covered one-fourth to 10 acres, and 15 burned over 10 acres or more. The total area burned was 2,611 acres and the damage to timber, reproduction, forage and watershed protection amounted to $3,708. Of the area burned, 1,267 acres were national forest land, 31 acres were land privately owned inside the forest boundaries and there were 1,313 acres of privately owned land burned outside the national forests. Of these fires, 83 were caused by lightning, 15 by railroads, 34 by campers, 49 by smokers, six by debris burning, one by lumbering operations, six by incendiaries, and 12 by miscellaneous other causes. The biggest increase in number of fires over 1930 was due to lightning. Numerous severe and very dry electrical storms occurred throughout the fire season. The balance of the increased number of fires was due to campers, smokers and debris burning. Railroads were responsible for fewer fires in 1931 than in the previous year. Campers and smokers in the forested areas continue to be careless with fire. During 1931, which was an exceptionally dry year, any one of these fires might have reached serious proportions had it not been for the alertness of forest officers and the local people. It cost the forest service $14,802 to suppress these fires in Colorado in 1931, in addition to which $560 was paid by other agencies. The largest fire occurred on the Grand Mesa national forest, where 1,510 acres of government and private land was burned over, due to the carelessness of smokers.

During the most hazardous part of the season it was necessary to close the Arapaho, Roosevelt, Routt and San Isabel national forests to camp fires, except in constructed fireplaces on improved campgrounds. All the forests were closed to fireworks during the Fourth of July period. Owing to the extreme hazard and the great number of visitors generally throughout most of the year, the Devils Head mountain area in the Pike national forest is permanently closed to camp fires, smoking and the discharge of firearms.

**Roads**—A comprehensive system of roads and trails has been adopted for the national forests, and the forest service alone or in co-operation with the state or counties is engaged in the improvement of roads on that system, using government and co-operative funds. The roads are divided into two major classes: Forest highways and forest development roads, which also include trails. Forest highways include roads that are of prime importance to the state, counties, and communities, and funds for their improvement are programmed upon joint recommendations by the state highway department, bureau of public roads, and forest service, based upon surveys and estimates prepared by the bureau of public roads, which also has direct supervision of their construction. Forest development roads and trails are of vital importance in the protection of the forests against fires, and are also used in administration and in the marketing of the forest crop. Such roads, with the exception of a few which require expert engineering, are of lower standard than forest highways and are constructed by the forest service organization. During the fiscal year 1931 a total of 79.3 miles of new roads were constructed by the expenditure of $745,315. A total of $595,390 was spent on the construction of forest highways, $149,925 on forest development roads, and $36,217 on trails, of which 422.4 miles were built during the year. In addition $79,758 was spent in the maintenance of roads and trails during 1931.

**Finances**—The receipts from the sale of timber, grazing, and special use permits and other uses amounted to $540,848 during the fiscal year 1931. Twenty-five per cent of this amount, or $135,212, was turned over to the counties in accordance with the law, for schools and roads. An additional 10 per cent, or $54,084.80, was spent directly by the forest service for roads and trails in the national forests, this also in accordance with a congressional act authorizing such expenditure.

During the year there was expended $1,013,564.31 of forest service funds appropriated by Congress for roads and trails in the national forests of Colorado. A total of $653,892.85 was disbursed for the protection, improvement and administration of the national forests in the state, making a grand total expenditure of $1,667,457.16. Although this amounts to about three times the total receipts, it will be noted that over two-thirds of the 1931 expenditures is in the nature of an investment by the government in roads and other improvements. Expenditures for these purposes were more than usual during the year because of congressional appropriations for unemployment relief.

# Tourist Attractions

COLORADO has in its incomparable climate and wonderful scenery a natural resource of almost incalculable value from an economic standpoint. At the same time it furnishes recreation facilities for thousands of people from all parts of the United States and foreign countries. The invigorating low-pressure atmosphere of high altitudes, the cool and refreshing nights, the days of continuous sunshine and the accessibility of the attractive regions make ideal conditions for the tourist and pleasure seeker. Camping, hunting, fishing, mountain climbing and other outdoor sports may be enjoyed in regions remote from the cities and towns or close to inhabited places, as the visitor may choose. Excellent highways make automobile touring a pleasure in the mountains, through the valleys and wherever one desires to go. Federal, state and municipal governments contribute toward the furnishing of accommodations for visitors and have organized means of adding to their comfort and pleasure.

It is impossible to enumerate, even partially, in a volume of this character, all the tourist attractions of the state. That is left to the railroads serving Colorado, the commercial clubs of the various cities and towns and similar corporations and organizations which publish annually hundreds of booklets and leaflets descriptive of the state's scenic attractions and recreation opportunities. Such literature may be obtained upon request from the various railroads and organizations. A list of the principal civic and commercial organizations of the state, with addresses, is published elsewhere in this volume.

Switzerland has been more successful than perhaps any other country in capitalizing its mountain scenery for profit.

Yet Colorado is nearly seven times as large as Switzerland, and its mountain area is fully six times as great. Colorado has at least 43 named peaks and equally as many unnamed peaks that tower more than 14,000 feet above sea level, while Switzerland has but eight. Colorado has fully 1,000 peaks 10,000 feet high and over, while Switzerland has fewer than one-eighteenth as many. Every peak in Colorado is accessible for any careful and reasonably strong mountain climber entirely to its summit, while the highest peaks in Switzerland are accessible to their summits only for hardy and expert climbers and then only under the direction of experienced guides.

There are thousands of beautiful lakes in the mountains of Colorado, many of them of large size and all of them of wonderful beauty. Some of Colorado's lakes, though far less famous than Lake Lucerne, are not surpassed by it in certain characteristics of natural beauty. If they were surrounded by beautiful villas and hotels scores of Colorado's lakes might soon have almost as many admirers as have the lakes of Switzerland. Some of the more easily accessible of our mountain lakes are beginning to be surrounded by the modern conveniences that many tourists and travelers demand, but there will always be in Colorado hundreds of picturesque lakes where fishing is good and where natural beauty is not too much marred by the art of man.

The United States government has recognized the value and importance of Colorado's scenery and natural recreation advantages by the creation of two national parks and five national monuments within the state.

These are described in more detail under the title, "National Parks and Monuments," in this volume. Hovenweep, another national monument, lies partly in Colorado and partly in Utah.

The government is constantly improving the highways, providing facilities for campers, automobile travelers and other visitors in these parks, while hotel and transportation facilities are all that may be desired.

The national park service reports that more than 300,000 visitors entered the national parks and monuments in Colorado in 1931.

Fourteen national forests are located wholly within the boundaries of the state and one—the La Sal—lies partially within its borders. These forests embrace 13,323,566 acres within the state and include nearly all the higher mountain peaks not within the national parks and a very large part of the most beautiful scenery in the state. The forest service is devoting more attention each year to popularizing these forests as national playgrounds and to improving them with roads, trails, shelter houses and other conveniences for travelers. The forest service places the number of people who viewed the scenery, fished in the streams and camped in the woods of the state of Colorado in 1931 at 2,265,070. This compares with 1,617,-147 in 1925 and indicates the growing popularity of the national forests.

A further description of the national forests, their uses for recreational purposes, hotels, resorts and residence sites therein, game, etc., will be found in another chapter under the title "National Forests."

Colorado has many hundreds of miles of streams at high and low altitudes which afford unusually good fishing grounds, and the state is noted for the excellent sport it affords the anglers. The streams are stocked annually by the state game and fish department, the number of trout planted increasing yearly. In recent years around 30,000,000 trout have been planted annually in the streams by this agency. Big game is abundant in Colorado and conditions are made as favorable as possible for the sportsmen. In another chapter in this book under "Fish and Game" there is much additional data on fishing and hunting opportunities.

In recent years excellent highways have been built into many of the most beautiful mountain districts, and many of the most magnificent mountain peaks which were unknown even to most of the people of Colorado are now coming to be almost as well known as Pikes peak, which in the past was practically the only mountain in Colorado known outside the state. Today there are five or more automobile routes across the state east and west, intersecting north and south highways, and travel is heavy on all of them. More tourists visit Colorado today by automobile than visit it by rail, and automobile travel to the state is increasing much more rapidly than travel by railroad.

The city of Denver owns a chain of mountain parks radiating from the municipality into the mountains to the west, which form one of the leading tourist attractions of the state. The city has expended around $2,000,000 in constructing highways, erecting shelter houses, opening picnic grounds and making the area accessible and attractive for visitors. A description of the municipal park system is given elsewhere in this volume.

Some of the mountain areas that are yet inaccessible because of lack of highways are of exceptional beauty and grandeur and Colorado will for many years be offering each season some new scenic attraction to its visitors. People no longer come to Colorado year after year to see Pikes peak alone, but each year they may visit some new peak, lake or mountain park and none of our visitors of today will live long enough to see all that is worth while in the Colorado Rockies by making one visit to the state each year.

The characteristics of the Colorado climate that make it so attractive to tourists and healthseekers are its dryness, high percentage of sunshine, moderate air movements, and moderate and equable temperatures. The high altitude affects the climate favorably for persons afflicted with pulmonary and similar diseases, the air being rarer, less humid and generally purer than the air in lower altitudes. A more detailed description of the climatic conditions in the state and their effect on health seekers will be found in another chapter in this volume under the title, "Climatological Data."

Colorado is rich in mineral waters, some of them acknowledged to be of high curative qualities. More than 250 mineral springs and wells in the state have been carefully studied and their waters analyzed by the state geological survey, and there are perhaps as many which have not been analyzed. The largest single group of mineral springs in Colorado is found in and about the city of Steamboat Springs, in Routt county. Among other well-known groups of mineral springs are those at Glenwood Springs, Idaho Springs, Pagosa Springs, Hot Sulphur Springs, Manitou and Canon City. Many of these places are well known health and tourist resorts, some of them having large bathing pools, sanitoria, hotels and other conveniences. One of the springs at Pagosa Springs has an average flow of about 700 gallons per minute, being one of the largest mineral springs in the United States. The waters of many of the Colorado mineral springs are highly radio-active, comparing favorably with the most notable springs in the world in this respect. Temperatures of the waters vary greatly, the highest being that of the Hortense hot springs, near Mt. Princeton, in Chaffee county.

The economic features of the tourist business are important and contribute materially to the prosperity of the state. Expenditures by tourists represent new capital coming in, which is quickly absorbed into all channels of trade and exceeds the state's income from precious minerals many times each year. Municipalities contribute liberally towards the convenience and comfort of tourists and in many of the cities and towns public camp grounds are maintained, where running water, comfort stations, shelters, cooking equipment and other facilities are provided.

The number of people entering Colorado from other states in any given period is difficult to determine, but estimates compiled by various agencies, based in part on counts made and in part by computation of available data, give a fairly reliable indication of the facts. One authority gives the approximate number of visitors in 1931 at 1,390,148. Of this number, 990,148 came by automobiles and 400,000 on the railroads. The automobile estimate is based on a count made by the state highway department for the months of June, July and August, which showed 192,206 cars entering the state, with an average of 3.06 passengers per car. These three months account for 60 per cent of the total travel for the year and the remaining nine months for 40 per cent. The estimate of people coming in by railroads is based on the average number of passengers on regular main-line passenger trains, adjusted to seasonal changes.

The estimates for 1931, calculated on the basis named, are as follows:

| | By Auto | By Rail | Total |
|---|---|---|---|
| 3 mos., June, July and Aug. | 588,150 | 202,000 | 790,150 |
| 9 other mos. | 401,998 | 198,000 | 599,998 |
| Total, year | 990,148 | 400,000 | 1,390,148 |

Expenditures by visitors in the state in 1931, estimated on the basis of questionnaires sent out in 1930, was $94,390,000. These questionnaires showed an average stay of 2.95 weeks in the state for each visitor at an average ex-

penditure of $5.58 per day. The estimate for 1931 is based on an average expenditure of $4.58 per person per day, the amount being reduced from that of the previous year by 18 per cent on account of prevailing conditions. Of the total of $94,390,000 for the year, $72,396,000 is accounted for during June, July and August and $21,994,000 during the other months of the year. Expenditures for oil and gas for automobiles from other states while visiting in Colorado are estimated at $2,248,000, including $436,142 for state gasoline tax.

It is estimated that the 588,150 persons who entered the state in June, July and August, 1931, in private automobiles and remained in Colorado an average of 2.95 weeks each, consumed 1,036 carloads of food products. This estimate is based on the apparent per capita consumption of principal foodstuffs in the United States as reported by the department of commerce. In the following table the first column gives the annual per capita consumption in the United States of the items mentioned and the second column gives the quantity apparently consumed by the auto visitors while in the state:

| | | |
|---|---|---|
| Wheat flour, pounds | 177.1 | 6,009,357 |
| Cornmeal, pounds | 5.4 | 183,232 |
| Dressed beef, pounds | 61.4 | 2,083,424 |
| Dressed mutton and lamb, pounds | 5.3 | 179,839 |
| Dressed veal, pounds | 8.0 | 271,456 |
| Dressed pork (not including lard), pounds | 70.2 | 2,382,026 |
| Butter, pounds | 17.4 | 590,416 |
| Cheese, pounds | 4.17 | 141,496 |
| Ice cream, gallons | 2.6 | 88,223 |
| Eggs, dozens | 17.9 | 607,382 |
| Dressed poultry, pounds | 19.8 | 671,853 |
| Apples, pounds | 67.7 | 2,297,196 |
| Peaches, pounds | 15.8 | 536,125 |
| Pears, pounds | 6.0 | 203,592 |
| Cantaloupes, melons | 5.42 | 183,911 |
| Onions, pounds | 10.48 | 355,607 |
| Potatoes, bushels | 3.06 | 103,831 |
| Lettuce, heads | 6.64 | 225,308 |
| Cabbage, pounds | 18.07 | 613,151 |
| Tomatoes, pounds | 29.70 | 1,007,780 |
| Dried beans, pounds | 9.12 | 309,459 |
| Sugar, pounds | 101.86 | 3,456,313 |
| Candy, pounds | 11.76 | 399,040 |

# Fish and Game

COLORADO has an elaborate and complete system for the propagation and protection of game and fish and as a result it has achieved an enviable reputation for its hunting and fishing opportunities. There were 113,081 licenses issued in 1931 to residents and non-residents, giving the holders the privilege of hunting or fishing in the state during the year. The revenues derived from the sale

of these licenses and permits, fines for violations of the laws, the sale of beaver pelts, etc., provide the funds for the operation of a state game and fish department, which has general supervision over the protection of game and fish, the stocking of streams and refuges, and the enforcement of the game laws. The expenditures for this work run from $275,000 to $318,000 each year without any appropriations being made out of the public funds.

The state owns and operates 15 hatcheries used in stocking the hundreds of miles of fishing streams with trout and one hatchery for propagation of bass, crappies, perch and other varieties of warm water fish. These hatcheries are among the most modern and complete in the United States and have a hatching capacity of 75,000,000 trout each year. The young trout are permitted to grow to a length of four to seven inches in retaining or nursing ponds before being planted in the streams, by which time they are sufficiently developed to take care of themselves in the swifter water.

The trout hatcheries, the counties in which they are located and the area of land included in each are as follows:

| Hatchery | County | Acres |
|---|---|---|
| Buena Vista | Chaffee | 205 |
| Cedaredge | Delta | 13 |
| Denver | Adams | 26 |
| Del Norte | Rio Grande | 10 |
| Durango | La Plata | 13 |
| Estes Park | Larimer | 10 |
| BelleVue | Larimer | 5 |
| Grand Lake | Grand | 1 |
| Glenwood Springs | Garfield | 5 |
| Grand Mesa | Delta | 10 |
| Pitkin | Gunnison | 20 |
| Rye | Pueblo | 5 |
| Steamboat Spgs | Routt | .. |
| Trappers Lake | Rio Blanco | 10 |
| Walden | Jackson | 10 |

The department has recently constructed four large reservoirs for egg-spawn taking purposes. In former years spawn was taken from wild lakes, but under this system the reservoirs will be used exclusively for that purpose and no trout will be taken from them. These reservoirs are expected to supply sufficient quantities of spawn to permit the operation of the hatcheries at their full capacity of 75,000,000 a year.

The location and description of these reservoirs is as follows:

Haviland reservoir, La Plata county, 80 acres of deeded land and 120 acres under government easement, 84 acres of water.

Parvin reservoir, Larimer county, 160 acres of deeded land, 90 acres of water.

Tarryall reservoir, Park county, 900 acres of land and 400 acres of water.

Cameron Pass reservoir, Jackson county, 160 acres under government easement, 60 acres of water.

The department has developed motor tanks for transporting trout, which by the use of compressed oxygen allowed to flow through ice-cooled compartments aerate the water. This method has resulted in approximately 85 per cent of the fingerlings planted in streams surviving. Ten of these tanks are operated by the department.

In 1929 the department planted 25,-583,000 trout in the streams of the state. The number in 1930 was 26,-083,000 and approximately the same number were planted in 1931. This number about represents present requirements and will not be increased until there is a larger demand. The department in 1930 removed approximately 40,000 surplus male rainbows, from 10 to 12 inches long, from the spawning lakes and reservoirs and planted them in streams. A similar number were transferred in 1931. It plans to expand this work as the excess of males over females increases and make the planting of trout of lawful size a regular feature.

Colorado ranks first among the states in the propagation of trout, and with its hundreds of miles of well-stocked streams, makes a fisherman's paradise.

The season for stream fishing in Colorado is from May 25 to October 31, inclusive, and all fishermen are required to obtain licenses. The game and fish department has planted more than 260,000,000 trout in the streams of the state in the past thirteen years. The following table shows the number planted by years:

| Year | Trout Distributed |
|---|---|
| 1919 | 10,389,000 |
| 1920 | 13,076,500 |
| 1921 | 12,011,000 |
| 1922 | 16,871,000 |
| 1923 | 18,117,000 |
| 1924 | 19,078,000 |
| 1925 | 19,921,000 |
| 1926 | 24,019,000 |
| 1927 | 24,094,100 |
| 1928 | 25,677,570 |
| 1929 | 25,583,172 |
| 1930 | 26,083,146 |
| 1931 (Est.) | 26,000,000 |

A table published herewith shows the distribution of trout by counties and by years.

The United States forest service also maintains hatcheries at several points in the state, from which it distributes fish fry into the streams in the national forests. The approximate number distributed by these hatcheries in recent years is as follows:

1928 .........................3,630,675
1929 .........................3,532,500
1930 .........................5,348,000
1931 .........................6,558,800

A number of private hatcheries are operated in the state for supplying trout for market purposes and for stocking private lakes and streams upon which summer resorts are located. The state game and fish department also supplies large quantities of bass and ring perch for lakes. An accompanying table shows the number of licenses of all classes issued by the game and fish department by years.

Big game still is found rather abundantly in Colorado, including deer, antelope, bear, elk, mountain lion, gray wolf and coyote. In an article in this book devoted to the national forests of the state will be found approximate estimates of the numbers of various kinds of big game found within the national forests. The numbers found outside the forest boundaries bring the totals considerably above the figures there given, but no accurate survey has been made except within the forests. There is also much small game, including sage hen, grouse, pheasant, dove, wild duck, rabbit, squirrel and other varieties. In recent years the state has exercised strict supervision over the killing of game, and such protective measures as have been adopted and enforced have had the effect of increasing the supply of many kinds of the larger game birds and animals which were in danger of extinction. There is open season on practically all game, and the regulations under which game may be killed may be obtained from the state game and fish commissioner at the state capitol.

**Game Refuges**—There are now within the state 23 protected areas in which game may not be killed at any time, except certain predatory animals, which may be trapped or hunted under special permits granted by the state game and fish commissioner. These areas comprise 3,551,970 acres, of which 2,666,484 acres are in national forests. The areas are known as game refuges, or sanctuaries, the following having been created by the state legislature in 1921:

The Colorado State game refuge, in Larimer and Boulder counties, surrounding the Rocky Mountain national park on the north, east and south. This refuge lies within the borders of the Colorado national forest.

The Pikes Peak game refuge, in El Paso and Teller counties, including much of the area about Pikes peak and being within the Pike national forest.

The Spanish Peaks game refuge, in the southwestern part of Huerfano county and extending into western Las Animas county, in the San Isabel national forest.

The Denver Mountain Parks game refuge, west of the city of Denver, in Jefferson, Clear Creek and Park counties, including the Denver mountain parks.

The Colorado Antelope refuge, comprising four townships in Larimer and Weld counties, north of Wellington.

Eight additional game reserves were created by the State legislature in 1923, as follows:

Royal Gorge game refuge, west of Canon City, in Fremont county.

Poncha Pass game refuge, in Gunnison and Saguache counties, west of Salida.

Cochetopa game refuge, in the Cochetopa national forest, in Saguache, Mineral and Hinsdale counties.

Ouray game refuge, between Ouray and Telluride, in San Juan county.

Gunnison game refuge, partly in the Gunnison national forest, in Gunnison county.

Snowmass game refuge, in the Sopris national forest, in Pitkin county.

Williams Fork game refuge, surrounding Hot Sulphur Springs, in Grand county.

North Park game refuge, in the central-north part of Jackson county, adjoining the Wyoming boundary.

The legislature in 1925 created five additional reserves, as follows:

Newlon Creek game refuge, Fremont county; Waugh Mountain game refuge, west of Cripple Creek, in Fremont county; Buffalo Peak game refuge, at Leadville, in Lake county; White River game refuge in White River national forest, Rio Blanco county; and the Cameron game refuge, in the south-central part of Jackson county.

The legislature in 1929 created two additional reserves, as follows:

Smith's Hollow game refuge, in Pueblo county, south of the city of Pueblo, and the Douglas Mountain refuge, in Moffat county, just east of the Utah boundary.

The legislature in 1930 enlarged the area of the Newlon Creek refuge in

Fremont county and created two new refuges, the Two Buttes refuge in southern Prowers county and the Carrizo refuge in the southwestern part of Baca county.

The inventory value of the property of the state game and fish department as of June 30, 1930, was $921,395, of which $150,000 was for land, $737,550 for buildings and improvements, $20,-000 for machinery, equipment and supplies, $2,500 for furniture and fixtures and $11,345 for autos and trucks.

Total disbursements by the state auditor on account of the game and fish department for fiscal years ending November 30, are as follows:

| | |
|---|---|
| 1919 | $ 76,835.52 |
| 1920 | 135,456.97 |
| 1921 | 144,938.81 |
| 1922 | 178,405.28 |
| 1923 | 150,526.06 |
| 1924 | 207,779.06 |
| 1925 | 186,589.50 |
| 1926 | 334,953.00 |
| 1927 | 276,413.75 |
| 1928 | 288,220.59 |
| *1929 to June 30 | 186,013.74 |
| *1930 (June 30) | 318,847.38 |
| 1931 | 276,421.79 |

*Fiscal year changed from November 30 to June 30. Figures for 1929 cover period from December 1, 1928, to June 30, 1929.

## HUNTING AND FISHING LICENSES SOLD IN COLORADO, BY YEARS

(State Game and Fish Commissioner)

| YEAR | Resident Licenses | | | Non-Resident Licenses | | | | |
|---|---|---|---|---|---|---|---|---|
| | Combination Hunting and Fishing | Big Game | Elk | Fishing | Hunting | Big Game | Elk | Total |
| 1920 | 86,371 | 15,951 | .... | 5,387 | 138 | 67 | .... | 107,914 |
| 1921 | 89,598 | 8,337 | .... | 2,445 | 117 | 42 | .... | 100,539 |
| 1922 | 72,333 | 6,960 | .... | 2,480 | 104 | 29 | .... | 81,906 |
| 1923 | 71,254 | 6,891 | .... | 2,954 | 102 | 26 | .... | 81,227 |
| 1924 | 80,735 | 7,979 | .... | 5,223 | 178 | 46 | .... | 94,161 |
| 1925 | 84,852 | 8,411 | .... | 6,459 | 249 | 47 | .... | 100,018 |
| 1926 | 88,570 | 8,956 | .... | 7,374 | 306 | 65 | .... | 105,271 |
| 1927 | 93,355 | 9,383 | .... | 8,653 | 353 | 70 | .... | 111,814 |
| 1928 | 95,512 | 11,793 | .... | 8,769 | 301 | 119 | .... | 116,494 |
| 1929 | 96,432 | 13,652 | .... | 9,882 | 227 | 170 | .... | 120,363 |
| 1930 | 96,495 | 14,393 | .... | 9,648 | 134 | 198 | .... | 120,86 |
| 1931 | 87,587 | 13,046 | 3,865 | 8,272 | 182 | 120 | 9 | 113,08 |

### HOLIDAYS IN COLORADO

The laws of Colorado provide for the following legal holidays in the state:

January 1—New Year's Day.

February 12—Lincoln's birthday.

February 22—Washington's birthday.

May 30—Memorial day.

July 4—Independence day.

August 1—Colorado day.

September—First Monday, Labor day.

October 12—Columbus day.

November—First Tuesday after first Monday, general election day.

November 11—Liberty day.

November—Thanksgiving day, by proclamation, last Thursday.

December 25—Christmas day.

Arbor day is not a legal holiday, but is set apart for observance by proclamation for the third Friday in April. It is a public school holiday.

Good Roads day is not a legal holiday, but is set apart by proclamation for the second Friday in May.

Saturday, from 12 o'clock noon until midnight, is a legal holiday during June, July and August in every city having 25,000 or more population.

### LEGAL EXECUTIONS

Thirty-six legal executions have taken place in Colorado between November 6, 1890, and November 30, 1930, inclusive. These were by years as follows:

| | |
|---|---|
| *1890 | 1 |
| 1891 | 3 |
| 1892 | 1 |
| 1895 | 3 |
| 1896 | 4 |
| 1905 | 4 |
| 1907 | 1 |
| 1908 | 2 |
| 1912 | 1 |
| 1915 | 1 |
| 1916 | 2 |
| 1920 | 1 |
| 1922 | 1 |
| 1924 | 1 |
| 1926 | 2 |
| 1928 | 2 |
| 1930 | 6 |
| 1931 | 4 |
| Total | 40 |

*For part of year.

### TROUT DISTRIBUTED IN COLORADO STREAMS, BY COUNTIES AND YEARS
(From the Records of the State Game and Fish Department)

| COUNTIES | 1930 | 1929 | 1928 | 1927 | 1926 | 1925 |
|---|---|---|---|---|---|---|
| Adams | 121,000 | ------ | ------ | 27,500 | ------ | ------ |
| Alamosa | ------ | ------ | ------ | 62,000 | ------ | ------ |
| Arapahoe | 22,440 | 10,000 | ------ | ------ | ------ | ------ |
| Archuleta | 412,350 | 359,000 | 724,320 | 269,000 | 560,000 | 309,000 |
| Baca | ------ | ------ | ------ | ------ | ------ | ------ |
| Bent | ------ | ------ | ------ | ------ | ------ | ------ |
| Boulder | 865,000 | 775,000 | 860,000 | 380,000 | 822,000 | 800,500 |
| Chaffee | 1,598,000 | 2,359,765 | 698,700 | 202,000 | 280,000 | 410,000 |
| Cheyenne | ------ | ------ | ------ | ------ | ------ | ------ |
| Clear Creek | 100,000 | 379,000 | 290,000 | 240,000 | 361,000 | 240,000 |
| Conejos | 615,000 | 1,160,600 | 822,000 | 574,500 | 844,300 | 800,000 |
| Costilla | 45,000 | 30,000 | 15,000 | 25,000 | 52,000 | 125,000 |
| Crowley | ------ | ------ | ------ | ------ | ------ | ------ |
| Custer | 325,000 | 20,000 | 86,500 | 25,000 | 30,000 | 240,000 |
| Delta | 1,159,000 | 966,000 | 1,119,000 | 2,465,700 | 993,800 | 1,300,000 |
| Denver | ------ | ------ | ------ | ------ | ------ | ------ |
| Dolores | 91,000 | 160,000 | 140,000 | 650,000 | 100,000 | 200,000 |
| Douglas | 122,260 | 67,500 | 199,500 | 115,000 | 310,000 | 300,000 |
| Eagle | 729,000 | 280,000 | 522,000 | 426,000 | 909,000 | 618,000 |
| Elbert | ------ | ------ | ------ | ------ | ------ | ------ |
| El Paso | 101,000 | 117,500 | 60,000 | 227,000 | 230,000 | 300,000 |
| Fremont | 250,036 | 400,000 | 546,000 | 180,000 | 346,000 | 250,000 |
| Garfield | 1,313,000 | 760,000 | 975,000 | 1,171,000 | 602,000 | 631,000 |
| Gilpin | 40,000 | 25,000 | 73,000 | 45,000 | 70,000 | 150,000 |
| Grand | 1,031,900 | 945,000 | 1,177,000 | 761,000 | 1,212,000 | 581,000 |
| Gunnison | 3,333,000 | 1,948,000 | 3,193,000 | 3,068,000 | 2,988,000 | 1,679,000 |
| Hinsdale | 848,000 | 868,120 | 489,000 | 160,000 | 300,000 | 200,000 |
| Huerfano | 134,000 | 230,000 | 65,500 | 137,500 | 200,000 | 180,000 |
| Jackson | 640,050 | 981,080 | 1,005,700 | 1,530,000 | 592,530 | 240,000 |
| Jefferson | 994,860 | 576,000 | 481,000 | 721,500 | 457,000 | 375,000 |
| Kiowa | ------ | ------ | ------ | ------ | ------ | ------ |
| Kit Carson | 35,000 | ------ | ------ | 10,000 | ------ | ------ |
| Lake | 320,000 | 449,757 | 255,000 | 30,000 | 130,000 | 260,000 |
| La Plata | 1,959,500 | 1,358,340 | 1,832,350 | 1,178,500 | 1,142,000 | 630,000 |
| Larimer | 1,948,000 | 2,861,100 | 2,270,000 | 1,885,000 | 2,388,000 | 1,457,600 |
| Las Animas | 65,000 | 150,000 | 57,500 | 172,500 | 140,000 | 350,000 |
| Lincoln | ------ | ------ | ------ | ------ | ------ | ------ |
| Logan | ------ | ------ | 80,000 | ------ | ------ | ------ |
| Mesa | 1,630,000 | 1,350,000 | 667,000 | 529,900 | 544,000 | 370,000 |
| Mineral | 584,500 | 520,950 | 324,500 | 314,500 | 595,000 | 552,000 |
| Moffat | ------ | 68,000 | 83,000 | 339,000 | 85,000 | 150,000 |
| Montezuma | 315,000 | 97,000 | 85,000 | 180,000 | 190,000 | 180,000 |
| Montrose | 214,000 | 767,000 | 367,000 | 193,500 | 302,000 | 310,000 |
| Morgan | ------ | ------ | ------ | ------ | ------ | ------ |
| Otero | ------ | ------ | ------ | ------ | ------ | ------ |
| Ouray | 220,000 | 84,000 | 154,000 | 112,000 | 68,000 | 190,000 |
| Park | 633,000 | 697,500 | 1,558,500 | 866,000 | 531,000 | 350,000 |
| Phillips | ------ | ------ | ------ | ------ | ------ | ------ |
| Pitkin | 398,000 | 120,000 | 463,000 | 365,000 | 796,000 | 560,000 |
| Prowers | ------ | ------ | ------ | ------ | ------ | ------ |
| Pueblo | 40,000 | 90,020 | 155,500 | 145,000 | 300,000 | 280,000 |
| Rio Blanco | 1,242,000 | 773,400 | 973,000 | 1,176,000 | 816,000 | 580,000 |
| Rio Grande | 325,000 | 365,000 | 239,500 | 481,500 | 398,000 | 595,000 |
| Routt | ------ | 787,000 | 946,000 | 932,000 | 938,000 | 853,000 |
| Saguache | 212,500 | 615,500 | 769,500 | 304,000 | 125,000 | 175,000 |
| San Juan | 199,000 | 363,600 | 266,000 | 720,000 | 80,000 | 170,000 |
| San Miguel | 453,750 | 325,840 | 242,000 | 419,000 | 260,000 | 190,000 |
| Sedgwick | ------ | ------ | ------ | 15,000 | ------ | ------ |
| Summit | 135,000 | 68,500 | 55,000 | 73,000 | 132,000 | 190,000 |
| Teller | 145,000 | 90,000 | 203,000 | 175,000 | 170,000 | 320,000 |
| Washington | ------ | ------ | ------ | ------ | ------ | ------ |
| Weld | ------ | 58,100 | 54,000 | ------ | ------ | ------ |
| Yuma | 83,000 | 65,000 | 25,000 | 15,000 | 30,000 | 80,000 |
| State | *26,083,146 | *25,583,172 | 25,667,570 | 24,094,100 | 22,419,630 | 18,721,100 |

*Includes 35,000 distributed in Texas in 1930; 40,000 at Del Norte in 1929

# Irrigation and Drainage

THE irrigation of land for the growing of crops by applying water to the soil as it is needed is as old as civilization itself, but in the United States the method is used, with few exceptions, only in the western half of the country in a district extending from the center of Kansas to the Pacific coast. The water used for this purpose is diverted to the soil direct from flowing streams, from reservoirs where it has been stored during flood seasons, or by pumping it from wells.

Farming under irrigation began in Colorado almost as soon as gold mining. Its development began on a small scale and was not very rapid at first but was steady and persistent, until today the annual output of the state's irrigated farms is more than ten times as great as that of its gold mines. Land in Colorado does not carry title to water rights unless so stated in the deed, and rights usually are acquired independent of the land. Water is pro-rated among users according to the priority of their rights as established by diversion and application to beneficial use.

Concerning the earliest record of irrigated farming, the History of Agriculture in Colorado, published in 1926 by the state board of agriculture, says: "While much must be left to conjecture in discussing Indian irrigation practice, there are authentic records as to the Spanish colonists from 1598 to the time when settlement in Colorado began. The first court decrees for irrigation rights in Colorado streams were granted to Spanish-American users in 1852, five years after the first Mormons arrived in the Salt Lake valley. While the Mormons were without previous experience in the use of water on crops, the early Spanish-American farmers who settled on what later became Colorado soil had long been accustomed to irrigation in the Taos country from which they came. In fact, the ancestors of these Colorado colonists came from a country where irrigation was practiced extensively at the time the first Spanish explorers crossed the Atlantic to the new world."

The first formal decree of appropriation for irrigation water, according to the same authority, was granted in Costilla and Conejos counties in April, 1852, the decree carrying 13.5 second-feet from the Culebra river. In northern Colorado David K. Wall, an outstanding figure in pioneer history, is popularly conceded to have been the first to divert water for agricultural purposes, his ditch drawing water from Clear Creek, in Jefferson county. Following these first ventures into the field of irrigated farming, development came rapidly.

Between 1860 and 1869 large community irrigation enterprises were undertaken. Up to this time only short ditches had been in operation, carrying water directly from the streams to the low lands lying in the narrow creek and river valleys. Most of these pioneer irrigation systems were individual enterprises, watering from 10 to 100 acres each. Irrigation on a large scale was first undertaken in the Greeley district, in northern Colorado, the water being taken from the South Platte river and its tributaries. The undertakings were generally successful and other districts immediately followed the example of northern Colorado. In 1889, when the United States census bureau made its first detailed report on irrigation enterprises, Colorado ranked second among the states in irrigation development, with 890,735 acres of land under ditch. California was first at that time, with 1,004,223 acres irrigated.

Colorado took first place in the area of land irrigated in 1899 and held that rank until 1919, when California went ahead of it as a result of the development of water from the drilling of wells. Colorado continues, however, to rank first among all the states in the area of land receiving its entire water supply from streams. The state lies at the top of the Continental Divide and its principal streams flow in all directions. To the east, the Arkansas and South Platte flow into Kansas and Nebraska; to the west, the Colorado flows into Utah; to the north, the North Platte flows into Wyoming; and to the south the Rio Grande del Norte flows into New Mexico. These streams.

with their numerous tributaries, form the foundation of the state's irrigation system, not only from the normal stream flow, but as the channels through which water from melting snow in the mountains passes down to the lower lands during the summer months.

The administration of the public water supplies of the state is in the hands of a state engineer. For the purpose of administering the waters, the state is divided into seven divisions, each in charge of a division engineer; the divisions in turn are divided into districts, of which there are 68 in the state, each in charge of a water commissioner. The state engineer is appointed by the governor, subject to civil service regulations; the division engineers are appointed by the governor, with the approval of the senate; and the water commissioners are appointed by the governor upon the recommendation of the county commissioners of the counties included in each district, all subject, of course, to civil service regulations prescribed by constitutional amendment and by statute, after the acts designating methods of appointing these officials were passed.

Under the laws of the state as they now stand, the state engineer has no authority to compel the furnishing of statistics, but through the co-operation of the division engineers and the water commissioners, the gathering of data each year has been put upon a more reliable basis. The records of the state engineer's office are complete and comprehensive as to stream discharges, quantity of water originating in Colorado and discharged into adjacent states, data on water returned to the streams, water in storage and other details of value in administering the irrigation laws. The 1,000 or more reservoirs in the state are inspected at regular periods, and a close check on all water users is maintained. There are at present in use in the state 209 automatic recording devices on ditches and canals, and 113 at stream gauging stations.

There were 59,956 farms in the state reported by the 1930 census, of which 31,288, or 52.2 per cent, were irrigated in whole or in part. All land in farms comprised 28,876,171 acres, of which 3,393,619 acres, or 11.8 per cent, was irrigated. The number of irriga-

tion enterprises in the state in 1930 was 6,509, representing an investment of $87,603,240. Of this number, 5,926 were individual and partnership enterprises; 531 were co-operative; 15 were irrigation districts; one was a Carey act project; 28 were commercial; and the remainder were United States reclamation, city and other projects. The co-operative projects represented an investment of $45,651,717. An accompanying table gives a summary of irrigation development in 1930, with comparative figures for 1920, and the amount and per cent of increase.

The irrigation works in the state, by character of enterprise, in 1930, were as follows:

Dams, number:
  Diversion .................... 3,672
  Storage .................... 706
Main canals:
  Capacity, sec.-ft............. 123,652
  Length, miles............... 15,355
Lateral canals:
  Length, miles............... 6,026
Reservoirs:
  Number .................... 765
  Capacity, acre-ft............1,924,982
Pipe lines:
  Length, miles............... 132
Flowing wells:
  Number .................... 621
  Capacity, g. p. m............. 39,644
Pumped wells:
  Number .................... 654
  Capacity, g. p. m.......... 237,903
Pumping plants:
  Number .................... 516
  No. pumps.................. 540
  Pump capacity, g. p. m...... 298,101

The investment in irrigation enterprises, as reported for census years, and the average per acre, based on the area the enterprises were capable of supplying with water, is as follows:

| Year | Investment | Average Per Acre |
|------|-----------|------------------|
| 1890 | $ 6,368,755 | $ 7.15 |
| 1900 | 11,758,703 | 7.30 |
| 1910 | 56,636,443 | 14.19 |
| 1920 | 88,302,442 | 22.90 |
| 1930 | 87,603,240 | 21.48 |

The investment of $87,603,240 in enterprises in 1930, distributed over the periods from the beginning of irrigation in the state, show that 27.2 per cent of the entire amount was invested in 1905 to 1909, inclusive, and 22.9 per cent between 1880 and 1889. This distribution does not agree with the figures reported by the 1920 census, and takes into account depreciation, abandonments, etc. The distribution of the investment in 1930 from the beginning is as follows:

| Date | Investment | Per Cent of Total |
|---|---|---|
| Before 1860........$ | 426,525 | 0.5 |
| 1860-1869 .......... | 5,213,823 | 6.0 |
| 1870-1879 .......... | 9,675,437 | 11.0 |
| 1880-1889 .......... | 20,071,653 | 22.9 |
| 1890-1899 .......... | 7,225,131 | 8.2 |
| 1900-1904 .......... | 12,791,634 | 14.6 |
| 1905-1909 .......... | 23,792,206 | 27.2 |
| 1910-1914 .......... | 5,613,651 | 6.4 |
| 1915-1919 .......... | 317,899 | 0.4 |
| 1920-1924 .......... | 869,698 | 1.0 |
| 1925-1929 .......... | 337,722 | 0.4 |
| Not Reported...... | 1,267,861 | 1.4 |
| Total ...........$ | 87,603,240 | 100.0 |

The progress of irrigation as indicated by the number of farms irrigated in whole or in part, the area irrigated, and percentages of increase by years are as follows:

| | Farms Irrig. | | Acres Irrig. | |
|---|---|---|---|---|
| Year | Number | Pct. Incr. | Number | Pct. Incr. |
| 1890 | .... 9,659 | ... | 890,735 | ... |
| 1900 | ....17,613 | 82.3 | 1,611,271 | 80.9 |
| 1910 | ....25,857 | 46.8 | 2,792,032 | 73.3 |
| 1920 | ....28,756 | 11.2 | 3,348,385 | 19.9 |
| 1930 | ....31,288 | 8.8 | 3,393,619 | 1.4 |

Soil to which water is applied by irrigation as needed produces larger yields per acre than non-irrigated crops as a rule. This fact may not be recognized readily from a study of crop reports unless the distinction is closely watched. For instance, the average yield per acre of irrigated winter wheat for five years ending with 1930 was 31.2 bushels, and non-irrigated 10.81 bushels. The average yield of wheat without taking into consideration whether it is irrigated or non-irrigated, would be somewhere between these two figures.

A table is given herewith showing the investment in irrigation enterprises in 1930 and 1920, by counties, the estimated final investment, and the average per acre in 1930.

Another table shows by counties the irrigation works in the state in 1930 and 1920, including the number of enterprises, mileage of canals and laterals, number of reservoirs and their capacity.

Another table gives the number of irrigated farms, land area, area irrigated and area enterprises are capable of supplying with water, by counties and years.

Drainage enterprises, which are operated in part in connection with irrigation systems, are described separately in an accompanying chapter.

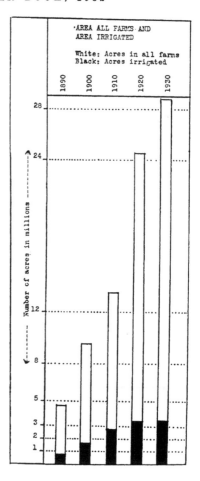

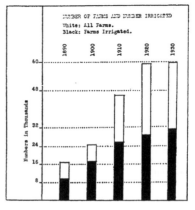

## IRRIGATION; SUMMARY OF STATE FOR 1930 AND 1920, WITH INCREASES
(Compiled from Census Reports)

| | 1930 | 1920 | Increase Amount | Per Cent |
|---|---|---|---|---|
| Land area of state, acres_____ | 66,341,120 | 66,341,120 | -------- | --- |
| Number farms_____ | 59,956 | 59,934 | 22 | --- |
| Acres in all farms_____ | 28,876,171 | 24,462,014 | 4,414,157 | 18.0 |
| Number irrigated farms_____ | 31,288 | 28,756 | 2,532 | 8.8 |
| Acres irrigated_____ | 3,393,619 | 3,348,385 | -------- | --- |
| Acres enterprises were capable of supplying with water_____ | 4,078,712 | 3,855,348 | 223,364 | 5.8 |
| *Acres in enterprises_____ | 4,528,251 | 5,220,588 | -------- | --- |
| Per cent irrigated: | | | | |
| All farms_____ | 52.2 | 48.0 | -------- | --- |
| All land in farms_____ | 11.8 | 13.7 | -------- | --- |
| All land in state_____ | 5.1 | 5.0 | -------- | --- |
| Excess of area enterprises were capable of supplying with water over irrigated area, acres_____ | 685,093 | 506,963 | 178,130 | 35.1 |
| *Excess of area in enterprises over area irrigated, acres_____ | 1,134,632 | 1,872,203 | -------- | --- |
| Area of irrigated land available, or to be available for settlement, acres___ | 88,731 | 274,282 | —185,551 | —67.6 |
| Value of irrigated farms (land, buildings, implements and machinery)____ | $414,180,910 | (†) | -------- | --- |
| Investment in irrigation enterprises___ | 87,603,240 | $ 88,302,442 | $ —699,202 | —0.8 |
| ‡Average per acre_____ | 21.48 | 22.90 | —1.42 | —6.2 |
| Est. final cost of existing enterprises_ | 91,845,804 | 95,198,423 | —3,352,619 | —3.5 |
| *Average per acre_____ | 20.28 | 18.24 | -------- | --- |
| Average annual cost, per acre, for maintenance and operation of irrigation works_____ | 0.85 | 0.87 | —0.02 | —2.3 |

*Irrigable area, 1930 ; total area, 1920.
†Figures not available.
‡Based on area enterprises were capable of supplying with water.
—Denotes decrease.

## COST OF TIMBERING MINES

It costs more than $1,000,000 a year to timber the walls and roofs of mines in Colorado to prevent caving. In 1923 a total of 5,404,933 cubic feet of round timber and 6,743,000 board feet of sawed timber was used for this purpose, the cost being $1,195,215. The bituminous coal mines of the state used 4,811,519 cubic feet of round timber and 1,281,000 board feet of sawed timber, at a cost of $883,820. The metal mines, other than iron mines, used 588,840 cubic feet of round and 5,453,000 board feet of sawed timber, the remainder of the total being used in the iron mines. The coal mines used almost four times as much timber in 1923 as in 1905, while the metal mines used only one-fifth the quantity of round timber and half the quantity of sawed timber used in 1905.

## PIKE'S PEAK

Pike's peak, in El Paso county, probably the most famed of Colorado peaks, was first seen by Lieut. Zebulon M. Pike, of the United States army, at 2 o'clock in the afternoon on November 15, 1806, from a point near the mouth of the Purgatoire river, in what is now Bent county. It subsequently was named in his honor and became the best known of all the high peaks by reason of the fact that it stands out to the view so prominently when the mountain range is approached from the east. In a table of the location and altitude of Colorado peaks published in this volume, there are 24 peaks which are higher above sea level than Pike's peak. Reports have been current at intervals that the peak is sinking gradually and that it has sunk nearly 40 feet in the last 25 or 30 years. This is denied by the United States geological survey, which in 1908 established its official altitude as 14,109 feet. These reports evidently arose over a confusion of the elevation with the data of old railroad or barometer figures, which gave it an elevation as high as 14,181 feet. Lieutenant Pike, shortly following his discovery, calculated the elevation of the peak at 18,581 feet.

## INVESTMENT IN IRRIGATION ENTERPRISES, 1930 AND 1920, BY COUNTIES
(Compiled from Census Reports)

| COUNTY | Investment to Jan. 1 | | Av. Per Acre, Based on Area Enterprises Were Capable of Supplying with Water | | Estimated Final Investment in Enterprises | | Av. Per Acre, Based on Est. Final Investment and Irri. Area 1930 |
|---|---|---|---|---|---|---|---|
| | 1930 | 1920 | 1930 | 1920 | 1930 | 1920 | |
| Adams | $ 2,758,737 | $ 2,436,771 | $ 24.53 | $ 35.80 | $ 2,759,587 | $ 2,557,121 | $ 21.06 |
| Alamosa | 586,296 | 416,305 | 3.75 | 2.47 | 587,296 | 458,952 | 3.23 |
| Arapahoe | 606,503 | 597,099 | 19.89 | 22.84 | 608,003 | 600,299 | 18.40 |
| Archuleta | 157,089 | 168,635 | 8.11 | 12.69 | 158,389 | 170,285 | 6.75 |
| Baca | 408,375 | 572,553 | 108.06 | 47.63 | 408,375 | 572,553 | 105.96 |
| Bent | 1,123,422 | 2,773,601 | 17.25 | 20.80 | 1,126,222 | 2,797,201 | 16.45 |
| Boulder | 1,703,651 | 1,774,922 | 9.37 | 10.16 | 1,790,211 | 1,850,662 | 9.72 |
| Chaffee | 517,909 | 261,368 | 16.82 | 8.68 | 518,909 | 265,083 | 15.41 |
| Conejos | 1,478,246 | 1,155,162 | 9.78 | 7.58 | 1,481,096 | 1,156,632 | 9.02 |
| Costilla | 1,687,160 | 1,389,816 | 15.34 | 31.65 | 1,692,260 | 1,403,066 | 14.98 |
| Crowley | 1,994,077 | 2,587,043 | 28.50 | 44.05 | 2,043,894 | 2,593,508 | 26.81 |
| Custer | 86,292 | 75,431 | 3.42 | 2.25 | 87,142 | 76,596 | 3.42 |
| Delta | 3,439,560 | 4,168,137 | 25.43 | 32.70 | 3,719,185 | 4,320,091 | 26.32 |
| Denver | 80,095 | 47,386 | 89.79 | 11.85 | 80,095 | 47,386 | 89.79 |
| *Dolores | 4,530 | 549,070 | 6.38 | 232.56 | 4,530 | 729,020 | 5.73 |
| Douglas | 392,242 | 207,786 | 41.04 | 20.00 | 392,642 | 208,286 | 39.35 |
| Eagle | 566,620 | 285,282 | 17.75 | 9.18 | 607,170 | 307,432 | 17.56 |
| Elbert | 130,450 | 25,561 | 20.77 | 14.28 | 130,450 | 39,961 | 19.76 |
| El Paso | 411,844 | 901,461 | 12.14 | 40.89 | 411,844 | 921,461 | 12.10 |
| Fremont | 945,663 | 1,761,518 | 29.59 | 49.35 | 951,418 | 1,889,558 | 25.80 |
| Garfield | 983,360 | 1,134,502 | 12.22 | 12.09 | 988,835 | 1,170,827 | 9.92 |
| Grand | 372,095 | 534,913 | 8.79 | 12.41 | 405,045 | 547,713 | 7.33 |
| Gunnison | 358,025 | 462,748 | 7.45 | 8.82 | 364,575 | 472,998 | 7.32 |
| Hinsdale | 1,269,972 | 395,752 | 212.23 | 102.00 | 1,319,972 | 395,752 | 199.90 |
| Huerfano | 283,324 | 1,061,777 | 6.42 | 33.06 | 287,824 | 1,083,232 | 6.22 |
| Jackson | 695,090 | 784,326 | 4.95 | 5.25 | 963,030 | 1,043,826 | 5.92 |
| Jefferson | 2,500,326 | 1,231,205 | 42.59 | 16.72 | 2,510,326 | 1,268,125 | 41.42 |
| Kiowa | 325,800 | 251,500 | 324.18 | 120.18 | 335,800 | 337,200 | 226.13 |
| Kit Carson | 1,910 | † | 2.89 | ---- | 1,910 | † | 2.79 |
| Lake | 8,970 | 33,696 | 2.11 | 4.75 | 8,970 | 33,696 | 2.11 |
| La Plata | 1,039,896 | 938,864 | 8.87 | 12.00 | 1,240,216 | 978,214 | 9.42 |
| Larimer | 7,514,401 | 6,236,866 | 41.54 | 33.17 | 7,516,971 | 6,473,663 | 40.95 |
| Las Animas | 2,058,902 | 401,720 | 42.76 | 9.16 | 2,319,602 | 455,470 | 42.90 |
| Lincoln | 2,950 | † | 6.56 | ---- | 2,950 | † | 3.17 |
| Logan | 3,072,572 | 3,593,889 | 24.86 | 33.93 | 3,081,072 | 3,596,039 | 24.20 |
| Mesa | 6,620,956 | 7,319,055 | 37.22 | 52.24 | 7,273,473 | 8,155,335 | 34.75 |
| Mineral | 24,250 | 81,683 | 7.65 | 8.21 | 32,050 | 102,243 | 6.39 |
| Moffat | 381,417 | 366,301 | 12.79 | 15.12 | 388,497 | 386,226 | 10.90 |
| Montezuma | 4,932,595 | 1,846,679 | 59.28 | 41.23 | 5,959,445 | 2,446,679 | 60.76 |
| Montrose | 6,944,017 | 6,788,758 | 66.07 | 54.79 | 7,139,617 | 7,286,466 | 62.27 |
| Morgan | 2,784,109 | 2,600,735 | 24.14 | 16.91 | 2,804,109 | 2,604,785 | 22.22 |
| Otero | 2,782,085 | 4,157,535 | 26.23 | 33.29 | 2,788,085 | 4,438,935 | 23.30 |
| Ouray | 213,491 | 197,689 | 9.11 | 8.56 | 216,016 | 197,758 | 6.87 |
| Park | 211,435 | 175,670 | 4.64 | 3.38 | 211,485 | 176,080 | 4.52 |
| Pitkin | 300,660 | 208,324 | 11.97 | 13.73 | 309,060 | 214,324 | 12.07 |
| Prowers | 2,319,500 | 1,160,422 | 18.27 | 14.24 | 2,319,825 | 1,163,412 | 17.68 |
| Pueblo | 2,459,925 | 3,645,462 | 25.33 | 41.10 | 2,748,525 | 3,919,262 | 22.24 |
| Rio Blanco | 488,770 | 355,617 | 14.19 | 10.86 | 515,990 | 372,882 | 13.09 |
| Rio Grande | 1,357,907 | 981,136 | 7.85 | 4.32 | 1,358,007 | 982,914 | 7.29 |
| Routt | 523,065 | 572,873 | 6.74 | 9.37 | 532,240 | 613,908 | 6.12 |
| Saguache | 587,809 | 450,609 | 3.30 | 2.94 | 588,409 | 531,614 | 3.19 |
| *San Miguel | 550,484 | 676,100 | 25.41 | 29.64 | 672,644 | 797,700 | 12.47 |
| Sedgwick | 802,360 | 716,215 | 33.45 | 31.07 | 802,860 | 716,215 | 32.66 |
| Summit | 84,960 | 103,581 | 7.48 | 9.43 | 84,960 | 103,631 | 7.48 |
| Teller | 3,965 | 12,141 | 6.29 | 7.88 | 3,965 | 12,141 | 5.71 |
| Washington | 988,116 | 78,966 | 84.42 | 7.82 | 992,116 | 80,166 | 84.40 |
| Weld | 12,621,370 | 16,417,224 | 25.26 | 41.52 | 13,144,670 | 18,892,937 | 23.13 |
| Yuma | 43,200 | 83,908 | 11.35 | 8.24 | 43,500 | 89,908 | 10.96 |
| All Other Counties | 10,440 | 89,094 | 17.03 | 63.91 | 10,440 | 90,994 | 17.03 |
| State | $87,603,240 | $88,302,442 | $ 21.48 | $ 22.90 | $91,845,804 | $95,198,423 | $ 20.2 |

*Part of Dolores annexed to San Miguel in 1925.
†Included in "All Other Counties."

## IRRIGATION WORKS IN 1930 AND 1920 BY COUNTIES *
(Compiled from Census Reports)

| COUNTY | Number Enterprises | | Length, Main Canals and Laterals (Miles) | | Number Reservoirs | | Capacity Reservoirs (Acre feet) | |
|---|---|---|---|---|---|---|---|---|
| | 1930 | 1920 | 1930 | 1920 | 1930 | 1920 | 1930 | 1920 |
| Adams | 150 | 59 | 304 | 366 | 7 | 11 | 44,245 | 68,551 |
| Alamosa | 49 | 57 | 548 | 355 | --- | 2 | ------ | 12,527 |
| Arapahoe | 24 | 37 | 97 | 218 | 1 | 6 | 232 | 73,866 |
| Archuleta | 124 | 97 | 201 | 185 | 3 | 5 | 869 | 665 |
| Baca | 4 | 7 | 29 | 27 | 1 | 4 | 35,000 | 33,726 |
| Bent | 37 | 30 | 719 | 1,110 | 3 | 17 | 62,756 | 339,402 |
| Boulder | 92 | 151 | 582 | 1,467 | 24 | 44 | 43,974 | 33,282 |
| Chaffee | 118 | 157 | 300 | 439 | 2 | 3 | 11,440 | 20 |
| Conejos | 172 | 159 | 662 | 683 | 2 | 5 | 24,000 | 34,968 |
| Costilla | 103 | 46 | 357 | 537 | 5 | 6 | 130,943 | 132,860 |
| Crowley | 22 | 24 | 116 | 212 | 19 | 18 | 66,577 | 8,593 |
| Custer | 126 | 202 | 238 | 338 | 2 | 1 | 280 | 5 |
| Delta | 276 | 298 | 799 | 997 | 129 | 115 | 35,537 | 39,284 |
| Denver | 5 | 4 | 14 | 20 | --- | --- | ------ | ------ |
| *Dolores | 10 | 22 | 13 | 58 | --- | 4 | ------ | 19,630 |
| Douglas | 95 | 94 | 126 | 213 | 9 | 17 | 15,335 | 4,287 |
| Eagle | 196 | 186 | 330 | 447 | 8 | 15 | 3,378 | 1,468 |
| Elbert | 17 | 22 | 54 | 62 | 9 | 5 | 4,537 | 6,755 |
| El Paso | 93 | 63 | 172 | 193 | 16 | 29 | 8,741 | 13,103 |
| Fremont | 186 | 179 | 245 | 330 | 20 | 31 | 7,260 | 6,972 |
| Garfield | 291 | 323 | 736 | 1,242 | 16 | 26 | 20,572 | 7,594 |
| Grand | 155 | 166 | 415 | 579 | 21 | 25 | 3,641 | 3,137 |
| Gunnison | 227 | 382 | 409 | 736 | 3 | 6 | 77 | 460 |
| Hinsdale | 53 | 52 | 51 | 104 | 5 | 2 | 126,400 | 43,500 |
| Huerfano | 313 | 267 | 388 | 621 | 12 | 34 | 1,446 | 12,027 |
| Jackson | 149 | 145 | 570 | 822 | 15 | 9 | 16,714 | 15,159 |
| Jefferson | 57 | 105 | 269 | 381 | 43 | 25 | 35,994 | 8,178 |
| Kiowa | 5 | 6 | 1 | 52 | 6 | 4 | 266,202 | 32,118 |
| Kit Carson | 6 | ‡ | 9 | ‡ | 2 | ‡ | 1 | ‡ |
| Lake | 24 | 30 | 24 | 52 | 2 | --- | 54,452 | ------ |
| La Plata | 324 | 211 | 769 | 704 | 1 | 5 | 30 | 15 |
| Larimer | 228 | 171 | 824 | 982 | 68 | 69 | 162,500 | 181,515 |
| Las Animas | 111 | 176 | 297 | 401 | 6 | 21 | 47,089 | 429,105 |
| Lincoln | 5 | ‡ | 20 | ‡ | 10 | ‡ | 804 | ‡ |
| Logan | 39 | 39 | 551 | 511 | 6 | 7 | 107,159 | 116,108 |
| Mesa | 221 | 213 | 761 | 1,012 | 58 | 60 | 16,584 | 19,201 |
| Mineral | 29 | 42 | 37 | 82 | --- | 2 | ------ | 2,311 |
| Moffat | 101 | 127 | 274 | 696 | 12 | 18 | 2,022 | 1,569 |
| Montezuma | 140 | 102 | 502 | 424 | 12 | 9 | 16,786 | 17,680 |
| Montrose | 76 | 103 | 841 | 813 | 14 | 14 | 13,144 | 8,335 |
| Morgan | 35 | 39 | 476 | 370 | 4 | 10 | 86,772 | 86,680 |
| Otero | 23 | 26 | 478 | 758 | 5 | 10 | 35,347 | 36,659 |
| Ouray | 152 | 96 | 255 | 213 | 2 | --- | 156 | ------ |
| Park | 199 | 213 | 341 | 460 | 2 | 1 | 26,002 | 8 |
| Pitkin | 104 | 76 | 254 | 228 | 2 | 3 | 1,011 | 19 |
| Prowers | 39 | 29 | 919 | 489 | 2 | 5 | 47,155 | 53,613 |
| Pueblo | 233 | 264 | 379 | 896 | 27 | 61 | 56,940 | 109,534 |
| Rio Blanco | 166 | 189 | 400 | 506 | 8 | 24 | 1,116 | 4,028 |
| Rio Grande | 206 | 159 | 773 | 721 | 2 | 4 | 54 | 30,150 |
| Routt | 374 | 310 | 700 | 687 | 30 | 50 | 19,951 | 5,432 |
| Saguache | 196 | 212 | 630 | 863 | 4 | 14 | 336 | 8,854 |
| *San Miguel | 64 | 67 | 235 | 413 | 6 | 3 | 6,046 | 5,066 |
| Sedgwick | 5 | 7 | 82 | 94 | --- | 2 | ------ | 27,219 |
| Summit | 64 | 79 | 99 | 157 | 1 | --- | 3 | ------ |
| Teller | 10 | 25 | 9 | 83 | --- | 1 | ------ | 40 |
| Washington | 6 | 8 | 52 | 60 | 1 | 3 | 32,300 | 268 |
| Weld | 225 | 238 | 1,606 | 1,990 | 88 | 103 | 224,056 | 310,059 |
| Yuma | 14 | 26 | 34 | 103 | 7 | 4 | 261 | 30 |
| All Other Counties | 17 | 17 | 5 | 31 | 2 | 7 | 755 | 737 |
| State | †6,585 | 6,634 | 21,381 | 27,593 | 765 | 979 | 1,924,982 | 2,406,372 |

*Part of Dolores annexed to San Miguel in 1925.
†Includes 63 intercounty projects counted in this table as 139 independent enterprises; corresponding figures for 1920 not available.
‡Included in "All Other Counties." All other counties include Cheyenne, Clear Creek, Gilpin, Phillips and San Juan.

**IRRIGATED FARMS; NUMBER, LAND AREA, AREA IRRIGATED, AND AREA ENTERPRISES WERE CAPABLE OF SUPPLYING WITH WATER, BY COUNTIES AND YEARS.**

(Compiled from Census Reports)

Note—This table includes only farms irrigated wholly or in part. Other tables in this volume give the number and area of all farms.

| COUNTY | Number of Irrigated Farms | | Land in Irrigated Farms 1930 (Acres) | Area Irrigated (Acres) | | Area Enterprises Were Capable of Supplying with Water (Acres) | | Irrigable Area in Enterprises 1930 (Acres) |
|---|---|---|---|---|---|---|---|---|
| | 1930 | 1920 | | 1929 | 1919 | 1930 | 1920 | |
| Adams | 1,057 | 740 | 135,866 | 66,826 | 66,407 | 112,471 | 68,065 | 131,00? |
| Alamosa | 484 | 281 | 207,907 | 141,489 | 89,805 | 156,249 | 168,625 | 182,06? |
| Arapahoe | 516 | 477 | 40,142 | 29,526 | 25,674 | 30,496 | 26,137 | 33,04? |
| Archuelta | 163 | 185 | 101,543 | 16,225 | 11,933 | 19,371 | 13,289 | 23,48? |
| Baca | 34 | 23 | 26,675 | 2,819 | 2,287 | 3,779 | 12,020 | 3,85? |
| Bent | 518 | 438 | 147,679 | 64,338 | 128,712 | 65,122 | 133,372 | 68,45? |
| Boulder | 1,201 | 1,200 | 152,867 | 159,428 | 159,781 | 181,896 | 174,736 | 184,18? |
| Chaffee | 291 | 313 | 68,015 | 26,938 | 29,623 | 30,797 | 30,113 | 33,67? |
| Conejos | 1,201 | 734 | 199,054 | 119,049 | 139,504 | 151,218 | 152,346 | 164,22? |
| Costilla | 551 | 431 | 319,786 | 48,272 | 36,771 | 109,957 | 43,906 | 112,96? |
| Crowley | 452 | 447 | 99,221 | 56,271 | 57,789 | 69,971 | 58,735 | 76,24? |
| Custer | 158 | 165 | 130,043 | 23,295 | 24,241 | 25,262 | 33,548 | 25,44? |
| Delta | 1,678 | 1,680 | 173,938 | 107,333 | 93,509 | 135,234 | 127,469 | 141,31? |
| Denver | 133 | 118 | 1,758 | 892 | 4,000 | 892 | 4,000 | 89? |
| *Dolores | 16 | 21 | 5,065 | 630 | 1,023 | 710 | 2,361 | 79? |
| Douglas | 96 | 108 | 109,233 | 6,474 | 8,696 | 9,557 | 10,391 | 9,97? |
| Eagle | 290 | 277 | 134,840 | 28,221 | 30,025 | 31,925 | 31,073 | 34,57? |
| Elbert | 7 | 12 | 12,411 | 2,487 | 1,175 | 6,282 | 1,790 | 6,60? |
| El Paso | 156 | 143 | 197,816 | 20,693 | 18,143 | 33,911 | 22,047 | 34,04? |
| Fremont | 1,015 | 827 | 188,410 | 25,655 | 29,884 | 31,957 | 35,697 | 36,87? |
| Garfield | 873 | 829 | 208,982 | 69,799 | 73,473 | 80,472 | 93,814 | 99,70? |
| Grand | 203 | 237 | 200,214 | 28,649 | 39,857 | 42,343 | 43,092 | 55,25? |
| Gunnison | 299 | 335 | 182,454 | 41,474 | 48,280 | 48,080 | 52,467 | 49,81? |
| Hinsdale | 34 | 29 | 15,633 | 5,212 | 3,675 | 5,984 | 3,880 | 6,60? |
| Huerfano | 383 | 418 | 300,088 | 30,974 | 29,081 | 44,129 | 32,119 | 46,26? |
| Jackson | 176 | 156 | 302,888 | 113,340 | 136,942 | 140,475 | 149,325 | 162,73 |
| Jefferson | 1,320 | 1,141 | 110,947 | 58,124 | 70,788 | 58,700 | 73,635 | 60,60 |
| Kiowa | 3 | 12 | 9,580 | 270 | 418 | 1,005 | 2,083 | 1,48 |
| Kit Carson | 5 | † | 11,340 | 650 | † | 660 | † | 68 |
| Lake | 27 | 29 | 15,034 | 4,242 | 6,397 | 4,242 | 7,088 | 4,24 |
| La Plata | 871 | 860 | 244,789 | 94,532 | 63,755 | 117,186 | 78,227 | 131,70 |
| Larimer | 1,499 | 1,486 | 537,255 | 173,078 | 169,356 | 180,879 | 188,047 | 183,57 |
| Las Animas | 531 | 530 | 633,022 | 32,092 | 40,400 | 48,153 | 43,857 | 54,07 |
| Lincoln | 7 | † | 84,490 | 185 | † | 450 | † | 93 |
| Logan | 617 | 397 | 260,966 | 111,378 | 85,079 | 123,616 | 105,916 | 127,31 |
| Mesa | 2,413 | 2,060 | 270,166 | 136,488 | 102,607 | 177,904 | 140,104 | 209,3 |
| Mineral | 32 | 28 | 20,810 | 2,563 | 6,865 | 3,172 | 9,950 | 5,0 |
| Moffat | 167 | 103 | 188,447 | 17,938 | 17,439 | 29,821 | 24,224 | 35,6 |
| Montezuma | 626 | 616 | 143,005 | 62,146 | 44,083 | 83,203 | 44,795 | 98,0 |
| Montrose | 1,238 | 1,294 | 199,966 | 84,058 | 94,757 | 105,100 | 123,905 | 114,6 |
| Morgan | 845 | 777 | 216,334 | 105,277 | 132,231 | 115,333 | 153,796 | 126,1 |
| Otero | 1,120 | 1,157 | 203,359 | 87,981 | 120,198 | 106,066 | 124,879 | 119,6 |
| Ouray | 156 | 142 | 95,820 | 20,401 | 14,016 | 23,431 | 23,092 | 31,4 |
| Park | 125 | 122 | 364,004 | 44,038 | 49,793 | 45,570 | 52,029 | 46,7 |
| Pitkin | 154 | 153 | 50,292 | 17,501 | 12,994 | 25,118 | 15,172 | 25,6 |
| Prowers | 729 | 660 | 168,730 | 111,634 | 76,322 | 126,955 | 81,508 | 131,1 |
| Pueblo | 935 | 995 | 749,730 | 69,211 | 75,454 | 97,122 | 88,699 | 123,5 |
| Rio Blanco | 234 | 278 | 209,671 | 30,526 | 28,046 | 34,438 | 32,742 | 39,4 |
| Rio Grande | 692 | 584 | 195,505 | 161,191 | 206,258 | 172,997 | 227,167 | 186,2 |
| Routt | 453 | 428 | 274,801 | 58,839 | 50,735 | 77,571 | 61,123 | 87,0 |
| Saguache | 416 | 390 | 400,113 | 163,815 | 137,581 | 178,052 | 153,391 | 184,4 |
| *San Miguel | 115 | 154 | 92,079 | 18,249 | 18,634 | 21,661 | 22,811 | 53,9 |
| Sedgwick | 161 | 130 | 93,891 | 22,375 | 21,510 | 23,985 | 23,050 | 24,5 |
| Summit | 52 | 67 | 28,836 | 9,204 | 9,831 | 11,354 | 10,986 | 11,3 |
| Teller | 12 | 26 | 12,830 | 550 | 1,464 | 630 | 1,540 | 6 |
| Washington | 68 | 51 | 27,515 | 11,120 | 9,335 | 11,705 | 10,095 | 11,7 |
| Weld | 3,612 | 3,398 | 761,920 | 443,915 | 382,701 | 499,675 | 395,444 | 568, |
| Yuma | 49 | 29 | 56,461 | 2,725 | 8,254 | 3,805 | 10,182 | 3, |
| All Other Counties | 19 | 35 | 16,054 | 514 | 794 | 613 | 1,394 | |
| State | 31,288 | 28,756 | 10,390,299 | 3,393,619 | 3,348,385 | 4,078,712 | 3,855,348 | 4 |

*Part of Dolores annexed to San Miguel in 1925.

†Included in "All Other Counties."

# Farm Drainage and Drainage Enterprises

THERE were 3,253 farms provided with drainage for 230,281 acres of land in the state on January 1, 1930, as reported by the census, and 58 drainage enterprises with drainage facilities for 366,719 acres. Drainage of agricultural land, as defined for census purposes, is the act or process of drawing off an excess of water by underground conduits, pipes, tiles, or by open or covered trenches in the surface of the ground for the purpose of improving the condition of the soil and crops. The purpose of drainage principally is for the prevention or removal of alkali and seepage resulting from irrigation and to protect land subject to overflow. Farm land provided with drainage is the work done by the farm owner and may be independent of or supplemental to the works of an organized enterprise. A drainage enterprise is an area organized according to law for the purpose of improving farm land for agricultural purposes.

Of the 366,719 acres under drainage enterprises on January 1, 1930, there were 250,238 acres in drainage districts organized under the drainage laws of the state, similar to irrigation districts; 99,130 acres under drainage projects controlled by irrigation enterprises; and 17,351 acres in individually owned enterprises. Of the 58 drainage enterprises in the state on January 1, 1930, there were 55 enterprises covering 293,489 acres of land, with an invested capital of $3,214,298, reported as completed, and three enterprises, covering 73,230 acres of land, with an invested capital of $1,144,568, upon which approximately $37,000 would be required to complete the drainage work under construction. The completed works included approximately 815 miles of ditches and 370 miles of tile drains.

**FARMS REPORTING DRAINAGE AND FARM LAND DRAINED, 1930 AND 1920; NUMBER OF FARMS AND LAND AREA, 1930**

(Compiled from Census Reports)

| COUNTY | Farms Reporting Drainage | | Number All Farms 1930 | Farm Land Provided with Drainage | | Land Area 1930 Acres |
|---|---|---|---|---|---|---|
| | Number 1930 | Number 1920 | | Acres 1930 | Acres 1920 | |
| Adams | 32 | 40 | 1,912 | 729 | 994 | 807,715 |
| Alamosa | 64 | 47 | 531 | 13,214 | 8,291 | 465,280 |
| Bent | 93 | 69 | 882 | 10,887 | 4,725 | 975,360 |
| Boulder | 221 | 358 | 1,473 | 5,312 | 11,499 | 488,960 |
| Conejos | 154 | 24 | 1,467 | 26,402 | 14,476 | 801,280 |
| Crowley | 260 | * | 626 | 22,473 | * | 517,120 |
| Delta | 82 | 122 | 1,744 | 1,743 | 2,427 | 768,640 |
| Gunnison | 5 | 19 | 370 | 558 | 539 | 2,034,560 |
| Jackson | 3 | 13 | 203 | 800 | 1,165 | 1,044,480 |
| Jefferson | 135 | 160 | 1,817 | 1,438 | 1,516 | 517,120 |
| Larimer | 233 | 396 | 1,838 | 8,125 | 12,711 | 1,682,560 |
| Logan | 57 | 16 | 1,845 | 3,956 | 2,393 | 1,166,080 |
| Mesa | 683 | 137 | 2,665 | 30,266 | 2,407 | 2,024,320 |
| Montrose | 99 | 161 | 1,318 | 3,364 | 3,836 | 1,448,960 |
| Otero | 120 | 107 | 1,298 | 9,599 | 5,144 | 805,760 |
| Prowers | 217 | 106 | 1,382 | 22,753 | 6,442 | 1,043,200 |
| Pueblo | 15 | 20 | 1,473 | 918 | 541 | 1,557,120 |
| Rio Grande | 156 | 18 | 730 | 39,993 | 6,080 | 574,720 |
| Saguache | 16 | 17 | 557 | 4,475 | 7,835 | 2,005,120 |
| Weld | 485 | 575 | 5,457 | 20,987 | 19,683 | 2,574,080 |
| All Other Counties | 123 | 344 | 30,368 | 2,289 | 14,333 | 43,038,685 |
| State | 3,253 | 2,749 | 59,956 | 230,281 | 127,037 | 66,341,120 |

Note—Farm land reported in this table may or may not be located within a drainage district, and usually such drainage is the result of work done by the farm owner, and may be independent of or supplemental to the works of an organized enterprise. Drainage enterprises are covered in another table.

No drainage on farms reported in Archuleta, Cheyenne, Costilla, Dolores, Elbert, Hinsdale, Kiowa, Kit Carson, Lake, Lincoln, Park, Phillips, San Juan, Sedgwick, Washington and Yuma Counties in 1930; and Baca, Cheyenne, Clear Creek, Dolores, Douglas, Elbert, Lincoln, Mineral, San Juan and Sedgwick Counties for 1920.

*Included in "All Other Counties."

## DRAINAGE ENTERPRISES BY COUNTIES, 1930 AND 1920

(Compiled from Census Reports)

| COUNTY | Land in Enter-prises (Acres) | Condition of Land | | Capital Invested in Enterprises | Estimated Cost When Completed | |
|---|---|---|---|---|---|---|
| | | Improved (Acres) | Unim-proved (Acres) | | Amount | Average Per Acre |
| Alamosa _____1930 | 33,845 | 19,443 | 14,402 | $ 308,494 | $ 308,494 | $ 9.11 |
| 1920 | † | † | ----- | † | † | † |
| Bent _____1930 | 23,112 | 22,772 | 340 | 259,150 | 259,150 | 11.21 |
| 1920 | 11,550 | 8,736 | ----- | 99,500 | 110,500 | 9.57 |
| Conejos _____1930 | 36,871 | 21,540 | 15,331 | 581,400 | 581,400 | 15.77 |
| 1920 | 17,100 | 9,163 | ----- | 253,907 | 343,907 | 20.11 |
| Crowley _____1930 | 28,867 | 28,282 | 585 | 519,000 | 519,000 | 17.98 |
| 1920 | † | † | ----- | † | † | † |
| Mesa _____1930 | 73,831 | 64,763 | 9,068 | 1,164,568 | 1,201,568 | 16.27 |
| 1920 | 50,640 | 30,640 | ----- | 224,805 | 312,000 | 6.16 |
| Otero _____1930 | 14,445 | 11,868 | 2,577 | 352,000 | 352,000 | 24.37 |
| 1920 | 4,539 | 4,196 | ----- | 141,000 | 156,000 | 34.37 |
| Prowers _____1930 | 47,593 | 47,593 | ----- | 539,050 | 539,050 | 11.33 |
| 1920 | 38,040 | 30,359 | ----- | 126,000 | 126,000 | 3.31 |
| Rio Grande_____1930 | 65,010 | 57,330 | 7,680 | 410,724 | 410,724 | 6.32 |
| 1920 | 27,000 | 23,650 | ----- | 108,200 | 108,200 | 4.01 |
| Saguache _____1930 | 33,220 | 19,240 | 13,980 | 82,080 | 82,080 | 2.47 |
| 1920 | † | † | ----- | † | † | † |
| *Other Counties_____1930 | 9,925 | 9,192 | 733 | 142,400 | 142,400 | 14.35 |
| 1920 | 22,787 | 16,287 | ----- | 128,463 | 128,463 | 5.64 |
| †State _____1930 | 366,719 | 302,023 | 64,696 | $4,358,866 | $4,395,866 | $11.99 |
| 1920 | 171,656 | 123,031 | ----- | 1,081,875 | 1,285,070 | 7.49 |

*Includes Logan, Morgan and Weld counties in 1930; and Alamosa, Crowley, Morgan and Saguache counties in 1920.
†Included in "Other Counties."

## RELATED RUN-OFF FOR COLORADO STREAMS

Period October 1, 1930, to September 30, 1931
(Compiled by State Engineer)

| STREAM | Total Runoff | | July to Sept. (Inclu.) | | No. Years Record |
|---|---|---|---|---|---|
| | Acre-Feet | % of Mean | Acre-Feet | % of Mean | |
| *South Platte River at South Platte _____ | 204,000 | 73 | 76,500 | 75 | 40 |
| Clear Creek near Golden_____ | 110,000 | 60 | 31,300 | 48 | 22 |
| St. Vrain River at Lyons_____ | 62,100 | 61 | 15,100 | 43 | 42 |
| Cache La Poudre River at the Canon Mouth_____ | 177,000 | 56 | 49,300 | 56 | 48 |
| Arkansas River at Canon City | 282,000 | 52 | 55,200 | 34 | 44 |
| Purgatoire River at Trinidad_ | 62,100 | 87 | 13,000 | 43 | 24 |
| Rio Grande near Del Norte___ | 353,000 | 42 | 77,200 | 43 | 42 |
| Saguache Creek near Saguache | 32,600 | 49 | 6,100 | 34 | 21 |
| Conejos River near Mogote___ | 136,000 | 48 | 31,600 | 52 | 29 |
| †Colorado River at Glenwood Springs _____ | 1,240,000 | 55 | 238,000 | 44 | 32 |
| Fraser River at West Portal__ | 21,100 | 64 | 5,630 | 57 | 21 |
| †Blue River near Dillon_____ | 65,000 | 69 | 18,000 | 59 | 21 |
| Dolores River at Dolores_____ | 130,000 | 39 | 18,900 | 36 | 22 |
| San Miguel River at Placer-ville _____ | 99,500 | 69 | 27,800 | 49 | 6 |
| Yampa River at Steamboat Springs _____ | 243,000 | 65 | 13,000 | 32 | 26 |
| White River at Meeker_____ | 361,000 | 73 | 61,400 | 64 | 28 |

*Corrected for Storage.
†Stations maintained by State Engineer's Office in co-operation with the U. S. Geological Survey.

# United States Reclamation Projects

THERE are in Colorado two great irrigation systems constructed by the United States reclamation service for the irrigation of arid lands in Mesa, Montrose and Delta counties, on the Western Slope. These two projects, which eventually will bring under irrigation approximately 135,000 acres, will represent a total investment of $11,000,000. At the present time they are maintaining a population of 6,835 on the farms, and including the towns within the districts, the population is well above 15,000.

The estimated farm value of the crops in recent years is as follows:

1928 ......................$2,817,798
1929 ...\.................... 2,785,257
1930 ...................... 2,078,435
1931 ...................... 1,724,040

The area farmed in 1931 was approximately 79,561 acres, which compares with 78,000 acres in 1930. Within their limits there were in 1931, 5,207 horses, 6,239 dairy cattle. 7,574 beef cattle, 10,276 swine, 34,961 sheep and 96,700 poultry.

More detailed information concerning each of the two projects is contained in the following data, obtained from the superintendent of each.

## THE GRAND VALLEY PROJECT

The area irrigated under this project lies in Mesa county, near Grand Junction, at an elevation of 4,700 feet. Water is secured by direct diversion from the Colorado river. The project will cost approximately $4,500,000 when completed. It includes the gravity division, now complete, and the pumping division, on which little construction work has been undertaken. The supply of water is adequate for the acreage to be irrigated

Approximately 18,800 acres of the gravity division is now being farmed and in 1931 produced crops with a value of $378,329, or an average of $24.82 per acre cropped. The principal crops were alfalfa, sugar beets, beans,

tomatoes, potatoes and grains. The livestock census for 1931 shows that there were on this area 1,000 horses and mules, 62 beef and 1,305 dairy cattle, 865 sheep, 2,105 swine, 3,000 turkeys and 14,180 hens. There are 275 families, with a total population of 1,281 residing on the farms.

At the present time there are 1,800 acres of government homestead land within the gravity division of the project and 3,800 acres within the pumping division, but none of the acreage is open to filing at this time. It is estimated that there are 3,000 acres of privately owned land within the gravity division and 4,700 acres under the pumping division which can be purchased with a small cash payment and liberal terms on the balance. The land is generally of good quality.

The cost of the water right for these lands has been established by contract with the United States at $83.45, probably reduced by certain credits and payable over a period of 40 years without interest. The average maintenance charge is $2.75 per acre annually, subject to change as operation and maintenance costs fluctuate.

In addition to this project the reclamation bureau has completed the reconstruction of the irrigation system for an area of 10,000 acres of land in the Orchard Mesa irrigation district. A total expenditure of nearly $1,000,000 insures an adequate and dependable water supply for the highly fertile land, of which more than one-half is now in a high state of cultivation, nearly 3,500 acres being idle. This district offers unusual opportunities for fruit growing and general farming.

Inquiries concerning these lands should be addressed to the Project Superintendent, Grand Valley Project, Grand Junction, Colorado.

## THE UNCOMPAHGRE PROJECT

The area irrigated under this project lies in Montrose and Delta counties at an elevation of 4,900 feet above sea level at the lower end and ranging up to 6,400 feet at the upper end. The water is secured by diversion from the Uncompahgre river, supplemented by water from the Gunnison river diverted through the Gunnison tunnel into the Uncompahgre valley. The system is complete and represents an expenditure of approximately $6,713,584. The water supply is considered adequate for the acreage to be irrigated.

A total of 60,761 acres was farmed under the project in 1931, and total crop production was valued at $1,345,711. The principal crops in the order of their importance were as follows: Alfalfa, wheat, potatoes, sugar beets, oats, corn, onions, apples and beans. Based on irrigable acreage, the average size of farms under the project is 40.0 acres, and based on acreage actually irrigated 35.5 acres. The livestock census within the area showed 4,207 horses, 4,934 dairy cattle, 7,512 beef cattle, 8,171 swine, 34,096 sheep and 79,520 hens and other poultry.

The farm population of the project is estimated at 5,554 and the town population, including Montrose, Olathe and Delta, at 7,097—a total population of 12,651 people wholly or partially dependent upon the irrigation of lands within its limits. The assessed valuation of all real and personal property in the project was about $6,000,000 in 1930.

There are only a few acres of government homestead land available in the project, but privately owned lands may be secured by purchase. The United States government exercises no restriction relative to the sale of such privately owned lands except that water rights for such land cannot be granted in excess of 160 irrigable acres. The terms upon which such land can be purchased depend entirely upon the individual transaction, and the price is based largely on the improvements, type of soil and location. The general character of the available land ranges from fair to excellent, two types of soil prevailing. On the west side of the Uncompahgre river the land consists generally of sandy loams, underlaid with gravel, while on the east side of the river the adobe type of soil predominates.

The approximate cost per acre for irrigation water is fixed by the adjusted cost of the project, the rate fixed at present being $52.00 for what is known as Class 1 land. In accordance with legislation passed by Congress on May 25, 1926, a contract was executed by the members of the Uncompahgre Valley Water Users association, providing for a reduction in the total cost per acre from $70.00 per acre to $52.00 per acre, and the term of payments is extended over a period of 40 years from December 1, 1922, instead of over a period of 20 years, as had been in effect.

Operation and maintenance charges in effect for 1932 provide for a minimum charge of $1.80 per acre annually for lands on the west side of the Uncompahgre river, entitling such lands to four acre-feet of water, and a minimum charge of $1.35 per acre annually for lands on the east side of the Uncompahgre river, entitling such lands to three acre-feet of water. Excess water over these amounts is furnished at the rate of 45 cents per acre-foot.

Inquiries concerning the lands within the project should be addressed to the Project Superintendent, Uncompahgre Project, Montrose, Colorado.

## Climatological Data

COLORADO is noted for its rare and exhilarating atmosphere. Visitors arriving in the state from low altitudes often feel a tendency to run, jump and indulge in other exercises. This is due to the fact that the atmosphere exerts less pressure against the body than in localities where it is more dense. The feeling is very much like that of having a load lifted from the body, and that is, in fact, what takes place.

Normal atmospheric pressure at sea level is 14.7 pounds to the square inch. In other words, that is the pressure exerted against the body by the weight, or density, of the atmosphere. The greater the altitude above sea level, the lighter becomes the pressure. The atmospheric pressure in Denver is only 83 per cent of that at sea level, or 12.2 pounds to the square inch. Denver is 5,280 feet above sea level. Wagon Wheel Gap is 9,200 feet above sea level. Atmospheric pressure at that point is only 72 per cent of that at sea level, or 10.5 pounds to the square inch. Denver's atmospheric pressure is 85 per cent of that at Indianapolis, Springfield and points of approximately the same altitude, and only 84 per cent of the average of the eight principal cities approximately on the same parallel due east from Denver to the sea coast.

A person breathes more deeply in a light atmosphere than in a locality where it is more dense, in order to fill the lungs with the quantity of oxygen necessary for the body. This is done automatically, without conscious effort, and causes all parts of the lungs to expand to full capacity. That is why climatic conditions in Colorado are considered especially beneficial to persons with a tendency toward pulmonary troubles. In lower altitudes parts of the lungs may lie dormant in persons of sedentary habits and thereby become susceptible to disease.

## TEMPERATURE

There is a wide variation in the normal monthly and annual mean temperature in different areas of the state, due to the high and low altitudes and other factors. It is apparent to a casual observer that it is much colder upon the top of a high mountain than in the lower plains. Altitude, therefore, is one factor. Exposed areas are more susceptible, also, to varying conditions than areas protected from severe winds by surrounding mountains. Because of these varying conditions, a general statement concerning the temperature of the state conveys little meaning. A table is published in this volume showing monthly and annual mean temperatures at 78 stations in as many different localities, which affords more comprehensive information upon the subject.

The weather-reporting station of lowest mean annual temperature is at Fraser, in Grand county, where the yearly average is 31.9 degrees, and the highest mean temperature is recorded at Lamar, in Prowers county, where the annual average is 54.4. At Fraser the month of January shows an average of 11.6 degrees, compared with 31.2 degrees at Lamar, while July averages 53.2 degrees, compared with 77.8 degrees at Lamar.

## HUMIDITY

Relative humidity of the atmosphere has no effect on the temperature but does have an important effect on the sensitiveness of the human body to the temperature. Colorado has a relatively low humidity and for that reason a person does not feel cold weather to as great an extent as he would in a place where the humidity is high. Relative humidity is the ratio of the vapor actually present in the atmosphere to the greatest amount the air could possibly contain at a given temperature. Complete saturation is designated as 100 per cent humidity. Relative humidity at Denver over a period of 53 years averages 53 per cent. In other words, the air at Denver contains just a little more than half of the moisture it could possibly contain.

Out of 70 typical cities of the United States, Denver has the lowest relative humidity of all of them with five exceptions. These are Phoenix, Arizona, 42 per cent; Santa Fe, New Mexico, 49 per cent; Winnemucca, Nevada, 52 per cent; El Paso, Texas, 40 per cent; and Salt Lake City 52 per cent. Denver's 53 per cent compares with some of the other cities as follows: Albany, 75 per cent; Atlanta, 72 per cent; Boston, 71 per cent; Chicago, 74 per cent; Galveston, 81 per cent; Kansas City, 64 per cent; Omaha, 69 per cent; Los Angeles, 64 per cent; San Francisco, 80 per cent.

Moist air is cold air, and moisture in the air takes heat away from the body. The greater the amount of moisture in the air, the colder a given temperature will feel. That explains why the people residing in Colorado do not feel cold temperature to as great an extent as people residing in areas of relative high humidity.

## SNOWFALL IN THE MOUNTAINS

Visitors to the high mountain passes in Colorado in the spring and early summer are often surprised by the enormous banks of snow which they may observe. These snow banks are of almost incalculable value not only to Colorado but to adjoining states. They are mostly deposited during the winter months and form a moisture reserve that feeds numerous small streams flowing in all directions. These streams combine into creeks which broaden out into rivers that flow into the Pacific ocean and the Gulf of Mexico, forming the principal rivers in Wyoming, Nebraska, Kansas, New Mexico and Utah.

The quantity of snow required to maintain the flow of these streams during the entire year as it gradually melts is difficult to comprehend. Some idea may be formed, however, from the measurements of river discharges, made by the government. The Arkansas river had a mean or average discharge of 756 cubic feet of water per second at Pueblo over a period of about nine years. That is equal to an average of approximately 21,236,000 gallons of water an hour, and the Arkansas is only one of the numerous rivers which have their origin in the mountains of Colorado.

The area of greatest snowfall in Colorado, as shown by actual measurements under the direction of the weather bureau, is at Wortman, in Lake county, at an altitude of 11,250 feet above sea level. The average annual snowfall at that point over a period of 10 years was 276.5 inches, or a fraction more than 23 feet a year. The snow drifts into canons and ravines, where it packs and is gradually released by the warm sun during the spring and summer months.

At Fairview, in Custer county, elevation 9,500 feet, the annual snowfall averages 241.6 inches. Lake Moraine, in El Paso county, 10,215 feet above sea level, is in a district where the snowfall has averaged 160.2 inches a year for a period of twenty-one years. Cumbres pass, in Conejos county, at an elevation of 10,015 feet, which is traversed by a railroad, averaged 217.9 inches over a period of eight years. Silverton, San Juan county, elevation 9,302 feet, averaged 223.2 inches for a period of six years. Telluride, San Miguel county, elevation 8,500 feet, averaged 171.0 inches for nine years. Breckenridge, in Summit county, elevation 9,579 feet, averaged 183.8 inches a year over a period of nineteen years.

## GLACIERS

The snow which falls in the mountains during the winter does not all melt in the following summer. When it packs hard in the ravines and remains for many years it forms glaciers. Colorado has a number of glaciers, one of the largest being the Arapahoe glacier at the crest of the Continental Divide between North and South Arapahoe peaks at an altitude of 13,500 feet, in the Roosevelt (formerly Colorado) national forest. In a former geological age it extended down towards the plains but now is about a mile wide. It flows at the rate of 27½ feet per year and its melting gives rise to a chain of beautiful lakes in the valley below. The St. Vrain glacier, on the east side of Mt. Hiamova, is supposed to contain the oldest ice of the group—that melting in current years having been deposited as snow many centuries ago.

## DENVER WEATHER CONDITIONS

Denver, being close to the center of the state and of approximately the same altitude as the principal cities, furnishes a fairly accurate index of weather conditions in Colorado. J. M. Sherier, meteorologist of the United States weather bureau, has compiled a chart showing average climatic data for Denver from 1872 to 1931, inclusive, a period of 60 years. The average temperature in degrees Fahrenheit for the 60 years is is follows:

| Month | Max. | Min. | Min. Av. |
|---|---|---|---|
| January | 42.7 | 17.9 | 30.4 |
| February | 44.6 | 20.7 | 32.7 |
| March | 51.3 | 26.9 | 39.1 |
| April | 59.6 | 35.2 | 47.4 |
| May | 68.8 | 44.1 | 56.5 |
| June | 80.1 | 53.0 | 66.6 |
| July | 85.3 | 58.9 | 72.1 |
| August | 84.2 | 57.7 | 70.9 |
| September | 76.5 | 48.8 | 62.5 |
| October | 64.4 | 37.8 | 51.1 |
| November | 52.4 | 27.4 | 39.9 |
| December | 44.1 | 19.8 | 31.9 |
| Year | 62.8 | 37.3 | 50.1 |

The highest temperature recorded in Denver during the 60 years was in August, 1878, when the thermometer registered 105 degrees, and the lowest was in January, 1875, when the temperature dropped to 29 degrees below zero. The thermometer never reached zero from April to September, inclusive, in the 60 years, and went below zero in October only once, in 1917, when it dropped to 2 degrees below. In 1888 the thermometer rose to 76 degrees in January.

The following chart shows the average maximum and minimum mean temperature over a period of 60 years, the solid black line being the average by months, and the dotted lines above and below, the maximum and minimum mean temperature by months.

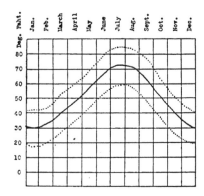

The average yearly rainfall in Denver during the 60 years was 14.20 inches. January is the driest month of the year, with February, November and December following in the order named, the precipitation averaging 1 inch or less per month six months out of the year. April and May are the months of greatest precipitation, with July, August and June following in the order named. The maximum precipitation recorded in any 24-hour period during the 60 years was 6.53 inches in May, 1876, and the maximum for any year was 22.96 inches, in 1909. The average snowfall is 55.7 inches, March, December and April being the months showing the heaviest records.

On July 14, 1912, a total of 0.91 inch of rain fell in Denver in five minutes, the absolute maximum over a period of 30 years. On the same day 1.36 inches fell in ten minutes, 1.54 inches in 15 minutes and 1.72 inches in 30 minutes. A rainfall of 2.20 inches in one hour occurred on May 23, 1921. The following chart shows the average monthly precipitation in inches for the period of 60 years.

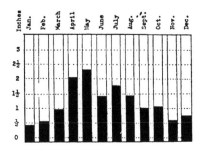

The sun shines 66 per cent of the time in Denver as shown by the records over a period of 60 years. The sky is clear on an average of 151 days out of every 365 and is cloudy only 61 days. It is partly cloudy 153 days in the year. The following chart shows the proportionate division of the year between clear, cloudy and partly cloudy days:

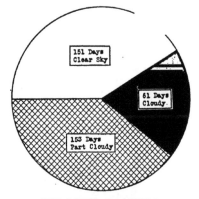

### VELOCITY OF WINDS

The average velocity of winds in Colorado as computed by the United States weather bureau from measurements taken at stations named, in miles per hour, is as follows:

| | |
|---|---|
| Denver | 7.3 |
| Pueblo | 7.2 |
| Wagon Wheel Gap | 6.3 |
| Durango | 5.6 |
| Grand Junction | 5.4 |
| Las Animas | 7.9 |
| Pikes Peak | 20.7 |

The average velocity of the wind in Denver is 7.3 miles per hour, the prevailing direction being from the south. March and April are the windiest months, the average being 8.1 and 8.3 miles per hour.

Revised weather bureau records show that the highest velocity ever recorded in Denver was 60 miles an hour, on August 6, 1877. Wind with a velocity of 3 to 5 miles an hour is classed as light air; of 10 miles an hour, a light breeze; of 20 miles an hour, a gentle breeze; of 70 miles an hour, a storm; and 80 miles an hour, a hurricane. Under this classification, it will be observed that the wind of August 6, 1877, did not quite reach the velocity of a storm. The force of that storm was approximately 15,000 pounds per square foot. The wind traveled at the rate of about 5,300 feet a minute.

### GROWING SEASONS

The records of the weather bureau show that Grand Junction has the longest growing season recorded anywhere in the state, the period between first and last frosts in that district averaging, over a period of 20 years, 184 days. In Canon City the average growing season is 163 days; in Boulder,

165; in Denver, 158; in Lamar, 168, and in Pueblo, 165. These are the regions of longest periods between late and early frosts, but in many of the higher altitudes, where the growing season is seemingly too short to make agriculture possible, crop growth is remarkably rapid and many of the crops mature in considerably less time than is required in other regions. This is true of potatoes, small grains, head lettuce and similar crops. While there are limited districts in the state where irrigation water is not available and the rainfall is not sufficient to carry crops through a long, warm summer, in most sections except the southwest proper soil treatment and the planting of crops which experience has shown to require comparatively little moisture have made non-irrigated farming highly successful.

## RELATIVE HUMIDITY OF 24 TYPICAL CITIES IN THE U. S.

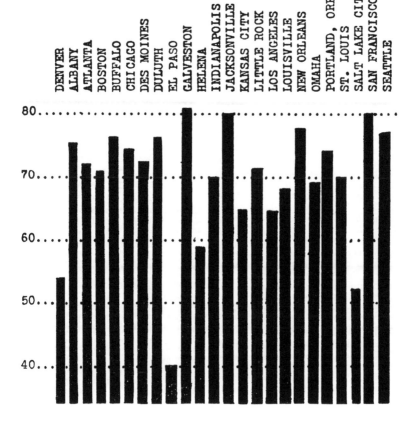

CHART SHOWING HOURS OF SUNRISE, SUNSET, DARKNESS, AND DAYLIGHT AT
DENVER, COLORADO SPRINGS, PUEBLO AND OTHER LOCATIONS ON
APPROXIMATELY THE SAME MERIDIAN.

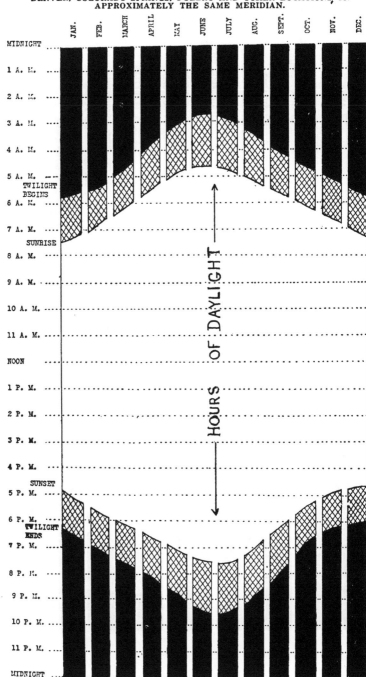

## CHART SHOWING AVERAGE ANNUAL RAINFALL IN INCHES
### IN 34 CITIES AND TOWNS

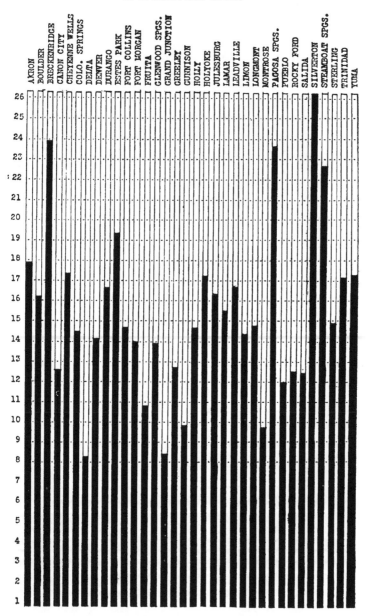

## NORMAL MONTHLY AND ANNUAL MEAN TEMPERATURE IN DEGREES FAHRENHEIT
(From the Records of the U. S. Weather Bureau)

| PLACE | COUNTY | Length of Record Years* | Jan. | Feb. | Mar. | Apr. | May | June | July | Aug. | Sept. | Oct. | Nov. | Dec. | Annual |
|---|---|---|---|---|---|---|---|---|---|---|---|---|---|---|---|
| Arriba | Lincoln | -- | 27.2 | 29.4 | 37.6 | 46.0 | 54.8 | 65.0 | 70.6 | 69.8 | 61.8 | 51.2 | 38.9 | 26.9 | 48.2 |
| Boulder | Boulder | 32 | 33.0 | 32.6 | 40.4 | 48.2 | 56.4 | 66.0 | 70.8 | 70.6 | 63.2 | 52.2 | 42.2 | 33.8 | 50.8 |
| Breckenridge | Summit | -- | 15.4 | 15.6 | 22.4 | 30.0 | 39.0 | 48.6 | 53.4 | 53.0 | 46.6 | 35.9 | 25.6 | 15.2 | 33.4 |
| Buena Vista | Chaffee | -- | 22.2 | 25.7 | 33.0 | 38.2 | 48.4 | 55.6 | 59.9 | 58.3 | 51.9 | 42.0 | 31.9 | 20.9 | 40.6 |
| Burlington | Kit Carson | 23 | 27.8 | 31.4 | 40.2 | 47.6 | 57.5 | 68.4 | 73.6 | 72.5 | 64.8 | 52.0 | 40.6 | 29.0 | 50.4 |
| Calhan | El Paso | 21 | 27.2 | 27.6 | 35.6 | 41.9 | 51.0 | 62.0 | 67.2 | 66.0 | 59.2 | 47.4 | 36.2 | 26.6 | 45.7 |
| Canon City | Fremont | 34 | 35.3 | 35.2 | 42.9 | 50.0 | 57.4 | 66.1 | 72.9 | 72.3 | 64.3 | 53.1 | 43.4 | 35.9 | 52.4 |
| Castle Rock | Douglas | 30 | 28.2 | 28.8 | 36.0 | 43.8 | 52.8 | 62.4 | 67.2 | 68.0 | 62.2 | 47.4 | 37.0 | 28.0 | 46.8 |
| Cedaredge | Delta | 26 | 26.0 | 29.9 | 38.6 | 47.0 | 55.2 | 63.9 | 69.8 | 68.4 | 60.4 | 49.2 | 38.2 | 26.9 | 47.8 |
| Cheyenne Wells | Cheyenne | 31 | 28.0 | 30.0 | 39.4 | 48.6 | 58.1 | 68.4 | 73.7 | 72.8 | 64.8 | 52.4 | 39.5 | 28.0 | 50.3 |
| Collbran | Mesa | 26 | 22.8 | 28.4 | 37.0 | 45.4 | 53.6 | 62.6 | 68.3 | 67.2 | 59.3 | 47.8 | 36.4 | 24.3 | 46.1 |
| Colorado Springs | El Paso | 34 | 30.0 | 29.6 | 37.5 | 44.6 | 53.1 | 62.0 | 67.0 | 66.2 | 59.6 | 48.8 | 38.7 | 30.6 | 47.3 |
| Cope | Washington | -- | 29.2 | 28.0 | 38.5 | 48.5 | 56.2 | 67.2 | 72.3 | 72.2 | 63.6 | 50.9 | 38.3 | 28.9 | 49.5 |
| Crawford | Montrose | -- | 25.4 | 26.9 | 35.2 | 42.9 | 52.0 | 61.9 | 67.8 | 65.9 | 58.4 | 48.2 | 37.2 | 25.4 | 45.6 |
| Crested Butte | Gunnison | 17 | 11.4 | 15.0 | 23.4 | 31.1 | 42.1 | 51.4 | 55.6 | 53.7 | 46.2 | 36.2 | 25.0 | 12.0 | 33.6 |
| Delta | Delta | 33 | 24.5 | 31.6 | 41.8 | 50.5 | 59.0 | 68.0 | 74.0 | 71.5 | 62.6 | 50.4 | 38.8 | 25.6 | 49.8 |
| Denver | Denver | 56 | 29.8 | 32.7 | 39.3 | 47.1 | 56.2 | 66.3 | 72.2 | 70.7 | 62.9 | 51.2 | 39.8 | 32.3 | 50.0 |
| Durango | La Plata | 34 | 24.5 | 29.9 | 37.5 | 46.4 | 55.0 | 62.7 | 68.7 | 66.3 | 58.2 | 48.9 | 37.2 | 28.3 | 47.0 |
| Eads | Kiowa | 16 | 29.0 | 31.8 | 42.0 | 48.4 | 59.9 | 71.0 | 76.1 | 74.3 | 66.2 | 52.6 | 40.0 | 28.9 | 51.6 |
| Fort Collins | Larimer | 33 | 26.2 | 27.4 | 36.0 | 44.3 | 53.8 | 63.1 | 68.0 | 67.5 | 59.2 | 48.0 | 36.1 | 27.2 | 46.4 |
| Fort Morgan | Morgan | 29 | 24.1 | 27.8 | 35.7 | 46.7 | 56.4 | 66.6 | 73.1 | 71.0 | 62.0 | 49.2 | 36.6 | 25.3 | 47.9 |
| Fraser | Grand | 18 | 11.6 | 14.2 | 21.2 | 30.0 | 39.4 | 48.2 | 53.2 | 51.2 | 45.0 | 34.4 | 23.0 | 12.2 | 31.9 |
| Fremont (Exp. Sta. | El Paso | 17 | 25.4 | 23.5 | 29.6 | 33.6 | 43.2 | 53.2 | 57.7 | 56.2 | 50.6 | 40.4 | 32.6 | 25.2 | 39.3 |
| Fruita | Mesa | 26 | 21.4 | 30.3 | 42.6 | 50.0 | 58.4 | 68.1 | 74.2 | 72.8 | 63.5 | 51.1 | 37.8 | 25.0 | 49.6 |
| Garnett | Alamosa | 29 | 17.2 | 23.8 | 32.8 | 41.2 | 49.2 | 58.6 | 62.6 | 61.2 | 54.5 | 43.1 | 30.7 | 20.2 | 41.2 |
| Glenwood Springs | Garfield | 24 | 22.6 | 27.1 | 37.3 | 45.0 | 52.6 | 60.6 | 65.5 | 65.0 | 57.9 | 47.1 | 35.8 | 23.8 | 45.0 |
| Grand Junction | Mesa | 36 | 24.0 | 32.9 | 43.6 | 52.4 | 61.1 | 71.4 | 77.7 | 75.4 | 66.2 | 52.8 | 39.3 | 27.5 | 52.0 |
| Grand Valley | Garfield | -- | 24.7 | 29.9 | 40.0 | 49.3 | 57.8 | 66.0 | 71.2 | 69.9 | 61.5 | 49.0 | 37.6 | 24.8 | 48.5 |
| Greeley | Weld | 33 | 26.0 | 27.8 | 38.0 | 47.4 | 56.8 | 66.6 | 70.9 | 70.0 | 61.2 | 49.1 | 36.6 | 26.0 | 48.0 |
| Grover | Weld | 17 | 24.2 | 26.8 | 34.6 | 42.0 | 52.0 | 62.6 | 68.6 | 66.8 | 58.9 | 47.2 | 35.4 | 25.0 | 45.4 |
| Gunnison | Gunnison | 34 | 7.2 | 12.4 | 25.6 | 39.2 | 47.6 | 57.6 | 61.4 | 59.8 | 52.0 | 41.4 | 27.6 | 10.8 | 36.9 |
| Hamps | Elbert | -- | 27.0 | 27.5 | 36.0 | 44.9 | 53.4 | 62.4 | 67.6 | 66.8 | 58.8 | 47.4 | 36.3 | 27.0 | 46.2 |
| Hermit | Hinsdale | 16 | 11.8 | 14.6 | 20.5 | 28.9 | 43.3 | 47.5 | 52.8 | 51.1 | 45.0 | 36.0 | 25.4 | 13.0 | 32.5 |
| Hoehne | Las Animas | -- | 32.2 | 33.2 | 40.8 | 48.4 | 56.7 | 66.8 | 71.4 | 70.2 | 63.2 | 52.3 | 42.4 | 31.1 | 50.8 |
| Holly | Prowers | 25 | 31.1 | 33.7 | 44.0 | 52.4 | 62.2 | 72.0 | 76.9 | 76.0 | 68.8 | 56.0 | 42.4 | 30.5 | 53.8 |
| Holyoke | Phillips | -- | 27.6 | 26.8 | 37.2 | 47.2 | 57.2 | 66.9 | 73.1 | 71.8 | 62.8 | 50.0 | 39.0 | 26.8 | 48.8 |
| Husted | El Paso | -- | 28.4 | 29.4 | 36.2 | 44.8 | 53.2 | 60.9 | 66.4 | 66.4 | 59.3 | 47.6 | 37.4 | 30.0 | 46.6 |
| Idaho Springs | Clear Creek | 24 | 28.0 | 28.3 | 34.4 | 39.8 | 48.2 | 58.3 | 63.0 | 62.0 | 55.3 | 45.0 | 35.1 | 28.0 | 43.8 |
| Lamar | Prowers | 34 | 31.2 | 33.8 | 44.8 | 53.4 | 61.9 | 73.4 | 77.8 | 76.8 | 68.9 | 55.7 | 42.4 | 32.2 | 54.4 |
| Las Animas | Bent | 41 | 28.0 | 29.2 | 42.1 | 51.4 | 61.0 | 71.8 | 76.0 | 72.8 | 66.1 | 53.2 | 40.2 | 29.7 | 51.8 |
| Lay | Moffat | 30 | 18.4 | 20.8 | 32.1 | 41.4 | 49.8 | 59.4 | 66.6 | 65.0 | 55.6 | 44.1 | 32.3 | 20.6 | 42.1 |
| Leadville | Lake | 22 | 17.4 | 18.6 | 24.1 | 30.8 | 39.9 | 49.5 | 55.2 | 53.8 | 47.4 | 36.9 | 27.3 | 18.2 | 34.9 |
| LeRoy | Logan | 28 | 26.8 | 28.0 | 36.6 | 45.2 | 55.2 | 65.4 | 71.7 | 71.2 | 63.0 | 50.2 | 37.2 | 28.0 | 48.2 |
| Limon | Lincoln | -- | 26.4 | 32.1 | 37.0 | 43.9 | 53.2 | 63.6 | 69.4 | 67.9 | 60.6 | 49.2 | 37.5 | 26.5 | 47.3 |
| Longmont | Boulder | 21 | 26.6 | 29.0 | 38.0 | 46.1 | 56.0 | 65.6 | 69.8 | 68.8 | 60.1 | 48.0 | 36.6 | 26.4 | 47.6 |
| Manassa | Conejos | 22 | 20.9 | 25.7 | 34.5 | 41.0 | 49.4 | 59.0 | 62.8 | 61.2 | 54.7 | 43.8 | 32.6 | 21.0 | 42.2 |
| Mancos | Montezuma | -- | 25.5 | 29.1 | 36.8 | 44.4 | 51.5 | 61.2 | 66.2 | 65.0 | 57.6 | 47.3 | 37.9 | 26.5 | 45.8 |
| Meeker | Rio Blanco | -- | 20.5 | 24.0 | 34.2 | 43.0 | 51.1 | 59.2 | 64.8 | 63.4 | 55.2 | 44.1 | 33.2 | 20.9 | 42.8 |
| Montrose | Montrose | 34 | 24.1 | 31.4 | 40.4 | 47.6 | 57.6 | 65.2 | 70.6 | 68.4 | 61.0 | 49.0 | 37.0 | 26.4 | 48.2 |
| Monument | El Paso | 17 | 27.1 | 28.0 | 33.4 | 39.3 | 49.5 | 59.0 | 64.4 | 62.8 | 56.0 | 45.5 | 35.3 | 27.8 | 44.0 |
| Nast | Pitkin | -- | 16.3 | 18.6 | 25.8 | 33.8 | 43.5 | 52.8 | 57.1 | 55.8 | 49.1 | 39.2 | 28.4 | 17.1 | 36.4 |
| Pagoda | Routt | -- | 21.1 | 22.4 | 32.4 | 42.2 | 49.6 | 57.4 | 63.8 | 63.4 | 55.5 | 44.6 | 33.0 | 21.0 | 42.2 |
| Pagosa Springs | Archuleta | -- | 19.8 | 22.2 | 34.2 | 42.0 | 47.9 | 56.4 | 63.4 | 61.8 | 55.0 | 43.2 | 32.8 | 18.4 | 41.6 |
| Palisades | Mesa | 15 | 22.6 | 33.2 | 42.2 | 51.6 | 60.6 | 69.7 | 76.2 | 74.6 | 65.7 | 50.6 | 39.9 | 28.8 | 51.4 |
| Paonia | Delta | 23 | 25.6 | 31.6 | 40.4 | 47.8 | 55.8 | 65.2 | 70.9 | 69.2 | 61.6 | 50.3 | 39.8 | 27.4 | 48.8 |
| Pueblo | Pueblo | 39 | 29.9 | 32.9 | 41.6 | 50.1 | 59.2 | 69.0 | 74.2 | 72.7 | 64.6 | 52.0 | 39.4 | 31.5 | 51.4 |
| Rangely | Rio Blanco | -- | 15.2 | 20.4 | 34.6 | 46.7 | 53.8 | 63.4 | 69.8 | 64.4 | 58.6 | 46.3 | 33.0 | 17.4 | 44.0 |
| Redvale | Montrose | -- | 22.6 | 28.3 | 36.4 | 44.5 | 54.0 | 63.2 | 68.0 | 66.4 | 58.6 | 47.3 | 36.8 | 25.4 | 46.0 |
| Rifle | Garfield | -- | 23.1 | 28.8 | 37.4 | 47.4 | 55.4 | 65.1 | 70.7 | 69.2 | 61.0 | 49.0 | 38.0 | 25.6 | 47.6 |
| Rocky Ford | Otero | 34 | 30.2 | 32.5 | 42.4 | 51.2 | 60.7 | 70.3 | 74.7 | 73.4 | 65.5 | 53.2 | 40.4 | 31.2 | 52.2 |
| Rugh Ranch | Larimer | 19 | 26.2 | 26.1 | 32.5 | 37.8 | 46.6 | 56.3 | 60.9 | 59.5 | 52.7 | 43.6 | 34.6 | 26.0 | 41.9 |
| Saguache | Saguache | 28 | 21.5 | 27.0 | 35.4 | 44.3 | 52.0 | 60.8 | 65.5 | 63.9 | 57.0 | 46.8 | 34.8 | 22.4 | 44.2 |
| Salida | Chaffee | 28 | 27.4 | 29.8 | 36.5 | 43.4 | 51.2 | 60.0 | 65.0 | 63.6 | 56.6 | 46.2 | 36.6 | 27.1 | 45.3 |
| San Luis | Costilla | 28 | 21.0 | 25.8 | 34.2 | 41.7 | 49.3 | 57.8 | 62.4 | 61.9 | 54.8 | 44.4 | 33.2 | 22.5 | 42.4 |
| Sapinero | Gunnison | 23 | 15.2 | 18.9 | 27.6 | 36.8 | 45.2 | 53.6 | 59.1 | 58.0 | 51.0 | 40.6 | 29.6 | 17.4 | 37.8 |
| Sedgwick | Sedgwick | -- | 25.2 | 28.2 | 38.4 | 47.0 | 57.2 | 68.0 | 73.6 | 71.3 | 62.8 | 50.5 | 39.3 | 24.2 | 48.6 |
| Silverton | San Juan | 21 | 16.2 | 17.9 | 24.1 | 31.2 | 40.0 | 48.9 | 55.1 | 52.8 | 46.6 | 37.7 | 26.6 | 16.8 | 34.5 |
| Spicer | Jackson | 23 | 18.1 | 21.1 | 26.1 | 35.3 | 43.2 | 54.2 | 59.6 | 57.5 | 49.7 | 38.5 | 29.0 | 17.8 | 37.5 |
| Steamboat Springs | Routt | 23 | 14.8 | 17.6 | 26.8 | 39.0 | 48.6 | 55.7 | 60.7 | 59.0 | 52.3 | 41.3 | 28.5 | 17.7 | 38.5 |
| Sterling | Logan | 18 | 24.1 | 28.9 | 38.0 | 46.9 | 56.6 | 67.2 | 72.2 | 70.2 | 62.2 | 49.8 | 37.0 | 24.2 | 48.2 |
| Telluride | San Miguel | -- | 21.4 | 23.6 | 28.2 | 36.2 | 45.4 | 54.0 | 58.8 | 57.0 | 51.2 | 41.3 | 31.5 | 23.0 | 39.3 |
| Trinidad | Las Animas | 24 | 34.0 | 35.4 | 42.2 | 48.3 | 57.4 | 66.5 | 71.0 | 69.9 | 63.0 | 52.8 | 41.9 | 34.0 | 51.4 |
| Two Buttes | Baca | 29 | 31.4 | 32.6 | 42.5 | 51.4 | 61.1 | 71.2 | 76.2 | 75.2 | 67.6 | 55.1 | 42.8 | 32.2 | 53.2 |
| Victor | Teller | 24 | 25.1 | 25.7 | 30.4 | 35.4 | 43.8 | 54.2 | 58.0 | 57.3 | 51.8 | 41.9 | 33.0 | 25.4 | 40.2 |
| Wagon Wheel Gap | Mineral | 20 | 14.2 | 17.4 | 25.6 | 34.2 | 42.4 | 51.0 | 56.6 | 54.6 | 48.1 | 37.6 | 26.8 | 14.2 | 35.2 |
| Waterdale | Larimer | 23 | 29.2 | 29.2 | 38.5 | 46.4 | 54.3 | 63.6 | 68.2 | 68.2 | 60.5 | 49.6 | 38.8 | 29.4 | 48.0 |
| Westcliffe | Custer | -- | 27.4 | 26.4 | 33.2 | 40.5 | 48.9 | 58.2 | 61.3 | 61.4 | 54.8 | 43.6 | 33.6 | 23.8 | 42.6 |
| Wray | Yuma | 28 | 29.2 | 30.4 | 39.8 | 48.8 | 59.0 | 69.2 | 74.4 | 73.1 | 64.4 | 51.8 | 39.4 | 29.8 | 50.8 |

*Period of years figured to 1930.

## NORMAL MONTHLY AND ANNUAL PRECIPITATION IN INCHES
### (From the Records of the U. S. Weather Bureau)

| PLACE | COUNTY | Length of Record Years* | Jan. | Feb. | Mar. | Apr. | May | June | July | Aug. | Sept. | Oct. | Nov. | Dec. | Annual |
|---|---|---|---|---|---|---|---|---|---|---|---|---|---|---|---|
| Akron | Washington | -- | 0.32 | 0.52 | 1.10 | 2.47 | 2.72 | 2.45 | 2.57 | 2.03 | 1.49 | 1.04 | 0.58 | 0.62 | 17.91 |
| Arriba | Lincoln | 10 | 0.12 | 0.57 | 0.70 | 2.15 | 2.05 | 2.02 | 2.70 | 2.50 | 1.67 | 1.21 | 0.41 | 0.89 | 16.99 |
| Auldhurst | Teller | 18 | 0.40 | 0.77 | 1.05 | 2.29 | 1.72 | 2.04 | 3.83 | 2.94 | 1.75 | 0.88 | 0.60 | 0.86 | 19.13 |
| Boulder | Boulder | 35 | 0.40 | 0.76 | 1.40 | 2.81 | 1.14 | 1.41 | 2.14 | 1.46 | 1.50 | 1.52 | 0.75 | 0.83 | 16.12 |
| Breckenridge | Summit | -- | 1.79 | 2.48 | 2.58 | 2.76 | 2.04 | 1.08 | 2.37 | 2.24 | 1.43 | 1.45 | 1.63 | 2.08 | 23.98 |
| Buena Vista | Chaffee | 18 | 0.43 | 0.67 | 0.61 | 0.82 | 0.74 | 0.57 | 1.63 | 1.31 | 0.69 | 0.73 | 0.49 | 0.50 | 9.19 |
| Burlington | Kit Carson | 38 | 0.27 | 0.46 | 0.80 | 2.12 | 2.19 | 2.83 | 2.77 | 2.59 | 1.33 | 0.92 | 0.46 | 0.61 | 17.35 |
| Calhan | El Paso | 21 | 0.38 | 0.67 | 0.67 | 2.20 | 1.91 | 1.68 | 2.91 | 2.97 | 1.27 | 0.82 | 0.57 | 0.76 | 16.81 |
| Canon City | Fremont | 39 | 0.37 | 0.59 | 0.81 | 1.67 | 1.60 | 1.14 | 1.86 | 1.88 | 0.82 | 0.84 | 0.52 | 0.54 | 12.64 |
| Castle Rock | Douglas | 36 | 0.45 | 0.66 | 1.13 | 2.26 | 2.40 | 1.85 | 2.71 | 2.15 | 1.15 | 1.19 | 0.54 | 0.82 | 17.31 |
| Cedaredge | Delta | 26 | 0.92 | 1.03 | 1.22 | 1.00 | 1.14 | 0.62 | 0.82 | 1.01 | 1.22 | 1.11 | 0.61 | 0.80 | 11.50 |
| Cheyenne Wells | Cheyenne | 34 | 0.31 | 0.53 | 0.79 | 1.99 | 2.14 | 2.60 | 2.98 | 2.57 | 1.35 | 0.85 | 0.46 | 0.61 | 17.18 |
| Collbran | Mesa | 35 | 1.26 | 1.13 | 1.64 | 1.62 | 1.49 | 0.78 | 1.18 | 1.53 | 1.48 | 1.11 | 1.04 | 1.15 | 15.44 |
| Colorado Springs | El Paso | 48 | 0.23 | 0.39 | 0.67 | 1.74 | 2.25 | 1.89 | 2.86 | 2.12 | 1.03 | 0.60 | 0.34 | 0.31 | 14.44 |
| Columbine | Routt | 17 | 1.99 | 2.69 | 2.35 | 2.13 | 1.96 | 1.07 | 1.77 | 1.48 | 1.88 | 1.48 | 1.39 | 2.43 | 22.69 |
| Cope | Washington | 29 | 0.37 | 0.60 | 1.21 | 2.59 | 3.15 | 3.01 | 2.82 | 2.10 | 1.25 | 0.96 | 0.52 | 0.64 | 19.22 |
| Crawford | Montrose | 9 | 0.77 | 0.53 | 0.55 | 0.84 | 0.93 | 0.81 | 1.20 | 1.15 | 1.20 | 1.11 | 0.83 | 0.81 | 10.72 |
| Crested Butte | Gunnison | 18 | 3.44 | 2.57 | 2.76 | 2.16 | 1.79 | 1.26 | 1.95 | 1.54 | 1.68 | 1.56 | 1.81 | 2.88 | 25.44 |
| Delta | Delta | 40 | 0.60 | 0.52 | 0.69 | 0.65 | 0.83 | 0.34 | 0.85 | 0.91 | 0.87 | 0.76 | 0.58 | 0.60 | 8.20 |
| Denver | Denver | 56 | 0.42 | 0.49 | 1.00 | 2.17 | 2.54 | 1.47 | 1.62 | 1.34 | 0.89 | 0.96 | 0.52 | 0.60 | 14.02 |
| Durango | La Plata | 35 | 1.28 | 1.39 | 1.46 | 1.14 | 1.14 | 0.78 | 1.55 | 1.79 | 1.85 | 1.75 | 1.14 | 1.40 | 16.67 |
| Eads | Kiowa | 17 | 0.22 | 0.47 | 0.37 | 1.46 | 2.09 | 1.73 | 2.58 | 1.24 | 0.86 | 1.21 | 0.36 | 0.38 | 12.97 |
| Estes Park (F.H.) | Larimer | 19 | 0.67 | 0.86 | 1.20 | 2.68 | 2.14 | 1.36 | 2.95 | 2.22 | 1.65 | 1.42 | 0.95 | 0.83 | 18.90 |
| Fort Collins | Larimer | 48 | 0.44 | 0.61 | 0.93 | 2.13 | 2.84 | 1.49 | 1.83 | 1.22 | 1.28 | 1.07 | 0.47 | 0.46 | 14.77 |
| Fort Lupton | Adams | 17 | 0.19 | 0.40 | 0.46 | 1.72 | 2.23 | 1.02 | 1.82 | 1.53 | 1.16 | 1.13 | 0.50 | 0.61 | 12.77 |
| Fort Morgan | Morgan | 4? | 0.28 | 0.41 | 0.69 | 1.77 | 2.36 | 1.83 | 2.49 | 1.65 | 0.92 | 0.85 | 0.35 | 0.38 | 13.96 |
| Fraser | Grand | 19 | 1.63 | 1.75 | 1.76 | 2.31 | 1.60 | 1.08 | 2.29 | 1.66 | 1.61 | 1.36 | 1.14 | 1.79 | 19.96 |
| Fruita | Mesa | 28 | 0.95 | 0.85 | 1.08 | 0.79 | 0.90 | 0.41 | 0.88 | 1.13 | 1.07 | 1.16 | 0.73 | 0.78 | 10.72 |
| Garnett | Alamosa | 36 | 0.14 | 0.22 | 0.28 | 0.56 | 0.13 | 0.70 | 1.24 | 1.14 | 0.76 | 0.54 | 0.27 | 0.23 | 6.21 |
| Glenwood Springs | Garfield | 24 | 1.29 | 1.00 | 1.29 | 1.26 | 1.11 | 0.72 | 1.25 | 1.57 | 1.14 | 1.05 | 0.96 | 1.26 | 13.94 |
| Grand Junction | Mesa | 36 | 0.49 | 0.63 | 0.71 | 0.76 | 0.92 | 0.40 | 0.50 | 1.04 | 0.95 | 0.91 | 0.55 | 0.44 | 8.30 |
| Grand Lake | Grand | 10 | 1.81 | 1.36 | 0.88 | 1.90 | 1.26 | 0.90 | 1.96 | 1.52 | 1.26 | 0.81 | 1.46 | 1.57 | 16.66 |
| Greeley | Weld | 39 | 0.32 | 0.41 | 0.73 | 1.71 | 2.47 | 1.41 | 1.85 | 1.13 | 0.96 | 0.92 | 0.33 | 0.41 | 12.60 |
| Grover | Weld | 26 | 0.36 | 0.63 | 0.65 | 2.01 | 2.35 | 1.75 | 2.21 | 1.63 | 1.14 | 0.76 | 0.32 | 0.61 | 14.42 |
| Gunnison | Gunnison | 36 | 0.80 | 0.70 | 0.60 | 0.85 | 0.78 | 0.64 | 1.44 | 1.32 | 0.81 | 0.61 | 0.56 | 0.71 | 9.82 |
| Hamps | Elbert | 26 | 0.24 | 0.46 | 0.90 | 2.03 | 1.99 | 1.71 | 2.54 | 2.22 | 0.98 | 0.56 | 0.25 | 0.47 | 14.35 |
| Hartsel | Park | 19 | 0.21 | 0.25 | 0.34 | 0.92 | 0.85 | 1.38 | 3.69 | 2.16 | 1.29 | 0.46 | 0.36 | 0.31 | 12.22 |
| Hermit | Hinsdale | 22 | 1.37 | 1.05 | 1.35 | 1.42 | 1.25 | 1.12 | 2.75 | 2.36 | 1.51 | 1.88 | 1.15 | 1.18 | 18.24 |
| Holly | Prowers | 32 | 0.26 | 0.62 | 0.46 | 1.80 | 1.91 | 2.06 | 2.54 | 2.24 | 1.21 | 0.61 | 0.50 | 0.46 | 14.66 |
| Holyoke | Phillips | 26 | 0.25 | 0.45 | 0.88 | 2.18 | 2.63 | 2.87 | 2.40 | 2.38 | 1.28 | 0.93 | 0.33 | 0.57 | 17.15 |
| Idaho Springs | Clear Creek | 38 | 0.39 | 0.50 | 1.08 | 2.23 | 2.13 | 1.34 | 2.79 | 2.05 | 1.53 | 1.31 | 0.53 | 0.62 | 16.56 |
| Julesburg | Sedgwick | 24 | 0.35 | 0.50 | 0.77 | 2.41 | 2.76 | 2.65 | 2.19 | 2.10 | 0.77 | 0.97 | 0.39 | 0.43 | 16.24 |
| Lamar | Prowers | 39 | 0.30 | 0.61 | 0.81 | 1.87 | 2.05 | 2.10 | 2.66 | 2.00 | 1.19 | 0.86 | 0.41 | 0.70 | 15.08 |
| Las Animas | Bent | 59 | 0.19 | 0.45 | 0.53 | 1.54 | 1.92 | 1.42 | 2.17 | 1.62 | 1.00 | 0.69 | 0.32 | 0.44 | 12.23 |
| Lay | Moffat | 36 | 1.12 | 1.25 | 1.45 | 1.21 | 1.28 | 0.72 | 0.97 | 1.02 | 1.30 | 1.10 | 0.84 | 0.96 | 13.22 |
| Leadville | Lake | 32 | 1.21 | 1.51 | 1.61 | 1.74 | 1.19 | 0.97 | 2.20 | 1.90 | 1.17 | 1.11 | 0.84 | 1.22 | 16.67 |
| LeRoy | Logan | 39 | 0.37 | 0.60 | 0.94 | 2.63 | 2.53 | 2.35 | 2.16 | 2.28 | 1.13 | 1.05 | 0.44 | 0.62 | 17.10 |
| Limon | Lincoln | 10 | 0.19 | 0.38 | 0.39 | 1.80 | 1.87 | 1.90 | 2.63 | 2.27 | 1.06 | 0.83 | 0.43 | 0.58 | 14.33 |
| Longmont | Boulder | 21 | 0.30 | 0.65 | 0.83 | 2.05 | 2.34 | 1.59 | 2.21 | 1.20 | 1.21 | 1.13 | 0.61 | 0.63 | 14.75 |
| Manassa | Conejos | 21 | 0.12 | 0.25 | 0.37 | 0.76 | 0.55 | 0.51 | 1.26 | 1.37 | 0.57 | 0.80 | 0.25 | 0.28 | 7.00 |
| Mancos | Montezuma | 20 | 1.36 | 1.46 | 2.02 | 1.77 | 1.19 | 0.77 | 1.91 | 2.01 | 1.55 | 1.55 | 1.08 | 1.23 | 17.12 |
| Meeker | Rio Blanco | 27 | 1.07 | 1.00 | 1.42 | 1.55 | 1.37 | 0.89 | 1.45 | 1.63 | 1.68 | 1.46 | 1.15 | 1.06 | 15.73 |
| Montrose | Montrose | 39 | 0.68 | 0.62 | 0.80 | 1.04 | 0.82 | 0.42 | 0.86 | 1.35 | 0.94 | 0.82 | 0.58 | 0.75 | 9.08 |
| Monument | El Paso | 17 | 0.55 | 0.84 | 1.10 | 3.23 | 2.13 | 2.05 | 3.23 | 2.82 | 1.33 | 1.05 | 0.65 | 1.01 | 19.90 |
| Pagoda | Routt | 12 | 1.31 | 1.85 | 1.95 | 1.87 | 1.44 | 1.09 | 1.31 | 1.58 | 1.82 | 1.68 | 0.97 | 1.62 | 18.49 |
| Pagosa Springs | Archuleta | 12 | 2.49 | 2.06 | 1.72 | 1.70 | 1.45 | 1.01 | 2.99 | 2.56 | 1.71 | 3.19 | 1.09 | 1.91 | 23.82 |
| Paonia | Delta | 35 | 1.32 | 1.25 | 1.49 | 1.41 | 1.43 | 0.59 | 1.05 | 1.29 | 1.30 | 1.44 | 1.01 | 1.11 | 14.69 |
| Pueblo | Pueblo | 39 | 0.35 | 0.47 | 0.86 | 1.43 | 1.68 | 1.47 | 1.97 | 1.57 | 0.62 | 0.70 | 0.37 | 0.46 | 11.95 |
| Redvale | Montrose | 6 | 1.22 | 0.83 | 0.94 | 1.37 | 1.03 | 0.84 | 2.20 | 1.66 | 0.97 | 1.68 | 1.08 | 1.20 | 15.02 |
| Rico | Dolores | 26 | 2.96 | 3.01 | 3.03 | 1.49 | 1.59 | 1.16 | 2.83 | 2.19 | 2.34 | 1.44 | 1.48 | 2.25 | 26.77 |
| Rifle | Garfield | 8 | 0.83 | 0.85 | 1.30 | 1.08 | 1.21 | 0.61 | 1.11 | 1.28 | 1.20 | 1.22 | 0.84 | 0.87 | 12.40 |
| Rocky Ford | Otero | 39 | 0.25 | 0.33 | 0.56 | 1.66 | 1.77 | 1.40 | 2.55 | 1.36 | 0.80 | 0.85 | 0.41 | 0.45 | 12.80 |
| Saguache | Saguache | 28 | 0.24 | 0.41 | 0.31 | 0.37 | 0.81 | 0.97 | 1.77 | 1.51 | 0.78 | 0.73 | 0.31 | 0.32 | 8.00 |
| Salida | Chaffee | -- | 0.55 | 0.83 | 0.73 | 1.54 | 0.86 | 1.05 | 1.85 | 1.49 | 1.02 | 0.93 | 0.73 | 0.73 | 12.51 |
| San Luis | Costilla | 27 | 0.42 | 0.50 | 0.66 | 0.95 | 1.12 | 0.75 | 2.23 | 1.50 | 2.89 | 1.02 | 0.42 | 0.61 | 13.07 |
| Sapinero | Gunnison | 26 | 0.90 | 2.05 | 2.07 | 2.21 | 1.64 | 0.97 | 1.43 | 1.85 | 1.49 | 1.46 | 1.23 | 1.68 | 18.48 |
| Sedgwick | Sedgwick | -- | 0.41 | 0.63 | 0.71 | 2.34 | 2.25 | 2.58 | 2.23 | 2.49 | 1.36 | 1.10 | 0.33 | 0.48 | 16.08 |
| Silverton | San Juan | 21 | 2.61 | 2.00 | 2.71 | 1.63 | 1.12 | 1.45 | 2.97 | 3.23 | 2.66 | 2.64 | 1.47 | 2.08 | 26.57 |
| Spicer | Jackson | -- | 0.79 | 0.77 | 0.65 | 0.84 | 0.80 | 0.77 | 1.16 | 1.01 | 1.14 | 0.96 | 0.83 | 0.76 | 10.46 |
| Springfield | Baca | 16 | 0.39 | 0.60 | 0.92 | 2.58 | 2.74 | 1.62 | 2.45 | 1.96 | 1.57 | 0.78 | 0.72 | 0.64 | 16.97 |
| Steamboat Springs | Routt | 25 | 2.51 | 2.67 | 1.89 | 2.06 | 1.91 | 1.34 | 1.46 | 1.59 | 1.53 | 1.79 | 1.58 | 2.55 | 22.88 |
| Sterling | Logan | 18 | 0.36 | 0.37 | 0.51 | 2.16 | 2.36 | 1.99 | 1.47 | 2.37 | 1.23 | 1.07 | 0.43 | 0.57 | 14.88 |
| Trinidad | Las Animas | 32 | 0.50 | 0.97 | 0.88 | 2.13 | 1.66 | 2.06 | 2.49 | 2.36 | 1.22 | 1.29 | 0.73 | 0.74 | 17.06 |
| Two Buttes | Baca | 29 | 0.29 | 0.61 | 0.73 | 1.79 | 2.23 | 2.19 | 2.59 | 1.86 | 1.33 | 0.74 | 0.41 | 0.58 | 15.55 |
| Westcliffe | Custer | -- | 0.55 | 0.62 | 1.15 | 1.90 | 1.37 | 1.37 | 2.57 | 1.61 | 1.13 | 1.24 | 0.86 | 0.73 | 15.10 |
| Wray | Yuma | 33 | 0.33 | 0.64 | 0.89 | 2.72 | 2.75 | 2.81 | 2.67 | 2.49 | 1.20 | 1.02 | 0.38 | 0.49 | 18.39 |
| Yampa | Routt | 9 | 2.04 | 1.83 | 1.15 | 1.30 | 0.88 | 0.85 | 1.88 | 1.49 | 1.43 | 1.17 | 0.97 | 1.57 | 16.54 |
| Yuma | Yuma | 26 | 0.36 | 0.56 | 1.03 | 2.30 | 2.35 | 2.74 | 2.52 | 2.48 | 1.01 | 0.98 | 0.40 | 0.55 | 17.88 |

*Period of years figured to 1930.

## LENGTH OF GROWING SEASON IN COLORADO

| | Number of days between killing frosts | | | Range of dates of last killing frost in spring and first in fall | |
|---|---|---|---|---|---|
| | Aver-age | Short-est | Long-est | Spring | Fall |
| Akron | 143 | 121 | 165 | Apr. 29 to June 5 | Sept. 15 to Oct. 24 |
| Arriba | 134 | 119 | 146 | May 4 to June 7 | Sept. 15 to Oct. 20 |
| Blanca | 105 | 81 | 126 | May 20 to June 23 | Sept. 12 to Oct. 1 |
| Boulder | 165 | 125 | 200 | Apr. 13 to June 2 | Sept. 15 to Nov. 10 |
| Buena Vista | 122 | 78 | 142 | May 22 to June 28 | Aug. 29 to Oct. 23 |
| Burlington | 154 | 111 | 170 | Apr. 22 to June 4 | Sept. 23 to Oct. 26 |
| Calhan | 137 | 108 | 167 | Apr. 29 to June 6 | Sept. 2 to Oct. 24 |
| Canon City | 163 | 124 | 200 | Apr. 4 to June 2 | Sept. 17 to Nov. 11 |
| Castle Rock | 131 | 99 | 154 | Apr. 19 to June 10 | Sept. 10 to Oct. 9 |
| Cedaredge | 136 | 95 | 164 | Apr. 19 to June 9 | Sept. 10 to Oct. 19 |
| Cheyenne Wells | 154 | 122 | 180 | Apr. 5 to June 4 | Sept. 12 to Oct. 26 |
| Collbran | 133 | 78 | 165 | Apr. 23 to July 3 | Sept. 12 to Oct. 24 |
| Colorado Springs | 146 | 112 | 179 | Apr. 16 to June 3 | Sept. 11 to Oct. 21 |
| Crawford | 137 | 111 | 171 | May 3 to June 12 | Sept. 14 to Oct. 26 |
| Delta | 140 | 111 | 187 | Apr. 14 to June 3 | Sept. 11 to Oct. 29 |
| Denver | 158 | 110 | 193 | Apr. 13 to June 6 | Sept. 12 to Oct. 29 |
| Dolores | 130 | 109 | 151 | May 4 to June 5 | Sept. 21 to Oct. 28 |
| Durango | 129 | 98 | 172 | Apr. 22 to June 5 | Sept. 11 to Oct. 16 |
| Eads | 156 | 143 | 179 | Apr. 26 to May 22 | Sept. 27 to Oct. 22 |
| Fort Collins | 142 | 124 | 181 | Apr. 12 to June 3 | Sept. 7 to Oct. 16 |
| Fort Morgan | 143 | 87 | 186 | Apr. 12 to June 30 | Aug. 25 to Oct. 26 |
| Fruita | 156 | 133 | 186 | Apr. 3 to June 1 | Sept. 15 to Oct. 30 |
| Garnett | 102 | 68 | 137 | May 3 to July 7 | Aug. 13 to Oct. 10 |
| Glenwood Springs | 114 | 58 | 134 | Apr. 4 to July 4 | Aug. 9 to Oct. 11 |
| Grand Junction | 184 | 144 | 233 | Mar. 23 to May 14 | Sept. 14 to Nov. 11 |
| Greeley | 149 | 112 | 180 | Apr. 14 to June 3 | Sept. 7 to Oct. 18 |
| Grover | 113 | 82 | 141 | May 6 to June 30 | Aug. 25 to Sept. 26 |
| Hamps | 134 | 98 | 164 | Apr. 25 to June 8 | Sept. 6 to Oct. 23 |
| Hayden | 91 | 64 | 128 | May 15 to July 3 | Aug. 31 to Sept. 20 |
| Hoehne | 140 | 73 | 201 | Apr. 18 to July 4 | Sept. 10 to Nov. 16 |
| Holly | 164 | 134 | 202 | Apr. 2 to June 2 | Sept. 17 to Oct. 31 |
| Holyoke | 138 | 108 | 167 | Apr. 18 to June 6 | Sept. 12 to Oct. 24 |
| Huerfano | 125 | 110 | 145 | May 10 to June 6 | Sept. 21 to Oct. 7 |
| Ignacio | 104 | 69 | 131 | May 28 to June 20 | Aug. 28 to Oct. 6 |
| Julesburg | 139 | 94 | 169 | Apr. 21 to June 19 | Sept. 19 to Oct. 24 |
| Lamar | 168 | 140 | 190 | Apr. 3 to May 14 | Sept. 17 to Oct. 29 |
| Las Animas | 159 | 123 | 191 | Apr. 9 to June 1 | Sept. 7 to Oct. 25 |
| Lay | 83 | 30 | 168 | Apr. 7 to June 19 | Aug. 11 to Sept. 26 |
| LeRoy | 150 | 100 | 182 | Apr. 13 to May 27 | Aug. 25 to Oct. 24 |
| Limon | 140 | 105 | 169 | Apr. 19 to June 5 | Sept. 14 to Oct. 25 |
| Longmont | 144 | 112 | 169 | Apr. 13 to June 2 | Sept. 14 to Oct. 12 |
| **Manassa** | 97 | 45 | 127 | May 19 to June 20 | Aug. 2 to Sept. 25 |
| Mancos | 110 | 70 | 143 | May 14 to July 6 | Aug. 27 to Oct. 24 |
| Meeker | 89 | 47 | 120 | May 17 to July 13 | Aug. 12 to Oct. 10 |
| Montrose | 145 | 112 | 186 | Apr. 10 to June 8 | Sept. 14 to Oct. 23 |
| Monument | 113 | 88 | 137 | May 10 to June 18 | Sept. 9 to Sept. 24 |
| Pagosa Springs | 76 | 50 | 89 | June 9 to July 29 | Sept. 5 to Sept. 18 |
| Palisades | 160 | 146 | 183 | Apr. 14 to May 26 | Sept. 15 to Oct. 27 |
| Paonia | 158 | 117 | 228 | Apr. 5 to June 2 | Sept. 21 to Nov. 11 |
| Platte Canon | 148 | 124 | 164 | Apr. 11 to June 2 | Sept. 14 to Oct. 26 |
| Pueblo | 165 | 131 | 193 | Apr. 9 to June 2 | Sept. 12 to Oct. 26 |
| Redvale | 130 | 93 | 163 | Apr. 27 to June 13 | Sept. 14 to Oct. 26 |
| Rifle | 144 | 123 | 165 | Apr. 17 to June 1 | Sept. 14 to Oct. 24 |
| Rocky Ford | 161 | 113 | 190 | Apr. 12 to June 2 | Sept. 17 to Oct. 27 |
| Saguache | 120 | 93 | 178 | Apr. 21 to June 26 | Aug. 28 to Oct. 16 |
| Salida | 112 | 68 | 148 | Apr. 28 to June 15 | Sept. 12 to Oct. 11 |
| San Luis | 108 | 68 | 128 | May 16 to July 6 | Sept. 5 to Oct. 11 |
| Sapinero | 93 | 63 | 117 | May 30 to July 5 | Sept. 6 to Sept. 28 |
| Sedgwick | 143 | 126 | 167 | Apr. 25 to May 27 | Sept. 14 to Oct. 24 |
| Sterling | 144 | 111 | 177 | Apr. 22 to June 3 | Sept. 20 to Oct. 24 |
| Trinidad | 161 | 130 | 194 | Apr. 16 to June 3 | Sept. 22 to Oct. 27 |
| Two Buttes | 164 | 124 | 192 | Apr. 11 to June 2 | Sept. 17 to Oct. 30 |
| Victor | 98 | 46 | 134 | May 22 to July 7 | Aug. 13 to Oct. 6 |
| Wagon Wheel Gap | 59 | 1 | 115 | May 26 to July 31 | Aug. 1 to Sept. 25 |
| Westcliffe | 95 | 3 | 131 | May 6 to July 29 | Aug. 1 to Oct. 10 |
| Wiggins | 130 | 114 | 149 | May 11 to June 2 | Sept. 14 to Oct. 7 |
| Wray | 152 | 124 | 179 | Apr. 11 to May 27 | Sept. 12 to Oct. 25 |

# Water Power Resources

WATER power has played an important part in the mining development of Colorado and was used for that purpose as far back as 1859, when the first ore mill was erected in the Blackhawk district, the oldest camp in the state. Its use for other industrial purposes started in the same year, when the Eggers saw mill in the same district was operated by water power. Today it is recognized as one of the most valuable of Colorado's natural resources.

Although the volume of water carried in the streams of the state generally is comparatively small, most of these streams have their sources at high altitudes and a vast quantity of power is developed as they descend over precipitous courses from the mountain sides to the plains below. The principal river systems having their origin in the state and developing sufficient water power to be utilized commercially are: The Colorado, on the western slope, the principal tributaries of which are the Yampa, White, Green, Gunnison, Dolores and San Juan; the Rio Grande, in the south, draining the San Luis valley; the Arkansas, in the southeast, and the Platte, in the northeast. These streams have scores of comparatively small tributaries rising in the mountains, which drop from 1,000 to 6,000 feet in their courses. There is considerable variation in the amount of power available in these streams, due to the fact that the volume of water they carry differs widely at different seasons of the year. A maximum development could be obtained only through the storage of water in reservoirs during the flood seasons.

The following figures, composed of estimates by the United States geological survey, furnish a good idea of the immense water power available for commercial uses in the state:

Horsepower available without storage for 90 per cent of the time ........................ 765,000
Horsepower available without storage for 50 per cent of the time ....................1,570,000
Horsepower available from storage of water................2,568,200

The federal government had 439,780 acres in power-site reserves in the state on June 30, 1931, according to the report of the commissioner of the general land office. This figure includes all areas reserved or classified

as valuable for power purposes and withheld subject to disposition only under the federal water power act of June 10, 1920. Designations, classifications and other types of reserves are included in the total area without distinction. The sites are available for leasing, subject to the approval of the federal power commission, under the act of 1920. Powersite reserves under the act of June 25, 1910, as amended by the act of August 24, 1912, on June 30, 1931, aggregated 218,941 acres. Miscellaneous withdrawals under the same act were 1,727 acres. Power-site classifications made under the act of March 3, 1879, aggregated 206,779 acres, and public water reserves under the act of June 25, 1910, aggregated 8,013 acres on June 30, 1931. Withdrawals under the act of June 17, 1902, aggregated 4,420 acres.

Applications for sites on the public domain should be made to the United States Geological Survey, 403 Post Office building, Denver. Applications for sites within the national forests should be made to the United States Forest Service, 462 Post Office building, Denver.

The development of water power in the state has not progressed as rapidly as in some other states, due in a large measure to the immense deposits of coal available in Colorado for the development of power. It is generally conceded that the initial cost of hydro-electric installation is greater than for steam power, though the cost of operation is considerably less.

The presence of the coal deposits, on the contrary, offers some advantage in that it permits the construction of auxiliary plants in connection with hydro-electric projects upon economical terms so as to insure uninterrupted operation.

Hydro-electric power developed in the state, in plants of 100 h. p. or over, according to the geological survey, is as follows:

| Use | Number Plants | Horse-power |
|---|---|---|
| Public utilities.......... | 30 | 86,961 |
| Individual mining plants | 24 | 9,182 |
| Irrigation pumping...... | 2 | 1,705 |
| Flour mills ............. | 1 | 188 |
| Private plants........... | 1 | 100 |
| Total ................ | 58 | 98,136 |

In addition, small plants of less than 100 horsepower in the state probably aggregate 5,000 horsepower.

# Agricultural Extension Service

CO-OPERATIVE extension work in agriculture and home economics in Colorado is conducted by the Colorado Agricultural college at Fort Collins in co-operation with the United States department of agriculture under the provisions of the Smith-Lever act. This act provides definitely for co-operation between the federal and state governments in carrying on a common enterprise and permitting participation by counties, local governments, associations and individuals.

In the extension service, scientific data developed by the state experimental station are given to the people through the demonstration method of teaching. This is mostly done through selected volunteer leaders in rural communities who agree to put into practice a method recommended by the extension service after it has been proved scientifically correct either by long farm practice elsewhere or through experiment station research. The service is headed by a director with a central office force of specialists and representatives in various agricultural counties which are organized for extension work. The county representatives are known as extension agents. The work is carried on intensively only in such counties as make financial provision for its support, a part of which is met out of federal funds under the agricultural extension act.

The extension service, in addition to demonstration work, maintains touch with the farmer and the farm home through direct correspondence and through the issuance of bulletins. The extension staff and list of county extension agents in the state, with their addresses, follow:

## EXTENSION SERVICE

### Colorado Agricultural College

F. A. Anderson...............Director
J. E. Morrison.......Assistant Director
F. C. Jans.....Administrative Assistant
C. W. Ferguson.......State Club Agent
Nora M. Hott........State Home Agent
E. D. Smith..........................
.....Extension Economist, Marketing
T. G. Stewart....Extension Agronomist
A. C. Allen...........................
.......Extension Animal Husbandman
C. A. Smith........Extension Dairyman

Thos. H. Summers.................
.Senior Economist, Farm Management
W. F. Droge (Montrose).............
.......Ext. Econ., Farm Management
J. L. Shields.......................
........Ext. Econ., Farm Management
Mary E. Sutherland.................
...Ext. Economist, Home Management
W. M. Case....Extension Horticulturist
Miriam J. Williams.................
.............Extension Nutritionist
O. C. Ufford......Extension Poultryman
I. G. Kinghorn..................Editor
Arthur Robinson.......Associate Editor

### COUNTY EXTENSION AGENTS

| County | Agent | Headquarters |
|---|---|---|
| Adams.......H. A. Sandhouse.Brighton |
| Alamosa.....M. C. Grandy....Alamosa |
| Arapahoe....A. H. Tedmon....Littleton |
| Boulder......R. E. Kiely.....Longmont |
| Costilla......E. W. Martin....San Luis |
| Delta........R. H. Tucker......Delta |
| El Paso.......A. J. Ryan.............  ......Colorado Springs |
| Garfield......A. V. Lough............  .....Glenwood Springs |
| Huerfano.....B. W. Allred..Walsenburg |
| Kiowa........J. G. Bishop.........Eads |
| La Plata.....W. B. Smith.....Durango |
| Larimer.....D. C. Bascom.Fort Collins |
| Las Animas..S. W. Morgan....Trinidad |
| Logan........H. E. Hogsett....Sterling |
| Mesa.........J. C. Foster............  ........Grand Junction |
| Moffat........T. J. Snyder........Craig |
| Montrose....H. D. Finch....Montrose |
| Prowers......F. R. Lamb........Lamar |
| Pueblo.......W H. Sawhill......Pueblo |
| Rio Grande...A. A. Goodman........  ..........Monte Vista |
| Routt........F. D. Moon.............  .....Steamboat Springs |
| San Miguel...J. H. Cheney.....Norwood |
| Sedgwick.....G. E. McCrimmon......  .............. Julesburg |
| Teller........A. F. Hoffman, Jr......  .........Cripple Creek |
| Washington..E. J. Meadows......Akron |
| Weld.........H. H. Simpson...Greeley |
| Weld (Asst.)..Walter S. Stratton, Jr...  ................ Greeley |
| Yuma........P. B. Miles.........Wray |

### HOME DEMONSTRATION AGENTS

| | | |
|---|---|---|
| Alamosa......Marie Neff.......Alamosa |
| El Paso......Bertha Boger Wear.....  .......Colorado Springs |
| Garfield......Gladys Bradley.........  .....Glenwood Springs |
| Larimer.....Delphine Dawson.......  .............Fort Collins |
| Logan........Exine Davenport..Sterling |
| Prowers.....Virginia Blackford.Lamar |
| Pueblo.......Jessie Reinholtz...Pueblo |
| Rio Grande...Nellie Mathews.........  ..........Monte Vista |
| Routt........Esther Elliott...........  ......Steamboat Springs |
| Washington..Opal Stafford.......Akron |

**SUMMARY OF THE ACREAGE, PRODUCTION AND VALUE OF PRINCIPAL CROPS IN THE UNITED STATES, 1931, 1930 AND 1929, AND COLORADO'S PROPORTION OF TOTALS**

| Crop and Year | Acreage | Production | Unit | Price Per Unit | Value | Colorado's Per Ce of U. S. Totals | | |
|---|---|---|---|---|---|---|---|---|
| | | | | | | Acreage | Production | V |
| **Corn:** | | | | | | | | |
| 1931 | 104,970,000 | 2,556,863,000 | Bu. | $ .360 | $ 920,142,000 | 1.75 | .75 | |
| 1930 | 100,743,000 | 2,060,185,000 | Bu. | .655 | 1,349,218,000 | 1.72 | 1.89 | |
| 1929 | 97,806,000 | 2,535,386,000 | Bu. | .774 | 1,962,832,000 | 1.57 | .88 | |
| **All Wheat:** | | | | | | | | |
| 1931 | 54,949,000 | 892,271,000 | Bu. | .443 | 395,600,000 | 2.54 | 1.86 | |
| 1930 | 61,138,000 | 858,160,000 | Bu. | .600 | 514,847,000 | 2.67 | 2.72 | |
| 1929 | 62,671,000 | 812,573,000 | Bu. | 1.035 | 841,385,000 | 2.46 | 2.21 | |
| **Oats (Grain):** | | | | | | | | |
| 1931 | 39,722,000 | 1,112,142,000 | Bu. | .231 | 256,483,000 | .37 | .31 | |
| 1930 | 39,729,000 | 1,277,764,000 | Bu. | .315 | 402,713,000 | .49 | .47 | |
| 1929 | 38,148,000 | 1,118,414,000 | Bu. | .426 | 475,998,000 | .53 | .53 | |
| **Barley:** | | | | | | | | |
| 1931 | 11,471,000 | 198,965,000 | Bu. | .352 | 70,119,000 | 3.99 | 3.57 | |
| 1930 | 12,662,000 | 304,601,000 | Bu. | .389 | 118,359,000 | 4.52 | 4.04 | |
| 1929 | 13,523,000 | 280,242,000 | Bu. | .544 | 152,334,000 | 4.50 | 3.91 | |
| **Rye:** | | | | | | | | |
| 1931 | 3,143,000 | 32,746,000 | Bu. | .387 | 12,673,000 | 1.69 | 1.13 | |
| 1930 | 3,543,000 | 45,379,000 | Bu. | .384 | 17,419,000 | 2.09 | 1.39 | |
| 1929 | 3,054,000 | 34,950,000 | Bu. | .849 | 29,685,000 | 2.10 | 1.46 | |
| **Flaxseed:** | | | | | | | | |
| 1931 | 2,313,000 | 11,018,000 | Bu. | 1.202 | 13,243,000 | --- | --- | |
| 1930 | 3,732,000 | 21,240,000 | Bu. | 1.398 | 29,684,000 | --- | --- | |
| 1929 | 3,047,000 | 15,910,000 | Bu. | 2.843 | 45,240,000 | --- | --- | |
| **Rice, 4 States:** | | | | | | | | |
| 1931 | 970,000 | 45,014,000 | Bu. | .609 | 27,402,000 | --- | --- | |
| 1930 | 959,000 | 44,299,000 | Bu. | .782 | 34,631,000 | --- | --- | |
| 1929 | 860,000 | 40,604,000 | Bu. | 1.002 | 40,666,000 | --- | --- | |
| **Tobacco:** | | | | | | | | |
| 1931 | 2,019,600 | 1,610,098,000 | Lbs. | .097 | 156,097,000 | --- | --- | |
| 1930 | 2,101,100 | 1,635,210,000 | Lbs. | .129 | 211,102,000 | --- | --- | |
| 1929 | 1,987,300 | 1,537,193,000 | Lbs. | .186 | 286,104,000 | --- | --- | |
| **Cotton:** | | | | | | | | |
| 1931 | 40,495,000 | 16,918,000 | Bale | .057 | 485,611,000 | --- | --- | |
| 1930 | 45,091,000 | 13,932,000 | Bale | .095 | 659,455,000 | --- | --- | |
| 1929 | 45,793,000 | 14,828,000 | Bale | .164 | 1,217,829,000 | --- | --- | |
| **Grain Sorghums:** | | | | | | | | |
| 1931 | 7,152,000 | 104,529,000 | Bu. | .300 | 31,370,000 | 2.67 | 2.01 | |
| 1930 | 6,586,000 | 64,416,000 | Bu. | .636 | 40,949,000 | 2.73 | 3.63 | |
| 1929 | 6,131,000 | 81,041,000 | Bu. | .705 | 57,127,000 | 2.85 | 2.27 | |
| **Hay, Tame:** | | | | | | | | |
| 1931 | 53,449,000 | 64,233,000 | Ton | 9.06 | 581,833,000 | 2.35 | 2.56 | |
| 1930 | 52,622,000 | 63,463,000 | Ton | 12.62 | 800,694,000 | 2.46 | 3.49 | |
| 1929 | 55,019,000 | 76,114,000 | Ton | 12.19 | 928,104,000 | 2.28 | 2.96 | |
| **Hay, Wild:** | | | | | | | | |
| 1931 | 11,977,000 | 8,133,000 | Ton | 6.18 | 50,277,000 | 3.02 | 3.57 | |
| 1930 | 13,793,000 | 10,751,000 | Ton | 7.10 | 76,345,000 | 2.65 | 3.40 | |
| 1929 | 13,586,000 | 11,194,000 | Ton | 8.04 | 89,975,000 | 2.66 | 3.07 | |
| **Sweet Sorghums (forage and hay):** | | | | | | | | |
| 1931 | 2,333,000 | 3,676,000 | Ton | 5.69 | 20,925,000 | 5.06 | 4.49 | |
| 1930 | 1,818,000 | 2,760,000 | Ton | 8.95 | 24,703,000 | 5.67 | 8.22 | |
| 1929 | 1,850,000 | 3,253,000 | Ton | 8.92 | 29,010,000 | 5.68 | 5.81 | |
| **Clover Seed (Red and Alsike):** | | | | | | | | |
| 1931 | 885,300 | 1,222,100 | Bu. | 7.15 | 8,732,000 | --- | --- | |
| 1930 | 1,076,000 | 1,523,100 | Bu. | 11.78 | 17,942,000 | --- | --- | |
| 1929 | 1,789,000 | 2,627,300 | Bu. | 10.28 | 26,997,000 | --- | --- | |
| **Alfalfa Seed:** | | | | | | | | |
| 1931 | 353,600 | 852,600 | Bu. | 6.51 | 5,550,000 | 5.66 | 7.04 | |
| 1930 | 419,900 | 1,145,400 | Bu. | 9.88 | 11,313,000 | 5.12 | 5.63 | |
| 1929 | 401,400 | 982,400 | Bu. | 11.17 | 10,977,000 | 3.24 | 5.29 | |
| **Dry Beans:** | | | | | | | | |
| 1931 | 1,860,000 | 12,705,000 | 100-lb. bag | 2.46 | 31,199,000 | 17.20 | 6.50 | |
| 1930 | 2,091,000 | 13,759,000 | 100-lb. bag | 3.90 | 53,719,000 | 20.66 | 18.84 | |
| 1929 | 1,836,000 | 12,240,000 | 100-lb. bag | 6.27 | 76,765,000 | 20.26 | 10.94 | |
| **Potatoes, White:** | | | | | | | | |
| 1931 | 3,382,000 | 376,248,000 | Bu. | .429 | 161,264,000 | 2.99 | 2.55 | |
| 1930 | 3,038,000 | 333,210,000 | Bu. | .890 | 296,505,000 | 3.03 | 5.25 | |
| 1929 | 2,978,000 | 329,134,000 | Bu. | 1.288 | 423,896,000 | 3.02 | 4.46 | |

UMMARY OF THE ACREAGE, PRODUCTION AND VALUE OF PRINCIPAL CROPS IN THE UNITED STATES, 1931, 1930 AND 1929, AND COLORADO'S PROPORTION OF TOTALS—Continued

| Crop and Year | Acreage | Production | Unit | Price Per Unit | Value | Colorado's Per Cent of U. S. Totals | | |
|---|---|---|---|---|---|---|---|---|
| | | | | | | Acre-age | Pro-duction | Value |
| **gar Beets:** | | | | | | | | |
| 1931 | 720,000 | 7,933,000 | Ton | $ 5,919 | $ 46,958,000 | 31.39 | 31.98 | 29.72 |
| 1930 | 775,000 | 9,199,000 | Ton | 7.142 | 65,697,000 | 31.23 | 36.00 | 34.82 |
| 1929 | 687,000 | 7,315,000 | Ton | 7.082 | 51,805,000 | 30.57 | 35.71 | 34.95 |
| **oomcorn:** | | | | | | | | |
| 1931 | 309,000 | 47,900 | Ton | 51.15 | 2,450,000 | 14.89 | 12.11 | 9.96 |
| 1930 | 391,000 | 49,800 | Ton | 73.61 | 3,666,000 | 19.69 | 20.88 | 14.46 |
| 1929 | 310,000 | 47,300 | Ton | 122.83 | 5,810,000 | 20.65 | 19.45 | 17.73 |
| **tUCK CROPS** | | | | | | | | |
| **ap Beans:** | | | | | | | | |
| 1931 | 168,110 | 184,500 | Ton | 87.42 | 15,970,000 | 1.75 | 3.61 | 2.08 |
| 1930 | 180,270 | 214,000 | Ton | 92.16 | 19,336,000 | 2.03 | 7.72 | 4.97 |
| 1929 | 159,420 | 199,500 | Ton | 101.84 | 20,322,000 | 2.38 | 6.47 | 3.52 |
| **bbage:** | | | | | | | | |
| 1931 | 146,010 | 992,800 | Ton | 10.03 | 9,758,000 | 2.60 | 3.18 | 4.81 |
| 1930 | 148,990 | 998,500 | Ton | 18.62 | 18,588,000 | 2.62 | 4.88 | 2.26 |
| 1929 | 142,820 | 1,035,600 | Ton | 18.51 | 19,169,000 | 2.31 | 3.38 | 3.73 |
| **ntaloupes:** | | | | | | | | |
| 1931 | 138,180 | 17,962,000 | Crate | 1.00 | 17,543,000 | 5.86 | 6.31 | 5.49 |
| 1930 | 129,210 | 15,951,000 | Crate | 1.21 | 19,283,000 | 7.74 | 12.54 | 12.45 |
| 1929 | 108,870 | 17,393,000 | Crate | 1.31 | 22,703,000 | 10.11 | 14.55 | 9.25 |
| **uliflower:** | | | | | | | | |
| 1931 | 27,910 | 7,087,000 | Crate | .74 | 5,270,000 | 13.97 | 14.31 | 13.47 |
| 1930 | 27,560 | 5,843,000 | Crate | .82 | 4,783,000 | 10.16 | 15.33 | 14.99 |
| 1929 | 25,070 | 6,797,000 | Crate | .78 | 5,288,000 | 12.76 | 16.95 | 15.24 |
| **ttuce:** | | | | | | | | |
| 1931 | 176,960 | 18,569,000 | Crate | 1.44 | 26,664,000 | 3.76 | 3.22 | 2.91 |
| 1930 | 172,620 | 19,591,000 | Crate | 1.71 | 33,582,000 | 4.31 | 3.42 | 1.70 |
| 1929 | 139,160 | 20,220,000 | Crate | 1.82 | 36,794,000 | 5.82 | 4.41 | 3.03 |
| **ions:** | | | | | | | | |
| 1931 | 76,680 | 18,857,000 | Bu. | .79 | 14,171,000 | 5.28 | 4.89 | 4.82 |
| 930 | 83,060 | 26,002,000 | Bu. | .51 | 13,186,000 | 6.74 | 6.63 | 4.19 |
| 929 | 87,340 | 25,489,000 | Bu. | .74 | 18,735,000 | 8.01 | 10.13 | 5.85 |
| **s, Green:** | | | | | | | | |
| 931 | 309,060 | 247,800 | Ton | 67.96 | 16,843,000 | 3.24 | 4.20 | 4.91 |
| 930 | 347,880 | 354,100 | Ton | 67.46 | 23,887,000 | 2.74 | 2.92 | 3.66 |
| 929 | 300,940 | 294,400 | Ton | 72.63 | 21,385,000 | 3.49 | 4.15 | 4.12 |
| **atoes:** | | | | | | | | |
| 931 | 448,220 | 1,475,500 | Ton | 20.62 | 30,425,000 | .85 | 1.89 | 1.33 |
| 930 | 560,000 | 2,216,700 | Ton | 24.26 | 53,778,000 | .62 | 1.36 | .97 |
| 929 | 460,910 | 1,981,900 | Ton | 27.17 | 53,849,000 | .67 | 1.36 | .96 |
| **UITS** | | | | | | | | |
| **ples:** | | | | | | | | |
| 1931 | ------ | 211,506,000 | Bu. | .577 | 122,091,000 | --- | .99 | 1.03 |
| 1930 | ------ | 155,982,000 | Bu. | .930 | 145,065,000 | --- | .68 | .62 |
| 1929 | ------ | 135,622,000 | Bu. | 1.310 | 177,719,000 | --- | 1.70 | 1.23 |
| **ches:** | | | | | | | | |
| 931 | ------ | 77,743,000 | Bu. | .562 | 41,377,000 | --- | 1.45 | 1.37 |
| 930 | ------ | 53,864,000 | Bu. | .887 | 43,825,000 | --- | 1.46 | 2.60 |
| 929 | ------ | 45,026,000 | Bu. | 1.354 | 60,982,000 | --- | 2.12 | 2.27 |
| **rs:** | | | | | | | | |
| 931 | ------ | 23,009,000 | Bu. | .602 | 13,567,000 | --- | 1.67 | 1.70 |
| 930 | ------ | 25,540,000 | Bu. | .749 | 18,158,000 | --- | .57 | 1.05 |
| 929 | ------ | 21,172,000 | Bu. | 1.427 | 30,202,000 | --- | 2.83 | 2.75 |
| **rries:** | | | | | | | | |
| 931 | ------ | 108,090 | Ton | 79.77 | 8,383,000 | --- | 2.31 | 2.09 |
| 930 | ------ | 115,250 | Ton | 129.47 | 14,921,000 | --- | 3.04 | 2.11 |
| 929 | ------ | 93,130 | Ton | 165.18 | 15,383,000 | --- | 5.48 | 3.98 |
| **ps not listed:** | | | | | | | | |
| 1931 | 6,707,370 | -------- | --- | ---- | 522,860,000 | --- | --- | --- |
| 1930 | 5,960,410 | -------- | --- | ---- | 681,496,000 | --- | --- | --- |
| 1929 | 4,925,770 | -------- | --- | ---- | 853,424,000 | --- | --- | --- |
| **als:** | | | | | | | | |
| 1931 | 350,672,000 | -------- | --- | ---- | $4,122,850,000 | 1.92 | --- | 1.54 |
| 1930 | 359,927,000 | -------- | --- | ---- | 5,818,849,000 | 2.01 | --- | 2.14 |
| 1929 | 357,827,000 | -------- | --- | ---- | 8,088,494,000 | 1.90 | --- | 1.66 |

# Agriculture

THE general decline of farm prices, together with reduced yields due to climatic conditions, resulted in another sharp decline in the value of farm crops in 1931. Total crop production for the year, on the basis of December 1 farm prices, is estimated to have had a gross value of $63,-489,000, compared with $124,442,000 in 1930 and $134,537,000 in 1929. These figures do not include some indirect values added to grain crops by feeding to livestock, but are based on prevailing market prices. The total is by far the lowest reported in Colorado in many years.

Yields in 1931 were uniformly lower than in the preceding year, and in addition only five of the 37 crops reported in Colorado showed higher market prices than in 1930. Similarly, only seven crops in the list showed aggregate values greater than in 1930. The same situation prevailed generally over the country, the department of agriculture reporting a marked decline in farm crop values in the nation as a whole.

The production of all crops was lower in 1931 than in 1930 with the exception of apples, peaches, pears, cauliflower and green peas for market. The increase in cauliflower and green pea production was due to increased acreage rather than larger yields.

The 1931 season was very unfavorable. Early spring conditions, however, were quite satisfactory. A late May freeze injured winter wheat in northeastern Colorado, fruit and alfalfa in northern Colorado, and alfalfa in Western Slope counties. The drouth started early in May and rainfall continued below normal during the entire season. Several rains fell during August but the relief was only temporary and did not check the rapid decline in crop condition. There was a general shortage of irrigation water in all areas, with the greatest deficiency in the San Luis valley and San Juan basin. Grasshoppers were numerous in eastern Colorado and caused heavy losses to alfalfa, dry beans, corn and other crops. October and November weather was unusually favorable for maturing and harvesting grain sorghums, sugar beets, and other late crops, and yields were somewhat above earlier expectations. Killing

freezes did not occur until the last of October.

The following table, which includes revisions of the 1929 and 1930 figures on the basis of the federal census, shows the number and average size of farms by years since the beginning of co-operative crop reporting in Colorado, and the acreage harvested and farm value of the crops by years:

| Year | No. Farms | Av. Size of Farms |
|------|-----------|-------------------|
| 1920 | 49,117 | 266.27 |
| 1921 | 52,245 | 294.62 |
| 1922 | 54,667 | 295.10 |
| 1923 | 51,589 | 290.36 |
| 1924 | 56,746 | 304.91 |
| 1925 | 53,190 | 313.17 |
| 1926 | 52,220 | 321.17 |
| 1927 | 50,230 | 303.97 |
| 1928 | 48,900 | 339.42 |
| 1929 | 46,200 | 347.52 |
| 1930 | 45,613 | 358.72 |
| 1931 | 46,250 | 330.18 |

| Year | Acreage | Crop Value |
|------|---------|------------|
| 1920 | 5,729,000 | $156,667,000 |
| 1921 | 5,823,000 | 91,270,000 |
| 1922 | 5,772,000 | 102,370,000 |
| 1923 | 6,144,000 | 131,275,000 |
| 1924 | 6,251,000 | 125,881,000 |
| 1925 | 6,143,000 | 139,722,000 |
| 1926 | 6,471,000 | 121,631,000 |
| 1927 | 6,226,000 | 125,524,000 |
| 1928 | 6,368,000 | 117,448,000 |
| 1929 | 6,811,000 | 134,537,000 |
| 1930 | 7,223,000 | 124,442,000 |
| 1931 | 6,735,000 | 63,489,000 |

Variations from the figures shown by the co-operative service appear in the federal census tables appearing elsewhere in this volume, but the discrepancies are not important and are due largely to different bases of collecting data. The total number of farms reported in the state is greater than the total shown by the co-operative service, largely because the census reports farms which produce nothing but pasture and because the census reports as individual farms the various units operated by one farmer, while the state service combines these into a single farm.

Note—In Colorado all crop and livestock data are compiled by the Colorado Co-Operative Crop Reporting service under a contract arrangement authorized by the federal and state governments. The co-operative service consists of the division of crop and livestock estimates, bureau of agricultural economics, United States department of agriculture, and the state board of immigration. Most of the information is based on reports secured through the assessors of the various counties, who are required by law to compile agricultural data upon blanks provided by the co-operative service.

## COLORADO CROP ACREAGE, PRODUCTION AND VALUE, 1931

| KIND OF CROP | Acreage | PRODUCTION | | FARM VALUE DECEMBER 1st | | |
|---|---|---|---|---|---|---|
| | | Per Acre | Total | Unit | Per Unit | Total |
| inter Wheat | 1,218,000 | 12.0 | 14,616,000 | Bus. | $ .43 | $ 6,285,000 |
| ring Wheat | 176,000 | 11.0 | 1,936,000 | Bus. | .46 | 891,000 |
| rn | 1,836,000 | 10.5 | 19,278,000 | Bus. | .40 | 7,711,000 |
| ts for Grain[1] | 148,000 | 23.0 | 3,404,000 | Bus. | .30 | 1,021,000 |
| rley for Grain | 455,000 | 15.5 | 7,099,000 | Bus. | .31 | 2,201,000 |
| e for Grain | 53,000 | 7.0 | 371,000 | Bus. | .31 | 115,000 |
| ain Sorghums | 191,000 | 11.0 | 2,101,000 | Bus. | .23 | 483,000 |
| eet Sorghums | 118,000 | 1.40 | 165,000 | Tons | 4.80 | 792,000 |
| oomcorn* | 46,000 | 250.0 | 5,800 | Tons | 42.00 | 241,000 |
| ld Peas | 49,000 | 9.0 | 441,000 | Bus. | .54 | 238,000 |
| y Beans | 320,000 | 2.58 | 826,000 | 100-lb. Bags. | 1.80 | 1,487,000 |
| tatoes | 101,000 | 95.0 | 9,595,000 | Bus. | .30 | 2,878,000 |
| gar Beets | 226,000 | 11.23 | 2,537,000 | Tons | 5.50 | 13,954,000 |
| bhage | 3,800 | 8.31 | 31,600 | Tons | 14.84 | 469,000 |
| ions | 4,050 | 228.0 | 923,000 | Bus. | .74 | 683,000 |
| uliflower | 3,900 | 260.0 | 1,014,000 | Crs. | .70 | 710,000 |
| matoes for Manufacturing | 2,500 | 7.0 | 17,500 | Tons | 10.50 | 184,000 |
| matoes for Market | 1,290 | 286.0 | 369,000 | Bus. | .60 | 221,000 |
| ntaloupes and Honeydew Melons for Market | 8,100 | 140.0 | 1,134,000 | Crs. | .85 | 964,000 |
| ntaloupes and Honeydew Melons for Seed | 1,800 | 227.0 | 408,050 | Lbs. | .28 | 114,260 |
| atermelons | 1,120 | 300.0 | 336,000 | Nos. | .15 | 5,000 |
| cumbers for Pickles | 1,820 | 128.0 | 233,000 | Bus. | .48 | 112,000 |
| cumbers for Seed | 2,200 | 313.0 | 688,400 | Lbs. | .25 | 172,110 |
| ap Beans for Manufacturing | 1,050 | 1.9 | 2,000 | Tons | 43.20 | 86,000 |
| ap Beans for Market | 1,890 | 154.0 | 291,000 | Bus. | .85 | 247,000 |
| as (Green) for Manufactur'g | 3,500 | 1480.0 | 5,180,000 | Lbs. | .023 | 119,000 |
| as (Green) for Market | 6,500 | 75.0 | 488,000 | Bus. | 1.45 | 708,000 |
| ttuce | 6,650 | 90.0 | 598,000 | Crs. | 1.30 | 777,000 |
| ery | 950 | 220.0 | 209,000 | ⅔ Crs. | 1.20 | 251,000 |
| nach | 500 | 150.0 | 75,000 | Bus. | .25 | 19,000 |
| let Seed[2] | 18,000 | 8.5 | 153,000 | Bus. | .41 | 62,700 |
| alfa Seed | 20,000 | 3.0 | 60,000 | Bus. | 6.50 | 390,000 |
| other Farm, Garden and eed Crops not listed separ-tely | 22,805 | ----- | -------- | ------ | ---- | 1,096,540 |
| e Hay, All Varieties | 1,258,000 | 1.32 | 1,647,000 | Tons | 7.60 | 12,517,000 |
| d Hay | 362,000 | .80 | 290,000 | Tons | 7.50 | 2,175,000 |
| les | ------ | ----- | 2,090,000 | Bus. | .60 | 1,254,000 |
| ches | ------ | ----- | 1,130,000 | Bus. | .50 | 565,000 |
| rs | ------ | ----- | 385,000 | Bus. | .60 | 231,000 |
| rries | ------ | ----- | 2,500 | Tons | 70.00 | 175,000 |
| cellaneous Fruits[3] | 32,500 | ----- | -------- | ------ | ---- | 128,000 |
| ar Beet Tops | ------ | ----- | -------- | ------ | ---- | 678,000 |
| for Pasture | 30,000 | ----- | -------- | ------ | ---- | 75,000 |
| Totals | 6,734,925 | ----- | -------- | ------ | ---- | $63,488,610 |

*County statistics for broomcorn in 1929-30-31 appear on page 92.

[1]In addition to the acreage harvested for grain, there is a large acreage of oats cut green for hay, s additional acreage appearing in the hay table.

[2]This acreage of millet saved for seed is in addition to the area harvested for hay as shown in the hay le.

[3]This acreage includes the total acreage of tree, bush and miscellaneous fruits for the state, but the ue shown in the last column includes only fruits not separately listed above.

## FARM VALUE OF CROPS BY COUNTIES, 1931

| COUNTY | Corn | Wheat | Oats | Barley | Rye | Potatoes | Dry Beans | Sorghums | Sugar Beets | All Hay | Fruits | Miscellaneous Crops | Totals |
|---|---|---|---|---|---|---|---|---|---|---|---|---|---|
| Adams | $142,040 | $225,760 | $13,920 | $54,140 | $1,640 | $5,810 | $87,770 | $27,620 | $705,430 | $257,890 | $6,900 | $567,770 | $2,096,690 |
| Alamosa | 60 | 9,540 | 14,280 | 17,930 | | 104,900 | 120 | | 15,340 | 274,620 | 160 | 101,420 | 538,360 |
| Arapahoe | 96,810 | 182,940 | 16,690 | 31,280 | 2,420 | 360 | 85,910 | 24,690 | 78,480 | 196,810 | 6,210 | 65,230 | 787,830 |
| Archuleta | 3,980 | 8,620 | 10,400 | 1,660 | | 8,820 | 180 | | | 159,170 | 270 | 2,200 | 195,200 |
| Baca | 481,140 | 1,638,600 | 1,310 | 16,600 | 1,660 | 80 | 33,220 | 213,480 | | 36,970 | 740 | 242,200 | 2,666,000 |
| Bent | 163,970 | 37,500 | 8,330 | 38,670 | 90 | 60 | 9,640 | 36,800 | 166,340 | 242,050 | 1,410 | 363,760 | 1,068,620 |
| Boulder | 141,780 | 153,860 | 68,070 | 98,490 | | 10,000 | 1,850 | 100 | 652,360 | 371,950 | 31,960 | 164,830 | 1,695,250 |
| Chaffee | 40 | 3,320 | 4,250 | 8,020 | | 9,760 | 330 | | | 72,800 | 5,700 | 102,390 | 206,610 |
| Cheyenne | 404,040 | 78,000 | 2,130 | 29,090 | 240 | 580 | 3,880 | 76,760 | | 25,740 | 340 | 4,910 | 625,710 |
| Clear Creek | 120 | | 40 | | | 450 | | | | 9,610 | | | 10,220 |
| Conejos | 1,010 | 36,280 | 25,380 | 57,230 | | 161,500 | 8,070 | | 1,870 | 308,220 | 180 | 316,730 | 916,470 |
| Costilla | 770 | 19,620 | 9,990 | 25,390 | | 25,060 | 4,690 | | | 118,160 | 160 | 506,660 | 710,190 |
| Crowley | 35,480 | 2,520 | 3,590 | 8,630 | 60 | 60 | 13,790 | 11,820 | 111,430 | 68,390 | 5,100 | 474,970 | 735,840 |
| Custer | 5,400 | 5,230 | 7,120 | 3,250 | 110 | 42,310 | | 70 | | 212,300 | 40 | 133,920 | 409,750 |
| Delta | 79,450 | 33,420 | 24,600 | 22,770 | | 52,630 | 1,840 | 60 | 160,760 | 404,910 | 854,520 | 93,340 | 1,728,300 |
| Denver | 4,560 | 10,610 | 1,050 | 270 | | 3,800 | 4,820 | 890 | | 9,730 | 210 | 1,400 | 37,340 |
| Dolores | | | | | | | | | | | | | |
| Douglas | 65,270 | 24,070 | 24,510 | 4,860 | 5,520 | 2,610 | 6,390 | 4,230 | | 166,980 | 1,000 | 5,380 | 310,820 |
| Eagle | 120 | 9,620 | 15,670 | 5,340 | 6,990 | 51,700 | | 19,680 | | 309,340 | 1,000 | 38,830 | 431,620 |
| Elbert | 217,620 | 101,750 | 14,160 | 17,330 | 7,680 | 8,140 | 202,160 | 30,380 | | 116,290 | 1,200 | 22,160 | 727,380 |
| El Paso | 178,690 | 22,200 | 25,280 | 3,780 | | 10,380 | 178,890 | | 53,130 | 138,270 | 1,200 | 45,490 | 695,370 |
| Fremont | 47,980 | 4,500 | 7,560 | 1,730 | 30 | 2,910 | 160 | 390 | | 164,840 | 158,900 | 272,100 | 661,100 |
| Garfield | 14,450 | 40,670 | 24,580 | 15,820 | 40 | 131,500 | 380 | 130 | 97,460 | 592,960 | 37,300 | 46,000 | 1,001,290 |
| Gilpin | | 40 | 250 | 40 | | 1,080 | 90 | | | 9,140 | | 2,190 | 12,830 |
| Grand | | 640 | 7,330 | 3,400 | 160 | 1,580 | | | | 259,870 | | 86,940 | 360,040 |
| Gunnison | 120 | 950 | 1,960 | 1,560 | 40 | 2,770 | | | | 409,940 | 180 | 3,210 | 420,610 |
| Hinsdale | | | 700 | | 10 | 180 | | | | 30,580 | | 450 | 31,910 |
| Huerfano | 30,890 | 9,890 | 8,430 | 1,560 | | 7,430 | 6,370 | 1,380 | 2,970 | 250,680 | 1,850 | 21,300 | 342,760 |
| Jackson | | | 760 | 320 | 150 | 1,230 | | | | 712,840 | | 1,220 | 510 |
| Jefferson | 37,480 | 73,910 | 28,100 | 32,980 | | 16,940 | 590 | 400 | 52,080 | 235,350 | 84,700 | 384,790 | 947,470 |
| Kiowa | 275,570 | 37,970 | 190 | 7,960 | 180 | 90 | 1,620 | 136,160 | | 14,270 | 200 | 11,200 | 485,410 |
| Kit Carson | 616,630 | 381,380 | 11,220 | 127,280 | 5,480 | 7,080 | 11,440 | 100,620 | | 68,820 | 680 | 18,580 | 1,349,110 |

| County | | | | | | | | | | | | |
|---|---|---|---|---|---|---|---|---|---|---|---|---|
| Lake | 15,190 | 74,630 | 49,010 | 22,820 | — | 62,480 | 3,830 | 490 | 41,030 | — | — | 200 | 41,230 |
| La | 107,710 | 200,400 | 58,390 | 175,770 | 60 | 33,280 | 8,990 | 2,540 | 333,560 | 1,574,380 | 15,840 | 18,560 | 86,470 |
| Larimer | 199,780 | 40,050 | 14,030 | 19,510 | 620 | 2,430 | 106,240 | 28,240 | 743,490 | 68,090 | 198,260 | 147,760 | 3,251,90 |
| Las Animas | 250,170 | 199,240 | 1,350 | 36,740 | 640 | 4,590 | 79,710 | 61,880 | 214,210 | — | 1,150 | 157,320 | 851,90 |
|  | 497,770 | 431,160 | 34,130 | 141,610 | 2,880 | 28,710 | 21,340 | 66,360 | 99,540 | 1,075,030 | 420 | 12,050 | 747,810 |
|  |  |  |  |  |  |  |  |  | 433,590 |  | 640 | 128,360 | 2,861,580 |
| Mesa | 138,970 | 40,820 | 22,880 | 14,100 | 90 | 89,960 | 49,740 | 1,040 | 520,430 | 106,590 | 833,770 | 211,730 | 2, 90,120 |
| Mineral | 7,930 | 29,890 | 20,780 | 5,020 | 2,240 | 110 | 380 | 1,070 | 20,690 | — | 540 | 20,690 | 20,800 |
|  | 31,720 | 37,350 | 43,470 | 10,370 | 160 | 13,520 | 47,460 | 2,000 | 243,470 | — | 86,890 | 24,530 | 349,370 |
|  | 67,250 | 80,910 | 39,270 | 22,330 | 20 | 45,380 | 4,190 | 10 | 249,640 | 48,730 | 33,340 | 15,000 | 69,440 |
| Morgan | 323,110 | 104,590 | 17,850 | 114,370 | 2,380 | 268,140 | 65,910 | 32,000 | 452,080 | 1,505,020 | 1,270 | 155,960 | 1,172,230 |
|  |  |  |  |  |  | 76,470 |  |  | 414,810 |  |  | 128,700 | 2,786,480 |
| Otero | 77,420 | 12,960 | 19,300 | 27,060 | 140 | 110 | 29,560 | 6,330 | 251,920 | 501,490 | 10,820 | 948,360 | 1,885,470 |
| Ouray | 1,040 | 7,700 | 9,610 | 2,430 | — | 8,350 | 40 | — | 122,040 | — | 640 | 400 | 152,250 |
| Park | — | 80 | 430 | 70 | — | 21,960 | — | — | 237,490 | — | 360 | 1,770 | 261,800 |
| Phillips | 364,840 | 378,060 | 21,120 | 36,060 | 2,650 | 1,880 | 940 | 39,790 | 44,440 | — | 460 | 17,260 | 907,400 |
| Pitkin | — | 2,930 | 4,280 | 600 | 20 | 36,330 | — | — | 67,850 | — | 680 | 920 | 113,90 |
| Prowers | 140,380 | 219,880 | 13,120 | 50,510 | 400 | 50 | 1,440 | 85,230 | 263,600 | 242,990 | 8,370 | 76,010 | 104,290 |
|  | 186,960 | 56,780 | 11,310 | 19,880 | 160 | 280 | 48,870 | 9,610 | 224,320 | 439,590 |  | 867,080 | 1,873,210 |
| Rio Blanco | — | 15,480 | 21,490 | 2,670 | 160 | 1,820 | — | — | 352,100 | — | 440 | 7,560 | 401,720 |
| Rio Grande | 160 | 20,980 | 24,490 | 26,140 | — | 337,660 | 1,200 | — | 291,270 | 2,750 | 720 | 374,710 | 196,080 |
| Routt | 40 | 24,610 | 44,640 | 19,410 | 560 | 12,940 | — | — | 394,070 | — | 1,860 | 188,560 | 66,50 |
| Saguache | 40 | 7,110 | 10,170 | 7,850 | 120 | 153,360 | 153,360 | — | 364,720 | — | 500 | 36,930 | 580,800 |
| San Juan | — | — | — | — | — | — | — | — | — | — | — | — | — |
| San | 2,290 | 6,280 | 2,430 | 1,990 | 60 | 4,640 | 4,640 | 170 | 77,340 | — | 280 | 1,410 | 97,760 |
| Sedgwick | 161,050 | 202,480 | 21,110 | 48,920 | 1,020 | 18,390 | 18,390 | 3,610 | 119,910 | 297,940 | 620 | 25,700 | 90,910 |
| Summit | — | 240 | 560 | 290 | 80 | 360 | 360 | — | 60,120 | — | 40 | 40 | 61,90 |
| Teller | 210 | 180 | 1,520 | 330 | 50 | 22,500 | 22,500 | — | 66,120 | — | — | 13,950 | 104, |
| Washington | 581,720 | 404,940 | 9,640 | 106,200 | 7,150 | 3,980 | 53,630 | 60,530 | 186,860 | 32,120 | 1,360 | 38,060 | 196, 90 |
| Weld | 545,350 | 818,760 | 112,330 | 596,830 | 12,040 | 951,700 | 294,450 | 45,750 | 1,435,800 | 5,961,630 | 8,240 | 865,930 | 11,648,810 |
| Yuma | 964,470 | 604,200 | 10,440 | 53,740 | 46,800 | 4,830 | 3,830 | 142,890 | 116,000 | — | 3,010 | 44,640 | 1,994,90 |
| State | $ 7,711,000 | $ 7,176,000 | $1,021,000 | $2,201,000 | $115,000 | $ 2,878,000 | $1,487,000 | $1,275,000 | $14,692,000 | $13,954,000 | $ 2,412,550 | $ 8,611,030 | $ 63,533,610 |

Note—Miscellaneous Crops include field peas, broomcorn, garden peas, snap beans, cantaloupes for market and seed, cucumbers for pickles and seed, cabbage and kraut, celery, lettuce, cauliflower, tomatoes, watermelons, onions, asparagus, garden beets, spinach, carrots, pumpkin and squash, sweet corn, sugar beet tops, rye for pasture, millet seed, alfalfa seed, sweet clover seed, red clover and other minor farm garden crops.
Fruits include apples, peaches, pears, cherries, grapes, plums, apricots, strawberries, etc.

### ACREAGE AND PRODUCTION OF WINTER WHEAT, 1931

| COUNTY | IRRIGATED | | | NON-IRRIGATED | | | TOTALS | |
|---|---|---|---|---|---|---|---|---|
| | Acreage | Average Yield | Production Bushels | Acreage | Average Yield | Production Bushels | Acreage | Production Bushels |
| Adams_____ | 2,930 | 23 | 67,390 | 45,170 | 9 | 406,530 | 48,100 | 473,920 |
| Alamosa_____ | 50 | 20 | 1,000 | ------ | -- | ------ | 50 | 1,000 |
| Arapahoe_____ | 1,170 | 26 | 30,420 | 35,330 | 10 | 353,300 | 36,500 | 383,720 |
| Archuleta_____ | 30 | 25 | 750 | 340 | 11 | 3,740 | 370 | 4,490 |
| Baca_____ | 710 | 28 | 19,880 | 236,690 | 16 | 3,787,040 | 237,400 | 3,806,920 |
| Bent_____ | 2,200 | 30 | 66,000 | 1,540 | 13 | 20,020 | 3,740 | 86,020 |
| Boulder_____ | 5,980 | 29 | 173,420 | 2,680 | 16 | 42,880 | 8,660 | 216,300 |
| Chaffee_____ | 30 | 18 | 540 | ------ | -- | ------ | 30 | 540 |
| Cheyenne_____ | ------ | -- | ------ | 15,230 | 11 | 167,530 | 15,230 | 167,530 |
| Clear Creek_____ | ------ | -- | ------ | ------ | -- | ------ | ------ | ------ |
| Conejos_____ | 140 | 22 | 3,080 | ------ | -- | ------ | 140 | 3,080 |
| Costilla_____ | 260 | 24 | 6,240 | ------ | -- | ------ | 260 | 6,240 |
| Crowley_____ | 90 | 28 | 2,520 | ------ | -- | ------ | 90 | 2,520 |
| Custer_____ | 220 | 26 | 5,720 | 200 | 13 | 2,600 | 420 | 8,320 |
| Delta_____ | 390 | 29 | 11,310 | ------ | -- | ------ | 390 | 11,310 |
| Denver_____ | ------ | -- | ------ | ------ | -- | ------ | ------ | ------ |
| Dolores_____ | 790 | 25 | 19,750 | 220 | 11 | 2,420 | 1,010 | 22,170 |
| Douglas_____ | 180 | 22 | 3,960 | 4,740 | 10 | 47,400 | 4,920 | 51,360 |
| Eagle_____ | 150 | 20 | 3,000 | 100 | 11 | 1,100 | 250 | 4,100 |
| Elbert_____ | 100 | 23 | 2,300 | 19,100 | 10 | 191,000 | 19,200 | 193,300 |
| El Paso_____ | 80 | 23 | 1,840 | 2,560 | 11 | 28,160 | 2,640 | 30,000 |
| Fremont_____ | 110 | 25 | 2,750 | 80 | 13 | 1,040 | 190 | 3,790 |
| Garfield_____ | 160 | 28 | 4,480 | 380 | 10 | 3,800 | 540 | 8,280 |
| Gilpin_____ | ------ | -- | ------ | ------ | -- | ------ | ------ | ------ |
| Grand_____ | 50 | 17 | 850 | 20 | 10 | 200 | 70 | 1,050 |
| Gunnison_____ | 40 | 18 | 720 | ------ | -- | ------ | 40 | 720 |
| Hinsdale_____ | ------ | -- | ------ | ------ | -- | ------ | ------ | ------ |
| Huerfano_____ | 280 | 24 | 6,720 | 480 | 15 | 7,200 | 760 | 13,920 |
| Jackson_____ | ------ | -- | ------ | ------ | -- | ------ | ------ | ------ |
| Jefferson_____ | 2,730 | 26 | 70,980 | 2,420 | 15 | 36,300 | 5,150 | 107,280 |
| Kiowa_____ | ------ | -- | ------ | 6,710 | 13 | 87,230 | 6,710 | 87,230 |
| Kit Carson_____ | 70 | 24 | 1,680 | 69,810 | 11 | 767,910 | 69,880 | 769,590 |
| Lake_____ | ------ | -- | ------ | ------ | -- | ------ | ------ | ------ |
| La Plata_____ | 470 | 21 | 9,870 | 490 | 9 | 4,410 | 960 | 14,280 |
| Larimer_____ | 5,710 | 26 | 148,460 | 12,780 | 17 | 217,260 | 18,490 | 365,720 |
| Las Animas_____ | 370 | 27 | 9,990 | 5,060 | 14 | 70,840 | 5,430 | 80,830 |
| Lincoln_____ | ------ | -- | ------ | 43,120 | 10 | 431,200 | 43,120 | 431,200 |
| Logan_____ | 480 | 24 | 11,520 | 119,700 | 8 | 957,600 | 120,180 | 969,120 |
| Mesa_____ | 1,380 | 31 | 42,780 | 340 | 13 | 4,420 | 1,720 | 47,200 |
| Mineral_____ | ------ | -- | ------ | ------ | -- | ------ | ------ | ------ |
| Moffat_____ | 50 | 18 | 900 | 3,860 | 11 | 42,460 | 3,910 | 43,360 |
| Montezuma_____ | 220 | 19 | 4,180 | 1,280 | 11 | 14,080 | 1,500 | 18,260 |
| Montrose_____ | 630 | 32 | 20,160 | 100 | 12 | 1,200 | 730 | 21,360 |
| Morgan_____ | 490 | 25 | 12,250 | 21,590 | 9 | 194,310 | 22,080 | 206,560 |
| Otero_____ | 740 | 30 | 22,200 | 80 | 14 | 1,120 | 820 | 23,320 |
| Ouray_____ | 30 | 26 | 780 | 310 | 11 | 3,410 | 340 | 4,190 |
| Park_____ | ------ | -- | ------ | ------ | -- | ------ | ------ | ------ |
| Phillips_____ | ------ | -- | ------ | 109,550 | 8 | 876,400 | 109,550 | 876,400 |
| Pitkin_____ | 30 | 21 | 630 | ------ | -- | ------ | 30 | 630 |
| Prowers_____ | 2,670 | 27 | 72,090 | 31,080 | 14 | 435,120 | 33,750 | 507,210 |
| Pueblo_____ | 540 | 26 | 14,040 | 8,080 | 13 | 105,040 | 8,620 | 119,080 |
| Rio Blanco_____ | 10 | 19 | 190 | 1,210 | 15 | 18,150 | 1,220 | 18,340 |
| Rio Grande_____ | 40 | 18 | 720 | ------ | -- | ------ | 40 | 720 |
| Routt_____ | 10 | 22 | 220 | 1,400 | 17 | 23,800 | 1,410 | 24,020 |
| Saguache_____ | 50 | 19 | 950 | ------ | -- | ------ | 50 | 950 |
| San Juan_____ | ------ | -- | ------ | ------ | -- | ------ | ------ | ------ |
| San Miguel_____ | 110 | 27 | 2,970 | 510 | 13 | 6,630 | 620 | 9,600 |
| Sedgwick_____ | 390 | 25 | 9,750 | 65,320 | 7 | 457,240 | 65,710 | 466,990 |
| Summit_____ | 20 | 18 | 360 | ------ | -- | ------ | 20 | 360 |
| Teller_____ | ------ | -- | ------ | 30 | 11 | 330 | 30 | 330 |
| Washington_____ | 240 | 26 | 6,240 | 81,430 | 11 | 895,730 | 81,670 | 901,970 |
| Weld_____ | 16,710 | 26 | 434,460 | 90,420 | 13 | 1,175,460 | 107,130 | 1,609,920 |
| Yuma_____ | 130 | 26 | 3,380 | 126,000 | 11 | 1,386,000 | 126,130 | 1,389,380 |
| State_____ | 50,460 | -- | 1,336,390 | 1,167,540 | -- | 13,279,610 | 1,218,000 | 14,616,000 |

Wheat | Corn | Oats | Barley | Potatoes | Rye | Sugar Beets | Sorghums | Dry Beans | Hay | Broomcorn | Field Peas | Snap Beans for Canning and Market | Lettuce | Celery | Cauliflower | Watermelons | Onions | GARDEN PEAS (For Market, For Mfg., Total) | CUCUMBERS (For Pickles, For Seed, Total) | CABBAGE (Early, Late, Total) | TOMATOES (For Market, For Mfg., Total) | CANTALOUPES AND HONEY DEW MELONS (For Market, For Seed, Total) | All Other Harvested Crops | Total Harvested Acreage | COUNTY

### ACREAGE AND PRODUCTION OF SPRING WHEAT, 1931

| ƆUNTY | IRRIGATED | | | NON-IRRIGATED | | | TOTALS | |
|---|---|---|---|---|---|---|---|---|
| | Acreage | Average Yield | Production Bushels | Acreage | Average Yield | Production Bushels | Acreage | Production Bushels |
| ms ------- | 1,590 | 20 | 31,800 | 3,990 | 4 | 15,960 | 5,580 | 47,760 |
| nosa ------ | 1,320 | 15 | 19,800 | ------ | -- | ------ | 1,320 | 19,800 |
| ɔahoe ----- | 740 | 20 | 14,800 | 4,840 | 5 | 24,200 | 5,580 | 39,000 |
| ıuleta ----- | 320 | 20 | 6,400 | 990 | 8 | 7,920 | 1,310 | 14,320 |
| ι ---------- | ------ | -- | ------ | 350 | 10 | 3,500 | 350 | 3,500 |
| ΅ ---------- | ------ | -- | ------ | 110 | 10 | 1,100 | 110 | 1,100 |
| lder ------- | 5,700 | 23 | 131,100 | 110 | 10 | 1,100 | 5,810 | 132,200 |
| ffee ------- | 480 | 14 | 6,720 | ------ | -- | ------ | 480 | 6,720 |
| ʏenne ----- | ------ | -- | ------ | 2,590 | 5 | 12,950 | 2,590 | 12,950 |
| r Creek---- | ------ | -- | ------ | ------ | -- | ------ | ------ | ------ |
| ejos ------- | 4,000 | 19 | 76,000 | ------ | -- | ------ | 4,000 | 76,000 |
| illa ------- | 1,840 | 20 | 36,800 | ------ | -- | ------ | 1,840 | 36,800 |
| vley ------- | 160 | 18 | 2,880 | 20 | 12 | 240 | 180 | 3,120 |
| :er -------- | 140 | 21 | 2,940 | 80 | 8 | 640 | 220 | 3,580 |
| a ---------- | 2,950 | 21 | 61,950 | 10 | 9 | 90 | 2,960 | 62,040 |
| ver | ------ | -- | ------ | ------ | -- | ------ | ------ | ------ |
| ɔres ------ | ------ | -- | ------ | 390 | 6 | 2,340 | 390 | 2,340 |
| glas ------- | 10 | 22 | 220 | 820 | 5 | 4,100 | 830 | 4,320 |
| le --------- | 670 | 25 | 16,750 | 30 | 11 | 330 | 700 | 17,080 |
| ɔrt -------- | ------ | -- | ------ | 6,750 | 6 | 40,500 | 6,750 | 40,500 |
| Paso ------- | 50 | 23 | 1,150 | 3,180 | 6 | 19,080 | 3,230 | 20,230 |
| nont ------ | 250 | 21 | 5,250 | 90 | 11 | 990 | ʼ340 | 6,240 |
| ɡeld ------- | 3,870 | 19 | 73,530 | 1,180 | 6 | 7,080 | 5,050 | 80,610 |
| in --------- | ------ | -- | ------ | 10 | 9 | 90 | 10 | 90 |
| ɧd --------- | 20 | 21 | 420 | ------ | -- | ------ | 20 | 420 |
| nison ----- | ·40 | 23 | 920 | 50 | 9 | 450 | 90 | 1,370 |
| ɛdale ------ | ------ | -- | ------ | ------ | -- | ------ | ------ | ------ |
| rfano ----- | 240 | 21 | 5,040 | 430 | 8 | 3,440 | 670 | 8,480 |
| ːson ------- | ------ | -- | ------ | ------ | -- | ------ | ------ | ------ |
| ɛrson ------ | 2,550 | 22 | 56,100 | 530 | 8 | 4,240 | 3,080 | 60,340 |
| va --------- | ------ | -- | ------ | 200 | 5 | 1,000 | 200 | 1,000 |
| Carson----- | ------ | -- | ------ | 18,280 | 6 | 109,680 | 18,280 | 109,680 |
| e ---------- | ------ | -- | ------ | ------ | -- | ------ | ------ | ------ |
| Plata------- | 7,070 | 20 | 141,400 | 820 | 9 | 7,380 | 7,890 | 148,780 |
| mer ------- | 3,680 | 23 | 84,640 | 1,140 | 8 | 9,120 | 4,820 | 93,760 |
| Animas---- | 330 | 23 | 7,590 | 490 | 8 | 3,920 | 820 | 11,510 |
| :oln ------- | ------ | -- | ------ | 7,510 | 4 | 30,040 | 7,510 | 30,040 |
| an -------- | 380 | 19 | 7,220 | 6,040 | 4 | 24,160 | 6,420 | 31,380 |
| ι ---------- | 2,260 | 19 | 42,940 | 230 | 7 | 1,610 | 2,490 | 44,550 |
| eral ------- | ------ | -- | ------ | ------ | -- | ------ | ------ | ------ |
| ʼat -------- | 110 | 18 | 1,980 | 2,810 | 8 | 22,480 | 2,920 | 24,460 |
| tezuma ---- | 3,390 | 14 | 47,460 | 2,770 | 6 | 16,620 | 6,160 | 64,080 |
| trose ----- | 6,930 | 22 | 152,460 | 480 | 7 | 3,360 | 7,410 | 155,820 |
| gan ------- | 100 | 27 | 2,700 | 7,890 | 4 | 31,560 | 7,990 | 34,260 |
| ʼo --------- | 330 | 19 | 6,270 | 10 | 9 | 90 | 340 | 6,360 |
| ay --------- | 560 | 20 | 11,200 | 270 | 6 | 1,620 | 830 | 12,820 |
| ɭ ---------- | ------ | -- | ------ | 20 | 9 | 180 | 20 | 180 |
| lips ------- | ------ | -- | ------ | 650 | 4 | 2,600 | 650 | 2,600 |
| in --------- | 250 | 23 | 5,750 | ------ | -- | ------ | 250 | 5,750 |
| vers ------- | 20 | 18 | 360 | 440 | 8 | 3,520 | 460 | 3,880 |
| ɔlo -------- | 300 | 26 | 7,800 | 620 | 7 | 4,340 | 920 | 12,140 |
| Blanco----- | 330 | 20 | 6,600 | 990 | 10 | 9,900 | 1,320 | 16,500 |
| Grande ---- | 3,210 | 14 | 44,940 | ------ | -- | ------ | 3,210 | 44,940 |
| ʇt --------- | 60 | 15 | 900 | 3,350 | 9 | 30,150 | 3,410 | 31,050 |
| ıache ------ | 1,120 | 13 | 14,560 | ------ | -- | ------ | 1,120 | 14,560 |
| Juan------ | ------ | -- | ------ | ------ | -- | ------ | ------ | ------ |
| Miguel---- | 200 | 20 | 4,000 | 80 | 8 | 640 | 280 | 4,640 |
| ːwick ------ | 160 | 21 | 3,360 | 60 | 5 | 300 | 220 | 3,660 |
| mit ------- | ------ | -- | ------ | 20 | 9 | 180 | 20 | 180 |
| ɛr --------- | ------ | -- | ------ | 10 | 9 | 90 | 10 | 90 |
| hington --- | ------ | -- | ------ | 9,280 | 4 | 37,120 | 9,280 | 37,120 |
| d --------- | 9,000 | 22 | 198,000 | 15,340 | 5 | 76,700 | 24,340 | 274,700 |
| ıa --------- | ------ | -- | ------ | 2,920 | 5 | 14,600 | 2,920 | 14,600 |
| ate ------- | 66,730 | -- | 1,342,700 | 109,270 | -- | 593,300 | 176,000 | 1,936,000 |

| COUNTY | PERCENTAGE DISTRIBUTION OF WHEAT ACREAGE, 1931 | | | | PERCENTAGE DISTRIBUTION OF WHEAT PRODUCTION, 1931 | | | |
|---|---|---|---|---|---|---|---|---|
| | Spring Wheat % Total Wheat Acreage | Winter Wheat % Total Wheat Acreage | Irrigated Wheat % Total Wheat Acreage | Non-Irrigated Wheat % Total Wheat Acreage | Spring Wheat % Total Wheat Prod. | Winter Wheat % Total Wheat Prod. | Irrigated Wheat % Total Wheat Prod. | Non-Irrigated Wheat % Total Wheat Prod. |
| Adams | 10.4 | 89.6 | 8.4 | 91.6 | 90.8 | 9.2 | 19.0 | 81.0 |
| Alamosa | 96.4 | 3.6 | 100.0 | ---- | 4.8 | 95.2 | 100.0 | ---- |
| Arapahoe | 13.3 | 86.7 | 4.5 | 95.5 | 90.8 | 9.2 | 10.7 | 89.3 |
| Archuleta | 78.0 | 22.0 | 20.8 | 79.2 | 23.9 | 76.1 | 38.0 | 62.0 |
| Baca | .1 | 99.9 | .3 | 99.7 | 99.9 | .1 | .5 | 99.5 |
| Bent | 2.9 | 97.1 | 57.1 | 42.9 | 98.7 | 1.3 | 75.8 | 24.2 |
| Boulder | 40.2 | 59.8 | 80.7 | 19.3 | 62.1 | 37.9 | 87.4 | 12.6 |
| Chaffee | 94.1 | 5.9 | 100.0 | ---- | 7.4 | 92.6 | 100.0 | ---- |
| Cheyenne | 14.5 | 85.5 | ---- | 100.0 | 92.8 | 7.2 | ---- | 100.0 |
| Clear Creek | ---- | ---- | ---- | ---- | ---- | ---- | ---- | ---- |
| Conejos | 96.6 | 3.4 | 100.0 | ---- | 3.9 | 96.1 | 100.0 | ---- |
| Costilla | 87.6 | 12.4 | 100.0 | ---- | 14.5 | 85.5 | 100.0 | ---- |
| Crowley | 66.7 | 33.3 | 92.6 | 7.4 | 44.7 | 55.3 | 95.7 | 4.3 |
| Custer | 34.4 | 65.6 | 56.2 | 43.8 | 69.9 | 30.1 | 72.8 | 27.2 |
| Delta | 88.4 | 11.6 | 99.7 | .3 | 15.4 | 84.6 | 99.9 | .1 |
| Denver | ---- | ---- | ---- | ---- | ---- | ---- | ---- | ---- |
| Dolores | 27.9 | 72.1 | 56.4 | 43.6 | 90.5 | 9.5 | 80.6 | 19.4 |
| Douglas | 14.4 | 85.6 | 3.3 | 96.7 | 92.2 | 7.8 | 7.5 | 92.5 |
| Eagle | 73.7 | 26.3 | 86.3 | 13.7 | 19.3 | 80.7 | 93.2 | 6.8 |
| Elbert | 26.0 | 74.0 | .4 | 99.6 | 82.7 | 17.3 | 1.0 | 99.0 |
| El Paso | 55.0 | 45.0 | 2.2 | 97.8 | 59.7 | 40.3 | 6.0 | 94.0 |
| Fremont | 64.2 | 35.8 | 67.9 | 32.1 | 37.8 | 62.2 | 79.8 | 20.2 |
| Garfield | 90.3 | 9.7 | 72.1 | 27.9 | 9.3 | 90.7 | 87.8 | 12.2 |
| Gilpin | 100.0 | ---- | ---- | 100.0 | ---- | 100.0 | ---- | 100.0 |
| Grand | 22.2 | 77.8 | 77.8 | 22.2 | 71.4 | 28.6 | 86.4 | 13.6 |
| Gunnison | 69.2 | 30.8 | 61.5 | 38.5 | 34.4 | 65.6 | 78.5 | 21.5 |
| Hinsdale | ---- | ---- | ---- | ---- | ---- | ---- | ---- | ---- |
| Huerfano | 46.9 | 53.1 | 36.4 | 63.6 | 62.1 | 37.9 | 52.5 | 47.5 |
| Jackson | ---- | ---- | ---- | ---- | ---- | ---- | ---- | ---- |
| Jefferson | 37.4 | 62.6 | 64.2 | 35.8 | 64.0 | 36.0 | 75.8 | 24.2 |
| Kiowa | 2.9 | 97.1 | ---- | 100.0 | 98.9 | 1.1 | ---- | 100.0 |
| Kit Carson | 20.7 | 79.3 | .1 | 99.9 | 87.5 | 12.5 | .2 | 99.8 |
| Lake | ---- | ---- | ---- | ---- | ---- | ---- | ---- | ---- |
| La Plata | 89.2 | 10.8 | 85.2 | 14.8 | 8.8 | 91.2 | 92.8 | 7.2 |
| Larimer | 20.7 | 79.3 | 40.3 | 59.7 | 57.8 | 42.2 | 50.7 | 49.3 |
| Las Animas | 13.1 | 86.9 | 11.2 | 88.8 | 87.5 | 12.5 | 19.0 | 81.0 |
| Lincoln | 14.8 | 85.2 | ---- | 100.0 | 93.5 | 6.5 | ---- | 100.0 |
| Logan | 5.1 | 94.9 | .7 | 99.3 | 96.9 | 3.1 | 1.9 | 98.1 |
| Mesa | 59.1 | 40.9 | 86.5 | 13.5 | 51.4 | 48.6 | 93.4 | 6.6 |
| Mineral | ---- | ---- | ---- | ---- | ---- | ---- | ---- | ---- |
| Moffat | 42.8 | 57.2 | 2.3 | 97.7 | 63.9 | 36.1 | 4.2 | 95.8 |
| Montezuma | 80.4 | 19.6 | 47.1 | 52.9 | 22.2 | 77.8 | 62.7 | 37.3 |
| Montrose | 91.0 | 9.0 | 92.9 | 7.1 | 12.1 | 87.9 | 97.4 | 2.6 |
| Morgan | 26.6 | 73.4 | 2.0 | 98.0 | 85.8 | 14.2 | 6.2 | 93.8 |
| Otero | 29.3 | 70.7 | 92.2 | 7.8 | 78.6 | 21.4 | 95.9 | 4.1 |
| Ouray | 70.9 | 29.1 | 50.4 | 49.6 | 24.6 | 75.4 | 70.4 | 29.6 |
| Park | 100.0 | ---- | ---- | 100.0 | ---- | 100.0 | ---- | 100.0 |
| Phillips | .6 | 99.4 | ---- | 100.0 | 99.7 | .3 | ---- | 100.0 |
| Pitkin | 89.3 | 10.7 | 100.0 | ---- | 9.9 | 90.1 | 100.0 | ---- |
| Prowers | 1.3 | 98.7 | 7.9 | 92.1 | 99.2 | .8 | 6.2 | 93.8 |
| Pueblo | 9.6 | 90.4 | 8.8 | 91.2 | 90.8 | 9.2 | 16.6 | 83.4 |
| Rio Blanco | 52.0 | 48.0 | 13.4 | 86.6 | 52.6 | 47.4 | 19.5 | 80.5 |
| Rio Grande | 98.8 | 1.2 | 100.0 | ---- | 1.6 | 98.4 | 100.0 | ---- |
| Routt | 70.7 | 29.3 | 1.5 | 98.5 | 43.6 | 56.4 | 2.0 | 98.0 |
| Saguache | 95.7 | 4.3 | 100.0 | ---- | 6.1 | 93.9 | 100.0 | ---- |
| San Juan | ---- | ---- | ---- | ---- | ---- | ---- | ---- | ---- |
| San Miguel | 31.1 | 68.9 | 34.4 | 65.6 | 67.4 | 32.6 | 48.9 | 51.1 |
| Sedgwick | .3 | 99.7 | .8 | 99.2 | 99.2 | .8 | 2.8 | 97.2 |
| Summit | 50.0 | 50.0 | 50.0 | 50.0 | 66.7 | 33.3 | 66.7 | 33.3 |
| Teller | 25.0 | 75.0 | ---- | 100.0 | 78.6 | 21.4 | ---- | 100.0 |
| Washington | 10.2 | 89.8 | .3 | 99.7 | 96.0 | 4.0 | .7 | 99.3 |
| Weld | 18.5 | 81.5 | 19.6 | 80.4 | 85.4 | 14.6 | 33.5 | 66.5 |
| Yuma | 2.3 | 97.7 | .1 | 99.9 | 99.0 | 1.0 | .2 | 99.8 |
| State | 12.6 | 87.4 | 8.4 | 91.6 | 88.3 | 11.7 | 16.2 | 83.8 |

## ACREAGE AND PRODUCTION OF CORN, 1931

| )UNTY | IRRIGATED | | | NON-IRRIGATED | | | TOTAL | |
|---|---|---|---|---|---|---|---|---|
| | Acreage | Average Yield | Production Bushels | Acreage | Average Yield | Production Bushels | Acreage | Production Bushels |
| ms _____ | 3,510 | 33 | 115,830 | 39,880 | 6 | 239,280 | 43,390 | 355,110 |
| nosa _____ | 10 | 16 | 160 | ------ | -- | ------ | 10 | 160 |
| )ahoe _____ | 990 | 32 | 31,680 | 30,050 | 7 | 210,350 | 31,040 | 242,030 |
| iuleta ____ | 30 | 29 | 870 | 910 | 10 | 9,100 | 940 | 9,970 |
| i _____ | 330 | 27 | 8,910 | 108,540 | 11 | 1,193,940 | 108,870 | 1,202,850 |
| ; _____ | 12,870 | 22 | 283,140 | 15,850 | 8 | 126,800 | 28,720 | 409,940 |
| der _____ | 11,520 | 28 | 322,560 | 2,900 | 11 | 31,900 | 14,420 | 354,460 |
| fee _____ | ------ | -- | ------ | 10 | 11 | 110 | 10 | 110 |
| 'enne _____ | ------ | -- | ------ | 101,010 | 10 | 1,010,100 | 101,010 | 1,010,100 |
| r Creek____ | 10 | 29 | 290 | ------ | -- | ------ | 10 | 290 |
| ijos _____ | 120 | 21 | 2,520 | ------ | -- | ------ | 120 | 2,520 |
| illa _____ | 80 | 24 | 1,920 | ------ | -- | ------ | 80 | 1,920 |
| vley _____ | 4,040 | 14 | 56,560 | 5,360 | 6 | 32,160 | 9,400 | 88,720 |
| er _____ | 130 | 29 | 3,770 | 650 | 15 | 9,750 | 780 | 13,520 |
| a _____ | 5,090 | 39 | 198,510 | 10 | 12 | 120 | 5,100 | 198,630 |
| /er _____ | ------ | -- | ------ | 1,140 | 10 | 11,400 | 1,140 | 11,400 |
| res _____ | ------ | -- | ------ | 1,140 | 10 | 11,400 | 1,140 | 11,400 |
| glas _____ | 230 | 29 | 6,670 | 17,390 | 9 | 156,510 | 17,620 | 163,180 |
| e _____ | 10 | 31 | 310 | ------ | -- | ------ | 10 | 310 |
| rt _____ | ------ | -- | ------ | 60,450 | 9 | 544,050 | 60,450 | 544,050 |
| Paso _____ | 560 | 31 | 17,360 | 61,340 | 7 | 429,380 | 61,900 | 446,740 |
| nont _____ | 3,100 | 34 | 105,400 | 1,040 | 14 | 14,560 | 4,140 | 119,960 |
| ield _____ | 920 | 37 | 34,040 | 160 | 13 | 2,080 | 1,080 | 36,120 |
| n _____ | ------ | -- | ------ | ------ | -- | ------ | ------ | ------ |
| id _____ | 10 | 29 | 290 | ------ | -- | ------ | 10 | 290 |
| nison _____ | ------ | -- | ------ | ------ | -- | ------ | ------ | ------ |
| dale _____ | ------ | -- | ------ | ------ | -- | ------ | ------ | ------ |
| rfano _____ | 860 | 27 | 23,220 | 4,500 | 12 | 54,000 | 5,360 | 77,220 |
| son _____ | ------ | -- | ------ | ------ | -- | ------ | ------ | ------ |
| rson _____ | 3,140 | 25 | 78,500 | 1,690 | 9 | 15,210 | 4,830 | 93,710 |
| a _____ | ------ | -- | ------ | 76,550 | 9 | 688,950 | 76,550 | 688,950 |
| Carson ____ | ------ | -- | ------ | 171,300 | 9 | 1,541,700 | 171,300 | 1,541,700 |
| lata _____ | 660 | 27 | 17,820 | 1,680 | 12 | 20,160 | 2,340 | 37,980 |
| er _____ | 8,110 | 27 | 218,970 | 5,590 | 9 | 50,310 | 13,700 | 269,280 |
| Animas_____ | 4,060 | 31 | 125,860 | 37,360 | 10 | 373,600 | 41,420 | 499,460 |
| ln _____ | ------ | -- | ------ | 89,350 | 7 | 625,450 | 89,350 | 625,450 |
| 1 _____ | 10,360 | 28 | 290,080 | 106,040 | 9 | 954,360 | 116,400 | 1,244,440 |
| _____ | 8,800 | 39 | 343,200 | 470 | 9 | 4,230 | 9,270 | 347,430 |
| 'al _____ | 10 | 29 | 290 | 1,630 | 12 | 19,560 | 1,640 | 19,850 |
| t _____ | 1,200 | 25 | 30,000 | 4,930 | 10 | 49,300 | 6,130 | 79,300 |
| ezuma _____ | 4,670 | 36 | 168,120 | ------ | -- | ------ | 4,670 | 168,120 |
| rose _____ | 9,410 | 32 | 301,120 | 72,380 | 7 | 506,660 | 81,790 | 807,780 |
| an _____ | 9,400 | 19 | 178,600 | 1,360 | 11 | 14,960 | 10,760 | 193,560 |
| y _____ | ------ | -- | ------ | 260 | 10 | 2,600 | 260 | 2,600 |
| ips _____ | ------ | -- | ------ | 82,920 | 11 | 912,120 | 82,920 | 912,120 |
| n _____ | ------ | -- | ------ | ------ | -- | ------ | ------ | ------ |
| ers _____ | 11,750 | 15 | 176,250 | 19,410 | 9 | 174,690 | 31,160 | 350,940 |
| lo _____ | 11,240 | 25 | 281,000 | 18,640 | 10 | 186,400 | 29,880 | 467,400 |
| Blanco ____ | ------ | -- | ------ | ------ | -- | ------ | ------ | ------ |
| Grande ____ | 30 | 13 | 390 | ------ | -- | ------ | 30 | 390 |
| t _____ | ------ | -- | ------ | ------ | -- | ------ | ------ | ------ |
| ache _____ | 10 | 11 | 110 | ------ | -- | ------ | 10 | 110 |
| Juan _____ | | | | | | | | |
| Miguel ____ | 80 | 34 | 2,720 | 300 | 10 | 3,000 | 380 | 5,720 |
| wick _____ | 2,470 | 26 | 64,220 | 33,840 | 10 | 338,400 | 36,310 | 402,620 |
| mit _____ | ------ | -- | ------ | ------ | -- | ------ | ------ | ------ |
| r _____ | ------ | -- | ------ | 40 | 13 | 520 | 40 | 520 |
| ington ___ | 480 | 29 | 13,920 | 160,050 | 9 | 1,440,450 | 160,530 | 1,454,370 |
| _____ | 26,150 | 32 | 836,800 | 75,230 | 7 | 526,610 | 101,380 | 1,363,410 |
| i _____ | 270 | 28 | 7,560 | 267,070 | 9 | 2,403,630 | 267,340 | 2,411,190 |
| te _____ | 156,720 | -- | 4,349,540 | 1,679,280 | -- | 14,928,460 | 1,836,000 | 19,278,000 |

## ACREAGE AND PRODUCTION OF OATS, 1931

| COUNTY | IRRIGATED | | | NON-IRRIGATED | | | TOTAL | |
|---|---|---|---|---|---|---|---|---|
| | Acreage | Average Yield | Production Bushels | Acreage | Average Yield | Production Bushels | Acreage | Product Bushel |
| Adams --------- | 1,280 | 34 | 43,520 | 320 | 9 | 2,880 | 1,600 | 46,4 |
| Alamosa ------ | 2,070 | 23 | 47,610 | ------ | -- | ------ | 2,070 | 47,6 |
| Arapahoe ----- | 1,170 | 38 | 44,460 | 1,240 | 9 | 11,160 | 2,410 | 55,6 |
| Archuleta ----- | 390 | ·39 | 15,210 | 1,770 | 11 | 19,470 | 2,160 | 34,6 |
| Baca --------- | 80 | 35 | 2,800 | 120 | 13 | 1,560 | 200 | 4,3 |
| Bent --------- | 790 | 35 | 27,650 | 10 | 11 | 110 | 800 | 27,7 |
| Boulder ------- | 5,260 | 43 | 226,180 | 50 | 15 | 750 | 5,310 | 226,9 |
| Chaffee ------- | 610 | 23 | 14,030 | 10 | 13 | 130 | 620 | 14,1 |
| Cheyenne ----- | ------ | -- | ------ | 790 | 9 | 7,110 | 790 | 7,1 |
| Clear Creek---- | ------ | -- | ------ | 10 | 12 | 120 | 10 | |
| Conejos ------- | 2,350 | 36 | 84,600 | ------ | -- | ------ | 2,350 | 84,6 |
| Costilla ------- | 900 | 37 | 33,300 | ------ | -- | ------ | 900 | 33,3 |
| Crowley ------- | 440 | 26 | 11,440 | 60 | 9 | 540 | 500 | 11,9 |
| Custer -------- | 400 | 31 | 12,400 | 810 | 14 | 11,340 | 1,210 | 23,7 |
| Delta --------- | 2,000 | 41 | 82,000 | ------ | -- | ------ | 2,000 | 82,0 |
| Denver -------- | ------ | -- | ------ | ------ | -- | ------ | ------ | ---- |
| Dolores ------- | ------ | -- | ------ | 500 | 7 | 3,500 | 500 | 3,5 |
| Douglas ------ | 160 | 39 | 6,240 | 6,860 | 11 | 75,460 | 7,020 | 81,7 |
| Eagle --------- | 1,180 | 44 | 51,920 | 20 | 16 | 320 | 1,200 | 52,2 |
| Elbert -------- | ------ | -- | ------ | 5,900 | 8 | 47,200 | 5,900 | 47,2 |
| El Paso ------- | 30 | 39 | 1,170 | 8,310 | 10 | 83,100 | 8,340 | 84,2 |
| Fremont ------- | 430 | 36 | 15,480 | 650 | 15 | 9,750 | 1,080 | 25,2 |
| Garfield ------- | 1,910 | 42 | 80,220 | 190 | 9 | 1,710 | 2,100 | 81,9 |
| Gilpin -------- | ------ | -- | ------ | 60 | 14 | 840 | 60 | 8 |
| Grand -------- | 670 | 35 | 23,450 | 70 | 14 | 980 | 740 | 24,4 |
| Gunnison ----- | 90 | 35 | 3,150 | 260 | 13 | 3,380 | 350 | 6,5 |
| Hinsdale ------ | 60 | 39 | 2,340 | ------ | -- | ------ | 60 | 2,3 |
| Huerfano ----- | 460 | 41 | 18,860 | 660 | 14 | 9,240 | 1,120 | 28,1 |
| Jackson ------- | 50 | 34 | 1,700 | 60 | 14 | 840 | 110 | 2,5 |
| Jefferson ------ | 1,860 | 36 | 66,960 | 1,910 | 14 | 26,740 | 3,770 | 93,7 |
| Kiowa --------- | ------ | -- | ------ | 80 | 8 | 640 | 80 | |
| Kit Carson----- | ------ | -- | ------ | 3,740 | 10 | 37,400 | 3,740 | 37, |
| Lake --------- | ------ | -- | ------ | ------ | -- | ------ | ------ | ---- |
| La Plata ------- | 3,380 | 45 | 152,100 | 940 | 12 | 11,280 | 4,320 | 163,3 |
| Larimer ------- | 4,380 | 42 | 183,960 | 630 | 17 | 10,710 | 5,010 | 194,6 |
| Las Animas --- | 870 | 36 | 31,320 | 1,720 | 9 | 15,480 | 2,590 | 46,8 |
| Lincoln ------- | ------ | -- | ------ | 500 | 9 | 4,500 | 500 | 4,5 |
| Logan -------- | 2,220 | 40 | 88,800 | 3,570 | 7 | 24,990 | 5,790 | 113,7 |
| Mesa --------- | 1,960 | 38 | 74,480 | 200 | 9 | 1,800 | 2,160 | 76,2 |
| Mineral ------- | ------ | -- | ------ | ------ | -- | ------ | ------ | ---- |
| Moffat -------- | 400 | 24 | 9,600 | 3,140 | 19 | 59,660 | 3,540 | 69,2 |
| Montezuma ---- | 3,660 | 34 | 124,440 | 1,580 | 13 | 20,540 | 5,240 | 144,9 |
| Montrose ------ | 3,610 | 36 | 129,960 | 70 | 14 | 980 | 3,680 | 130,9 |
| Morgan ------- | 1,200 | 44 | 52,800 | 840 | 8 | 6,720 | 2,040 | 59,5 |
| Otero --------- | 1,690 | 38 | 64,220 | 10 | 13 | 130 | 1,700 | 64,3 |
| Ouray -------- | 790 | 39 | 30,810 | 110 | 11 | 1,210 | 900 | 32,0 |
| Park --------- | ------ | -- | ------ | 130 | 11 | 1,430 | 130 | 1,4 |
| Phillips ------- | ------ | -- | ------ | 6,400 | 11 | 70,400 | 6,400 | 70,4 |
| Pitkin -------- | 420 | 34 | 14,280 | ------ | -- | ------ | 420 | 14,2 |
| Prowers ------- | 1,090 | 35 | 38,150 | 510 | 11 | 5,610 | 1,600 | 43,7 |
| Pueblo -------- | 870 | 34 | 29,580 | 740 | 11 | 8,140 | 1,610 | 37,7 |
| Rio Blanco----- | 1,540 | 41 | 63,140 | 530 | 16 | 8,480 | 2,070 | 71,6 |
| Rio Grande ---- | 3,710 | 22 | 81,620 | ------ | -- | ------ | 3,710 | 81,6 |
| Routt --------- | 230 | 37 | 8,510 | 8,770 | 16 | 140,320 | 9,000 | 148,8 |
| Saguache ------ | 2,260 | 15 | 33,900 | ------ | -- | ------ | 2,260 | 33,9 |
| San Juan ------ | ------ | -- | ------ | ------ | -- | ------ | ------ | --- |
| San Miguel ---- | 150 | 41 | 6,150 | 150 | 13 | 1,950 | 300 | 8,1 |
| Sedgwick ----- | 860 | 39 | 33,540 | 3,350 | 11 | 36,850 | 4,210 | 70, |
| Summit ------- | 40 | 29 | 1,160 | 50 | 14 | 700 | 90 | 1,8 |
| Teller -------- | ------ | -- | ------ | 390 | 13 | 5,070 | 390 | 5,0 |
| Washington --- | 220 | 41 | 9,020 | 3,300 | 7 | 23,100 | 3,520 | 32,1 |
| Weld --------- | 9,120 | 38 | 346,560 | 3,110 | 9 | 27,990 | 12,230 | 374,5 |
| Yuma --------- | ------ | -- | ------ | 3,490 | 10 | 34,900 | 3,490 | 34,9 |
| State ------- | 69,310 | -- | 2,524,790 | 78,690 | -- | 879,210 | 148,000 | |

## ACREAGE AND PRODUCTION OF BARLEY, 1931

| OUNTY | IRRIGATED | | | NON-IRRIGATED | | | TOTAL | |
|---|---|---|---|---|---|---|---|---|
| | Acreage | Average Yield | Production Bushels | Acreage | Average Yield | Production Bushels | Acreage | Production Bushels |
| ms _____ | 2,910 | 37 | 107,670 | 9,570 | 7 | 66,990 | 12,480 | 174,660 |
| nosa _____ | 2,410 | 24 | 57,840 | ------ | -- | ------ | 2,410 | 57,840 |
| )ahoe _____ | 1,140 | 37 | 42,180 | 8,390 | 7 | 58,730 | 9,530 | 100,910 |
| iuleta _____ | 120 | 32 | 3,840 | 190 | 8 | 1,520 | 310 | 5,360 |
| i _____ | 270 | 27 | 7,290 | 6,610 | 7 | 46,270 | 6,880 | 53,560 |
| ; _____ | 4,580 | 27 | 123,660 | 180 | 6 | 1,080 | 4,760 | 124,740 |
| ider _____ | 8,920 | 35 | 312,200 | 500 | 11 | 5,500 | 9,420 | 317,700 |
| fee _____ | 1,170 | 22 | 25,740 | 10 | 12 | 120 | 1,180 | 25,860 |
| 'enne _____ | ------ | -- | ------ | 11,730 | 8 | 93,840 | 11,730 | 93,840 |
| r Creek____ | ------ | -- | ------ | ------ | -- | ------ | ------ | ------ |
| :jos _____ | 7,100 | 26 | 184,600 | ------ | -- | ------ | 7,100 | 184,600 |
| illa _____ | 3,150 | 26 | 81,900 | ------ | -- | ------ | 3,150 | 81,900 |
| vley _____ | 1,200 | 23 | 27,600 | 40 | 6 | 240 | 1,240 | 27,840 |
| er _____ | 440 | 15 | 6,600 | 430 | 9 | 3,870 | 870 | 10,470 |
| a _____ | 2,040 | 36 | 73,440 | ------ | -- | ------ | 2,040 | 73,440 |
| ver _____ | ------ | -- | ------ | 110 | 8 | 880 | 110 | 880 |
| res _____ | ------ | -- | ------ | | | | | |
| zlas _____ | 150 | 29 | 4,350 | 1,260 | 9 | 11,340 | 1,410 | 15,690 |
| le _____ | 500 | 33 | 16,500 | 60 | 12 | 720 | 560 | 17,220 |
| rt _____ | ------ | -- | ------ | 7,980 | 7 | 55,860 | 7,980 | 55,860 |
| Paso_____ | 140 | 28 | 3,920 | 1,180 | 7 | 8,260 | 1,320 | 12,180 |
| nont _____ | 260 | 18 | 4,680 | 130 | 7 | 910 | 390 | 5,590 |
| ield _____ | 1,750 | 28 | 49,000 | 170 | 12 | 2,040 | 1,920 | 51,040 |
| in _____ | ------ | -- | ------ | 10 | 12 | 120 | 10 | 120 |
| id _____ | 320 | 32 | 10,240 | 60 | 12 | 720 | 380 | 10,960 |
| nison _____ | 100 | 30 | 3,000 | 170 | 12 | 2,040 | 270 | 5,040 |
| sdale _____ | ------ | -- | ------ | ------ | -- | ------ | ------ | ------ |
| rfano _____ | 130 | 27 | 3,510 | 190 | 8 | 1,520 | 320 | 5,030 |
| :son _____ | 50 | 21 | 1,050 | ------ | -- | ------ | 50 | 1,050 |
| :rson _____ | 3,180 | 31 | 98,580 | 780 | 10 | 7,800 | 3,960 | 106,380 |
| va _____ | ------ | -- | ------ | 4,280 | 6 | 25,680 | 4,280 | 25,680 |
| Carson ____ | 120 | 25 | 3,000 | 58,180 | 7 | 407,260 | 58,300 | 410,260 |
| e _____ | ------ | -- | ------ | ------ | -- | ------ | ------ | ------ |
| Plata_____ | 1,920 | 36 | 69,120 | 560 | 8 | 4,480 | 2,480 | 73,600 |
| imer _____ | 13,990 | 39 | 545,610 | 2,140 | 10 | 21,400 | 16,130 | 567,010 |
| Animas ___ | 1,680 | 25 | 42,000 | 2,990 | 7 | 20,930 | 4,670 | 62,930 |
| :oln _____ | 80 | 27 | 2,160 | 19,390 | 6 | 116,340 | 19,470 | 118,500 |
| an _____ | 9,750 | 27 | 263,250 | 32,260 | 6 | 193,560 | 42,010 | 456,810 |
| a _____ | 1,660 | 27 | 44,820 | 60 | 11 | 660 | 1,720 | 45,480 |
| eral _____ | ------ | -- | ------ | ------ | -- | ------ | ------ | ------ |
| 'at _____ | 140 | 34 | 4,760 | 880 | 13 | 11,440 | 1,020 | 16,200 |
| tezuma ____ | 950 | 25 | 23,750 | 970 | 10 | 9,700 | 1,920 | 33,450 |
| trose _____ | 2,220 | 32 | 71,040 | 100 | 10 | 1,000 | 2,320 | 72,040 |
| gan _____ | 8,300 | 39 | 323,700 | 7,540 | 6 | 45,240 | 15,840 | 368,940 |
| :o _____ | 3,320 | 26 | 86,320 | 160 | 6 | 960 | 3,480 | 87,280 |
| ay _____ | 150 | 23 | 5,750 | 260 | 8 | 2,080 | 410 | 7,830 |
| k _____ | ------ | -- | ------ | 20 | 12 | 240 | 20 | 240 |
| lips _____ | ------ | -- | ------ | 16,620 | 7 | 116,340 | 16,620 | 116,340 |
| :in _____ | 60 | 32 | 1,920 | ------ | -- | ------ | 60 | 1,920 |
| vers _____ | 5,590 | 23 | 128,570 | 4,910 | 7 | 34,370 | 10,500 | 162,940 |
| blo _____ | 2,310 | 26 | 60,060 | 680 | 6 | 4,080 | 2,990 | 64,140 |
| Blanco_____ | 90 | 34 | 3,060 | 370 | 15 | 5,550 | 460 | 8,610 |
| Grande ____ | 4,960 | 17 | 84,320 | ------ | -- | ------ | 4,960 | 84,320 |
| tt _____ | 50 | 31 | 1,550 | 4,360 | 14 | 61,040 | 4,410 | 62,590 |
| iache _____ | 1,810 | 14 | 25,340 | ------ | -- | ------ | 1,810 | 25,340 |
| Juan _____ | ------ | -- | ------ | ------ | -- | ------ | ------ | ------ |
| Miguel____ | 100 | 22 | 2,200 | 470 | 9 | 4,230 | 570 | 6,430 |
| rwick _____ | 2,490 | 29 | 72,210 | 12,230 | 7 | 85,610 | 14,720 | 157,820 |
| imit _____ | 10 | 24 | 240 | 70 | 10 | 700 | 80 | 940 |
| er _____ | ------ | -- | ------ | 90 | 12 | 1,080 | 90 | 1,080 |
| ihington ___ | 820 | 35 | 28,700 | 44,840 | 7 | 313,880 | 45,660 | 342,580 |
| d _____ | 44,840 | 39 | 1,748,760 | 25,120 | 7 | 175,840 | 69,960 | 1,924,600 |
| na _____ | ------ | -- | ------ | 19,260 | 9 | 173,340 | 19,260 | 173,340 |
| tate _____ | 149,440 | -- | 4,891,600 | 308,560 | -- | 2,207,400 | 458,000 | 7,099,000 |

## ACREAGE AND PRODUCTION OF POTATOES, 1931

| COUNTY | IRRIGATED | | | NON-IRRIGATED | | | TOTAL | |
|---|---|---|---|---|---|---|---|---|
| | Acreage | Average Yield | Production Bushels | Acreage | Average Yield | Production Bushels | Acreage | Producti Bushel |
| Adams | 210 | 85 | 17,850 | 30 | 51 | 1,530 | 240 | 19,3 |
| Alamosa | 5,640 | 62 | 349,680 | ------ | -- | ------ | 5,640 | 349,6 |
| Arapahoe | 5 | 120 | 600 | 10 | 60 | 600 | 15 | 1,2 |
| Archuleta | 80 | 120 | 9,600 | 330 | 60 | 19,800 | 410 | 29,4 |
| Baca | ------ | -- | ------ | 5 | 50 | 250 | 5 | 2 |
| Bent | ------ | -- | ------ | 5 | 40 | 200 | 5 | 2 |
| Boulder | 245 | 135 | 33,075 | 5 | 55 | 275 | 250 | 33,3 |
| Chaffee | 465 | 70 | 32,550 | ------ | -- | ------ | 465 | 32,5 |
| Cheyenne | ------ | -- | ------ | 65 | 30 | 1,950 | 65 | 1,9 |
| Clear Creek | 5 | 60 | 300 | 30 | 40 | 1,200 | 35 | 1,5 |
| Conejos | 7,180 | 75 | 538,500 | ------ | -- | ------ | 7,180 | 538,5 |
| Costilla | 1,670 | 50 | 83,500 | ------ | -- | ------ | 1,670 | 83,5 |
| Crowley | ------ | -- | ------ | 5 | 40 | 200 | 5 | 2 |
| Custer | 215 | 70 | 15,050 | 3,405 | 37 | 125,985 | 3,620 | 141,0 |
| Delta | 1,290 | 136 | 175,440 | ------ | -- | ------ | 1,290 | 175,4 |
| Denver | ------ | -- | ------ | | | | | |
| Dolores | ------ | -- | ------ | 195 | 65 | 12,675 | 195 | 12,6 |
| Douglas | ------ | -- | ------ | 290 | 30 | 8,700 | 290 | 8,7 |
| Eagle | 1,145 | 150 | 171,750 | 10 | 60 | 600 | 1,155 | 172,3 |
| Elbert | ------ | -- | ------ | 775 | 35 | 27,125 | 775 | 27,1 |
| El Paso | 5 | 80 | 400 | 760 | 45 | 34,200 | 765 | 34,6 |
| Fremont | 20 | 65 | 1,300 | 240 | 35 | 8,400 | 260 | 9,7 |
| Garfield | 2,860 | 152 | 434,720 | 60 | 60 | 3,600 | 2,920 | 438,3 |
| Gilpin | ------ | -- | ------ | 80 | 45 | 3,600 | 80 | 3,6 |
| Grand | 20 | 70 | 1,400 | 110 | 35 | 3,850 | 130 | 5,2 |
| Gunnison | 70 | 70 | 4,900 | 135 | 32 | 4,320 | 205 | 9,2 |
| Hinsdale | 5 | 120 | 600 | ------ | -- | ------ | 5 | 6 |
| Huerfano | .95 | 90 | 8,550 | 295 | 55 | 16,225 | 390 | 24,7 |
| Jackson | 10 | 80 | 800 | 60 | 55 | 3,300 | 70 | 4, |
| Jefferson | 235 | 130 | 30,550 | 370 | 70 | 25,900 | 605 | 56, |
| Kiowa | ------ | -- | ------ | 10 | 30 | 300 | 10 | |
| Kit Carson | ------ | -- | ------ | 590 | 40 | 23,600 | 590 | 23, |
| Lake | ------ | -- | ------ | ------ | -- | ------ | ------ | |
| La Plata | 1,375 | 150 | 206,250 | 30 | 67 | 2,010 | 1,405 | 208, |
| Larimer | 795 | 135 | 107,325 | 60 | 60 | 3,600 | 855 | 110, |
| Las Animas | 20 | 105 | 2,100 | 150 | 40 | 6,000 | 170 | 8, |
| Lincoln | ------ | -- | ------ | 340 | 45 | 15,300 | 340 | 15, |
| Logan | 370 | 90 | 33,300 | 1,040 | 60 | 62,400 | 1,410 | 95, |
| Mesa | 1,770 | 155 | 274,350 | 340 | 75 | 25,500 | 2,110 | 299, |
| Mineral | 5 | 75 | 375 | ------ | -- | ------ | 5 | |
| Moffat | 90 | 90 | 8,100 | 860 | 43 | 36,980 | 950 | 45, |
| Montezuma | 830 | 120 | 99,600 | 795 | 65 | 51,675 | 1,625 | 151, |
| Montrose | 5,180 | 172 | 890,960 | 50 | 60 | 3,000 | 5,230 | 893, |
| Morgan | 1,740 | 145 | 252,300 | 40 | 65 | 2,600 | 1,780 | 254, |
| Otero | 5 | 70 | 350 | ------ | -- | ------ | 5 | |
| Ouray | 165 | 135 | 22,275 | 90 | 62 | 5,580 | 255 | 27, |
| Park | ------ | -- | ------ | 1,830 | 40 | 73,200 | 1,830 | 73, |
| Phillips | ------ | -- | ------ | 125 | 50 | 6,250 | 125 | 6, |
| Pitkin | 865 | 140 | 121,100 | ------ | -- | ------ | 865 | 121, |
| Prowers | ------ | -- | ------ | 5 | 36 | 180 | 5 | |
| Pueblo | ------ | -- | ------ | 20 | 47 | 940 | 20 | |
| Rio Blanco | 75 | 70 | 5,250 | 20 | 40 | 800 | 95 | 6 |
| Rio Grande | 14,630 | 77 | 1,126,510 | ------ | -- | ------ | 14,630 | 1,126 |
| Routt | 50 | 65 | 3,250 | 1,140 | 35 | 39,900 | 1,190 | 43 |
| Saguache | 7,100 | 72 | 511,200 | ------ | -- | ------ | 7,100 | 511 |
| San Juan | ------ | -- | ------ | | | | ------ | |
| San Miguel | 20 | 145 | 2,900 | 170 | 74 | 12,580 | 190 | 15 |
| Sedgwick | 560 | 95 | 53,200 | 180 | 45 | 8,100 | 740 | 61 |
| Summit | ------ | -- | ------ | 30 | 40 | 1,200 | 30 | 1 |
| Teller | ------ | -- | ------ | 1,875 | 40 | 75,000 | 1,875 | 75 |
| Washington | 15 | 70 | 1,050 | 330 | 37 | 12,210 | 345 | 13 |
| Weld | 25,350 | 123 | 3,118,050 | 780 | 70 | 54,600 | 26,130 | 3,172 |
| Yuma | 30 | 110 | 3,300 | 320 | 40 | 12,800 | 350 | 16 |
| State | 82,510 | -- | 8,754,210 | 18,490 | -- | 840,790 | 101,000 | |

## ACREAGE AND PRODUCTION OF SUGAR BEETS AND RYE, 1931

| COUNTY | SUGAR BEETS | | | RYE FOR GRAIN | | | Acreage Rye for Pasture | Total Rye Acreage |
|---|---|---|---|---|---|---|---|---|
| | Acreage | Average Yield | Production Tons | Acreage | Average Yield | Production Bushels | | |
| Adams | 11,350 | 11.3 | 128,260 | 660 | 8 | 5,280 | 520 | 1,180 |
| Alamosa | 680 | 4.1 | 2,790 | ----- | -- | ------ | ----- | ------ |
| Arapahoe | 1,170 | 12.2 | 14,270 | 780 | 10 | 7,800 | 330 | 1,110 |
| Archuleta | ----- | --- | ------ | ----- | -- | ------ | ----- | ------ |
| Baca | ----- | --- | ------ | 670 | 8 | 5,360 | 120 | 790 |
| Bent | 4,320 | 7.0 | 30,240 | 30 | 10 | 300 | 15 | 45 |
| Boulder | 10,590 | 11.2 | 118,610 | ----- | -- | ------ | 30 | 30 |
| Chaffee | ----- | --- | ------ | ----- | -- | ------ | ----- | ------ |
| Cheyenne | ----- | --- | ------ | 110 | 7 | 770 | 50 | 160 |
| Clear Creek | ----- | --- | ------ | ----- | -- | ------ | ----- | ------ |
| Conejos | 50 | 6.9 | 340 | ----- | -- | ------ | ----- | ------ |
| Costilla | ----- | --- | ------ | ----- | -- | ------ | ----- | ------ |
| Crowley | 5,790 | 3.5 | 20,260 | 25 | 8 | 200 | 5 | 30 |
| Custer | ----- | --- | ------ | 35 | 10 | 350 | 60 | 95 |
| Delta | 2,320 | 12.6 | 29,230 | ----- | -- | ------ | ----- | ------ |
| Denver | ----- | --- | ------ | ----- | -- | ------ | ----- | ------ |
| Dolores | ----- | --- | ------ | ----- | -- | ------ | 60 | 60 |
| Douglas | ----- | --- | ------ | 2,225 | 8 | 17,800 | 350 | 2,575 |
| Eagle | ----- | --- | ------ | ----- | -- | ------ | ----- | ------ |
| Elbert | ----- | --- | ------ | 3,220 | 7 | 22,540 | 860 | 4,080 |
| El Paso | 1,110 | 8.7 | 9,660 | 3,540 | 7 | 24,780 | 1,225 | 4,765 |
| Fremont | ----- | --- | ------ | 10 | 9 | 90 | 40 | 50 |
| Garfield | 1,720 | 10.3 | 17,720 | 15 | 8 | 120 | 30 | 45 |
| Gilpin | ----- | --- | ------ | ----- | -- | ------ | ----- | ------ |
| Grand | ----- | --- | ------ | 50 | 10 | 500 | 30 | 80 |
| Gunnison | ----- | --- | ------ | 15 | 8 | 120 | 5 | 20 |
| Hinsdale | ----- | --- | ------ | ----- | -- | ------ | ----- | ------ |
| Huerfano | 40 | 13.4 | 540 | 5 | 8 | 40 | 30 | 35 |
| Jackson | ----- | --- | ------ | ----- | -- | ------ | 10 | 10 |
| Jefferson | 740 | 12.8 | 9,470 | 70 | 7 | 490 | 20 | 90 |
| Kiowa | ----- | --- | ------ | 85 | 7 | 595 | ----- | 85 |
| Kit Carson | ----- | --- | ------ | 2,525 | 7 | 17,675 | 1,260 | 3,785 |
| Lake | ----- | --- | ------ | ----- | -- | ------ | ----- | ------ |
| La Plata | ----- | --- | ------ | 35 | 6 | 210 | 10 | 45 |
| Larimer | 22,190 | 12.9 | 286,250 | 250 | 8 | 2,000 | 50 | 300 |
| Las Animas | 1,190 | 10.4 | 12,380 | 260 | 8 | 2,080 | 160 | 420 |
| Lincoln | ----- | --- | ------ | 1,140 | 6 | 6,840 | 580 | 1,720 |
| Logan | 18,440 | 10.6 | 195,460 | 1,550 | 6 | 9,300 | 4,500 | 6,050 |
| Mesa | 1,730 | 11.2 | 19,380 | 35 | 8 | 280 | 30 | 65 |
| Mineral | ----- | --- | ------ | ----- | -- | ------ | ----- | ------ |
| Moffat | ----- | --- | ------ | 1,040 | 7 | 7,280 | 1,260 | 2,300 |
| Montezuma | ----- | --- | ------ | 75 | 7 | 525 | 20 | 95 |
| Montrose | 820 | 10.8 | 8,860 | 5 | 13 | 65 | 15 | 20 |
| Morgan | 23,190 | 11.8 | 273,640 | 1,275 | 6 | 7,650 | 3,650 | 4,925 |
| Otero | 11,690 | 7.8 | 91,180 | 40 | 11 | 440 | 20 | 60 |
| Ouray | ----- | --- | ------ | ----- | -- | ------ | ----- | ------ |
| Park | ----- | --- | ------ | ----- | -- | ------ | ----- | ------ |
| Phillips | ----- | --- | ------ | 1,220 | 7 | 8,540 | 2,260 | 3,480 |
| Pitkin | ----- | --- | ------ | 5 | 14 | 70 | 130 | 135 |
| Prowers | 7,890 | 5.6 | 44,180 | 160 | 8 | 1,280 | 35 | 195 |
| Pueblo | 7,540 | 10.6 | 79,920 | 50 | 10 | 500 | 65 | 115 |
| Rio Blanco | ----- | --- | ------ | 65 | 8 | 520 | 40 | 105 |
| Rio Grande | 80 | 6.2 | 500 | ----- | -- | ------ | ----- | ------ |
| Routt | ----- | --- | ------ | 150 | 12 | 1,800 | 30 | 180 |
| Saguache | ----- | --- | ------ | ----- | -- | ------ | ----- | ------ |
| San Juan | ----- | --- | ------ | ----- | -- | ------ | ----- | ------ |
| San Miguel | ----- | --- | ------ | 25 | 8 | 200 | 45 | 70 |
| Sedgwick | 4,880 | 11.1 | 54,170 | 550 | 6 | 3,300 | 1,200 | 1,750 |
| Summit | ----- | --- | ------ | 25 | 10 | 250 | 15 | 40 |
| Teller | ----- | --- | ------ | 10 | 15 | 150 | 80 | 90 |
| Washington | 460 | 12.7 | 5,840 | 3,845 | 6 | 23,070 | 2,880 | 6,725 |
| Weld | 86,020 | 12.6 | 1,083,850 | 5,550 | 7 | 38,850 | 5,560 | 11,110 |
| Yuma | ----- | --- | ------ | 21,570 | 7 | 150,990 | 2,315 | 23,885 |
| State | 226,000 | --- | 2,537,000 | 53,000 | -- | 371,000 | 30,000 | 83,000 |

ACREAGE AND PRODUCTION OF GRAIN AND SWEET SORGHUMS, 1931

| COUNTY | GRAIN SORGHUMS | | | SWEET SORGHUMS | | | Total Acreage All Sorghums |
|---|---|---|---|---|---|---|---|
| | Acreage | Average Yield | Production Bushels | Acreage | Average Yield | Production Tons | |
| Adams | 1,530 | 10 | 15,300 | 3,860 | 1.3 | 5,020 | 5,39 |
| Alamosa | | -- | | | -- | | |
| Arapahoe | 1,610 | 9 | 14,490 | 3,420 | 1.3 | 4,450 | 5,03 |
| Archuleta | | -- | | | -- | | |
| Baca | 66,720 | 12 | 800,640 | 3,830 | 1.6 | 6,130 | 70,55 |
| Bent | 12,390 | 11 | 136,290 | 950 | 1.2 | 1,140 | 13,34 |
| Boulder | | -- | | 10 | 1.5 | 20 | 1 |
| Chaffee | | | | | | | |
| Cheyenne | 12,050 | 13 | 156,650 | 5,660 | 1.5 | 8,490 | 17,71 |
| Clear Creek | | -- | | | -- | | |
| Conejos | | -- | | | -- | | |
| Costilla | | -- | | | -- | | |
| Crowley | 840 | 9 | 7,560 | 2,100 | 1.0 | 2,100 | 2,94 |
| Custer | 25 | 12 | 300 | | -- | | 2 |
| Delta | 5 | 11 | 55 | 5 | 1.5 | 10 | 1 |
| Denver | | -- | | | -- | | |
| Dolores | 25 | 12 | 300 | 115 | 1.5 | 170 | 14 |
| Douglas | 110 | 10 | 1,100 | 640 | 1.3 | 830 | 75 |
| Eagle | | -- | | | -- | | |
| Elbert | 770 | 10 | 7,700 | 3,370 | 1.1 | 3,710 | 4,14 |
| El Paso | 1,210 | 10 | 12,100 | 4,420 | 1.3 | 5,750 | 5,63 |
| Fremont | 20 | 11 | 220 | 50 | 1.4 | 70 | 7 |
| Garfield | 10 | 12 | 120 | 15 | 1.5 | 20 | 2 |
| Gilpin | | -- | | | -- | | |
| Grand | | -- | | | -- | | |
| Gunnison | | -- | | | -- | | |
| Hinsdale | | -- | | | -- | | |
| Huerfano | 30 | 12 | 360 | 270 | 1.0 | 270 | 30 |
| Jackson | | -- | | | -- | | |
| Jefferson | 75 | 12 | 900 | 25 | 1.5 | 40 | 10 |
| Kiowa | 10,420 | 12 | 125,040 | 17,215 | 1.3 | 22,380 | 27,63 |
| Kit Carson | 11,660 | 12 | 139,920 | 9,490 | 1.5 | 14,240 | 21,15 |
| Lake | | -- | | | -- | | |
| La Plata | 30 | 10 | 300 | 60 | 1.5 | 90 | 9 |
| Larimer | 130 | 11 | 1,430 | 310 | 1.5 | 460 | 44 |
| Las Animas | 5,560 | 10 | 55,600 | 2,680 | 1.2 | 3,220 | 8,24 |
| Lincoln | 12,650 | 9 | 113,850 | 6,775 | 1.1 | 7,440 | 19,42 |
| Logan | 2,140 | 10 | 21,400 | 7,530 | 1.7 | 12,800 | 9,67 |
| Mesa | 145 | 11 | 1,595 | 95 | 1. | 140 | 24 |
| Mineral | | -- | | | -- | | |
| Moffat | 20 | 12 | 240 | 150 | 1 | 210 | 17 |
| Montezuma | 225 | 9 | 2,025 | 215 | 1:6 | 320 | 44 |
| Montrose | 5 | 10 | 50 | | -- | | |
| Morgan | 2,690 | 10 | 26,900 | 3,590 | 1.5 | 5,380 | 6,28 |
| Otero | 1,220 | 12 | 14,640 | 410 | 1.5 | 620 | 1,6 |
| Ouray | | -- | | | -- | | |
| Park | | -- | | | -- | | |
| Phillips | 960 | 10 | 9,600 | 5,220 | 1.5 | 7,830 | 6,11 |
| Pitkin | | -- | | | -- | | |
| Prowers | 22,500 | 10 | 225,000 | 4,650 | 1.5 | 6,980 | 27,1 |
| Pueblo | 2,560 | 8 | 20,480 | 730 | 1.4 | 1,020 | 3,2 |
| Rio Blanco | | -- | | | -- | | |
| Rio Grande | | -- | | | -- | | |
| Routt | | -- | | | -- | | |
| Saguache | | -- | | | -- | | |
| San Juan | | -- | | | -- | | |
| San Miguel | 45 | 11 | 495 | 5 | 1.5 | 10 | |
| Sedgwick | 330 | 11 | 3,630 | 420 | 1.4 | 580 | 7 |
| Summit | | -- | | | -- | | |
| Teller | | -- | | | -- | | |
| Washington | 6,470 | 9 | 58,230 | 7,555 | 1.3 | 9,820 | 14,0 |
| Weld | 2,110 | 10 | 21,100 | 5,680 | 1.5 | 8,520 | 7,7 |
| Yuma | 11,710 | 9 | 105,390 | 16,480 | 1.5 | 24,720 | 28,1 |
| State | 191,000 | -- | 2,101,000 | 118,000 | -- | 165,000 | 309,0 |

## ACREAGE AND PRODUCTION OF DRY BEANS, 1931

| COUNTY | IRRIGATED | | | NON-IRRIGATED | | | TOTAL | |
|---|---|---|---|---|---|---|---|---|
| | Acreage | Average Yield | Production Pounds | Acreage | Average Yield | Production Pounds | Acreage | Production Pounds |
| Adams _____ | 510 | 610 | 311,100 | 25,080 | 182 | 4,564,560 | 25,590 | 4,875,660 |
| Alamosa _____ | 10 | 650 | 6,500 | ------ | --- | ------ | 10 | 6,500 |
| Arapahoe _____ | 200 | 700 | 140,000 | 20,140 | 230 | 4,632,200 | 20,340 | 4,772,200 |
| Archuleta _____ | ------ | --- | ------ | 40 | 251 | 10,040 | 40 | 10,040 |
| Baca _____ | 60 | 510 | 30,600 | 6,050 | 300 | 1,815,000 | 6,110 | 1,845,600 |
| Bent _____ | 290 | 550 | 159,500 | 1,790 | 210 | 375,900 | 2,080 | 535,400 |
| Boulder _____ | 100 | 610 | 61,000 | 320 | 130 | 41,600 | 420 | 102,600 |
| Chaffee _____ | 40 | 460 | 18,400 | ------ | --- | ------ | 40 | 18,400 |
| Cheyenne _____ | ------ | --- | ------ | 980 | 220 | 215,600 | 980 | 215,600 |
| Clear Creek____ | ------ | --- | ------ | ------ | --- | ------ | ------ | ------- |
| Conejos _____ | 540 | 830 | 448,200 | ------ | --- | ------ | 540 | 448,200 |
| Costilla _____ | 420 | 620 | 260,400 | ------ | --- | ------ | 420 | 260,400 |
| Crowley _____ | 300 | 520 | 156,000 | 2,440 | 250 | 610,000 | 2,740 | 766,000 |
| Custer _____ | ------ | --- | ------ | ------ | --- | ------ | ------ | ------- |
| Delta _____ | 130 | 730 | 94,900 | 30 | 240 | 7,200 | 160 | 102,100 |
| Denver _____ | ------ | --- | ------ | | | | | |
| Dolores _____ | ------ | --- | ------ | 1,070 | 250 | 267,500 | 1,070 | 267,500 |
| Douglas _____ | ------ | --- | ------ | 1,690 | 210 | 354,900 | 1,690 | 354,900 |
| Eagle _____ | ------ | --- | ------ | | | | | |
| Elbert _____ | ------ | --- | ------ | 51,020 | 220 | 11,224,400 | 51,020 | 11,224,400 |
| El Paso _____ | 410 | 630 | 258,300 | 40,330 | 240 | 9,679,200 | 40,740 | 9,937,500 |
| Fremont _____ | 10 | 410 | 4,100 | 30 | 160 | 4,800 | 40 | 8,900 |
| Garfield _____ | 30 | 710 | 21,300 | ------ | --- | ------ | 30 | 21,300 |
| Gilpin _____ | ------ | --- | ------ | 20 | 260 | 5,200 | 20 | 5,200 |
| Grand _____ | ------ | --- | ------ | ------ | --- | ------ | ------ | ------- |
| Gunnison _____ | ------ | --- | ------ | ------ | --- | ------ | ------ | ------- |
| Hinsdale _____ | ------ | --- | ------ | ------ | --- | ------ | ------ | ------- |
| Huerfano _____ | 90 | 410 | 36,900 | 1,220 | 260 | 317,200 | 1,310 | 354,100 |
| Jackson _____ | ------ | --- | ------ | | | | | |
| Jefferson _____ | 40 | 610 | 24,400 | 70 | 120 | 8,400 | 110 | 32,800 |
| Kiowa _____ | ------ | --- | ------ | 450 | 200 | 90,000 | 450 | 90,000 |
| Kit Carson ____ | 30 | 580 | 17,400 | 3,090 | 200 | 618,000 | 3,120 | 635,400 |
| Lake _____ | ------ | --- | ------ | | | | | |
| La Plata _____ | 80 | 420 | 33,600 | 640 | 280 | 179,200 | 720 | 212,800 |
| Larimer _____ | 710 | 550 | 390,500 | 680 | 160 | 108,800 | 1,390 | 499,300 |
| Las Animas____ | 2,750 | 630 | 1,732,500 | 13,450 | 310 | 4,169,500 | 16,200 | 5,902,000 |
| Lincoln _____ | ------ | --- | ------ | 26,040 | 170 | 4,426,800 | 26,040 | 4,426,800 |
| Logan _____ | 320 | 480 | 153,600 | 4,300 | 240 | 1,032,000 | 4,620 | 1,185,600 |
| Mesa _____ | 2,870 | 930 | 2,669,100 | 470 | 200 | 94,000 | 3,340 | 2,763,100 |
| Mineral _____ | ------ | --- | ------ | | | | | |
| Moffat _____ | ------ | --- | ------ | 70 | 300 | 21,000 | 70 | 21,000 |
| Montezuma ___ | 1,320 | 470 | 620,400 | 7,470 | 270 | 2,016,900 | 8,790 | 2,637,300 |
| Montrose _____ | 330 | 700 | 231,000 | 10 | 200 | 2,000 | 340 | 233,000 |
| Morgan _____ | 1,100 | 530 | 583,000 | 14,660 | 210 | 3,078,600 | 15,760 | 3,661,600 |
| Otero _____ | 2,780 | 580 | 1,612,400 | 120 | 250 | 30,000 | 2,900 | 1,642,400 |
| Ouray _____ | ------ | --- | ------ | 10 | 200 | 2,000 | 10 | 2,000 |
| Park _____ | ------ | --- | ------ | | | | | |
| Phillips _____ | ------ | --- | ------ | 210 | 250 | 52,500 | 210 | 52,500 |
| Pitkin _____ | ------ | --- | ------ | | | | | |
| Prowers _____ | 90 | 570 | 51,300 | 150 | 190 | 28,500 | 240 | 79,800 |
| Pueblo _____ | 1,530 | 520 | 795,600 | 13,710 | 140 | 1,919,400 | 15,240 | 2,715,000 |
| Rio Blanco ____ | ------ | --- | ------ | ------ | --- | ------ | ------ | ------- |
| Rio Grande ____ | 110 | 610 | 67,100 | ------ | --- | ------ | 110 | 67,100 |
| Routt _____ | ------ | --- | ------ | | | | | |
| Saguache _____ | 10 | 650 | 6,500 | ------ | --- | ------ | 10 | 6,500 |
| San Juan_____ | ------ | --- | ------ | | | | | |
| San Miguel ____ | ------ | --- | ------ | 230 | 210 | 48,300 | 230 | 48,300 |
| Sedgwick _____ | ------ | --- | ------ | 60 | 150 | 9,000 | 60 | 9,000 |
| Summit _____ | ------ | --- | ------ | ------ | --- | ------ | ------ | ------- |
| Teller _____ | ------ | ---- | ------ | ------ | --- | ------ | ------ | ------- |
| Washington ___ | ------ | --- | ------ | 16,520 | 180 | 2,973,600 | 16,520 | 2,973,600 |
| Weld _____ | 13,160 | 780 | 10,264,800 | 33,850 | 180 | 6,093,000 | 47,010 | 16,357,800 |
| Yuma _____ | ------ | --- | ------ | 1,120 | 190 | 212,800 | 1,120 | 212,800 |
| State _____ | 30,370 | --- | 21,260,400 | 289,630 | --- | 61,339,600 | 320,000 | 82,600,000 |

### ACREAGE AND PRODUCTION OF BROOMCORN, 1931, 1930 AND 1929

| COUNTY | 1931 | | | 1930 | | | 1929 | | |
|---|---|---|---|---|---|---|---|---|---|
| | Acreage | Average Yield | Production Pounds | Acreage | Average Yield | Production Pounds | Acreage | Average Yield | Producti Pound |
| Adams | 20 | 190 | 3,800 | 25 | 260 | 6,500 | 35 | 300 | 10,5 |
| Alamosa | ----- | ----- | -------- | ----- | ------ | -------- | ----- | ------ | ------ |
| Arapahoe | ----- | ----- | -------- | ----- | ------ | -------- | ----- | ------ | ------ |
| Archuleta | ----- | ----- | -------- | ----- | ------ | -------- | ----- | ------ | ------ |
| Baca | 39,560 | 260 | 10,285,600 | 55,630 | 270 | 15,020,100 | 52,565 | 287 | 15,086,1 |
| Bent | 610 | 240 | 146,400 | 740 | 257 | 190,180 | 145 | 371 | 53,7 |
| Boulder | ----- | ----- | -------- | ----- | ------ | -------- | ----- | ------ | ------ |
| Chaffee | ----- | ----- | -------- | ----- | ------ | -------- | ----- | ------ | ------ |
| Cheyenne | ----- | ----- | -------- | 760 | 269 | 204,440 | ----- | ------ | ------ |
| Clear Creek | ----- | ----- | -------- | ----- | ------ | -------- | ----- | ------ | ------ |
| Conejos | ----- | ----- | -------- | ----- | ------ | -------- | ----- | ------ | ------ |
| Costilla | ----- | ----- | -------- | ----- | ------ | -------- | ----- | ------ | ------ |
| Crowley | ----- | ----- | -------- | ----- | ------ | -------- | ----- | ------ | ------ |
| Custer | ----- | ----- | -------- | ----- | ------ | -------- | ----- | ------ | ------ |
| Delta | 60 | 240 | 14,400 | ----- | ------ | -------- | ----- | ------ | ------ |
| Denver | ----- | ----- | -------- | ----- | ------ | -------- | ----- | ------ | ------ |
| Dolores | 10 | 230 | 2,300 | ----- | ------ | -------- | ----- | ------ | ------ |
| Douglas | ----- | ----- | -------- | ----- | ------ | -------- | ----- | ------ | ------ |
| Eagle | ----- | ----- | -------- | ----- | ------ | -------- | ----- | ------ | ------ |
| Elbert | ----- | ----- | -------- | ----- | ------ | -------- | ----- | ------ | ------ |
| El Paso | ----- | ----- | -------- | ----- | ------ | -------- | ----- | ------ | ------ |
| Fremont | ----- | ----- | -------- | ----- | ------ | -------- | ----- | ------ | ------ |
| Garfield | ----- | ----- | -------- | ----- | ------ | -------- | ----- | ------ | ------ |
| Gilpin | ----- | ----- | -------- | ----- | ------ | -------- | ----- | ------ | ------ |
| Grand | ----- | ----- | -------- | ----- | ------ | -------- | ----- | ------ | ------ |
| Gunnison | ----- | ----- | -------- | ----- | ------ | -------- | ----- | ------ | ------ |
| Hinsdale | ----- | ----- | -------- | ----- | ------ | -------- | ----- | ------ | ------ |
| Huerfano | ----- | ----- | -------- | ----- | ------ | -------- | ----- | ------ | ------ |
| Jackson | ----- | ----- | -------- | ----- | ------ | -------- | ----- | ------ | ------ |
| Jefferson | ----- | ----- | -------- | ----- | ------ | -------- | ----- | ------ | ------ |
| Kiowa | 720 | 150 | 108,000 | 1,710 | 303 | 518,180 | 650 | 291 | 189, |
| Kit Carson | 60 | 140 | 8,400 | ----- | ------ | -------- | 10 | 299 | 2, |
| Lake | ----- | ----- | -------- | ----- | ------ | -------- | ----- | ------ | ------ |
| La Plata | ----- | ----- | -------- | ----- | ------ | -------- | ----- | ------ | ------ |
| Larimer | ----- | ----- | -------- | ----- | ------ | -------- | ----- | ------ | ------ |
| Las Animas | 1,050 | 200 | 210,000 | 1,240 | 214 | 265,360 | 1,060 | 271 | 287, |
| Lincoln | ----- | ----- | -------- | ----- | ------ | -------- | 25 | 490 | 12, |
| Logan | ----- | ----- | -------- | ----- | ------ | -------- | ----- | ------ | ------ |
| Mesa | ----- | ----- | -------- | ----- | ------ | -------- | ----- | ------ | ------ |
| Mineral | ----- | ----- | -------- | ----- | ------ | -------- | ----- | ------ | ------ |
| Moffat | ----- | ----- | -------- | ----- | ------ | -------- | ----- | ------ | ------ |
| Montezuma | ----- | ----- | -------- | ----- | ------ | -------- | ----- | ------ | ------ |
| Montrose | ----- | ----- | -------- | ----- | ------ | -------- | ----- | ------ | ------ |
| Morgan | ----- | ----- | -------- | ----- | ------ | -------- | ----- | ------ | ------ |
| Otero | ----- | ----- | -------- | 10 | 257 | 2,570 | ----- | ------ | ------ |
| Ouray | ----- | ----- | -------- | ----- | ------ | -------- | ----- | ------ | ------ |
| Park | ----- | ----- | -------- | ----- | ------ | -------- | ----- | ------ | ------ |
| Phillips | ----- | ----- | -------- | ----- | ------ | -------- | ----- | ------ | ------ |
| Pitkin | ----- | ----- | -------- | ----- | ------ | -------- | ----- | ------ | ------ |
| Prowers | 3,910 | 210 | 821,100 | 16,885 | 272 | 4,592,720 | 9,510 | 290 | 2,757, |
| Pueblo | ----- | ----- | -------- | ----- | ------ | -------- | ----- | ------ | ------ |
| Rio Blanco | ----- | ----- | -------- | ----- | ------ | -------- | ----- | ------ | ------ |
| Rio Grande | ----- | ----- | -------- | ----- | ------ | -------- | ----- | ------ | ------ |
| Routt | ----- | ----- | -------- | ----- | ------ | -------- | ----- | ------ | ------ |
| Saguache | ----- | ----- | -------- | ----- | ------ | -------- | ----- | ------ | ------ |
| San Juan | ----- | ----- | -------- | ----- | ------ | -------- | ----- | ------ | ------ |
| San Miguel | ----- | ----- | -------- | ----- | ------ | -------- | ----- | ------ | ------ |
| Sedgwick | ----- | ----- | -------- | ----- | ------ | -------- | ----- | ------ | ------ |
| Summit | ----- | ----- | -------- | ----- | ------ | -------- | ----- | ------ | ------ |
| Teller | ----- | ----- | -------- | ----- | ------ | -------- | ----- | ------ | ------ |
| Washington | ----- | ----- | -------- | ----- | ------ | -------- | ----- | ------ | ---- |
| Weld | ----- | ----- | -------- | ----- | ------ | -------- | ----- | ------ | ---- |
| Yuma | ----- | ----- | -------- | ----- | ------ | -------- | ----- | ------ | ---- |
| State | 46,000 | ----- | 11,600,000 | 77,000 | ------ | 20,800,000 | 64,000 | ------ | ------ |

## ACREAGE OF HAY CROPS, 1931

| COUNTY | Alfalfa | All Clover and Timothy, Alone or Mixed | Millet and Sudan Grass | All Other Tame Hay* | Total Tame Hay | Wild Grass Cut for Hay | Total Hay |
|---|---|---|---|---|---|---|---|
| Adams | 16,820 | 170 | 3,660 | 570 | 21,220 | 2,660 | 23,880 |
| Alamosa | 11,850 | 1,890 | ----- | 10,430 | 24,170 | 13,450 | 37,620 |
| Arapahoe | 12,950 | 150 | 1,210 | 2,890 | 17,200 | 2,300 | 19,500 |
| Archuleta | 4,780 | 9,210 | 20 | 1,170 | 15,180 | 1,540 | 16,720 |
| Baca | 1,610 | 710 | 1,690 | 60 | 4,070 | 490 | 4,560 |
| Bent | 25,910 | 170 | 290 | 30 | 26,400 | 290 | 26,690 |
| Boulder | 24,530 | 870 | 30 | 760 | 26,190 | 4,280 | 30,470 |
| Chaffee | 4,250 | 3,110 | ----- | 1,390 | 8,750 | 840 | 9,590 |
| Cheyenne | 590 | 40 | 1,790 | 110 | 2,530 | 1,450 | 3,980 |
| Clear Creek | 10 | 200 | ----- | 760 | 970 | 310 | 1,280 |
| Conejos | 15,250 | 2,210 | ----- | 2,740 | 20,200 | 20,710 | 40,910 |
| Costilla | 6,020 | 2,290 | ----- | 2,690 | 11,000 | 1,580 | 12,580 |
| Crowley | 8,540 | 40 | 210 | 160 | 8,950 | 60 | 9,010 |
| Custer | 2,210 | 3,780 | 40 | 10,710 | 16,740 | 3,580 | 20,320 |
| Delta | 27,080 | 610 | 40 | 1,780 | 29,510 | 180 | 29,690 |
| Denver | ----- | ----- | ----- | ----- | ----- | ----- | ----- |
| Dolores | 310 | 320 | ----- | 470 | 1,100 | 80 | 1,180 |
| Douglas | 8,910 | 1,590 | 1,170 | 4,070 | 15,740 | 2,190 | 17,930 |
| Eagle | 9,890 | 12,230 | 20 | 1,490 | 23,630 | 490 | 24,120 |
| Elbert | 9,490 | 480 | 4,320 | 7,740 | 22,030 | 4,210 | 26,240 |
| El Paso | 5,880 | 1,210 | 7,120 | 8,990 | 23,200 | 6,180 | 29,380 |
| Fremont | 7,390 | 1,530 | 90 | 4,490 | 13,500 | 130 | 13,630 |
| Garfield | 38,450 | 970 | 30 | 1,270 | 40,720 | 710 | 41,430 |
| Gilpin | ----- | 30 | ----- | 750 | 780 | 510 | 1,290 |
| Grand | 850 | 13,520 | ----- | 12,240 | 26,610 | 4,240 | 30,850 |
| Gunnison | 2,290 | 21,340 | ----- | 10,410 | 34,040 | 15,200 | 49,240 |
| Hinsdale | 70 | 2,590 | ----- | 290 | 2,950 | 700 | 3,650 |
| Huerfano | 14,460 | 3,780 | 100 | 1,990 | 20,330 | 920 | 21,250 |
| Jackson | 10 | 960 | ----- | 2,380 | 3,350 | 89,650 | 93,000 |
| Jefferson | 15,340 | 1,090 | 180 | 1,930 | 18,540 | 1,210 | 19,750 |
| Kiowa | 1,630 | 80 | 1,170 | 140 | 3,020 | 110 | 3,130 |
| Kit Carson | 1,620 | 40 | 7,150 | 2,470 | 11,280 | 1,840 | 13,120 |
| Lake | ----- | 20 | ----- | 1,660 | 1,680 | 5,630 | 7,310 |
| La Plata | 20,990 | 3,370 | 20 | 4,370 | 28,750 | 780 | 29,530 |
| Larimer | 43,150 | 3,230 | 1,570 | 9,790 | 57,740 | 5,020 | 62,760 |
| Las Animas | 16,150 | 4,070 | 370 | 4,010 | 24,600 | 1,430 | 26,030 |
| Lincoln | 1,950 | 140 | 7,310 | 3,920 | 13,320 | 4,940 | 18,260 |
| Logan | 24,150 | 880 | 5,940 | 1,170 | 32,140 | 12,810 | 44,950 |
| Mesa | 32,940 | 610 | 140 | 2,280 | 35,970 | 160 | 36,130 |
| Mineral | 10 | 1,220 | ----- | 940 | 2,170 | 940 | 3,110 |
| Moffat | 13,150 | 3,870 | 90 | 8,870 | 25,980 | 3,890 | 29,870 |
| Montezuma | 19,460 | 880 | 30 | 1,460 | 21,830 | 90 | 21,920 |
| Montrose | 34,120 | 1,810 | 20 | 1,160 | 37,110 | 110 | 37,220 |
| Morgan | 22,940 | 410 | 4,360 | 1,330 | 29,040 | 10,590 | 39,630 |
| Otero | 18,850 | 950 | 110 | 3,670 | 23,580 | 150 | 23,730 |
| Ouray | 3,560 | 5,450 | ----- | 1,270 | 10,280 | 1,300 | 11,580 |
| Park | 20 | 220 | ----- | 6,920 | 7,160 | 35,920 | 43,080 |
| Phillips | 440 | 50 | 4,370 | 850 | 5,710 | 200 | 5,910 |
| Pitkin | 3,140 | 6,210 | ----- | 330 | 9,680 | 250 | 9,930 |
| Prowers | 36,150 | 90 | 1,140 | 620 | 38,000 | 540 | 38,540 |
| Pueblo | 17,940 | 990 | 510 | 410 | 19,850 | 1,750 | 21,600 |
| Rio Blanco | 18,790 | 8,840 | ----- | 8,430 | 36,060 | 2,580 | 38,640 |
| Rio Grand | 9,150 | 6,090 | ----- | 24,340 | 39,580 | 3,910 | 43,490 |
| Routt | 9,870 | 31,140 | 100 | 4,780 | 45,890 | 1,390 | 47,280 |
| Saguache | 7,140 | 3,130 | ----- | 19,590 | 29,860 | 45,750 | 75,610 |
| San Juan | ----- | ----- | ----- | ----- | ----- | ----- | ----- |
| San Miguel | 4,020 | 1,290 | ----- | 3,690 | 9,000 | 200 | 9,200 |
| Sedgwick | 4,650 | 220 | 720 | 2,290 | 7,880 | 5,010 | 12,890 |
| Summit | 30 | 7,320 | ----- | 690 | 8,040 | 760 | 8,800 |
| Teller | 160 | 120 | ----- | 9,770 | 10,050 | 1,110 | 11,160 |
| Washington | 3,060 | 90 | 16,360 | 3,640 | 23,150 | 10,250 | 33,400 |
| Weld | 95,540 | 1,570 | 11,640 | 9,720 | 118,470 | 14,200 | 132,670 |
| Yuma | 2,490 | 510 | 6,870 | 1,660 | 11,530 | 8,250 | 19,780 |
| State | 743,000 | 182,000 | 92,000 | 241,000 | 1,258,000 | 362,000 | 1,620,000 |

*Includes grains cut green.

## ACREAGE AND PRODUCTION OF HAY, 1931

| COUNTY | TAME HAY | | | WILD HAY | | | TOTAL HAY | |
|---|---|---|---|---|---|---|---|---|
| | Acreage | Yield | Production Tons | Acreage | Yield | Production Tons | Acreage | Produ tion Ton |
| Adams _____ | 21,220 | 1.5 | 31,830 | 2,660 | .8 | 2,130 | 23,880 | 33, |
| Alamosa _____ | 24,170 | 1.2 | 29,000 | 13,450 | .5 | 7,230 | 37,620 | 36, |
| Arapahoe _____ | 17,200 | 1.4 | 24,080 | 2,300 | .8 | 1,840 | 19,500 | 25, |
| Archuleta _____ | 15,180. | 1.3 | 19,730 | 1,540 | .8 | 1,230 | 16,720 | 20, |
| Baca _____ | 4,070 | 1.1 | 4,480 | 490 | .8 | 390 | 4,560 | 4, |
| Bent _____ | 26,400 | 1.2 | 31,680 | 290 | .6 | 170 | 26,690 | 31, |
| Boulder _____ | 26,190 | 1.7 | 44,520 | 4,280 | 1.0 | 4,480 | 30,470 | 49, |
| Chaffee _____ | 8,750 | 1.0 | 8,750 | 840 | 1.0 | 840 | 9,590 | 9, |
| Cheyenne _____ | 2,530 | 1.0 | 2,530 | 1,450 | .6 | 870 | 3,980 | 3, |
| Clear Creek ____ | 970 | .9 | 870 | 310 | 1.3 | 400 | 1,280 | 1, |
| Conejos _____ | 20,200 | 1.3 | 26,260 | 20,710 | .7 | 14,490 | 40,910 | 40, |
| Costilla _____ | 11,000 | 1.3 | 14,300 | 1,580 | .8 | 1,270 | 12,580 | 15, |
| Crowley _____ | 8,950 | 1.0 | 8,950 | 60 | .8 | 50 | 9,010 | 9, |
| Custer _____ | 16,740 | 1.5 | 25,110 | 3,580 | .8 | 2,860 | 20,320 | 27, |
| Delta _____ | 29,510 | 1.8 | 53,120 | 180 | .9 | 160 | 29,690 | 53, |
| Denver _____ | ------ | -- | ------ | ------ | -- | ------ | ------ | --- |
| Dolores _____ | 1,100 | 1.1 | 1,210 | 80 | .9 | 70 | 1,180 | 1, |
| Douglas _____ | 15,740 | 1.3 | 20,460 | 2,190 | .7 | 1,530 | 17,930 | 21, |
| Eagle _____ | 23,630 | 1.7 | 40,170 | 490 | 1.1 | 540 | 24,120 | 40, |
| Elbert _____ | 22,030 | .6 | 13,220 | 4,210 | .5 | 2,110 | 26,240 | 15, |
| El Paso _____ | 23,200 | .6 | 13,920 | 6,180 | .7 | 4,330 | 29,380 | 18, |
| Fremont _____ | 13,500 | 1.6 | 21,600 | 130 | .7 | 90 | 13,630 | 21, |
| Garfield _____ | 40,720 | 1.9 | 77,370 | 710 | .9 | 660 | 41,430 | 78, |
| Gilpin _____ | 780 | .9 | 700 | 510 | 1.0 | 510 | 1,290 | 1, |
| Grand _____ | 26,610 | 1.1 | 29,270 | 4,240 | 1.1 | 4,990 | 30,850 | 34, |
| Gunnison _____ | 34,040 | 1.1 | 37,440 | 15,200 | 1.1 | 16,720 | 49,240 | 54, |
| Hinsdale _____ | 2,950 | 1.2 | 3,540 | 700 | .7 | 490 | 3,650 | 4, |
| Huerfano _____ | 20,330 | 1.6 | 32,530 | 920 | .5 | 460 | 21,250 | 32, |
| Jackson _____ | 3,350 | 1.0 | 3,350 | 89,650 | 1.0 | 91,650 | 93,000 | 95, |
| Jefferson _____ | 18,540 | 1.6 | 29,660 | 1,210 | 1.1 | 1,330 | 19,750 | 30, |
| Kiowa _____ | 3,020 | .6 | 1,810 | 110 | .6 | 70 | 3,130 | 1, |
| Kit Carson _____ | 11,280 | .7 | 7,900 | 1,840 | .5 | 1,170 | 13,120 | 9 |
| Lake _____ | 1,680 | .9 | 1,510 | 5,630 | .7 | 3,940 | 7,310 | 5 |
| La Plata_____ | 28,750 | 1.5 | 43,120 | 780 | 1.0 | 780 | 29,530 | 43 |
| Larimer _____ | 57,740 | 1.6 | 92,380 | 5,020 | 1.1 | 5,520 | 62,760 | 97 |
| Las Animas____ | 24,600 | 1.1 | 27,060 | 1,430 | .8 | 1,140 | 26,030 | 28 |
| Lincoln _____ | 13,320 | .8 | 10,660 | 4,940 | .5 | 2,470 | 18,260 | 13 |
| Logan _____ | 32,140 | 1.5 | 48,210 | 12,810 | .7 | 8,960 | 44,950 | 57 |
| Mesa _____ | 35,970 | 1.9 | 68,340 | 160 | .9 | 140 | 36,130 | 68 |
| Mineral _____ | 2,170 | 1.0 | 2,170 | 940 | .6 | 560 | 3,110 | 2 |
| Moffat _____ | 25,980 | 1.1 | 28,580 | 3,890 | .9 | 3,500 | 29,870 | 32 |
| Montezuma ____ | 21,830 | 1.5 | 32,740 | 90 | 1.2 | 110 | 21,920 | 32 |
| Montrose _____ | 37,110 | 1.6 | 59,380 | 110 | 1.0 | 110 | 37,220 | 59 |
| Morgan _____ | 29,040 | 1.7 | 49,370 | 10,590 | .8 | 5,280 | 39,630 | 54 |
| Otero _____ | 23,580 | 1.4 | 33,000 | 150 | 1.0 | 150 | 23,730 | 33 |
| Ouray _____ | 10,280 | 1.4 | 14,390 | 1,300 | 1.3 | 1,690 | 11,580 | 16 |
| Park _____ | 7,160 | .9 | 6,440 | 35,920 | .7 | 25,140 | 43,080 | 31 |
| Phillips _____ | 5,710 | 1.0 | 5,710 | 200 | .7 | 140 | 5,910 | 5 |
| Pitkin _____ | 9,680 | .9 | 8,710 | 250 | .9 | 220 | 9,930 | 8 |
| Prowers _____ | 38,000 | .9 | 34,200 | 540 | .9 | 490 | 38,540 | 34 |
| Pueblo _____ | 19,850 | 1.4 | 27,790 | 1,750 | 1.0 | 1,750 | 21,600 | 29 |
| Rio Blanco_____ | 36,060 | 1.2 | 43,270 | 2,580 | 1.2 | 3,100 | 38,640 | 46 |
| Rio Grande_____ | 39,580 | .9 | 35,620 | 3,910 | .7 | 2,740 | 43,490 | 38 |
| Routt _____ | 45,890 | 1.1 | 50,480 | 1,390 | 1.0 | 1,390 | 47,280 | 5 |
| Saguache _____ | 29,860 | .7 | 20,900 | 45,750 | .6 | 27,450 | 75,610 | 4 |
| San Juan_____ | ------ | -- | ------ | ------ | -- | ------ | ------ | -- |
| San Miguel_____ | 9,000 | 1.1 | 9,900 | 200 | 1.4 | 280 | 9,200 | 1 |
| Sedgwick _____ | 7,880 | 1.5 | 11,820 | 5,010 | .8 | 4,010 | 12,890 | 1 |
| Summit _____ | 8,040 | .9 | 7,240 | 760 | .9 | 680 | 8,800 | |
| Teller _____ | 10,050 | .8 | 8,040 | 1,110 | .6 | 670 | 11,160 | |
| Washington ____ | 23,150 | .8 | 18,520 | 10,250 | .6 | 6,150 | 33,400 | 2 |
| Weld _____ | 118,470 | 1.5 | 177,710 | 14,200 | .8 | 11,360 | 132,670 | 18 |
| Yuma _____ | 11,530 | .9 | 10,380 | 8,250 | .6 | 4,950 | 19,780 | 1 |
| State_____ | 1,258,000 | -- | 1,647,000 | 362,000 | -- | 290,000 | 1,620,000 | 1,93 |

| COUNTY | Hay | Broom-corn | Field Peas | Beans grown for Canning and Market | Lettuce | Celery | Cauli-flower | Water-melons | Onions | GARDEN PEAS | | | CUCUMBERS | | | CABBAGE | | | TOMATOES | | | CANTALOUPES AND HONEY DEW MELONS | | | All Other Crops | Total Harvested Acreage |
|---|---|---|---|---|---|---|---|---|---|---|---|---|---|---|---|---|---|---|---|---|---|---|---|---|---|---|
| | | | | | | | | | | For Market | For Mfg. | Total | For Pickles | For Seed | Total | Early | Late | Total | For Market | For Mfg. | Total | For Market | For Seed | Total | | |

Not seed, garden crops to be consumed by the farmer, and commercial crops such as Asparagus, garden beets, spinach, carrots, pumpkin and squash, etc.

## COLORADO CROP ACREAGE, PRODUCTION AND VALUE, 1930

| KIND OF CROP | Acreage | PRODUCTION | | FARM VALUE, DECEMBER 1ST | | |
|---|---|---|---|---|---|---|
| | | Per Acre | Total | Unit | Per Unit | Total |
| inter Wheat | 1,324,000 | 14.5 | 19,198,000 | Bus. | $ 0.53 | $ 10,175,000 |
| oring Wheat | 308,000 | 13.5 | 4,158,000 | Bus. | .54 | 2,245,000 |
| orn | 1,732,000 | 22.5 | 38,970,000 | Bus. | .62 | 24,161,000 |
| ats for Grain[1] | 195,000 | 31.0 | 6,045,000 | Bus. | .36 | 2,176,000 |
| arley for Grain | 572,000 | 21.5 | 12,298,000 | Bus. | .40 | 4,919,000 |
| ye for Grain | 74,000 | 8.5 | 629,000 | Bus. | .37 | 233,000 |
| rain Sorghums | 180,000 | 13.0 | 2,340,000 | Bus. | .50 | 1,170,000 |
| veet Sorghums | 103,000 | 2.2 | 227,000 | Tons | 6.00 | 1,430,000 |
| roomcorn* | 77,000 | 270 | 10,400 | Tons | 51.00 | 530,000 |
| eld Peas | 49,000 | 12 | 588,000 | Bus. | .90 | 529,000 |
| ry Beans | 432,000 | 6.00 | 2,592,000 | 100-lb. Bags | 2.25 | 5,832,000 |
| otatoes | 92,000 | 190.0 | 17,480,000 | Bus. | .60 | 10,488,000 |
| ugar Beets | 242,000 | 13.69 | 3,312,000 | Tons | 6.94 | 22,873,000 |
| abbage | 3,900 | 12.48 | 48,700 | Tons | 8.62 | 420,000 |
| nions | 5,600 | 308 | 1,725,000 | Bus. | .32 | 552,000 |
| auliflower | 2,800 | 320 | 896,000 | Crs. | .80 | 717,000 |
| omatoes for Mfg. | 2,230 | 8.5 | 19,000 | Tons | 10.90 | 207,000 |
| omatoes for Market | 1,230 | 320 | 394,000 | Bus. | .80 | 315,000 |
| antaloupes and Honeydew Melons for Market | 10,000 | 200 | 2,000,000 | Std. Crs. | 1.20 | 2,400,000 |
| antaloupes and Honeydew Melons for Seed | 2,400 | 250 | 600,040 | Lbs. | .28 | 168,010 |
| atermelons | 1,070 | 320 | 342,000 | Nos. | .17 | 58,000 |
| ucumbers for Pickles | 2,800 | 130 | 364,000 | Bus. | .53 | 193,000 |
| ucumbers for Seed | 4,400 | 461 | 2,026,880 | Lbs. | .029 | 587,800 |
| nap Beans for Mfg. | 2,100 | 4.0 | 8,400 | Tons | 60.00 | 504,000 |
| nap Beans for Market | 1,750 | 290 | 508,000 | Bus. | .90 | 457,000 |
| eas (Green) for Mfg. | 3,700 | 1820 | 6,734,000 | Lbs. | .023 | 155,000 |
| eas (Green) for Market | 5,820 | 75 | 436,000 | Bus. | 1.65 | 719,000 |
| ettuce | 7,440 | 90 | 670,000 | Crs. | .85 | 570,000 |
| elery | 950 | 260 | 247,000 | ⅔ Crs. | .90 | 222,000 |
| pinach | 450 | 180 | 81,000 | Bus. | .40 | 32,000 |
| illet Seed[2] | 22,000 | 16.3 | 358,600 | Bus. | .58 | 208,000 |
| alfa Seed | 21,500 | 3.0 | 64,500 | Bus. | 8.40 | 542,000 |
| l Other Farm, Garden and Seed Crops not listed separately | 22,890 | ---- | ------ | | ---- | 1,347,510 |
| me Hay, All Varieties | 1,292,000 | 1.71 | 2,215,000 | Tons | 9.20 | 20,378,000 |
| ild Hay | 366,000 | 1.00 | 366,000 | Tons | 8.80 | 3,221,000 |
| pples | ------ | ---- | 1,060,000 | Bus. | .85 | 901,000 |
| aches | ------ | ---- | 787,000 | Bus. | 1.45 | 1,141,000 |
| ars | ------ | ---- | 146,000 | Bus. | 1.30 | 190,000 |
| erries | ------ | ---- | 3,500 | Tons | 90.00 | 315,000 |
| iscellaneous Fruits[3] | 32,500 | ---- | ------ | | ---- | 206,000 |
| gar Beet Tops | ------ | ---- | ------ | | ---- | 847,000 |
| e for Pasture | 27,000 | ---- | ------ | | ---- | 108,000 |
| otals | 7,222,530 | ---- | ------ | | ---- | $124,442,320 |

*County statistics for broomcorn in 1929-30-31 appear on page 92.

[1]In addition to the acreage harvested for grain, there is a large acreage of oats cut green for hay, this additional acreage appearing in the hay table.

[2]This acreage of millet saved for seed is in addition to the area harvested for hay as shown in the hay table.

[3]This acreage includes the total acreage of tree, bush and miscellaneous fruits for the state, but the value shown in the last column includes only fruits not separately listed above.

Note—On this and the following five pages, including inserts, appear revisions of crop statistics for the state for 1930 and 1929. The reports for both years were revised in the light of the 1930 federal census. Only state figures are shown in most of these published revisions, but county totals as revised will be found in "Agricultural Statistics" for 1931.

## FARM VALUE OF CROPS BY COUNTIES, 1930

| COUNTY | Corn | Wheat | Oats | Barley | Rye | Potatoes | Dry Beans | Sorghums | Sugar Beets | All Hay | Fruits | Miscellaneous Crops | Totals |
|---|---|---|---|---|---|---|---|---|---|---|---|---|---|
| Adams | 460,260 | 470,970 | 29,50 | 132,290 | 2,370 | 30,900 | 302,920 | 59,260 | 1,029,960 | 325,620 | 9,940 | 706,190 | 3,560,260 |
| Alamosa | 260 | 22,790 | 60,50 | 28,50 | 90 | 833,910 | 180 | — | 54,140 | 487,980 | 250 | 117,060 | 1,596,870 |
| Arapahoe | 348,560 | 341,820 | 24,40 | 48,60 | 3,170 | 13,740 | 280,580 | 20,430 | 114,920 | 243,190 | 8,760 | 68,570 | 1,504,280 |
| Archuleta | 19,850 | 15,670 | 14,190 | 3,80 | — | — | 60 | — | — | 318,270 | 320 | 3,180 | 389,250 |
| Baca | 681,880 | 732,350 | 40 | 20,80 | 2,390 | 30 | 51,460 | 280,450 | — | 31,950 | 1,100 | 418,740 | 2,221,90 |
| Bent | 481,200 | 56,760 | 19,50 | 72,520 | 180 | 30 | 20,480 | 97,010 | 458,420 | 552,810 | 1,650 | 552,470 | 2,313,90 |
| Boulder | 201,430 | 266,760 | 64,80 | 129,360 | — | 24,700 | 6,800 | — | 876,030 | 481,900 | 26,170 | 188,650 | 2,254,90 |
| Chaffee | 250 | 8,400 | 26,160 | 28,280 | — | 60,020 | 1,010 | — | — | 153,270 | 2,790 | 108,460 | 390,850 |
| Cheyenne | 1,167,400 | 70,870 | 5,80 | 60,260 | 1,130 | 5,230 | 11,460 | 98,430 | 2,210 | 51,000 | 260 | 14,220 | 1,485,520 |
| Clear Creek | 270 | — | — | — | — | 1,420 | — | — | — | 8,930 | — | — | 10,70 |
| Conejos | 3,300 | 77,890 | 61,90 | 129,600 | 220 | 90 | 13,110 | — | 13,260 | 565,510 | 220 | 403,690 | 2,159,740 |
| Costilla | 2,230 | 30,020 | 21,920 | 25,420 | 110 | 74,580 | 10,920 | — | 1,040 | 151,620 | 200 | 573,300 | 891,360 |
| Crowley | 234,170 | 3,570 | 14,860 | 26,240 | 30 | 30 | 69,450 | 38,540 | 453,030 | 280,760 | 5,640 | 1,195,680 | 2,322,300 |
| Custer | 16,500 | 8,840 | 20,430 | 8,400 | 210 | 244,580 | — | 13,220 | — | 297,470 | 50 | 118,030 | 727,760 |
| Delta | 134,540 | 52,930 | 37,490 | 34,170 | — | 104,840 | 4,800 | — | 172,720 | 652,860 | 651,200 | 159,460 | 2,005,010 |
| Denver | 8,030 | 12,980 | 3,560 | 1,150 | 330 | 9,310 | 20,790 | 2,130 | — | 12,310 | 200 | 3,100 | 73,890 |
| Dolores | — | — | — | — | — | — | — | — | — | — | — | — | — |
| Douglas | 241,210 | 36,400 | 58,470 | 13,600 | 6,670 | 12,240 | 33,900 | 6,770 | — | 253,290 | 1,260 | 7,710 | 91,520 |
| Eagle | 500 | 22,880 | 30,530 | 4,520 | 7,600 | 214,930 | — | — | — | 317,380 | 820 | 30,470 | 622,80 |
| Elbert | 678,760 | 131,270 | 48,100 | 31,440 | 7,130 | 43,160 | 804,990 | 51,750 | — | 279,400 | 1,540 | 34,150 | 2,112,60 |
| El Paso | 864,730 | 32,460 | 77,530 | 16,850 | — | 40,550 | 883,030 | 40,470 | 49,650 | 328,140 | 1,520 | 52,910 | 2,394,90 |
| Fremont | 83,320 | 5,100 | 19,320 | 5,570 | 90 | 12,750 | 3,140 | 60 | 4,490 | 243,740 | 198,000 | 346,220 | 921,80 |
| Garfield | 19,030 | 82,950 | 46,340 | 30,220 | 530 | 373,240 | 1,880 | 250 | 176,790 | 815,290 | 46,940 | 55,450 | 1,648,910 |
| Gilpin | — | — | 190 | 70 | — | 4,120 | — | — | — | 10,420 | — | 2,370 | 17,170 |
| Grand | — | 1,100 | 12,500 | 8,160 | 180 | 5,760 | — | — | — | 396,470 | — | 62,730 | 486,900 |
| Gunnison | — | 1,050 | 3,890 | 2,270 | 60 | 22,730 | — | — | — | 540,590 | 220 | 4,040 | 574,850 |
| Hinsdale | — | — | 1,730 | — | — | 850 | — | — | — | 41,290 | — | 540 | 44,410 |
| Huerfano | 64,490 | 17,060 | 10,960 | 3,670 | 160 | 14,650 | 19,270 | 5,630 | 1,800 | 253,380 | 2,210 | 25,940 | 419,120 |
| Jackson | — | — | 1,740 | 120 | — | 7,770 | — | — | — | 905,630 | — | 1,660 | 916,820 |
| Jefferson | 93,170 | 165,600 | 49,070 | 44,110 | 190 | 35,300 | 4,020 | 130 | 53,380 | 340,330 | 98,420 | 458,320 | 1,342,040 |
| Kiowa | 763,310 | 24,610 | 730 | 23,180 | 260 | 490 | 3,910 | 254,600 | — | 30,410 | 260 | 26,360 | 1,128,120 |
| Kit Carson | 2,378,130 | 485,070 | 30,540 | 467,600 | 7,700 | 30,690 | 37,600 | 233,780 | — | 159,860 | 820 | 30,740 | 3,862,530 |

| County | | | | | | | | | | | | | | | |
|---|---|---|---|---|---|---|---|---|---|---|---|---|---|---|---|
| Lake | 25,670 | 75,310 | 22,840 | 190 | 87,060 | 16,470 | | | 940 | | | 57,990 | | 250 | 68, 30 |
| La Plata | 287,670 | 90,230 | 284,900 | 560 | 65,610 | 15,990 | 2,202,120 | | 480 | 570,180 | 13,960 | 23,910 | 96,910 | 20 |
| Larimer | 266,970 | 19,610 | 12,300 | 1,580 | 11,780 | 186,670 | | 56,950 | 1,008,630 | 218,000 | 253,130 | 4,819, 50 |
| Las Animas | 1,104,730 | 4,810 | 93,220 | 6,270 | 16,470 | 370,880 | 58,980 | 192,680 | 327,390 | 1,920 | 92,060 | 45, 50 |
| Lincoln | 1,721,520 | 87,160 | 520,640 | 23,110 | 83,480 | 100,550 | 1,910,060 | 130,580 | 198,150 | 630 | 20,410 | 29, 90 |
| Logan | | | | | | | | | 720,540 | 860 | 173,110 | 6,601, 50 |
| Mesa | 310,030 | 59,210 | 19,730 | 180 | 168,520 | 156,900 | 110,910 | 1,380 | 673,660 | 1,377,640 | 264,500 | 3,193, 30 |
| Mineral | | | | | 600 | | | | 23,830 | | | 24, 30 |
| Moffat | 17,400 | 66,760 | 10,120 | 3,730 | 37,810 | 620 | | 800 | 475,450 | 720 | 34,410 | 69, 90 |
| Montezuma | 58,180 | 80,650 | 14,740 | 870 | 73,580 | 64,540 | | 1,870 | 416,890 | 23,800 | 20,150 | 80, 90 |
| Montrose | 104,840 | 77,110 | 37,380 | 300 | 516,430 | 19,660 | 138,680 | | 791,050 | 37,300 | 227,480 | 2, 88, 80 |
| Morgan | 1,095,960 | 42,850 | 230,630 | 7,880 | 153,860 | 328,950 | 2,688,090 | 86,560 | 578,250 | 1,940 | 164,520 | 5, 69, 30 |
| Otero | 401,890 | 40,320 | 42,860 | 160 | 340 | 82,260 | 1,200,820 | 16,690 | 404,170 | 15,250 | 1,793,040 | 4, 89, 80 |
| Ouray | 12,760 | 15,700 | 3,650 | | 24,800 | 220 | | | 141,110 | 740 | 570 | 22, 50 |
| Park | | 60 | 220 | | 107,910 | | | | 330,430 | | 3,990 | 43, 30 |
| Phillips | 1,148,290 | 1,375,880 | 203,780 | 12,070 | 11,520 | 7,440 | | 113,480 | 87,030 | 520 | 30,520 | 65, 90 |
| Pitkin | | 4,900 | 1,120 | 40 | 95,480 | | | | 129,320 | 510 | 750 | 83, 90 |
| Prowers | 556,230 | 186,430 | 106,960 | 470 | 330 | 6,680 | 571,820 | 173,700 | 857,110 | 1,000 | 191,020 | 64, 90 |
| Pueblo | 387,290 | 84,010 | 27,600 | 60 | 520 | 363,780 | 602,880 | 25,000 | 415,490 | 8,540 | 1,126,710 | 55, 60 |
| Rio Blanco | | 31,250 | 4,890 | 300 | 8,150 | | | | 591,610 | 520 | 10,410 | 63, 90 |
| Rio Grande | 760 | 40,890 | 56,360 | 100 | 2,149,330 | 2,940 | 270 | | 561,170 | 940 | 452,980 | 3, 39, 90 |
| Routt | | 55,320 | 128,380 | 480 | 90,260 | | | | 645,930 | 2,500 | 178,990 | 1, 41, 90 |
| Saguache | 240 | 14,260 | 19,580 | 300 | 869,400 | 180 | | | 835,520 | 600 | 55,800 | 1, 89, 90 |
| San Juan | | 60 | | | | | | | | | | |
| San Miguel | 5,710 | 6,840 | 5,040 | 370 | 15,080 | 1,820 | | 150 | 132,760 | 400 | 1,930 | 76, 80 |
| Sedgwick | 508,030 | 890,610 | 183,830 | 6,960 | 64,740 | 2,760 | 451,170 | 23,070 | 178,130 | 840 | 29,680 | 2, 97, 90 |
| Summit | | 790 | 1,020 | 60 | 3,090 | | | | 85,600 | | 30 | 93, 70 |
| Teller | 650 | 4,320 | 750 | | 120,650 | | | | 118,550 | | 10,180 | 85, 00 |
| Washington | 2,189,460 | 25,100 | 314,920 | 14,520 | 30,040 | 176,970 | 37,090 | 210,690 | 354,310 | 1,510 | 85,760 | 4, 65, 80 |
| Weld | 1,359,230 | 221,680 | 1,052,930 | 25,800 | 2,628,080 | 1,286,980 | 9,438,270 | 115,450 | 2,106,850 | 11,240 | 1,233,490 | 21,171, 50 |
| Yuma | 3,650,710 | 42,040 | 207,900 | 85,810 | 36,770 | 53,390 | | 246,720 | 250,830 | 4,860 | 103,820 | 6, 24, 20 |
| State | $24,161,000 | $12,176,000 | $4,919,000 | $233,000 | $10,488,000 | $5,832,000 | $22,873,000 | $2,600,000 | $23,599,000 | $2,787,510 | $12,353,810 | $124,442,320 |

Note—Miscellaneous Crops include field peas, broomcorn, garden peas, snap beans, cantaloupes for market and seed, cucumbers for pickles and seed, cabbage and kraut, celery, lettuce, cauliflower, tomatoes, watermelons, onions, asparagus, garden beets, spinach, carrots, pumpkin and squash, sweet corn, sugar beet tops, rye for pasture, millet seed, alfalfa seed, sweet clover seed, red clover and other minor farm garden and commercial crops.

Fruits include apples, peaches, pears, cherries, grapes, plums, apricots, strawberries, etc.

FARM VALUE OF CROPS BY COUNTIES, 1929

| COUNTY | Corn | Wheat | Oats | Barley | Rye | Potatoes | Dry Beans | Sorghums | Sugar Beets | All Hay | Fruits | Miscellaneous Crops | Totals |
|---|---|---|---|---|---|---|---|---|---|---|---|---|---|
| Adams | 333,280 | 1,072,150 | 8,090 | 170,330 | 4,370 | 43,550 | 305,570 | 71,200 | 941,440 | 504,910 | 33,660 | 847,750 | 4,  27,80 |
| Alamosa | 220 | 47,360 | 8,550 | 35,930 | 110 | 1,218,620 | 760 | --- | 760 | 541,350 | 480 | 128,310 | 2,  01,60 |
| Arapahoe | 263,910 | 703,700 | 9,350 | 99,660 | 7,840 | 2,660 | 273,870 | 46,270 | 143,450 | 361,450 | 27,260 | 120,520 | 2,  89,90 |
| Archuleta | 9,690 | 25,090 | 2,810 | 3,630 | --- | 18,830 | 1,430 | 80 | --- | 305,230 | 230 | 3,370 | 89,90 |
| Baca | 770,350 | 967,100 | 1,720 | 81,330 | 2,840 | 390 | 92,050 | 453,320 | --- | 42,200 | 1,400 | 870,800 | 3,  83,60 |
| Bent | 474,600 | 137,960 | 15,240 | 77,530 | 110 | 750 | 37,430 | 109,520 | 305,610 | 759,390 | 4,620 | 563,000 | 2,  85,60 |
| Boulder | 175,500 | 90 | 8,560 | 167,160 | --- | 24,500 | 7,390 | 1,040 | 788,290 | 641,360 | 91,420 | 194,360 | 2,627,230 |
| Chaffee | 617,510 | 23,980 | 2,800 | 32,080 | 930 | 3,680 | 1,980 | 164,040 | --- | 178,540 | 7,800 | 142,020 | 47,80 |
| Cheyenne | 450 | 76,360 | 6,290 | 76,520 | --- | 5,150 | 24,100 | --- | --- | 34,650 | 450 | 9,480 | 1,  95,80 |
| Clear Creek | --- | --- | --- | --- | --- | 1,910 | --- | --- | --- | 7,940 | 690 | 690 | 11,90 |
| Conejos | 3,360 | 136,800 | 102,530 | 131,700 | 360 | 1,064,820 | 22,360 | --- | 10,310 | 711,170 | 440 | 540,210 | 2,  74,80 |
| Costilla | 2,250 | 43,750 | 25,410 | 30,050 | 50 | 47,380 | 22,270 | --- | --- | 175,300 | 2,120 | 708,710 | 1,  87,90 |
| Crowley | 163,460 | 5,480 | 16,130 | 31,160 | 140 | 390 | 0,380 | 51,680 | 446,290 | 437,070 | 19,360 | 897,130 | 2,  73,90 |
| Custer | 5,640 | 15,500 | 13,990 | 10,800 | 390 | 180,700 | 140 | 140 | --- | 259,620 | --- | 109,740 | 96,90 |
| Delta | 103,660 | 108,990 | 65,910 | 60,840 | --- | 150,980 | 6,030 | 250 | 170,270 | 929,070 | 1,592,590 | 203,710 | 3,392,300 |
| Denver | 19,460 | 29,010 | 11,050 | 2,070 | 420 | 13,090 | 28,840 | 4,300 | --- | 17,640 | 80 | 2,250 | 128,310 |
| Douglas | 141,980 | 101,310 | 39,730 | 20,260 | 10,800 | 13,200 | 34,000 | 6,510 | --- | 255,260 | 2,150 | 9,420 | 634,620 |
| Eagle | 450 | 45,320 | 44,430 | 9,950 | --- | 0,860 | 639,820 | 40,080 | --- | 498,100 | 140 | 73,280 | 93,80 |
| Elbert | 378,020 | 90 | 51,500 | 50,240 | 27,590 | 29,170 | 730,470 | 49,100 | --- | 316,070 | 2,830 | 37,800 | 1,884,60 |
| El Paso | 456,520 | 50,510 | 81,760 | 17,100 | 20,730 | 36,380 | --- | --- | 27,030 | 288,730 | 2,440 | 74,190 | 1,834,90 |
| Fremont | 79,400 | 12,220 | 15,880 | 8,710 | 70 | 30,270 | 4,980 | 1,760 | 6,580 | 213,980 | 273,840 | 296,680 | 94,20 |
| Garfield | 12,620 | 158,890 | 66,550 | 38,690 | 1,200 | 590,140 | 6,770 | 360 | 133,190 | 1,005,350 | 113,680 | 61,020 | 2,188,40 |
| Gilpin | --- | --- | 330 | 90 | --- | 4,780 | --- | --- | --- | 113,690 | --- | 3,800 | 22,80 |
| Grand | --- | 600 | 10,940 | 6,050 | 780 | 8,450 | --- | --- | --- | 411,720 | 10 | 89,400 | 87,80 |
| Gunnison | --- | 2,150 | 4,970 | 2,020 | 220 | 28,510 | --- | --- | --- | 726,470 | 50 | 6,000 | 70,90 |
| Hinsdale | --- | --- | --- | --- | --- | 50 | --- | --- | --- | 54,780 | --- | --- | 57,80 |
| Huerfano | 66,540 | 32,750 | 25,310 | 17,100 | 170 | 19,600 | 39,910 | 6,460 | --- | 360,400 | 11,800 | 57,040 | 87,80 |
| Jackson | --- | --- | 890 | 240 | --- | 4,710 | --- | --- | --- | 925,220 | --- | 1,880 | 932,940 |
| Jefferson | 86,770 | 264,980 | 53,170 | 66,000 | 160 | 47,500 | 2,150 | 340 | 42,830 | 411,160 | 268,980 | 505,060 | 1,749,100 |
| Kiowa | 534,110 | 63,130 | 520 | 21,480 | 730 | 90 | 3,200 | 255,200 | --- | 23,360 | 50 | 22,540 | 926,020 |
| Kit Carson | 993,130 | 90 | 25,670 | 364,500 | 12,710 | 20,000 | 31,140 | 189,280 | --- | 98,690 | 120 | 36,070 | 2,494,150 |

| County | (1) | (2) | (3) | (4) | (5) | (6) | (7) | (8) | (9) | (10) | (11) | (12) | Total |
|---|---|---|---|---|---|---|---|---|---|---|---|---|---|
| Lake | 55,130 | | 90,030 | 30,040 | 490 | 91,700 | 22,880 | 1,370 | | 48,440 | | 300 | 48,740 |
| La Plata | 160,790 | 225,690 | 114,990 | 376,200 | 450 | 55,200 | 19,900 | 1,500 | 1,792,650 | 619,910 | 47,230 | 20,660 | 1,215,130 |
| Larimer | 256,260 | 616,760 | 32,960 | 28,160 | 1,920 | 9,500 | 438,110 | 129,200 | | 970,180 | 445,940 | 227,560 | 4,782,120 |
| Las Animas | 659,260 | 76,980 | 6,910 | 70,350 | 9,350 | 20,460 | 369,750 | 140,440 | 53,360 | 416,870 | 4,570 | 94,480 | 1,542,370 |
| Lincoln | 916,050 | 549,790 | 99,490 | 617,030 | 22,720 | 82,700 | 113,270 | 141,200 | | 147,200 | 1,430 | 24,370 | 1,999,310 |
| Logan | 1,196,200 | | | | | | | | 1,137,070 | 891,370 | 5,700 | 157,670 | 5,380,470 |
| Mesa | 217,660 | 140,600 | 74,420 | 28,000 | 490 | 93,060 | 360,480 | 3,200 | 116,020 | 1,137,580 | 2,324,930 | 231,560 | 4,988,200 |
| Mineral | | | | | | 1,060 | | | | 31,820 | | 70 | |
| Moffat | 11,360 | 165,980 | 53,780 | 16,820 | 8,230 | 55,880 | 300 | 1,240 | | 504,030 | 2,090 | 29,030 | |
| Montezuma | 77,420 | 137,600 | 77,280 | 16,070 | 1,760 | 90,750 | 96,770 | 4,360 | | 479,100 | 149,270 | 23,040 | |
| Montrose | 96,560 | 227,170 | 100,160 | 48,280 | 850 | 68,410 | 26,770 | 100 | 133,400 | 962,630 | 143,100 | 377,920 | |
| Morgan | 799,160 | 439,610 | 60,340 | 303,890 | 16,900 | 22,140 | 247,910 | 63,420 | 1,657,860 | 824,990 | 4,520 | 144,300 | |
| Otero | 297,680 | 56,190 | 55,890 | 59,090 | 780 | 630 | 126,590 | 22,820 | 954,680 | 614,190 | 21,120 | 2,058,330 | |
| Ouray | 2,880 | 19,680 | 26,280 | 5,120 | | 33,210 | 880 | | | 209,660 | 2,230 | 700 | |
| Park | | 100 | 1,800 | 270 | 20,480 | 13,280 | 11,000 | 86,080 | | 395,680 | 1,920 | 5,350 | |
| Phillips | 927,940 | 1,154,980 | 87,350 | 196,570 | 190 | 15,780 | | | | 66,180 | 670 | 28,700 | |
| Pitkin | 260 | 7,930 | 26,110 | 2,260 | 1,350 | 98,030 | | | | 218,730 | | 3,650 | |
| Prowers | 639,040 | 298,770 | 27,070 | 172,330 | 410 | 630 | 5,870 | 212,360 | 523,080 | 1,378,380 | 4,420 | 229,680 | |
| Pueblo | 346,530 | 111,030 | 16,700 | 49,030 | | 1,020 | 308,380 | 29,520 | 576,440 | 536,940 | 22,810 | 891,580 | |
| Rio Blanco | | 56,020 | 41,620 | 6,730 | 570 | 11,500 | | | | 745,170 | 1,320 | 8,050 | |
| Rio Grande | 960 | 89,770 | 128,230 | 91,950 | 130 | 4,856,540 | 10,080 | | 8,300 | 708,370 | 1,770 | 656,730 | |
| Routt | 2,180 | 128,490 | 137,640 | 66,190 | 1,300 | 131,380 | | | | 1,166,950 | 4,980 | 275,590 | |
| Saguache | 230 | 31,080 | 73,590 | 30,250 | 850 | 1,762,800 | 350 | | | 822,580 | 1,790 | 88,290 | |
| San Juan | | | | | | | | | | | | | |
| San Miguel | 4,310 | 12,780 | 7,500 | 10,180 | 900 | 17,130 | 760 | 900 | | 164,800 | 940 | 2,800 | |
| Sedgwick | 358,330 | 776,100 | 57,900 | 255,300 | 11,930 | 42,680 | 2,170 | 10,750 | 327,440 | 225,460 | 1,740 | 35,820 | |
| Summit | | 470 | 3,460 | 780 | 140 | 4,980 | | | | 128,960 | | 50 | |
| Teller | 220 | | 5,300 | 900 | 70 | 120,530 | | | | 97,620 | 13,120 | | |
| Washington | 1,217,200 | 678,670 | 24,790 | 245,370 | 18,390 | 27,940 | 150,770 | 184,820 | 144,560 | 300,710 | 2,030 | 84,400 | |
| Weld | 1,132,190 | 2,511,670 | 355,640 | 1,345,010 | 54,040 | 2,920,020 | 1,213,230 | 147,070 | 7,613,390 | 2,894,960 | 29,290 | 1,270,220 | |
| Yuma | 2,708,520 | 1,292,140 | 69,610 | 204,620 | 96,600 | 44,080 | 72,880 | 360,720 | 10,120 | 255,670 | 12,640 | 107,920 | |
| **State** | **$16,671,000** | **$16,632,000** | **$2,826,000** | **$5,910,000** | **$364,000** | **$16,137,000** | **$6,026,000** | **$2,982,000** | **$18,106,000** | **$29,475,000** | **$5,700,000** | **$13,708,170** | **$134,537,170** |

Note—Miscellaneous Crops include field peas, broomcorn, garden peas, snap beans, cantaloupes for market and seed, cucumbers for pickles and seed, cabbage and kraut, celery, cauliflower, lettuce, tomatoes, watermelons, onions, asparagus, garden beets, spinach, carrots, pumpkin and squash, sweet corn, sugar beet tops, rye for pasture, millet seed, alfalfa seed, sweet clover seed, red clover and other minor farm garden and commercial crops.

Fruits include apples, peaches, pears, cherries, grapes, plums, apricots, strawberries, etc.

## COLORADO CROP ACREAGE, PRODUCTION AND VALUE, 1929

| KIND OF CROP | Acreage | PRODUCTION | | FARM VALUE DECEMBER 1S | | |
| --- | --- | --- | --- | --- | --- | --- |
| | | Per Acre | Total | Unit | Per Unit | Total |
| Winter Wheat | 1,204,000 | 11.0 | 13,244,000 | Bus. | $ 0.93 | $ 12,317, |
| Spring Wheat | 335,000 | 14.0 | 4,690,000 | Bus. | .92 | 4,315, |
| Corn | 1,533,000 | 14.5 | 22,228,000 | Bus. | .75 | 16,671, |
| Oats for Grain[1] | 203,000 | 29.0 | 5,887,000 | Bus. | .48 | 2,826, |
| Barley for Grain | 608,000 | 18.0 | 10,944,000 | Bus. | .54 | 5,910, |
| Rye for Grain | 64,000 | 8.0 | 512,000 | Bus. | .71 | 364, |
| Grain Sorghums | 175,000 | 10.5 | 1,838,000 | Bus. | .80 | 1,470, |
| Sweet Sorghums | 105,000 | 1.80 | 189,000 | Tons | 8.00 | 1,512, |
| Broomcorn* | 64,000 | 286 | 9,200 | Tons | 112.00 | 1,030, |
| Field Peas | 49,000 | 12.0 | 588,000 | Bus. | 1.20 | 706, |
| Dry Beans | 372,000 | 3.60 | 1,339,000 | 100-lb. Bags | 4.50 | 6,026, |
| Potatoes | 90,000 | 163.0 | 14,670,000 | Bus. | 1.10 | 16,137, |
| Sugar Beets | 210,000 | 12.44 | 2,612,000 | Tons | 6.95 | 18,106, |
| Cabbage | 3,300 | 10.6 | 35,000 | Tons | 20.43 | 715, |
| Onions[2] | 7,000 | 369 | 2,583,000 | Bus. | .45 | 1,097, |
| Cauliflower | 3,200 | 360 | 1,152,000 | Crs. | .70 | 806, |
| Tomatoes for Mfg. | 2,030 | 8.7 | 17,700 | Tons | 11.00 | 195, |
| Tomatoes for Market | 1,070 | 310 | 332,000 | Bus. | .97 | 322, |
| Cantaloupes and Honeydew Melons for Market | 11,000 | 230 | 2,530,000 | Crs. | .83 | 2,100, |
| Cantaloupes and Honeydew Melons for Seed | 1,700 | 237.6 | 403,920 | Lbs. | .30 | 121, |
| Watermelons | 1,070 | 300 | 321,000 | Nos. | .165 | 53, |
| Cucumbers for Pickles | 2,000 | 115 | 230,000 | Bus. | .60 | 138, |
| Cucumbers for Seed | 3,800 | 259.5 | 986,170 | Lbs. | .28 | 276, |
| Snap Beans for Mfg. | 2,300 | 3.0 | 6,900 | Tons | 58.00 | 400, |
| Snap Beans for Market | 1,500 | 250 | 375,000 | Bus. | .84 | 315, |
| Peas (Green) for Mfg. | 3,400 | 1776 | 6,038,000 | Lbs. | .022 | 133, |
| Peas (Green) for Market | 7,100 | 81 | 575,000 | Bus. | 1.30 | 748, |
| Lettuce | 8,100 | 110 | 891,000 | Crs. | 1.25 | 1,114, |
| Celery | 1,100 | 240 | 264,000 | Crs. | 1.10 | 290, |
| Spinach | 400 | 240 | 96,000 | Bus. | .70 | 67, |
| Millet Seed[3] | 18,000 | 11.5 | 207,000 | Bus. | .75 | 155, |
| Alfalfa Seed | 13,000 | 4.0 | 52,000 | Bus. | 10.10 | 525, |
| All Other Farm, Garden and Seed Crops not listed separately | 28,350 | ---- | ------ | | ---- | 1,741, |
| Tame Hay, All Varieties | 1,255,000 | 1.8 | 2,255,000 | Tons | 11.50 | 25,932, |
| Wild Hay | 362,000 | .95 | 344,000 | Tons | 10.30 | 3,543, |
| Apples | ------ | ---- | 2,300,000 | Bus. | .95 | 2,185, |
| Peaches | ------ | ---- | 953,000 | Bus. | 1.45 | 1,382, |
| Pears | ------ | ---- | 600,000 | Bus. | 1.50 | 900, |
| Cherries | ------ | ---- | 5,100 | Tons | 120 | 612, |
| Miscellaneous Fruits[4] | 32,500 | ---- | ------ | | ---- | 291, |
| Sugar Beet Tops | ------ | ---- | ------ | | ---- | 840, |
| Rye for Pasture | 30,000 | ---- | ------ | | ---- | 150, |
| Totals | 6,810,920 | ---- | ------ | | ---- | $134,537, |

*County statistics for broomcorn in 1929-30-31 appear on page 92.

[1]In addition to the acreage harvested for grain, there is a large acreage of oats cut green for hay, additional acreage appearing in the hay table.

[2]Including 146,000 bushels onions lost by freeze but not included in computing value.

[3]This acreage of millet saved for seed is in addition to the area harvested for hay as shown in hay table.

[4]This acreage includes the total acreage of tree, bush and miscellaneous fruits for the state, but value shown in the last column includes only fruits not separately listed above.

| Dry Beans | Hay | Broom-corn | Field Peas | Snap Beans for Canning and Market | Lettuce | Celery | Cauli-flower | Water-melons | Onions | GARDEN PEAS | | | CUCUMBERS | | | CABBAGE (including Kraut) | | | TOMATOES | | | CANTALOUPES AND HONEY DEW MELONS | | | All Other Crops | Total Harvested Acreage | COUNTY |
|---|---|---|---|---|---|---|---|---|---|---|---|---|---|---|---|---|---|---|---|---|---|---|---|---|---|---|---|
| | | | | | | | | | | For Market | For Mfg. | Total | For Pickles | For Seed | Total | Early | Late | Total | For Market | For Mfg. | Total | For Market | For Seed | Total | | | |

seed, millet seed, garden crops to be consumed by the farmer, and commercial crops such as asparagus, garden beets, spinach, carrots, parsnips, pumpkins and squash, etc.

## RANK OF COUNTIES IN THE PRODUCTION OF PRINCIPAL CROPS, 1931

| COUNTY | Corn | All Wheat | Oats for Grain | Barley | Rye for Grain | Grain Sorghums | Sweet Sorghums | Dry Beans | Potatoes | Sugar Beets | All Hay | All Fruits | Bees and Honeydews | Field Peas | Broomcorn | Lettuce | ths |
|---|---|---|---|---|---|---|---|---|---|---|---|---|---|---|---|---|---|
| .ms | 18 | 8 | 28 | 9 | 15 | 15 | 14 | 5 | 33 | 5 | 22 | 10 | 8 | 28 | 8 | 8 | 8 |
| mosa | 48 | 41 | 25 | 28 | -- | -- | -- | 43 | 7 | 22 | 19 | -- | -- | 5 | -- | 14 | -- |
| pahoe | 23 | 13 | 23 | 17 | 10 | 17 | 15 | 6 | 50 | 16 | 33 | 15 | -- | -- | -- | 17 | 11 |
| huleta | 38 | 42 | 33 | 48 | -- | -- | -- | 40 | 28 | -- | 37 | 24 | -- | -- | -- | -- | -- |
| a | 6 | 1 | 51 | 30 | -- | 1 | 11 | 13 | 57 | -- | 54 | 29 | -- | 17 | 1 | -- | -- |
| t | 16 | 26 | 39 | 13 | 30 | 5 | 19 | 18 | 58 | 11 | 27 | 18 | 3 | -- | 4 | -- | 7 |
| lder | 19 | 14 | 2 | 7 | 14 | -- | 33 | 29 | 26 | 6 | 12 | 9 | 12 | 10 | -- | 25 | -- |
| ffee | 49 | 48 | 44 | 35 | -- | -- | -- | 39 | 27 | -- | 46 | 39 | -- | 6 | -- | 5 | -- |
| yenne | 7 | 17 | 47 | 18 | 21 | 3 | 7 | 26 | 48 | -- | 56 | 36 | -- | -- | -- | -- | -- |
| ir Creek | 46 | -- | 59 | -- | -- | -- | -- | -- | 49 | -- | 60 | -- | -- | -- | -- | -- | -- |
| ejos | 41 | 28 | 10 | 8 | -- | -- | -- | 20 | 4 | 25 | 16 | -- | -- | 3 | -- | 6 | -- |
| tilla | 42 | 35 | 35 | 21 | -- | -- | -- | 24 | 18 | -- | 41 | -- | -- | 2 | -- | 4 | -- |
| wley | 30 | 50 | 45 | 34 | 35 | 21 | 18 | 16 | 59 | 13 | 48 | 17 | 2 | -- | -- | -- | 6 |
| ter | 36 | 46 | 42 | 43 | 29 | 30 | -- | -- | 14 | -- | 32 | 37 | -- | 9 | -- | 11 | -- |
| a | 24 | 29 | 12 | 23 | -- | 36 | 35 | 30 | 11 | 12 | 10 | 2 | 11 | 23 | 6 | -- | 5 |
| ores | 37 | 38 | 52 | 55 | -- | 32 | 28 | 23 | 38 | -- | 59 | 14 | -- | -- | 9 | -- | -- |
| glas | 27 | 31 | 14 | 40 | 6 | 26 | 21 | 21 | 41 | -- | 35 | 28 | -- | -- | -- | -- | -- |
| le | 45 | 40 | 24 | 38 | -- | -- | -- | -- | 12 | -- | 17 | 32 | -- | 16 | -- | 7 | -- |
| ert | 12 | 16 | 26 | 29 | 5 | 20 | 16 | 2 | 30 | -- | 42 | 34 | -- | 15 | -- | -- | -- |
| Paso | 15 | 33 | 11 | 41 | 3 | 18 | 12 | 3 | 25 | 18 | 38 | 19 | -- | 26 | -- | 23 | 15 |
| nont | 28 | 47 | 40 | 47 | 39 | 34 | 31 | 42 | 39 | -- | 36 | 4 | 6 | 14 | -- | 10 | 12 |
| field | 34 | 24 | 13 | 31 | 37 | 35 | 34 | 37 | 6 | 15 | 4 | 6 | -- | 25 | -- | 15 | -- |
| in | -- | 56 | 57 | 57 | -- | -- | -- | 45 | 47 | -- | 61 | -- | -- | 18 | -- | 18 | -- |
| nd | 47 | 52 | 41 | 42 | 25 | -- | -- | -- | 45 | -- | 21 | -- | -- | -- | -- | 3 | -- |
| nison | -- | 51 | 48 | 49 | 38 | -- | -- | -- | 40 | -- | 9 | -- | -- | -- | -- | -- | -- |
| sdale | -- | -- | 54 | -- | -- | -- | -- | -- | 53 | -- | 55 | -- | -- | -- | -- | -- | -- |
| rfano | 32 | 39 | 38 | 50 | 42 | 29 | 26 | 22 | 31 | 23 | 24 | 21 | -- | 12 | -- | -- | -- |
| son | -- | -- | 53 | 53 | -- | -- | -- | -- | 46 | -- | 3 | -- | -- | -- | -- | -- | -- |
| rson | 29 | 19 | 9 | 16 | 27 | 27 | 32 | 36 | 22 | 19 | 29 | 5 | 13 | -- | -- | 12 | 10 |
| ra | 10 | 25 | 58 | 36 | 22 | 6 | 2 | 21 | 56 | -- | 58 | 35 | 14 | -- | 5 | -- | -- |
| Carson | 2 | 6 | 31 | 4 | 7 | 4 | 3 | 17 | 32 | -- | 47 | 38 | -- | 30 | 7 | -- | -- |
| | | | | | | | | | | | 53 | | | | | | |
| Plata | 33 | 20 | 4 | 22 | 33 | 31 | 30 | 27 | 10 | -- | 15 | 7 | -- | 19 | -- | 24 | -- |
| mer | 22 | 12 | 3 | 2 | 18 | 25 | 24 | 19 | 16 | 2 | 2 | 3 | 17 | 7 | -- | -- | 13 |
| Animas | 13 | 22 | 27 | 26 | 17 | 10 | 17 | 4 | 42 | 17 | 31 | 30 | 9 | 13 | 3 | 9 | -- |
| oln | 11 | 11 | 50 | 14 | 13 | 7 | 9 | 7 | 36 | -- | 44 | 33 | -- | -- | -- | -- | -- |
| n | 5 | 4 | 8 | 3 | 8 | 12 | 4 | 15 | 17 | 4 | 7 | 23 | 15 | -- | -- | -- | 14 |
| | 21 | 23 | 16 | 32 | 31 | 24 | 29 | 10 | 8 | 14 | 5 | 1 | 5 | -- | -- | 21 | 9 |
| ral | -- | -- | -- | -- | -- | -- | -- | -- | 54 | -- | 57 | -- | -- | -- | -- | -- | -- |
| it | 35 | 30 | 20 | 39 | 12 | 33 | 27 | 38 | 23 | -- | 26 | 31 | -- | 27 | -- | -- | -- |
| ezuma | 31 | 27 | 6 | 33 | 23 | 23 | 25 | 12 | 13 | -- | 25 | 11 | 10 | 21 | -- | -- | -- |
| rose | 26 | 18 | 7 | 24 | 41 | 37 | -- | 25 | 3 | 20 | 6 | 8 | -- | 29 | -- | -- | 2 |
| an | 9 | 15 | 22 | 5 | 11 | 11 | 13 | 8 | 9 | 3 | 8 | 26 | 16 | 8 | -- | -- | -- |
| o | 25 | 37 | 21 | 19 | 28 | 16 | 22 | 14 | 55 | 7 | 23 | 16 | 1 | 24 | -- | -- | 1 |
| y | 40 | 43 | 37 | 45 | -- | -- | -- | 46 | 29 | -- | 39 | -- | -- | -- | -- | -- | -- |
| | -- | 55 | 56 | 56 | -- | -- | -- | -- | 20 | -- | 28 | -- | -- | -- | -- | 22 | -- |
| ips | 8 | 7 | 18 | 15 | 9 | 19 | 8 | 34 | 43 | -- | 52 | 36 | -- | 22 | -- | -- | -- |
| n | -- | 49 | 43 | 51 | 40 | -- | -- | -- | 15 | -- | 49 | 39 | -- | -- | -- | -- | -- |
| ers | 20 | 9 | 29 | 11 | 20 | 2 | 10 | 32 | 60 | 10 | 20 | 20 | 18 | -- | 2 | -- | -- |
| lo | 14 | 21 | 30 | 25 | 26 | 14 | 20 | 11 | 52 | 8 | 30 | 13 | 4 | -- | -- | 20 | 3 |
| Blanco | -- | 36 | 17 | 44 | 24 | -- | -- | -- | 44 | -- | 14 | 36 | -- | -- | -- | -- | -- |
| Grande | 40 | 34 | 15 | 20 | -- | -- | -- | 33 | 2 | 24 | 18 | -- | -- | 1 | -- | 1 | -- |
| t | -- | 32 | 5 | 27 | 19 | -- | -- | -- | 24 | -- | 11 | 27 | -- | 20 | -- | 2 | -- |
| ache | 50 | 44 | 34 | 37 | -- | -- | -- | 44 | 5 | -- | 13 | -- | -- | 4 | -- | 19 | -- |
| Miguel | 39 | 45 | 46 | 46 | 34 | 28 | 36 | 35 | 35 | -- | 45 | 38 | -- | -- | -- | -- | -- |
| wick | 17 | 10 | 19 | 12 | 16 | 22 | 23 | 41 | 21 | 9 | 40 | 39 | -- | -- | -- | -- | -- |
| it | -- | 53 | 55 | 54 | 32 | -- | -- | -- | 51 | -- | 51 | -- | -- | -- | -- | -- | -- |
| r | 43 | 54 | 49 | 52 | 36 | -- | -- | -- | 19 | -- | 50 | -- | -- | -- | -- | 13 | -- |
| ington | 3 | 5 | 36 | 6 | 4 | 9 | 5 | 9 | 37 | 21 | 34 | 25 | -- | 11 | -- | -- | -- |
| | 4 | 2 | 1 | 1 | 2 | 13 | 6 | 1 | 1 | 1 | 1 | 12 | 7 | -- | -- | 16 | 4 |
| a | 1 | 3 | 32 | 10 | 1 | 8 | 1 | 28 | 34 | -- | 43 | 22 | -- | -- | -- | -- | -- |

ote—Denver and San Juan are omitted as no agricultural statistics are collected for those counties.

## CARLOT SHIPMENTS OF COLORADO FRUITS AND VEGETABLES

| CROP OF | 1931 | 1930 | 1929 | 1928 | 1927 | 1926 | 1925 | 1924 | 1923 | 1922 | 1921 | 192 |
|---|---|---|---|---|---|---|---|---|---|---|---|---|
| **Fruits** | | | | | | | | | | | | |
| Apples | 1,096 | 1,082 | 2,322 | 2,804 | 2,228 | 2,877 | 3,193 | 2,404 | 2,718 | 3,385 | 3,882 | 3,0 |
| Peaches | 1,503 | 1,369 | 1,765 | 1,117 | 1,709 | 1,271 | 884 | 1,772 | 1,254 | 1,428 | 1,223 | 1,0 |
| Pears | 396 | 249 | 1,082 | 264 | 737 | 750 | 717 | 955 | 696 | 774 | 745 | 6 |
| Mixed Deciduous Fruits | 18 | 25 | 34 | 22 | 37 | 44 | 26 | 62 | 60 | 99 | ---- | -- |
| **Vegetables** | | | | | | | | | | | | |
| Potatoes | 7,481 | 18,080 | 15,366 | 13,714 | 17,328 | 14,200 | 15,422 | 12,386 | 13,870 | 15,467 | 17,697 | 11,2 |
| Cabbage | 611 | 1,164 | 810 | 1,162 | 683 | 1,274 | 1,432 | 1,473 | 3,174 | 1,964 | 2,523 | 1,8 |
| Celery | 53 | 136 | 149 | 188 | 161 | 211 | 399 | 197 | 125 | 222 | 211 | 3 |
| Onions | 1,482 | 2,124 | 4,035 | 2,244 | 1,460 | 1,758 | 1,809 | 1,064 | 928 | 651 | 447 | 1 |
| Lettuce | 1,001 | 1,610 | 2,109 | 2,368 | 2,848 | 2,795 | 3,096 | 1,036 | 1,436 | 812 | 234 | 1 |
| Mixed Vegetables | 3,613 | 4,215 | 4,079 | 3,780 | 3,444 | 3,473 | 4,111 | 3,428 | 2,880 | 2,178 | 1,042 | 1,3 |
| Cauliflower | 1,455 | 1,309 | 1,500 | 843 | 411 | 220 | 191 | 61 | 101 | 4 | 3 | -- |
| Cantaloupes | 2,772 | 4,094 | 3,195 | 2,110 | 2,993 | 3,574 | 3,224 | 2,654 | 2,195 | 4,420 | 3,288 | 2,4 |
| Watermelons | 87 | 90 | 31 | 35 | 34 | 71 | 80 | 56 | 55 | 148 | 149 | |
| Miscellaneous Melons | 265 | 178 | 1,469 | 679 | 985 | 1,534 | 613 | 575 | 111 | ---- | ---- | -- |
| Dry Beans | 1,628 | 4,312 | 2,347 | 1,575 | 1,710 | 1,866 | 2,927 | 1,316 | 1,732 | 427 | 486 | 3 |
| Peas, Green | 559 | 463 | 459 | 348 | 149 | 58 | 35 | ---- | ---- | ---- | ---- | -- |
| Carrots | 41 | 43 | 96 | 216 | 10 | 62 | 29 | 26 | 12 | 4 | 9 | |
| Spinach | 50 | 28 | 67 | 6 | 8 | 6 | 14 | 3 | ---- | ---- | ---- | -- |
| Tomatoes | 195 | 138 | 55 | 59 | 20 | 27 | 195 | 77 | 128 | 94 | 38 | 1 |
| Beans, String | 76 | 165 | 58 | 3 | 5 | 1 | 5 | ---- | ---- | ---- | ---- | -- |

Note—Shipments of 1931 crops of dry beans cover period from September 1, 1931, to June 1, 193 and potato shipments cover period from July 1, 1931, to June 28, 1932.

## COLORADO'S BEAN SHIPMENTS, CAR LOTS, CROP YEAR BASIS—SEPT. 1 TO AUG. 31

### CROP OF

| | | | | | | | | |
|---|---|---|---|---|---|---|---|---|
| Adams | 11 | 72 | 27 | 20 | 23 | 23 | 18 | 1 |
| Arapahoe | 85 | 444 | 196 | 81 | 155 | 103 | 158 | 6 |
| †Baca | 45 | 91 | 74 | --- | --- | --- | --- | -- |
| Crowley | 8 | 50 | 38 | 48 | 32 | 11 | 40 | |
| El Paso | 274 | 498 | 306 | 262 | 315 | 255 | 427 | 21 |
| Elbert | 224 | 562 | 227 | 147 | 138 | 117 | 255 | 18 |
| †Kit Carson | 5 | 32 | 21 | --- | --- | --- | --- | -- |
| ‡Larimer | 3 | --- | --- | --- | --- | --- | --- | |
| Las Animas | 57 | 95 | 100 | 37 | 14 | 37 | 17 | 2 |
| Lincoln | 96 | 246 | 105 | 114 | 99 | 51 | 87 | 5 |
| Logan | 2 | 35 | 37 | 13 | 16 | 20 | 37 | 1 |
| Mesa | 85 | 130 | 119 | 116 | 68 | 30 | 23 | |
| †Montezuma | 24 | 123 | 83 | --- | --- | --- | --- | - |
| Morgan | 142 | 429 | 179 | 146 | 223 | 180 | 309 | 1 |
| Otero | 65 | 196 | 131 | 119 | 172 | 133 | 98 | |
| Pueblo | 25 | 135 | 106 | 20 | 84 | 49 | 79 | |
| †Washington | 24 | 96 | 30 | --- | --- | --- | --- | - |
| Weld | 443 | 1,021 | 501 | 394 | 344 | 827 | 1,336 | 5 |
| †Yuma | --- | 28 | 38 | --- | --- | --- | --- | - |
| Other Counties | 10 | 29 | 29 | 58 | 27 | 30 | 43 | |
| Total Colorado | 1,628 | 4,312 | 2,347 | 1,575 | 1,710 | 1,866 | 2,927 | |
| United States | 14,039 | 18,253 | 18,422 | 15,003 | 13,643 | 17,086 | 19,725 | |

*1931 crop shipments only to June 1, 1932.
†Shipments previous to 1929 crop included in "Other Counties."
‡Shipments previous to 1931 included in "Other Counties."

## NUMBER AND SIZE OF FARMS AND FARM TENURE, 1931

| COUNTY | No. of Farms | Average No. of Acres Per Farm | Total Farm Acreage | Owners | Renters | Home-steaders | Owners and Renters |
|---|---|---|---|---|---|---|---|
| Adams _____ | 1,430 | 240.93 | 344,530 | 789 | 541 | --- | 100 |
| Alamosa _____ | 370 | 287.54 | 106,390 | 234 | 118 | --- | 18 |
| Arapahoe _____ | 750 | 396.75 | 297,560 | 346 | 285 | 2 | 117 |
| Archuleta _____ | 330 | 321.64 | 106,140 | 279 | 41 | 2 | 8 |
| Baca _____ | 1,420 | 583.93 | 829,180 | 459 | 548 | 5 | 408 |
| Bent _____ | 790 | 344.14 | 271,870 | 284 | 372 | 14 | 120 |
| Boulder _____ | 980 | 138.88 | 136,100 | 505 | 443 | --- | 32 |
| Chaffee _____ | 200 | 234.25 | 46,850 | 151 | 45 | --- | 4 |
| Cheyenne _____ | 470 | 483.19 | 227,100 | 197 | 190 | --- | 83 |
| Clear Creek_____ | 30 | 231.00 | 6,930 | 24 | 5 | 1 | --- |
| Conejos _____ | 680 | 113.46 | 77,150 | 541 | 117 | --- | 22 |
| Costilla _____ | 330 | 75.12 | 24,790 | 193 | 128 | --- | 9 |
| Crowley _____ | 560 | 176.07 | 99,040 | 192 | 323 | 3 | 42 |
| Custer _____ | 320 | 465.31 | 148,900 | 233 | 72 | 7 | 8 |
| Delta _____ | 1,430 | 83.69 | 119,670 | 1,016 | 393 | 4 | 17 |
| Denver* _____ | ----- | ------- | ------- | ----- | ----- | --- | --- |
| Dolores _____ | 150 | 298.33 | 44,750 | 142 | 8 | --- | --- |
| Douglas _____ | 400 | 633.95 | 253,580 | 231 | 162 | --- | 7 |
| Eagle _____ | 360 | 249.06 | 89,660 | 310 | 41 | 8 | 1 |
| Elbert _____ | 1,070 | 583.74 | 624,600 | 550 | 375 | --- | 145 |
| El Paso _____ | 950 | 491.26 | 466,700 | 499 | 367 | --- | 84 |
| Fremont _____ | 890 | 98.33 | 87,510 | 645 | 173 | 2 | 70 |
| Garfield _____ | 780 | 196.58 | 153,330 | 538 | 207 | 7 | 28 |
| Gilpin _____ | 30 | 360.33 | 10,810 | 18 | 10 | 2 | --- |
| Grand _____ | 230 | 586.22 | 134,830 | 200 | 27 | --- | 3 |
| Gunnison _____ | 290 | 553.93 | 160,640 | 251 | 28 | 3 | 8 |
| Hinsdale _____ | 30 | 338.00 | 10,140 | 30 | ----- | --- | --- |
| Huerfano _____ | 490 | 534.73 | 262,020 | 485 | 5 | --- | --- |
| Jackson _____ | 240 | 856.33 | 205,520 | 225 | 13 | 2 | --- |
| Jefferson _____ | 1,400 | 143.39 | 200,740 | 965 | 370 | --- | 65 |
| Kiowa _____ | 540 | 541.33 | 292,320 | 228 | 196 | --- | 116 |
| Kit Carson_____ | 1,460 | 533.86 | 779,430 | 424 | 703 | 2 | 331 |
| Lake _____ | 30 | 688.33 | 20,650 | 24 | 6 | --- | --- |
| La Plata _____ | 760 | 260.07 | 197,650 | 427 | 224 | --- | 109 |
| Larimer _____ | 1,450 | 186.52 | 270,450 | 666 | 695 | --- | 89 |
| Las Animas _____ | 880 | 287.15 | 252,690 | 593 | 222 | 9 | 56 |
| Lincoln _____ | 1,020 | 482.75 | 492,400 | 499 | 372 | 1 | 148 |
| Logan _____ | 1,830 | 412.93 | 755,660 | 498 | 886 | --- | 446 |
| Mesa _____ | 2,350 | 69.09 | 162,350 | 1,766 | 484 | 8 | 92 |
| Mineral _____ | 30 | 582.67 | 17,480 | 25 | 3 | 2 | --- |
| Moffat _____ | 700 | 487.23 | 341,060 | 545 | 67 | 42 | 46 |
| Montezuma _____ | 590 | 206.92 | 122,080 | 375 | 156 | 12 | 47 |
| Montrose _____ | 1,020 | 123.06 | 125,520 | 562 | 374 | --- | 84 |
| Morgan _____ | 1,360 | 331.82 | 451,280 | 501 | 695 | 1 | 163 |
| Otero _____ | 930 | 114.62 | 106,600 | 436 | 425 | --- | 69 |
| Ouray _____ | 150 | 246.33 | 36,950 | 106 | 42 | --- | 2 |
| Park _____ | 230 | 729.04 | 167,680 | 174 | 42 | 13 | 1 |
| Phillips _____ | 690 | 494.96 | 341,520 | 143 | 305 | 1 | 241 |
| Pitkin _____ | 130 | 325.31 | 42,290 | 111 | 19 | --- | --- |
| Prowers _____ | 1,080 | 313.09 | 338,140 | 397 | 532 | 2 | 149 |
| Pueblo _____ | 1,190 | 290.10 | 345,220 | 604 | 406 | --- | 180 |
| Rio Blanco _____ | 350 | 605.66 | 211,980 | 348 | 2 | --- | --- |
| Rio Grande _____ | 450 | 300.56 | 135,250 | 274 | 128 | --- | 48 |
| Routt _____ | 640 | 378.83 | 242,450 | 434 | 187 | 5 | 14 |
| Saguache _____ | 350 | 464.43 | 162,550 | 163 | 165 | --- | 22 |
| San Juan _____ | ----- | ------ | ------- | ----- | ----- | --- | --- |
| San Miguel _____ | 210 | 502.14 | 105,450 | 177 | 25 | 5 | 3 |
| Sedgwick _____ | 550 | 433.85 | 238,620 | 172 | 270 | --- | 108 |
| Summit _____ | 60 | 396.67 | 23,800 | 56 | 4 | --- | --- |
| Teller _____ | 180 | 343.00 | 61,740 | 129 | 47 | 3 | 1 |
| Washington _____ | 1,600 | 578.88 | 926,210 | 424 | 682 | 2 | 492 |
| Weld _____ | 4,420 | 242.90 | 1,073,600 | 1,594 | 2,443 | 1 | 382 |
| Yuma _____ | 1,620 | 543.62 | 880,670 | 648 | 638 | --- | 334 |
| State _____ | 46,250 | 330.18 | 15,268,770 | 24,055 | 16,852 | 171 | 5,172 |

*No farm reports are taken by the assessor of the City and County of Denver. Its farms are allotted by the Crop Reporting Service to neighboring counties on the best authority available.

## NUMBER OF FARMS BY COUNTIES, 1930, 1925, 1920
### (Census Reports)

| COUNTY | Number of Farms | | | *Increase 1925-1930 | | *Increase 1920-1930 | |
|---|---|---|---|---|---|---|---|
| | 1930 April 1 | 1925 Jan. 1 | 1920 Jan. 1 | Number | Per Cent | Number | Per Cent |
| Adams | 1,912 | 1,873 | 1,753 | 39 | 2.1 | 159 | 9.1 |
| Alamosa | 531 | 300 | 302 | 231 | 77.0 | 229 | 75.8 |
| Arapahoe | 1,225 | 1,174 | 1,025 | 51 | 4.3 | 200 | 19.5 |
| Archuleta | 389 | 329 | 420 | 60 | 18.2 | —31 | —7.4 |
| Baca | 1,750 | 1,706 | 1,858 | 44 | 2.6 | —108 | —5.8 |
| Bent | 882 | 900 | 1,056 | —18 | —2.0 | —174 | —16.5 |
| Boulder | 1,473 | 1,492 | 1,420 | —19 | —1.3 | 53 | 3.7 |
| Chaffee | 307 | 247 | 326 | 60 | 24.3 | —19 | —5.8 |
| Cheyenne | 625 | 625 | 674 | ---- | -- | —49 | —7.3 |
| Clear Creek | 34 | 16 | 27 | 18 | 112.5 | 7 | 25.9 |
| Conejos | 1,467 | 680 | 814 | 787 | 115.7 | 653 | 80.2 |
| Costilla | 648 | 329 | 443 | 319 | 97.0 | 205 | 46.3 |
| Crowley | 626 | 622 | 743 | 4 | 0.6 | —117 | —15.7 |
| Custer | 406 | 367 | 353 | 39 | 10.6 | 53 | 15.0 |
| Delta | 1,744 | 1,636 | 1,707 | 108 | 6.6 | 37 | 2.2 |
| Denver | 257 | 307 | 239 | —50 | —16.3 | 18 | 7.5 |
| Dolores | 194 | 177 | 186 | 17 | 9.6 | 8 | 4.3 |
| Douglas | 438 | 401 | 462 | 37 | 9.2 | —24 | —5.2 |
| Eagle | 374 | 350 | 301 | 24 | 6.9 | 73 | 24.3 |
| Elbert | 1,241 | 1,281 | 1,308 | —40 | —3.1 | —67 | —5.1 |
| El Paso | 1,463 | 1,580 | 1,571 | —117 | —7.4 | —108 | —6.9 |
| Fremont | 1,270 | 1,127 | 1,014 | 143 | 12.7 | 256 | 25.2 |
| Garfield | 1,015 | 928 | 930 | 87 | 9.4 | 85 | 9.1 |
| Gilpin | 34 | 47 | 41 | —13 | —27.7 | —7 | —17.1 |
| Grand | 229 | 269 | 265 | —40 | —14.9 | —36 | —13.6 |
| Gunnison | 370 | 358 | 376 | 12 | 3.4 | —6 | —1.6 |
| Hinsdale | 44 | 38 | 40 | 6 | 15.8 | 4 | 10.0 |
| Huerfano | 760 | 1,003 | 954 | —243 | —24.2 | —194 | —20.3 |
| Jackson | 203 | 156 | 182 | 47 | 30.1 | 21 | 11.5 |
| Jefferson | 1,817 | 1,951 | 1,446 | —134 | —6.9 | 371 | 25.7 |
| Kiowa | 579 | 692 | 668 | —113 | —16.3 | —89 | —13.3 |
| Kit Carson | 1,630 | 1,500 | 1,461 | 130 | 8.7 | 169 | 11.6 |
| Lake | 44 | 27 | 30 | 17 | 63.0 | 14 | 46.7 |
| La Plata | 1,161 | 973 | 1,069 | 188 | 19.3 | 92 | 8.6 |
| Larimer | 1,838 | 1,816 | 1,921 | 22 | 1.2 | —83 | —4.3 |
| Las Animas | 1,758 | 1,943 | 2,286 | —185 | —9.5 | —528 | —23.1 |
| Lincoln | 1,232 | 1,279 | 1,385 | —47 | —3.7 | —153 | —11.0 |
| Logan | 1,845 | 1,916 | 1,874 | —71 | —3.7 | —29 | —1.5 |
| Mesa | 2,665 | 2,199 | 2,207 | 466 | 21.2 | 458 | 20.8 |
| Mineral | 50 | 27 | 34 | 23 | 85.2 | 16 | 47.1 |
| Moffat | 797 | 712 | 1,023 | 85 | 11.9 | —226 | —22.1 |
| Montezuma | 978 | 728 | 904 | 250 | 34.3 | 74 | 8.2 |
| Montrose | 1,318 | 1,423 | 1,368 | —105 | —7.4 | —50 | —3.7 |
| Morgan | 1,569 | 1,692 | 1,720 | —123 | —7.3 | —151 | —8.8 |
| Otero | 1,298 | 1,419 | 1,486 | —121 | —8.5 | —188 | —12.7 |
| Ouray | 178 | 162 | 180 | 16 | 9.9 | —2 | —1.1 |
| Park | 394 | 219 | 286 | 175 | 79.9 | 108 | 37.8 |
| Phillips | 766 | 843 | 680 | —77 | —9.1 | 86 | 12.6 |
| Pitkin | 180 | 166 | 179 | 14 | 8.4 | 1 | 0.6 |
| Prowers | 1,382 | 1,194 | 1,469 | 188 | 15.7 | —87 | —5.9 |
| Pueblo | 1,473 | 1,534 | 1,826 | —61 | —4.0 | —353 | —19.3 |
| Rio Blanco | 433 | 422 | 537 | 11 | 2.6 | —104 | —19.4 |
| Rio Grande | 730 | 535 | 603 | 195 | 36.4 | 127 | 21.1 |
| Routt | 928 | 834 | 926 | 94 | 11.3 | 2 | 0.2 |
| Saguache | 557 | 346 | 432 | 211 | 61.0 | 125 | 28.9 |
| San Juan | ** | ** | ** | ---- | ---- | ---- | ---- |
| San Miguel | 263 | 366 | 334 | —103 | —28.1 | —71 | —21.3 |
| Sedgwick | 560 | 632 | 487 | —72 | —11.4 | 73 | 15.0 |
| Summit | 61 | 69 | 72 | —8 | —11.6 | —11 | —15.3 |
| Teller | 238 | 186 | 250 | 52 | 28.0 | —12 | —4.8 |
| Washington | 1,753 | 1,984 | 2,057 | —231 | —11.6 | —304 | —14.8 |
| Weld | 5,457 | 5,610 | 5,765 | —153 | —2.7 | —308 | —5.3 |
| Yuma | 2,113 | 2,303 | 2,179 | —190 | —8.3 | —66 | —3.0 |
| State | 59,956 | 58,020 | 59,934 | 1,936 | 3.3 | 22 | 0.04 |

*A minus sign (—) denotes a decrease.
**No farms reported.
The figures for 1930 are preliminary and subject to correction.
La Plata county includes two San Juan county farms.

## NUMBER OF FARMS AND FARM ACREAGE, BY COUNTIES, 1930
(Compiled from Census Reports)

| COUNTY | Number of Farms April 1, 1930 | All Land in Farms (Acres) | Crop Land Crops Harvested (Acres) | Crop Land Crop Failure (Acres) | Crop Land Idle or Fallow (Acres) | Pasture Land (Acres) | Woodland Not Used for Pasture (Acres) | All Other Land in Farms (Acres) |
|---|---|---|---|---|---|---|---|---|
| Adams _____ | 1,912 | 557,561 | 220,918 | 30,074 | 54,987 | 225,330 | 386 | 25,866 |
| Alamosa _____ | 531 | 225,192 | 59,476 | 1,617 | 5,274 | 151,591 | 131 | 7,103 |
| Arapahoe _____ | 1,225 | 459,673 | 154,367 | 9,066 | 14,238 | 269,875 | 406 | 11,721 |
| Archuleta _____ | 389 | 163,442 | 21,416 | 614 | 2,819 | 127,841 | 1,478 | 9,274 |
| Baca _____ | 1,750 | 1,126,576 | 276,792 | 20,969 | 99,002 | 698,948 | 753 | 30,112 |
| Bent _____ | 882 | 540,938 | 87,492 | 4,200 | 6,872 | 435,701 | 373 | 6,300 |
| Boulder _____ | 1,473 | 203,313 | 84,531 | 3,656 | 7,541 | 98,065 | 697 | 8,823 |
| Chaffee _____ | 307 | 74,023 | 19,004 | 417 | 1,915 | 47,096 | 948 | 4,643 |
| Cheyenne _____ | 625 | 494,428 | 128,309 | 28,828 | 17,380 | 309,369 | 183 | 10,359 |
| Clear Creek____ | 34 | 14,454 | 884 | 20 | 176 | 11,533 | 1,528 | 313 |
| Conejos _____ | 1,467 | 252,552 | 93,448 | 1,413 | 12,190 | 133,320 | 357 | 11,824 |
| Costilla _____ | 648 | 349,527 | 33,279 | 2,817 | 8,198 | 296,960 | 2,024 | 6,249 |
| Crowley _____ | 626 | 328,113 | 49,126 | 9,254 | 4,236 | 261,040 | 83 | 4,374 |
| Custer _____ | 406 | 260,169 | 25,209 | 2,131 | 5,177 | 221,120 | 3,303 | 3,229 |
| Delta _____ | 1,744 | 187,965 | 60,218 | 1,648 | 4,589 | 62,103 | 2,199 | 57,208 |
| Denver _____ | 257 | 3,789 | 1,857 | 390 | 551 | 609 | 2 | 380 |
| Dolores _____ | 194 | 71,455 | 9,310 | 1,417 | 4,770 | 33,416 | 3,523 | 19,019 |
| Douglas _____ | 438 | 347,283 | 51,607 | 5,287 | 4,518 | 278,415 | 1,677 | 5,779 |
| Eagle _____ | 374 | 170,616 | 29,706 | 430 | 2,336 | 125,706 | 2,169 | 10,269 |
| Elbert _____ | 1,241 | 966,899 | 200,154 | 51,948 | 16,498 | 695,306 | 4,330 | 18,663 |
| El Paso_____ | 1,463 | 1,071,111 | 172,117 | 18,900 | 17,410 | 832,236 | 2,331 | 28,117 |
| Fremont _____ | 1,270 | 366,717 | 23,388 | 2,187 | 3,206 | 325,738 | 950 | 11,298 |
| Garfield _____ | 1,015 | 251,791 | 61,118 | 1,233 | 3,301 | 160,520 | 3,602 | 22,017 |
| Gilpin _____ | 34 | 14,374 | 1,287 | 115 | 3 | 11,587 | 1,167 | 215 |
| Grand _____ | 229 | 212,341 | 28,692 | 537 | 1,891 | 170,372 | 4,496 | 6,353 |
| Gunnison _____ | 370 | 215,849 | 46,100 | 511 | 1,666 | 149,416 | 2,149 | 16,007 |
| Hinsdale _____ | 44 | 18,142 | 3,564 | 75 | 764 | 12,695 | 145 | 899 |
| Huerfano _____ | 760 | 495,851 | 38,524 | 4,592 | 8,441 | 424,601 | 6,425 | 13,268 |
| Jackson _____ | 203 | 321,277 | 89,876 | 230 | 258 | 227,200 | 1,220 | 2,493 |
| Jefferson _____ | 1,817 | 259,690 | 54,328 | 2,564 | 6,931 | 174,987 | 7,939 | 12,941 |
| Kiowa _____ | 579 | 461,829 | 90,329 | 9,548 | 15,277 | 338,699 | ---- | 7,976 |
| Kit Carson_____ | 1,630 | 969,104 | 348,842 | 117,390 | 37,286 | 437,538 | 1,998 | 26,050 |
| Lake _____ | 44 | 20,681 | 5,162 | 122 | 5 | 13,723 | 510 | 1,159 |
| La Plata_____ | 1,161 | 359,127 | 57,100 | 3,719 | 8,567 | 257,769 | 6,999 | 24,973 |
| Larimer _____ | 1,838 | 698,304 | 148,159 | 8,283 | 24,330 | 486,427 | 1,046 | 30,059 |
| Las Animas ____ | 1,758 | 1,927,923 | 96,633 | 11,061 | 22,067 | 1,775,168 | 4,088 | 18,906 |
| Lincoln _____ | 1,232 | 1,195,717 | 266,824 | 55,121 | 33,599 | 812,135 | 1,618 | 26,420 |
| Logan _____ | 1,845 | 961,377 | 371,372 | 79,557 | 28,990 | 451,512 | 1,906 | 28,040 |
| Mesa _____ | 2,665 | 345,098 | 77,639 | 1,990 | 8,295 | 225,988 | 889 | 30,297 |
| Mineral _____ | 50 | 25,511 | 2,895 | 312 | 539 | 19,786 | 772 | 1,207 |
| Moffat _____ | 797 | 642,257 | 50,992 | 2,216 | 15,647 | 559,602 | 2,158 | 11,642 |
| Montezuma ____ | 978 | 285,730 | 48,116 | 2,984 | 7,971 | 167,924 | 11,901 | 46,834 |
| Montrose _____ | 1,318 | 231,065 | 67,018 | 1,396 | 4,152 | 109,794 | 883 | 47,822 |
| Morgan _____ | 1,569 | 632,615 | 235,876 | 22,325 | 10,767 | 339,282 | 1,776 | 22,589 |
| Otero _____ | 1,298 | 467,846 | 73,665 | 4,235 | 6,046 | 362,536 | 516 | 20,848 |
| Ouray _____ | 178 | 100,925 | 14,401 | 73 | 1,120 | 77,177 | 424 | 7,730 |
| Park _____ | 394 | 535,826 | 43,577 | 1,444 | 2,906 | 477,823 | 3,741 | 6,335 |
| Phillips _____ | 766 | 390,370 | 253,517 | 15,961 | 16,313 | 94,822 | 328 | 9,429 |
| Pitkin _____ | 180 | 59,888 | 13,526 | 131 | 721 | 40,085 | 324 | 5,101 |
| Prowers _____ | 1,382 | 564,644 | 167,000 | 9,637 | 20,518 | 356,998 | 276 | 10,211 |
| Pueblo _____ | 1,473 | 1,245,441 | 98,746 | 16,533 | 19,991 | 1,088,192 | 1,634 | 20,345 |
| Rio Blanco____ | 433 | 336,640 | 43,891 | 932 | 5,663 | 277,933 | 1,692 | 6,529 |
| Rio Grande_____ | 730 | 202,094 | 95,974 | 1,875 | 6,659 | 87,490 | 661 | 9,555 |
| Routt _____ | 928 | 527,847 | 80,276 | 1,799 | 9,814 | 420,757 | 3,432 | 11,769 |
| Saguache _____ | 557 | 454,726 | 100,443 | 3,499 | 5,266 | 331,059 | 1,501 | 12,868 |
| San Juan _____ | ---- | ------ | ------- | ---- | ---- | ------ | ---- | ---- |
| San Miguel_____ | 263 | 171,070 | 12,438 | 793 | 2,913 | 144,218 | 3,960 | 6,748 |
| Sedgwick _____ | 560 | 307,410 | 147,367 | 8,801 | 20,378 | 123,304 | ---- | 7,560 |
| Summit _____ | 61 | 32,231 | 8,604 | 25 | 1,290 | 20,945 | 705 | 662 |
| Teller _____ | 238 | 134,249 | 11,594 | 558 | 1,477 | 113,189 | 3,008 | 4,423 |
| Washington ___ | 1,753 | 1,237,648 | 376,171 | 138,955 | 46,908 | 653,001 | 4,595 | 18,018 |
| Weld _____ | 5,457 | 1,977,783 | 744,533 | 83,447 | 98,065 | 964,516 | 1,752 | 85,470 |
| Yuma _____ | 2,113 | 1,348,084 | 471,617 | 66,240 | 39,676 | 736,289 | 8,562 | 25,700 |
| State _____ | 59,956 | 28,876,171 | 6,750,398 | 858,052 | 840,234 | 19,338,377 | 130,719 | 958,391 |

### FARM PROPERTY VALUES BY COUNTIES, 1925 AND 1910

(From Reports of the U. S. Census Bureau)

| COUNTY | Land | Buildings | Implements and Mach. | Livestock | Total All Property 1925 | Total All Property 1910 |
|---|---|---|---|---|---|---|
| Adams | $ 17,401,203 | $ 3,470,786 | $ 953,480 | $ 1,608,369 | $ 23,433,838 | $ 15,767,956 |
| Alamosa | 5,414,522 | 726.035 | 252,080 | 995,775 | 7,388,412 | (a) |
| Arapahoe | 11,209,376 | 3,812,726 | 809,190 | 1,104,901 | 16,936,193 | 11,351,431 |
| Archuleta | 1,667,621 | 325,115 | 121,768 | 620,609 | 2,735,113 | 1,965,568 |
| Baca | 7,281,358 | 947,975 | 505,719 | 1,577,122 | 10,312,174 | 2,027,854 |
| Bent | 9.243,993 | 1,374,712 | 545,152 | 2,493,928 | 13,657,785 | 7,731,767 |
| Boulder | 14,589,625 | 4,028,005 | 907,505 | 1,540,040 | 21,065,175 | 16,478.541 |
| Chaffee | 1,939,545 | 576,200 | 185.552 | 393,272 | 3,094,569 | 1,987,810 |
| Cheyenne | 7,191,317 | 889,150 | 698,297 | 896,436 | 9,675,200 | 3,576,820 |
| Clear Creek | 185,400 | 67,000 | 8,150 | 12,498 | 273,048 | 216,018 |
| Conejos | 5,947,694 | 732,323 | 277,314 | 1,661,549 | 8,618,880 | 8,430,531 |
| Costillo | 3,901,484 | 445,470 | 210,960 | 604,623 | 5,162,537 | 3,714.504 |
| Crowley | 5,634,640 | 745,380 | 244,750 | 527,742 | 7,152,512 | (a) |
| Custer | 2,114,645 | 518,650 | 199,395 | 459,652 | 3,292,342 | 2,067,447 |
| Delta | 9,323,430 | 2,274,839 | 730,725 | 1,536,480 | 13,865,474 | 21,024,102 |
| Denver | 1,980,200 | 1,514,900 | 146,855 | 79,806 | 3,721,761 | 3,406,332 |
| Dolores | 245,285 | 62,845 | 35,040 | 146,984 | 490,154 | 248,501 |
| Douglas | 4,975,845 | 1,238,245 | 360,472 | 722,846 | 7,297,408 | 5,622,844 |
| Eagle | 3,214,334 | 762,636 | 293,197 | 653,227 | 4,923,394 | 3,691,648 |
| Elbert | 13,421,607 | 2,287,918 | 805,820 | 1,651,064 | 18,166,409 | 9,624,465 |
| El Paso | 13,860,102 | 3,058,480 | 819,442 | 1,556,672 | 19,294,696 | 13,117,316 |
| Fremont | 4,618,950 | 1,728,600 | 353,310 | 798,420 | 7,499,280 | 7,130,241 |
| Garfield | 6,788,140 | 1,508,150 | 507,437 | 1,930,768 | 10,734,495 | 11,017,329 |
| Gilpin | 138,100 | 36,775 | 9,130 | 24,296 | 208,301 | 195,481 |
| Grand | 2,311,960 | 500,930 | 161,235 | 534,145 | 3,508,270 | 2,625,740 |
| Gunnison | 2,751,125 | 678,450 | 238,013 | 1,232,679 | 4,900,267 | 3,352,823 |
| Hinsdale | 254,270 | 52,650 | 22,985 | 101,794 | 431,699 | 126,608 |
| Huerfano | 3,792,890 | 707,657 | 260,404 | 1,114,948 | 5,875,899 | 3,640,602 |
| Jackson | 2,703,020 | 428,600 | 158,606 | 1,096,140 | 4,386,366 | 4,416,646 |
| Jefferson | 16,310,465 | 5,562,780 | 734,575 | 966,210 | 23,574,030 | 17,616,573 |
| Kiowa | 5,182,425 | 659,875 | 373,915 | 968,292 | 7,183,507 | 3,031,538 |
| Kit Carson | 12,036,558 | 1,705,760 | 954,449 | 1,533,726 | 16,230,493 | 7,951,330 |
| Lake | 119,050 | 37,250 | 14,295 | 32,559 | 203,154 | 466,646 |
| La Plata | 4,195,120 | 1,319,445 | 298,695 | 1,212,839 | 7,026,099 | 5,812,793 |
| Larimer | 25,803,740 | 4,556,703 | 1,582,892 | 6,239,118 | 38,182,453 | 25,930,176 |
| Las Animas | 7,635,351 | 1,163,629 | 444,808 | 2,410,507 | 11,654,295 | 6,495,792 |
| Lincoln | 15,307,702 | 1,563,708 | 689,612 | 1,717,957 | 19,278,979 | 9,735,622 |
| Logan | 20,247,215 | 3,387,348 | 1,450,900 | 2,426,350 | 27,511,816 | 10,866,393 |
| Mesa | 9,745,965 | 3,244,609 | 981,843 | 2,088,683 | 16,061,100 | 30,209,338 |
| Mineral | 228,990 | 60,225 | 25,010 | 104,656 | 418,881 | 537,691 |
| Moffat | 3,426,540 | 700,855 | 306,480 | 1,041,637 | 5,475,512 | (a) |
| Montezuma | 2,722,808 | 755,815 | 201,760 | 1,336,695 | 5,017,078 | 6,996,047 |
| Montrose | 6,295,044 | 2,079,059 | 655,901 | 1,494,115 | 10,524,119 | 13,858,109 |
| Morgan | 15,065,041 | 2,998,970 | 1,172,956 | 3,483,644 | 22,720,611 | 11,548,557 |
| Otero | 11,730,057 | 2,725,477 | 927,872 | 1,922,835 | 17,306,241 | 19,738,280 |
| Ouray | 1,277,150 | 302,600 | 98,395 | 300,559 | 1,978,704 | 1,786,767 |
| Park | 2,737,184 | 687,236 | 255,634 | 952,930 | 4,632,984 | 2,925,215 |
| Phillips | 11,423,930 | 2,117,155 | 885,100 | 939,485 | 15,365,670 | 6,394,186 |
| Pitkin | 1,318,040 | 243,750 | 114,720 | 291,398 | 1,967,908 | 1,903,709 |
| Prowers | 10,174,623 | 1,720,780 | 557,718 | 1,551,563 | 14,004,684 | 13,938,513 |
| Pueblo | 11,823,044 | 2,236,450 | 718,040 | 1,558,817 | 16,336,351 | 9,940,218 |
| Rio Blanco | 3,442,895 | 798,010 | 294,660 | 1,464,338 | 5,999,903 | 4,350,437 |
| Rio Grande | 8,333,907 | 1,842,178 | 664,153 | 1,245,521 | 12,085,759 | 10,771,802 |
| Routt | 6,276,965 | 1,155,180 | 505,857 | 1,705,920 | 9,643,922 | 13,454,136 |
| Saguache | 6,571,414 | 887,420 | 358,658 | 1,774,186 | 9,591,678 | 9,299,491 |
| San Juan | (b) | ------ | ------ | ------ | ------ | ------ |
| San Miguel | 2,006,015 | 428,525 | 174,995 | 705,723 | 3,315,258 | 1,507,239 |
| Sedgwick | 7,648,345 | 1,354,950 | 483,350 | 739,972 | 10,226,617 | 5,439,388 |
| Summit | 610,850 | 142,950 | 46,525 | 143,861 | 944,186 | 602,166 |
| Teller | 1,045,945 | 249,595 | 96,745 | 262,026 | 1,654,311 | 1,268,472 |
| Washington | 18,627,450 | 2,672,079 | 1,334,048 | 2,426,687 | 25,060,264 | 8,266,561 |
| Weld | 59,480,778 | 10,497,342 | 3,760,667 | 11,096,378 | 84,835,165 | 56,363,139 |
| Yuma | 21,021,648 | 3,123,260 | 1,485,529 | 2,540,802 | 28,171,239 | 10,908,457 |
| State | $493,973,938 | $ 98,481,170 | $ 33,472,740 | $ 86,356,774 | $712,284,622 | $494,471,706 |

(a) County formed out of parts of other counties subsequent to 1910 census.
(b) County has no farms.

## SPECIFIED FARM VALUES IN COLORADO, APRIL 1, 1930, AND 1920
(Compiled from Census Reports)

| COUNTY | Farm Land and Buildings | | Farm Implements and Machinery | |
|---|---|---|---|---|
| | 1930 | 1920 | 1930 | 1920 |
| Adams ............... | $ 23,143,053 | $ 26,901,211 | $ 1,760,342 | $ 1,663,876 |
| Alamosa ............. | 6,777,009 | 6,164,415 | 573,907 | 296,947 |
| Arapahoe ............ | 17,884,017 | 17,174,405 | 1,212,567 | 957,668 |
| Archuleta ........... | 2,028,562 | 2,851,960 | 181,099 | 241,003 |
| Baca ................ | 17,158,962 | 12,511,397 | 1,590,569 | 947,605 |
| Bent ................ | 10,112,517 | 14,515,674 | 823,895 | 862,049 |
| Boulder ............. | 18,128,233 | 23,343,151 | 1,078,663 | 1,517,998 |
| Chaffee ............. | 3,132,970 | 3,173,885 | 257,144 | 223,023 |
| Cheyenne ............ | 5,867,516 | 15,180,510 | 522,367 | 446,526 |
| Clear Creek.......... | 592,238 | 548,600 | 15,440 | 29,960 |
| Conejos ............. | 9,478,459 | 11,498,311 | 706,953 | 594,970 |
| Costilla ............ | 4,145,803 | 6,211,797 | 394,569 | 262,236 |
| Crowley ............. | 6,952,382 | 11,007,264 | 449,892 | 538,004 |
| Custer .............. | 2,909,693 | 3,218,293 | 347,175 | 240,746 |
| Delta ............... | 10,538,579 | 14,371,545 | 954,450 | 932,502 |
| Denver .............. | 2,848,287 | 3,107,646 | 121,654 | 110,226 |
| Dolores ............. | 502,800 | 753,480 | 105,321 | 41,300 |
| Douglas ............. | 8,058,665 | 10,448,835 | 598,865 | 524,880 |
| Eagle ............... | 4,314,696 | 4,233,125 | 366,904 | 248,818 |
| Elbert .............. | 13,170,272 | 27,590,814 | 1,195,865 | 1,050,184 |
| El Paso.............. | 17,319,833 | 21,631,734 | 1,031,391 | 1,104,639 |
| Fremont ............. | 7,189,054 | 6,140,674 | 431,583 | 416,303 |
| Garfield ............ | 8,472,775 | 11,271,300 | 591,639 | 798,828 |
| Gilpin .............. | 149,870 | 193,985 | 15,240 | 18,751 |
| Grand ............... | 3,172,663 | 3,284,240 | 185,745 | 175,390 |
| Gunnison ............ | 4,129,000 | 4,235,182 | 296,685 | 329,398 |
| Hinsdale ............ | 385,645 | 353,800 | 32,885 | 19,900 |
| Huerfano`............ | 4,760,629 | 7,071,363 | 358,398 | 427,318 |
| Jackson ............. | 3,430,876 | 5,680,992 | 225,160 | 193,195 |
| Jefferson ........... | 24,106,053 | 19,286,253 | 972,824 | 1,046,930 |
| Kiowa ............... | 5,529,623 | 8,160,370 | 436,017 | 326,083 |
| Kit Carson........... | 14,396,018 | 20,550,988 | 1,304,837 | 961,266 |
| Lake ................ | 241,389 | 221,800 | 30,890 | 548,944 |
| La Plata............. | 6,643,259 | 7,310,267 | 630,904 | 22,090 |
| Larimer ............. | 28,541,224 | 39,420,325 | 1,941,348 | 2,013,478 |
| Las Animas........... | 12,260,863 | 14,064,697 | 836,040 | 714,441 |
| Lincoln ............. | 13,345,855 | 24,078,168 | 1,196,093 | 1,029,670 |
| Logan ............... | 25,931,038 | 41,462,007 | 2,269,144 | 2,384,869 |
| Mesa ................ | 16,205,224 | 16,034,577 | 1,313,813 | 1,209,883 |
| Mineral ............. | 643,255 | 359,300 | 39,870 | 27,695 |
| Moffat .............. | 5,670,029 | 8,394,431 | 476,867 | 688,784 |
| Montezuma ........... | 5,046,342 | 5,543,230 | 576,628 | 480,902 |
| Montrose ............ | 7,832,094 | 13,690,795 | 776,623 | 1,032,848 |
| Morgan .............. | 19,736,549 | 27,648,440 | 1,709,789 | 1,614,576 |
| Otero ............... | 13,360,386 | 20,067,756 | 961,300 | 1,194,335 |
| Ouray ............... | 1,652,268 | 1,925,035 | 151,715 | 126,208 |
| Park ................ | 4,018,412 | 3,505,286 | 305,954 | 229,513 |
| Phillips ............ | 11,796,670 | 21,154,427 | 1,201,783 | 1,139,690 |
| Pitkin .............. | 1,684,765 | 2,000,210 | 135,715 | 142,165 |
| Prowers ............. | 14,871,233 | 21,321,622 | 1,208,892 | 1,012,076 |
| Pueblo .............. | 15,323,482 | 27,664,475 | 1,122,781 | 1,201,273 |
| Rio Blanco........... | 5,077,685 | 5,755,348 | 398,142 | 427,346 |
| Rio Grande........... | 14,933,998 | 17,340,043 | 1,230,645 | 1,052,876 |
| Routt ............... | 8,424,669 | 10,763,065 | 665,166 | 786,106 |
| Saguache ............ | 8,650,968 | 10,954,145 | 597,750 | 465,275 |
| San Juan............. | ........ | ........ | ........ | ........ |
| San Miguel........... | 1,699,841 | 2,165,750 | 171,480 | 159,875 |
| Sedgwick ............ | 10,680,721 | 13,012,585 | 1,138,368 | 794,150 |
| Summit .............. | 729,900 | 741,250 | 62,660 | 64,901 |
| Teller .............. | 1,377,791 | 1,575,701 | 105,696 | 103,045 |
| Washington .......... | 15,063,272 | 32,740,702 | 1,372,716 | 2,081,929 |
| Weld ................ | 74,876,659 | 112,249,669 | 6,446,662 | 7,194,455 |
| Yuma ................ | 22,240,082 | 40,181,355 | 2,025,958 | 2,312,589 |
| State ............... | $629,346,675 | $866,013,660 | $ 50,241,437 | $ 49,804,509 |

Note—The total value of all farm property in 1920, including land and buildings, livestock and farm implements and machinery, was $1,076,794,749, classified as follows: Land in farms, $763,722,716; farm buildings, $102,290,944; implements and machinery, $49,804,509; livestock, $160,976,580. Total value all farm property in 1925 was $712,439,922 and in 1910, $494,471,706. The figures for 1925 and 1910, by counties, are given in a separate table.

FARM ACREAGE REPORTED UNDER VARIOUS TENURES AND TOTAL ACREAGE
HARVESTED, 1931

| COUNTY | Acreage Owners | Acreage Renters | Acreage Homesteaders | Acreage Owners and Renters | Total Farm Acreage | Total Harvested Acreage | Harv. Area % of Total Area |
|---|---|---|---|---|---|---|---|
| Adams | 156,169 | 141,191 | ---- | 47,170 | 344,530 | 183,920 | 22.77 |
| Alamosa | 70,870 | 27,818 | ---- | 7,702 | 106,390 | 54,050 | 11.62 |
| Arapahoe | 118,118 | 115,865 | 94 | 63,483 | 297,560 | 132,950 | 24.67 |
| Archuleta | 86,608 | 14,060 | 324 | 5,148 | 106,140 | 22,390 | 2.87 |
| Baca | 228,882 | 267,010 | 1,246 | 332,042 | 829,180 | 476,180 | 29.15 |
| Bent | 94,592 | 94,309 | 6,458 | 76,511 | 271,870 | 91,470 | 9.38 |
| Boulder | 62,114 | 67,858 | ---- | 6,128 | 136,100 | 88,590 | 18.12 |
| Chaffee | 37,274 | 8,348 | ---- | 1,228 | 46,850 | 14,655 | 2.11 |
| Cheyenne | 94,875 | 81,529 | ---- | 50,696 | 227,100 | 154,955 | 13.68 |
| Clear Creek | 5,947 | 886 | 97 | ------ | 6,930 | 1,335 | 0.53 |
| Conejos | 59,159 | 13,719 | ---- | 4,272 | 77,150 | 72,465 | 9.04 |
| Costilla | 12,624 | 10,550 | ---- | 1,616 | 24,790 | 35,250 | 4.65 |
| Crowley | 36,680 | 56,830 | 845 | 4,685 | 99,040 | 36,550 | 7.07 |
| Custer | 116,408 | 26,924 | 2,134 | 3,434 | 148,900 | 29,095 | 6.09 |
| Delta | 79,072 | 37,854 | 859 | 1,885 | 119,670 | 55,985 | 7.28 |
| Denver | ------ | ------ | ---- | ------ | ------ | ------ | ---- |
| Dolores | 43,035 | 1,715 | ---- | ------ | 44,750 | 5,840 | 0.87 |
| Douglas | 144,435 | 103,582 | ---- | 5,563 | 253,580 | 55,230 | 10.21 |
| Eagle | 76,998 | 10,444 | 2,087 | 131 | 89,660 | 28,460 | 2.74 |
| Elbert | 305,476 | 186,968 | ---- | 132,156 | 624,600 | 187,520 | 15.78 |
| El Paso | 224,055 | 176,715 | ---- | 65,930 | 466,700 | 160,600 | 11.83 |
| Fremont | 61,124 | 19,013 | 27 | 7,346 | 87,510 | 26,030 | 2.61 |
| Garfield | 106,033 | 39,036 | 2,599 | 5,662 | 153,330 | 59,140 | 2.97 |
| Gilpin | 6,853 | 3,597 | 360 | ------ | 10,810 | 1,540 | 1.82 |
| Grand | 119,042 | 12,233 | ---- | 3,555 | 134,830 | 33,090 | 2.77 |
| Gunnison | 136,752 | 13,089 | 1,120 | 9,679 | 160,640 | 50,300 | 2.47 |
| Hinsdale | 10,140 | ------ | ---- | ------ | 10,140 | 3,725 | 0.60 |
| Huerfano | 260,192 | 1,828 | ---- | ------ | 262,020 | 32,210 | 3.36 |
| Jackson | 195,171 | 9,057 | 1,292 | ------ | 205,520 | 93,270 | 8.93 |
| Jefferson | 133,462 | 60,439 | ---- | 6,839 | 200,740 | 46,590 | 9.01 |
| Kiowa | 114,113 | 101,514 | ---- | 76,693 | 292,320 | 120,390 | 10.46 |
| Kit Carson | 207,693 | 333,255 | 84 | 238,398 | 779,430 | 364,640 | 26.39 |
| Lake | 16,520 | 4,130 | ---- | ------ | 20,650 | 7,315 | 3.08 |
| La Plata | 107,885 | 48,983 | ---- | 40,782 | 197,650 | 51,145 | 4.32 |
| Larimer | 141,946 | 115,927 | ---- | 12,577 | 270,450 | 152,010 | 9.03 |
| Las Animas | 158,037 | 63,773 | 1,600 | 29,280 | 252,690 | 111,030 | 3.61 |
| Lincoln | 241,861 | 144,894 | 281 | 105,364 | 492,400 | 226,440 | 13.77 |
| Logan | 189,289 | 297,906 | ---- | 268,465 | 755,660 | 379,780 | 32.57 |
| Mesa | 113,189 | 35,629 | 862 | 12,670 | 162,350 | 72,670 | 3.59 |
| Mineral | 16,815 | 498 | 167 | ------ | 17,480 | 3,115 | 0.5 |
| Moffat | 245,296 | 37,876 | 20,279 | 37,609 | 341,060 | 47,180 | 1.5 |
| Montezuma | 73,221 | 31,239 | 2,997 | 14,623 | 122,080 | 55,715 | 4.2 |
| Montrose | 69,272 | 45,529 | ---- | 10,719 | 125,520 | 65,690 | 4.5 |
| Morgan | 147,876 | 191,857 | 162 | 111,385 | 451,280 | 223,855 | 27.2 |
| Otero | 52,371 | 45,790 | ---- | 8,439 | 106,600 | 72,125 | 8.9 |
| Ouray | 26,786 | 9,694 | ---- | 470 | 36,950 | 14,645 | 4.4 |
| Park | 132,655 | 26,490 | 7,707 | 828 | 167,680 | 45,105 | 3.1 |
| Phillips | 63,109 | 132,736 | 118 | 145,557 | 341,520 | 233,295 | 52.9 |
| Pitkin | 35,826 | 6,464 | ---- | ------ | 42,290 | 11,710 | 1.8 |
| Prowers | 120,325 | 145,635 | 265 | 71,915 | 338,140 | 157,910 | 15.1 |
| Pueblo | 137,468 | 94,180 | ---- | 113,572 | 345,220 | 99,595 | 6.4 |
| Rio Blanco | 210,734 | 1,246 | ---- | ------ | 211,980 | 44,490 | 21.5 |
| Rio Grande | 84,086 | 32,805 | ---- | 18,359 | 135,250 | 89,950 | 15.6 |
| Routt | 164,019 | 65,122 | 2,835 | 10,474 | 242,450 | 68,890 | 4.6 |
| Saguache | 116,278 | 33,636 | ---- | 12,636 | 162,550 | 94,955 | 4.7 |
| San Juan | ------ | ------ | ---- | ------ | ------ | ------ | ---- |
| San Miguel | 96,563 | 6,144 | 1,575 | 1,168 | 105,450 | 11,945 | 1.4 |
| Sedgwick | 54,848 | 101,968 | ---- | 81,804 | 238,620 | 142,605 | 41.9 |
| Summit | 21,638 | 2,162 | ---- | ------ | 23,800 | 9,080 | 2.1 |
| Teller | 46,759 | 13,816 | 406 | 759 | 61,740 | 13,835 | 3.9 |
| Washington | 189,861 | 334,929 | 589 | 400,831 | 926,210 | 376,510 | 23.3 |
| Weld | 327,653 | 506,572 | 167 | 239,208 | 1,073,600 | 635,770 | 24.7 |
| Yuma | 325,629 | 293,302 | ---- | 261,739 | 880,670 | 498,150 | 32.8 |
| State | 7,131,781 | 4,908,168 | 59,636 | 3,169,185 | 15,268,770 | 6,734,925 | |

## NUMBER OF FARMS REPORTING PRINCIPAL CROPS IN 1931

| COUNTY | Corn | Oats | Barley | Winter Wheat | Spring Wheat | Potatoes | All Sor- ghums | Alfalfa | Sugar Beets |
|---|---|---|---|---|---|---|---|---|---|
| Adams ---------- | 979 | 208 | 640 | 464 | 278 | 63 | 331 | 567 | 361 |
| Alamosa -------- | --- | 231 | 241 | --- | 139 | 303 | --- | 303 | 47 |
| Arapahoe ------- | 609 | 124 | 385 | 284 | 145 | 15 | 332 | 276 | 47 |
| Archuleta ------ | 14 | 245 | 58 | 52 | 133 | 271 | --- | 272 | --- |
| Baca ----------- | 1,124 | 7 | 247 | 648 | 6 | --- | 1,185 | 25 | --- |
| Bent ----------- | 742 | 79 | 320 | 92 | 3 | 1 | 351 | 471 | 234 |
| Boulder -------- | 782 | 471 | 768 | 370 | 394 | 22 | 2 | 895 | 503 |
| Chaffee -------- | 2 | 122 | 128 | --- | 118 | 169 | --- | 150 | 4 |
| Cheyenne ------- | 463 | 25 | 223 | 42 | 27 | --- | 430 | 2 | --- |
| Clear Creek----- | --- | 1 | 1 | --- | 1 | 20 | --- | 2 | --- |
| Conejos -------- | --- | 238 | 435 | 18 | 314 | 509 | --- | 321 | 9 |
| Costilla ------- | 35 | 40 | 147 | 17 | 165 | 207 | --- | 155 | 1 |
| Crowley -------- | 475 | 82 | 211 | 4 | 15 | 4 | 177 | 385 | 273 |
| Custer --------- | 39 | 187 | 142 | 16 | 42 | 172 | 1 | 21 | --- |
| Delta ---------- | 889 | 375 | 294 | 44 | 532 | 396 | 2 | 1,197 | 183 |
| Denver --------- | --- | --- | --- | --- | --- | --- | --- | --- | --- |
| Dolores -------- | 131 | 70 | 40 | 38 | 40 | 99 | 40 | 5 | --- |
| Douglas -------- | 353 | 300 | 98 | 98 | 41 | 85 | 59 | 217 | 1 |
| Eagle ---------- | --- | 140 | 67 | --- | 96 | 143 | --- | 247 | --- |
| Elbert --------- | 1,021 | 429 | 301 | 219 | 235 | 432 | 416 | 243 | --- |
| El Paso -------- | 856 | 414 | 88 | 49 | 109 | 267 | 222 | 53 | 8 |
| Fremont -------- | 546 | 186 | 124 | 23 | 105 | 55 | 23 | 470 | 2 |
| Garfield ------- | 263 | 335 | 256 | 33 | 413 | 453 | 6 | 715 | 110 |
| Gilpin --------- | --- | 29 | 4 | --- | 3 | 29 | --- | --- | --- |
| Grand ---------- | --- | 65 | 31 | 6 | 6 | 90 | --- | 20 | --- |
| Gunnison ------- | 1 | 55 | 49 | 1 | 31 | 230 | --- | 28 | --- |
| Hinsdale ------- | --- | 1 | --- | --- | --- | 8 | --- | 4 | --- |
| Huerfano ------- | 331 | 185 | 114 | 34 | 64 | 11 | 37 | 246 | --- |
| Jackson -------- | --- | 9 | 6 | 3 | --- | 13 | --- | --- | --- |
| Jefferson ------ | 690 | 551 | 271 | 199 | 281 | 307 | 15 | 777 | 55 |
| Kiowa ---------- | 516 | 8 | 78 | 42 | 3 | --- | 498 | 26 | --- |
| Kit Carson------ | 1,414 | 288 | 1,154 | 521 | 270 | 878 | 1,213 | 21 | --- |
| Lake ----------- | --- | --- | --- | --- | --- | --- | --- | --- | --- |
| La Plata-------- | 338 | 445 | 357 | 31 | 510 | 440 | 10 | 636 | --- |
| Larimer -------- | 848 | 551 | 1,027 | 295 | 305 | 159 | 30 | 1,174 | 907 |
| Las Animas----- | 774 | 223 | 161 | 101 | 93 | 33 | 395 | 204 | 35 |
| Lincoln -------- | 966 | 35 | 461 | 216 | 225 | 472 | 710 | 31 | --- |
| Logan ---------- | 1,592 | 492 | 1,351 | 783 | 186 | 709 | 672 | 595 | 470 |
| Mesa ----------- | 1,622 | 646 | 412 | 241 | 658 | 886 | 57 | 1,769 | 128 |
| Mineral -------- | --- | --- | --- | --- | --- | 1 | --- | 1 | --- |
| Moffat --------- | 217 | 341 | 139 | 186 | 200 | 352 | 33 | 399 | 5 |
| Montezuma ----- | 389 | 323 | 182 | 16 | 332 | 447 | 68 | 374 | --- |
| Montrose ------- | 694 | 489 | 280 | 36 | 700 | 735 | 1 | 911 | 120 |
| Morgan -------- | 1,168 | 177 | 775 | 162 | 141 | 220 | 372 | 647 | 588 |
| Otero ---------- | 775 | 316 | 417 | 65 | 73 | 4 | 117 | 749 | 600 |
| Ouray ---------- | 1 | 71 | 37 | 10 | 82 | 96 | --- | 90 | --- |
| Park ----------- | --- | 169 | 76 | 3 | 7 | 183 | --- | 1 | --- |
| Phillips ------- | 644 | 324 | 438 | 591 | 15 | 21 | 460 | 17 | --- |
| Pitkin --------- | --- | 104 | 18 | --- | 71 | 105 | --- | 69 | --- |
| Prowers -------- | 888 | 97 | 526 | --- | 9 | 1 | 688 | 552 | 267 |
| Pueblo --------- | 974 | 236 | 258 | 134 | 117 | 10 | 271 | 717 | 270 |
| Rio Blanco ----- | 2 | 185 | 39 | 49 | 134 | 237 | --- | 272 | --- |
| Rio Grande ----- | --- | 289 | 308 | --- | 152 | 433 | --- | 279 | 8 |
| Routt ---------- | --- | 393 | 294 | 72 | 194 | 222 | --- | 252 | 1 |
| Saguache ------- | --- | 189 | 199 | 15 | 61 | 102 | --- | 123 | --- |
| San Juan ------- | --- | --- | --- | --- | --- | --- | --- | --- | --- |
| San Miguel ----- | 37 | 71 | 80 | 34 | 39 | 39 | 13 | 91 | --- |
| Sedgwick ------- | 456 | 194 | 371 | 347 | 6 | 177 | 81 | 164 | 130 |
| Summit --------- | --- | 14 | 9 | --- | 5 | 28 | --- | 2 | --- |
| Teller --------- | 1 | 169 | 38 | 1 | 3 | 167 | --- | 3 | --- |
| Washington ---- | 1,361 | 198 | 1,076 | 650 | 226 | 318 | 881 | 76 | 52 |
| Weld ---------- | 2,912 | 1,151 | 3,070 | 905 | 826 | 1,892 | 347 | 2,852 | 2,767 |
| Yuma ---------- | 1,523 | 234 | 528 | 771 | 66 | 471 | 1,240 | 40 | --- |
| State --------- | 30,457 | 13,626 | 19,848 | 9,031 | 9,445 | 14,212 | 11,786 | 21,204 | 8,186 |

PER CENT OF HARVESTED AREA DEVOTED TO PRINCIPAL CROPS IN 1931

| COUNTY | Corn | Oats | Barley | Winter Wheat | Spring Wheat | Pota- toes | Dry Beans | All Sor- ghums | Al- falfa | Sugar Beets |
|---|---|---|---|---|---|---|---|---|---|---|
| Adams | 23.59 | 0.87 | 6.79 | 26.15 | 3.03 | 0.13 | 13.91 | 2.93 | 9.15 | 6.17 |
| Alamosa | 0.02 | 3.83 | 4.46 | 0.09 | 2.44 | 10.43 | 0.02 | ---- | 21.92 | 1.26 |
| Arapahoe | 23.35 | 1.81 | 7.17 | 27.45 | 4.20 | 0.01 | 15.30 | 3.78 | 9.74 | 0.88 |
| Archuleta | 4.20 | 9.62 | 1.38 | 1.65 | 5.85 | 1.83 | 0.18 | ---- | 21.35 | ---- |
| Baca | 22.86 | 0. 4 | 1.44 | 49.86 | 0.07 | ---- | 1.28 | 14.82 | 0.34 | ---- |
| Bent | 31.40 | 0. 7 | 5.20 | 4.09 | 0.12 | 0.01 | 2.27 | 14.58 | 28.33 | 4.72 |
| Boulder | 16.28 | 5.29 | 10.63 | 9.78 | 6.56 | 0.28 | 0.47 | 0.01 | 27.69 | 11.95 |
| Chaffee | 0.07 | 4.23 | 8.05 | 0.20 | 3.28 | 3.17 | 0.27 | ---- | 29.00 | ---- |
| Cheyenne | 65.18 | 0.51 | 7.57 | 9.83 | 1.67 | 0.04 | 0.63 | 11.43 | 0.38 | ---- |
| Clear Creek | 0.75 | 0.75 | ---- | ---- | ---- | 2.62 | ---- | ---- | 0.74 | ---- |
| Conejos | 0.17 | 3.24 | 9.80 | 0.19 | 52 | 9.91 | 0.75 | ---- | 21.04 | 0.07 |
| Costilla | 0.23 | 2.55 | 8.94 | 0.74 | .22 | 4.74 | 1.19 | ---- | 17.08 | ---- |
| Crowley | 25.72 | 1.37 | 3.39 | 0.25 | 5.49 | 0.01 | 7.50 | 8.04 | 23.37 | 15.83 |
| Custer | 2.68 | 4.16 | 2.99 | 1.44 | 6.76 | 12.44 | ---- | 0.09 | 7.60 | ---- |
| Delta | 9.11 | 3.57 | 3.64 | 0.70 | 5.29 | 2.30 | 0.29 | 0.02 | 48.37 | 4.14 |
| Denver | ---- | ---- | ---- | ---- | ---- | ---- | ---- | ---- | ---- | ---- |
| Dolores | 19.52 | 8.56 | 1.88 | 17.29 | 6 | 3.34 | 18.32 | 2.40 | 5.31 | ---- |
| Douglas | 31.90 | 12.71 | 2.55 | 8.91 | 1.80 | 0.53 | 3.06 | 1.36 | 16.13 | ---- |
| Eagle | 0.04 | 4.22 | 1.97 | 0.88 | 2.46 | 4.06 | ---- | ---- | 34.75 | ---- |
| Elbert | 32.24 | 3.15 | 4.26 | 10.24 | 3.60 | 0.41 | 27.21 | 2.21 | 5.06 | ---- |
| El Paso | 38.54 | 5.19 | 0.82 | 1.64 | 2.01 | 0.48 | 25.37 | 3.51 | 3.66 | 0.69 |
| Fremont | 15.90 | 4.15 | 1.50 | 0.45 | 1.31 | 1.00 | 0.15 | 0.27 | 28.39 | ---- |
| Garfield | 1.83 | 3.55 | 3.25 | 0.91 | 8.5 | 4.94 | 0.05 | 0.04 | 65.02 | 2.91 |
| Gilpin | ---- | 3.90 | 0.65 | ---- | 0.6 | 5.19 | 1.30 | ---- | ---- | ---- |
| Grand | 0.03 | 2.24 | 1.15 | 0.21 | 0.0 | 0.39 | ---- | ---- | 2.57 | ---- |
| Gunnison | ---- | 0.79 | 0.54 | 0.08 | 0.14 | 0.41 | ---- | ---- | 4.55 | ---- |
| Hinsdale | ---- | 1.61 | ---- | ---- | ---- | 0.13 | ---- | ---- | 1.88 | ---- |
| Huerfano | 16.64 | 3.48 | 0.99 | 2.36 | 2.08 | 1.21 | 4.07 | 0.93 | 44.89 | 0.12 |
| Jackson | ---- | 0.12 | 0.05 | ---- | ---- | 0.08 | ---- | ---- | 0.01 | ---- |
| Jefferson | 10.37 | 8.09 | 8.50 | 11.05 | 6.61 | 1.30 | 0.24 | 0.21 | 32.93 | 1.59 |
| Kiowa | 63.59 | 0.07 | 3.56 | 5.57 | 0.17 | 0.01 | 0.37 | 22.95 | 1.35 | ---- |
| Kit Carson | 46.97 | 1.03 | 15.99 | 17.52 | 5.01 | 0.16 | 0.86 | 5.80 | 0.44 | ---- |
| Lake | ---- | ---- | ---- | ---- | ---- | ---- | ---- | ---- | ---- | ---- |
| La Plata | 4.58 | 8.45 | 4.85 | 1.88 | 15.43 | 2.75 | 1.41 | 0.18 | 41.04 | ---- |
| Larimer | 9.01 | 3.30 | 10.61 | 12.16 | 3.17 | 0.56 | 0.91 | 0.29 | 28.39 | 14.6 |
| Las Animas | 37.31 | 2.33 | 4.21 | 4.89 | 0.74 | 0.15 | 14.59 | 7.42 | 14.55 | 1.0 |
| Lincoln | 39.46 | 0.22 | 8.60 | 19.04 | 3.32 | 0.15 | 11.50 | 8.58 | 0.86 | --- |
| Logan | 20.65 | 1.52 | 11.06 | 31.64 | 1.69 | 0.37 | 1.22 | 2.55 | 6.36 | 4.8 |
| Mesa | 12.76 | 2.97 | 2.37 | 2.37 | 3.43 | 2.90 | 4.60 | 0.33 | 45.33 | 2.3 |
| Mineral | --- | ---- | ---- | ---- | ---- | 0.16 | ---- | ---- | 0.32 | --- |
| Moffat | 3.48 | 7.50 | 2.16 | 8.29 | 6.19 | 2.01 | 0.15 | 0.36 | 27.87 | --- |
| Montezuma | 11.00 | 9.41 | 3.45 | 2.69 | 11.06 | 2.92 | 15.78 | 0.79 | ---- | --- |
| Montrose | 7.11 | 5.60 | 3.53 | 1.11 | 11.28 | 7.96 | 0.52 | 0.01 | 51.94 | 1.2 |
| Morgan | 36.54 | 0.91 | 7.08 | 9.86 | 3.57 | 0.80 | 7.04 | 2.81 | 10.25 | 10.3 |
| Otero | 14.92 | 2.36 | 4.82 | 1.14 | 0.47 | 0.01 | 4.02 | 2.26 | 26.14 | 16.2 |
| Ouray | 1.78 | 6.15 | 2.80 | 2.32 | 5.67 | 1.74 | 0.07 | ---- | 24.31 | --- |
| Park | ---- | 0.29 | 0.04 | ---- | 0.04 | 4.06 | ---- | ---- | 0.04 | --- |
| Phillips | 35.54 | 2.74 | 7.12 | 46.96 | 0.28 | 0.05 | 0.09 | 2.65 | 0.19 | --- |
| Pitkin | ---- | 3.59 | 0.51 | 0.26 | 2.13 | 7.39 | ---- | ---- | 26.81 | --- |
| Prowers | 19.73 | 1.01 | 6.65 | 21.37 | 0.29 | ---- | 0.15 | 17.19 | 22.89 | 5.0 |
| Pueblo | 30.00 | 1.62 | 3.00 | 8.66 | 0.92 | 0.02 | 15.30 | 3.30 | 18.01 | 7.5 |
| Rio Blanco | ---- | 4.65 | 1.03 | 2.74 | 2.97 | 0.21 | ---- | ---- | 42.23 | ---- |
| Rio Grande | 0.03 | 4.12 | 5.51 | 0.04 | 3.57 | 16.26 | 0.12 | ---- | 10.17 | 0.0 |
| Routt | ---- | 13.06 | 6.40 | 2.05 | 4.95 | 1.73 | ---- | ---- | 14.33 | --- |
| Saguache | 0.01 | 2.38 | 1.91 | 0.05 | 1.18 | 7.48 | 0.01 | ---- | 7.52 | --- |
| San Juan | --- | ---- | ---- | ---- | ---- | ---- | ---- | ---- | ---- | --- |
| San Miguel | 3.18 | 2.51 | 4.77 | 5.19 | 2.34 | 1.59 | 1.93 | 0.42 | 33.65 | --- |
| Sedgwick | 25.46 | 2.95 | 10.32 | 46.08 | 0.15 | 0.52 | 0.04 | 0.53 | 3.26 | 3.4 |
| Summit | ---- | 0.99 | 0.88 | 0.22 | 0.22 | 0.33 | ---- | ---- | 0.33 | --- |
| Teller | 0.29 | 2.82 | 0.65 | 0.22 | 0.07 | 13.55 | ---- | ---- | 1.16 | --- |
| Washington | 42.64 | 0.93 | 12.13 | 21.69 | 2.46 | 0.09 | 4.39 | 3.72 | 0.81 | 0.1 |
| Weld | 15.95 | 1.92 | 11.00 | 16.85 | 3.83 | 4.11 | 7.39 | 1.23 | 15.03 | 13.5 |
| Yuma | 53.67 | 0.70 | 3.87 | 25.32 | 0.59 | 0.07 | 0.22 | 5.66 | 0.50 | --- |
| State | 27.26 | 2.20 | 6.80 | 18.08 | 2.61 | 1.50 | 4.75 | 4.59 | 11.03 | |

### PERCENTAGE OF CROPS GROWN WITH AND WITHOUT IRRIGATION, 1931

| OUNTY | CORN | | OATS | | BARLEY | | POTATOES | | DRY BEANS | |
|---|---|---|---|---|---|---|---|---|---|---|
| | % Irrigated | % Non-Irrigated | % Irrigated | % Non-Irrigated | % Irrigated | % Non-Irrigated | % Irrigated | % Non-Irrigated | % Irrigated | % Non-Irrigated |
| ms ____ | 8.1 | 91.9 | 80.3 | 19.7 | 23.3 | 76.7 | 88.0 | 12.0 | 2.0 | 98.0 |
| mosa ____ | 100.0 | ---- | 100.0 | ---- | 100.0 | ---- | 100.0 | ---- | 100.0 | ---- |
| pahoe __ | 3.2 | 96.8 | 48.5 | 51.5 | 12.0 | 88.0 | 20.0 | 80.0 | 1.0 | 99.0 |
| huleta __ | 2.9 | 97.1 | 17.8 | 82.2 | 39.3 | 60.7 | 20.0 | 80.0 | 8.0 | 92.0 |
| a _____ | .3 | 99.7 | 38.1 | 61.9 | 3.9 | 96.1 | ---- | 100.0 | 1.0 | 99.0 |
| t _____ | 44.8 | 55.2 | 98.8 | 1.2 | 96.3 | 3.7 | ---- | 100.0 | 14.0 | 86.0 |
| lder ____ | 79.9 | 20.1 | 99.1 | .9 | 94.7 | 5.3 | 98.0 | 2.0 | 24.0 | 76.0 |
| ffee ____ | ---- | 100.0 | 98.6 | 1.4 | 99.0 | 1.0 | 100.0 | ---- | 100.0 | ---- |
| yenne __ | ---- | 100.0 | ---- | 100.0 | ---- | 100.0 | ---- | 100.0 | ---- | 100.0 |
| r Creek_ | 100.0 | ---- | ---- | 100.0 | ---- | ---- | 23.0 | 77.0 | ---- | ---- |
| ejos ____ | 100.0 | ---- | 100.0 | ---- | 100.0 | ---- | 100.0 | ---- | 100.0 | ---- |
| illa ____ | 100.0 | ---- | 100.0 | ---- | 100.0 | ---- | 100.0 | ---- | 100.0 | ---- |
| wley ___ | 43.0 | 57.0 | 86.9 | 13.1 | 97.0 | 3.0 | ---- | 100.0 | 11.0 | 89.0 |
| ter _____ | 16.8 | 83.2 | 33.4 | 66.6 | 50.1 | 49.9 | 6.0 | 94.0 | ---- | ---- |
| a _____ | 99.9 | .1 | 100.0 | ---- | 100.0 | ---- | 100.0 | ---- | 82.0 | 18.0 |
| ver ____ | ---- | ---- | ---- | ---- | ---- | ---- | ---- | ---- | ---- | ---- |
| ores ____ | ---- | 100.0 | ---- | 100.0 | ---- | 100.0 | ---- | 100.0 | ---- | 100.0 |
| glas ___ | 1.3 | 98.7 | 2.3 | 97.7 | 10.5 | 89.5 | ---- | 100.0 | ---- | 100.0 |
| le _____ | 80.0 | 20.0 | 98.2 | 1.8 | 89.6 | 10.4 | 99.0 | 1.0 | ---- | ---- |
| ert _____ | ---- | 100.0 | ---- | 100.0 | ---- | 100.0 | ---- | 100.0 | ---- | 100.0 |
| Paso ____ | .9 | 99.1 | .4 | 99.6 | 10.5 | 89.5 | 1.0 | 99.0 | 1.0 | 99.0 |
| mont ___ | 74.8 | 25.2 | 39.9 | 60.1 | 67.4 | 32.6 | 7.0 | 93.0 | 36.0 | 64.0 |
| field ___ | 85.5 | 14.5 | 91.0 | 9.0 | 91.3 | 8.7 | 98.0 | 2.0 | 100.0 | ---- |
| in _____ | ---- | ---- | ---- | 100.0 | ---- | 100.0 | ---- | 100.0 | ---- | 100.0 |
| nd _____ | 100.0 | ---- | 90.4 | 9.6 | 85.2 | 14.8 | 13.0 | 87.0 | ---- | ---- |
| nison __ | ---- | ---- | 25.5 | 74.5 | 35.2 | 64.8 | 35.0 | 65.0 | ---- | ---- |
| sdale ___ | ---- | ---- | 100.0 | ---- | ---- | ---- | 75.0 | 25.0 | ---- | ---- |
| rfano __ | 16.1 | 83.9 | 41.2 | 58.8 | 41.3 | 58.7 | 24.0 | 76.0 | 7.0 | 93.0 |
| kson ___ | ---- | ---- | 49.0 | 51.0 | 92.6 | 7.4 | 18.0 | 82.0 | ---- | ---- |
| erson __ | 65.0 | 35.0 | 49.2 | 50.8 | 80.4 | 19.6 | 39.0 | 61.0 | 34.0 | 66.0 |
| wa _____ | ---- | 100.0 | ---- | 100.0 | ---- | 100.0 | ---- | 100.0 | ---- | 100.0 |
| Carson_ | ---- | 100.0 | ---- | 100.0 | .2 | 99.8 | ---- | 100.0 | 1.0 | 99.0 |
| e _____ | ---- | ---- | ---- | ---- | ---- | ---- | ---- | ---- | ---- | ---- |
| Plata___ | 28.0 | 72.0 | 78.3 | 21.7 | 77.4 | 22.6 | 98.0 | 2.0 | 11.0 | 89.0 |
| imer ___ | 59.2 | 40.8 | 87.5 | 12.5 | 86.7 | 13.3 | 93.0 | 7.0 | 51.0 | 49.0 |
| Animas_ | 9.8 | 90.2 | 33.5 | 66.5 | 35.9 | 64.1 | 11.0 | 89.0 | 17.0 | 83.0 |
| oln ____ | ---- | 100.0 | ---- | 100.0 | .4 | 99.6 | ---- | 100.0 | ---- | 100.0 |
| an _____ | 8.9 | 91.1 | 38.3 | 61.7 | 23.2 | 76.8 | 26.0 | 74.0 | 7.0 | 93.0 |
| a _____ | 94.9 | 5.1 | 90.7 | 9.3 | 96.2 | 3.8 | 84.0 | 16.0 | 86.0 | 14.0 |
| eral ___ | ---- | ---- | ---- | ---- | ---- | ---- | 100.0 | ---- | ---- | ---- |
| at _____ | .4 | 99.6 | 11.3 | 88.7 | 12.7 | 87.3 | 9.0 | 91.0 | ---- | 100.0 |
| tezuma _ | 19.6 | 80.4 | 69.8 | 30.2 | 49.7 | 50.3 | 51.0 | 49.0 | 15.0 | 85.0 |
| trose __ | 100.0 | ---- | 98.1 | 1.9 | 95.4 | 4.6 | 99.0 | 1.0 | 98.0 | 2.0 |
| gan ___ | 11.5 | 88.5 | 58.9 | 41.1 | 52.4 | 47.6 | 98.0 | 2.0 | 7.0 | 93.0 |
| o _____ | 87.4 | 12.6 | 99.7 | .3 | 95.5 | 4.5 | 100.0 | ---- | 96.0 | 4.0 |
| ay _____ | ---- | 100.0 | 87.9 | 12.1 | 37.2 | 62.8 | 64.0 | 36.0 | ---- | 100.0 |
| c _____ | ---- | ---- | ---- | 100.0 | ---- | 100.0 | ---- | 100.0 | ---- | ---- |
| lips ____ | ---- | 100.0 | ---- | 100.0 | ---- | 100.0 | ---- | 100.0 | ---- | 100.0 |
| in _____ | ---- | ---- | 100.0 | ---- | 100.0 | ---- | 100.0 | ---- | ---- | ---- |
| vers ___ | 37.7 | 62.3 | 68.0 | 32.0 | 53.2 | 46.8 | ---- | 100.0 | 36.0 | 64.0 |
| olo ____ | 37.6 | 62.4 | 54.1 | 45.9 | 77.4 | 22.6 | ---- | 100.0 | 10.0 | 90.0 |
| Blanco _ | ---- | ---- | 74.4 | 25.6 | 19.9 | 80.1 | 81.0 | 19.0 | ---- | ---- |
| Grande_ | 100.0 | ---- | 100.0 | ---- | 100.0 | ---- | 100.0 | ---- | 100.0 | ---- |
| t _____ | ---- | ---- | 2.6 | 97.4 | 1.2 | 98.8 | 4.0 | 96.0 | ---- | ---- |
| ache __ | 100.0 | ---- | 100.0 | ---- | 100.0 | ---- | 100.0 | ---- | 100.0 | ---- |
| Juan __ | ---- | ---- | ---- | ---- | ---- | ---- | ---- | ---- | ---- | ---- |
| Miguel_ | 22.1 | 77.9 | 50.1 | 49.9 | 17.4 | 82.6 | 10.0 | 90.0 | ---- | 100.0 |
| wick __ | 6.8 | 93.2 | 20.3 | 79.7 | 16.9 | 83.1 | 76.0 | 24.0 | ---- | 100.0 |
| mit ___ | ---- | ---- | 39.3 | 60.7 | 12.0 | 88.0 | ---- | 100.0 | ---- | ---- |
| r _____ | ---- | 100.0 | ---- | 100.0 | ---- | 100.0 | ---- | 100.0 | ---- | ---- |
| hington_ | .3 | 99.7 | 6.1 | 93.9 | 1.8 | 98.2 | 4.0 | 96.0 | ---- | 100.0 |
| l _____ | 25.8 | 74.2 | 74.6 | 25.4 | 64.1 | 35.9 | 97.0 | 3.0 | 28.0 | 72.0 |
| a _____ | .1 | 99.9 | ---- | 100.0 | ---- | 100.0 | 9.0 | 91.0 | ---- | 100.0 |
| tate____ | 8.5 | 91.5 | 46.8 | 53.2 | 32.6 | 67.4 | 81.7 | 18.3 | 9.5 | 90.5 |

**AVERAGE YIELD, IN BUSHELS, OF PRINCIPAL CROPS PER ACRE FOR FIVE YEARS ENDING WITH 1931**

| COUNTY | CORN | | BARLEY | | WINTER WHEAT | | SPRING WHEAT | | POTATOES | |
|---|---|---|---|---|---|---|---|---|---|---|
| | Irri-gated | Non-Irri-gated | Irri-gated | Non-Irri-gated | Irri-gated | Non-Irri-gated | Irri-gated | Non-Irri-gated | Irri-gated | Non-Irri-gate |
| Adams | 34.34 | 12.29 | 38.22 | 14.07 | 28.21 | 11.02 | 28.53 | 8.34 | 117.82 | 43. |
| Alamosa | 29.33 | ---- | 28.63 | ---- | 25.25 | ---- | 22.44 | ---- | 159.22 | -- |
| Arapahoe | 33.21 | 12.93 | 37.45 | 13.34 | 28.55 | 11.81 | 26.40 | 8.41 | 112.31 | 55. |
| Archuleta | 31.34 | 12.21 | 32.80 | 16.12 | 27.27 | 12.30 | 26.70 | 10.77 | 113.84 | 70. |
| Baca | 29.54 | 12.78 | 27.07 | 9.11 | 28.18 | 11.90 | 21.00 | 4.89 | ---- | 76. |
| Bent | 35.68 | 12.53 | 34.70 | 12.23 | 32.67 | 11.80 | 27.87 | 8.33 | 99.00 | 53. |
| Boulder | 32.90 | 14.99 | 39.35 | 18.19 | 31.11 | 15.78 | 28.81 | 12.68 | 133.24 | 51. |
| Chaffee | 41.00 | 11.50 | 32.44 | 12.00 | 25.00 | 18.00 | 24.56 | ---- | 122.25 | -- |
| Cheyenne | ---- | 12.36 | ---- | 10.72 | ---- | 7.91 | ---- | 6.23 | ---- | 59. |
| Clear Creek | 29.67 | 22.00 | 34.00 | 21.00 | ---- | ---- | ---- | ---- | 100.00 | 54. |
| Conejos | 28.90 | ---- | 31.48 | ---- | 24.89 | ---- | 22.98 | ---- | 155.27 | -- |
| Costilla | 30.37 | 11.00 | 29.53 | ---- | 30.61 | ---- | 22.56 | 12.00 | 106.39 | 40 |
| Crowley | 35.84 | 11.80 | 34.59 | 9.86 | 30.63 | ---- | 23.60 | 12.00 | 60.00 | 48 |
| Custer | 34.48 | 14.88 | 29.06 | 12.63 | 28.80 | 14.09 | 25.48 | 11.07 | 114.05 | 85 |
| Delta | 40.43 | 17.03 | 39.45 | 18.20 | 31.62 | 14.59 | 28.94 | 10.09 | 128.32 | 66. |
| Denver | ---- | ---- | ---- | ---- | ---- | ---- | ---- | ---- | ---- | |
| Dolores | ---- | 13.30 | ---- | 14.29 | 25.00 | 11.21 | ---- | 9.54 | ---- | 56. |
| Douglas | 30.29 | 14.79 | 29.95 | 17.00 | 24.57 | 12.94 | 24.90 | 10.49 | ---- | 60 |
| Eagle | 34.20 | ---- | 40.75 | 18.87 | 23.60 | 16.74 | 31.62 | 15.17 | 207.22 | 75 |
| Elbert | ---- | 13.10 | 38.00 | 12.19 | 23.00 | 10.96 | 27.00 | 8.64 | ---- | 59 |
| El Paso | 31.40 | 12.42 | 31.80 | 11.59 | 28.71 | 12.26 | 24.75 | 7.89 | 91.43 | 63 |
| Fremont | 39.24 | 14.70 | 36.17 | 14.04 | 29.36 | 11.00 | 25.58 | 10.28 | 104.00 | 61 |
| Garfield | 37.37 | 15.37 | 36.42 | 16.54 | 31.87 | 14.33 | 29.21 | 13.52 | 180.12 | 68 |
| Gilpin | ---- | ---- | ---- | 15.88 | ---- | ---- | ---- | 9.00 | ---- | 52 |
| Grand | 29.00 | ---- | 39.62 | 15.22 | 29.14 | 12.33 | 29.10 | 14.00 | 131.84 | 41 |
| Gunnison | 30.00 | ---- | 35.67 | 15.24 | 20.33 | 13.71 | 28.56 | 14.09 | 142.79 | 69 |
| Hinsdale | ---- | ---- | 35.00 | ---- | ---- | ---- | ---- | ---- | 129.26 | -- |
| Huerfano | 29.03 | 12.40 | 36.15 | 14.94 | 28.57 | 11.60 | 23.07 | 8.37 | 114.58 | 79 |
| Jackson | 21.00 | ---- | 32.77 | 23.00 | ---- | ---- | 28.00 | ---- | 94.00 | 101 |
| Jefferson | 30.29 | 14.25 | 35.81 | 14.27 | 30.81 | 15.26 | 28.69 | 11.65 | 132.39 | 68 |
| Kiowa | ---- | 12.12 | 33.00 | 8.99 | 30.00 | 10.89 | 26.67 | 4.45 | 115.00 | 50 |
| Kit Carson | 30.00 | 12.67 | 32.00 | 11.74 | 24.00 | 8.64 | 24.00 | 6.37 | ---- | 52 |
| Lake | ---- | ---- | ---- | ---- | ---- | ---- | ---- | ---- | ---- | 7 |
| La Plata | 30.97 | 14.89 | 34.78 | 14.38 | 29.71 | 12.73 | 25.09 | 11.14 | 145.22 | 7 |
| Larimer | 33.06 | 14.88 | 43.04 | 16.94 | 32.00 | 16.72 | 29.94 | 12.57 | 140.92 | 6 |
| Las Animas | 35.02 | 11.02 | 31.38 | 8.81 | 26.87 | 8.41 | 23.42 | 5.42 | 138.60 | 6 |
| Lincoln | 32.00 | 12.33 | 28.36 | 9.61 | 30.00 | 9.02 | 20.47 | 6.56 | 85.00 | 5 |
| Logan | 33.23 | 14.88 | 37.64 | 15.39 | 29.39 | 11.52 | 27.40 | 9.16 | 129.45 | 6 |
| Mesa | 39.49 | 13.89 | 34.76 | 15.21 | 31.33 | 12.76 | 27.35 | 9.90 | 107.30 | 5 |
| Mineral | ---- | ---- | 37.40 | ---- | ---- | ---- | ---- | ---- | 135.29 | |
| Moffat | 25.36 | 14.84 | 39.87 | 20.57 | 29.60 | 16.02 | 28.63 | 13.49 | 132.78 | 6 |
| Montezuma | 30.04 | 14.66 | 31.07 | 13.78 | 26.03 | 12.56 | 23.35 | 10.47 | 129.90 | 6 |
| Montrose | 38.74 | 15.96 | 36.55 | 13.39 | 32.67 | 14.11 | 30.16 | 9.32 | 145.67 | 4 |
| Morgan | 35.60 | 12.65 | 41.40 | 14.68 | 27.45 | 10.66 | 28.11 | 7.99 | 161.28 | 5 |
| Otero | 36.99 | 12.86 | 34.28 | 10.14 | 33.21 | 11.01 | 27.95 | 6.04 | 84.50 | 5 |
| Ouray | 40.03 | 10.00 | 38.15 | 15.51 | 28.38 | 14.28 | 29.21 | 12.03 | 137.84 | 5 |
| Park | ---- | ---- | ---- | 17.46 | ---- | 10.14 | ---- | 9.15 | 80.00 | 6 |
| Phillips | ---- | 16.47 | ---- | 16.81 | ---- | 12.69 | ---- | 8.55 | ---- | 7 |
| Pitkin | 35.00 | ---- | 36.98 | 18.00 | 28.43 | 20.00 | 32.67 | 14.00 | 183.20 | |
| Prowers | 32.56 | 11.21 | 33.91 | 9.82 | 29.99 | 10.96 | 29.20 | 4.79 | 84.80 | 4 |
| Pueblo | 35.89 | 12.01 | 35.58 | 11.34 | 30.13 | 10.32 | 28.95 | 7.09 | 75.00 | 6 |
| Rio Blanco | 25.76 | 14.58 | 36.42 | 22.30 | 31.78 | 18.12 | 26.33 | 15.15 | 121.10 | 5 |
| Rio Grande | 29.00 | ---- | 28.38 | ---- | 30.27 | ---- | 22.40 | ---- | 177.77 | |
| Routt | 27.33 | 15.00 | 42.17 | 24.07 | 30.61 | 20.47 | 27.05 | 18.48 | 167.94 | 5 |
| Saguache | 26.33 | ---- | 27.90 | ---- | 32.83 | ---- | 19.75 | ---- | 163.32 | |
| San Juan | ---- | ---- | ---- | ---- | ---- | ---- | ---- | ---- | ---- | |
| San Miguel | 35.34 | 14.42 | 37.43 | 16.82 | 27.47 | 14.66 | 25.81 | 10.74 | 141.72 | |
| Sedgwick | 33.83 | 16.33 | 37.64 | 18.26 | 31.17 | 13.55 | 24.98 | 10.20 | 137.65 | |
| Summit | ---- | ---- | 34.77 | 15.11 | 26.43 | 10.18 | 25.50 | 9.00 | 138.11 | |
| Teller | ---- | 17.00 | ---- | 17.74 | ---- | 17.28 | ---- | 11.12 | ---- | |
| Washington | 33.56 | 13.66 | 37.15 | 12.57 | 28.28 | 8.93 | 25.62 | 5.93 | 106.71 | |
| Weld | 34.14 | 12.53 | 41.85 | 14.49 | 30.06 | 12.74 | 27.58 | 9.55 | 144.75 | |
| Yuma | 29.05 | 14.70 | 38.23 | 13.85 | 26.00 | 12.12 | 26.62 | 6.78 | 126.86 | |
| State | 34.99 | 13.43 | 37.76 | 13.48 | 30.35 | 11.41 | 27.26 | 8.63 | 156.37 | |

ACREAGE, PRODUCTION AND VALUE OF WHEAT IN COLORADO, 1880-1931

| YEAR | Acres | Yield per Acre, Bushels | Production, Bushels | Price per Bushels | Value | Value per Acre |
|---|---|---|---|---|---|---|
| 1880 | 65,300 | 17.0 | 1,110,100 | $ .95 | $ 1,054,595 | $16.15 |
| 1881 | 66,000 | 19.8 | 1,310,000 | 1.33 | 1,742,300 | 26.40 |
| 1882 | 95,000 | 16.8 | 1,598,200 | .94 | 1,502,308 | 15.81 |
| 1883 | 114,000 | 21.0 | 2,394,000 | .95 | 2,298,240 | 20.16 |
| 1884 | 117,430 | 20.0 | 2,348,000 | .56 | 1,314,880 | 11.20 |
| 1885 | 120,943 | 19.8 | 2,395,000 | .82 | 1,963,900 | 16.24 |
| 1886 | 122,152 | 19.8 | 2,419,000 | .72 | 1,693,300 | 13.87 |
| 1887 | 119,709 | 21.0 | 2,514,000 | .75 | 1,885,500 | 15.75 |
| 1888 | 134,074 | 17.5 | 2,346,000 | .90 | 2,111,400 | 15.75 |
| 1889 | 87,300 | 21.2 | 1,851,000 | .72 | 1,332,547 | 15.26 |
| 1890 | 96,000 | 18.5 | 1,777,000 | .81 | 1,439,010 | 14.99 |
| 1891 | 100,832 | 20.2 | 2,037,000 | .73 | 1,486,808 | 14.74 |
| 1892 | 131,082 | 19.1 | 2,504,000 | .58 | 1,452,126 | 11.08 |
| 1893 | 137,636 | 13.2 | 1,816,795 | .52 | 944,733 | 6.86 |
| 1894 | 119,777 | 17.9 | 2,144,000 | .65 | 1,393,600 | 11.62 |
| 1895 | 119,500 | 23.5 | 2,808,250 | .56 | 1,572,000 | 13.16 |
| 1896 | 159,839 | 17.5 | 2,797,182 | .61 | 1,706,281 | 10.67 |
| 1897 | 213,231 | 24.0 | 5,117,544 | .70 | 3,582,281 | 16.80 |
| 1898 | 255,877 | 26.3 | 6,729,565 | .56 | 3,768,556 | 14.73 |
| 1899 | 309,611 | 23.7 | 7,337,781 | .57 | 4,182,535 | 13.51 |
| 1900 | 318,899 | 22.6 | 7,207,117 | .59 | 4,252,199 | 13.33 |
| 1901 | 312,521 | 24.1 | 7,531,756 | .67 | 5,046,277 | 16.15 |
| 1902 | 293,770 | 18.0 | 5,287,800 | .75 | 3,965,895 | 13.50 |
| 1903 | 279,082 | 26.6 | 7,423,581 | .66 | 4,899,563 | 17.56 |
| 1904 | 259,546 | 22.8 | 5,917,649 | .91 | 5,385,061 | 20.75 |
| 1905 | 254,355 | 25.0 | 6,358,875 | .70 | 4,451,212 | 17.50 |
| 1906 | 254,555 | 32.5 | 8,266,538 | .65 | 5,373,250 | 21.12 |
| 1907 | 293,000 | 29.0 | 8,497,000 | .78 | 6,628,000 | 22.62 |
| 1908 | 293,000 | 21.0 | 6,153,000 | .88 | 5,415,000 | 18.48 |
| 1909 | 341,000 | 21.2 | 7,224,000 | .93 | 6,718,000 | 19.70 |
| 1910 | 403,000 | 22.3 | 8,994,000 | .82 | 7,376,000 | 18.30 |
| 1911 | 438,000 | 18.9 | 8,274,000 | .84 | 6,950,000 | 15.87 |
| 1912 | 453,000 | 24.2 | 10,968,000 | .73 | 8,006,000 | 17.67 |
| 1913 | 460,000 | 21.0 | 9,680,000 | .78 | 7,551,000 | 16.42 |
| 1914 | 475,000 | 23.8 | 11,312,000 | .87 | 9,842,000 | 20.72 |
| 1915 | 570,000 | 24.2 | 13,770,000 | .80 | 11,016,000 | 19.32 |
| 1916 | 600,000 | 19.8 | 11,885,000 | 1.50 | 17,828,000 | 29.70 |
| 1917 | 600,000 | 22.6 | 13,536,000 | 1.93 | 26,124,000 | 43.55 |
| 1918 | 1,250,000 | 12.3 | 15,400,000 | 1.95 | 30,030,000 | 24.02 |
| 1919 | 1,329,000 | 13.7 | 18,196,000 | 2.02 | 36,755,000 | 27.66 |
| 1920 | 1,405,000 | 18.0 | 25,273,000 | 1.35 | 34,118,000 | 24.28 |
| 1921 | 1,719,000 | 13.5 | 23,239,000 | .76 | 17,662,000 | 10.27 |
| 1922 | 1,620,000 | 13.4 | 21,776,000 | .89 | 19,380,000 | 11.96 |
| 1923 | 1,407,000 | 13.0 | 18,272,000 | .83 | 15,166,000 | 10.78 |
| 1924 | 1,360,000 | 14.4 | 19,520,000 | 1.18 | 23,033,000 | 16.94 |
| 1925 | 1,268,000 | 11.8 | 14,988,000 | 1.36 | 20,345,000 | 16.04 |
| 1926 | 1,364,000 | 13.5 | 18,427,000 | 1.07 | 19,728,000 | 14.47 |
| 1927 | 1,419,000 | 14.2 | 20,112,000 | 1.03 | 20,818,000 | 14.67 |
| 1928 | 1,339,000 | 13.9 | 18,564,000 | .85 | 15,815,000 | 11.81 |
| 1929 | 1,539,000 | 11.7 | 17,934,000 | .93 | 16,632,000 | 10.81 |
| 1930 | 1,632,000 | 14.3 | 23,356,000 | .53 | 12,420,000 | 7.61 |
| 1931 | 1,394,000 | 11.9 | 16,552,000 | .43 | 7,176,000 | 5.15 |

### ACREAGE, PRODUCTION AND VALUE OF CORN IN COLORADO, 1880-1931

| YEAR | Acres | Yield per Acre, Bushels | Production, Bushels | Price per Bushel | Value | Value per Acre |
|------|-------|----------------|----------------|----------|-------|----------|
| 1880 | 13,795 | 18.5 | 255,207 | $ .77 | $ 196,500 | $14.24 |
| 1881 | 13,800 | 25.5 | 352,000 | 1.05 | 369,600 | 26.78 |
| 1882 | 21,076 | 20.0 | 422,400 | .90 | 380,160 | 18.03 |
| 1883 | 21,287 | 25.0 | 532,100 | .85 | 452,285 | 21.24 |
| 1884 | 25,300 | 28.1 | 710,000 | .65 | 461,500 | 18.24 |
| 1885 | 27,830 | 34.5 | 959,000 | .68 | 652,120 | 23.43 |
| 1886 | 29,778 | 31.5 | 938,000 | .50 | 469,000 | 15.75 |
| 1887 | 31,267 | 30.0 | 938,000 | .63 | 590,940 | 18.90 |
| 1888 | 34,394 | 22.6 | 777,000 | .57 | 442,890 | 12.87 |
| 1889 | 42,993 | 25,4 | 1,092,000 | .58 | 633,373 | 14.73 |
| 1890 | 42,133 | 18.2 | 767.000 | .63 | 483,097 | 11.47 |
| 1891 | 43,397 | 21.5 | 933,000 | .53 | 494,509 | 11.39 |
| 1892 | 124,350 | 22.3 | 2,773,000 | .40 | 1,109,202 | 8.92 |
| 1893 | 123,107 | 16.5 | 2,031,266 | .51 | 1,035,946 | 8.41 |
| 1894 | 125,569 | 19.7 | 2,473,709 | .61 | 1,508,962 | 12.01 |
| 1895 | 178,308 | 20.7 | 3,690,976 | .41 | 1,513,300 | 8.48 |
| 1896 | 178,308 | 16.0 | 2,852,928 | .36 | 1,027,054 | 5.76 |
| 1897 | 176,525 | 19.0 | 3,353,975 | .38 | 1,274,510 | 7.22 |
| 1898 | 172,99´ | 18.0 | 3,113,892 | .40 | 1,245,557 | 7.20 |
| 1899 | 171,264 | 17.0 | 2,911,488 | .43 | 1,251,940 | 7.31 |
| 1900 | 167,839 | 19.0 | 3,188,941 | .48 | 1,530,692 | 9.11 |
| 1901 | 107,127 | 17.1 | 1,831,872 | .74 | 1,355,585 | 12.65 |
| 1902 | 115,697 | 16.5 | 1,909,000 | .59 | 1,126,310 | 9.73 |
| 1903 | 112,226 | 19.8 | 2,222,075 | .54 | 1,199,920 | 10.69 |
| 1904 | 117,837 | 20.5 | 2,415,658 | .54 | 1,304,455 | 11.07 |
| 1905 | 116,659 | 23.8 | 2,776,484 | .47 | 1,304,947 | 11.18 |
| 1906 | 113,159 | 27.9 | 3,157,136 | .50 | 1,578,568 | 13.95 |
| 1907 | 111,000 | 23.5 | 2,608,000 | .65 | 1,695,000 | 15.27 |
| 1908 | 128,000 | 20.2 | 2,586,000 | .71 | 1,836,000 | 14.34 |
| 1909 | 327,000 | 15.0 | 4,903,000 | .70 | 3,432,000 | 10.45 |
| 1910 | 346,000 | 19.9 | 6,885,000 | .60 | 4,131,000 | 11.94 |
| 1911 | 373,000 | 14.0 | 5,222,000 | .78 | 4,073,000 | 10.92 |
| 1912 | 420,000 | 20.8 | 8,736,000 | .50 | 4,368,000 | 10.40 |
| 1913 | 420,000 | 15.0 | 6,300,000 | .73 | 4,599,000 | 10.90 |
| 1914 | 462,000 | 23.0 | 10,626,000 | 60 | 6,376,000 | 13.80 |
| 1915 | 470,000 | 24.0 | 11,280,000 | .55 | 6,204,000 | 13.20 |
| 1916 | 475,000 | 15.5 | 7,362,000 | .90 | 6,626,000 | 13.90 |
| 1917 | 532,000 | 20.0 | 10,640,000 | 1.25 | 13,300,000 | 25.00 |
| 1918 | 610,000 | 17.5 | 10,675,000 | 1.35 | 14,411,000 | 23.63 |
| 1919 | 1,021,000 | 15.0 | 15,315,000 | 1.42 | 21,747,000 | 21.3 |
| 1920 | 1,182,000 | 20.5 | 24,231,000 | .70 | 16,962,000 | 14.3 |
| 1921 | 1,102,000 | 14.5 | 15,979,000 | .31 | 4,953,000 | 4.4 |
| 1922 | 1,145,000 | 16.0 | 18,320,000 | .66 | 12,091,000 | 10.5 |
| 1923 | 1,505,000 | 25.0 | 37,625,000 | .65 | 24,456,000 | 16.2 |
| 1924 | 1,450,000 | 10.0 | 14,500,000 | .88 | 12,760,000 | 8.8 |
| 1925 | 1,410,000 | 15.0 | 21,150,000 | .70 | 14,805,000 | 10.5 |
| 1926 | 1,396,000 | 7.0 | 9,772,000 | .71 | 6,938,000 | 4.9 |
| 1927 | 1,284,000 | 15.5 | 19,902,000 | .68 | 13,533,000 | 10.5 |
| 1928 | 1,438,000 | 13.0 | 18,694,000 | .68 | 12,712,000 | 8.8 |
| 1929 | 1,533,000 | 14.5 | 22,228,000 | .75 | 16,671,000 | 10.8 |
| 1930 | 1,732,000 | 22.5 | 38,970,000 | .62 | 24,161,000 | 13.9 |
| 1931 | 1,836,000 | 10.5 | 19,278,000 | .40 | 7,711,000 | 4.2 |

ACREAGE, PRODUCTION AND VALUE OF OATS FOR GRAIN IN COLORADO, 1880-1931

| YEAR | Acres | Yield per Acre, Bushels | Production, Bushels | Price per Bushel | Value | Value per Acre |
|---|---|---|---|---|---|---|
| 1880 | 24,000 | 27.0 | 648,000 | $ .65 | $ 421,200 | $17.55 |
| 1881 | 28,100 | 27.4 | 771,000 | 81 | 624,510 | 22.22 |
| 1882 | 27,500 | 28.4 | 780,000 | .65 | 507,000 | 18.44 |
| 1883 | 41,250 | 29.3 | 1,209,000 | .60 | 725,400 | 17.58 |
| 1884 | 43,312 | 35.0 | 1,516,000 | .40 | 606,400 | 14.00 |
| 1885 | 45,478 | 37.3 | 1,698,000 | .46 | 781,080 | 17.17 |
| 1886 | 48,207 | 33.0 | 1,591,000 | .42 | 668,220 | 13.86 |
| 1887 | 50,617 | 31.0 | 1,569,000 | .45 | 706,050 | 13.95 |
| 1888 | 60,740 | 27.4 | 1,664,000 | .42 | 698,880 | 11.50 |
| 1889 | 97,791 | 32.0 | 3,129,000 | .40 | 1,251,725 | 12.80 |
| 1890 | 100,725 | 24.8 | 2,498,000 | .50 | 1,248,990 | 12.40 |
| 1891 | 109,790 | 32.6 | 3,579,000 | .38 | 1,360,079 | 12.39 |
| 1892 | 98,811 | 28.7 | 2,836,000 | .34 | 964,198 | 9.76 |
| 1893 | 104,740 | 26.7 | 2,796,558 | .37 | 1,034,726 | 9.88 |
| 1894 | 93,219 | 13.5 | 1,258,457 | .46 | 578,890 | 6.21 |
| 1895 | 98,812 | 34.3 | 3,389,252 | .28 | 948,991 | 9.61 |
| 1896 | 92,883 | 28.0 | 2,600,724 | .30 | 780,217 | 8.40 |
| 1897 | 87,310 | 34.0 | 2,968,540 | .32 | 949,933 | 10.88 |
| 1898 | 85,564 | 35.8 | 3,063,191 | .41 | 1,255,908 | 14.67 |
| 1899 | 90,698 | 27.0 | 2,448,846 | .42 | 1,028,515 | 11.34 |
| 1900 | 99,768 | 32.8 | 3,272,390 | .43 | 1,407,128 | 14.10 |
| 1901 | 135,224 | 33.8 | 4,570,571 | .50 | 2,285,286 | 16.90 |
| 1902 | 136,576 | 26.8 | 3,660,237 | .51 | 1,866,721 | 13.68 |
| 1903 | 137,942 | 33.3 | 4,593,469 | .41 | 1,883,322 | 13.65 |
| 1904 | 136,563 | 35.4 | 4,834,330 | .46 | 2,223,792 | 16.36 |
| 1905 | 137,929 | 35.0 | 4,827,515 | .41 | 1,979,281 | 14.36 |
| 1906 | 147,584 | 40.4 | 5,962,394 | .45 | 2,683,077 | 18.18 |
| 1907 | 155,000 | 38.0 | 5,890,000 | .50 | 2,945,000 | 19.00 |
| 1908 | 178,000 | 39.5 | 7,031,000 | .54 | 3,797,000 | 21.33 |
| 1909 | 276,000 | 27.7 | 7,643,000 | .53 | 4,051,000 | 14.68 |
| 1910 | 284,000 | 39.1 | 11,104,000 | .46 | 5,108,000 | 17.99 |
| 1911 | 290,000 | 35.0 | 10,150,000 | .48 | 4,872,000 | 16.80 |
| 1912 | 290,000 | 42.8 | 12,412,000 | .38 | 4,717,000 | 16.26 |
| 1913 | 305,000 | 35.0 | 10,675,000 | .44 | 4,697,000 | 15.40 |
| 1914 | 325,000 | 40.0 | 13,000,000 | .45 | 5,850,000 | 18.00 |
| 1915 | 300,000 | 39.0 | 11,700,000 | .41 | 4,797,000 | 15.99 |
| 1916 | 290,000 | 33.0 | 9,570,000 | .60 | 5,742,000 | 19.80 |
| 1917 | 293,000 | 38.0 | 11,134,000 | .76 | 8,462,000 | 28.89 |
| 1918 | 251,000 | 30.0 | 7,530,000 | .80 | 6,024,000 | 24.00 |
| 1919 | 174,000 | 26.2 | 4,559,000 | .90 | 4,103,000 | 23.58 |
| 1920 | 204,000 | 31.5 | 6,426,000 | .60 | 3,856,000 | 18.90 |
| 1921 | 217,000 | 31.0 | 6,727,000 | .33 | 2,220,000 | 10.23 |
| 1922 | 185,000 | 25.0 | 4,625,000 | .45 | 2,081,000 | 11.25 |
| 1923 | 226,000 | 32.0 | 7,232,000 | .46 | 3,327,000 | 14.72 |
| 1924 | 232,000 | 25.0 | 5,800,000 | .58 | 3,364,000 | 14.50 |
| 1925 | 214,000 | 27.0 | 5,778,000 | .50 | 2,889,000 | 13.50 |
| 1926 | 195,000 | 24.0 | 4,680,000 | .44 | 2,059,000 | 10.56 |
| 1927 | 189,000 | 29.0 | 5,481,000 | .48 | 2,631,000 | 13.92 |
| 1928 | 193,000 | 31.0 | 5,983,000 | .45 | 2,692,000 | 13.95 |
| 1929 | 335,000 | 14.0 | 4,690,000 | .92 | 2,826,000 | 8.44 |
| 1930 | 308,000 | 13.5 | 4,158,000 | .54 | 2,176,000 | 7.06 |
| 1931 | 176,000 | 14.0 | 1,936,000 | .46 | 1,021,000 | 5.80 |

## ACREAGE, PRODUCTION AND VALUE OF BARLEY IN COLORADO, 1880-1931

| YEAR | Acres | Yield per Acre, Bushels | Production, Bushels | Price per Bushel | Value | Value per Acre |
|------|-------|------|------|------|------|------|
| 1880 | 4,700 | 19.0 | 89,300 | $ .90 | $    80,370 | $17.1 |
| 1881 | 4,900 | 18.0 | 88,000 | 1.15 | 101,200 | 20.6 |
| 1882 | 4,851 | 19.0 | 92,400 | .92 | 85,000 | 17.8 |
| 1883 | 6,064 | 25.9 | 157,080 | .75 | 117,810 | 19.4 |
| 1884 | 6,367 | 29.5 | 188,000 | .57 | 107,160 | 16.8 |
| 1885 | 6,494 | 24.0 | 156,000 | .60 | 93,510 | 14.3 |
| 1886 | 6,876 | 28.1 | 193,000 | .62 | 119,660 | 17.4 |
| 1887 | 6,876 | 25.6 | 176,000 | .62 | 109,120 | 15.8 |
| 1888 | 12,377 | 25.8 | 319,000 | .70 | 223,530 | 18.0 |
| 1889 | 12,086 | 27.4 | 331,560 | .63 | 208,880 | 17.3 |
| 1890 | 12,086 | 24.5 | 296,110 | .76 | 225,040 | 18.6 |
| 1891 | 12,328 | 26.5 | 326,700 | .56 | .     182,950 | 14.8 |
| 1892 | 12,944 | 24.0 | 310,660 | .54 | 167,750 | 12.9 |
| 1893 | 12,944 | 28.3 | 366,320 | .50 | 183,160 | 14.1 |
| 1894 | 12,426 | 27.9 | 345,440 | .58 | 200,360 | 16.1 |
| 1895 | 14,290 | 31.3 | 447,280 | .60 | 268,360 | 18.7 |
| 1896 | 12,861 | 20.0 | 257,220 | .46 | 118,320 | 9.2 |
| 1897 | 12,089 | 28.0 | 338,490 | .51 | 172,630 | 14.2 |
| 1898 | 11,005 | 32.1 | 353,950 | .46 | 162,820 | 14.8 |
| 1899 | 12,070 | 28.0 | 337,930 | .55 | 185,860 | 15.4 |
| 1900 | 12,672 | 24.8 | 314,270 | .50 | 157,130 | 12.4 |
| 1901 | 20,811 | 28.7 | 597,280 | .63 | 376,280 | 18.0 |
| 1902 | 21,020 | 26.3 | 552,800 | .60 | 331,680 | 15.7 |
| 1903 | 18,920 | 38.3 | 724,520 | .61 | 441,960 | 23.3 |
| 1904 | 19,295 | 37.1 | 715,840 | .57 | 408,030 | 21.1 |
| 1905 | 18,910 | 33.0 | 624,000 | .53 | 330,720 | 15.3 |
| 1906 | 18,531 | 41.0 | 759,770 | .54 | 410,270 | 22.1 |
| 1907 | 25,000 | 40.0 | 1,000,000 | .60 | 600,000 | 24.0 |
| 1908 | 24,000 | 33.0 | 792,000 | .65 | 515,000 | 21.4 |
| 1909 | 71,000 | 26.5 | 1,889,000 | .66 | 1,247,000 | 17.1 |
| 1910 | 75,000 | 32.0 | 2,400,000 | .60 | 1,440,000 | 19.2 |
| 1911 | 74,000 | 29.0 | 2,146,000 | .69 | 1,481,000 | 20.0 |
| 1912 | 76,000 | 39.0 | 2,964,000 | .50 | 1,482,000 | 19. |
| 1913 | 100,000 | 32.5 | 3,250,000 | .56 | 1,820,000 | 18.2 |
| 1914 | 103,000 | 38.5 | 3,966,000 | .55 | 2,181,000 | 21. |
| 1915 | 120,000 | 36.0 | 4,320,000 | .48 | 2,074,000 | 17. |
| 1916 | 160,000 | 32.0 | 5,120,000 | .82 | 4,198,000 | 26. |
| 1917 | 168,000 | 33.0 | 5,544,000 | 1.04 | 5,766,000 | 34. |
| 1918 | 206,000 | 18.0 | 3,708,000 | 1.13 | 4,190,000 | 20. |
| 1919 | 153,000 | 19.0 | 2,907,000 | 1.20 | 3,488,000 | 22. |
| 1920 | 216,000 | 24.5 | 5,292,000 | .75 | 3,969,000 | 18. |
| 1921 | 202,000 | 22.0 | 4,444,000 | .37 | 1,644,000 | 8. |
| 1922 | 186,000 | 19.0 | 3,534,000 | .59 | 2,085,000 | 11. |
| 1923 | 300,000 | 29.0 | 8,700,000 | .54 | 4,698,000 | 15. |
| 1924 | 327,000 | 20.0 | 6,540,000 | .72 | 4,709,000 | 14. |
| 1925 | 410,000 | 21.0 | 8,610,000 | .58 | 4,994,000 | 12. |
| 1926 | 380,000 | 16.0 | 6,080,000 | .55 | 3,344,000 | 8 |
| 1927 | 410,000 | 22.0 | 9,020,000 | .56 | 5,051,000 | 12 |
| 1928 | 547,000 | 24.0 | 13,128,000 | .54 | 7,089,000 | 12 |
| 1929 | 608,000 | 18.0 | 10,944,000 | .54 | 5,910,000 | 9. |
| 1930 | 572,000 | 21.5 | 12,298,000 | .40 | 4,919,000 | 8. |
| 1931 | 458,000 | 15.5 | 7,099,000 | .31 | 2,201,000 | 4. |

ACREAGE, PRODUCTION AND VALUE OF RYE IN COLORADO, 1880-1931

| YEAR | Acres | Yield per Acre, Bushels | Production, Bushels | Price per Bushel | Value | Value per Acre |
|---|---|---|---|---|---|---|
| 380 | 1,500 | 17.0 | 25,500 | $ .67 | $ 17,085 | $11.39 |
| 381 | 1,400 | 20.0 | 28,000 | .97 | 27,160 | 19.40 |
| 382 | 1,592 | 17.7 | 28,224 | .90 | 25,405 | 15.96 |
| 383 | 1,783 | 17.4 | 31,046 | .80 | 24,837 | 13.93 |
| 384 | 1,872 | 17.6 | 33,000 | .60 | 19,800 | 10.58 |
| 385 | 1,966 | 17.8 | 35,000 | .68 | 23.710 | 12.06 |
| 386 | 1,909 | 22.0 | 42,000 | .72 | 30,240 | 15.84 |
| 387 | 1,966 | 14.2 | 28,000 | .78 | 21,840 | 11.11 |
| 388 | 2,379 | 12.2 | 29,000 | .66 | 19,127 | 8.04 |
| 389 | 4,615 | 11.7 | 54,158 | .57 | 30,870 | 6.69 |
| 390 | 4,707 | 14.5 | 68,252 | .65 | 44,364 | 9.42 |
| 391 | 4,942 | 20.6 | 101,805 | .62 | 63,119 | 12.77 |
| 392 | 5,683 | 14.6 | 82,972 | .52 | 43,145 | 7.59 |
| 393 | 5,683 | 21.0 | 119,343 | .50 | 59,672 | 10.50 |
| 394 | 4,035 | 15.6 | 62,946 | .66 | 41,544 | 10.29 |
| 395 | 3,389 | 14.5 | 49,141 | .48 | 23,588 | 6.96 |
| 396 | 2,779 | 23.5 | 65,306 | .62 | 40,490 | 14.56 |
| 397 | 2,612 | 15.0 | 39,180 | .52 | 20,374 | 7.80 |
| 398 | 2,638 | 18.0 | 47,484 | .50 | 23,742 | 9.00 |
| 399 | 2,374 | 14.0 | 33,236 | .48 | 15,953 | 6.72 |
| 100 | 2,350 | 16.8 | 39,480 | .54 | 21,319 | 9.07 |
| 101 | 2,659 | 16.1 | 42,810 | .62 | 26,542 | 9.98 |
| 102 | 2,872 | 15.9 | 45,665 | .56 | 25,572 | 8.90 |
| 103 | 2,843 | 18.3 | 52,027 | .61 | 31,736 | 11.16 |
| 104 | 2,786 | 19.1 | 53,213 | .65 | 34,588 | 12.41 |
| 105 | 2,368 | 19.0 | 44,992 | .56 | 25,196 | 10.64 |
| 106 | 2,179 | 20.0 | 43,580 | .56 | 24,405 | 11.20 |
| 107 | 2,300 | 20.5 | 47,000 | .62 | 29,000 | 12.61 |
| 108 | 3,000 | 15.5 | 46,000 | .70 | 32,000 | 10.67 |
| 109 | 16,000 | 12.6 | 198,000 | .73 | 145,000 | 9.06 |
| 110 | 20,000 | 14.0 | 280,000 | .67 | 188,000 | 9.40 |
| 111 | 21,000 | 12.0 | 252,000 | .70 | 176,000 | 8.38 |
| 112 | 25,000 | 19.5 | 488,000 | .55 | 268,000 | 10.72 |
| 113 | 20,000 | 17.0 | 340,000 | .60 | 204,000 | 10.20 |
| 114 | 21,000 | 17.5 | 368,000 | .65 | 239,000 | 11.38 |
| 115 | 30,000 | 17.5 | 525,000 | .70 | 368,000 | 12.27 |
| 116 | 28,000 | 14.0 | 392,000 | 1.05 | 412,000 | 14.71 |
| 17 | 27,000 | 16.0 | 432,000 | 1.46 | 631,000 | 23.37 |
| 18 | 149,000 | 7.0 | 1,043,000 | 1.40 | 1,460,000 | 9.80 |
| 19 | 124,000 | 8.8 | 1,088,000 | 1.30 | 1,414,000 | 11.40 |
| 20 | 100,000 | 11.8 | 1,180,000 | 1.05 | 1,239,000 | 12.39 |
| 21 | 92,000 | 11.5 | 1,058,000 | .60 | 635,000 | 6.89 |
| 22 | 97,000 | 9.0 | 873,000 | .66 | 576,000 | 5.94 |
| 23 | 77,000 | 12.0 | 924,000 | .56 | 517,000 | 6.71 |
| 24 | 80,000 | 9.0 | 720,000 | .85 | 612,000 | 7.65 |
| 25 | 85,000 | 10.0 | 850,000 | .67 | 570,000 | 6.70 |
| 26 | 85,000 | 11.5 | 977,000 | .71 | 694,000 | 8.17 |
| 27 | 76,000 | 10.5 | 798,000 | .70 | 559,000 | 7.34 |
| 28 | 74,000 | 11.0 | 814,000 | .70 | 570,000 | 7.70 |
| 29 | 64,000 | 8.0 | 512,000 | .71 | 364,000 | 5.69 |
| 30 | 74,000 | 8.5 | 629,000 | .37 | 233,000 | 3.15 |
| 31 | 53,000 | 7.0 | 371,000 | .31 | 115,000 | 2.17 |

ACREAGE, PRODUCTION AND VALUE OF POTATOES IN COLORADO, 1880-1931

| YEAR | Acres | Yield per Acre, Bushels | Production, Bushels | Price per Bushel | Value | Value per Acre |
|---|---|---|---|---|---|---|
| 1880 | 1,640 | 46.0 | 75,440 | $1.10 | $    82,984 | $ 50.6( |
| 1881 | 5,357 | 80.0 | 428,560 | 1.30 | 557,128 | 104.0( |
| 1882 | 5,730 | 76.3 | 437,000 | .72 | 314,640 | 54.9| |
| 1883 | 5,959 | 85.0 | 506,515 | .65 | 329,235 | 55.2| |
| 1884 | 7,151 | 90.0 | 644,000 | .60 | 386,400 | 54.0: |
| 1885 | 7,860 | 95.0 | 747,000 | .61 | 455,487 | 57.9| |
| 1886 | 8,096 | 78.0 | 631,000 | .57 | 359,670 | 44.4: |
| 1887 | 8,258 | 105.0 | 867,000 | .56 | 485,520 | 58.7| |
| 1888 | 28,903 | 94.0 | 2,717,000 | .45 | 1,222,600 | 42.3( |
| 1889 | 31,588 | 70.0 | 2,211,160 | .50 | 1,105,580 | 34.9| |
| 1890 | 33,483 | 73.0 | 2,444,250 | .75 | 1,833,200 | 54.7: |
| 1891 | 35,827 | 115.0 | 4,120,100 | .28 | · 1,153,630 | 32.2: |
| 1892 | 34,036 | 99.0 | 3,369,560 | .61 | 2,055,430 | 60.3: |
| 1893 | 33,096 | 94.0 | 3,167,424 | .54 | 1,710,410 | 51.6| |
| 1894 | 34,033 | 85.0 | 2,892,800 | .55 | 1,591,040 | 46.7| |
| 1895 | 36,756 | 95.0 | 3,491,800 | .33 | 1,152,300 | 31.3| |
| 1896 | 32,345 | 88.0 | 2,846,360 | .47 | 1,337,790 | 41.3( |
| 1897 | 32,022 | 97.0 | 3,106,130 | .56 | 1,739,440 | 54.3: |
| 1898 | 33,303 | 77.0 | 2,564,330 | .54 | 1,384,740 | 41.5: |
| 1899 | 32,304 | 84.0 | 2,713,540 | .55 | 1,492,450 | 46.2( |
| 1900 | 33,273 | 56.0 | 1,863,290 | .82 | 1,527,900 | 45.9: |
| 1901 | 43,923 | 120.0 | 5,270,760 | .90 | 4,743,680 | 107.9! |
| 1902 | 47,437 | 100.0 | 4,743,700 | .51 | 2,419,290 | 51.0( |
| 1903 | 50,758 | 145.0 | 7,359,910 | .60 | 4,415,950 | 87.0. |
| 1904 | 54,311 | 159.0 | 8,635,440 | .37 | 3,195,120 | 58.8 |
| 1905 | 51,052 | 160.0 | 8,168,320 | .57 | 4,655,940 | 91.1 |
| 1906 | 46,968 | 125.0 | 5,871,000 | .45 | 2,641,950 | 56.2 |
| 1907 | 47,000 | 150.0 | 7,050,000 | .66 | 4,653,000 | 99.0 |
| 1908 | 56,000 | 125.0 | 7,000,000 | .60 | 4,200,000 | 75.0 |
| 1909 | 86,000 | 137.0 | 11,781,000 | .57 | 6,715,000 | 78.0 |
| 1910 | 86,000 | 100.0 | 8,600,000 | .55 | 4,730,000 | 55.0 |
| 1911 | 90,000 | 35.0 | 3,150,000 | .99 | 3,118,000 | 34.6 |
| 1912 | 85,000 | 95.0 | 8,075,000 | .41 | 3,311,000 | 38.9 |
| 1913 | 80,000 | 115.0 | 9,200,000 | .65 | 5,980,000 | 74.7 |
| 1914 | 50,000 | 120.0 | · 6,000,000 | .50 | 3,000,000 | 60.0 |
| 1915 | 53,000 | 135.0 | 7,155,000 | .55 | 3,935,000 | 74.2 |
| 1916 | 50,000 | 138.0 | 6,900,000 | 1.35 | 9,315,000 | 186.! |
| 1917 | 80,000 | 160.0 | 12,800,000 | .91 | 11,648,000 | 145.( |
| 1918 | 99,000 | 160.0 | 15,840,000 | .99 | 15,682,000 | 158.( |
| 1919 | 77,000 | 115.0 | 8,855,000 | 1.70 | 15,054,000 | 195.( |
| 1920 | 73,000 | 130.0 | 9,490,000 | .80 | 7,592,000 | 104.( |
| 1921 | 113,000 | 132.0 | 14,916,000 | .73 | 10,889,000 | 96.: |
| 1922 | 142,000 | 130.0 | 18,460,000 | .37 | 6,830,000 | 48.( |
| 1923 | 110,000 | 123.0 | 13,530,000 | .53 | 7,171,000 | 65.: |
| 1924 | 71,000 | 145.0 | 10,295,000 | .60 | 6,177,000 | 87.( |
| 1925 | 62,000 | 195.0 | 12,090,000 | 1.55 | 18,740,000 | 302.: |
| 1926 | 82,000 | 145.0 | 11,890,000 | 1.30 | 15,457,000 | 188. |
| 1927 | 96,000 | 150.0 | 14,400,000 | .55 | 7,920,000 | 82. |
| 1928 | 110,000 | 122.0 | 13,420,000 | .45 | 6,039,000 | 54. |
| 1929 | 90,000 | 163.0 | 14,670,000 | 1.10 | 16,137,000 | 179.' |
| 1930 | 92,000 | 190.0 | 17,480,000 | .60 | 10,488,000 | 114.' |
| 1931 | 101,000 | 95.0 | 9,595,000 | .30 | 2,878,000 | 28. |

## ACREAGE, PRODUCTION AND VALUE OF TAME HAY IN COLORADO, 1880-1931

| YEAR | Acres | Yield per Acre, Tons | Production, Tons | Price per Ton | Value | Value per Acre |
|------|------|------|------|------|------|------|
| 1880 | 44,119 | .94 | 41,472 | $25.62 | $ 1,062,513 | $24.08 |
| 1881 | 71,594 | 1.20 | 85,913 | 20.00 | 1,718,260 | 24.00 |
| 1882 | 73,026 | 1.24 | 90,209 | 13.75 | 1,240,374 | 16.99 |
| 1883 | 81,780 | 1.40 | 114,505 | 13.50 | 1,545,818 | 18.90 |
| 1884 | 73,000 | 1.30 | 94,900 | 12.00 | 1,138,800 | 15.60 |
| 1885 | 87,000 | 1.00 | 87,000 | 9.96 | 867,240 | 9.96 |
| 1886 | 115,000 | 1.00 | 115,000 | 9.80 | 1,127,000 | 9.80 |
| 1887 | 149,500 | 1.20 | 179,400 | 10.75 | 1,928,550 | 12.90 |
| 1888 | 246,675 | 1.50 | 370,013 | 11.40 | 4,218,148 | 17.10 |
| 1889 | 481,621 | 1.48 | 714,555 | 9.10 | 6,502,450 | 13.51 |
| 1890 | 530,684 | 1.37 | 727,037 | 9.00 | 6,543,333 | 12.33 |
| 1891 | 636,821 | 1.88 | 1,197,223 | 8.00 | 9,577,784 | 15.04 |
| 1892 | 764,185 | 2.00 | 1,528,370 | 6.50 | 9,934,405 | 13.00 |
| 1893 | 794,752 | 1.19 | 945,755 | 6.98 | 6,601,370 | 8.30 |
| 1894 | 786,804 | 2.27 | 1,786,045 | 7.54 | 13,466,779 | 17.11 |
| 1895 | 810,408 | 2.42 | 1,961,187 | 5.87 | 11,512,168 | 14.20 |
| 1896 | 761,784 | 2.20 | 1,675,925 | 6.22 | 10,424,254 | 13.68 |
| 1897 | 784,638 | 2.25 | 1,765,436 | 5.50 | 9,709,808 | 12.39 |
| 1898 | 800,331 | 2.20 | 1,760,728 | 5.40 | 9,507,931 | 11.88 |
| 1899 | 776,321 | 2.10 | 1,630,274 | 7.35 | 11,982,514 | 15.43 |
| 1900 | 799,611 | 2.23 | 1,783,133 | 7.60 | 13,551,811 | 16.96 |
| 1901 | 617,233 | 2.08 | 1,283,845 | 9.04 | 11,605,959 | 18.80 |
| 1902 | 592,544 | 1.92 | 1,137,684 | 9.89 | 11,251,695 | 18.99 |
| 1903 | 622,171 | 2.56 | 1,592,758 | 7.48 | 11,913,830 | 19.15 |
| 1904 | 671,945 | 1.85 | 1,243,098 | 6.71 | 8,341,188 | 12.41 |
| 1905 | 665,226 | 2.65 | 1,762,849 | 8.20 | 14,455,362 | 21.74 |
| 1906 | 638,617 | 2.50 | 1,596,542 | 9.50 | 15,167,149 | 23.75 |
| 1907 | 677,000 | 2.70 | 1,828,000 | 9.50 | 17,366.000 | 25.65 |
| 1908 | 670,000 | 2.50 | 1,675,000 | 8.75 | 14,656,000 | 21.87 |
| 1909 | 785,000 | 2.13 | 1,674,000 | 10.00 | 16,740,000 | 21.32 |
| 1910 | 781,000 | 2.00 | 1,562,000 | 10.80 | 16,870,000 | 21.60 |
| 1911 | 785,000 | 2.00 | 1,570,000 | 9.30 | 14,601,000 | 18.60 |
| 1912 | 870,000 | 2.19 | 1,905,000 | 8.70 | 16,574,000 | 19.05 |
| 1913 | 890,000 | 2.05 | 1,824,000 | 10.00 | 18,240,000 | 20.49 |
| 1914 | 970,000 | 2.40 | 2,328,000 | 7.40 | 17,227,000 | 17.76 |
| 1915 | 970,000 | 2.20 | 2,134,000 | 7.60 | 16,218,000 | 16.72 |
| 1916 | 970,000 | 2.05 | 1,988,000 | 11.00 | 21,868,000 | 22.54 |
| 1917 | 970,000 | 2.45 | 2,376,000 | 16.60 | 39,442,000 | 40.66 |
| 1918 | 1,030,000 | 2.22 | 2,287,000 | 15.50 | 35,448,000 | 34.41 |
| 1919 | 1,227,000 | 2.06 | 2,527,000 | 18.50 | 46,750,000 | 38.10 |
| 1920 | 1,256,000 | 2.40 | 3,019,000 | 12.00 | 36,228,000 | 28.84 |
| 1921 | 1,195,000 | 2.15 | 2,576,000 | 6.90 | 17,774,000 | 14.87 |
| 1922 | 1,191,000 | 1.91 | 2,273,000 | 11.20 | 25,458,000 | 21.38 |
| 1923 | 1,203,000 | 2.05 | 2,463,000 | 11.30 | 27,832,000 | 23.13 |
| 1924 | 1,262,000 | 2.11 | 2,661,000 | 11.00 | 29,271,000 | 23.18 |
| 1925 | 1,253,000 | 2.15 | 2,694,000 | 12.00 | 32,328,000 | 25.80 |
| 1926 | 1,210,000 | 2.31 | 2,795,000 | 8.60 | 24,037,000 | 19.86 |
| 1927 | 1,225,000 | 2.17 | 2,658,000 | 9.20 | 24,454,000 | 19.96 |
| 1928 | 1,183,000 | 2.08 | 2,467,000 | 11.70 | 28,864,000 | 24.41 |
| 1929 | 1,255,000 | 1.80 | 2,255,000 | 11.50 | 25,932,000 | 20.66 |
| 1930 | 1,292.000 | 1.71 | 2,215,000 | 9.20 | 20,378,000 | 15.77 |
| 1931 | 1,258,000 | 1.31 | 1,647,000 | 7.60 | 12,517,000 | 9.95 |

SUGAR BEET PRODUCTION IN COLORADO, 1905 TO 1931, INCLUSIVE

| Year | Acres Harvested | Average Yield, Tons | Production Tons | Farm Price | Value* | Value* per Acre | Average Sugar Content | Tons Sugar Mfr'd | No. of Factories Operating† |
|---|---|---|---|---|---|---|---|---|---|
| 1905 | 86,000 | 10.19 | 875,154 | $ --- | $ --- | $ --- | 14.71 | 91,608 | 12 |
| 1906 | 111,000 | 13.41 | 1,487,383 | --- | --- | --- | 14.70 | 167,193 | 15 |
| 1907 | 128,000 | 11.93 | 1,523,300 | --- | --- | --- | 15.30 | 169,287 | 16 |
| 1908 | 119,500 | 9.28 | 1,109,000 | --- | --- | --- | 13.85 | 122,280 | 15 |
| 1909 | 121,700 | 10.33 | 1,266,700 | --- | --- | --- | 14.24 | 149,405 | 16 |
| 1910 | 81,400 | 10.62 | 864,500 | 5.55 | 5,312,000 | 61.46 | 15.19 | 103,092 | 16 |
| 1911 | 86,400 | 11.07 | 957,100 | 5.96 | 9,785,000 | 67.49 | 15.44 | 124,800 | 14 |
| 1912 | 100 | 11.32 | 1,642,000 | | | | 16.19 | 216,010 | 17 |
| 1913 | 168,400 | 10.93 | 1,340,700 | 5.67 | 10,437,000 | 61.97 | 11.92 | 229,274 | 14 |
| 1914 | 135,400 | 12.60 | 100 | 5.68 | 9,692,000 | 71.58 | 15.35 | 220,799 | 13 |
| 1915 | 171,200 | 11.03 | 1,886,900 | 5.88 | 11,106,000 | 64.87 | 16.53 | 278,780 | 14 |
| 1916 | 189,000 | 10.70 | 2,018,300 | 6.06 | 12,231,000 | 64.86 | 15.00 | 252,147 | 14 |
| 1917 | 161,000 | 11.50 | 1,857,700 | 7.28 | 13,526,000 | 83.75 | 15.40 | 234,303 | 15 |
| 1918 | 126,000 | 11.47 | 1,444,000 | 10.02 | 14,474,000 | 114.83 | 16.10 | 192,000 | 14 |
| 1919 | 183,000 | 9.66 | 1,765,000 | 10.85 | 19,143,000 | 104.65 | 13.62 | 194,000 | 15 |
| 1920 | 220,000 | 10.58 | 2,325,000 | 11.88 | 27,627,000 | 125.25 | 15.81 | 294,000 | 17 |
| 1921 | 200,000 | 11.39 | 2,279,000 | 6.37 | 14,521,000 | 72.61 | 15.66 | 295,000 | 15 |
| 1922 | 148,000 | 9.93 | 1,466,000 | 7.79 | 11,426,000 | 77.16 | 14.66 | 183,000 | 15 |
| 1923 | 164,000 | 12.15 | 1,996,000 | 8.15 | 16,276,000 | 99.19 | 14.59 | 240,000 | 16 |
| 1924 | 225,000 | 11.32 | 2,540,000 | 7.59 | 19,329,000 | 85.89 | 16.65 | 364,000 | 16 |
| 1925 | 130,000 | 12.60 | 1,640,000 | 5.98 | 9,815,000 | 75.50 | 14.25 | 200,000 | 16 |
| 1926 | 211,000 | 13.80 | 2,312,000 | 7.92 | 23,050,000 | 109.24 | 15.05 | 377,000 | 17 |
| 1927 | 218,000 | 12.70 | 2,774,000 | 7.84 | 21,758,000 | 99.81 | 15.25 | 373,900 | 18 |
| 1928 | 100 | 13.40 | 2,394,000 | 6.97 | 16,687,000 | 93.22 | 16.51 | 384,261 | 18 |
| 1929 | 100 | 12.44 | 2,612,000 | 6.95 | 18,106,000 | 86.22 | 14.51 | 348,000 | 18 |
| 1930 | 242,000 | 13.69 | 3,312,000 | 6.94 | 22,873,000 | 94.52 | 130 | 407,000 | 17 |
| 1931 | 226,000 | 11.23 | 2,537,000 | 5.50 | 13,954,000 | 61.74 | 15.50 | 360,000 | 17 |

NOTE—Compiled from reports of the United States Department of Agriculture and the Colorado Co-Operative Crop Reporting Service. Data on prices and farm value prior to 1911 not available. †Including barium by-products plant at Johnstown.

*Exclusive of beet tops, which have a high feed value.

## COLORADO'S POSITION IN SUGAR BEET PRODUCTION OF THE UNITED STATES, 1911-1930 INCLUSIVE

| | Acres Harvest-ed | % of U. S. Total | Av. Yield Tons | Tons Beets Harvested | % of U. S. Total | Total Farm Value[3] | % of U. S. Total | Av. Value Per Acre[3] |
|---|---|---|---|---|---|---|---|---|
| Colorado | 3,522,000 | 26.7 | 11.76 | 41,485,000 | 30.9 | $ 307,598,000 | 30.3 | $87.34 |
| Michigan | 2,191,000 | 16.6 | 7.99 | 17,499,000 | 13.1 | 132,918,000 | 13.1 | 60.67 |
| California | 1,863,000 | 14.1 | 9.23 | 17,190,000 | 12.8 | 140,398,000 | 13.8 | 75.36 |
| Utah | 1,313,000 | 10.0 | 11.42 | 14,995,000 | 11.2 | 112,146,000 | 11.0 | 85.41 |
| Nebraska | 999,000 | 7.6 | 11.74 | 11,731,000 | 8.7 | 90,969,000 | 9.0 | 91.06 |
| Idaho | 661,000 | 5.0 | 9.79 | 6,474,000 | 4.8 | 48,337,000 | 4.8 | 73.13 |
| Montana and Wyoming[1] | 555,000 | 4.2 | 11.19 | 6,209,000 | 4.6 | 46,705,000 | 4.6 | 84.15 |
| Other States[2] | 2,076,000 | 15.8 | 8.91 | 18,498,000 | 13.9 | 135,839,000 | 13.4 | 65.43 |
| United States | 13,180,000 | 100.0 | 10.17 | 134,081,000 | 100.0 | $1,014,910,000 | 100.0 | $77.00 |

## COLORADO'S POSITION IN PRODUCTION AND MANUFACTURE OF BEET SUGAR IN THE UNITED STATES, 1911-1930 INCLUSIVE

| | No. Fac-tories[4] | Av. Lbs. Sugar Per Acre | Tons Sugar Manufactured | % of U. S. Total | Lbs. Sugar Per Ton of Beets | Farm Recpt. in Cts. Per Lb. of Sugar |
|---|---|---|---|---|---|---|
| Colorado | 17 | 3,078.4 | 5,421,000 | 30.7 | 261.3 | 2.84 |
| Michigan | 10 | 1,974.4 | 2,163,000 | 12.3 | 247.2 | 3.07 |
| California | 5 | 2,958.7 | 2,756,000 | 15.6 | 320.6 | 2.55 |
| Utah | 8 | 2,875.9 | 1,888,000 | 10.7 | 251.8 | 2.97 |
| Nebraska | 7 | 2,924.9 | 1,461,000 | 8.3 | 249.1 | 3.11 |
| Idaho | 7 | 2,835.1 | 937,000 | 5.3 | 289.5 | 2.58 |
| Montana and Wyoming[1] | 9 | 3,023.4 | 839,000 | 4.8 | 270.3 | 2.78 |
| Other States[2] | 15 | 2,054.4 | 2,174,000 | 12.3 | 235.1 | 3.12 |
| United States | 78 | 2,676.6 | 17,659,000 | 100.0 | 263.1 | 2.88 |

[1]Montana and Wyoming first appeared in sugar beet statistics in 1922. Data from these states continue from that year.

[2]Includes Iowa, Minnesota, Kansas, Indiana, South Dakota, Ohio, Wisconsin and Washington.

[3]Value is exclusive of beet tops, which have a high feed value.

[4]Numbers include factories operating in the season of 1930-1931; output of the Johnstown, Colo., molasses refinery not included.

Note—Figures begin with 1911 because data as to price and value are not available for years prior to that time. All figures have been rounded to even thousands. All available data for Colorado in years prior to 1911 will be found in the state table on the preceding page.

## ACREAGE, PRODUCTION AND VALUE OF WILD HAY IN COLORADO, 1909-1931

| Year | Acres | Yield per Acre, Tons | Production, Tons | Price per Ton | Value | Value per Acre |
|------|-------|------|------|------|------|------|
| 1909 | 395,000 | 0.93 | 368,000 | $ ---- | $ ------- | $ --- |
| 1910 | 395,000 | 0.90 | 356,000 | ----- | --------- | ---- |
| 1911 | 395,000 | 0.90 | 356,000 | ----- | --------- | ---- |
| 1912 | 466,000 | 1.10 | 513,000 | ----- | --------- | ---- |
| 1913 | 419,000 | 0.95 | 398,000 | ----- | --------- | ---- |
| 1914 | 444,000 | 1.20 | 533,000 | 8.80 | 4,690,000 | 10.5 |
| 1915 | 460,000 | 1.12 | 515,000 | 7.96 | 4,068,000 | 8.8 |
| 1916 | 460,000 | 0.92 | 423,000 | 11.40 | 4,822,000 | 10.4 |
| 1917 | 451,000 | 1.02 | 460,000 | 17.50 | 8,050,000 | 17.8 |
| 1918 | 400,000 | 0.94 | 376,000 | 17.50 | 6,580,000 | 16.4 |
| 1919 | 411,000 | 0.89 | 366,000 | 18.40 | 6,734,000 | 16.3 |
| 1920 | 419,000 | 1.05 | 440,000 | 14.00 | 6,160,000 | 14.7 |
| 1921 | 407,000 | 1.00 | 407,000 | 6.00 | 2,442,000 | 6.0 |
| 1922 | 366,000 | 0.97 | 355,000 | 9.00 | 3,195,000 | 8.7 |
| 1923 | 373,000 | 1.05 | 392,000 | 10.50 | 4,116,000 | 11.0 |
| 1924 | 360,000 | 1.00 | 360,000 | 9.70 | 3,492,000 | 9.7 |
| 1925 | 360,000 | 1.00 | 360,000 | 10.80 | 3,888,000 | 10.8 |
| 1926 | 360,000 | 1.00 | 360,000 | 8.00 | 2,880,000 | 8.0 |
| 1927 | 396,000 | 1.00 | 396,000 | 8.40 | 3,326,000 | 8.4 |
| 1928 | 376,000 | 0.90 | 338,000 | 10.30 | 3,481,000 | 9.2 |
| 1929 | 362,000 | .95 | 344,000 | 10.30 | 3,543,000 | 9.7 |
| 1930 | 366,000 | 1.00 | 366,000 | 8.80 | 3,221,000 | 8.8 |
| 1931 | 362,000 | .80 | 290,000 | 7.50 | 2,175,000 | 6.0 |

Note—Data concerning price and value not available for earlier years.

## ACREAGE, PRODUCTION AND VALUE OF DRY BEANS IN COLORADO, 1914-1931

| Year | Acres | Yield per Acre | Production | Price per Ton | Value | Value per Acre |
|------|-------|------|------|------|------|------|
| 1914 | 20,000 | 15.0 | 300,000 | $2.00 | $ 600,000 | $30.00 |
| 1915 | 21,000 | 16.2 | 340,000 | 2.28 | 775,000 | 36.90 |
| 1916 | 38,000 | 11.2 | 424,000 | 4.20 | 1,781,000 | 46.87 |
| 1917 | 250,000 | 7.8 | 1,950,000 | 4.80 | 9,360,000 | 37.44 |
| 1918 | 252,000 | 6.5 | 1,638,000 | 4.40 | 7,207,000 | 28.60 |
| 1919 | 66,000 | 6.5 | 429,000 | 3.50 | 1,502,000 | 22.76 |
| 1920 | 52,000 | 8.0 | 416,000 | 3.15 | 1,310,000 | 25.19 |
| 1921 | 39,000 | 8.0 | 312,000 | 2.70 | 842,000 | 21.58 |
| 1922 | 81,000 | 5.0 | 405,000 | 4.40 | 1,782,000 | 22.00 |
| 1923 | 170,000 | 8.0 | 1,360,000 | 3.70 | 5,032,000 | 29.60 |
| 1924 | 280,000 | 3.4 | 952,000 | 3.10 | 2,951,000 | 10.54 |
| 1925 | 320,000 | 7.0 | 2,240,000 | 2.40 | 5,376,000 | 16.80 |
| 1926 | 378,000 | 3.6 | 1,361,000 | 2.80 | 3,811,000 | 10.08 |
| 1927 | 281,000 | 5.5 | 1,546,000 | 2.70 | 4,174,000 | 14.85 |
| 1928 | 309,000 | 4.5 | 1,390,000 | 3.40 | 4,726,000 | 15.29 |
| 1929 | 372,000 | 6.0 | 2,232,000 | 2.70 | 6,026,000 | 16.20 |
| 1930 | 432,000 | 10.0 | 4,320,000 | 1.35 | 5,832,000 | 13.50 |
| 1931 | 320,000 | 4.3 | 1,376,000 | 1.08 | 1,487,000 | 4.65 |

Note—The decline in average yield and value per acre is due almost wholly to the large acreage of non-irrigated land which has been devoted to this crop in recent years. Nearly 85 per cent of crop is now produced without irrigation.

## ACREAGE, PRODUCTION AND VALUE OF BROOM CORN IN COLORADO, 1915-1931

| Year | Acres | Yield per Acre, Pounds | Production, Tons | Price per Ton | Value | Value per Acre |
|---|---|---|---|---|---|---|
| 1915 | 18,000 | 500 | 4,550 | $ 75.00 | $ 341,000 | $18.74 |
| 1916 | 25,000 | 224 | 2,835 | 156.00 | 442,000 | 17.54 |
| 1917 | 30,000 | 310 | 4,600 | 282.00 | 1,297,000 | 43.23 |
| 1918 | 30,000 | 350 | 5,200 | 175.00 | 910,000 | 30.33 |
| 1919 | 11,000 | 350 | 1,900 | 100.00 | 190,000 | 17.27 |
| 1920 | 7,000 | 370 | 1,300 | 70.00 | 91,000 | 13.00 |
| 1921 | 9,000 | 400 | 1,800 | 45.00 | 81,000 | 9.00 |
| 1922 | 10,000 | 350 | 1,800 | 195.00 | 351,000 | 35.10 |
| 1923 | 48,000 | 365 | 8,760 | 145.00 | 1,270,000 | 26.47 |
| 1924 | 19,000 | 261 | 2,480 | 60.00 | 148,800 | 7.83 |
| 1925 | 15,000 | 250 | 1,875 | 140.00 | 263,000 | 17.53 |
| 1926 | 30,000 | 225 | 3,375 | 83.00 | 280,000 | 9.33 |
| 1927 | 28,000 | 315 | 4,400 | 120.00 | 528,000 | 18.86 |
| 1928 | 52,000 | 360 | 9,400 | 85.00 | 799,000 | 15.37 |
| 1929 | 64,000 | 286 | 9,200 | 112.00 | 1,030,000 | 16.09 |
| 1930 | 77,000 | 270 | 10,400 | 51.00 | 530,000 | 6.88 |
| 1931 | 46,000 | 250 | 5,800 | 42.00 | 244,000 | 5.30 |

## ACREAGE, PRODUCTION AND VALUE OF DRY ONIONS IN COLORADO, 1918-1931

| Year | Acres | Yield per Acre, Bus. | Production, Bus. | Price per Bu. | Value | Value per Acre |
|---|---|---|---|---|---|---|
| 1918 | 700 | 244 | 171,000 | $1.00 | $ 171,000 | $244.30 |
| 1919 | 830 | 250 | 208,000 | 1.62 | 337,000 | 406.02 |
| 1920 | 760 | 340 | 258,000 | .72 | 186,000 | 244.73 |
| 1921 | 1,300 | 300 | 390,000 | 1.53 | 597,000 | 460.00 |
| 1922 | 1,900 | 280 | 532,000 | .52 | 277,000 | 145.79 |
| 1923 | 2,620 | 250 | 655,000 | 1.08 | 707,000 | 269.85 |
| 1924 | 3,410 | 270 | 921,000 | .58 | 534,000 | 156.60 |
| 1925 | 3,520 | 325 | 1,144,000 | .78 | 892,000 | 253.41 |
| 1926 | 3,700 | 275 | 1,018,000 | .50 | 509,000 | 135.57 |
| 1927 | 4,300 | 320 | 1,376,000 | .45 | 474,000 | 110.23 |
| 1928 | 3,760 | 330 | 1,241,000 | 1.42 | 1,762,000 | 468.62 |
| 1929 | 7,000 | 369 | 2,583,000 | .45 | 1,097,000 | 156.71 |
| 1930 | 5,600 | 308 | 1,725,000 | .32 | 552,000 | 98.57 |
| 1931 | 4,050 | 228 | 923,000 | .74 | 683,000 | 168.64 |

## ACREAGE, PRODUCTION AND VALUE OF WATERMELONS IN COLORADO, 1918-1931

| Year | Acres | Yield per Acre, Number | Production, Carloads | Price per Car | Value | Value per Acre |
|---|---|---|---|---|---|---|
| 1918 | 375 | 360 | 135 | $150 | $ 20,000 | $53.33 |
| 1919 | 408 | 375 | 153 | 175 | 27,000 | 66.17 |
| 1920 | 830 | 315 | 261 | 150 | 39,000 | 47.00 |
| 1921 | 780 | 375 | 292 | 200 | 58,000 | 74.36 |
| 1922 | 660 | 350 | 231 | 180 | 42,000 | 63.63 |
| 1923 | 400 | 135 | 140 | 167 | 23,000 | 57.50 |
| 1924 | 380 | 300 | 114 | 128 | 15,000 | 39.90 |
| 1925 | 300 | 323 | 97 | 168 | 16,000 | 53.33 |
| 1926 | 300 | 361 | 108 | 95 | 10,000 | 33.33 |
| 1927 | 700 | 150 | 105 | 242 | 25,000 | 35.71 |
| 1928 | 570 | 319 | 182 | 150 | 27,000 | 47.37 |
| 1929 | 1,070 | 300 | 321 | 165 | 53,000 | 49.53 |
| 1930 | 1,070 | 320 | 342 | 170 | 58,000 | 54.21 |
| 1931 | 1,120 | 300 | 336 | 150 | 50,000 | 44.64 |

## PRODUCTION, MARKET PRICE AND VALUE OF APPLES AND PEACHES IN COLORADO
### 1910-1931

| Year | APPLES | | | PEACHES | | |
|------|--------|--|--|---------|--|--|
| | Production, Bus. | Price per Bu. | Value | Production, Bus. | Price per Bu. | Value |
| 1910 | 1,500,000 | $1.15 | $ 1,725,000 | 390,000 | $1.80 | $ 702,00 |
| 1911 | 2,700,000 | 1.22 | 3,294,000 | 410,000 | 1.75 | 718,00 |
| 1912 | 3,100,000 | .80 | 2,480,000 | 1,100,000 | 1.00 | 1,100,00 |
| 1913 | 3,300,000 | 1.08 | 3,564,000 | 390,000 | 1.24 | 484,00 |
| 1914 | 4,500,000 | .70 | 3,150,000 | 1,025,000 | .60 | 615,00 |
| 1915 | 2,080,000 | .95 | 1,976,000 | 650,000 | 1.25 | 813,00 |
| 1916 | 2,541,000 | .94 | 2,389,000 | 405,000 | 1.25 | 506,00 |
| 1917 | 2,190,000 | .80 | 1,752,000 | 1,096,000 | 2.00 | 2,192,00 |
| 1918 | 2,067,000 | 1.70 | 3,514,000 | 959,000 | 2.00 | 1,918,00 |
| 1919 | 3,418,000 | 1.85 | 6,323,000 | 722,000 | 2.50 | 1,805,00 |
| 1920 | 2,830,000 | 1.40 | 3,962,000 | 670,000 | 2.50 | 1,675,00 |
| 1921 | 3,200,000 | 1.70 | 5,440,000 | 810,000 | 1.75 | 1,417,50 |
| 1922 | 4,250,000 | .75 | 3,188,000 | 900,000 | 1.00 | 900,00 |
| 1923 | 3,010,000 | .95 | 2,860,000 | 750,000 | 1.71 | 1,282,00 |
| 1924 | 3,024,000 | 1.30 | 3,931,000 | 920,000 | 1.60 | 1,472,00 |
| 1925 | 3,200,000 | 1.10 | 3,520,000 | 450,000 | 1.90 | 855,00 |
| 1926 | 3,444,000 | .70 | 2,411,000 | 976,000 | 1.10 | 1,074,00 |
| 1927 | 2,592,000 | 1.10 | 2,851,000 | 892,000 | 1.20 | 1,070,00 |
| 1928 | 3,020,000 | .65 | 1,963,000 | 650,000 | 1.20 | 780,00 |
| 1929 | 2,300,000 | .95 | 2,185,000 | 953,000 | 1.45 | 1,382,00 |
| 1930 | 1,060,000 | .85 | 901,000 | 787,000 | 1.45 | 1,141,00 |
| 1931 | 2,090,000 | .60 | 1,254,000 | 1,130,000 | .50 | 565,00 |

## PRODUCTION, PRICE AND VALUE OF PEARS IN COLORADO, 1910-1931

| Year | Bus. | | |
|------|------|--|--|
| 1910 | 121,000 | ---- | ------ |
| 1911 | 160,000 | $1.55 | $ 248,00 |
| 1912 | 193,000 | .93 | 179,00 |
| 1913 | 130,000 | 1.75 | 227,00 |
| 1914 | 206,000 | ---- | ------ |
| 1915 | 99,000 | ---- | ------ |
| 1916 | 99,000 | ---- | ------ |
| 1917 | 320,000 | 2.10 | 672,00 |
| 1918 | 194,000 | 1.50 | 291,00 |
| 1919 | 345,000 | 2.20 | 759,00 |
| 1920 | 386,000 | 1.90 | 733,00 |
| 1921 | 502,000 | 2.20 | 1,104,0 |
| 1922 | 519,000 | .75 | 389,0 |
| 1923 | 400,000 | 1.56 | 624,0 |
| 1924 | 550,000 | 1.40 | 770,0 |
| 1925 | 510,000 | 1.15 | 586,0 |
| 1926 | 564,000 | .65 | 367,0 |
| 1927 | 480,000 | 1.40 | 672,0 |
| 1928 | 185,000 | 1.05 | 194,0 |
| 1929 | 600,000 | 1.50 | 900,0 |
| 1930 | 146,000 | 1.30 | 190,0 |
| 1931 | 385,000 | .60 | 231,0 |

No prices published for 1914-15-16.

## ACREAGE, PRODUCTION AND VALUE OF CUCUMBERS FOR PICKLES IN COLORADO, 1918-1931

| Year | Acres | Yield per Acre, Bus. | Production, Bus. | Price per Bu. | Value | Value per Acre |
|------|-------|------|------|------|-------|------|
| 1918 | 2,140 | 74 | 158,000 | ---- | -------- | ----- |
| 1919 | 2,140 | 69 | 148,000 | ---- | -------- | ----- |
| 1920 | 1,880 | 81 | 152,000 | ---- | -------- | ----- |
| 1921 | 3,850 | 75 | 289,000 | ---- | -------- | ----- |
| 1922 | 3,080 | 65 | 200,000 | $1.45 | $ 290,000 | $ 91.16 |
| 1923 | 3,250 | 78 | 254,000 | 1.55 | 394,000 | 121.24 |
| 1924 | 2,800 | 35 | 98,000 | 1.00 · | 98,000 | 35.00 |
| 1925 | 3,500 | 102 | 357,000 | 1.00 | 357,000 | 102.00 |
| 1926 | 2,900 | 61 | 177,060 | .87 | 154,000 | 53.10 |
| 1927 | 3,130 | 50 | 156,000 | .75 | 117,000 | 37.39 |
| 1928 | 2,300 | 101 | 232,000 | .60 | 139,000 | 60.43 |
| 1929 | 2,000 | 115 | 230,000 | .60 | 138,000 | 69.00 |
| 1930 | 2,800 | 130 | 364,000 | .53 | 193,000 | 68.93 |
| 1931 | 1,820 | 128 | 233,000 | .48 | 112,000 | 61.54 |

Price data for 1918-1921, inclusive, not available.

## ACREAGE, PRODUCTION AND VALUE OF SNAP BEANS FOR MANUFACTURE IN COLORADO, 1918-1931

| Year | Acres | Yield per Acre, Tons | Production, Tons | Price per Ton | Value | Value per Acre |
|------|-------|------|------|------|-------|------|
| 1918 | 840 | 3.3 | 2,800 | ------ | --------- | ------ |
| 1919 | 1,040 | 4.1 | 4,300 | --- -- | --------- | ------ |
| 1920 | 980 | 2.4 | 2,400 | ------ | --------- | ------ |
| 1921 | 700 | 3.3 | 2,300 | ------ | --------- | ------ |
| 1922 | 610 | 2.5 | 1,500 | $56.67 | $ 85,000 | $139.35 |
| 1923 | 750 | 3.5 | 2,600 | 60.00 | 156,000 | 208.00 |
| 1924 | 1,200 | 3.0 | 3,600 | 60.00 | 216,000 | 180.00 |
| 1925 | 1,800 | 3.0 | 5,400 | 56.67 | 306,000 | 170.00 |
| 1926 | 700 | 3.2 | 2,200 | 53.33 | 117,000 | 167.15 |
| 1927 | 900 | 2.4 | 2,200 | 60.00 | 132,000 | 146.67 |
| 1928 | 1,600 | 2.1 | 3,400 | 60.00 | 204,000 | 127.50 |
| 1929 | 2,300 | 3.0 | 6,900 | 58.00 | 400,000 | 173.91 |
| 1930 | 2,100 | 4.0 | 8,400 | 60.00 | 504,000 | 240.00 |
| 1931 | 1,050 | 1.9 | 2,000 | 43.20 | 86,000 | 81.90 |

Price data for 1918-1921, inclusive, not available.

## ACREAGE, PRODUCTION AND VALUE OF CANTALOUPES IN COLORADO, 1918-1931

| Year | Acres Harvested | Yield per Acre, Crates | Production, Crates | Price per Crate | Value | Value per Acre |
|------|-------|------|------|------|-------|------|
| 1918 | 4,600 | 176 | 809,000 | $1.50 | $ 1,214,000 | $263.91 |
| 1919 | 6,690 | 165 | 1,104,000 | 1.25 | 1,380,000 | 206.30 |
| 1920 | 8,280 | 150 | 1,242,000 | 1.60 | 1,987,000 | 239.97 |
| 1921 | 8,200 | 182 | 1,492,000 | .84 | 1,253,000 | 152.80 |
| 1922 | 14,000 | 100 | 1,400,000 | 1.75 | 2,450,000 | 175.00 |
| 1923 | 8,620 | 125 | 1,078,000 | 1.69 | 1,822,000 | 211.35 |
| 1924 | 8,040 | 145 | 1,166,000 | 1.19 | 1,388,000 | 172.64 |
| 1925 | 7,900 | 181 | 1,430,000 | .91 | 1,301,000 | 164.72 |
| 1926 | 11,670 | 170 | 1,984,000 | 1.17 | 2,321,000 | 198.89 |
| 1927 | 12,100 | 127 | 1,537,000 | 1.05 | 1,614,000 | 133.39 |
| 1928 | 9,000 | 130 | 1,170,000 | .94 | 1,100,000 | 122.00 |
| 1929 | 11,000 | 230 | 2,530,000 | .83 | 2,100,000 | 190.91 |
| 1930 | 10,000 | 200 | 2,000,000 | 1.20 | 2,400,000 | 240.00 |
| 1931 | 8,100 | 140 | 1,134,000 | .85 | 964,000 | 119.01 |

ACREAGE, PRODUCTION AND VALUE OF TOMATOES IN COLORADO FOR TABLE USE.
1918-1931

| Year | Acres | Yield per Acre, Bus. | Production, Bushels | Price per Bu. | Value | Value per Acre |
|---|---|---|---|---|---|---|
| 1918 | 610 | 286 | 174,000 | $1.60 | $ 278,000 | $455.71 |
| 1919 | 650 | 321 | 209,000 | 1.29 | 270,000 | 415.41 |
| 1920 | 630 | 250 | 158,000 | 1.60 | 253,000 | 401.61 |
| 1921 | 180 | 250 | 45,000 | 1.65 | 74,000 | 411.11 |
| 1922 | 490 | 303 | 148,000 | 1.29 | 191,000 | 889.91 |
| 1923 | 970 | 214 | 208,000 | 1.76 | 366,000 | 377.31 |
| 1924 | 350 | 228 | 80.000 | 1.13 | 90,000 | 257.11 |
| 1925 | 580 | 303 | 176,000 | 1.20 | 211,000 | 868.81 |
| 1926 | 410 | 268 | 110,000 | .76 | 84,000 | 204.81 |
| 1927 | 800 | 200 | 160,000 | .85 | 136,000 | 170.00 |
| 1928 | 600 | 264 | 158,000 | .91 | 144,000 | 240.00 |
| 1929 | 1,070 | 310 | 332,000 | .97 | 322,000 | 300.93 |
| 1930 | 1,230 | 320 | 394,000 | .89 | 315,000 | 256.10 |
| 1931 | 1,290 | 286 | 369,000 | .60 | 221,000 | 171.32 |

ACREAGE, PRODUCTION AND VALUE OF TOMATOES IN COLORADO FOR
MANUFACTURE, 1918-1931

| Year | Acres | Yield per Acre, Tons | Production, Tons | Price per Ton | Value | Value per Acre |
|---|---|---|---|---|---|---|
| 1918 | 2,440 | 8.0 | 19,500 | $15.12 | $ 295,000 | $120.90 |
| 1919 | 2,600 | 9.1 | 23,700 | 12.90 | 306,000 | 117.70 |
| 1920 | 2,530 | 6.3 | 15,900 | 15.00 | 238,000 | 94.01 |
| 1921 | 730 | 6.0 | 4,400 | 9.00 | 40,000 | 54.80 |
| 1922 | 2,200 | 8.2 | 18,000 | 8.67 | 156,000 | 70.9 |
| 1923 | 2,860 | 5.0 | 14,300 | 9.00 | 129,000 | 45.1 |
| 1924 | 2,000 | 7.2 | 14,400 | 10.25 | 148,000 | 74.0 |
| 1925 | 3,040 | 8.5 | 25,800 | 11.50 | 297,000 | 97.7 |
| 1926 | 2,350 | 7.5 | 17,600 | 12.00 | 211,000 | 89.7 |
| 1927 | 2,000 | 7.0 | 14,000 | 12.00 | 168,000 | 84.0 |
| 1928 | 1,600 | 7.4 | 11,800 | 11.00 | 130,000 | 81.2 |
| 1929 | 2,030 | 8.7 | 17,700 | 11.00 | 195,000 | 96.0 |
| 1930 | 2,230 | 8.5 | 19,000 | 10.90 | 207,000 | 92.8 |
| 1931 | 2,500 | 7.0 | 17,500 | 10.50 | 184,000 | 73.6 |

ACREAGE, PRODUCTION AND VALUE OF CELERY IN COLORADO, 1918-1931

| 1918 | 200 | 313 | 63,000 | $2.00 | $ 126,000 | $630.0 |
|---|---|---|---|---|---|---|
| 1919 | 350 | 330 | 116,000 | 2.00 | 232,000 | 662.8 |
| 1920 | 410 | 300 | 123,000 | 1.67 | 205,000 | 500.0 |
| 1921 | 400 | 330 | 132,000 | 1.33 | 176,000 | 440.0 |
| 1922 | 600 | 300 | 180,000 | 1.91 | 344,000 | 573.3 |
| 1923 | 670 | 300 | 201,000 | 1.41 | 283,000 | 422.3 |
| 1924 | 720 | 345 | 248,000 | 2.51 | 622,000 | 863.8 |
| 1925 | 920 | 420 | 386,000 | 3.16 | 1,220,000 | 1,326.1 |
| 1926 | 940 | 300 | 282,000 | 1.22 | 344,000 | 366.0 |
| 1927 | 240 | 300 | 282.000 | 1.70 | 479,000 | 509.5 |
| 1928 | 900 | 300 | 270,000 | 1.65 | 446,000 | 495.5 |
| 1929 | 1,100 | 240 | 264,000 | 1.10 | 290,000 | 263.6 |
| 1930 | 950 | 260 | 247,000 | .90 | 222,000 | 233.6 |
| 1931 | 950 | 220 | 209,000 | 1.20 | 251,000 | 264.2 |

## ACREAGE, PRODUCTION AND VALUE OF GREEN PEAS GROWN IN COLORADO FOR TABLE USE, 1922-1931

| Year | Acres | Yield per Acre, Hampers | Production, Hampers | Price per Hamper | Value | Value per Acre |
|------|-------|------------------------|---------------------|------------------|-------|----------------|
| 1922 | 300 | 45 | 14,000 | $1.55 | $ 22,000 | $ 73.33 |
| 1923 | 380 | 75 | 28,000 | 1.44 | 40,000 | 105.27 |
| 1924 | 850 | 80 | 68,000 | 1.85 | 126,000 | 150.00 |
| 1925 | 2,560 | 100 | 256,000 | 3.07 | 786,000 | 307.00 |
| 1926 | 1,940 | 62 | 120,000 | 1.94 | 233,000 | 120.10 |
| 1927 | 4,000 | 50 | 200,000 | 2.84 | 568,000 | 142.00 |
| 1928 | 6,500 | 55 | 358,000 | 1.60 | 573,000 | 87.85 |
| 1929 | 7,100 | 81 | 575,000 | 1.30 | 748,000 | 105.35 |
| 1930 | 5,820 | 75 | 436,000 | 1.65 | 719,000 | 123.54 |
| 1931 | 6,500 | 75 | 488,000 | 1.45 | 708,000 | 108.92 |

## ACREAGE, PRODUCTION AND VALUE OF GREEN PEAS FOR MANUFACTURE IN COLORADO, 1922-1931

| Year | Acres | Yield per Acre, Pounds | Production, Tons | Price per Ton | Value | Value per Acre |
|------|-------|------------------------|------------------|---------------|-------|----------------|
| 1922 | 2,940 | 1,400 | 2,100 | $65.00 | $136,000 | $46.24 |
| 1923 | 3,680 | 1,000 | 1,800 | 69.00 | 124,000 | 33.70 |
| 1924 | 3,140 | 1,600 | 2,500 | 52.54 | 131,000 | 41.72 |
| 1925 | 3,520 | 1,800 | 3,200 | 60.00 | 192,000 | 54.55 |
| 1926 | 2,570 | 1,800 | 2,313 | 60.10 | 139,000 | 54.09 |
| 1927 | 1,900 | 1,800 | 1,710 | 60.00 | 103,000 | 54.21 |
| 1928 | 3,000 | 1,900 | 2,850 | 50.00 | 142,000 | 47.33 |
| 1929 | 3,400 | 1,776 | 3,019 | 44.00 | 133,000 | 39.12 |
| 1930 | 3,700 | 1,820 | 3,367 | 46.00 | 155,000 | 41.89 |
| 1931 | 3,500 | 1,480 | 2,590 | 46.00 | 119,000 | 34.00 |

## ACREAGE, PRODUCTION AND VALUE OF CABBAGE IN COLORADO, 1918-1931

| Year | Acres Harvested | Yield per Acre, Tons | Production, Tons | Price per Ton | Value | Av. Value per Acre |
|------|-----------------|----------------------|------------------|---------------|-------|--------------------|
| 1918 | 4,220 | 9.0 | 38,000 | $24.50 | $ 931,000 | $220.61 |
| 1919 | 4,000 | 10.0 | 40,000 | 20.00 | 800,000 | 200.00 |
| 1920 | 4,390 | 15.1 | 66,300 | 9.04 | 599,400 | 136.54 |
| 1921 | 3,995 | 11.7 | 46,730 | 24.55 | 1,147,000 | 287.09 |
| 1922 | 5,240 | 12.0 | 62,900 | 4.27 | 269,000 | 51.32 |
| 1923 | 5,270 | 14.3 | 75,400 | 7.40 | 558,000 | 105.91 |
| 1924 | 4,010 | 11.0 | 44,100 | 11.38 | 502,000 | 125.20 |
| 1925 | 2,000 | 11.5 | 23,000 | 18.96 | 436,000 | 218.00 |
| 1926 | 3,220 | 13.6 | 43,800 | 7.29 | 319,000 | 99.08 |
| 1927 | 2,300 | 14.6 | 33,500 | 13.97 | 468,000 | 203.48 |
| 1928 | 2,600 | 14.4 | 37,500 | 13.39 | 502,000 | 193.08 |
| 1929 | 2,800 | 10.7 | 30,000 | 21.30 | 639,000 | 228.21 |
| 1930 | 3,400 | 12.6 | 42,900 | 8.83 | 379,000 | 111.47 |
| 1931 | 3,550 | 8.2 | 29,200 | 15.55 | 454,000 | 127.89 |

### ACREAGE, PRODUCTION AND VALUE OF LETTUCE IN COLORADO, 1918-1931

| Year | Acres | Yield per Acre, Crates | Production, Crates | Price per Crate | Value | Value per Acre |
|---|---|---|---|---|---|---|
| 1918 | 140 | 255 | 36,000 | $3.50 | $ 126,000 | $900.00 |
| 1919 | 190 | 235 | 45,000 | 3.00 | 135,000 | 710.55 |
| 1920 | 730 | 250 | 182,000 | 1.80 | 328,000 | 449.32 |
| 1921 | 900 | 270 | 243,000 | 1.50 | 364,000 | 404.45 |
| 1922 | 6,000 | 180 | 1,080,000 | 1.71 | 1,847,000 | 307.83 |
| 1923 | 6,710 | 145 | 973,000 | 1.60 | 1,557,000 | 231.99 |
| 1924 | 5,600 | 85 | 476,000 | 2.16 | 1,028,000 | 183.57 |
| 1925 | 10,500 | 133 | 1,396,000 | 1.58 | 2,206,000 | 210.09 |
| 1926 | 13,240 | 115 | 1,523,000 | 1.43 | 2,178,000 | 164.50 |
| 1927 | 13,240 | 110 | 1,456,000 | 1.63 | 2,373,000 | 179.24 |
| 1928 | 9,800 | 115 | 1,127,000 | 1.07 | 1,206,000 | 123.05 |
| 1929 | 8,100 | 110 | 891,000 | 1.25 | 1,114,000 | 137.53 |
| 1930 | 7,440 | 90 | 670,000 | .85 | 570,000 | 76.61 |
| 1931 | 6,650 | 90 | 598,000 | 1.30 | 777,000 | 116.84 |

### ACREAGE, PRODUCTION AND VALUE OF CAULIFLOWER IN COLORADO, 1922-1931

| 1922 | 260 | 277 | 72,000 | $1.82 | $ 131,000 | $504.00 |
|---|---|---|---|---|---|---|
| 1923 | 400 | 160 | 64,000 | 1.11 | 71,000 | 177.50 |
| 1924 | 400 | 160 | 64,000 | 1.80 | 115,000 | 288.00 |
| 1925 | 1,000 | 160 | 160,000 | .71 | 114,000 | 114.00 |
| 1926 | 1,100 | 90 | 99,000 | 1.15 | 114,000 | 103.64 |
| 1927 | 1,160 | 290 | 336,000 | 1.78 | 598,000 | 515.52 |
| 1928 | 1,700 | 300 | 510,000 | 1.20 | 612,000 | 360.00 |
| 1929 | 3,200 | 360 | 1,152,000 | .70 | 806,000 | 251.88 |
| 1930 | 2,800 | 320 | 896,000 | .80 | 717,000 | 256.07 |
| 1931 | 3,900 | 260 | 1,014,000 | .70 | 710,000 | 182.05 |

### ACRES, PRODUCTION AND VALUE OF GRAIN SORGHUMS IN COLORADO, 1919-1931

| Year | Acres | Yield per Acre, Bus. | Production, Bushels | Price per Bu. | Value | Value per Acre |
|---|---|---|---|---|---|---|
| 1919 | 283,000 | 16 | 4,528,000 | $1.20 | $ 5,434,000 | $19.20 |
| 1920 | 282,000 | 15 | 4,230,000 | .84 | 3,553,000 | 12.60 |
| 1921 | 265,000 | 13 | 3,445,000 | .52 | 1,791,000 | 6.76 |
| 1922 | 247,000 | 14 | 3,458,000 | .70 | 2,421,000 | 9.80 |
| 1923 | 320,000 | 18 | 5,760,000 | .80 | 4,608,000 | 14.40 |
| 1924 | 233,000 | 8 | 1,864,000 | .90 | 1,678,000 | 7.20 |
| 1925 | 246,000 | 11 | 2,706,000 | .71 | 1,921,000 | 7.81 |
| 1926 | 227,000 | 5 | 1,135,000 | .60 | 681,000 | 3.00 |
| 1927 | 284,000 | 10 | 2,840,000 | .65 | 1,846,000 | 6.50 |
| 1928 | 256,000 | 10.5 | 2,688,000 | .60 | 1,613,000 | 6.30 |
| 1929 | 175,000 | 10.5 | 1,838,000 | .80 | 1,470,000 | 8.40 |
| 1930 | 180,000 | 13.0 | 2,340,000 | .50 | 1,170,000 | 6.50 |
| 1931 | 191,000 | 11.0 | 2,101,000 | .23 | 483,000 | 2.53 |

Note—The acreage includes both sorghums threshed for grain and that portion cut for forage, both being considered on the basis of grain values.

## ACRES OF ALL FARM LAND* RETURNED ANNUALLY FOR ASSESSMENT IN COLORADO FOR 1915, 1920, 1928, 1929, 1930 AND 1931

| COUNTY | 1931 | 1930 | 1929 | 1928 | 1920 | 1915 |
|---|---|---|---|---|---|---|
| Adams | 739,019 | 742,427 | 750,104 | 750,430 | 737,123 | 629,707 |
| Alamosa | 299,085 | 316,144 | 322,280 | 321,286 | 307,800 | 334,500 |
| Arapahoe | 501,362 | 497,502 | 491,810 | 492,410 | 490,550 | 441,447 |
| Archuleta | 253,445 | 246,445 | 311,076 | 323,702 | 257,141 | 249,577 |
| Baca | 1,533,545 | 1,533,420 | 1,532,020 | 1,529,257 | 1,137,896 | 540,620 |
| Bent | 785,185 | 790,914 | 772,596 | 750,115 | 446,787 | 189,325 |
| Boulder | 262,248 | 260,922 | 264,239 | 258,880 | 251,790 | 232,766 |
| Chaffee | 101,315 | 99,954 | 98,053 | 94,626 | 83,363 | 80,687 |
| Cheyenne | 1,074,538 | 1,072,229 | 1,075,601 | 1,074,814 | 1,044,149 | 888,535 |
| Clear Creek | 37,543 | 32,897 | 33,046 | 41,433 | 33,857 | 30,828 |
| Conejos | 257,976 | 257,386 | 256,646 | 252,638 | 225,604 | 216,263 |
| Costilla | 780,400 | 374,160 | 374,180 | 376,180 | 219,200 | 769,456 |
| Crowley | 429,793 | 424,921 | 425,311 | 418,361 | 307,539 | 131,443 |
| Custer | 261,840 | 257,318 | 254,901 | 251,240 | 140,405 | 117,653 |
| Delta | 268,124 | 359,446 | 258,689 | 130,001 | 218,167 | 189,239 |
| Denver | 5,855 | 5,928 | 5,706 | 6,074 | 7,519 | 7,843 |
| Dolores | 203,387 | 191,787 | 190,558 | 188,894 | 37,035 | 10,257 |
| Douglas | 380,345 | 379,997 | 379,358 | 379,332 | 375,584 | 367,270 |
| Eagle | 159,769 | 148,314 | 155,146 | 138,772 | 98,394 | 85,392 |
| Elbert | 1,081,576 | 1,081,479 | 1,077,854 | 1,073,216 | 1,034,431 | 952,091 |
| El Paso | 989,529 | 988,889 | 990,870 | 991,474 | 951,958 | 799,156 |
| Fremont | 368,841 | 372,416 | 359,693 | 354,360 | 214,408 | 182,330 |
| Garfield | 340,952 | 327,139 | 328,812 | 323,568 | 259,122 | 204,520 |
| Gilpin | 29,133 | 28,502 | 28,073 | 26,883 | 18,091 | 15,936 |
| Grand | 265,893 | 265,109 | 262,169 | 253,131 | 172,269 | 128,246 |
| Gunnison | 336,513 | 330,832 | 309,367 | 293,927 | 151,927 | 122,701 |
| Hinsdale | 20,990 | 20,102 | 15,622 | 18,427 | 14,759 | 12,081 |
| Huerfano | 668,867 | 657,567 | 654,232 | 651,264 | 366,959 | 340,211 |
| Jackson | 316,027 | 306,734 | 300,497 | 291,040 | 214,044 | 193,940 |
| Jefferson | 336,652 | 334,422 | 346,325 | 341,323 | 322,343 | 296,175 |
| Kiowa | 1,039,593 | 1,050,114 | 1,030,751 | 1,036,847 | 960,670 | 680,986 |
| Kit Carson | 1,306,444 | 1,307,131 | 1,307,131 | 1,307,011 | 1,265,961 | 1,128,158 |
| Lake | 28,713 | 28,966 | 28,327 | 23,912 | 27,011 | 26,658 |
| La Plata | 430,339 | 432,180 | 436,714 | 423,906 | 328,843 | 265,834 |
| Larimer | 763,389 | 761,541 | 761,535 | 762,364 | 666,173 | 621,368 |
| Las Animas | 2,584,673 | 2,576,249 | 2,637,187 | 2,549,571 | 1,078,269 | 765,310 |
| Lincoln | 1,487,988 | 1,496,195 | 1,496,898 | 1,495,256 | 1,409,418 | 1,058,771 |
| Logan | 990,201 | 988,921 | 988,321 | 987,641 | 966,630 | 680,036 |
| Mesa | 483,418 | 480,507 | 474,647 | 457,564 | 338,284 | 287,055 |
| Mineral | 26,892 | 26,744 | 26,599 | 27,331 | 20,551 | 19,256 |
| Moffat | 1,000,559 | 981,949 | 960,114 | 940,924 | 229,710 | 129,754 |
| Montezuma | 317,504 | 315,366 | 289,569 | 302,906 | 209,902 | 160,104 |
| Montrose | 406,823 | 411,824 | 407,347 | 398,129 | 293,693 | 230,329 |
| Morgan | 744,607 | 743,898 | 742,845 | 742,305 | 634,280 | 367,245 |
| Otero | 650,337 | 648,908 | 623,031 | 606,039 | 323,442 | 240,275 |
| Ouray | 150,040 | 149,895 | 147,958 | 144,817 | 155,440 | 83,793 |
| Park | 467,485 | 466,040 | 459,728 | 445,722 | 192,192 | 196,132 |
| Phillips | 407,977 | 403,618 | 408,372 | 408,372 | 395,780 | 385,671 |
| Pitkin | 70,181 | 70,147 | 70,485 | 70,485 | 58,078 | 50,701 |
| Prowers | 967,521 | 973,008 | 964,067 | 958,253 | 811,164 | 448,925 |
| Pueblo | 1,173,513 | 1,169,258 | 1,165,970 | 1,164,642 | 867,047 | 688,441 |
| Rio Blanco | 355,341 | 355,341 | 345,955 | 341,487 | 194,466 | 139,814 |
| Rio Grande | 222,153 | 220,244 | 219,255 | 215,973 | 185,285 | 170,680 |
| Routt | 565,056 | 559,221 | 543,945 | 518,558 | 345,619 | 261,047 |
| Saguache | 555,892 | 553,117 | 539,530 | 542,679 | 453,873 | 407,323 |
| San Juan | 200 | 200 | 200 | 200 | 200 | 200 |
| San Miguel | 230,627 | 229,052 | 229,683 | 223,005 | 125,269 | 87,098 |
| Sedgwick | 305,933 | 305,777 | 304,112 | 303,383 | 297,652 | 280,973 |
| Summit | 39,780 | 38,075 | 37,740 | 37,706 | 28,945 | 22,610 |
| Teller | 150,363 | 149,691 | 149,911 | 149,560 | 112,470 | 99,807 |
| Washington | 1,482,039 | 1,481,907 | 1,487,261 | 1,485,598 | 1,393,009 | 914,615 |
| Weld | 2,272,958 | 2,266,855 | 2,270,582 | 2,262,005 | 2,171,570 | 1,631,321 |
| Yuma | 1,440,993 | 1,438,893 | 1,433,522 | 1,425,885 | 1,296,745 | 993,616 |
| State | 36,209,279 | 35,791,134 | 35,614,126 | 35,163,103 | 27,977,855 | 22,284,101 |

*Includes fruit, irrigated, natural hay, dry farming, grazing and waste and seep land.

## DISTRIBUTION OF AGRICULTURAL LAND
(From County Assessors' Reports, 1931)

| COUNTY | Area Acres | Agricultural Land | Per Cent of Total Area | Irrigated Land* | Per Cent of Agricultural Land | Grazing Land† | Per Cent of Agricultural Land | Dry Farming Land | Per Cent of Agricultural Land |
|---|---|---|---|---|---|---|---|---|---|
| Adams | 807,680 | 749,89 | 92.84 | 109,381 | .59 | 124,824 | 16.65 | 515,634 | 68.76 |
| Alamosa | 465,280 | 299,85 | 64.28 | 66,000 | 22.07 | 117,285 | 39.21 | 115,800 | 38.72 |
| Arapahoe | 538,880 | 511,529 | 4092 | 28,876 | 5.65 | 69,942 | 13.67 | 412,711 | 80.68 |
| Archuleta | 780,800 | 253,445 | 32.46 | 11,049 | 4.36 | 232,239 | 91.63 | 10,157 | 4.01 |
| Baca | 1,633,280 | 1,533,545 | 93.88 | 2,750 | 0.18 | 556,255 | 36.27 | 974,540 | 63.55 |
| Bent | 975,360 | 785,185 | 80.50 | 48,670 | 6.19 | 679,384 | 86.53 | 57,131 | 7.28 |
| Boulder | 488,960 | 265,134 | 54.22 | 102,951 | .83 | 132,678 | 50.04 | 29,505 | 11.13 |
| Chaffee | 693,120 | 101,315 | 14.62 | 24,569 | 24.25 | 76,746 | 75.75 | | |
| Cheyenne | 1,137,280 | 1,074,554 | 94.48 | 16 | 0.05 | 235,871 | 21.92 | 838,967 | 78.03 |
| Clear Creek | 249,600 | 37,83 | 15.04 | | | 37,543 | 100.00 | | |
| Conejos | 801,280 | 257,96 | 32.20 | 96,400 | 37.37 | 161,576 | 62.63 | 6,264 | 0.80 |
| Costilla | 758,400 | 780,400 | 102.90 | 97,756 | 12.53 | 676,280 | 86.67 | 9,947 | 2.31 |
| Crowley | 517,120 | 429,793 | 83.11 | 42,185 | 9.82 | 377,661 | 87.87 | 6,805 | 2.60 |
| Custer | 478,080 | 261,840 | 54.77 | 17,509 | 6.69 | 237,526 | 90.71 | | |
| Delta | 768,640 | 268,124 | 48 | 61,631 | 22.98 | 184,757 | 68.91 | 21,736 | 8.11 |
| Denver | 37,120 | 5,85 | 15.77 | 5,855 | 100.00 | | | | |
| Dolores | 67,520 | 203,387 | 30.47 | 595 | 0.29 | 182,579 | 89.77 | 20,213 | 9.94 |
| Douglas | 540,80 | 80,345 | 70.33 | 13,853 | 3.64 | 299,944 | 78.86 | 66,548 | 17.50 |
| Eagle | 1,066,800 | 159,769 | 15.41 | 27,933 | 17.48 | 130,623 | 81.76 | 1,213 | 0.76 |
| Elbert | 1,188,480 | 1,081,576 | 91.00 | 11,808 | 1.10 | 725,666 | 67.09 | 344,102 | 31.81 |
| El Paso | 1,87,140 | 90,954 | 73.00 | 24,015 | 2.42 | 750,519 | 75.74 | 216,420 | 21.84 |
| Fremont | 96,480 | 68,841 | 37.01 | 17,731 | 4.81 | 302,933 | 82.13 | 48,177 | 13.06 |
| Garfield | 1,988,480 | 340,952 | 17.15 | 53,934 | 15.82 | 259,016 | 75.97 | 28,002 | 8.21 |
| Gilpin | 84,480 | 29,133 | 34.49 | | | 29,133 | 100.00 | | |
| Grand | 1,194,240 | 265,893 | 22.26 | 31,525 | 11.86 | 234,368 | 88.14 | | |
| Gunnison | 2,034,50 | 336,513 | 16.54 | 37,286 | 11.08 | 299,227 | 88.92 | | |
| Hinsdale | 621,140 | 20,90 | 3.38 | 2,365 | 11.26 | 18,265 | 87.02 | 360 | 1.72 |
| Huerfano | 60,00 | 668,867 | 69.67 | 15,757 | 2.36 | 630,702 | 94.29 | 22,408 | 3.35 |
| Jackson | 1,044,480 | 316,027 | 30.26 | 69,191 | 21.90 | 246,764 | 78.08 | 72 | 0.02 |
| Jefferson | 517,120 | 348,612 | 67.41 | 62,960 | 18.06 | 256,847 | 73.68 | 28,805 | 8.26 |

| County | | | | | | | | | |
|---|---|---|---|---|---|---|---|---|---|
| Kiowa | 1,150,720 | 1,039,593 | 90.34 | | — | 93,361 | 28.22 | 746,232 | 71.78 |
| Kit Carson | 1,381,760 | 1,306,444 | 94.55 | 4,047 | 3.10 | 97,513 | 22.77 | 1,004,884 | 76.87 |
| Lake | 237,440 | 28,713 | 12.09 | 4,836 | 16.84 | 23,387 | 83.16 | | — |
| La Plata | 1,184,640 | 430,822 | 36.37 | 42,976 | 9.98 | 59,317 | 83.40 | 28,529 | 6.62 |
| Larimer | 1,682,560 | 764,767 | 45.45 | 123,195 | 16.11 | 617,832 | 80.75 | 24,050 | 3.14 |
| Las Animas | 3,077,760 | 2,585,314 | 84.00 | 32,675 | 1.26 | 2,483,098 | 96.07 | 68,930 | 2.67 |
| Lincoln | 1,644,800 | 1,487,988 | 90.47 | 3,090 | 0.21 | 581,832 | 39.08 | 903,406 | 60.71 |
| Logan | 1,166,080 | 990,201 | 84.92 | 88,761 | 8.87 | 33,340 | 33.67 | 568,000 | 57.46 |
| Mesa | 2,024,320 | 483,870 | 23.90 | 51,581 | 10.66 | 82,855 | 91.2 | 49,434 | 10.22 |
| Mineral | 554,240 | 26,892 | 4.85 | 4,099 | 15.24 | 22,293 | 84.76 | 34,434 | — |
| Moffat | 2,981,120 | 1,000,559 | 33.56 | 14,928 | 1.49 | 951,197 | 95.07 | 44,294 | 3.44 |
| Montezuma | 1,312,640 | 317,504 | 24.19 | 36,978 | 11.65 | 26,832 | 74.40 | 23,850 | 13.95 |
| Montrose | 1,448,960 | 406,823 | 28.08 | 64,581 | 5.78 | 318,832 | 78.35 | 36,860 | 15.87 |
| Morgan | 823,040 | 744,607 | 90.47 | 83,292 | 11.18 | 414,865 | 55.69 | 36,860 | 33.13 |
| Otero | 805,760 | 652,397 | 80.97 | 78,162 | 11.98 | 54,605 | 86.46 | 10,140 | 1.56 |
| Ouray | 332,160 | 150,040 | 45.17 | 11,960 | 7.97 | 134,860 | 89.76 | 3,860 | .27 |
| Park | 1,434,880 | 467,485 | 32.58 | 22,700 | 4.86 | 89,601 | 94.04 | 5,184 | 1.10 |
| Phillips | 440,320 | 407,977 | 92.65 | | — | 31,883 | 7.74 | 36,84 | 92.26 |
| Pitkin | 652,160 | 70,181 | 10.76 | 16,248 | 23.15 | 53,683 | 76.61 | 170 | .04 |
| Prowers | 1,043,200 | 967,938 | 92.79 | 95,947 | 9.92 | 20,866 | 24.86 | 631,325 | 65.22 |
| Pueblo | 1,557,120 | 1,178,023 | 75.65 | 44,680 | 3.79 | 1,063,003 | 89.39 | 80,340 | 6.82 |
| Rio Blanco | 2,062,720 | 355,341 | 17.23 | 23,734 | 6.68 | 310,368 | 87.43 | 20,929 | .59 |
| Rio Grande | 574,720 | 222,153 | 38.65 | 91,557 | 41.21 | 130,896 | 58.79 | | — |
| Routt | 1,477,760 | 565,056 | 38.24 | 41,583 | 7.36 | 471,850 | 83.46 | 51,893 | 9.18 |
| Saguache | 2,005,120 | 555,892 | 27.72 | 86,640 | 15.59 | 49,382 | 84.41 | | — |
| San Juan | 289,920 | 200 | 0.07 | | — | 50,890 | 100.00 | | — |
| San Miguel | 824,320 | 230,627 | 27.98 | 7,118 | 3.09 | 216,850 | 93.90 | 6,959 | 3.01 |
| Sedgwick | 339,840 | 305,933 | 90.02 | 25,303 | 8.27 | 92,883 | 30.33 | 187,842 | 61.40 |
| Summit | 415,360 | 39,780 | 9.58 | 6,210 | 15.61 | 33,850 | 84.39 | | — |
| Teller | 350,080 | 150,363 | 42.95 | 2,042 | 1.36 | 127,179 | 84.58 | 21,142 | 14.06 |
| Washington | 1,613,440 | 1,482,039 | 91.86 | 7,641 | 0.52 | 30,827 | 22.28 | 44,71 | 77.20 |
| Weld | 2,574,080 | 2,275,122 | 88.23 | 355,930 | 15.64 | 1,167,394 | 51.33 | 751,398 | 33.03 |
| Yuma | 1,514,880 | 1,440,993 | 95.12 | 7,397 | 0.51 | 63,894 | 53.02 | 669,612 | 46.47 |
| State | 66,341,120 | 36,258,658 | 54.65 | 2,564,442 | 7.07 | 22,215,437 | 61.27 | 11,478,779 | 31.66 |

*Includes acreage classed by assessors as fruit land, natural hay land, and suburban tracts.
†Includes acreage classed by assessors as waste and seep land.
Note: Due to errors in assessment, agricultural land in Costilla county shows more acreage than the total area for the county.

ASSESSED VALUE OF FARM PROPERTY IN COLORADO, 1930 AND 1931

(Compiled from Records of the State Tax Commission)

| COUNTY | 1931 | | | | | | | | 1930 |
|---|---|---|---|---|---|---|---|---|---|
| | Farm Land* | Livestock† | Poultry and Bees | Equities in State Lands | Improvements on Patented Land | Improvements on Public Land | Agricultural Implements | Total | Total |
| Adams | $11,422,100 | 82, 55 | 80, 95 | $60,970 | $2,149, 90 | $97,260 | 88, 95 | $14,831, 55 | $19, 90, 90 |
| Alamosa | 3,324,278 | 83, 80 | 9, 86 | 39,945 | 93, 86 | 23,829 | 72, 80 | 4,166, 24 | 5,105, 60 |
| Arapahoe | 3,262,665 | 82, 30 | 42,110 | 51,500 | 2,211, 05 | | 126, 90 | 8,197, 80 | 10, 02,155 |
| Archuleta | 992,987 | 47,616 | 4, 60 | 2,880 | 89, 215 | 1,600 | 20, 65 | 1, 69,513 | 1, 89,717 |
| Baca | 6,421,754 | 90, 89 | 33, 95 | 156,375 | 69, 80 | 15,425 | 51, 95 | 8, 49, 33 | 10,124, 33 |
| Bent | 4,920,305 | 63, 85 | 29, 90 | 25,045 | 90, 50 | 9,450 | 56, 25 | 6,191, 80 | 7, 84, 90 |
| Boulder | 8,179,480 | 66, 40 | 39, 80 | 6,080 | 2,730, 80 | | 128, 80 | 11, 49, 90 | 14, 04,410 |
| Chaffee | 1,120,510 | 80, 80 | 3,135 | | 441, 80 | 29,345 | 21, 95 | 1, 85, 95 | 2, 87, 40 |
| Cheyenne | 6,295,815 | 84,195 | 13,016 | 26,785 | 62,610 | 2,010 | 75, 85 | 7, 99, 95 | 9, 83, 20 |
| Clear Creek | 329,820 | 23, 55 | 295 | 9,990 | 121,135 | 1,830 | 2, 95 | 83, 00 | 87,175 |
| Conejos | 3,496,135 | 73, 25 | 11,580 | 39,610 | 89, 90 | 4,615 | 96, 90 | 4, 81,615 | 6, 02,130 |
| Costilla | 2,460,935 | 210,615 | 4,135 | | 193, 40 | 11,775 | 32, 80 | 93, 80 | 3, 25,815 |
| Crowley | 4,061,100 | 90, 95 | 24,695 | 11,835 | 571, 90 | 33,460 | 90,140 | 5,194, 95 | 6, 80,133 |
| Custer | 1,147,552 | 89, 55 | 2,875 | | 85, 58 | 7,218 | 35, 85 | 1, 08, 83 | 2,112, 85 |
| Delta | 4,030,780 | 1, 89, 65 | 33,385 | | 96, 30 | 12,460 | 142, 80 | 6,155, 80 | 7, 65, 90 |
| Denver | 3,442,950 | 49, 80 | | | 5,453, 90 | 8, 00 | 8, 00 | 8, 94, 00 | 9, 64, 50 |
| Dolores | 613,485 | 28, 25 | 1,250 | | 59,112 | 7,032 | 10, 60 | 90, 24 | 1,136, 95 |
| Douglas | 2,617,965 | 82,100 | 12,640 | | 1,552, 55 | 27,625 | 86, 30 | 5,129,815 | 6,120,610 |
| Eagle | 1,761,982 | 745,196 | 4,330 | 1,120 | 38, 00 | 16,595 | 62, 95 | 2,910,168 | 3, 53, 64 |
| Elbert | 6,800,490 | 1,028,077 | 25,207 | 112,137 | 86,418 | 61,421 | 199, 62 | 9, 03,312 | 11,310,516 |
| El Paso | 6,047,730 | 1,193,050 | 36,150 | 59,680 | 1,975, 80 | 39,300 | 79, 50 | 9,431, 00 | 12,132, 00 |
| Fremont | 2,799,002 | 96, 98 | 25,998 | 11,660 | 1,718, 00 | 5,560 | 34,186 | 4,951, 84 | 6, 32,916 |
| Garfield | 4,146,060 | 1, 80,105 | 27,425 | | 713, 50 | 74,600 | 441, 85 | 6, 83,125 | 8, 90, 80 |
| Gilpin | 70,752 | 34, 86 | | 3,673 | 22, 80 | | 1, 60 | 133,021 | 143, 88 |
| Grand | 1,466,440 | 82, 90 | 1,665 | 13,680 | 83, 80 | 69,250 | 37, 00 | 2, 84, 85 | 2, 90, 95 |
| Gunnison | 1,968,040 | 1,149,130 | 2,625 | 6,780 | 56,140 | 15,785 | 48,150 | 3, 66, 60 | 4,615, 74 |
| Hinsdale | 93,690 | 59, 65 | | | 19, 85 | 7,550 | 1, 95 | 184, 90 | 352,108 |
| Huerfano | 2,030,149 | 86, 96 | 5,715 | 2,435 | 86, 04 | 28,845 | 58, 40 | 2, 82, 96 | 3,680,272 |
| Jackson | 1,230,270 | 1,002, 80 | 1,480 | 7,770 | 217, 40 | 14,570 | 44, 90 | 2,517, 60 | 3,035,100 |
| Jefferson | 5,748,025 | 63, 85 | 63,700 | 36,420 | 5,195,197 | 18,340 | 121, 85 | 11,816, 22 | 17,839,090 |

| County | | | | | | | | | |
|---|---|---|---|---|---|---|---|---|
| Kiowa | 6,396,210 | 45, 85 | 13,850 | 50,450 | 225,090 | 1,760 | 32, 35 | 7,175, 20 | 8,944,555 |
| Kit Carson | 9,575,480 | 1, 1, 66 | 47,022 | 56,710 | 1,072,200 | 119,730 | 35, 23 | 12,317, 76 | 15,778,631 |
| Lake | 140,130 | 29, 90 | ----- | 505 | 96,805 | ----- | 7, 65 | 24, 85 | 89, 85 |
| La Plata | 3,038,975 | 64,315 | 22,370 | 1,035 | 741,535 | 3,350 | 58,100 | 4, 89, 80 | 5,708, 80 |
| Larimer | 10,397,250 | 1,213,160 | 49,620 | 40,970 | 3,580,210 | 27,750 | 96, 90 | 15, 76, 80 | 20,690, 40 |
| Las Animas | 7,508,769 | 1,719, 85 | 12,434 | ----- | 1,420,027 | 16,000 | 99, 65 | 10, 24, 80 | 13,310, 88 |
| Lincoln | 8,474,265 | 1, 00, 85 | 31,240 | 52,530 | 467,510 | 82,975 | 115, 85 | 15, 33, 20 | 12,743, 85 |
| Logan | 11,747,940 | 1, 26,195 | 55,985 | 121,780 | 1,560,440 | 30,740 | 30,140 | 19,251, 88 | 19,251, 88 |
| Mesa | 7,407,874 | 1,619,145 | 69,445 | ----- | 1,540,510 | 15,730 | 215, 55 | 10, 88, 29 | 13,895, 85 |
| Mineral | 139,495 | 89, 85 | 295 | 720 | 127,030 | 6,225 | 2, 85 | 86,165 | 67, 45 |
| Moffat | 2,656,167 | 861, 95 | 7,550 | 35,035 | 426,128 | 21,672 | 86, 50 | 4, 65,147 | 5,138, 00 |
| Montezuma | 2,131,285 | 619,165 | 18,940 | 41,600 | 419,660 | 19,630 | 61, 30 | 3,311, 80 | 4,041,130 |
| Montrose | 3,525,385 | 998,930 | 31,045 | ----- | 684,045 | 4,375 | 138, 90 | 5, 82, 20 | 6,710, 66 |
| Morgan | 8,319,790 | 854,540 | 38,810 | 63,660 | 1,280,930 | 33,860 | 33, 90 | 10, 94, 90 | 13,860, 90 |
| Otero | 6,668,190 | 754,615 | 50,795 | 10,855 | 3,027,480 | 353,145 | 29, 85 | 11, 04, 65 | 13,937, 80 |
| Ouray | 793,234 | 269,640 | 2,250 | ----- | 107,760 | 400 | 21, 60 | 1,194, 54 | 311, 43 |
| Park | 1,754,600 | 664,710 | 2,560 | 19,400 | 500,355 | 22,360 | 61,120 | 3, 65,105 | 3,630, 20 |
| Phillips | 7,817,340 | 401,660 | 24,105 | 43,085 | 526,790 | 123,770 | 88, 60 | 9,145,310 | 11,343, 85 |
| Pitkin | 825,380 | 218,825 | 1,210 | ----- | 149,560 | 23,120 | 40, 40 | 1, 88, 55 | 1,645, 80 |
| Prowers | 7,884,580 | 848,447 | 45,963 | 50,700 | 1,175,000 | 42,810 | 186, 53 | 10, 24, 63 | 12,698, 60 |
| Pueblo | 7,165,250 | 949,195 | 37,670 | 217,009 | 11,692,730 | 66,500 | 144, 30 | 20, 22, 65 | 23,794, 75 |
| Rio Blanco | 2,030,960 | 1,167,290 | 3,490 | 203,710 | 405,330 | 11,260 | 66, 50 | 3, 34, 90 | 4,613,615 |
| Rio Grande | 3,845,415 | 597,660 | 5,231 | 67,810 | 575,715 | 100,620 | 76, 80 | 5, 45,231 | 6, 94, 82 |
| Routt | 3,536,960 | 1,440,060 | 11,030 | ----- | 754,700 | 102,130 | 162, 30 | 6, 65, 20 | 7, 92, 80 |
| Saguache | 3,207,790 | 1,042,561 | 4,570 | 57,429 | 397,157 | 29,095 | 50,170 | 4, 83, 72 | 6, 98, 38 |
| San Juan | 1,120 | 47,744 | ----- | ----- | ----- | 175 | 175 | 49, 89 | 58, 83 |
| San Miguel | 879,710 | 330,835 | 2,260 | 4,470 | 197,770 | 6,630 | 19,315 | 1, 40, 90 | 1, 87, 45 |
| Sedgwick | 4,906,960 | 398,155 | 15,730 | 51,020 | 613,025 | 6,080 | 176, 95 | 6,167, 55 | 7, 65, 50 |
| Summit | 287,165 | 116,485 | 300 | ----- | 47,050 | 500 | 6, 90 | 57, 80 | 618,100 |
| Teller | 438,790 | 183,760 | 845 | ----- | 88,930 | 5,860 | 16, 30 | 34, 35 | 888,285 |
| Washington | 7,796,021 | 1,149,216 | 49,035 | 38,610 | 638,132 | 6,805 | 24, 35 | 9,921, 64 | 12,220,587 |
| Weld | 32,751,570 | 2,704,630 | 103,940 | 102,190 | 4,678,060 | 51,420 | 85, 90 | 41,217, 90 | 52,149,094 |
| Yuma | 12,637,610 | 1,418,540 | 52,050 | 49,980 | 972,220 | 20,450 | 30,510 | 15,491, 80 | 19,176,010 |
| State | $291,040,936 | $44,732,602 | $1,322,666 | $2,075,701 | $71,455,744 | $1,992,502 | $8,087,584 | $420,707,825 | $527,187,096 |

*Excluding valuation of suburban tracts and mountain home sites.

†Excluding valuation of cattle and sheep fed in transit.

## ACREAGE OF IRRIGATED LAND AS RETURNED BY COUNTY ASSESSORS FOR ASSESS. MENT FOR 1914, 1920, 1925, 1929, 1930 AND 1931

| COUNTY | 1931 | 1930 | 1929 | 1925 | 1920 | 1914 |
|---|---|---|---|---|---|---|
| Adams ____ | 81,329 | 82,499 | 93,389 | 87,343 | 102,073 | 100,381 |
| Alamosa ___ | 28,500 | 28,500 | 27,500 | 26,800 | 26,000 | 65,900 |
| Arapahoe __ | 18,709 | 18,694 | 27,750 | 29,876 | 33,180 | 38,625 |
| Archuleta __ | 10,479 | 10,479 | 10,598 | 10,712 | 11,826 | 8,918 |
| Baca _____ | 2,750 | 2,950 | 2,950 | 3,540 | 9,000 | ------ |
| Bent _____ | 48,670 | 48,170 | 47,550 | 47,909 | 46,732 | 46,234 |
| Boulder ____ | 81,955 | 79,127 | 79,059 | 83,563 | 86,407 | 98,323 |
| Chaffee ____ | 24,569 | 25,062 | 24,543 | 22,526 | 20,045 | 19,037 |
| Cheyenne __ | ----- | ----- | ----- | ----- | ----- | ----- |
| Clear Creek_ | ----- | ----- | ----- | ----- | ----- | ----- |
| Conejos ____ | 86,480 | 86,480 | 85,840 | 86,950 | 87,300 | 97,656 |
| Costilla ____ | 76,760 | 78,060 | 78,580 | 80,825 | 83,000 | 92,239 |
| Crowley ___ | 42,072 | 40,007 | 40,198 | 40,330 | 54,050 | 45,336 |
| Custer _____ | 5,632 | 5,968 | 5,916 | 10,208 | 11,965 | 7,083 |
| Delta _____ | 53,420 | 56,034 | 55,159 | 55,208 | 64,849 | 56,123 |
| Denver ____ | 5,855 | 5,928 | 5,706 | 6,606 | 7,519 | 7,724 |
| Dolores ____ | 595 | 1,083 | 836 | 832 | 2,065 | 1,858 |
| Douglas ___ | 6,205 | 6,414 | 6,335 | 6,856 | 7,715 | 7,075 |
| Eagle _____ | 27,933 | 25,276 | 25,379 | 23,557 | 22,259 | 19,778 |
| Elbert _____ | ----- | ----- | ----- | ----- | 830 | 220 |
| El Paso_____ | 20,510 | 20,426 | 20,400 | 20,400 | 20,500 | 19,120 |
| Fremont ___ | 14,492 | 14,975 | 14,869 | 21,659 | 20,633 | 15,337 |
| Garfield ____ | 53,187 | 53,240 | 53,925 | 51,588 | 59,278 | 53,278 |
| Gilpin _____ | ----- | ----- | ----- | ----- | ----- | ----- |
| Grand _____ | 31,525 | 32,234 | 32,854 | 29,592 | 31,097 | 25,111 |
| Gunnison __ | 37,286 | 38,096 | 36,845 | 39,405 | 35,955 | 32,497 |
| Hinsdale ___ | 2,365 | 2,489 | 2,206 | 2,180 | 2,233 | 1,445 |
| Huerfano __ | 12,415 | 12,897 | 16,106 | 5,223 | 21,802 | 19,037 |
| Jackson ___ | ----- | ----- | ----- | 71,635 | 67,685 | 59,710 |
| Jefferson __ | 51,000 | 51,400 | 51,759 | 48,263 | 49,397 | 40,200 |
| Kiowa _____ | ----- | ----- | ----- | ----- | ----- | ----- |
| Kit Carson_ | 471 | 506 | 583 | 145 | 180 | 750 |
| Lake _____ | ----- | ----- | ----- | ----- | ----- | ----- |
| La Plata___ | 42,394 | 51,708 | 53,080 | 56,788 | 57,881 | 44,995 |
| Larimer ___ | 105,383 | 105,532 | 105,679 | 111,589 | 106,921 | 111,278 |
| Las Animas | 25,963 | 23,552 | 20,893 | 28,830 | 22,931 | 23,876 |
| Lincoln ___ | ----- | ----- | ----- | ----- | ----- | ----- |
| Logan _____ | 72,681 | 70,481 | 70,481 | 67,000 | 59,472 | 63,344 |
| Mesa _____ | 44,880 | 93,653 | 31,049 | 97,692 | 89,452 | 82,589 |
| Mineral ___ | 1,712 | 1,707 | 1,847 | 993 | 370 | 1,309 |
| Moffat _____ | 11,308 | 11,420 | 13,261 | 18,187 | 16,247 | 15,168 |
| Montezuma . | 36,311 | 36,850 | 36,925 | 37,579 | 37,077 | 38,660 |
| Montrose __ | 63,573 | 64,557 | 65,459 | 69,748 | 79,240 | 73,129 |
| Morgan ____ | 81,092 | 81,062 | 81,085 | 78,692 | 76,269 | 74,580 |
| Otero _____ | 75,733 | 78,464 | 78,307 | 76,492 | 79,015 | 70,201 |
| Ouray _____ | 9,620 | 9,625 | 9,824 | 10,060 | 11,655 | 10,143 |
| Park _____ | ----- | ----- | ----- | ----- | ----- | ----- |
| Phillips ___ | ----- | ----- | ----- | ----- | ----- | ----- |
| Pitkin _____ | 16,248 | 17,088 | 18,127 | 16,163 | 15,407 | 14,081 |
| Prowers ___ | 92,880 | 93,702 | 90,282 | 95,744 | 89,851 | 96,585 |
| Pueblo ____ | 40,170 | 40,258 | 40,225 | 40,376 | 40,788 | 47,641 |
| Rio Blanco_ | 21,824 | 21,824 | 22,321 | 23,552 | 22,990 | 19,973 |
| Rio Grande_ | 66,016 | 63,908 | 63,641 | 72,403 | 42,721 | 80,861 |
| Routt _____ | 41,583 | 41,873 | 42,614 | 42,494 | 47,864 | 36,159 |
| Saguache __ | 37,640 | 37,640 | 37,640 | 37,640 | 37,480 | 26,496 |
| San Juan___ | ----- | ----- | ----- | ----- | ----- | ----- |
| San Miguel_ | 7,118 | 7,180 | 7,544 | 8,857 | 9,390 | 6,631 |
| Sedgwick __ | 19,529 | 19,825 | 19,872 | 19,816 | 20,054 | 20,396 |
| Summit ___ | 6,210 | 6,770 | 6,760 | 7,011 | 6,225 | 4,970 |
| Teller _____ | ----- | ----- | ----- | ----- | ----- | ----- |
| Washington | 7,641 | 7,648 | 7,786 | 6,885 | 6,682 | 7,050 |
| Weld _____ | 347,512 | 346,795 | 357,505 | 339,139 | 343,808 | 283,058 |
| Yuma _____ | 2,658 | 3,678 | 3,624 | 5,600 | 3,550 | 4,332 |
| State_____ | 2,102,843 | 2,163,794 | 2,192,666 | 2,283,111 | 2,308,415 | 2,236,000 |

## ACREAGE OF DRY FARMING LAND AS RETURNED BY COUNTY ASSESSORS FOR ASSESSMENT FOR 1914, 1920, 1925, 1929, 1930 AND 1931

| COUNTY | 1931 | 1930 | 1929 | 1925 | 1920 | 1914 |
|---|---|---|---|---|---|---|
| Adams | 515,634 | 509,427 | 443,523 | 502,099 | 442,385 | 135,930 |
| Alamosa | 115,800 | 115,500 | 115,500 | 112,150 | 102,000 | ------ |
| Arapahoe | 412,711 | 411,717 | 380,330 | 379,940 | 375,440 | 42,760 |
| Archuleta | 10,157 | 10,157 | 10,482 | 10,760 | 10,876 | 3,938 |
| Baca | 974,540 | 968,045 | 968,045 | 955,977 | 1,080,212 | ------ |
| Bent | 57,131 | 59,237 | 60,580 | 4,730 | 6,435 | ------ |
| Boulder | 29,505 | 22,375 | 23,119 | 23,496 | 22,838 | ------ |
| Chaffee | ----- | ----- | ------ | ------ | ------ | ------ |
| Cheyenne | 838,967 | 840,946 | 845,120 | 851,476 | 1,044,149 | ------ |
| Clear Creek | ----- | ----- | ------ | ------ | ------ | ------ |
| Conejos | ----- | ----- | ------ | ------ | ------ | ------ |
| Costilla | 6,264 | 10,500 | 10,000 | 10,000 | 1,000 | ------ |
| Crowley | 9,947 | 9,409 | 11,699 | 12,584 | 2,351 | 1,751 |
| Custer | 6,805 | 5,718 | 6,711 | 2,386 | 12,101 | ------ |
| Delta | 21,736 | 21,945 | 24,108 | 25,116 | 38,075 | ------ |
| Denver | ----- | ----- | ------ | ------ | ------ | ------ |
| Dolores | 20,213 | 73,352 | 17,866 | 65,219 | 14,292 | ------ |
| Douglas | 66,548 | 89,807 | 89,030 | 84,078 | 89,217 | 23,666 |
| Eagle | 1,213 | 1,065 | 844 | ------ | ------ | ------ |
| Elbert | 344,102 | 347,495 | 352,362 | 366,242 | 407,190 | 65,512 |
| El Paso | 216,420 | 216,890 | 217,010 | 218,560 | 213,520 | 193,150 |
| Fremont | 48,177 | 42,666 | 45,185 | 68,583 | 21,366 | 17,510 |
| Garfield | 28,002 | 29,036 | 29,458 | 32,006 | 32,961 | 39,602 |
| Gilpin | ----- | ----- | ------ | ------ | ------ | ------ |
| Grand | ----- | 297 | 285 | ------ | ------ | ------ |
| Gunnison | ----- | | | ------ | ------ | ------ |
| Hinsdale | 360 | ----- | ------ | 316 | ------ | ------ |
| Huerfano | 22,408 | 22,190 | 25,102 | 27,093 | 5,012 | ------ |
| Jackson | 72 | 102 | ------ | ------ | ------ | ------ |
| Jefferson | 28,805 | 28,700 | 28,816 | 25,624 | 29,029 | 30,970 |
| Kiowa | 746,232 | 758,754 | 746,389 | 789,526 | ------ | ------ |
| Kit Carson | 1,004,884 | 1,012,673 | 1,013,515 | 1,040,810 | 1,033,286 | 59,947 |
| Lake | ----- | | | ------ | ------ | ------ |
| La Plata | 28,529 | 20,301 | 19,243 | 17,593 | 15,289 | 6,045 |
| Larimer | 24,050 | 24,000 | 24,019 | 22,910 | 22,520 | 20,004 |
| Las Animas | 68,930 | 61,659 | 58,161 | 86,656 | 27,293 | 12,507 |
| Lincoln | 903,406 | 911,351 | 909,372 | 859,969 | 914,318 | ------ |
| Logan | 568,000 | 570,000 | 570,000 | 580,000 | 584,019 | 252,429 |
| Mesa | 49,434 | ----- | ------ | ------ | ------ | ------ |
| Mineral | | | | | | |
| Moffat | 34,434 | 35,237 | 39,112 | 130,879 | 79,808 | 4,936 |
| Montezuma | 44,294 | 42,383 | 40,394 | 38,781 | 28,468 | 30,413 |
| Montrose | 23,500 | 23,690 | 23,412 | 29,528 | 37,621 | 25,261 |
| Morgan | 246,680 | 244,460 | 244,450 | 254,545 | 236,392 | 41,578 |
| Otero | 10,140 | 10,612 | 11,209 | 24,197 | 20,316 | 19,550 |
| Ouray | 3,400 | 3,510 | 3,510 | 3,387 | 2,986 | 1,778 |
| Park | 5,184 | 5,460 | 5,482 | 6,508 | 6,021 | 3,483 |
| Phillips | 376,384 | 373,650 | 374,362 | 371,670 | 366,420 | 426,161 |
| Pitkin | 170 | 140 | 300 | 300 | 480 | 480 |
| Prowers | 631,325 | 639,367 | 635,900 | 597,977 | 5,090 | ------ |
| Pueblo | 80,340 | 81,960 | 81,890 | 80,260 | 72,942 | 62,485 |
| Rio Blanco | 20,929 | 20,929 | 19,074 | 18,240 | 18,684 | 5,076 |
| Rio Grande | ----- | ----- | ------ | ------ | 28,400 | ------ |
| Routt | 51,893 | 52,866 | 55,449 | 60,241 | 42,015 | 22,376 |
| Saguache | ----- | ----- | ------ | ------ | ------ | ------ |
| San Juan | ----- | | | | | |
| San Miguel | 6,959 | 6,419 | 7,036 | 8,469 | 7,452 | 4,500 |
| Sedgwick | 187,842 | 188,752 | 187,800 | 187,150 | 179,121 | 177,345 |
| Summit | ----- | ----- | ------ | ------ | ------ | ------ |
| Teller | 21,142 | 22,224 | 23,018 | 23,226 | 18,281 | 6,749 |
| Washington | 1,144,171 | 1,137,091 | 1,167,884 | 1,158,074 | 1,215,046 | 859,538 |
| Weld | 751,398 | 747,340 | 737,825 | 719,947 | 806,842 | 62,564 |
| Yuma | 669,612 | 685,119 | 681,815 | 751,188 | 620,238 | 617,925 |
| State | 11,478,779 | 11,516,523 | 11,385,796 | 11,640,466 | 10,339,797 | 3,277,919 |

## ACREAGE OF IMPROVED FRUIT LAND AND NATURAL HAY LAND AS RETURNED BY COUNTY ASSESSORS FOR 1914, 1920, 1930, 1931

| COUNTY | IMPROVED FRUIT LAND | | | | NATURAL HAY LAND | | | |
|---|---|---|---|---|---|---|---|---|
| | 1931 | 1930 | 1920 | 1914 | 1931 | 1930 | 1920 | 1914 |
| Adams_____ | ----- | ----- | ----- | ----- | 17,232 | 10,259 | ----- | ----- |
| Alamosa_____ | ----- | ----- | ----- | ----- | 37,500 | 37,500 | 37,000 | 12,368 |
| Arapahoe_____ | ----- | ----- | ----- | ----- | ----- | ----- | ----- | ----- |
| Archuleta_____ | ----- | ----- | ----- | ----- | 570 | 570 | ----- | ----- |
| Baca_____ | ----- | ----- | ----- | ----- | ----- | ----- | ----- | ----- |
| Bent_____ | ----- | ----- | ----- | ----- | ----- | ----- | ----- | ----- |
| Boulder_____ | ----- | ----- | ----- | ----- | 18,110 | ----- | 2,904 | ----- |
| Chaffee_____ | ----- | ----- | ----- | 150 | ----- | ----- | ----- | ----- |
| Cheyenne_____ | ----- | ----- | ----- | ----- | ----- | ----- | ----- | ----- |
| Clear Creek_____ | ----- | ----- | ----- | ----- | ----- | ----- | ----- | ----- |
| Conejos_____ | ----- | ----- | ----- | ----- | 9,920 | 9,920 | 9,400 | 10,000 |
| Costilla_____ | ----- | ----- | ----- | ----- | 20,996 | 5,600 | 5,200 | 5,300 |
| Crowley_____ | 113 | 123 | 535 | 540 | ----- | ----- | ----- | ----- |
| Custer_____ | ----- | ----- | ----- | ----- | 11,877 | 11,596 | ----- | 9,306 |
| Delta_____ | 8,211 | 7,458 | 10,303 | 4.630 | ----- | ----- | ----- | ----- |
| Denver_____ | ----- | ----- | ----- | ----- | ----- | ----- | ----- | ----- |
| Dolores_____ | ----- | ----- | ----- | ----- | ----- | ----- | ----- | 142 |
| Douglas_____ | ----- | ----- | ----- | ----- | 7,648 | 5,853 | 5,453 | 3,388 |
| Eagle_____ | ----- | ----- | ----- | ----- | ----- | ----- | ----- | ----- |
| Elbert_____ | ----- | ----- | ----- | ----- | 11,808 | 11,756 | 11,587 | 6,454 |
| El Paso_____ | 170 | 170 | 320 | 380 | 1,910 | 1,910 | 1,910 | 1,240 |
| Fremont_____ | 2.039 | 2,051 | 2,371 | 2,803 | 1,200 | 1,200 | 1,200 | 1,910 |
| Garfield_____ | 747 | 798 | 898 | 1,509 | ----- | ----- | ----- | ----- |
| Gilpin_____ | ----- | ----- | ----- | ----- | ----- | ----- | ----- | ----- |
| Grand_____ | ----- | ----- | ----- | ----- | ----- | ----- | ----- | ----- |
| Gunnison_____ | ----- | ----- | ----- | ----- | ----- | ----- | ----- | ----- |
| Hinsdale_____ | ----- | ----- | ----- | ----- | ----- | ----- | ----- | ----- |
| Huerfano_____ | 37 | 36 | 20 | ----- | 3,305 | 3,499 | ----- | ----- |
| Jackson_____ | ----- | ----- | ----- | ----- | 69,191 | 69,361 | ----- | ----- |
| Jefferson_____ | ----- | ----- | ----- | ----- | ----- | ----- | ----- | ----- |
| Kiowa_____ | ----- | ----- | ----- | ----- | ----- | ----- | ----- | ----- |
| Kit Carson_____ | ----- | ----- | ----- | ----- | 3,576 | 3,701 | 3,666 | 600 |
| Lake_____ | ----- | ----- | ----- | ----- | 4,836 | 5,089 | ----- | ----- |
| La Plata_____ | 90 | 120 | 88 | 83 | 15,350 | 15,400 | 15,400 | 15,025 |
| Larimer_____ | 1,084 | 1,004 | ----- | 2,011 | 6,071 | 6,445 | 4,016 | 3,436 |
| Las Animas_____ | ----- | ----- | ----- | ----- | 3,090 | 3,102 | 3,310 | ----- |
| Lincoln_____ | ----- | ----- | ----- | ----- | 16,080 | 15,000 | 13,424 | ----- |
| Logan_____ | ----- | ----- | ----- | ----- | ----- | ----- | ----- | ----- |
| Mesa_____ | 6.249 | 6,215 | 8,070 | 7,024 | ----- | ----- | ----- | ----- |
| Mineral_____ | ----- | ----- | ----- | ----- | 2,387 | 2,657 | 2,885 | 1,400 |
| Moffat_____ | ----- | ----- | ----- | ----- | 3,620 | 3,720 | ----- | ----- |
| Montezuma_____ | 667 | 700 | 806 | 1,017 | ----- | ----- | ----- | ----- |
| Montrose_____ | 1,008 | 1,102 | 1,743 | 1,450 | ----- | ----- | ----- | ----- |
| Morgan_____ | ----- | ----- | ----- | ----- | 2,200 | 2,200 | 2,700 | 4,064 |
| Otero_____ | 369 | 437 | 1,051 | 1,553 | ----- | ----- | ----- | ----- |
| Ouray_____ | ----- | ----- | ----- | ----- | 2,340 | 2,228 | 1,424 | ----- |
| Park_____ | ----- | ----- | ----- | ----- | 22,700 | 23,480 | 22,662 | 21,311 |
| Phillips_____ | ----- | ----- | ----- | ----- | ----- | ----- | ----- | ----- |
| Pitkin_____ | ----- | ----- | ----- | 45 | 2,650 | 3,440 | 3,647 | 5,973 |
| Prowers_____ | ----- | ----- | ----- | ----- | ----- | ----- | ----- | ----- |
| Pueblo_____ | ----- | ----- | 5,910 | ----- | ----- | ----- | ----- | ----- |
| Rio Blanco_____ | ----- | ----- | ----- | ----- | 1,910 | 1,910 | 1,010 | 3,599 |
| Rio Grande_____ | ----- | ----- | ----- | ----- | 25,541 | 29,557 | 8,870 | ----- |
| Routt_____ | ----- | ----- | 33 | 305 | ----- | ----- | ----- | 90 |
| Saguache_____ | ----- | ----- | ----- | ----- | 49,000 | 49,000 | 48,750 | 71,124 |
| San Juan_____ | ----- | ----- | ----- | ----- | ----- | ----- | ----- | ----- |
| San Miguel_____ | ----- | ----- | ----- | ----- | ----- | ----- | ----- | ----- |
| Sedgwick_____ | ----- | ----- | ----- | ----- | 5,774 | 5,750 | 5,469 | 5,165 |
| Summit_____ | ----- | ----- | ----- | ----- | ----- | ----- | ----- | ----- |
| Teller_____ | ----- | ----- | ----- | ----- | 2,042 | 2,036 | 2,322 | 1,580 |
| Washington_____ | ----- | ----- | ----- | ----- | ----- | ----- | ----- | 1,755 |
| Weld_____ | ----- | ----- | ----- | ----- | 6,254 | 6,673 | 9,631 | 5,635 |
| Yuma_____ | ----- | ----- | ----- | ----- | 4,739 | 4,780 | 4,490 | ----- |
| State_____ | 20,793 | 20,214 | 32,148 | 23,500 | 391,427 | 55,192 | 228,330 | 190,865 |

## ACREAGE OF GRAZING LAND AS RETURNED BY COUNTY ASSESSORS FOR ASSESS-
### MENT FOR 1914, 1920, 1925, 1929, 1930, 1931

| COUNTY | 1931 | 1930 | 1929 | 1925 | 1920 | 1914 |
|---|---|---|---|---|---|---|
| Adams | 119,994 | 96,220 | 155,407 | 151,609 | 192,665 | 355,512 |
| Alamosa | 117,285 | 134,644 | 141,980 | 156,049 | 142,800 | 218,392 |
| Arapahoe | 69,942 | 67,091 | 83,730 | 83,690 | 81,930 | 331,884 |
| Archuleta | 222,369 | 215,369 | 280,673 | 274,067 | 234,439 | 226,948 |
| Baca | 556,255 | 562,425 | 561,025 | 564,369 | 48,684 | 474,067 |
| Bent | 669,471 | 675,362 | 656,320 | 636,392 | 393,620 | 137,772 |
| Boulder | 130,190 | 156,732 | 156,456 | 149,213 | 139,641 | 133,820 |
| Chaffee | 76,746 | 74,892 | 73,510 | 66,879 | 63,318 | 61,359 |
| Cheyenne | 235,571 | 219,599 | 230,481 | 221,327 | ------ | 821,560 |
| Clear Creek | 37,543 | 32,897 | 32,587 | 37,260 | 33,857 | 30,828 |
| Conejos | 161,576 | 160,986 | 160,886 | 151,843 | 128,904 | 91,054 |
| Costilla | 219,235 | 60,000 | 60,000* | 290,000 | 130,000 | 674,084 |
| Crowley | 374,486 | 375,382 | 373,222 | 350,808 | 250,603 | 75,500 |
| Custer | 237,526 | 234,036 | 230,627 | 194,530 | 116,339 | 101,572 |
| Delta | 58,673 | 61,258 | 48,674 | 48,748 | 104,940 | 127,328 |
| Denver | | | | | | |
| Dolores | 182,579 | 117,352 | 171,856 | 87,946 | 20,678 | 8,237 |
| Douglas | 299,944 | 277,923 | 278,263 | 282,858 | 273,199 | 338,854 |
| Eagle | 130,623 | 121,973 | 128,923 | 88,891 | 76,135 | 62,290 |
| Elbert | 725,666 | 722,228 | 713,991 | 686,187 | 615,324 | 843,349 |
| El Paso | 745,040 | 744,620 | 745,180 | 743,305 | 715,708 | 542,483 |
| Fremont | 302,533 | 311,124 | 296,112 | 220,187 | 168,838 | 135,289 |
| Garfield | 259,016 | 244,065 | 244,664 | 213,934 | 165,985 | 104,888 |
| Gilpin | 29,133 | 28,502 | 28,073 | 20,649 | 18,091 | 16,754 |
| Grand | 234,368 | 232,875 | 229,315 | 205,423 | 141,172 | 107,020 |
| Gunnison | 293,655 | 285,052 | 266,228 | 206,500 | 115,972 | 82,036 |
| Hinsdale | 18,265 | 17,253 | 13,026 | 14,002 | 12,526 | 9,882 |
| Huerfano | 630,702 | 618,945 | 552,865 | 567,857 | 340,125 | 291,720 |
| Jackson | 246,764 | 237,271 | 230,961 | 182,740 | 146,359 | 122,151 |
| Jefferson | 256,847 | 254,322 | 253,947 | 222,534 | 243,917 | 224,048 |
| Kiowa | 290,001 | 287,815 | 281,017 | 245,296 | 960,670 | 607,114 |
| Kit Carson | 297,513 | 290,251 | 289,431 | 267,112 | 228,829 | 998,347 |
| Lake | 23,877 | 23,877 | 23,877 | 27,624 | 27,011 | 26,652 |
| La Plata | 359,317 | 360,051 | 363,563 | 318,219 | 255,585 | 186,040 |
| Larimer | 612,622 | 610,855 | 609,473 | 566,771 | 521,332 | 469,678 |
| Las Animas | 2,483,709 | 2,484,593 | 2,551,240 | 2,173,614 | 1,024,029 | 716,102 |
| Lincoln | 581,492 | 581,742 | 584,409 | 621,622 | 491,790 | 993,743 |
| Logan | 333,440 | 333,440 | 332,840 | 323,800 | 309,715 | 329,042 |
| Mesa | 382,855 | 380,639 | 373,663 | 324,859 | 240,762 | 183,083 |
| Mineral | 16,211 | 15,798 | 15,768 | 23,801 | 17,296 | 20,891 |
| Moffat | 946,011 | 928,300 | 901,430 | 584,609 | 133,655 | 100,246 |
| Montezuma | 232,037 | 231,233 | 207,518 | 207,255 | 143,551 | 84,736 |
| Montrose | 206,152 | 213,885 | 210,393 | 259,615 | 175,089 | 121,579 |
| Morgan | 414,635 | 416,176 | 415,110 | 400,909 | 318,919 | 179,079 |
| Otero | 542,535 | 539,351 | 530,980 | 468,799 | 221,636 | 126,795 |
| Ouray | 129,430 | 129,276 | 127,276 | 122,696 | 118,137 | 64,273 |
| Park | 439,601 | 437,100 | 430,800 | 324,539 | 186,171 | 173,917 |
| Phillips | 31,593 | 34,968 | 34,010 | 31,800 | 29,360 | |
| Pitkin | 53,763 | 52,919 | 52,058 | 51,093 | 42,191 | 36,988 |
| Prowers | 230,275 | 223,014 | 215,314 | 263,262 | 712,576 | 322,898 |
| Pueblo | 1,042,823 | 1,037,930 | 1,030,720 | 1,013,869 | 749,407 | 559,892 |
| Rio Blanco | 310,678 | 310,678 | 302,513 | 239,475 | 151,782 | 99,872 |
| Rio Grande | 130,596 | 126,779 | 128,196 | 124,089 | 105,294 | 87,613 |
| Routt | 469,375 | 462,095 | 443,671 | 358,516 | 255,707 | 188,763 |
| Saguache | 266,025 | 266,025 | 260,250 | 421,079 | 367,643 | 226,221 |
| San Juan | 200 | 200 | 200 | 200 | 200 | 200 |
| San Miguel | 216,550 | 215,453 | 215,103 | 178,088 | 108,427 | 69,054 |
| Sedgwick | 92,788 | 91,450 | 91,003 | 88,166 | 93,008 | 73,794 |
| Summit | 33,570 | 31,305 | 30,980 | 29,452 | 22,720 | 16,922 |
| Teller | 127,179 | 125,431 | 124,794 | 115,923 | 91,867 | 88,437 |
| Washington | 330,227 | 337,168 | 311,591 | 319,209 | 171,281 | ------ |
| Weld | 1,167,794 | 1,166,047 | 1,167,763 | 1,182,871 | 1,011,289 | 1,192,886 |
| Yuma | 763,984 | 745,316 | 744,131 | 744,607 | 668,467 | 285,540 |
| State | 21,200,855 | 20,836,558 | 20,800,067 | 19,542,636 | 15,071,165 | 15,381,078 |

## ASSESSED VALUE OF ALL FARM LAND IN COLORADO AS RETURNED BY COUNTY ASSESSORS FOR 1915, 1920, 1929, 1930, 1931

| COUNTY | 1931 | 1930 | 1929 | 1920 | 1915 |
|---|---|---|---|---|---|
| Adams | $11,422,100 | $14,240,100 | $ 15,289,070 | $ 17,346,280 | $ 11,731,350 |
| Alamosa | 3,324,278 | 4,178,428 | 4,283,748 | 4,509,139 | 2,275,990 |
| Arapahoe | 5,262,665 | 6,597,630 | 8,176,965 | 9,915,770 | 6,473,900 |
| Archuleta | 992,987 | 1,201,821 | 1,327,595 | 1,382,773 | 907,132 |
| Baca | 6,421,754 | 8,028,385 | 8,022,685 | 6,233,251 | 1,689,437 |
| Bent | 4,920,305 | 6,090,800 | 6,396,760 | 7,206,575 | 8,942,210 |
| Boulder | 8,179,480 | 10,278,710 | 10,880,210 | 11,971,220 | 8,726,800 |
| Chaffee | 1,120,510 | 1,368,195 | 1,411,485 | 1,428,500 | 1,275,335 |
| Cheyenne | 6,295,815 | 7,877,170 | 7,878,575 | 13,228,595 | 4,442,677 |
| Clear Creek | 329,820 | 334,405 | 395,530 | 309,815 | 107,510 |
| Conejos | 3,496,135 | 4,394,140 | 4,354,680 | 4,532,364 | 4,240,655 |
| Costilla | 2,460,935 | 2,670,950 | 2,701,045 | 2,966,242 | 3,150,750 |
| Crowley | 4,061,100 | 4,946,033 | 5,339,385 | 6,108,970 | 4,669,539 |
| Custer | 1,147,552 | 1,440,525 | 1,439,420 | 1,223,170 | 1,088,200 |
| Delta | 4,030,780 | 5,043,125 | 5,184,940 | 8,152,925 | 6,721,485 |
| Denver | 3,442,950 | 3,714,910 | 4,045,340 | 3,617,390 | 3,858,530 |
| Dolores | 613,485 | 811,653 | 676,820 | 277,415 | 71,848 |
| Douglas | 2,617,965 | 3,281,495 | 3,271,450 | 4,179,510 | 2,628,305 |
| Eagle | 1,761,982 | 2,176,172 | 2,151,336 | 1,873,775 | 1,602,427 |
| Elbert | 6,800,490 | 8,513,870 | 9,618,963 | 11,706,966 | 5,551,416 |
| El Paso | 6,047,730 | 7,554,450 | 8,718,520 | 11,096,370 | 6,124,770 |
| Fremont | 2,799,002 | 3,494,180 | 3,531,433 | 3,254,630 | 8,215,976 |
| Garfield | 4,146,060 | 5,148,460 | 5,185,805 | 5,232,570 | 4,883,820 |
| Gilpin | 70,752 | 87,618 | 89,625 | 54,273 | 47,808 |
| Grand | 1,466,440 | 1,853,890 | 1,879,365 | 1,599,980 | 1,102,450 |
| Gunnison | 1,968,040 | 2,459,059 | 2,435,210 | 2,160,525 | 2,014,878 |
| Hinsdale | 93,690 | 120,679 | 85,970 | 79,425 | 38,083 |
| Huerfano | 2,030,149 | 2,466,052 | 2,609,999 | 2,231,420 | 1,699,296 |
| Jackson | 1,230,270 | 1,541,700 | 1,555,750 | 2,727,695 | 1,468,864 |
| Jefferson | 5,748,025 | 7,562,040 | 10,686,670 | 10,013,595 | 8,069,735 |
| Kiowa | 6,396,240 | 7,988,890 | 8,238,510 | 10,179,094 | 3,413,286 |
| Kit Carson | 9,575,480 | 12,248,283 | 12,541,358 | 20,453,265 | 5,679,205 |
| Lake | 140,130 | 174,230 | 176,545 | 193,530 | 172,825 |
| La Plata | 3,038,975 | 3,795,810 | 3,974,335 | 3,927,655 | 3,298,920 |
| Larimer | 10,397,250 | 12,818,790 | 13,282,070 | 16,959,870 | 11,923,983 |
| Las Animas | 7,508,769 | 9,374,230 | 9,182,098 | 6,835,416 | 5,017,713 |
| Lincoln | 8,474,265 | 10,598,070 | 12,705,860 | 16,343,285 | 5,315,710 |
| Logan | 11,747,940 | 14,684,910 | 14,922,105 | 22,884,010 | 7,885,974 |
| Mesa | 7,407,874 | 9,290,110 | 9,390,730 | 9,979,585 | 10,159,695 |
| Mineral | 139,495 | 175,110 | 178,260 | 162,875 | 138,635 |
| Moffat | 2,656,167 | 3,320,210 | 3,376,180 | 2,424,190 | 1,198,940 |
| Montezuma | 2,131,285 | 2,689,065 | 2,662,455 | 2,310,452 | 1,951,590 |
| Montrose | 3,525,385 | 4,429,575 | 4,483,638 | 7,298,220 | 5,872,205 |
| Morgan | 8,319,790 | 10,409,740 | 10,863,300 | 12,371,500 | 5,313,540 |
| Otero | 6,668,190 | 8,566,595 | 9,309,264 | 11,136,010 | 8,733,185 |
| Ouray | 793,234 | 994,893 | 1,013,888 | 1,320,604 | 724,900 |
| Park | 1,754,600 | 2,170,700 | 2,154,350 | 1,570,285 | 1,881,540 |
| Phillips | 7,817,340 | 9,767,105 | 9,825,830 | 11,735,765 | 3,776,655 |
| Pitkin | 825,380 | 1,049,895 | 1,058,490 | 1,038,980 | 934,290 |
| Prowers | 7,884,580 | 9,880,170 | 10,376,560 | 11,796,415 | 7,483,880 |
| Pueblo | 7,165,250 | 8,975,125 | 9,903,075 | 9,169,292 | 7,739,328 |
| Rio Blanco | 2,080,960 | 2,601,200 | 2,610,800 | 2,707,495 | 2,107,221 |
| Rio Grande | 3,845,415 | 5,002,467 | 4,803,465 | 5,344,250 | 3,577,850 |
| Routt | 3,536,960 | 4,430,550 | 4,675,600 | 4,682,835 | 3,009,790 |
| Saguache | 3,207,790 | 3,986,452 | 4,126,793 | 4,726,651 | 4,473,019 |
| San Juan | 1,120 | 1,280 | 1,280 | 1,280 | 1,280 |
| San Miguel | 879,710 | 1,087,810 | 1,144,445 | 1,094,880 | 735,710 |
| Sedgwick | 4,906,960 | 6,107,975 | 6,126,305 | 7,047,526 | 3,009,920 |
| Summit | 287,165 | 354,345 | 352,775 | 303,300 | 188,232 |
| Teller | 438,790 | 521,770 | 531,570 | 420,900 | 275,100 |
| Washington | 7,796,021 | 9,754,564 | 11,036,811 | 24,176,680 | 6,306,191 |
| Weld | 32,751,570 | 40,962,382 | 43,018,520 | 56,135,660 | 32,081,740 |
| Yuma | 12,637,610 | 15,830,760 | 16,140,050 | 17,065,095 | 4,990,032 |
| State | $291,040,936 | $363,520,306 | $383,811,664 | $460,417,978 | $262,693,260 |

## AVERAGE VALUE OF IRRIGATED AND DRY FARMING LAND PER ACRE AS RETURNED ANNUALLY BY COUNTY ASSESSORS FOR 1914, 1920, 1930, 1931

| COUNTY | IRRIGATED LAND | | | | DRY FARMING LAND | | | |
|---|---|---|---|---|---|---|---|---|
| | 1931 | 1930 | 1920 | 1914 | 1931 | 1930 | 1920 | 1914 |
| Adams | $72.32 | $ 90.41 | $ 92.94 | $ 77.78 | $ 8.73 | $ 11.17 | $ 13.76 | $ 15.67 |
| Alamosa | 30.00 | 35.00 | 48.00 | 13.44 | 11.00 | 15.00 | 15.00 | ---- |
| Arapahoe | 89.68 | 111.15 | 126.09 | 99.52 | 8.09 | 10.20 | 13.50 | 12.74 |
| Archuleta | 32.57 | 40.47 | 41.35 | 24.74 | 8.26 | 10.33 | 10.21 | 7.44 |
| Baca | 10.00 | 12.50 | 25.00 | ---- | 5.00 | 6.25 | 5.42 | ---- |
| Bent | 63.90 | 77.21 | 110.96 | 65.04 | 4.36 | 7.16 | 15.00 | ---- |
| Boulder | 79.27 | 103.13 | 113.09 | 71.42 | 23.59 | 33.60 | 36.05 | ---- |
| Chaffee | 35.32 | 44.08 | 56.93 | 52.31 | ---- | ---- | ---- | ---- |
| Cheyenne | ---- | ---- | ---- | ---- | 6.61 | 8.29 | 12.67 | ---- |
| Clear Creek | ---- | ---- | ---- | ---- | ---- | ---- | ---- | ---- |
| Conejos | 35.78 | 45.00 | 45.00 | 36.22 | ---- | ---- | ---- | ---- |
| Costilla | 24.08 | 29.15 | 30.00 | 21.69 | 2.61 | 3.00 | 10.00 | ---- |
| Crowley | 67.27 | 85.39 | 89.32 | 87.77 | 6.59 | 8.98 | 20.53 | 18.93 |
| Custer | 31.94 | 30.07 | 40.00 | 34.16 | 9.59 | 14.83 | 20.88 | ---- |
| Delta | 52.35 | 64.25 | 89.09 | 76.00 | 14.01 | 16.63 | 24.74 | ---- |
| Denver | 588.04 | 626.67 | 481.10 | 481.77 | ---- | ---- | ---- | ---- |
| Dolores | 12.04 | 17.36 | 20.00 | 18.00 | 6.75 | 6.46 | 10.01 | ---- |
| Douglas | 61.57 | 75.16 | 79.03 | 45.70 | 12.78 | 15.90 | 18.09 | 10.22 |
| Eagle | 47.12 | 65.08 | 69.89 | 71.33 | 24.42 | 30.65 | ---- | ---- |
| Elbert | ---- | ---- | 46.06 | 40.00 | 9.51 | 11.84 | 16.54 | 6.01 |
| El Paso | 60.00 | 75.00 | 75.00 | 78.00 | 9.39 | 11.74 | 13.96 | 12.00 |
| Fremont | 64.28 | 77.62 | 66.94 | 76.68 | 6.34 | 8.94 | 8.74 | 9.46 |
| Garfield | 56.52 | 70.54 | 70.73 | 71.70 | 16.88 | 19.90 | 15.89 | 17.22 |
| Gilpin | ---- | ---- | ---- | ---- | ---- | ---- | ---- | ---- |
| Grand | 27.91 | 34.81 | 35.67 | 20.00 | ---- | 15.61 | ---- | ---- |
| Gunnison | 33.34 | 41.54 | 46.76 | 34.07 | ---- | ---- | ---- | ---- |
| Hinsdale | 20.59 | 24.44 | 14.00 | 10.94 | 10.00 | ---- | ---- | ---- |
| Huerfano | 33.46 | 42.89 | 38.20 | 31.94 | 5.99 | 7.20 | 7.00 | ---- |
| Jackson | ---- | ---- | 29.77 | 15.00 | 8.05 | 10.00 | ---- | ---- |
| Jefferson | 78.56 | 103.10 | 148.00 | 150.32 | 16.10 | 21.69 | 33.00 | 25.00 |
| Kiowa | ---- | ---- | ---- | ---- | 7.21 | 8.85 | ---- | ---- |
| Kit Carson | 25.60 | 31.99 | 75.00 | 20.00 | 8.76 | 11.12 | 17.78 | 4.00 |
| Lake | ---- | ---- | ---- | ---- | ---- | ---- | ---- | ---- |
| La Plata | 38.29 | 42.66 | 45.95 | 45.40 | 12.77 | 15.33 | 16.83 | 15.28 |
| Larimer | 77.01 | 94.50 | 131.00 | 72.06 | 13.62 | 17.50 | 24.96 | 13.83 |
| Las Animas | 39.40 | 52.51 | 59.00 | 48.22 | 8.00 | 10.00 | 20.00 | 16.38 |
| Lincoln | ---- | ---- | ---- | ---- | 7.04 | 8.67 | 13.11 | ---- |
| Logan | 55.30 | 71.28 | 82.79 | 45.65 | 11.49 | 14.31 | 26.01 | 9.92 |
| Mesa | 78.38 | 68.54 | 77.93 | 94.53 | 31.29 | ---- | ---- | ---- |
| Mineral | 11.46 | 14.24 | 11.35 | 17.78 | ---- | ---- | ---- | ---- |
| Moffat | 30.16 | 36.21 | 49.54 | 37.55 | 8.91 | 10.48 | 12.04 | 15.40 |
| Montezuma | 27.72 | 35.18 | 37.70 | 37.00 | 11.63 | 14.95 | 15.04 | 17.00 |
| Montrose | 39.35 | 48.93 | 71.51 | 55.08 | 12.70 | 15.42 | 18.07 | 15.14 |
| Morgan | 62.60 | 78.35 | 93.02 | 49.54 | 7.72 | 9.70 | 13.84 | 14.47 |
| Otero | 69.93 | 87.19 | 122.48 | 100.47 | 10.91 | 12.24 | 15.82 | 14.48 |
| Ouray | 39.54 | 49.51 | 68.29 | 40.15 | 8.50 | 10.00 | 12.50 | 16.23 |
| Park | ---- | ---- | ---- | ---- | 12.00 | 15.00 | 15.00 | 15.00 |
| Phillips | ---- | ---- | ---- | ---- | 20.53 | 25.83 | 31.30 | 7.49 |
| Pitkin | 42.20 | 51.33 | 58.08 | 53.97 | 8.00 | 10.00 | 22.92 | 24.00 |
| Prowers | 51.19 | 63.67 | 86.78 | 59.75 | 4.12 | 5.10 | 26.65 | ---- |
| Pueblo | 75.80 | 94.72 | 98.82 | 102.49 | 12.35 | 15.43 | 16.81 | 15.56 |
| Rio Blanco | 47.00 | 59.64 | 67.45 | 64.95 | 11.00 | 14.62 | 22.43 | 27.63 |
| Rio Grande | 48.55 | 64.00 | 87.40 | 39.18 | ---- | ---- | 24.00 | ---- |
| Routt | 36.02 | 45.03 | 41.58 | 38.01 | 15.93 | 19.92 | 27.22 | 19.90 |
| Saguache | 35.20 | 44.00 | 39.53 | 42.00 | ---- | ---- | ---- | ---- |
| San Juan | ---- | ---- | ---- | ---- | ---- | ---- | ---- | ---- |
| San Miguel | 28.70 | 35.65 | 40.00 | 34.50 | 13.81 | 18.07 | 24.00 | 21.00 |
| Sedgwick | 64.42 | 76.16 | 63.61 | 43.06 | 17.18 | 21.55 | 29.16 | 8.00 |
| Summit | 29.34 | 35.00 | 35.00 | 24.92 | ---- | ---- | ---- | ---- |
| Teller | ---- | ---- | ---- | ---- | 8.00 | 9.73 | 10.18 | 10.00 |
| Washington | 49.90 | 60.58 | 117.94 | 70.00 | 5.66 | 7.06 | 17.86 | 6.74 |
| Weld | 66.65 | 85.18 | 110.64 | 72.20 | 8.92 | 10.35 | 13.75 | 11.05 |
| Yuma | 37.13 | 38.70 | 61.00 | 22.21 | 15.30 | 18.35 | 21.00 | 6.12 |
| State | $57.39 | $ 70.92 | $ 83.52 | $ 62.11 | $ 8.81 | $ 10.84 | $ 16.16 | $ 8.91 |

**AVERAGE VALUE OF GRAZING AND NATURAL HAY LAND PER ACRE AS RETURNED ANNUALLY BY COUNTY ASSESSORS FOR 1914, 1920, 1930, 1931**

| COUNTY | GRAZING LAND | | | | NATURAL HAY LAND | | | |
|---|---|---|---|---|---|---|---|---|
| | 1931 | 1930 | 1920 | 1914 | 1931 | 1930 | 1920 | 1914 |
| Adams | $6.09 | $ 6. 1 | $ 9.20 | $ 5.33 | $16.01 | $21.31 | ---- | ---- |
| Alamosa | 2.20 | 2. 0 | 4.35 | 5.08 | 25.00 | 30.00 | $30.00 | $18.00 |
| Arapahoe | 3.52 | 4.95 | 8.10 | 4.91 | ---- | ---- | ---- | ---- |
| Archuleta | 2.45 | 3.90 | 3.42 | 2.41 | 23.57 | 29.48 | ---- | ---- |
| Baca | 2.73 | 3.45 | 3.25 | 3.12 | ---- | ---- | ---- | ---- |
| Bent | 2.29 | 2.87 | 5.05 | 6.81 | ---- | ---- | ---- | ---- |
| Boulder | 4.71 | 8.46 | 9.49 | 10.37 | 19.43 | ---- | 17.71 | ---- |
| Chaffee | 3.29 | 3.52 | 4.53 | 4.05 | ---- | ---- | ---- | ---- |
| Cheyenne | 3.20 | 4.01 | ---- | 5.00 | ---- | ---- | ---- | ---- |
| Clear Creek | 8.79 | 10.17 | 9.15 | 4.04 | ---- | ---- | ---- | ---- |
| Conejos | 1.50 | 1.89 | 3.07 | 6.00 | 16.00 | 20.00 | 22.06 | 25.00 |
| Costilla | 1.55 | 3.00 | 3.00 | 1.80 | 6.06 | 20.00 | 20.00 | 20.00 |
| Crowley | 3.12 | 3.82 | 4.66 | 9.74 | ---- | ---- | ---- | ---- |
| Custer | 2.38 | 3.04 | 4.23 | 4.45 | 28.37 | 40.00 | ---- | 41.17 |
| Delta | 3.39 | 4.09 | 3.09 | 11.65 | ---- | ---- | ---- | ---- |
| Denver | ---- | ---- | ---- | ---- | ---- | ---- | ---- | ---- |
| Dolores | 2.57 | 2.72 | 4.50 | 4.96 | ---- | ---- | ---- | 10.00 |
| Douglas | 3.85 | 4.14 | 6.16 | 5.94 | 29.93 | 37.77 | 50.04 | 28.02 |
| Eagle | 3.19 | 4.08 | 4.18 | 2.79 | ---- | ---- | ---- | ---- |
| Elbert | 4.32 | 5.41 | 7.03 | 5.59 | 33.33 | 41.43 | 37.30 | 24.90 |
| El Paso | 3.59 | 4.49 | 8.99 | 5.95 | 37.20 | 46.50 | 46.50 | 35.00 |
| Fremont | 2.86 | 3.48 | 4.15 | 4.10 | 29.67 | 35.00 | 35.00 | 28.00 |
| Garfield | 2.43 | 2.98 | 2.52 | 1.30 | ---- | ---- | ---- | ---- |
| Gilpin | 2.43 | 3.07 | 3.00 | 3.00 | ---- | ---- | ---- | ---- |
| Grand | 2.50 | 3.14 | 3.47 | 4.92 | ---- | ---- | ---- | ---- |
| Gunnison | 2.46 | 3.02 | 4.13 | 3.34 | ---- | ---- | ---- | ---- |
| Hinsdale | 2.27 | 3.00 | 3.71 | 2.15 | ---- | ---- | ---- | ---- |
| Huerfano | 2.18 | 2.62 | 4.00 | 3.01 | 31.28 | 36.82 | ---- | ---- |
| Jackson | 1.62 | 2.11 | 4.86 | 2.02 | 12.00 | 15.00 | ---- | ---- |
| Jefferson | 4.97 | 6.46 | 7.07 | 6.00 | ---- | ---- | ---- | ---- |
| Kiowa | 3.49 | 4.39 | 10.60 | 4.37 | ---- | ---- | ---- | ---- |
| Kit Carson | 2.34 | 3.04 | 8.45 | 3.47 | 17.57 | 22.36 | 37.08 | 10.00 |
| Lake | 3.70 | 4.95 | 7.16 | 6.41 | 10.70 | 11.01 | ---- | ---- |
| La Plata | 2.90 | 3.52 | 3.90 | 4.60 | ---- | ---- | ---- | ---- |
| Larimer | 2.48 | 3.12 | 3.81 | 3.66 | 16.26 | 20.00 | 25.00 | 26.00 |
| Las Animas | 2.34 | 2.96 | 4.60 | 4.74 | 19.60 | 24.71 | 31.00 | 28.23 |
| Lincoln | 3.45 | 4.49 | 8.65 | 5.01 | 24.49 | 28.96 | 29.01 | ---- |
| Logan | 2.80 | 3.50 | 7.84 | 4.46 | 16.79 | 22.50 | 25.54 | ---- |
| Mesa | 3.52 | 4.39 | 5.82 | 6.22 | ---- | ---- | ---- | ---- |
| Mineral | 3.93 | 4.94 | 5.00 | 4.02 | 21.34 | 24.88 | 25.00 | 25.00 |
| Moffat | 2.03 | 2.63 | 4.76 | 5.98 | 21.68 | 25.63 | ---- | ---- |
| Montezuma | 2.49 | 3.11 | 3.01 | 3.99 | ---- | ---- | ---- | ---- |
| Montrose | 2.56 | 3.08 | 4.04 | 3.84 | ---- | ---- | ---- | ---- |
| Morgan | 3.13 | 3.93 | 6.09 | 4.04 | 18.80 | 23.50 | 23.51 | 16.16 |
| Otero | 2.26 | 2.86 | 4.22 | 4.74 | ---- | ---- | ---- | ---- |
| Ouray | 2.76 | 3.50 | 4.00 | 3.85 | 9.14 | 12.00 | 10.35 | ---- |
| Park | 2.30 | 2.79 | 3.42 | 3.18 | 30.03 | 37.00 | 37.16 | 36.36 |
| Phillips | 2.87 | 3.24 | 9.14 | ---- | ---- | ---- | ---- | ---- |
| Pitkin | 2.58 | 3.24 | 3.15 | 2.51 | ---- | ---- | ---- | ---- |
| Prowers | 1.79 | 2.27 | 5.26 | 3.15 | 17.50 | 22.37 | 30.32 | 27.72 |
| Pueblo | 2.99 | 3.74 | 4.03 | 3.35 | ---- | ---- | ---- | ---- |
| Rio Blanco | 2.30 | 2.95 | 4.60 | 4.33 | 31.00 | 39.77 | 38.96 | 48.95 |
| Rio Grande | 2.40 | 3.00 | 6.08 | 5.46 | 12.80 | 18.00 | 32.50 | ---- |
| Routt | 2.57 | 3.22 | 6.00 | 5.15 | ---- | ---- | ---- | 28.88 |
| Saguache | 2.80 | 3.75 | 5.10 | 2.32 | 18.80 | 23.50 | 28.10 | 18.00 |
| San Juan | 5.60 | 6.40 | 6.40 | 6.40 | ---- | ---- | ---- | ---- |
| San Miguel | 2.68 | 3.52 | 4.96 | 5.49 | ---- | ---- | ---- | ---- |
| Sedgwick | 3.55 | 4.63 | 5.00 | 4.00 | 15.91 | 18.56 | 15.25 | 15.18 |
| Summit | 3.12 | 3.75 | 3.75 | 3.76 | ---- | ---- | ---- | ---- |
| Teller | 1.92 | 2.18 | 2.16 | 2.01 | 12.56 | 15.50 | 15.38 | 14.95 |
| Washington | 2.85 | 3.73 | 9.80 | ---- | ---- | ---- | ---- | 16.00 |
| Weld | 2.40 | 3.06 | 5.93 | 4.45 | 13.69 | 17.59 | 24.50 | 18.47 |
| Yuma | 2.86 | 3.55 | 5.50 | 2.71 | 23.75 | 26.76 | 29.00 | ---- |
| State | $2.76 | $ 3.48 | $ 5.87 | $ 4.41 | $18.53 | $23.95 | $29.25 | $23.78 |

ESTIMATED PRICE OF FARM PRODUCTS RECEIVED BY PRODUCERS
AS OF THE 15TH OF THE MONTH

### WHEAT
(Cents per bushel)

| Year | Jan. | Feb. | Mar. | April | May | June | July | Aug. | Sept. | Oct. | Nov. | Dec. |
|------|------|------|------|-------|-----|------|------|------|-------|------|------|------|
| 1910 | 98 | 99 | 98 | 97 | 96 | 98 | 96 | 94 | 90 | 86 | 84 | 80 |
| 1911 | 78 | 77 | 77 | 79 | 82 | 83 | 88 | 86 | 80 | 80 | 82 | 84 |
| 1912 | 84 | 84 | 87 | 92 | 94 | 94 | 92 | 82 | 76 | 76 | 76 | 70 |
| 1913 | 72 | 75 | 75 | 75 | 74 | 73 | 72 | 72 | 74 | 74 | 76 | 76 |
| 1914 | 74 | 75 | 76 | 78 | 78 | 77 | 76 | 78 | 81 | 81 | 84 | 90 |
| 1915 | 107 | 121 | 118 | 118 | 120 | 104 | 95 | 92 | 82 | 84 | 83 | 84 |
| 1916 | 93 | 97 | 94 | 91 | 91 | 88 | 92 | 112 | 128 | 135 | 145 | 145 |
| 1917 | 148 | 152 | 156 | 180 | 220 | 242 | 232 | 210 | 200 | 194 | 190 | 192 |
| 1918 | 190 | 190 | 192 | 193 | 192 | 195 | 200 | 198 | 194 | 192 | 194 | 194 |
| 1919 | 198 | 195 | 194 | 201 | 203 | 206 | 204 | 196 | 194 | 198 | 200 | 210 |
| 1920 | 216 | 212 | 212 | 215 | 225 | 234 | 226 | 212 | 196 | 178 | 152 | 136 |
| 1921 | 138 | 138 | 130 | 108 | 112 | 118 | 96 | 86 | 86 | 82 | 76 | 78 |
| 1922 | 80 | 94 | 102 | 99 | 99 | 90 | 84 | 84 | 78 | 84 | 90 | 92 |
| 1923 | 95 | 96 | 99 | 100 | 100 | 94 | 80 | 72 | 79 | 84 | 84 | 86 |
| 1924 | 84 | 83 | 84 | 82 | 84 | 82 | 95 | 105 | 100 | 115 | 118 | 127 |
| 1925 | 142 | 163 | 155 | 133 | 139 | 141 | 128 | 145 | 138 | 129 | 136 | 145 |
| 1926 | 152 | 147 | 135 | 131 | 132 | 127 | 111 | 108 | 105 | 107 | 110 | 109 |
| 1927 | 110 | 113 | 109 | 111 | 109 | 119 | 118 | 109 | 107 | 105 | 103 | 107 |
| 1928 | 108 | 109 | 115 | 118 | 132 | 127 | 114 | 83 | 80 | 85 | 85 | 87 |
| 1929 | 89 | 93 | 95 | 89 | 84 | 80 | 91 | 101 | 100 | 98 | 91 | 95 |
| 1930 | 96 | 90 | 84 | 89 | 84 | 84 | 68 | 64 | 63 | 57 | 53 | 54 |
| 1931 | 52 | 51 | 51 | 51 | 52 | 45 | 32 | 28 | 30 | 33 | 46 | 42 |
| 1932 | 43 | 42 | 40 | -- | -- | -- | -- | -- | -- | -- | -- | -- |

### CORN
(Cents per bushel)

| Year | Jan. | Feb. | Mar. | April | May | June | July | Aug. | Sept. | Oct. | Nov. | Dec. |
|------|------|------|------|-------|-----|------|------|------|-------|------|------|------|
| 1910 | 70 | 70 | 68 | 66 | 72 | 72 | 70 | 73 | 70 | 64 | 62 | 58 |
| 1911 | 56 | 54 | 53 | 54 | 59 | 62 | 64 | 68 | 72 | 75 | 76 | 76 |
| 1912 | 75 | 76 | 74 | 79 | 83 | 86 | 85 | 80 | 75 | 72 | 62 | 44 |
| 1913 | 41 | 44 | 50 | 52 | 50 | 52 | 54 | 62 | 72 | 76 | 74 | 71 |
| 1914 | 70 | 69 | 70 | 70 | 70 | 72 | 72 | 71 | 72 | 72 | 66 | 62 |
| 1915 | 66 | 68 | 70 | 68 | 66 | 65 | 66 | 68 | 66 | 56 | 52 | 55 |
| 1916 | 58 | 62 | 64 | 66 | 66 | 66 | 72 | 76 | 78 | 77 | 83 | 90 |
| 1917 | 92 | 92 | 98 | 120 | 145 | 161 | 174 | 186 | 184 | 155 | 130 | 122 |
| 1918 | 128 | 144 | 150 | 150 | 147 | 148 | 152 | 156 | 154 | 146 | 138 | 140 |
| 1919 | 142 | 136 | 134 | 143 | 150 | 156 | 166 | 168 | 172 | 164 | 146 | 141 |
| 1920 | 133 | 120 | 124 | 144 | 155 | 160 | 160 | 150 | 126 | 98 | 80 | 61 |
| 1921 | 48 | 43 | 42 | 48 | 50 | 48 | 49 | 42 | 36 | 33 | 31 | 32 |
| 1922 | 34 | 39 | 44 | 48 | 50 | 51 | 50 | 45 | 44 | 55 | 66 | 64 |
| 1923 | 61 | 62 | 66 | 78 | 84 | 82 | 78 | 74 | 73 | 75 | 70 | 68 |
| 1924 | 60 | 60 | 58 | 59 | 65 | 62 | 90 | 95 | 93 | 94 | 90 | 104 |
| 1925 | 115 | 115 | 106 | 87 | 100 | 110 | 108 | 99 | 98 | 92 | 70 | 70 |
| 1926 | 72 | 65 | 60 | 57 | 62 | 65 | 68 | 72 | 75 | 79 | 76 | 73 |
| 1927 | 70 | 71 | 72 | 73 | 79 | 91 | 97 | 97 | 94 | 83 | 70 | 69 |
| 1928 | 69 | 72 | 80 | 87 | 93 | 94 | 92 | 85 | 83 | 80 | 73 | 73 |
| 1929 | 76 | 80 | 80 | 78 | 79 | 78 | 80 | 87 | 87 | 88 | 80 | 76 |
| 1930 | 71 | 71 | 66 | 68 | 68 | 71 | 68 | 77 | 77 | 70 | 61 | 55 |
| 1931 | 48 | 44 | 42 | 44 | 43 | 40 | 42 | 42 | 38 | 34 | 41 | 37 |
| 1932 | 36 | 35 | 33 | -- | -- | -- | -- | -- | -- | -- | -- | -- |

ESTIMATED PRICE OF FARM PRODUCTS RECEIVED BY PRODUCERS
AS OF THE 15TH OF THE MONTH—Continued

OATS
(Cents per bushel)

| Year | Jan. | Feb. | Mar. | April | May | June | July | Aug. | Sept. | Oct. | Nov. | D. |
|------|------|------|------|-------|-----|------|------|------|-------|------|------|----|
| 1910 | 54 | 54 | 56 | 56 | 56 | 58 | 58 | 56 | 52 | 46 | 46 | |
| 1911 | 44 | 44 | 44 | 47 | 50 | 50 | 53 | 55 | 52 | 50 | 49 | |
| 1912 | 48 | 47 | 52 | 58 | 60 | 60 | 57 | 47 | 41 | 39 | 37 | |
| 1913 | 38 | 40 | 40 | 38 | 40 | 42 | 44 | 47 | 47 | 46 | 45 | |
| 1914 | 45 | 46 | 47 | 48 | 50 | 50 | 45 | 42 | 46 | 48 | 46 | |
| 1915 | 49 | 48 | 48 | 52 | 53 | 50 | 50 | 48 | 43 | 42 | 42 | |
| 1916 | 42 | 45 | 50 | 52 | 54 | 55 | 56 | 54 | 54 | 58 | 58 | |
| 1917 | 64 | 64 | 69 | 84 | 97 | 98 | 92 | 86 | 82 | 72 | 71 | |
| 1918 | 76 | 80 | 96 | 101 | 100 | 96 | 90 | 92 | 90 | 84 | 80 | |
| 1919 | 90 | 86 | 82 | 89 | 96 | 90 | 89 | 87 | 83 | 84 | 86 | |
| 1920 | 90 | 92 | 97 | 99 | 100 | 110 | 104 | 90 | 84 | 74 | 64 | |
| 1921 | 53 | 51 | 56 | 53 | 51 | 56 | 53 | 48 | 40 | 36 | 34 | |
| 1922 | 32 | 36 | 40 | 43 | 44 | 44 | 44 | 42 | 38 | 38 | 43 | |
| 1923 | 49 | 53 | 58 | 64 | 66 | 67 | 66 | 58 | 50 | 46 | 46 | |
| 1924 | 48 | 47 | 50 | 48 | 45 | 49 | 55 | 56 | 54 | 50 | 54 | |
| 1925 | 60 | 63 | 65 | 67 | 62 | 63 | 58 | 53 | 49 | 49 | 49 | |
| 1926 | 46 | 47 | 47 | 49 | 48 | 48 | 47 | 44 | 43 | 44 | 43 | |
| 1927 | 47 | 49 | 48 | 50 | 50 | 55 | 56 | 50 | 49 | 45 | 46 | |
| 1928 | 50 | 50 | 55 | 58 | 62 | 60 | 62 | 47 | 43 | 44 | 45 | |
| 1929 | 48 | 52 | 53 | 54 | 54 | 50 | 53 | 49 | 47 | 45 | 47 | |
| 1930 | 45 | 44 | 45 | 45 | 45 | 44 | 39 | 38 | 37 | 35 | 35 | |
| 1931 | 34 | 32 | 35 | 34 | 33 | 32 | 29 | 26 | 26 | 23 | 29 | |
| 1932 | 29 | 30 | 30 | -- | -- | -- | -- | -- | -- | -- | -- | |

BARLEY
(Cents per bushel)

| Year | Jan. | Feb. | Mar. | April | May | June | July | Aug. | Sept. | Oct. | Nov. |
|------|------|------|------|-------|-----|------|------|------|-------|------|------|
| 1910 | 68 | 68 | 72 | 66 | 70 | 76 | 74 | 69 | 62 | 60 | 60 |
| 1911 | 64 | 58 | 56 | 60 | 62 | 65 | 68 | 68 | 68 | 66 | 67 |
| 1912 | 65 | 68 | 76 | 86 | 86 | 81 | 81 | 60 | 55 | 49 | 52 |
| 1913 | 46 | 48 | 44 | 48 | 49 | 48 | 48 | 52 | 56 | 55 | 54 |
| 1914 | 59 | 59 | 58 | 60 | 60 | 58 | 56 | 57 | 60 | 64 | 60 |
| 1915 | 60 | 66 | 66 | 66 | 64 | 60 | 58 | 58 | 52 | 48 | 50 |
| 1916 | 58 | 57 | 62 | 66 | 64 | 64 | 62 | 69 | 76 | 76 | 81 |
| 1917 | 88 | 88 | 101 | 128 | 146 | 142 | 125 | 119 | 114 | 105 | 104 |
| 1918 | 123 | 134 | 151 | 159 | 149 | 135 | 124 | 125 | 132 | 120 | -- |
| 1919 | 128 | 133 | 131 | 116 | 122 | 138 | 152 | 143 | 126 | 130 | 128 |
| 1920 | 122 | 124 | 136 | 146 | 147 | 148 | 144 | 137 | 106 | -- | 73 |
| 1921 | 62 | 60 | -- | -- | 62 | 63 | -- | 60 | 55 | -- | -- |
| 1922 | 41 | 44 | 46 | 46 | 46 | 48 | 50 | 50 | 45 | 49 | 58 |
| 1923 | 60 | 61 | 65 | 75 | 78 | 67 | 58 | 54 | 50 | 52 | 54 |
| 1924 | 49 | 51 | 53 | 52 | 55 | 57 | 64 | 68 | 65 | 70 | 71 |
| 1925 | 86 | 90 | 90 | 79 | 79 | 84 | 75 | 67 | 60 | 62 | 58 |
| 1926 | 57 | 57 | 56 | 58 | 61 | 55 | 56 | 48 | 55 | 54 | 54 |
| 1927 | 58 | 59 | 61 | 64 | 65 | 69 | 70 | 62 | 58 | 55 | 54 |
| 1928 | 59 | 63 | 67 | 73 | 75 | 76 | 74 | 51 | 46 | 48 | 52 |
| 1929 | 60 | 60 | 63 | 62 | 61 | 58 | 57 | 54 | 54 | 56 | 56 |
| 1930 | 56 | 52 | 53 | 53 | 55 | 53 | 42 | 44 | 43 | 41 | 39 |
| 1931 | 35 | 34 | 35 | 35 | 35 | 32 | 30 | 23 | 25 | 22 | 29 |
| 1932 | 30 | 29 | 29 | -- | -- | -- | -- | -- | -- | -- | -- |

## ESTIMATED PRICE OF FARM PRODUCTS RECEIVED BY PRODUCERS AS OF THE 15TH OF THE MONTH—Continued

### RYE
(Cents per bushel)

| Year | Jan. | Feb. | Mar. | April | May | June | July | Aug. | Sept. | Oct. | Nov. | Dec. |
|------|------|------|------|-------|-----|------|------|------|-------|------|------|------|
| 10_____ | 74 | 74 | 74 | 71 | 75 | 79 | 78 | 78 | 70 | 68 | 68 | 66 |
| 11_____ | 64 | 63 | 64 | 65 | 64 | 61 | 60 | 72 | 76 | 68 | 68 | 68 |
| 12_____ | 68 | 72 | 80 | 82 | 78 | 75 | 76 | 70 | 59 | 54 | 54 | 54 |
| 13_____ | 53 | 52 | 50 | 52 | 57 | 62 | 64 | 63 | 62 | 59 | 58 | 60 |
| 14_____ | 62 | 58 | 56 | 62 | 64 | 60 | 62 | 61 | 59 | 60 | 62 | 64 |
| 15_____ | 69 | 80 | 90 | 98 | 96 | 84 | 78 | 78 | 70 | 64 | 67 | 72 |
| 16_____ | 72 | 74 | 76 | 75 | 74 | 71 | 72 | 79 | 84 | 94 | 105 | 100 |
| 17_____ | 104 | 110 | 108 | 128 | 148 | 148 | 146 | 135 | 142 | 151 | 144 | 140 |
| 18_____ | 136 | 139 | 162 | 176 | 163 | 138 | 138 | 165 | 166 | 151 | 141 | 138 |
| 19_____ | 128 | 125 | 138 | 151 | 144 | 134 | 140 | 151 | 147 | 132 | 129 | 131 |
| 20_____ | 142 | 136 | 125 | 152 | 172 | 194 | 184 | 150 | 138 | 121 | 110 | 98 |
| 21_____ | 101 | 92 | 90 | 96 | 95 | 90 | 77 | 68 | 70 | 67 | 60 | 58 |
| 22_____ | 58 | 62 | 66 | 68 | 70 | 72 | 68 | 57 | 51 | 60 | 68 | 67 |
| 23_____ | 67 | 65 | 65 | 70 | 75 | 70 | 56 | 50 | 56 | 60 | 58 | 56 |
| 24_____ | 54 | 58 | 58 | 60 | 60 | 55 | 59 | 70 | -- | 83 | 85 | 95 |
| 25_____ | 103 | 118 | 112 | 89 | 82 | 95 | 82 | 83 | 82 | 69 | 63 | 70 |
| 26_____ | 70 | 71 | 61 | 59 | 58 | 61 | 65 | 70 | 70 | 73 | 71 | 65 |
| 27_____ | 68 | 73 | 72 | 70 | 72 | 78 | 80 | 72 | 71 | 68 | 67 | 72 |
| 28_____ | 73 | 73 | 79 | 80 | 89 | 87 | 85 | 67 | 67 | 70 | 71 | 71 |
| 29_____ | 72 | 76 | 75 | 75 | 70 | 66 | 69 | 76 | 73 | 73 | 71 | 73 |
| 30_____ | 71 | 66 | 59 | 63 | 61 | 57 | 38 | 42 | 46 | 41 | 33 | 33 |
| 31_____ | 31 | 30 | 28 | 31 | 32 | 29 | 22 | 20 | 21 | 24 | 32 | 32 |
| 32_____ | 32 | 32 | 33 | -- | -- | -- | -- | -- | -- | -- | -- | -- |

### POTATOES
(Cents per bushel)

| Year | Jan. | Feb. | Mar. | April | May | June | July | Aug. | Sept. | Oct. | Nov. | Dec. |
|------|------|------|------|-------|-----|------|------|------|-------|------|------|------|
| 10_____ | 62 | 59 | 54 | 35 | 26 | 32 | 50 | 75 | 80. | 70 | 60 | 53 |
| 11_____ | 54 | 60 | 60 | 70 | 77 | 122 | 170 | 162 | 135 | 98 | 90 | 94 |
| 12_____ | 90 | 95 | 102 | 120 | 146 | 140 | 115 | 94 | 70 | 55 | 46 | 38 |
| 13_____ | 35 | 39 | 42 | 36 | 30 | 34 | 49 | 69 | 70 | 62 | 63 | 62 |
| 14_____ | 60 | 60 | 60 | 58 | 58 | 74 | 86 | 88 | 81 | 72 | 62 | 48 |
| 15_____ | 50 | 58 | 57 | 63 | 71 | 73 | 86 | 82 | 54 | 42 | 48 | 58 |
| 16_____ | 70 | 76 | 80 | 95 | 105 | 118 | 133 | 130 | 100 | 103 | 130 | 130 |
| 17_____ | 138 | 194 | 220 | 228 | 258 | 257 | 244 | 186 | 113 | 88 | 90 | 94 |
| 18_____ | 106 | 104 | 85 | 64 | 51 | 51 | 120 | 168 | 132 | 97 | 88 | 88 |
| 19_____ | 76 | 70 | 66 | 77 | 83 | 76 | 120 | 160 | 155 | 150 | 158 | 162 |
| 20_____ | 181 | 226 | 274 | 330 | 428 | 450 | 400 | 265 | 123 | 94 | 76 | 70 |
| 21_____ | 60 | 56 | 64 | 68 | 67 | 81 | 96 | 110 | 103 | 90 | 81 | 66 |
| 22_____ | 77 | 80 | 70 | 64 | 55 | 62 | 70 | 88 | 76 | 48 | 41 | 32 |
| 23_____ | 41 | 40 | 34 | 45 | 43 | 41 | 96 | 128 | 95 | 74 | 65 | 64 |
| 24_____ | 71 | 65 | 65 | 70 | 71 | 180 | 150 | 120 | 60 | 53 | 51 | 52 |
| 25_____ | 63 | 64 | 80 | 77 | 85 | 113 | 166 | 152 | 114 | 110 | 188 | 173 |
| 26_____ | 193 | 178 | 175 | 230 | 180 | 145 | 140 | 105 | 110 | 115 | 130 | 125 |
| 27_____ | 130 | 110 | 110 | 115 | 135 | 170 | 200 | 140 | 85 | 65 | 60 | 60 |
| 28_____ | 55 | 55 | 80 | 80 | 60 | 55 | 75 | 65 | 55 | 35 | 45 | 45 |
| 29_____ | 45 | 40 | 45 | 45 | 45 | 50 | 100 | 120 | 115 | 110 | 115 | 115 |
| 30_____ | 110 | 115 | 120 | 120 | 140 | 150 | 115 | 105 | 85 | 70 | 70 | 60 |
| 31_____ | 60 | 55 | 50 | 60 | 55 | 50 | 75 | 70 | 35 | 30 | 30 | 30 |
| 32_____ | 29 | 26 | 27 | -- | -- | -- | -- | -- | -- | -- | -- | -- |

## ESTIMATED PRICE OF FARM PRODUCTS RECEIVED BY PRODUCERS AS OF THE 15TH OF THE MONTH—Continued

### HAY (LOOSE)
(Dollars per ton)

| Year | Jan. | Feb. | Mar. | April | May | June | July | Aug. | Sept. | Oct. | Nov. | Dec. |
|---|---|---|---|---|---|---|---|---|---|---|---|---|
| 1910 | 11.25 | 11.00 | 10.55 | 10.00 | 10.00 | 10.30 | 10.05 | 10.40 | 10.45 | 10.30 | 10.60 | 10.6 |
| 1911 | 10.75 | 10.60 | 10.55 | 10.40 | 10.70 | 10.50 | 10.20 | 10.05 | 9.55 | 9.95 | 9.65 | 9.4 |
| 1912 | 9.80 | 10.30 | 11.55 | 13.00 | 13.75 | 12.85 | 10.55 | 9.25 | 8.70 | 8.80 | 8.95 | 8.8 |
| 1913 | 8.85 | 8.50 | 8.30 | 8.30 | 8.30 | 8.60 | 8.70 | 8.45 | 8.35 | 9.30 | 9.65 | 9.8 |
| 1914 | 10.15 | 11.10 | 10.65 | 9.65 | 9.80 | 9.55 | 8.50 | 8.20 | 8.20 | 8.25 | 7.95 | 7.4 |
| 1915 | 7.45 | 7.50 | 7.30 | 7.30 | 7.85 | 8.40 | 8.65 | 8.15 | 7.45 | 7.40 | 7.60 | 7.9 |
| 1916 | 8.55 | 9.15 | 9.55 | 9.65 | 10.00 | 10.35 | 10.10 | 9.40 | 8.75 | 9.35 | 10.60 | 11.0 |
| 1917 | 11.55 | 12.55 | 13.65 | 15.95 | 18.95 | 19.60 | 16.00 | 13.75 | 14.50 | 15.15 | 16.20 | 16.8 |
| 1918 | 18.05 | 17.85 | 15.50 | 15.65 | 16.00 | 15.15 | 14.65 | 13.85 | 14.15 | 15.10 | 15.55 | 15.3 |
| 1919 | 14.70 | 15.75 | 17.15 | 20.05 | 21.80 | 19.40 | 18.50 | 18.60 | 18.25 | 17.50 | 17.75 | 18.0 |
| 1920 | 18.50 | 18.75 | 18.15 | 18.65 | 20.60 | 20.60 | 18.75 | 17.55 | 16.00 | 13.20 | 11.50 | 11.5 |
| 1921 | 10.55 | 10.20 | 9.95 | 9.35 | 8.85 | 9.20 | 8.90 | 8.20 | 7.30 | 6.70 | 7.05 | 6.6 |
| 1922 | 6.40 | 6.50 | 6.95 | 7.32 | 7.02 | 6.40 | 6.80 | 7.95 | 8.70 | 9.15 | 10.20 | 10.6 |
| 1923 | 10.95 | 12.05 | 12.30 | 13.15 | 14.20 | 13.05 | 10.30 | 9.00 | 9.15 | 9.15 | 10.15 | 12.9 |
| 1924 | 11.00 | 10.50 | 10.50 | 10.00 | 10.00 | 10.50 | 9.50 | 10.80 | 10.00 | 11.50 | 11.30 | 12.0 |
| 1925 | 12.30 | 12.30 | 13.60 | 11.60 | 12.00 | 12.00 | 13.70 | 12.00 | 11.60 | 10.70 | 12.00 | 12.2 |
| 1926 | 11.50 | 10.70 | 11.30 | 10.50 | 11.90 | 11.10 | 10.50 | 9.80 | 9.50 | 9.30 | 8.90 | 9.0 |
| 1927 | 8.00 | 7.60 | 7.50 | 8.50 | 9.00 | 8.50 | 8.70 | 8.40 | 8.80 | 9.00 | 9.30 | 9.2 |
| 1928 | 8.50 | 8.10 | 9.00 | 10.00 | 11.00 | 10.60 | 9.70 | 9.30 | 10.60 | 10.80 | 11.00 | 11.0 |
| 1929 | 11.00 | 12.00 | 13.00 | 12.20 | 12.70 | 12.70 | 11.70 | 11.70 | 11.00 | 10.90 | 10.90 | 10.6 |
| 1930 | 10.80 | 10.00 | 9.60 | 8.90 | 9.30 | 9.30 | 8.90 | 9.90 | 10.20 | 8.90 | 9.00 | 8.6 |
| 1931 | 9.00 | 8.00 | 7.60 | 7.90 | 8.10 | 7.30 | 7.10 | 7.80 | 7.60 | 7.50 | 7.80 | 8.4 |
| 1932 | 8.30 | 8.80 | 8.60 | --- | --- | --- | --- | --- | --- | --- | --- | -- |

### APPLES
(Dollars per bushel)

| Year | Jan. | Feb. | Mar. | April | May | June | July | Aug. | Sept. | Oct. | Nov. | |
|---|---|---|---|---|---|---|---|---|---|---|---|---|
| 1910 | 1.17 | 1.14 | --- | 1.27 | 1.25 | 1.13 | 1.61 | 1.17 | 1.25 | 1.00 | 1.10 | 1. |
| 1911 | 1.35 | 1.54 | 1.50 | 2.47 | 2.09 | 2.50 | 1.25 | 1.03 | .77 | .96 | 1.17 | 1. |
| 1912 | 1.00 | 1.15 | 1.17 | 1.60 | 1.80 | 2.00 | 1.96 | .85 | .88 | .97 | .83 | . |
| 1913 | .90 | .75 | .90 | .65 | 1.25 | 2.07 | 1.40 | .82 | .85 | 1.00 | 1.05 | 1. |
| 1914 | 1.00 | 1.20 | 1.20 | 1.30 | 1.50 | 1.50 | --- | .80 | .75 | .60 | .75 | . |
| 1915 | .65 | .70 | .80 | 1.05 | 1.05 | --- | 1.30 | 1.00 | 1.00 | .85 | .95 | . |
| 1916 | .90 | 1.00 | .95 | 1.00 | 1.05 | 1.40 | 2.00 | 1.20 | .95 | .85 | 1.00 | 1. |
| 1917 | 1.20 | 1.30 | 1.40 | 1.60 | 2.50 | 3.20 | --- | 1.20 | 1.20 | .90 | 1.10 | 1. |
| 1918 | 1.25 | 1.30 | 1.15 | 1.40 | 2.60 | --- | 1.80 | 1.70 | 1.50 | 1.50 | 1.70 | 2. |
| 1919 | 2.25 | 2.10 | 2.50 | 2.10 | 2.70 | 2.60 | 2.30 | 1.50 | 1.70 | 1.60 | 2.00 | 2. |
| 1920 | 2.20 | 2.10 | 2.30 | 2.25 | 3.60 | 2.40 | 2.70 | 2.00 | 1.50 | 1.60 | 1.70 | 1. |
| 1921 | .65 | 1.00 | .98 | 1.40 | 1.60 | 1.25 | 1.00 | 1.50 | 1.70 | 1.70 | 1.60 | 1. |
| 1922 | 1.50 | 1.50 | 1.80 | 1.80 | 1.60 | 2.20 | 1.90 | .75 | .65 | .75 | .70 | . |
| 1923 | 1.00 | 1.10 | 1.18 | 1.30 | 2.38 | 3.20 | 1.90 | 1.76 | 1.26 | 1.24 | 1.23 | 1. |
| 1924 | 1.25 | 1.00 | 1.00 | 1.10 | --- | 1.00 | 2.00 | .94 | 1.00 | 1.09 | 1.26 | 1. |
| 1925 | 1.41 | 1.43 | 1.62 | 1.71 | --- | 2.50 | 1.61 | 1.19 | 1.24 | 1.22 | 1.39 | 1. |
| 1926 | 1.64 | 1.27 | 1.14 | 1.58 | --- | 1.60 | 1.80 | 1.10 | .80 | .75 | .65 | . |
| 1927 | .90 | .95 | .90 | 1.00 | 1.05 | 1.50 | 1.60 | 1.25 | 1.10 | 1.15 | 1.20 | 1 |
| 1928 | 1.30 | 1.35 | 1.30 | 1.35 | 1.55 | 1.55 | 1.45 | 1.25 | .95 | .90 | .85 | |
| 1929 | .80 | .90 | .95 | .90 | .95 | 1.20 | 1.70 | 1.30 | 1.15 | 1.10 | 1.05 | 1 |
| 1930 | 1.10 | 1.20 | 1.10 | 1.20 | 1.20 | 1.45 | 1.70 | 1.45 | 1.00 | .80 | .85 | |
| 1931 | 1.05 | .85 | .95 | 1.00 | 1.00 | 1.05 | 1.25 | 1.00 | .70 | .55 | .55 | |
| 1932 | .70 | .65 | .60 | --- | --- | --- | --- | --- | --- | --- | --- | |

### ESTIMATED PRICE OF FARM PRODUCTS RECEIVED BY PRODUCERS AS OF THE 15TH OF THE MONTH—Continued

#### COLORADO HOG PRICES BY MONTHS
(Dollars per 100 pounds)

| Year | Jan. | Feb. | Mar. | April | May | June | July | Aug. | Sept. | Oct. | Nov. | Dec. |
|---|---|---|---|---|---|---|---|---|---|---|---|---|
| 1910 | 7.60 | 7.50 | 9.00 | 8.80 | 8.20 | 9.00 | 8.50 | 7.80 | 8.50 | 8.20 | 8.00 | 7.70 |
| 1911 | 7.60 | 7.60 | 7.20 | 6.30 | 6.20 | 5.60 | 5.70 | 6.90 | 7.00 | 6.20 | 6.00 | 6.10 |
| 1912 | 6.00 | 5.90 | 6.00 | 6.90 | 7.00 | 6.90 | 6.80 | 7.20 | 7.40 | 7.60 | 7.60 | 7.50 |
| 1913 | 7.20 | 7.10 | 7.50 | 7.90 | 7.80 | 7.70 | 7.80 | 7.80 | 7.60 | 7.70 | 7.70 | 7.40 |
| 1914 | 7.30 | 7.70 | 7.60 | 7.70 | 7.70 | 7.70 | 7.70 | 8.10 | 8.30 | 7.70 | 7.50 | 6.80 |
| 1915 | 6.90 | 6.40 | 6.50 | 6.60 | 6.80 | 6.90 | 7.00 | 7.20 | 6.80 | 7.10 | 6.50 | 6.10 |
| 1916 | 6.00 | 6.60 | 7.70 | 7.80 | 8.20 | 8.10 | 8.30 | 8.50 | 9.00 | 8.30 | 8.60 | 8.70 |
| 1917 | 9.10 | 10.10 | 12.20 | 14.00 | 14.20 | 14.30 | 13.50 | 14.90 | 16.20 | 17.30 | 15.50 | 15.70 |
| 1918 | 15.20 | 14.80 | 15.70 | 15.60 | 15.80 | 15.40 | 15.50 | 17.00 | 17.30 | 16.20 | 15.50 | 15.60 |
| 1919 | 15.30 | 15.00 | 15.20 | 17.20 | 17.90 | 17.90 | 19.20 | 19.40 | 16.50 | 14.50 | 12.80 | 12.70 |
| 1920 | 12.70 | 13.20 | 13.30 | 13.00 | 12.90 | 12.50 | 13.00 | 12.90 | 13.70 | 13.70 | 11.50 | 8.40 |
| 1921 | 7.30 | 7.80 | 8.60 | 7.80 | 7.10 | 6.60 | 8.00 | 8.60 | 7.10 | 6.80 | 6.80 | 5.80 |
| 1922 | 6.00 | 7.50 | 9.00 | 8.90 | 8.80 | 9.00 | 8.90 | 8.70 | 8.50 | 8.20 | 7.50 | 7.00 |
| 1923 | 7.30 | 7.20 | 7.10 | 7.10 | 6.50 | 6.00 | 6.30 | 6.50 | 7.70 | 7.00 | 6.50 | 6.10 |
| 1924 | 6.30 | 6.00 | 6.10 | 6.30 | 6.10 | 6.00 | 6.00 | 8.30 | 8.00 | 8.70 | 8.20 | 7.80 |
| 1925 | 8.80 | 9.30 | 12.20 | 11.50 | 10.00 | 10.40 | 12.20 | 12.10 | 11.70 | 11.20 | 10.60 | 10.30 |
| 1926 | 10.60 | 11.60 | 11.60 | 11.30 | 11.70 | 12.60 | 13.10 | 11.90 | 12.00 | 12.30 | 11.70 | 10.70 |
| 1927 | 10.60 | 10.80 | 10.60 | 10.40 | 9.30 | 8.50 | 8.60 | 9.60 | 10.20 | 10.50 | 9.10 | 8.50 |
| 1928 | 7.70 | 7.50 | 7.50 | 7.50 | 8.40 | 8.60 | 9.60 | 9.90 | 11.00 | 9.60 | 8.70 | 7.80 |
| 1929 | 8.00 | 8.70 | 9.70 | 10.00 | 9.70 | 9.70 | 10.30 | 10.50 | 9.80 | 9.40 | 8.80 | 8.40 |
| 1930 | 8.70 | 9.00 | 9.30 | 8.90 | 8.80 | 8.90 | 8.20 | 8.50 | 9.40 | 8.80 | 8.30 | 7.40 |
| 1931 | 7.20 | 6.70 | 6.80 | 6.00 | 6.20 | 5.60 | 6.00 | 6.20 | 5.40 | 4.40 | 4.30 | 3.50 |
| 1932 | 3.40 | 3.20 | 3.70 | --- | --- | --- | --- | --- | --- | --- | --- | --- |

#### BEEF CATTLE
(Dollars per 100 pounds)

| Year | Jan. | Feb. | Mar. | April | May | June | July | Aug. | Sept. | Oct. | Nov. | Dec. |
|---|---|---|---|---|---|---|---|---|---|---|---|---|
| 1910 | 5.70 | 6.00 | 4.80 | 6.00 | 5.80 | 6.20 | 5.50 | 4.60 | 4.50 | 4.90 | 4.50 | 4.20 |
| 1911 | 5.00 | 5.00 | 5.00 | 5.00 | 4.90 | 5.00 | 4.80 | 4.40 | 4.70 | 4.00 | 4.60 | 4.60 |
| 1912 | 4.80 | 4.90 | 5.20 | 5.70 | 6.00 | 5.90 | 5.70 | 5.40 | 5.60 | 5.80 | 5.50 | 6.10 |
| 1913 | 6.00 | 6.10 | 6.30 | 6.50 | 6.90 | 6.70 | 6.70 | 6.50 | 6.30 | 6.30 | 6.70 | 6.60 |
| 1914 | 6.50 | 6.90 | 6.70 | 6.90 | 6.90 | 7.00 | 7.00 | 6.50 | 6.70 | 6.00 | 6.30 | 6.50 |
| 1915 | 6.60 | 6.70 | 6.60 | 6.50 | 7.00 | 7.00 | 6.60 | 6.60 | 6.20 | 6.20 | 6.30 | 6.00 |
| 1916 | 6.30 | 6.50 | 6.70 | 7.00 | 7.10 | 7.40 | 7.50 | 7.30 | 6.70 | 6.60 | 6.60 | 7.10 |
| 1917 | 7.80 | 7.80 | 8.40 | 9.30 | 9.30 | 10.20 | 10.00 | 10.00 | 8.50 | 8.70 | 9.00 | 8.80 |
| 1918 | 8.60 | 9.50 | 9.90 | 11.00 | 12.40 | 11.80 | 11.00 | 10.90 | 9.00 | 9.20 | 9.90 | 9.90 |
| 1919 | 11.00 | 11.10 | 11.20 | 12.20 | 12.00 | 11.80 | 10.50 | 10.50 | 9.20 | 9.20 | 9.00 | 8.70 |
| 1920 | 9.00 | 8.90 | 9.20 | 9.20 | 9.40 | 10.00 | 9.50 | 8.80 | 8.70 | 6.70 | 7.20 | 6.20 |
| 1921 | 6.30 | 5.60 | 6.90 | 6.40 | 6.10 | 5.80 | 5.80 | 5.40 | 4.60 | 4.50 | 4.60 | 4.60 |
| 1922 | 4.90 | 5.50 | 5.80 | 6.00 | 6.20 | 6.40 | 6.30 | 5.80 | 5.70 | 5.60 | 5.50 | 5.70 |
| 1923 | 5.80 | 5.70 | 6.20 | 6.30 | 6.50 | 6.50 | 6.40 | 5.70 | 6.00 | 5.30 | 5.30 | 5.20 |
| 1924 | 6.00 | 6.00 | 6.00 | 6.40 | 6.50 | 6.40 | 6.20 | 5.60 | 5.70 | 5.30 | 5.00 | 5.50 |
| 1925 | 5.60 | 5.60 | 6.80 | 7.80 | 6.90 | 7.10 | 6.80 | 7.10 | 6.30 | 6.30 | 6.40 | 6.20 |
| 1926 | 6.50 | 7.10 | 7.30 | 7.70 | 7.00 | 7.40 | 7.10 | 7.10 | 6.80 | 6.50 | 6.60 | 6.50 |
| 1927 | 6.60 | 6.80 | 7.20 | 8.00 | 7.90 | 8.00 | 8.20 | 7.70 | 7.30 | 8.10 | 8.00 | 8.90 |
| 1928 | 9.00 | 9.40 | 8.80 | 9.10 | 10.10 | 9.80 | 9.50 | 10.10 | 10.40 | 10.10 | 9.80 | 9.10 |
| 1929 | 9.40 | 9.30 | 10.10 | 10.40 | 10.30 | 10.20 | 10.90 | 11.20 | 9.70 | 9.30 | 9.20 | 9.20 |
| 1930 | 9.30 | 9.10 | 9.20 | 9.20 | 9.10 | 9.00 | 7.90 | 7.00 | 7.10 | 7.20 | 7.10 | 7.30 |
| 1931 | 7.20 | 6.50 | 6.50 | 6.50 | 5.90 | 5.30 | 5.60 | 5.70 | 5.50 | 5.00 | 4.90 | 4.00 |
| 1932 | 3.90 | 3.60 | 4.10 | --- | --- | --- | --- | --- | --- | --- | --- | --- |

ESTIMATED PRICE OF FARM PRODUCTS RECEIVED BY PRODUCERS
AS OF THE 15TH OF THE MONTH—Continued

VEAL CALVES
(Dollars per 100 pounds)

| Year | Jan. | Feb. | Mar. | April | May | June | July | Aug. | Sept. | Oct. | Nov. | Dec. |
|------|------|------|------|-------|-----|------|------|------|-------|------|------|------|
| 1910 | 9.30 | 7.60 | 6.00 | 10.10 | 11.00 | 9.50 | 8.50 | 7.60 | 7.30 | 6.70 | 5.90 | 7.0 |
| 1911 | 7.00 | 6.50 | 7.30 | 7.30 | 6.60 | 6.70 | 7.30 | 7.20 | 7.00 | 6.10 | 6.20 | 6.8 |
| 1912 | 6.30 | 6.70 | 6.70 | 7.20 | 7.30 | 7.70 | 7.40 | 7.70 | 7.20 | 7.20 | 7.00 | 7.7 |
| 1913 | 7.90 | 8.00 | 8.30 | 8.80 | 9.00 | 8.60 | 9.30 | 9.50 | 8.20 | 8.30 | 8.70 | 8.2 |
| 1914 | 8.40 | 9.00 | 8.60 | 8.70 | 9.00 | 9.30 | 9.40 | 8.20 | 8.60 | 7.50 | 8.00 | 8.3 |
| 1915 | 8.50 | 8.70 | 8.90 | 9.00 | 9.50 | 9.00 | 8.40 | 8.50 | 8.30 | 9.00 | 8.10 | 8.4 |
| 1916 | 8.00 | 8.70 | 8.90 | 9.80 | 9.60 | 9.70 | 10.10 | 10.00 | 9.30 | 9.20 | 8.60 | 9.0 |
| 1917 | 9.30 | 9.80 | 10.30 | 11.00 | 12.50 | 11.90 | 13.40 | 11.50 | 11.70 | 11.10 | 10.20 | 11.0 |
| 1918 | 11.30 | 11.80 | 12.60 | 12.70 | 13.40 | 12.70 | 12.80 | 12.50 | 11.80 | 10.50 | 10.50 | 11.8 |
| 1919 | 12.10 | 12.60 | 13.30 | 12.70 | 12.60 | 12.90 | 12.50 | 11.80 | 11.40 | 11.60 | 11.60 | 11.0 |
| 1920 | 12.00 | 12.10 | 12.80 | 12.50 | 12.90 | 11.90 | 12.80 | 11.00 | 11.10 | 9.90 | 9.50 | 7.9 |
| 1921 | 8.00 | 8.00 | 8.80 | 8.90 | 8.20 | 8.10 | 7.60 | 7.00 | 7.00 | 6.80 | 6.50 | 6.5 |
| 1922 | 7.10 | 7.50 | 7.20 | 7.50 | 7.70 | 7.70 | 7.30 | 6.80 | 6.60 | 6.60 | 6.30 | 6.4 |
| 1923 | 6.90 | 8.00 | 8.20 | 8.50 | 8.40 | 8.50 | 8.10 | 7.40 | 8.00 | 7.30 | 6.80 | 7.1 |
| 1924 | 7.90 | 7.80 | 8.20 | 8.50 | 8.30 | 8.30 | 8.40 | 7.80 | 7.80 | 7.30 | 7.00 | 7.3 |
| 1925 | 7.90 | 7.90 | 8.80 | 8.70 | 9.00 | 8.60 | 8.20 | 8.50 | 7.90 | 8.60 | 8.60 | 7.8 |
| 1926 | 8.60 | 9.90 | 10.00 | 10.10 | 10.00 | 10.50 | 10.20 | 9.10 | 9.80 | 9.50 | 9.10 | 9.4 |
| 1927 | 9.50 | 10.00 | 9.80 | 10.50 | 10.40 | 10.30 | 10.70 | 10.50 | 10.60 | 10.50 | 10.80 | 11.8 |
| 1928 | 10.70 | 11.50 | 11.50 | 11.80 | 11.30 | 12.70 | 12.90 | 12.90 | 13.00 | 12.70 | 11.80 | 11.4 |
| 1929 | 12.10 | 12.10 | 12.70 | 13.50 | 13.80 | 13.20 | 13.20 | 13.30 | 13.60 | 13.00 | 12.40 | 12.3 |
| 1930 | 12.20 | 11.90 | 11.70 | 11.60 | 11.40 | 11.70 | 10.80 | 9.70 | 9.80 | 10.30 | 10.20 | 9.9 |
| 1931 | 9.70 | 8.90 | 9.10 | 8.70 | 8.10 | 8.00 | 7.50 | 7.50 | 7.20 | 6.50 | 6.50 | 6.0 |
| 1932 | 6.00 | 5.80 | 6.30 | --- | --- | --- | --- | --- | --- | --- | --- | -- |

SHEEP
(Dollars per 100 pounds)

| Year | Jan. | Feb. | Mar. | April | May | June | July | Aug. | Sept. | C | | |
|------|------|------|------|-------|-----|------|------|------|-------|------|------|------|
| 1910 | 6.20 | 6.50 | 3.50 | 8.20 | 5.20 | 6.00 | 5.20 | 5.00 | 5.00 | 4.20 | 4.60 | 4. |
| 1911 | 4.60 | 4.70 | 4.20 | 4.40 | 4.90 | 4.00 | 4.10 | 4.70 | 4.10 | 3.80 | 3.30 | 4. |
| 1912 | 4.00 | 4.00 | 4.50 | 5.20 | 5.50 | 5.10 | 5.00 | 4.30 | 4.40 | 4.30 | 4.10 | 4. |
| 1913 | 5.00 | 4.90 | 5.40 | 6.00 | 5.20 | 5.10 | 5.00 | 4.70 | 4.10 | 4.00 | 4.50 | 4. |
| 1914 | 5.30 | 4.60 | 5.10 | 5.50 | 6.00 | 4.50 | 5.00 | 5.50 | 4.50 | 4.40 | 5.00 | 5. |
| 1915 | 4.80 | 5.30 | 5.90 | 6.30 | 6.40 | 6.10 | 6.60 | 5.90 | 5.00 | 5.00 | 5.60 | 5. |
| 1916 | 5.60 | 6.20 | 7.00 | 7.80 | 7.80 | 7.80 | 7.70 | 6.90 | 6.60 | 6.90 | 6.90 | 8. |
| 1917 | 8.40 | 9.30 | 9.80 | 10.90 | 11.40 | 12.20 | 10.80 | 11.30 | 11.30 | 11.40 | 10.80 | 11. |
| 1918 | 11.90 | 12.00 | 12.60 | 13.90 | 14.40 | 12.60 | 12.40 | 13.20 | 13.90 | 11.00 | 9.60 | 10. |
| 1919 | 10.20 | 10.30 | 10.50 | 11.90 | 11.70 | 12.50 | 10.30 | 10.80 | 10.90 | 9.20 | 9.40 | 9. |
| 1920 | 10.00 | 11.60 | 11.70 | 11.20 | 11.60 | 10.00 | 10.00 | 6.80 | 7.00 | 7.10 | 7.30 | 5. |
| 1921 | 4.50 | 5.00 | 6.40 | 5.60 | 5.60 | 5.10 | 5.00 | 4.50 | 4.40 | 4.50 | 4.50 | 4. |
| 1922 | 6.70 | 7.50 | 7.40 | 7.40 | 7.20 | 6.20 | 7.20 | 6.70 | 6.40 | 6.20 | 6.20 | 7. |
| 1923 | 7.20 | 8.10 | 7.80 | 8.20 | 7.70 | 8.00 | 7.00 | 6.40 | 7.30 | 7.30 | 6.70 | 6. |
| 1924 | 7.50 | 7.60 | 8.00 | 8.30 | 8.50 | 8.60 | 7.60 | 6.60 | 6.80 | --- | 6.80 | 8. |
| 1925 | 8.40 | 9.00 | 8.60 | 10.00 | 9.00 | 8.60 | 8.20 | 8.00 | 8.50 | 7.60 | 7.70 | 7. |
| 1926 | 9.30 | 9.20 | 8.80 | 8.50 | 8.40 | 8.90 | 6.90 | 6.50 | 7.60 | 6.10 | 6.80 | 8. |
| 1927 | 7.00 | 7.00 | 8.00 | 8.70 | 8.10 | 8.00 | 6.70 | 6.70 | 6.70 | 6.00 | 7.30 | 7. |
| 1928 | 7.40 | 7.20 | 8.40 | 7.90 | 8.80 | 7.60 | 7.60 | 7.60 | 7.70 | 7.00 | 7.30 | 7. |
| 1929 | 7.40 | 7.90 | 8.40 | 9.10 | 8.70 | 8.20 | 7.20 | 6.40 | 5.70 | 5.80 | 6.10 | 6. |
| 1930 | 6.40 | 6.40 | 5.60 | 5.70 | 5.70 | 5.40 | 4.50 | 4.40 | 4.30 | 3.40 | 3.20 | 3. |
| 1931 | 3.80 | 4.20 | 4.50 | 4.30 | 3.80 | 3.60 | 2.60 | 3.00 | 2.60 | 2.50 | 2.20 | 2. |
| 1932 | 2.10 | 2.20 | 2.40 | --- | --- | --- | --- | --- | --- | --- | --- | - |

ESTIMATED PRICE OF FARM PRODUCTS RECEIVED BY PRODUCERS
AS OF THE 15TH OF THE MONTH—Continued

LAMBS

(Dollars per 100 pounds)

| Year | Jan. | Feb. | Mar. | April | May | June | July | Aug. | Sept. | Oct. | Nov. | Dec. |
|------|------|------|------|-------|-----|------|------|------|-------|------|------|------|
| 1910 | 7.00 | 7.50 | 4.30 | --- | 5.90 | 7.40 | 6.70 | 5.80 | 6.00 | 6.30 | 5.30 | 5.60 |
| 1911 | 6.50 | 5.80 | 4.80 | 5.60 | 6.20 | 5.10 | 5.30 | 6.50 | 5.40 | 4.50 | 4.60 | 5.10 |
| 1912 | 5.00 | 5.30 | 6.10 | 6.60 | 7.50 | 6.80 | 7.00 | 6.00 | 5.80 | 5.60 | 5.80 | 6.20 |
| 1913 | 6.70 | 6.60 | 7.00 | 7.30 | 6.60 | 6.00 | 6.50 | 6.30 | 5.60 | 5.50 | 5.70 | 5.70 |
| 1914 | 6.70 | 6.50 | 6.80 | 7.30 | 7.00 | 7.20 | 7.40 | 7.20 | 6.00 | 6.00 | 6.10 | 7.40 |
| 1915 | 7.20 | 7.20 | 7.60 | 8.10 | 8.40 | 8.00 | 7.90 | 7.20 | 7.00 | 7.00 | 7.30 | 7.70 |
| 1916 | 7.70 | 8.50 | 9.50 | 8.70 | 10.00 | 10.00 | 9.80 | 9.30 | 8.50 | 9.00 | 9.00 | 10.00 |
| 1917 | 11.40 | 12.00 | 12.20 | 12.90 | 14.20 | 15.30 | 13.70 | 13.50 | 14.60 | 16.30 | 15.50 | 15.70 |
| 1918 | 15.80 | 16.00 | 14.80 | 17.80 | 17.10 | 15.70 | 15.70 | 15.50 | 16.60 | 14.30 | 13.00 | 13.60 |
| 1919 | 14.20 | 14.30 | 14.50 | 15.70 | 14.60 | 15.20 | 13.80 | 15.50 | 14.60 | 12.30 | 12.80 | 13.20 |
| 1920 | 14.80 | 16.70 | 16.40 | 15.70 | 16.20 | 16.10 | 13.40 | 11.10 | 11.30 | 11.10 | 11.10 | 8.20 |
| 1921 | 8.40 | 7.30 | 8.00 | 7.30 | 7.90 | 8.00 | 8.10 | 7.00 | 5.50 | 6.00 | 5.80 | 6.00 |
| 1922 | 8.00 | 10.40 | 12.40 | 12.40 | 12.00 | 10.70 | 11.10 | 10.50 | 10.30 | 10.80 | 11.00 | 11.00 |
| 1923 | 11.20 | 11.50 | 12.30 | 12.00 | 12.70 | 12.00 | 11.20 | 10.50 | 11.50 | 11.80 | 11.00 | 11.50 |
| 1924 | 11.40 | 11.60 | 12.00 | 12.50 | 13.00 | 12.70 | 11.50 | 11.00 | 11.20 | 11.40 | 11.80 | 12.20 |
| 1925 | 14.00 | 14.50 | 14.70 | 12.60 | 12.70 | 12.80 | 12.50 | 12.90 | 13.20 | 12.90 | 13.40 | 13.40 |
| 1926 | 14.30 | 12.60 | 12.00 | 11.30 | 12.00 | 12.90 | 12.60 | 11.50 | 12.00 | 12.00 | 11.80 | 11.70 |
| 1927 | 11.20 | 11.30 | 12.40 | 13.00 | 13.00 | 13.50 | 13.00 | 12.60 | 11.90 | 12.00 | 12.80 | 11.80 |
| 1928 | 11.80 | 13.00 | 13.30 | 14.10 | 12.80 | 15.20 | 12.50 | 12.90 | 12.90 | 12.40 | 12.00 | 12.10 |
| 1929 | 12.90 | 13.40 | 14.00 | 14.60 | 14.20 | 13.10 | 12.80 | 12.30 | 11.90 | 12.00 | 11.70 | 11.40 |
| 1930 | 11.70 | 10.00 | 9.20 | 8.70 | 9.10 | 9.80 | 9.00 | 7.60 | 7.30 | 6.50 | 6.70 | 6.60 |
| 1931 | 7.10 | 7.60 | 7.70 | 7.80 | 8.10 | 7.30 | 6.20 | 5.90 | 5.40 | 5.00 | 4.70 | 3.80 |
| 1932 | 4.30 | 4.80 | 5.80 | --- | --- | --- | --- | --- | --- | --- | --- | --- |

MILK COWS

(Dollars per head)

| Year | Jan. | Feb. | Mar. | April | May | June | July | Aug. | Sept. | Oct. | Nov. | Dec. |
|------|------|------|------|-------|-----|------|------|------|-------|------|------|------|
| 1910 | 42.90 | 39.70 | 44.70 | 47.00 | 42.80 | 48.00 | 51.00 | 45.00 | 45.00 | 45.50 | 46.50 | 46.00 |
| 1911 | 51.00 | 49.00 | 49.10 | 48.00 | 50.00 | 52.00 | 50.00 | 48.00 | 48.30 | 47.00 | 49.00 | 49.70 |
| 1912 | 49.30 | 51.00 | 52.90 | 54.00 | 55.00 | 55.20 | 55.00 | 57.20 | 55.80 | 56.20 | 57.30 | 59.20 |
| 1913 | 59.00 | 58.20 | 63.50 | 66.40 | 67.80 | 66.90 | 62.20 | 67.00 | 67.00 | 69.00 | 66.60 | 60.70 |
| 1914 | 67.50 | 68.00 | 69.00 | 70.00 | 68.60 | 70.00 | 75.00 | 70.00 | 73.00 | 77.00 | 76.10 | 72.90 |
| 1915 | 76.00 | 76.00 | 75.40 | 72.20 | 72.30 | 73.00 | 73.60 | 72.00 | 73.50 | 74.10 | 78.50 | 77.10 |
| 1916 | 72.10 | 72.00 | 76.00 | 75.00 | 75.80 | 78.00 | 76.60 | 82.00 | 75.20 | 72.70 | 75.00 | 80.00 |
| 1917 | 79.00 | 80.20 | 83.40 | 84.00 | 88.50 | 92.00 | 90.00 | 88.80 | 90.20 | 87.40 | 90.50 | 91.50 |
| 1918 | 89.30 | 92.20 | 87.90 | 92.10 | 96.50 | 95.50 | 88.40 | 94.30 | 93.00 | 90.00 | 97.80 | 92.00 |
| 1919 | 93.00 | 91.30 | 92.00 | 90.20 | 96.00 | 95.00 | 91.00 | 96.00 | 96.40 | 91.70 | 86.50 | 92.80 |
| 1920 | 86.10 | 92.60 | 96.50 | 97.00 | 97.20 | 92.80 | 92.60 | 100.70 | 87.00 | 85.00 | 82.00 | 65.50 |
| 1921 | 69.00 | 64.00 | 69.00 | 68.00 | 63.00 | 62.50 | 63.00 | 63.00 | 60.00 | 62.00 | 60.00 | 58.00 |
| 1922 | 60.00 | 60.00 | 63.50 | 65.00 | 68.00 | 68.00 | 65.00 | 63.00 | 59.00 | 55.00 | 53.00 | 56.00 |
| 1923 | 56.00 | 59.20 | 56.70 | 55.50 | 58.50 | 60.00 | 58.00 | 57.20 | 60.00 | 57.50 | 53.00 | 53.10 |
| 1924 | 55.00 | 55.00 | 57.00 | 58.00 | 58.00 | 57.90 | 55.00 | 57.00 | 56.50 | 53.00 | 51.00 | 48.00 |
| 1925 | 50.00 | 48.00 | 54.40 | 53.50 | 53.40 | 52.60 | 52.50 | 56.60 | 51.50 | 51.60 | 54.00 | 52.80 |
| 1926 | 58.20 | 59.60 | 61.00 | 61.00 | 61.00 | 61.00 | 63.00 | 64.00 | 58.00 | 56.00 | 59.00 | 63.00 |
| 1927 | 61.00 | 64.00 | 68.00 | 71.00 | 70.00 | 69.00 | 69.00 | 69.00 | 69.00 | 72.00 | 74.00 | 72.00 |
| 1928 | 75.00 | 80.00 | 82.00 | 82.00 | 84.00 | 86.00 | 88.00 | 88.00 | 93.00 | 92.00 | 89.00 | 84.00 |
| 1929 | 86.00 | 86.00 | 87.00 | 88.00 | 91.00 | 92.00 | 93.00 | 93.00 | 92.00 | 87.00 | 89.00 | 84.00 |
| 1930 | 85.00 | 80.00 | 74.00 | 73.00 | 75.00 | 76.00 | 68.00 | 63.00 | 64.00 | 62.00 | 61.00 | 59.00 |
| 1931 | 58.00 | 56.00 | 56.00 | 56.00 | 52.00 | 50.00 | 49.00 | 48.00 | 45.00 | 42.00 | 40.00 | 38.00 |
| 1932 | 38.00 | 36.00 | 36.00 | --- | --- | --- | --- | --- | --- | --- | --- | --- |

ESTIMATED PRICE OF FARM PRODUCTS RECEIVED BY PRODUCERS
AS OF THE 15TH OF THE MONTH—Continued

### HORSES
(Dollars per head)

| Year | Jan. | Feb. | Mar. | April | May | June | July | Aug. | Sept. | Oct. | Nov. | Dec. |
|------|------|------|------|-------|-----|------|------|------|-------|------|------|------|
| 1910 | 134 | 125 | 136 | 139 | 112 | 133 | 128 | 128 | 125 | 122 | 125 | 115 |
| 1911 | 129 | 120 | 125 | 125 | 122 | 130 | 115 | 121 | 129 | 111 | 115 | 118 |
| 1912 | 105 | 110 | 115 | 118 | 119 | 119 | 117 | 118 | 123 | 115 | 124 | 122 |
| 1913 | 122 | 118 | 122 | 122 | 119 | 120 | 115 | 112 | 116 | 105 | 101 | 105 |
| 1914 | 110 | 108 | 103 | 98 | 102 | 102 | 110 | 105 | 105 | 105 | 103 | 110 |
| 1915 | 111 | 120 | 118 | 114 | 116 | 112 | 114 | 103 | 110 | 120 | 125 | 112 |
| 1916 | 115 | 114 | 119 | 115 | 118 | 113 | 115 | 118 | 119 | 112 | 120 | 125 |
| 1917 | 123 | 121 | 125 | 126 | 125 | 136 | 119 | 126 | 126 | 136 | 126 | 127 |
| 1918 | 137 | 135 | 135 | 134 | 129 | 125 | 124 | 126 | 122 | 124 | 123 | 122 |
| 1919 | 124 | 124 | 123 | 121 | 128 | 120 | 113 | 120 | 109 | 113 | 105 | 112 |
| 1920 | 105 | 125 | 117 | 112 | 112 | 106 | 110 | 119 | 103 | 104 | 95 | 80 |
| 1921 | 71 | 77 | 79 | 82 | 82 | 80 | 81 | 79 | 78 | 68 | 63 | 60 |
| 1922 | 67 | 72 | 72 | 78 | 78 | 80 | 78 | 74 | 67 | 67 | 53 | 52 |
| 1923 | 60 | 64 | 66 | 70 | 70 | 70 | 65 | 67 | 70 | 66 | 60 | 55 |
| 1924 | 54 | 55 | 57 | 58 | 60 | 59 | 60 | 60 | 62 | 58 | 60 | 55 |
| 1925 | 56 | 63 | 70 | 75 | 64 | 62 | 62 | 69 | 66 | 53 | 61 | 58 |
| 1926 | 68 | 67 | 67 | 72 | 71 | 75 | 69 | 71 | 61 | 61 | 59 | 61 |
| 1927 | 60 | 63 | 70 | 69 | 72 | 60 | 65 | 68 | 63 | 65 | 60 | 61 |
| 1928 | 60 | 61 | 60 | 63 | 51 | 65 | 65 | 62 | 61 | 61 | 61 | 56 |
| 1929 | 54 | 55 | 59 | 62 | 57 | 62 | 61 | 63 | 63 | 60 | 56 | 55 |
| 1930 | 55 | 54 | 55 | 57 | 53 | 54 | 46 | 48 | 47 | 46 | 44 | 49 |
| 1931 | 45 | 48 | 48 | 48 | 50 | 45 | 42 | 40 | 40 | 39 | 37 | 37 |
| 1932 | 37 | 37 | 40 | -- | -- | -- | -- | -- | -- | -- | -- | -- |

### CHICKENS
(Cents per pound)

| Year | Jan. | Feb. | Mar. | April | May | June | July | Aug. | Sept. | Oct. | Nov. | Dec. |
|------|------|------|------|-------|-----|------|------|------|-------|------|------|------|
| 1910 | 13.0 | 13.3 | 13.5 | 13.4 | 14.1 | 14.6 | 15.0 | 15.0 | 13.6 | 13.5 | 13.2 | 12. |
| 1911 | 12.8 | 13.2 | 13.1 | 12.5 | 12.4 | 13.1 | 13.8 | 14.0 | 13.7 | 13.4 | 12.3 | 12. |
| 1912 | 12.6 | 12.8 | 13.1 | 13.0 | 12.8 | 13.1 | 13.2 | 13.2 | 12.7 | 12.6 | 12.6 | 12. |
| 1913 | 13.0 | 13.1 | 13.2 | 13.1 | 12.4 | 12.8 | 13.4 | 14.1 | 13.0 | 12.2 | 11.9 | 12. |
| 1914 | 11.3 | 12.7 | 12.2 | 12.2 | 12.6 | 12.3 | 15.0 | 12.5 | 13.0 | 12.0 | 11.4 | 10. |
| 1915 | 12.0 | 11.9 | 12.3 | 12.1 | 12.6 | 13.2 | 10.8 | 11.7 | 10.6 | 11.4 | 12.2 | 11. |
| 1916 | 11.5 | 11.6 | 11.8 | 11.6 | 13.0 | 12.8 | 12.6 | 13.3 | 13.1 | 12.1 | 12.0 | 11. |
| 1917 | 12.7 | 13.2 | 14.0 | 15.0 | 16.3 | 17.2 | 14.6 | 15.5 | 16.5 | 17.7 | 15.5 | 16. |
| 1918 | 16.4 | 19.5 | 17.9 | 19.3 | 20.0 | 21.0 | 21.5 | 22.0 | 22.1 | 21.0 | 19.2 | 17. |
| 1919 | 17.6 | 18.0 | 20.5 | 22.5 | 24.0 | 22.5 | 23.0 | 25.0 | 33.0 | 22.0 | 20.0 | 20. |
| 1920 | 20.0 | 22.0 | 23.8 | 24.6 | 25.4 | 25.1 | 26.5 | 28.0 | 22.0 | 22.0 | 21.0 | 17. |
| 1921 | 19.0 | 19.0 | 20.0 | 20.0 | 19.0 | 19.0 | 21.0 | 21.0 | 18.0 | 17.0 | 17.0 | 16. |
| 1922 | 17.0 | 16.0 | 17.0 | 18.0 | 18.0 | 18.0 | 17.0 | 17.0 | 16.0 | 16.0 | 15.0 | 14. |
| 1923 | 15.7 | 15.0 | 16.1 | 16.0 | 16.0 | 16.9 | 19.1 | 18.0 | 17.0 | 17.4 | 15.5 | 14. |
| 1924 | 15.3 | 15.2 | 16.3 | 17.0 | 18.0 | 17.3 | 19.3 | 18.6 | 17.8 | 15.2 | 15.4 | 14. |
| 1925 | 16.3 | 14.8 | 17.8 | 16.9 | 17.9 | 18.4 | 19.0 | 20.1 | 17.8 | 16.8 | 17.6 | 17. |
| 1926 | 18.5 | 18.1 | 19.6 | 21.3 | 20.3 | 20.3 | 21.7 | 20.7 | 19.4 | 18.5 | 18.4 | 18. |
| 1927 | 18.4 | 19.2 | 18.6 | 20.4 | 19.7 | 17.4 | 19.9 | 18.5 | 19.0 | 18.3 | 18.4 | 18. |
| 1928 | 17.7 | 17.5 | 17.7 | 18.5 | 20.2 | 18.7 | 20.8 | 18.9 | 20.0 | 19.0 | 19.3 | 18. |
| 1929 | 18.7 | 19.3 | 19.4 | 19.9 | 20.6 | 21.2 | 21.0 | 21.0 | 20.2 | 18.8 | 18.4 | 16. |
| 1930 | 17.2 | 17.2 | 18.0 | 18.6 | 18.0 | 17.1 | 14.9 | 15.2 | 16.5 | 15.2 | 14.0 | 14. |
| 1931 | 13.8 | 13.2 | 14.1 | 14.9 | 13.8 | 13.3 | 14.6 | 14.0 | 13.5 | 12.8 | 12.9 | 12. |
| 1932 | 12.0 | 11.1 | 11.0 | --- | --- | --- | --- | --- | --- | -- | --- | - |

## ESTIMATED PRICE OF FARM PRODUCTS RECEIVED BY PRODUCERS
### AS OF THE 15TH OF THE MONTH—Continued

#### BUTTER
(Cents per pound)

| ear | Jan. | Feb. | Mar. | April | May | June | July | Aug. | Sept. | Oct. | Nov. | Dec. |
|---|---|---|---|---|---|---|---|---|---|---|---|---|
| 0_____ | 33 | 33 | 32 | 28 | 28 | 28 | 28 | 30 | 31 | 32 | 32 | 32 |
| 1_____ | 32 | 28 | 27 | 26 | 24 | 24 | 24 | 25 | 27 | 28 | 30 | 32 |
| 2_____ | 33 | 32 | 30 | 29 | 28 | 27 | 26 | 27 | 28 | 30 | 32 | 31 |
| 3_____ | 31 | 30 | 30 | 28 | 27 | 28 | 28 | 28 | 29 | 31 | 32 | 31 |
| 4_____ | 31 | 30 | 28 | 28 | 26 | 25 | 25 | 26 | 29 | 30 | 31 | 32 |
| 5_____ | 32 | 30 | 28 | 27 | 26 | 26 | 24 | 26 | 26 | 28 | 29 | 30 |
| 6_____ | 30 | 28 | 28 | 28 | 28 | 27 | 27 | 28 | 30 | 32 | 34 | 36 |
| 7_____ | 36 | 34 | 34 | 36 | 38 | 36 | 36 | 38 | 41 | 43 | 44 | 46 |
| 8_____ | 46 | 45 | 44 | 42 | 40 | 40 | 40 | 42 | 45 | 51 | 56 | 58 |
| 9_____ | 58 | 50 | 46· | 52 | 51 | 48 | 50 | 52 | 54 | 57 | 62 | 66 |
| 0_____ | 63 | 56 | 57 | 59 | 56 | 52 | 53 | 54 | 56 | 57 | 58 | 53 |
| 1_____ | 46 | 42 | 40 | 40 | 34 | 27 | 29 | 34 | 37 | 40 | 42 | 39 |
| 2_____ | 32 | 28 | 29 | 30 | 30 | 29 | 29 | 30 | 32 | 36 | 42 | 46 |
| 3_____ | 45 | 44 | 44 | 42 | 41 | 40 | 38 | 38 | 41 | 43 | 45 | 45 |
| 4_____ | 45 | 44 | 42 | 40 | 36 | 35 | 38 | 36 | 33 | 38 | 36 | 40 |
| 5_____ | 40 | 35 | 37 | 36 | 37 | 37 | 38 | 40 | 41 | 43 | 49 | 45 |
| 6_____ | 50 | 41 | 40 | 42 | 40 | 41 | 39 | 39 | 42 | 42 | 43 | 46 |
| 7_____ | 45 | 44 | 45 | 45 | 43 | 41 | 40 | 40 | 42 | 45 | 44 | 46 |
| 8_____ | 47 | 45 | 45 | 45 | 43 | 43 | 42 | 43 | 44 | 46 | 46 | 47 |
| 9_____ | 47 | 46 | 46 | 45 | 45 | 44 | 43 | 44 | 45 | 45 | 42 | 42 |
| 0_____ | 38 | 37 | 37 | 37 | 39 | 33 | 31 | 37 | 40 | 38 | 37 | 33 |
| 1_____ | 29 | 28 | 29 | 29 | 26 | 25 | 24 | 27 | 29 | 33 | 29 | 28 |
| 2_____ | 23. | 22 | 22 | -- | -- | -- | -- | -- | -- | -- | -- | -- |

#### EGGS
(Cents per dozen)

| ear | Jan. | Feb. | Mar. | April | May | June | July | Aug. | Sept. | Oct. | Nov. | Dec. |
|---|---|---|---|---|---|---|---|---|---|---|---|---|
| 0_____ | 36 | 30 | 24 | 22 | 22 | 24 | 24 | 26 | 28 | 31 | 33 | 35 |
| 1_____ | 34 | 28 | 22 | 18 | 18 | 18 | 20 | 22 | 24 | 27 | 31 | 36 |
| 2_____ | 36 | 30 | 26 | 22 | 20 | 20 | 21 | 23 | 25 | 29 | 33 | 34 |
| 3_____ | 32 | 27 | 22 | 17 | 15 | 17 | 19 | 21 | 22 | 29 | 35 | 37 |
| 4_____ | 38 | 26 | 20 | 16 | 16 | 17 | 20 | 19 | 24 | 24 | 30 | 33 |
| 5_____ | 32 | 24 | 18 | 16 | 15 | 17 | 17 | 20 | 21 | 27 | 33 | 36 |
| 6_____ | 32 | 30 | 16 | 15 | 17 | 20 | 20 | 22 | 27 | 30 | 40 | 45 |
| 7_____ | 40 | 37 | 25 | 27 | 29 | 31 | 29 | 34 | 40 | 40 | 45 | 50 |
| 8_____ | 46 | 49 | 30 | 29 | 29 | 30 | 32 | 39 | 41 | 47 | 54 | 62 |
| 9_____ | 59 | 36 | 35 | 33 | 36 | 35 | 36 | 42 | 45 | 53 | 62 | 72 |
| _____ | 60 | 45 | 38 | 36 | 37 | 35 | 39 | 47 | 50 | 56 | 60 | 72 |
| _____ | 59 | 30 | 25 | 20 | 17 | 19 | 25 | 25 | 25 | 38 | 48 | 52 |
| _____ | 34 | 29 | 19 | 17 | 22 | 19 | 19 | 21 | 25 | 33 | 44 | 48 |
| _____ | 37 | 28 | 20 | 19 | 19 | 19 | 20 | 25 | 31 | 37 | 46 | 48 |
| _____ | 39 | 33 | 18 | 19 | 20 | 21 | 23 | 26 | 32 | 36 | 45 | 51 |
| _____ | 53 | 32 | 23 | 24 | 23 | 25 | 27 | 33 | 33 | 37 | 50 | 48 |
| _____ | 36 | 27 | 21 | 23 | 23 | 23 | 25 | 27 | 30 | 37 | 47 | 50 |
| _____ | 37 | 28 | 20 | 19 | 18 | 18 | 21 | 23 | 28 | 36 | 43 | 43 |
| _____ | 39 | 26 | 22 | 20 | 22 | 22 | 24 | 28 | 30 | 35 | 43 | 48 |
| _____ | 35 | 32 | 28 | 22 | 21 | 22 | 25 | 28 | 31 | 37 | 46 | 49 |
| _____ | 35 | 33 | 20 | 20 | 19 | 18 | 18 | 20 | 25 | 29 | 34 | 32 |
| _____ | 21 | 14 | 15.5 | 5.6 | 11.5 | 12.6 | 14.5 | 17.8 | 18.7 | 23.0 | 28.0 | 31.0 |
| _____ | 19.0 | 14.0 | 9.0 | --- | --- | --- | --- | --- | --- | --- | --- | --- |

ESTIMATED PRICE OF FARM PRODUCTS RECEIVED BY PRODUCERS
AS OF THE 15TH OF THE MONTH—Continued

## ALFALFA
(Dollars per ton)

| Year | Jan. | Feb. | Mar. | April | May | June | July | Aug. | Sept. | Oct. | Nov. | De |
|---|---|---|---|---|---|---|---|---|---|---|---|---|
| 1910 | --- | --- | --- | --- | --- | --- | --- | --- | --- | --- | --- | |
| 1911 | --- | --- | --- | --- | --- | --- | --- | --- | --- | --- | --- | |
| 1912 | --- | --- | --- | --- | --- | --- | --- | --- | --- | --- | --- | |
| 1913 | --- | --- | --- | --- | --- | --- | --- | --- | --- | --- | --- | |
| 1914 | --- | --- | --- | --- | --- | --- | --- | --- | --- | 6.60 | 7.70 | 7 |
| 1915 | 8.50 | 7.80 | 8.30 | 8.50 | 9.00 | 7.80 | 7.70 | 7.40 | 7.50 | 7.50 | 8.70 | 8 |
| 1916 | 9.00 | 8.80 | 9.50 | 9.70 | 10.50 | 11.50 | 10.20 | 10.50 | 9.60 | 9.70 | 9.85 | 11 |
| 1917 | 12.10 | 12.60 | 13.20 | 14.60 | 20.10 | 19.30 | 13.60 | 14.80 | 15.00 | 15.30 | 17.40 | 18 |
| 1918 | 18.20 | 18.20 | 16.80 | 15.60 | 15.50 | 14.50 | 14.30 | 15.26 | 17.00 | 17.20 | 17.20 | 17 |
| 1919 | 17.00 | 18.20 | 20.50 | 21.00 | 22.70 | 20.10 | 18.20 | 18.00 | 18.10 | 18.10 | 17.50 | 19 |
| 1920 | 19.50 | 19.90 | 19.00 | 20.10 | 22.60 | 21.60 | 18.30 | 17.20 | 14.50 | 14.00 | 12.50 | 11 |
| 1921 | 8.50 | 8.00 | 8.80 | 8.50 | 8.75 | 8.50 | 6.00 | 5.50 | 5.00 | 5.70 | 5.00 | 4 |
| 1922 | 4.40 | 6.50 | 7.00 | 7.50 | 7.50 | 7.00 | 7.00 | 9.00 | 9.80 | 9.80 | 10.40 | 11 |
| 1923 | 12.30 | 12.20 | 13.40 | 13.80 | 16.00 | 14.60 | 12.00 | 11.00 | 10.10 | 10.00 | 12.40 | 11 |
| 1924 | 11.00 | 11.50 | 11.00 | 11.00 | 11.30 | 11.00 | 10.00 | 10.30 | 11.00 | 11.50 | 11.70 | 11 |
| 1925 | 12.50 | 12.80 | 12.90 | 11.40 | 12.60 | 11.70 | 12.20 | 12.60 | 12.40 | 12.00 | 12.60 | 11 |
| 1926 | 13.30 | 11.80 | 11.30 | 12.10 | 10.80 | 10.10 | 9.60 | 9.80 | 9.40 | 9.70 | 10.00 | 10 |
| 1927 | 9.00 | 8.30 | 8.50 | 9.00 | 8.70 | 9.50 | 8.50 | 9.00 | 9.10 | 9.50 | 9.60 | 9 |
| 1928 | 9.10 | 9.00 | 10.00 | 10.20 | 11.90 | 11.20 | 10.20 | 10.40 | 11.40 | 12.30 | 12.30 | 11 |
| 1929 | 13.80 | 14.30 | 14.80 | 14.60 | 14.50 | 13.50 | 12.40 | 11.70 | 12.30 | 12.10 | 12.10 | 11 |
| 1930 | 11.60 | 11.30 | 10.30 | 9.70 | 9.90 | 9.50 | 9.20 | 9.00 | 9.80 | 10.00 | 9.20 | 9 |
| 1931 | 9.00 | 8.20 | 7.80 | 8.00 | 8.20 | 7.60 | 6.80 | 8.10 | 7.40 | 7.20 | 8.00 | 8 |
| 1932 | 8.60 | 8.60 | 8.70 | --- | --- | --- | --- | --- | --- | --- | --- | |

## BEANS, DRY
(Dollars per 100 pounds)

| Year | Jan. | Feb. | Mar. | April | May | June | July | Aug. | Sept. | Oct. | Nov. |
|---|---|---|---|---|---|---|---|---|---|---|---|
| 1910 | --- | --- | --- | --- | --- | --- | --- | --- | 4.32 | 4.50 | 4.33 |
| 1911 | 4.15 | 5.08 | 4.93 | 4.77 | 4.87 | 5.07 | 5.08 | 5.27 | 5.42 | 4.72 | 5.13 |
| 1912 | 4.60 | 4.43 | 4.42 | 4.82 | 4.65 | 4.25 | 4.23 | 3.92 | 3.83 | 3.93 | 3.18 |
| 1913 | 3.50 | 3.58 | 2.88 | 3.00 | 2.80 | 3.33 | 3.33 | 2.92 | 3.17 | 4.08 | 4.17 |
| 1914 | 3.58 | 3.42 | 3.50 | 3.83 | 3.75 | 3.75 | 3.50 | 4.17 | 4.90 | 3.83 | 3.33 |
| 1915 | 3.58 | 4.38 | 4.43 | 3.87 | 4.40 | 4.83 | 3.75 | 3.83 | 3.33 | 3.83 | 3.80 |
| 1916 | 4.73 | 4.78 | 4.27 | 4.87 | 5.17 | 5.17 | 5.83 | 5.83 | 7.00 | 5.00 | 5.83 |
| 1917 | 7.50 | 7.50 | 7.92 | 9.00 | 13.67 | 14.33 | 13.17 | 10.50 | 9.67 | 8.67 | 8.00 |
| 1918 | 8.00 | 8.17 | 8.33 | 8.33 | 8.67 | 8.67 | 8.58 | 7.92 | 8.00 | 7.33 | 7.33 |
| 1919 | 6.67 | 5.92 | 5.33 | 5.00 | 5.00 | 5.33 | 5.33 | 5.83 | 6.17 | 5.50 | 5.83 |
| 1920 | 6.42 | 6.33 | 5.83 | 5.92 | 6.17 | 6.17 | 6.17 | 6.17 | 6.00 | 5.50 | 5.25 |
| 1921 | 3.00 | 3.67 | 3.75 | 4.00 | 3.67 | 4.33 | 4.50 | 4.50 | 4.50 | 4.50 | 4.50 |
| 1922 | 4.50 | 4.83 | 5.50 | 5.58 | 5.83 | 6.00 | 5.83 | 5.42 | 5.33 | 5.42 | 7.33 |
| 1923 | 7.50 | 8.67 | 8.33 | 8.33 | 8.08 | 8.33 | 7.67 | 7.83 | 6.57 | 7.00 | 6.17 |
| 1924 | 5.00 | 4.92 | 4.92 | 4.50 | 4.33 | 4.50 | 4.33 | 4.75 | 5.00 | 5.67 | 5.17 |
| 1925 | 5.33 | 5.83 | 6.00 | 6.33 | 6.83 | 6.05 | 6.33 | 6.50 | 4.75 | 4.98 | 4.00 |
| 1926 | 3.70 | 3.98 | 3.80 | 3.90 | 4.20 | 4.50 | 5.00 | 4.70 | 4.30 | 4.40 | 4.80 |
| 1927 | 4.90 | 4.90 | 5.00 | 5.50 | 5.60 | 5.80 | 5.90 | 6.10 | 6.15 | 5.10 | 4.40 |
| 1928 | 4.95 | 5.40 | 5.60 | 6.10 | 6.10 | 6.30 | 6.20 | 5.40 | 4.75 | 5.00 | 5.20 |
| 1929 | 5.80 | 5.95 | 5.90 | 6.25 | 6.05 | 6.20 | 6.25 | 6.25 | 6.25 | 5.30 | 4.90 |
| 1930 | 4.30 | 4.20 | 4.30 | 4.15 | 4.30 | 4.30 | 4.00 | 4.25 | 4.40 | 3.20 | 2.45 |
| 1931 | 2.15 | 2.15 | 2.10 | 1.95 | 1.80 | 1.65 | 1.60 | 1.50 | 1.50 | 1.30 | 1.95 |
| 1932 | 1.45 | 1.25 | 1.20 | 1.25 | --- | --- | --- | --- | --- | --- | --- |

COLORADO: FARM VALUE, GROSS INCOME AND CASH INCOME FROM FARM PRODUCTION,
BY COMMODITIES, 1925-1927
In Thousands of Dollars

CROPS

| COMMODITIES | 1925 | | | 1926 | | | 1927 | | |
|---|---|---|---|---|---|---|---|---|---|
| | Farm Value | Gross Income | Cash Income | Farm Value | Gross Income | Cash Income | Farm Value | Gross Income | Cash Income |
| Corn | 14,382 | 3,325 | 3,320 | 7,437 | 1,689 | 1,684 | 14,727 | 3,793 | 3,788 |
| Wheat | 20,683 | 16,252 | 16,114 | 20,296 | 16,475 | 16,367 | 21,922 | 17,266 | 17,157 |
| Oats | 2,831 | 991 | 991 | 2,153 | 667 | 667 | 2,795 | 783 | 783 |
| Barley | 5,252 | 1,471 | 1,471 | 3,405 | 1,021 | 1,021 | 5,412 | 1,624 | 1,624 |
| Rye | 629 | 390 | 390 | 694 | 440 | 440 | 575 | 343 | 343 |
| Flaxseed | 7 | 4 | 4 | ---- | ---- | ---- | ---- | ---- | ---- |
| Grain sorghums | 1,921 | 43 | 43 | 681 | 25 | 25 | 2,442 | 134 | 134 |
| Emmer and Speltz | 73 | ---- | ---- | 45 | ---- | ---- | 79 | ---- | ---- |
| Hay | 34,328 | 8,579 | 8,579 | 27,984 | 6,996 | 6,996 | 28,250 | 7,067 | 7,067 |
| Sweet sorghum forage | 1,344 | 134 | 134 | 1,132 | 115 | 115 | 1,258 | 128 | 128 |
| Cloverseed, sweet* | 228 | 200 | 200 | 292 | 256 | 256 | 248 | 225 | 225 |
| Alfalfa seed | 235 | 192 | 192 | 137 | 99 | 99 | 108 | 66 | 66 |
| Dry edible beans | 5,533 | 4,645 | 4,621 | 3,552 | 2,664 | 2,638 | 4,452 | 3,496 | 3,468 |
| Broomcorn | 266 | 266 | 266 | 282 | 282 | 282 | 528 | 528 | 528 |
| Potatoes, white | 18,860 | 14,641 | 14,210 | 13,911 | 11,315 | 11,006 | 10,512 | 7,975 | 7,747 |
| Truck crops | 9,625 | 9,625 | 9,167 | 7,775 | 7,775 | 7,405 | 8,644 | 8,644 | 8,232 |
| Apples | 4,160 | 4,014 | 3,786 | 2,686 | 2,552 | 2,355 | 3,136 | 3,042 | 2,842 |
| Peaches | 855 | 855 | 821 | 1,074 | 1,042 | 1,005 | 1,070 | 1,070 | 1,049 |
| Pears | 586 | 569 | 557 | 367 | 352 | 344 | 672 | 652 | 640 |
| Plums (prunes), cherries and apricots | 342 | 342 | 328 | 430 | 417 | 402 | 428 | 428 | 420 |
| Grapes | 22 | 21 | 1 | 12 | 12 | 3 | 17 | 17 | 4 |
| Strawberries | 61 | 61 | 57 | 52 | 52 | 48 | 63 | 63 | 60 |
| Small fruits | 64 | 64 | 61 | 55 | 55 | 52 | 66 | 66 | 64 |
| Sugar beets, for sugar | 9,815 | 9,815 | 9,815 | 23,050 | 23,050 | 23,050 | 21,758 | 21,758 | 21,758 |
| Forest products | 327 | 327 | 177 | 318 | 318 | 172 | 309 | 309 | 167 |
| Farm gardens | 1,810 | 1,810 | ---- | 1,706 | 1,706 | ---- | 1,596 | 1,596 | ---- |
| Nursery products | 83 | 83 | 83 | 83 | 83 | 83 | 83 | 83 | 83 |
| Greenhouse products | 1,062 | 1,062 | 1,062 | 1,062 | 1,062 | 1,062 | 1,062 | 1,062 | 1,062 |
| Total | 135,384 | 79,781 | 76,450 | 120,671 | 80,520 | 77,577 | 132,212 | 82,218 | 79,439 |

LIVESTOCK AND LIVESTOCK PRODUCTS

| | | | | | | | | | |
|---|---|---|---|---|---|---|---|---|---|
| Cattle and calves | 21,808 | 25,729 | 25,146 | 21,729 | 21,421 | 20,787 | 24,469 | 30,264 | 29,573 |
| Hogs | 14,466 | 15,332 | 13,414 | 13,492 | 13,667 | 11,587 | 12,053 | 11,067 | 9,473 |
| Sheep and lambs | 9,738 | 9,965 | 9,807 | 8,826 | 14,486 | 14,340 | 9,029 | 1,374 | 1,234 |
| Horses | 1,320 | 713 | 713 | 1,105 | 734 | 734 | 915 | 580 | 580 |
| Mules | 348 | 226 | 226 | 284 | 300 | 300 | 284 | 292 | 292 |
| Chickens | 3,588 | 3,487 | 1,771 | 4,288 | 4,053 | 2,314 | 4,146 | 4,092 | 2,120 |
| Eggs (chicken) | 6,850 | 6,550 | 4,300 | 6,967 | 6,664 | 4,660 | 6,240 | 5,990 | 4,014 |
| Milk | 16,776 | 16,200 | 12,276 | 19,475 | 18,867 | 14,725 | 22,021 | 21,356 | 17,214 |
| Wool | 2,676 | 2,676 | 2,676 | 2,632 | 2,632 | 2,632 | 2,273 | 2,273 | 2,273 |
| Honey | 270 | 270 | 231 | 289 | 289 | 253 | 345 | 345 | 310 |
| Beeswax | 7 | 7 | 7 | 8 | 8 | 8 | 11 | 11 | 11 |
| Total | 77,847 | 81,155 | 70,567 | 79,095 | 83,121 | 72,340 | 81,786 | 77,644 | 67,094 |
| Grand Total | ---- | 160,936 | 147,017 | ---- | 163,641 | 149,917 | ---- | 159,862 | 146,533 |

*Cloverseed (red and alsike) included in sweet cloverseed.

Farm value relates to the evaluation of the total outturn of the given commodity, irrespective of use, whether sold, consumed by the farm family, or consumed in the production of further farm products on the farm where grown.

Cash income relates to the value of quantities actually sold off the farms of the State where these were produced.

Gross income relates to cash income plus the value of the products consumed in the farm household on the farm where the commodities were produced.

The farm value, gross income, and cash income of crops are credited to the year in which the commodities were produced, evaluated at prices received during the marketing season for the particular crop.

Farm value, gross income, and cash income from livestock production are computed on a calendar-year basis, evaluated at average prices for the calendar year.

## COLORADO: FARM VALUE, GROSS INCOME AND CASH INCOME FROM FARM PRODUCTION, BY COMMODITIES, 1928-1930
### In Thousands of Dollars

### CROPS

| COMMODITIES | 1928 | | | 1929 (Revised) | | | 1930 (Preliminary) | | |
|---|---|---|---|---|---|---|---|---|---|
| | Farm Value | Gross Income | Cash Income | Farm Value | Gross Income | Cash Income | Farm Value | Gross Income | Cash Income |
| Corn | 14,581 | 4,035 | 4,029 | 16,671 | 4,118 | 4,118 | 24,161 | 7,079 | 7,05( |
| Wheat | 15,779 | 12,260 | 12,175 | 16,632 | 12,973 | 12,873 | 12,420 | 9,315 | 9,24( |
| Oats | 2,872 | 804 | 804 | 2,826 | 706 | 706 | 2,176 | 653 | 65: |
| Barley | 6,958 | 2,505 | 2,505 | 5,910 | 1,773 | 1,773 | 4,919 | 1,722 | 1,72: |
| Rye | 562 | 337 | 337 | 364 | 236 | 236 | 233 | 149 | 14( |
| Grain sorghums | 1,640 | 149 | 149 | 1,470 | 193 | 193 | 1,170 | 246 | 24( |
| Emmer and speltz | 86 | ---- | ---- | 98 | ---- | ---- | 79 | ---- | --- |
| Hay | 31,640 | 9,498 | 9,498 | 29,475 | 7,369 | 7,369 | 27,183 | 8,155 | 8,15( |
| Sweet sorghum forage | 1,230 | 123 | 123 | 1,512 | 150 | 150 | 1,430 | 142 | 14: |
| Popcorn | ---- | ---- | ---- | 44 | 44 | 44 | 59 | 59 | 5( |
| Cloverseed (red and alsike) | 78 | 62 | 62 | 140 | 128 | 128 | 99 | 89 | 8( |
| Cloverseed, sweet | 92 | 74 | 74 | 34 | 25 | 25 | 68 | 50 | 5( |
| Alfalfa seed | 274 | 225 | 225 | 525 | 471 | 471 | 542 | 505 | 50( |
| Dry edible beans | 4,365 | 3,387 | 3,357 | 6,026 | 5,110 | 5,086 | 5,832 | 5,371 | 5,35( |
| Broomcorn | 799 | 799 | 799 | 1,030 | 1,030 | 1,030 | 530 | 530 | 53( |
| Potatoes, white | 6,112 | 3,997 | 3,818 | 16,137 | 13,394 | 12,974 | 10,488 | 8,642 | 8,40: |
| Truck crops | 8,082 | 8,082 | 7,697 | 9,633 | 9,633 | 9,071 | 8,853 | 8,853 | 8,42( |
| Apples | 2,688 | 2,567 | 2,371 | 2,185 | 2,109 | 1,932 | 901 | 874 | 76( |
| Peaches | 780 | 756 | 731 | 1,382 | 1,341 | 1,307 | 1,141 | 1,118 | 1,09( |
| Pears | 194 | 188 | 178 | 900 | 872 | 860 | 190 | 184 | 18( |
| Plums (prunes) | 78 | 76 | 73 | 145 | 141 | 137 | 118 | 116 | 11( |
| Grapes | 17 | 16 | 5 | 18 | 17 | 6 | 8 | 8 | |
| Apricots | 36 | 36 | 35 | 48 | 48 | 47 | 24 | 24 | 2 |
| Cherries | 234 | 234 | 210 | 612 | 612 | 550 | 315 | 315 | 27 |
| Strawberries | 39 | 39 | 36 | 39 | 39 | 36 | 39 | 39 | 3 |
| Small fruits | 41 | 41 | 39 | 41 | 41 | 39 | 41 | 41 | 3 |
| Sugar beets, for sugar | 16,687 | 16,687 | 16,687 | 18,106 | 18,106 | 18,106 | 22,873 | 22,873 | 22,87 |
| Forest products | 310 | 310 | 167 | 321 | 321 | 173 | 299 | 299 | 16 |
| Farm gardens | 1,820 | 1,820 | ---- | 1,809 | 1,809 | ---- | 1,380 | 1,380 | --- |
| Nursery products | 83 | 83 | 83 | 83 | 83 | 83 | 83 | 83 | 8 |
| Greenhouse products | 1,062 | 1,062 | 1,062 | 1,062 | 1,062 | 1,062 | 1,062 | 1,062 | 1,06 |
| Total | 119,219 | 70,252 | 67,329 | 135,278 | 83,954 | 80,585 | 128,716 | 79,976 | |
| Cattle and calves | 31,189 | 31,040 | 30,371 | 30,510 | 29,558 | 28,943 | 25,403 | 23,201 | 22,56 |
| Hogs | 11,900 | 11,813 | 10,312 | 13,363 | 14,063 | 12,228 | 12,167 | 11,962 | 10,29 |
| Sheep and lambs | 10,273 | 9,720 | 9,573 | 10,407 | 5,539 | 5,394 | 7,903 | 11,739 | 11,52 |
| Horses | 923 | 428 | 428 | 882 | 348 | 348 | 806 | 318 | 31 |
| Mules | 296 | 234 | 234 | 327 | 206 | 206 | 262 | 207 | 20 |
| Chickens | 4,184 | 4,253 | 2,486 | 4,686 | 4,412 | 2,477 | 3,416 | 3,508 | 1,81 |
| Eggs (chickens) | 7,245 | 6,952 | 4,972 | 8,155 | 7,829 | 5,825 | 6,797 | 6,566 | 4,83 |
| Milk | 21,552 | 20,738 | 16,558 | 22,729 | 21,929 | 17,413 | 17,395 | 16,790 | 13,30 |
| Wool | 3,285 | 3,285 | 3,285 | 2,894 | 2,894 | 2,894 | 2,160 | 2,160 | 2,16 |
| Honey | 251 | 251 | 219 | 323 | 323 | 291 | 247 | 247 | 21 |
| Beeswax | 9 | 9 | 9 | 10 | 10 | 10 | 6 | 6 | |
| Total | 91,107 | 88,723 | 78,447 | 94,286 | 87,111 | 76,029 | 76,562 | 76,704 | |
| Grand Total | ---- | 158,975 | 145,776 | ---- | 171,065 | 156,614 | ---- | 156,680 | 1 |

(See explanatory footnotes on preceding page.)

# Colorado Livestock

THE estimated number of livestock in Colorado on January 1, 1932, compared with January 1, 1931, shows an increase in swine, range cattle, milk cows, sheep and lambs on feed, no change in the number of farm and range sheep, and a decreased number of horses, mules, and cattle on feed. Colorado livestock on January 1, 1932, were valued at $60,656,000, compared with $97,617,000 on January 1, 1931, and $130,515,000 on January 1, 1930.

When the numbers of all livestock are combined into units, which allows for difference in size and feed requirements among the several species, the total number of animal units on January 1, 1932, was about 1 per cent more than on January 1, 1931. In spite of increased numbers of all livestock declining prices have drastically reduced inventory values. Feed supplies are very limited. On May 1, 1932, farm hay stocks were 5 per cent of the total 1931 production, compared with 12.5 per cent a year ago, and 11 per cent of the five-year (1927-1931) average.

Cattle—Cattle numbers remain unchanged from a year ago and are estimated at 1,541,000 head. This is a reduction of 216,000 head from 1,757,000 on hand January 1, 1920. Colorado cattle and calves were valued at $34,670,000 on January 1, 1932, compared with $58,324,000 on January 1, 1931, and $73,985,000 on January 1, 1930. There has been a gradual increase in milk cow numbers since 1920 and on January 1, 1932, it was estimated there were 266,000 cows and heifers two years old and over being kept for milk. This compares with 260,000 on January 1, 1931, and is an increase of 64,000 over the 202,000 head on farms January 1, 1920. Beef cattle showed a slight decrease, with a marked reduction from the year before in the number of cattle and calves on feed on January 1, 1932. Colorado has 1,135,000 beef cattle and calves. The 1931 marketings of cattle and calves were about 583,000, of which 529,000 were cattle and 54,000 were calves. In 1930, 458,000 cattle and 50,000 calves were marketed, and in 1929, 529,000 cattle and 55,000 calves.

Sheep—The Colorado sheep population on January 1, 1932, was 3,361,000 head, compared with 3,351,000 sheep and lambs on hand January 1, 1931, and 3,750,000 on January 1, 1930. Colorado sheep and lambs on January 1, 1932, were valued at $10,575,000, compared with $18,659,000 the previous year and $33,843,000 on January 1, 1930. The number of farm and range sheep was estimated at 1,801,000 head on January 1, 1932, or no change from a year earlier, and compares with 1,715,000 on hand January 1, 1930. Stock sheep have shown a steady increase since 1922, when Colorado had 900,000 head. The 1931 lamb crop was 1,230,000 head, compared with 1,245,000 in 1930 and 1,033,000 in 1929. The numbers of lambs saved, per one hundred ewes, one year old and over, on hand January 1, was 82 in 1931 compared with 85 in 1930 and 78 in 1929. Colorado had 1,560,000 sheep and lambs on feed on January 1, 1932. This compares with 1,550,000 on January 1, 1931, and 2,035,000 on January 1, 1930, which was the largest number on record.

Wool—Colorado wool clip in 1931 was estimated at 13,541,000 pounds; in 1930 was 13,446,000 pounds. Fleeces in 1931 averaged 7.8 pounds and in 1930, 8.1 pounds.

Hogs—Colorado hogs, including pigs, were estimated at 624,000 head on January 1, 1932, compared with 520,000 on January 1, 1931, and 495,000 on January 1, 1930. On January 1, 1932, hogs were valued at $3,271,000, compared with $5,769,000 the previous year and $5,943,000 on January 1, 1930. Marketings of hogs in 1931 amounted to 380,000 head compared with 391,000 head in 1930, and 451,000 head in 1929. The June, 1931, pig survey indicated that about 118.1 per cent as many sows farrowed in the spring of 1931 as the previous spring, with an average of 5.5 pigs saved per litter, compared with 5.6 pigs per litter in the spring of 1930, making the total pig crop 116.7 per cent of the spring crop in 1930. The pig survey in the fall of 1931, showed that 144.5 per cent as many sows were farrowed as in the fall of 1930, with an average of 5.8 pigs per litter, or the same as the fall of 1930. This indicates that 144 per cent as many pigs were saved in the fall of 1931 as in the fall of 1930. The survey also indicated that the number of sows bred for next spring's farrowing was 126.6 per cent of the number farrowed in the spring of 1931.

**Horses**—There has been a gradual reduction in the number of work stock in Colorado, and it is estimated that 324,000 horses and colts were on farms on January 1, 1932, compared with 331,000 on January 1, 1931, and 338,000 on January 1, 1930. There were 421,000 horses and colts on Colorado farms January 1, 1920. January 1, 1932, horses and colts were valued at $11,008,000 compared with $13,420,000 on January 1, 1931; $15,023,000 on January 1, 1930, and $33,375,000 on January 1, 1920.

## CATTLE AND SHEEP FEEDING

**Cattle Feeding**—Cattle feeding is an important part of the agriculture in the irrigated sections of northern Colorado, the Arkansas valley and the Western Slope. The feeding of cattle provides an outlet for by-products from the sugar beet factories, surplus alfalfa hay, grains and other feeds.

It is estimated that there were 74,000 cattle and calves on feed for market January 1, 1932, compared with 142,000 on January 1, 1931.

### Estimated Number of Cattle on Feed by Sections

| | 1932 | 1931 | 1930 | 1929 | 1928 | 1927 |
|---|---|---|---|---|---|---|
| Northern Colorado | 60,000 | 120,000 | 105,000 | 120,000 | 120,000 | 130,000 |
| Arkansas Valley | 9,000 | 14,000 | 14,000 | 13,000 | 12,000 | 12,000 |
| Western Slope | 2,000 | 3,000 | 3,000 | 3,000 | 4,000 | 4,000 |
| Other Sections | 3,000 | 5,000 | 3,000 | 4,000 | 4,000 | 4,000 |
| State Total | 74,000 | 142,000 | 125,000 | 140,000 | 140,000 | 150,000 |

**Lamb Feeding**—Colorado is the leading lamb feeding state and had 1,560,000 lambs on feed January 1, 1932, compared with 1,550,000 on January 1, 1931, and 2,035,000 on January 1, 1930.

On January 1, 1932, Colorado had 25.2 per cent of the lambs on feed in the United States.

Northern Colorado and the Arkansas valley are the leading lamb feeding areas, with smaller operations in the San Luis valley and Western Slope sections.

During the past 10 years northern Colorado has averaged about 1,100,000 lambs on feed. Larimer and Weld counties are the leading counties in lamb feeding, each county having fed annually from 400,000 to 500,000 lambs. This is a larger number than is fed in any Corn Belt state except Nebraska.

Lamb feeding operations have increased during the past few years in the Fort Morgan-Sterling section of northeastern Colorado.

### ESTIMATED NUMBER OF SHEEP AND LAMBS ON FEED JANUARY 1

| Year | Colorado Number | Per cent of total in United States | United States Number |
|---|---|---|---|
| 1914 | 1,300,000 | ----- | -------- |
| 1915 | 1,116,000 | ----- | -------- |
| 1916 | 1,150,000 | ----- | -------- |
| 1917 | 1,250,000 | ----- | -------- |
| 1918 | 1,135,000 | ----- | -------- |
| 1919 | 940,000 | ----- | -------- |
| 1920 | 950,000 | ----- | -------- |
| 1921 | 1,283,000 | ----- | -------- |
| 1922 | 1,040,000 | ----- | -------- |
| 1923 | 1,500,000 | 34.5% | 4,351,000 |
| 1924 | 1,400,000 | 32.6% | 4,297,000 |
| 1925 | 1,600,000 | 39.7% | 4,028,000 |
| 1926 | 1,475,000 | 31.7% | 4,646,000 |
| 1927 | 770,000 | 18.0% | 4,284,000 |
| 1928 | 1,580,000 | 35.2% | 4,488,000 |
| 1929 | 1,520,000 | 31.5% | 4,822,000 |
| 1930 | 2,035,000 | 34.6% | 5,886,000 |
| 1931 | 1,550,000 | 28.6% | 5,428,000 |
| 1932 | 1,560,000 | 25.2% | 6,186,000 |

Note: United States estimates were not made prior to January 1, 1923.

### ESTIMATED NUMBER OF SHEEP AND LAMBS ON FEED JANUARY 1 OF EACH YEAR —BY SECTIONS

| Year | Northern Colorado | Arkansas Valley | San Luis Valley | Western Slope | Miscellaneous Sections | State Total |
|---|---|---|---|---|---|---|
| 1922 | 760,000 | 225,000 | 30,000 | 25,000 | ...... | 1,040,000 |
| 1923 | 1,175,000 | 235,000 | 65,000 | 25,000 | ...... | 1,500,000 |
| 1924 | 1,150,000 | 170,000 | 55,000 | 25,000 | ...... | 1,400,000 |
| 1925 | 1,250,000 | 265,000 | 60,000 | 25,000 | ...... | 1,600,000 |
| 1926 | 1,090,000 | 285,000 | 75,000 | 25,000 | ...... | 1,475,000 |
| 1927 | 520,000 | 177,000 | 54,000 | 19,000 | ...... | 770,000 |
| 1928 | 1,265,000 | 275,000 | 30,000 | 10,000 | ...... | 1,580,000 |
| 1929 | 1,100,000 | 385,000 | 22,000 | 13,000 | ...... | 1,520,000 |
| 1930 | 1,490,000 | 475,000 | 45,000 | 25,000 | ...... | 2,035,000 |
| 1931 | 975,000 | 360,000 | 90,000 | 80,000 | 45,000 | 1,550,000 |
| 1932 | 1,100,000 | 360,000 | 35,000 | 25,000 | 40,000 | 1,560,000 |

Note—"Miscellaneous Sections" division first established in 1931.

## WOOL PRODUCTION

| Year | COLORADO | | UNITED STATES | | |
|---|---|---|---|---|---|
| | Production Pounds | Weight Per Fleece | Production | | Weight Per Fleece |
| | | | Shorn, Lbs. | Pulled, Lbs. | |
| 1920 | 6,266,000 | 6.5 | 244,179,000 | 42,900,000 | 7.3 |
| 1921 | 6,325,000 | 6.7 | 235,129,000 | 48,500,000 | 7.3 |
| 1922 | 6,138,000 | 6.6 | 221,713,000 | 42,000,000 | 7.3 |
| 1923 | 6,486,000 | 6.9 | 225,696,000 | 42,500,000 | 7.5 |
| 1924 | 6,486,000 | 6.9 | 235,575,000 | 43,800,000 | 7.6 |
| 1925 | 6,956,000 | 7.4 | 252,832,000 | 46,800,000 | 7.6 |
| 1926 | 8,132,000 | 7.6 | 268,900,000 | 49,600,000 | 7.7 |
| 1927 | 8,877,000 | 7.3 | 289,909,000 | 50,100,000 | 7.7 |
| 1928 | 11,300,000 | 8.1 | 314,588,000 | 51,900,000 | 7.9 |
| 1929 | 12,269,000 | 7.8 | 327,566,000 | 54,500,000 | 7.8 |
| 1930 | 13,446,000 | 8.1 | 351,521,000 | 61,900,000 | 7.9 |
| 1931 | 13,541,000 | 7.8 | 369,315,000 | 66,100,000 | 8.0 |

## ESTIMATED CREAMERY BUTTER PRODUCTION

| Year | Colorado Pounds | Per cent of Preceding Year | United States Pounds | Per cent of Preceding Year |
|---|---|---|---|---|
| 1919 | 13,144,000 | .... | 868,125,000 | .... |
| 1920 | 12,979,000 | 98.7 | 863,577,000 | 99.5 |
| 1921 | 15,290,000 | 117.8 | 1,054,938,000 | 122.2 |
| 1922 | 16,410,000 | 107.3 | 1,153,515,000 | 109.3 |
| 1923 | 18,625,000 | 113.5 | 1,242,214,000 | 107.7 |
| 1924 | 18,130,000 | 97.3 | 1,356,080,000 | 109.2 |
| 1925 | 18,794,000 | 103.7 | 1,361,526,000 | 100.4 |
| 1926 | 18,255,000 | 97.1 | 1,451,766,000 | 106.6 |
| 1927 | 20,871,000 | 114.3 | 1,496,495,000 | 103.1 |
| 1928 | 21,614,000 | 103.6 | 1,487,049,000 | 99.4 |
| 1929 | 21,924,000 | 101.4 | 1,597,027,000 | 107.4 |
| 1930 | 22,643,000 | 103.3 | 1,595,231,000 | 97.4 |
| 1931 | 22,287,000 | 98.4 | 1,626,338,000 | 101.9 |

## CORN AND HOG RATIOS FOR THE UNITED STATES, 1910-1932

Number of Bushels of Corn Required to Buy 100 Pounds of Live Hogs Based on Averages of Farm Prices of Corn and Hogs for the Month

| Year | January | February | March | April | May | June | July | August | September | October | November | December | Average |
|---|---|---|---|---|---|---|---|---|---|---|---|---|---|
| | Bus. | Bus. | Bus. | Bus. | Bus. | Bus. | Bus. | Bus. | Bus. | Bus. | Bus. | Bus. | Bus. |
| 1910 | 12.2 | 12.0 | 11.7 | 13.0 | 14.4 | 13.3 | 12.9 | 12.2 | 11.7 | 13.0 | 14.2 | 15.1 | 14.9 | 13.3 |
| 1911 | 15.3 | 14.4 | 13.7 | 12.1 | 10.7 | 9.8 | 9.4 | 9.9 | 9.9 | 9.3 | 9.3 | 9.3 | 11.1 |
| 1912 | 9.1 | 8.8 | 8.6 | 9.0 | 8.4 | 8.1 | 8.3 | 9.1 | 10.1 | 12.0 | 13.2 | 14.1 | 9.9 |
| 1913 | 13.6 | 13.9 | 14.4 | 14.4 | 12.7 | 12.3 | 12.1 | 11.1 | 10.2 | 10.4 | 10.5 | 10.3 | 12.2 |
| 1914 | 10.8 | 11.3 | 11.2 | 10.9 | 10.3 | 9.9 | 10.1 | 10.3 | 10.2 | 10.0 | 10.4 | 10.2 | 10.5 |
| 1915 | 9.5 | 8.6 | 8.4 | 8.5 | 8.7 | 8.7 | 8.7 | 8.5 | 9.2 | 10.8 | 10.6 | 10.1 | 9.2 |
| 1916 | 9.8 | 10.5 | 11.4 | 11.5 | 11.4 | 11.0 | 10.9 | 10.6 | 11.1 | 10.4 | 10.1 | 9.8 | 10.7 |
| 1917 | 9.9 | 10.5 | 11.5 | 10.3 | 8.8 | 8.3 | 7.4 | 7.7 | 9.0 | 10.1 | 11.2 | 12.0 | 9.7 |
| 1918 | 11.2 | 10.3 | 10.1 | 10.2 | 10.3 | 10.0 | 9.9 | 10.1 | 10.8 | 11.0 | 11.5 | 11.3 | 10.6 |
| 1919 | 11.1 | 11.3 | 11.2 | 11.1 | 10.8 | 10.2 | 10.5 | 10.2 | 9.3 | 9.7 | 9.2 | 9.2 | 10.3 |
| 1920 | 9.3 | 9.2 | 8.9 | 8.4 | 7.6 | 7.1 | 7.8 | 8.5 | 10.1 | 13.0 | 15.0 | 13.2 | 9.8 |
| 1921 | 13.5 | 13.5 | 14.3 | 13.0 | 12.5 | 11.6 | 13.1 | 14.8 | 14.0 | 15.9 | 16.0 | 15.2 | 14.0 |
| 1922 | 15.4 | 16.5 | 15.8 | 15.7 | 15.0 | 14.7 | 14.7 | 13.7 | 13.4 | 13.4 | 12.8 | 11.7 | 14.4 |
| 1923 | 11.1 | 10.9 | 10.2 | 9.8 | 8.8 | 7.9 | 7.5 | 7.7 | 8.5 | 8.8 | 8.2 | 9.0 | 9.0 |
| 1924 | 9.0 | 8.5 | 8.6 | 8.6 | 8.5 | 8.1 | 6.7 | 8.0 | 7.7 | 8.7 | 8.7 | 7.9 | 8.2 |
| 1925 | 8.3 | 8.4 | 10.6 | 11.2 | 10.0 | 9.7 | 11.5 | 11.4 | 11.6 | 13.4 | 14.3 | 14.9 | 11.3 |
| 1926 | 15.8 | 17.2 | 17.5 | 17.5 | 17.8 | 18.7 | 17.7 | 14.7 | 15.8 | 16.2 | 17.3 | 17.0 | 16.9 |
| 1927 | 17.1 | 16.8 | 16.7 | 15.9 | 12.9 | 9.4 | 9.3 | 9.5 | 10.3 | 11.6 | 12.2 | 10.8 | 12.7 |
| 1928 | 10.3 | 9.6 | 8.7 | 8.4 | 8.6 | 8.5 | 9.4 | 10.2 | 11.7 | 11.3 | 11.3 | 10.4 | 9.9 |
| 1929 | 10.2 | 10.2 | 11.3 | 11.7 | 11.6 | 11.3 | 11.3 | 10.7 | 9.8 | 9.9 | 10.5 | 10.9 | 10.8 |
| 1930 | 11.4 | 12.2 | 12.8 | 11.7 | 11.6 | 11.5 | 10.9 | 9.5 | 10.3 | 10.7 | 12.4 | 11.5 | 11.4 |
| 1931 | 11.8 | 11.6 | 12.0 | 12.0 | 11.3 | 10.6 | 11.5 | 12.3 | 12.6 | 14.1 | 11.9 | 10.9 | 11.9 |
| 1932 | 11.2 | 10.9 | --- | --- | --- | --- | --- | --- | --- | --- | --- | --- | --- |

## ESTIMATED NUMBERS AND VALUES OF LIVESTOCK ON FARMS JANUARY 1

### ALL CATTLE AND CALVES

| Year | COLORADO | | | | UNITED STATES | | | |
|---|---|---|---|---|---|---|---|---|
| | Numbers | | Values, Dollars | | Numbers | | Values, Dollars | |
| | Per Cent Prec'd'g Year | Total Number | Per Head | Aggregate | Per Cent Prec'd'g Year | Total Number | Per Head | Aggregate |
| 1910 | ---- | 1,130,000 | $27.50 | $31,075,000 | ---- | 61,803,000 | $ 24.50 | $1,513,063,000 |
| 1920 | 155.5 | 1,757,000 | 49.70 | 87,323,000 | 113.8 | 70,325,000 | 52.67 | 3,703,896,000 |
| 1921 | 95.8 | 1,683,000 | 36.90 | 62,103,000 | 97.6 | 68,633,000 | 39.10 | 2,683,246,000 |
| 1922 | 99.8 | 1,680,000 | 29.40 | 49,392,000 | 100.0 | 68,663,000 | 30.41 | 2,087,807,000 |
| 1923 | 96.1 | 1,614,000 | 28.30 | 45,676,000 | 98.1 | 67,384,000 | 31.69 | 2,135,710,000 |
| 1924 | 95.4 | 1,540,000 | 27.70 | 42,658,000 | 97.7 | 65,832,000 | 32.14 | 2,116,009,000 |
| 1925 | 95.1 | 1,465,000 | 26.00 | 38,090,000 | 95.9 | 63,115,000 | 31.77 | 2,005,351,000 |
| 1926 | 96.0 | 1,406,000 | 32.00 | 44,992,000 | 95.0 | 59,977,000 | 36.94 | 2,215,400,000 |
| 1927 | 100.0 | 1,406,000 | 36.20 | 50,897,000 | 95.9 | 57,528,000 | 40.11 | 2,307,401,000 |
| 1928 | 97.9 | 1,377,000 | 46.70 | 64,306,000 | 98.6 | 56,701,000 | 50.81 | 2,880,802,000 |
| 1929 | 103.2 | 1,421,000 | 55.30 | 78,581,000 | 102.1 | 57,878,000 | 58.77 | 3,401,534,000 |
| 1930 | 102.3 | 1,454,000 | 50.90 | 73,985,000 | 103.2 | 59,730,000 | 56.69 | 3,386,010,000 |
| 1931 | 106.0 | 1,541,000 | 37.80 | 58,324,000 | 102.0 | 60,915,000 | 39.31 | 2,394,411,000 |
| 1932 | 100.0 | 1,541,000 | 22.50 | 34,670,000 | 102.4 | 62,407,000 | 26.64 | 1,662,222,000 |

### COWS AND HEIFERS 2 YEARS OLD AND OVER KEPT FOR MILK

| Year | Per Cent Prec'd'g Year | Total Number | Per Head | Aggregate | Per Cent Prec'd'g Year | Total Number | Per Head | Aggregate |
|---|---|---|---|---|---|---|---|---|
| 1910 | ---- | 145,000 | ---- | -------- | ---- | 20,625,000 | $ 35.29 | $ 727,856,000 |
| 1920 | 158.6 | 230,000 | $86.00 | $19,780,000 | 104.0 | 21,455,000 | 81.51 | 1,748,820,000 |
| 1921 | 101.7 | 234,000 | 69.00 | 16,146,000 | 99.9 | 21,440,000 | 61.20 | 1,312,100,000 |
| 1922 | 102.6 | 240,000 | 56.00 | 13,440,000 | 101.8 | 21,822,000 | 48.69 | 1,062,478,000 |
| 1923 | 102.1 | 245,000 | 52.00 | 12,740,000 | 101.3 | 22,099,000 | 48.68 | 1,075,752,000 |
| 1924 | 102.0 | 250,000 | 49.00 | 12,250,000 | 100.9 | 22,288,000 | 49.94 | 1,113,127,000 |
| 1925 | 102.4 | 256,000 | 44.00 | 11,264,000 | 101.0 | 22,505,000 | 48.38 | 1,088,900,000 |
| 1926 | 100.0 | 256,000 | 49.00 | 12,544,000 | 99.1 | 22,311,000 | 54.73 | 1,221,113,000 |
| 1927 | 100.4 | 257,000 | 56.00 | 14,392,000 | 99.3 | 22,159,000 | 59.24 | 1,312,673,000 |
| 1928 | 100.0 | 257,000 | 69.00 | 17,733,000 | 99.9 | 22,129,000 | 73.47 | 1,625,875,000 |
| 1929 | 100.4 | 258,000 | 77.00 | 19,866,000 | 100.9 | 22,330,000 | 83.99 | 1,875,538,000 |
| 1930 | 100.4 | 259,000 | 72.00 | 18,648,000 | 102.6 | 22,910,000 | 82.80 | 1,897,011,000 |
| 1931 | 100.4 | 260,000 | 56.00 | 14,560,000 | 102.8 | 23,558,000 | 57.11 | 1,345,479,000 |
| 1922 | 102.3 | 266,000 | 36.00 | 9,576,000 | 103.5 | 24,379,000 | 39.61 | 965,758,000 |

### HEIFERS 1 TO 2 YEARS OLD BEING KEPT FOR MILK COWS

| Year | Per Cent Prec'd'g Year | Total Number | Per Head | Aggregate | Per Cent Prec'd'g Year | Total Number | Per Head | Aggregate |
|---|---|---|---|---|---|---|---|---|
| 1920 | ---- | 46,000 | ---- | -------- | ---- | 4,420,000 | ---- | -------- |
| 1921 | 102.2 | 47,000 | ---- | -------- | 94.2 | 4,164,000 | ---- | -------- |
| 1922 | 102.1 | 48,000 | ---- | -------- | 95.4 | 3,972,000 | ---- | -------- |
| 1923 | 102.1 | 49,000 | ---- | -------- | 104.6 | 4,155,000 | ---- | -------- |
| 1924 | 102.0 | 50,000 | ---- | -------- | 99.7 | 4,143,000 | ---- | -------- |
| 1925 | 110.0 | 55,000 | ---- | -------- | 100.7 | 4,171,000 | ---- | -------- |
| 1926 | 100.0 | 55,000 | ---- | -------- | 97.0 | 4,045,000 | ---- | -------- |
| 1927 | 100.0 | 55,000 | ---- | -------- | 100.1 | 4,048,000 | ---- | -------- |
| 1928 | 101.8 | 56,000 | ---- | -------- | 102.7 | 4,158,000 | ---- | -------- |
| 1929 | 101.8 | 57,000 | ---- | -------- | 105.9 | 4,404,000 | ---- | -------- |
| 1930 | 100.0 | 57,000 | ---- | -------- | 106.7 | 4,700,000 | ---- | -------- |
| 1931 | 100.0 | 57,000 | ---- | -------- | 101.6 | 4,777,000 | ---- | -------- |
| 1932 | 103.5 | 59,000 | ---- | -------- | 97.7 | 4,665,000 | ---- | -------- |

### ALL SHEEP AND LAMBS, INCLUDING SHEEP AND LAMBS ON FEED

| Year | Per Cent Prec'd'g Year | Total Number | Per Head | Aggregate | Per Cent Prec'd'g Year | Total Number | Per Head | Aggregate |
|---|---|---|---|---|---|---|---|---|
| 1910 | ---- | 1,426,000 | $ 4.80 | $ 6,845,000 | ---- | 52,488,000 | $ 4.12 | $ 216,030,000 |
| 1920 | 137.7 | 1,964,000 | 9.10 | 17,872,000 | 77.4 | 40,643,000 | 10.45 | 424,644,000 |
| 1921 | 114.4 | 2,247,000 | 5.40 | 12,134,000 | 96.9 | 39,378,000 | 6.27 | 246,744,000 |
| 1922 | 86.3 | 1,940,000 | 4.70 | 9,118,000 | 93.5 | 36,821,000 | 4.79 | 176,447,000 |
| 1923 | 126.2 | 2,449,000 | 7.40 | 18,123,000 | 99.7 | 36,695,000 | 7.49 | 274,993,000 |
| 1924 | 95.0 | 2,327,000 | 7.40 | 17,220,000 | 100.9 | 37,020,000 | 7.88 | 291,840,000 |
| 1925 | 110.2 | 2,565,000 | 10.30 | 26,420,000 | 103.7 | 38,392,000 | 9.68 | 371,639,000 |
| 1926 | 100.0 | 2,565,000 | 10.50 | 26,933,000 | 104.7 | 40,183,000 | 10.48 | 421,086,000 |
| 1927 | 80.0 | 2,051,000 | 9.40 | 19,279,000 | 105.3 | 42,302,000 | 9.67 | 409,184,000 |
| 1928 | 147.2 | 3,020,000 | 9.60 | 28,992,000 | 106.7 | 45,121,000 | 10.22 | 461,193,000 |
| 1929 | 103.3 | 3,118,000 | 10.60 | 33,051,000 | 106.9 | 48,249,000 | 10.59 | 510,869,000 |
| 1930 | 120.3 | 3,750,000 | 9.00 | 33,843,000 | 106.5 | 51,383,000 | 8.94 | 459,208,000 |
| 1931 | 89.4 | 3,351,000 | 5.60 | 18,659,000 | 102.7 | 52,745,000 | 5.35 | 282,352,000 |
| 1932 | 100.3 | 3,361,000 | 3.10 | 10,575,000 | 102.2 | 53,912,000 | 3.40 | 183,255,000 |

## ESTIMATED NUMBERS AND VALUES OF LIVESTOCK ON FARMS JANUARY 1

### SWINE, INCLUDING PIGS

| Year | COLORADO | | | | UNITED STATES | | | |
|---|---|---|---|---|---|---|---|---|
| | Numbers | | Values, Dollars | | Numbers | | Values, Dollars | |
| | Per Cent Prec'd'g Year | Total Number | Per Head | Aggregate | Per Cent Prec'd'g Year | Total Number | Per Head | Aggregate |
| 1910 | ---- | 179,000 | $ 8.75 | $ 1,566,000 | ---- | 58,186,000 | $ 9.17 | $ 533,309,000 |
| 1920 | 251.4 | 450,000 | 17.80 | 8,010,000 | 103.4 | 60,159,000 | 20.00 | 1,203,052,000 |
| 1921 | 92.0 | 414,000 | 12.20 | 5,051,000 | 98.0 | 58,942,000 | 13.63 | 803,544,000 |
| 1922 | 109.9 | 455,000 | 9.50 | 4,322,000 | 101.5 | 59,849,000 | 10.58 | 633,313,000 |
| 1923 | 130.1 | 592,000 | 10.40 | 6,157,000 | 115.8 | 69,304,000 | 12.29 | 851,838,000 |
| 1924 | 97.1 | 575,000 | 9.40 | 5,405,000 | 96.1 | 66,576,000 | 10.30 | 685,574,000 |
| 1925 | 85.7 | 493,000 | 10.90 | 5,374,000 | 83.8 | 55,770,000 | 13.15 | 733,220,000 |
| 1926 | 89.8 | 443,000 | 13.60 | 6,025,000 | 93.4 | 52,085,000 | 15.66 | 815,412,000 |
| 1927 | 100.0 | 443,000 | 16.00 | 7,088,000 | 106.5 | 55,468,000 | 17.19 | 953,495,000 |
| 1928 | 114.8 | 509,000 | 13.10 | 6,668,000 | 111.4 | 61,772,000 | 13.17 | 813,639,000 |
| 1929 | 108.0 | 550,000 | 12.10 | 6,655,000 | 95.2 | 58,789,000 | 12.94 | 760,695,000 |
| 1930 | 90.0 | 495,000 | 12.00 | 5,943,000 | 94.1 | 55,301,000 | 13.46 | 744,308,000 |
| 1931 | 105.0 | 520,000 | 11.10 | 5,769,000 | 98.3 | 54,374,000 | 11.36 | 617,668,000 |
| 1932 | 120.0 | 624,000 | 5.20 | 3,271,000 | 109.4 | 59,511,000 | 6.14 | 365,133,000 |

### HORSES AND COLTS

| 1910 | ---- | 294,000 | $93.13 | $27,380,000 | ---- | 19,833,000 | $108.00 | $2,141,964,000 |
|---|---|---|---|---|---|---|---|---|
| 1920 | 143.1 | 421,000 | 79.00 | 33,259,000 | 101.3 | 20,092,000 | 96.48 | 1,938,447,000 |
| 1921 | 100.0 | 421,000 | 63.00 | 26,523,000 | 96.4 | 19,366,000 | 84.54 | 1,637,181,000 |
| 1922 | 98.6 | 415,000 | 56.00 | 23,240,000 | 96.9 | 18,760,000 | 71.05 | 1,332,822,000 |
| 1923 | 96.4 | 400,000 | 48.00 | 19,200,000 | 96.6 | 18,123,000 | 70.51 | 1,277,873,000 |
| 1924 | 96.3 | 385,000 | 45.00 | 17,325,000 | 95.8 | 17,365,000 | 65.42 | 1,135,967,000 |
| 1925 | 95.3 | 367,000 | 43.00 | 15,781,000 | 95.8 | 16,640,000 | 64.28 | 1,069,654,000 |
| 1926 | 98.1 | 360,000 | 47.00 | 16,920,000 | 96.6 | 16,067,000 | 65.32 | 1,049,442,000 |
| 1927 | 96.1 | 346,000 | 44.00 | 15,224,000 | 95.6 | 15,368,000 | 63.74 | 979,509,000 |
| 1928 | 99.1 | 348,000 | 43.00 | 14,749,000 | 96.0 | 14,768,000 | 66.68 | 984,763,000 |
| 1929 | 100.0 | 343,000 | 47.00 | 16,121,000 | 96.2 | 14,203,000 | 69.63 | 988,953,000 |
| 1930 | 98.5 | 338,000 | 44.00 | 15,023,000 | 96.3 | 13,684,000 | 69.86 | 955,964,000 |
| 1931 | 97.9 | 331,000 | 41.00 | 13,420,000 | 96.2 | 13,165,000 | 60.43 | 795,541,000 |
| 1932 | 98.0 | 324,000 | 34.00 | 11,008,000 | 96.3 | 12,679,000 | 53.37 | 676,698,000 |

### MULES AND MULE COLTS

| 1910 | ---- | 14,700 | $122.03 | $ 1,794,000 | ---- | 4,210,000 | $120.20 | $ 506,042,000 |
|---|---|---|---|---|---|---|---|---|
| 1920 | 210.9 | 31,000 | 102.00 | 3,162,000 | 134.3 | 5,656,000 | 148.25 | 838,530,000 |
| 1921 | 103.2 | 32,000 | 91.00 | 2,912,000 | 102.1 | 5,772,000 | 117.37 | 677,475,000 |
| 1922 | 106.3 | 34,000 | 70.00 | 2,380,000 | 101.0 | 5,827,000 | 88.99 | 518,558,000 |
| 1923 | 105.9 | 36,000 | 62.00 | 2,232,000 | 101.2 | 5,895,000 | 86.86 | 512,067,000 |
| 1924 | 105.6 | 38,000 | 61.00 | 2,318,000 | 100.2 | 5,908,000 | 85.89 | 507,435,000 |
| 1925 | 100.0 | 38,000 | 57.00 | 2,166,000 | 100.2 | 5,918,000 | 82.91 | 490,668,000 |
| 1926 | 97.3 | 37,000 | 59.00 | 2,183,000 | 99.7 | 5,903,000 | 81.51 | 481,153,000 |
| 1927 | 94.6 | 35,000 | 55.00 | 1,925,000 | 98.3 | 5,801,000 | 74.50 | 432,181,000 |
| 1928 | 91.6 | 32,000 | 56.00 | 1,792,000 | 97.3 | 5,647,000 | 79.79 | 450,585,000 |
| 1929 | 96.9 | 31,000 | 58.00 | 1,798,000 | 97.3 | 5,496,000 | 82.39 | 452,825,000 |
| 1930 | 96.8 | 30,000 | 57.00 | 1,721,000 | 97.6 | 5,366,000 | 83.76 | 449,480,000 |
| 1931 | 93.3 | 28,000 | 52.00 | 1,445,000 | 97.2 | 5,215,000 | 69.17 | 360,736,000 |
| 1932 | 96.0 | 27,000 | 42.00 | 1,132,000 | 97.4 | 5,082,000 | 60.69 | 308,440,000 |

### TOTAL VALUE OF ALL LIVESTOCK JANUARY 1

| | Colorado | United States | | Colorado | United States |
|---|---|---|---|---|---|
| 1910 | $ 68,660,000 | $4,910,408,000 | 1926 | $ 97,053,000 | $4,982,493,000 |
| 1920 | 149,626,000 | 8,108,569,000 | 1927 | 94,413,000 | 5,081,770,000 |
| 1921 | 108,723,000 | 6,048,190,000 | 1928 | 116,507,000 | 5,590,982,000 |
| 1922 | 88,452,000 | 4,748,947,000 | 1929 | 136,206,000 | 6,114,876,000 |
| 1923 | 91,388,000 | 5,052,481,000 | 1930 | 130,515,000 | 5,994,970,000 |
| 1924 | 84,926,000 | 4,736,825,000 | 1931 | 97,617,000 | 4,450,708,000 |
| 1925 | 87,831,000 | 4,670,532,000 | 1932 | 60,656,000 | 3,195,748,000 |

## COLORADO LIVESTOCK ASSESSMENTS

| | HORSES | | | MULES | | | RANGE CATTLE | | |
|---|---|---|---|---|---|---|---|---|---|
| Year | Number | Assessed Value | Aver. Per Head | Number | Assessed Value | Aver. Per Head | Number | Assessed Value | Aver. Per Head |
| 1910 | 246,975 | $7,506,000 | $30.39 | 14,277 | $ 524,559 | $36.74 | 720,297 | -------- | ---- |
| 1911 | 259,990 | 7,752,000 | 29.81 | 16,741 | 601,292 | 35.91 | 715,315 | -------- | ---- |
| 1912 | 255,511 | 7,254,000 | 28.38 | 16,821 | 600,442 | 85.69 | 701,542 | -------- | ---- |
| 1913 | 281,704 | 18,028,000 | 63.99 | 19,329 | 1,568,328 | 81.12 | 793,957 | $23,912,000 | $30.11 |
| 1914 | 279,826 | 18,211,000 | 65.05 | 19,635 | 1,669,737 | 85.03 | 868,261 | 30,167,000 | 34.73 |
| 1915 | 296,368 | 20,031,000 | 67.59 | 23,284 | 1,991,820 | 85.54 | 997,823 | 37,548,000 | 37.63 |
| 1916 | 308,062 | 21,729,000 | 70.54 | 26,280 | 2,303,481 | 87.64 | 1,063,153 | 41,864,000 | 39.38 |
| 1917 | 326,002 | 23,837,000 | 73.12 | 29,269 | 2,716,010 | 92.80 | 1,147,432 | 46,533,000 | 40.56 |
| 1918 | 352,794 | 26,836,000 | 76.05 | 29,838 | 2,843,990 | 95.31 | 1,262,616 | 55,236,000 | 43.75 |
| 1919 | 354,868 | 25,254,000 | 71.16 | 30,045 | 2,660,731 | 88.56 | 1,286,547 | 56,989,000 | 44.30 |
| 1920 | 337,903 | 22,856,000 | 67.65 | 28,682 | 2,476,076 | 86.33 | 1,187,480 | 51,334,000 | 42.88 |
| 1921 | 333,669 | 18,495,000 | 55.42 | 29,539 | 2,054,836 | 69.56 | 1,123,594 | 31,856,000 | 28.35 |
| 1922 | 318,808 | 15,350,168 | 48.15 | 31,741 | 1,787,269 | 56.31 | 1,112,299 | 29,719,000 | 26.72 |
| 1923 | 304,262 | 11,901,589 | 39.12 | 32,528 | 1,499,818 | 46.10 | 1,060,189 | 26,084,000 | 24.60 |
| 1924 | 290,784 | 10,722,327 | 36.87 | 35,325 | 1,495,797 | 42.34 | 972,984 | 20,619,000 | 21.20 |
| 1925 | 280,094 | 10,248,460 | 36.59 | 32,939 | 1,417,710 | 43.04 | 905,618 | 18,023,000 | 19.90 |
| 1926 | 268,346 | 9,634,799 | 35.90 | 31,653 | 1,335,301 | 42.19 | 828,797 | 17,095,126 | 20.62 |
| 1927 | 250,008 | 8,764,003 | 35.06 | 30,306 | 1,250,836 | 41.27 | 804,545 | 18,212,260 | 21.98 |
| 1928 | 239,759 | 8,207,666 | 34.23 | 26,189 | 1,116,295 | 42.63 | 796,725 | 23,622,220 | 29.64 |
| 1929 | 233,855 | 7,893,333 | 33.75 | 25,318 | 1,072,270 | 41.92 | 793,974 | 27,050,976 | 34.07 |
| 1930 | 225,609 | 7,294,217 | 32.33 | 21,994 | 917,187 | 41.70 | 800,198 | 27,312,372 | 34.13 |
| 1931 | 216,811 | 6,704,193 | 30.92 | 20,588 | 803,274 | 39.02 | 864,846 | 23,119,472 | 26.78 |

| | DAIRY CATTLE | | | RANGE OR STOCK SHEEP | | | SWINE | | |
|---|---|---|---|---|---|---|---|---|---|
| Year | Number | Assessed Value | Aver. Per Head | Number | Assessed Value | Aver. Per Head | Number | Assessed Value | Aver. Per Head |
| 1910 | 63,671 | -------- | ---- | 1,463,861 | $ 2,165,838 | $ 1.48 | 60,871 | $ 253,678 | $ 4.16 |
| 1911 | 70,996 | -------- | ---- | 1,757,771 | 2,400,404 | 1.36 | 75,954 | 281,762 | 3.68 |
| 1912 | 66,273 | -------- | ---- | 1,352,900 | 1,788,897 | 1.32 | 70,261 | 245,102 | 3.48 |
| 1913 | 73,768 | $3,324,000 | $45.06 | 1,579,560 | 4,776,626 | 3.02 | 83,859 | 630,919 | 7.52 |
| 1914 | 97,732 | 4,994,869 | 51.10 | 1,555,165 | 4,853,413 | 3.12 | 112,342 | 883,609 | 7.86 |
| 1915 | 101,037 | 5,786,218 | 57.26 | 1,157,544 | 4,032,950 | 3.48 | 163,143 | 1,183,742 | 7.25 |
| 1916 | 110,298 | 6,727,172 | 60.99 | 1,044,380 | 5,092,433 | 4.88 | 181,169 | 1,359,799 | 7.50 |
| 1917 | 124,342 | 7,919,512 | 63.69 | 1,003,168 | 7,182,427 | 7.16 | 165,329 | 1,630,154 | 9.86 |
| 1918 | 137,126 | 9,449,630 | 68.91 | 1,164,411 | 12,659,415 | 10.87 | 194,576 | 2,768,632 | 14.23 |
| 1919 | 143,106 | 10,170,007 | 71.06 | 1,089,037 | 11,386,972 | 10.46 | 199,988 | 2,955,440 | 15.14 |
| 1920 | 143,981 | 10,169,207 | 70.56 | 915,394 | 9,230,084 | 10.08 | 182,097 | 2,129,493 | 12.00 |
| 1921 | 145,070 | 7,981,591 | 55.02 | 855,873 | 3,216,728 | 3.76 | 175,064 | 1,619,404 | 9.37 |
| 1922 | 149,119 | 7,295,697 | 48.92 | 815,714 | 3,441,985 | 4.22 | 209,017 | 1,882,647 | 9.14 |
| 1923 | 143,163 | 6,245,287 | 43.62 | 830,483 | 4,390,920 | 5.57 | 259,917 | 2,211,060 | 8.61 |
| 1924 | 149,425 | 6,038,056 | 40.40 | 809,784 | 4,691,228 | 5.79 | 246,163 | 1,794,677 | 7.29 |
| 1925 | 147,411 | 5,789,318 | 39.27 | 860,600 | 6,188,636 | 7.19 | 183,176 | 1,450,864 | 7.92 |
| 1926 | 147,176 | 5,795,951 | 39.38 | 1,014,931 | 7,421,145 | 7.31 | 140,768 | 1,246,258 | 8.85 |
| 1927 | 162,268 | 6,467,821 | 39.86 | 1,212,716 | 9,028,761 | 7.45 | 164,058 | 1,637,001 | 9.98 |
| 1928 | 148,474 | 7,390,272 | 49.78 | 1,260,863 | 10,234,087 | 8.12 | 172,209 | 1,675,270 | 9.73 |
| 1929 | 177,856 | 8,505,365 | 47.82 | 1,436,385 | 10,644,536 | 7.41 | 184,530 | 1,802,999 | 9.77 |
| 1930 | 171,382 | 8,092,468 | 47.22 | 1,486,492 | 8,340,788 | 5.61 | 178,906 | 1,746,068 | 9.76 |
| 1931 | 168,487 | 6,548,819 | 38.87 | 1,508,675 | 5,446,916 | 3.61 | 184,383 | 1,652,581 | 8.96 |

Note: The discrepancy between census and assessors' figures is less than appears from the totals, as enumerations are made at different seasons and not on an identical basis. In 1913 Colorado's assessment basis was raised from one-third of actual value to full value, accounting for the large increase in 1913 values.

| | CATTLE FED IN TRANSIT | | SHEEP FED IN TRANSIT | |
|---|---|---|---|---|
| Year | Number | Assessed Value | Number | Assessed Value |
| 1916 | 47,292 | $ 927,860 | 767,468 | $ 591,870 |
| 1917 | 77,211 | 1,149,145 | 946,156 | 929,650 |
| 1918 | 78,651 | 1,447,860 | 806,560 | 1,420,495 |
| 1919 | 84,907 | 1,643,400 | 656,455 | 1,151,155 |
| 1920 | 73,163 | 1,286,830 | 666,810 | 929,150 |
| 1921 | 77,813 | 1,077,590 | 1,029,242 | 679,600 |
| 1922 | 82,430 | 685,285 | 762,872 | 730,805 |
| 1923 | 83,248 | 581,495 | 1,187,399 | 1,115,046 |
| 1924 | 85,829 | 708,895 | 1,137,349 | 1,135,710 |
| 1925 | 92,357 | 760,645 | 1,370,479 | 1,485,685 |
| 1926 | 96,495 | 928,495 | 1,311,481 | 1,270,847 |
| 1927 | 122,462 | 1,156,235 | 678,984 | 883,156 |
| 1928 | 101,377 | 1,239,890 | 1,392,935 | 1,660,625 |
| 1929 | 127,500 | 1,889,000 | 1,582,282 | 1,750,968 |
| 1930 | 123,823 | 1,274,389 | 1,863,330 | 1,424,824 |
| 1931 | 136,268 | 1,576,450 | 1,302,892 | 997,090 |

Note: Assessment made on April 1. Cattle Fed in Transit covers cattle in feed lots after January 1. Sheep Fed in Transit covers sheep and lambs in feed lots after January 1 and also some sheep on summer range.

## STOCKYARD RECEIPTS OF LIVESTOCK FROM COLORADO*
### SHEEP AND LAMBS†
(Number of Head)

| MONTH | 1926 | 1927 | 1928 | 1929 | 1930 | 1931 |
|---|---|---|---|---|---|---|
| January | 170,690 | 65,858 | 150,706 | 189,086 | 232,923 | 131,753 |
| February | 295,756 | 90,911 | 425,693 | 328,893 | 381,263 | 271,120 |
| March | 518,824 | 278,440 | 515,871 | 401,271 | 624,761 | 494,331 |
| April | 415,676 | 308,161 | 445,345 | 443,237 | 607,367 | 536,617 |
| May | 135,790 | 95,345 | 90,024 | 247,337 | 238,165 | 207,353 |
| June | 18,709 | 19,637 | 13,985 | 42,926 | 15,891 | 10,586 |
| July | 28,562 | 17,098 | 38,272 | 20,708 | 20,697 | 10,677 |
| August | 49,991 | 52,419 | 58,690 | 47,280 | 46,132 | 48,632 |
| September | 290,935 | 238,242 | 289,489 | 245,997 | 304,553 | 290,428 |
| October | 397,272 | 493,764 | 584,920 | 492,127 | 444,945 | 403,409 |
| November | 93,019 | 122,274 | 110,833 | 115,765 | 130,233 | 128,602 |
| December | 51,974 | 75,100 | 65,263 | 70,479 | 68,353 | 112,046 |
| Total | 2,467,198 | 1,857,249 | 2,789,691 | 2,645,106 | 3,115,288 | 2,645,554 |

### CATTLE
(Number of Head)

| MONTH | 1926 | 1927 | 1928 | 1929 | 1930 | 1931 |
|---|---|---|---|---|---|---|
| January | 36,071 | 55,566 | 49,754 | 44,856 | 44,553 | 34,305 |
| February | 24,073 | 43,742 | 32,689 | 23,999 | 29,933 | 24,547 |
| March | 42,269 | 46,279 | 35,956 | 44,521 | 49,664 | 37,000 |
| April | 37,514 | 40,950 | 44,566 | 47,698 | 42,769 | 46,360 |
| May | 32,794 | 43,940 | 28,890 | 43,182 | 36,801 | 53,807 |
| June | 22,983 | 17,699 | 18,256 | 22,388 | 27,181 | 40,049 |
| July | 14,052 | 10,279 | 13,958 | 20,410 | 14,890 | 30,208 |
| August | 16,766 | 17,777 | 16,925 | 16,801 | 12,110 | 24,925 |
| September | 41,541 | 32,721 | 42,622 | 37,162 | 30,848 | 33,486 |
| October | 81,706 | 117,551 | 95,378 | 94,258 | 66,681 | 68,451 |
| November | 101,461 | 100,513 | 92,206 | 88,951 | 63,023 | 99,913 |
| December | 39,712 | 40,531 | 54,516 | 44,372 | 39,160 | 35,828 |
| Total | 490,942 | 567,548 | 525,716 | 528,598 | 457,613 | 528,879 |

### CALVES
(Number of Head)

| MONTH | 1926 | 1927 | 1928 | 1929 | 1930 | 1931 |
|---|---|---|---|---|---|---|
| January | 4,617 | 4,809 | 6,728 | 6,535 | 5,834 | 5,858 |
| February | 3,072 | 3,224 | 3,376 | 2,779 | 3,487 | 2,300 |
| March | 3,903 | 3,315 | 3,188 | 3,778 | 4,024 | 2,945 |
| April | 3,443 | 3,393 | 4,447 | 5,302 | 3,297 | 3,507 |
| May | 4,777 | 3,543 | 3,394 | 4,268 | 2,943 | 3,971 |
| June | 3,600 | 2,955 | 2,570 | 3,220 | 2,854 | 2,942 |
| July | 2,262 | 2,117 | 2,392 | 2,705 | 2,034 | 2,480 |
| August | 3,605 | 3,256 | 2,729 | 2,741 | 1,867 | 3,424 |
| September | 4,375 | 3,119 | 3,397 | 3,038 | 2,509 | 4,327 |
| October | 5,009 | 9,602 | 11,804 | 6,031 | 7,061 | 6,404 |
| November | 7,173 | 10,223 | 9,457 | 10,235 | 8,569 | 10,762 |
| December | 3,189 | 3,160 | 4,636 | 4,530 | 5,034 | 5,172 |
| Total | 49,025 | 52,716 | 58,118 | 55,162 | 49,513 | 54,092 |

### HOGS
(Number of Head)

| MONTH | 1926 | 1927 | 1928 | 1929 | 1930 | 1931 |
|---|---|---|---|---|---|---|
| January | 27,336 | 34,695 | 44,572 | 57,733 | 47,997 | 39,582 |
| February | 27,703 | 33,984 | 44,919 | 49,897 | 44,382 | 35,781 |
| March | 36,124 | 37,934 | 40,940 | 46,125 | 38,581 | 31,312 |
| April | 33,736 | 26,656 | 35,468 | 42,897 | 41,505 | 29,908 |
| May | 24,102 | 31,112 | 32,107 | 39,845 | 37,425 | 34,980 |
| June | 21,434 | 25,147 | 29,534 | 32,575 | 33,320 | 34,298 |
| July | 13,138 | 15,578 | 24,138 | 31,733 | 26,941 | 31,496 |
| August | 18,813 | 15,975 | 16,589 | 28,034 | 20,030 | 29,889 |
| September | 16,911 | 14,737 | 21,737 | 28,035 | 24,529 | 25,334 |
| October | 11,707 | 14,739 | 27,429 | 30,306 | 24,792 | 30,055 |
| November | 21,064 | 21,470 | 30,626 | 26,969 | 23,289 | 27,612 |
| December | 23,727 | 24,071 | 39,492 | 37,230 | 28,630 | 29,894 |
| Total | 275,795 | 296,098 | 387,551 | 451,379 | 391,421 | 380,141 |

*Some duplication between markets has been eliminated. The figures include all stockyards receipts of Colorado livestock, whether shipped to Colorado stockyards or to yards in other states.

†Net receipts include some New Mexico, Wyoming and Utah sheep shipped from Colorado points.

## HORSES IN COLORADO, 1930 AND 1931
### (From Reports of County Assessors to State Tax Commission)

| COUNTY | 1931 | | | 1930 | | |
|---|---|---|---|---|---|---|
| | Number | Assessed Value | Average Per Head | Number | Assessed Value | Average Per Head |
| Adams | 5,669 | $ 186,290 | $32.86 | 5,772 | $ 203,530 | $35.26 |
| Alamosa | 1,460 | 81,795 | 56.02 | 1,656 | 97,580 | 58.93 |
| Arapahoe | 2,646 | 85,705 | 32.39 | 2,660 | 96,280 | 36.20 |
| Archuleta | 1,275 | 38,345 | 30.08 | 1,161 | 36,635 | 31.55 |
| Baca | 7,167 | 135,745 | 18.94 | 6,864 | 124,238 | 18.10 |
| Bent | 4,207 | 110,765 | 26.33 | 4,412 | 117,265 | 26.57 |
| Boulder | 3,591 | 129,120 | 35.96 | 3,473 | 141,440 | 40.73 |
| Chaffee | 893 | 32,680 | 36.60 | 921 | 38,120 | 41.39 |
| Cheyenne | 2,370 | 60,395 | 25.49 | 2,801 | 70,345 | 25.11 |
| Clear Creek | 210 | 7,515 | 35.79 | 124 | 5,125 | 41.33 |
| Conejos | 2,146 | 90,660 | 42.25 | 2,151 | 85,960 | 39.96 |
| Costilla | 1,885 | 47,100 | 25.03 | 1,345 | 47,665 | 35.44 |
| Crowley | 2,597 | 87,515 | 33.73 | 2,576 | 88,100 | 34.20 |
| Custer | 1,092 | 31,730 | 29.06 | 1,111 | 32,865 | 29.58 |
| Delta | 3,975 | 129,345 | 32.54 | 3,848 | 134,765 | 35.02 |
| Denver | 556 | 24,510 | 44.08 | 613 | 28,180 | 45.97 |
| Dolores | 415 | 9,985 | 24.06 | 464 | 10,950 | 23.60 |
| Douglas | 1,591 | 83,125 | 52.24 | 1,945 | 99,150 | 50.98 |
| Eagle | 2,297 | 78,040 | 33.97 | 2,348 | 88,965 | 37.89 |
| Elbert | 5,454 | 173,096 | 31.74 | 5,928 | 190,985 | 32.22 |
| El Paso | 4,987 | 140,000 | 28.19 | 4,670 | 138,360 | 29.63 |
| Fremont | 1,299 | 37,685 | 29.01 | 1,432 | 42,395 | 29.61 |
| Garfield | 5,316 | 193,995 | 36.50 | 4,691 | 193,685 | 41.29 |
| Gilpin | 130 | 4,130 | 31.77 | 125 | 3,735 | 29.88 |
| Grand | 1,859 | 48,700 | 26.20 | 2,201 | 59,070 | 26.84 |
| Gunnison | 2,523 | 93,900 | 37.22 | 2,528 | 99,190 | 39.24 |
| Hinsdale | 196 | 4,590 | 23.42 | 159 | 5,185 | 32.61 |
| Huerfano | 1,810 | 51,085 | 28.98 | 1,856 | 51,475 | 27.73 |
| Jackson | 2,862 | 58,430 | 20.41 | 2,580 | 50,440 | 19.55 |
| Jefferson | 2,921 | 79,950 | 27.37 | 2,912 | 96,645 | 33.19 |
| Kiowa | 957 | 38,280 | 40.00 | 1,110 | 44,360 | 39.96 |
| Kit Carson | 7,622 | 234,091 | 30.71 | 7,393 | 265,736 | 35.94 |
| Lake | 150 | 6,225 | 41.50 | 234 | 8,360 | 35.73 |
| La Plata | 2,856 | 71,400 | 25.00 | 2,931 | 83,005 | 28.32 |
| Larimer | 7,452 | 250,540 | 33.62 | 7,764 | 267,700 | 34.48 |
| Las Animas | 6,310 | 126,091 | 19.98 | 6,908 | 139,139 | 20.14 |
| Lincoln | 4,945 | 114,790 | 23.21 | 5,487 | 131,835 | 24.03 |
| Logan | 9,503 | 295,280 | 31.07 | 9,831 | 319,250 | 32.47 |
| Mesa | 5,325 | 185,150 | 34.77 | 5,510 | 200,655 | 36.41 |
| Mineral | 280 | 8,395 | 29.98 | 323 | 9,195 | 28.46 |
| Moffat | 4,571 | 88,320 | 19.32 | 5,284 | 104,380 | 19.75 |
| Montezuma | 1,725 | 65,355 | 37.88 | 2,315 | 67,875 | 29.32 |
| Montrose | 3,703 | 130,990 | 35.38 | 4,724 | 148,010 | 31.33 |
| Morgan | 7,598 | 239,010 | 31.46 | 8,187 | 269,310 | 32.90 |
| Otero | 5,204 | 160,990 | 30.93 | 5,557 | 188,445 | 33.91 |
| Ouray | 600 | 16,800 | 28.00 | 590 | 16,570 | 28.08 |
| Park | 1,774 | 60,760 | 34.25 | 1,643 | 58,860 | 35.83 |
| Phillips | 3,283 | 106,215 | 32.35 | 3,264 | 105,175 | 32.22 |
| Pitkin | 822 | 21,320 | 25.94 | 847 | 27,400 | 32.35 |
| Prowers | 8,515 | 175,085 | 20.56 | 8,814 | 185,516 | 21.05 |
| Pueblo | 4,244 | 141,180 | 33.27 | 4,405 | 155,295 | 35.25 |
| Rio Blanco | 2,465 | 81,760 | 33.17 | 2,660 | 88,115 | 33.13 |
| Rio Grande | 2,196 | 85,075 | 38.74 | 2,437 | 106,085 | 43.53 |
| Routt | 5,399 | 190,990 | 35.38 | 5,638 | 209,750 | 37.20 |
| Saguache | 2,100 | 71,020 | 33.82 | 2,415 | 80,918 | 33.50 |
| San Juan | 37 | 1,785 | 48.24 | 44 | 2,255 | 51.25 |
| San Miguel | 609 | 24,925 | 40.93 | 627 | 29,215 | 46.59 |
| Sedgwick | 2,399 | 90,515 | 37.73 | 2,506 | 98,440 | 39.28 |
| Summit | 449 | 15,655 | 34.87 | 465 | 17,670 | 38.00 |
| Teller | 664 | 21,560 | 32.47 | 689 | 19,450 | 28.23 |
| Washington | 8,378 | 202,935 | 24.22 | 8,728 | 218,945 | 25.09 |
| Weld | 21,071 | 791,850 | 37.58 | 22,000 | 848,670 | 38.58 |
| Yuma | 8,197 | 253,240 | 30.89 | 8,952 | 300,310 | 33.55 |
| State | 216,811 | $6,704,193 | $30.92 | 225,609 | $7,294,217 | $32.33 |

## MULES IN COLORADO, 1930 AND 1931
### (From Reports of County Assessors to State Tax Commission)

| COUNTY | 1931 | | | 1930 | | |
|---|---|---|---|---|---|---|
| | Number | Assessed Value | Average Per Head | Number | Assessed Value | Average Per Head |
| Adams | 329 | $ 12,565 | $38.20 | 352 | $ 13,540 | $38.46 |
| Alamosa | 114 | 8,200 | 71.93 | 147 | 10,675 | 72.62 |
| Arapahoe | 214 | 8,345 | 39.00 | 200 | 8,215 | 41.08 |
| Archuleta | 58 | 1,875 | 32.33 | 59 | 2,240 | 37.97 |
| Baca | 878 | 22,445 | 25.56 | 650 | 16,510 | 25.40 |
| Bent | 440 | 16,165 | 36.74 | 465 | 18,635 | 40.07 |
| Boulder | 335 | 16,270 | 48.57 | 382 | 19,580 | 51.26 |
| Chaffee | 21 | 840 | 40.00 | 18 | 770 | 42.78 |
| Cheyenne | 242 | 7,365 | 30.43 | 302 | 10,085 | 33.40 |
| Clear Creek | ----- | ------- | ---- | 2 | 30 | 15.00 |
| Conejos | 262 | 12,870 | 49.12 | 234 | 11,680 | 50.00 |
| Costilla | 84 | 4,020 | 47.85 | 76 | 2,780 | 36.58 |
| Crowley | 399 | 15,755 | 39.48 | 377 | 17,390 | 46.13 |
| Custer | 33 | 960 | 29.08 | 29 | 1,000 | 34.48 |
| Delta | 341 | 13,650 | 40.03 | 304 | 13,480 | 44.34 |
| Denver | 53 | 1,660 | 31.32 | 53 | 2,450 | 46.23 |
| Dolores | 55 | 1,620 | 29.45 | 79 | 2,320 | 29.37 |
| Douglas | 86 | 4,280 | 49.76 | 69 | 3,550 | 51.45 |
| Eagle | 95 | 4,415 | 46.47 | 82 | 4,190 | 51.10 |
| Elbert | 720 | 25,090 | 34.85 | 735 | 28,375 | 38.61 |
| El Paso | 1,119 | 36,260 | 32.40 | 1,124 | 39,450 | 35.10 |
| Fremont | 141 | 5,360 | 38.02 | 130 | 6,796. | 52.28 |
| Garfield | 270 | 12,220 | 45.26 | 264 | 12,300 | 46.60 |
| Gilpin | 1 | 25 | 25.00 | 1 | 30 | 30.00 |
| Grand | 14 | 495 | 35.36 | 18 | 540 | 30.00 |
| Gunnison | 256 | 10,110 | 39.49 | 256 | 12,900 | 50.40 |
| Hinsdale | 2 | 30 | 15.00 | ----- | ------ | ---- |
| Huerfano | 215 | 9,575 | 44.53 | 416 | 32,605 | 78.37 |
| Jackson | 27 | 730 | 27.04 | 55 | 1,460 | 26.54 |
| Jefferson | 111 | 4,175 | 37.61 | 144 | 6,345 | 44.06 |
| Kiowa | 171 | 6,840 | 40.00 | 166 | 6,640 | 40.00 |
| Kit Carson | 911 | 30,550 | 33.53 | 1,021 | 37,825 | 37.05 |
| Lake | ----- | ------- | ---- | 2 | 100 | 50.00 |
| La Plata | 167 | 4,195 | 25.12 | 171 | 4,900 | 28.65 |
| Larimer | 660 | 27,240 | 41.27 | 810 | 30,980 | 38.25 |
| Las Animas | 860 | 51,485 | 59.87 | 1,160 | 68,920 | 59.41 |
| Lincoln | 611 | 17,805 | 29.14 | 685 | 21,075 | 30.77 |
| Logan | 700 | 28,460 | 40.66 | 800 | 32,855 | 41.07 |
| Mesa | 302 | 11,920 | 39.47 | 430 | 18,310 | 42.58 |
| Mineral | 15 | 740 | 49.33 | 12 | 710 | 59.16 |
| Moffat | 137 | 4,410 | 32.19 | 215 | 6,905 | 32.11 |
| Montezuma | 249 | 11,020 | 44.25 | 277 | 9,100 | 32.85 |
| Montrose | 253 | 8,690 | 34.35 | 247 | 9,340 | 37.81 |
| Morgan | 733 | 30,780 | 41.99 | 764 | 34,320 | 44.92 |
| Otero | 964 | 45,740 | 47.45 | 926 | 46,155 | 49.84 |
| Ouray | 36 | 900 | 25.00 | 46 | 1,250 | 27.17 |
| Park | 74 | 3,220 | 43.51 | 63 | 3,430 | 54.44 |
| Phillips | 389 | 16,010 | 41.15 | 388 | 16,160 | 41.65 |
| Pitkin | 12 | 380 | 31.67 | 14 | 340 | 24.29 |
| Prowers | 1,049 | 29,364 | 27.99 | 1,084 | 31,551 | 29.11 |
| Pueblo | 393 | 18,190 | 46.28 | 396 | 18,645 | 47.09 |
| Rio Blanco | 172 | 6,480 | 37.67 | 179 | 6,935 | 38.74 |
| Rio Grande | 432 | 19,555 | 45.26 | 480 | 24,730 | 51.52 |
| Routt | 36 | 1,440 | 40.00 | 30 | 1,500 | 50.00 |
| Saguache | 211 | 8,065 | 38.22 | 240 | 9,265 | 38.60 |
| San Juan | 30 | 940 | 31.33 | 30 | 1,220 | 40.66 |
| San Miguel | 24 | 920 | 38.33 | 31 | 1,230 | 39.68 |
| Sedgwick | 251 | 11,935 | 47.55 | 275 | 12,240 | 44.51 |
| Summit | 2 | 70 | 35.00 | 3 | 90 | 30.00 |
| Teller | 34 | 1,420 | 41.77 | 40 | 2,430 | 60.75 |
| Washington | 609 | 16,160 | 26.54 | 628 | 17,335 | 27.60 |
| Weld | 2,030 | 88,780 | 43.73 | 2,132 | 93,060 | 43.65 |
| Yuma | 1,156 | 42,200 | 36.51 | 1,226 | 47,720 | 38.92 |
| State | 20,588 | $803,274 | $39.02 | 21,994 | $917,187 | $41.70 |

### DAIRY CATTLE IN COLORADO, 1930 AND 1931
#### (From Reports of County Assessors to State Tax Commission)

| COUNTY | 1931 | | | 1930 | | |
|---|---|---|---|---|---|---|
| | Number | Assessed Value | Average Per Head | Number | Assessed Value | Average Per Head |
| Adams | 6,661 | $ 270,525 | $40.61 | 6,760 | $ 321,010 | $47.49 |
| Alamosa | 1,116 | 48,775 | 43.71 | 1,164 | 58,190 | 49.99 |
| Arapahoe | 4,511 | 204,115 | 45.25 | 4,359 | 227,770 | 52.25 |
| Archuleta | 806 | 40,380 | 50.10 | 651 | 32,695 | 50.22 |
| Baca | 1,759 | 55,981 | 31.83 | 1,535 | 65,430 | 42.63 |
| Bent | 1,616 | 59,010 | 36.52 | 1,489 | 69,435 | 46.63 |
| Boulder | 5,774 | 211,320 | 36.60 | 5,800 | 257,480 | 44.39 |
| Chaffee | 864 | 31,075 | 35.97 | 904 | 45,020 | 49.80 |
| Cheyenne | 978 | 29,690 | 30.36 | 853 | 44,500 | 52.17 |
| Clear Creek | 71 | 3,260 | 45.92 | 100 | 4,970 | 49.70 |
| Conejos | 1,749 | 73,675 | 42.12 | 1,564 | 78,650 | 50.29 |
| Costilla | 225 | 11,190 | 49.73 | 383 | 19,190 | 50.10 |
| Crowley | 1,230 | 47,200 | 38.37 | 939 | 47,140 | 50.20 |
| Custer | 808 | 34,170 | 42.29 | 803 | 35,070 | 43.67 |
| Delta | 4,899 | 197,190 | 40.25 | 4,195 | 209,750 | 50.00 |
| Denver | 337 | 17,410 | 51.66 | 350 | 15,290 | 43.69 |
| Dolores | 172 | 6,295 | 36.60 | 323 | 13,126 | 40.64 |
| Douglas | 4,541 | 229,735 | 50.59 | 4,805 | 240,310 | 50.01 |
| Eagle | 1,210 | 48,400 | 40.00 | 1,192 | 59,600 | 50.00 |
| Elbert | 3,845 | 155,000 | 40.31 | 6,152 | 308,325 | 50.12 |
| El Paso | 8,153 | 310,020 | 38.03 | 7,480 | 360,420 | 48.18 |
| Fremont | 1,436 | 64,865 | 45.17 | 1,684 | 89,832 | 53.34 |
| Garfield | 3,481 | 158,200 | 45.45 | 3,313 | 166,670 | 50.31 |
| Gilpin | 38 | 1,600 | 42.11 | 39 | 1,720 | 44.10 |
| Grand | 1,307 | 39,420 | 30.16 | 1,215 | 60,950 | 50.16 |
| Gunnison | 1,232 | 48,955 | 39.74 | 1,269 | 63,470 | 50.02 |
| Hinsdale | 76 | 3,080 | 40.53 | 266 | 10,704 | 40.24 |
| Huerfano | 1,667 | 58,985 | 35.38 | 1,756 | 76,123 | 43.35 |
| Jackson | 681 | 27,240 | 40.00 | 696 | 34,800 | 50.00 |
| Jefferson | 4,672 | 205,070 | 43.89 | 4,596 | 236,420 | 51.44 |
| Kiowa | 516 | 25,800 | 50.00 | 563 | 28,150 | 50.00 |
| Kit Carson | 5,083 | 194,064 | 38.18 | 5,403 | 272,145 | 50.37 |
| Lake | 161 | 8,075 | 50.16 | 163 | 8,150 | 50.00 |
| La Plata | 2,523 | 101,640 | 40.29 | 2,448 | 123,490 | 50.44 |
| Larimer | 6,230 | 292,600 | 46.97 | 6,618 | 319,990 | 48.31 |
| Las Animas | 2,344 | 101,475 | 43.29 | 3,737 | 162,068 | 43.37 |
| Lincoln | 3,278 | 109,550 | 33.42 | 2,950 | 136,835 | 46.38 |
| Logan | 7,349 | 236,655 | 32.20 | 7,040 | 302,035 | 42.90 |
| Mesa | 6,023 | 253,990 | 42.17 | 6,490 | 324,830 | 50.05 |
| Mineral | 84 | 3,620 | 43.10 | 83 | 3,910 | 47.11 |
| Moffat | 1,266 | 46,090 | 36.41 | 1,400 | 67,080 | 47.91 |
| Montezuma | 2,767 | 101,235 | 36.59 | 2,538 | 127,120 | 50.09 |
| Montrose | 3,529 | 132,455 | 37.53 | 3,184 | 159,235 | 50.01 |
| Morgan | 5,836 | 201,960 | 34.61 | 6,069 | 250,290 | 41.24 |
| Otero | 3,232 | 119,415 | 36.95 | 3,261 | 169,715 | 52.04 |
| Ouray | 479 | 17,370 | 36.26 | 483 | 22,460 | 46.50 |
| Park | 731 | 30,350 | 41.52 | 692 | 34,710 | 50.16 |
| Phillips | 2,992 | 100,810 | 33.69 | 2,877 | 115,070 | 40.00 |
| Pitkin | 442 | 13,280 | 30.05 | 503 | 20,120 | 40.00 |
| Prowers | 4,209 | 138,129 | 32.82 | 3,673 | 157,470 | 42.87 |
| Pueblo | 4,454 | 178,470 | 40.07 | 4,371 | 202,685 | 46.36 |
| Rio Blanco | 719 | 31,690 | 44.08 | 711 | 39,555 | 55.63 |
| Rio Grande | 1,296 | 57,090 | 44.05 | 1,302 | 65,100 | 50.00 |
| Routt | 3,033 | 122,330 | 40.33 | 3,320 | 166,630 | 50.19 |
| Saguache | 681 | 27,150 | 39.87 | 801 | 40,080 | 50.04 |
| San Juan | 42 | 1,975 | 47.02 | 27 | 1,140 | 42.22 |
| San Miguel | 728 | 28,230 | 38.78 | 619 | 30,785 | 49.73 |
| Sedgwick | 2,208 | 84,850 | 38.43 | 2,078 | 91,180 | 43.88 |
| Summit | 308 | 12,320 | 40.00 | 360 | 14,400 | 40.00 |
| Teller | 549 | 22,730 | 41.40 | 570 | 24,100 | 42.28 |
| Washington | 4,157 | 152,540 | 36.69 | 2,380 | 119,180 | 50.08 |
| Weld | 20,962 | 774,540 | 36.95 | 20,167 | 916,770 | 45.46 |
| Yuma | 4,361 | 134,510 | 30.84 | 7,866 | 321,980 | 40.93 |
| State | 168,487 | $6,548,819 | $38.87 | 171,382 | $8,092,468 | $47.22 |

RANGE CATTLE IN COLORADO, 1930 AND 1931
(From Reports of County Assessors to State Tax Commission)

| COUNTY | 1931 | | | 1930 | | |
|---|---|---|---|---|---|---|
| | Number | Assessed Value | Average Per Head | Number | Assessed Value | Average Per Head |
| Adams | 6,087 | $ 167,290 | $27.48 | 5,537 | $ 182,910 | $33.03 |
| Alamosa | 7,314 | 198,775 | 27.18 | 6,369 | 209,185 | 32.84 |
| Arapahoe | 5,676 | 154,900 | 27.29 | 6,238 | 220,825 | 35.40 |
| Archuleta | 10,076 | 263,526 | 26.15 | 8,901 | 306,237 | 34.40 |
| Baca | 24,153 | 633,508 | 26.23 | 21,902 | 747,781 | 34.14 |
| Bent | 14,214 | 363,055 | 25.54 | 13,083 | 445,300 | 34.04 |
| Boulder | 6,084 | 164,700 | 27.07 | 5,832 | 193,650 | 33.20 |
| Chaffee | 5,350 | 150,375 | 28.11 | 4,980 | 171,825 | 34.50 |
| Cheyenne | 18,351 | 469,845 | 25.60 | 19,821 | 666,365 | 33.62 |
| Clear Creek | 371 | 9,575 | 25.81 | 196 | 6,920 | 35.31 |
| Conejos | 10,192 | 265,465 | 26.05 | 10,370 | 369,580 | 35.64 |
| Costilla | 1,806 | 46,195 | 25.58 | 1,977 | 66,390 | 33.58 |
| Crowley | 8,000 | 207,480 | 25.94 | 9,689 | 325,450 | 33.59 |
| Custer | 6,529 | 169,740 | 26.00 | 6,150 | 205,975 | 33.49 |
| Delta | 17,830 | 477,225 | 26.77 | 16,890 | 571,085 | 33.81 |
| Denver | ----- | ------- | ---- | ----- | ------- | ---- |
| Dolores | 3,973 | 108,360 | 27.27 | 2,800 | 98,643 | 35.23 |
| Douglas | 14,677 | 456,950 | 31.13 | 12,368 | 469,570 | 37.97 |
| Eagle | 18,186 | 499,940 | 27.49 | 16,340 | 575,899 | 35.24 |
| Elbert | 22,235 | 588,235 | 26.46 | 19,162 | 642,369 | 33.52 |
| El Paso | 20,399 | 610,720 | 29.94 | 20,722 | 731,380 | 35.29 |
| Fremont | 8,384 | 227,460 | 27.13 | 8,049 | 273,975 | 34.04 |
| Garfield | 27,458 | 730,720 | 26.61 | 24,666 | 856,320 | 34.72 |
| Gilpin | 938 | 24,274 | 25.88 | 494 | 16,001 | 32.39 |
| Grand | 11,997 | 333,480 | 27.80 | 10,820 | 393,185 | 36.34 |
| Gunnison | 30,413 | 792,860 | 26.07 | 28,027 | 954,250 | 34.05 |
| Hinsdale | 1,320 | 34,505 | 26.14 | 1,371 | 46,279 | 33.76 |
| Huerfano | 11,158 | 297,450 | 26.66 | 11,109 | 391,233 | 35.22 |
| Jackson | 28,841 | 810,740 | 28.11 | 26,766 | 901,880 | 33.69 |
| Jefferson | 9,650 | 271,110 | 28.09 | 9,038 | 312,800 | 34.61 |
| Kiowa | 12,506 | 342,305 | 27.37 | 13,161 | 443,650 | 33.71 |
| Kit Carson | 19,286 | 506,406 | 26.26 | 16,750 | 562,024 | 33.55 |
| Lake | 403 | 13,990 | 34.71 | 394 | 14,090 | 35.76 |
| La Plata | 12,577 | 320,605 | 25.49 | 11,776 | 392,345 | 33.32 |
| Larimer | 19,983 | 557,420 | 27.89 | 17,975 | 613,450 | 34.13 |
| Las Animas | 44,388 | 1,128,320 | 25.42 | 40,426 | 1,447,187 | 35.80 |
| Lincoln | 25,201 | 669,035 | 26.55 | 25,193 | 846,085 | 33.58 |
| Logan | 20,595 | 538,435 | 26.14 | 18,385 | 628,355 | 34.18 |
| Mesa | 33,825 | 905,480 | 26.77 | 33,071 | 1,093,920 | 33.08 |
| Mineral | 1,139 | 30,695 | 26.95 | 1,381 | 49,320 | 35.71 |
| Moffat | 14,274 | 385,700 | 27.02 | 12,595 | 426,265 | 33.84 |
| Montezuma | 9,976 | 267,760 | 26.84 | 8,475 | 268,960 | 31.74 |
| Montrose | 17,157 | 441,370 | 25.73 | 15,095 | 502,305 | 33.28 |
| Morgan | 11,893 | 302,690 | 25.45 | 10,210 | 331,580 | 32.48 |
| Otero | 10,805 | 287,170 | 26.58 | 11,407 | 374,875 | 32.86 |
| Ouray | 7,085 | 182,800 | 25.80 | 6,150 | 198,585 | 32.29 |
| Park | 12,679 | 378,130 | 29.82 | 11,520 | 398,740 | 34.61 |
| Phillips | 3,666 | 101,430 | 27.67 | 3,524 | 114,980 | 32.63 |
| Pitkin | 5,090 | 140,200 | 27.54 | 4,828 | 165,025 | 34.18 |
| Prowers | 16,564 | 423,951 | 25.58 | 14,051 | 464,309 | 33.04 |
| Pueblo | 20,620 | 549,405 | 26.64 | 18,567 | 642,980 | 34.63 |
| Rio Blanco | 30,140 | 795,170 | 26.38 | 26,922 | 898,900 | 33.39 |
| Rio Grande | 9,271 | 235,490 | 25.40 | 9,397 | 309,480 | 32.93 |
| Routt | 28,913 | 813,470 | 28.13 | 24,429 | 905,390 | 37.06 |
| Saguache | 25,316 | 662,728 | 26.18 | 25,122 | 838,623 | 33.38 |
| San Juan | 195 | 4,983 | 25.55 | 143 | 5,030 | 35.17 |
| San Miguel | 5,471 | 139,900 | 25.57 | 5,117 | 169,525 | 33.13 |
| Sedgwick | 5,945 | 155,470 | 26.15 | 5,386 | 180,540 | 33.52 |
| Summit | 3,021 | 77,930 | 25.80 | 3,478 | 117,530 | 33.79 |
| Teller | 4,400 | 131,965 | 29.99 | 4,478 | 158,865 | 35.48 |
| Washington | 23,510 | 599,031 | 25.48 | 22,641 | 757,627 | 33.46 |
| Weld | 25,336 | 680,620 | 26.86 | 21,548 | 740,890 | 34.38 |
| Yuma | 31,954 | 820,960 | 25.69 | 26,936 | 897,680 | 33.33 |
| State | 864,846 | $23,119,472 | $26.73 | 800,198 | $27,312,372 | $34.13 |

## SHEEP IN COLORADO, 1930 AND 1931
### (From Reports of County Assessors to State Tax Commission)

| COUNTY | 1931 | | | 1930 | | |
|---|---|---|---|---|---|---|
| | Number | Assessed Value | Average Per Head | Number | Assessed Value | Average Per Head |
| Adams | 3,412 | $ 11,965 | $ 3.51 | 5,002 | $ 27,500 | $ 5.50 |
| Alamosa | 13,998 | 51,980 | 3.71 | 8,472 | 51,920 | 6.13 |
| Arapahoe | 7,850 | 27,500 | 3.50 | 7,843 | 43,415 | 5.54 |
| Archuleta | 32,765 | 114,680 | 3.50 | 22,365 | 123,770 | 5.53 |
| Baca | 7,520 | 26,320 | 3.50 | 7,560 | 41,580 | 5.50 |
| Bent | 13,949 | 48,820 | 3.50 | 17,533 | 96,435 | 5.50 |
| Boulder | 3,800 | 13,600 | 3.58 | 5,698 | 31,340 | 5.50 |
| Chaffee | 6,394 | 23,185 | 3.63 | 6,154 | 34,165 | 5.55 |
| Cheyenne | 9,755 | 34,215 | 3.51 | 10,414 | 57,435 | 5.52 |
| Clear Creek | 846 | 2,960 | 3.50 | 1,917 | 10,545 | 5.50 |
| Conejos | 85,130 | 305,725 | 3.59 | 82,154 | 452,440 | 5.51 |
| Costilla | 25,150 | 88,045 | 3.50 | 23,226 | 127,740 | 5.50 |
| Crowley | 7,270 | 25,755 | 3.54 | 6,069 | 33,470 | 5.52 |
| Custer | 4,058 | 14,210 | 3.50 | 4,286 | 23,570 | 5.50 |
| Delta | 56,435 | 200,765 | 3.56 | 52,303 | 289,350 | 5.53 |
| Denver | ------ | ------ | ---- | ------ | ------ | |
| Dolores | 22,559 | 100,510 | 4.46 | 16,761 | 92,185 | 5.50 |
| Douglas | 5,980 | 21,815 | 3.65 | 1,070 | 8,390 | 7.84 |
| Eagle | 26,721 | 106,884 | 4.00 | 26,813 | 147,498 | 5.50 |
| Elbert | 11,320 | 41,247 | 3.64 | 10,424 | 58,140 | 5.58 |
| El Paso | 6,657 | 26,300 | 3.95 | 6,024 | 33,360 | 5.53 |
| Fremont | 2,850 | 10,248 | 3.60 | 2,850 | 15,925 | 5.59 |
| Garfield | 101,097 | 355,035 | 3.51 | 87,834 | 484,930 | 5.52 |
| Gilpin | 41 | 145 | 3.54 | ------ | ------ | ---- |
| Grand | 13,409 | 47,755 | 3.56 | 16,796 | 94,875 | 5.65 |
| Gunnison | 56,534 | 199,020 | 3.52 | 48,659 | 274,100 | 5.63 |
| Hinsdale | 4,980 | 17,430 | 3.50 | 3,958 | 21,545 | 5.44 |
| Huerfano | 23,819 | 84,366 | 3.54 | 25,429 | 140,199 | 5.51 |
| Jackson | 29,343 | 103,030 | 3.51 | 25,678 | 141,190 | 5.50 |
| Jefferson | 1,705 | 6,410 | 3.76 | 3,008 | 16,535 | 5.50 |
| Kiowa | 6,078 | 21,275 | 3.50 | 8,490 | 46,695 | 5.50 |
| Kit Carson | 3,511 | 13,210 | 3.76 | 4,340 | 23,874 | 5.50 |
| Lake | 400 | 1,400 | 3.50 | 412 | 2,265 | 5.50 |
| La Plata | 30,470 | 106,645 | 3.50 | 31,388 | 172,575 | 5.50 |
| Larimer | 14,794 | 51,780 | 3.50 | 15,625 | 93,470 | 5.98 |
| Las Animas | 82,107 | 287,365 | 3.50 | 78,992 | 486,043 | 6.15 |
| Lincoln | 11,423 | 40,040 | 3.51 | 10,373 | 57,180 | 5.51 |
| Logan | 2,711 | 9,500 | 3.50 | 3,537 | 19,453 | 5.50 |
| Mesa | 63,470 | 230,800 | 3.64 | 98,660 | 552,640 | 5.60 |
| Mineral | 13,096 | 45,870 | 3.50 | 11,723 | 67,195 | 5.73 |
| Moffat | 91,845 | 329,900 | 3.59 | 88,721 | 496,840 | 5.60 |
| Montezuma | 32,364 | 153,865 | 4.75 | 42,731 | 235,020 | 5.50 |
| Montrose | 74,757 | 259,900 | 3.48 | 62,660 | 344,630 | 5.50 |
| Morgan | 2,837 | 9,720 | 3.43 | 1,546 | 8,500 | 5.50 |
| Otero | 30,079 | 105,275 | 3.50 | 29,527 | 162,400 | 5.50 |
| Ouray | 14,414 | 50,450 | 3.50 | 13,746 | 75,600 | 5.50 |
| Park | 48,903 | 189,895 | 3.88 | 42,040 | 246,370 | 5.86 |
| Phillips | 303 | 1,115 | 3.68 | 212 | 1,275 | 6.00 |
| Pitkin | 11,447 | 40,065 | 3.50 | 6,194 | 35,375 | 5.71 |
| Prowers | 9,101 | 31,854 | 3.50 | 13,933 | 76,631 | 5.50 |
| Pueblo | 10,234 | 36,530 | 3.57 | 12,432 | 68,440 | 5.50 |
| Rio Blanco | 71,247 | 249,450 | 3.50 | 69,975 | 395,460 | 5.65 |
| Rio Grande | 45,560 | 159,600 | 3.50 | 51,219 | 281,705 | 5.50 |
| Routt | 76,165 | 291,430 | 3.83 | 79,579 | 456,820 | 5.74 |
| Saguache | 74,361 | 262,994 | 3.54 | 79,230 | 447,967 | 5.65 |
| San Juan | 10,874 | 38,061 | 3.50 | 8,595 | 47,318 | 5.51 |
| San Miguel | 38,352 | 134,325 | 3.50 | 40,070 | 221,585 | 5.53 |
| Sedgwick | 437 | 1,530 | 3.50 | 1,137 | 6,255 | 5.50 |
| Summit | 2,817 | 9,862 | 3.50 | 2,130 | 11,720 | 5.50 |
| Teller | 330 | 1,170 | 3.55 | 358 | 1,980 | 5.53 |
| Washington | 18,206 | 64,890 | 3.56 | 13,541 | 74,550 | 5.51 |
| Weld | 28,518 | 99,820 | 3.50 | 23,755 | 130,650 | 5.50 |
| Yuma | 2,117 | 7,410 | 3.50 | 3,321 | 18,760 | 5.65 |
| State | 1,508,675 | $5,446,916 | $ 3.61 | 1,486,492 | $8,340,788 | $ 5.61 |

## SWINE IN COLORADO, 1930 AND 1931
### (From Reports of County Assessors to State Tax Commission)

| COUNTY | 1931 | | | 1930 | | |
|---|---|---|---|---|---|---|
| | Number | Assessed Value | Average Per Head | Number | Assessed Value | Average Per Head |
| Adams | 11,020 | $ 101,375 | $ 9.20 | 11,788 | $ 91,390 | $ 7.75 |
| Alamosa | 1,176 | 13,535 | 11.51 | 1,444 | 16,840 | 11.66 |
| Arapahoe | 1,890 | 17,370 | 9.19 | 1,357 | 13,765 | 10.14 |
| Archuleta | 564 | 3,415 | 6.05 | 414 | 3,184 | 7.69 |
| Baca | 6,921 | 53,125 | 7.68 | 6,027 | 52,797 | 8.76 |
| Bent | 2,550 | 21,570 | 8.46 | 1,842 | 20,440 | 11.10 |
| Boulder | 1,802 | 17,590 | 9.76 | 1,432 | 14,870 | 10.39 |
| Chaffee | 1,277 | 9,190 | 7.20 | 1,459 | 12,345 | 8.46 |
| Cheyenne | 3,066 | 22,685 | 7.40 | 2,682 | 26,845 | 10.01 |
| Clear Creek | ---- | ------ | ---- | ---- | ------- | ---- |
| Conejos | 2,215 | 25,330 | 11.44 | 2,652 | 30,205 | 11.39 |
| Costilla | 1,800 | 12,425 | 6.90 | 1,267 | 12,315 | 9.72 |
| Crowley | 1,675 | 16,470 | 9.84 | 1,730 | 17,015 | 9.84 |
| Custer | 394 | 2,765 | 7.02 | 301 | 2,200 | 7.31 |
| Delta | 2,341 | 17,280 | 7.38 | 2,342 | 22,180 | 9.47 |
| Denver | ---- | ------ | ---- | ---- | ------- | ---- |
| Dolores | 107 | 875 | 8.18 | 134 | 1,885 | 14.07 |
| Douglas | 833 | 8,310 | 9.97 | 744 | 7,830 | 10.52 |
| Eagle | 506 | 6,072 | 12.00 | 468 | 5,616 | 12.00 |
| Elbert | 4,196 | 42,439 | 10.11 | 3,698 | 39,547 | 10.69 |
| El Paso | 3,617 | 31,490 | 8.71 | 3,327 | 33,430 | 10.05 |
| Fremont | 1,297 | 10,830 | 8.35 | 1,388 | 12,398 | 8.93 |
| Garfield | 2,724 | 23,935 | 8.79 | 2,711 | 25,825 | 9.53 |
| Gilpin | ---- | ------ | ---- | 3 | 35 | 11.67 |
| Grand | 91 | 900 | 9.89 | 160 | 1,600 | 10.00 |
| Gunnison | 167 | 1,205 | 7.22 | 227 | 2,085 | 9.19 |
| Hinsdale | ---- | ------ | ---- | ---- | ------- | ---- |
| Huerfano | 436 | 3,480 | 7.98 | 448 | 4,060 | 9.06 |
| Jackson | 72 | 720 | 10.00 | 84 | 840 | 10.00 |
| Jefferson | 779 | 7,795 | 10.00 | 1,143 | 8,850 | 7.74 |
| Kiowa | 1,198 | 11,620 | 9.70 | 1,004 | 12,625 | 12.57 |
| Kit Carson | 15,207 | 132,752 | 8.73 | 12,424 | 127,292 | 10.24 |
| Lake | ---- | ------ | ---- | ---- | ------- | ---- |
| La Plata | 1,679 | 12,895 | 7.68 | 1,580 | 10,755 | 6.81 |
| Larimer | 2,619 | 24,950 | 9.52 | 2,581 | 24,520 | 9.50 |
| Las Animas | 1,150 | 9,828 | 8.55 | 1,167 | 12,892 | 11.05 |
| Lincoln | 5,786 | 49,625 | 8.58 | 5,264 | 49,595 | 9.42 |
| Logan | 14,000 | 124,185 | 8.87 | 12,479 | 121,065 | 9.70 |
| Mesa | 3,154 | 29,865 | 9.47 | 3,350 | 37,890 | 11.31 |
| Mineral | ---- | ------ | ---- | ---- | ------- | ---- |
| Moffat | 792 | 7,140 | 9.02 | 650 | 6,845 | 10.53 |
| Montezuma | 828 | 7,660 | 9.25 | 1,021 | 6,850 | 6.71 |
| Montrose | 2,812 | 22,500 | 8.00 | 4,000 | 38,920 | 9.73 |
| Morgan | 7,401 | 66,180 | 8.94 | 9,225 | 75,110 | 8.14 |
| Otero | 4,138 | 35,685 | 8.62 | 3,920 | 37,725 | 9.62 |
| Ouray | 220 | 1,320 | 6.00 | 203 | 1,421 | 7.00 |
| Park | 64 | 485 | 7.58 | 42 | 460 | 11.00 |
| Phillips | 8,454 | 75,645 | 8.95 | 7,901 | 79,385 | 10.05 |
| Pitkin | 220 | 2,250 | 10.23 | 315 | 2,640 | 8.38 |
| Prowers | 5,655 | 49,544 | 8.76 | 6,972 | 60,696 | 8.71 |
| Pueblo | 2,958 | 21,725 | 7.34 | 3,251 | 24,605 | 7.57 |
| Rio Blanco | 298 | 2,740 | 9.19 | 321 | 3,210 | 10.00 |
| Rio Grande | 2,094 | 26,360 | 12.59 | 2,643 | 36,240 | 13.71 |
| Routt | 1,609 | 14,850 | 9.23 | 1,428 | 13,250 | 9.28 |
| Saguache | 835 | 9,493 | 11.37 | 1,190 | 15,095 | 12.68 |
| San Juan | ---- | ------ | ---- | ---- | ------- | ---- |
| San Miguel | 135 | 1,120 | 8.30 | 169 | 1,635 | 9.67 |
| Sedgwick | 4,563 | 51,650 | 11.32 | 3,382 | 43,395 | 12.83 |
| Summit | 29 | 348 | 12.00 | 31 | 375 | 12.00 |
| Teller | 67 | 535 | 7.99 | 50 | 505 | 10.10 |
| Washington | 13,182 | 113,535 | 8.61 | 12,859 | 126,250 | 9.82 |
| Weld | 11,593 | 114,550 | 9.88 | 10,716 | 111,280 | 10.38 |
| Yuma | 18,127 | 159,370 | 8.79 | 17,496 | 183,150 | 10.47 |
| State | 184,383 | $1,652,581 | $ 8.96 | 178,906 | $1,746,068 | $ 9.76 |

## FOXES AND GOATS IN COLORADO, 1931
### (From Reports of County Assessors to State Tax Commission)

| COUNTY | FOXES, 1931 | | | GOATS, 1931 | | |
|---|---|---|---|---|---|---|
| | Number | Assessed Value | Average Per Head | Number | Assessed Value | Average Per Head |
| Adams | ----- | ------- | ---- | ----- | ------- | --- |
| Alamosa | ----- | ------- | ---- | ----- | ------- | --- |
| Arapahoe | 57 | $ 2,640 | $46.32 | 138 | $ 700 | $ 5.0 |
| Archuleta | ----- | ------- | ---- | 1,654 | 5,235 | 3.1 |
| Baca | 27 | 1,365 | 50.56 | ----- | ------- | --- |
| Bent | ----- | ------- | ---- | ----- | ------- | --- |
| Boulder | 281 | 12,430 | 44.24 | ----- | ------- | --- |
| Chaffee | ----- | ------- | ---- | 40 | 200 | 5.0 |
| Cheyenne | ----- | ------- | ---- | ----- | ------- | --- |
| Clear Creek | 4 | 160 | 40.00 | 28 | 280 | 10.0 |
| Conejos | ----- | ------- | ---- | ----- | ------- | --- |
| Costilla | 20 | 1,000 | 50.00 | 91 | 455 | 5.0 |
| Crowley | ----- | ------- | ---- | 23 | 95 | 4.1 |
| Custer | 120 | 6,000 | 50.00 | ----- | ------- | --- |
| Delta | ----- | ------- | ---- | 3,554 | 3,745 | 1.0 |
| Denver | ----- | ------- | ---- | ----- | ------- | --- |
| Dolores | ----- | ------- | ---- | 200 | 1,080 | 5.4 |
| Douglas | 204 | 9,460 | 46.37 | 470 | 2,135 | 4.5 |
| Eagle | 28 | 1,400 | 50.00 | 9 | 45 | 5.0 |
| Elbert | 40 | 2,000 | 50.00 | ----- | ------- | --- |
| El Paso | 434 | 21,700 | 50.00 | 319 | 2,790 | 8.7 |
| Fremont | ----- | ------- | ---- | 100 | 350 | 3.5 |
| Garfield | 123 | 6,000 | 48.78 | ----- | ------- | --- |
| Gilpin | 74 | 4,220 | 57.02 | 14 | 42 | 3.0 |
| Grand | 18 | 900 | 50.00 | ----- | ------- | --- |
| Gunnison | 58 | 2,600 | 44.86 | 153 | 390 | 2.5 |
| Hinsdale | ----- | ------- | ---- | ----- | ------- | --- |
| Huerfano | 20 | 1,000 | 50.00 | 236 | 635 | 2.6 |
| Jackson | 5 | 150 | 30.00 | 4 | 40 | 10.0 |
| Jefferson | 1,221 | 54,590 | 44.71 | 261 | 1,425 | 5.4 |
| Kiowa | ----- | ------- | ---- | ----- | ------- | --- |
| Kit Carson | ----- | ------- | ---- | 52 | 172 | 3.3 |
| Lake | ----- | ------- | ---- | ----- | ------- | --- |
| La Plata | 110 | 5,500 | 50.00 | 909 | 1,265 | 1.3 |
| Larimer | 166 | 8,300 | 50.00 | 55 | 330 | 6.0 |
| Las Animas | ----- | ------- | ---- | 5,590 | 14,976 | 2.6 |
| Lincoln | ----- | ------- | ---- | ----- | ------- | --- |
| Logan | ----- | ------- | ---- | ----- | ------- | --- |
| Mesa | 8 | 640 | 80.00 | 415 | 1,300 | 3.1 |
| Mineral | ----- | ------- | ---- | 9 | 225 | 25.0 |
| Moffat | ----- | ------- | ---- | 120 | 365 | 3.0 |
| Montezuma | ----- | ------- | ---- | 140 | 620 | 4.4 |
| Montrose | 60 | 3,025 | 50.41 | ----- | ------- | --- |
| Morgan | 84 | 4,200 | 50.00 | ----- | ------- | --- |
| Otero | ----- | ------- | ---- | ----- | ------- | --- |
| Ouray | ----- | ------- | ---- | ----- | ------- | --- |
| Park | 20 | 1,000 | 50.00 | 73 | 300 | 4. |
| Phillips | ----- | ------- | ---- | ----- | ------- | --- |
| Pitkin | 23 | 1,150 | 50.00 | ----- | ------- | --- |
| Prowers | ----- | ------- | ---- | 153 | 520 | 3. |
| Pueblo | 18 | 900 | 50.00 | 304 | 1,340 | 4. |
| Rio Blanco | ----- | ------- | ---- | ----- | ------- | -- |
| Rio Grande | 192 | 8,840 | 43.44 | ----- | ------- | -- |
| Routt | 42 | 1,380 | 32.86 | ----- | ------- | -- |
| Saguache | ----- | ------- | ---- | ----- | ------- | -- |
| San Juan | ----- | ------- | ---- | ----- | ------- | -- |
| San Miguel | ----- | ------- | ---- | ----- | ------- | -- |
| Sedgwick | 30 | 1,500 | 50.00 | ----- | ------- | -- |
| Summit | 6 | 300 | 50.00 | ----- | ------- | -- |
| Teller | 104 | 3,580 | 34.42 | 84 | 280 | 3. |
| Washington | ----- | ------- | ---- | ----- | ------- | -- |
| Weld | ----- | ------- | ---- | ----- | ------- | -- |
| Yuma | ----- | ------- | ---- | 5 | 10 | 2. |
| State | 3,597 | $167,430 | $46.55 | 15,203 | $ 41,345 | $ 2. |

**AVERAGE VALUE OF HORSES AND MULES PER HEAD AS RETURNED BY COUNTY ASSESSORS FOR 1914, 1919, 1930, 1931.**

| COUNTY | HORSES | | | | MULES | | | |
|---|---|---|---|---|---|---|---|---|
| | 1931 | 1930 | 1919 | 1914 | 1931 | 1930 | 1919 | 1914 |
| Adams | $32.86 | $35.26 | $87.30 | $73.58 | $38.20 | $38.47 | $113.50 | $93.64 |
| Alamosa | 56.02 | 58.93 | 73.33 | 43.74 | 71.93 | 72.62 | 111.90 | 81.57 |
| Arapahoe | 32.39 | 36.20 | 68.36 | 62.86 | 39.00 | 41.08 | 84.73 | 82.05 |
| Archuleta | 30.08 | 31.55 | 61.72 | 44.12 | 32.33 | 37.97 | 60.00 | 63.71 |
| Baca | 18.94 | 18.10 | 45.00 | 34.20 | 25.56 | 25.40 | 60.00 | 45.97 |
| Bent | 36.33 | 26.57 | 57.71 | 58.20 | 36.74 | 40.07 | 70.25 | 68.11 |
| Boulder | 35.96 | 40.73 | 113.04 | 83.55 | 48.57 | 51.26 | 114.81 | 88.59 |
| Chaffee | 36.60 | 41.39 | 62.88 | 55.67 | 40.00 | 42.78 | 85.00 | 100.00 |
| Cheyenne | 25.49 | 25.11 | 59.09 | 40.61 | 30.43 | 33.40 | 81.56 | 73.34 |
| Clear Creek | 35.79 | 41.33 | 66.39 | 70.03 | .... | 15.00 | 62.50 | 112.50 |
| Conejos | 42.25 | 39.96 | 75.40 | 66.50 | 49.12 | 50.00 | 87.00 | 98.53 |
| Costilla | 25.03 | 35.44 | 74.50 | 46.12 | 47.85 | 36.58 | 76.68 | 100.73 |
| Crowley | 33.73 | 34.20 | 67.61 | 70.03 | 39.48 | 46.13 | 84.74 | 94.80 |
| Custer | 29.06 | 29.58 | 67.51 | 60.36 | 29.08 | 34.48 | 67.80 | 53.21 |
| Delta | 32.54 | 35.02 | 85.01 | 75.17 | 40.03 | 44.34 | 95.20 | 102.97 |
| Denver | 44.08 | 45.97 | 100.00 | 63.79 | 31.32 | 46.23 | 100.00 | 77.16 |
| Dolores | 24.06 | 23.60 | 78.72 | 67.70 | 29.45 | 29.37 | 105.78 | 80.83 |
| Douglas | 52.24 | 50.98 | 68.79 | 64.17 | 49.76 | 51.45 | 97.10 | 63.15 |
| Eagle | 33.97 | 37.89 | 81.94 | 66.91 | 46.47 | 51.10 | 78.30 | 96.15 |
| Elbert | 31.74 | 32.22 | 68.20 | 56.00 | 34.85 | 38.61 | 87.89 | 72.37 |
| El Paso | 28.19 | 29.63 | 67.00 | 60.19 | 32.40 | 35.10 | 89.00 | 82.92 |
| Fremont | 29.01 | 29.61 | 53.72 | 56.64 | 38.02 | 52.28 | 78.00 | 72.75 |
| Garfield | 36.50 | 41.29 | 72.03 | 65.20 | 45.26 | 46.60 | 96.42 | 78.77 |
| Gilpin | 31.77 | 29.88 | 60.48 | 58.22 | 25.00 | 30.00 | 75.00 | 56.00 |
| Grand | 26.20 | 26.84 | 64.08 | 55.01 | 35.36 | 30.00 | 62.66 | 67.27 |
| Gunnison | 37.22 | 39.24 | 70.06 | 61.99 | 39.49 | 50.40 | 104.89 | 100.48 |
| Hinsdale | 23.42 | 32.61 | 58.00 | 52.09 | 15.00 | .... | 53.00 | 66.66 |
| Huerfano | 28.08 | 27.73 | 64.50 | 74.11 | 44.53 | 78.37 | 122.00 | 97.91 |
| Jackson | 20.41 | 19.55 | 48.88 | 61.53 | 27.04 | 26.54 | 84.68 | 72.76 |
| Jefferson | 27.37 | 33.19 | 71.19 | 75.13 | 37.61 | 44.06 | 102.45 | 110.00 |
| Kiowa | 40.00 | 39.96 | 59.65 | 45.57 | 40.00 | 40.00 | 95.04 | 93.09 |
| Kit Carson | 30.71 | 35.94 | 52.13 | 58.58 | 33.53 | 37.05 | 58.04 | 66.02 |
| Lake | 41.50 | 35.73 | 73.95 | 88.15 | .... | 50.00 | 73.20 | .... |
| La Plata | 25.00 | 28.32 | 69.20 | 67.54 | 25.12 | 28.65 | 72.28 | 64.73 |
| Larimer | 33.62 | 34.48 | 112.00 | 87.30 | 41.27 | 38.25 | 123.40 | 111.74 |
| Las Animas | 19.98 | 20.14 | 49.70 | 61.00 | 59.87 | 59.41 | 103.00 | 93.16 |
| Lincoln | 23.21 | 24.03 | 54.83 | 52.33 | 29.14 | 30.77 | 89.52 | 67.20 |
| Logan | 31.07 | 32.47 | 93.29 | 66.24 | 40.66 | 41.07 | 106.98 | 87.25 |
| Mesa | 34.77 | 36.41 | 73.29 | 60.26 | 39.47 | 42.58 | 87.82 | 86.92 |
| Mineral | 29.98 | 28.46 | 54.71 | 48.72 | 49.33 | 59.16 | 84.00 | 35.00 |
| Moffat | 19.32 | 19.75 | 63.00 | 50.60 | 32.19 | 32.11 | 85.40 | 105.84 |
| Montezuma | 37.88 | 29.32 | 71.20 | 90.00 | 44.25 | 32.85 | 82.60 | 100.00 |
| Montrose | 35.38 | 31.33 | 81.39 | 71.77 | 34.35 | 37.81 | 98.89 | 94.19 |
| Morgan | 31.46 | 32.90 | 87.84 | 80.40 | 41.99 | 44.92 | 95.56 | 105.34 |
| Otero | 30.93 | 33.91 | 74.41 | 75.82 | 47.45 | 49.84 | 98.78 | 103.63 |
| Ouray | 28.00 | 28.08 | 55.95 | 68.87 | 25.00 | 27.17 | 62.04 | 71.71 |
| Park | 34.25 | 35.83 | 71.14 | 60.99 | 43.51 | 54.44 | 81.80 | 117.20 |
| Phillips | 32.35 | 32.22 | 66.40 | 58.09 | 41.15 | 41.65 | 83.87 | 74.07 |
| Pitkin | 25.94 | 32.35 | 71.29 | 64.98 | 31.67 | 24.29 | 101.33 | 50.00 |
| Prowers | 20.56 | 21.05 | 62.00 | 61.15 | 27.99 | 29.11 | 80.00 | 78.79 |
| Pueblo | 33.27 | 35.25 | 68.70 | 60.07 | 46.28 | 47.09 | 100.89 | 83.09 |
| Rio Blanco | 33.17 | 33.13 | 57.94 | 55.86 | 37.67 | 38.74 | 92.30 | 93.57 |
| Rio Grande | 38.74 | 43.53 | 75.70 | 72.30 | 45.26 | 51.52 | 113.08 | 107.43 |
| Routt | 35.38 | 37.20 | 75.58 | 68.79 | 40.00 | 50.00 | 93.00 | 90.27 |
| Saguache | 33.82 | 33.50 | 51.00 | 36.94 | 38.22 | 38.60 | 80.00 | 62.76 |
| San Juan | 48.24 | 51.25 | 68.25 | 72.57 | 31.33 | 40.66 | 76.81 | 74.25 |
| San Miguel | 40.93 | 46.59 | 81.00 | 70.99 | 38.33 | 39.68 | 79.59 | 81.00 |
| Sedgwick | 37.73 | 39.28 | 62.05 | 68.45 | 47.55 | 44.51 | 88.10 | 81.10 |
| Summit | 34.87 | 38.00 | 80.24 | 64.78 | 35.00 | 30.00 | 75.00 | 77.14 |
| Teller | 32.47 | 25.09 | 57.06 | 54.38 | 41.77 | 60.75 | 83.20 | 74.03 |
| Washington | 24.22 | 25.08 | 59.19 | 62.47 | 26.54 | 27.60 | 79.02 | 84.53 |
| Weld | 37.58 | 38.58 | 89.34 | 80.86 | 43.73 | 43.65 | 100.26 | 101.33 |
| Yuma | 30.89 | 33.55 | 60.00 | 58.03 | 36.51 | 38.92 | 72.00 | 67.58 |
| State | $30.92 | $32.33 | $71.16 | $65.08 | $39.02 | $41.70 | $88.56 | $85.03 |

**AVERAGE VALUE OF RANGE CATTLE AND DAIRY CATTLE PER HEAD AS RETURNED BY COUNTY ASSESSORS FOR 1914, 1919, 1930, 1931**

| COUNTY | RANGE CATTLE | | | | DAIRY CATTLE | | | |
|---|---|---|---|---|---|---|---|---|
| | 1931 | 1930 | 1919 | 1914 | 1931 | 1930 | 1919 | 1914 |
| Adams | $27.48 | $33.03 | $43.00 | $32.01 | $40.61 | $47.49 | $78.28 | $52.17 |
| Alamosa | 27.18 | 32.80 | 44.24 | 35.05 | 43.71 | 49.99 | 75.14 | 53.00 |
| Arapahoe | 27.29 | 35.40 | 41.29 | 30.79 | 45.25 | 52.25 | 78.30 | 55.40 |
| Archuleta | 26.15 | 34.39 | 45.00 | 25.40 | 50.10 | 50.22 | 67.20 | 42.31 |
| Baca | 26.23 | 34.14 | 41.00 | 26.56 | 31.83 | 42.63 | 66.00 | .... |
| Bent | 25.54 | 34.04 | 41.88 | 35.45 | 36.52 | 46.63 | 62.26 | 58.25 |
| Boulder | 27.07 | 33.20 | 52.08 | 28.67 | 36.60 | 44.39 | 74.60 | 50.84 |
| Chaffee | 28.11 | 34.48 | 42.47 | 32.49 | 35.97 | 49.80 | 68.29 | 48.62 |
| Cheyenne | 25.60 | 33.62 | 45.87 | 39.85 | 30.36 | 52.17 | 65.27 | .... |
| Clear Creek | 25.81 | 35.31 | 41.44 | 40.39 | 45.92 | 49.70 | 65.10 | 50.00 |
| Conejos | 26.05 | 35.64 | 42.00 | 37.46 | 42.12 | 47.73 | 65.00 | 45.00 |
| Costilla | 25.58 | 33.92 | 43.00 | 36.62 | 49.73 | 50.10 | 76.23 | 50.27 |
| Crowley | 25.94 | 33.59 | 44.85 | 34.70 | 38.37 | 50.20 | 66.77 | 48.29 |
| Custer | 26.00 | 33.49 | 41.85 | 35.06 | 42.29 | 43.67 | 60.13 | 43.98 |
| Delta | 26.77 | 33.81 | 45.05 | 35.42 | 40.25 | 50.00 | 78.66 | 63.00 |
| Denver | .... | .... | .... | .... | 51.66 | 43.69 | 80.00 | 47.95 |
| Dolores | 27.27 | 35.23 | 45.57 | 33.67 | 36.60 | 40.64 | 69.86 | 44.59 |
| Douglas | 31.13 | 37.97 | 47.50 | 32.34 | 50.59 | 50.01 | 77.62 | 50.52 |
| Eagle | 27.49 | 35.24 | 44.87 | 33.50 | 40.00 | 50.00 | 71.75 | 46.53 |
| Elbert | 26.46 | 33.52 | 43.66 | 26.27 | 40.31 | 50.12 | 68.47 | 43.16 |
| El Paso | 29.94 | 35.29 | 42.71 | 31.96 | 38.03 | 48.18 | 61.00 | 52.74 |
| Fremont | 27.13 | 34.04 | 42.70 | 30.26 | 45.17 | 53.34 | 72.00 | 44.71 |
| Garfield | 26.61 | 34.72 | 42.61 | 34.50 | 45.45 | 50.31 | 68.39 | 48.25 |
| Gilpin | 25.88 | 32.39 | 40.00 | 30.14 | 42.11 | 44.10 | 60.00 | .... |
| Grand | 27.80 | 36.34 | 45.27 | 37.24 | 30.16 | 50.17 | 66.38 | 50.00 |
| Gunnison | 26.07 | 34.05 | 47.97 | 36.66 | 39.74 | 50.02 | 71.00 | .... |
| Hinsdale | 26.14 | 33.71 | 42.00 | 30.29 | 40.53 | 40.24 | 64.00 | 50.16 |
| Huerfano | 26.66 | 35.22 | 42.00 | 36.61 | 35.38 | 43.35 | 95.00 | .... |
| Jackson | 28.11 | 33.69 | 44.99 | 39.99 | 40.00 | 50.00 | 65.00 | 55.00 |
| Jefferson | 28.09 | 34.60 | 46.17 | 35.91 | 43.89 | 51.44 | 80.00 | 60.13 |
| Kiowa | 27.37 | 33.71 | 44.92 | 35.25 | 50.00 | 50.00 | 64.75 | .... |
| Kit Carson | 26.26 | 33.55 | 42.95 | 29.53 | 38.18 | 50.37 | 61.14 | 42.63 |
| Lake | 34.71 | 35.76 | 42.53 | 34.60 | 50.16 | 49.97 | 64.92 | 58.24 |
| La Plata | 25.49 | 33.32 | 40.40 | 30.26 | 40.29 | 50.24 | 69.77 | 50.49 |
| Larimer | 27.89 | 34.13 | 42.25 | 31.83 | 46.97 | 48.35 | 77.00 | 51.30 |
| Las Animas | 25.42 | 35.80 | 44.00 | 32.50 | 43.29 | 43.37 | 74.00 | 56.89 |
| Lincoln | 26.55 | 33.58 | 44.13 | 33.15 | 33.42 | 46.38 | 65.06 | .... |
| Logan | 26.14 | 34.18 | 48.21 | 35.14 | 32.20 | 42.90 | 72.61 | 50.25 |
| Mesa | 26.77 | 32.90 | 43.20 | 36.66 | 42.17 | 50.05 | 70.16 | 48.67 |
| Mineral | 26.95 | 35.71 | 40.00 | 29.98 | 43.10 | 47.11 | 65.77 | 46.40 |
| Moffat | 27.02 | 33.21 | 42.50 | 39.01 | 36.41 | 47.91 | 65.00 | .... |
| Montezuma | 26.84 | 31.74 | 42.33 | 32.71 | 36.59 | 50.09 | 66.81 | 45.02 |
| Montrose | 25.73 | 33.28 | 46.44 | 35.42 | 37.53 | 50.01 | 72.54 | 58.26 |
| Morgan | 25.45 | 32.48 | 41.71 | 41.77 | 34.61 | 41.24 | 65.38 | 48.14 |
| Otero | 26.58 | 32.86 | 43.22 | 42.35 | 36.95 | 52.04 | 71.36 | 58.50 |
| Ouray | 25.80 | 32.29 | 42.26 | 35.07 | 36.26 | 46.50 | 64.83 | 44.88 |
| Park | 29.82 | 34.61 | 44.09 | 35.00 | 41.52 | 50.16 | 65.00 | 55.00 |
| Phillips | 27.67 | 32.63 | 45.26 | 35.01 | 33.69 | 40.00 | 62.85 | 48.69 |
| Pitkin | 27.54 | 34.18 | 48.20 | 30.60 | 30.05 | 40.00 | 75.00 | 55.00 |
| Prowers | 25.58 | 33.04 | 41.70 | 32.23 | 32.82 | 42.87 | 73.50 | 59.26 |
| Pueblo | 26.64 | 34.63 | 45.73 | 36.02 | 40.07 | 46.36 | 72.52 | 51.39 |
| Rio Blanco | 26.38 | 33.39 | 44.00 | 35.73 | 44.08 | 54.23 | 70.23 | 53.57 |
| Rio Grande | 25.40 | 32.93 | 40.61 | 34.78 | 44.05 | 50.00 | 70.00 | 50.64 |
| Routt | 28.13 | 37.06 | 58.65 | 36.65 | 40.33 | 50.19 | 72.45 | 50.50 |
| Saguache | 26.18 | 33.38 | 39.55 | 33.67 | 39.87 | 50.04 | 60.00 | .... |
| San Juan | 25.55 | 35.17 | 47.21 | .... | 47.02 | 42.22 | 65.16 | 57.10 |
| San Miguel | 25.57 | 33.13 | 47.96 | 38.00 | 38.78 | 49.73 | 76.90 | 63.86 |
| Sedgwick | 26.15 | 33.52 | 41.60 | 35.21 | 38.43 | 43.88 | 69.13 | 49.58 |
| Summit | 25.80 | 33.79 | 54.66 | 35.16 | 40.00 | 40.00 | 75.00 | .... |
| Teller | 29.99 | 35.48 | 40.17 | 33.41 | 41.40 | 42.28 | 60.09 | 46.05 |
| Washington | 25.48 | 33.46 | 41.88 | 35.22 | 36.69 | 35.26 | 75.30 | 61.76 |
| Weld | 26.86 | 34.38 | 44.38 | 35.35 | 36.95 | 45.46 | 75.18 | 51.87 |
| Yuma | 25.69 | 33.33 | 41.25 | 35.23 | 30.84 | 40.93 | 65.37 | .... |
| State | $26.73 | $34.13 | $44.30 | $34.74 | $38.87 | $46.94 | $71.06 | $51.10 |

## AVERAGE VALUE OF SHEEP AND SWINE PER HEAD AS RETURNED BY COUNTY ASSESSORS IN 1914, 1919, 1930, 1931

| COUNTY | SHEEP | | | | SWINE | | | |
|---|---|---|---|---|---|---|---|---|
| | 1931 | 1930 | 1919 | 1914 | 1931 | 1930 | 1919 | 1914 |
| Adams | $ 3.51 | $ 5.50 | $ 7.39 | $ 3.02 | $ 9.20 | $ 7.75 | $15.06 | $ 9.03 |
| Alamosa | 3.71 | 6.13 | 10.20 | 2.47 | 11.51 | 11.66 | 16.96 | 8.30 |
| Arapahoe | 3.50 | 5.54 | 10.00 | 3.50 | 9.19 | 10.14 | 15.00 | 9.31 |
| Archuleta | 3.50 | 5.53 | 10.00 | 3.00 | 6.05 | 7.69 | 10.50 | 5.89 |
| Baca | 3.50 | 5.50 | 9.00 | 2.50 | 7.68 | 8.76 | 12.00 | 4.45 |
| Bent | 3.50 | 5.50 | 9.40 | 2.64 | 8.46 | 11.10 | 9.77 | 5.89 |
| Boulder | 3.58 | 5.50 | 9.34 | 3.33 | 9.76 | 10.39 | 16.47 | 10.29 |
| Chaffee | 3.63 | 5.55 | 16.00 | 3.88 | 7.20 | 8.46 | 11.19 | 6.21 |
| Cheyenne | 3.51 | 5.52 | 10.01 | 3.00 | 7.40 | 10.01 | 20.67 | 7.58 |
| Clear Creek | 3.50 | 5.50 | 10.00 | .... | .... | .... | 18.12 | .... |
| Conejos | 3.59 | 5.51 | 10.00 | 2.74 | 11.44 | 11.39 | 13.00 | 6.48 |
| Costilla | 3.50 | 5.50 | 10.27 | 3.00 | 6.90 | 9.72 | 14.00 | 7.17 |
| Crowley | 3.54 | 5.52 | 8.23 | 3.06 | 9.84 | 9.84 | 12.93 | 5.94 |
| Custer | 3.50 | 5.50 | 10.00 | 2.62 | 7.02 | 7.31 | 13.48 | 5.10 |
| Delta | 3.56 | 5.53 | 11.16 | 3.99 | 7.38 | 9.47 | 12.53 | 7.66 |
| Denver | .... | .... | .... | .... | .... | .... | .... | .... |
| Dolores | 4.46 | 5.50 | 10.53 | 4.00 | 8.18 | 14.07 | 12.90 | 7.33 |
| Douglas | 3.65 | 7.84 | 10.00 | .... | 9.97 | 10.52 | 15.04 | 7.90 |
| Eagle | 4.00 | 5.50 | 9.80 | 2.99 | 12.00 | 12.00 | 12.16 | 5.41 |
| Elbert | 3.64 | 5.58 | 9.55 | 2.39 | 10.11 | 10.69 | 16.35 | 7.09 |
| El Paso | 3.95 | 5.53 | 10.00 | 2.49 | 8.71 | 10.05 | 16.47 | 7.44 |
| Fremont | 3.60 | 5.59 | .... | .... | 8.35 | 8.93 | 13.80 | 6.59 |
| Garfield | 3.51 | 5.52 | 10.00 | 3.96 | 8.79 | 9.53 | 10.70 | 5.17 |
| Gilpin | 3.54 | .... | 10.00 | .... | .... | 11.60 | 20.00 | .... |
| Grand | 3.56 | 5.65 | 10.00 | 2.51 | 9.89 | 10.00 | 13.96 | 5.00 |
| Gunnison | 3.52 | 5.63 | 11.91 | 4.00 | 7.22 | 9.19 | 13.59 | 7.61 |
| Hinsdale | 3.50 | 5.44 | 10.00 | 3.64 | .... | .... | 7.00 | 5.00 |
| Huerfano | 3.54 | 5.51 | 10.00 | 3.04 | 7.98 | 9.06 | 15.00 | 6.23 |
| Jackson | 3.51 | 5.50 | 10.07 | 2.70 | 10.00 | 10.00 | 12.24 | 10.00 |
| Jefferson | 3.76 | 5.50 | 10.00 | 4.02 | 10.00 | 7.74 | 17.00 | 9.00 |
| Kiowa | 3.50 | 5.50 | 10.00 | 3.00 | 9.70 | 12.57 | 17.75 | 7.54 |
| Kit Carson | 3.76 | 5.50 | 10.88 | 3.03 | 8.73 | 10.24 | 15.94 | 7.88 |
| Lake | 3.50 | 5.50 | 11.60 | 2.55 | .... | .... | .... | .... |
| La Plata | 3.50 | 5.50 | 10.15 | 2.74 | 7.68 | 6.81 | 11.47 | 6.26 |
| Larimer | 3.50 | 5.98 | 10.26 | 2.48 | 9.52 | 9.50 | 19.00 | 8.12 |
| Las Animas | 3.50 | 6.15 | 10.00 | 3.49 | 8.55 | 11.05 | 9.00 | 12.65 |
| Lincoln | 3.51 | 5.51 | 10.07 | 2.49 | 8.58 | 9.42 | 15.35 | 6.77 |
| Logan | 3.50 | 5.50 | 10.81 | 4.06 | 8.87 | 9.70 | 15.63 | 9.11 |
| Mesa | 3.64 | 5.60 | 10.85 | 3.93 | 9.47 | 11.31 | .... | 6.82 |
| Mineral | 3.50 | 5.73 | 10.00 | 3.49 | .... | .... | 11.25 | .... |
| Moffat | 3.59 | 5.60 | 11.20 | 3.99 | 9.02 | 10.53 | 12.00 | 5.93 |
| Montezuma | 4.75 | 5.50 | 10.35 | 4.00 | 9.25 | 6.71 | 11.21 | 10.00 |
| Montrose | 3.48 | 5.50 | 13.03 | 3.57 | 8.00 | 9.73 | 12.86 | 5.71 |
| Morgan | 3.43 | 5.50 | 10.00 | 2.65 | 8.94 | 8.14 | 14.14 | 8.08 |
| Otero | 3.50 | 5.50 | 9.72 | 2.71 | 8.62 | 9.62 | 13.57 | 7.26 |
| Ouray | 3.50 | 5.50 | 15.70 | 3.96 | 6.00 | 7.00 | 10.52 | 6.24 |
| Park | 3.88 | 5.86 | 9.47 | 2.75 | 7.58 | 11.00 | 15.40 | 11.78 |
| Phillips | 3.68 | 6.00 | .... | .... | 8.95 | 10.05 | 16.56 | 9.90 |
| Pitkin | 3.50 | 5.71 | 10.00 | 1.84 | 10.23 | 8.38 | 14.00 | 5.51 |
| Prowers | 3.50 | 5.50 | 8.16 | 2.35 | 8.76 | 8.71 | 14.20 | 6.13 |
| Pueblo | 3.57 | 5.50 | 12.75 | 3.71 | 7.34 | 7.57 | 14.19 | 6.17 |
| Rio Blanco | 3.50 | 5.65 | 12.02 | .... | 9.19 | 10.00 | 13.27 | 7.59 |
| Rio Grande | 3.50 | 5.50 | 10.03 | 3.56 | 12.59 | 13.71 | 16.10 | 8.41 |
| Routt | 3.83 | 5.74 | 12.50 | 3.50 | 9.23 | 9.28 | 17.95 | 8.20 |
| Saguache | 3.54 | 5.65 | 10.00 | 2.47 | 11.37 | 12.68 | 15.52 | 8.30 |
| San Juan | 3.50 | 5.51 | 10.01 | 3.97 | .... | .... | .... | .... |
| San Miguel | 3.50 | 5.53 | 10.72 | 2.69 | 8.30 | 9.67 | 14.25 | 7.44 |
| Sedgwick | 3.50 | 5.50 | 5.97 | 2.79 | 11.32 | 12.83 | 18.23 | 10.65 |
| Summit | 3.50 | 5.50 | 10.00 | 4.00 | 12.00 | 12.00 | 15.00 | 10.00 |
| Teller | 3.55 | 5.53 | .... | .... | 7.99 | 10.10 | 10.93 | 5.90 |
| Washington | 3.56 | 5.51 | 9.05 | 3.39 | 8.61 | 9.82 | 15.79 | 8.83 |
| Weld | 3.50 | 5.50 | 11.14 | 2.67 | 9.88 | 10.38 | 14.90 | 8.44 |
| Yuma | 3.50 | 5.65 | 10.10 | 2.88 | 8.79 | 10.47 | 18.90 | 8.24 |
| State | $ 3.61 | $ 5.61 | $10.46 | $ 3.12 | $ 8.96 | $ 9.76 | $15.14 | $ 7.86 |

## ASSESSED VALUE OF LIVESTOCK IN COLORADO, 1931 AND 1930
(Compiled from Records of the State Tax Commission)

| COUNTY | Horses 1931 | Mules 1931 | Range Cattle 1931 | Dairy Cattle 1931 | Sheep 1931 | Swine 1931 | Foxes 1931 | Goats 1931 | All Other Animals 1931* | Total 1931 | Total 1930 |
|---|---|---|---|---|---|---|---|---|---|---|---|
| Adams | $ 186,290 | $ 12,565 | $ 167,290 | $ 270,525 | $ 165 | $ 101,375 | $ | | $ 2,745 | $ 752,755 | $ 853,490 |
| Alamosa | 81,795 | 8,200 | 198,775 | 48,775 | 51,980 | 13,535 | | | | 403,060 | 444,390 |
| Arapahoe | 85,705 | 8,345 | 154,900 | 204,115 | 27,500 | 17,370 | 2,640 | 700 | 955 | 502,230 | 621,685 |
| Archuleta | 38,345 | 1,875 | 263,526 | 40,380 | 14,680 | 3,415 | | 5,235 | 160 | 467,616 | 508,356 |
| Baca | 135,745 | 22,445 | 633,508 | 55,981 | 26,320 | 53,125 | 1,365 | | 2,000 | 930,489 | 1,051,986 |
| Bent | 110,765 | 16,165 | 363,055 | 59,010 | 48,820 | 21,570 | | | | 619,385 | 767,510 |
| Boulder | 129,120 | 16,270 | 164,700 | 211,320 | 13,600 | 17,590 | 12,430 | | 1,440 | 566,470 | 676,940 |
| Chaffee | 32,680 | 840 | 150,375 | 31,075 | 23,185 | 9,190 | | 200 | 2,035 | 249,580 | 303,320 |
| Cheyenne | 60,395 | 7,365 | 469,845 | 29,690 | 34,215 | 22,685 | 160 | | | 624,195 | 875,575 |
| Clear Creek | 7,515 | | 9,575 | 3,260 | 2,960 | | | 280 | 5 | 23,775 | 27,610 |
| Conejos | 90,660 | 12,870 | 265,465 | 73,675 | 305,725 | 25,330 | 160 | | | 773,725 | 1,028,515 |
| Costilla | 17,190 | 4,020 | 46,195 | 11,190 | 88,045 | 12,425 | 1,000 | 455 | 95 | 210,615 | 277,845 |
| Crowley | 87,515 | 15,755 | 207,480 | 47,200 | 25,755 | 16,470 | | 95 | 625 | 400,895 | 529,455 |
| Custer | 31,730 | 960 | 169,740 | 34,170 | 14,210 | 2,765 | 6,000 | | | 259,575 | 306,530 |
| Delta | 129,345 | 13,650 | 477,225 | 197,190 | 200,765 | 17,280 | | 3,745 | 105 | 1,039,305 | 1,255,845 |
| Denver | 24,510 | 1,660 | | 17,410 | | | | 1,080 | 5,680 | 49,260 | 52,410 |
| Dolores | 9,985 | 1,620 | 108,360 | 6,295 | 100,510 | 875 | | 2,135 | | 228,725 | 220,201 |
| Douglas | 83,125 | 4,280 | 456,950 | 229,735 | 21,815 | 8,310 | 9,460 | | 16,290 | 832,100 | 861,350 |
| Eagle | 78,040 | 4,415 | 199,940 | 48,400 | 106,884 | 6,072 | 1,400 | 45 | | 445,196 | 833,833 |
| Elbert | 173,096 | 25,090 | 588,235 | 155,000 | 41,247 | 42,439 | 2,000 | | 970 | 1,028,077 | 1,270,726 |
| El Paso | 140,600 | 36,260 | 610,720 | 310,020 | 26,300 | 31,490 | 21,700 | 2,790 | 13,170 | 1,193,050 | 1,373,170 |
| Fremont | 37,685 | 5,360 | 227,460 | 64,865 | 10,248 | 10,830 | | 350 | | 356,798 | 444,406 |
| Garfield | 193,995 | 12,220 | 730,720 | 158,200 | 355,035 | 23,935 | 6,000 | | | 1,480,105 | 1,749,395 |
| Gilpin | 4,130 | 25 | 24,274 | 1,600 | 145 | | 4,220 | 42 | | 34,436 | 25,643 |
| Grand | 48,700 | 495 | 333,480 | 39,420 | 47,755 | 900 | 900 | | 990 | 472,640 | 611,500 |
| Gunnison | 93,900 | 10,110 | 792,860 | 48,955 | 199,020 | 1,205 | 2,600 | 390 | 90 | 1,149,130 | 1,410,835 |
| Hinsdale | 4,590 | 30 | 34,505 | 3,080 | 17,430 | | | | | 59,635 | 83,738 |
| Huerfano | 51,085 | 9,575 | 297,450 | 58,985 | 84,366 | 3,480 | 1,000 | 635 | | 506,576 | 696,470 |
| Jackson | 58,430 | 730 | 810,740 | 27,240 | 103,030 | 720 | 150 | 40 | 1,000 | 1,002,080 | 1,131,690 |
| Jefferson | 79,950 | 4,175 | 271,110 | 205,070 | 6,410 | 7,795 | 54,590 | 1,425 | 2,560 | 633,085 | 773,160 |

| County | | | | | | | | | | | |
|---|---|---|---|---|---|---|---|---|---|---|---|
| Kiowa | 38,280 | 6,840 | 342,305 | 25,800 | 21,275 | 11,620 | | | 9,185 | 455,305 | 590,580 |
| Kit Carson | 234,091 | 30,550 | 506,406 | 194,064 | 13,210 | 132,752 | | 172 | 161 | 1,111,406 | 1,289,283 |
| Lake | 6,225 | | 13,990 | 8,075 | 1,400 | | | | | 29,690 | 32,965 |
| La Plata | 71,400 | 4,195 | 320,605 | 101,640 | 106,645 | 12,395 | 5,500 | 1,265 | | 624,315 | 794,845 |
| Larimer | 250,540 | 27,240 | 557,420 | 292,600 | 51,780 | 24,950 | 8,300 | 330 | 170 | 1,213,160 | 1,360,610 |
| Las Animas | 126,091 | 51,485 | 1,128,320 | 101,475 | 287,365 | 9,828 | | 14,976 | | 1,719,865 | 2,331,101 |
| Lincoln | 114,790 | 17,805 | 669,035 | 109,550 | 40,040 | 49,625 | | | 325 | 1,000,845 | 1,242,603 |
| Logan | 295,280 | 28,460 | 538,435 | 236,655 | 9,500 | 124,185 | | | 3,680 | 1,236,195 | 1,432,038 |
| Mesa | 185,150 | 11,920 | 905,480 | 253,990 | 230,800 | 29,865 | 640 | 1,300 | | 1,619,145 | 2,228,980 |
| Mineral | 8,395 | 740 | 30,695 | 3,620 | 45,870 | | | 225 | | 89,545 | 130,555 |
| Moffat | 88,320 | 4,410 | 385,700 | 46,090 | 329,900 | 7,140 | | 365 | | 861,925 | 1,109,125 |
| Montezuma | 65,355 | 11,020 | 267,760 | 101,235 | 153,865 | 7,660 | | 620 | | 619,165 | 718,420 |
| Montrose | 130,990 | 8,690 | 441,370 | 132,455 | 259,990 | 22,500 | 3,025 | | 11,650 | 998,930 | 1,207,540 |
| Morgan | 239,010 | 30,780 | 302,690 | 201,960 | 9,720 | 66,180 | 4,200 | | | 854,540 | 972,980 |
| Otero | 160,990 | 45,740 | 287,170 | 119,415 | 105,275 | 35,685 | | | 340 | 754,615 | 981,260 |
| Ouray | 16,800 | 90 | 182,800 | 17,370 | 50,450 | 1,320 | | | | 269,640 | 315,911 |
| Park | 60,760 | 3,220 | 378,130 | 30,350 | 189,895 | 485 | 1,000 | 300 | 570 | 664,710 | 746,110 |
| Phillips | 106,215 | 16,010 | 101,430 | 100,810 | 1,115 | 75,645 | | | 435 | 401,660 | 432,425 |
| Pitkin | 21,320 | 380 | 140,200 | 13,280 | 40,065 | 2,250 | 1,150 | 520 | 180 | 218,825 | 253,265 |
| Prowers | 175,085 | 29,364 | 423,951 | 138,129 | 31,854 | 49,544 | | | | 848,447 | 976,408 |
| Pueblo | 141,180 | 18,190 | 549,405 | 178,470 | 36,530 | 21,725 | 900 | 1,340 | 1,455 | 949,195 | 1,116,635 |
| Rio Blanco | 81,760 | 6,480 | 795,170 | 31,690 | 249,450 | 2,740 | | | | 1,167,290 | 1,432,175 |
| Rio Grande | 85,075 | 19,555 | 235,490 | 57,090 | 159,600 | 26,350 | 8,340 | 6,150 | 6,150 | 597,660 | 843,285 |
| Routt | 190,990 | 1,440 | 813,470 | 122,330 | 291,430 | 14,850 | 1,380 | 4,170 | 4,170 | 1,440,060 | 1,755,930 |
| Saguache | 71,020 | 8,065 | 662,728 | 27,150 | 262,994 | 9,493 | | | 1,111 | 1,042,561 | 1,433,713 |
| San Juan | 1,785 | 940 | 4,983 | 1,975 | 38,061 | | | | | 47,744 | 56,963 |
| San Miguel | 24,925 | 920 | 139,900 | 28,230 | 134,325 | 1,120 | | 1,415 | 1,415 | 330,835 | 458,035 |
| Sedgwick | 90,515 | 11,935 | 155,470 | 84,850 | 1,530 | 51,650 | 1,500 | 705 | 705 | 398,155 | 433,695 |
| Summit | 15,655 | 70 | 77,930 | 12,320 | 9,862 | 348 | 300 | | | 162,485 | 162,835 |
| Teller | 21,560 | 1,420 | 131,965 | 22,730 | 1,170 | 535 | 3,580 | 280 | 520 | 183,760 | 214,355 |
| Washington | 202,935 | 16,160 | 599,031 | 152,540 | 64,890 | 113,535 | | 125 | 125 | 1,149,216 | 1,314,712 |
| Weld | 791,850 | 88,780 | 680,620 | 774,540 | 99,820 | 114,550 | | 154,470 | 154,470 | 2,704,630 | 3,050,800 |
| Yuma | 253,240 | 42,200 | 820,960 | 134,510 | 7,410 | 159,370 | 10 | 840 | 840 | 1,418,540 | 1,771,180 |
| State | $6,704,193 | $803,274 | $23,119,472 | $6,548,819 | $5,446,916 | $1,652,581 | $167,430 | $41,345 | $248,572 | $44,732,602 | $54,308,893 |

Note—This table does not include sheep and cattle fed in transit.
*Includes burros, rabbits and smaller animals.

# Co-operative Marketing Associations

CO-OPERATIVE marketing of Colorado agricultural products has become increasingly general during the past 10 years through the rapid expansion of farmer-owned merchandising associations. Although a few of these associations antedate the passage of the state co-operative marketing act of 1923, most of them have been formed since that time. Almost all of them are incorporated under its provisions.

There were 35 associations in the state reporting to the director of markets as of March 1, 1932. These had a total membership of 20,730, an average of 592 members per association, and an increase of 6,478 or 45.5 per cent, compared with 1931. The gross business reported in 1931 was $21,064,538. This does not, however, represent the total business of all of the associations for the reason that many associations do not actually handle the commodities for their members, but sell on contract in such a manner that the gross volume cannot be reported. During 1931 the Pinto Bean Growers association, the Colorado Bean Growers association and the Interstate Bean Growers association were merged and their business is shown in the report of the Pinto Bean Growers association. Four associations became inoperative during the year, one of these, the Delta Onion Growers association, turning its production over to the Colorado Potato Growers exchange. The indebtedness of all associations reporting to the director of markets as of January 1, 1932, was $435,998, a large per cent of which is represented by commodities in the hands of the association on that date. The above summary does not take into account business done by farmers' organizations which are not incorporated under the co-operative marketing act. An accompanying table lists the names of associations, the number of members, gross returns in 1931, and the name and address of the manager of each association.

Differing in their details of operation, all of the marketing associations have one common purpose: the merchandising of their members' products in an orderly manner over a definite period of time. Many of them make "advances" to the members at delivery time; and the total returns always are prorated between all the members on a basis of volume and grade. Thus the farmer receives the average price which his association received for all of the crop, less the usual handling charges and association overhead.

Since the passage of the agricultural marketing act and the formation of the federal farm board, a number of Colorado associations have become affiliated with the national co-operative sales organizations sponsored by the government department. These sales organizations are designed to coordinate the activities of the state and regional associations of each commodity, and handle the entire sales of the co-operative members.

The national sales organizations, like the local and statewide associations, are owned and controlled by the members. Each member has one vote in his local association, and each local has its representative share of control in the regional and national groups.

In Colorado many of the associations own or lease their own handling facilities, and are thus able to handle their members' products at actual cost.

Besides the co-operative marketing associations, Colorado farmers also own a number of co-operative purchasing concerns. Some of these are buying subsidiaries of the marketing associations, formed for the purpose of purchasing supplies required in the growing, processing or packaging of the crop. Others are purely purchasing organizations for handling oil, fertilizers, or other agricultural requirements.

The census reported on sales through farmers' organizations in census years as follows:

**Farms reporting:**

| | |
|---|---:|
| 1930 | 6,783 |
| 1925 | 10,828 |
| 1920 | 5,847 |

**Sales:**

| | |
|---|---:|
| 1929 | $ 8,399,417 |
| 1924 | 21,090,456 |
| 1919 | 9,303,346 |

Purchases made by farmers through farmers' organizations in census years are as follows:

**Farms reporting:**

| | |
|---|---:|
| 1930 | 3,339 |
| 1925 | 3,703 |
| 1920 | 5,613 |

**Purchases:**

| | |
|---|---:|
| 1929 | $ 804,378 |
| 1924 | 883,318 |
| 1919 | 1,658,358 |

## COLORADO CO-OPERATIVE MARKETING ASSOCIATIONS, MARCH 1, 1932

(From the Reports of the Director of Markets)

| Name of Association | Members | Gross Returns | Manager | Address |
|---|---|---|---|---|
| Arkansas Valley Poultry Producers Association | 26 | $ 10,613.95 | Mrs. J. A. Taggart | Pueblo |
| *Avon Lettuce Association | | | Fred Kroelling | Avon |
| Crowley ...ty Melon ...rs Association | | 2,044.63 | E. M. Haise | Manzanola |
| Colorado Co-operative Lettuce Association | 25 | 5,539.04 | F. S. Tompkins | Buena Vista |
| Colorado Dairymen's Co-operative, Inc | 2,400 | † | B. C. Stanton, Sec | Denver |
| Colorado-New ...No Wool Marketing Association | | | A. H. Long, Sec | Durango |
| Colorado Poultry Association | 420 | ‡ | John Mack | Delta |
| Colorado Potato Growers Exchange | 2,304 | 3,464,649.43 | W. F. Heppe | Denver |
| Colorado ...Nut ...rs Association | 1,350 | 634,879.22 | H. C. Stephens | Denver |
| Colorado Wool Marketing Association | 1,150 | 728,000.00 | L. W. Clough | Denver |
| Conejos ...ty Vegetable ...rs Association | 214 | 64,275.61 | A. O. Johnson | La Jara |
| Culebra ...k Vegetable Association | 55 | 19,267.79 | Vincente Gonzales | San ...o |
| Del Norte Vegetable Growers Association | 125 | 29,101.08 | M. I. ...h | Del Norte |
| §Delta Onion Growers Association | | | | |
| Equity Co-operative Oil Company | 412 | 74,659.18 | J. H. Liston | Yuma |
| Intermountain Livestock Marketing Association | 701 | 1,851,510.61 | C. W. ... | Denver |
| Kiowa County Turkey Pr...(...urs Association | 226 | 21,956.07 | W. H. Bradley | Eads |
| Mesa County Livestock Shipping Association | 701 | 74,071.90 | E. A. Burch | Grand Junction |
| ...Min Vegetable ...rs Co-operative Association | 7 | 28,695.21 | S. Yaritomo | Blanca |
| Montezuma Creamery Association | 202 | 6,827.37 | T. P. Kuhre | Cortez |
| ...Min States Beet Growers Marketing Association | 5,453 | 12,200,000.00 | J. D. Pancake | Greeley |
| Montrose Co-operative Creamery Association | 194 | £ | H. R. Burritt | Montrose |
| North Fork Creamery Association | 165 | 47,452.33 | Mrs. ...Me Henry | Hotchkiss |
| *Pueblo Milk Producers Co-operative Association | | | A. B. Thomas | Pueblo |
| Pinto-Colorado-Interstate Bean ...rs Association | 2,084 | 640,737.62 | D. W. Aupperle | Grand Junction |
| Pikes Peak Certified Seed Potato Association | 14 | | George Pierce | Divide |
| Plateau ...r ...ty Association | 126 | 3,506.75 | George LaGrange | ...an |
| Surface Creek Co-operative Association | 135 | 56,740.40 | G. G. Williams | Eckert |
| Southern Colorado Beet ...rs Association | 825 | 500,000.00 | H. H. Hampton | Rocky Ford |
| United Fruit Growers | 292 | 246,500.00 | H. G. Crissey | Palisade |
| Vegetable Producers Co-operative Associati...a | 387 | 112,215.27 | C. A. Gerall | Denver |
| Western Colorado Honey Exchange | 85 | 111,551.58 | W. H. Kendle | Montrose |
| Western Livestock Association | 457 | 129,743.00 | J. F. Wilson | ...e |
| *Yampa Valley Lettuce Association | 47 | | R. C. Kauffman | Yampa |
| Pueblo Vegetable Growers Association | 148 | 100,000.00 | Chas. O'Connor | Pueblo |
| Totals | 20,730 | $21,064,538.04 | | |

*Inoperative. †Began business January 1, 1932. ‡Began business in September, 1931. §Products handled by the Colorado Potato Growers Exchange. ‡Began business in November, 1931.

# Dairying

DAIRYING ranks as one of Colorado's most important industries. The annual production of milk and butter, ice cream, cheese, and evaporated, condensed and malted milk ranges from $23,000,000 to $34,000,000 a year in value. The total value of all dairy products in the fiscal year ending June 30, 1931, as reported by the state dairy commissioner, was $24,164,509. This compares with $28,635,025 in 1930, a decrease of $4,470,516, and $33,134,695 in 1929, the year of peak production, a decrease of $9,070,186. The decrease in value in 1931, as compared with 1930, was due principally to lower prices, which resulted in decreased production. These totals include milk used on the farm and butter churned on the farm as well as the output of the factories.

The value of all dairy products, including the products of the factories, as reported by the state dairy commissioner for fiscal years ending on June 30, was as follows:

| | |
|---|---|
| 1923 | $23,348,356 |
| 1924 | 28,543,590 |
| 1925 | 25,832,969 |
| 1926 | 26,430,336 |
| 1927 | 28,902,412 |
| 1928 | 31,453,025 |
| 1929 | 33,134,695 |
| 1930 | 28,635,025 |
| 1931 | 24,164,509 |

In the fiscal year ending June 30, 1931, there were 168 plants in the state engaged in manufacturing dairy products under licenses from the state dairy commissioner. The products manufactured by these plants included butter, ice cream, condensed and evaporated milk, malted milk, dried or powdered skim milk, condensed or evaporated buttermilk, dried or powdered buttermilk and six varieties of cheese. The value of these products for 1931 was $12,690,913, a decrease of $2,617,473, compared with 1930, and of $5,862,927 compared with 1929.

The value of factory products, butter, cheese, condensed milk, etc., as reported by the state dairy inspector for the fiscal years ending June 30, was as follows:

| | |
|---|---|
| 1923 | $11,354,477 |
| 1924 | 14,004,422 |
| 1925 | 12,114,710 |
| 1926 | 13,450,855 |
| 1927 | 14,533,764 |
| 1928 | 17,117,396 |
| 1929 | 18,553,840 |
| 1930 | 15,308,386 |
| 1931 | 12,690,913 |

Butter produced in the factories in 1931 was 21,550,119 pounds, valued at $7,311,952, a decrease of 1,454,657 pounds in quantity and $1,199,815 in value compared with 1930. The full cream cheddar (American) cheese totaled 2,466,772 pounds, valued at $340,415, a decrease of 594,411 pounds in quantity and $271,822 in value. The total output of cheese of all varieties was 4,765,004 pounds, valued at $609,638. This compares with 5,553,597 pounds in 1930, 5,344,006 pounds in 1929, and 3,842,816 pounds in 1928. The value in 1931 of $609,638 compares with $986,762 in 1930, $1,023,190 in 1929, $748,131 in 1928 and $407,868 in 1927.

A table published herewith shows in detail the dairy operations of the state for 1931, with comparisons for 1930 and 1929.

The number of plants in the state identified with dairying as of June 30 of the years named as reported by the state dairy inspector is as follows:

| | 1931 | 1930 | 1929 |
|---|---|---|---|
| Creameries (butter).. | 75 | 76 | 81 |
| Ice cream plants..... | 78 | 82 | 84 |
| Cheese factories ..... | 17 | 19 | 18 |
| Malted and dried milk plants ............ | 1 | 1 | 4 |
| Condensaries and evaporated milk plants ............ | 5 | 5 | 0 |
| Cottage cheese factories ............. | 23 | 23 | .. |
| Receiving stations.... | 359 | 384 | 404 |
| Licensed plants ...... | 168 | 180 | 178 |
| Licensed operators ...1,114 | 1,238 | 1,265 |

Of those licensed in 1931, 30 creameries made no product other than butter, 41 ice cream plants made no product other than ice cream, 13 cheese factories made only cheese, one plant made no product other than malted milk and seven plants made only cottage cheese.

Milk and cream exported from the state in 1931 amounted to 3,942,245 pounds, a decrease of 2,377,597 pounds compared with 1930 and imports amounted to 2,359,814 pounds, an increase of 13,104 pounds.

The census bureau of the department of commerce, which gathers statistics for calendar years, and under a somewhat different classification from that used by the state dairy commissioner, reports that the number of cows and heifers milked in Colorado in 1929 was 234,530. Milk produced was 121,905,777 gallons. Whole milk sold during the year amounted to 36,-

082,195 gallons, butter churned on farms, 3,578,682 pounds; butter sold, 582,962 pounds; cream sold as butterfat, 17,208,287 pounds; and cream sold, not as butterfat, 250,768 gallons. The value of the 3,578,682 pounds of butter churned on the farms was $1,587,465. The total value of butter, cream and whole milk sold in 1929 was $14,606,564, divided as follows:

| | |
|---|---:|
| Butter sold..................$ | 258,996 |
| Cream sold as butterfat...... | 7,149,445 |
| Cream sold not as butterfat.. | 376,022 |
| Whole milk sold............ | 6,822,101 |
| Total ....................$ | 14,606,564 |

A table published herewith shows the quantity of specified dairy products produced and sold in the state in census years. Another table gives the distribution of these items for 1929 by counties, and a third table shows the value of these products by counties for the same year.

The figures from the census given herein apply to the dairy business as a part of agricultural development. The production of dairy products in factories is treated as a manufacturing industry and further information on that subject will be found in the chapter on manufactures. Two items which appeared in the census for the first time in 1930 were the number of cows and heifers being milked daily and the daily production of milk on April 1, 1930, the date of the enumeration. These showed that 186,637 cows and heifers were being milked on that date and that the daily production of milk was 406,827 gallons. That was equal to a daily average of 2.18 gallons per cow.

The average production per year of dairy cows milked in 1924, the latest figures released by the census bureau, was 421 gallons, which compares with 348 gallons average in 1919 and 357 gallons in 1909.

All of the 63 counties in the state reported cows and heifers milked in 1929. Nineteen counties, however, had 64 per cent of all cows and heifers milked. These counties and the number milked in 1924, are as follows:

| County | Number 1929 | 1924 |
|---|---:|---:|
| Adams ................ | 7,221 | 7,664 |
| Baca ................. | 6,832 | 7,056 |
| Boulder .............. | 6,386 | 6,397 |
| Delta ................ | 5,710 | 5,041 |
| Douglas .............. | 5,985 | 5,470 |
| Elbert ............... | 8,671 | 9,339 |
| El Paso............... | 9,996 | 10,315 |
| Kit Carson........... | 8,416 | 6,539 |
| Larimer ............. | 6,606 | 5,978 |
| Las Animas........... | 5,708 | 4,894 |
| Lincoln ............. | 6,024 | 6,514 |
| Logan ............... | 7,244 | 6,653 |
| Mesa ................ | 6,543 | 6,854 |
| Morgan .............. | 6,323 | 6,252 |
| Prowers ............. | 5,635 | 5,317 |
| Pueblo .............. | 5,880 | 6,700 |
| Washington .......... | 8,270 | 8,360 |
| Weld ................ | 22,428 | 23,606 |
| Yuma ................ | 9,907 | 9,018 |
| | 149,785 | 147,967 |
| Total, state.......... | 234,530 | 229,700 |
| Per cent............. | 63.9 | 64.4 |

The most rapid development in the dairy industry during the past decade has been in the non-irrigated districts of eastern Colorado. This has been due largely to a change in general farming methods in these districts. Forage crops now are being grown extensively and nearly all farmers are keeping a few dairy cattle to consume this forage. Silos for storing forage for winter feed have been built quite extensively in this region as a part of the dairying program. In 1929 there were 2,028 silos, with an aggregate capacity of 221,133 tons, reported in the state.

A table published herewith gives the mean average prices paid to the producers of milk and cream in 1931, 1930 and 1929 as reported by the state dairy commissioner.

**DAIRY PRODUCTS: QUANTITIES PRODUCED IN COLORADO IN CENSUS YEARS**
(From Census Reports on Agriculture)

| ITEM | 1929 | 1924 | 1919 | 1909 | 1899 |
|---|---:|---:|---:|---:|---:|
| Milk produced, gallons_____ | 121,905,777 | 96,649,262 | 79,492,631 | 51,670,038 | 38,440,111 |
| Whole milk sold, gallons_____ | 36,082,195 | 17,703,304 | 16,086,983 | 10,037,067 | 13,170,810 |
| Butter churned on farms, pounds _____ | 3,578,682 | 5,245,186 | 5,775,602 | 5,856,132 | 4,932,482 |
| Butter sold, pounds_____ | 582,962 | * | 1,739,147 | 2,914,143 | 2,756,798 |
| Cream sold as butterfat, pounds | 17,208,287 | 14,081,231 | 5,804,055 | 1,087,681 | * |
| Cream sold not as butterfat, gallons _____ | 259,768 | 851,437 | 1,381,758 | 440,257 | 132,297 |

*Not reported.

### MEAN AVERAGE PRICES PAID PRODUCERS FOR MILK AND CREAM IN FISCAL YEARS

(From Report of the State Dairy Commissioner)

|  | 1931 | 1930 | 1929 |
|---|---|---|---|
| Sour cream, cream station price per lb. b. f. | $0.23½ | $0.30 | $0.43 |
| Sour cream, track price per lb. b. f. | .26¾ | .33 | .45 |
| Sweet cream, delivered, per lb. | .31 | .38 | .49 |
| Milk for fluid use, per cwt. | 2.03 | 2.25 | 2.18 |
| Milk for manufacturing use, per cwt. | 1.23 | 1.43 | 1.92 |

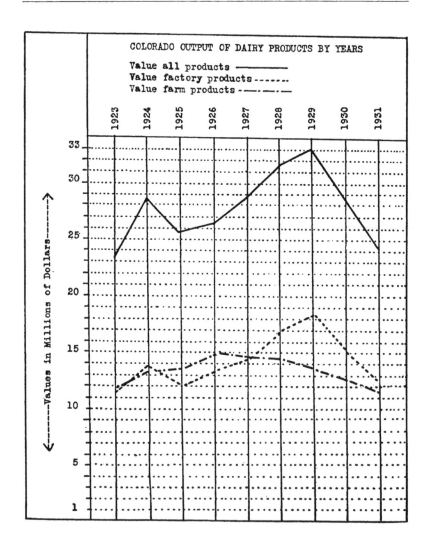

## DAIRY INDUSTRY FOR YEARS ENDING JUNE 30, 1929, 1930 AND 1931
(State Dairy Commissioner)

| | 1931 | | 1930 | | 1929 | |
|---|---|---|---|---|---|---|
| | Quantity | Value | Quantity | Value | Quantity | Value |
| Butter, lbs. | 21,550,119 | $ 7,311,952 | 23,004,776 | $ 8,511,767 | 21,747,865 | $10,547,715 |
| Ice cream, gals. | 2,244,288 | 2,247,295 | 2,567,803 | 2,696,193 | 2,609,031 | 2,609,031 |
| Cheddar (whole milk) cheese, lb. | 2,466,772 | 340,415 | 3,061,183 | 612,237 | 3,004,618 | 639,984 |
| Cheddar (part skim) cheese, lb. | 1,192,975 | 128,841 | 1,139,493 | 193,714 | 1,281,746 | 240,968 |
| Brick and Munster cheese, lbs. | 25,735 | 3,989 | 24,080 | 4,575 | 23,815 | 4,763 |
| Limburger cheese, lbs. | 7,170 | 1,111 | 4,610 | 876 | 4,460 | 892 |
| Italian varieties (including goat cheese) lbs. | 165,000 | 26,400 | 330,000 | 66,000 | 39,500 | 7,900 |
| Cottage cheese, lbs. | 907,352 | 108,882 | 994,231 | 109,366 | 989,867 | 128,683 |
| Condensed milk (sweetened) lbs. | 52,265 | 3,397 | 185,337 | 11,120 | 138,413 | 11,073 |
| Evaporated milk (unsweetened) lbs. | 23,370,665 | 1,916,395 | 24,044,376 | 2,091,861 | 32,028,612 | 3,523,147 |
| Condensed skim milk (sweetened) lbs. | 138,265 | 6,222 | 335,041 | 9,026 | 488,201 | 30,513 |
| Evaporated skim milk (unsweetened) lbs. | 614,391 | 9,216 | 916,767 | 18,335 | 965,299 | 26,063 |
| Condensed or evaporated buttermilk; lbs. | 3,813,007 | 89,606 | 156,221 | 9,373 | 213,341 | 7,637 |
| Dried or powdered skim, lbs. | 156,327 | 8,692 | 216,110 | 14,047 | 283,403 | 31,174 |
| Dried or powdered buttermilk, lbs. | 910,194 | 40,959 | 570,012 | 34,201 | 569,856 | 34,191 |
| Malted milk, lbs. | 2,196,723 | 447,541 | 3,702,781 | 925,695 | 2,536,092 | 710,106 |
| Value factory products | | $12,690,913 | | $15,308,386 | | $18,553,840 |
| Milk for fluid use (est.) | 57,765,495 | $10,065,011 | 57,237,877 | $11,075,529 | 60,905,042 | $11,418,477 |
| Farm butter (est.) | 4,250,000 | 1,442,025 | 4,600,000 | 1,702,000 | 4,916,992 | 2,384,741 |
| Total | | $11,507,036 | | $12,777,529 | | $13,803,218 |
| Milk exported, lbs. | 1,847,655 | $ 37,507 | 2,778,627 | $ 62,519 | 2,028,640 | $ 44,224 |
| Cream exported (B. F.) lbs. | 2,094,590 | 560,303 | 3,541,215 | 1,133,189 | 3,806,766 | 1,674,977 |
| Value exports | | $ 597,810 | | $ 1,195,708 | | $ 1,719,201 |
| Milk imported, lbs. | | | 349,678 | $ 7,868 | 1,379,858 | $ 30,081 |
| Cream imported (B. F.) lbs. | 2,359,814 | 631,250 | 1,996,032 | 638,730 | 2,071,553 | 911,483 |
| Value imports | | $ 631,250 | | $ 646,598 | | $ 941,564 |
| Recapitulation: | | | | | | |
| Factory products | | $12,690,913 | | $15,308,386 | | $18,553,840 |
| Produced and used on farms | | 11,507,036 | | 12,777,529 | | 13,803,218 |
| Excess exports over imports | | *—33,440 | | 549,110 | | 777,637 |
| Value all dairy products | | $24,164,509 | | $28,635,025 | | $33,134,695 |

*Minus sign (—) denotes imports in excess of exports.

## VALUE COLORADO DAIRY PRODUCTS SOLD AND BUTTER CHURNED IN 1929, BY COUNTIES

(From Census Reports on Agriculture)

| COUNTY | Butter Sold | Cream Sold as Butterfat | Cream Sold Not as Butterfat | Whole Milk Sold | Total Butter, Cream and Whole Milk Sold | Value Butter Churned |
|---|---|---|---|---|---|---|
| Adams | $ 5,524 | $ 104,918 | $ 4,389 | $ 532,877 | $ 647,708 | $ 27,044 |
| Alamosa | 2,714 | 76,895 | 19,534 | 56,568 | 155,711 | 11,438 |
| Arapahoe | 3,954 | 121,290 | 33,615 | 382,038 | 540,897 | 25,206 |
| Archuleta | 210 | 50,127 | 832 | 2,662 | 53,831 | 7,642 |
| Baca | 1,801 | 200,796 | 1,809 | 23,706 | 228,112 | 40,771 |
| Bent | 3,911 | 56,733 | 9,965 | 62,638 | 133,247 | 20,722 |
| Boulder | 14,149 | 70,319 | 6,252 | 482,647 | 573,367 | 26,938 |
| Chaffee | 3,431 | 33,691 | 9,027 | 33,383 | 79,532 | 8,335 |
| Cheyenne | 860 | 139,021 | 770 | 2,782 | 143,433 | 20,741 |
| Clear Creek | 154 | 490 | 272 | 5,130 | 6,046 | 817 |
| Conejos | 4,139 | 37,847 | 1,254 | 135,105 | 178,345 | 16,410 |
| Costilla | 1,664 | 19,546 | 2,168 | 1,000 | 24,378 | 6,578 |
| Crowley | 849 | 68,266 | 1,232 | 9,692 | 80,039 | 14,837 |
| Custer | 2,444 | 33,547 | 2,468 | 51,613 | 90,072 | 10,072 |
| Delta | 12,045 | 229,824 | 6,984 | 123,370 | 372,223 | 55,120 |
| Denver | 17 | 586 | 2,136 | 73,660 | 76,399 | 774 |
| Dolores | 493 | 10,644 | 341 | 1,105 | 12,583 | 5,504 |
| Douglas | 1,023 | 134,513 | 13,115 | 352,359 | 501,010 | 7,244 |
| Eagle | 2,503 | 66,171 | 4,369 | 9,835 | 82,878 | 19,265 |
| Elbert | 2,117 | 419,942 | 817 | 68,353 | 491,229 | 41,617 |
| El Paso | 5,955 | 288,183 | 10,318 | 473,546 | 778,002 | 40,645 |
| Fremont | 6,207 | 37,657 | 4,920 | 91,720 | 140,504 | 23,652 |
| Garfield | 5,165 | 166,336 | 8,902 | 27,686 | 208,089 | 35,975 |
| Gilpin | 163 | 319 | 3,883 | 5,029 | 9,394 | 499 |
| Grand | 2,265 | 50,201 | 3,876 | 20,503 | 76,845 | 12,961 |
| Gunnison | 6,125 | 54,373 | 7,122 | 13,572 | 81,192 | 18,820 |
| Hinsdale | 662 | 2,284 | 188 | 3,314 | 6,448 | 1,582 |
| Huerfano | 4,133 | 42,287 | 3,181 | 57,793 | 107,394 | 13,211 |
| Jackson | 1,231 | 33,837 | 1,030 | 2,774 | 38,872 | 9,713 |
| Jefferson | 7,781 | 38,629 | 30,386 | 492,447 | 569,243 | 24,451 |
| Kiowa | 2,947 | 105,746 | 93 | 3,637 | 112,423 | 18,305 |
| Kit Carson | 4,098 | 312,490 | 5,050 | 14,408 | 336,046 | 55,086 |
| Lake | 69 | 2,702 | 272 | 20,127 | 23,170 | 734 |
| *La Plata | 12,528 | 235,291 | 15,602 | 45,219 | 308,640 | 49,469 |
| Larimer | 13,635 | 87,227 | 3,251 | 489,823 | 593,936 | 37,799 |
| Las Animas | 7,852 | 138,106 | 11,143 | 73,641 | 230,742 | 36,110 |
| Lincoln | 2,472 | 224,524 | 1,052 | 13,181 | 241,229 | 47,159 |
| Logan | 4,713 | 261,033 | 5,841 | 52,686 | 324,273 | 70,791 |
| Mesa | 12,578 | 325,236 | 6,806 | 75,813 | 420,433 | 68,260 |
| Mineral | 515 | 727 | 868 | 1,706 | 3,816 | 810 |
| Moffat | 3,723 | 95,019 | 2,279 | 15,580 | 116,601 | 27,253 |
| Montezuma | 6,983 | 192,511 | 4,222 | 12,307 | 216,023 | 40,008 |
| Montrose | 5,442 | 167,082 | 2,173 | 79,689 | 254,386 | 35,674 |
| Morgan | 1,332 | 206,325 | 7,344 | 108,727 | 323,728 | 32,386 |
| Otero | 5,918 | 108,460 | 4,274 | 92,023 | 210,675 | 28,329 |
| Ouray | 3,226 | 35,503 | 3,793 | 5,178 | 47,700 | 9,700 |
| Park | 951 | 27,360 | 344 | 2,622 | 31,277 | 10,340 |
| Phillips | 1,291 | 131,858 | 2,643 | 11,830 | 147,622 | 28,381 |
| Pitkin | 1,389 | 29,949 | 1,560 | 5,531 | 38,429 | 8,085 |
| Prowers | 5,893 | 104,279 | 7,423 | 171,690 | 289,285 | 29,134 |
| Pueblo | 3,490 | 180,785 | 14,067 | 280,721 | 479,063 | 28,020 |
| Rio Blanco | 150 | 39,196 | 1,050 | 4,745 | 45,141 | 10,269 |
| Rio Grande | 7,671 | 55,747 | 7,753 | 88,214 | 159,385 | 23,873 |
| Routt | 7,249 | 236,198 | 8,205 | 31,110 | 282,762 | 41,516 |
| Saguache | 3,720 | 47,905 | 2,166 | 16,236 | 70,027 | 16,747 |
| *San Juan | ------ | ------ | ------ | ------ | ------ | ------ |
| San Miguel | 1,377 | 55,171 | 2,713 | 4,447 | 63,708 | 8,501 |
| Sedgwick | 3,792 | 71,047 | 17,689 | 12,259 | 104,787 | 22,768 |
| Summit | 2,953 | 17,959 | 840 | 5,768 | 27,520 | 5,914 |
| Teller | 868 | 24,160 | 5,102 | 28,340 | 58,470 | 5,917 |
| Washington | 2,389 | 338,536 | 6,623 | 14,487 | 362,035 | 65,526 |
| Weld | 19,732 | 372,879 | 9,810 | 1,418,255 | 1,820,676 | 100,703 |
| Yuma | 4,361 | 329,162 | 18,816 | 23,194 | 375,533 | 75,314 |
| State | $258,996 | $7,149,445 | $376,022 | $6,822,101 | $14,606,564 | $1,587,465 |

*Includes statistics for two farms reported for San Juan in 1930, to avoid disclosure of individual operations.

## COWS MILKED AND DAIRY PRODUCTS IN COLORADO IN 1929, BY COUNTIES
(From Census Reports on Agriculture)

| COUNTY | Number Cows and Heifers Milked | Gallons of Milk Produced | Gallons Whole Milk Sold | Pounds Butter Churned | Pounds Butter Sold | Pounds Cream Sold as Butterfat | Pounds Cream Sold Not as Butterfat |
|---|---|---|---|---|---|---|---|
| Adams | 7,221 | 4,582,017 | 2,960,425 | 64,390 | 13,152 | 249,804 | 3,027 |
| Alamosa | 2,169 | 1,209,930 | 314,264 | 25,418 | 6,031 | 183,083 | 13,472 |
| Arapahoe | 5,644 | 3,724,903 | 2,122,433 | 57,287 | 8,987 | 295,830 | 24,900 |
| Archuleta | 1,127 | 571,942 | 12,098 | 16,614 | 456 | 119,351 | 537 |
| Baca | 6,832 | 2,515,161 | 131,700 | 92,661 | 4,094 | 489,747 | 1,292 |
| Bent | 2,980 | 1,337,269 | 391,489 | 46,049 | 8,690 | 135,078 | 7,118 |
| Boulder | 6,386 | 3,921,278 | 2,631,370 | 64,139 | 33,687 | 167,427 | 4,312 |
| Chaffee | 1,010 | 565,370 | 166,915 | 18,120 | 7,458 | 78,352 | 5,642 |
| Cheyenne | 3,841 | 1,434,889 | 13,910 | 47,139 | 1,955 | 339,075 | 570 |
| Clear Creek | 97 | 48,240 | 25,650 | 1,777 | 335 | 1,140 | 170 |
| Conejos | 2,525 | 1,485,397 | 711,079 | 36,466 | 9,197 | 90,113 | 865 |
| Costilla | 750 | 356,502 | 5,265 | 14,617 | 3,697 | 46,538 | 1,495 |
| Crowley | 1,729 | 856,443 | 48,460 | 32,972 | 1,387 | 162,537 | 880 |
| Custer | 1,584 | 706,891 | 286,741 | 22,383 | 5,431 | 79,873 | 1,763 |
| Delta | 5,710 | 3,260,273 | 685,391 | 119,826 | 26,184 | 547,201 | 4,506 |
| Denver | 557 | 445,169 | 409,223 | 1,842 | 40 | 1,395 | 1,473 |
| Dolores | 437 | 187,151 | 5,261 | 12,231 | 1,095 | 25,960 | 235 |
| Douglas | 5,985 | 3,204,585 | 1,957,548 | 16,464 | 2,324 | 328,080 | 9,045 |
| Eagle | 1,447 | 813,080 | 49,174 | 41,881 | 5,441 | 157,550 | 2,819 |
| Elbert | 8,671 | 4,313,831 | 379,739 | 94,584 | 4,812 | 1,024,249 | 605 |
| El Paso | 9,996 | 5,290,288 | 2,152,480 | 92,376 | 13,535 | 702,886 | 7,116 |
| Fremont | 1,836 | 1,158,003 | 436,760 | 52,560 | 13,794 | 89,659 | 3,393 |
| Garfield | 3,612 | 1,920,476 | 125,844 | 78,207 | 11,228 | 396,039 | 5,743 |
| Gilpin | 126 | 54,745 | 25,145 | 1,134 | 370 | 742 | 2,427 |
| Grand | 1,411 | 632,652 | 102,514 | 27,002 | 4,719 | 119,526 | 2,673 |
| Gunnison | 1,674 | 704,029 | 67,860 | 40,912 | 13,315 | 126,448 | 4,451 |
| Hinsdale | 145 | 56,022 | 16,568 | 3,440 | 1,439 | 5,312 | 121 |
| Huerfano | 2,366 | 1,029,478 | 339,960 | 30,025 | 9,393 | 103,138 | 2,272 |
| Jackson | 888 | 410,825 | 12,061 | 20,235 | 2,565 | 80,564 | 644 |
| Jefferson | 5,303 | 3,686,841 | 2,735,814 | 55,570 | 17,685 | 91,974 | 20,956 |
| Kiowa | 3,110 | 1,140,290 | 18,186 | 41,603 | 6,697 | 257,917 | 69 |
| Kit Carson | 8,416 | 3,535,239 | 72,042 | 125,196 | 9,313 | 762,170 | 3,741 |
| Lake | 244 | 141,525 | 100,635 | 1,595 | 150 | 6,284 | 170 |
| La Plata* | 4,759 | 2,807,199 | 215,668 | 109,931 | 27,840 | 573,782 | 10,760 |
| Larimer | 6,606 | 3,956,027 | 2,449,115 | 87,904 | 31,709 | 207,684 | 2,032 |
| Las Animas | 5,708 | 2,290,359 | 387,583 | 82,068 | 17,845 | 336,844 | 7,959 |
| Lincoln | 6,024 | 2,531,147 | 65,907 | 107,180 | 5,618 | 547,619 | 779 |
| Logan | 7,244 | 3,373,098 | 277,297 | 168,551 | 11,222 | 621,507 | 4,028 |
| Mesa | 6,543 | 3,919,882 | 379,067 | 148,391 | 27,343 | 774,371 | 4,391 |
| Mineral | 82 | 29,598 | 8,530 | 1,760 | 1,120 | 1,690 | 560 |
| Moffat | 2,332 | 1,205,308 | 67,740 | 59,246 | 8,093 | 226,236 | 1,519 |
| Montezuma | 3,390 | 2,104,339 | 58,604 | 88,906 | 15,518 | 469,538 | 2,912 |
| Montrose | 4,102 | 2,423,152 | 398,446 | 77,552 | 11,831 | 397,814 | 1,402 |
| Morgan | 6,323 | 3,254,215 | 639,573 | 77,110 | 3,171 | 491,251 | 5,065 |
| Otero | 3,654 | 1,899,796 | 511,237 | 62,954 | 13,150 | 258,238 | 3,053 |
| Ouray | 830 | 428,732 | 25,891 | 21,087 | 7,014 | 82,565 | 2,447 |
| Park | 895 | 367,838 | 13,108 | 22,478 | 2,068 | 63,627 | 215 |
| Phillips | 3,035 | 1,497,828 | 59,150 | 64,502 | 2,934 | 321,604 | 1,953 |
| Pitkin | 754 | 368,063 | 27,655 | 17,575 | 3,020 | 69,649 | 975 |
| Prowers | 5,635 | 2,504,699 | 953,836 | 64,743 | 13,095 | 248,283 | 5,302 |
| Pueblo | 5,880 | 3,362,097 | 1,336,766 | 62,267 | 7,756 | 430,440 | 10,048 |
| Rio Blanco | 1,256 | 523,522 | 21,567 | 22,324 | 325 | 93,323 | 724 |
| Rio Grande | 2,588 | 1,390,075 | 490,077 | 53,052 | 17,047 | 132,731 | 5,347 |
| Routt | 4,438 | 2,485,432 | 135,262 | 86,491 | 15,103 | 562,375 | 5,128 |
| Saguache | 1,531 | 752,273 | 90,200 | 37,215 | 8,266 | 114,060 | 1,494 |
| San Juan* | ---- | ----- | ----- | ----- | ---- | ----- | ---- |
| San Miguel | 1,047 | 583,142 | 21,174 | 18,891 | 3,060 | 134,564 | 1,871 |
| Sedgwick | 2,082 | 1,050,302 | 61,293 | 54,209 | 9,028 | 169,159 | 12,199 |
| Summit | 504 | 220,197 | 28,840 | 12,856 | 6,420 | 41,765 | 525 |
| Teller | 854 | 432,090 | 141,699 | 12,864 | 1,888 | 56,185 | 3,189 |
| Washington | 8,270 | 3,704,912 | 72,437 | 148,923 | 5,429 | 825,698 | 4,906 |
| Weld | 22,428 | 12,918,243 | 7,464,501 | 239,769 | 46,982 | 887,808 | 6,540 |
| Yuma | 9,907 | 4,221,478 | 115,968 | 171,168 | 9,911 | 802,835 | 13,938 |
| State | 234,530 | 121,905,777 | 36,082,195 | 3,578,682 | 582,962 | 17,208,287 | 259,768 |

*Statistics for two farms included with data for La Plata, to avoid disclosure of individual operations.

**BUTTER, CHEESE AND CONDENSED MILK, BY YEARS**

Note.—This table is compiled from reports of census bureau on manufactures and consists of establishments not on farms. Farm production of butter and cheese is treated as an agricultural operation and is not, therefore, covered by the census of manufactures.

|                               | 1927        | 1925        | 1923        | 1921       | 1919       |
|-------------------------------|-------------|-------------|-------------|------------|------------|
| Number establishments.........| 79          | 68          | 72          | 69         | 78         |
| Persons engaged................| 916         | 730         | 738         | 689        | 705        |
| Salaries paid....................| $ 419,299   | $ 332,173   | $ 356,963   | $ 361,208  | $ 401,322  |
| Wages .........................| 703,697     | 536,462     | 596,646     | 546,245    | 454,200    |
| Cost of materials..............| 11,325,801  | 10,050,581  | 10,046,537  | 7,881,073  | 9,947,799  |
| Value of products.............| 13,977,398  | 12,030,768  | 11,968,458  | 9,845,569  | 11,905,940 |
| Value added by manufacture....| 2,489,432   | 1,980,187   | 1,921,921   | 1,964,496  | 1,958,141  |

# Poultry

CLIMATIC conditions are especially favorable for poultry raising in Colorado and as a result the industry has shown a substantial growth in recent years. The comparatively light rainfall and abundance of sunshine in the poultry raising areas, which make it possible for fowls to spend much of the time out of doors, are important factors contributing to the success of the industry. Diseases are less prevalent than in most sections of the country and young fowls make rapid and vigorous growth.

Poultry raisers have found, also, that climatic conditions are favorable for the production of a good quality of fowl for the table, and the eggs are graded as being of extra quality and are in demand as far east as New York, to which state large quantities are exported annually.

Almost all sections of the state with the exception of the mountainous counties, where the climate is too severe, are adapted to the raising of poultry. The state has not produced in the past sufficient quantities of chickens and eggs to meet the demand, and imports from adjoining states have been large, sometimes aggregating as much as $5,000,000 in value a year. This condition has been overcome by the establishment of commercial poultry farms to which the owners devote all of their time instead of regarding poultry as a side line, and Colorado now is an exporting state. The introduction of the commercial poultry farm has had much to do with improving the quality of the poultry and products. In 1919, according to census reports, average egg production per hen was 59, but this has been increased to an average of more than 70 per hen.

The value of all poultry raised and of eggs produced in 1929, as reported by the census, was $13,677,213, distributed as follows:

Chickens raised..............$ 4,768,549
Turkeys raised .............. 1,443,913
Ducks raised ................ 58,742
Geese raised ................ 36,786

All poultry.................$ 6,307,990
Eggs produced ............. 7,369,223

Poultry and eggs...........$13,677,213

The number of chickens on the farms on April 1, 1930, was 3,653,054. These included only chickens over three months old. The figures are not exactly comparable with those of former census years, due to a difference in the dates upon which the census was taken. The number on farms on April 1, 1925, was 3,751,618. A considerable number of chickens are killed between January 1 and April 1. The number of chickens on farms, by years, as reported by the census were as follows:

| Year | Number |
|------|--------|
| 1900 (June 1) .................. | *968,761 |
| 1910 (April 15)................ | 1,644,471 |
| 1920 (Jan. 1)................. | 2,874,721 |
| 1925 (Jan. 1)................. | 3,751,618 |
| 1930 (April 1)................ | 3,653,054 |

*Includes guinea fowls.

The number of chickens raised in 1929 was 6,333,339, with a value of $4,768,549. This was an increase of 26.5 per cent over 1924 and 63.2 per cent over 1919 in the number of chickens raised and 42.6 per cent over 1924 and 53.6 per cent over 1919 in the value. The number of chickens raised and their value, by census years, are as follows:

| Year | Number | Value |
|------|--------|-------|
| 1909............. | 2,585,132 | $1,277,417 |
| 1919............. | 3,880,873 | 3,104,698 |
| 1924............. | 5,005,977 | 3,343,769 |
| 1929............. | 6,333,339 | 4,768,549 |

The number of eggs produced (in dozens) in 1929 was 27,343,356, with a value of $7,369,223. This was an increase of 32.1 per cent over 1924 and 92.9 per cent over 1919 in the dozens of eggs produced and 44.6 per cent over 1924 and 29.9 per cent over 1919 in their value. The daily production of chicken eggs on April 1, 1930, was 1,830,917 and the average for 1929 was 898,959 daily. The dozens of eggs produced and their value in census years are as follows:

| Year | Number (doz.) | Value |
|---|---|---|
| 1899 | 5,704,290 | ...... |
| 1909 | 10,577,829 | $2,444,006 |
| 1919 | 14,172,375 | 5,668,950 |
| 1924 | 18,561,043 | 5,094,348 |
| 1929 | 27,343,356 | 7,369,223 |

The raising of baby chicks has grown into a substantial industry, and it is estimated that 5,000,000 are being produced annually. This number includes exports. The census gives 3,061,768 as the number of baby chicks purchased in the state by farmers in 1929.

Turkey raising has increased steadily, the number reported in 1929 being 547,789, with a value of $1,443,913. Comparative figures as to the number raised are not available, but on January 1, 1920, there were 57,687, with a value of $183,113, reported on the farms. The number on the farms on April 15, 1910, was 26,430.

The turkey industry was a leading phase of agricultural activity in southwestern Colorado in former years, but more recently it has been more widely distributed, and in 1929 turkeys were reported in every county but two. There are a number of ranches in the state where the birds range much as other classes of livestock, in some instances the flocks being of sufficient size to warrant the use of horses in herding them. Carload shipments of the birds at certain seasons are not uncommon. Approximately 40 per cent of the crop is marketed for Thanksgiving, 49 per cent for Christmas and 11 per cent later. A more general use of turkey meat at other than the special seasons has been a noticeable development in the past few years.

There is published herewith a table showing the number of chickens raised, their value and the number on farms by years and by counties. Another table gives the egg production and value by years and counties and a third table shows the number and value of turkeys, ducks and geese raised by counties in 1929 and the value of all poultry in that year. Another table shows the assessed valuation of poultry by counties for taxation purposes as reported by county assessors for 1930 and 1931.

## STANDARD MOUNTAIN TIME

The 105th meridian west of Greenwich, which divides standard central time from standard mountain time as determined by congress, passes in a north and south line through Denver. However, congress gave authority to the interstate commerce commission to readjust the boundaries of time zones and under a readjustment made by the commission, all of Colorado operates on standard mountain time. The eastern boundary of this zone goes through Mandan, North Dakota; Pierre, South Dakota; McCook, Nebraska; Dodge City, Kansas, and along the western boundaries of Oklahoma and Texas. The western boundary is along the western boundary of Montana; follows the Salmon river westward; western boundary of Idaho westward; southern boundary of Idaho eastward; passes southward through Ogden and Salt Lake City, Utah, and Parker and Yuma, Arizona.

Twelve o'clock noon, U. S. standard mountain time in Colorado, compares with clocks in other cities of the United States and foreign countries as follows:

| | |
|---|---|
| Boston | 2:00 P. M. |
| Chicago | 1:00 P. M. |
| Cincinnati | 1:00 P. M. |
| Dallas | 1:00 P. M. |
| El Paso | 12:00 Noon |
| Kansas City | 1:00 P. M. |
| London | 7:00 P. M. |
| Los Angeles | 11:00 A. M. |
| Melbourne | *1:00 A. M. |
| Memphis | 1:00 P. M. |
| New Orleans | 1:00 P. M. |
| New York | 2:00 P. M. |
| Rome | 8:00 P. M. |
| Paris | 7:00 P. M. |
| Salt Lake | 12:00 Noon |
| Seattle | 11:00 A. M. |
| Washington | 2:00 P. M. |
| Yokohoma | 12:00 Midn. |

*Next day.

## STATES WITH STRAIGHT-LINE BOUNDARIES

Colorado and Wyoming are the only states in the Union having unbroken straight-line boundaries on all sides. Each covers the same number of degrees of latitude and longitude, namely, four of latitude and seven of longitude, yet because of the convergence of the meridians towards the north the area of Wyoming is 6,034 square miles less than that of Colorado.

## CHICKENS IN COLORADO, BY COUNTIES AND YEARS
### (Compiled from Census Reports)

| COUNTY | Number of Chickens Raised | | | Value of Chickens Raised | | Number on Farms April 1, 1930 |
|---|---|---|---|---|---|---|
| | 1929 | 1924 | 1919 | 1929 | 1924 | |
| Adams | 237,665 | 195,426 | 122,011 | $183,002 | $134,844 | 134,488 |
| Alamosa | 32,813 | 17,511 | 16,115 | 23,297 | 10,507 | 23,707 |
| Arapahoe | 255,509 | 137,121 | 85,655 | 183,966 | 95,985 | 137,378 |
| Archuleta | 13,393 | 8,618 | 13,626 | 10,447 | 5,688 | 10,517 |
| Baca | 172,776 | 141,215 | 126,106 | 138,221 | 91,790 | 102,199 |
| Bent | 105,951 | 37,926 | 70,793 | 81,582 | 57,152 | 64,452 |
| Boulder | 257,479 | 206,947 | 127,924 | 198,259 | 142,793 | 133,980 |
| Chaffee | 19,188 | 22,815 | 14,612 | 14,967 | 15,971 | 11,982 |
| Cheyenne | 93,728 | 67,852 | 41,124 | 67,484 | 47,496 | 57,691 |
| Clear Creek | 1,422 | 270 | 993 | 1,109 | 189 | 1,147 |
| Conejos | 39,099 | 23,458 | 26,561 | 27,760 | 14,075 | 30,193 |
| Costilla | 15,504 | 21,144 | 13,343 | 11,008 | 12,686 | 13,913 |
| Crowley | 60,414 | 63,478 | 43,016 | 46,519 | 41,261 | 32,403 |
| Custer | 13,598 | 10,232 | 16,462 | 10,470 | 6,139 | 11,280 |
| Delta | 144,447 | 94,722 | 99,576 | 114,113 | 58,728 | 75,482 |
| Denver | 47,692 | 22,472 | 18,120 | 36,723 | 15,506 | 19,003 |
| Dolores | 6,897 | 5,170 | 5,936 | 5,311 | 3,412 | 5,159 |
| Douglas | 50,614 | 39,429 | 33,508 | 36,442 | 27,600 | 30,847 |
| Eagle | 20,344 | 13,192 | 14,251 | 16,072 | 8,179 | 13,332 |
| Elbert | 132,605 | 101,223 | 84,100 | 95,476 | 70,854 | 80,271 |
| El Paso | 217,045 | 162,200 | 108,246 | 156,272 | 113,540 | 114,045 |
| Fremont | 112,745 | 86,640 | 58,186 | 86,814 | 60,648 | 63,059 |
| Garfield | 72,977 | 54,855 | 51,646 | 57,652 | 34,010 | 43,400 |
| Gilpin | 1,159 | 1,138 | 1,594 | 904 | 797 | 827 |
| Grand | 7,165 | 7,145 | 6,940 | 5,732 | 4,501 | 5,610 |
| Gunnison | 10,312 | 9,226 | 8,873 | 8,043 | 5,720 | 6,442 |
| Hinsdale | 616 | 637 | 654 | 480 | 420 | 563 |
| Huerfano | 41,600 | 40,149 | 75,068 | 33,280 | 24,089 | 28,142 |
| Jackson | 4,924 | 5,281 | 4,925 | 3,939 | 3,327 | 2,978 |
| Jefferson | 304,414 | 209,982 | 128,936 | 234,399 | 146,987 | 158,856 |
| Kiowa | 78,905 | 78,554 | 43,519 | 56,812 | 51,060 | 50,812 |
| Kit Carson | 209,906 | 142,359 | 99,180 | 151,132 | 99,651 | 127,318 |
| Lake | 220 | 134 | 232 | 172 | 94 | 267 |
| La Plata | 65,852 | 49,544 | 52,568 | 50,706 | 32,699 | 43,540 |
| Larimer | 258,137 | 163,576 | 124,934 | 198,765 | 112,867 | 122,393 |
| Las Animas | 121,714 | 101,824 | 102,494 | 97,371 | 66,186 | 69,252 |
| Lincoln | 155,171 | 133,950 | 75,260 | 111,723 | 93,765 | 102,570 |
| Logan | 283,205 | 227,244 | 148,264 | 218,068 | 149,981 | 152,839 |
| Mesa | 208,685 | 129,744 | 122,663 | 164,861 | 80,441 | 111,261 |
| Mineral | 905 | 572 | 421 | 706 | 378 | 608 |
| Moffat | 40,071 | 31,599 | 40,851 | 32,057 | 19,907 | 26,046 |
| Montezuma | 46,358 | 35,867 | 46,858 | 35,696 | 23,672 | 34,179 |
| Montrose | 100,114 | 78,657 | 74,312 | 79,090 | 48,767 | 57,613 |
| Morgan | 198,091 | 214,323 | 114,762 | 152,530 | 141,453 | 122,137 |
| Otero | 143,307 | 166,797 | 193,040 | 110,346 | 108,418 | 74,307 |
| Ouray | 10,207 | 6,354 | 7,401 | 7,961 | 4,194 | 7,163 |
| Park | 8,612 | 5,091 | 6,168 | 6,717 | 3,564 | 6,07 |
| Phillips | 119,565 | 112,727 | 50,348 | 86,087 | 74,400 | 73,15 |
| Pitkin | 8,805 | 6,411 | 7,359 | 6,868 | 3,975 | 5,94 |
| Prowers | 204,641 | 131,229 | 104,617 | 157,574 | 85,299 | 114,67 |
| Pueblo | 157,738 | 148,398 | 130,499 | 121,458 | 96,459 | 94,74 |
| Rio Blanco | 24,216 | 32,195 | 28,902 | 19,373 | 20,283 | 16,07 |
| Rio Grande | 49,202 | 35,790 | 39,930 | 34,933 | 21,474 | 34,82 |
| Routt | 56,180 | 43,848 | 49,328 | 44,944 | 27,024 | 34,13 |
| Saguache | 25,991 | 18,181 | 22,495 | 18,454 | 10,909 | 16,91 |
| San Juan | ----- | ----- | ----- | ----- | ----- | |
| San Miguel | 8,593 | 10,098 | 11,857 | 6,617 | 6,665 | 7,02 |
| Sedgwick | 78,200 | 64,303 | 39,765 | 60,214 | 42,440 | 45,47 |
| Summit | 1,315 | 1,024 | 1,933 | 1,026 | 717 | 1,19 |
| Teller | 5,032 | 5,262 | 6,813 | 3,925 | 3,683 | 3,80 |
| Washington | 226,461 | 211,967 | 144,226 | 163,052 | 139,898 | 151,66 |
| Weld | 611,638 | 523,623 | 396,031 | 440,379 | 362,680 | 335,38 |
| Yuma | 332,207 | 235,261 | 174,938 | 239,189 | 155,272 | 196,31 |
| State | 6,333,339 | 5,005,977 | 3,880,873 | $4,768,549 | $3,343,769 | |

Note: Values of chickens raised in 1919 not segregated.

## CHICKEN EGGS PRODUCED, BY COUNTIES AND YEARS
(Compiled from Census Reports)

| COUNTY | Number Eggs Produced (Dozens) | | | Value Eggs Produced | | Value Eggs Sold in 1929 |
|---|---|---|---|---|---|---|
| | 1929 | 1924 | 1919 | 1929 | 1924 | |
| Adams | 1,067,698 | 643,911 | 435,917 | $288,278 | $173,856 | $187,761 |
| Alamosa | 172,512 | 71,050 | 58,504 | 53,479 | 20,605 | 29,132 |
| Arapahoe | 1,078,271 | 639,062 | 338,060 | 280,350 | 178,937 | 214,929 |
| Archuleta | 69,235 | 48,733 | 68,663 | 22,848 | 14,620 | 7,550 |
| Baca | 671,542 | 479,120 | 369,555 | 174,601 | 134,154 | 103,693 |
| Bent | 496,805 | 306,934 | 257,829 | 134,137 | 85,942 | 76,229 |
| Boulder | 1,050,737 | 788,479 | 462,695 | 283,699 | 212,889 | 210,135 |
| Chaffee | 93,146 | 49,809 | 62,339 | 30,738 | 14,943 | 15,669 |
| Cheyenne | 440,085 | 250,861 | 154,566 | 114,422 | 70,241 | 88,999 |
| Clear Creek | 7,356 | 1,875 | 3,971 | 2,207 | 563 | 1,679 |
| Conejos | 188,789 | 175,962 | 142,833 | 58,525 | 51,029 | 29,364 |
| Costilla | 90,411 | 37,562 | 65,732 | 28,027 | 10,893 | 11,030 |
| Crowley | 249,052 | 189,399 | 133,436 | 67,244 | 53,032 | 40,758 |
| Custer | 71,768 | 48,213 | 54,977 | 19,377 | 13,982 | 8,661 |
| Delta | 633,130 | 367,057 | 393,455 | 164,614 | 102,776 | 101,574 |
| Denver | 181,598 | 104,680 | 71,970 | 49,031 | 28,264 | 36,850 |
| Dolores | 31,818 | 17,063 | 15,202 | 9,545 | 5,119 | 4,646 |
| Douglas | 224,532 | 124,126 | 132,531 | 58,378 | 34,755 | 36,467 |
| Eagle | 94,380 | 77,689 | 74,177 | 26,426 | 21,753 | 10,457 |
| Elbert | 592,478 | 487,325 | 262,280 | 154,044 | 136,451 | 99,837 |
| El Paso | 1,055,632 | 582,012 | 387,608 | 274,464 | 162,963 | 198,764 |
| Fremont | 539,955 | 340,420 | 208,945 | 151,187 | 102,126 | 102,923 |
| Garfield | 350,692 | 217,954 | 235,306 | 98,194 | 61,027 | 51,170 |
| Gilpin | 6,369 | 8,062 | 4,125 | 1,911 | 2,419 | 532 |
| Grand | 38,651 | 33,945 | 29,409 | 12,368 | 9,505 | 2,931 |
| Gunnison | 45,590 | 34,514 | 45,858 | 13,677 | 9,664 | 4,314 |
| Hinsdale | 4,569 | 3,049 | 1,881 | 1,508 | 915 | 366 |
| Huerfano | 198,430 | 116,770 | 137,595 | 57,545 | 33,863 | 30,387 |
| Jackson | 21,595 | 23,745 | 16,973 | 6,910 | 6,649 | 1,024 |
| Jefferson | 1,392,032 | 905,557 | 500,420 | 375,849 | 271,667 | 295,256 |
| Kiowa | 364,893 | 241,903 | 146,826 | 94,872 | 67,733 | 66,897 |
| Kit Carson | 845,558 | 495,525 | 470,932 | 219,845 | 138,747 | 156,997 |
| Lake | 2,017 | 2,714 | 2,211 | 666 | 814 | 133 |
| La Plata | 335,211 | 207,187 | 226,338 | 100,566 | 62,156 | 54,156 |
| Larimer | 949,129 | 590,609 | 460,039 | 256,265 | 159,464 | 163,396 |
| Las Animas | 522,837 | 291,851 | 265,958 | 146,394 | 81,718 | 75,041 |
| Lincoln | 751,277 | 453,344 | 325,585 | 195,332 | 126,936 | 143,142 |
| Logan | 1,066,991 | 817,630 | 543,118 | 288,088 | 204,408 | 179,727 |
| Mesa | 888,865 | 610,793 | 472,609 | 231,105 | 171,022 | 141,418 |
| Mineral | 5,170 | 4,531 | 2,049 | 1,706 | 1,359 | 817 |
| Moffat | 205,369 | 109,620 | 155,248 | 65,718 | 30,694 | 29,161 |
| Montezuma | 258,965 | 129,331 | 198,802 | 77,690 | 38,799 | 40,697 |
| Montrose | 443,737 | 362,687 | 325,610 | 115,372 | 101,538 | 62,081 |
| Morgan | 864,844 | 544,964 | 438,773 | 233,508 | 136,241 | 142,157 |
| Otero | 600,370 | 582,285 | 335,867 | 156,096 | 163,040 | 96,668 |
| Ouray | 56,752 | 27,702 | 38,284 | 17,026 | 8,311 | 7,877 |
| Park | 39,719 | 27,740 | 30,432 | 11,916 | 8,322 | 4,487 |
| Phillips | 489,978 | 306,866 | 190,336 | 127,394 | 76,717 | 96,598 |
| Pitkin | 35,715 | 15,077 | 34,600 | 10,715 | 4,222 | 4,468 |
| Prowers | 819,396 | 520,668 | 401,577 | 213,043 | 145,787 | 141,569 |
| Pueblo | 725,152 | 609,854 | 405,318 | 195,791 | 170,759 | 150,617 |
| Rio Blanco | 111,267 | 66,184 | 99,099 | 33,380 | 18,532 | 13,057 |
| Rio Grande | 225,121 | 120,845 | 141,036 | 69,788 | 35,045 | 39,010 |
| Routt | 243,871 | 242,201 | 170,716 | 78,039 | 67,816 | 36,893 |
| Saguache | 117,204 | 64,166 | 77,474 | 36,333 | 18,608 | 16,853 |
| San Juan | ------ | ------ | ------ | ------ | ------ | ------ |
| San Miguel | 52,931 | 60,172 | 51,350 | 14,821 | 18,052 | 6,683 |
| Sedgwick | 297,211 | 221,920 | 155,404 | 74,303 | 55,480 | 48,600 |
| Summit | 7,839 | 9,015 | 7,505 | 2,587 | 2,705 | 529 |
| Teller | 26,094 | 22,783 | 30,700 | 7,306 | 6,835 | 2,948 |
| Washington | 1,038,846 | 936,747 | 695,992 | 270,100 | 234,187 | 190,566 |
| Weld | 2,391,050 | 2,019,418 | 1,425,802 | 645,584 | 545,243 | 358,229 |
| Yuma | 1,401,119 | 669,823 | 719,973 | 364,291 | 167,456 | 238,638 |
| State | 27,343,356 | 18,561,043 | 14,172,375 | $7,369,223 | $5,094,348 | $4,713,227 |

Note—Values of eggs produced in 1919 not segregated.

**TURKEYS, DUCKS AND GEESE; NUMBER RAISED AND VALUE, 1929**
(Compiled from Census Reports)

| COUNTY | TURKEYS | | DUCKS | | GEESE | | Value All Poultry Including Chickens |
|---|---|---|---|---|---|---|---|
| | Number Raised | Value | Number Raised | Value | Number Raised | Value | |
| Adams | 14,993 | $ 38,832 | 5,210 | $ 4,429 | 1,601 | $ 2,642 | $ 228,905 |
| Alamosa | 3,694 | 9,974 | 198 | 164 | 154 | 277 | 33,712 |
| Arapahoe | 9,819 | 24,253 | 4,323 | 3,372 | 858 | 1,416 | 213,007 |
| Archuleta | 8,413 | 23,556 | 27 | 22 | 27 | 49 | 34,074 |
| Baca | 8,104 | 20,665 | 343 | 274 | 296 | 444 | 159,604 |
| Bent | 21,923 | 55,904 | 376 | 301 | 264 | 436 | 138,223 |
| Boulder | 7,464 | 19,332 | 2,863 | 2,434 | 958 | 1,677 | 221,702 |
| Chaffee | 1,714 | 4,799 | 259 | 215 | 101 | 182 | 20,163 |
| Cheyenne | 5,430 | 13,412 | 344 | 268 | 143 | 222 | 81,386 |
| Clear Creek | 46 | 129 | 8 | 7 | ---- | ---- | 1,245 |
| Conejos | 5,609 | 15,144 | 218 | 181 | 123 | 221 | 43,306 |
| Costilla | 853 | 2,303 | 46 | 38 | 42 | 76 | 13,425 |
| Crowley | 19,022 | 48,506 | 329 | 263 | 154 | 262 | 95,550 |
| Custer | 1,437 | 3,664 | 149 | 119 | 105 | 189 | 14,442 |
| Delta | 34,992 | 99,727 | 897 | 745 | 486 | 875 | 215,460 |
| Denver | 191 | 495 | 771 | 655 | 96 | 168 | 38,041 |
| Dolores | 900 | 2,430 | 3 | 2 | ---- | ---- | 7,743 |
| Douglas | 5,946 | 14,687 | 592 | 462 | 129 | 219 | 51,810 |
| Eagle | 3,585 | 10,217 | 81 | 67 | 23 | 41 | 26,397 |
| Elbert | 9,717 | 24,001 | 846 | 660 | 238 | 381 | 120,518 |
| El Paso | 9,074 | 22,413 | 1,029 | 803 | 200 | 340 | 179,828 |
| Fremont | 4,832 | 12,322 | 1,705 | 1,364 | 332 | 598 | 101,098 |
| Garfield | 8,376 | 23,872 | 821 | 681 | 328 | 590 | 82,795 |
| Gilpin | ------ | ------ | 20 | 17 | 1 | 2 | 923 |
| Grand | 648 | 1,782 | 33 | 30 | 4 | 7 | 7,551 |
| Gunnison | 857 | 2,400 | 56 | 46 | 23 | 41 | 10,530 |
| Hinsdale | 173 | 484 | 12 | 10 | 23 | 41 | 1,015 |
| Huerfano | 2,223 | 5,669 | 186 | 149 | 72 | 122 | 39,220 |
| Jackson | 113 | 311 | 30 | 27 | 2 | 4 | 4,281 |
| Jefferson | 9,925 | 25,706 | 6,401 | 5,441 | 1,740 | 3,045 | 268,591 |
| Kiowa | 6,396 | 15,798 | 268 | 209 | 189 | 293 | 73,112 |
| Kit Carson | 5,895 | 14,561 | 1,321 | 1,030 | 448 | 694 | 167,417 |
| Lake | 2 | 6 | 5 | 4 | ---- | ---- | 182 |
| La Plata | 27,638 | 74,623 | 699 | 580 | 350 | 630 | 126,539 |
| Larimer | 10,508 | 27,216 | 2,816 | 2,394 | 1,074 | 1,880 | 230,255 |
| Las Animas | 7,031 | 17,929 | 530 | 424 | 103 | 165 | 115,889 |
| Lincoln | 9,706 | 23,974 | 1,445 | 1,127 | 358 | 573 | 137,397 |
| Logan | 12,411 | 32,144 | 4,805 | 4,084 | 1,506 | 2,334 | 256,630 |
| Mesa | 47,688 | 135,911 | 1,949 | 1,618 | 932 | 1,678 | 304,068 |
| Mineral | 20 | 56 | 19 | 16 | 6 | 11 | 789 |
| Moffat | 3,404 | 9,361 | 617 | 555 | 154 | 277 | 42,250 |
| Montezuma | 14,918 | 40,279 | 529 | 439 | 287 | 517 | 76,931 |
| Montrose | 22,876 | 65,197 | 1,249 | 1,037 | 457 | 823 | 146,147 |
| Morgan | 11,862 | 30,723 | 2,768 | 2,353 | 555 | 916 | 186,522 |
| Otero | 36,441 | 92,925 | 716 | 573 | 432 | 756 | 204,600 |
| Ouray | 2,555 | 7,154 | 92 | 76 | 14 | 25 | 15,216 |
| Park | 585 | 1,638 | 138 | 115 | 33 | 59 | 8,525 |
| Phillips | 3,202 | 7,909 | 959 | 748 | 318 | 493 | 95,237 |
| Pitkin | 1,435 | 4,018 | 68 | 56 | ---- | ---- | 10,942 |
| Prowers | 22,615 | 57,668 | 969 | 775 | 385 | 597 | 216,614 |
| Pueblo | 8,576 | 21,869 | 655 | 524 | 256 | 461 | 144,311 |
| Rio Blanco | 2,961 | 8,143 | 114 | 103 | 61 | 110 | 27,729 |
| Rio Grande | 4,139 | 11,175 | 364 | 302 | 176 | 317 | 46,727 |
| Routt | 3,917 | 10,772 | 515 | 464 | 196 | 353 | 56,533 |
| Saguache | 2,536 | 6,847 | 212 | 176 | 121 | 218 | 25,690 |
| San Juan | ------ | ------ | ------ | ------ | ------ | ------ | ---- |
| San Miguel | 1,319 | 3,561 | 158 | 131 | 23 | 41 | 10,355 |
| Sedgwick | 3,305 | 8,560 | 843 | 717 | 336 | 521 | 70,015 |
| Summit | 94 | 263 | 4 | 3 | 10 | 18 | 1,315 |
| Teller | 639 | 1,725 | 42 | 35 | 9 | 16 | 5,705 |
| Washington | 16,074 | 39,703 | 2,153 | 1,679 | 1,031 | 1,650 | 206,085 |
| Weld | 37,542 | 97,234 | 13,717 | 11,659 | 3,154 | 5,204 | 554,475 |
| Yuma | 19,426 | 47,982 | 1,910 | 1,490 | 380 | 589 | 289,250 |
| State | 547,789 | $1,443,913 | 70,825 | $58,742 | 21,877 | $36,786 | $6,307,997 |

## POULTRY (DOZENS) IN COLORADO, 1930 AND 1931
### (From Reports of County Assessors to State Tax Commission)

| COUNTY | 1931 | | | '1930 | | |
|---|---|---|---|---|---|---|
| | Number | Assessed Value | Average Per Dozen | Number | Assessed Value | Average Per Dozen |
| Adams | 7,958 | $ 42,940 | $ 5.40 | 8,691 | $ 46,790 | $ 5.38 |
| Alamosa | 782 | 3,910 | 5.00 | 728 | 3,685 | 5.06 |
| Arapahoe | 7,878 | 40,095 | 5.09 | 8,712 | 43,560 | 5.00 |
| Archuleta | 698 | 4,580 | 6.56 | 580 | 3,970 | 6.84 |
| Baca | 6,697 | 33,935 | 5.07 | 5,564 | 27,820 | 5.00 |
| Bent | 4,605 | 23,350 | 5.07 | 4,750 | 23,785 | 5.00 |
| Boulder | 6,279 | 31,950 | 5.09 | 5,673 | 31,210 | 5.50 |
| Chaffee | 571 | 2,865 | 5.02 | 553 | 3,365 | 6.08 |
| Cheyenne | 2,567 | 13,015 | 5.07 | 3,281 | 16,615 | 5.05 |
| Clear Creek | 59 | 295 | 5.00 | 78 | 390 | 5.00 |
| Conejos | 1,150 | 5,800 | 5.04 | 1,041 | 5,205 | 5.00 |
| Costilla | 744 | 3,865 | 5.19 | 550 | 2,790 | 5.07 |
| Crowley | 2,854 | 17,210 | 6.03 | 2,845 | 16,805 | 5.91 |
| Custer | 543 | 2,715 | 5.00 | 554 | 2,770 | 5.00 |
| Delta | 4,174 | 23,720 | 5.68 | 4,668 | 23,340 | 5.00 |
| Denver | ----- | ------- | ---- | ----- | ------- | ---- |
| Dolores | 250 | 1,250 | 5.00 | 295 | 1,540 | 5.22 |
| Douglas | 2,125 | 11,465 | 5.40 | 2,157 | 12,235 | 5.67 |
| Eagle | 785 | 3,970 | 5.06 | 778 | 3,890 | 5.00 |
| Elbert | 4,897 | 24,952 | 5.10 | 5,190 | 27,021 | 5.21 |
| El Paso | 6,880 | 34,890 | 5.07 | 6,740 | 33,700 | 5.00 |
| Fremont | 4,800 | 24,014 | 5.00 | 4,421 | 22,108 | 5.00 |
| Garfield | 3,113 | 17,185 | 5.52 | 3,339 | 17,980 | 5.38 |
| Gilpin | ----- | ------- | ---- | ----- | ------- | ---- |
| Grand | 333 | 1,665 | 5.00 | 313 | 1,565 | 5.00 |
| Gunnison | 498 | 2,625 | 5.27 | 515 | 2,830 | 5.50 |
| Hinsdale | ----- | ------- | ---- | 11 | 55 | 5.00 |
| Huerfano | 1,109 | 5,565 | 5.02 | 1,236 | 6,255 | 5.06 |
| Jackson | 297 | 1,480 | 5.00 | 206 | 1,030 | 5.00 |
| Jefferson | 11,560 | 59,295 | 5.13 | 11,583 | 58,015 | 5.00 |
| Kiowa | 2,770 | 13,850 | 5.00 | 2,971 | 14,855 | 5.00 |
| Kit Carson | 8,954 | 47,022 | 5.25 | 8,954 | 45,373 | 5.07 |
| Lake | ----- | ------- | ---- | ----- | ------- | ---- |
| La Plata | 2,525 | 15,120 | 5.99 | 2,355 | 15,290 | 6.49 |
| Larimer | 8,412 | 42,060 | 5.00 | 8,712 | 43,560 | 5.00 |
| Las Animas | 2,040 | 10,654 | 5.22 | 2,358 | 13,237 | 5.61 |
| Lincoln | 6,248 | 31,240 | 5.00 | 6,992 | 34,960 | 5.00 |
| Logan | 10,760 | 53,800 | 5.00 | 11,072 | 55,360 | 5.00 |
| Mesa | 10,867 | 54,335 | 5.00 | 11,426 | 57,130 | 5.00 |
| Mineral | 59 | 295 | 5.00 | 65 | 325 | 5.00 |
| Moffat | 1,362 | 7,430 | 5.46 | 1,322 | 7,190 | 5.43 |
| Montezuma | 2,203 | 11,015 | 5.00 | 1,973 | 9,865 | 5.00 |
| Montrose | 3,715 | 18,565 | 5.00 | 4,094 | 20,470 | 5.00 |
| Morgan | 6,831 | 35,400 | 5.18 | 8,646 | 43,230 | 5.00 |
| Otero | 6,442 | 37,690 | 5.85 | 6,899 | 39,380 | 5.71 |
| Ouray | 255 | 1,350 | 5.30 | 241 | 1,205 | 5.00 |
| Park | 512 | 2,560 | 5.00 | 536 | 3,210 | 6.00 |
| Phillips | 4,744 | 24,105 | 5.08 | 5,119 | 25,595 | 5.00 |
| Pitkin | 242 | 1,210 | 5.00 | 255 | 1,275 | 5.00 |
| Prowers | 7,414 | 41,725 | 5.63 | 7,947 | 45,617 | 5.74 |
| Pueblo | 6,260 | 32,925 | 5.26 | 6,503 | 32,560 | 5.01 |
| Rio Blanco | 694 | 3,490 | 5.03 | 735 | 3,675 | 5.00 |
| Rio Grande | 683 | 3,415 | 5.00 | 746 | 3,730 | 5.00 |
| Routt | 2,206 | 11,030 | 5.00 | 2,000 | 10,000 | 5.00 |
| Saguache | 700 | 3,500 | 5.00 | 768 | 3,840 | 5.00 |
| San Juan | ----- | ------- | ---- | ----- | ------- | ---- |
| San Miguel | 342 | 1,710 | 5.00 | 420 | 2,100 | 5.00 |
| Sedgwick | 2,893 | 14,780 | 5.11 | 3,081 | 15,405 | 5.00 |
| Summit | 60 | 300 | 5.00 | 64 | 320 | 5.00 |
| Teller | 155 | 845 | 5.45 | 158 | 855 | 5.41 |
| Washington | 9,419 | 49,035 | 5.21 | 9,832 | 53,290 | 5.42 |
| Weld | 18,134 | 91,450 | 5.04 | 19,594 | 99,860 | 5.10 |
| Yuma | 9,936 | 51,930 | 5.23 | 11,150 | 59,110 | 5.30 |
| State | 222,043 | $1,152,437 | $ 5.19 | 232,040 | $1,202,196 | $ 5.18 |

# Bees and Honey

COLORADO produces approximately 2,500,000 to 3,500,000 pounds of honey annually, the crop varying according to climatic conditions and the flora available for nectar secretions. In 1929, according to census reports, the state's crop was 3,509,510 pounds, valued at $396,270. This was an increase of 1,015,560 pounds, compared with 1919, and a decrease of $177,340 in value. The crop in 1930 was estimated at approximately 3,000,000 pounds and 1931 showed a small decrease, due principally to a dry year and the absence of an ample supply of nectar secretions. Under normal conditions there is a demand for all the honey produced and a considerable proportion of the output is exported to other states.

The high altitude, dry climate and types of sources provide a honey of flavor and body unexcelled anywhere in the United States. The color varies somewhat but as a rule ranges from white to a light amber and commands top prices on eastern markets. Amber honey, which has a stronger flavor and a deeper color, and which is used largely for baking and candy making, also is produced in considerable quantities. Honey is produced in the state from the lowest elevations of the valleys up to and including 7,500 to 8,000 feet above sea level.

A table is published herewith showing the number of stands of bees assessed for taxation purposes in 1931 and 1930, by counties, their assessed value and the average per stand. These figures, as reported by the county assessors, are of value principally as indicating the trend and distribution of the industry in non-census years, as they are necessarily incomplete and below the actual number.

The number of hives as reported by the census bureau for the state, by years, is as follows:

| Year | Hives |
|------|-------|
| 1900, June 1 | 59,756 |
| 1910, Jan. 15 | 71,434 |
| 1920, Jan. 1 | 63,253 |
| 1930, April 1 | 67,289 |

The production, in pounds, and the value of the crop, by years, as reported by the census, is as follows:

| Year | Pounds | Value |
|------|--------|-------|
| 1899 | 1,732,630 | *$171,740 |
| 1909 | 2,306,492 | 225,883 |
| 1919 | 2,493,950 | 573,610 |
| 1929 | 3,509,510 | 396,270 |

*Includes wax.

An accompanying table shows the number of bee hives and the value of the bees on April 1, 1930, and January 1, 1920, by counties, and the quantity and value of the honey produced in 1929 and 1919, by counties. The figures are not exactly comparable, due to the different dates upon which the census was taken, as the normal life of a bee is only 35 days.

The surplus production of honey per hive has not been so favorable for the past few years, due to the curtailment of the quantity of native flora.

In 1921, the surplus production of honey per hive was estimated at 58 pounds, compared with an average of about 44.2 pounds for the country. In 1922 the surplus honey per stand was approximately 55 pounds, but in the following year it dropped to 31 pounds, where it remained in 1923, and in 1924 the average was about 30 pounds. Since the beginning of 1925 the average is estimated at around 40 pounds.

Approximately 60 per cent of the honey production of the state is in the hands of professional bee keepers.

Fifty of the 63 counties in the state reported honey production in 1929. While this indicates a wide distribution of the industry, 13 counties actually produced nearly 75 per cent of the total output. The counties comprising the principal honey-producing areas, their output and the value of production in 1929, are as follows:

| County | Pounds | Value |
|--------|--------|-------|
| Alamosa | 128,048 | $ 13,445 |
| Boulder | 162,842 | 20,355 |
| Conejos | 120,953 | 12,700 |
| Crowley | 163,095 | 19,571 |
| Delta | 357,040 | 35,704 |
| Garfield | 163,562 | 17,992 |
| La Plata | 201,305 | 20,131 |
| Mesa | 299,620 | 29,962 |
| Montrose | 205,694 | 20,569 |
| Morgan | 134,071 | 16,759 |
| Otero | 317,421 | 38,091 |
| Prowers | 114,400 | 13,728 |
| Weld | 252,416 | 31,552 |
| Total, 13 counties | 2,620,467 | $290,559 |
| Total, state | 3,509,510 | 396,270 |
| Per cent of total | 74.7 | 73.3 |

The principal producing areas are in the sections devoted to the growing of alfalfa and sweet clover in the irrigated districts. The non-irrigated areas of the state, as distinguished from the irrigated districts, are not so inviting to the commercial apiarists, owing to the scarcity of flowers to furnish the nectar.

## BEES AND HONEY; NUMBER, VALUE AND PRODUCTION, BY COUNTIES AND YEARS
(Compiled from Census Reports)

| COUNTY | Hives of Bees (Number) | | Value of Bees | | Honey Produced (Pounds) | | Value Honey Produced | |
|---|---|---|---|---|---|---|---|---|
| | 1930 | 1920 | 1930 | 1920 | 1929 | 1919 | 1929 | 1919 |
| Adams | 1,698 | 847 | $ 8,320 | $ 5,607 | 51,442 | 15,556 | $ 6,430 | $ 3,594 |
| Alamosa | 1,237 | 518 | 5,814 | 2,402 | 125,048 | 10,021 | 13,445 | 2,323 |
| Arapahoe | 1,673 | 2,589 | 7,863 | 19,956 | 62,169 | 125,235 | 8,393 | 29,182 |
| Archuleta | 125 | 540 | 638 | 2,629 | 3,780 | 34,165 | 416 | 7,938 |
| Baca | 26 | ---- | 112 | ------ | 1,056 | ------ | 127 | ------ |
| Bent | 1,357 | 916 | 6,378 | 5,634 | 95,521 | 29,710 | 11,463 | 6,945 |
| Boulder | 3,212 | 3,535 | 15,739 | 24,951 | 162,842 | 160,955 | 20,355 | 37,536 |
| Chaffee | 38 | 120 | 179 | 669 | 703 | 2,607 | 81 | 640 |
| Cheyenne | 1 | ---- | 4 | ------ | ------ | ------ | ------ | ------ |
| Clear Creek | ---- | ---- | ------ | ------ | ------ | ------ | ------ | ------ |
| Conejos | 1,543 | 1,667 | 7,869 | 7,707 | 120,953 | 47,152 | 12,700 | 11,533 |
| Costilla | 135 | 126 | 635 | 534 | 4,685 | 2,391 | 492 | 550 |
| Crowley | 1,544 | 1,736 | 7,257 | 14,600 | 163,095 | 43,924 | 19,571 | 10,290 |
| Custer | 172 | 193 | 808 | 1,138 | 6,399 | 6,146 | 768 | 1,436 |
| Delta | 5,551 | 5,434 | 26,090 | 47,185 | 357,040 | 315,544 | 35,704 | 73,873 |
| Denver | 293 | 22 | 1,436 | 144 | 18,111 | 388 | 2,264 | 89 |
| Dolores | 13 | 48 | 68 | 505 | 450 | 852 | 45 | 196 |
| Douglas | 220 | 571 | 1,034 | 2,936 | 3,662 | 14,641 | 494 | 3,387 |
| Eagle | 125 | 166 | 588 | 932 | 1,769 | 4,895 | 195 | 1,160 |
| Elbert | 344 | 702 | 1,617 | 3,568 | 4,515 | 12,753 | 610 | 3,049 |
| El Paso | 580 | 347 | 2,726 | 1,818 | 17,459 | 4,351 | 2,357 | 1,008 |
| Fremont | 889 | 772 | 4,178 | 3,856 | 44,623 | 18,128 | 5,355 | 4,272 |
| Garfield | 2,881 | 4,541 | 13,541 | 28,796 | 163,562 | 181,950 | 17,992 | 42,479 |
| Gilpin | ---- | ---- | ------ | ------ | ------ | ------ | ------ | ------ |
| Grand | ---- | ---- | ------ | ------ | ------ | ------ | ------ | ------ |
| Gunnison | ---- | 6 | ------ | 60 | ------ | 96 | ------ | 23 |
| Hinsdale | 1 | 2 | 5 | 10 | ------ | ------ | ------ | ------ |
| Huerfano | 346 | 461 | 1,626 | 2,185 | 10,700 | 14,330 | 1,284 | 3,516 |
| Jackson | ---- | ---- | ------ | ------ | ------ | ------ | ------ | ------ |
| Jefferson | 1,737 | 4,292 | 8,511 | 35,672 | 55,916 | 175,200 | 6,990 | 40,717 |
| Kiowa | ---- | 12 | ------ | 36 | 76 | 100 | 10 | 23 |
| Kit Carson | 2 | ---- | 9 | | 250 | ------ | 34 | |
| Lake | ---- | 2,829 | ------ | 14,905 | ------ | 106,457 | ------ | 25,185 |
| La Plata | 4,300 | ---- | 24,510 | ------ | 201,305 | ------ | 20,131 | ------ |
| Larimer | 2,223 | 3,451 | 10,448 | 23,109 | 87,597 | 157,879 | 10,950 | 37,212 |
| Las Animas | 809 | 1,065 | 3,802 | 6,007 | 28,322 | 19,531 | 3,399 | 4,543 |
| Lincoln | 114 | 30 | 536 | 150 | 1,688 | 1,000 | 228 | 230 |
| Logan | 930 | 1,304 | 4,371 | 9,493 | 70,424 | 40,044 | 8,803 | 9,450 |
| Mesa | 10,048 | 6,210 | 47,226 | 40,714 | 299,620 | 294,178 | 29,962 | 68,803 |
| Mineral | ---- | ---- | ------ | ------ | ------ | ------ | ------ | ------ |
| Moffat | 159 | 36 | 747 | 283 | 6,000 | 940 | 660 | 217 |
| Montezuma | 3,611 | 1,560 | 20,583 | 11,627 | 75,757 | 85,157 | 7,576 | 20,037 |
| Montrose | 4,186 | 3,454 | 19,674 | 24,782 | 205,694 | 110,705 | 20,569 | 26,382 |
| Morgan | 1,608 | 1,699 | 7,558 | 15,289 | 134,074 | 83,043 | 16,759 | 19,738 |
| Otero | 4,097 | 79 | 19,256 | 407 | 317,421 | 990 | 38,091 | 228 |
| Ouray | 380 | 163 | 1,786 | 892 | 21,445 | 5,990 | 2,359 | 1,392 |
| Park | ---- | 1 | ------ | 12 | ------ | 18 | ------ | 4 |
| Phillips | ---- | ---- | ------ | ------ | ------ | ------ | ------ | ------ |
| Pitkin | 108 | 34 | 508 | 158 | 622 | 850 | 68 | 196 |
| Prowers | 1,724 | 1,913 | 7,413 | 13,533 | 114,400 | 57,132 | 13,728 | 13,356 |
| Pueblo | 1,717 | 2,109 | 8,070 | 14,805 | 87,969 | 56,649 | 10,556 | 13,282 |
| Rio Blanco | 438 | 580 | 2,059 | 3,194 | 9,504 | 13,889 | 1,045 | 3,227 |
| Rio Grande | 488 | 512 | 2,294 | 2,488 | 31,350 | 19,542 | 3,292 | 4,620 |
| Routt | 33 | 9 | 155 | 35 | 1,250 | 85 | 138 | 20 |
| Saguache | 734 | 227 | 3,450 | 1,459 | 47,377 | 5,347 | 4,975 | 1,257 |
| San Juan | ---- | ---- | ------ | ------ | ------ | ------ | ------ | ------ |
| San Miguel | 378 | 45 | 1,852 | 360 | 29,110 | 770 | 2,911 | 185 |
| Sedgwick | 173 | 78 | 813 | 655 | 4,805 | 1,950 | 601 | 489 |
| Summit | ---- | ---- | ------ | ------ | ------ | ------ | ------ | ------ |
| Teller | 3 | ---- | 14 | ------ | 7 | ------ | 1 | ------ |
| Washington | 12 | 13 | 56 | 65 | 262 | 80 | 35 | 18 |
| Weld | 3,177 | 5,674 | 14,932 | 35,254 | 252,416 | 210,530 | 31,552 | 49,064 |
| Yuma | 96 | 19 | 413 | 133 | 2,265 | 104 | 306 | 25 |
| State | 67,289 | 63,253 | $325,571 | $433,339 | 3,509,510 | 2,493,950 | $396,270 | *$584,924 |

Note—Number of hives of bees owned on farms, or elsewhere, are as of April 1, 1930, and January 1, 1920.
*Includes value of 28,282 pounds of wax produced, valued at $11,314. The value of honey produced was $573,610.

## BEES (STANDS) IN COLORADO, 1930 AND 1931
### (From Reports of County Assessors to State Tax Commission)

| COUNTY | 1931 | | | 1930 | | |
|---|---|---|---|---|---|---|
| | Number | Assessed Value | Average Per Stand | Number | Assessed Value | Average Per Stand |
| Adams | 2,452 | $ 7,355 | $ 3.00 | 2,500 | $ 10,000 | $ 4.00 |
| Alamosa | 1,847 | 5,896 | 3.19 | 1,420 | 5,825 | 4.10 |
| Arapahoe | 663 | 2,015 | 3.04 | 630 | 2,520 | 4.00 |
| Archuleta | ----- | ------- | ---- | 57 | 230 | 4.00 |
| Baca | ----- | ------- | ---- | ----- | ------- | ---- |
| Bent | 2,146 | 6,440 | 3.00 | 1,658 | 6,675 | 4.00 |
| Boulder | 2,445 | 7,370 | 3.01 | 2,695 | 10,780 | 4.00 |
| Chaffee | 90 | 270 | 3.00 | 82 | 330 | 4.02 |
| Cheyenne | ----- | ------- | ---- | ----- | ------- | ---- |
| Clear Creek | ----- | ------- | ---- | ----- | ------- | ---- |
| Conejos | 1,927 | 5,780 | 3.00 | 2,025 | 8,065 | 4.00 |
| Costilla | 90 | 270 | 3.00 | 91 | 365 | 4.01 |
| Crowley | 2,490 | 7,485 | 3.01 | 2,378 | 9,545 | 4.01 |
| Custer | 53 | 160 | 3.00 | 47 | 185 | 4.00 |
| Delta | 3,122 | 9,665 | 3.10 | 2,817 | 12,235 | 4.34 |
| Denver | ----- | ------- | ---- | ----- | ------- | ---- |
| Dolores | ----- | ------- | ---- | 4 | 20 | 5.00 |
| Douglas | 392 | 1,175 | 3.00 | 22 | 90 | 4.00 |
| Eagle | 120 | 360 | 3.00 | 51 | 204 | 4.00 |
| Elbert | 77 | 255 | 3.31 | 35 | 152 | 4.34 |
| El Paso | 303 | 1,260 | 4.16 | 405 | 1,680 | 4.11 |
| Fremont | 662 | 1,984 | 3.00 | 871 | 3,486 | 4.00 |
| Garfield | 3,308 | 10,240 | 3.10 | 3,002 | 12,430 | 4.14 |
| Gilpin | ----- | ------- | ---- | ----- | ------- | ---- |
| Grand | ----- | ------- | ---- | ----- | ------- | ---- |
| Gunnison | ----- | ------- | ---- | ----- | ------- | ---- |
| Hinsdale | ----- | ------- | ---- | ----- | ------- | ---- |
| Huerfano | 32 | 150 | 4.69 | 125 | 575 | 4.60 |
| Jackson | ----- | ------- | ---- | ----- | ------- | ---- |
| Jefferson | 1,418 | 4,405 | 3.11 | 1,445 | 6,005 | 4.11 |
| Kiowa | ----- | ------- | ---- | ----- | ------- | ---- |
| Kit Carson | ----- | ------- | ---- | ----- | ------- | ---- |
| Lake | ----- | ------- | ---- | ----- | ------- | ---- |
| La Plata | 2,399 | 7,250 | 3.02 | 2,466 | 9,835 | 3.99 |
| Larimer | 2,520 | 7,560 | 3.00 | 1,760 | 7,040 | 4.00 |
| Las Animas | 505 | 1,780 | 3.52 | 576 | 2,305 | 4.00 |
| Lincoln | ----- | ------- | ---- | ----- | ------- | ---- |
| Logan | 728 | 2,185 | 3.00 | 618 | 2,475 | 4.00 |
| Mesa | 5,036 | 15,110 | 3.00 | 4,235 | 16,955 | 4.0 |
| Mineral | ----- | ------- | ---- | ----- | ------- | ---- |
| Moffat | 30 | 120 | 4.00 | 36 | 150 | 4.1 |
| Montezuma | 2,062 | 7,925 | 3.84 | 2,704 | 10,960 | 4.0 |
| Montrose | 4,160 | 12,480 | 3.00 | 4,569 | 18,276 | 4.0 |
| Morgan | 1,133 | 3,410 | 3.01 | 905 | 3,620 | 4.0 |
| Otero | 4,368 | 13,105 | 3.00 | 5,184 | 21,075 | 4.0 |
| Ouray | 225 | 900 | 4.00 | 231 | 924 | 4.0 |
| Park | ----- | ------- | ---- | ----- | ------- | ---- |
| Phillips | ----- | ------- | ---- | 54 | 270 | 5.0 |
| Pitkin | ----- | ------- | ---- | ----- | ------- | ---- |
| Prowers | 1,376 | 4,228 | 3.07 | 1,372 | 5,484 | 4.0 |
| Pueblo | 1,422 | 4,645 | 3.27 | 1,481 | 5,935 | 4.0 |
| Rio Blanco | ----- | ------- | ---- | ----- | ------- | ---- |
| Rio Grande | 605 | 1,816 | 3.00 | 590 | 2,360 | 4.0 |
| Routt | ----- | ------- | ---- | ----- | ------- | ---- |
| Saguache | 356 | 1,070 | 3.00 | 262 | 1,048 | 4.0 |
| San Juan | ----- | ------- | ---- | ----- | ------- | ---- |
| San Miguel | 150 | 550 | 3.67 | 150 | 600 | 4.0 |
| Sedgwick | 298 | 950 | 3.19 | 315 | 1,285 | 4.0 |
| Summit | ----- | ------- | ---- | ----- | ------- | ---- |
| Teller | ----- | ------- | ---- | ----- | ------- | ---- |
| Washington | ----- | ------- | ---- | ----- | ------- | ---- |
| Weld | 4,144 | 12,490 | 3.01 | 3,840 | 13,410 | 4.0 |
| Yuma | 40 | 120 | 3.00 | 33 | 140 | 4.2 |
| State | 55,194 | $170,229 | $ 3.08 | 53,241 | $215,544 | $ 4.0 |

# Horticulture and Floriculture

THE value of Colorado's orchard crop, exclusive of berries and some small fruits, varies year by year according to climatic conditions and the seasonal farm value. In a 13-year period ending with 1931, the maximum output was established in 1919 when the crop was valued at $9,451,800, and the minimum was established in 1931, in which year the crop was valued at $2,353,000. The value of the crop by years is as follows:

| Year | Value |
|------|-------|
| 1919 | $9,451,800 |
| 1920 | 6,143,700 |
| 1921 | 8,953,000 |
| 1922 | 5,910,750 |
| 1923 | 5,987,620 |
| 1924 | 6,801,000 |
| 1925 | 6,068,000 |
| 1926 | 5,239,000 |
| 1927 | 5,647,000 |
| 1928 | 3,786,000 |
| 1929 | 5,370,000 |
| 1930 | 2,753,000 |
| 1931 | 2,353,000 |

Soil and climatic conditions in certain areas of Colorado are especially suited to the production of nearly all orchard and small fruits adapted to this latitude. The quality of the soil in the fruit-growing districts, the abundance of sunshine, water for irrigation, and atmospheric conditions existing in relatively high altitudes combine to make an excellent grade of fruit that commands favorable prices on account of its quality. The areas in which the industry is profitable are restricted as to size, and the fruit orchards are located mostly in the valleys surrounded by mountain ranges which protect them from hard winters and early and late frosts.

Apples, peaches and pears are the principal orchard fruits grown. Other fruits and berries grown include plums, apricots, grapes, strawberries, raspberries, loganberries, blackberries and currants. Cherries are grown extensively in certain areas and rank next to the three principal fruits in value and volume of production.

The locations of the principal orchards of the state and the areas in which small fruits are grown are shown in two tables published herewith. One of these gives the number of apple, peach and pear trees of bearing age, by counties, in 1930 and 1920, and production in 1929, as shown by the census reports. Another shows the number of cherry and plum and prune trees and grape vines of bearing age, by counties, for the same years.

Another table gives state totals on trees of bearing age in 1930 and 1920, trees not of bearing age and production of fruit for these years.

Other tables give state totals on the number of farms reporting strawberries, raspberries, blackberries and dewberries, currants, gooseberries and other small fruits in 1929 and 1919, the acreage cultivated and the production for these years; the quantity and value of the fruit crops for 1931, 1930 and 1929 as reported by the Colorado Co-Operative Crop Reporting service, and the average prices for apples, peaches and pears in Colorado and the United States, as of December 1, for the years 1927 to 1931, inclusive.

The most important fruit-growing districts are the western slope, in the valleys of the Grand and Gunnison rivers and tributary streams, comprising parts of Garfield, Mesa, Delta and Montrose counties; the Canon City district, comprising a part of Fremont county; the Arkansas valley, comprising parts of Crowley, Otero, Pueblo, Bent and Prowers counties; southwestern Colorado, comprising parts of La Plata and Montezuma counties, and comparatively small areas near the foothills along the eastern side of the mountains. The western slope area ranks first in importance from the standpoint of production, with the Canon City district second. Apples, peaches and pears are the principal fruit crops in the Grand valley and in the valleys of tributary streams, though practically all fruits grown in the state are produced here. This district produces nearly all the commercial peach crop of the state and a very large proportion of the apple crop. Southwest Colorado produces as fine a variety of all kinds of fruit as is grown in any part of the state, but lack of adequate transportation facilities has retarded development of the fruit-growing industry in this district. In the Canon City district the principal crop is apples, with a considerable production of cherries and small fruits. Some apples, cherries and small fruits are grown in the Arkansas valley, especially in Crowley and Otero counties, and cherries are grown rather extensively in several of the counties just east of the mountains, particularly .in Larimer county. Apples have been grown to considerable extent in this same area for a good many years, but the yield is not so dependable as on the western slope and the quality of the fruit is not so high. In the irrigated district immediately north of Denver, including parts of Boulder, Adams, Larimer and Weld counties, berries and other small fruits are grown successfully and always find a good market in Denver. Routt county is especially famous for its strawberries, which come into market late in the summer, after the berries from most other districts are gone, and for that reason command exceptionally high prices.

Some attention has been paid in the past few years to the growing of orchards in the non-irrigated districts of eastern Colorado, and a few small trees of hardy varieties are being grown on many of the farms. In the irrigated sections of eastern Colorado apples and some other tree fruits are grown successfully. Late spring frosts frequently damage fruits in all sections of the state, but the organization of community forces in the principal fruit-producing districts to heat orchards with specially devised heaters on nights when the temperature falls below the frost point has in a large measure eliminated the danger of loss from this source.

### FLORICULTURE

The floral industry in Colorado, including flowers, plants and vegetables grown under glass and flowers grown in the open; the operation of nurseries and bulb farms and the production of flower and vegetable seed, has developed into one of the state's important industries.

The bureau of the census took a census of the industry in 1930, the reports covering operations in 1929. This was done at the request of the industry and was conducted by mail. The results, as given in the preliminary figures, showed an investment of $4,981,-990 in land, buildings and equipment, and $2,795,685 in greenhouses, a total of $7,777,675, by 204 establishments reporting. Total receipts of these establishments for the year were $3,535,862. The receipts are below estimates made by the industry in the state in the same year, these estimates placing the annual business at approximately $5,-000,000. A summary of the census report is published in an accompanying table.

Climatic conditions, which are favorable for producing blooms of unusual brilliance in colors, large size and lasting quality, have had much to do with the development of the industry, which finds a market for its product not only in most parts of the United States, but in several foreign countries. The glass area of Colorado's flower houses is estimated at 3,527,000 square feet.

Carnations lead the list of products, the output being in excess of 12,000,000 a year. Ten states depend upon Colorado for their entire supply of this flower and shipments have been made to Cuba, New York and London. Orchid production is conducted upon a large scale by a few growers, there being one commercial collection in Denver comprising more than 500 varieties and valued at a million dollars.

The greenhouses in this state produce a cut of 5,000,000 roses annually. The quality of these flowers compares favorably with that of the blooms grown in eastern and middle western sections of the country. In fact, the excellence of the quality of both roses and carnations is sustained during the entire year; whereas, in some sections of the country during certain seasons the heat is so excessive as to impair materially the standard required for good keeping and shipping qualities.

Because of favorable climatic conditions, Gypsophila is considered to be in its best environment in Colorado. It is one of the outdoor products and is being grown in constantly increasing quantities. More than 150,000 bushes of Gypsophila, or baby breath, as it is commonly called, are cut and dried annually. A large percentage of this product is sent to eastern states where it is used in wreaths and for other decorative purposes.

Sweet peas are grown under glass from September until June, and soon after that are produced out of doors. The mountain peas, grown in July, August and September, are of unusual quality in size and color, and are famous also in that they keep and ship well.

About 5,500,000 gladioli are grown annually in and around Denver. Asters, peonies, marigolds, daisies and many other annuals and perennials are grown in large quantities, one of the foremost in number being the dahlias, which are increasing in number and beauty each year.

About 65,000,000 bedding plants are produced and sold annually. These include the different varieties of flowers such as petunias, geraniums, salvias, heliotrope, fuchsias and many kinds of decorative greens and foliage used so extensively in landscape gardening in parks, floral gardens, etc.

It is a recognized fact that climatic conditions in Colorado are most favorable for the growing of potted plants. This is especially true of cyclamen. Many thousands of this variety are sold in small pots to the surrounding states, and the sale of full-grown plants during the Christmas season is very large.

An average of 100,000 Easter lilies are grown for the Easter season, and 400,000 chrysanthemums are sold during the Thanksgiving days.

An important item of the floral industry is the forcing of Dutch bulbs, such as tulips, hyacinths and narcissi, about 500,000 being forced each season.

Colorado is taking a place rapidly as one of the most important, if not the leading state in the Union in the production of quality flowers.

### FRUIT PRODUCTION AND VALUE BY YEARS

| | 1931 | | 1930 | | 1929 | |
|---|---|---|---|---|---|---|
| | Quantity | Value | Quantity | Value | Quantity | Value |
| Apples (Bu.) | 2,090,000 | $1,254,000 | 1,060,000 | $ 901,000 | 2,300,000 | $2,185,000 |
| Peaches (Bu.) | 1,130,000 | 565,000 | 787,000 | 1,141,000 | 953,000 | 1,382,000 |
| Pears (Bu.) | 385,000 | 231,000 | 146,000 | 190,000 | 600,000 | 900,000 |
| Cherries (Tons) | 2,500 | 175,000 | 3,500 | 315,000 | 5,100 | 612,000 |
| Miscellaneous fruits | -------- | ˙128,000 | -------- | 206,000 | -------- | 291,000 |
| | -------- | $2,353,000 | -------- | $2,753,000 | -------- | $5,370,000 |

### SMALL FRUITS: ACREAGE AND PRODUCTION IN COLORADO
(Bureau of the Census)

| | Straw-berries | Rasp-berries | Black-berries and Dew-berries | Currants | Goose-berries | Other Small Fruits |
|---|---|---|---|---|---|---|
| **Farms reporting:** | | | | | | |
| 1929 | 1,588 | 1,890 | 195 | 361 | 240 | 36 |
| 1919 | 1,513 | 1,356 | 251 | 751 | ------ | ------ |
| **Acreage:** | | | | | | |
| 1929 | 658 | 973 | 112 | 85 | 88 | 9 |
| 1919 | 653 | 600 | 91 | 141 | ------ | ------ |
| **Production (Quarts):** | | | | | | |
| 1929 | 900,765 | 982,546 | 78,951 | 54,648 | 146,390 | 7,600 |
| 1919 | 944,276 | 633,766 | 76,234 | 137,634 | ------ | ------ |

### COLORADO FRUIT TREES AND PRODUCTION, CENSUS YEARS
(Bureau of the Census)

| | Apples | Peaches | Pears | Plums and Prunes | Cherries | †Grapes | Apricots |
|---|---|---|---|---|---|---|---|
| **Trees not of bearing age, number:** | | | | | | | |
| 1930 | 97,053 | 334,565 | 47,809 | 17,923 | 230,218 | 37,434 | 10,974 |
| 1920 | 183,315 | 32,158 | 39,979 | 28,055 | 74,799 | 15,836 | 575 |
| **Trees of bearing age:** | | | | | | | |
| 1930 | 993,186 | 454,101 | 155,300 | 60,148 | 286,111 | 168,307 | 15,015 |
| 1920 | 1,777,737 | 446,943 | 136,117 | 80,027 | 348,832 | 125,027 | 5,904 |
| **Production (bushels):** | | | | | | | |
| 1929 | 2,251,330 | 953,175 | 527,900 | 26,890 | 182,606 | *963,202 | 22,176 |
| 1919 | 3,417,682 | 721,480 | 269,465 | 44,944 | 165,087 | *526,509 | 9,154 |

*Pounds.  †Vines.

**APPLE, PEACH AND PEAR TREES, 1930 AND 1920, AND PRODUCTION IN 1929, BY COUNTIES**
(Compiled from Census Reports)

| COUNTY | Apples | | | Peaches | | | Pears | | |
|---|---|---|---|---|---|---|---|---|---|
| | No. Trees | | Production 1929 (Bu.) | No. Trees | | Production 1929 (Bu.) | No. Trees | | Production 1929 (Bu.) |
| | 1930 | 1920 | | 1930 | 1920 | | 1930 | 1920 | |
| Adams | 6,463 | 14,999 | 18,940 | 35 | 114 | 8 | 37 | 44 | 17 |
| Alamosa | 82 | ----- | 89 | ----- | ----- | ----- | ----- | ----- | ----- |
| Arapahoe | 4,357 | 12,895 | 9,006 | 51 | 17 | 7 | 148 | 125 | 45 |
| Archuleta | 676 | 3,680 | 75 | ----- | 37 | ----- | 26 | 147 | 58 |
| Baca | 400 | 934 | 82 | 1,753 | 2,709 | 390 | 90 | 312 | 19 |
| Bent | 1,586 | 5,709 | 754 | 675 | 1,776 | 514 | 84 | 77 | 22 |
| Boulder | 21,150 | 40,285 | 58,711 | 34 | 173 | 23 | 25 | 143 | 30 |
| Chaffee | 10,067 | 11,645 | 5,841 | 1 | ----- | ----- | 23 | 24 | 13 |
| Cheyenne | 175 | 232 | 31 | 119 | 529 | 28 | 22 | 25 | 2 |
| Clear Creek | 6 | ----- | 2 | ----- | ----- | ----- | ----- | ----- | ----- |
| Conejos | 133 | 62 | 188 | ----- | ----- | ----- | ----- | ----- | ----- |
| Costilla | 934 | 260 | 1,434 | ----- | ----- | ----- | 51 | 23 | 91 |
| Crowley | 8,829 | 19,626 | 6,706 | 138 | 336 | 184 | 30 | 16 | 3 |
| Custer | 616 | 1,301 | 483 | 10 | 63 | 5 | 14 | 23 | ----- |
| Delta | 423,932 | 482,644 | 1,189,442 | 148,089 | 163,488 | 78,373 | 9,375 | 8,449 | 18,327 |
| Denver | 255 | 904 | 310 | ----- | ----- | ----- | ----- | 19 | ----- |
| Dolores | 105 | 70 | 14 | 45 | 10 | 39 | 4 | 10 | ----- |
| Douglas | 3,094 | 2,276 | 1,183 | 2 | 50 | ----- | 4 | 5 | 6 |
| Eagle | 479 | 1,221 | 620 | 1 | ----- | 1 | 5 | 52 | 5 |
| Elbert | 408 | 681 | 252 | 17 | 16 | 3 | 38 | 14 | 3 |
| El Paso | 1,408 | 2,557 | 620 | 35 | 19 | 7 | 15 | 40 | 21 |
| Fremont | 115,003 | 195,010 | 124,991 | 176 | 1,691 | 118 | 1,351 | 1,379 | 2,045 |
| Garfield | 37,439 | 67,685 | 54,450 | 5,212 | 7,885 | 2,206 | 587 | 2,033 | 778 |
| Gilpin | ----- | ----- | ----- | ----- | ----- | ----- | ----- | ----- | ----- |
| Grand | ----- | ----- | ----- | ----- | ----- | ----- | ----- | ----- | ----- |
| Gunnison | 320 | 8 | 400 | ----- | ----- | ----- | ----- | ----- | ----- |
| Hinsdale | ----- | ----- | ----- | ----- | ----- | ----- | ----- | ----- | ----- |
| Huerfano | 4,485 | 7,422 | 10,672 | 14 | 15 | 6 | 31 | 118 | 57 |
| Jackson | ----- | ----- | ----- | ----- | ----- | ----- | ----- | ----- | ----- |
| Jefferson | 31,294 | 56,646 | 28,899 | 154 | 539 | 60 | 105 | 202 | 23 |
| Kiowa | 132 | 199 | 50 | 110 | 152 | 21 | 15 | 13 | 3 |
| Kit Carson | 327 | 635 | 57 | 177 | 909 | 36 | 35 | 21 | 3 |
| Lake | ----- | 22,651 | ----- | ----- | 233 | ----- | ----- | 1,291 | ----- |
| La Plata | 16,689 | ----- | 31,618 | 268 | ----- | 247 | 1,446 | ----- | 1,905 |
| Larimer | 53,012 | 65,585 | 170,081 | 9 | 200 | 4 | 72 | 424 | 143 |
| Las Animas | 2,034 | 5,019 | 3,474 | 88 | 27 | 47 | 41 | 45 | 12 |
| Lincoln | 370 | 116 | 198 | 225 | 152 | 47 | 12 | 4 | 8 |
| Logan | 1,134 | 1,476 | 1,059 | 134 | 68 | 88 | 60 | 72 | 23 |
| Mesa | 108,950 | 477,800 | 284,250 | 285,754 | 242,200 | 862,316 | 139,114 | 115,525 | 501,167 |
| Mineral | ----- | ----- | ----- | ----- | ----- | ----- | ----- | ----- | ----- |
| Moffat | 269 | 66 | 524 | 5 | ----- | 15 | 8 | ----- | 18 |
| Montezuma | 48,403 | 67,471 | 122,816 | 3,593 | 7,001 | 5,249 | 998 | 2,250 | 1,620 |
| Montrose | 51,903 | 106,774 | 94,702 | 4,431 | 8,217 | 1,101 | 768 | 2,071 | 1,037 |
| Morgan | 788 | 1,357 | 640 | 14 | 49 | 6 | 60 | 24 | 16 |
| Otero | 9,530 | 36,878 | 1,338 | 364 | 1,248 | 401 | 37 | 65 | 23 |
| Ouray | 343 | 522 | 219 | 33 | 22 | 3 | 7 | 18 | 1 |
| Park | ----- | ----- | ----- | ----- | ----- | ----- | ----- | ----- | ----- |
| Phillips | 163 | 158 | 60 | 47 | 57 | 9 | 20 | 1 | 4 |
| Pitkin | 286 | 296 | 265 | ----- | ----- | ----- | 1 | 10 | ----- |
| Prowers | 3,564 | 9,726 | 1,054 | 982 | 2,923 | 786 | 74 | 192 | 17 |
| Pueblo | 11,250 | 27,585 | 11,916 | 87 | 214 | 40 | 54 | 217 | 28 |
| Rio Blanco | 620 | 959 | 570 | 1 | ----- | ----- | 2 | ----- | ----- |
| Rio Grande | 187 | 103 | 444 | ----- | ----- | ----- | ----- | ----- | ----- |
| Routt | 90 | 33 | 130 | ----- | 4 | ----- | ----- | ----- | ----- |
| Saguache | 525 | 442 | 1,041 | 1 | ----- | 1 | 3 | 6 | 1 |
| San Juan | ----- | ----- | ----- | ----- | ----- | ----- | ----- | ----- | ----- |
| San Miguel | 505 | 1,250 | 364 | 8 | 45 | 11 | 25 | 70 | 2 |
| Sedgwick | 163 | 135 | 239 | 106 | 54 | ----- | 14 | 26 | 2 |
| Summit | ----- | ----- | ----- | ----- | ----- | ----- | ----- | ----- | ----- |
| Teller | 28 | 3,017 | ----- | ----- | 100 | ----- | ----- | 25 | ----- |
| Washington | 489 | 164 | 163 | 242 | 209 | 18 | 60 | 15 | 2 |
| Weld | 6,137 | 15,640 | 8,363 | 28 | 202 | 22 | 150 | 108 | 15 |
| Yuma | 1,599 | 2,928 | 1,500 | 833 | 3,190 | 735 | 159 | 344 | 9 |
| State | 993,186 | 1,777,737 | 2,251,330 | 454,101 | 446,943 | 953,175 | 155,300 | 136,117 | 527,90 |

Note—Table shows only trees of bearing age for 1930 and 1920  A separate table gives stat totals for trees of non-bearing age.

**CHERRY, PLUM AND PRUNE TREES AND GRAPE VINES, 1930 AND 1920, AND PRODUCTION IN 1929, BY COUNTIES**

(Compiled from Census Reports)

| COUNTY | Cherries | | | Plums and Prunes | | | Grapes | | |
|---|---|---|---|---|---|---|---|---|---|
| | No. Trees | | Produc-tion 1929 (Bushels) | No. Trees | | Produc-tion 1929 (Bushels) | No. Vines | | Produc-tion 1929 (Pounds) |
| | 1930 | 1920 | | 1930 | 1920 | | 1930 | 1920 | |
| Adams | 3,670 | 12,071 | 1,466 | 1,270 | 1,755 | 471 | 408 | 75 | 531 |
| Alamosa | 2 | ---- | ---- | ---- | ---- | ---- | ---- | ---- | ---- |
| Arapahoe | 1,840 | 3,788 | 922 | 789 | 1,017 | 655 | 260 | 27 | 985 |
| Archuleta | 18 | 151 | ---- | 52 | 101 | 12 | 3 | ---- | ---- |
| Baca | 1,153 | 1,073 | 69 | 720 | 740 | 101 | 556 | 1,125 | 1,360 |
| Bent | 737 | 1,477 | 322 | 1,000 | 1,299 | 798 | 830 | 1,280 | 1,895 |
| Boulder | 3,566 | 7,719 | 2,217 | 1,262 | 3,462 | 775 | 6,324 | 5,662 | 36,013 |
| Chaffee | 123 | 126 | 51 | 60 | 221 | 38 | ---- | ---- | ---- |
| Cheyenne | 224 | 244 | 55 | 319 | 1,286 | 67 | 53 | 128 | 30 |
| Clear Creek | ---- | ---- | ---- | ---- | ---- | ---- | ---- | ---- | ---- |
| Conejos | 17 | ---- | 5 | 2 | 9 | 1 | ---- | 6 | ---- |
| Costilla | 45 | 7 | 21 | 59 | 105 | 35 | ---- | ---- | ---- |
| Crowley | 1,606 | 30,691 | 1,238 | 251 | 790 | 160 | 12,235 | 7,492 | 91,925 |
| Custer | 29 | 206 | 16 | 34 | 94 | 3 | ---- | 4 | ---- |
| Delta | 10,418 | 13,846 | 15,014 | 4,225 | 11,025 | 2,116 | 19,728 | 9,067 | 154,580 |
| Denver | 142 | 497 | 103 | 11 | 66 | 10 | 104 | ---- | 200 |
| Dolores | 14 | 6 | 7 | 28 | 41 | 6 | 6 | 6 | 75 |
| Douglas | 63 | 142 | 13 | 144 | 82 | 17 | 21 | ---- | ---- |
| Eagle | 84 | 211 | 25 | 47 | 57 | 27 | ---- | ---- | ---- |
| Elbert | 940 | 1,429 | 595 | 247 | 383 | 51 | 6 | 29 | ---- |
| El Paso | 1,495 | 17,261 | 240 | 298 | 219 | 148 | 150 | 250 | 600 |
| Fremont | 36,638 | 43,151 | 47,260 | 2,079 | 3,625 | 428 | 16,076 | 23,404 | 56,610 |
| Garfield | 3,193 | 4,053 | 3,866 | 2,322 | 2,395 | 1,977 | 22,343 | 9,544 | 95,794 |
| Gilpin | ---- | ---- | ---- | ---- | ---- | ---- | ---- | ---- | ---- |
| Grand | ---- | ---- | ---- | ---- | ---- | ---- | ---- | ---- | ---- |
| Gunnison | ---- | 3 | ---- | ---- | ---- | ---- | ---- | ---- | ---- |
| Hinsdale | ---- | ---- | ---- | ---- | ---- | ---- | ---- | ---- | ---- |
| Huerfano | 191 | 558 | 114 | 86 | 511 | 56 | ---- | 2 | ---- |
| Jackson | ---- | ---- | ---- | ---- | ---- | ---- | ---- | ---- | ---- |
| Jefferson | 42,577 | 50,245 | 12,349 | 6,667 | 8,581 | 1,744 | 12,484 | 11,990 | 32,693 |
| Kiowa | 141 | 372 | 77 | 172 | 1,435 | 25 | 191 | 150 | 200 |
| Kit Carson | 891 | 1,114 | 253 | 1,086 | 1,199 | 72 | 125 | 2,413 | 20 |
| Lake | ---- | 2,064 | ---- | ---- | 1,487 | ---- | ---- | 37 | ---- |
| La Plata | 1,446 | ---- | 1,202 | 1,468 | ---- | 800 | 271 | ---- | 1,699 |
| Larimer | 145,957 | 73,169 | 76,689 | 3,535 | 4,412 | 1,844 | 1,526 | 262 | 2,005 |
| Las Animas | 1,281 | 428 | 128 | 619 | 1,166 | 118 | 36 | 12 | 46 |
| Lincoln | 693 | 364 | 234 | 488 | 294 | 75 | 73 | 224 | 150 |
| Logan | 1,512 | 1,354 | 395 | 2,472 | 1,437 | 1,186 | 129 | ---- | 980 |
| Mesa | 3,763 | 9,639 | 3,438 | 3,356 | 4,565 | 2,865 | 38,375 | 18,390 | 267,723 |
| Mineral | ---- | ---- | ---- | ---- | ---- | ---- | ---- | ---- | ---- |
| Moffat | 38 | 1 | 19 | 184 | 14 | 46 | 54 | ---- | 500 |
| Montezuma | 1,188 | 2,233 | 1,496 | 1,727 | 2,643 | 2,253 | 10,085 | 4,838 | 70,638 |
| Montrose | 1,601 | 4,137 | 1,683 | 1,451 | 3,025 | 2,449 | 8,087 | 4,581 | 50,533 |
| Morgan | 1,165 | 1,790 | 398 | 11,000 | 2,166 | 946 | 71 | 157 | 250 |
| Otero | 3,600 | 35,085 | 2,617 | 991 | 3,964 | 665 | 13,504 | 16,090 | 76,430 |
| Ouray | 12 | 33 | ---- | 95 | 74 | 47 | 88 | 12 | 500 |
| Park | ---- | ---- | ---- | ---- | ---- | ---- | ---- | ---- | ---- |
| Phillips | 971 | 583 | 307 | 525 | 202 | 171 | 32 | ---- | 155 |
| Pitkin | 17 | 23 | 8 | ---- | 14 | ---- | ---- | ---- | ---- |
| Prowers | 720 | 2,375 | 191 | 1,377 | 1,730 | 390 | 126 | 394 | 305 |
| Pueblo | 3,249 | 11,907 | 2,122 | 757 | 2,519 | 581 | 3,588 | 6,507 | 15,475 |
| Rio Blanco | 22 | 39 | 15 | 52 | 22 | 58 | ---- | ---- | ---- |
| Rio Grande | 1 | ---- | ---- | 15 | ---- | 5 | ---- | ---- | ---- |
| Routt | 38 | 2 | 5 | 4 | 2 | 1 | ---- | ---- | ---- |
| Saguache | 14 | 105 | 2 | 16 | 22 | 9 | ---- | ---- | ---- |
| San Juan | ---- | ---- | ---- | ---- | ---- | ---- | ---- | ---- | ---- |
| San Miguel | 32 | 82 | 21 | 29 | 53 | 15 | 10 | 20 | 50 |
| Sedgwick | 360 | 608 | 226 | 660 | 392 | 260 | 35 | ---- | 93 |
| Summit | ---- | ---- | ---- | ---- | ---- | ---- | ---- | ---- | ---- |
| Teller | 1 | 1,000 | ---- | ---- | 100 | ---- | ---- | ---- | ---- |
| Washington | 1,343 | 826 | 263 | 1,257 | 1,185 | 152 | 34 | 83 | 25 |
| Weld | 3,497 | 5,944 | 2,999 | 2,199 | 6,372 | 1,403 | 207 | 250 | 1,823 |
| Yuma | 3,764 | 4,600 | 1,850 | 2,641 | 1,669 | 758 | 73 | 516 | 306 |
| State | 286,111 | 348,832 | 182,606 | 60,148 | 80,027 | 26,890 | 168,307 | 125,027 | 963,202 |

Note—Table shows only trees or vines of bearing age for 1930 and 1920. A separate table shows ate totals for trees or vines of non-bearing age.

## AVERAGE PRICES OF APPLES, PEACHES AND PEARS ON DECEMBER 1

|  | 1931 | | 1930 | | 1929 | | 1928 | | 1927 | |
|---|---|---|---|---|---|---|---|---|---|---|
|  | Colo. | U. S. | Colo. | U. S. | Colo. | U. S. | Colo. | U. S. | Colo. | U. S. |
| Applies _____ | .60 | .58 | .85 | .93 | .95 | 1.31 | .65 | 1.00 | 1.10 | 1.38 |
| Peaches _____ | .50 | .56 | 1.45 | .89 | 1.45 | 1.35 | 1.20 | .99 | 1.20 | 1.18 |
| Pears _____ | .60 | .60 | 1.30 | .75 | 1.50 | 1.48 | 1.05 | 1.02 | 1.40 | 1.32 |

## CENSUS OF HORTICULTURE IN COLORADO, 1930

Note—These are preliminary figures of the 1930 census covering operations in 1929, which was conducted by mail by the census bureau. It was primarily a census of production.

**Flowers, plants and vegetables grown under glass and flowers grown in the open in Colorado in 1929:**

| | |
|---|---|
| Number of establishments reporting (growing flowers only, 127; vegetables only, 35; flowers and Vegetables, 42) ..................... | 204 |
| Acres used in production ............................................. | 570 |
| Value of land, buildings and equipment............................ | $4,143,359 |
| Square feet in greenhouses (3,217,796 feet for florists' crops; 295,785 for Vegetable crops)........................................... | 3,519,888 |
| Total value of greenhouses ......................................... | $2,792,385 |
| Maximum number of persons employed any time in 1929............. | 1,181 |
| Total receipts of growers from sales of flowers, plants and vegetables grown under glass and flowers grown in the open......... | $2,137,912 |

**Nurseries in Colorado in 1929:**

| | |
|---|---|
| Number reporting ................................................. | 46 |
| Acres used for nursery purposes.................................. | 272 |
| Value of land, buildings and equipment........................... | $325,266 |
| Square feet in greenhouses ....................................... | 6,953 |
| Total value of greenhouses ....................................... | $3,300 |
| Maximum number of persons employed any time in 1929............. | 191 |
| Total receipts by growers from sales of nursery stock grown in Colorado ......................................................... | $228,059 |

**Bulb Farms in Colorado in 1929:**

| | |
|---|---|
| Number reporting ................................................. | 12 |
| Acres used in production .......................................... | 28 |
| Value of land, buildings and equipment........................... | $22,415 |
| Maximum number of persons employed any time in 1929............. | 28 |
| Total receipts of growers.......................................... | $21,913 |

**Flower and vegetable seed production in Colorado in 1929:**

| | |
|---|---|
| Number of seed farms reporting.................................... | 18 |
| Acres used in growing seed........................................ | 2,536 |
| Value of land, buildings and equipment........................... | $490,950 |
| Maximum number of persons employed any time in 1929............. | 149 |
| Total receipts by growers from sale of flower and Vegetable seed..... | $1,147,978 |

Note—A report was received from one farm producing mushrooms, but the data cannot be published without disclosing operations of the individual establishment.

# Manufacturing

THE manufacturing industry in Colorado has progressed steadily from its inception down to and including 1929, as shown by the reports of the bureau of the census, with the exception that in 1921 and 1923 there were decreases in the value of products when compared with the output in 1919, when the industry still felt the stimulus of war conditions and high prices. The ground lost during the business depression of 1921-1922 was more than regained in the following years, and beginning with 1925 the value of output in the census years was greater than during the war period.

The last census of manufactures.was taken in 1930 and covered activities in 1929. Final figures for the state by industries and counties have not as yet been released, except for some of the major industries. A table published herewith shows the final state totals for 1929 and figures for 1927 and 1919. The data for 1929 and 1919 are fairly comparable, although there are some slight differences in the forms in which they were taken.

The value of products by census years and increase over previous census year are as follows:

| Year | Value | Per Cent Increase |
|------|-------|-------------------|
| 1869 | ...........$  2,852,820 | ..... |
| 1879 | ...........  14,260,159 | 399.86 |
| 1889 | ...........  42,480,205 | 197.89 |
| 1899 | ...........  89,068,000 | 109.66 |
| 1904 | ...........  100,144,000 | 12.44 |
| 1909 | ...........  130,044,312 | 29.89 |
| 1914 | ...........  136,839,321 | 5.23 |
| 1919 | ...........  275,622,335 | 101.42 |
| 1921 | ...........  219,225,800 | —20.46 |
| 1923 | ...........  255,189,812 | 16.41 |
| 1925 | ...........  278,778,008 | 9.24 |
| 1927 | ...........  278,221,431 | —0.20 |
| 1929 | ...........  304,654,661 | 9.50 |
| 1929 | ...........  306,071,031 | 10.00 |

(—) Denotes decrease.

The manufacturing industry ranks first in comparison to agriculture and mining on the basis of value of products. That basis is not, however, a true measure of the relative importance of the industries, inasmuch as many of the products of agriculture and mining go into manufacturing. A much better measure of the actual value created by manufacturing processes is the "value added by manufacture." On that basis agriculture ranks ahead of manufacturing in Colorado, while the latter is ahead of mining. The relative position of the three industries for 1929, using the "value added by manufacture" for that industry, is as follows:

Agricultural products.......$134,537,170
Manufactures .............. 122,331,478
Mineral output ............. 55,331,911

The accompanying tables show the number of persons engaged in the manufacturing industry in the state, including officers and salaried employes. The following shows the average number of wage earners by years:

1914 .............................27,278
1919 .............................35,254
1921 .............................27,469
1923 .............................31,060
1925 .............................31,967
1927 .............................31,997
1929 .............................32,890

Colorado ranked thirty-fourth among the states in the value of its manufactured products in 1929, the same position it occupied in 1919. The increase in 1929 as compared with 1919 was 11.0 per cent. The increase for the United States in the same ten-year period was 13.5 per cent.

A table published herewith shows that the number of manufacturing establishments dropped from 2,631 in 1919 to 1,479 in 1921. This was due to the inclusion in 1919 of all plants with an output of $500, or more, in value, and in subsequent years only plants with an output of $5,000 or more were included. The change made little difference in the comparability of figures for census years except in the number of establishments.

A table which accompanies this chapter gives manufacturing by industries in Colorado in 1927. The values of manufactured products of some of the largest individual industries in the state for that year are not segregated. The figures for 1925 were broken down so as to include these, and the statistics for that year are used to show the relative rank of the more important industries of Colorado among the states of the Union, which follows:

| Group | Rank |
|-------|------|
| Sugar, beet......................... | 1 |
| Mining machinery................... | 4 |
| Canned beans....................... | 9 |
| Cheese ............................ | 11 |
| Ketchup ........................... | 11 |
| Pickles ............................ | 11 |
| Concrete products.................. | 12 |
| Pottery ........................... | 12 |
| Condensed and evaporated milk...... | 14 |
| Butter ............................ | 16 |
| Paints and varnishes............... | 17 |
| Jewelry ........................... | 18 |
| Clay products...................... | 18 |
| Bread and other bakery products.... | 20 |

Group                   Rank

Slaughtering and meat packing.......20
Canning and preserving..............21
Confectionery ......................21
Food preparations...................22
Book and job printing...............23
Flour and grain mill products........24
Foundry and machine shop products..25
Electrical machinery................26
Car construction and repair shops,
    steam railroads....................27
Men's clothing......................31
Beverages ..........................35

Colorado produces large quantities of manufactured products which are listed in the tables under "miscellaneous" in order not to disclose the operations of individual concerns. Some of these are manufactured on an extensive scale and include such products as iron and steel, rubber goods, cement, chemicals, coke, etc. The principal factory products, segregated by groups in the order of their importance, beginning with the largest as reported in 1925, were beet sugar, slaughtering and meat packing products, iron and steel, printing and publishing, flour and grain mill products, steam railroad car construction and repair shops work, butter, cheese and condensed and evaporated milk, bread and bakery products, foundry and machine shop products, clay products, canning and preserving, food preparations, manufactured gas and confectionery.

Altho the manufacture of beet sugar was not segregated in the 1927 and 1929 census reports, to avoid disclosing the operations of individual manufacturers, it still continues to be the leading industry of the state in the value of finished products. The number of factories operated, the amount of sugar manufactured and other data relating to the industry appear in the historical tables following the agricultural production data in this volume.

Data on manufacturing possibilities in Colorado may be obtained from other articles in this volume. The state contains most of the raw materials, agricultural products, minerals, clays, timber, stone, iron, coal and other products used in manufacture, and these, with water power, railroad facilities, taxes and other data, will be found described in considerable detail on other pages.

Tables published herewith show the progress of manufacturing in Colorado by years, the number of establishments, persons engaged, salaries and wages paid, value of products and value added by manufacture; manufactures by counties in 1919 and 1929, value of products of principal manufacturing industries by years; manufacturing by industries in 1927; and tables on manufacturing in the principal cities. Also, there are charts showing the rank of principal manufacturing industries in the state; growth of the industry by years, and the relationship of manufacturing to mining and agriculture. Several industries not included in the above tables are listed under separate heads, such as rubber manufactures, dairying, the printing and publishing industry and the manufacture of beverages.

## RUBBER MANUFACTURES

One of the important manufacturing industries of Colorado which the bureau of the census lists under the item "All Other Industries" in order to avoid the disclosure of individual operations is that of rubber manufactures. The largest rubber manufacturing plant between Akron, Ohio, and the Pacific coast, a position maintained over a period of years, is that of the Gates Rubber company, in Denver. The value of its products is in excess of $8,000,000 annually. Its distribution is general throughout the United States and more than 50 foreign countries. The average number of wage earners in 1930 was 1,350 and wages paid exceed $2,100,000 annually. More than one-half of gross expenditures remain in the state in the form of wages, salaries, raw materials, supplies and taxes.

## MANUFACTURE OF BEVERAGES

The following table shows the number of gallons of cereal beverages containing less than one-half of one per cent of alcohol by volume manufactured in Colorado in fiscal years ending on June 30:

| Year | Gallons |
|------|---------|
| 1925 | 1,153,744 |
| 1926 | 1,133,389 |
| 1927 | 905,226 |
| 1928 | 1,098,112 |
| 1929 | 1,017,203 |
| 1930 | 900,481 |
| 1931 | 675,924 |

There were three plants in operation engaged in the manufacture of beverages in 1931, which compares with four in 1930. Materials used in producing the 1931 output included 560,777 pounds of malt, 151,340 pounds of corn and corn products, 11,123 pounds of hops and hop extracts, and 124,892 pounds of syrups.

## MANUFACTURING IN COLORADO, 1929, 1927 AND 1919
(Compiled from Census Reports)

Note.—Data for "Automobile Repairing" and for establishments with products valued at $500 or more, but less than $5,000, for all industries are included in the figures for 1919, but omitted for 1927 and 1929.

|  | 1929 | 1927 | 1919 |
|---|---|---|---|
| Number of establishments.............. | 1,548 | 1,483 | 2,631 |
| Persons engaged: |  |  |  |
| Proprietors and firm members....... | 867 | ...... | 2,234 |
| Salaried employes* ................. | 6,223 | ...... | 7,241 |
| Wage earners (average for year).... | 32,890 | 32,001 | 35,254 |
| Total ...................... | 39,980 | ...... | 44,729 |
| Horsepower ......................... | 233,726 | 254,530 | 206,110 |
| Salaries ............................ | $ 13,580,172 | ...... | $ 13,045,975 |
| Wages .............................. | 43,640,403 | $ 43,193,765 | 42,974,879 |
| Cost of materials, containers for products, fuel and purchased electric energy: |  |  |  |
| Materials and containers........... | 170,113,113 | 155,046,508 | 160,204,060 |
| Fuel and purchased energy........ | 13,626,440 | 18,230,891 | 14,666,215 |
| Total ........................ | $183,739,553 | $173,277,399 | $174,870,275 |
| Value of products..................... | $306,071,031 | $278,221,431 | $275,622,335 |
| Value added by manufacture†.......... | 122,331,478 | 104,944,032 | 100,752,060 |

*Not including number or compensation of employes of central administrative offices located elsewhere than at the factories.

†Value of products less cost of materials, containers for products, fuel and purchased electric energy. Manufacturers' profits cannot be calculated from census statistics, for the reason that these statistics do not show total production costs, which include depreciation, interest, rent, taxes and other miscellaneous expense items.

## MANUFACTURING IN COLORADO BY YEARS
(From Census Reports)

| YEAR | Number of Establishments | Persons Engaged | Salaries and Wages Paid | Value of Products | Value Added by Manufacture |
|---|---|---|---|---|---|
| 1869......... | 256 | 876 | $ 528,221 | $ 2,852,820 | $ 1,259,540 |
| 1879......... | 599 | 5,074 | 2,314,427 | 14,260,159 | 5,453,397 |
| 1889......... | 1,518 | 17,067 | 12,285,734 | 42,480,205 | 21,631,889 |
| 1899......... | 1,323 | 22,768 | 13,767,000 | 89,068,000 | 28,317,000 |
| 1904......... | 1,606 | 25,888 | 18,649,000 | 100,144,000 | 37,030,000 |
| 1909......... | 2,034 | 34,115 | 25,560,026 | 130,044,312 | 49,553,408 |
| 1914......... | 2,126 | 33,715 | 26,576,617 | 136,839,321 | 47,083,019 |
| 1919......... | 2,631 | 44,729 | 56,020,854 | 275,622,335 | 100,752,060 |
| 1921......... | 1,479 | 34,396 | 50,090,546 | 219,225,800 | 73,477,610 |
| 1923......... | 1,377 | 38,353 | 53,254,702 | 255,189,812 | 105,097,059 |
| 1925......... | 1,416 | (*) | (*) | 278,778,008 | 107,586,465 |
| 1927......... | 1,483 | (*) | (*) | 278,221,431 | 104,944,032 |
| 1929......... | 1,548 | 39,980 | 57,220,575 | 306,071,031 | 122,331,478 |

(*) Proprietors and salaried employes are not included in state tables for these years.

Note—Number of establishments in the biennial census of 1921 and subsequent years does not include factories with output of less than $5,000, but Wage earners and Value of products are included. Number of Wage earners of factories with less than $5,000 output were omitted in 1923 and 1925, but Value of products is included.

**MANUFACTURING IN COLORADO BY INDUSTRIES, 1927**
(Compiled from Census Reports)

| INDUSTRY | Number Estab- lish- ments | Wage Earners (Average Number) | Wages | Cost of Materials, Fuel and Power | Value of Products |
|---|---|---|---|---|---|
| Awnings, tents, etc. | 10 | 156 | $157,495 | $606,719 | $1,094,042 |
| Beverages | 36 | 151 | 166,459 | 572,186 | 1,318,105 |
| Boxes, paper and other | 4 | 170 | 149,663 | 295,724 | 642,953 |
| Boxes, wooden, except cigar boxes | 4 | 81 | 73,618 | 253,137 | 350,644 |
| Brass, bronze, non-ferrous alloys | 10 | 103 | 139,057 | 680,824 | 952,199 |
| Bread and bakery products | 172 | 1,461 | 1,743,307 | 5,732,444 | 12,994,347 |
| Butter | 66 | 498 | 561,758 | 8,914,266 | 10,942,919 |
| Canning and preserving | 21 | 558 | 399,250 | 2,106,636 | 3,487,252 |
| Car and general construction and repairs, electric railroad repair shops | 4 | 226 | 370,606 | 177,678 | 594,474 |
| Car and general construction and repairs, steam railroad repair shops | 29 | 4,792 | 7,031,034 | 5,510,337 | 13,396,090 |
| Caskets, coffins, burial cases, and morticians' goods | 6 | 35 | 42,603 | 171,372 | 345,909 |
| Cheese | 8 | 23 | 28,401 | 427,802 | 553,105 |
| Chemicals, not elsewhere classified | 5 | 159 | 224,961 | 1,299,380 | 2,115,992 |
| Clay products (other than pottery) and non-clay refractories | 30 | 971 | 1,134,988 | 1,090,555 | 3,348,514 |
| Clothing, women's | 5 | 165 | 100,638 | 329,869 | 621,080 |
| Clothing, men's | 4 | 439 | 422,600 | 865,319 | 1,579,410 |
| Coffee and spice, roasting and grinding | 13 | 131 | 128,516 | 2,307,187 | 3,111,027 |
| Concrete products | 10 | 44 | 45,693 | 77,024 | 200,352 |
| Confectionery | 45 | 515 | 452,279 | 1,551,170 | 3,044,635 |
| Copper, tin, sheet-iron work | 17 | 257 | 346,416 | 974,641 | 1,647,190 |
| Dental goods | 8 | 61 | 103,670 | 124,529 | 311,654 |
| Druggists' preparations | 5 | 21 | 30,121 | 137,375 | 209,756 |
| Electrical machinery, apparatus and supplies | 8 | 53 | 68,898 | 112,643 | 377,432 |
| Engraving, steel and copperplate, and plate printing | 4 | 43 | 46,605 | 51,679 | 154,214 |
| Feeds, prepared, for animals and fowls | 20 | 239 | 249,907 | 2,000,854 | 2,517,550 |
| Flour and other grain-mill products | 66 | 437 | 633,736 | 11,234,450 | 13,267,581 |
| Food preparations | 12 | 117 | 126,220 | 939,877 | 1,323,581 |
| Foundry and machine-products, not elsewhere classified | 68 | 1,436 | 1,979,850 | 2,616,974 | 8,109,546 |
| Furniture, including store and of- fice fixtures | 11 | 116 | 194,272 | 448,486 | 837,562 |
| Gas, manufactured, illuminating and heating | 9 | 500 | 588,909 | 1,621,009 | 3,655,607 |
| Grease and tallow, not including lubricating greases | 7 | 56 | 72,062 | 192,624 | 377,390 |
| Ice Cream | 24 | 114 | 169,601 | 875,447 | 1,546,173 |
| Ice, manufactured | 27 | 220 | 323,528 | 310,779 | 1,380,014 |
| Instruments, professional and sci- entific | 3 | 34 | 53,254 | 16,868 | 122,296 |
| Jewelry | 11 | 54 | 82,401 | 82,214 | 266,215 |
| Lime | 3 | 33 | 33,904 | 41,165 | 97,241 |
| Lumber and timber products, not elsewhere classified | 62 | 1,190 | 1,278,036 | 442,773 | 2,368,366 |
| Marble, granite, slate and other stone products | 16 | 75 | 148,625 | 214,911 | 556,476 |
| Mattresses and bed springs | 4 | 154 | 175,034 | 501,661 | 878,109 |
| Motor-vehicle bodies and motor- vehicle parts | 10 | 103 | 170,675 | 175,773 | 489,466 |
| Oils, not elsewhere classified | 3 | 8 | 10,562 | 105,525 | 211,435 |
| Paints and varnishes | 7 | 173 | 224,588 | 1,465,263 | 2,131,261 |
| Patent and proprietary medicines and compounds | 10 | 18 | 14,984 | 97,846 | 214,887 |

MANUFACTURING IN COLORADO BY INDUSTRIES, 1927—Continued
(Compiled from Census Reports)

| INDUSTRY | Number Estab- lish- ments | Wage Earners (Average Number) | Wages | Cost of Materials, Fuel and Power | Value of Products |
|---|---|---|---|---|---|
| Photo-engraving, not done in print- ing establishments | 7 | 70 | $ 123,449 | $ 71,247 | $ 390,005 |
| Planing-mill products, not made in planing mills connected with sawmills | 29 | 363 | 507,630 | 754,072 | 1,678,548 |
| Pottery, including porcelain ware | 4 | 186 | 159,775 | 75,074 | 321,043 |
| Printing and publishing, book and job | 99 | 896 | 1,366,004 | 1,540,287 | 5,062,522 |
| Printing and publishing, news- paper and periodical | 166 | 1,239 | 2,347,209 | 3,182,953 | 11,039,597 |
| Saddlery and harness | 9 | 92 | 135,027 | 255,974 | 540,007 |
| Signs and advertising novelties | 12 | 45 | 62,224 | 97,322 | 342,515 |
| Slaughtering and meat packing, wholesale | 25 | 1,246 | 1,552,897 | 27,325,998 | 30,538,016 |
| Sporting and athletic goods, not including firearms or ammunition | 5 | 42 | 37,811 | 15,182 | 90,327 |
| Structural and ornamental iron and steel work, not made in rolling mills | 11 | 195 | 255,771 | 1,048,845 | 1,886,543 |
| Surgical appliances | 4 | 13 | 19,192 | 14,679 | 56,294 |
| Toys (not including children's wheel goods or sleds), games and playground equipment | 3 | 8 | 7,952 | 13,226 | 28,383 |
| All other industries* | 212 | 11,416 | 16,120,040 | 81,127,545 | 122,503,580 |
| Total, State | 1,483 | 32,001 | $43,193,765 | $173,277,399 | $278,221,431 |

*Items included under "All Other Industries" embrace cement, steel rails and other products which would disclose individual operations if segregated; also the following, with value of products: Bookbinding and blank book making, $167,509; brushes, other than rubber, $43,250; cigars and cigarets, $292,739; cleaning and polishing preparations, $101,673; models and patterns, $61,805; steam and other packing, $52,921.

CHART SHOWING RANK OF PRINCIPAL MANUFACTURING INDUSTRIES, VALUE OF PRODUCTS AND PER CENT OF TOTAL FOR ALL INDUSTRIES, 1925.

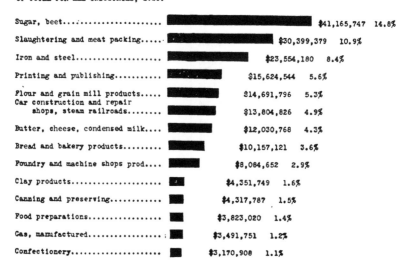

| | | |
|---|---|---|
| Sugar, beet | $41,165,747 | 14.8% |
| Slaughtering and meat packing | $30,399,379 | 10.9% |
| Iron and steel | $23,554,180 | 8.4% |
| Printing and publishing | $15,624,544 | 5.6% |
| Flour and grain mill products | $14,691,796 | 5.3% |
| Car construction and repair shops, steam railroads | $13,804,826 | 4.9% |
| Butter, cheese, condensed milk | $12,030,768 | 4.3% |
| Bread and bakery products | $10,157,121 | 3.6% |
| Foundry and machine shops prod | $8,084,652 | 2.9% |
| Clay products | $4,351,749 | 1.6% |
| Canning and preserving | $4,317,787 | 1.5% |
| Food preparations | $3,823,020 | 1.4% |
| Gas, manufactured | $3,491,751 | 1.2% |
| Confectionery | $3,170,908 | 1.1% |

## MANUFACTURES BY COUNTIES, U. S. CENSUS, 1919 AND 1929

Note.—Number of establishments in 1929 does not include those with an annual output of less than $5,000. The 1929 figures are preliminary and state totals vary slightly from final figures for that year given in other tables.

| COUNTY | No. Establishments | | Wages Paid | | Value of Products | |
|---|---|---|---|---|---|---|
| | 1919 | 1929 | 1919 | 1929 | 1919 | 1929 |
| Adams | 37· | 20 | $ 987,790 | $ 804,580 | $ 4,791,206 | $ 5,949,286 |
| Alamosa | 14 | 12 | 48,456 | 409,999 | 423,618 | 1,617,218 |
| Arapahoe | 24 | 11 | 165,436 | 1,015,268 | 860,974 | 3,965,492 |
| Archuleta | 12 | 7 | 106,990 | 56,080 | 367,853 | 151,877 |
| Baca | 8 | *___ | 20,919 | *_____ | 82,170 | *_____ |
| Bent | 15 | 8 | 50,419 | 52,680 | 317,540 | 545,540 |
| Boulder | 95 | 37 | 976,334 | 670,986 | 9,660,142 | 6,366,986 |
| Chaffee | 20 | 10 | 592,904 | 429,184 | 3,935,183 | 1,986,870 |
| Cheyenne | 4 | *___ | 1,832 | *_____ | 9,975 | *_____ |
| Clear Creek | 13 | *___ | 89,517 | *_____ | 97,788 | *_____ |
| Conejos | 15 | *___ | 417,381 | *_____ | 1,081,839 | *_____ |
| Costilla | 5 | *___ | 47,679 | *_____ | 180,892 | *_____ |
| Crowley | 19 | *___ | 141,211 | *_____ | 1,380,221 | *_____ |
| Custer | 9 | *___ | 6,722 | *_____ | 12,581 | *_____ |
| Delta | 24 | 19 | 37,130 | 113,908 | 344,786 | 1,670,071 |
| Denver | 1,097 | 781 | 19,341,915 | 20,910,625 | 125,411,270 | 144,664,746 |
| Douglas | 8 | *___ | 244,164 | *_____ | 1,783,316 | *_____ |
| Eagle | 4 | *___ | 12,700 | *_____ | 31,016 | *_____ |
| Elbert | 8 | *___ | 3,469 | *_____ | 11,480 | *_____ |
| El Paso | 141 | 69 | 996,090 | 1,184,507 | 4,788,504 | 7,508,593 |
| Fremont | 45 | 23 | 1,023,831 | 532,220 | 6,787,570 | 4,107,320 |
| Garfield | 23 | *___ | 68,215 | *_____ | 333,815 | *_____ |
| Gilpin | 7 | *___ | 9,854 | *_____ | 35,093 | *_____ |
| Grand | 14 | *___ | 636,170 | *_____ | 998,783 | *_____ |
| Gunnison | 27 | 13 | 82,067 | 120,626 | 179,044 | 219,246 |
| Huerfano | 21 | 9 | 43,271 | 37,551 | 274,222 | 295,213 |
| Jackson | 5 | *___ | 37,855 | *_____ | 92,518 | *_____ |
| Jefferson | 23 | 16 | 213,940 | 248,443 | 907,169 | 1,531,056 |
| Kiowa | 6 | *___ | 11,616 | *_____ | 24,594 | *_____ |
| Kit Carson | 19 | *___ | 31,572 | *_____ | 146,018 | *_____ |
| Lake | 14 | *___ | 569,798 | *_____ | 4,243,184 | *_____ |
| La Plata | 32 | *___ | 372,747 | *_____ | 3,384,123 | *_____ |
| Larimer | 87 | 50 | 1,278,179 | 1,188,271 | 13,440,083 | 13,296,364 |
| Las Animas | 60 | 31 | 844,712 | 714,002 | 3,943,416 | 3,344,790 |
| Lincoln | 17 | 7 | 53,916 | 18,576 | 508,365 | 70,513 |
| Logan | 29 | *___ | 498,753 | *_____ | 2,814,130 | *_____ |
| Mesa | 38 | 30 | 555,320 | 519,246 | 3,347,570 | 2,863,052 |
| Moffat | 6 | *___ | 5,963 | *_____ | 39,318 | *_____ |
| Montezuma | 16 | *___ | 31,707 | *_____ | 184,354 | *_____ |
| Montrose | 26 | 11 | 109,732 | 33,716 | 701,936 | 357,255 |
| Morgan | 31 | *___ | 453,029 | *_____ | 4,823,336 | *_____ |
| Otero | 57 | 34 | 1,667,381 | 1,224,144 | 8,766,757 | 7,127,828 |
| Ouray | 7 | *___ | 38,184 | *_____ | 78,777 | *_____ |
| Park | 13 | *___ | 58,141 | *_____ | 105,831 | *_____ |
| Phillips | 8 | 5 | 21,136 | 11,266 | 336,371 | 94,996 |
| Pitkin | 6 | *___ | 11,797 | *_____ | 33,976 | *_____ |
| Prowers | 49 | 19 | 231,635 | 248,231 | 3,825,014 | 3,801,893 |
| Pueblo | 143 | 84 | 8,229,412 | 8,713,761 | 47,568,936 | 55,997,697 |
| Rio Blanco | 10 | *___ | 35,390 | *_____ | 126,378 | *_____ |
| Rio Grande | 24 | 14 | 76,890 | 99,789 | 673,531 | 707,947 |
| Routt | 18 | 17 | 219,926 | 122,403 | 627,229 | 353,252 |
| Saguache | 10 | *___ | 59,001 | *_____ | 209,173 | *_____ |
| San Juan | 6 | *___ | 8,885 | *_____ | 25,121 | *_____ |
| San Miguel | 12 | 3 | 51,933 | 15,456 | 150,636 | 29,853 |
| Sedgwick | 3 | *___ | 7,476 | *_____ | 30,896 | *_____ |
| Summit | 4 | *___ | 418 | *_____ | 9,290 | *_____ |
| Teller | 9 | *___ | 45,002 | *_____ | 206,129 | *_____ |
| Washington | 7 | *___ | 15,640 | *_____ | 90,591 | *_____ |
| Weld | 98 | 50 | 923,739 | 1,328,323 | 9,743,802 | 13,582,776 |
| Yuma | 24 | 5 | 43,319 | 11,415 | 210,229 | 57,242 |
| All other counties* | 5 | 150 | 8,269 | 2,593,818 | 22,673 | 22,389,689 |
| †State | 2,631 | 1,545 | $ 42,974,879 | $ 43,429,074 | $275,622,335 | $304,654,661 |

*Included under "All Other Counties" in order to avoid disclosing data for individual establishments. No manufacturing establishments were reported from Kiowa or Mineral counties in 1929. Dolores, Hinsdale and Mineral counties are included under "All Other Counties" for 1919.

†See note at head of the table.

## VALUE OF PRODUCTS OF PRINCIPAL MANUFACTURING INDUSTRIES, BY YEARS

| INDUSTRY | 1927 | 1925 | 1923 | 1921 | 1919 |
|---|---|---|---|---|---|
| Awnings, tents, etc.--------------- | $ 1,094,042 | $ 1,049,462 | $ 1,249,798 | $ 934,392 | $ 1,021,654 |
| Bread and other bakery products | 12,994,347 | 10,157,121 | 8,575,077 | 9,309,156 | 9,807,799 |
| Brick, tile and terra cotta and fire-clay products-------------- | 3,669,557 | 4,351,749 | 4,295,427 | 2,480,517 | 2,504,658 |
| Butter, cheese and condensed milk | (a)11,496,024 | 12,030,768 | 11,968,458 | 9,845,569 | 14,504,639 |
| Canning and preserving--------- | 3,487,252 | 4,317,787 | 3,122,338 | 2,936,283 | 2,970,113 |
| Car and general shop construction and repairs, steam rail-- roads ----------------------- | 13,396,000 | 13,804,826 | 15,649,087 | 13,502,349 | 15,130,423 |
| Clothing, men's------------------- | 1,579,410 | 1,538,271 | 1,341,186 | 1,116,208 | 1,033,729 |
| Confectionery and ice cream------ | 4,590,808 | 4,413,505 | 4,943,305 | 4,188,040 | 5,003,989 |
| Copper, tin and sheet iron work | 1,647,190 | 1,696,427 | 1,435,029 | 1,287,835 | 1,411,036 |
| Flour mill products------------- | 13,267,581 | 14,691,796 | 11,574,113 | 16,044,754 | 19,954,119 |
| Food preparations--------------- | 1,323,581 | 3,823,020 | 3,031,719 | 2,028,641 | 4,381,012 |
| Foundry and machine shop products ----------------------- | 8,109,546 | 8,084,652 | 10,967,650 | 7,687,058 | 11,199,721 |
| Ice, manufactured--------------- | 1,546,173 | 1,643,997 | 1,376,565 | 1,237,804 | 1,045,477 |
| Printing and publishing, books and job----------------------- | 5,062,522 | 5,491,213 | (*) | 4,292,467 | 3,985,230 |
| Printing and publishing, newspapers and periodicals--------- | 11,039,597 | 10,123,331 | (*) | 9,507,737 | 7,533,978 |
| Paints ----------------------- | 2,131,261 | 2,493,943 | 2,387,100 | 827,289 | 1,168,001 |
| Slaughtering and meat packing- | 30,538,016 | 30,399,379 | 23,290,903 | 22,494,615 | 41,007,531 |
| Sugar, beet--------------------- | (b) | 41,165,742 | 30,165,810 | 37,558,657 | (not seg.) |

(*) Not segregated in 1923. Combined products of book and job printing and newspaper and periodical publishing in that year were valued at $13,743,497.
(a) Exclusive of evaporated and condensed milk.
(b) Not segregated in 1927.
Note: 1929 figures not yet made public.

## SUMMARY OF MANUFACTURES FOR CITIES HAVING 10,000 INHABITANTS OR MORE, 1925 AND 1929

| CITY | Number Establishments | Wage Earners Av. No. | Wages | Cost of Materials | Value of Products |
|---|---|---|---|---|---|
| **Boulder:** | | | | | |
| 1929.............. | 17 | 155 | $ 181,401 | $ 336,820 | $ 828,913 |
| 1925.............. | 21 | 160 | 203,823 | 391,967 | 801,860 |
| **Colorado Springs:** | | | | | |
| 1929.............. | 55 | 547 | 775,811 | 2,539,577 | 4,948,810 |
| 1925.............. | 60 | 451 | 611,423 | 1,943,266 | 3,727,458 |
| **Denver:** | | | | | |
| 1929.............. | 781 | 16,235 | 20,910,625 | 83,251,524 | 144,664,746 |
| 1925.............. | 686 | 15,077 | 19,970,520 | 72,530,686 | 125,762,865 |
| **Greeley:** | | | | | |
| 1929.............. | 22 | 152 | 215,546 | 1,208,311 | 1,935,244 |
| 1925.............. | 19 | 190 | 216,322 | 1,364,752 | 2,141,906 |
| **Pueblo:*** | | | | | |
| 1925.............. | 84 | 1,240 | 1,761,604 | 4,015,041 | 7,733,113 |
| **Trinidad:** | | | | | |
| 1929.............. | 25 | 297 | 391,903 | 1,149,145 | 2,036,363 |
| 1925.............. | 24 | 313 | 464,329 | 970,046 | 1,866,754 |
| **Remainder of state:** | | | | | |
| 1929.............. | 648 | 15,504 | 21,165,117 | 95,254,176 | 151,656,955 |
| 1925.............. | 522 | 14,536 | 19,779,653 | 89,975,785 | 136,744,052 |
| **Entire state:** | | | | | |
| 1929.............. | 1,548 | 32,890 | 43,640,403 | 183,739,553 | 306,071,031 |
| 1925.............. | 1,416 | 31,967 | 43,007,674 | 171,191,543 | 278,778,008 |

*Included under "Remainder of state" for 1929.
Note.—The 1929 figures are preliminary and subject to revision for the cities, but final for the entire state. Grand Junction and Fort Collins were in the above classification in 1929, but segregated figures have not yet been released. The above statistics are for industries actually within the boundaries of the cities.

PROGRESS OF MANUFACTURING IN COLORADO

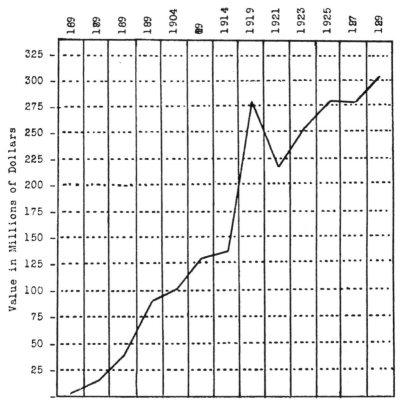

### BREAD AND OTHER BAKERY PRODUCTS

THERE were 180 establishments in the state in 1929 engaged in the production of bread and other bakery products. They employed 178 salaried officials and employes and an average of 1,689 wage earners. Salaries for the year amounted to $418,117 and wages to $2,005,840. The cost of materials, containers for their products, and fuel and purchased energy was $5,648,904 and the value of their products was $11,773,612, of which $6,124,708 was added by manufacture. A table published herewith gives the operations of these establishments in detail for 1929, with comparative figures for 1927 and 1919.

The principal materials consumed by this industry in 1929, showing the quantity and cost, were as follows:

| | Quantity | Cost |
|---|---|---|
| Flour (bbls.): | | |
| White ........... | 290,473 | $1,779,162 |
| Graham and Whole Wheat ........ | 15,591 | 101,059 |
| Rye ............. | 8,026 | 48,158 |
| Other ........... | 4,109 | 35,355 |
| Sugar (lbs.)........ | 7,807,127 | 431,636 |
| Eggs, fresh, frozen and dried........ | ...... | 217,643 |
| Butter, oleomargarine, and other butter substitutes (lbs.) ........... | 165,552 | 50,071 |
| Lard (lbs.)......... | 2,730,220 | 318,800 |

The products of the bakeries included 67,980,435 pounds of bread, rolls, coffee cake, etc., valued at $4,821,382; $1,699,483 worth of pound cake, package cake, fruit cake, etc.; 1,851,117 pounds of doughnuts, crullers and other fried cakes valued at $354,520; $669,877 worth of pies and $2,962,972 worth of other products.

## BREAD AND OTHER BAKERY PRODUCTS PRODUCED IN COLORADO, 1929, 1927 AND 1919
(Compiled from Census Reports)

Note.—Data for establishments with products under $5,000 in value are included for 1919, but not for subsequent years.

|  | 1929 | 1927 | 1919 |
|---|---|---|---|
| Number of establishments............... | 180 | 172 | 252 |
| Salaried officers and employes............ | 178 | 166 | 439 |
| Wage earners (average for the year)....... | 1,689 | 1,461 | 1,340 |
| Horsepower (rated capacity) of power equipment: | | | |
| Prime movers........................ | 395 | 359 | 134 |
| Motors run by purchased energy....... | 2,452 | 1,876 | 1,325 |
| Total ........................... | 2,847 | 2,235 | 1,459 |
| Salaries .................................. | $ 418,117 | $ 372,878 | $ 511,342 |
| Wages .................................. | 2,005,840 | 1,743,307 | 1,308,559 |
| Cost of materials, containers for products, fuel and purchased energy: | | | |
| Materials and containers............. | 5,424,373 | 5,512,745 | 5,909,476 |
| Fuel and purchased energy............. | 224,531 | 219,699 | 150,491 |
| Total ........................... | $ 5,648,904 | $ 5,732,444 | $ 6,059,967 |
| Value of products........................ | $11,773,612 | $12,994,347 | $ 9,807,799 |
| Value added by manufacture............... | 6,124,708 | 7,261,903 | 3,747,832 |

## WHEAT GROUND AND WHEAT-MILLING PRODUCTS, BY YEARS

Note.—The data used in this table is compiled from monthly returns of Colorado mills to the bureau of the census of the Department of Commerce—mills that manufacture 5,000 or more barrels annually.

|  | 1931 | 1930 | 1929 | 1928 | 1927 |
|---|---|---|---|---|---|
| Average number of mills reporting ............ | 21 | 21 | 21 | 21 | 21 |
| Wheat ground (bushels) ...... | 6,180,720 | 7,809,098 | 7,812,213 | 7,707,198 | 7,113,524 |
| Production: Wheat flour (barrels) ...... | 1,377,207 | 1,740,616 | 1,735,062 | 1,719,686 | 1,585,632 |
| Offal (pounds). | 102,933,698 | 130,268,076 | 130,785,718 | 128,198,598 | 118,695,711 |
| Average daily 24-hour capacity in Wheat flour (barrels) ...... | 9,406 | 9,267 | 8,463 | 8,911 | 9,172 |
| Average pounds of wheat per barrel of flour..... | 269.3 | 269.2 | 270.2 | 268.9 | 269.2 |
| Average pounds of offal per barrel of flour ........ | 74.7 | 74.8 | 75.4 | 74.5 | 16.7 |

Production of wheat in Colorado in bushels, as reported by the Co-operative Crop Reporting Service, was as follows: 1931, 16,552,000; 1930, 23,356,000; 1929, 17,934,000; 1928, 18,564,000; 1927, 20,112,000.

**COLORADO PRINTING AND PUBLISHING INDUSTRY, BY CENSUS YEARS**
(Compiled from Census Reports)

| | 1929 | 1927 | 1925 | 1923 | 1919 |
|---|---|---|---|---|---|
| **Book and Job:** | | | | | |
| Number establishments_____ | 109 | 99 | 99 | 87 | 120 |
| Salaried officers and employes | 273 | 314 | 285 | 229 | 231 |
| Wage earners (Average No.)_ | 1,034 | 896 | 946 | 896 | 952 |
| Salaries _____ | $ 669,273 | $ 681,123 | $ 580,680 | $ 499,750 | $ 395,249 |
| Wages _____ | 1,597,046 | 1,366,004 | 1,451,658 | 1,295,231 | 1,117,478 |
| Cost materials_____ | 1,630,725 | 1,540,287 | 1,863,076 | 1,433,818 | 1,368,854 |
| Value of products_____ | 5,353,011 | 5,062,522 | 5,491,213 | 4,417,139 | 3,985,230 |
| Value added by manufacture_ | 3,722,286 | 3,522,235 | 3,628,137 | 2,983,321 | 2,616,376 |
| | | | | | |
| **Newspapers and periodicals:** | | | | | |
| Number establishments_____ | 169 | 166 | 154 | 139 | 333 |
| Salaried officers and employes | 1,019 | 1,240 | 891 | 788 | 763 |
| Wage earners (Average No.)_ | 1,121 | 1,239 | 980 | 1,106 | 1,079 |
| Salaries _____ | $1,966,200 | $1,919,938 | $1,442,899 | $1,327,044 | $1,137,345 |
| Wages _____ | 1,871,851 | 2,347,209 | 1,666,006 | 1,707,026 | 1,321,725 |
| Cost materials_____ | 2,649,044 | 3,182,953 | 2,607,746 | 2,567,763 | 2,315,211 |
| Value of products_____ | 12,526,112 | 11,039,597 | 10,123,331 | 9,326,355 | 7,533,978 |
| Value added by manufacture_ | 9,877,068 | 7,856,644 | 7,515,585 | 6,758,592 | 5,218,767 |

Note —Establishments with products of $5,000, or less, are omitted in the census for 1923, 1925 and 1927, but are included for 1919 and 1929.

## PRINTING AND PUBLISHING INDUSTRY

The printing industry, comprising establishments printing and publishing newspapers and periodicals and book and job printing, had an output of products valued at $17,879,123 in 1929, as revealed by the census reports. This compares with $16,102,119 in 1927 and $11,519,208 in 1919. The output for 1929 showed an increase of $1,777,004, or 11.0 per cent, over 1927 and $6,359,915, or 55.2 per cent over 1919. Allied industries, including book-binding establishments operated separately, steel and copper plate engraving and photoengraving plants, turned out products valued at $785,067 in 1929. This figure is not included in the totals for the printing and publishing industry.

The value of products of the printing and publishing industry in 1929, by classes, is as follows:

Newspapers:
- Subscriptions and sales....$ 2,7 1,630
- Advertising .............. 7,969,789

Periodicals:
- Subscriptions and sales.... 413,166
- Advertising .............. 621,778

Books and pamphlets printed and published............ 145,654

Commercial printing:
- Newspapers and periodicals printed for publication by others .................. 313,161
- Books and pamphlets printed for publication by others .................. 202,728
- General job printing, composition, etc. ............ 5,039,543

Other products............. 421,674

Total .....................$17,879,123

A table published herewith shows the industry in detail for the census years of 1929, 1927, 1925, 1923 and 1919.

In the following tabulation of newspapers and periodicals, morning, evening and Sunday papers are counted as separate publications, though issued by the same publisher in many instances:

| | No. of Publications | Gross Circulation |
|---|---|---|
| **Daily newspapers:*** | | |
| 1919 ................. | 32 | 302,078 |
| 1921 ................. | 38 | 307,968 |
| 1923 ................. | 38 | 314,679 |
| 1925 ................. | 32 | 302,078 |
| 1927 ................. | 34 | 365,768 |
| 1929 ................. | 29 | 298,528 |

*Exclusive of Sunday circulation.

| **Sunday newspapers:** | | |
|---|---|---|
| 1921 ................. | 12 | 298,663 |
| 1923 ................. | 11 | 311,263 |
| 1925 ................. | 11 | 344,358 |
| 1927 ................. | 9 | 404,193 |
| 1929 ................. | 8 | 400,913 |

| **Weekly newspapers:** | | |
|---|---|---|
| 1921 ................. | 97 | 115,089 |
| 1923 ................. | 100 | 124,852 |
| 1925 ................. | 112 | 206,537 |
| 1927 ................. | 117 | 183,874 |
| 1929 ................. | 121 | 185,472 |

## CIGARS AND TOBACCO

There were 4,491,487 cigars manufactured in Colorado in the calendar year of 1930, a decrease of 1,833,345 compared with 1929. The industry has shown a steady decline in recent years, the number of cigars manufactured having decreased from 34,902,482 in 1920 to the figure named for 1930. More than half of this number were manufactured to retail at not more than five cents each. There were 85,265 pounds of tobacco used in manufacturing this output.

There were 35 cigar factories in the state on January 1, 1930. During the year four were opened and 10 closed, leaving 29 factories on January 1, 1931.

The number of factories on January 1 of the years named were as follows:

| | | | |
|---|---|---|---|
| 1921 | 57 | 1926 | 52 |
| 1922 | 67 | 1927 | 64 |
| 1923 | 64 | 1928 | 47 |
| 1924 | 56 | 1929 | 41 |
| 1925 | 53 | 1930 | 35 |
| | | 1931 | 29 |

Quantities of tobacco used and number of cigars manufactured in Colorado in the calendar years named were as follows:

| Year | Tobacco, Pounds | Number of Cigars |
|---|---|---|
| 1920 | 732,179 | 34,902,482 |
| 1921 | 556,467 | 27,272,697 |
| 1922 | 359,930 | 16,643,058 |
| 1923 | 394,816 | 18,219,382 |
| 1924 | 317,189 | 15,324,979 |
| 1925 | 274,940 | 13,843,994 |
| 1926 | 216,365 | 10,216,392 |
| 1927 | 117,370 | 5,602,215 |
| 1928 | 152,717 | 7,673,536 |
| 1929 | 122,523 | 6,324,832 |
| 1930 | 85,265 | 4,491,487 |

There were two factories in the state on January 1, 1931, engaged in the manufacture of tobacco, in which there was used 8,919 pounds of tobacco. Tobacco is not grown commercially in Colorado, and experimental crops have been planted in only a few known instances and then on a small scale. There is no plant in the state engaged in the manufacture of cigarettes. There were 112 factories in the United States engaged in manufacturing cigarettes on January 1, 1931, and the output of cigarettes in 1930 was 123,802,186,217, an increase of 1,409,-805,371, compared with 1929. This was equal to 1,008 cigarettes for each man, woman and child in continental United States on the basis of the 1930 census. The total number of cigars weighing more than three pounds per thousand manufactured in the United States in 1930 was 5,893,890,418, a decrease of 624,642,624 in 1929. This was at the rate of 48 cigars per capita.

## OLEOMARGARINE PRODUCED

The manufacture of colored and uncolored oleomargarine in Colorado, as reported by the commissioner of internal revenue, showed a rapid and substantial increase in recent years up to 1931, when a decrease was reported. A proportionate decrease in 1931 was reported for the entire country. The Colorado output for the fiscal year ending June 30, 1931, was 855,989 pounds, which compares with 1,618,741 pounds in the preceding year, in which year the state had the largest production of any year since 1921.

Production in pounds, in fiscal years ending June 30, of years named, was as follows:

| Year | Colored | Uncolored |
|---|---|---|
| 1921 | 53,060 | 477,656 |
| 1922 | 8,280 | 167,080 |
| 1924 | 20,760 | 369,260 |
| 1925 | 14,570 | 408,460 |
| 1926 | 50,510 | 586,640 |
| 1927 | 49,826 | 662,784 |
| 1928 | 71,160 | 954,900 |
| 1929 | 53,887 | 1,048,006 |
| 1930 | 128,825 | 1,489,916 |
| 1931 | 59,730 | 796,259 |

## BUTTER AND CHEESE MANUFACTURES IN COLORADO, 1929, 1927 AND 1919
(Compiled from Census Reports)

Note —Census figures for 1927 cover only establishments reporting products to the value of $5,000 or more. For 1919 and 1929, establishments reporting products valued at $500 or more are covered   Statistics for 1929 and 1919 are not exactly comparable, due to a widening of the scope of the 1929 census and changing the value of products to those shipped or delivered instead of produced. Other items, however, mostly offset these differences. The industries included in this table are factories not located on farms. Farm production of butter and cheese is treated as an agricultural operation and is described in detail in the chapter in this volume under "Dairying." The following table does not include condensed and evaporated milk, which are not segregated, but grouped with other states in order not to disclose individual operations.

| | Butter | | | Cheese | | |
|---|---|---|---|---|---|---|
| | 1929 | 1927 | 1919 | 1929 | 1927 | 1919 |
| Number of establishments | 60 | 66 | 65 | 16 | 8 | 8 |
| Salaried officers and employes | 142 | 221 | 137 | 4 | 3 | 23 |
| Wage earners (average) | 1,092 | 1,211 | 1,268 | 29 | 23 | 49 |
| Horsepower (rated capacity of equipment) | 6,921 | 8,300 | 4,650 | 149 | 100 | 110 |
| Salaries | $ 280,682 | $ 367,725 | $ 291,614 | $ 6,750 | $ 3,852 | $ 50,135 |
| Wages | 340,492 | 561,758 | 281,539 | 44,825 | 28,401 | 46,413 |
| Cost of materials, containers for products, fuel and purchased electric energy | 8,039,080 | 8,914,266 | 7,363,502 | 713,432 | 427,802 | 532,107 |
| Value of products | 9,854,633 | 10,942,919 | 8,768,394 | 846,964 | 553,105 | 732,260 |
| Value added by manufacture | 1,815,553 | 2,028,653 | 1,404,892 | 133,532 | 125,303 | 200,153 |

Creamery butter produced in 1929 in the factories incorporated in above table amounted to 22,020,043 pounds valued at $9,083,253, which compares with 20,998,638 pounds valued at $9,201,-904 in 1927.

# Revenue and Taxation

THE exact amount of money collected from the people of Colorado in the form of taxes and from permits, licenses and fees of all kinds is difficult to determine for any given period because of the variety of collection agencies representing different civil divisions and sub-divisions, lack of uniformity in fiscal years, and the interlocking of funds.

The department of commerce made a compilation as of 1922 which gave a total of $48,930,000 in revenue from taxes, licenses and permits and special assessments of state, counties, incorporated places and local civil divisions. This was equal to $62.41 per capita. The distribution of these revenues for that year is shown in two accompanying tables. A third table includes United States internal revenue and customs receipts, which bring the total up to $65,119,000, or $66.77 per capita. No similar compilation has been made for any year subsequent to 1922, the figures given being the latest available.

Revenues with which to defray governmental costs are derived from two principal sources, both of which are extensively sub-divided. The first of these is called taxes and includes revenues from a general property tax, the inheritance tax, sales taxes and corporation and business taxes. The other includes revenues from special assessments, fees collected by various departments and agencies of government for specific purposes, fines, gifts, escheated property, earnings of public service organizations, interest on investments and other sources.

All taxable property of persons and corporations in the state is listed and appraised as to value for taxation purposes as of April 1 each year. This work is done through the county assessors as to most property within the taxing districts of the counties. The assessments on intercounty property, such as railroads, telephone and telegraph lines, power lines, express companies, etc., are made by the state tax commission. These valuations are certified to the county treasurers, who are the tax-collecting agents.

The state, the counties, cities and towns and school districts levy taxes on property situated within their respective boundaries. These levies are spread equally over all property in the district subject to the jurisdiction of the levying agent, in amount sufficient to raise the revenues required to defray the governmental cost of the taxing district. The levies are certified to the county treasurers, who apply them to each and every parcel of property assessed. The aggregate rate at which any one parcel of property is taxed is equal to the total of all levies made by all the taxing agents.

Taxes thus levied for any given year become due on January 1 of the following year. They may be paid in two installments. To avoid penalties, the first half must be paid by March 1 and the second half by August 1. All unpaid taxes become delinquent on August 1 and bear interest thereafter at the rate of 10 per cent per annum until the property is sold. From March 1 to December 1 the first half bears interest at the rate of 10 per cent.

The assessed value of all property in Colorado for taxation purposes as of April 1, 1931, as determined by the county assessors and tax commission, after all corrections and revisions, was $1,438,448,065, which compares with $1,586,462,903 in 1930, a decrease of $148,014,838. Subsequent to these final determinations, the county treasurers submit to the tax commission final statements of assessments which include some items not taken by the assessors. The figures for 1931, as shown by treasurers' statements, and upon which all levies are made, aggregate a total of $1,447,169,719, which compares with $1,590,674,097 for 1930, a decrease of $143,504,378. The anticipated revenues to be derived from this direct taxation by levies, as reported by the tax commission, are $44,863,801, compared with $49,206,717 from the 1930 levies. The distribution of the revenues from the 1931 levies is as follows:

|  | Amount | Per Cent |
|---|---|---|
| State | $ 5,050,622 | 11.26 |
| County | 8,733,128 | 19.47 |
| Town | 8,753,896 | 19.51 |
| General school | 5,557,516 | 12.38 |
| Special school | 16,768,639 | 37.38 |
| Total | $44,863,801 | 100.00 |

The assessed valuation of $1,438,-448,065, as reported by the county assessors and tax commission, is distributed as follows:

|  | Per Cent |
| --- | --- |
| Land and improvements.......... | 26.02 |
| Metal mining properties.......... | 1.41 |
| Timber, oil and coal properties.... | 1.41 |
| Town and city lots and improvements ...................... | 34.92 |
| Live stock....................... | 3.38 |
| Merchandise .................... | 4.60 |
| Manufactures ................... | 2.31 |
| Bank stock...................... | 1.66 |
| Money, credits and accounts (less exemptions) .................. | 0.88 |
| Miscellaneous (less exemptions).. | 5.94 |
| Corporations assessed by tax commission ...................... | 17.47 |
| Total ..................... | 100.00 |

In addition to taxes collected through levies, revenues are derived from taxes on gasoline sales, inheritances, motor vehicle licenses, fishing and hunting licenses and business licenses. Counties share in the revenues from most of these sources. School districts also receive revenue from the state school fund and from tuition, and some of the state institutions from federal land grants. Some county offices are conducted on a fee basis, such as the clerk and recorder and sheriff, their receipts going into the county treasury. Cities and towns also collect additional revenues from licenses, fees and special assessments of improvement districts, and the federal government contributes considerable funds for highway and other purposes, parts of revenues from the forests, and royalties and bonuses from mineral land production.

Published elsewhere in this volume are numerous tables showing assessed valuations by years and by counties, levies for sundry purposes, detailed tables on gasoline and inheritance taxes, motor vehicle licenses, school, county and town taxes, and other sources of revenue mentioned in this text.

**PER CAPITA GOVERNMENTAL-COST PAYMENTS (EXCLUSIVE OF INTEREST) FOR OPERATION AND MAINTENANCE OF GENERAL DEPARTMENTS OF STATE GOVERNMENT**

(From Financial Statistics of States Compiled by the Bureau of the Census)

| DEPARTMENT | 1929 | 1928 | 1927 | 1926 | 1925 | 1924 | All States 1929 |
| --- | --- | --- | --- | --- | --- | --- | --- |
| General government.......... | $ 0.95 | $ 0.87 | $ 0.90 | $ 0.74 | $ 0.91 | $ 0.80 | $ 0.95 |
| Protection to person and property: | | | | | | | |
| Militia and armories....... | 0.11 | 0.13 | 0.11 | 0.09 | 0.09 | 0.10 | 0.09 |
| Regulation ................ | 0.28 | 0.31 | 0.27 | 0.30 | 0.31 | 0.34 | 0.29 |
| All others................ | 0.28 | 0.37 | 0.30 | 0.30 | 0.14 | 0.12 | 0.21 |
| Conservation of health and sanitation: | | | | | | | |
| Prevention and treatment of communicable diseases.... | 0.02 | 0.02 | 0.02 | 0.03 | 0.04 | 0.04 | 0.14 |
| All others................ | 0.11 | 0.11 | 0.10 | 0.10 | 0.11 | 0.11 | 0.12 |
| Development and conservation of natural resources: | | | | | | | |
| Agriculture .............. | 0.75 | 0.73 | 0.61 | 0.62 | 0.48 | 0.58 | 0.47 |
| All others..... .......... | 0.25 | 0.14 | 0.19 | 0.29 | 0.19 | 0.25 | 0.11 |
| Highways ................. | 2.55 | 2.11 | 2.29 | 1.59 | 2.58 | 2.54 | 1.82 |
| Charities, hospitals and corrections ................ | 2.38 | 2.20 | 2.03 | 1.92 | 1.63 | 1.89 | 1.79 |
| Education: | | | | | | | |
| Schools .................. | 4.08 | 4.04 | 3.37 | 3.45 | 3.74 | 3.40 | 4.27 |
| Libraries ................ | (a) | (a) | (a) | (a) | (a) | (a) | (a) |
| Recreation ................ | 0.02 | 0.01 | 0.01 | 0.01 | 0.02 | 0.02 | 0.04 |
| Miscellaneous .............. | 0.30 | 0.27 | 0.22 | 0.23 | 0.29 | 0.22 | 0.44 |
| All general departments*.... | $12.08 | $11.31 | $10.42 | $ 9.67 | $10.53 | $10.41 | $10.74 |

*The totals upon which the per capita figures are based are same as in table on disbursement of state government for expenses and interest, less payments for interest, and do not include outlays for permanent improvements and investments.
(a) Less than one-half of one cent.

**ABSTRACT OF ASSESSED VALUE OF ALL REAL AND PERSONAL PROPERTY
IN COLORADO, 1930 AND 1931**

(From Report of the State Tax Commission)

Note.—This table shows the gross and net value of all property in Colorado as assessed for taxation purposes in 1931 and 1930 by the county assessors and the state tax commission, after all corrections and revisions. Distributions of the major items by counties, with mill levies for various purposes, will be found in separate tables. To these figures are added certain amounts by county treasurers which slightly increase the totals and comprise the amounts upon which all levies are made.

| CLASS OF PROPERTY | Assessed Value | |
| --- | --- | --- |
| | 1931 | 1930 |
| **Real Estate and Improvements as Returned by County Assessors to the Tax Commission:** | | |
| Agricultural land............................. | $ 290,247,090 | $ 362,508,726 |
| Waste and seep land.......................... | 793,846 | 1,011,580 |
| Suburban land................................ | 6,733,668 | 7,956,388 |
| Mountain home sites.......................... | 1,003,355 | 976,510 |
| Improvements on above land.................. | 71,455,744 | 83,298,510 |
| Improvements on public and state lands....... | 1,992,502 | 2,364,376 |
| Equities in state and school lands............ | 2,075,791 | 2,437,164 |
| Timber land ................................. | 764,110 | 1,130,282 |
| Improvements on timber land................. | 62,615 | 17,615 |
| Productive coal land......................... | 3,105,705 | 3,058,686 |
| Non-productive coal land..................... | 6,849,808 | 7,218,845 |
| Coal reserves ............................... | 2,385,369 | 2,512,957 |
| Improvements on coal lands.................. | 5,131,513 | 6,033,220 |
| Oil land .................................... | 331,747 | 483,543 |
| Oil shale land............................... | 733,555 | 788,875 |
| Oil reserves................................. | 482,475 | 512,470 |
| Improvements on oil lands.................... | 422,457 | 452,424 |
| Metalliferous mining claims (non-producing)... | 10,994,235 | 11,347,178 |
| Placer mining claims......................... | 801,474 | 777,929 |
| Output of producing metalliferous mines...... | 1,845,509 | 2,890,798 |
| Mineral reserves (other than coal and oil)..... | 1,868,680 | 1,854,900 |
| Improvements on all metalliferous mines...... | 5,058,612 | 5,055,926 |
| Town and city lots........................... | 174,612,399 | 184,533,058 |
| Improvements on town and city lots.......... | 327,706,895 | 347,577,974 |
| Total value, real estate and improvements.. | $ 917,459,154 | $1,036,799,934 |
| **Personal Property as Returned by County Assessors to Tax Commission:** | | |
| Livestock ................................... | $ 48,628,808 | $ 58,425,846 |
| Bicycles .................................... | 11,345 | 8,739 |
| Motorcycles ................................. | 23,340 | 28,841 |
| Automobiles and trucks...................... | 45,234,099 | 50,510,390 |
| Tractors .................................... | 3,272,816 | 3,133,650 |
| Carriages and vehicles of every description..... | 871,598 | 959,336 |
| Aeroplanes ................................. | 85,020 | 94,800 |
| Agricultural implements, harness, etc......... | 8,087,584 | 8,207,996 |
| Manufacturing machinery and equipment....... | 22,365,833 | 20,590,580 |
| Musical instruments.......................... | 5,462,757 | 6,162,411 |
| Radios ...................................... | 3,132,122 | 2,653,868 |
| Clocks and watches.......................... | 379,065 | 408,906 |
| Jewelry and silverware...................... | 1,332,545 | 1,390,275 |
| Household property........................... | 35,599,352 | 35,249,542 |
| Electric refrigerators........................ | 675,280 | 313,080 |
| Store and office fixtures and furniture........ | 13,404,567 | 13,661,330 |
| Libraries ................................... | 404,770 | 440,424 |
| Stocks of merchandise........................ | 66,090,039 | 74,751,964 |
| Capital employed in manufacture............. | 10,752,855 | 13,495,823 |
| Bank stock ................................. | 23,874,937 | 24,706,898 |

**ABSTRACT OF ASSESSED VALUE OF ALL REAL AND PERSONAL PROPERTY
IN COLORADO, 1930 AND 1931—Continued**

| CLASS OF PROPERTY | Assessed Value | |
|---|---|---|
| | 1931 | 1930 |
| **Personal Property as Returned by County Assessors to Tax Commission—Continued:** | | |
| Gross Value bank deposits in and out of state.. | 18,296,101 | 18,049,516 |
| Gross Value of money, credits and bank accounts | 36,309,591 | 36,540,160 |
| Gross Value promissory notes, bonds and debentures .................................... | 15,736,570 | 17,307,281 |
| Cash Value special privileges, franchises, etc... | 142,000 | 139,270 |
| All other property........................... | 2,803,921 | 2,572,160 |
| Gross value, personal property............ | $ 362,976,915 | $ 389,803,086 |
| **Corporation Valuations by Tax Commission:** | | |
| Railroads, telegraph and telephone........... | $ 190,250,040 | $ 192,023,550 |
| Railway Express Agency...................... | 217,170 | 273,920 |
| Self-Winding clocks .......................... | 20,865 | 22,530 |
| Pullman .................................... | 927,000 | 1,125,020 |
| Local public utilities......................... | 58,102,070 | 57,886,530 |
| Private car lines............................. | 1,193,440 | 1,060,700 |
| Motor Vehicle carriers (bus and truck lines).... | 599,560 | 692,730 |
| Total value, corporations.................. | $ 251,310,145 | $ 253,084,980 |
| **Recapitulation:** | | |
| Real estate and improvements................. | $ 917,459,154 | $1,036,799,934 |
| Personal property............................ | 362,976,915 | 389,803,086 |
| Corporations ................................ | 251,310,145 | 253,084,980 |
| Gross value, all property.................. | $1,531,746,214 | $1,679,688,000 |
| Exemptions allowed by law............... | 93,298,149 | 93,225,097 |
| Final net value, all property.............. | $1,438,448,065 | $1,586,462,903 |

**EXPENDITURES DENVER, PUEBLO AND COLORADO SPRINGS,
1915 AND 1925**
(Schools Not Included)
(Financial Statistics of Cities)
(Amounts in Thousands)

| | General Gov. | Prot. to Pers. & Prop. | Health and San. | Highways | Charities Hosp. Correction | Libraries | Recreation | General & Miscel. | Total |
|---|---|---|---|---|---|---|---|---|---|
| **1915:** | | | | | | | | | |
| Denver ................. | $798 | $739 | $239 | $598 | $270 | $50 | $415 | $128 | $3,237 |
| Pueblo ................. | 43 | 150 | 31 | 88 | 2 | 6 | 20 | 16 | 356 |
| Colorado Springs......... | 48 | 81 | 29 | 73 | 3 | 7 | 30 | 2 | 273 |
| Total ............. | $889 | $970 | $299 | $759 | $275 | $ 63 | $465 | $146 | $3,866 |
| Per Capita (Pop. 328,458) | $2.71 | $2.95 | $ .91 | $2.31 | $ .84 | $ .19 | $1.42 | $ .44 | $11.77 |
| U. S. | | | | | | | | | |
| Group I.............. | 2.94 | 4.90 | 2.30 | 2.20 | 1.84 | .26 | .89 | .98 | 16.31 |
| Group V ............. | 1.12 | 2.71 | 1.12 | 1.70 | .48 | .20 | .35 | .22 | 7.90 |
| **1925:** | | | | | | | | | |
| Denver ................. | $1,040 | $1,881 | $614 | $1,048 | $709 | $149 | $614 | $379 | $6,434 |
| Pueblo ................. | 74 | 219 | 58 | 131 | 3 | 9 | 51 | 18 | 563 |
| Colorado Springs......... | 59 | 151 | 43 | 92 | 5 | 13 | 88 | 18 | 469 |
| Total ............. | $1,173 | $2,251 | $715 | $1,271 | $717 | $171 | $753 | $415 | $7,466 |
| Per Capita (Pop. 354,803) | $3.32 | $6.36 | $2.02 | $3.59 | $2.02 | $ .48 | $2.12 | $1.17 | $21.10 |
| U. S. | | | | | | | | | |
| Group I.............. | $4.46 | $8.99 | $4.83 | $3.67 | $3.09 | $ .52 | $1.47 | $2.77 | $29.80 |
| Group V ............. | 1.77 | 5.19 | 2.24 | 2.89 | 1.01 | .38 | .79 | .88 | 15.13 |

## RECEIPTS OF STATE GOVERNMENT FOR 1923 TO 1929, INCLUSIVE

NOTE.—This table is compiled from reports of the bureau of the census of the United States department of commerce. Owing to the use of different classifications and inclusion of items not handled through the state auditing department, the figures are not comparable with the auditor's reports. The reports are for fiscal years. Prior to 1929 the Colorado fiscal year ended November 30. Beginning with 1929 it ends June 30.

| REVENUE RECEIPTS | 1929 | 1928 | 1927 | 1926 | 1925 | 1924 | 1923 |
|---|---|---|---|---|---|---|---|
| Taxes: | | | | | | | |
| General property | $ 5,624,518 | $5,971,509 | $ 5,611,972 | $ 5,659,605 | $ 5,844,144 | $ 6,215,155 | $ 6,913,075 |
| Special: | | | | | | | |
|   Property | | | | 183,679 | 182,517 | 190,682 | 200,225 |
|   Inheritance | 919,984 | 869,408 | 674,690 | 876,009 | 911,039 | 864,161 | 703,731 |
|   All others | 274,847 | 281,365 | 272,093 | 86,600 | 93,715 | 102,169 | 89,190 |
|   Poll | | | 15 | 122 | 166 | 131 | 342 |
| Business license taxes: | | | | | | | |
|   Gasoline | 4,162,842 | 4,118,399 | 3,012,626 | 2,085,833 | 1,847,641 | *2,373,889 | *1,406,599 |
|   All others | 898,816 | 869,001 | 763,558 | 724,291 | 672,989 | | |
| Non-business license taxes: | | | | | | | |
|   Motor vehicles | 1,017,362 | 980,491 | 876,413 | 828,884 | 789,358 | 660,958 | 635,590 |
|   All others | 289,393 | 287,484 | 269,857 | 229,956 | 242,555 | 213,959 | 205,736 |
|   Permits | 5,008 | 2,036 | 6,194 | 6,208 | 9,610 | 9,573 | 8,872 |
| Special assessments and special charges for outlays | 36,655 | 41,520 | 93,927 | 53,558 | 883,414 | 871,404 | 932,282 |
| Fines, forfeits, escheats | 38,353 | 41,595 | 4,596 | 4,029 | 18,416 | 19,054 | 19,431 |
| Subventions and grants, donations and pension assessments: | | | | | | | |
|   From U. S. Government | 2,148,589 | 2,053,964 | 1,445,798 | 1,424,488 | 1,662,461 | 1,791,013 | 1,508,439 |
|   From private persons and corporations | 48,583 | 40,899 | 57,200 | 121,296 | 17,226 | 191,170 | 55,597 |
| Rents and interest: | | | | | | | |
|   Sinking and trust funds | 425,702 | 449,669 | 473,766 | 322,398 | 540,730 | 447,066 | 477,043 |
|   Interest | 674,820 | 687,450 | 660,160 | 709,399 | 521,033 | 542,280 | 523,534 |
| Earnings of general departments | 2,160,565 | 2,113,490 | 2,125,555 | 1,979,621 | 1,651,102 | 1,572,353 | 1,394,289 |
| Total revenue receipts | $18,726,037 | $18,805,280 | $16,348,420 | $15,295,976 | $15,888,116 | $16,065,017 | $15,073,975 |

* Not segregated.

## DISBURSEMENTS OF STATE GOVERNMENT FOR 1923 TO 1929, INCLUSIVE

| EXPENSES | 1929 | 1928 | 1927 | 1926 | 1925 | 1924 | 1923 |
|---|---|---|---|---|---|---|---|
| General government | $ 977,083 | $ 887,149 | $ 968,797 | $ 781,274 | $ 926,138 | $ 797,949 | $ 903,618 |
| Protection to persons and property: | | | | | | | |
| Militia and armories | 109,131 | 129,529 | 114,294 | 99,705 | 86,746 | 104,096 | 118,198 |
| Regulation | 286,916 | 318,098 | 294,975 | 317,954 | 314,166 | 336,870 | 344,030 |
| All others | 288,455 | 375,976 | 318,051 | 314,952 | 140,687 | 120,528 | 142,097 |
| Development and conservation of natural resources: | | | | | | | |
| Agriculture | 771,762 | 742,380 | 657,135 | 654,219 | 492,808 | 585,513 | 533,595 |
| All others | 255,344 | 739,589 | 203,139 | 301,319 | 197,283 | 252,508 | 190,527 |
| Conservation of health and sanitation: | | | | | | | |
| Prevention and treatment of communicable diseases | 22,497 | 23,982 | 24,904 | 27,692 | 36,407 | 37,096 | 36,691 |
| All others | 111,107 | 103,971 | 106,558 | 101,944 | 115,127 | 106,348 | 102,521 |
| Highways | 2,612,572 | 2,148,055 | 2,455,574 | 1,679,991 | 2,623,880 | 2,552,989 | 2,194,606 |
| Charities, hospitals and corrections | 2,438,489 | 2,236,081 | 2,174,161 | 2,026,190 | 1,655,808 | 1,901,758 | 1,585,162 |
| Education: | | | | | | | |
| Schools | 4,179,245 | 4,117,355 | 3,614,122 | 3,646,272 | 3,810,044 | 3,411,549 | 3,361,76 |
| Libraries | 3,313 | 1,660 | 973 | 575 | 892 | 2,200 | 2,00 |
| Recreation | 16,006 | 15,085 | 12,610 | 12,829 | 16,716 | 19,206 | 17,33 |
| Miscellaneous | 306,488 | 275,482 | 240,197 | 240,659 | 293,227 | 217,455 | 252,53 |
| Interest | 513,423 | 557,468 | 620,860 | 578,273 | 542,154 | 490,318 | 438,737 |
| Total expenses and interest | $12,891,851 | $12,076,860 | $11,806,350 | $10,783,848 | $11,251,083 | $10,936,383 | $10,223,64 |
| Outlays (permanent improvements and investments): | | | | | | | |
| Agriculture | $ 12,943 | $ 4,097 | $ 20,238 | $ 31,324 | $ 22,778 | $ 17,507 | $ 60,431 |
| Fish and game | 113,592 | 112,267 | 93,360 | 118,644 | 31,379 | | |
| Highways | 4,299,597 | 4,919,584 | 3,348,800 | 3,910,519 | 3,761,659 | 4,774,445 | 4,538,231 |
| Hospitals and corrections | 169,260 | 15,528 | 30,642 | 221,819 | 38,659 | 103,652 | 267,615 |
| Education | 224,957 | 399,463 | 711,052 | 704,690 | 1,532,915 | 1,807,411 | 1,293,314 |
| Miscellaneous | 117 | 4,050 | 136,752 | 59,279 | 6,373 | 7,164 | 31,608 |
| Total governmental costs | $17,712,317 | $17,531,849 | $16,147,194 | $15,830,123 | $16,644,846 | $17,646,562 | $16,414,903 |

## DETAILED STATEMENT OF ASSESSMENT FOR 1931
### (From the Records of the State Tax Commission)

| COUNTY | Valuation by County Assessor | Valuation by Tax Commission | | | | | | | | | Total Valuation by Tax Commission |
|---|---|---|---|---|---|---|---|---|---|---|---|
| | | Railroad Companies | Telephone Companies | Telegraph Companies | Express Companies | Pullman Company | Private Car Lines | Self-Winding Clocks | Local Utility Companies | Motor eMcle Carriers (Bus and Trck) Lines | |
| Adams | $ 23,063,560 | $ 4,269,160 | $ 273,040 | $ 116,620 | $5,660 | $36,200 | $31,670 | $240 | $210 | $38,340 | $4,975,640 |
| lamosa | 7,218,176 | 1,594,030 | 57,860 | 9,430 | 2,360 | 4,780 | 6,960 | 270 | 161,930 | 5,420 | 1,843,040 |
| Arapahoe | 17,382,145 | 2,588,750 | 416,790 | 68,960 | 3,960 | 27,600 | 17,960 | 255 | 1,005,360 | 14,790 | 4,144,425 |
| lleta | 2,286,334 | 1,954,970 | 12,850 | 9,000 | 2,870 | ----- | 250 | ----- | 16,380 | ----- | 1,996,320 |
| Baca | 10,655,590 | 2,093,840 | 38,890 | 2,340 | 2,260 | ----- | 16,240 | ----- | 130,980 | ----- | 2,283,510 |
| Bent | 8,486,685 | 3,439,060 | 88,690 | 31,120 | 3,530 | 14,010 | 28,260 | ----- | 191,610 | 12,160 | 3,808,330 |
| Boulder | 34,563,280 | 3,725,390 | 501,780 | 26,770 | 4,570 | 14,080 | 31,360 | 375 | 4,809,820 | 43,820 | 9,157,965 |
| Chaffee | 6,249,755 | 2,384,070 | 76,200 | 38,080 | 3,200 | 17,920 | 15,730 | 195 | 535,480 | 1,390 | 3,072,265 |
| Cheyenne | 8,791,698 | 2,838,940 | 37,720 | 57,020 | 2,870 | 23,940 | 22,700 | ----- | 34,900 | 7,150 | 3,025,240 |
| Clear Creek | 3,888,650 | 894,010 | 38,550 | 3,240 | 1,370 | ----- | 100 | ----- | 430,420 | 16,890 | 1,384,580 |
| Conejos | 6,100,165 | 1,674,580 | 38,600 | 10,490 | 2,460 | ----- | 500 | ----- | 38,390 | 480 | 1,765,500 |
| tilla | 3,407,520 | 1,044,530 | 35,600 | 6,260 | 2,890 | 12,170 | 13,340 | 150 | 25,530 | 1,710 | 1,142,030 |
| Crowley | 7,105,550 | 1,103,010 | 43,060 | 6,660 | 1,430 | 11,890 | 8,810 | ----- | 189,080 | 1,240 | 1,365,320 |
| Custer | 2,228,332 | 391,920 | 11,480 | 2,530 | 580 | ----- | 4,250 | 150 | 15,170 | ----- | 425,930 |
| Delta | 10,599,290 | 2,153,260 | 11,230 | 21,370 | 3,140 | ----- | 25,740 | 210 | 146,860 | 7,690 | 2,489,500 |
| Denver | 399,549,240 | 2,422,430 | 6,860 | 165,320 | 3,450 | 16,130 | 13,570 | 11,385 | 24,867,970 | 17,230 | 36,083,445 |
| Dolores | 1,384,094 | 70,880 | 8,270 | 1,670 | 810 | ----- | 780 | ----- | 22,720 | ----- | 100,130 |
| Douglas | 380 | 3,480,390 | 127,470 | 146,170 | 4,300 | 43,890 | 29,990 | ----- | 525,350 | 26,940 | 4,384,500 |
| Eagle | 4,363,468 | 2,533,140 | 32,020 | 45,450 | 3,740 | 24,320 | 26,560 | ----- | H0 | ----- | 2,861,330 |
| Elbert | 10,471,133 | 3,291,550 | 84,010 | 48,060 | 5,080 | 32,170 | 26,820 | 1,680 | 79,620 | 6,700 | 3,573,910 |
| El Paso | 61,184,340 | 6,667,860 | 1,036,800 | 195,890 | 9,700 | 72,710 | 56,260 | ----- | 1,191,890 | 39,690 | 9,272,470 |
| Fremont | 15,384,832 | 3,407,150 | 158,420 | 41,760 | 3,800 | 26,930 | 35,730 | 195 | 1,544,920 | 5,660 | 5,224,565 |
| Garfield | 11,613,825 | 2,999,620 | 103,250 | 57,630 | 5,260 | 25,470 | 29,300 | 300 | 1,702,570 | 6,070 | 4,929,470 |
| Gilpin | 1,844,336 | 220 | 26,580 | 3,490 | 1,690 | ----- | 3,360 | ----- | 97,880 | ----- | 1,308,220 |
| Grand | 3,858,775 | 2,327,480 | 43,550 | ----- | 2,420 | ----- | 15,640 | ----- | 12,240 | 13,640 | 2,414,970 |
| Gunnison | 8,768,205 | 480 | 51,270 | 15,830 | 5,320 | ----- | 1,570 | 225 | 70,560 | 220 | 5,760,175 |
| Hinsdale | 652,502 | 291,230 | 2,110 | ----- | 40 | ----- | ----- | ----- | 9,760 | ----- | 308,530 |
| Huerfano | 8,698,863 | 4,082,100 | 101,630 | 77,580 | 4,910 | 37,190 | 45,090 | ----- | 874,770 | 21,720 | 5,244,990 |

| County | A | B | C | D | E | F | G | H | I | J | K |
|---|---|---|---|---|---|---|---|---|---|---|---|
| Jackson | 2,976,710 | 179,460 | 8,630 | | 1,990 | | 1,040 | | | | 191,120 |
| Jefferson | 20,351,755 | 3,382,020 | 393,370 | 37,900 | 5,220 | 2,170 | 9,970 | | 1,257,850 | 17,220 | 190 |
| Kiowa | 7,955,685 | 3,078,210 | 64,980 | 17,850 | 3,980 | 33,180 | 29,500 | | | | 3,227,700 |
| Kit Carson | 14,797,154 | 2,091,290 | 31,870 | 30,460 | 2,740 | 22,820 | 19,840 | 210 | 33,740 | 8,210 | 2,241,180 |
| Lake | 4,998,183 | 1,714,680 | 58,210 | 22,930 | 2,440 | 10,890 | 12,220 | 270 | 536,220 | 500 | 2,358,360 |
| La Plata | 9,826,175 | 2,946,120 | 80,190 | 16,540 | 5,510 | | 5,340 | 405 | 959,940 | 5,880 | 4,019,925 |
| Larimer | 38,854,150 | 5,125,430 | 519,620 | 21,460 | 4,620 | 19,730 | 47,980 | 480 | 858,310 | 40,150 | 6,637,780 |
| Las Animas | 25,222,367 | 9,019,400 | 246,910 | 144,510 | 8,250 | 52,960 | 65,640 | 495 | 2,886,760 | 18,770 | 12,443,695 |
| Lincoln | 12,303,560 | 2,991,390 | 100,760 | 54,160 | 3,400 | 28,340 | 22,820 | 120 | 120,920 | 8,200 | 3,330,110 |
| Logan | 24,721,875 | 6,438,690 | 201,340 | 56,580 | 6,890 | 37,560 | 46,380 | 285 | 628,740 | 11,390 | 7,427,855 |
| Mesa | 22,671,940 | 3,232,350 | 252,140 | 75,220 | 5,110 | 26,650 | 39,030 | 615 | 772,610 | 7,520 | 4,411,245 |
| Mineral | 911,860 | 539,090 | 8,900 | 1,740 | 790 | | 5,900 | | | | 556,420 |
| Moffat | 5,823,718 | 225,050 | 32,840 | | 340 | | 1,680 | | 109,870 | | 369,780 |
| Montezuma | 4,799,855 | 260,760 | 32,900 | 5,960 | 2,850 | | 2,570 | | 97,540 | 3,320 | 395,900 |
| Montrose | 8,563,700 | 1,621,910 | 116,090 | 14,010 | 2,380 | | 5,940 | 270 | 121,870 | 3,230 | 1,885,700 |
| Morgan | 19,898,770 | 4,271,560 | 211,700 | 85,380 | 4,280 | 35,500 | 30,420 | 180 | 161,670 | 17,530 | 4,818,220 |
| Otero | 23,813,695 | 4,101,820 | 169,280 | 63,550 | 4,210 | 28,400 | 33,740 | 180 | 786,010 | 13,120 | 5,200,310 |
| Ouray | 2,515,324 | 799,870 | 34,890 | 7,200 | 1,700 | | 1,540 | | 150,790 | 4,220 | 1, 9,210 |
| Park | 4,665,550 | 3,296,130 | 51,520 | 59,860 | 2,960 | | 370 | | 38,000 | | 3,448,340 |
| Phillips | 11,504,435 | 1,763,320 | 32,000 | 3,630 | 1,650 | | 12,220 | a | | | 1,812,820 |
| Pitkin | 2,537,400 | 649,230 | 23,050 | 2,860 | 930 | | 5,370 | | 75,260 | | 756,700 |
| Prowers | 15,244,180 | 3,587,980 | 202,940 | 33,010 | 3,670 | 14,600 | 27,470 | 90 | 233,380 | 4,440 | 4,107,580 |
| Pueblo | 63,269,640 | 7,203,850 | 1,115,730 | 191,340 | 9,980 | 76,160 | 63,870 | 1,140 | 4,878,700 | 49,300 | 13,590,070 |
| Rio Blanco | 4,635,355 | 92,130 | 27,480 | | 350 | | 14,260 | | 58,490 | | 119,960 |
| Rio Grande | 7,910,257 | 1,360,900 | 63,460 | 5,020 | 1,860 | | 23,110 | 135 | 576,840 | 2,350 | 1,506,475 |
| Routt | 11,994,210 | 2,732,420 | 60,010 | | 4,140 | | | | | | 3,396,520 |
| Saguache | 6,018,829 | 2,781,620 | 51,440 | 14,760 | 3,750 | | 350 | | 53,100 | 10,360 | 2,915,380 |
| San Juan | 2,753,277 | 553,360 | 24,340 | 1,310 | 600 | | | | 159,050 | 3,980 | 742,640 |
| San Miguel | 3,046,995 | 190,800 | 31,060 | 5,210 | 2,110 | | 2,160 | | 753,960 | | 985,300 |
| Sedgwick | 9,671,450 | 1,418,990 | 64,740 | 26,180 | 1,430 | 11,610 | 9,360 | | 41,670 | 4,440 | 1,578,420 |
| Summit | 2,342,237 | 1,543,480 | 27,250 | 8,600 | 2,050 | | | | 395,040 | | 176,420 |
| Teller | 3,135,220 | 662,760 | 107,660 | | | | | | 548,690 | | 1,319,110 |
| Washington | 11,206,456 | 1,976,150 | 38,010 | 41,260 | 1,960 | 16,390 | 12,850 | | 123,540 | 7,290 | 2,217,450 |
| Weld | 71,561,860 | 16,112,350 | 604,150 | 263,150 | 17,130 | 54,310 | 120,350 | 510 | 1,549,740 | 63,470 | 18,585,160 |
| Yuma | 18,583,570 | 1,962,920 | 50,240 | 40,650 | 1,840 | 15,330 | 12,670 | | | 5,720 | 2,089,270 |
| State | $1,187,137,920 | $170,411,240 | $17,279,370 | $2,559,430 | $217,170 | $ 927,000 | $1,193,440 | $20,865 | $58,102,070 | $599,560 | $251,310,145 |

VALUATION AND TAXES LEVIED, TOGETHER WITH MILL LEVIES FOR COUNTY, AVERAGE LEVIES FOR TOWN AND SCHOOL PURPOSES, AND THE AVERAGE TOTAL LEVIES FOR THE YEAR 1930.* STATE LEVY 3.59 MILLS

| COUNTY | Valuation | Revenue | County Levy | Average Town Levy | Average School Levy | Average Total Levy |
|---|---|---|---|---|---|---|
| Adams | $ 32,063,560 | $ 812,128.85 | 6.29 | 19.64 | 12.98 | 25.33 |
| Alamosa | 10,095,070 | 359,263.26 | 5.82 | 19.53 | 20.12 | 35.59 |
| Arapahoe | 23,971,995 | 753,988.39 | 5.67 | 17.95 | 18.10 | 31.45 |
| Archuleta | 4,723,143 | 111,551.57 | 7.55 | 17.50 | 10.56 | 23.62 |
| Baca | 14,318,800 | 424,443.74 | 7.41 | 20.63 | 16.78 | 29.64 |
| Bent | 13,759,870 | 360,425.40 | 7.80 | 14.00 | 13.12 | 26.19 |
| Boulder | 47,422,306 | 1,378,397.62 | 6.31 | 9.73 | 14.86 | 29.07 |
| Chaffee | 9,872,389 | 329,945.46 | 11.30 | 11.94 | 13.63 | 33.42 |
| Cheyenne | 13,862,418 | 249,486.46 | 2.65 | 18.00 | 10.98 | 18.00 |
| Clear Creek | 5,452,455 | 155,417.63 | 10.40 | 12.09 | 10.44 | 28.50 |
| Conejos | 9,197,160 | 305,827.98 | 10.00 | 13.92 | 17.83 | 33.25 |
| Costilla | 5,293,410 | 201,943.59 | 14.00 | 9.00 | 20.06 | 38.15 |
| Crowley | 9,802,780 | 260,648.63 | 3.65 | 15.03 | 16.74 | 26.60 |
| Custer | 3,074,735 | 84,670.26 | 10.00 | 10.21 | 12.92 | 27.54 |
| Delta | 14,690,545 | 592,322.06 | 12.84 | 11.48 | 20.19 | 40.32 |
| Denver | 464,482,500 | 15,026,008.87 | 4.76 | 10.20 | 13.80 | 32.35 |
| Dolores | 1,887,958 | 71,693.26 | 19.40 | 11.00 | 13.80 | 37.97 |
| Douglas | 11,829,775 | 229,107.65 | 6.10 | 20.00 | 8.79 | 19.37 |
| Eagle | 8,058,056 | 242,881.71 | 11.60 | 16.94 | 13.48 | 30.14 |
| Elbert | 16,482,668 | 357,886.74 | 5.06 | 14.73 | 12.58 | 21.71 |
| El Paso | 75,588,010 | 2,529,519.08 | 4.75 | 12.82 | 17.23 | 33.46 |
| Fremont | 22,873,857 | 745,274.69 | 5.92 | 12.85 | 18.12 | 32.58 |
| Garfield | 18,285,280 | 634,545.09 | 11.00 | 19.13 | 16.25 | 34.70 |
| Gilpin | 3,208,733 | 96,379.25 | 13.00 | 23.47 | 10.25 | 30.03 |
| Grand | 6,884,270 | 135,321.56 | 8.04 | 16.92 | 7.04 | 19.66 |
| Gunnison | 15,661,565 | 374,642.56 | 8.74 | 12.98 | 9.59 | 23.32 |
| Hinsdale | 1,170,628 | 44,414.91 | 19.00 | 16.00 | 13.54 | 37.94 |
| Huerfano | 16,069,091 | 580,857.07 | 11.30 | 11.54 | 18.42 | 36.15 |
| Jackson | 3,690,870 | 58,650.73 | 4.40 | 18.00 | 6.99 | 15.89 |
| Jefferson | 28,626,045 | 797,948.16 | 7.11 | 14.94 | 15.12 | 27.87 |
| Kiowa | 13,018,460 | 222,170.78 | 1.41 | 18.35 | 11.39 | 17.06 |
| Kit Carson | 21,126,843 | 563,840.47 | 6.09 | 16.38 | 14.66 | 26.69 |
| Lake | 7,530,705 | 274,214.89 | 11.61 | 35.00 | 13.65 | 36.41 |
| La Plata | 15,360,005 | 538,383.51 | 9.39 | 12.47 | 17.97 | 35.05 |
| Larimer | 52,101,980 | 1,601,873.12 | 8.39 | 14.25 | 13.80 | 30.74 |
| Las Animas | 42,016,901 | 1,423,274.49 | 7.30 | 18.14 | 18.32 | 33.87 |
| Lincoln | 18,383,215 | 478,542.26 | 5.67 | 12.93 | 15.44 | 26.03 |
| Logan | 36,588,130 | 1,067,625.45 | 6.32 | 17.65 | 15.54 | 29.18 |
| Mesa | 30,755,190 | 1,048,148.93 | 7.00 | 14.75 | 17.96 | 34.08 |
| Mineral | 1,667,299 | 35,540.14 | 8.67 | 22.00 | 6.50 | 21.32 |
| Moffat | 7,304,600 | 249,571.92 | 13.25 | 19.00 | 14.59 | 34.16 |
| Montezuma | 6,221,605 | 240,941.92 | 13.63 | 14.84 | 18.35 | 38.72 |
| Montrose | 12,057,750 | 471,389.62 | 12.10 | 15.08 | 19.21 | 39.00 |
| Morgan | 27,748,752 | 798,836.81 | 6.97 | 11.73 | 15.78 | 28.70 |
| Otero | 32,087,645 | 935,011.52 | 4.95 | 14.61 | 15.88 | 29.14 |
| Ouray | 4,092,453 | 128,523.61 | 13.60 | 17.13 | 11.08 | 31.41 |
| Park | 8,707,710 | 133,131.65 | 4.80 | 8.81 | 6.59 | 15.29 |
| Phillips | 15,414,635 | 327,412.74 | 4.92 | 11.48 | 11.25 | 21.24 |
| Pitkin | 3,773,985 | 123,087.92 | 16.00 | 43.00 | 9.53 | 32.61 |
| Frowers | 21,788,035 | 631,695.30 | 7.02 | 12.85 | 15.67 | 28.99 |
| Pueblo | 82,824,353 | †3,085,943.17 | 4.46 | 23.50 | 17.50 | 37.25 |
| Rio Blanco | 5,793,850 | 165,516.58 | 9.16 | 21.00 | 13.37 | 28.57 |
| Rio Grande | 10,893,956 | 429,630.37 | 7.75 | 16.84 | 24.51 | 39.44 |
| Routt | 16,839,880 | 487,450.57 | 7.95 | 20.15 | 14.74 | 28.95 |
| Saguache | 10,584,427 | 278,985.32 | 7.40 | 12.60 | 14.21 | 26.36 |
| San Juan | 3,796,488 | 110,790.85 | 12.90 | 15.00 | 10.01 | 29.18 |
| San Miguel | 4,638,715 | 160,060.43 | 13.41 | 11.65 | 15.11 | 34.51 |
| Sedgwick | 12,968,138 | 342,399.10 | 6.05 | 16.85 | 13.97 | 26.40 |
| Summit | 4,481,396 | 112,680.59 | 10.38 | 14.16 | 9.73 | 25.14 |
| Teller | 5,002,390 | 210,718.95 | 13.10 | 46.96 | 16.41 | 42.12 |
| Washington | 15,921,474 | 473,914.45 | 7.40 | 12.93 | 17.62 | 29.77 |
| Weld | 102,176,120 | 3,132,736.45 | 6.48 | 14.62 | 17.39 | 30.66 |
| Yuma | 24,607,070 | 617,077.52 | 4.50 | 12.59 | 15.47 | 25.08 |
| State | $1,590,674,097 | $49,206,716.63 | 8.60 | 16.53 | ‡14.40 | 30.93 |

*From County Treasurers' Annual Statements.
†Includes Revenues of Water and Park Districts.
‡Exclusive of Educational Institutions.
Note—County levy does not include general school tax levy, shown in another table.

**DISTRIBUTION OF GENERAL TAX IN COLORADO FOR 1911***

(From the Records of the State Tax Commission)

| COUNTY | Assessed Valuation | Per Cent of Total Value of State | State Revenue | Per Cent of Total State Revenue | County Revenue | Per Cent of Total Tax of County | Town Revenue | Per Cent of Total Tax of County | School Revenue | Per Cent of Total Tax of County | Total County Property Tax | Per Cent of Total Property Tax of State |
|---|---|---|---|---|---|---|---|---|---|---|---|---|

*From County Treasurers' Annual Statements.
†Includes water and park districts.
‡Includes water and park districts.

## MILEAGE AND VALUE OF RAILROADS, TELEGRAPH AND TELEPHONE LINES AS RETURNED BY STATE TAX COMMISSION FOR 1931

| COUNTY | Miles of Railroad | Value | Miles of Telephone | Value | Miles of Telegraph | Value |
|---|---|---|---|---|---|---|
| Adams | 92.06 | $4,269,160 | 7,640.66 | $273,040 | 1,288.76 | $115,620 |
| Alamosa | 51.45 | 1,594,030 | 1,716.50 | 57,860 | 94.35 | 9,430 |
| Arapahoe | 62.94 | 2,588,750 | 11,381.57 | 416,790 | 742.86 | 68,960 |
| Archuleta | 63.10 | 1,954,970 | 315.25 | 12,850 | 90.04 | 9,000 |
| Baca | 47.24 | 2,093,840 | 1,163.00 | 38,890 | 23.44 | 2,340 |
| Bent | 77.59 | 3,439,060 | 2,374.00 | 88,690 | 482.55 | 31,120 |
| Boulder | 98.15 | 3,725,390 | 14,929.24 | 501,780 | 267.90 | 26,770 |
| Chaffee | 76.95 | 2,384,070 | 2,279.00 | 76,200 | 389.53 | 38,080 |
| Cheyenne | 63.12 | 2,838,940 | 894.88 | 37,720 | 570.70 | 57,020 |
| Clear Creek | 26.03 | 894,010 | 1,153.00 | 38,550 | 32.42 | 3,240 |
| Conejos | 54.05 | 1,674,580 | 1,167.00 | 38,600 | 105.01 | 10,490 |
| Costilla | 63.63 | 1,044,530 | 1,075.05 | 55,600 | 62.69 | 6,260 |
| Crowley | 31.35 | 1,103,010 | 1,168.20 | 43,050 | 66.70 | 6,660 |
| Custer | 12.65 | 391,920 | 347.00 | 11,480 | 25.30 | 2,530 |
| Delta | 69.50 | 2,153,260 | 4,063.00 | 131,230 | 213.86 | 21,370 |
| Denver | 55.18 | 2,422,430 | 256,014.40 | 8,566,960 | 1,736.87 | 165,320 |
| Dolores | 17.72 | 70,880 | 46.00 | 3,270 | 16.67 | 1,670 |
| Douglas | 94.39 | 3,480,390 | 3,393.60 | 127,470 | 1,749.71 | 146,170 |
| Eagle | 82.21 | 2,533,140 | 995.50 | 32,020 | 454.91 | 45,450 |
| Elbert | 83.24 | 3,291,550 | 1,720.20 | 84,010 | 480.98 | 48,060 |
| El Paso | 190.52 | 6,667,860 | 30,262.32 | 1,036,800 | 2,309.38 | 195,890 |
| Fremont | 101.38 | 3,407,150 | 4,768.00 | 158,420 | 473.52 | 41,760 |
| Garfield | 118.04 | 2,999,620 | 3,107.25 | 103,250 | 577.84 | 57,630 |
| Gilpin | 36.99 | 1,175,220 | 795.00 | 26,580 | 34.94 | 3,490 |
| Grand | 76.58 | 2,327,480 | 1,304.00 | 43,550 | ----- | ----- |
| Gunnison | 184.03 | 5,615,180 | 1,479.66 | 51,270 | 186.78 | 15,830 |
| Hinsdale | 9.40 | 291,230 | 77.00 | 2,110 | ----- | ----- |
| Huerfano | 127.75 | 4,082,100 | 2,803.84 | 101,630 | 830.86 | 77,580 |
| Jackson | 43.88 | 179,460 | 258.00 | 8,630 | ----- | ----- |
| Jefferson | 98.65 | 3,382,020 | 11,790.00 | 393,370 | 379.35 | 37,900 |
| Kiowa | 87.49 | 3,078,210 | 1,261.88 | 64,980 | 178.70 | 17,850 |
| Kit Carson | 60.18 | 2,091,290 | 975.50 | 31,870 | 804.84 | 30,460 |
| Lake | 53.69 | 1,714,680 | 1,741.00 | 58,210 | 229.55 | 22,930 |
| La Plata | 121.00 | 2,946,120 | 2,446.25 | 80,190 | 165.52 | 16,540 |
| Larimer | 141.54 | 5,125,430 | 14,952.48 | 519,620 | 214.77 | 21,460 |
| Las Animas | 231.93 | 9,019,400 | 6,841.60 | 246,910 | 1,849.05 | 144,510 |
| Lincoln | 73.33 | 2,991,390 | 2,093.98 | 100,760 | 542.03 | 54,160 |
| Logan | 133.60 | 6,438,690 | 5,115.02 | 201,340 | 786.84 | 56,580 |
| Mesa | 112.25 | 3,232,350 | 7,508.88 | 252,140 | 752.84 | 75,220 |
| Mineral | 17.40 | 539,090 | 266.00 | 8,900 | 17.41 | 1,740 |
| Moffat | 7.49 | 225,050 | 976.00 | 32,840 | ----- | ----- |
| Montezuma | 62.69 | 250,760 | 984.00 | 32,900 | 59.67 | 5,960 |
| Montrose | 52.35 | 1,621,910 | 3,497.50 | 116,090 | 140.23 | 14,010 |
| Morgan | 90.53 | 4,271,560 | 5,657.30 | 211,700 | 1,028.89 | 85,380 |
| Otero | 92.58 | 4,101,820 | 4,906.20 | 169,280 | 1,000.57 | 63,550 |
| Ouray | 37.40 | 799,870 | 1,043.00 | 34,890 | 72.05 | 7,200 |
| Park | 95.97 | 3,296,130 | 1,535.00 | 51,520 | 594.17 | 59,360 |
| Phillips | 36.31 | 1,763,320 | 701.97 | 32,000 | 36.30 | 3,630 |
| Pitkin | 39.14 | 649,230 | 695.00 | 23,050 | 37.33 | 2,860 |
| Prowers | 80.95 | 3,587,980 | 4,848.18 | 202,940 | 509.49 | 33,010 |
| Pueblo | 211.17 | 7,203,850 | 32,529.38 | 1,115,730 | 2,269.96 | 191,340 |
| Rio Blanco | 7.80 | 92,130 | 829.50 | 27,480 | ----- | ----- |
| Rio Grande | 52.51 | 1,360,900 | 1,884.00 | 63,460 | 50.25 | 5,020 |
| Routt | 90.94 | 2,732,420 | 1,793.25 | 60,010 | ----- | ----- |
| Saguache | 90.15 | 2,781,620 | 1,597.50 | 51,440 | 163.79 | 14,760 |
| San Juan | 28.72 | 553,360 | 728.00 | 24,340 | 13.10 | 1,310 |
| San Miguel | 47.70 | 190,800 | 929.00 | 31,060 | 52.11 | 5,210 |
| Sedgwick | 31.48 | 1,418,990 | 1,523.86 | 64,740 | 357.70 | 26,180 |
| Summit | 44.94 | 1,543,480 | 848.00 | 27,250 | 86.04 | 8,600 |
| Teller | 39.55 | 662,760 | 3,220.00 | 107,660 | ----- | ----- |
| Washington | 40.44 | 1,976,150 | 968.45 | 38,010 | 424.40 | 41,260 |
| Weld | 401.40 | 16,112,350 | 17,294.36 | 604,150 | 3,185.59 | 263,150 |
| Yuma | 40.42 | 1,962,920 | 1,439.27 | 50,240 | 405.89 | 40,550 |
| State | 4,964.81 | $170,411,240 | 504,113.43 | $17,279,370 | 29,217.00 | $2,559,430 |

## COMPARATIVE ASSESSED VALUATION AS REPORTED BY TAX COMMISSION,
### 1923, 1924, 1925, 1929, 1930, 1931

| COUNTY | 1931 | 1930 | 1929 | 1925 | 1924 | 1923 |
|---|---|---|---|---|---|---|
| Adams | $ 28,039,200 | $ 32,186,300 | $ 32,229,890 | $ 31,771,520 | $ 31,770,460 | $ 32,493 |
| Alamosa | 9,061,216 | 10,095,070 | 9,997,212 | 9,346,936 | 9,260,459 | 9,234 |
| Arapahoe | 21,526,570 | 23,956,229 | 23,152,000 | 21,175,010 | 21,301,925 | 20,847 |
| Archuleta | 4,282,654 | 4,636,869 | 4,665,810 | 4,550,250 | 4,603,580 | 4,701 |
| Baca | 12,939,100 | 14,318,800 | 13,389,800 | 10,004,707 | 9,710,749 | 10,465 |
| Bent | 12,294,915 | 13,759,870 | 13,741,575 | 13,588,251 | 13,512,295 | 13,945 |
| Boulder | 43,721,245 | 47,414,950 | 46,872,840 | 47,273,532 | 46,753,280 | 46,767 |
| Chaffee | 9,322,020 | 9,858,980 | 9,610,955 | 10,489,660 | 10,590,445 | 10,566 |
| Cheyenne | 11,816,838 | 13,853,688 | 13,784,464 | 16,937,730 | 18,303,302 | 19,873 |
| Clear Creek | 5,273.230 | 5,434,895 | 5,411,690 | 5,424,380 | 5,488,825 | 5,533 |
| Conejos | 7,865,665 | 9,205,570 | 9,291,400 | 8,482,960 | 8,433,945 | 8,717 |
| Costilla | 4,549,550 | 5,293,410 | 5,312,665 | 5,244,260 | 5,401,112 | 5,666 |
| Crowley | 8,470,870 | 9,743,528 | 10,185,080 | 9,798,990 | 9,808,585 | 9,547 |
| Custer | 2,654,262 | 3,075,435 | 3,055,645 | 3,114,268 | 3,096,800 | 3,111 |
| Delta | 13,088.790 | 14,688,795 | 15,079,260 | 15,555,771 | 16,445,405 | 17,009 |
| Denver | 435,632,685 | 459,992,853 | 453,835,330 | 416,604,690 | 405,106,910 | 388,170 |
| Dolores | 1,484.224 | 2,066,877 | 1,825,115 | 1,630,444 | 1,560,443 | 1,745 |
| Douglas | 10,584,880 | 11,837,705 | 11,474,840 | 10,738,479 | 11,217,455 | 11,564 |
| Eagle | 7,224,798 | 8,058,056 | 7,176,615 | 6,652,163 | 6,385,168 | 6,551 |
| Elbert | 14,045.043 | 16,478,763 | 17,708,317 | 17,998,235 | 18,259,814 | 18,798 |
| El Paso | 70,456,810 | 75,322,405 | 75,393,330 | 70,999,530 | 70,661,250 | 70,056 |
| Fremont | 20,609,397 | 22,871,813 | 23,383,340 | 21,496,797 | 21,470,829 | 21,578 |
| Garfield | 16,543,295 | 19,212,475 | 18,036,195 | 16,760,930 | 16,770,960 | 17,472 |
| Gilpin | 3,152,556 | 3,204,732 | 2,877,759 | 2,636,555 | 2,831,029 | 2,820 |
| Grand | 6,273.745 | 6,888,680 | 5,813,895 | 4,683,230 | 4,539,060 | 4,675 |
| Gunnison | 14,528,380 | 15,659,405 | 15,956,050 | 15,633,235 | 15,855,290 | 16,005 |
| Hinsdale | 956,032 | 1,178,983 | 982,553 | 940,990 | 926,077 | 932 |
| Huerfano | 13,943,853 | 16,069,091 | 16,605,932 | 15,960,350 | 16,141,453 | 15,905 |
| Jackson | 3,167,830 | 3,670,740 | 3,855,680 | 3,677,870 | 3,846,730 | 4,238 |
| Jefferson | 25,457,475 | 28,644,700 | 27,775,520 | 25,711,450 | 24,692,740 | 24,158 |
| Kiowa | 11,183,385 | 13,004,770 | 13,187,310 | 14,353,803 | 14,161,089 | 14,401 |
| Kit Carson | 17,038,334 | 21,154,833 | 21,295,855 | 26,076,536 | 26,110,941 | 28,394 |
| Lake | 7,356,543 | 7,487,005 | 7,610,450 | 7,706,810 | 7,744,325 | 8,087 |
| La Plata | 13,846,100 | 15,351,155 | 15,520,611 | 15,264,755 | 15,084,263 | 15,070 |
| Larimer | 45,491,930 | 52,357,595 | 53,346,290 | 55,278,060 | 53,362,355 | 52,035 |
| Las Animas | 37,666,062 | 41,974,002 | 41,622,162 | 42,308,393 | 42,939,525 | 43,448 |
| Lincoln | 15,633,670 | 18,393,217 | 20,406,035 | 22,623,650 | 23,143,320 | 23,578 |
| Logan | 32,149,730 | 36,555,861 | 36,916,775 | 36,891,095 | 38,102,560 | 40,243 |
| Mesa | 27,083,185 | 30,755,510 | 30,225,510 | 29,712,195 | 29,447,230 | 29,623 |
| Mineral | 1,468,280 | 1,667,299 | 1,566,140 | 1,486,650 | 1,474,705 | 1,361 |
| Moffat | 6,193,498 | 7,261,564 | 7,374,850 | 6,572,136 | 6,128,905 | 6,181 |
| Montezuma | 5,195,755 | 6,241,295 | 6,564,155 | 6,296,535 | 6,120,240 | 6,310 |
| Montrose | 10,449,400 | 12,050,922 | 12,204,332 | 12,464,845 | 12,976,810 | 14,361 |
| Morgan | 24,716,990 | 27,718,762 | 28,881,820 | 28,299,506 | 28,626,940 | 28,911 |
| Otero | 29,014,005 | 32,118,810 | 32,013,510 | 34,495,560 | 33,694,130 | 33,700 |
| Ouray | 3,515,534 | 4,092,453 | 4,084,281 | 4,020,672 | 4,128,887 | 4,531 |
| Park | 8,113,890 | 8,696,650 | 8,895,205 | 8,510,030 | 8,481,555 | 8,831 |
| Phillips | 13,317,255 | 15,414,635 | 15,435,890 | 14,914,375 | 15,910,370 | 17,283 |
| Pitkin | 3,294,100 | 3,816,490 | 3,915,120 | 4,448,460 | 4,560,290 | 4,621 |
| Prowers | 19,351,760 | 21,564,010 | 21,831,630 | 21,770,175 | 22,862,215 | 23,156 |
| Pueblo | 76,859,710 | 83,025,130 | 81,257,860 | 74,263,765 | 73,445,919 | 72,711 |
| Rio Blanco | 4,805,315 | 5,796,095 | 6,074,325 | 5,291,040 | 4,914,165 | 5,145 |
| Rio Grande | 9,416,732 | 11,137,246 | 10,931,025 | 10,483,371 | 10,701,820 | 11,489 |
| Routt | 15,390,730 | 16,802,930 | 15,907,960 | 14,605,133 | 14,446,455 | 14,910 |
| Saguache | 8,934,209 | 10,583,464 | 11,435,834 | 11,151,184 | 11,278,995 | 11,331 |
| San Juan | 3,495,917 | 3,796,488 | 3,440,058 | 3,613,684 | 3,297,850 | 3,281 |
| San Miguel | 4,032,295 | 4,635,150 | 5,447,270 | 6,742,990 | 7,129,420 | 7,706 |
| Sedgwick | 11,249,870 | 12,970,688 | 13,273,730 | 9,985,115 | 10,372,865 | 11,116 |
| Summit | 4,318,657 | 4,481,396 | 4,616,006 | 4,501,909 | 4,522,946 | 5,240 |
| Teller | 4,454,330 | 5,038,070 | 5,674,560 | 7,004,030 | 6,860,590 | 6,931 |
| Washington | 13,423,906 | 15,921,474 | 17,244.308 | 23,503,472 | 25,859,305 | 27,254 |
| Weld | 90,347,020 | 102,130,907 | 105,179,350 | 106,102,390 | 110,485,890 | 113,711 |
| Yuma | 20,672,840 | 24,797,360 | 25,058,795 | 25,236,990 | 24,973,470 | 25,451 |
| State | $1,438,448,065 | $1,586,462,903 | $1,586,919,769 | $1,540,732,487 | $1,538,096,720 | $1,543,5 |

ACRES, VALUE PER ACRE AND TOTAL VALUE OF AGRICULTURAL LANDS AS RETURNED FOR ASSESSMENT IN COLORADO, 1913-1931, INCLUSIVE

| YEAR | Fruit Land | | | Irrigated Land | | | Natural Hay Land | | | Dry Farming Land | | | Grazing Land | | | Total Including Grazing Land | |
|---|---|---|---|---|---|---|---|---|---|---|---|---|---|---|---|---|---|
| | Acres | Value | Val. per Acre | Acres | Value | Val. Per Acre | Acres | Value | Val. per Acre | Acres | Value | Val. per Acre | Acres | Value | Val. per Acre | Acres | Value |
| 1913 | | | | | | | | | | | | | | | | | |
| 1914 | | | | | | | | | | | | | | | | | |
| 1915 | | | | | | | | | | | | | | | | | |
| 1916 | | | | | | | | | | | | | | | | | |
| 1917 | | | | | | | | | | | | | | | | | |
| 1918 | | | | | | | | | | | | | | | | | |
| 1919 | | | | | | | | | | | | | | | | | |
| 1920 | | | | | | | | | | | | | | | | | |
| 1921 | | | | | | | | | | | | | | | | | |
| 1922 | | | | | | | | | | | | | | | | | |
| 1923 | | | | | | | | | | | | | | | | | |
| 1924 | | | | | | | | | | | | | | | | | |
| 1925 | | | | | | | | | | | | | | | | | |
| 1926 | | | | | | | | | | | | | | | | | |
| 1927 | | | | | | | | | | | | | | | | | |
| 1928 | | | | | | | | | | | | | | | | | |
| 1929 | | | | | | | | | | | | | | | | | |
| 1930 | | | | | | | | | | | | | | | | | |
| 1931 | | | | | | | | | | | | | | | | | |

### 31 COUNTY TAX LEVIES, IN MILLS, FOR ALL COUNTY PURPOSES; TAX COLLECTED IN 1932

| COUNTY | General School | Roads and Bridges | Ordinary County, Including Poor and Contingent | Mothers' Compensation and Blind Benefits† | County Fair and Advertising‡ | Bonds, Interest and Registered Warrants | Building | Total |
|---|---|---|---|---|---|---|---|---|
| lams | 4.48 | 1.50 | 4.06 | .18 | --- | --- | --- | 10.22 |
| amosa | 5.00 | --- | 4.50 | .01 | .15 | .58 | .20 | 10.44 |
| apahoe | 5.00 | 1.45 | 3.90 | .12 | .14 | --- | --- | 10.61 |
| chuleta | 4.00 | 2.00 | 5.00 | .10 | --- | --- | --- | 11.10 |
| ca | 5.00 | 2.25 | 4.12 | --- | --- | .14 | --- | 11.51 |
| nt | 5.00 | 1.75 | 4.11 | .06 | .20 | 1.00 | --- | 12 12 |
| ulder | 4 00 | 1.78 | 3.00 | .12 | .10 | --- | --- | 9.00 |
| affee | 4.80 | --- | 7.50 | --- | --- | 2.20 | .80 | 15.30 |
| eyenne | 2.57 | --- | 2.76 | --- | --- | --- | --- | 5.33 |
| ear Creek | 4.10 | 2.10 | 8.20 | .10 | --- | 1.00 | --- | 15.50 |
| nejos | 5.00 | .50 | 6.10 | .05 | --- | 1.85 | --- | 13.50 |
| stilla | 5.00 | 1.50 | 10.00 | --- | --- | 3.50 | --- | 20.00 |
| owley | 4.00 | 1.00 | 2.80 | .10 | .10 | --- | --- | 8.00 |
| ster | 5.00 | 1.00 | 9.00 | --- | --- | --- | --- | 15.00 |
| lta | 5.00 | 5.45 | 6.15 | .27 | .15 | .28 | --- | 17.30 |
| nver | 2.44 | 2.41 | 4.39 | .12 | --- | --- | --- | 9.36 |
| lores | 5.00 | 4.90 | 9.50 | --- | .50 | 4.50 | --- | 24.40 |
| uglas | 3.40 | 2.35 | 3.75 | --- | --- | --- | --- | 9.50 |
| gle | 4.00 | 3.00 | 7.50 | .05 | --- | --- | 1.05 | 15.60 |
| bert | 5.00 | 3.00 | 2.68 | .13 | --- | --- | --- | 10.81 |
| Paso | 3.72 | .90 | 3.72 | .12 | --- | --- | --- | 8.46 |
| emont | 5.00 | 1.00 | 4.71 | --- | --- | --- | --- | 10.71 |
| rfield | 5.00 | 3.53 | 5.85 | .12 | .20 | 1.30 | --- | 16.00 |
| lpin | 3.50 | 3.50 | 8.50 | 4.00 | --- | 2.00 | --- | 21.50 |
| and | 3.00 | 1.60 | 5.00 | .03 | .20 | .25 | .50 | 10.58 |
| nnison | 2.21 | 1.00 | 3.82 | .13 | .10 | 3.70 | --- | 10.96 |
| nsdale | 5.00 | 2.00 | 11.00 | --- | --- | 4.14 | --- | 22.14 |
| erfano | 5.00 | 2.50 | 6.80 | --- | --- | 1.00 | --- | 15.30 |
| ckson | 2.00 | --- | 4.00 | --- | --- | .40 | --- | 6.40 |
| fferson | 4.90 | 2.90 | 4.21 | --- | --- | --- | --- | 12.01 |
| owa | 3.38 | --- | 4.00 | --- | .30 | --- | --- | 7.68 |
| t Carson | 5.00 | 2.00 | 4.02 | .07 | --- | --- | --- | 11.09 |
| ke | 3.90 | 2.88 | 8.00 | 2.28 | .15 | --- | --- | 17.21 |
| Plata | 5.00 | 3.75 | 5.22 | .10 | .20 | .70 | --- | 14.97 |
| rimer | 4.44 | 3.35 | 3.16 | .16 | .04 | 1.17 | --- | 12.32 |
| s Animas | 5.00 | 3.65 | 4.51 | .02 | .11 | --- | .01 | 13.30 |
| acoln | 5.00 | 1.00 | 4.23 | --- | --- | .44 | --- | 10.67 |
| gan | 5.00 | 1.56 | 3.18 | .12 | --- | .15 | --- | 10.01 |
| sa | 5.00 | 2.30 | 4.00 | .10 | --- | .60 | --- | 12.00 |
| neral | 3.50 | --- | 7.50 | .17 | --- | --- | --- | 11.17 |
| ffat | 5.00 | 3.00 | 6.00 | .20 | --- | 2.80 | --- | 17.00 |
| ntezuma | 5.00 | 3.00 | 8.30 | .05 | .27 | 2.51 | .50 | 19.63 |
| ntrose | 5.00 | 3.44 | 5.91 | .11 | --- | 1.92 | --- | 16.38 |
| rgan | 4.86 | 1.00 | 3.52 | .13 | --- | --- | --- | 9.51 |
| ero | 4.27 | 1.75 | 3.05 | .10 | .05 | --- | --- | 9.22 |
| ray | 4.00 | 2.00 | 5.80 | --- | .10 | 6.10 | .10 | 18.10 |
| rk | 3.00 | 1.00 | 5.30 | .10 | --- | --- | --- | 9.40 |
| illips | 4.00 | 1.25 | 3.23 | .08 | .10 | .24 | --- | 8.90 |
| kin | 4.00 | 1.00 | 5.88 | .12 | --- | 7.12 | --- | 18.12 |
| wers | 5.00 | 1.00 | 5.60 | .21 | .07 | --- | .02 | 11.90 |
| eblo | 4.73 | .75 | 3.51 | .20 | --- | --- | --- | 9.19 |
| Blanco | 5.00 | 2.20 | 5.60 | --- | .15 | --- | 1.11 | 14.06 |
| Grande | 5.00 | 1.00 | 5.00 | --- | --- | --- | --- | 6.50 |
| att | 5.00 | 2.50 | 3.80 | --- | .10 | 1.50 | --- | 12.90 |
| uache | 3.00 | 1.00 | 5.00 | --- | --- | --- | --- | 9.00 |
| Juan | 3.25 | 3.00 | 8.50 | .12 | --- | 1.70 | --- | 16.57 |
| Miguel | 5.00 | 2.50 | 8.01 | --- | .80 | 6.20 | --- | 22.51 |
| gwick | 3.86 | 2.50 | 3.20 | .16 | .90 | --- | --- | 10.62 |
| mit | 3.00 | 2.50 | 7.75 | .13 | --- | --- | --- | 13.38 |
| ler | 5.00 | --- | 8.00 | .10 | --- | 5.00 | --- | 18.10 |
| shington | 5.00 | 2.25 | 3.78 | .12 | --- | --- | --- | 11.15 |
| ld | 4.20 | 2.11 | 2.08 | .02 | --- | --- | --- | 8.41 |
| na | 5.00 | 1.50 | 2.65 | .10 | --- | --- | --- | 9.25 |
| tate Av | 3.84 | 1.36 | 4.19 | .12 | .03 | .31 | .02 | 9.87 |

†Revenue includes Old Age Pension in Gilpin and Lake Counties and advertising is included in linary County for Weld County.
‡Revenue for San Miguel County includes Rodent fund.

DETAILED ASSESSMENT FOR ALL COLORADO PROPERTY, 1912-1931, INCLUSIVE, BY CLASSES OF PROPERTY

(Assessments by County Assessors, Exclusive of Agricultural Land and Improvements)

| Year | Non-Ag. Land and Imp. | Mineral Land and Imp. | Town Lots and Improvements | Livestock, Poultry and Bees | Bicycles, Motorcycles, Automobiles, Planes | Bank Deposits | Ag. Imp., Tractors, Harness | Amount Invested in Mdse. | Capital in Manufacturing | All Other Property | Total Net Assessment by Assessors |
|---|---|---|---|---|---|---|---|---|---|---|---|
| 1912 | $2,630,95? | $25,957,136 | $168,979,728 | $18,004,084 | $2,051,141 | $ 9890 | $ 468,314 | $16,691,083 | $ 3,507,675 | $48,854,820 | $ 361,428,891 |
| 1913 | 5,946,033 | 6?54,447 | 366,684,421 | 52,677,676 | 4,364,644 | 2,068,865 | 3,143,115 | 39,039,676 | 10,769,114 | 75,339,545 | 859,743,039 |
| 1914 | 5,472,154 | 60,879,869 | 375,237,261 | 61,455,511 | 5,865,126 | 12,601,812 | 6,609,377 | 39,336,101 | 8,185,690 | 78,6?76 | 912,486,185 |
| 1915 | 5,053,479 | 5?29,297 | 374,735,282 | 72,682,153 | 7,978,314 | 11,130,408 | 7,433,882 | 40,666,917 | 12,048,092 | 78,055,300 | 936,284,863 |
| 1916 | 5,451,655 | 0,801,642 | 378,961,582 | 81,548,335 | 11,399,299 | 13,677,436 | 7,555,631 | 41,655,204 | 19,413,290 | 79,092,969 | 967,109,979 |
| 1917 | 7,274,740 | 60,241,450 | 370,415,144 | 93,174,264 | 17,549,202 | 18,305,192 | 9,872,963 | 55,139,090 | 25,214,748 | 92, 1?403 | *1,057,718,759 |
| 1918 | 7,466,631 | 59,279,676 | 381,243,444 | 114,622,555 | 26,831,349 | 20,993,169 | 9,872,712 | 79,846,131 | 29,341,520 | 109, 3?10 | 1,176,456,535 |
| 1919 | 7,760,066 | 55,506,510 | 385,779,834 | 114,571,936 | 32,291,605 | 16,845,540 | 12,189,286 | 92,462,521 | 31,936,595 | 29?71 | 1,263,435,529 |
| 1920 | 8,650,543 | 52,417,510 | 407,973,988 | 102,802,539 | 46,479,662 | 19,341,727 | 14,379,817 | 92,129,113 | 39,428,674 | 129,308,176 | 1,362,813,477 |
| 1921 | 8,776,117 | 51,040,844 | 418,796,292 | 68,921,432 | 51,112,260 | 8,217,902 | 14,077,186 | 87,361,814 | 41,037,125 | 95,580,457 | 1,361,837,539 |
| 1922 | 8,517,485 | 48,708,999 | 429,160,986 | 62,821,752 | 43,887,596 | 7,426,325 | 12,402,950 | 79,842,423 | 38,705,447 | 95, ?655 | 1,322,490,909 |
| 1923 | 8,258,774 | 50,426,361 | 446,281,329 | 55,741,929 | 41,108,338 | 3?78 | 10,570,140 | 79,756,623 | 37,350,254 | 95,777,622 | ?23 |
| 1924 | 7,515,499 | 49,337,483 | 462,432,766 | 48,859,346 | 43,361,435 | 8,560,386 | 9,880,861 | 80,238,703 | 39,702,880 | 91,015,179 | 1,312,730,329 |
| 1925 | 7,361,755 | 50,239,825 | 578,594,338 | 47,022,156 | 47,330,833 | 7,399,164 | 9,985,965 | 81,065,785 | 38,336,462 | 89,246,313 | 1,813,345,047 |
| 1926 | 7,013,614 | 49,242,857 | 503,718,773 | 46,406,718 | 46,035,357 | 9,262,190 | 10,190,859 | 76,264,162 | 36,716,344 | 82,902,047 | 1,320,890,766 |
| 1927 | 6,538,305 | 48,629,088 | 513,552,845 | 49,337,956 | 48,085,926 | 8,138,408 | 10,198,982 | 76,648,132 | 37,919,838 | 84,385,349 | 1,332,474,176 |
| 1928 | 6,220,581 | 47,313,344 | 526,006,389 | 57,129,404 | 47,576,260 | 14,281,445 | 10,467,523 | 77,131,541 | 37,390,163 | 83,413,727 | 1,334,532,680 |
| 1929 | 6,262,518 | 43,956,226 | 529,374,806 | 62,350,561 | 53,685,246 | 15,277,173 | 10,646,398 | 73,714,596 | 12,464,438 | 5?42 | 1,346,069,169 |
| 1930 | 5,949,43? | 42,988,351 | 532,111,032 | 55,726,631 | 50,642,770 | 18,049,516 | 11,341,646 | 74,751,964 | 13,495,823 | 163,095,621 | 1,333,377,923 |
| 1931 | 4,895,018 | 39,011,139 | 502,319,294 | 46,065,268 | 45,363,804 | 18,296,101 | 11,360,400 | 66,090,039 | 10,752,855 | 162,494,908 | ?,187,137,920 |
| Per Cent of increase or decrease, 1913 to 1931 | D. 17.68 | D. 37.24 | I. 36.99 | D. 12.57 | I. 939.12 | I. 784.35 | I. 261.44 | I. 69.29 | D. 0.15 | I. 115.68 | I. 38.08 |

*Includes $1,219,265 increase ordered by Tax Commission.

Note—Assessment prior to 1913 was on the basis of one-third of actual value. Commencing with 1913 a full cash value basis was used.

## ASSESSMENTS OF PUBLIC UTILITIES BY COLORADO TAX COMMISSION, 1912 TO 1931

| Year | RAILROADS | | | TELEPHONE LINES | | | TELEGRAPH LINES | | | All Other Property | Total by Tax Commission | Total Assessment Including County Assessors' |
|---|---|---|---|---|---|---|---|---|---|---|---|---|
| | Miles | Value | Val. Per Mile | Miles | Value | Val. Per Mile | Miles | Value | Val. Per Mile | | | |
| 1912 | 35.0 | $ 54,567,795 | $10,172 | 214,878 | $ 3,872,576 | $18.02 | 29, 0 | $ 0,110 | $31.15 | $ 1,665,128 | $ 61,011,609 | $ 422,440, 0 |
| 1913 | 5,655 | 174,774,505 | 30,906 | 247,283 | 10,842,640 | 43.85 | 28,252 | 1,507, 0 | 53.34 | 73,117,780 | 260,241,995 | 1,119,985,034 |
| 1914 | 5,814 | 179,460,890 | 30,867 | 253,524 | 10,842,490 | 42.77 | 28,304 | 1,495, 0 | 52.84 | 71,871, 0 | 263,669,985 | 1,176,156,170 |
| 1915 | 5.8 | 173,499,550 | 30,950 | 255,407 | 10,558,510 | 41.34 | 28,279 | 1,477,640 | 52.25 | 68,149, 0 | 253,685,650 | 1,189,970,513 |
| 1916 | 5,588 | 168,911,680 | 30,227 | 276,4 0 | 12,741, 0 | 46.08 | 28,008 | 1,607,850 | 57.41 | 59,190,084 | 242,451,164 | 1,209,561,143 |
| 1917 | 5,587 | 169,795,900 | 30,391 | 278,072 | 12,890,130 | 46.35 | 28,055 | 2, 6,320 | 73. 0 | 62,830,300 | 247,567,650 | 1, 6,286,409 |
| 1918 | 5,542 | 169,086,470 | 30,510 | 28 5,04 | 12,666,340 | 44.3 | 26,114 | 2,184,780 | 83.66 | 61,719,150 | 245,656,740 | 1,422,113,275 |
| 1919 | 5,500 | 165,833,130 | 30,151 | 307,613 | 12,722,800 | 41.36 | 26,916 | 2,221,400 | 82.53 | 50,999, 0 | 231,777,130 | 1,495,213,659 |
| 1920 | 5,406 | 161,6 7, 0 | 29,907 | 2 851 | 12,976,670 | 24.94 | 25,456 | 2, 6,850 | . 0 | 50,408,880 | 227,454,190 | 1, 6,267,567 |
| 1921 | 5,327 | 160,314, 0 | 30,094 | 321,374 | 13,214,700 | 41.12 | 26,020 | 2,431,240 | 93.44 | 50,468,340 | 226,418,960 | 1,578,256,499 |
| 1922 | 5,164 | 160,487,520 | 31,078 | 33,567 | 13,332,880 | 9.95 | 26,809 | 2, 6,820 | 89.03 | 49,919,450 | 226,126,970 | 1,548,617,879 |
| 1923 | 50 | 160,693,730 | 31,589 | 13,700 | 13,544,500 | 36.44 | 27,724 | 2,484,100 | 89.60 | 51,244,150 | 227,966,480 | 1,543,589, 0 |
| 1924 | 5,459 | 160,6 950 | 29,432 | 64,136 | 13,879,710 | 33.35 | 26,971 | 2, 6,740 | 92.91 | 5, 704,760 | 227,770,150 | 1,540, 6,479 |
| 1925 | 5,045 | 160,404,460 | 32,516 | 14,231 | 13,945,600 | 3. 0 | 28,113 | 2,479, 0 | 88.18 | 50,565,380 | 227,387,440 | 1,540,732,487 |
| 1926 | 50 | 158,898,470 | 31,552 | 469,564 | 14,146,180 | 30.12 | 28,283 | 2,634,790 | 93.16 | 50,259,840 | 225,939,280 | 1,546,830,046 |
| 1927 | 4,826 | 164,118,640 | 34,007 | 34,000 | 14,313,420 | 29.03 | 28, 0 | 2,669,170 | 94.30 | 51,715,260 | 232,816,490 | 1, 6,290,666 |
| 1928 | 4,995 | 161,387,910 | 32,309 | 490,555 | 14,499,940 | 29.56 | 27,852 | 2, 6, 0 | 4. 0 | 54,499,920 | 233,027,700 | 1,577, 6, 0 |
| 1929 | 4,992 | 165,567,770 | 33,168 | 74,453 | 15, 76,400 | 35.00 | 27,931 | 2,658, 0 | 95.18 | 56,949,040 | 240,851,600 | 1,586,919,769 |
| 1930 | 4,961 | 172,658,060 | 34, 0 | 478,850 | 16,686,810 | 34.85 | 27,394 | 2,678, 0 | 97.78 | 61,061,430 | 253,084,980 | 1,586,462, 0 |
| 1931 | 4,973 | 170,411,240 | 34,267 | 504,175 | 17,279,370 | 34.27 | 29,217 | 2, 6,430 | 87.60 | 61,060,105 | 251,310,145 | 1,438,448, 0 |
| Per cent of increase or decrease, 1913 to 1931 | D.12.06 | D.2.56 | I.10.87 | I.103.89 | I.59.36 | D.21.85 | I.3.42 | I.69.83 | I.64.23 | D.16.49 | D.3.43 | I.28.43 |

Note—Assessment prior to 1913 was on the basis of one-third of actual value. Commencing with 1913 a full cash value basis was used.

## COMPARISON OF INCREASES OR DECREASES IN ASSESSMENTS, 1913 AND 1931

| Classes of Property | Acres or Miles Per Cent | | Total Value Per Cent | | Av. Value Per Acre or Per Mile Per Cent | |
|---|---|---|---|---|---|---|
| | Increase | Decrease | Increase | Decrease | Increase | Decrease |
| **Assessments by Assessors** | | | | | | |
| Fruit Land | ---- | 12.77 | ---- | 60.83 | ---- | 55.31 |
| Irrigated Land | ---- | 6.47 | ---- | 2.51 | 4.25 | ---- |
| Natural Hay Land | 238.59 | ---- | 171.88 | ---- | ---- | 19.71 |
| Dry Farming Land | 242.34 | ---- | 270.33 | ---- | 8.23 | ---- |
| Grazing Land | 52.79 | ---- | 8.92 | ---- | ---- | 28.68 |
| Total Lands | 79.41 | ---- | 135.45 | ---- | ---- | 24.45 |
| Non-Ag. Land and Improvements | ---- | ---- | ---- | 17.68 | ---- | ---- |
| Mineral Land and Improvements | ---- | ---- | ---- | 37.24 | ---- | ---- |
| Town Lots and Improvements | ---- | ---- | 36.99 | ---- | ---- | ---- |
| Livestock, Poultry and Bees | ---- | ---- | ---- | 12.57 | ---- | ---- |
| All Motor Vehicles | ---- | ---- | 939.12 | ---- | ---- | ---- |
| Bank Deposits | ---- | ---- | 784.35 | ---- | ---- | ---- |
| Agricultural Implements | ---- | ---- | 261.44 | ---- | ---- | ---- |
| Money in Merchandise | ---- | ---- | 69.29 | ---- | ---- | ---- |
| Capital in Manufacturing | ---- | ---- | ---- | 0.15 | ---- | ---- |
| All Other Property | ---- | ---- | 115 68 | ---- | ---- | ---- |
| Total by Assessors | ---- | ---- | 38.08 | ---- | ---- | ---- |
| **Assessments by Tax Commission** | | | | | | |
| Railroads | ---- | 12.06 | ---- | 2.56 | 10.87 | ---- |
| Telephone Lines | 103.89 | ---- | 59.36 | ---- | 21.85 | 21.85 |
| Telegraph Lines | 3.42 | ---- | 69.83 | ---- | 64.23 | ---- |
| All Other Property | ---- | ---- | ---- | 16.49 | ---- | ---- |
| Total by Tax Commission | ---- | ---- | ---- | 3.43 | ---- | ---- |
| Total Assessment for State | ---- | ---- | 28.43 | ---- | ---- | ---- |

## DISTRIBUTION OF STATE LEVY, AND ESTIMATED RECEIPTS THEREFROM, 1912-1931, INCLUSIVE

| | General State | | State University | | Agricultural Coll. | | School of Mines | |
|---|---|---|---|---|---|---|---|---|
| | Levy, Mills | Revenue | Levy, Mills | Revenue | Levy, Mills | Revenue | Levy, Mills | Revenue |
| 1912 | 2.30950 | $ 975,380 | 0.40000 | $ 168,923 | 0.20000 | $ 84,466 | 0.20000 | $ 84,466 |
| 1913 | 0.71920 | 939,623 | 0.13650 | 178,264 | 0.06820 | 89,132 | 0.06820 | 89,132 |
| 1914 | 0.75220 | 985,059 | 0.14275 | 186,942 | 0.07138 | 93,471 | 0.06800 | 89,050 |
| 1915 | 0.73000 | 911,887 | 0.20450 | 255,386 | 0.14480 | 180,928 | 0.07150 | 89,263 |
| 1916 | 0.70000 | 848,159 | 0.20450 | 247,719 | 0.14480 | 175,497 | 0.07150 | 86,588 |
| 1917 | 0.80230 | 1,047,218 | 0.39170 | 511,385 | 0.30340 | 396,011 | 0.08840 | 115,374 |
| 1918 | 0.74500 | 1,059,745 | 0.38660 | 549,788 | 0.30150 | 428,767 | 0.08270 | 117,609 |
| 1919 | 0.86540 | 1,294,017 | 0.38660 | 578,050 | 0.28650 | 428,379 | 0.08270 | 123,654 |
| 1920 | 0.85720 | 1,363,177 | 0.38360 | 607,800 | 0.28430 | 450,444 | 0.08180 | 130,084 |
| 1921 | 0.89310 | 1,409,463 | 0.74770 | 1,179,496 | 0.42440 | 670,784 | 0.13290 | 209,798 |
| 1922 | 0.91840 | 1,422,188 | 0.74770 | 1,157,338 | 0.42440 | 658,194 | 0.13290 | 205,858 |
| 1923 | 0.88520 | 1,366,081 | 0.59770 | 922,380 | 0.41780 | 644,768 | 0.13290 | 205,139 |
| 1924 | 0.65570 | 1,010,137 | 0.59770 | 920,757 | 0.42530 | 655,292 | 0.13290 | 204,779 |
| 1925 | 0.64950 | 1,000,706 | 0.59770 | 920,895 | 0.41780 | 643,733 | 0.13290 | 204,810 |
| 1926 | 0.53016 | 820,047 | 0.60324 | 933,086 | 0.42004 | 649,716 | 0.13842 | 214,107 |
| 1927 | 0.65082 | 1,018,723 | 0.61989 | 970,308 | 0.38132 | 596,877 | 0.17534 | 274,458 |
| 1928 | 0.52892 | 834,403 | 0.61989 | 977,914 | 0.38132 | 601,555 | 0.17534 | 276,609 |
| 1929 | 1.02672 | 1,629,240 | 0.61989 | 983,666 | 0.38132 | 605,094 | 0.17534 | 278,236 |
| 1930 | 1.04172 | 1,652,650 | 0.61989 | 983,433 | 0.38132 | 604,950 | 0.17534 | 278,170 |
| 1931 | 0.94172 | 1,354,615 | 0.61989 | 891,680 | 0.38132 | 548,509 | 0.17534 | 252,217 |

Note.—General State includes ordinary governmental costs and the cost of maintenance and operation of the Capitol buildings. State University includes the university and Colorado General hospital. Agricultural College includes the college, the experiment station and Fort Lewis school. School of Mines includes the experiment station. All building levies for the educational institutions are included with maintenance and operation levies, but some of them have special funds not included in the ordinary state levy and hence not included here.

DISTRIBUTION OF STATE LEVY, AND ESTIMATED RECEIPTS THEREFROM, 1912-1931,
INCLUSIVE—Continued

| | Teachers College | | Western State Coll. | | Insane Hospital | | Deaf & Blind School | |
|---|---|---|---|---|---|---|---|---|
| | Levy, Mills | Revenue | Levy, Mills | Revenue | Levy, Mills | Revenue | Levy, Mills | Revenue |
| 1912 | 0.20000 | $  84,466 | ------ | ------- | 0.20000 | $ 84,466 | 0.20000 | $  84,466 |
| 1913 | 0.06820 | 89,132 | ------ | ------- | 0.06820 | 89,132 | 0.06820 | 89,132 |
| 1914 | 0.07138 | 93,471 | ------ | ------- | 0.07138 | 93,471 | 0.07138 | 93,471 |
| 1915 | 0.10230 | 127,838 | 0.03000 | $ 37,476 | 0.07480 | 93,485 | 0.10230 | 127,838 |
| 1916 | 0.10230 | 124,000 | 0.03000 | 36,351 | 0.07480 | 90,679 | 0.10230 | 124,000 |
| 1917 | 0.19590 | 255,692 | 0.06500 | 84,843 | 0.27300 | 356,278 | 0.10040 | 131,116 |
| 1918 | 0.19400 | 275,890 | 0.06500 | 92,438 | 0.26600 | 378,282 | 0.09400 | 133,679 |
| 1919 | 0.19400 | 290,072 | 0.08000 | 119,617 | 0.26600 | 397,727 | 0.09400 | 140,550 |
| 1920 | 0.19250 | 305,013 | 0.07600 | 125,868 | 0.26300 | 418,240 | 0.09300 | 147,895 |
| 1921 | 0.27190 | 433,656 | 0.10280 | 162,107 | 0.26530 | 418,711 | 0.13820 | 218,115 |
| 1922 | 0.27490 | 425,515 | 0.10280 | 159,063 | 0.26530 | 410,848 | 0.13820 | 214,019 |
| 1923 | 0.27500 | 424,305 | 0.09530 | 147,037 | 0.26530 | 409,414 | 0.13820 | 213,272 |
| 1924 | 0.27500 | 423,561 | 0.09530 | 146,777 | 0.26530 | 408,695 | 0.13820 | 212,897 |
| 1925 | 0.27500 | 423,624 | 0.11030 | 169,912 | 0.26530 | 408,756 | 0.13820 | 212,929 |
| 1926 | 0.27702 | 428,493 | 0.10285 | 159,088 | 0.26822 | 414,881 | 0.14022 | 216,891 |
| 1927 | 0.26042 | 407,633 | 0.10044 | 157,218 | 0.26822 | 419,842 | 0.14022 | 219,485 |
| 1928 | 0.26042 | 410,828 | 0.10044 | 158,450 | 0.26822 | 423,133 | 0.14022 | 221,206 |
| 1929 | 0.26042 | 413,245 | 0.12544 | 199,053 | 0.26822 | 425,622 | 0.14022 | 222,507 |
| 1930 | 0.26042 | 413,147 | 0.12544 | 199,006 | 0.26822 | 425,521 | 0.14022 | 222,454 |
| 1931 | 0.26042 | 374,601 | 0.10044 | 144,478 | 0.26822 | 385,821 | 0.14022 | 201,699 |

DISTRIBUTION OF STATE LEVY, AND ESTIMATED RECEIPTS THEREFROM, 1912-1931,
INCLUSIVE—Continued

| | Bonds and Interest | | Highways | | Miscellaneous | | State Totals | |
|---|---|---|---|---|---|---|---|---|
| | Levy, Mills | Revenue | Levy, Mills | Revenue | Levy, Mills | Revenue | Total Levy | Total Revenue |
| 1912 | 0.27940 | $ 117,984 | ------ | ------- | 0.06670 | $ 28,155 | 4.0556 | $1,712,772 |
| 1913 | 0.08290 | 108,300 | ------ | ------- | 0.02040 | 26,600 | 1.3000 | 1,698,447 |
| 1914 | 0.12125 | 158,794 | ------ | ------- | 0.02028 | 26,558 | 1.3900 | 1,820,287 |
| 1915 | 0.11950 | 149,280 | 0.5000 | $ 624,600 | 0.02030 | 25,334 | 2.1000 | 2,623,320 |
| 1916 | 0.11950 | 144,797 | 0.5000 | 605,849 | 0.02030 | 24,573 | 2.0700 | 2,508,212 |
| 1917 | 0.11950 | 155,981 | 0.5000 | 652,643 | 0.28040 | 365,951 | 3.1200 | 4,072,492 |
| 1918 | 0.10650 | 151,455 | 0.5000 | 711,057 | 0.02870 | 40,815 | 2.7700 | 3,939,525 |
| 1919 | 0.09800 | 146,531 | 1.0000 | 1,495,214 | 0.11680 | 174,581 | 3.4700 | 5,188,392 |
| 1920 | 0.11990 | 190,673 | 0.9886 | 1,572,139 | 0.13010 | 206,895 | 3.4700 | 5,518,228 |
| 1921 | 0.23180 | 365,807 | 0.9973 | 1,573,932 | 0.14160 | 223,544 | 4.3500 | 6,865,413 |
| 1922 | 0.27500 | 425,870 | 0.9973 | 1,544,375 | 0.20310 | 314,540 | 4.4800 | 6,937,808 |
| 1923 | 0.39800 | 614,198 | 0.5000 | 771,606 | 0.22460 | 346,620 | 3.9300 | 6,064,820 |
| 1924 | 0.39400 | 606,958 | 0.5000 | 770,250 | 0.22060 | 339,850 | 3.7000 | 5,699,953 |
| 1925 | 0.38600 | 594,723 | 0.5000 | 770,366 | 0.22730 | 350,255 | 3.7000 | 5,700,709 |
| 1926 | 0.54600 | 844,549 | 0.5000 | 773,396 | 0.14380 | 222,475 | 3.6700 | 5,676,729 |
| 1927 | 0.54000 | 845,257 | 0.5000 | 782,645 | 0.20330 | 318,271 | 3.8400 | 6,010,717 |
| 1928 | 0.40190 | 634,021 | 0.5000 | 788,780 | 0.18330 | 289,214 | 3.5600 | 5,616,113 |
| 1929 | 0.38410 | 609,505 | ------ | ------- | 0.27830 | 441,665 | 3.6600 | 5,807,833 |
| 1930 | 0.39410 | 625,225 | ------ | ------- | 0.18333 | 290,846 | 3.5900 | 5,695,402 |
| 1931 | 0.41910 | 602,854 | ------ | ------- | 0.18333 | 263,710 | 3.4900 | 5,020,184 |

Note—The Miscellaneous column contains levies for stock inspection, 0.03333; war and other military uses, 0.07; the state fair tax, 0.03; Adams State Normal, 0.05.

## INHERITANCE TAXES

The thirteenth general assembly of the Colorado legislature enacted a law in 1901 as a part of the revenue act, providing for the imposition of a tax on transfers of property by inheritance through will or gift, or instrument made in contemplation of death, or intended to take effect at or after the death of the maker thereof. This law, which was approved by Governor James B. Orman on April 5, 1901, was declared unconstitutional by the state supreme court. The law was re-enacted, with changes, at an extra session of the legislature and the new act was approved on March 22, 1902. The law of 1921 was re-enacted with a considerable number of changes in 1927 and went into effect July 4, 1927, its rates and requirements applying only to estates of persons dying on or after that date.

The administration of the law is vested in an inheritance tax commissioner appointed by the attorney general, as an assistant attorney general, charged with the special duty of representing him in all matters connected with the administration and enforcement of the provisions of the law. The commissioner holds office at the pleasure of the attorney general.

The law is complicated and cannot be reviewed in detail here. It divides beneficiaries into five classes. Class A includes the father, mother, husband, wife, child, or any lineal descendant. The law allows exemptions of $20,000 for widows and $10,000 for all others in this class. The tax amounts to two per cent above the exemptions up to $50,000 and from four to seven and one-half per cent for amounts above that sum. Class B includes the wife or widow of son, husband or widower of daughter, grandparent, brother, sister and mutually acknowledged child. The exemptions in this class amount to $2,000 and the tax ranges from three to 10 per cent on amounts above the exemption. Class C includes uncle, aunt, niece, nephew, or lineal descendant of same. There is no exemption in this class, but there is no tax on $500, or less, and the tax rate ranges from four per cent up to 14 per cent. Class D includes strangers and all others not exempt. There is no exemption and no tax on $500 or less. The rate for Class D ranges from seven to 16 per cent.

Inheritance taxes go into the general state fund and are a part of the general revenues of the state.

Collections by years ending November 30, as reported by the inheritance tax commissioner, are as follows:

| Year | Amount |
|---|---|
| 1921 | $ 500,476.52 |
| 1922 | 512,687.63 |
| 1923 | 703,730.82 |
| 1924 | 864,161.04 |
| 1925 | 911,210.88 |
| 1926 | 876,008.95 |
| 1927 | 674,685.20 |
| 1928 | 869,407.88 |
| 1929 | 938,609.40 |
| 1930 | 1,126,377.20 |
| 1931 | 782,570.43 |

## Taxable and Non-Taxable Property

THE actual value of all property in Colorado, taxable and non-taxable, cannot be determined with any great degree of accuracy, but by using the best figures available from all sources of information a fairly reliable estimate of all wealth may be obtained. This estimate gives a total value of at least $2,679,794,177, of which $1,-438,448,065 is the assessed value of property on the tax rolls of the state in 1931, as reported by the state tax commission, and $1,241,346,112 is the estimated value of property not assessed for the payment of taxes. The taxable property comprises 53.7 per cent of the total and the non-taxable property 46.3 per cent. The per capita value, based on the population in 1930, is $2,587.19, of which $1,388.74 per capita is for taxable property and $1,198.45 for non-taxable property. An estimate compiled on the same basis in 1931 gave a total of $2,855,175,481 for all property, of which $1,586,462,903 was the assessed value of property taxed and $1,268,712,578 was the estimated value of non-taxable property. Adjustments due to changes in conditions and values showed a decrease of $205,381,304 in the total in 1932 as compared with 1931. Of this amount $148,014,838 is credited to reductions in the assessed value of property on the tax rolls and $26,366,466 to adjustments in the value of exempt property.

The value of these figures lies principally in their indication of the relative position of taxable and non-taxable property, and they are not intended to establish the total wealth of

the state. In order to arrive at the total wealth, adjustments would be necessary. Property on the tax rolls, for instance, while theoretically assessed at full value, would have to be revised upward to reflect the real value, as it is safe to assume that the assessed value does not exceed 60 per cent of the actual value. Bank deposits in the state on December 31, 1930, for example, aggregated $209,991,122, but only $18,049,516 in bank deposits actually was assessed in 1930. Also, taxes are not collected on all the property assessed, as the law allows $200 exemption on the personal property of heads of families. There were 268,531 families in the state in 1930, according to the census and, assuming that all were assessed, the exemption would amount to $53,706,200.

The department of commerce does attempt to adjust values to determine the total wealth of the country and its figures are given consideration in another chapter in this volume on "Colorado's Total Wealth."

The figures show that almost one-half of all the property in the state is not assessed for taxes through the customary channels for collecting revenue. However, a considerable portion of the non-taxable property does render some return to the state in an indirect manner, such as the national forests and federal mineral lands, portions of the revenue from the same either being spent in the state or remitted direct to the state.

The following table, made up from various sources explained in the text, gives the estimated value of the non-taxable property of the state:

| Class of Property | Est. Val. |
|---|---|
| Federal property: | |
| Unappropriated land..... $ | 11,485,710 |
| Government land filed upon but not patented...... | 3,197,206 |
| National forests........ | 70,000,000 |
| Reclamation projects.... | 11,000,000 |
| Coal lands.............. | 523,450,000 |
| Indian property......... | 3,544,917 |
| Shale land.............. | 25,430,000 |
| Oil reserves............. | 2,173,040 |
| Government buildings.... | 21,389,487 |
| National parks and monuments .......... | 1,500,000 |
| Power, water and reservoir reserves.......... | 25,000,000 |
| Total federal.......... $ | 698,170,360 |
| State and local public property : | |
| State property.......... $ | 230,076,103 |
| Municipal property...... | 80,000,000 |
| County property......... | 8,932,000 |
| Public schools.......... | 63,615,455 |
| Total public.......... $ | 382,623,558 |

| Class of Property | Est. Val. |
|---|---|
| Private property: | |
| Colleges and universities (private) ........... $ | 10,905,738 |
| Churches and rectories.. | 26,646,456 |
| Hospitals .............. | 12,000,000 |
| Cemeteries ............ | 2,000,000 |
| Irrigation works........ | 90,000,000 |
| County fair associations. | 1,000,000 |
| Fraternal organizations.. | 10,000,000 |
| Charity organizations.... | 3,000,000 |
| Miscellaneous ......... | 5,000,000 |
| Total private........ $ | 160,552,194 |
| Total exempt........... | $1,241,346,112 |
| Taxable (assessed val.).. | 1,438,448,065 |
| Grand total all property. | $2,679,794,177 |

Unappropriated government land and land filed on but not yet patented are estimated at $1.50 per acre.

The national forests include 13,-323,566 acres. The estimate of value is arrived at by using a flat price of a little more than $5 per acre. Estimates based on stumpage value of timber sold and capitalization of returns yield approximately the same total. While the national forests are not taxable, they yield considerable revenue to the state, the total expended in 1931 being $1,667,457, of which $1,013,564 was appropriated by congress. Twenty-five per cent of the gross revenues from the forests goes to the counties in which the forests are located in the form of cash for roads and school purposes, and 10 per cent goes on roads and trails in the forests, while the counties also benefit from road funds appropriated by congress.

The federal reclamation projects and their irrigation works yield no direct return to the state in the form of taxes, but indirectly they increase the taxes on private property coming within the districts by creating a greater taxable value for them. The estimates on these two items are based on their costs, which are more fully reported in another place in this volume under the heading, "United States Reclamation Projects."

The United States geological survey has appraised Colorado coal land at $100 to $400 per acre, based on the extent of the deposits and their accessibility to markets, while the state land board appraises coal land at a little more than $200 an acre. The estimate in the above table is made on a basis of $100 an acre, giving cognizance to changed conditions resulting from the more widespread use of natural gas and fuel oil, and there is included 2,142,200 acres of withdrawn coal land and 3,092,300 acres of the public domain classified as coal land but not withdrawn from entry.

The value of Indian property, both tribal and individual, is taken from the annual report of the commissioner for Indian affairs for the fiscal year 1927. Oil land reserves are estimated at $10 per acre and shale land at $25 per acre, including the withdrawn areas and 952,239 acres classified as shale land but not withdrawn. The government returns to the state 37½ per cent of revenue received in the form of bonuses and royalties from the leasing of these lands.

The federal government buildings include not only the Denver postoffice, custom house, mint, Fort Logan army post and Fitzsimons general hospital, but postoffices in various towns of the state. Their value is based on cost. In many instances, the sites were donated in whole or in part, and their present true value is in excess of the figure used. This item comprises property valued at $7,089,487 under the jurisdiction of the treasury department and $14,300,000 under the army, veterans' bureau and other departments, but does not include $1,860,000 of government-owned property used by the national guard. The value of buildings other than those under the jurisdiction of the treasury department shows a decrease of $3,000,000 from last year, due to revised figures on the veterans' hospital at Fort Lyon.

The value of state property is that shown by an inventory as of 1930, details of which are available in a table published elsewhere in this volume.

The estimate on municipal property is based on the census of 1913, plus 100 per cent for increase in value in 18 years. When it is recalled that Denver alone had added nearly one-half of the total increase through the purchase of its own water system, the estimate may be considered conservative. The census bureau reported a total value of $53,389,144 for municipal property owned in 1928 by Denver, Colorado Springs and Pueblo, or two-thirds of the total used in the above estimate.

The value of county property is based on a 100 per cent increase over the 1913 census figures, several of the counties having built court houses in the interval, which will justify the estimate.

The value of public school property is taken from the report of the state superintendent of public instruction for 1931.

The value given to colleges and universities in the above table includes only the seven privately controlled institutions reporting to the United States bureau of education in 1928 and is for land, buildings and equipment valued at $5,680,123 and productive funds to the amount of $5,225,615. Parochial and several other privately controlled institutions are not included in this total.

The state colleges and universities are included in the value of state property. The value of church property and rectories is that given by the census bureau for 1926 plus an average for the 57 churches not reporting.

Property of fraternal organizations includes only those portions not taxed. Buildings owned by Masonic, Elks, Woodmen and other organizations are not taxed except for those portions used for income purposes. Under this heading are included such institutions as the Printers' home and the Woodmen of the World sanitarium at Colorado Springs, Masonic temples, buildings of the Young Men's Christian association, etc.

# Mineral Resources

COLORADO has produced annually in the 25 years ending with 1929 an average of $62,639,877 in minerals, including both metals and non-metals. The maximum output during that period was in 1917, when war demands and high prices established a record of $80,296,218. The minimum production in value during the 25 years was in 1914, when the output was $52,522,-416. Figures have never been compiled and are not available showing the value of the production of all minerals since the industry was first established, but from such records as have been kept, the total is estimated at not far short of three billion dollars. Reliable data on the seven principal minerals, including five metals, show that the output of these from the beginning down to the end of 1931 (some of the figures for the last year being preliminary) was $2,419,005,276. The values making up this total, as reported by various agencies, are distributed as follows:

| | |
|---|---:|
| Coal ...................... $ | 729,816,680 |
| Gold ...................... | 720,245,420 |
| Silver ................... | 519,126,832 |
| Lead ..................... | 217,578,011 |
| Zinc ..................... | 156,992,432 |
| Copper ................... | 47,050,242 |
| Petroleum ................ | 28,195,659 |
| | |
| Total .................. | $2,419,005,276 |

On the basis of industries canvassed for 1929 by the bureau of the census Colorado ranked 15th among the states in value of mineral products and 12th in number of wage earners employed in mining and quarrying industries. Since the scope of the censuses for 1919 and 1929 was not the same as to the industries covered, comparisons as to the magnitude of the mining and quarrying industries cannot be made directly between the statistics for the two years; but by revision of the figures to exclude data for all industries not canvassed at both censuses, comparison of the activities of the remaining industries is made possible. On this basis the value of products in 1929 was $41,208,031, compared with $51,063,444 in 1919, a decrease of 19.3 per cent. This decrease is accounted for principally in the gold and silver mining industries. Comparative figures for gold and silver (lode) industries in 1929 and 1919 show decreases of 72.2 per cent in the number of enterprises; 52.8 per cent in the average number of wage earners; 46 per cent in salaries; 53.9 per cent in wages and 74 per cent in the value of products. A table is published herewith showing a summary of operations in 1929 and 1919, with adjusted figures for 1929 for comparative purposes. Another table gives detailed statistics for selected industries. In none of the tables presented are statistics for non-producing (development only) enterprises given. A summary of these is as follows:

| | 1929 |
|---|---:|
| Number of enterprises........ | 117 |
| Number of mines and quarries. | 123 |
| Wage earners (average)....... | 537 |
| Power equipment (total horsepower) .................. | 7,610 |
| Principal expenses: | |
| Salaries .................... | $146,845 |
| Wages ...................... | 699,931 |
| Contract work.............. | 77,450 |
| Supplies, fuel and purchased electric energy .......... | 363,068 |
| Expenditures for development (included in above).......... | 1,158,744 |

Colorado occupies a unique position among the states of the Union in the variety and extent of its mineral resources, both metal and non-metal. This is due largely to the extreme irregularity of the state's surface and the wide range of geological formations exposed for examination

and development. Approximately 250 useful metallic and non-metallic minerals and compounds have been reported in the state, and undoubtedly numerous others are yet to be found. Up to the present time approximately 30 metals have been produced in commercial quantities, of which gold, silver, copper, lead and zinc are the most important. The range of useful non-metals found in Colorado is almost as wide as that of the metals, but their production has not been so extensive, with the exception of coal, until recent years. Beginning with 1918, production of minerals other than gold, silver, copper, lead and zinc has been in excess of the combined output of these five principal metals in value.

Colorado's relative position among the states in the mining industry is indicated by the following table:

| Resource | Rank |
|---|---:|
| Coal (reserves)..................... | 1 |
| Molybdenum (value, 1929).......... | 1 |
| Uranium and vanadium ores (value, 1929) ........................... | 1 |
| Tungsten ore (value, 1929)......... | 2 |
| FluorSpar (value, 1929)............ | 3 |
| Arsenious oxides (value, 1929)...... | 3 |
| Manganiferous ores (quantity, 1929) | 4 |
| Gold (value, 1929)................. | 5 |
| Silver (value, 1929)................ | 6 |
| Coal (value, 1929)................. | 8 |
| Copper (pounds, 1929).............. | 10 |
| Coke (tons, 1929).................. | 14 |
| Petroleum (barrels, 1929)........... | 16 |
| Natural gas (cu. ft., 1929).......... | 17 |
| Clay products (value, 1929)........ | 20 |
| All minerals (value, 1925)......... | 22 |
| All minerals (value, 1928)......... | 20 |
| All minerals (value, 1929)......... | 21 |
| Lime (value, 1929).................. | 28 |

The director of the United States mint in his annual report gives the estimated value of the world's production of gold since Columbus discovered America in 1492 at $21,940,679,-253. Colorado's output from 1858 to 1930, inclusive, amounted to $715,-747,032, or 3.3 per cent of the world's production over a period of 438 years. The same authority gives the value of silver production since the discovery of America at $19,364,192,748. Colorado produced in 72 years silver valued at $518,525,201, or 2.7 per cent of the world's supply since 1492.

The capital invested in mining in Colorado is estimated at $150,000,000. The bureau of the census reported for 1930 a total of 17,488 persons engaged in the extraction of minerals. The occupation statistics include all persons who usually follow a gainful occupation without regard to whether they were employed at the time the census was taken. The distribution of these workers is as follows:

Operators ........................ 505
Managers and officials........... 399
Foremen and overseers........... 386
Inspectors ....................... 90
Coal-mine operatives.............10,134
Copper-mine operatives........... 27
Gold and silver-mine operatives... 2,538
Iron-mine operatives............. 25
Lead and zinc-mine operatives.... 358
Other specified mine operatives... 583
Not specified mine peratives..... 1,731
Quarry operatives................ 380
Oil and gas-well operatives....... 331
Salt-Well and works operatives... 1

Total........................17,488

The United States bureau of mines reported 313 lode and 21 placer mines operating in the state in 1930. The state coal mine inspector reported 318 coal mines operated in 1931. There were 213 oil wells being produced in the state on January 1, 1931. Colorado's output of minerals in 1929 was equal in value to 1.07 per cent of the value of all minerals produced in the country, including Alaska.

A table published herewith shows the value of all minerals produced in Colorado by years from 1905 to 1929, inclusive. Production by states was not segregated prior to 1905. The table gives the value each year of the output of gold, silver, copper, lead and zinc, and of all other minerals, with the percentages of the totals. It shows that in 1905 minerals other than the five principal metals yielded only 24.6 per cent of the total value of all mineral production in that year and 72.4 per cent of the total in 1929. On the contrary, the five principal metals supplied 75.4 per cent of the total in 1905 and only 27.6 per cent in 1929. This indicates that while metal mining as a whole declined in the 25-year period, the output of other minerals increased and made up for the decrease. A readjustment in mining, rather than a decrease, is apparent. A chart illustrating these changes is published herewith. It will be noted that there was a distinct upward movement in the five principal metals and other minerals in the war period of 1915-1918, inclusive. This was an abnormal period, in which production values were affected by market prices, and in order to illustrate the effect of one on the other a table of average prices for the period appears below.

There is also published on page 228 a table giving mineral production of the state in 1925 to 1929, inclusive, the latest figures in that form available. Duplications are eliminated in this table. An examination of its various items discloses a long list of minerals which are rarely considered in that

classification by the public. Clay products, for instance, account for $3,117,-000, natural gas for nearly three-quarters of a million dollars, stone for nearly $1,000,000, and many others of the less widely known minerals—such as fluorspar, lime, manganese ores, molybdenum, tungsten, uranium and vanadium, marble, basalt and sand and gravel—add largely to the total of values taken from the ground in Colorado. While many of these are not reported separately, to avoid disclosing individual operations, their total value is impressive.

Average prices per ounce for silver and per pound for copper, lead and zinc in Colorado in the years 1905 to 1930, inclusive, as reported by the United States bureau of mines, were as follows:

| Year | Silver | Copper | Lead | Zinc |
|------|--------|--------|------|------|
| 1905..... | $0.61 | $0.156 | $0.047 | $0.059 |
| 1906..... | .68 | .193 | .057 | .061 |
| 1907..... | .66 | .20 | .053 | .059 |
| 1908..... | .53 | .132 | .042 | .047 |
| 1909..... | .52 | .13 | .043 | .054 |
| 1910..... | .54 | .127 | .044 | .054 |
| 1911..... | .53 | .125 | .045 | .057 |
| 1912..... | .615 | .165 | .045 | .069 |
| 1913..... | .604 | .155 | .044 | .056 |
| 1914..... | .553 | .133 | .039 | .051 |
| 1915..... | .507 | .175 | .047 | .124 |
| 1916..... | .658 | .246 | .069 | .134 |
| 1917..... | .824 | .273 | .086 | .102 |
| 1918..... | 1.00 | .247 | .071 | .091 |
| 1919..... | 1.12 | .186 | .053 | .073 |
| 1920..... | 1.09 | .184 | .08 | .081 |
| 1921..... | 1.00 | .129 | .045 | .05 |
| 1922..... | 1.00 | .135 | .055 | .057 |
| 1923..... | .82 | .147 | .070 | .068 |
| 1924..... | .67 | .131 | .08 | .065 |
| 1925..... | .694 | .142 | .087 | .076 |
| 1926..... | .624 | .14 | .08 | .075 |
| 1927..... | .567 | .131 | .063 | .064 |
| 1928..... | .585 | .144 | .058 | .061 |
| 1929..... | .533 | .176 | .063 | .066 |
| 1930..... | .385 | .124 | .052 | .047 |
| 1931..... | .290 | .091 | .037 | .038 |

Metals, non-metals, stone, coal, petroleum and other minerals are discussed in detail in sub-chapters published herewith.

## COLORADO SCHOOL OF MINES

Colorado's state school of mines, located at Golden, ranks as one of the foremost institutions of its character in the entire country. Its numerous courses deal with all branches of the mineral industry, including practical mining, assaying, identifying the various minerals, mine engineering, etc., as well as all branches of the petroleum industry and all other subjects dealing with the metallic and non-metallic minerals which abound in Colorado. The school was established in 1874 and has a present enrollment of about 470 students.

## MINING AND QUARRYING IN COLORADO, 1929 AND 1919
(Compiled from Census Reports)

Note—The statistics given in this table include data for all mineral-producing activities in Colorado with the following exceptions: The production of petroleum and natural gas, salt, marls, natural mineral waters, certain minor and rare minerals and non-commercial clay (clay mined by clay-products manufacturers and used in their own production); production of coal by enterprises whose output was less than 1,000 tons; the production of sand and gravel by enterprises whose output was less than 25,000 tons; the production of other mining or quarrying industries whose output was valued at less than $2,500; production by governmental (state, county and municipal) enterprises. The scope of the census for 1929 differed considerably from that of 1919, as follows: Petroleum and natural gas were canvassed for 1919, but not for 1929; the sand and gravel, glass sand, and moulding sand industries were canvassed for the first time in 1929; the quarrying of limestone carried on in connection with the manufacture of lime and cement was also covered for the first time in 1929 census; data for the production of sandstone ground into sand are included in the statistics for glass-sand, the sand and gravel, or the silica industry, according to the nature of the product, whereas in other censuses these data have been included in the statistics for the sandstone industry.

| | All Mining and Quarrying Industries | | 1919 | Per Cent of Increase or Decrease (—) |
|---|---|---|---|---|
| | 1929 | | | |
| | All Industries | *Revised (for comparative Purposes) | | |
| Number of enterprises | 314 | 311 | 466 | —33.3 |
| Number of mines and quarries | 343 | 333 | 523 | —36.3 |
| Persons engaged: | | | | |
| Proprietors and firm members | 142 | 142 | 370 | —61.6 |
| Salaried employes | 863 | 843 | 1,321 | —36.2 |
| Wage earners (av. no. for year) | 14,562 | 14,493 | 16,710 | —13.3 |
| Total, persons engaged | 15,567 | 15,478 | 18,401 | —15.9 |
| Power equipment (total horsepower) | 118,330 | 116,592 | 114,448 | 1.9 |
| Principal expenses: | | | | |
| Salaries | $ 2,305,888 | $ 2,250,319 | $ 2,766,151 | —18.6 |
| Wages | 22,374,765 | 22,266,604 | 25,263,057 | —11.9 |
| Contract work | 536,454 | 536,454 | 307,930 | 34.8 |
| Supplies and materials | 5,970,812 | 5,939,045 | 11,826,142 | —49.8 |
| Fuel | 717,683 | 715,183 | 1,232,647 | —42.0 |
| Purchased electric energy | 1,659,708 | 1,629,428 | 1,448,975 | 12.5 |
| Value of products | 41,530,446 | 41,205,031 | 51,063,444 | —19.3 |

*Revised by omission of all data for all industries not canvassed in both censuses, for comparative purposes.

## MINES AND QUARRIES: STATISTICS FOR SELECTED INDUSTRIES, 1929
(Compiled from Census Reports)

Note—This table presents statistics for each industry for which it is possible to give separate figures without disclosing data for individual enterprises. Certain of the "other industries," however, were of greater importance in the state than some of the industries shown separately.

| | Number of Enterprises | Persons Engaged in Industry | Principal Expenses | | Expenditures for Development* | Value of Products | Machinery and Other Equipment Purchased During Year (Cost) |
|---|---|---|---|---|---|---|---|
| | | | Salaries and Wages | Contract Work, Supplies, Fuel and Purchased Electric Energy | | | |
| Coal, bituminous | 173 | 10,957 | $16,899,610 | $3,924,836 | $ 703,000 | $26,553,407 | $ 635,679 |
| Gold, lode | 44 | 1,651 | 2,745,928 | 1,705,910 | 1,401,000 | 4,057,060 | 646,720 |
| Lead | 18 | 787 | 1,574,917 | 774,420 | 377,000 | 2,946,136 | 159,273 |
| Copper | 3 | 562 | 891,264 | 580,158 | 325,000 | 1,697,051 | 6,537 |
| Zinc | 9 | 263 | 409,612 | 237,015 | 125,000 | 906,538 | 8,746 |
| Limestone | 14 | 257 | 308,653 | 76,986 | 3,000 | 489,236 | 70,365 |
| Sand and gravel | 3 | 89 | 163,730 | 64,547 | ------ | 325,415 | 52,000 |
| Silver | 11 | 168 | 230,445 | 114,387 | 129,000 | 303,251 | 19,410 |
| Granite | 4 | 90 | 150,832 | 52,488 | ------ | 270,073 | 28,232 |
| Clay | 9 | 62 | 57,304 | 5,577 | 1,000 | 115,537 | 117 |
| Fluorspar | 3 | 30 | 48,264 | 7,781 | 1,000 | 51,239 | 1,650 |
| Gypsum | 3 | 13 | 15,772 | 5,651 | ------ | 27,867 | 6,500 |
| Sandstone | 3 | 18 | 11,083 | 7,185 | ------ | 21,562 | ------ |
| Other industries | 17 | 625 | 1,172,339 | 1,327,716 | 246,000 | 3,766,074 | 161,156 |
| Totals | 314 | 15,567 | $24,630,653 | $8,884,657 | $3,311,000 | $41,530,446 | $1,796,385 |

*Included in items under "Principal Expenses."

## MINERAL PRODUCTION OF COLORADO IN 1929, 1928, 1927, 1926 AND 1925
### (U. S. Bureau of Mines)

| PRODUCT | 1929 Quantity | 1929 Value | 1928 Quantity | 1928 Value | 1927 Quantity | 1927 Value | 1926 Quantity | 1926 Value | 1925 Quantity | 1925 Value |
|---|---|---|---|---|---|---|---|---|---|---|
| Arsenious oxide____Short tons | 163 | $ 13,201 | 115 | $ 9,501 | ---- | ---- | ---- | ---- | ---- | ---- |
| Barite _____do | ---- | (1) | 40 | 346 | ---- | ---- | ---- | (1) | ---- | (1) |
| Cement _____Barrels | (1) | ³ 7,064 | (1) | (1) | (1) | ᵇ$2,?986 | (1) | ²3,381,776 | (1) | ²$4,126,945 |
| Clay Products_____ | ---- | ᵇ215,409 | ---- | ²2,998,242 | ---- | ---- | ---- | ᵇ254,523 | ---- | ᵇ358,687 |
| Clay, raw_____Short tons | 162,008 | | 155,075 | ᵇ256,548 | 218,255 | ³319,994 | 199,367 | | 254,521 | |
| Coal _____do | 9,920,741 | 26,254,000 | 9,847,707 | 27,613,000 | 9,274,075 | 27,044,000 | 10,637,225 | 29,529,000 | 10,310,551 | 30,322,000 |
| Coke _____do | 721,457 | (1 3) | 769,622 | (1 3) | 788,586 | (1 3) | 790,118 | (1 3) | 644,481 | (1 3) |
| Copper _____Pounds | 8,905,074 | 7,803 | 8,504,646 | 1,237,629 | 5,670,581 | 2,846 | 3,403,850 | 689 | 2,360,500 | 355,191 |
| Feldspar (crude)____Long tons | (1) | (1) | (1) | (1) | (1) | (0) | (1) | (1) | (1) | (1) |
| Ferro-alloys _____do | (1 3) | (1 3) | (1 3) | (1 3) | ---- | ---- | ---- | ---- | (1 3) | (1 3) |
| Fluorspar _____Short tons | 4,808 | 56,607 | 1,815 | 18,046 | 6,432 | (1) | 10,440 | (1) | 11,776 | 31,507 |
| Fuller's earth_____do | (1) | (1) | (1) | (1) | ---- | ---- | ---- | ---- | ---- | ---- |
| Gems and precious stones____ | (4) | (4) | ---- | (4) | ---- | (4) | ---- | (4) | ---- | (4) |
| Gold _____Troy ounces | 290 | 4,417,358 | 256,623 | 5,304,876 | 255,377 | 5,279,118 | 23,400 | 7,078,033 | 349,607 | 7,227,022 |
| Gypsum _____Short tons | (1) | (1) | (1) | (1) | (1) | (1) | (1) | (1) | (1) | (1) |
| Iron ore_____Long tons | 50,754 | (1) | 52,713 | (1) | 32,206 | (1) | 35,535 | (1) | 8,642 | (1) |
| Iron, pig_____do | (1 3) | (1 3) | (1 3) | (1 3) | (1 3) | (1 3) | (1 3) | (1 3) | (1 3) | (1 5) |
| Lead _____Short tons | 24,445 | 3,080,064 | 26,751 | 3,103,100 | 33,386 | 4,206,671 | 34,494 | 5,519,024 | 31,483 | 6,478,042 |
| Lime _____do | 7,046 | 76,791 | 8,114 | 88,775 | 11,900 | 125,875 | 12,470 | 7,975 | 743 | 5,127 |
| Manganese ore_____Long tons | ---- | ---- | ---- | ---- | (1) | (1) | ---- | ---- | ---- | ---- |
| Manganiferous ore: | | | | | | | | | | |
| For fluxing_____do | ---- | ---- | 48 | (1) | 1,029 | (1) | 6,656 | 9,208 | 11,366 | 16,749 |
| For other purposes_____do | 17,770 | (1) | 18,599 | 99,823 | 26,828 | 126,938 | 2,925 | (1) | 7,352 | 26,565 |

| Item | Unit | I Qty | I Value | II Qty | II Value | III Qty | III Value | IV Qty | IV Value | V Qty | V Value |
|---|---|---|---|---|---|---|---|---|---|---|---|
| Mica: Scrap | Short tons | (1) | (1) | (1) | (1) | (1) | (1) | (1) | (1) | (1) | (1) |
| Sheet | Pounds | --- | --- | --- | --- | --- | --- | --- | --- | --- | --- |
| Micaceous (vermiculite) | Short tons | (1) | --- | 1 | --- | 64 | --- | --- | --- | --- | --- |
| Mineral paints, zinc and lead pigments | do | (1 3) | (1 3) | (1 3) | (1 3) | (1 3) | (1 3) | 13,751 | [2]1,713,367 | 16,301 | [2]2,007,495 |
| Mineral waters | Gallons sold | (4) | (4) | (4) | (4) | (4) | (4) | (4) | (4) | (4) | (4) |
|  | Pounds | (1) | (1) | (1) | (1) | (1) | (1) | (1) | (1) | (1) | (1) |
| Natural gas | M cubic feet | 2700 | 675,000 | 2,931,000 | 786,000 | 1,725,400 | 290,000 | 553,800 | 130,000 | 574,460 | 61,100 |
| Natural gas-gasoline | Gallons | 1,630,000 | 118,000 | 1,909,000 | 136,000 | 912,000 | 64,000 | 276,000 | 17,000 | 35,000 | 4,000 |
| Ores (crude) etc.: Copper | Short tons | 36,539 | (9) | 11,983 | (9) | 467 | (9) | --- | --- | --- | --- |
| gold-lead | do | 81 | (9) | 366 | (9) | 410 | (9) | --- | --- | --- | --- |
| Dry and siliceous (gold and silver) | do | 640,442 | (9) | [3]894,455 | (9) | 1,035,305 | (9) | --- | --- | --- | --- |
| Lead | do | 36,880 | (9) | [3]26,687 | (9) | 61,275 | (9) | --- | --- | --- | --- |
| Lead-zinc | do | 458,251 | (9) | [3]492,593 | (9) | 508,679 | (9) | --- | --- | --- | --- |
| Zinc | do | --- | (9) | --- | (9) | 392 | (9) | --- | --- | --- | --- |
| Petroleum | Barrels | 2,358,000 | --- | 2,380,000 | 2,774,000 | 2,750,000 | 2,331,000 | 2,768,000 | 5,100,000 | 1,226,000 | 1,810,000 |
| Sand and gravel | Short tons | --- | 492,587 | 903,846 | 806,051 | 605,511 | 465,818 | 764,523 | 590,695 | 692,395 | 547,944 |
| Shale oil | Gallons | --- | --- | --- | (10) | --- | --- | --- | --- | --- | --- |
| Silver | Troy ounces | 4,397,377 | 2,343,802 | 4,052,253 | 2,370,568 | 784,605 | 2,145,871 | 4,704,122 | 2,935,372 | 4,506,940 | 3,127,816 |
| Stone | Short tons | [8]834,260 | --- | [8]966,380 | [8]882,140 | [8]933,241 | [8]975,953 | 911,450 | 1,107,867 | [5]674,610 | [8]881,756 |
| Tungsten ore (60 per cent concentrates) | do | 152 | 124,416 | 332 | 149,423 | 229 | 209,007 | 232 | 148,200 | 201 | (1) |
| Uranium and vanadium ores | do | (1) | (1) | (1) | (1) | (1) | (1) | 20,511 | 292,000 | (1) | (1) |
| Zinc | do | 29,431 | 3,884,826 | 35,731 | 4,359,182 | 35,865 | 4,590,656 | 32,500 | 4,875,000 | 30,811 | 4,683,196 |
| Miscellaneous (6) |  |  | 17,741,885 |  | 16,433,270 |  | 19,176,739 |  | 15,439,688 |  | 15,275,625 |
| Total value, eliminating duplications |  |  | $55,331,911 |  | $58,594,688 |  | $58,855,263 |  | $65,597,487 |  | $63,148,959 |

[1]Value included under "Miscellaneous."
[2]Figures obtained through co-operation with bureau of the census.
[3]Value not included in total value for state.
[4]No canvass.
[5]Exclusive of basalt and marble, value for which is included under "Miscellaneous."
[6]Includes minerals indicated by "1," "5," and "8" above.
[7]Exclusive of pottery, value of which is included under "Miscellaneous."
[8]Exclusive of marble, value for which is included under "Miscellaneous."
[9]Not valued as ore; value of recoverable metal content included under the metals.
[10]No data available.

## VALUE OF ALL MINERALS PRODUCED IN COLORADO BY YEARS FROM 1905 TO 1929, INCLUSIVE

(Compiled from reports of the U. S. Bureau of Mines)

| YEAR | Gold, silver, copper, lead and zinc | | All other minerals | | Total value all mineral production |
|---|---|---|---|---|---|
| | Value | Per ct. of total | Value | Per ct. of total | |
| 1905................ | $ 44,699,700 | 75.4 | $ 14,581,244 | 24.6 | $ 59,280,944 |
| 1906................ | 43,899,199 | 62.9 | 25,935,382 | 37.1 | 69,834,581 |
| 1907................ | 39,466,900 | 55.5 | 31,638,228 | 44.5 | 71,105,128 |
| 1908................ | 32,718,573 | 55.8 | 25,910,914 | 44.2 | 58,629,487 |
| 1909................ | 33,901,891 | 57.3 | 25,288,533 | 42.7 | 59,190,424 |
| 1910................ | 33,671,502 | 55.8 | 26,686,213 | 44.2 | 60,357,715 |
| 1911................ | 32,418,218 | 61.7 | 20,104,198 | 38.3 | 52,522,416 |
| 1912................ | 37,320,966 | 64.1 | 20,846,433 | 35.9 | 58,167,399 |
| 1913................ | 35,450,585 | 65.3 | 18,843,696 | 34.7 | 54,294,281 |
| 1914................ | 33,460,126 | 64.1 | 18,701,534 | 35.9 | 52,161,660 |
| 1915................ | 46,426,697 | 72.2 | 17,868,422 | 27.8 | 64,295,119 |
| 1916................ | 49,200,697 | 63.3 | 28,442,081 | 36.7 | 77,642,778 |
| 1917................ | 42,084,668 | 52.4 | 38,211,550 | 47.6 | 80,296,218 |
| 1918................ | 34,160,172 | 43.2 | 44,843,756 | 56.8 | 79,003,928 |
| 1919................ | 21,679,614 | 36.1 | 38,250,665 | 63.9 | 59,930,279 |
| 1920................ | 21,898,974 | 28.8 | 54,138,922 | 71.2 | 76,037,896 |
| 1921................ | 14,005,500 | 26.0 | 40,039,556 | 74.0 | 54,045,056 |
| 1922................ | 15,301,698 | 27.9 | 39,504,579 | 72.1 | 54,806,277 |
| 1923................ | 18,471,590 | 30.1 | 12,907,556 | 69.9 | 61,379,146 |
| 1924................ | 18,620,796 | 30.3 | 42,867,086 | 69.7 | 61,487,882 |
| 1925................ | 20,851,267 | 33.0 | 42,297,692 | 67.0 | 63,148,959 |
| 1926................ | 20,883,968 | 31.8 | 44,713,519 | 68.2 | 65,597,487 |
| 1927................ | 16,965,162 | 28.8 | 41,890,101 | 71.2 | 58,855,263 |
| 1928................ | 16,375,355 | 27.9 | 42,219,333 | 72.1 | 58,594,688 |
| 1929................ | 15,293,343 | 27.6 | 40,038,568 | 72.4 | 55,331,911 |
| Total 25 years.. | $739,227,161 | 47.2 | $826,769,761 | 52.8 | $1,565,996,922 |

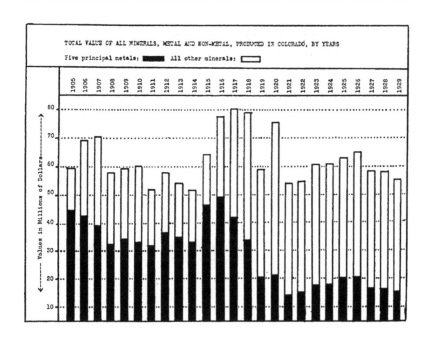

TOTAL VALUE OF ALL MINERALS, METAL AND NON-METAL, PRODUCED IN COLORADO, BY YEARS

Five principal metals: ▮ All other minerals: ☐

## METALS

The principal metals produced in Colorado, in point of value, are gold, silver, copper, lead and zinc. The total value of the output of these five metals from the beginning of the industry in the state down to the close of 1931 was $1,660,992,937. This total includes the preliminary figures for 1931 as reported by *C. W.* Henderson, of the United States bureau of mines, which are not included in permanent tables published elsewhere in this volume on account of their being subject to revision. The 1931 preliminary figures are as follows:

|  | Quantity | Value |
|---|---|---|
| Gold ................... | ....... | $4,766,388 |
| Silver, ounces..... | 2,074,591 | 601,631 |
| Copper, pounds.... | 7,722,000 | 640,926 |
| Lead, pounds...... | 13,457,000 | 511,366 |
| Zinc, pounds ...... | 31,975,000 | 1,215,050 |
| Total ........... | ....... | $7,735,361 |

The advance figures for 1931, by counties, are given in detail in a table accompanying this chapter.

The number of mines producing in the years named are as follows:

| Year | Lode | Placer | Total |
|---|---|---|---|
| 1917 ............... | 715 | 33 | 748 |
| 1918 ............... | 576 | 12 | 588 |
| 1919 ............... | 453 | 11 | 464 |
| 1920 ............... | 405 | 11 | 416 |
| 1921 ............... | 367 | 15 | 382 |
| 1922 ............... | 460 | 20 | 480 |
| 1923 ............... | 400 | 17 | 417 |
| 1924 ............... | 340 | 18 | 358 |
| 1925 ............... | 412 | 30 | 442 |
| 1926 ............... | 387 | 31 | 418 |
| 1927 ............... | 330 | 19 | 349 |
| 1928 ............... | 336 | 23 | 359 |
| 1929 ............... | 290 | 13 | 303 |
| 1930 ............... | 313 | 21 | 334 |

Gold was first mined in Colorado in 1858 and the production of silver began shortly thereafter. Copper has been produced steadily since 1868 and lead since 1869. The first zinc was produced in 1885. Metal mining is the state's oldest industry.

While Colorado's distinction as a mining state was built up principally on the production of these five metals, it has in recent years achieved a pre-eminent position in the production of other metals. The world's largest molybdenum mine is located at Climax, in Lake county, operated by the Climax-Molybdenum company, and in 1929 treated 408,000 tons of ore. Competent authorities estimate the output of this property at 85 per cent of the world's entire supply. A similar distinction is given to a property at Rifle, in Garfield county, where the United State Vanadium corporation operates the largest vanadium mine in the world. This property is credited with an output four times greater than the entire production of the mines of Peru in 1928, which in former years were the source of the world's principal supply of vanadium. A third mine credited with being in the same class as these two, though its output is included with the state's five principal metals, is the property of the Empire Zinc company, located at Gilman, in Eagle county, said to be one of the largest zinc mines in the world. This mine also recovers silver from its dry ore, copper ore and lead-zinc ore, and in 1929 ranked 17th among the larger producers of silver in the United States.

Gold leads the five principal metals in the value of total output, the production to the end of 1931 being valued at more than $720,245,000. Colorado held first place among the gold producing states for many years, but this position was surrendered to California in 1916. In 1928 Colorado ranked fourth, its output being exceeded only by Alaska, California and South Dakota. In 1929 Utah went slightly ahead of Colorado and the state dropped to fifth place. The peak in gold production in the state was reached in 1900, when the output was valued at $28,762,063. In the 70-year period ending with 1927 in which Colorado has produced gold, its output was equal to 15.8 per cent of all the gold produced in the United States between 1792 and 1927, inclusive, a period of 136 years. The third largest producer of gold in the United States in 1929 was the Golden Cycle Mining & Reduction company, which produced gold in the Cripple Creek district, its output being exceeded only by one operator in South Dakota and another in Alaska. The value of all gold produced in the world since Columbus discovered America is placed at $21,940,679,253. In the 72 years in which Colorado has been producing gold its output was equal to 3.3 per cent of the world's output since 1492.

Silver production in Colorado from the beginning of the industry to the end of 1931 was in excess of $519,126,000. The state ranks sixth among the states in annual output, being exceeded in 1929 only by Arizona, Idaho, Montana, Nevada and Utah. In that year Colorado produced 7.2 per cent of the country's output, which compares with 7.5 per cent in 1928, 6.5 per cent in 1927, 8.0 per cent in 1926 and 6.8 per cent in 1925. The peak in silver production was reached in 1891, in which year the output was valued at $20,948,401. World production of silver since the discovery of America is $19,364,192,748. In the 72 years in which Colorado has been producing silver its output is equal to 2.6 per cent of the world's output since 1492.

The value of the copper output of the state in 1868 was only $11,500. The peak was reached in 1917, when the output was $2,217,307. Total value of the output to the end of 1931 was $47,050,215. In 1925 the output reached the lowest point in 36 years, but in 1926 it began to increase and in 1929 the production was more than four times greater than in 1925. Nine states exceed Colorado in copper production.

In 1924 lead took second place in annual output, being ahead of silver and next to gold. It retained that place in 1925 and 1926, but in 1927 it yielded second place to zinc. The aggregate production of lead to the end of 1931 was $217,578,011, this giving it third place among the five principal metals. Colorado is one of the five largest lead producing states, its output being exceeded only by Idaho, Missouri, Oklahoma and Utah.

Zinc production reached a maximum output of 134,285,463 pounds in 1916, following which year there was a pronounced decline until 1921, when the output was only 2,360,000 pounds, the smallest in 24 years. Production showed a large gain in 1922 and gradually climbed back to 72,518,000 pounds in 1930. Due to adverse business conditions in 1931 the output again dropped in that year. The aggregate value of output from 1885, when commercial production began, to the end of 1931, was more than $156,992,000. The value of the 1885 output was only $4,300. In 1927 it took second place in value among the five principal minerals, being next to gold, and maintained that relative position in 1931.

While the five metals named above furnish the largest portion of the metal output, almost every useful metal found in the United States exists here. Tungsten has been produced commercially when market conditions warranted since 1904, and the state ranked third in 1925 in quantity and value of output. Uranium, vanadium and radium have been produced

since 1906, and the state ranks first in the output of vanadium. At this time it is producing about 85 per cent of the world's supply of molybdenum. There are 92 known deposits of manganese ores in the state which have been examined and reported upon by the United States geological survey.

The peak production of gold, silver, copper, lead and zinc in the state was reached in 1900, when the aggregate value of the output was $50,614,424. There was a downward tendency in the output until the bottom was reached in 1921, with a total output for the year of $14,005,500. The next five years showed increases, but in 1930 and 1931 the output dropped below the 1921 figures.

The production of metals in Colorado is confined largely to the mountainous counties in the central and western parts of the state. The metals occur usually in compound ores found in well-defined veins or lodes. Free gold is the principal output of the placer mines, and Summit county has led all other counties in the state for 50 years in the output of its placer mines. There is a wide variety in the gold ores found in Colorado. Among the compound ores from which gold is obtained are amalgam, calaverite, petzite and sylvanite.

Zinc is the predominant metal in many of the ores which carry gold. The principal compound ores carrying zinc are aurichalcite, calamine, chalcophanite, hetaerolite, hydrozincite, nicholsonite, smithsonite and sphalerite.

Silver is found very commonly associated with both zinc and gold as well as with lead. The principal compound ores in which silver is found are acanthite, amalgam, calaverite, cosalite, galena, massicot, mimehessite, krennerite, pearceite, petzite, polybasite, proustite, pyrargyrite, stephenite, stromeyerite and sylvanite.

Lead is perhaps more widely distributed than any other metal found in the state, and is often associated with both gold and silver. The principal compound ores from which lead is produced are altaite, anglesite, cerusite, cosalite, galena, massicot, mimetite, minium, plumbojarsite and pyromorphite.

Copper is very widely distributed, but usually occurs in comparatively small quantities. The principal compound ores containing copper are azurite, bornite, brochantite, chalcanthite, chalcocite, chacopyrite, chrysocolla, covellite, cuprite, enargite, malachite, melaconite, stromeyerite, tenantite and tetrahedrite.

Of the total values of gold, silver, copper, lead and zinc reported by the United States bureau of mines up to the end of 1930, as shown on pages 236-237 of this volume, the largest total came from Lake county, which furnished more than one-fourth of the total for the state. Silver was the dominant metal in the development of the mines of that county, with zinc, lead, gold and copper following in that order. Lake county produced $446,-233,628 in the five metals up to the end of 1930.

Teller county ranked second in the development of the metal mining industry during that period, its production having been $350,612,298 in the period from 1891 to 1930. Gold was almost exclusively responsible for the county's position, silver values totaling only $1,236,038 and the values of other metals being negligible. San Miguel county ranked third, Pitkin county fourth and Gilpin county fifth in the value of the five metals taken from the mines up to the end of 1930.

Of the state's total values produced to that time, gold led in importance, accounting for nearly half the total. Silver, valued at more than $518,000,-000, was second, with lead, zinc and copper following in the order named.

## PRINCIPAL METALS

The following tabulation gives the principal metals found in Colorado and the counties in which they occur:

**Aluminum** (alunite, bauxite, cryolite)—Chaffee, Conejos, Custer, El Paso, Fremont, Gunnison, Hinsdale, Lake, Mineral, Ouray, Rio Grande, Saguache.

**Antimony** (bournonite, polybasite, stibnite)—Boulder, Clear Creek, Dolores, Grand, Gunnison, Ouray, Pitkin, San Juan, San Miguel, Teller.

**Arsenic** (arsenopyrite)—Gilpin, Gunnison, Pitkin, San Juan, San Miguel.

**Barium** (barite)—Boulder, Mineral, Pitkin, San Miguel.

**Bismuth** (beegerite, bismuthinite, bismutite, cosalite, tetradymite)—Boulder, Chaffee, Fremont, Grand, Gunnison, Jefferson, Lake, La Plata, Larimer, Montezuma, Ouray, Park, San Miguel.

**Cadmium** (greenockite)—Lake.

**Cerium** (allanite, gadolinite, monazite)—Boulder, Chaffee, Costilla, Douglas, Routt, Washington.

**Cobalt** (erythrite, smaltite)—Gunnison.

**Copper**—Archuleta, Baca, Boulder, Chaffee, Clear Creek, Conejos, Custer, Dolores, Eagle, Fremont, Garfield, Gilpin, Grand, Gunnison, Hinsdale, Huerfano, Jackson, Jefferson, Lake, La Plata, Larimer, Mesa, Mineral, Moffat, Montezuma, Montrose, Ouray, Park, Pitkin, Rio Grande, Routt, Saguache, San Juan, San Miguel, Summit, Teller.

**Gold**—Archuleta, Boulder, Chaffee, Clear Creek, Conejos, Costilla, Custer, Dolores, Douglas, Eagle, Fremont, Garfield, Gilpin, Grand, Gunnison, Hinsdale, Huerfano, Jackson, Jefferson, Lake, La Plata, Mineral, Moffat, Montezuma, Montrose, Ouray, Park, Pitkin, Rio Grande, Routt, Saguache, San Juan, San Miguel, Summit, Teller.

**Iron** (brown iron ore, hematite, magnetite, marasite, pyrite, pyrrhotite, siderite) — Chaffee, Costilla, Dolores, Fremont, Gunnison, Hinsdale, Jefferson, Lake, Ouray, Pitkin, Routt, Saguache, San Juan, San Miguel, Summit, Teller. Pyrite is found in nearly every metal producing county in the state.

**Lead**—Archuleta, Boulder, Chaffee, Clear Creek, Custer, Dolores, Eagle, Fremont, Gilpin, Gunnison, Hinsdale, Lake, La Plata, Mineral, Montezuma, Ouray, Park, Pitkin, Routt, Saguache, San Juan, Summit, Teller.

**Lithium** (amblygonite)—Fremont.

**Manganese** (alabandite, chalcophanite, psilomelane, pyrolusite, rhodochrosite)—Boulder, Chaffee, Custer, Dolores, Eagle, Gunnison, Hinsdale, Lake, Park, Saguache, San Juan, Summit.

**Mercury** (amalgam, cinnabar, quicksilver)—Boulder, La Plata.

**Molybdenum** (molybdenite)—Boulder, Chaffee, Clear Creek, Grand, Gunnison, Lake, San Juan, Summit, Teller.

**Nickel** (annabergite, nicolite)—Custer, Fremont, Gunnison.

**Platinum**—Clear Creek, Chaffee, Gunnison, Pitkin, Saguache, San Miguel.

**Radium, Uranium, Vanadium** (carnotite, pitchblende, volborthite) — Clear Creek, Custer, Dolores, Eagle, Garfield, Huerfano, Jefferson, La Plata, Mesa, Moffat, Montrose, Park, Rio Blanco, San Miguel.

**Silver** — Archuleta, Baca, Boulder, Chaffee, Clear Creek, Conejos, Costilla, Custer, Dolores, Douglas, Eagle, Fremont, Garfield, Gilpin, Grand, Gunnison, Hinsdale, Jackson, Lake, La Plata, Mineral, Moffat, Montezuma, Montrose, Ouray, Park, Pitkin, Rio Grande, Routt, Saguache, San Juan, San Miguel, Summit, Teller.

**Tantalum** (columbite)—Fremont, Jefferson, Teller.

**Tellurium**—Boulder, Teller.

**Tin** (cassiterite)—Garfield.

**Titanium** (ilmenite, rutile, perofskite)—El Paso, Gunnison.

**Tungsten** (ferberite, hubernite, scheelite)—Boulder, Chaffee, Clear Creek, Gilpin, Gunnison, Lake, Ouray, San Juan, San Miguel, Summit.

**Yttrium** (allanite, gadolinite)—Boulder, Douglas, Washington.

**Zinc**—Archuleta, Chaffee, Clear Creek, Conejos, Dolores, Eagle, Fremont, Gilpin, Hinsdale, Lake, Mineral, Ouray, Park, Pitkin, Saguache, San Juan, San Miguel, Summit.

**Zircon**—El Paso.

MINE PRODUCTION OF GOLD, SILVER, COPPER, LEAD AND ZINC IN COLORADO BY YEARS—1858-1930

(U. S. Bureau of Mines)

| YEAR | GOLD Total Value | SILVER Fine Ounces | SILVER Value | COPPER Pounds | COPPER Value | LEAD Pounds | LEAD Value | ZINC Pounds | ZINC Value | Total Value |
|---|---|---|---|---|---|---|---|---|---|---|
| 1858-67 | $25,021,784 | 302,829 | $406,139 | ----- | ----- | ----- | ----- | ----- | ----- | $25,427,923 |
| 1868 | 2,010,000 | 200,716 | 266,150 | 50,000 | $11,500 | ----- | ----- | ----- | ----- | 2,287,650 |
| 1869 | 3,180,000 | 475,472 | 630,000 | 102,000 | 24,735 | 150,000 | $9,000 | ----- | ----- | 3,843,735 |
| 1870 | 3,016,000 | 496,988 | 660,000 | 182,500 | 38,654 | 250,000 | 15,000 | ----- | ----- | 3,728,654 |
| 1871 | 3,633,951 | 776,648 | 1,029,059 | 183,000 | 44,140 | 555,000 | 33,300 | ----- | ----- | 4,740,450 |
| 1872 | 2,646,463 | 1,524,206 | 2,015,000 | 204,000 | 72,542 | 1,150,000 | 73,600 | ----- | ----- | 4,807,605 |
| 1873 | 2,018,931 | 1,543,047 | 2,001,331 | 379,493 | 2,258 | 1,236,400 | 74,184 | ----- | ----- | 4,200,704 |
| 1874 | 2,152,487 | 2,348,174 | 3,000,966 | 475,541 | 4,019 | 1,277,933 | 76,676 | ----- | ----- | 5,334,748 |
| 1875 | 2,224,568 | 2,330,291 | 2,889,560 | 280,815 | 63,745 | 1,636,000 | 94,888 | ----- | ----- | 5,272,761 |
| 1876 | 2,726,311 | 2,564,403 | 2,974,707 | 333,333 | 7,000 | 1,334,020 | 81,375 | ----- | ----- | 5,852,393 |
| 1877 | 3,148,708 | 2,882,121 | 3,458,546 | 493,664 | 93,796 | 4,286,364 | 235,750 | ----- | ----- | 6,936,800 |
| 1878 | 3,240,348 | 4,672,961 | 5,373,904 | 536,145 | 89,000 | 13,722,222 | 494,000 | ----- | ----- | 9,197,252 |
| 1879 | 3,193,500 | 11,899,335 | 13,327,257 | 704,301 | 1,900 | 47,348,000 | 1,941,268 | ----- | ----- | 18,593,025 |
| 1880 | 3,252,514 | 14,397,539 | 16,557,170 | 859,000 | 3,826 | 71,348,000 | 3,567,400 | ----- | ----- | 23,560,910 |
| 1881 | 3,300,000 | 13,272,188 | 14,997,572 | 884,000 | 0,883 | 81,094,000 | 3,892,512 | ----- | ----- | 22,350,972 |
| 1882 | 3,360,000 | 12,761,719 | 14,548,359 | 1,494,000 | 285,354 | 110,114,000 | 5,390,000 | ----- | ----- | 23,583,713 |
| 1883 | 4,100,000 | 13,434,610 | 14,912,417 | 1,152,652 | 0,988 | 141,114,000 | 0,067,902 | ----- | ----- | 25,270,507 |
| 1884 | 4,300,000 | 12,375,000 | 13,736,251 | 2,013,125 | 2,506 | 126,330,000 | 4,674,209 | ----- | ----- | 22,972,166 |
| 1885 | 4,203,425 | 12,220,982 | 13,076,451 | 1,146,460 | 3,818 | 106,692,000 | 4,160,989 | 100,000 | $4,300 | 21,568,983 |
| 1886 | 4,460,000 | 12,375,000 | 12,251,250 | 1,6,460 | 7,257 | 118,000 | 5,428,000 | 100,000 | 4,400 | 22,260,907 |
| 1887 | 4,000,000 | 11,601,563 | 11,369,534 | 2,012,027 | 72,060 | 126,000,000 | 5,670,000 | 100,000 | 4,600 | 21,321,794 |
| 1888 | 3,768,099 | 14,695,313 | 13,813,596 | 1,6,300 | 272,345 | 128,404,000 | 5,649,777 | 300,000 | 14,700 | 23,508,617 |
| 1889 | 3,883,859 | 18,375,136 | 17,272,629 | 1,170,053 | 7,856 | 133,940,000 | 5,223,660 | 300,000 | 15,000 | 26,563,104 |
| 1890 | 4,151,132 | 18,800,000 | 19,740,000 | 3,585,691 | 55,868 | 109,192,000 | 4,913,639 | 300,000 | 16,500 | 29,380,639 |
| 1891 | 4,600,000 | 21,160,000 | 20,948,401 | 6,336,878 | 79,121 | 126,256,000 | 5,429,009 | 300,000 | 15,000 | 31,803,531 |
| 1892 | 5,300,000 | 24,000,000 | 20,880,000 | 7,593,674 | 00,866 | 110,000,0 | 4,800,001 | 1,125,000 | 51,750 | 31,912,617 |
| 1893 | 7,527,000 | 25,838,600 | 20,154,107 | 7,695,826 | 831,149 | 110,000,0 | 4,070,000 | 1,650,000 | 66,000 | 32,648,256 |
| 1894 | 9,491,514 | 23,281,398 | 14,667,281 | 9,481,413 | 65,134 | 101,226,000 | 3,340,458 | 1,650,000 | 52,500 | 28,167,487 |
| 1895 | 13,305,100 | 23,398,500 | 15,209,024 | 9,079,243 | 650,479 | 93,968,000 | 3,006,975 | 1,671,000 | 60,156 | 32,231,734 |
| 1896 | 14,911,000 | 22,573,000 | 15,349,642 | 9,022,176 | 650,395 | 89,000 | 2,688,178 | 1,292,000 | 50,388 | 33,649,603 |
| 1897 | 19,679,433 | 21,278,202 | 12,766,919 | 9,149,967 | 1,097,995 | 80,794,286 | 2,908,592 | 2,683,989 | 1,144 | 36,462,983 |
| 1898 | 23,534,532 | 23,602,601 | 13,866,532 | 10,870,701 | 1,347,965 | 113,416,138 | 4,309,813 | 3,900,656 | 179,430 | 43,238,272 |
| 1899 | 26,508,675 | 23,114,688 | 13,868,811 | 7,356,970 | 1,258,041 | 138,048,416 | 0,212,178 | 11,300,656 | 655,438 | 48,503,143 |
| 1900 | 28,762,036 | 20,336,512 | 12,608,637 | 7,826,815 | 1,299,261 | 164,274,762 | 7,223,090 | 16,282,055 | 716,410 | 50,614,424 |

| Year | | | | | | | | | | |
|---|---|---|---|---|---|---|---|---|---|---|
| 1901 | 27,679,443 | 18,492,663 | 11,095,638 | 7,872,529 | 1,814,712 | 148,111,020 | 6,368,772 | 26,843,731 | 1,100,593 | 47,559,058 |
| 1902 | 28,516,914 | 15,941,523 | 8,449,008 | 8,463,938 | 1,132,601 | 106,296,827 | 4,358,169 | 52,582,510 | 2,523,963 | 44,980,655 |
| 1903 | 21,605,357 | 13,245,438 | 7,162,536 | 7,809,920 | 1,069,958 | 101,513,414 | 4,263,566 | 80,616,000 | 4,353,263 | 38,444,680 |
| 1904 | 24,242,485 | 12,960,792 | 7,517,260 | 9,412,707 | 1,204,828 | 107,498,854 | 4,622,453 | 66,771,590 | 3,405,353 | 40,992,379 |
| 1905 | 25,295,222 | 12,339,435 | 7,527,056 | 9,661,546 | 1,507,201 | 115,746,777 | 5,440,098 | 83,561,396 | 4,930,123 | 44,699,700 |
| 1906 | 22,905,671 | 12,339,052 | 8,390,553 | 6,618,332 | 1,277,338 | 106,646,506 | 6,078,850 | 86,012,903 | 5,246,787 | 43,899,199 |
| 1907 | 20,307,648 | 11,599,514 | 7,655,679 | 8,826,254 | 1,765,251 | 89,065,232 | 4,720,457 | 85,048,564 | 5,017,865 | 39,466,900 |
| 1908 | 22,595,571 | 9,002,316 | 4,771,227 | 10,201,123 | 1,346,547 | 61,645,671 | 2,589,118 | 30,130,002 | 1,416,110 | 32,718,573 |
| 1909 | 21,984,008 | 8,904,701 | 4,630,444 | 10,916,191 | 1,419,105 | 72,162,326 | 3,102,980 | 51,210,260 | 2,765,354 | 33,901,891 |
| 1910 | 20,505,614 | 8,508,942 | 4,594,829 | 8,359,307 | 1,061,632 | 76,058,775 | 3,346,586 | 77,089,648 | 4,162,841 | 33,671,502 |
| 1911 | 19,001,975 | 7,330,168 | 3,884,989 | 8,024,488 | 1,003,061 | 69,679,289 | 3,135,568 | 94,607,456 | 5,392,625 | 32,418,218 |
| 1912 | 18,588,562 | 8,212,070 | 5,050,423 | 7,107,303 | 1,172,705 | 75,242,257 | 3,385,502 | 132,222,812 | 9,123,374 | 37,320,966 |
| 1913 | 18,146,916 | 9,325,255 | 5,632,454 | 7,227,826 | 1,120,313 | 87,897,773 | 3,867,502 | 119,346,429 | 6,683,400 | 35,450,985 |
| 1914 | 19,883,105 | 8,796,065 | 4,864,224 | 6,639,173 | 883,010 | 74,211,898 | 2,594,264 | 96,774,960 | 4,935,523 | 33,460,126 |
| 1915 | 22,414,944 | 7,027,972 | 3,563,182 | 7,112,537 | 1,244,694 | 68,810,597 | 3,234,098 | 104,594,994 | 12,969,779 | 43,426,697 |
| 1916 | 19,153,821 | 7,656,544 | 5,038,006 | 8,624,081 | 2,121,524 | 70,914,087 | 4,893,072 | 134,285,463 | 17,994,252 | 43,75 |
| 1917 | 15,729,224 | 7,304,353 | 6,018,787 | 8,122,004 | 2,217,307 | 67,990,012 | 5,847,141 | 120,315,775 | 12,272,209 | 42,084,663 |
| 1918 | 12,761,718 | 7,063,554 | 7,063,554 | 6,277,332 | 1,550,501 | 65,960,760 | 4,663,214 | 89,133,901 | 8,111,185 | 34,160,172 |
| 1919 | 9,886,627 | 5,758,010 | 6,448,971 | 3,560,207 | 662,198 | 37,070,241 | 1,964,722 | 37,220,493 | 2,717,096 | 21,679,614 |
| 1920 | 7,576,319 | 5,409,335 | 5,896,175 | 4,043,734 | 744,047 | 46,629,788 | 3,730,383 | 48,796,742 | 3,952,050 | 21,898,974 |
| 1921 | 6,835,328 | 5,631,657 | 5,631,657 | 4,153,442 | 535,794 | 19,660,466 | 884,721 | 2,360,000 | 118,000 | 14,005,500 |
| 1922 | 6,373,419 | 5,855,911 | 5,855,911 | 3,373,454 | 455,416 | 23,477,200 | 1,291,246 | 23,258,000 | 1,325,706 | 15,301,698 |
| 1923 | 6,591,629 | 5,334,488 | 4,374,280 | 4,248,109 | 624,472 | 45,698,185 | 3,198,873 | 54,152,000 | 3,632,336 | 18,471,190 |
| 1924 | 8,593,116 | 3,254,370 | 2,180,428 | 2,713,219 | 355,432 | 47,557,061 | 3,804,565 | 56,727,000 | 3,687,255 | 18,620,796 |
| 1925 | 7,227,022 | 4,505,940 | 3,127,816 | 2,360,500 | 335,191 | 62,966,000 | 5,478,042 | 61,621,000 | 4,683,196 | 20,851,267 |
| 1926 | 7,078,033 | 4,704,122 | 2,935,372 | 3,403,850 | 476,539 | 63,987,800 | 5,519,024 | 65,000,000 | 4,875,000 | 20,883,968 |
| 1927 | 5,279,118 | 3,784,605 | 2,145,871 | 5,670,581 | 742,846 | 66,772,557 | 4,206,671 | 71,729,000 | 4,590,656 | 16,965,162 |
| 1928 | 6,304,876 | 4,052,253 | 2,370,668 | 8,594,646 | 1,237,629 | 53,501,723 | 3,103,100 | 71,462,000 | 4,359,182 | 16,375,365 |
| 1929 | 4,417,358 | 4,397,377 | 2,343,802 | 8,905,074 | 1,567,293 | 48,889,906 | 3,080,064 | 58,861,000 | 3,884,826 | 15,293,343 |
| 1930 | 4,517,619 | 4,382,852 | 1,687,398 | 10,514,000 | 1,366,820 | 44,260,000 | 2,213,000 | 72,518,000 | 3,480,864 | 13,265,701 |
| | $715,479,032 | 657,931,919 | $518,525,200 | 305,240,430 | $46,409,315 | 4,593,572,583 | $217,066,644 | 2,197,752,985 | $155,777,382 | $1,653,257,574 |

Note—1931 figures, shown in the text, are preliminary and subject to revision, so are not included here.

## TOTAL PRODUCTION OF GOLD, SILVER, COPPER, LEAD AND ZINC IN COLORADO BY COUNTIES TO THE END OF 1930

| Period | County | GOLD Value | SILVER Fine Ounces | SILVER Value | COPPER Pounds | COPPER Value | LEAD Pounds | LEAD Value | ZINC Pounds | ZINC Value | Total, Gold, Silver, Copper, Lead and Zinc Value |
|---|---|---|---|---|---|---|---|---|---|---|---|
| 1922-1930 | Adams | $ 21,470 | 154 | $ | | | | | | | $ 21,561 |
| 1928 | Alamosa | 11 | | | | | | | | | 11 |
| 1868-1930 | Arapahoe | 8,251 | 101 | 64 | | | | | | | 8,315 |
| 1897-1904 | Archuleta | 1,489 | 505 | 302 | | | | | | | 1,791 |
| 1900-1917 | Baca | 292 | 356 | 226 | 21,511 | 4,441 | | | | | 4,959 |
| 1859-1930 | Boulder | 16,382,700 | 8,227,008 | 7,715,323 | 978,655 | 150,014 | 7,214,963 | $ 399,496 | | | 24,647,533 |
| 1859-1930 | Chaffee | 7,416,773 | 5,244,775 | 4,248,750 | 9,666,962 | 1,730,319 | 131,066,764 | 5,790,052 | 28,865,705 | $2,511,825 | 21,697,719 |
| 1859-1930 | Cr Creek | 2,062 | 58,722,611 | 52,928,159 | 12,057,161 | 1,947,912 | 181,089,219 | 8,317,797 | 31,510,221 | 2,287,772 | 88,502,802 |
| 1861-1906 | Conejos | 38,445 | 55,823 | 33,278 | 4,815 | 797 | 3,400 | 149 | | | 72,663 |
| 1875-1929 | tola | 43,569 | 2,726 | 1,598 | 1,827 | 239 | 50,048 | 1,302 | | | 47,208 |
| 1872-1929 | Custer | 2,189,664 | 4,578,537 | 4,570,122 | 567,125 | 106,940 | 39,715,009 | 1,997,817 | 217,227 | 14,787 | 8,879,330 |
| 1894-1910 | Delta | 4,273 | 306 | 176 | | | | | | | 4,449 |
| 1929 | Denver | 115 | | | | | | | | | 115 |
| 1879-1930 | Dolores | 2,036,635 | 12,696,697 | 9,775,758 | 3,064,339 | 1,415,626 | 72,404,485 | 3,974,965 | 45,878,116 | 3,029,755 | 20,232,739 |
| 1858-1928 | Douglas | 4,981 | 161 | 128 | | | | | | | 5,109 |
| 1879-1930 | Eagle | 3,271,654 | 10,928,995 | 8,137,272 | 17,621,373 | 2,601,865 | 108,284,592 | 5,304,094 | 247,534,129 | 19,662,530 | 38,977,415 |
| 1926 | Elbert | 148 | | | | | | | | | 148 |
| 1913-1914 | El Paso | | | | 13,276 | 2,000 | | | | | 2,000 |
| 1881-1928 | Fremont | 81,186 | 92,319 | 85,742 | 667,955 | 120,562 | 691,477 | 29,243 | 1,494,769 | 108,255 | 424,988 |
| 1885-1927 | Garfield | 16,935 | 722 | 437 | 1,044 | 150 | 142 | 639 | | | 18,164 |
| 1859-1930 | Gilpin | 84,630,142 | 10,668,511 | 8,631,502 | 25,688,887 | 4,209,933 | 36,514,280 | 1,632,042 | 405,113 | 32,495 | 99,136,114 |
| 1896-1925 | Grand | 13,186 | 4,656 | 3,538 | 5,171 | 805 | 4,345 | 248 | | | 17,777 |
| 1861-1930 | Gunnison | 2,297,296 | 5,608,800 | 5,014,765 | 1,031,565 | 187,511 | 49,561,769 | 2,474,492 | 26,028,150 | 2,148,973 | 12,123,037 |
| 1875-1929 | Hinsdale | 1,459,279 | 5,736,350 | 4,645,172 | 2,906,838 | 409,419 | 98,296,199 | 4,073,481 | 1,283,634 | 70,273 | 10,657,624 |
| 1875-1907 | Huerfano | 3,474 | 1,176 | 698 | 92 | 11 | 1,067 | 38 | | | 4,221 |
| 1858-1928 | Jefferson | 62,396 | 7,058 | 4,631 | 20,695 | 3,347 | 10,863 | 398 | | | 70,772 |

| Period | County | | | | | | | | | | |
|---|---|---|---|---|---|---|---|---|---|---|---|
| 1859-1931 | Lake | 53,808,070 | 234,410,008 | 191,725,530 | 101,576,281 | 14,543,623 | 2,015,276,847 | 91,709,037 | 1,377,052,034 | 94,447,368 | 446,233,628 |
| 1925-1931 | La Plata | 225,924 | 144,693 | 82,163 | 97 | 14 | 136,600 | 8,331 | | | 316,432 |
| 1878-1924 | La Plata-Montezuma | 3,612,156 | 1,766,360 | 1,137,638 | 278,979 | 45,087 | 260,093 | 12,185 | | | 4,807,066 |
| 1895-1917 | Jackson | 24,304 | 2,502 | 1,735 | 235,328 | 38,647 | | | 30,722 | 1,650 | 66,345 |
| 1887-1899 | Las Animas | 2,094 | 20 | 15 | | | | | | | 2,109 |
| 1885-1928 | Mesa | 5,040 | 5,044 | 3,033 | 37,375 | 5,512 | 20 | 1 | | | 13,586 |
| 1891-1930 | Mineral | 2,731,645 | 47,529,941 | 30,932,303 | 275,088 | 44,187 | 199,542,449 | 8,873,457 | 27,662,407 | 1,518,005 | 44,099,597 |
| 1924-1930 | Montezuma | 1,119 | 127 | 60 | 26,000 | 4,162 | | | | | 5,341 |
| 1929 | Montezuma | 151 | | | | | | | | | 151 |
| 1886-1930 | Montrose | 48,389 | 212,958 | 137,345 | 532,502 | 93,899 | 64 | 3 | | | 279,636 |
| 1878-1930 | Ouray | 36,051,144 | 42,214,992 | 32,543,211 | 23,556,530 | 3,396,697 | 164,165,498 | 7,297,625 | 1,500,650 | 122,736 | 79,411,413 |
| 1859-1930 | Pitkin | 11,618,598 | 7,028,502 | 6,954,470 | 2,108,888 | 396,583 | 42,096,625 | 1,886,336 | 2,993,532 | 196,964 | 21,054,951 |
| 1880-1930 | Pitkin | 578,133 | 98,646,546 | 73,976,431 | 1,128,463 | 197,445 | 579,603,279 | 26,806,734 | 19,127,002 | 1,222,195 | 102,780,936 |
| 1894-1901 | | 793 | 90 | 55 | 210 | 35 | | | | | 882 |
| 1870-1930 | Rio Grande | 2,899,087 | 184,082 | 174,565 | 129,397 | 20,807 | 109,847 | 6,133 | | | 3,100,592 |
| 1866-1922 | Routt-Moffat | 388,865 | 28,941 | 19,696 | 78,570 | 16,704 | 139,536 | 5,205 | | | 430,476 |
| 1889-1930 | Saguache | 349,624 | 5,128,825 | 3,378,760 | 13,902,054 | 2,065,369 | 34,060,256 | 2,062,110 | 3,035,548 | 215,762 | 8,071,625 |
| 1873-1930 | San Juan | 25,395,726 | 34,512,099 | 23,769,385 | 62,828,513 | 9,551,151 | 444,047,095 | 24,210,774 | 205,387,684 | 14,118,831 | 97,045,867 |
| 1875-1930 | San Miguel | 65,430,543 | 47,745,134 | 34,749,390 | 18,051,570 | 2,929,552 | 223,326,702 | 12,447,650 | 19,545,182 | 1,418,619 | 116,975,554 |
| 1859-1930 | Summit | 19,917,398 | 13,883,411 | 11,904,495 | 1,174,743 | 167,867 | 165,888,438 | 7,742,262 | 158,191,160 | 12,648,578 | 52,380,600 |
| 1891-1930 | Teller | 349,376,118 | 1,908,083 | 1,236,048 | 451 | 83 | 612 | 49 | | | 350,612,298 |
| 1888- | Miscellaneous | 8,785 | 1,214 | 1,141 | | | | | | | 9,926 |
| | Totals | $715,479,032 | $657,931,919 | $518,525,201 | 305,240,420 | $46,409,316 | 4,693,572,583 | $217,066,645 | 2,197,752,985 | $155,777,382 | $1,653,257,576 |

## MINE PRODUCTION OF GOLD, SILVER, COPPER, LEAD AND ZINC IN COLORADO IN 1930, BY COUNTIES

(In terms of recovered or recoverable metals)

(Final figures by Chas. W. Henderson, of the United States Bureau of Mines, Department of Commerce)

| COUNTY | Placer | Lode | Total | GOLD Value | SILVER Fine Ounces | SILVER Value | COPPER Pounds | COPPER Value | LEAD Pounds | LEAD Value | ZINC Pounds | ZINC Value | Total Value |
|---|---|---|---|---|---|---|---|---|---|---|---|---|---|
| das | 2 | -- | 2 | $ 2,125 | 13 | $ 5 | -- | -- | -- | -- | -- | -- | $ 2,130 |
| Arapahoe | 1 | -- | 1 | 104 | -- | -- | -- | -- | -- | -- | -- | -- | D4 |
| Boulder | -- | 36 | 36 | 16,516 | 3,304 | 1,272 | -- | -- | 4,900 | $ 245 | -- | -- | 18,033 |
| Chaffee | 3 | 3 | 5 | 1,574 | 1,348 | 519 | 1,500 | $ 195 | 44,000 | 2,200 | -- | -- | 4,488 |
| Clear Creek | -- | 47 | 47 | 102,141 | 38,556 | 14,844 | 23,000 | 2,990 | 184,500 | 9,225 | 21,000 | $ 1,008 | 130,203 |
| Dolores | -- | 13 | 13 | 8,605 | 82,678 | 31,831 | 309,000 | 40,170 | 1,355,200 | 67,760 | 1,190,000 | 57,120 | 205,486 |
| Eagle | -- | 4 | 4 | 117,133 | 1,620,574 | 623,921 | 5,849,000 | 760,370 | 5,642,000 | 282,100 | 28,544,000 | 1,370,112 | 3,163,636 |
| Gilpin | 6 | 25 | 31 | 139,710 | 21,696 | 8,353 | 90,300 | 11,739 | 94,300 | 4,715 | 7,000 | 336 | 164,853 |
| ion | -- | 6 | 6 | 16,743 | 2,265 | 872 | -- | -- | 35,600 | 1,780 | 41,000 | 1,968 | 21,363 |
| Lake | -- | 42 | 42 | D4,276 | 616,800 | 237,468 | 252,000 | 32,760 | 13,626,000 | 681,300 | 23,038,000 | 1,105,824 | 2,161,628 |
| La Plata | -- | 12 | 12 | 8,482 | 2,969 | 1,143 | -- | -- | 600 | 30 | -- | -- | 9,655 |
| Mineral | -- | 5 | 5 | 2,364 | 396,044 | 152,477 | 9,000 | 1,170 | 148,600 | 7,430 | -- | -- | 162,271 |
| Moffat | 1 | 1 | 1 | 7 | 52 | 20 | -- | -- | -- | -- | -- | -- | 1,197 |
| Montrose | 1 | -- | 1 | 32 | -- | -- | -- | -- | -- | -- | -- | -- | 32 |
| Ouray | -- | 8 | 8 | 149,384 | 18,122 | 6,977 | 26,000 | 3,380 | 171,000 | 8,650 | -- | -- | 168,291 |
| Park | 1 | 7 | 8 | 452,142 | 11,709 | 4,508 | 8,100 | 1,053 | 328,800 | 16,440 | -- | -- | 474,143 |
| Pitkin | -- | 7 | 7 | 98 | 65,522 | 25,226 | -- | -- | 795,000 | 39,750 | -- | -- | 65,074 |
| Rio Grande | -- | 2 | 2 | 8,590 | 239 | 92 | -- | -- | 1,500 | 75 | -- | -- | 8,757 |
| Saguache | -- | 3 | 3 | 11,373 | 333,722 | 128,483 | 1,234,000 | 160,420 | 2,343,000 | 117,150 | -- | -- | 417,426 |
| San Juan | -- | 12 | 12 | 661,376 | 1,067,496 | 410,986 | 2,678,000 | 348,140 | 17,788,600 | 889,430 | 19,677,000 | 944,496 | 3,254,428 |
| San Miguel | 7 | 12 | 12 | 45,506 | 87,556 | 33,709 | 34,100 | 4,433 | 1,637,800 | 81,890 | -- | -- | 165,538 |
| Summit | -- | 5 | 12 | 137,306 | 3,496 | 1,346 | -- | -- | 58,600 | 2,930 | -- | -- | 141,582 |
| Teller | -- | 63 | 63 | 2,532,032 | 8,691 | 3,346 | -- | -- | -- | -- | -- | -- | 2,535,378 |
| Total, 1930 | 21 | 313 | 334 | *$4,517,619 | †4,382,852 | $1,687,398 | 10,514,000 | $1,366,820 | 44,260,000 | $2,213,000 | 72,518,000 | $3,480,864 | $13,265,701 |
| Total, 1929 | 13 | 290 | 303 | 4,417,358 | 4,397,377 | 2,343,802 | 8,905,074 | 1,567,293 | 48,889,906 | 3,080,064 | 58,861,000 | 3,584,826 | 15,293,343 |

*Placer gold, $188,243.     †Placer silver, 1,657 ounces.

## GOLD, SILVER, COPPER, LEAD AND ZINC MINED IN COLORADO IN 1931*, BY COUNTIES

(In terms of recovered or recoverable metals)

(Preliminary figures by Chas. W. Henderson, United States Bureau of Mines, Department of Commerce)

| COUNTY | Gold† Value | SILVER† Fine Ounces | SILVER† Value | COPPER Pounds | COPPER Value | LEAD Pounds | LEAD Value | ZINC Pounds | ZINC Value | Total Value |
|---|---|---|---|---|---|---|---|---|---|---|
| Adams | $ 1,716 | 13 | $ 4 | | | | | | | $ 1,720 |
| Arapahoe | 227 | | | | | | | | | 227 |
| Boulder | 31,070 | 3,302 | 958 | | | 17,000 | $ 646 | | | 32,674 |
| Chaffee | 2,419 | 53 | 15 | | | | | | | 2,434 |
| Clear Creek | 76,817 | 23,669 | 6,864 | 9,000 | $ 747 | 98,000 | 3,724 | | | 88,152 |
| Custer | 661 | 409 | 119 | | | 16,000 | 570 | | | 1,350 |
| Delta | 496 | 2 | 1 | | | | | | | 497 |
| Dolores | 124 | 770 | 223 | | | | | | | 965 |
| Douglas | 331 | | | | | 16,000 | 608 | | | 331 |
| Eagle | 72,372 | 1,394,956 | 404,537 | 6,315,000 | 524,145 | 6,684,000 | 253,992 | 26,182,000 | $ 994,916 | 2,249,962 |
| Elbert | 41 | | | | | | | | | 41 |
| Gilpin | 329,116 | 20,483 | 5,940 | 100,000 | 8,300 | 63,000 | 2,394 | | | 345,750 |
| Gunnison | 9,137 | 2,963 | 859 | | | 26,000 | 988 | | | 10,984 |
| Hinsdale | 269 | 200 | 58 | | | | | | | 327 |
| Jefferson | 41 | | | | | | | | | 41 |
| Lake | 128,724 | 0,910 | 26,190 | 34,000 | 2,822 | 3,914,000 | 148,732 | 5,793,000 | 220,134 | 526,602 |
| La Plata | 10,398 | 1,882 | 546 | | | | | | | 10,944 |
| Moffat | 269 | 1 | 62 | | | | | | | 269 |
| Montezuma | 496 | 80 | | | | | | | | 648 |
| Ouray | 200,579 | 42,293 | 12,265 | 68,000 | 5,644 | 382,000 | 14,516 | | | 233,001 |
| Park | 770,377 | 23,937 | 6,942 | | | 695,000 | 26,410 | | | 803,729 |
| Pitkin | 1,778 | 0,338 | 8,914 | | | 257,000 | 9,766 | | | 20,458 |
| Rio Grande | 1,116 | 87 | 25 | | | | | | | 1,141 |
| Routt | 103 | | | | | | | | | 103 |
| Saguache | 517 | 2,812 | 815 | 8,000 | 664 | 74,000 | 2,812 | | | 4,808 |
| San Juan | 665,716 | 414,298 | 120,146 | 1,180,000 | 97,940 | 1,009,000 | 38,342 | | | 922,144 |
| San Miguel | 47,421 | 9,294 | 2,692 | 5,000 | 415 | 179,000 | 6,802 | | | 57,330 |
| Summit | 19,556 | 3,944 | 1,145 | 3,000 | 249 | 28,000 | 1,064 | | | 22,014 |
| Teller | 2,394,501 | 8,50 | 2,321 | | | | | | | 2,396,822 |
| Total, 1931‡ | $4,766,388 | 2,074,591 | $ 601,631 | 7,722,000 | $ 640,926 | 13,457,000 | $ 511,366 | 31,975,000 | $1,215,050 | $7,735,361 |
| Total, 1930§ | 4,516,196 | 4,290,587 | 1,651,876 | 9,787,000 | 1,272,310 | 45,635,000 | 2,276,750 | 72,657,000 | 3,482,736 | 13,199,868 |
| Increase or decrease from 1930 | +$250,192 | -2,215,996 | -$1,050,245 | -2,065,000 | -$631,384 | -32,078,000 | -$1,765,384 | -40,682,000 | -$2,267,686 | -$5,464,507 |

*Actual 11 months figures, with estimate for December. †Includes placer production. ‡Average value of metals: Gold, $20.671835 per ounce; silver, $0.29 per ounce; copper, $0.083 per pound; lead, $0.038 per pound; zinc, $0.05 per pound. §Average value of metals: Gold, $20.671835 per ounce; silver, $0.385 per ounce; copper, $0.13 per pound; lead, $0.05 per pound; zinc, $0.048 per pound.

## COAL

The annual output of coal in Colorado exceeds in volume and value that of any other product of the mines. Since 1914 the volume has ranged from a maximum of 12,658,055 tons in 1918 to a minimum of 6,604,063 tons in 1931, and the value from a maximum of $42,829,000 in 1920,. to a minimum of $13,599,264 in 1915. The value of all coal produced in the state from the beginning of the industry down to the end of 1931 is estimated at $729,-816,680, which compares with $720,-245,420, total value of all gold produced in the state in the same period. Gold held first place in total value of output up to 1931, in which year that position was surrendered to coal.

The coal resources of the state, that is, coal in the ground unmined, are greater than in any other state in the Union, according to Clark B. Carpenter, associate professor of metallurgy of the Colorado School of Mines, who places Colorado first in the estimates of the country's available supply, with Illinois, West Virginia and Pennsylvania following in the order named. The state ranked third at the end of 1912, according to estimates made by the United States geological survey. Colorado ranks eighth among the states in the value of the annual output.

M. R. Campbell, senior geologist of the United States geological survey, estimates that the quantity of coal in the state unmined at the end of 1925 was approximately 417,982,149,000 short tons. This estimate is based on areas given by him in the "Coal Resources of the World" before the Twelfth International Geological Congress at Ottawa, Canada, in 1913, from which is deducted the coal mined up to the end of 1925 and estimated amount lost in mining. The areas mentioned comprised 19,754 square miles. These figures are given in detail in the following table:

| | Area Sq. Mi. | Tonnage |
|---|---|---|
| Denver region.... | 6,860 | 36,297,700,000 |
| Canon City field.. | 40 | 932,800,000 |
| Trinidad ........ | 1,115 | 22,198,000,000 |
| North Park...... | 100 | 2,588,600,000 |
| Yampa field....... | 3,130 | 122,999,800,000 |
| Uinta basin...... | 6,500 | 206,283,400,000 |
| South Park....... | 73 | 18,100,000 |
| Durango field..... | 1,860 | 26,197,800,000 |
| Tongue Mesa..... | 40 | 842,300,000 |
| Area north of Mancos and West of Telluride ...... | 36 | 74,000,000 |
| Total .........19,754 | | 418,432,500,000 |

| Coal mined up to end of 1925 ......300,351,000 | |
|---|---|
| Est. loss in mining ....150,000,000 | |
| Total exhaustion ...... | 450,351,000 |
| Coal unmined | 417,982,149,000 |

Of the area given in the above table, Mr. Campbell segregates 14,341 square miles as area in which coal probably is present and 5,413 square miles in which coal possibly is present. In the Denver region 5,380 square miles is classed as probable and 1,480 square miles as possible coal area, and in the Uinta basin, 2,780 square miles as probable and 3,720 square miles as possible coal area. The figures do not represent coal that is available at the present time, but coal that will ultimately be mined.

Professor Carpenter's estimates place the total considerably in excess of the geological survey, his estimate being 503,895,000,000 tons exclusive of the Denver and North Park regions. His estimates are as follows:

| Field | Area Sq. Mi. | Tonnage |
|---|---|---|
| Canon City........ | 40 | 932,000,000 |
| Trinidad ..........| 1,035 | 22,198,000,000 |
| Yampa ...........| 3,130 | 85,045,000,000 |
| Uinta Basin......| 2,780 | 76,282,000,000 |
| South Park........ | 3 | 18,000,000 |
| Durango ..........| 1,840 | 8,504,000,000 |
| Tongue Mesa...... | 40 | 842,000,000 |
| Southwest Colorado | 36 | 74,000,000 |
| Yampa and Uinta (below 3,000 ft.) .... | | 310,000,000,000 |
| Total ...........| 8,904 | 503,895,000,000 |

The Colorado state geological survey estimates on area and available supply are as follows:

| Field | Area Sq. Mi. | Tonnage |
|---|---|---|
| Denver region.... | 4,300 | 13,590,000,000 |
| Durango field..... | 1,900 | 21,428,000,000 |
| North Park....... | 500 | 453,000,000 |
| Trinidad ......... | 1,080 | 24,462,000,000 |
| Uinta region...... | 6,000 | 271,810,000,000 |
| Yampa field...... | 3,700 | 39,639,000,000 |
| Scattered fields... | 350 | 388,000,000 |
| Total .........| 17,830 | 371,770,000,000 |

Colorado, through its ownership of state school land, profits extensively from its coal deposits, its holdings of coal lands being estimated at 473,732 acres, of which 15,774 acres was under lease on November 30, 1930. From these leases 1,227,158 tons of coal was mined in the biennial period ending November 30, 1930, the amount received therefrom during the period being $197,916. Additional data on state school land will be found in the chapter under that heading.

In order to present the magnitude of the Colorado coal deposits, Professor Carpenter points out that at an estimated value of only one cent a ton the value of the state's coal resources is at least three times greater than the total value of all metals ever produced in the state. On the basis of coal consumption in 1925 the state has sufficient coal to provide for the entire United States for more than seven centuries.

Colorado coal ranges in quality from black lignite and sub-bituminous varieties through various grades of bituminous to true anthracite. The bituminous varieties include high-grade coking coal found in the Trinidad district, in the Glenwood Springs area and in Gunnison county. High-grade bituminous coal is also found in Jackson, Routt, Moffat, Rio Blanco, Mesa, Delta, Montezuma, La Plata, Fremont and Huerfano counties. True anthracite coal is found near Crested Butte, in Gunnison county, and is found in several localities in Routt and Moffat counties.

Tables published herewith are as follows:

Summary of state coal mining industry, by years.

Colorado coal production and value, by years.

Coal production by counties in 1920, and 1926 to 1931, inclusive.

Production, value, men employed, days worked and output per man per day at Colorado coal mines in 1930, as reported by the bureau of mines of the department of commerce.

## COAL PRODUCTION BY COUNTIES
(From the Report of the State Coal Mine Inspector)

| COUNTY | Tons 1931 | Tons 1930 · | Tons 1929 | Tons 1928 | Tons 1927 | Tons 1926 | Tons 1920* |
|---|---|---|---|---|---|---|---|
| Archuleta | 1,106 | 948 | 408 | 515 | 414 | 1,106 | -------- |
| Boulder | 499,133 | 428,051 | 479,643 | 434,995 | 433,661 | 600,849 | 1,230,347 |
| Delta | 60,202 | 70,323 | 72,273 | 68,745 | 87,883 | 69,838 | 123,478 |
| Dolores | -------- | 6,085 | 11,732 | 8,354 | 9,200 | 5,220 | -------- |
| Elbert | 3,136 | 2,158 | 3,003 | 4,249 | 3,615 | 3,254 | -------- |
| El Paso | 345,978 | 345,344 | 361,595 | 352,589 | 349,386 | 352,300 | 379,869 |
| Fremont | 347,356 | 411,455 | 526,927 | 480,069 | 449,769 | 572,631 | 874,766 |
| Garfield | 30,447 | 33,841 | 44,430 | 33,498 | 30,654 | 31,292 | 28,507 |
| Gunnison | 404,209 | 498,724 | 521,401 | 460,805 | 555,837 | 566,315 | 620,632 |
| Huerfano | 975,397 | 1,374,491 | 1,783,744 | 1,800,105 | 1,814,629 | 1,967,437 | 2,448,733 |
| Jackson | 44,298 | 48,762 | 56,318 | 66,832 | 69,799 | 59,192 | 50,905 |
| Jefferson | 140,374 | 121,085 | 98,755 | 101,169 | 79,380 | 102,416 | 176,427 |
| La Plata | 31,662 | 57,011 | 74,464 | 89,701 | 92,215 | 102,998 | 132,497 |
| Larimer | 1,914 | -------- | -------- | -------- | -------- | -------- | -------- |
| Las Animas | 1,333,999 | 1,970,599 | 2,564,897 | 2,944,211 | 3,231,872 | 3,299,803 | 4,345,110 |
| Mesa | 92,679 | 96,337 | 118,567 | 163,861 | 118,495 | 127,096 | 174,801 |
| Moffat | 3,953 | 8,445 | 6,025 | 7,396 | 5,357 | 6,196 | 3,173 |
| Montezuma | 4,985 | 6,456 | 6,663 | 7,399 | 7,928 | 6,156 | 4,147 |
| Montrose | 1,143 | 3,470 | 1,278 | 1,354 | 1,346 | 1,091 | 2,105 |
| Ouray | 1,742 | 1,180 | -------- | 373 | 250 | -------- | 500 |
| Park | 200 | -------- | -------- | -------- | -------- | -------- | -------- |
| Pitkin | 10,175 | 14,011 | 18,757 | 16,198 | 2,224 | 3,002 | 913 |
| Rio Blanco | 7,947 | 6,304 | 6,771 | 5,942 | 5,042 | 6,175 | 6,068 |
| Routt | 574,211 | 837,801 | 1,006,740 | 928,855 | 921,614 | 917,717 | 966,912 |
| San Miguel | 1,504 | 1,433 | 557 | 1,057 | 1,096 | 1,047 | -------- |
| Weld | 1,686,313 | 1,893,780 | 2,169,116 | 1,943,313 | 1,509,914 | 1,813,629 | 944,803 |
| Total | 6,604,063 | 8,238,094 | 9,934,064 | 9,921,585 | 9,781,580 | 10,616,760 | 12,514,693 |

*Year of peak output.

## SUMMARY OF STATE COAL MINING INDUSTRY
(From Records of the State Coal Mine Inspector)

| Year | Tons of Coal Produced | No. of Men Employed | No. of Fatal Accidents | Killed Per 1,000 Employed | Tons Coal Produced Per Fatal Accident | Total No. of Mines State |
|------|------|------|------|------|------|------|
| 1913....... | 9,268,939 | 12,871 | 110 | 8.6 | 84,263 | 178 |
| 1914....... | 8,201,423 | 10,596 | 75 | 7.0 | 109,352 | 188 |
| 1915....... | 8,715,397 | 12,563 | 64 | 5.1 | 136,178 | 199 |
| 1916....... | 10,522,185 | 13,315 | 44 | 3.35 | 239,095 | 219 |
| 1917....... | 12,515,305 | 13,970 | 188 | 13.5 | 66,571 | 238 |
| 1918....... | 12,658,055 | 14,374 | 71 | 4.94 | 177,578 | 249 |
| 1919....... | 10,406,543 | 12,799 | 91 | 7.1 | 114,357 | 241 |
| 1920....... | 12,514,693 | 13,665 | 70 | 5.1 | 178,781 | 231 |
| 1921....... | 9,141,947 | 14,164 | 52 | 3.6 | 175,807 | 249 |
| 1922....... | 10,003,610 | 13,436 | 74 | 5.51 | 135,184 | 275 |
| 1923....... | 10,336,735 | 13,277 | 66 | 4.97 | 156,617 | 276 |
| 1924....... | 10,501,088 | 12,703 | 44 | 3.48 | 238,661 | 271 |
| 1925....... | 10,440,387 | 12,228 | 57 | 4.66 | 183,165 | 283 |
| 1926....... | 10,616,760 | 11,768 | 52 | 4.42 | 204,168 | 261 |
| 1927....... | 9,781,580 | 11,453 | 54 | 4.7 | 181,140 | 266 |
| 1928....... | 9,921,585 | 11,474 | 35 | 3.05 | 283,474 | 266 |
| 1929....... | 9,934,064 | 11,196 | 53 | 4.73 | 187,435 | 264 |
| 1930....... | 8,238,094 | 10,683 | 36 | 3.38 | 228,836 | 275 |
| 1931....... | 6,604,063 | 10,015 | 22 | 2.20 | 300,184 | 318 |
| Average ... | 10,016,971 | 12,450 | 66.2 | 5.32 | 151,290 | 250 |

## COLORADO COAL PRODUCTION BY YEARS

| Year | Tons | Value | Year | Tons | Value |
|------|------|------|------|------|------|
| 1864 to 1872... | 53,700 | $ 127,400 | 1904 .......... | 6,776,551 | $ 8,751,821 |
| 1873 .......... | 69,977 | 139,954 | 1905 .......... | 8,989,631 | 10,810,978 |
| 1874 .......... | 87,372 | 179,740 | 1906 .......... | 10,308,421 | 12,735,616 |
| 1875 .......... | 98,838 | 197,676 | 1907 .......... | 10,965,640 | 15,079,449 |
| 1876 .......... | 117,666 | 235,332 | 1908 .......... | 9,773,007 | 13,586,988 |
| 1877 .......... | 160,000 | 320,000 | 1909 .......... | 10,772,400 | 14,206,012 |
| 1878 .......... | 200,630 | 451,417 | 1910 .......... | 12,104,887 | 17,026,934 |
| 1879 .......... | 322,732 | 726,154 | 1911 .......... | 10,197,000 | 14,747,764 |
| 1880 .......... | 375,000 | 844,100 | 1912 .......... | 11,016,948 | 16,345,336 |
| 1881 .......... | 706,744 | 1,590,178 | 1913 .......... | 9,268,939 | 14,035,090 |
| 1882 .......... | 1,161,479 | 2,388,328 | 1914 .......... | 8,201,423 | 13,601,718 |
| 1883 .......... | 1,220,593 | 2,766,584 | 1915 .......... | 8,715,397 | 13,599,264 |
| 1884 .......... | 1,130,024 | 2,542,554 | 1916 .......... | 10,522,185 | 16,964,104 |
| 1885 .......... | 1,398,796 | 3,051,589 | 1917 .......... | 12,515,305 | 27,669,129 |
| 1886 .......... | 1,436,211 | 3,215,594 | 1918 .......... | 12,658,055 | 33,404,743 |
| 1887 .......... | 1,791,735 | 3,941,817 | 1919 .......... | 10,406,543 | 28,748,534 |
| 1888 .......... | 2,185,477 | 4,808,049 | 1920 .......... | 12,514,693 | 42,829,000 |
| 1889 .......... | 2,400,629 | 3,843,992 | 1921 .......... | 9,141,947 | 32,377,000 |
| 1890 .......... | 3,075,781 | 4,344,196 | 1922 .......... | 10,003,610 | 31,701,000 |
| 1891 .......... | 3,512,632 | 4,800,000 | 1923 .......... | 10,346,218 | 33,299,000 |
| 1892 .......... | 3,771,234 | 5,685,112 | 1924 .......... | 10,501,088 | 32,133,000 |
| 1893 .......... | 3,947,056 | 5,104,602 | 1925 .......... | 10,440,387 | *30,694,738 |
| 1894 .......... | 3,021,928 | 4,078,000 | 1926 .......... | 10,616,760 | *29,514,593 |
| 1895 .......... | 3,339,495 | 4,519,000 | 1927 .......... | 9,781,580 | *27,192,792 |
| 1896 .......... | 3,371,633 | 4,560,000 | 1928 .......... | 9,921,585 | *27,780,438 |
| 1897 .......... | 3,565,660 | 4,475,000 | 1929 .......... | 9,934,064 | *26,325,269 |
| 1898 .......... | 4,174,037 | 5,215,000 | 1930 .......... | 8,238,094 | *19,705,845 |
| 1899 .......... | 4,826,939 | 5,363,667 | 1931 .......... | 6,604,063 | 15,586,808 |
| 1900 .......... | 5,495,734 | 5,858,036 | Total .......359,575,783 | | $729,816,680 |
| 1901 .......... | 6,021,405 | 6,441,891 | | | |
| 1902 .......... | 7,522,923 | 8,397,812 | | | |
| 1903 .......... | 7,775,302 | 9,150,943 | *Revised. | | |

## PRODUCTION, VALUE, MEN EMPLOYED, DAYS WORKED AND OUTPUT PER MAN PER DAY AT COAL MINES IN COLORADO IN 1930*

Note.—Information in this table is that reported by the Bureau of Mines of the United States Department of Commerce and is exclusive of product of wagon mines producing less than 1,000 tons. The statistics of the state coal mine inspector include all mines and, therefore, the two reports do not agree in detail.

| COUNTY | Net Tons — Loaded at Mines for Shipment | Sold to Local Trade and Used by Employes | Used at Mines for Power and Heat | Made into Coke at Mines | Total Quantity | Value — Total | Average Per Ton | Number of Employees — Underground: Miners, Loaders and Shot Firers | Haulage and Track | All Others | Surface | Total | Average Number of Days Worked | Average Tons Per Man Per Day |
|---|---|---|---|---|---|---|---|---|---|---|---|---|---|---|
| Boulder | 261,248 | 144,540 | 23,409 | — | 429,197 | $1,151,000 | $2.68 | 356 | 59 | 26 | 76 | 517 | 134 | 4.28 |
| Delta | 40,501 | 29,355 | 500 | — | 70,356 | 207,000 | 2.94 | 52 | 1 | 8 | 23 | 84 | 131 | 6.42 |
| Dolores, Montrose, and Ouray | — | 8,295 | 170 | — | 8,465 | 20,000 | 2.36 | 10 | 3 | 3 | 3 | 19 | 164 | 2.72 |
| El Paso | 118,975 | 215,567 | 10,447 | — | 344,989 | 754,000 | 2.19 | 212 | 32 | 21 | 48 | 313 | 257 | 4.29 |
| Fremont | 337,539 | 60,838 | 4,601 | — | 402,978 | 1,523,000 | 3.80 | 522 | 106 | 97 | 132 | 857 | 180 | 2.61 |
| Garfield | 10,546 | 25,429 | 300 | — | 36,275 | 99,000 | 2.73 | 30 | 5 | 3 | 9 | 47 | 89 | 1.09 |
| Gunnison | 461,617 | 7,560 | 30,450 | — | 499,627 | 1,228,000 | 2.46 | 355 | 78 | 58 | 105 | 596 | 189 | 4.44 |
| Huerfano | 1,333,286 | 23,436 | 18,734 | — | 1,375,456 | 4,088,000 | 2.97 | 1,493 | 251 | 204 | 320 | 2,268 | 168 | 3.60 |
| Jefferson | 99,169 | 21,752 | 2,550 | — | 123,471 | 264,000 | 2.14 | 74 | 16 | 5 | 22 | 117 | 232 | 4.55 |
| La Plata | 25,565 | 20,929 | 31 | 10,351 | 56,876 | 154,000 | 2.71 | 59 | 9 | 10 | 19 | 97 | 151 | 3.89 |
| Las Animas | 1,753,654 | 53,822 | 27,331 | 110,483 | 1,945,290 | 4,747,000 | 2.44 | 2,171 | 293 | 231 | 369 | 3,064 | 115 | 3.84 |
| Mesa | 53,256 | 35,320 | 2,607 | — | 91,183 | 195,000 | 2.14 | 97 | 10 | 14 | 21 | 142 | 176 | 3.65 |
| Moffat | — | 7,637 | — | — | 7,637 | 18,000 | 2.36 | 9 | 1 | 1 | 1 | 12 | 176 | 3.63 |
| Montezuma | 525 | 4,444 | — | — | 4,969 | 20,000 | 4.02 | 11 | 1 | 1 | 3 | 16 | 214 | 1.93 |
| Rio Blanco | — | 5,599 | — | — | 5,699 | 15,000 | 2.68 | 9 | 1 | 1 | 3 | 12 | 137 | 2.55 |
| Routt | 791,610 | 19,908 | 27,310 | — | 838,828 | 2,819,000 | 3.36 | 728 | 110 | 123 | 257 | 1,218 | 100 | 6.89 |
| Weld | 1,662,093 | 199,944 | 29,062 | — | 1,891,099 | 4,014,000 | 2.12 | 1,168 | 150 | 145 | 155 | 1,618 | 134 | 6.36 |
| Other counties (Elbert, Jackson and Pitkin) | 54,926 | 7,072 | 2,617 | — | 64,615 | 159,000 | 2.46 | 57 | 8 | 7 | 22 | 94 | 238 | 2.89 |
| Total 1930 | 7,064,510 | 891,447 | 180,119 | 120,834 | 8,196,910 | $21,485,000 | $2.62 | 7,411 | 1,134 | 958 | 1,558 | 11,091 | 169 | 4.38 |
| Total 1929 | 8,664,817 | 824,049 | 183,746 | 248,129 | 9,920,741 | 26,254,000 | 2.65 | 7,981 | 1,227 | 1,226 | 1,623 | 12,057 | 187 | 4.40 |

*The figures relate only to active mines of commercial size that produced coal in 1930. The number of such mines in Colorado was 218 in 1930; 214 in 1929; and 215 in 1928.

Methods of mining in 1930: The tonnage by hand was 2,623,860; shot off the solid, 858,869; cut by machines, 4,681,537; not specified, 32,644.

Size classes of commercial mines in 1930: There were 8 mines in Class 1 B (200,000 to 500,000 tons) producing 28.8 per cent of the tonnage; 21 in Class 2 (100,000 to 200,000 tons) with 37.2 per cent; 20 in Class 3 (50,000 to 100,000 tons) with 16.9 per cent; 40 in Class 4 (10,000 to 50,000 tons) with 13.5 per cent; and 129 in Class 5 (less than 10,000 tons) producing 3.6 per cent.

†In this county certain mines have in recent times followed the practice of reducing their forces in periods of dull market and of working every day underground when the tipple works only one, two, or three days a week. As the figures of days worked represent tipple time, the result is not comparable with the returns for other counties, and the average for the State is affected also.

## COKÉ PRODUCTION

The production of coke in Colorado in the calendar year of 1931 as reported by the state coal mine inspector was 264,269 tons, a decrease of 194,174 tons compared with the output in 1930, and of 848,180 tons compared with 1917, when the maximum in output was established. There were 266 coke ovens operated during the year, employing an average of 76 men, and 439,189 tons of coal were made into coke.

The production of coke began in Colorado in 1880, when the total output was 25,568 tons. A steady increase in output continued up to 1891, in which year the quantity was 277,074 tons. During the next 20 years Colorado's output was not reported separately, but included Utah production. The maximum output for Colorado was in 1917, when the total was 1,112,-449 tons.

By-product coke ovens have been gradually replacing the old bee-hive type in the state, and as a result of this change the output of benzol, ammonium sulphate and other by-products has been steadily increasing. In 1929 the Colorado Fuel & Iron company appropriated $1,100,000 for the construction of 42 additional by-product ovens and auxiliary equipment, which brought the total number operated by that company alone up to 162.

Operations by calendar years were as follows:

| Year | No. Ovens | Tons Coal Used | Tons Coke |
|---|---|---|---|
| 1923 | 545 | 1,068,354 | 648,851 |
| 1924 | 559 | 1,260,209 | 738,345 |
| 1925 | .. | 945,957 | 644,481 |
| 1926 | 600 | 1,324,465 | 792,517 |
| 1927 | 492 | 1,332,038 | 790,573 |
| 1928 | 493 | 1,265,105 | 750,022 |
| 1929 | 562 | 1,103,308 | 722,072 |
| 1930 | 295½ | 687,800 | 458,443 |
| 1931 | 266 | 439,189 | 264,269 |

## STONE AND OTHER NON-METALS

Colorado ranks first among the states in the wide variety and volume of deposits of high grade stone which are to be found within its boundaries. The state is so rich in beautifully colored and marked building and decorative stones that if its resources are properly developed, according to competent authorities, it will, in time, be the stone and marble center of the United States. Building stones in Colorado are divided into five general classes by Justin H. Haynes, consulting engineer, of Denver. These are the granites, marbles, limestones, sandstones and lavas. In addition, there are special stones, due to some particular characteristic or specified method of formation. Among these are travertine, which formerly was classed by some as a marble and by others as a limestone; dolomites and olivines.

Colorado is rich in the decorative marbles and particularly so in the vicinity of Salida, Cotopaxi and Wet Mountain valley. Very little work has been done on them and many are open to location.

Granites are found widely scattered throughout the state, notably at Lyons, Gunnison, Silver Plume, Salida, Cotopaxi and Platte canyon.

Sandstones are found on the sedimentary uplifts on both sides of the main range, from north to south. The principal quarries have been at Lyons, Colorado Springs, Glenwood Springs and Stone City.

Lavas are not so abundant but commercial quarries have been operated at Castle Rock and Del Norte.

Limestones occur mostly in Colorado as a sedimentary deposit on both sides of the main range. Some of the limestone quarries are along the Arkansas river between Pueblo and Salida, and in the vicinity of Colorado Springs and Fort Collins.

The limestones have in all cases been quarried for their lime content and not as building stone and, therefore, must be eliminated from the building stones unless deposits are found that are free from fracture and capable of being cut into large blocks.

Travertine, which was used largely in building ancient Rome, the Colosseum being the outstanding example, is found in Colorado in several deposits. The best known and the only one that has been worked to any appreciable extent is located about six miles southeast of Salida. It is from this deposit that the stone for the interior of the new Denver municipal building was obtained. There are numerous installations of Colorado travertine in the United States, among these being the Sunnyside mausoleum in Long Beach, California, and the department of commerce building in Washington, D. C. Colorado travertine has been specified for about 12 government buildings to be erected in 1932 and 1933. Marble from quarries near the town of Marble was used in the construction of the Lincoln memorial in the nation's capital, New York City's municipal building and structures in other large cities.

The value of stone sold or used by producers in the years named as reported by the United States bureau of mines, was as follows:

|  | 1926 | 1927 | 1928 |
|---|---|---|---|
| Stone | $1,107,867 | $ 975,953 | $ 933,241 |
| Granite | 194,386 | 179,591 | 205,785 |
| Limestone | 740,138 | 681,742 | 563,215 |
| Sandstone | 71,085 | 77,004 | 69,470 |
| Total | *$2,113,476 | *$1,914,290 | *$1,771,711 |

*Does not include basalt, marble and miscellaneous.

The value of the output of stone, granite, limestone and sandstone by years is as follows:

| | |
|---|---|
| 1920 | $1,621,180 |
| 1921 | 1,111,954 |
| 1922 | 1,111,388 |
| 1923 | 1,485,369 |
| 1924 | 2,114,960 |
| 1925 | 1,733,842 |
| 1926 | 2,113,476 |
| 1927 | 1,914,290 |
| 1928 | 1,771,711 |

In 1928 there were 43 active plants producing stone, eight producing granite, 17 producing limestone and 13 producing sandstone.

Minerals used in the manufacture of cement are being developed in the state on an extensive scale. Figures on production are not segregated, but annual output is in excess of $3,000,000 in value. Brick clay is found in almost every county in the state and has been dug to some extent in at least two-thirds of the counties. The importance of this industry is indicated by the census bureau's figures on manufactures for 1925, which credit Colorado with 30 establishments engaged in manufacturing clay products (other than pottery) and non-clay refractories. These establishments employed an average of 1,182 wage earners, distributed $1,414,974 in wages, and had an output of products valued at $4,351,749. In addition, there were four plants producing pottery and porcelain ware, with an output of products valued at $287,820. Fire clay, plastic clay and kaolin, also, are widely distributed.

The accompanying tabulation shows the principal valuable non-metals found in the state, together with the counties where they have been reported:

**Abrasive Stone**—Gunnison.
**Amber**—Boulder.
**Asbestos**—Boulder, Chaffee, Fremont, Rio Grande.
**Asphalt**—Garfield, Grand, Jefferson, Mesa, Routt, Rio Blanco.
**Basalt**—Boulder, Delta, Eagle, Garfield, Grand, Huerfano, Jefferson, Las Animas, Mesa, Rio Blanco.
**Cement Materials**—Boulder, Chaffee, Fremont, Larimer, and many others.
**Corundum**—Chaffee, Clear Creek.
**Coal**—Adams, Arapahoe, Archuleta, Boulder, Delta, Dolores, Douglas, Elbert, El Paso, Fremont, Garfield, Gunnison,

Huerfano, Jackson, Jefferson, La Plata, Las Animas, Larimer, Mesa, Moffat, Montezuma, Montrose, Ouray, Park, Pitkin, Rio Blanco, Routt, Weld.
**Feldspar**—El Paso.
**Fire Clay**—Bent, Boulder, Custer, Douglas, El Paso, Fremont, Garfield, Gunnison, Huerfano, Jefferson, Larimer, Las Animas, Pueblo.
**Fluorspar**—Boulder, Chaffee, Clear Creek, Custer, Dolores, Douglas, El Paso, Fremont, Gilpin, Jefferson, Lake, Larimer, Mineral, Montezuma, Montrose, Park, San Juan, Saguache, San Miguel, Teller.
**Fuller's Earth**—Chaffee, Washington.
**Gem Stones**—Chaffee, Clear Creek. Eagle, El Paso, Fremont, Hinsdale, Jefferson, Lake, Larimer, Moffat, Park, Saguache, Teller.
**Glass Sand**—Bent, Fremont, Prowers, Pueblo.
**Granite**—Archuleta, Boulder, Chaffee, Clear Creek, Conejos, Costilla, Custer, Delta, Dolores, Douglas, Eagle, El Paso, Fremont, Garfield, Gunnison, Jackson, Jefferson, La Plata, Larimer, Las Animas, Mineral, Moffat, Ouray, Park, Pueblo, Rio Blanco, Rio Grande.
**Graphite**—Chaffee, Gunnison, Las Animas.
**Gypsum** — Custer, Delta, Dolores, Eagle, El Paso, Fremont, Garfield, Jefferson, Larimer, Montrose.
**Kaolin**—Boulder, El Paso, Fremont, Huerfano, Jefferson, La Plata, Morgan, Pueblo.
**Limestone**—Boulder, Chaffee, Douglas, Fremont, Gunnison, Jefferson, La Plata, Larimer, Las Animas, Mesa, Mineral, Ouray, Park, Pueblo, Rio Blanco.
**Marble**—Boulder, Chaffee, Gunnison, Larimer, Pueblo.
**Mica**—Clear Creek, Fremont, Larimer, Mesa.
**Oil Shale**—Garfield, Gunnison, Mesa, Moffat, Montrose, Rio Blanco.
**Onyx**—Gunnison.
**Petroleum**—Boulder, Fremont, Larimer, Mesa, Moffat, Montrose, Pueblo, Rio Blanco, Routt.
**Potash**—Costilla, Delta.
**Sandstone**—Archuleta, Boulder, Chaffee, Conejos, Costilla, Custer, Delta, Dolores, Douglas, Eagle, Elbert, El Paso, Fremont, Garfield, Gunnison, Jackson, La Plata, Larimer, Las Animas, Mesa, Mineral, Ouray, Park, Pueblo, Rio Blanco.
**Salts of Sodium**—Alamosa, Saguache.
**Slate**—Gunnison.
**Sulphur**—Gunnison, Mineral.

## RADIUM

A relatively small area of land in southwestern Colorado and extending into southeastern Utah has furnished almost half of the world's supply of radium, a brilliant white metal that melts sharply at about 700 degrees centigrade, but which is produced in such minute quantities that it is handled in the form of a compound and packed in small glass tubes encased in lead as protection to those who must handle it. World production of radium element from 1898 to 1928, inclusive, is given by the United States bureau of mines at 575 grams, of which 250 grams was produced in this country, mostly from ores mined in the Paradox valley in southwestern Colorado.

Radium is one of the most precious articles of commerce, costing many times as much as ordinary fine-quality gems. During the world war the price of the product reached $125,000 and occasionally $135,000 or more a gram. The price at present is $70,000 a gram except for large orders for charitable institutions. Emeralds and rubies rarely exceed a value of $1,000 a carat, or $5,000 a gram. One gram of radium is 14 times more valuable than a gram of these gems. A gram of gold is worth only 66 cents. For about 10 years, 1913 to 1922, the Colorado deposits practically dominated the world situation, but since 1923 very little radium has been isolated in this country. This was due to economic conditions and not to any exhaustion of supply. In 1923 a Belgium company, a subsidiary of a government-controlled concern, cut the price of radium from $100,000 and more to $70,000 a gram, approximately the cost of producing it from carnotite ores in this country.

Ores from Colorado, including pitcheblende from Gilpin county and carnotite from Montrose county, were used in perfecting the discovery of radium. The way to the discovery was opened in 1895 by Roentgen, who found that a glow from a Crooke's tube contained penetrating rays which he called X-rays. It was then found that uranium salts produced photographic impressions even when enveloped with opaque substances. To Marie Sklovouski, a young Polish student, who later became Madam Curie, was delegated the task of learning how and why uranium possessed powers to emit these peculiar rays. Out of these investigations resulted in the discovery of radium and a world search for radioactive substances began. As early as 1881 the yellow ore which became known as carnotite was mined in western Colorado for small quantities of gold found in pockets. In 1896, after being informed by the Smithsonian institution that specimens they had sent in contained uranium, Kimball and Logan mined 10 tons of the ore and sold it in Denver for $2,700. In 1899 Poule and Voillegue sent specimens to France and there the new ore was named carnotite in honor of M. Carnot, then president of the Republic.

"Radioactivity" is a term generally applied to a class of substances, such as uranium, thorium, radium and their compounds, that possess the property of spontaneously emitting radiations capable of passing through plates of metals and other substances opaque to ordinary light. This is a result of the explosion of atoms. In a single gram of uranium, 5,000 atoms break down each second. Nevertheless, it is estimated that in spite of the large number of atoms that break down each second, it would take five billion years for even one-half of a given piece of uranium to dissipate itself spontaneously. The half-life of radium is placed at 1,520 to 2,500 years. The principal use of radium is for the treatment of cancer. It is also employed for the manufacture of luminous paints used on watch and clock dials, electric switch buttons, keyholes and like products. It was extensively used during the world war to eliminate lights that might betray to the enemy the presence of troops.

## PETROLEUM

Colorado has the distinction of being the second oldest oil producing state in the United States and at the same time being among the latest to attract the attention of the oil operators of the country as a probable source of a considerable part of the nation's future crude oil supply.

This situation arises out of the fact that the oil industry of Colorado is divided into two distinct periods of development. The first period embraces the era from the first discovery in 1862 down to the time when the search for new fields had practically ceased. The second period opened in 1923, when some of the major producing companies of the country commenced an exploratory campaign which resulted in discoveries that promise to put the state in the front rank among the oil producers.

The first attempts to open up a supply of crude oil in Colorado were mostly economic failures. The second period has yielded more favorable results. Between the two periods the oil industry made rapid progress in development in the way of geological knowledge and in methods for drilling to greater depths, and this advance undoubtedly has been a big factor in changing the outlook for the future.

The first discovery of oil in Colorado in a well drilled for that purpose was made in the spring of 1862 by A. M. Cassedy, a pioneer in the Pennsylvania fields. This well came in as a producer at 50 feet and was located on Oil creek, six miles north of Canon City, near an oil spring, in what is now Fremont county, in the south-central part of the state, but what was then a part of Colorado territory. When it is recalled that the first well sunk for oil to come in as a producer in this country was drilled near Titusville, Pa., by Col. E. L. Drake, founder of the petroleum industry, in August, 1859, it will be seen that Colorado's oil development began when the business was in its infancy.

Prospecting continued in the state for a number of years after the Florence discovery and a small pool was found in Boulder county, some shallow wells with small production were drilled in the Rangely district in Rio Blanco county, and some discoveries were made near DeBeque in Mesa and Garfield counties, but these were of importance mostly in pointing to the possibilities of the future.

The present oil activity dates from November 11, 1923, when the Union Oil Company of California brought in a large gas and oil well on the Wellington dome, 15 miles north of Fort Collins, in Larimer county. This was followed by the Texas company's completion of a large oil producer on the Moffat dome, 16 miles south of Craig, in Moffat county, on March 3, 1924. These developments opened a new era of prospecting in the state under the auspices of many of the leading oil companies of the country.

Exploration up to the beginning of 1930 resulted in the discovery of 11 oil pools. The location of these pools along the edges of large natural basins and parallel to the Rocky Mountain range, or near the edges of smaller basins surrounded by mountains, at first led to the conclusion that conditions were unfavorable for the occurrence of oil far out from the mountains in the plains region of eastern Colorado. This theory was upset on October 10, 1930, when the Platte Valley Petroleum company, drilling on the Greasewood dome in Weld county, 60 miles east of the mountain range, made a commercial discovery which inaugurated a third era in oil prospecting in the state. Three producing wells had been completed in this pool up to the beginning of 1932 and three other tests drilled defined the productive area on the west and south, but the possibilities to the north and east of the producers have not been determined.

The location of the producing pools, the dates of their discovery, the formations from which they are producing, the average depth of wells and the quality of the crude are given in an accompanying table.

A table is published herewith showing the extent of drilling operations and results by years beginning with 1926. Prior to the last named year no official records of exploration for oil were compiled by the state. The immigration department has compiled, however, such records as are available of wells drilled in earlier periods and while these are incomplete they furnish an index to past drilling activities in the state. Logs of these wells are not available in many instances; some of them were drilled only to shallow depths and abandoned without making tests of the objective horizons, and many went only to horizons that were then considered likely to contain oil. In later years formations below those formerly drilled have been found productive in several areas of the state. This record, as far as the information is available, has been published in a separate volume entitled "Mineral, Oil and Shale Resources," copies of which may be obtained upon request to the department. Altogether, approximately 2,000 wells have been drilled in 42 counties of the state up to the present in search of oil.

The number of producing wells in the state on December 31 of the year named and average production in barrels per well per day, as reported by the United States bureau of mines, was as follows:

| Year | No. Wells | Av. Prod. |
|---|---|---|
| 1921 | 80 | 3.2 |
| 1922 | 75 | 3.2 |
| 1923 | 60 | 3.5 |
| 1924 | 70 | 25.8 |
| 1925 | 80 | 64.1 |
| 1926 | 130 | 60.3 |
| 1927 | 170 | 51.7 |
| 1928 | 210 | 39.9 |
| 1929 | 220 | 30.0 |
| 1930 | 240 | 19.7 |

The average production per well per day in Colorado compares with 7.4 barrels for the United States in 1926, 7.7 barrels in 1927, 7.6 barrels in 1928, 8.4 barrels in 1929, and 7.5 barrels in 1930. Colorado's average per well per day was the highest in the country in 1926, third highest in 1927 and 1928 and fifth highest in 1929 and 1930.

The total production of crude oil in Colorado from 1862 to 1931, inclusive, a period of 70 years, was 27,544,538 barrels, with a value of $28,195,659. An accompanying chart shows the trend of production and values by years. The following table gives the gross output by years and the estimated value at the well:

### PRODUCTION OF CRUDE OIL IN COLORADO

| Year | Barrels | Value |
|---|---|---|
| 1862-86 | 350,000 | $ 245,000 |
| 1887 | 154,000 | 123,200 |
| 1888 | 298,000 | 262,240 |
| 1889 | 317,000 | 280,240 |
| 1890 | 369,000 | 324,720 |
| 1891 | 666,000 | 559,005 |
| 1892 | 824,000 | 692,160 |
| 1893 | 594,000 | 497,581 |
| 1894 | 516,000 | 423,420 |
| 1895 | 438,000 | 359,160 |
| 1896 | 361,000 | 295,020 |
| 1897 | 385,000 | 346,500 |
| 1898 | 444,000 | 444,000 |
| 1899 | 390,000 | 404,110 |
| 1900 | 317,000 | 323,434 |
| 1901 | 461,000 | 461,030 |
| 1902 | 397,000 | 486,583 |
| 1903 | 484,000 | 431,723 |
| 1904 | 501,000 | 587,035 |
| 1905 | 376,000 | 337,606 |

### PRODUCTION OF CRUDE OIL IN COLORADO

| Year | Barrels | Value |
|---|---|---|
| 1906 | 328,000 | 262,675 |
| 1907 | 332,000 | 272,813 |
| 1908 | 380,000 | 346,403 |
| 1909 | 311,000 | 317,712 |
| 1910 | 240,000 | 243,402 |
| 1911 | 227,000 | 228,104 |
| 1912 | 206,000 | 199,661 |
| 1913 | 189,000 | 174,779 |
| 1914 | 223,000 | 200,894 |
| 1915 | 208,000 | 208,474 |
| 1916 | 197,000 | 217,139 |
| 1917 | 121,000 | 128,100 |
| 1918 | 143,000 | 188,472 |
| 1919 | 121,000 | 183,000 |
| 1920 | 111,000 | 199,000 |
| 1921 | 108,000 | 132,000 |
| 1922 | 97,000 | 114,000 |
| 1923 | 86,000 | 129,000 |
| 1924 | 445,000 | 667,500 |
| 1925 | 1,211,702 | 1,817,553 |
| 1926 | 2,692,892 | 4,577,916 |
| 1927 | 2,722,670 | 2,611,058 |
| 1928 | 2,750,060 | 2,655,670 |
| 1929 | 2,273,723 | 2,120,425 |
| 1930 | 1,627,987 | 1,242,257 |
| 1931 | 1,550,504 | 873,885 |
| Total | 27,544,538 | $28,195,659 |

Note—Above figures up to 1925 are from reports of the U. S. geological survey. Figures for years beginning with 1925 were compiled by the state immigration department.

### PRODUCING OIL POOLS IN JANUARY, 1932

| POOL | County | Date Opened | Av. Gr. of Oil | Depth to Sands (feet) | Producing Formations | No. Wells Jan. 1, 1930 | Av. Daily Production Jan., 1932 |
|---|---|---|---|---|---|---|---|
| Fort Collins | Larimer | 1924 | 37.5 | 4,550 | Dakota | 13 | 190 |
| Wellington | Larimer | 1923 | 33.5 | 4,400 | Dakota | 22 | 840 |
| Moffat | Moffat | 1924 | 41.6 38.0 | 3,800 4,200 4,400 | Dakota Morrison Sundance | 12 | 780 |
| Iles | Moffat | 1927 | 32.5 | 3,200 3,400 | Morrison Sundance | 17 | 858 |
| Florence-Canon City | Fremont | 1887 1926 | 31.0 | 1,000 to 2,300 | Pierre shale | 105 | 318 |
| Walden | Jackson | 1926 | 54.0 | 5,100 | Dakota | 1 | * |
| Tow Creek | Routt | 1924 | 36.0 | 2,500 to 3,100 | Shale above Dakota | 15 | 295 |
| Rangely | Rio Blanco | 1902 | 52.0 | 600 | Mancos shale | 4 | 20 |
| Boulder | Boulder | 1901 | 38.6 | 2,500 | Shale | 7 | 20 |
| Berthoud | Larimer | 1925 | 40.0 | 3,750 | Dakota | 3 | 38 |
| Greasewood | Weld | 1930 | 42.0 | 6,650 | Dakota (?) | 3 | 615 |
| Mancos Creek | Montezuma | 1927 | --- | 350 | Mancos shale | 11 | 3 |
| Total | | | | | | 213 | 3,977 |

*Shut in.

## OIL WELL DRILLING OPERATIONS, BY YEARS

| YEAR | Wells Completed or Abandoned | | | | Initial Production (Bbls.) | | Footage Drilled | |
|------|------|------|------|------|------|------|------|------|
| | Oil Wells | Gas Wells | Dry or Abandoned | Total | Total | Av. per Well | Total | Av. per Well |
| 1926 | 37 | 7 | 53 | 97 | ----- | ---- | 314,609 | 3,243 |
| 1927 | 56 | 7 | 77 | 140 | 11,708 | 209 | 352,612 | 2,519 |
| 1928 | 58 | 2 | 70 | 130 | 8,949 | 154.3 | 347,831 | 2,676 |
| 1929 | 28 | 5 | 57 | 90 | 3,668 | 131.0 | 204,108 | 2,266 |
| 1930 | 16 | 10 | 31 | 57 | 1,752 | 109.5 | 152,839 | 2,681 |
| 1931 | 8 | 4 | 19 | 31 | .2,240 | 280.0 | 76,963 | 2,483 |

## WELLS COMPLETED OR ABANDONED IN 1931
(Wells completed in 1930 are listed in the 1931 Year Book)

| Well Number and County | Location | Operator | Result | Depth (Feet) |
|------|------|------|------|------|
| ARCHULETA: | | | | |
| Brooks No. 1 | 2-32N-2E | Standard Oil Co. of Colo. | Abandoned | 81 |
| BACA: | | | | |
| Boice Cattle No. 1 | 50-34S-42 | A. R. Jones Oil & Oper. Co. | Abandoned | 4,965 |
| BOULDER: | | | | |
| Blair-Winter No. 1 | 25-3N-71 | Independent Oil & Ref. Co. | Abandoned | 200 |
| FREMONT: | | | | |
| Hassler No. 6 | 21-20-69 | Thomas A. Davis | Producer | 2,700 |
| Travis No. 24 | 28-20-69 | Vogel-Raddatz Corp. | Producer | 2,160 |
| Griffith No. 2 | 5-20-69 | M. L. Eno | Abandoned | 1,470 |
| LA PLATA: | | | | |
| Sanchez No. 1 | 27-33-12 | McGarr Pet. Co. | Producer | 3,320 |
| LARIMER: | | | | |
| Hall No. 1 | 20-4N-69 | Standard Oil Co. of Colo. | Gas | 730 |
| Hertha No. 1 | 21-4N-69 | Standard Oil Co. of Colo. | Producer | 3,792 |
| Red Rock No. 1 | 20-4N-69 | Raddatz Corp. | Abandoned | 1,000 |
| Maxwell No. 1 | 25-8N-70 | Consolidated Drilling Co. | Abandoned | 400 |
| MESA: | | | | |
| Hoel No. 1 | 23-8S-104 | Argo Oil Co. | Abandoned | 3,000 |
| MOFFAT: | | | | |
| Burton Musser No. 1 | 5-11N-97 | Mountain Fuel Co. | Gas | 2,152 |
| Hannewalt No. 24 | 4-6N-92 | Midwest Refining Co. | Abandoned | 3,040 |
| Parkinson No. 7-M | 23-4N-92 | Midwest Refining Co. | Producer | 3,479 |
| State No. 2 | 37-12N-100 | Mountain Fuel Supply Co. | Gas | 2,287 |
| Wick No. 4 | 10-4N-91 | Texas Production Co. | Producer | 4,759 |
| MONTEZUMA: | | | | |
| Carr No. 2 | 33-36N-14W | Fred C. Haller | Abandoned | 240 |
| Carr No. 2A | 33-36N-14W | Fred C. Haller, et al. | Abandoned | 745 |
| Haller No. 3 | 33-36-14 | Mesa Verde Ranch Co. | Abandoned | 900 |
| Haller No. 4 | 34-26-14 | Fred C. Haller | Abandoned | 585 |
| Stephens No. 1 | 33-36N-14W | Fred C. Haller | Gas | 750 |
| No. 1 | 7-35N-16W | G. H. Talcott, et al. | Abandoned | 594 |
| MORGAN: | | | | |
| Mortier No. 1 | 2-5N-60 | Prairie Oil & Gas Co. | Abandoned | 6,588 |
| State No. 1 | 16-1N-57 | Indian Territory I. Oil Co. | Abandoned | 5,920 |
| Pumphrey No. 1 | 14-4N-58 | Colorado Associated Oil Co. | Abandoned | 6,176 |
| PUEBLO: | | | | |
| Beecher No. 1 | 7-22S-66 | Kuykendall Oil Corp. | Abandoned | 1,312 |
| WELD: | | | | |
| Ida Johnson No. 1 | 24-6N-61 | Reiter-Foster Oil Corp. | Producer | 6,678 |
| Briggs No. 1 | 13-6N-61 | Continental Oil Co. | Producer | 6,675 |
| State No. 1 | 16-6N-61 | Aztec Corp. | Abandoned | 100 |
| Steele No. 1 | 14-2N-67 | Eastman Oil Co. | Abandoned | 165 |

Number of wells completed in 1931: Oil wells, 8; gas wells, 4; dry and abandoned, 19; total 31. Total footage drilled, 76,963 feet. Initial production of oil wells, 2,240 barrels per day; of gas wells, 53,248,000 cubic feet.

**COLORADO CRUDE OIL PRODUCTION IN 1931, BY FIELDS AND MONTHS, IN BARRELS**

| Month | Fort Collins | Welling-ton | Moffat | Iles |
|---|---|---|---|---|
| January | 10,833 | 24,523 | 28,310 | 29,459 |
| February | 8,739 | 21,087 | 30,051 | 27,470 |
| March | 8,295 | 21,841 | 30,640 | 31,613 |
| April | 7,320 | 22,188 | 28,686 | 30,457 |
| May | 7,327 | 23,645 | 25,634 | 30,578 |
| June | 8,282 | 21,388 | 25,404 | 43,359 |
| July | 7,252 | 29,976 | 25,449 | 38,645 |
| August | 6,644 | 16,585 | 24,907 | 37,140 |
| September | 6,352 | 25,512 | 20,685 | 29,027 |
| October | 6,508 | 21,722 | 23,683 | 30,501 |
| November | 6,013 | 21,053 | 22,218 | 27,661 |
| December | 5,833 | 26,083 | 24,105 | 26,593 |
| Totals | 89,398 | 275,603 | 309,772 | 382,503 |

| Month | Florence-Canon City | Tow Creek | Rangely | Berthoud |
|---|---|---|---|---|
| January | 15,618 | 10,990 | 2,005 | 868 |
| February | 12,912 | 10,221 | 2,779 | 784 |
| March | 12,557 | 11,432 | 2,621 | 850 |
| April | 13,209 | 10,946 | 2,765 | 840 |
| May | 11,822 | 11,850 | 3,206 | 870 |
| June | 10,603 | 9,941 | 3,358 | 835 |
| July | 9,165 | 9,176 | 3,246 | 1,240 |
| August | 9,308 | 10,443 | 3,063 | 1,178 |
| September | 10,417 | 8,886 | 3,031 | 1,140 |
| October | 11,769 | 10,209 | 2,899 | 1,180 |
| November | 8,849 | 9,289 | 2,621 | 1,145 |
| December | 9,737 | 9,158 | 2,764 | 1,175 |
| Totals | 135,966 | 122,541 | 34,358 | 12,105 |

| Month | Boulder | Grease-wood | Walden | Mancos | Totals |
|---|---|---|---|---|---|
| January | 610 | 11,418 | .... | 30 | 134,664 |
| February | 560 | 8,660 | .... | 35 | 123,298 |
| March | 618 | 10,222 | .... | 75 | 130,764 |
| April | 600 | 10,757 | .... | 95 | 127,863 |
| May | 620 | 9,964 | .... | 100 | 125,616 |
| June | 590 | 9,006 | 2,440 | 105 | 135,311 |
| July | 620 | 9,444 | 4,194 | 95 | 138,502 |
| August | 615 | 12,509 | 1,708 | 100 | 124,200 |
| September | 595 | 17,660 | 428 | 105 | 123,838 |
| October | 620 | 32,117 | .... | 95 | 141,303 |
| November | 600 | 20,470 | .... | 85 | 120,004 |
| December | 610 | 19,053 | .... | 30 | 125,141 |
| Totals | 7,258 | 171,280 | 8,770 | 950 | 1,550,504 |

Note—Figures for the Boulder and Berthoud fields are estimated. Monthly distribution only for Mancos field is estimated.

### CRUDE OIL PRODUCTION BY FIELDS AND YEARS, IN BARRELS

| FIELD | 1931 | 1930 | 1929 | 1928 | 1927 | 1926 |
|---|---|---|---|---|---|---|
| Fort Collins. | 89,398 | 112,135 | 159,228 | 241,830 | *1,161,332 | 466,931 |
| Wellington . | 275,603 | 376,595 | 662,998 | 790,210 | (*) | 754,044 |
| Moffat ...... | 309,772 | 362,551 | 410,430 | 442,530 | 663,810 | 1,167,184 |
| Iles ....... | 382,503 | 368,360 | 503,366 | 596,040 | 248,200 | 23,486 |
| Florence-Canon City. | 135,966 | 199,418 | 336,825 | 451,510 | 293,844 | 95,902 |
| Tow Creek... | 122,541 | 150,736 | 172,492 | 189,960 | 263,462 | 139,720 |
| Rangely .... | 34,358 | 32,850 | 19,090 | 23,800 | 36,500 | 36,500 |
| Boulder .... | 7,258 | 6,935 | 8,325 | 9,310 | 9,125 | 9,125 |
| Walden .... | 8,770 | ...... | 969 | 4,870 | 46,397 | ...... |
| Berthoud ... | 12,105 | 5,110 | ...... | ...... | ...... | ...... |
| Greasewood.. | 171,280 | 13,297 | ...... | ...... | ...... | ...... |
| Mancos..... | 950 | ...... | ...... | ...... | ...... | ...... |
| Totals .... | 1,550,504 | 1,627,987 | 2,273,723 | 2,750,060 | 2,722,670 | 2,692,892 |
| Est. value... | $873,885 | $1,242,257 | $2,120,425 | $2,655,670 | $2,611,058 | $4,577,916 |
| Av. value per bbl.(a). | $0.56 | $0.76 | $0.93 | $0.97 | $0.96 | $1.70 |

(*)Wellington and Fort Collins productions for 1927 are combined under "Fort Collins."

(a)These averages, based on the posted and contract prices, vary slightly from the averages of the U. S. Bureau of Mines.

Note—Rangely and Boulder output is estimated.

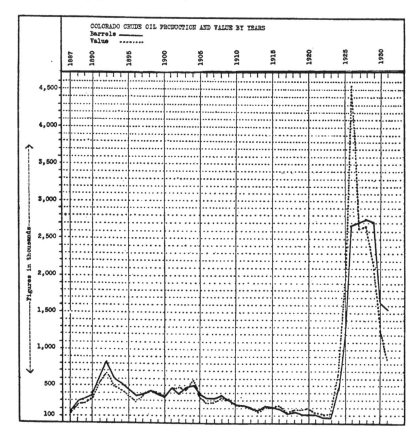

## PETROLEUM INDUSTRY

Statistics showing the total number of persons engaged in the petroleum industry and all allied branches, capital invested, value of all products, etc., have never been compiled, but the following data from various sources contributes information on the subject.

The census for 1930 on gainful workers reported the following in its occupational statistics for Colorado:

Oil and gas wells, operatives........331
Petroleum refineries, operatives..... 36
Petroleum refineries, laborers....... 62

The census on retail distribution in Colorado in 1930 shows 1,368 filling stations in the state, which had net sales in 1929 of $21,737,497. Of that number, 690 handled gas, oil and fuel oil and had net sales of $10,601,593; 461 also handled tires and accessories and had net sales of $8,881,651; and 217 also handled candy, lunch counters, tobacco, groceries or other merchandise, and had net sales of $2,-254,253.

The 1930 census of wholesale distribution reported 80 establishments handling petroleum and petroleum products, employing 288 persons and paying $435,739 in salaries and wages and $706,406 in other expenses. These establishments had net sales in 1929 of $10,794,626.

## NATURAL GAS

The production and use of natural gas in Colorado for domestic and industrial purposes began, as far as available records indicate, either in 1892 or in the following year, when the Florence Oil & Refining company supplied about half a dozen residences in Florence with the output of its No. 16 well in that district. Shortly thereafter two wells were drilled near Garcia in Las Animas county, which produced sufficient gas to heat and illuminate the buildings upon the ranches upon which they were located. Ten or more years later some natural gas was used for domestic purposes in and near Boulder, following the opening of that field in the early 90s, and there are a few other instances of gas being used commercially in small quantities in isolated districts. The first major natural gas discovery was made, however, on November 11, 1923, when the Union Oil company of California brought in its discovery well on the Wellington dome in Larimer county. This gas was piped first to Fort Collins and

subsequently a line was laid to Cheyenne, Wyoming.

In the year of the major discovery, 1923, the total quantity of gas produced and marketed in the state was 800,000 cubic feet, valued at the point of consumption at $400, as reported by the United States bureau of mines. The development since then has been rapid, and in 1930 the production in the state amounted to 3,312,000,000 cubic feet. Production of natural gas in the state by years, as reported by the bureau of mines, is as follows:

|  | M cu. ft. |
|---|---|
| 1923 | 800 |
| 1924 | 47,600 |
| 1925 | 574,400 |
| 1926 | 553,800 |
| 1927 | 1,725,400 |
| 1928 | 2,931,000 |
| 1929 | 2,787,000 |
| 1930 | 3,312,000 |

The principal areas in which gas is produced and marketed commercially are the Hiawatha district in northern Moffat county, the Wellington and Berthoud districts in Larimer county, and, beginning with 1932, the Craig district in Moffat county. Gas in large quantities has been discovered on the Rangely, Piceance Creek and White River domes in Rio Blanco county; on the Thornburg dome in Moffat county, and in smaller quantities in several other districts, but the wells are shut in and the product is not being marketed. Helium gas was developed and refined for commercial purposes on the Model dome in Las Animas county for several years, until the government began producing helium in its own refinery. Carbon dioxide gas has been found in very large quantities on the McCallum dome in Jackson county, but experiments made to separate this gas from crude oil and use it in the manufacture of "dry" ice so far have not been successful.

Consumption of natural gas by years, as reported by the bureau of mines, is as follows:

|  | M cu. ft. |
|---|---|
| 1923 | 800 |
| 1924 | 47,600 |
| 1925 | 574,400 |
| 1926 | 503,800 |
| 1927 | 1,544,000 |
| 1928 | 6,347,000 |
| 1929 | 14,362,000 |
| 1930 | 16,642,000 |

In 1930 Colorado exported 439,000,-000 cubic feet into Wyoming and 1,-287,000,000 cubic feet through Wyoming into Utah. In the same year Colorado imported from New Mexico 142,-000,000 cubic feet and through New

Mexico from Texas 14,914,000,000 cubic feet. The value of gas produced in Colorado in 1930 was $80,000 at the well and $958,000 at the point of consumption. The value of gas consumed, including receipts from other states, was $5,445,000, of which $3,-905,000 was from domestic and commercial consumers and $1,540,000 was from industrial consumers. A table published herewith gives production, consumption, total and average values, and distribution by years.

The Colorado Interstate Gas company and associated interests completed in 1928 a 340-mile pipe line from the Amarillo field in Texas to Denver. This line directly and indirectly serves the steel mills at Pueblo and the cities of Denver, Colorado Springs and Pueblo. Since its completion it has been extended eastward to supply La Junta, Rocky Ford, Swink and other towns in the Arkansas valley, and westward to supply industrial plants and communities in Fremont county. The Colorado-Wyoming Gas company

constructed in 1929 an extension of the Texas system to convey gas to Boulder, Fort Collins and other cities and towns in northern Colorado. Through pipe lines originally constructed to pipe gas from the Wellington dome to Cheyenne and Fort Collins, the new line now carries Texas gas as far north as Cheyenne. The Western Public Service company in 1929 constructed a system comprising 345 miles of line from the Hiawatha dome in northern Moffat county to Salt Lake City and Ogden, Utah, and is marketing gas from that structure and other gas domes. This line eventually is to be extended into southern Idaho. Durango and industries in that vicinity are being supplied with natural gas from northern New Mexico through a 36-mile line completed in 1929 by the Mesa Grande Gas company. In 1930 the Colorado Gas & Utilities company constructed a system to supply Lamar, Holly, Springfield and other towns in southeastern Colorado with natural gas from the Hugoton, Kansas, field.

**NATURAL GAS PRODUCTION AND CONSUMPTION IN COLORADO**
(From Reports of the U. S. Bureau of Mines)

|  | 1930 | 1929 | 1928 | 1927 |
|---|---|---|---|---|
| Quantity produced and delivered to consumers, including deliveries in other states, M cubic feet | 3,312,000 | 2,787,000 | 2,931,000 | 1,725,400 |
| Estimated Value at the Wells: |  |  |  |  |
| Total | $ 80,000 | $ 71,000 | $ 293,000 | $ 173,000 |
| Average per M cu. ft. (cts.) | 2.4 | 2.5 | 10.0 | 10.0 |
| Value at points of consumption: |  |  |  |  |
| Total | $ 958,000 | $ 675,000 | $ 786,000 | $ 290,000 |
| Average per M cu. ft. (cts.) | 28.9 | 24.2 | 26.8 | 16.8 |
| Consumed, including receipts from other states: |  |  |  |  |
| Quantity, M cubic feet | 16,642,000 | 14,362,000 | 6,347,000 | 1,544,000 |
| Value at point of consumption: |  |  |  |  |
| Total | $5,445,000 | $4,539,000 | $1,847,000 | $ 277,000 |
| Average per M cu. ft. (cts.) | 32.7 | 31.6 | 29.1 | 17.9 |
| Distribution of consumption: |  |  |  |  |
| Domestic, including commercial: |  |  |  |  |
| Number consumers | 86,640 | 77,150 | 69,030 | 2,050 |
| Quantity consumed, M cu. ft. | 5,141,000 | 2,731,000 | 629,000 | 179,000 |
| Value at point of consumption: |  |  |  |  |
| Total | $3,905,000 | $2,524,000 | $ 697,000 | $ 105,000 |
| Average per M cu ft. (cts.) | 76.0 | 92.4 | 110.8 | 58.7 |
| Industrial consumption: |  |  |  |  |
| M cu. ft. consumed | 11,501,000 | 11,631,000 | 5,718,000 | 1,365,000 |
| Value at point of consumption: |  |  |  |  |
| Total | $1,540,000 | $2,015,000 | $1,150,000 | $ 172,000 |
| Average per M cu. ft. (cts.) | 13.4 | 17.3 | 20.1 | 12.6 |
| Domestic (household) consumption only:* |  |  |  |  |
| Quantity consumed, M cu. ft. | 3,775,000 | ........* | ........‾ | ........‾ |
| Value at point of consumption: |  |  |  |  |
| Total | $3,221,000 | ........* | ........* | ........* |
| Average per M cu. ft. (cts.) | 85.3 | ........* | ........* | ........* |

*Domestic and commercial not separately reported prior to 1930.

## OIL SHALE

One of the greatest undeveloped natural resources in Colorado is the immense acreage of oil shale land, located upon the western slope of the main range of the Rocky mountains, mostly in Mesa, Garfield and Rio Blanco counties. The shales do not contain crude oil similar to that which comes from petroleum wells, but the material from which crude oil is made and which in the course of time would become petroleum if nature were permitted to complete its processes. Engineers and scientists have devised methods by which nature's work can be hastened and the shales made to yield the oil in a short time by the application of heat and pressure. The shale beds lie mostly in horizontal strata ranging in thickness from a few feet to 50 feet or more, some strata being exposed at the surface and others lying at varying depths beneath the surface.

The area of land in Colorado classified by the United States geological survey as oil shale land is 952,239 acres. In 1928 the federal oil conservation board made a report to the president on general petroleum problems in the United States which contained a statement on oil possibilities of the shales by Dean E. Winchester. This statement estimates the oil in the Colorado shales at 79,625,998,000 barrels, of which 47,625,598,000 barrels is recoverable. In arriving at these figures Mr. Winchester adopted the following limiting factors:

No oil shale less than one foot in thickness is considered minable.

No shale which will yield less than 15 gallons of oil to the ton is considered minable.

No oil shale which will yield less than 3,000 barrels of shale oil per acre of shale land is considered minable.

It was also assumed that not more than 60 per cent of the shale in the ground will reach the retorts and be treated, although in the best operations, using the most economical wholesale mining methods, this percentage doubtless will be very greatly increased and it is not at all impossible that 95 per cent of the shale included in the estimates will be treated. At the present rate of production of crude oil, Mr. Winchester's estimate of recoverable oil in the Colorado shales alone is equal to the entire output of crude oil in the United States for a period of 50 years.

Production of oil from shale has been in progress in Scotland and other European countries for many years upon a profitable basis, but it is a comparatively new and undeveloped industry in this country, though considerable progress has been made in recent years in working out processes, acquiring shale lands and other preliminary operations. Many of the larger oil producing and refining companies of the country have extensive investments in Colorado oil shale land which they are holding for development at such time as the price of crude oil and the demands of the industry justify the operation of the properties.

The federal government has two shale reserves in Colorado, which were set aside primarily with a view to insuring an ample supply of oil for the future needs of the navy. President Wilson created Naval Oil Shale Reserve No. 1 in Colorado by an executive order issued on December 6, 1916. This reserve is located in Garfield county near Rifle and Grand Valley and embraces 45,440 acres, which the geological survey estimates to contain at least 2,500,000,000 barrels of crude oil. President Coolidge issued a similar order on November 22, 1924, creating No. 3 reserve adjoining No. 1 and containing approximately 22,000 acres. No. 2 reserve is located in Utah. Since the first withdrawal was made 3,880 acres in No. 1 reserve have been restored to the public domain, as investigations disclosed that the acreage is not oil shale land.

The federal government has been active in experimenting with methods and developing processes for the recovery of oil from shale, and in 1926 placed in operation on one of its reserves at Rulison a plant equipped with a full-sized Pumpherston retort of the Scottish type and another of American development and make. In this plant the shale was handled in a small way the same as the product would be worked by a larger unit, so that actual results in the recovery of oil, the cost of mining, transporting and crushing the shale, and other details can be determined. This was followed by the construction at Boulder by the bureau of mines, in cooperation with the state government, of a small refinery for the treating of crude oil from the Rulison plant to recover gasoline and other products. The Rulison plant commenced producing oil on September 17, 1926, and at a subsequent date runs of oil were made in the refinery at Boulder. Small quantities of the crude were supplied by the government to private operators for experimental refining purposes. The operation subsequently was discontinued.

The principal hindrance to development has been the low price of well oil compared with the cost of producing oil from shale. The cost of the latter has been computed mostly on a theoretical basis, due to the very limited number of commercial plants actually operated, and the government plant was constructed principally for the purpose of determining these factors by actual operations.

Colorado's oil shales are found principally in what is known as the Green River formation. Tests made by the United States geological survey have shown a recovery of 10 to 68 gallons of oil from a ton of shale. Many by-products are recoverable from shale, among which is ammonium sulphate. The survey estimates that 300,000,000 tons of that product can be recovered in the process of recovering the other contents.

## NATURAL GASOLINE PLANTS

Colorado had three natural gasoline plants for the recovery of gasoline from natural gas on January 1, 1932, of which two were in active operation and one was shut down. All three plants are of the absorption type and have a capacity for recovering 12,000 gallons of gasoline per day.

## PETROLEUM REFINERIES

There are six petroleum refineries and several small skimming plants in Colorado. The largest is at Florence and is owned by the Continental Oil company. It has a daily charging capacity of 3,000 barrels of crude oil and recovers gasoline, kerosene, gas, fuel oil, lubricating oil, wax and other products. Included with the equipment is a unit of Burton cracking stills with a capacity of 1,500 barrels daily. The cracking unit is owned by the Standard Oil Co. of Indiana. The same company placed in operation in 1930 a new refinery at Denver with a charging capacity of 1,500 barrels of crude oil per day and a Cross cracking unit of 800-barrel capacity. The Texas company operates a complete plant at Craig, in Moffat county, with a daily charging capacity of 1,500 barrels and a Holmes-Manley cracking unit with a capacity of 1,000 barrels daily. The Mountain States Refining company has under construction at Denver a plant with a charging capacity of 1,000 barrels per day, which will recover gasoline, kerosene and fuel oil. The Mountain States Refining company operates a 200-barrel skimming plant at Orchard, in Weld county, and the Raven Oil & Refining company has a 100-barrel plant at Rangely, in Rio Blanco county, which runs crude oil from shallow wells in the Rangely oil field. There are several small skimming plants of lesser capacity than those named, operated at Berthoud, Boulder and in Montezuma county.

## FUEL OIL DISTRIBUTION IN COLORADO

(Compiled from surveys of gas-oil and fuel-oil distribution in the United States made by the United States Bureau of Mines, co-operatively with the American Petroleum Institute. Quantities are in barrels of 42 gallons each.)

| USES | 1930 | 1929 | 1928 | 1927 | 1926 |
|---|---|---|---|---|---|
| Railroads .................... | 40,576 | 19,065 | 17,900 | 19,883 | 11,107 |
| Gas and electric power plants. | 10,957 | 24,467 | 60,420 | 83,270 | 94,241 |
| Smelters and mines........... | 388 | 18,115 | 16,493 | 62,928 | 9,419 |
| Steel mills and foundries..... | 2,020 | 53,310 | 276,014 | 443,425 | 146,559 |
| Automotive industries........ | 582 | 2,246 | 144 | ...... | 476 |
| Textiles and their products... | ...... | 245 | ...... | ...... | ...... |
| Chemical and allied industries. | ...... | 285 | 432 | 165 | ...... |
| Sugar refineries.............. | ...... | ...... | ...... | ...... | 6,190 |
| Cement and lime plants....... | ...... | 2,752 | 344 | 216 | 152 |
| Ceramic industries........... | 771 | 28,327 | 41,680 | 50,093 | 49,429 |
| Commercial heating........... | 41,385 | 4,934 | 754 | 35,847 | ...... |
| Domestic heating............. | 95,331 | 73,803 | 9,435 | 2,500 | 2,157 |
| Food industries.............. | 2,067 | 53,083 | 28,876 | 30,871 | ...... |
| Other manufacturing......... | 1,697 | 5,984 | 3,538 | 2,539 | 7,093 |
| Used as fuel by oil companies. | 159,865 | 147,800 | 125,205 | 89,252 | 80,869 |
| Miscellaneous ................ | 12,144 | 11,543 | 4,380 | 63,019 | 12,778 |
| Totals ................... | 367,783 | 445,959 | 585,615 | 884,008 | 420,470 |

# Colorado's Educational System

COLORADO ranks favorably among the states of the Union in educational facilities and in some specialized lines it stands near the top of the list. The state has a large and elaborate public school system, which is undergoing rapid extension. In addition, it has a number of colleges, universities and professional schools for the higher education of students and numerous commercial and business colleges, nurses' training schools and parochial schools and private institutions offering specialized courses in music, the arts and sciences.

Illiteracy, the inability to read or write any language, is steadily declining in the state as shown by the federal census, due, in a large measure, to the state's excellent educational system. In 1920 the percentage of illiterates 10 years of age and over was only 3.2 per cent, compared with 3.7 per cent in 1910 and 4.2 per cent in 1900. The 3.2 per cent illiteracy in Colorado in 1920 compares with 6.0 per cent for the entire country. Twenty-nine states had a larger per cent of illiterates in that year than Colorado, while 18 states had a smaller per cent. Comparative figures for 1930 have not as yet been released by the bureau of the census.

The enrollment in the schools, colleges and universities of the state in the school year of 1930-1931 was 286,-164, or 27.6 per cent of the entire population of the state, an increase of 8,521, or 3.1 per cent, compared with 1929-1930. This is exclusive of duplications, summer schools and commercial and business schools. There are several of the latter in the state for which reliable statistics are not available. There was a decrease of 2,714 in the number enrolled in 1929-1930 as compared with 1928-1929, in which school year there was an increase of 5,130 over 1927-1928. This increase was accounted for in part by the inclusion of two institutions with an enrollment of 204 in the tabulations for 1928-1929 which were not in the figures for the preceding school year.

Enrollment by sexes showed a small gain in males over females in the school year of 1930-1931, the total number of males being 3,998 larger than the number of females. In the school year of 1929-1930 there were 2,691 more males than females, which compares with 1,821 more females than males in 1928-1929 and 2,518 more males than females in 1927-1928.

Enrollment by sex and classes of institutions for the school year of 1930-1931 was as follows:

|  | Male | Female | Total |
|---|---|---|---|
| Public schools | 132,415 | 128,220 | 260,635 |
| State controlled colleges and universities | 4,610 | 3,423 | 8,033 |
| Privately controlled colleges and universities | 2,214 | 2,535 | 4,749 |
| Parochial, etc. | 5,842 | 6,905 | 12,747 |
| Total | 145,081 | 141,083 | 286,164 |

Total enrollment by years was as follows:

|  | Male | Female | Total |
|---|---|---|---|
| 1924-1925 | ....* | ....* | 266,938 |
| 1925-1926 | ....* | ....* | 278,696 |
| 1926-1927 | ....* | ....* | 274,637 |
| 1927-1928 | 138,873 | 136,354 | 275,227 |
| 1928-1929 | 139,268 | 141,089 | 280,357 |
| 1929-1930 | 140,167 | 137,476 | 277,643 |
| 1930-1931 | 145,081 | 141,083 | 286,164 |

*Not segregated for these years.

The cool summers and other attractive features in Colorado afford unusually desirable opportunities for summer schools, and a number of the larger institutions make these regular and important features of their programs. Many students from eastern states, where the summer period is too oppressive for effective work in the school room, attend the summer terms of Colorado institutions and combine education with recreation.

Ten of the colleges and universities of the state, both publicly and privately controlled, conducted summer schools in 1931, in which there were enrolled 9,099 students, of whom 2,672 were males and 6,427 were females. This was equal to 69.9 per cent of the total enrollment in the preceding regular school year. The total summer school enrollment of these institutions by years was as follows:

| 1928 | 8,522 |
|---|---|
| 1929 | 8,680 |
| 1930 | 8,825 |
| 1931 | 9,099 |

The value of all property in the state used for educational purposes, based on inventories of state institutions and investment in public schools and private colleges and universities, is $90,-333,585. This total is compiled on the following basis:

Public schools (1931).........$63,615,456
State universities and colleges
(1930) .................... 16,052,420
County high schools.......... 1,695,336
Private universities and col-
leges (1928).............. *5,479,373
Private high schools and
academies (1930).......... 3,491,000

Total ....................$90,333,585

*Includes value of libraries, grounds, buildings and equipment, but excludes productive funds amounting to $5,225,615.

The cost of operating the educational institutions of the state, including both publicly and privately controlled, is estimated at $40,000,000 annually. The expenditures for the public schools in 1931 amounted to $26,172,932 and of state owned institutions in 1928, $4,776,245. Data on private universities and colleges and parochial schools are not available, but estimated on a per capita basis at slightly less than the per capita costs of publicly controlled institutions, indicate an annual outlay of close to $10,000,000.

The public schools, colleges, universities and private schools of all classes included in this summary reported a total of 11,370 instructors and teachers employed during the regular school year of 1930-1931, of whom 2,523 were men and 8,847 were women. These are exclusive of instructors and teachers employed in the summer schools. The figures by classes for 1930-1931 are as follows:

|  | Male | Female | Total |
|---|---|---|---|
| Public schools | 1,779 | 8,081 | 9,860 |
| State colleges and universities | 441 | 180 | 621 |
| Private colleges and universities | 222 | 129 | 351 |
| Parochial | 81 | 457 | 538 |
| Total | 2,523 | 8,847 | 11,370 |

The total number of instructors and teachers, by years, is as follows:

|  | Male | Female | Total |
|---|---|---|---|
| 1925-26 | 2,469 | 8,565 | 11,034 |
| 1927-28 | 2,379 | 8,660 | 11,039 |
| 1928-29 | 2,377 | 8,616 | 10,993 |
| 1929-30 | 2,338 | 8,832 | 11,170 |
| 1930-31 | 2,523 | 8,847 | 11,370 |

Additional information on public schools, colleges and universities and private schools will be found in chapters under those headings.

## PUBLIC SCHOOL SYSTEM

The state has a large and elaborate public school system which affords ample facilities to all for acquiring a fundamental education. The system embraces kindergarten, elementary, junior high and senior high schools in both urban and rural communities, and in some of the larger cities special facilities in opportunity, manual training and night schools.

The state is divided into 2,033 school districts, the schools in each district being under the supervision of a local school board elected by the district. Each county has a superintendent of schools who is chosen at the general elections and who has limited advisory powers and certain powers for organizing new districts, consolidated schools and inter-district movements. A state superintendent of public instruction is chosen at each biennial general election.

The revenues for the operation of the schools are derived from three sources. The largest revenue is derived from district school levies. The directors in each district make annual budgets of funds required and their budgets are certified by the county superintendents to the county commissioners, who make levies through the regular tax-collecting channels. In addition, the state is a large owner of school land, from the sale and operation of which funds are derived. These revenues are maintained in a permanent school fund and the interest therefrom becomes available for the support of the state educational institutions. The third source of revenue is from levies made by counties under a minimum teachers' salary law which is limited to not to exceed five mills a year. School districts may authorize the issuance of school bonds upon vote of taxpaying electors, and many of the school buildings of the state have been and are being constructed through bond issues.

The state superintendent of public instruction reported a total of 3,305 schools in the state in 1930, a high school, an elementary school and a kindergarten housed in the same building being counted as three schools. These are classified as follows:

Senior high schools........... 322
Junior high schools........... 158
Elementary schools........... 690
Kindergarten schools........... 56
Rural schools....................2,079

Total ........................3,305

In 1930 there was a total of 3,208 school houses, classified as follows:

Sod, adobe or log............. 227
Frame .......................1,929
Brick or stone...............1,052

Total ........................3,208

The number of school houses in use in 1930 was 2,989.

The growth in the number of school districts, schools and buildings in recent years is shown in the following table:

| Year | Dists. | Schools | Bldgs. |
|---|---|---|---|
| 1921 | 1,900 | .... | 3,742 |
| 1922 | 1,912 | 2,884 | 3,510 |
| 1923 | 1,944 | 3,243 | 3,635 |
| 1924 | 1,992 | 3,391 | 3,587 |
| 1925 | 2,003 | 3,396 | 4,116 |
| 1926 | 2,019 | *3,302 | *3,800 |
| 1927 | 2,029 | 3,439 | 4,380 |
| 1928 | 2,032 | 3,317 | 4,636 |
| 1929 | 2,040 | 3,334 | 3,543 |
| 1930 | 2,041 | 3,305 | 3,208 |
| 1931 | 2,033 | 3,300 | 3,199 |

*Apparent decrease is due to failure of Washington county superintendent to report in 1926, that county reporting 121 schools and 313 buildings in 1925.

The total value of public school property in 1931, as reported by the state superintendent of public instruction, was $63,615,456, of which $5,820,296 was in land, $51,177,335 in buildings and $6,617,825 in equipment.

The valuation placed upon school property by years and amount invested per pupil enrolled was as follows:

| | Valuation | |
|---|---|---|
| | Total | Per Pupil |
| 1922 | $33,518,134 | ..... |
| 1924 | 43,100,821 | ..... |
| 1925 | 48,803,695 | $284.48 |
| 1926 | 54,643,685 | 218.63 |
| 1927 | 56,232,651 | 259.72 |
| 1928 | 59,738,453 | 237.88 |
| 1929 | 60,656,164 | 236.80 |
| 1930 | 62,147,540 | 246.00 |
| 1931 | 63,615,456 | 244.08 |

Total enrollment by years, with increases, is as follows:

| Year | Enrollment | Increase |
|---|---|---|
| 1920 | 229,508 | ..... |
| 1921 | 232,757 | 3,249 |
| 1922 | 243,004 | 10,247 |
| 1923 | 249,813 | 6,809 |
| 1924 | 247,195 | *2,618 |
| 1925 | 255,115 | 7,920 |
| 1926 | 250,087 | *5,208 |
| 1927 | 251,615 | 528 |
| 1928 | 251,131 | *484 |
| 1929 | 256,134 | 5,003 |
| 1930 | 252,718 | *3,416 |
| 1931 | 260,635 | 7,917 |

*Decrease.

A statement of the school fund derived from the sale and leasing of state land and amounts apportioned to the counties for school purposes will be found in the chapter on state or school lands. Distributions to the schools from the income fund for the biennial periods ending on November 30 of the years named were as follows:

| Year | Amount |
|---|---|
| 1918 | $1,156,943 |
| 1920 | 1,520,396 |
| 1922 | 1,582,097 |
| 1924 | 1,777,314 |
| 1926 | 1,868,083 |
| 1928 | 1,672,690 |
| 1930 | 1,631,566 |

The total indebtedness of the public school districts, exclusive of bonds for county high schools, on June 30, 1930, was $32,743,730, of which $30,266,091 was for bonds, and the remainder for registered and unregistered warrants. There is published elsewhere in this volume a detailed statement by counties of bonded indebtedness as of January 1, 1932.

The annual per capita cost of education in the public schools, as reported by the state superintendent of public instruction, based on enrollment and average attendance, is as follows:

| Year | Enrollment | Attendance |
|---|---|---|
| 1921 | $ 70.56 | $ 97.97 |
| 1922 | 80.57 | 114.88 |
| 1923 | 83.53 | 119.59 |
| 1924 | 94.03 | 129.51 |
| 1925 | 104.74 | 143.53 |
| 1926 | 107.51 | 183.51 |
| 1927 | 97.44 | 135.83 |
| 1928 | 101.10 | 135.82 |
| 1929 | 98.22 | 129.36 |
| 1930 | 103.73 | 137.43 |
| 1931 | 133.80 | 177.12 |

Receipts for school purposes, including county high schools, and the sources of revenue, for the year ending June 30, 1930, as reported by the state superintendent, were as follows:

| | |
|---|---|
| Balance on hand | $ 3,426,306 |
| General fund, by apportionment | 925,877 |
| County levy, teachers minimum salary | 5,848,944 |
| Special tax | 16,847,257 |
| Tuition | 506,030 |
| All other sources | 2,265,860 |
| Total | $29,820,274 |

Total receipts from all sources for the fiscal year of 1931 amounted to $28,929,241.

Disbursements for the year ending June 30, 1930, were as follows:

| | |
|---|---|
| Teachers' salaries | $14,539,403 |
| Current expenses | 6,250,305 |
| Permanent improvements | 1,790,813 |
| Library purposes | 125,851 |
| Redemption of bonds | 1,042,136 |
| Payment overdrafts | 583,556 |
| Interest: | |
| Bonds | 1,460,800 |
| Warrants | 121,026 |
| Abatement and fees | 299,727 |
| Total | $26,213,617 |

Total disbursements for the fiscal year of 1931 amounted to $26,172,932.

Receipts, including balances on hand at the beginning of the fiscal year, and disbursements, by years, were as follows:

| | Receipts | Disbursem'ts |
|---|---|---|
| 1925 | $27,158,849 | $26,720,801 |
| 1926 | 25,204,797 | 26,888,074 |
| 1927 | 27,650,274 | 24,518,450 |
| 1928 | 28,356,121 | 25,410,668 |
| 1929 | 28,544,910 | 25,157,462 |
| 1930 | 29,820,274 | 26,213,617 |
| 1931 | 28,929,241 | 26,172,932 |

## COLLEGES AND UNIVERSITIES

Among the principal universities, colleges and professional schools of the state devoted to higher education are the following:

| Name | Location | Year of Opening |
|---|---|---|
| University of Colorado | Boulder | 1877 |
| Agricultural college | Fort Collins | 1879 |
| School of Mines | Golden | 1874 |
| Western State college | Gunnison | 1909 |
| State Normal | Alamosa | 1925 |
| Teachers college | Greeley | 1890 |
| Fort Lewis School | Hesperus | 1911 |
| Colorado college | Colorado Springs | 1874 |
| Regis college | Denver | 1888 |
| Colorado Woman's college | Denver | 1909 |
| University of Denver | Denver | 1864 |
| Loretto Heights college | Loretto | 1918 |
| Iliff School of Theology | Denver | 1892 |
| Westminster Law School | Denver | 1912 |

The first seven named above are publicly controlled and are largely supported by legislative appropriations and state tax levies. The Agricultural college and State university derive some revenue from the sale and administration of school land grants made by the federal government for their benefit. These funds are administered through the state land board in the same manner as the public school land funds.

The number of students enrolled in the colleges and universities included in this survey for the regular school year 1930-1931, by sex, was as follows:

| Name | Male | Female | Total |
|---|---|---|---|
| University of Colorado | 2,245 | 1,205 | 3,450 |
| Agricultural college | 1,055 | 447 | 1,502 |
| School of Mines | 503 | ... | 503 |
| Western State college | 163 | 207 | 370 |
| State Normal | 57 | 148 | 205 |
| Teachers college | 529 | 1,365 | 1,894 |
| Fort Lewis School | 58 | 51 | 109 |
| Colorado college | 349 | 298 | 647 |
| Regis college | 193 | 82 | 275 |
| Colorado Woman's college | ... | 265 | 265 |
| University of Denver | 1,562 | 1,758 | 3,320 |
| Loretto Heights college | ... | 113 | 113 |
| Iliff School of Theology | 50 | 9 | 59 |
| Westminster Law School | 60 | 10 | 70 |
| Total | 6,824 | 5,958 | 12,782 |

## PAROCHIAL SCHOOLS

The Roman Catholic educational institutions in Colorado include 48 parochial schools, four academies for girls, one special school for boys, four orphan asylums, one seminary and one industrial and reform school. Total enrollment in these institutions in the school year of 1930-1931 was 12,747, of whom 5,842 were males and 6,905 were females. The parochial schools accounted for 11,460 of these, the academies for 369 and the orphan asylums for 626. The number of teachers employed was 528, of whom 81 were males and 447 were females. The parochial schools accounted for 407 of these, the academies for 42 and the orphan asylums for 54.

The office of education of the United States department of commerce, in its survey of education in the United States for 1928-1930, reported upon 25 private high schools and academies in the state in 1929-1930. These included not only those conducted by the Catholics, but others. The 25 institutions reporting had 65,652 bound volumes in their libraries. The value of buildings and grounds was $3,240,000 and of scientific apparatus, furniture, etc., $251,000.

## PRIVATE COMMERCIAL AND BUSINESS SCHOOLS

Data on private commercial and business schools in the state are not included in the general summary of Colorado's educational system, due to the difficulty of compiling information that is comparable. Thirteen of these institutions reported to the federal bureau of education for the school year of 1924-1925. These schools had an enrollment of 4,861 students, of whom 3,118 were in the day courses and 1,743 in the night courses. The number of instructors and professors employed by these schools was 115, of whom 62 were men and 53 were women.

In addition to the public schools, universities, colleges and professional schools mentioned herewith, there are in the state a number of nurses' schools, law schools, theological universities, schools of music and art, and private business schools which are not included in this report.

## OTHER STATE SCHOOLS

In addition to the state educational institutions listed in this chapter Colorado carries on a definite program of education in separate institutions for the mute, the blind and the deaf. Likewise consistent educational programs are carried on at the industrial schools for boys and girls, the reform schools and various other institutions of involuntary confinement. The pupils in these schools are not counted, as they are included among the inmates of the institutions named, in the chapter under the heading "State Institutions."

## AVERAGE ANNUAL PER CAPITA COST OF EDUCATION IN PUBLIC SCHOOLS
(From Records of the State Superintendent of Public Instruction)

| COUNTY | 1931 | | 1930 | | 1929 | | 1928 | | 1927 | |
|---|---|---|---|---|---|---|---|---|---|---|
| | Based on Enrollment | Based on Average Attendance | Based on Enrollment | Based on Average Attendance | Based on Enrollment | Based on Average Attendance | Based on Enrollment | Based on Average Attendance | Based on Enrollment | Based on Average Attendance |
| Adams | $114.84 | $152.40 | $ 78.10 | $117.42 | $ 74.01 | $110.22 | $ 88.49 | $127.64 | $ 99.04 | $151.37 |
| Alamosa | 140.76 | 188.04 | 86.70 | 126.04 | 93.29 | 128.93 | 93.53 | 133.91 | 150.46 | 220.76 |
| Arapahoe | 114.00 | 139.56 | 84.82 | 115.69 | 78.56 | 106.00 | 83.00 | 109.32 | 79.27 | 103.67 |
| Archuleta | 74.88 | 102.72 | 57.62 | 80.31 | 57.58 | 71.14 | 56.45 | 82.75 | 53.72 | 81.10 |
| Baca | 123.96 | 165.60 | 83.35 | 117.77 | 84.82 | 116.79 | 62.63 | 93.63 | 70.24 | 97.71 |
| Bent | 104.16 | 143.40 | 89.77 | 138.54 | 91.76 | 120.14 | 82.58 | 95.15 | 91.11 | 124.88 |
| Boulder | 129.12 | 161.64 | 101.33 | 129.31 | 100.81 | 126.69 | 96.69 | 124.45 | 98.44 | 124.25 |
| Chaffee | 119.64 | 147.36 | 89.96 | 111.41 | 79.33 | 92.50 | 89.79 | 112.87 | 64.46 | 79.18 |
| Cheyenne | 201.60 | 260.40 | 154.19 | 192.55 | 158.64 | 202.09 | 147.51 | 192.58 | 130.04 | 193.02 |
| Clear Creek | 154.20 | 179.64 | 102.33 | 132.60 | 106.22 | 135.30 | 100.98 | 125.82 | 101.20 | 128.73 |
| Conejos | 84.72 | 112.32 | 63.88 | 85.13 | 58.71 | 95.76 | 55.41 | 79.29 | 55.09 | 80.04 |
| Costilla | 69.12 | 107.76 | 50.30 | 81.92 | 50.98 | 82.28 | 60.34 | 85.56 | 51.97 | 81.84 |
| Crowley | 148.32 | 169.80 | 127.32 | 153.49 | 103.10 | 143.59 | 102.55 | 142.93 | 89.20 | 132.16 |
| Custer | 99.60 | 137.64 | 89.87 | 124.51 | 82.40 | 139.13 | 65.11 | 93.19 | 75.23 | 111.32 |
| Delta | 90.36 | 115.08 | 91.26 | 117.79 | 87.96 | 114.97 | 75.93 | 107.92 | 79.57 | 110.44 |
| Denver | 142.20 | 190.92 | 114.23 | 149.09 | 104.37 | 144.40 | 119.72 | 157.20 | 105.15 | 146.27 |
| Dolores | 71.64 | 89.16 | 78.01 | 108.09 | 101.05 | ____ | 54.47 | 76.98 | 79.33 | 102.99 |
| Douglas | 175.32 | 225.60 | 134.19 | 170.48 | 122.20 | 163.20 | 102.81 | 145.36 | 98.92 | 137.44 |
| Eagle | 138.96 | 172.56 | 109.75 | 140.49 | 106.18 | 142.71 | 92.96 | 131.28 | 97.95 | 135.70 |
| Elbert | 160.80 | 195.84 | 123.49 | 151.83 | 122.75 | 153.01 | 110.53 | 139.30 | 100.32 | 120.75 |
| El Paso | 180.60 | 232.32 | 129.37 | 166.66 | 125.82 | 150.00 | 130.32 | 182.48 | 122.56 | 162.43 |
| Fremont | 175.56 | 216.72 | 105.90 | 133.93 | 91.82 | 115.10 | 89.11 | 116.21 | 81.80 | 103.78 |
| Garfield | 141.60 | 198.00 | 115.06 | 122.70 | 98.68 | 140.34 | 77.38 | 99.33 | 71.57 | 98.04 |
| Gilpin | 171.60 | 225.60 | 90.55 | 124.87 | 175.50 | 202.78 | 112.38 | 163.45 | 78.77 | 124.04 |
| Grand | 126.00 | 182.16 | 108.97 | 148.31 | 106.57 | 147.18 | 68.38 | 105.40 | 69.81 | 97.47 |
| Gunnison | 138.12 | 212.04 | 111.61 | 150.29 | 113.65 | 146.11 | 91.51 | 107.27 | 93.34 | 118.05 |
| Hinsdale | 171.60 | 216.00 | 104.68 | 120.79 | 103.82 | 112.57 | 88.89 | 101.05 | 84.14 | 106.86 |
| Huerfano | 92.40 | 128.28 | 85.62 | 126.81 | 68.50 | 102.84 | 61.27 | 100.99 | 67.26 | 101.96 |
| Jackson | 130.44 | 153.24 | 100.81 | 145.67 | 99.40 | 141.08 | 101.51 | 134.98 | 94.19 | 128.70 |
| Jefferson | 114.36 | 147.36 | 82.80 | 109.11 | 78.50 | 91.91 | 83.87 | 135.97 | 74.46 | 99.22 |
| Kiowa | 229.92 | 222.96 | 137.11 | 172.56 | 135.00 | 171.62 | 139.40 | 180.51 | 102.84 | 131.32 |
| Kit Carson | 146.52 | 212.64 | 124.08 | 155.92 | 106.14 | 137.01 | 107.85 | 136.45 | 103.72 | 133.05 |
| Lake | 130.32 | 155.28 | 98.02 | 117.75 | 91.76 | 113.08 | 86.81 | 105.42 | 86.89 | 106.19 |
| La Plata | 110.40 | 147.36 | 82.60 | 113.34 | 74.87 | 99.92 | 76.58 | 108.50 | 74.79 | 104.43 |
| Larimer | 127.44 | 160.44 | 102.46 | 134.00 | 97.01 | 125.46 | 95.89 | 125.44 | 88.56 | 158.69 |
| Las Animas | 108.48 | 140.40 | 26.06 | 39.12 | 80.56 | 110.35 | 66.83 | 93.14 | 74.16 | 85.90 |
| Lincoln | 156.00 | 185.28 | 126.69 | 145.63 | 114.34 | 128.43 | 127.55 | 152.87 | 108.39 | 132.72 |
| Logan | 141.36 | 219.00 | 120.91 | 158.89 | 97.59 | 129.46 | 100.91 | 125.28 | 92.33 | 114.68 |
| Mesa | 104.52 | 139.20 | 76.79 | 103.14 | 75.51 | 95.31 | 75.38 | 98.14 | 75.78 | 99.88 |
| Mineral | 151.92 | 186.00 | 125.64 | 169.40 | 98.09 | 126.78 | 65.56 | 69.45 | 68.98 | 77.74 |
| Moffat | 126.12 | 225.12 | 90.65 | 113.27 | 90.93 | 120.94 | 89.38 | 124.65 | 91.34 | 124.93 |
| Montezuma | 89.16 | 116.04 | 74.60 | 91.54 | 71.10 | 95.49 | 82.36 | 119.13 | 77.24 | 105.78 |
| Montrose | 91.20 | 121.80 | 74.20 | 95.42 | 75.15 | 98.12 | 69.10 | 97.81 | 65.95 | 90.21 |
| Morgan | 117.84 | 173.16 | 110.17 | 152.40 | 128.94 | 193.36 | 90.04 | 127.75 | 82.98 | 120.52 |
| Otero | 105.24 | 140.64 | 84.89 | 113.49 | 83.93 | 107.16 | 86.33 | 116.61 | 89.60 | 116.07 |
| Ouray | 157.32 | 190.44 | 130.89 | 159.07 | 108.88 | 142.35 | 73.29 | 95.29 | 60.43 | 68.26 |
| Park | 193.32 | 339.00 | 131.86 | 246.09 | 177.85 | 253.37 | 137.95 | 210.91 | 145.55 | 224.96 |
| Phillips | 126.60 | 156.00 | 97.04 | 117.20 | 93.72 | 115.53 | 78.99 | 102.04 | 79.05 | 101.75 |
| Pitkin | 127.20 | 141.24 | 95.91 | 113.53 | 86.31 | 98.95 | 81.03 | 108.31 | 78.17 | 98.54 |
| Prowers | 130.68 | 175.08 | 99.82 | 131.83 | 94.03 | 130.76 | 112.44 | 145.42 | 107.34 | 149.95 |
| Pueblo | 136.92 | 178.44 | 98.40 | 135.16 | 92.16 | 97.73 | 99.71 | 134.49 | 115.28 | 161.53 |
| Rio Blanco | 142.32 | 149.76 | 114.51 | 144.45 | 84.91 | 107.78 | 111.52 | 140.85 | 86.67 | 112.18 |
| Rio Grande | 139.56 | 197.40 | 114.52 | 136.11 | 86.07 | 114.65 | 103.91 | 153.50 | 112.10 | 157.65 |
| Routt | 141.00 | 182.40 | 106.08 | 135.06 | 104.73 | 163.69 | ____ | ____ | 86.78 | 125.38 |
| Saguache | 134.16 | 192.00 | 113.96 | 155.21 | 109.83 | 153.13 | 113.70 | 169.71 | 126.69 | 185.52 |
| San Juan | 128.40 | 174.00 | 110.13 | 116.63 | 167.21 | 214.71 | 172.35 | 218.09 | 139.57 | 178.49 |
| San Miguel | 174.00 | 218.76 | 158.33 | 198.58 | 91.30 | 118.02 | 86.91 | 117.89 | 77.75 | 97.68 |
| Sedgwick | 156.48 | 201.84 | 74.09 | 97.64 | 117.12 | 158.48 | 79.94 | 109.60 | 73.90 | 126.33 |
| Summit | 234.00 | 288.00 | 178.07 | 200.45 | 143.30 | 193.70 | 143.78 | 180.84 | 122.10 | 171.99 |
| Teller | 109.68 | 181.80 | 91.58 | 109.93 | 93.43 | 118.77 | 98.08 | 105.62 | 93.45 | 117.26 |
| Washington | 147.12 | 194.76 | 116.78 | 147.88 | 118.44 | 136.67 | 97.62 | 120.02 | 92.37 | 119.52 |
| Weld | 143.04 | 192.96 | 116.70 | 165.31 | 117.23 | 160.69 | 117.59 | 161.41 | 111.70 | 154.39 |
| Yuma | 148.56 | 145.20 | 101.09 | 125.58 | 101.55 | 127.89 | 72.34 | 93.59 | 70.16 | 88.02 |
| State | $133.80 | $177.12 | $103.73 | $137.43 | $ 98.22 | $129.36 | $101.10 | $135.82 | $ 97.44 | $135.83 |
| *Co. H.Sc. | ____ | ____ | ____ | ____ | ____ | ____ | 168.31 | 196.87 | 177.37 | 207.18 |
| Total | $133.80 | $177.12 | $103.73 | $137.43 | $ 98.22 | $129.36 | $ 99.69 | $134.24 | $ 95.67 | $133.93 |

*County High Schools included in county totals for 1929 and subsequent years.

## VALUE OF PUBLIC SCHOOL PROPERTY, 1931, BY COUNTIES
(From Records of Superintendent of Public Instruction)

| COUNTY | Buildings | Land | Equipment | Total | Per Pupil Enrolled |
|---|---|---|---|---|---|
| Adams | $ 859,485.00 | $ 201,265.00 | $ 100,680.00 | $ 1,161,430.00 | $215.20 |
| Alamosa | 352,751.35 | 35,690.00 | 54,229.53 | 442,670.88 | 185.70 |
| Arapahoe | 874,300.00 | 125,164.00 | 108,980.45 | 1,108,444.45 | 213.75 |
| Archuleta | 156,864.25 | 20,278.00 | 29,784.62 | 186,926.87 | 196.15 |
| Baca | 342,699.00 | 11,924.00 | 48,791.10 | 403,414.10 | 118.13 |
| Bent | 329,081.77 | 19,940.00 | 47,470.00 | 396,491.77 | 150.35 |
| Boulder | 1,423,238.00 | 178,078.00 | 149,614.00 | 1,750,930.00 | 222.60 |
| Chaffee | 253,150.00 | 12,125.00 | 34,910.00 | 300,185.00 | 176.20 |
| Cheyenne | 249,500.00 | 16,416.50 | 56,895.00 | 322,811.50 | 287.25 |
| Clear Creek | 146,400.00 | 8,635.00 | 12,425.00 | 167,460.00 | 396.50 |
| Conejos | 283,650.00 | 10,725.00 | 51,000.00 | 345,375.00 | 115.00 |
| Costilla | 81,475.00 | 5,775.00 | 11,450.00 | 98,700.00 | 63.60 |
| Crowley | 393,580.00 | 15,875.00 | 36,000.00 | 445,455.00 | 272.28 |
| Custer | 60,150.00 | 3,770.00 | 11,848.95 | 75,768.95 | 167.25 |
| Delta | 630,934.00 | 37,705.00 | 71,142.95 | 739,781.95 | 169.54 |
| Denver | 16,884,048.58 | 2,751,993.61 | 1,953,866.25 | 21,589,908.44 | 337.65 |
| Dolores | -------- | -------- | -------- | -------- | ------ |
| Douglas | 168,021.23 | 8,241.00 | 18,269.00 | 194,531.23 | 220.30 |
| Eagle | 156,376.00 | 10,665.00 | 43,406.00 | 210,447.00 | 200.00 |
| Elbert | 200,062.00 | 5,225.00 | 39,268.00 | 244,555.00 | 160.57 |
| El Paso | 2,725,004.93 | 458,747.96 | 340,225.20 | 3,523,978.09 | 322.03 |
| Fremont | 950,124.52 | 33,485.00 | 109,135.00 | 1,092.744.52 | 249.09 |
| Garfield | 611,375.00 | 114,545.00 | 87,063.00 | 812,983.00 | 314.00 |
| Gilpin | 46,040.00 | 2,155.00 | 6,450.00 | 54,645.00 | 241.80 |
| Grand | 61,400.00 | 3,185.00 | 13,435.00 | 78,020.00 | 144.00 |
| Gunnison | 477,367.34 | 13,075.00 | 30,855.00 | 521,297.34 | 385.55 |
| Hinsdale | 11,000.00 | 1,050.00 | 1,000.00 | 13,050.00 | 124.00 |
| Huerfano | 444,400.00 | 19,365.00 | 40,550.00 | 504,315.00 | 107.00 |
| Jackson | 31,475.00 | 2,325.00 | 10,950.00 | 44,750.00 | 159.25 |
| Jefferson | 965,462.00 | 73,675.00 | 141,999.00 | 1,181,136.00 | 233.46 |
| Kiowa | 207,615.00 | 8,080.00 | 30,681.00 | 246,376.00 | 221.00 |
| Kit Carson | 387,066.43 | 12,451.00 | 71,107.14 | 470,624.57 | 119.81 |
| Lake | 117,401.00 | 625.00 | 28,767.00 | 146,793.00 | 167.00 |
| La Plata | 613,825.75 | 58,858.00 | 62,117.39 | 734,801.14 | 204.15 |
| Larimer | 1,533,566.75 | 224,876.40 | 175,003.60 | 1,933,446.75 | 221.95 |
| Las Animas | 1,111,055.00 | 106,310.25 | 138,448.80 | 1,355,814.05 | 140.12 |
| Lincoln | 380,950.00 | 10,688.00 | 64,071.00 | 455,709.00 | 175.07 |
| Logan | 857,825.05 | 79,262.00 | 164,270.00 | 1,101,357.05 | 198.00 |
| Mesa | 1,072,950.00 | 92,501.00 | 167,125.00 | 1,332,576.00 | 190.00 |
| Mineral | 8,000.00 | 800.00 | 1,300.00 | 10,100.00 | 85.00 |
| Moffat | 145,035.00 | 10,050.00 | 29,120.00 | 184,205.00 | 143.90 |
| Montezuma | 193,575.00 | 19,735.00 | 40,950.00 | 254,260.00 | 120.45 |
| Montrose | 486,100.00 | 26,855.00 | 75,375.00 | 588,330.00 | 172.37 |
| Morgan | 1,031,617.00 | 83,930.00 | 124,857.60 | 1,240,404.00 | 147.10 |
| Otero | 1,252,231.79 | 107,087.00 | 148,111.40 | 1,507,430.19 | 214.45 |
| Ouray | 45,687.00 | 2,760.00 | 8,115.00 | 56,562.00 | 151.90 |
| Park | 56,275.00 | 5,100.00 | 9,945.00 | 71,320.00 | 200.00 |
| Phillips | 305,800.00 | 22,830.00 | 40,455.00 | 369,085.00 | 217.10 |
| Pitkin | 62,200.00 | 8,900.00 | 10,026.00 | 81,126.00 | 260.80 |
| Prowers | 678,029.35 | 27,336.00 | 84,299.35 | 789,664.70 | 175.40 |
| Pueblo | 3,812,936.62 | 351,345.08 | 475,330.39 | 4,639,612.09 | 316.20 |
| Rio Blanco | 164,235.00 | 12,880.00 | 21,225.00 | 198,340.00 | 283.00 |
| Rio Grande | 440,888.80 | 28,850.00 | 109,350.00 | 579,088.80 | 203.50 |
| Routt | 475,918.11 | 25,930.00 | 60,974.51 | 562,822.62 | 231.33 |
| Saguache | 283,175.13 | 10,050.00 | 54,600.00 | 347,825.13 | 181.35 |
| San Juan | 60,000.00 | 10,000.00 | 1,000.00 | 71,000.00 | 245.00 |
| San Miguel | 188,530.39 | 3,595.00 | 16,351.34 | 208,476.73 | 345.15 |
| Sedgwick | 476,921.95 | 27,953.21 | 65,646.62 | 570,521.78 | 328.83 |
| Summit | 114,100.00 | 1,700.00 | 14,200.00 | 130,000.00 | 669.00 |
| Teller | 88,050.00 | 1,150.00 | 9,525.00 | 98,725.00 | 122.00 |
| Washington | 388,025.00 | 23,843.00 | 61,972.00 | 473,840.00 | 173.00 |
| Weld | 3,181,017.45 | 185,065.29 | 421,105.52 | 3,787,188.26 | 207.30 |
| Yuma | 807,316.00 | 27,802.00 | 170,707.00 | 1,005,825.00 | 248.30 |
| State | $51,177,334.54 | $ 5,820,296.30 | $ 6,617,825.11 | $63,615,455.95 | $244.08 |

## PUBLIC SCHOOLS, TEACHERS AND SCHOOL POPULATION, 1931

| COUNTY | Total Number | | | Teachers | | | School Population | | |
|---|---|---|---|---|---|---|---|---|---|
| | No. of School Districts | Schools | School Bldgs. | Male | Female | Total | Persons of School Age | Enrollm't in Public Schools | Aver. Daily Attend. |
| Adams | 42 | 79 | 79 | 34 | 179 | 213 | 5,979 | 5,397 | 4,067 |
| Alamosa | 14 | 23 | 20 | 16 | 68 | 84 | 2,626 | 2,383 | 1,784 |
| Arapahoe | 29 | 49 | 47 | 30 | 161 | 191 | 6,176 | 5,186 | 4,238 |
| Archuleta | 22 | 27 | 28 | 3 | 41 | 44 | 1,031 | 953 | 698 |
| Baca | 63 | 92 | 85 | 39 | 101 | 140 | 3,308 | 3,415 | 2,541 |
| Bent | 38 | 49 | 48 | 23 | 92 | 115 | 2,624 | 2,637 | 1,916 |
| Boulder | 57 | 72 | 76 | 56 | 258 | 314 | 9,602 | 7,866 | 6,284 |
| Chaffee | 25 | 31 | 31 | 10 | 61 | 71 | 2,270 | 1,703 | 1,383 |
| Cheyenne | 9 | 29 | 46 | 17 | 49 | 66 | 1,181 | 1,123 | 866 |
| Clear Creek | 9 | 12 | 10 | 5 | 21 | 26 | 512 | 432 | 363 |
| Conejos | 30 | 39 | 34 | 32 | 86 | 118 | 3,719 | 3,004 | 2,265 |
| Costilla | 14 | 25 | 18 | 13 | 31 | 44 | 1,909 | 1,552 | 995 |
| Crowley | 9 | 21 | 20 | 15 | 53½ | 68½ | 2,007 | 1,837 | 1,380 |
| Custer | 23 | 24 | 22 | 5 | 28 | 33 | 535 | 453 | 326 |
| Delta | 18 | 40 | 39 | 34 | 125 | 159 | 5,160 | 4,014 | 3,126 |
| Denver | 1 | 77 | 95 | 217 | 1,381 | 1,598 | 79,039 | 63,941 | 47,624 |
| Dolores | 10 | 18 | 18 | 3 | 16 | 19 | 392 | 374 | 300 |
| Douglas | 33 | 36 | 36 | 11 | 52 | 63 | 900 | 910 | 707 |
| Eagle | 23 | 39 | 36 | 7 | 55 | 62 | 996 | 1,057 | 850 |
| Elbert | 47 | 89 | 86 | 14 | 103 | 117 | 2,025 | 1,673 | 1,373 |
| El Paso | 38 | 99 | 86 | 85 | 337 | 422 | 12,325 | 10,943 | 8,627 |
| Fremont | 33 | 51 | 51 | 41 | 149 | 190 | 5,552 | 4,387 | 3,554 |
| Garfield | 42 | 57 | 57 | 26 | 102 | 128 | 3,137 | 2,591 | 1,852 |
| Gilpin | 11 | 8 | 12 | 2 | 12 | 14 | 251 | 226 | 171 |
| Grand | 17 | 27 | 24 | 5 | 32 | 37 | 518 | 542 | 376 |
| Gunnison | 26 | 41 | 36 | 16 | 53 | 69 | 1,523 | 1,352 | 881 |
| Hinsdale | 4 | 5 | 4 | 2 | 7 | 9 | 124 | 105 | 83 |
| Huerfano | 51 | 82 | 80 | 23 | 156 | 179 | 6,967 | 4,711 | 3,379 |
| Jackson | 6 | 11 | 10 | 2 | 13 | 15 | 348 | 281 | 239 |
| Jefferson | 47 | 67 | 59 | 30 | 171 | 201 | 5,815 | 5,150 | 3,996 |
| Kiowa | 18 | 31 | 27 | 18 | 44 | 62 | 1,335 | 1,110 | 904 |
| Kit Carson | 83 | 104 | 90 | 42 | 109 | 151 | 3,324 | 2,845 | 2,554 |
| Lake | 9 | 17 | 17 | 8 | 30 | 38 | 1,494 | 879 | 738 |
| La Plata | 38 | 66 | 62 | 26 | 111 | 137 | 4,343 | 3,599 | 2,697 |
| Larimer | 46 | 84 | 73 | 49 | 281 | 330 | 9,923 | 8,812 | 6,858 |
| Las Animas | 120 | 169 | 163 | 76 | 318 | 394 | 12,828 | 9,662 | 7,449 |
| Lincoln | 45 | 81 | 81 | 39 | 89 | 128 | 2,813 | 2,313 | 1,950 |
| Logan | 57 | 98 | 92 | 45 | 207 | 252 | 7,057 | 5,557 | 3,588 |
| Mesa | 36 | 67 | 69 | 51 | 214 | 265 | 8,181 | 7,014 | 5,510 |
| Mineral | 3 | 3 | 3 | 2 | 5 | 7 | 136 | 120 | 98 |
| Moffat | 36 | 67 | 67 | 19 | 73 | 92 | 1,506 | 1,215 | 720 |
| Montezuma | 30 | 43 | 40 | 16 | 67 | 83 | 2,405 | 2,111 | 1,621 |
| Montrose | 26 | 37 | 40 | 22 | 103 | 125 | 3,924 | 3,413 | 2,554 |
| Morgan | 19 | 58 | 63 | 38 | 161 | 199 | 6,178 | 5,479 | 3,727 |
| Otero | 20 | 47 | 42 | 47 | 188 | 235 | 7,918 | 7,029 | 5,261 |
| Ouray | 12 | 19 | 15 | 3 | 21 | 24 | 465 | 346 | 286 |
| Park | 20 | 38 | 36 | 6 | 36 | 42 | 494 | 398 | 223 |
| Phillips | 38 | 40 | 37 | 21 | 63 | 84 | 1,751 | 1,654 | 1,338 |
| Pitkin | 15 | 12 | 13 | 4 | 19 | 23 | 448 | 311 | 380 |
| Prowers | 50 | 72 | 69 | 38 | 135 | 173 | 4,992 | 4,502 | 3,360 |
| Pueblo | 47 | 111 | 102 | 75 | 528½ | 603½ | 20,348 | 15,625 | 11,267 |
| Rio Blanco | 18 | 33 | 33 | 6 | 40 | 46 | 883 | 701 | 665 |
| Rio Grande | 8 | 16 | 18 | 15 | 74 | 89 | 3,280 | 2,846 | 2,012 |
| Routt | 44 | 68 | 66 | 19 | 108 | 127 | 2,792 | 2,433 | 1,881 |
| Saguache | 8 | 25 | 23 | 18 | 54 | 72 | 2,070 | 1,808 | 1,248 |
| San Juan | 1 | 3 | 5 | 6 | 6 | 12 | 319 | 286 | 211 |
| San Miguel | 14 | 24 | 22 | 4 | 31 | 35 | 713 | 570 | 462 |
| Sedgwick | 24 | 32 | 32 | 19 | 64 | 83 | 1,887 | 1,735 | 1,345 |
| Summit | 9 | 12 | 9 | 2 | 14 | 16 | 229 | 194 | 156 |
| Teller | 11 | 15 | 14 | 5 | 30 | 35 | 1,052 | 809 | 495 |
| Washington | 84 | 123 | 123 | 33 | 138 | 171 | 3,250 | 2,741 | 2,222 |
| Weld | 136 | 230 | 222 | 141 | 563½ | 704½ | 21,384 | 18,269 | 13,545 |
| Yuma | 117 | 136 | 138 | 50½ | 162½ | 213 | 4,455 | 4,051 | 3,435 |
| State | 2,033 | 3,300 | 3,199 | 1,779½ | 8,081 | 9,860½ | 312,728 | 260,635 | 197,013 |

## RECEIPTS AND EXPENDITURES OF PUBLIC SCHOOL SYSTEM BY COUNTIES

(From Reports of State Superintendent of Public Instruction)

Note—Receipts include balances on hand at beginning of fiscal years.

| COUNTY | 1931 Receipts | 1931 Expenditures | 1930 Receipts | 1930 Expenditures |
|---|---|---|---|---|
| Adams | $ 609,155.49 | $ 464,734.37 | $ 560,961.74 | $ 445,021.95 |
| Alamosa | 288,943.86 | 251,563.32 | 260,466.63 | 195,858.49 |
| Arapahoe | 500,178.34 | 443,374.93 | 478,981.96 | 427,139.44 |
| Archuleta | 71,917.05 | 53,545.25 | 81,282.11 | 54,047.42 |
| Baca | 277,300.30 | 317,552.36 | 292,203.66 | 239,892.99 |
| Bent | 218,452.28 | 206,010.39 | 236,232.15 | 212,666.15 |
| Boulder | 853,136.88 | 761,980.37 | 886,240.59 | 786,847.75 |
| Chaffee | 168,180.36 | 149,449.15 | 161,584.05 | 147,724.98 |
| Cheyenne | 202,992.12 | 169,805.75 | 218,686.54 | 158,665.02 |
| Clear Creek | 51,324.95 | 44,897.51 | 53,843.78 | 47,071.30 |
| Conejos | 234,313.58 | 190,836.40 | 226,579.55 | 189,414.22 |
| Costilla | 111,791.87 | 80,413.61 | 82,158.01 | 74,137.46 |
| Crowley | 250,675.90 | 204,415.85 | 260,209.61 | 222,553.62 |
| Custer | 40,938.06 | 33,664.57 | 46,921.88 | 39,094.81 |
| Delta | 361,556.69 | 330,230.20 | 416,722.59 | 371,986.42 |
| Denver | 6,981,209.21 | 7,200,366.32 | 6,868,081.13 | 6,792,827.22 |
| Dolores | 37,746.95 | 20,072.61 | 38,027.51 | 22,699.90 |
| Douglas | 145,170.06 | 119,672.02 | 144,545.25 | 114,733.77 |
| Eagle | 159,328.87 | 110,139.93 | 171,676.36 | 107,340.17 |
| Elbert | 266,868.18 | 201,685.48 | 280,400.05 | 207,096.27 |
| El Paso | 1,437,112.69 | 1,329,718.12 | 1,537,461.40 | 1,410,951.20 |
| Fremont | 661,665.86 | 577,590.94 | 550,545.39 | 482,150.68 |
| Garfield | 363,474.20 | 275,318.06 | 358,298.16 | 297,780.87 |
| Gilpin | 38,159.97 | 29,065.23 | 38,780.19 | 22,726.99 |
| Grand | 64,019.81 | 51,271.21 | 63,884.93 | 50,127.21 |
| Gunnison | 172,078.22 | 140,105.73 | 170,815.17 | 147,889.10 |
| Hinsdale | 13,506.99 | 13,484.81 | 14,403.83 | 10,991.78 |
| Huerfano | 420,174.95 | 325,094.85 | 546,702.37 | 424,571.52 |
| Jackson | 37,665.50 | 27,482.47 | 37,864.37 | 26,513.15 |
| Jefferson | 544,671.91 | 439,377.78 | 498,934.06 | 411,033.11 |
| Kiowa | 160,384.56 | 151,377.54 | 168,315.54 | 146,846.07 |
| Kit Carson | 420,022.92 | 329,755.69 | 417,878.18 | 325,709.27 |
| Lake | 100,031.22 | 85,940.62 | 107,285.76 | 88,315.03 |
| La Plata | 319,135.73 | 298,130.18 | 325,957.87 | 290,162.56 |
| Larimer | 1,006,336.85 | 832,402.11 | 1,081,229.63 | 896,332.29 |
| Las Animas | 873,469.26 | 785,671.10 | 987,199.87 | 853,469.99 |
| Lincoln | 350,217.62 | 270,591.40 | 379,448.59 | 290,378.83 |
| Logan | 699,438.55 | 589,287.32 | 804,170.42 | 668,766.09 |
| Mesa | 598,205.35 | 549,690.40 | 601,628.15 | 536,518.81 |
| Mineral | 25,100.29 | 13,675.43 | 27,599.06 | 15,076.68 |
| Moffat | 145,757.74 | 121,187.57 | 142,833.37 | 108,058.98 |
| Montezuma | 175,207.06 | 141,056.35 | 195,878.65 | 148,301.24 |
| Montrose | 291,759.30 | 233,382.01 | 324,258.78 | 253,529.75 |
| Morgan | 547,014.29 | 484,138.49 | 643,942.90 | 576,215.05 |
| Otero | 615,176.18 | 555,160.04 | 672,122.86 | 590,353.66 |
| Ouray | 50,928.56 | 40,844.92 | 52,191.61 | 48,038.92 |
| Park | 68,783.41 | 57,718.15 | 61,857.97 | 49,710.32 |
| Phillips | 255,830.77 | 157,059.55 | 243,237.88 | 157,402.81 |
| Pitkin | 41,042.72 | 29,668.21 | 50,307.08 | 37,693.55 |
| Prowers | 465,662.56 | 441,422.12 | 476,920.37 | 427,527.02 |
| Pueblo | 1,602,588.40 | 1,507,760.47 | 1,656,144.28 | 1,552,141.54 |
| Rio Blanco | 99,351.56 | 74,813.25 | 100,962.40 | 75,692.57 |
| Rio Grande | 391,703.02 | 297,836.08 | 428,258.61 | 308,970.26 |
| Routt | 310,331.08 | 257,338.53 | 313,455.68 | 251,618.38 |
| Saguache | 228,669.31 | 182,006.09 | 272,436.81 | 203,639.21 |
| San Juan | 48,308.26 | 27,547.90 | 50,924.64 | 31,606.14 |
| San Miguel | 83,088.04 | 74,345.92 | 111,018.93 | 93,729.87 |
| Sedgwick | 230,793.17 | 203,642.03 | 157,807.30 | 127,806.54 |
| Summit | 52,151.84 | 35,443.10 | 56,283.92 | 38,285.19 |
| Teller | 73,996.20 | 66,524.32 | 83,832.60 | 73,540.00 |
| Washington | 394,153.12 | 302,398.31 | 416,931.96 | 312,613.50 |
| Weld | 2,116,690.41 | 1,960,601.67 | 2,354,422.12 | 2,103,092.01 |
| Yuma | 554,140.43 | 451,645.17 | 530,034.85 | 390,920.17 |
| State | $28,929,240.88 | $26,172,931.63 | $29,820,273.66 | $26,213,617.76 |

## AVERAGE YEARLY SALARIES OF TEACHERS IN PUBLIC SCHOOLS, 1931

(From Records of the State Superintendent of Public Instruction)

| COUNTY | Senior High Schools | | Junior High Schools | | Three or More Teacher Schools | | Two-Teacher Schools | |
|---|---|---|---|---|---|---|---|---|
| | Men | Women | Men | Women | Men | Women | Men | Women |
| Adams | $1,827.30 | $1,363.50 | _____ | $1,428.18 | $1,407.00 | $1,216.80 | $1,167.50 | $1,078.25 |
| Alamosa | 2,181.00 | 1,378.00 | $1,600.00 | 1,500.00 | 1,086.00 | 1,054.00 | _____ | 1,146.00 |
| Arapahoe | 2,000.00 | 1,390.00 | _____ | 1,705.00 | 1,660.00 | 1,062.00 | _____ | 1,032.00 |
| Archuleta | 1,640.00 | 1,365.00 | 1,200.00 | _____ | _____ | 1,079.37 | _____ | 1,080.00 |
| Baca | 1,392.00 | 1,301.00 | 1,057.00 | 1,140.00 | 1,080.00 | 1,266.00 | 1,188.00 | 950.00 |
| Bent | 1,510.00 | 1,485.00 | 1,910.00 | 1,360.00 | 1,530.00 | 1,194.00 | 1,206.00 | 1,083.00 |
| Boulder | 1,823.00 | 1,443.00 | 1,650.00 | 1,410.00 | 1,405.00 | 1,177.00 | 1,166.00 | 1,027.00 |
| Chaffee | 1,875.00 | 1,450.00 | _____ | 1,425.00 | _____ | 1,084.50 | 950.00 | _____ |
| Cheyenne | 1,671.40 | 1,538.88 | _____ | _____ | 1,136.00 | 1,090.00 | 990.00 | 939.00 |
| Clear Creek | 1,900.00 | 1,350.00 | 1,400.00 | 1,333.00 | _____ | 1,116.00 | _____ | _____ |
| Conejos | 1,627.00 | 1,236.00 | _____ | _____ | 1,028.00 | 868.00 | 926.00 | 813.00 |
| Costilla | 1,575.00 | _____ | _____ | 1,125.00 | 994.68 | 899.89 | 927.50 | 869.20 |
| Crowley | 2,051.50 | 1,360.30 | 1,688.60 | 1,309.30 | 1,400.00 | 1,084.00 | _____ | 1,035.00 |
| Custer | 1,420.00 | 1,925.00 | 1,125.00 | _____ | _____ | _____ | 1,350.00 | 900.00 |
| Delta | 1,844.09 | 1,395.00 | 1,808.00 | 1,350.00 | 950.00 | 1,139.00 | 1,200.00 | 874.40 |
| Denver | 2,501.66 | 2,668.00 | 2,270.45 | 2,505.32 | 1,980.00 | 2,231.28 | _____ | 2,231.28 |
| Dolores | _____ | _____ | _____ | _____ | 1,700.00 | 1,275.00 | 1,125.00 | 900.00 |
| Douglas | 2,037.50 | 1,340.00 | _____ | _____ | 1,675.00 | 1,256.00 | _____ | 1,145.00 |
| Eagle | 2,160.00 | 1,350.00 | _____ | _____ | _____ | 1,271.00 | _____ | 1,037.45 |
| Elbert | 1,853.00 | 1,313.00 | _____ | _____ | 1,185.00 | 1,113.00 | _____ | 880.00 |
| El Paso | 1,804.47 | 1,490.95 | 1,980.73 | 1,703.00 | 1,242.26 | 1,166.86 | 1,500.00 | 1,324.75 |
| Fremont | 1,925.00 | 1,409.00 | 1,750.00 | 1,414.50 | 1,580.00 | 1,163.90 | 1,337.50 | 1,086.00 |
| Garfield | 1,797.00 | 1,372.00 | _____ | 1,100.00 | 1,864.00 | 1,198.00 | 1,050.00 | 1,050.00 |
| Gilpin | 1,800.00 | 1,400.00 | _____ | _____ | 1,200.00 | 1,200.00 | _____ | 1,287.00 |
| Grand | 1,400.00 | 1,300.00 | 1,350.00 | _____ | 1,400.00 | 1,100.00 | _____ | 1,068.00 |
| Gunnison | 1,784.00 | 1,726.00 | _____ | 1,487.00 | 2,000.00 | 1,345.00 | _____ | _____ |
| Hinsdale | 1,575.00 | _____ | _____ | _____ | 1,575.00 | 1,065.00 | _____ | _____ |
| Huerfano | 1,859.00 | 1,467.00 | 2,060.00 | 1,400.00 | 1,852.00 | 1,220.00 | 900.00 | 1,006.00 |
| Jackson | 2,600.00 | 1,700.00 | _____ | _____ | _____ | 1,205.00 | 1,305.00 | 1,125.00 |
| Jefferson | 2,038.00 | 1,414.00 | 1,654.00 | 1,270.00 | _____ | 1,123.00 | 1,575.00 | 987.00 |
| Kiowa | 1,718.00 | 1,177.00 | _____ | _____ | 1,375.00 | 1,067.80 | 945.00 | 917.50 |
| Kit Carson | 1,737.08 | 1,376.20 | 1,253.61 | 1,336.66 | 1,553.57 | 1,126.60 | 1,032.50 | 906.25 |
| Lake | 1,870.00 | 1,634.00 | _____ | _____ | 1,616.00 | 1,280.00 | _____ | 1,275.00 |
| La Plata | 1,963.00 | 1,788.00 | 1,775.00 | 1,310.00 | 1,350.00 | 1,071.00 | 900.00 | 1,042.00 |
| Larimer | 2,507.60 | 1,490.00 | 1,735.50 | 1,432.60 | 1,441.00 | 1,221.00 | _____ | 991.00 |
| Las Animas | 1,714.00 | 1,493.00 | 1,550.00 | 1,252.00 | 1,060.00 | 1,230.00 | 1,137.00 | 1,029.00 |
| Lincoln | 1,796.50 | 1,271.40 | _____ | _____ | 1,342.00 | 1,099.50 | 1,128.75 | 1,025.00 |
| Logan | 2,195.00 | 1,531.00 | 1,585.00 | 1,310.00 | 1,162.00 | 1,232.00 | 955.80 | 919.00 |
| Mesa | 1,694.00 | 1,395.00 | 1,450.00 | 1,630.00 | 1,600.00 | 1,105.00 | 1,160.00 | 1,020.00 |
| Mineral | 1,500.00 | 1,300.00 | _____ | _____ | 1,400.00 | 1,000.00 | _____ | _____ |
| Moffat | 2,240.00 | 1,636.66 | 1,500.00 | 945.00 | _____ | 1,007.00 | 1,230.00 | 850.00 |
| Montezuma | 1,844.00 | 1,253.00 | 1,350.00 | 1,071.00 | 1,282.00 | 1,051.00 | 1,136.00 | 912.00 |
| Montrose | 1,892.00 | 1,535.00 | _____ | _____ | 1,392.00 | 1,070.00 | 1,400.00 | 1,026.00 |
| Morgan | 1,942.00 | 1,405.00 | 1,760.00 | 1,538.00 | 1,414.00 | 1,087.00 | 1,153.00 | 1,022.00 |
| Otero | 1,881.00 | 1,455.00 | 1,676.00 | 1,298.00 | 1,483.00 | 1,107.00 | _____ | 1,049.00 |
| Ouray | 1,750.00 | 1,350.00 | _____ | 1,200.00 | 1,350.00 | 1,035.00 | _____ | 1,000.00 |
| Park | 1,575.00 | 1,350.00 | _____ | _____ | _____ | _____ | 1,192.50 | 1,114.00 |
| Phillips | 1,811.00 | 1,369.00 | _____ | _____ | 1,277.00 | 987.00 | 810.00 | 918.00 |
| Pitkin | 1,675.00 | 1,350.00 | _____ | 1,000.00 | 1,000.00 | 925.00 | _____ | 900.00 |
| Prowers | 1,827.00 | 1,437.00 | 1,644.00 | 1,418.00 | 1,403.00 | 1,208.00 | 1,350.00 | 976.00 |
| Pueblo | 1,904.00 | 1,348.00 | 2,298.00 | 1,409.00 | 1,789.00 | 2,901.00 | 1,371.00 | 1,048.00 |
| Rio Blanco | 1,825.00 | 1,575.00 | _____ | _____ | _____ | 1,157.00 | _____ | _____ |
| Rio Grande | 2,259.00 | 1,482.00 | 1,850.00 | 1,495.00 | 1,200.00 | 1,259.00 | _____ | 922.00 |
| Routt | 2,231.00 | 1,389.60 | 2,250.00 | 1,383.75 | 2,133.33 | 1,266.83 | _____ | 1,053.75 |
| Saguache | 1,956.00 | 1,335.00 | 1,550.00 | 1,375.00 | 1,492.00 | 1,126.00 | 1,500.00 | 1,055.00 |
| San Juan | 1,500.00 | 1,400.00 | _____ | _____ | 1,390.00 | 1,340.00 | 1,560.00 | 1,260.00 |
| San Miguel | 2,025.00 | 1,600.00 | _____ | _____ | 1,495.00 | 1,500.00 | _____ | _____ |
| Sedgwick | 1,896.00 | 1,410.00 | _____ | _____ | 1,381.00 | 1,103.00 | _____ | 945.00 |
| Summit | 2,125.00 | 1,230.00 | _____ | 1,200.00 | 2,125.00 | 1,237.00 | _____ | 1,005.00 |
| Teller | 1,800.00 | 1,400.00 | 1,700.00 | 1,250.00 | _____ | 1,140.00 | _____ | 995.00 |
| Washington | 2,009.00 | 1,400.00 | _____ | _____ | 1,529.00 | 1,112.00 | 1,013.00 | 912.00 |
| Weld | 1,872.00 | 1,389.00 | 1,467.00 | 1,344.00 | 1,273.00 | 1,137.00 | 1,127.00 | 1,070.00 |
| Yuma | 1,778.00 | 1,440.00 | _____ | _____ | 1,185.00 | 1,145.00 | 925.00 | 1,145.00 |
| Average | $1,868.00 | $1,449.00 | $1,653.00 | $1,373.00 | $1,431.00 | $1,055.00 | $1,159.00 | $1,040.00 |

Note.—Space does not permit publication of average salaries for one-teacher schools. However, the state average is $894.00 for men and $915.00 for women; kindergarten state average for women, $1,422.00.

# State Institutions

THE state of Colorado maintains 18 penal, eleemosynary and educational institutions. The penal and reform institutions, and their locations, are as follows:

Penitentiary..................Canon City
Industrial school for boys.......Golden
Industrial school for girls.....Morrison
Reformatory...............Buena Vista

The eleemosynary institutions, and their locations, are as follows:

Home for dependent and neglected
  children ......................Denver
Insane hospital...................Pueblo
Home and training school for mental
  defectives.............Grand Junction
Home and training school for mental
  defectives .....................Ridge
Soldiers and sailors home...Monte Vista
Industrial workshop for the blind.Denver

The educational institutions, and their locations, are as follows:

Agricultural college........Fort Collins
School of mines.................Golden
Teachers college..............Greeley
University of Colorado..........Boulder
Western state college.........Gunnison
Adams normal school...........Alamosa
Deaf and blind school..Colorado Springs
Fort Lewis school.............Hesperus

The governing boards of all state institutions are appointed by the governor, with the exceptions of the state university at Boulder, which is under the supervision of a board of regents elected by the voters of the state.

The disbursements of state institutions for salaries, maintenance, equipment, lands, buildings, etc., for the year ending November 30, 1928, amounted to $6,856,759, of which $5,054,540 was distributed by the educational institutions. An accompanying table shows these disbursements by items and institutions and another gives the total disbursements by institutions by years.

Beginning with 1929 the fiscal year was changed by the legislature to end with June 30, instead of November 30. Comparative figures for 1929 and 1930, therefore, are not available, but the auditor reports expenditures of $3,221,350 for state institutions, of which $2,018,789 was for educational institutions and $1,202,561 for penal and eleemosynary institutions, in the period from December 1, 1928, to June 30, 1929. For the fiscal year ending June 30, 1930, the expenses of state institutions were $6,151,822, of which $3,975,318 was for the educational institutions and $2,176,504 for the penal and eleemosynary institutions.

The inventory value on June 30,

1930, including land, buildings, and equipment of above named institutions, as reported by the public examiner, was $23,888,910. This compares with an inventory value of $22,750,651 in 1928, $23,558,543 in 1926 and $17,973,107 in 1924. A table giving details of valuations of state institutions is published in a succeeding table under the heading "Inventory Value of State Property." Additional information on the state educational institutions will be found in the chapter elsewhere in this volume under "Educational," and of individual institutions by name under sub-headings.

The total population of state institutions, exclusive of universities and colleges, has shown a steady increase in recent years. It increased from 2,602 in 1914 to 5,729 in 1931. Population by years and institutions is shown in a separate table.

## STATE PENITENTIARY

The Colorado state penitentiary is located at Canon City, in Fremont county. It is operated under the supervision of the state board of corrections and is in charge of a warden. The inventory value of the institution on June 30, 1930, as reported by the public examiner, was as follows:

Lands .......................$ 75,000
Buildings and improvements.. 1,250,000
Machinery ...................    45,000
Tools and equipment..........    60,000
Furniture and fixtures.......     5,000
Libraries, etc...............       200
Autos, etc...................    12,500
General supplies.............    14,000
Livestock ...................    26,800
Rights in land...............     4,000
Cash ........................    15,326

  Total ...................$1,507,826

The population of the penitentiary on November 30, of the years named, was as follows:

| Year | Male | Female | Total |
|------|------|--------|-------|
| 1924............ | 845 | 37 | 882 |
| 1925............ | 917 | 35 | 952 |
| 1926............ | 927 | 31 | 958 |
| 1927............ | 1,024 | 41 | 1,065 |
| 1928............ | 1,005 | 31 | 1,036 |
| 1929............ | 1,037 | 24 | 1,061 |
| 1930............ | 1,108 | 16 | 1,124 |
| 1931............ | 1,126 | 16 | 1,142 |

The number of prisoners received at the penitentiary during the fiscal years ending November 30, for the years named, was as follows:

| Year | Male | Female | Total |
|------|------|--------|-------|
| 1926 | 508 | 28 | 536 |
| 1927 | 558 | 38 | 596 |
| 1928 | 497 | 38 | 535 |
| 1929 | 532 | 18 | 550 |
| 1930 | 515 | 19 | 534 |
| 1931 | 737 | 16 | 753 |

Disbursements on account of the penitentiary for the year ended November 30, 1928, in detail, and totals by years, are given in separate tables under the heading "Disbursements of State Institutions."

In connection with the penitentiary there are operated several ranches and gardens in which convicts are employed and which supply food products for the prisoners. A dairy herd owned by the state furnishes milk and butter, and a fruit and vegetable canning plant is operated each season by the inmates. The method employed for executing prisoners sentenced to death is by hanging. A record of legal executions in the state by years is reported under a separate heading.

The total cost of operating the institution for the two-year period ending November 30, 1930, was $879,695, of which $53,862 was in food products raised and consumed and $10,134 came from the convict labor fund, leaving a net cost to the state of $815,699. The per capita annual expenditure was $374.17, based on a daily average population of 1,090.

Of 1,065 prisoners received in the two years ending November 30, 1930, 905 were native born and 160 were foreign born. Forty-five states were represented among the native born, Missouri with 83 having the largest outside of Colorado. Twenty-five foreign countries were listed as birthplaces of the foreign born, Mexico, with 41, having the largest representation, and Jugo-Slavia, with 26, being second. Of the 1,065 prisoners received during the period, 286 were farmers, 145 were laborers, 53 were cooks, 52 were miners, 34 were ranchers, 23 were housewives and the remainder were scattered among more than 150 occupations. Of those received, 559 were sentenced for crimes against property, 338 for crimes against persons and 118 for crimes against property and persons. Three hundred and three of the prisoners received, or almost one-third, were under 25 years of age, 90 were more than 50 years old and 672 were between the ages of 25 and 50 years. Ten prisoners were received for execution and 11 for life. The average minimum sentence was four years, nine months and 16 days and the average

maximum sentence was eight years and 22 days. Of the 1,065 prisoners received, 728 were serving their first sentence, 204 their second term, 84 their third, 37 their fourth, 6 their fifth, three their sixth and three their seventh term. Of the total, 434 were single, 496 married, 40 were widowers, five were widows and 90 were separated. Four could read but not write, 61 could neither read nor write, 62 could read and write a foreign language only and 938 could read and write English. Only 119 had received no religious instruction.

## HOSPITAL FOR INSANE

The value of the state hospital for the insane at Pueblo on June 30, 1930, as reported by the public examiner, was as follows:

| | |
|---|---|
| Lands | $ 208,000 |
| Buildings and improvements | 1,602,500 |
| Machinery | 105,000 |
| Tools and equipment | 52,000 |
| Furniture and fixtures | 195,000 |
| Libraries, etc. | 600 |
| Autos, etc. | 7,000 |
| General supplies | 21,452 |
| Livestock | 37,471 |
| Rights in lands | 19,725 |
| Cash | 6,000 |
| **Total** | **$2,254,748** |

The population of the hospital on November 30, of the years named, was as follows:

| Year | Male | Female | Total |
|------|------|--------|-------|
| 1914 | 704 | 472 | 1,176 |
| 1924 | 1,366 | 1,059 | 2,425 |
| 1925 | 1,348 | 1,113 | 2,461 |
| 1926 | 1,441 | 1,176 | 2,617 |
| 1927 | 1,525 | 1,225 | 2,750 |
| 1928 | 1,572 | 1,271 | 2,843 |
| 1929 | 1,586 | 1,312 | 2,898 |
| 1930 | 1,596 | 1,348 | 2,944 |
| 1931 | 1,636 | 1,389 | 3,025 |

The number received during the year ending November 30, for the years named, was as follows:

| Year | Male | Female | Total |
|------|------|--------|-------|
| 1925 | 223 | 159 | 382 |
| 1926 | 259 | 165 | 424 |
| 1927 | 288 | 187 | 475 |
| 1928 | 278 | 181 | 459 |
| 1929 | 266 | 201 | 467 |
| 1930 | 291 | 180 | 471 |
| 1931 | 294 | 189 | 483 |

Disbursements on account of the hospital in 1928, in detail, and totals by years, are given in separate tables under the headings "Disbursements of State Institutions."

There were 938 patients admitted to the hospital in the two years ending November 30, 1930, of whom 557 were male and 381 female.

## POPULATION OF STATE INSTITUTIONS
(November 30 of Years Named)

| INSTITUTION | 1931 | 1930 | 1929 | 1928 | 1927 | 1926 | 1925 | 1919 | 1914 |
|---|---|---|---|---|---|---|---|---|---|
| Industrial school for boys___ | 266 | 237 | 247 | 274 | 289 | 257 | 193 | 337 | 293 |
| Industrial school for girls___ | 141 | 130 | 135 | 125 | 141 | 139 | 125 | 136 | 122 |
| Reformatory _____ | 230 | 215 | 155 | 159 | 189 | 171 | 222 | 157 | 137 |
| Home and training schools: | | | | | | | | | |
| Grand Junction_____ | 270 | 263 | 260 | 252 | 254 | 271 | 250 | * | * |
| Ridge _____ | 187 | 148 | 108 | 89 | 74 | 78 | 80 | 73 | 80 |
| Soldiers' and Sailors' Home__ | 118 | 230 | 185 | 160 | 160 | 203 | 219 | 153 | 188 |
| Insane hospital_____ | 3,025 | 2,944 | 2,898 | 2,843 | 2,750 | 2,617 | 2,461 | 1,926 | 1,176 |
| Penitentiary _____ | 1,142 | 1,124 | 1,061 | 1,036 | 1,065 | 958 | 964 | 571 | 352 |
| Workshop for blind_____ | 36 | 27 | 27 | 16 | 16 | 13 | 13 | 18 | 18 |
| Home for dependent and neglected children_____ | 314 | 309 | 198 | 192 | 158 | 135 | 147 | 192 | 236 |
| Totals _____ | 5,729 | 5,627 | 5,274 | 5,146 | 5,096 | 4,842 | 4,674 | 3,563 | 2,602 |

## DISBURSEMENTS OF STATE INSTITUTIONS, BY YEARS
(From Report of Public Examiner)

| INSTITUTION | 1928 | 1927 | 1926 | 1925 | 1924 |
|---|---|---|---|---|---|
| **Educational:** | | | | | |
| Agricultural college_____ | $1,312,323 | $1,382,488 | $1,258,758 | $1,161,255 | $1,152,161 |
| Fort Lewis school_____ | 120,502 | 84,596 | 133,230 | 119,187 | 107,402 |
| Alamosa Normal_____ | †88,650 | 24,015 | 8,219 | 21,616 | 67,265 |
| School of Mines_____ | 363,773 | 298,938 | 296,018 | 273,950 | 280,735 |
| Teachers college_____ | 645,789 | 738,917 | 722,698 | 587,813 | 664,759 |
| University _____ | 2,082,894 | 1,983,946 | 1,803,371 | 2,221,773 | 2,861,333 |
| Western State college_____ | 190,170 | 228,648 | 262,624 | 244,841 | 240,349 |
| Deaf and Blind school_____ | 250,439 | 182,122 | 277,143 | 173,435 | 165,601 |
| Total _____ | $5,054,540 | $4,923,670 | $4,762,061 | $4,803,870 | $5,539,605 |
| **Eleemosynary:** | | | | | |
| Dependent and Neglected Children_____ | $  80,039 | $  99,444 | $  83,302 | $  91,353 | $ 116,626 |
| Insane Hospital_____ | 608,153 | 639,158 | 544,263 | 552,111 | 510,058 |
| Mental Defectives (Ridge)_____ | 35,324 | 40,603 | 83,477 | 33,135 | 37,833 |
| Mental Defectives (Grand Junction)____ | 98,399 | 100,586 | 77,377 | 85,303 | 71,181 |
| Soldiers' and Sailors' Home_____ | 98,631 | 116,195 | 117,400 | 132,576 | 126,773 |
| Workshop for Blind_____ | 43,183 | 27,416 | 29,386 | 32,298 | 50,390 |
| Detention Home_____ | ------ | ------ | 750 | 10,694 | 10,790 |
| Total _____ | $ 963,729 | $1,023,402 | $ 935,955 | $ 937,470 | $ 923,651 |
| **Penal and Reform:** | | | | | |
| Penitentiary _____ | $ 478,753 | $ 413,311 | $ 406,931 | $ 405,304 | $ 272,011 |
| Industrial School, boys_____ | 166,654 | 163,229 | 182,451 | 147,985 | 195,018 |
| Industrial School, girls_____ | 62,380 | 54,844 | 62,796 | 55,600 | 66,501 |
| Reformatory _____ | 130,703 | 130,938 | 109,208 | 116,781 | 81,621 |
| Total _____ | $ 838,490 | $ 762,322 | $ 761,386 | $ 725,670 | $ 615,151 |
| **Recapitulation:** | | | | | |
| Educational _____ | $5,054,540 | $4,923,670 | $4,762,061 | $4,803,870 | $5,539,605 |
| Eleemosynary _____ | 963,729 | 1,023,402 | 935,955 | 937,470 | 923,651 |
| Penal and reform_____ | 838,490 | 762,322 | 761,386 | 725,670 | 615,151 |
| Grand total_____ | $6,856,759 | $6,709,394 | $6,459,402 | $6,467,010 | $7,078,407 |

†Includes deficiency for previous years.

Note.—Figures used in above table are for fiscal years ending November 30. Due to change in fiscal year, 1929 figures, which cover only seven months, are not comparable and are omitted. No report for subsequent years is yet available.

## DISBURSEMENTS OF STATE INSTITUTIONS FOR YEAR ENDING NOVEMBER 30, 1928

(From Report of the Public Examiner)

| INSTITUTION | Salaries Amount | Per Cent | Maintenance Amount | Per Cent | Equipment Amount | Per Cent | Lands, Bldgs. Amount | Per Cent | Miscellaneous Amount | Per Cent | Total |
|---|---|---|---|---|---|---|---|---|---|---|---|
| **Educational:** | | | | | | | | | | | |
| Agricultural college | $ 812,725.38 | 61.9 | $ 305,557.56 | 23.3 | $ 19,918.52 | 1.5 | $ 90,602.03 | 6.9 | $ 83,519.51 | 6.4 | $1,312,323.00 |
| Fort Lewis | 45,364.32 | 37.7 | 32,337.60 | 26.8 | 4,800.00 | 4.0 | 38,000.00 | 31.9 | 46.00 | 0.1 | 120,501.92 |
| Adams Normal | 50,110.59 | 82.4 | 6,999.12 | 11.5 | 2,537.92 | 4.2 | 1,100.45 | 1.8 | --- | --- | 60,794.08 |
| School of Mines | 201,571.20 | 54.4 | 88,739.79 | 24.4 | --- | 0.0 | 24,718.60 | 6.8 | 48,743.43 | 13.4 | 363,773.02 |
| Teachers college | 396,739.21 | 61.4 | 94,635.44 | 14.7 | 17,135.13 | 2.7 | 44,878.62 | 6.9 | 92,400.87 | 14.3 | 645,789.27 |
| University of Colorado | 1,181,781.90 | 56.7 | 621,933.64 | 29.9 | 19,288.41 | 0.9 | 170,909.09 | 8.7 | 79,980.97 | 3.8 | 2,082,894.01 |
| Western State | 125,148.67 | 65.8 | 28,386.46 | 14.9 | 652.28 | 0.4 | 4,594.62 | 2.4 | 31,387.52 | 16.5 | 190,169.55 |
| Deaf and Blind | 117,576.84 | 47.0 | 51,667.19 | 20.6 | 3,432.52 | 1.4 | 72,455.14 | 28.9 | 5,316.99 | 2.1 | 250,438.68 |
| Adams Normal Deficiency | --- | 0.0 | 27,856.39 | 100.0 | --- | 0.0 | --- | --- | --- | --- | 27,856.39 |
| Total | $2,931,018.11 | 58.0 | $1,258,103.19 | 24.9 | $ 67,764.78 | 1.3 | $ 456,258.55 | 9.0 | $ 341,395.29 | 6.8 | $5,054,539.92 |
| **Penal and Reform:** | | | | | | | | | | | |
| Penitentiary | $ 129,725.29 | 27.1 | $ 274,173.94 | 57.3 | $ 25,000.00 | 5.2 | $ --- | --- | $ 49,853.80 | 10.4 | $ 478,753.03 |
| Reformatory | 41,465.56 | 31.7 | 72,884.43 | 55.8 | 6,120.90 | 4.7 | 6,500.00 | 5.0 | 3,732.42 | 2.8 | 130,703.31 |
| Boys' Industrial School | 59,220.58 | 25.5 | 98,928.28 | 59.4 | 1,121.79 | 0.7 | 3,945.89 | 2.4 | 3,437.25 | 2.0 | 166,653.79 |
| Girls' Industrial School | 25,441.79 | 40.8 | 32,851.70 | 52.7 | 845.30 | 1.3 | 2,113.31 | 3.4 | 1,128.26 | 1.8 | 62,380.36 |
| Total | $ 255,853.22 | 30.5 | $ 478,838.35 | 57.1 | $ 33,087.99 | 3.9 | $ 12,555.20 | 1.5 | $ 58,151.73 | 7.0 | $ 838,490.49 |
| **Eleemosynary:** | | | | | | | | | | | |
| Dependent and neglected children | $ 28,613.48 | 35.8 | $ 51,227.12 | 64.0 | $ --- | --- | $ 35.55 | --- | $ 163.27 | 0.2 | $ 80,039.42 |
| Insane asylum | 210,790.70 | 34.7 | 379,200.54 | 62.4 | 1,000.00 | 0.1 | 10,944.41 | 1.8 | 6,217.63 | 1.0 | 608,153.28 |
| Mental defectives, Ridge | 15,557.92 | 44.0 | 19,763.86 | 56.0 | --- | --- | --- | --- | 2.43 | --- | 35,324.21 |
| Mental defectives, Grand Junction | 28,427.55 | 28.9 | 67,379.40 | 68.4 | 544.20 | 0.6 | 2,047.20 | 2.1 | --- | --- | 98,398.35 |
| Soldiers' and Sailors' Home | 29,431.02 | 29.8 | 50,503.23 | 51.2 | 7,005.40 | 7.1 | 11,690.64 | 11.9 | --- | --- | 98,630.29 |
| Workshop for blind | 18,323.16 | 42.4 | 4,041.50 | 9.4 | --- | --- | --- | --- | 20,818.39 | 48.2 | 43,183.05 |
| Total | $ 331,143.83 | 34.4 | $ 572,115.65 | 59.4 | $ 8,549.60 | 0.8 | $ 24,717.80 | 2.6 | $ 27,201.72 | 2.8 | $ 963,728.60 |
| **Recapitulation:** | | | | | | | | | | | |
| Educational | $2,931,018.11 | 58.0 | $1,258,103.19 | 24.9 | $ 67,764.78 | 1.3 | $ 456,258.55 | 9.6 | $ 341,395.29 | 6.8 | $5,054,539.92 |
| Penal and reform | 255,853.22 | 30.5 | 478,838.35 | 57.1 | 33,087.99 | 3.9 | 12,559.20 | 1.5 | 58,151.73 | 7.0 | 838,490.49 |
| Eleemosynary | 331,143.83 | 34.4 | 572,115.65 | 59.4 | 8,549.60 | 0.8 | 24,717.80 | 2.6 | 27,201.72 | 2.8 | 963,728.60 |
| Grand total | $3,518,015.16 | 51.3 | $2,309,057.19 | 33.7 | $ 109,402.37 | 1.6 | $ 493,535.55 | 7.2 | $ 426,748.74 | 6.2 | $6,856,759.01 |

Note.—Due to change in fiscal years, no report later than 1928 is yet available.

## INVENTORY OF STATE PROPERTY, JUNE 30, 1930

(From Report of State Auditor)

| INSTITUTION | Lands | Buildings and Improvements | Machinery, Equipment and Supplies | Furniture and Fixtures | Libraries and Collections | Autos, Trucks and Tractors | Live Stock | Water, Coal and Mineral Rights | Cash on Hand | Total |
|---|---|---|---|---|---|---|---|---|---|---|
| Adams Normal School | $ 18,614 | $ 184,495 | $ 3,619 | $ 12,733 | $ 6,098 | $ 912 | $ ------- | $ ------- | $ 3,467 | $ 229,938 |
| Fort Lewis School | 102,400 | 369,200 | 48,243 | 26,081 | 2,781 | 14,163 | 15,237 | ------- | ------- | 578,105 |
| al college | 350,000 | 3,100,000 | 247,946 | 127,204 | 194,133 | 14,741 | 48,962 | ------- | 107,997 | 4,190,983 |
| Deaf and blind school | 45,800 | 920,722 | 68,085 | 66,989 | 1,500 | 3,000 | 5,742 | ------- | 1,000 | 1,112,838 |
| School of Mines | 186,705 | 473,876 | 329,940 | 106,377 | 60,801 | 1,873 | ------- | ------- | 32,062 | 1,141,634 |
| State university | 406,036 | 5,376,277 | 561,953 | 267,620 | 479,159 | 25,663 | ------- | ------- | 344,904 | 7,461,612 |
| Teachers college | 210,000 | 1,276,433 | 26,500 | 324,536 | 40,000 | 1,800 | ------- | ------- | 1,000 | 1,879,269 |
| Wn. State college | 8,255 | 419,942 | 36,760 | 50,659 | 34,079 | 1,652 | ------- | ------- | 19,532 | 570,879 |
| Penitentiary | 75,000 | 1,250,000 | 119,000 | 5,000 | 200 | 12,500 | 26,800 | $ 4,000 | 15,326 | 1,507,826 |
| Reformatory | 26,775 | 248,450 | 35,325 | 14,000 | 2,000 | 9,753 | 73,000 | 11,500 | 1,000 | 421,803 |
| Industrial school, boys | 63,175 | 383,654 | 70,729 | 10,398 | 1,562 | 6,733 | 14,439 | 9,000 | 3,909 | 563,599 |
| Industrial school, girls | 10,500 | 266,970 | 28,775 | 16,975 | 500 | 700 | 1,505 | 4,950 | 2,744 | 333,619 |
| Dependent and neglected children | 37,500 | 196,614 | 27,449 | 17,780 | 1,200 | 1,379 | 7,650 | ------- | 1,738 | 291,210 |
| Hospital for the insane | 208,000 | 1,602,500 | 178,462 | 195,000 | 600 | 7,000 | 37,471 | 19,725 | 6,000 | 2,254,748 |
| Mental defectives, Grand Junction | 18,320 | 394,124 | 19,045 | 60,000 | 200 | 2,459 | 4,800 | 1,600 | 1,000 | 501,548 |
| Mental defectives, Ridge | 62,279 | 237,743 | 14,393 | 14,556 | 428 | 300 | 3,665 | 7,700 | ------- | 341,064 |
| Soldiers' and Sailors' home | 37,000 | 317,233 | 68,273 | 27,935 | 313 | 7,028 | 7,000 | 8,800 | 1,000 | 474,582 |
| Workshop for the blind | ------- | 12,000 | 20,000 | 1,500 | ------- | ------- | ------- | ------- | 153 | 33,653 |
| Sool managers | 1,198,500 | 7,600,000 | 126,375 | 365,557 | ------- | ------- | ------- | ------- | ------- | 9,290,432 |
| Game and fish department | 150,000 | 737,550 | 20,000 | 2,500 | ------- | 11,345 | ------- | ------- | ------- | 921,395 |
| Highway commission | 5,000 | 36,338,809 | 11,000 | 20,500 | ------- | 535,740 | 500 | ------- | 14,400 | 36,925,949 |
| Land board | 46,979,584 | ------- | 3,429 | 11,510 | 115 | 1,458 | ------- | 100,000,000 | 167 | 146,996,263 |
| Military department | 166,086 | 846,043 | 13,409 | 7,125 | 150 | 725 | ------- | ------- | ------- | 1,033,538 |
| State fair | 22,500 | 250,000 | 5,000 | 2,000 | ------- | ------- | ------- | ------- | 624 | 280,124 |
| Miscellaneous departments | ------- | ------- | 59,124 | 64,576 | 444,268 | 16,832 | ------- | ------- | 10,154,692 | 10,739,492 |
| Totals | $50,338,029 | $62,801,535 | $ 2,142,824 | $ 1,819,111 | $ 1,270,087 | $ 677,756 | $ 246,771 | $100,067,275 | $ 10,712,715 | $230,076,103 |

## INVENTORY VALUE OF STATE PROPERTY

(From Reports of State Examiner)

Note.—Another table shows inventory as of June 30, 1930, classified as to institutions and departments.

| Classification | June 30, 1930 | Nov. 30, 1928 | Nov. 30, 1926 |
|---|---|---|---|
| Lands | $ 50,338,029 | $ 45,988,877 | $ 45,015,148 |
| Buildings and improvements | 62,801,535 | 57,840,578 | 55,086,235 |
| Machinery | 610,414 | 651,445 | 605,796 |
| Tools and equipment | 1,216,291 | 1,860,859 | 1,043,260 |
| Furniture and office equipment | 1,819,111 | 1,617,706 | 1,361,230 |
| Libraries and collections | 1,270,087 | 1,364,061 | 1,261,301 |
| Automobiles, trucks, etc. | 686,756 | 186,286 | 173,021 |
| General supplies | 307,119 | 292,569 | 367,729 |
| Livestock | 246,771 | 239,042 | 204,713 |
| Land, water and mineral rights | 100,067,275 | 100,045,748 | 103,246,680 |
| Cash in funds, institutions and departments | 10,712,715 | 7,192,439 | 4,551,094 |
| Totals | $230,076,103 | $217,279,610 | $212,916,207 |

# Highways and Highway Revenues

COLORADO has been conducting an aggressive highway construction program for a number of years, which is resulting in giving the state a system of highways comparable with any in the Union. It is estimated that more than $153,000,000 was expended for this purpose by all agencies in the state from 1910 to 1931, inclusive, covering the building of new roads, maintenance and administrative expenses. This is exclusive of street construction in cities and towns and in the Denver mountain parks system.

The state at the beginning of 1932 had 72,456 miles of state and county roads, according to surveys made by the United States bureau of public roads and the state highway department. This is an increase of 3,716 miles as compared with January 1, 1931, of which 3,695 miles is in county roads. The gain in reported mileage is due primarily to the inclusion of some county roads omitted in former surveys. Of the 72,456 miles of roads on January 1, 1932, 63,201.7 miles are classified as county roads and 9,254.9 miles as state highways.

The classification of county roads as reported by the United States bureau of public roads is as follows:

**Earth roads:**      **Miles**

Unimproved and partly graded. 38,979.0

Improved to establish grade and drained. 18,411.9

Total non-surfaced. 57,390.9

**Surfaced roads:**

Sand-clay and top soil. 1,869.5

Treated, gravel, chert, etc. 3,937.5

Bituminous. 0.6

Concrete. 3.2

Total surfaced. 5,810.8

Grand total. 63,201.7

The classification of state highways, including federal aid projects, as reported by the state highway department, is as follows:

                     **Miles**

Projected. 246.2

Graded. 4,359.2

Surfaced. 3,948.3

Oiled. 254.1

Paved. 447.1

Total. *9,254.9

*Includes 3,493.7 miles designated as federal aid projects.

The location of roads in the state in relation to farms, as reported by the federal census in 1930, is as follows:

**Farms located on—**      **Number**

Concrete road. 839

Brick road. 1

Asphalt road. 28

Macadam road. 149

Gravel road. 14,262

Sand-clay road. 161

Improved dirt road. 22,602

Unimproved dirt road. 18.072

All others. 3,842

Total. 59,956

Highway construction and maintenance in the state are carried on through several agencies. The principal agency is the state highway department, which consists of the governor, the state highway engineer, highway advisory board, and such assistants, clerks and employes as are necessary to comply with the state highway act.

The advisory board consists of one member from each of seven districts into which the state is divided, whose term is for three years and whose successor is appointed by the governor. The administrative head of the state highway department is the state highway engineer. The senior assistant engineer has complete charge of the office and routine problems connected therewith. The assistant engineer has charge of all engineering covering location, design and construction. The maintenance engineer has direct control of all maintenance work, as well as mechanical equipment. The auditor has charge of all accounting. A division engineer, in charge of location and construction, and a maintenance superintendent are assigned to each of the seven divisions.

The personnel of the state highway department is as follows:

STATE HIGHWAY ENGINEER

Charles D. Vail

ADVISORY BOARD

Dist.
1 Peter Seerie, Chairman......Denver
2 William Weiser......Grand Junction
3 I. F. Beauchamp.............Trinidad
4 E. G. Middlekamp...........Pueblo
5 Jefferson H. Davis..Colorado Springs
6 L. C. Moore.............Fort Collins
7 Frank H. Blair.............Sterling

GENERAL OFFICE

O. T. Reedy...Senior Assistant Engineer
J. E. Maloney........Assistant Engineer
Robt. H. Higgins..Supt. of Maintenance
John P. Donovan..Maintenance Engineer
Paul Bailey.............Bridge Engineer
Roy Randall.............Office Engineer
John Marshall........Chief Draftsman
Edwin Mitchell................Auditor
Roy F. Smith..............Chief Clerk

DIVISION ENGINEERS

Div.
1 E. E. Montgomery...........Denver
2 J. J. Vandermoer.....Grand Junction
3 J. R. Cheney.............Durango
4 James D. Bell..............Pueblo
5 Ernest Montgomery.Colorado Springs
6 H. L. Jenness......Glenwood Springs
7 A. B. Collins................Greeley

Owing to geographical conditions and mountain barriers, the highway advisory board districts do not correspond with the engineering and maintenance divisions. There are seven districts which have representation on the advisory board, seven districts having division engineers and nine districts having assistant superintendents of maintenance.

The assistant superintendents of maintenance, the division in which they serve and their headquarters are as follows:

Div. Asst. Supt. Headquarters
1 W. T. Murnan...............Denver
2 J. P. Shea............Grand Junction
3 Temporary Vacancy........Durango
4 D. N. Stewart................Pueblo
5 Robt. E. Norvell.............Hugo
6 Frank M. Drescher............Craig
7 John Stamm................Denver
8 E. R. Bowie............Buena Vista
9 C. M. Terrel..............Alamosa

The United States bureau of public roads co-operates with the state highway department and maintains a district office in Denver. The federal government joins with the state in the cost of construction of numerous projects and furnishes a large part of the funds used for that purpose. In 1931 the government provided 51.6 per cent of the total revenues of the state highway department, while 71.9 per cent of the total expenditure by the department was on federal aid projects.

The United States forest service constructs numerous roads and trails in and adjacent to the national forests, and expended for that purpose in 1931 a total of $745,315. This department co-operates with the counties and state in this work and a certain per cent of its revenues from the operation of the forests goes to the counties for road purposes. Additional information on forest road construction will be found elsewhere in this volume under "National Forests."

The boards of county commissioners of the several counties have absolute jurisdiction over the construction and maintenance of county roads. The funds for this work come out of county revenues. The state highway department does all of the maintenance work on all of the federal aid highways and the counties maintain the remainder of the state highways which are not part of the federal aid system. There are 16 counties which have little or no federal aid road. In these 16 counties the counties maintain the state highways and the state pays one-half of the cost.

The total cost of highway construction in Colorado in 1931, exclusive of streets in cities and towns and highways in the Denver mountain park system, as reported by all agencies, was $15,915,375. County disbursements, as shown by a table published herewith, amounted to $5,802,630. This item includes, however, $760,713 which was transferred from the state highway fund to county road funds. This item appears in accompanying tables of disbursement, since it was handled by both agencies. After eliminating the duplications, the expenditures were as follows:

By counties.................$ 5,041,917
By state highway department 10,128,143
By forest service............ 745,315
Total ...................$15,915,375

The total expenditures by these agencies, by years, before eliminating the duplications, are as follows:

```
1925 .........................$11,538,804
1926 ......................... 10,248,179
1927 .................... (not compiled)
1928 ......................... 12,502,418
1929 ......................:.... 11,607,043
1930 ......................... 13,465,628
1931 ......................... 16,676,089
```

The figures of the state highway department for 1929 used in this chapter cover 13 months, the fiscal year being changed to the calendar year in order to put the department on the same basis as other states for comparative purposes.

The sources of state highway funds, by years, are shown in a table published herewith, and disbursements by years and classification are given in another table.

The status of state highway funds for 1931 was as follows:

```
Balance, January 1........$   905,763.57
Receipts ..................  9,285,220.83
                           ──────────────
    Total ..................$10,190,984.40
Disbursements ...........  10,128,143.83
                           ──────────────
    Balance, December 31....$    62,840.57
```

The following chart shows the division of the dollar as expended by the state highway department in 1931.

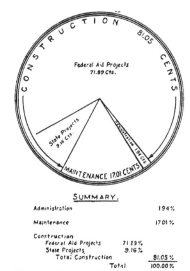

SUMMARY.

Administration                    194%

Maintenance                      1701%

Construction
    Federal Aid Projects    71.89%
    State Projects            9.16%
        Total Construction              81.05%
                Total              100.00%

The funds supplied by the government towards the construction of federal aid projects are governed by certain regulations which result in a division of costs that varies on different projects but, as a rule, the government pays about 56.22 per cent of the construction cost of the projects. The state does the locating and engineering work at its own expense, and after a project is approved by the bureau of roads the government stands half the cost, not to exceed $30,000 a mile.

### SOURCES OF STATE HIGHWAY DEPARTMENT FUNDS, BY YEARS

| SOURCE | 1931 | 1930 | 1929* | 1928 | 1927 |
|---|---|---|---|---|---|
| Taxes: | | | | | |
|   Half-mill levy........ | ........ | ........ | $ 432,872 | $ 787,946 | $ 762,527 |
|   Gasoline tax.......... | $4,219,681 | $4,171,887 | 3,908,623 | 2,665,355 | 1,740,051 |
| U. S. Government: | | | | | |
|   Federal aid........... | 4,793,420 | 2,298,636 | 1,879,435 | 1,730,450 | 1,148,156 |
|   Internal improvement. | 45,500 | 75,000 | 64,300 | 69,200 | 70,600 |
| Bus licenses........... | 43,945 | 70,999 | 35,534 | ........ | ........ |
| County aid and mis- | | | | | |
|   cellaneous........... | 182,675 | 58,376 | 38,767 | 62,276 | 109,800 |
|     Total .............. | $9,285,221 | $6,674,898 | $6,359,531 | $5,315,227 | $3,831,134 |

*Figures for 1929 cover thirteen months in order to make fiscal year correspond with the calendar year.

## DISBURSEMENTS OF STATE HIGHWAY FUNDS, BY YEARS

| PURPOSE | 1931 | 1930 | 1929* | 1928 | 1927 |
|---|---|---|---|---|---|
| Federal aid projects.... | $ 7,213,340 | $4,343,773 | $3,218,109 | $3,650,829 | $2,522,026 |
| State projects .......... | 917,454 | 701,518 | 547,925 | 665,702 | 591,607 |
| Maintenance .......... | 1,364,421 | 1,558,698 | 1,195,481 | 917,287 | 852,123 |
| Federal aid renewals... | ........ | ...... | 140,034 | ...... | 6,559 |
| Maintenance equipment and repairs.......... | 292,270 | 236,220 | 360,185 | 486,951 | ...... |
| Property and equipment.. | 47,707 | 30,388 | 74,930 | 28,935 | 24,756 |
| Surveys .............. | 46,268 | 7,914 | 26,157 | 31,119 | 15,824 |
| Road signs and traffic census............... | 21,311 | 23,042 | 21,771 | 6,755 | 30,532 |
| Administration ........ | 196,139 | 172,947 | 174,024 | 115,394 | 101,593 |
| Compensation insurance. | 27,166 | 24,771 | 10,618 | 13,030 | 19,784 |
| Legislative relief........ | 2,067 | ...... | ...... | ...... | ...... |
| Total .............. | $10,128,143 | $7,099,271 | $5,769,234 | $5,916,002 | $4,164,804 |

*Figures for 1929 cover thirteen months in order to make the fiscal year the same as the calendar year.

## CHART SHOWING BOUNDARIES OF THE HIGHWAY DISTRICTS HAVING REPRESENTATION ON THE ADVISORY BOARD

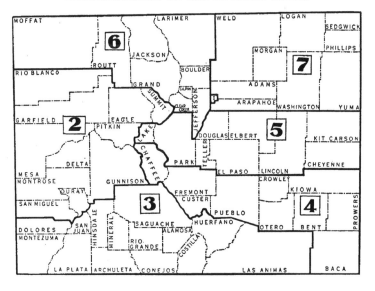

## COUNTY REVENUE FOR HIGHWAY PURPOSES IN 1931

(Supplied by the United States Bureau of Public Roads)

| COUNTY | Balance on Hand | General County Road Taxes | Motor Vehicle Fees | Gasoline Taxes | Funds from State | Miscellaneous | Totals |
|---|---|---|---|---|---|---|---|
| Adams | $ 42,888.10 | $ 96,196.68 | $ 23,000.00 | $ 12,000.00 | $ | $ 5,000.00 | $ 179,084.78 |
| Alamosa | 33,029.03 | | 7,927.33 | 20,775.43 | 2,000.00 | 1,305.67 | 65,037.46 |
| Arapahoe | 5,787.09 | 52,556.16 | 21,291.96 | 19,707.81 | 11,857.56 | 1,108.22 | 112,308.80 |
| Archuleta | 4,183.31 | 10,191.60 | 2,282.12 | 18,570.20 | | 4,118.00 | 39,345.23 |
| Baca | | | 10,953.92 | 38,934.42 | 22,862.41 | 256.79 | 73,007.54 |
| Bent | 204.43 | 39,117.17 | 6,641.47 | 13,007.17 | 386.28 | 8,287.17 | 67,234.83 |
| Boulder | 716.66 | 123,922.72 | 31,465.06 | 24,994.63 | 5,332.39 | 7,315.00 | 193,746.46 |
| Chaffee | —130.49 | 9,085.80 | 5,621.86 | 16,707.01 | 4,945.12 | 11,403.07 | 47,632.37 |
| Cheyenne | 22,620.18 | | 4,228.95 | 22,796.57 | | 1,038.38 | 50,683.08 |
| Clear Creek | 6,369.13 | 12,847.58 | 2,042.21 | 19,285.67 | 8,810.26 | | 49,354.85 |
| Conejos | 9,674.80 | 9,671.06 | 5,513.09 | 23,334.31 | 378.75 | 6,900.65 | 55,472.66 |
| Costilla | —3,183.76 | 3,570.69 | 3,103.38 | 23,103.37 | | 59.70 | 26,663.23 |
| Crowley | 18,165.32 | 10,773.95 | 5,008.91 | 11,399.13 | | 261.55 | 45,598.86 |
| Custer | —5,726.40 | 8,303.98 | 2,725.92 | 17,062.89 | 5,296.03 | 2,205.79 | 29,868.21 |
| Delta | | 84,856.09 | 11,926.53 | 21,573.43 | 10,647.23 | 10,537.07 | 139,540.35 |
| Denver | 4,703.09 | 6,871.75 | 1,110.17 | 12,774.82 | | 12,420.68 | 47,361.51 |
| Dolores | 5,957.40 | 31,872.67 | 3,533.97 | 27,705.53 | 9,481.00 | 14,204.23 | 83,273.80 |
| Eagle | 1,704.30 | 39,091.36 | 3,875.25 | 22,943.86 | 150.00 | 11,367.59 | 79,132.36 |
| Elbert | 18,618.44 | 91,935.40 | 46,288.72 | 44,167.10 | 20,748.67 | 6,276.12 | 228,034.45 |
| El Paso | 10,794.23 | 57,518.69 | 5,513.85 | 23,012.73 | 14,576.13 | | 111,415.63 |
| Fremont | | 58,858.31 | 15,577.93 | 32,244.35 | 11,078.81 | 1,261.09 | 119,020.49 |
| Garfield | | 78,967.65 | 7,346.07 | 30,813.07 | | 11,963.99 | 129,090.78 |
| Gilpin | | 5,000.00 | 800.00 | 300.00 | 5,000.00 | | 11,100.00 |
| Grand | 2,952.83 | 13,358.67 | 3,057.01 | 34,484.17 | | 3,941.18 | 57,793.86 |
| Gunnison | | 32,219.40 | 5,140.58 | 45,999.00 | 10,000.00 | 11,126.00 | 104,484.98 |
| Hinsdale | 191.45 | 816.40 | 351.44 | 8,782.50 | 6,029.60 | 9,259.99 | 26,242.23 |
| Huerfano | 5,422.93 | 44,806.22 | 9,474.48 | 25,530.82 | 11,381.79 | 1,456.36 | 98,072.60 |
| Jackson | 3,033.62 | 3,825.39 | 1,546.94 | 24,337.88 | 1,170.99 | 1,510.01 | 35,424.83 |
| Jefferson | 17,356.59 | 94,554.93 | 25,585.48 | 42,722.79 | 15,000.00 | | 195,219.79 |
| Kiowa | 43,880.64 | 5.06 | 4,587.23 | 26,103.60 | 18,369.30 | 1,4 4.877 | 94,420.70 |
| Kit Carson | —6,333.47 | 47,576.96 | 9,926.38 | 31,231.45 | 5,204.11 | 1,206.91 | 88,902.34 |

| County | | | | | | | |
|---|---|---|---|---|---|---|---|
| Lake | 4,986.20 | 64,232.77 | 8,913.62 | 18,176.77 | 381.24 | 8,718.86 | 105,409.46 |
| La Plata | —8,072.72 | 2,354.21 | 2,666.03 | 13,346.57 | | 692.17 | 19,048.98 |
| Larimer | 8,072.72 | 171,707.52 | 34,355.35 | 46,854.74 | 34,231.91 | 25,051.62 | 319,273.86 |
| Las Animas | —22,670.03 | 113,220.94 | 20,394.87 | 48,730.00 | 28,845.52 | 18,331.98 | 206,853.28 |
| Lincoln | 38.71 | 38,422.37 | 8,346.33 | 57,335.05 | 7,953.39 | 986.93 | 113,082.78 |
| Logan | —2,094.60 | 76,589.13 | 20,454.22 | 31,258.92 | 13,964.93 | 2,565.52 | 142,738.12 |
| Mesa | 3,124.20 | 81,344.80 | 22,062.88 | 40,111.32 | 30,035.38 | 1,831.47 | 178,510.05 |
| Mineral | 13,666.84 | 2,859.94 | 495.45 | 11,988.65 | 14,000.00 | 3,231.83 | 46,242.71 |
| Moffat | 2,323.13 | 22,691.61 | 2,639.27 | 31,467.21 | 22,671.68 | 13,998.60 | 95,671.50 |
| Montezuma | | 21,194.29 | 7,543.12 | 25,426.18 | 11,749.96 | 8,643.47 | 74,557.02 |
| Montrose | —3,330.04 | 30,069.17 | 8,623.30 | 42,142.90 | 4,568.02 | 13,033.91 | 102,167.34 |
| Morgan | —21,500.01 | 64,876.13 | 15,961.64 | 27,461.80 | 31,420.94 | 12,146.50 | 130,367.00 |
| Otero | 6,523.20 | 60,841.07 | 19,811.11 | 17,178.22 | | 2,624.49 | 106,978.09 |
| Ouray | 5,121.19 | 10,458.85 | 1,129.21 | 8,844.18 | 2,866.97 | 2,736.14 | 31,156.54 |
| Park | 7,727.03 | 13,000.00 | 2,643.97 | 33,789.37 | 25,020.10 | 919.87 | 75,373.31 |
| Phillips | 7,382.65 | 22,450.00 | 7,361.47 | 17,995.13 | 3,894.46 | 5,680.76 | 65,108.85 |
| Pitkin | 15,676.04 | 3,268.17 | 916.53 | 15,724.33 | 564.05 | 2,276.24 | 30,131.97 |
| Prowers | | 54,722.02 | 13,545.91 | 34,520.34 | 23,118.50 | 665.09 | 142,247.90 |
| Pueblo | | 113,358.08 | 44,992.34 | 35,586.33 | 993.00 | 484.33 | 195,414.08 |
| Rio Blanco | 6,102.41 | 13,118.15 | 2,139.27 | 36,859.59 | 5,000.00 | 5,948.24 | 69,167.66 |
| Rio Grande | 9,029.09 | 20,360.11 | 10,045.32 | 15,616.32 | 4,107.87 | 6,972.05 | 66,130.76 |
| Routt | 8,505.62 | 35,848.16 | 6,433.86 | 30,646.61 | 29,970.50 | 15,655.30 | 127,060.05 |
| Saguache | —5,581.27 | 26,793.72 | 5,274.72 | 30,159.59 | | 5,549.93 | 62,196.69 |
| San Juan | | | | | | 22,000.00 | 22,000.00 |
| San Miguel | 12,325.87 | 18,540.60 | 1,205.00 | 25,119.01 | 21,314.18 | | 66,178.79 |
| Sedgwick | 9,733.94 | 35,317.27 | 6,471.66 | 13,720.96 | 9,955.30 | | 77,791.06 |
| Summit | | 8,892.90 | 629.31 | 15,571.72 | 9,299.90 | 21.40 | 45,149.17 |
| Teller | 2,006.32 | | 3,500.91 | 18,438.78 | 10,865.48 | 1,863.56 | 35,674.05 |
| Washington | 9,432.27 | 45,853.53 | 8,740.42 | 46,485.96 | | 4,099.32 | 114,611.50 |
| Weld | 82,509.58 | 292,221.93 | 63,577.43 | 63,059.82 | 179,544.95 | 10,903.20 | 756,496.10 |
| Yuma | 16,100.08 | 47,543.91 | 11,257.37 | 44,212.90 | 33,178.56 | 4,862.53 | 157,165.35 |
| State | $ 424,440.81 | $2,580,423.59 | $ 649,570.10 | $1,634,213.98 | $ 760,713.22 | $ 349,751.39 | *$6,464,503.13 |

Minus sign (—) means deficit.

*Total includes $810.85 in Hinsdale County for "Local Bond Sale Receipts" and $64,579.19 in Weld county for "Note Sale Receipts." "Appropriations from Local Funds" included in "Funds from State," as follows: Alamosa, $2,000.00; Baca, $21,659.31; Jefferson, $15,000.00; Logan, $2,094.60; Morgan, $20,000.00; Routt, $19,970.50; Teller, $719.22; Weld, $162,000.00.

## DISBURSEMENTS BY COUNTIES FOR HIGHWAY PURPOSES IN 1931

(Supplied by the United States Bureau of Public Roads)

| COUNTY | Construction Roads and Bridges | Maintenance Roads and Bridges | Administration Overhead | Interest on Bonds & Notes | Retirement of Notes | County Funds to State | Miscellaneous | Total Disbursements | Balance End of Year | Total |
|---|---|---|---|---|---|---|---|---|---|---|
| Adams | | $ 898 | | | | | $ 46,897.41 | $ 107,487.39 | $ 71,597.39 | $ 179,084.78 |
| Alamosa | $ 5,000.00 | 38,560.49 | | | | | | 43,560.49 | 21,476.97 | 65,037.46 |
| Arapahoe | 10,000.00 | 95,208.18 | | | | | | 105,208.18 | 7,100.62 | 112,308.80 |
| Archuleta | 3,000.00 | 33,880.44 | | | | | | 36,880.44 | 2,464.79 | 39,345.23 |
| Baca | 56,970.45 | 16,037.09 | $ 2,395.43 | | | | | 73,007.54 | 992.02 | 73,007.54 |
| Bent | 7,694.59 | 48,717.80 | | $ 2,646.96 | | | 4,788.03 | 66,242.81 | | 67,234.83 |
| Boulder | 22,436.27 | 154,948.37 | | 5,600.00 | | | | 182,984.64 | 10,761.82 | 193,746.46 |
| Chaffee | | 42,981.90 | | | | | | 42,981.90 | 4,650.47 | 47,632.37 |
| Cheyenne | 1,150.00 | 37,894.97 | | | | | | 39,044.97 | 11,638.11 | 50,683.08 |
| Clear Creek | 21,000.00 | 21,805.01 | | | | | | 42,805.01 | 6,649.84 | 49,364.85 |
| Conejos | | 39,535.19 | | | | | 15,000.00 | 54,535.19 | 937.47 | 55,472.66 |
| Costilla | | 27,022.63 | | | | | | 27,022.63 | —369.35 | 26,663.23 |
| Crowley | 24,065.82 | 8,063.05 | | | | | | 32,128.87 | 13,469.99 | 45,598.86 |
| Custer | | 36,589.63 | | | | | | 36,589.63 | —6,721.42 | 29,868.21 |
| Delta | 14,000.00 | 120,271.46 | | 4,275.45 | | $ 1,500.00 | | 138,546.90 | 993.45 | 139,540.35 |
| Denver | | | | | | | | | | |
| Dolores | | 34,896.04 | | | | | | 34,896.04 | 12,465.47 | 47,361.51 |
| Douglas | | 75,042.70 | | 1,114.10 | | | 10,235.79 | 86,392.59 | —3,118.79 | 83,273.80 |
| Eagle | 17,000.00 | 35,985.07 | 7,746.68 | | | | 20,092.33 | 62,231.75 | 16,900.61 | 79,132.36 |
| Elbert | 57,223.96 | 133,522.56 | 10,080.33 | | | | | 220,919.18 | 7,115.27 | 228,034.45 |
| El Paso | | 113,769.29 | | | | | | 113,769.29 | —2,353.66 | 111,415.63 |
| Fremont | 22,157.70 | 87,057.12 | 2,234.75 | | | | | 111,449.57 | 7,570.92 | 119,020.49 |
| Garfield | 11,500.00 | 70,977.66 | 6,000.00 | | | | 20,162.00 | 108,633.66 | 20,451.12 | 129,090.78 |
| Gilpin | 3,500.00 | 10,000.00 | | | | | 5,000.00 | 18,500.00 | —7,400.00 | 11,100.00 |
| Grand | | 64,736.93 | | | | | | 64,736.93 | —6,943.07 | 57,793.86 |
| Gunnison | 36,600.00 | 33,430.93 | | | | | 54,413.42 | 123,444.35 | —18,959.37 | 104,484.98 |
| Hinsdale | | 6,914.71 | 38.44 | | | 18,901.24 | | 25,854.39 | 387.84 | 26,242.23 |
| Huerfano | | 85,558.88 | 1,500.00 | | | | | 87,058.88 | 11,013.72 | 98,072.60 |
| Jackson | | 31,664.90 | | | | 2,500.00 | | 34,064.90 | 1,359.93 | 35,424.83 |
| Jefferson | 9,864.71 | 137,917.32 | | | | | 13,519.73 | 161,301.76 | 33,918.03 | 195,219.79 |

| County | | | | | | | | | | |
|---|---|---|---|---|---|---|---|---|---|---|
| Kiowa | 5,108.79 | 46,074.28 | — | — | $2,772.07 | — | 10,000.00 | 63,965.14 | 30,465.56 | 94,420.70 |
| Kit Carson | 20,500.00 | 40,360.00 | — | — | — | — | 3,002.01 | 63,852.01 | 25,050.33 | 88,902.34 |
| Lake | — | 79,774.66 | 1,000.00 | — | — | — | — | 80,774.66 | 24,634.80 | 105,409.46 |
| La Plata | — | 19,048.98 | — | — | — | — | — | 19,048.98 | — | 19,048.98 |
| Larimer | 103,000.00 | 96,567.56 | — | 14,208.00 | 85,792.65 | — | — | 299,568.21 | 19,705.65 | 319,273.86 |
| Las Animas | 50,000.00 | 156,989.93 | — | — | — | — | — | 206,989.93 | —136.65 | 206,853.23 |
| Lincoln | 20,442.74 | 56,738.77 | — | 1,062.12 | 20,941.01 | — | 11,436.45 | 110,621.09 | 2,461.69 | 113,082.78 |
| Logan | 14,500.00 | 102,365.27 | 2,620.45 | — | — | — | 6,313.88 | 125,799.60 | 16,938.52 | 142,738.12 |
| Mesa | 60,000.00 | 118,510.05 | — | — | — | — | — | 178,510.05 | — | 178,510.05 |
| Mineral | 10,800.54 | 23,978.51 | — | — | — | — | 4,342.49 | 39,121.54 | 7,121.17 | 46,242.71 |
| Moffat | 7,500.00 | 31,921.21 | — | — | — | — | 2,265.11 | 41,686.32 | 53,985.18 | 95,671.50 |
| Montezuma | — | 64,229.38 | — | — | — | — | — | 64,229.38 | 10,327.64 | 74,557.02 |
| Montrose | 22,000.00 | 67,827.94 | — | — | — | — | — | 89,827.94 | 12,339.40 | 102,167.34 |
| Morgan | 49,497.67 | 55,500.00 | 3,000.00 | — | — | — | 37,224.42 | 145,222.09 | —14,855.09 | 130,367.00 |
| Otero | — | 88,528.97 | — | — | — | 10,000.00 | — | 98,528.97 | 8,449.12 | 106,978.09 |
| Ouray | 6,539.59 | 17,362.74 | — | — | — | — | — | 23,902.33 | 7,254.21 | 31,156.54 |
| Park | 29,097.63 | 48,860.62 | — | — | — | — | — | 77,968.25 | —2,584.94 | 75,373.31 |
| Phillips | — | 47,578.49 | — | — | — | — | — | 47,578.49 | 17,530.36 | 65,108.85 |
| Pitkin | — | 16,163.73 | — | — | — | 9,000.00 | — | 25,163.73 | 4,968.24 | 30,131.97 |
| Prowers | 78,981.22 | 36,972.08 | 2,368.35 | — | 5,636.26 | — | 5,476.16 | 129,424.07 | 12,823.83 | 142,247.90 |
| Pueblo | 40,138.33 | 151,818.58 | 3,216.57 | — | — | — | 180.60 | 195,414.08 | — | 195,414.03 |
| Rio Blanco | 1,000.00 | 59,726.17 | — | — | — | — | — | 60,726.17 | 8,441.49 | 69,167.66 |
| Rio Grande | — | 56,171.05 | — | — | — | — | — | 56,171.05 | 9,959.71 | 66,130.76 |
| Routt | 21,000.00 | 79,484.77 | 5,000.00 | — | — | — | — | 105,484.77 | 21,575.28 | 127,060.05 |
| Saguache | 20,389.00 | 33,846.43 | — | — | — | — | — | 54,235.48 | 7,961.21 | 62,196.69 |
| San Juan | — | 22,000.00 | — | — | — | — | — | 22,000.00 | — | 22,000.00 |
| San Miguel | 11,000.00 | 36,772.35 | — | — | — | — | 5,562.18 | 53,334.53 | 12,844.26 | 66,178.79 |
| Sedgwick | 13,114.04 | 13,663.80 | — | — | — | — | 40,780.30 | 67,558.14 | 10,232.92 | 77,791.06 |
| Summit | 5,446.80 | 12,970.88 | — | — | 1,880.00 | — | 12,972.43 | 33,270.11 | 11,879.06 | 45,149.17 |
| Teller | — | 27,784.54 | — | — | — | — | — | 27,784.54 | 8,889.51 | 36,674.05 |
| Washington | 46,039.60 | 49,773.75 | — | 1,808.04 | — | — | 3,932.88 | 101,553.77 | 13,057.73 | 114,611.50 |
| Weld | 298,600.00 | 136,210.64 | 17,618.30 | 5,753.10 | 169,748.38 | — | 43,689.10 | 671,619.52 | 84,576.58 | 756,496.10 |
| Yuma | 75,766.51 | 63,662.95 | — | — | — | — | — | 139,429.46 | 17,725.89 | 157,155.35 |
| State | $1,332,625.96 | $3,662,709.42 | $ 64,869.30 | $ 36,467.77 | $286,770.37 | $41,901.24 | $377,286.22 | $5,802,630.28 | $661,872.85 | $6,464,503.13 |

Minus sign (—) indicates deficit.

## MILEAGE OF HIGHWAYS IN COLORADO AT BEGINNING OF 1932

(Compiled from Records of U. S. Bureau of Public Roads and State Highway Commission)

| COUNTY | State Roads | | | | | County Roads | | | | Total State & County |
|---|---|---|---|---|---|---|---|---|---|---|
| | Paved | Sur-faced† | Graded | Pro-jected | Total State | Sur-faced | Graded | Pro-jected | Total County | |
| Adams | 26.9 | 68.7 | ---- | ---- | 95.6 | 332.0 | 385.0 | 743.0 | 1,460.0 | 1,555.6 |
| Alamosa | 0.2 | 32.6 | 72.9 | 8.5 | 114.2 | 69.0 | ---- | 347.0 | 416.0 | 530.2 |
| Arapahoe | 13.5 | 90.8 | ---- | ---- | 104.3 | 97.0 | ---- | 400.0 | 500.0 | 604.3 |
| Archuleta | ---- | 30.4 | 72.6 | ---- | 103.0 | 15.0 | 35.0 | 356.7 | 406.7 | 509.7 |
| Baca | ---- | 16.1 | 222.5 | ---- | 238.6 | ---- | 620.5 | 531.0 | 1,151.5 | 1,390.1 |
| Bent | 9.8 | 27.5 | 33.4 | ---- | 70.7 | ---- | 47.0 | 753.0 | 800.0 | 870.7 |
| Boulder | 33.0 | 55.7 | 51.2 | ---- | 139.9 | 431.0 | 80.0 | 31.0 | 542.0 | 681.9 |
| Chaffee | ---- | 53.1 | 40.2 | ---- | 93.3 | 17.0 | 195.0 | 44.4 | 256.4 | 349.7 |
| Cheyenne | ---- | 100.4 | 27.3 | ---- | 127.7 | ---- | 335.0 | 280.0 | 615.0 | 742.7 |
| Clear Creek | 1.9 | 49.5 | 52.8 | 3.8 | 108.0 | ---- | 8.0 | 98.0 | 106.0 | 214.0 |
| Conejos | ---- | 38.6 | 92.0 | ---- | 130.6 | 7.1 | ---- | 484.9 | 492.0 | 622.6 |
| Costilla | ---- | 43.4 | 64.4 | 21.5 | 129.3 | ---- | 13.0 | 169.0 | 182.0 | 311.3 |
| Crowley | ---- | 39.6 | 24.2 | ---- | 63.8 | 110.0 | 140.0 | 600.0 | 850.0 | 913.8 |
| Custer | ---- | 8.5 | 87.0 | ---- | 95.5 | 35.0 | 265.5 | 400.0 | 700.5 | 796.0 |
| Delta | ---- | 57.2 | 62.6 | ---- | 119.8 | 14.0 | 21.5 | 440.0 | 475.5 | 595.3 |
| Denver | ---- | ---- | ---- | ---- | ---- | ---- | ---- | ---- | ---- | ---- |
| Dolores | ---- | ---- | 71.5 | ---- | 71.5 | ---- | 6.0 | 150.0 | 156.0 | 227.5 |
| Douglas | 36.4 | 88.1 | 29.9 | ---- | 154.4 | 385.0 | 115.0 | ---- | 500.0 | 654.4 |
| Eagle | ---- | 48.2 | 87.3 | 8.9 | 144.4 | 10.0 | 7.0 | 244.8 | 261.8 | 406.2 |
| Elbert | ---- | 57.7 | 69.6 | ---- | 127.3 | 348.7 | 926.0 | 1,785.8 | 3,060.5 | 3,187.8 |
| El Paso | 49.6 | 120.4 | 70.6 | 6.0 | 246.6 | ---- | 60.0 | 1,632.0 | 1,692.0 | 1,938.6 |
| Fremont | 2.1 | 82.5 | 82.8 | 16.0 | 183.4 | ---- | 12.0 | 160.0 | 172.0 | 355.4 |
| Garfield | ---- | 79.1 | 77.3 | 7.5 | 163.9 | ---- | 15.0 | 1,340.0 | 1,355.0 | 1,518.9 |
| Gilpin | ---- | 4.0 | 32.1 | ---- | 36.1 | 32.0 | ---- | 32.0 | 64.0 | 100.1 |
| Grand | ---- | 74.6 | 118.2 | 0.1 | 192.9 | ---- | ---- | 185.0 | 185.0 | 377.9 |
| Gunnison | ---- | 66.7 | 169.3 | 21.7 | 257.7 | 18.0 | ---- | 218.0 | 236.0 | 493.7 |
| Hinsdale | ---- | ---- | 48.6 | ---- | 48.6 | ---- | ---- | 90.0 | 90.0 | 138.6 |
| Huerfano | ---- | 47.6 | 86.1 | 6.4 | 140.1 | 8.0 | ---- | 380.0 | 388.0 | 528.1 |
| Jackson | ---- | 68.0 | 68.2 | ---- | 136.2 | ---- | ---- | 250.0 | 250.0 | 386.2 |
| Jefferson | 22.5 | 130.2 | 73.4 | 14.0 | 240.1 | 6.5 | 184.5 | 900.0 | 1,091.0 | 1,331.1 |
| Kiowa | ---- | 57.4 | 88.7 | ---- | 146.1 | 48.0 | ---- | 615.0 | 663.0 | 809.1 |
| Kit Carson | ---- | 114.9 | 59.4 | ---- | 174.3 | ---- | 540.0 | 965.0 | 1,505.0 | 1,679.3 |
| Lake | ---- | 52.7 | 22.0 | ---- | 74.7 | 65.0 | 25.1 | 1,400.0 | 1,490.1 | 1,564.8 |
| La Plata | ---- | 80.0 | 20.9 | ---- | 100.9 | ---- | ---- | 80.0 | 80.0 | 180.9 |
| Larimer | 25.4 | 125.7 | 103.9 | 1.3 | 256.3 | 325.0 | 175.0 | 570.0 | 1,070.0 | 1,326.3 |
| Las Animas | 27.5 | 102.0 | 126.5 | 15.0 | 271.0 | 32.0 | 1,000.0 | 4,715.0 | 5,747.0 | 6,018.0 |
| Lincoln | ---- | 108.0 | 212.8 | ---- | 320.8 | ---- | 38.0 | 941.0 | 979.0 | 1,299.8 |
| Logan | 15.7 | 159.7 | ---- | ---- | 175.4 | 389.0 | 2,372.0 | 1,000.0 | 3,761.0 | 3,936.4 |
| Mesa | 5.9 | 81.9 | 135.2 | ---- | 223.0 | 92.0 | 2,543.0 | ---- | 2,635.0 | 2,858.0 |
| Mineral | ---- | 17.4 | 47.8 | ---- | 65.2 | 40.0 | ---- | ---- | 40.0 | 105.2 |
| Moffat | ---- | 59.3 | 122.3 | ---- | 181.6 | 8.0 | 22.0 | 790.0 | 820.0 | 1,001.6 |
| Montezuma | ---- | 53.1 | 84.6 | ---- | 137.7 | 6.2 | 303.8 | 800.0 | 1,110.0 | 1,247.7 |
| Montrose | ---- | 60.6 | 158.1 | 16.2 | 234.9 | 7.0 | 73.2 | 879.8 | 960.0 | 1,194.9 |
| Morgan | 35.0 | 84.2 | 8.0 | 9.0 | 136.2 | 253.0 | 180.0 | 400.0 | 833.0 | 969.2 |
| Otero | 19.6 | 9.4 | 63.6 | ---- | 92.6 | 167.2 | 771.4 | 525.0 | 1,463.6 | 1,556.2 |
| Ouray | ---- | 24.7 | 24.8 | ---- | 49.5 | 52.0 | 21.4 | 192.6 | 266.0 | 315.5 |
| Park | ---- | 105.1 | 79.2 | 8.7 | 193.0 | ---- | 13.0 | 585.0 | 598.0 | 791.0 |
| Phillips | ---- | 100.4 | ---- | ---- | 100.4 | 100.0 | 300.0 | 600.0 | 1,000.0 | 1,100.4 |
| Pitkin | ---- | ---- | 81.3 | 6.7 | 88.0 | ---- | 10.0 | 114.0 | 124.0 | 212.0 |
| Prowers | 6.4 | 78.6 | 108.3 | ---- | 193.3 | 108.5 | 900.0 | 400.0 | 1,408.5 | 1,601.8 |
| Pueblo | 35.3 | 97.8 | 66.1 | ---- | 199.2 | 560.0 | 1,900.0 | 540.0 | 3,000.8 | 3,200.0 |
| Rio Blanco | ---- | 41.5 | 151.5 | 13.3 | 206.3 | ---- | 164.0 | 95.0 | 259.0 | 465.3 |
| Rio Grande | 1.9 | 47.4 | 34.8 | ---- | 84.1 | ---- | 409.0 | 91.0 | 500.0 | 584.1 |
| Routt | ---- | 51.2 | 113.8 | 16.2 | 181.2 | 7.0 | 20.0 | 1,748.0 | 1,775.0 | 1,956.2 |
| Saguache | ---- | 84.1 | 85.9 | ---- | 170.0 | 61.0 | 44.0 | 994.3 | 1,099.3 | 1,269.3 |
| San Juan | ---- | 35.1 | 9.0 | 4.5 | 48.6 | 4.0 | ---- | 88.7 | 92.7 | 141.3 |
| San Miguel | ---- | 8.3 | 122.7 | 12.0 | 143.0 | ---- | ---- | 200.0 | 200.0 | 343.0 |
| Sedgwick | ---- | 63.1 | 9.0 | ---- | 72.1 | 208.0 | ---- | 310.0 | 518.0 | 590.1 |
| Summit | ---- | 28.7 | 51.7 | 12.3 | 92.7 | 20.0 | ---- | 13.0 | 33.0 | 125.7 |
| Teller | ---- | 52.7 | 38.2 | 12.3 | 103.2 | 20.8 | 39.0 | 202.0 | 261.8 | 365.0 |
| Washington | 7.4 | 180.6 | 71.9 | ---- | 259.9 | 3.0 | 49.0 | 2,802.0 | 2,854.0 | 3,113.9 |
| Weld | 71.1 | 216.1 | 63.2 | 4.3 | 354.7 | 1,220.0 | 2,028.0 | 2,752.0 | 6,000.0 | 6,354.7 |
| Yuma | ---- | 241.5 | 6.0 | ---- | 247.5 | 75.0 | 1,000.0 | 525.0 | 1,600.0 | 1,847.5 |
| State | 447.1 | 4,202.4 | 4,359.2 | 246.2 | 9,254.9 | 5,807.0 | 18,411.9 | 38,979.0 | *63,201.7 | 72,456.6 |

This table does not include forest service roads or city streets. *Total includes hard surfaced county roads, omitted from table to save space, as follows: Arapahoe, 3.0 miles and Pueblo, 0.8 miles. †Includes oiled roads as follows: Adams, 4.0 miles; Alamosa, 10.2 miles; Arapahoe, 9.7 miles; Bent, 22.8 miles; Boulder, 12.0 miles; Conejos, 14.4 miles; Elbert, 4.9 miles; Fremont, 18.2 miles; Garfield, 2.0 miles; Jefferson, 40.3 miles; Larimer, 24.0 miles; Las Animas, 6.0 miles; Otero, 9.4 miles; Prowers, 21.8 miles; Pueblo, 18.4 miles; Rio Grande, 5.9 miles; Weld, 30.1 miles.

## MOTOR VEHICLE LICENSES

There were 276,376 motor vehicle licenses for passenger cars and 32,082 for trucks issued in Colorado in 1931 through the office of the secretary of state, the registration agency for the state. This was a decrease of 471 in the number of passenger cars, the first reported since registration was inaugurated in 1913, and an increase of 420, or 1.33 per cent, in the number of trucks in 1931 as compared with 1930. There was an increase of 2,887, or 1.05 per cent, in passenger cars and 3,161, or 11.09 per cent, in trucks in 1930 as compared with 1929. The increase in passenger cars in 1929 over 1928 was 5.39 per cent and in trucks 18.95 per cent, and 1928 showed an increase over 1927 of 6.05 per cent in passenger cars and 2.46 per cent in trucks.

The number of motorcycle licenses issued has shown a steady decrease since the peak was reached in 1916, in which year there were 4,731. The number in 1931 was 962.

Receipts for motor vehicle licenses in 1931 aggregated $1,910,740, the highest in any year since registration under the present system began in 1913. In that year the fees amounted to $60,833. The total amount of fees collected for the 19 years ending December 31, 1931, was $18,693,660. After deducting the cost of administration, the motor vehicle license fees are divided equally between the state highway department for state highway purposes and counties for local road purposes.

There were 7.8 persons per passenger car in the state in 1920 and 3.7 persons per car in 1930.

Commencing in 1932, the system of licensing cars in Colorado was changed, and thereafter each county is indicated by an initial number, followed by the number of each particular license from 1 up to the maximum for that county. The identifying key numbers are as follows:

1, Denver; 2, Pueblo; 3, Weld; 4, El Paso; 5, Las Animas; 6, Larimer; 7, Boulder; 8, Mesa; 9, Otero; 10, Arapahoe; 11, Jefferson; 12, Adams; 13, Logan; 14, Fremont; 15, Morgan; 16, Huerfano; 17, Prowers; 18, Delta; 19, Yuma; 20, La Plata; 21, Montrose; 22, Baca; 23, Rio Grande; 24, Garfield; 25, Conejos; 26, Kit Carson; 27, Washington; 28, Routt; 29, Bent; 30, Alamosa; 31, Chaffee; 32, Montezuma; 33, Lincoln; 34, Elbert; 35, Saguache; 36, Crowley; 37, Phillips; 38, Costilla; 39, Sedgwick; 40, Gunnison; 41, Lake; 42, Moffat; 43, Teller; 44, Eagle; 45, Kiowa; 46, Cheyenne; 47, Douglas; 48, Archuleta; 49, Rio Blanco; 50, San Miguel; 51, Clear Creek; 52, Custer; 53, Grand; 54, Park; 55, San Juan; 56, Ouray; 57, Pitkin; 58, Dolores; 59, Jackson; 60, Gilpin; 61, Summit; 62, Mineral; 63, Hinsdale.

Beginning with 1932, all drivers of passenger cars are required to take out individual drivers' licenses.

Two tables published herewith show registrations and fees collected for the state by years and by counties in 1931.

### REGISTRATION AND RECEIPTS BY YEARS SINCE STATE ASSUMED CONTROL OF LICENSING

| YEAR | Passenger Cars | Trucks | Motor-cycles | Drivers | Total Receipts |
|---|---|---|---|---|---|
| 1913 ............... | 13,135 | * | 2,753 | 1,980 | $ 60,833.00 |
| 1914 ............... | 17,756 | * | 3,683 | 2,058 | 80,047.00 |
| 1915 ............... | 27.568 | * | 4,268 | 3,536 | 120,800.84 |
| 1916 ............... | 43,296 | * | 4,731 | 6,754 | 197,794.75 |
| 1917 ............... | 66,850 | * | 4,505 | 9,291 | 297,292.21 |
| 1918 ............... | 83,244 | * | 3,872 | 9,686 | 372,490.25 |
| 1919 ............... | 104,865 | * | 3,636 | 10,291 | 491,713.36 |
| 1920 ............... | 119,964 | 7,585 | 3,364 | 9,814 | 815,100.10 |
| 1921 ............... | 136,336 | 9,403 | 2,868 | 7,340 | 906,059.27 |
| 1922 ............... | 151,499 | 10,829 | 2,770 | 7,058 | 991,677.22 |
| 1923 ............... | 175,669 | 13,287 | 2,473 | 7,736 | 1,126,218.55 |
| 1924 ............... | 197,361 | 15,886 | 2,226 | 7,559 | 1,258,204.80 |
| 1925 ............... | 221,513 | 18,584 | 1,862 | 7,776 | 1,430,299.47 |
| 1926 ............... | 232,308 | 20,905 | 1,480 | 7,162 | 1,507,379.19 |
| 1927 ............... | 245,107 | 23,385 | 1,362 | 7,664 | 1,600,221.73 |
| 1928 ............... | 259,948 | 23,961 | 1,234 | 7.977 | 1,790,182.73 |
| 1929 ............... | 273,960 | 28,501 | 1,142 | 7,916 | 1,835,385.53 |
| 1930 ............... | 276,847 | 31,662 | 1,059 | 7,296 | 1,901,219.94 |
| 1931 ............... | 276,376 | 32,082 | 962 | 6,255 | 1,910,740.49 |

Total .........................................................................$18,693,660.43

*Trucks included with passenger cars for these years.

## MOTOR VEHICLE REGISTRATION AND FEES COLLECTED, 1931, BY COUNTIES
### (From the records of the Secretary of State)

| COUNTY | Owners | Trucks and Trailers | Dealers | Motor-cycles | Drivers | Permits, Re-issues and Misc. | Guests | Fees Collected |
|---|---|---|---|---|---|---|---|---|
| Adams_____ | 6,175 | 1,189 | 27 | 17 | 146 | 1,199 | 24 | $ 46,561.07 |
| Alamosa_____ | 2,147 | 349 | 44 | 4 | 29 | 312 | 16 | 15,983.78 |
| Arapahoe_____ | 7,123 | 622 | 79 | 26 | 182 | 1,292 | 55 | 45,667.11 |
| Archuleta_____ | 461 | 52 | 2 | 2 | 5 | 116 | 2 | 2,881.80 |
| Baca_____ | 2,776 | 794 | 12 | 6 | 7 | 375 | 6 | 23,843.96 |
| Bent_____ | 2,278 | 206 | 21 | 10 | 11 | 341 | 3 | 14,502.17 |
| Boulder_____ | 10,316 | 1,075 | 128 | 50 | 207 | 4,523 | 1,308 | 69,119.74 |
| Chaffee_____ | 1,858 | 160 | 41 | 3 | 37 | 257 | 23 | 12,309.14 |
| Cheyenne_____ | 1,070 | 160 | 21 | 4 | 14 | 112 | 11 | 7,604.17 |
| Clear Creek____ | 619 | 66 | 11 | 1 | 26 | 89 | 6 | 4,422.85 |
| Conejos_____ | 1,426 | 260 | 13 | 2 | 16 | 70 | ----- | 10,295.46 |
| Costilla_____ | 767 | 117 | 5 | 3 | 4 | 127 | ----- | 5,303.21 |
| Crowley_____ | 1,557 | 243 | 14 | 2 | 10 | 311 | 20 | 10,997.25 |
| Custer_____ | 559 | 140 | ----- | 2 | 6 | 77 | 3 | 4,750.50 |
| Delta_____ | 3,557 | 581 | 45 | 8 | 30 | 486 | 36 | 25,019.53 |
| Denver_____ | 80,807 | 5,561 | 966 | 361 | 3,207 | 26,202 | 3,483 | 538,750.78 |
| Dolores_____ | 243 | 40 | ----- | 1 | 1 | 26 | 1 | 1,648.78 |
| Douglas_____ | 1,158 | 119 | 5 | 1 | 29 | 159 | 15 | 7,606.40 |
| Eagle_____ | 1,012 | 134 | 2 | 3 | 29 | 157 | 4 | 6,940.87 |
| Elbert_____ | 1,717 | 236 | 10 | 2 | 4 | 157 | ----- | 11,608.10 |
| El Paso_____ | 15,330 | 1,034 | 151 | 52 | 292 | 2,715 | 3,124 | 102,661.47 |
| Fremont_____ | 4,749 | 539 | 82 | 10 | 46 | 541 | 22 | 32,613.16 |
| Garfield_____ | 2,318 | 275 | 40 | 2 | 59 | 297 | 2 | 16,094.86 |
| Gilpin_____ | 337 | 34 | ----- | ----- | 9 | 30 | 2 | 2,067.92 |
| Grand_____ | 678 | 109 | 8 | 1 | 7 | 46 | 5 | 4,484.25 |
| Gunnison_____ | 1,329 | 101 | 18 | 1 | 24 | 204 | 12 | 7,894.25 |
| Hinsdale_____ | 83 | 11 | ----- | ----- | 4 | 8 | ----- | 544.90 |
| Huerfano_____ | 3,100 | 236 | 34 | 5 | 17 | 265 | 9 | 19,226.42 |
| Jackson_____ | 491 | 60 | 4 | ----- | 8 | 27 | 1 | 3,274.36 |
| Jefferson_____ | 7,129 | 755 | 38 | 22 | 172 | 1,189 | 34 | 47,330.26 |
| Kiowa_____ | 1,143 | 184 | 10 | ----- | 5 | 113 | ----- | 8,178.94 |
| Kit Carson_____ | 2,870 | 564 | 34 | 9 | 70 | 325 | 5 | 21,409.06 |
| Lake_____ | 975 | 25 | 23 | 1 | 50 | 96 | 6 | 5,680.52 |
| La Plata_____ | 2,776 | 265 | 41 | 5 | 109 | 256 | 13 | 18,270.76 |
| Larimer_____ | 10,403 | 1,415 | 97 | 53 | 153 | 3,663 | 310 | 73,286.44 |
| Las Animas____ | 6,444 | 729 | 76 | 22 | 150 | 885 | 24 | 44,621.30 |
| Lincoln_____ | 2,133 | 315 | 23 | 3 | 15 | 362 | 8 | 14,874.24 |
| Logan_____ | 5,732 | 1,102 | 55 | 18 | 46 | 1,224 | 60 | 43,019.56 |
| Mesa_____ | 6,862 | 768 | 76 | 21 | 76 | 910 | 38 | 45,657.47 |
| Mineral_____ | 146 | 25 | ----- | ----- | ----- | 16 | ----- | 1,063.15 |
| Moffat_____ | 1,165 | 162 | 13 | ----- | 30 | 92 | 16 | 7,863.02 |
| Montezuma_____ | 1,558 | 290 | 20 | 7 | 27 | 206 | 22 | 11,971.29 |
| Montrose_____ | 2,722 | 345 | 40 | 3 | 30 | 324 | 21 | 18,059.63 |
| Morgan_____ | 5,218 | 1,087 | 68 | 13 | 47 | 860 | 42 | 39,840.96 |
| Otero_____ | 6,212 | 831 | 83 | 29 | 25 | 1,858 | ----- | 43,060.84 |
| Ouray_____ | 419 | 36 | ----- | ----- | 18 | 24 | ----- | 2,425.28 |
| Park_____ | 663 | 120 | 13 | ----- | 4 | 71 | 7 | 5,129.05 |
| Phillips_____ | 2,044 | 439 | 29 | 4 | 13 | 359 | ----- | 16,039.27 |
| Pitkin_____ | 311 | 26 | 1 | ----- | 11 | 43 | 1 | 1,955.53 |
| Prowers_____ | 4,172 | 439 | 84 | 4 | 47 | 491 | 18 | 27,386.38 |
| Pueblo_____ | 15,016 | 1,372 | 208 | 106 | 168 | 2,937 | 152 | 99,308.90 |
| Rio Blanco_____ | 693 | 80 | 10 | 1 | 9 | 45 | ----- | 4,574.61 |
| Rio Grande____ | 2,602 | 571 | 37 | 1 | 81 | 299 | 11 | 21,325.76 |
| Routt_____ | 2,170 | 208 | 36 | 1 | 25 | 232 | 17 | 13,047.28 |
| Saguache_____ | 1,222 | 203 | 13 | ----- | 38 | 178 | 1 | 9,744.03 |
| San Juan_____ | 273 | 15 | 1 | ----- | 9 | 65 | ----- | 1,725.82 |
| San Miguel____ | 402 | 48 | 3 | 2 | 5 | 26 | ----- | 2,695.09 |
| Sedgwick_____ | 1,735 | 424 | 26 | 6 | 8 | 213 | 3 | 14,135.38 |
| Summit_____ | 296 | 11 | 2 | ----- | 6 | 32 | 1 | 1,622.85 |
| Teller_____ | 993 | 97 | 17 | 3 | 15 | 149 | 6 | 6,431.96 |
| Washington____ | 2,362 | 542 | 21 | 1 | 22 | 325 | 2 | 18,802.56 |
| Weld_____ | 17,626 | 3,681 | 161 | 37 | 240 | 4,993 | 1,023 | 137,540.71 |
| Yuma_____ | 3,848 | 663 | 37 | 12 | 65 | 511 | 6 | 27,984.33 |
| Totals_____ | 276,376 | *32,340 | †3,184 | 963 | 6,255 | ‡63,893 | 10,040 | $1,910,740.49 |

*Includes 32,082 trucks and 258 trailers. †Includes 3,121 auto dealers and 63 truck dealers. ‡Includes 40,825 motor vehicle re-issues, 2,848 replacements, 27,596 special permits and 1,625 special engine numbers.

## GASOLINE CONSUMPTION, TAX AND DISTRIBUTION

Colorado commenced the collection of a tax of one cent a gallon on gasoline to provide revenues for highway construction on May 11, 1919. This tax was increased to two cents a gallon on April 30, 1923, 50 per cent of the amount collected going to the state highway fund and the remaining 50 per cent being apportioned among the counties according to the mileage of state highways. On May 1, 1927, the tax was increased to three cents a gallon and the division of revenues changed so that 70 per cent went to the highway fund and 30 per cent to the counties. The tax again was increased to four cents in 1929, 70 per cent going to the state highway fund, 27 per cent to the counties for highway purposes, and three per cent into a special highway fund for construction and maintenance purposes in cities and towns. Dealers pay the tax direct to the state inspector.

Collections, tax only, exclusive of inspection fees, for calendar years were as follows:

| Year | | % Increase Over Previous Year |
|---|---|---|
| 1919 (8 mos.)......$ | 274,401 | .... |
| 1920 .............. | 458,395 | 67.1 |
| 1921 .............. | 566,570 | 23.6 |
| 1922 .............. | 644,912 | 13.8 |
| 1923 .............. | 922,643 | 43.1 |
| 1924 .............. | 1,773,362 | 92.2 |
| 1925 .............. | 1,845,471 | 4.1 |
| 1926 .............. | 2,169,456 | 17.6 |
| 1927 .............. | 3,272,537 | 50.8 |
| 1928 .............. | 4,115,299 | 25.8 |
| 1929 .............. | 5,560,348 | 35.1 |
| 1930 .............. | 6,642,208 | 19.5 |
| 1931 .............. | 6,857,517 | 3.2 |

Total ............$35,103,119

Gasoline consumption in Colorado by years, as reported by the state oil inspector, was as follows:

| Year | Gallons | Per Ct. Inc. Over Former Yr. |
|---|---|---|
| 1913.............. | 5,860,855 | .... |
| 1914.............. | 10,372,238 | 76.97 |
| 1915.............. | 14,482,629 | 39.63 |
| 1916.............. | 19,988,001 | 38.01 |
| 1917.............. | 29,879,153 | 49.49 |
| 1918.............. | 32,800,910 | 9.78 |
| 1919.............. | 42,361,550 | 29.15 |
| 1920.............. | 51,917,098 | 22.56 |
| 1921.............. | 60,390,692 | 16.32 |
| 1922.............. | 65,891,200 | 9.11 |
| 1923.............. | 75,258,403 | 14.22 |
| 1924.............. | 94,031,766 | 24.95 |
| 1925.............. | 98,741,301 | 5.01 |
| 1926.............. | 112,380,309 | 13.81 |
| 1927.............. | 128,304,024 | 14.16 |
| 1928.............. | 142,027,665 | 10.69 |
| 1929.............. | 155,507,842 | 9.49 |
| 1930.............. | 170,855,026 | 9.86 |
| 1931.............. | 176,493,739 | 3.30 |

Colorado was the source of supply for 26,284,127 gallons of the 176,493,739 gallons of gasoline, or 14.89 per cent of the total, consumed in the state in 1931, according to the records of the state inspector of oils. In addition, 989,918 gallons was exported out of the state during the year. An accompanying table gives the source of Colorado's gasoline supply by states and years. The following table shows the quantity Colorado supplied by years and the per cent of the state's total consumption:

| Year | Quantity (Gals.) | Per Cent of Total Consumption |
|---|---|---|
| 1915............. | 332,168 | 2.29 |
| 1916............. | 395,035 | 1.98 |
| 1917............. | 3,546,823 | 11.87 |
| 1918............. | 5,701,883 | 17.38 |
| 1919............. | 6,454,277 | 15.24 |
| 1920............. | 6,610,291 | 12.73 |
| 1921............. | 5,222,884 | 8.65 |
| 1922............. | 7,019,477 | 10.65 |
| 1923............. | 7,010,704 | 9.32 |
| 1924.............10,282,726 | | 10.94 |
| 1925............. | 5,659,669 | 5.73 |
| 1926............. | 9,555,417 | 8.50 |
| 1927.............15,465,893 | | 12.05 |
| 1928.............18,164,163 | | 12.79 |
| 1929.............19,029,208 | | 12.24 |
| 1930.............18,171,350 | | 10.64 |
| 1931.............26,284,127 | | 14.89 |

Refunds by calendar years of taxes on gasoline used for agricultural, industrial, contractors and aviation purposes and by the United States government are as follows:

| Year | Amount |
|---|---|
| 1924 ...........................$ 33,167 |
| 1925 ........................... 31,628 |
| 1926 ........................... 63,261 |
| 1927 ........................... 143,919 |
| 1928 ........................... 265,709 |
| 1929 ........................... 412,410 |
| 1930 ........................... 630,231 |
| 1931 ........................... 730,289 |

The average consumption of gasoline in gallons in Colorado per motor vehicle registered has shown a steady increase from an average of 408.1 gallons in 1925 to 570.4 gallons in 1931. The state inspector of oils credits this increase to a large increase of bus lines, heavy truck lines, taxicabs, closed cars and the general use of tractors and gasoline-operated machinery. The lowest average gasoline consumption per registered motor vehicle in the 18 years ending with 1931, was 376.5 gallons in 1918 and the highest was 570.4 gallons in 1931.

An accompanying table shows gasoline consumption and road taxes distributed, by counties, for 1930 and 1931. Another gives the amounts of the tax distributed to counties and to the general and special highway funds by years.

## GASOLINE CONSUMPTION BY AND TAX DISTRIBUTION TO COUNTIES
(From Reports of the State Oil Inspector)

| COUNTY | Gallons Consumed | | Road Tax Distributed | |
|---|---|---|---|---|
| | 1931 | 1930 | 1931 | 1930 |
| Adams | 3,004,727 | 3,250,700 | $ 17,093.83 | $ 16,995.83 |
| Alamosa | 2,577,753 | 2,451,279 | 20,086.61 | 19,971.43 |
| Arapahoe | 2,217,276 | 2,097,994 | 18,467.09 | 18,360.98 |
| Archuleta | 208,148 | 211,995 | 18,185.35 | 18,081.02 |
| Baca | 3,230,858 | 3,848,286 | 42,004.07 | 41,535.61 |
| Bent | 1,185,788 | 1,256,740 | 12,816.01 | 12,742.45 |
| Boulder | 6,904,915 | 6,555,376 | 24,628.63 | 24,469.81 |
| Chaffee | 3,032,286 | 3,811,581 | 16,460.15 | 16,383.13 |
| Cheyenne | 967,835 | 982,450 | 22,463.21 | 22,299.39 |
| Clear Creek | ........ | ........ | 19,100.77 | 18,991.12 |
| Conejos | 615,114 | 550,104 | 22,991.39 | 22,859.31 |
| Costilla | 285,515 | 291,401 | 22,762.50 | 22,649.34 |
| Crowley | 683,979 | 828,599 | 11,231.60 | 11,167.14 |
| Custer | 162,621 | 195,941 | 16,812.11 | 16,715.75 |
| Delta | 1,549,402 | 1,506,577 | 21,090.16 | 20,864.13 |
| Denver | 52,848,456 | 50,091,295 | ........ | ........ |
| Dolores | 33,705 | 15,368 | 12,587.09 | 12,514.86 |
| Douglas | 576,140 | 656,116 | 27,181.13 | 28,565.52 |
| Eagle | 335,962 | 322,863 | 22,603.99 | 22,509.36 |
| Elbert | 1,021,828 | 1,151,516 | 22,674.52 | 22,544.47 |
| El Paso | 11,230,327 | 10,037,736 | 43,518.06 | 43,268.46 |
| Fremont | 2,817,120 | 2,444,452 | 31,846.40 | 30,665.97 |
| Garfield | 1,958,181 | 1,877,136 | 27,480.43 | 27,322.82 |
| Gilpin | 82,772 | 88,807 | 6,355.32 | 6,318.83 |
| Grand | 973,061 | 741,101 | 33,976.53 | 33,799.07 |
| Gunnison | 405,448 | 352,714 | 45,472.16 | 43,250.91 |
| Hinsdale | ........ | ........ | 8,555.70 | 8,506.64 |
| Huerfano | 2,146,054 | 2,233,828 | 24,699.01 | 24,662.46 |
| Jackson | 230,642 | 299,707 | 23,959.50 | 23,822.12 |
| Jefferson | 621,073 | 584,442 | 42,268.07 | 39,750.20 |
| Kiowa | 932,970 | 851,001 | 25,719.95 | 25,572.56 |
| Kit Carson | 2,552,258 | 2,697,572 | 30,772.45 | 30,595.90 |
| Lake | 707,456 | 679,558 | 13,150.41 | 13,075.10 |
| La Plata | 1,056,768 | 754,145 | 17,850.78 | 17,731.01 |
| Larimer | 7,643,970 | 6,406,084 | 45,172.84 | 45,018.75 |
| Las Animas | 3,516,741 | 3,688,960 | 47,743.09 | 47,416.68 |
| Lincoln | 2,083,072 | 2,045,915 | 56,492.41 | 56,168 46 |
| Logan | 4,081,918 | 4,144,281 | 30,878.11 | 29,668.27 |
| Mesa | 3,883,491 | 3,470,604 | 39,521.81 | 39,295.20 |
| Mineral | 34,734 | 55,525 | 11,812.45 | 11,744.74 |
| Moffat | 1,257,486 | 1,152,340 | 30,948.51 | 32,416.22 |
| Montezuma | 467,015 | 427,500 | 24,241.23 | 24,102.25 |
| Montrose | 1,546,694 | 1,327,940 | 41,247.11 | 41,290.60 |
| Morgan | 4,224,808 | 3,796,778 | 23,977.23 | 20,986.53 |
| Otero | 4,300,433 | 3,955,455 | 16,354.50 | 16,278.11 |
| Ouray | 66,130 | 32,476 | 8,714.21 | 8,664.19 |
| Park | ........ | ........ | 34,029.37 | 37,667.35 |
| Phillips | 2,474,764 | 2,263,026 | 17,674.72 | 18,308.46 |
| Pitkin | 63,054 | 58,799 | 15,491.90 | 15,420.53 |
| Prowers | 3,101,220 | 3,219,006 | 34,011.66 | 33,834.19 |
| Pueblo | 9,278,180 | 9,407,953 | 35,138.43 | 33,956.61 |
| Rio Blanco | 51,979 | 40,368 | 36,317.87 | 36,109.56 |
| Rio Grande | 1,985,488 | 1,975,839 | 15,174.90 | 15,087.91 |
| Routt | 903,041 | 935,684 | 32,339.30 | 30,263.43 |
| Saguache | 702,839 | 817,947 | 29,716.23 | 29,545.80 |
| San Juan | 46,706 | 83,225 | 7,851.62 | 7,806.59 |
| San Miguel | 125,816 | 69,796 | 25,174.22 | 25,047.27 |
| Sedgwick | 1,458,667 | 1,597,545 | 12,692.78 | 12,637.43 |
| Summit | ........ | ........ | 16,319.20 | 16,225.60 |
| Teller | 470,408 | 391,371 | 18,167.80 | 18,063.76 |
| Washington | 1,229,206 | 1,193,506 | 45,736.16 | 46,349.05 |
| Weld | 11,934,534 | 12,006,918 | 62,319.54 | 59,511.61 |
| Yuma | 2,404,907 | 2,541,805 | 43,570.91 | 43,320.99 |
| Totals | 176,493,739 | 170,855,026 | $1,625,695.09 | $1,610,768.57 |

## DISTRIBUTION OF GASOLINE TAXES

Note.—Amounts given are those distributed to the various agencies by the state auditor and do not show total taxes collected or balances on hand.

| YEAR | To Counties | To Highway Fund | To Special Fund |
|------|-------------|-----------------|-----------------|
| *1927 .............................. | $1,505,651 | $1,740,651 | ....... |
| *1928 .............................. | 1,122,438 | 2,665,355 | ....... |
| 1929 .............................. | 1,455,430 | 3,719,623 | $ 102,969 |
| 1930 .............................. | 1,603,082 | 4,171,888 | 178,531 |
| 1931 .............................. | 1,649,511 | 4,219,681 | 180,820 |

*For fiscal year ending November 30. Others are for calendar years.

## SOURCES OF COLORADO'S GASOLINE SUPPLY, BY YEARS
(From State Oil Inspector's Reports; in Gallons)

|  | 1931 | 1930 | 1929 | 1928 | 1927 | 1926 |
|--|------|------|------|------|------|------|
| Arkansas .. | 125,395 | 38,509 | ........ | ........ | ........ | ........ |
| California . | ........ | 47,282 | ........ | ........ | 41,055 | 187,409 |
| Colorado .. | 26,284,127 | 18,171,350 | 19,029,208 | 18,164,163 | 15,465,893 | 9,555,417 |
| Kansas ... | 34,020,492 | 30,866,498 | 23,998,336 | 18,491,680 | 14,135,557 | 6,844,453 |
| Missouri .. | 4,116 | ........ | ........ | ........ | ........ | ........ |
| Nebraska .. | 209,239 | 166,991 | 111,438 | 129,657 | 95,105 | 35,539 |
| New Mexico | 3,196,318 | 2,798,901 | 2,382,770 | 2,617,796 | 2,314,029 | 2,014,429 |
| Oklahoma . | 34,327,531 | 34,568,177 | 31,802,699 | 26,082,400 | 29,875,514 | 19,276,048 |
| Texas ..... | 21,483,690 | 17,966,408 | 5,840,205 | 2,409,842 | 1,673,332 | 945,848 |
| Utah ...... | 204,444 | 194,836 | 30,195 | 24,419 | 409,386 | 101,459 |
| Wyoming . | 56,638,387 | 66,036,074 | 72,259,543 | 74,107,708 | 64,294,153 | 73,419,707 |
| Louisiana . | ........ | ........ | 53,448 | ........ | ........ | ........ |
| Totals... | 176,493,739 | 170,855,026 | 155,507,842 | 142,027,665 | 128,304,024 | 112,380,309 |

# Federal Operations in Colorado

DENVER is the center from which numerous activities of the United States government in western states are conducted and has the largest representation of the government of any city in the country with the exception of the capital city of Washington. This has led to the frequent characterization of Denver as the western capital of the United States. A survey made by the immigration department in 1927 shows that there are 75 departmental, district and local agencies of the federal government in Colorado, counting all the postoffices in the state as a single unit, most of which have their headquarters in or adjacent to Denver.

There are under the jurisdiction of the Colorado agencies 7,418 salaried officials and employes, of whom 6,922 are located within the state. These figures are exclusive of several departments, such as the secret service, which are forbidden by regulations to give out information of this nature, and of more than 1,000 seasonal employes. Additional information on this subject will be found in another chapter entitled "Persons in Governmental Service."

The value of federal government property in Colorado is estimated at approximately $698,170,360. Wherever possible, official figures were used in making this estimate and where such figures were not available the amount was computed on the basis of value of similar property for taxation purposes, or fixed by private ownership. These estimates are as follows:

| | |
|--|--|
| National forests............ | $ 70,000,000 |
| Reclamation projects........ | 11,000,000 |
| Unappropriated land........ | 11,485,710 |
| Land filed upon but not patented ................. | 3,197,206 |
| Coal land (reserved and classified) .............. | 523,450,000 |
| Oil reserves............... | 2,173,040 |
| Oil shale land (reserves and classified) .............. | 25,430,000 |
| Buildings .................. | 21,389,487 |
| Parks and monuments...... | 1,500,000 |
| Power, water, reservoir, etc. | 25,000,000 |
| Indian property........... | 3,544,917 |
| Total.................. | $698,170,360 |

The method of arriving at these estimates is given in detail in the chapter, "Taxable and Non-taxable

Property," published elsewhere in this volume.

The area, location, and value of these various holdings are given in more detail in other chapters in this volume.

The total expenditures of the federal government in Colorado in the fiscal year ending June 30, 1926, the only year for which such a compilation has been made, aggregated $21,-545,903, and receipts from all sources, $23,565,513. Buildings of the government in and adjacent to Denver, with their estimated value, are as follows:

| | |
|---|---:|
| Fitzsimons general hospital (160 bldgs.) | $10,000,000 |
| Postoffice and federal courthouse | 3,000,000 |
| Mint | 4,000,000 |
| Customs house (old) | 1,000,000 |
| Customs house (new) | 1,200,000 |
| Army post (Fort Logan, 136 bldgs.) | 1,300,000 |
| Total | $20,500,000 |

The above table does not include postoffice buildings and sites in various cities and towns of the state, which are included in a table published elsewhere, covering operations of the postoffice department.

Information concerning federal operations in Colorado is given in more detail under sub-headings in this chapter.

## PENSIONS AND COMPENSATION PAID ON ACCOUNT OF WARS

The United States government distributed $7,991,691 to 13,980 residents of Colorado in the fiscal year ending June 30, 1931, in pensions, disability compensation and death benefits arising out of the wars in which the country has engaged. These payments went to survivors or the dependents of veterans. The aggregate payments from 1918 to 1931, inclusive, amounted to $74,049,954.

The distribution of disbursements in the fiscal year ending June 30, 1931, is as follows:

| | |
|---|---:|
| Disability compensation | $4,455,648.34 |
| Army and navy pensions | 2,514,623.32 |
| Disability allowance | 350,048.09 |
| Death compensation | 339,593.45 |
| Retired emergency officers | 331,777.98 |
| Total | $7,991,691.18 |

Disability compensation is paid to the veterans of the world war. The army and navy pensions went to survivors or dependents of veterans of wars other than the world war. Disability allowance represents payments to veterans of the world war for disabilities encountered since the war ended. The item of death compensa-

tion applies to world war veterans. Payments of disability allowance and to retired emergency officers are made under a new law which went into effect July 1, 1930.

Pension payments formerly were handled by the bureau of pensions and compensation to world war veterans by the veterans' bureau. These two agencies were consolidated July 1, 1930, under the veterans' administration.

The number of persons in the state receiving army and navy pensions has decreased steadily in recent years. There were 4,967 on the rolls on June 30, 1931, a decrease of 148, compared with the same date in 1930, and a decrease of 311 compared with 1929. The amount paid in pensions increased $222,983 in 1931, compared with 1930, and $129,848 compared with 1929. The aggregate amount of army and navy pensions paid to residents of the state in the years 1918 to 1931, inclusive, was $33,118,368. The beneficiaries include survivors or dependents of veterans of the civil war, the war with Spain, the Indian wars and the regular establishment who receive pensions through the United States veterans' administration.

The following table shows the number of pensioners in Colorado on June 30 of the year given and the amounts paid:

| Year | Number | Amount |
|---|---:|---:|
| 1918 | 6,369 | $1,769,946 |
| 1919 | 6,328 | 2,252,895 |
| 1920 | 6,002 | 2,160,440 |
| 1921 | 5,640 | 2,577,818 |
| 1922 | 5,296 | 2,460,019 |
| 1923 | 6,105 | 2,933,758 |
| 1924 | 5,837 | 2,356,452 |
| 1925 | 5,711 | 2,237,270 |
| 1926 | 5,590 | 2,352,265 |
| 1927 | 5,450 | 2,420,010 |
| 1928 | 5,432 | 2,406,457 |
| 1929 | 5,278 | 2,384,775 |
| 1930 | 5,115 | 2,291,640 |
| 1931 | 4,967 | 2,514,623 |
| Total, 14 years | | $33,118,368 |

Deaths of veterans of the world war are increasing gradually. Death compensation was being paid to the beneficiaries of 963 veterans on June 30, 1931, which compares with 914, an increase of 49, in 1930, and 877, an increase of 86, compared with 1929. The number on June 30, 1919, was 222, indicating an increase of 741 since the close of the war. The aggregate disbursements from 1919 to 1931, inclusive, were $3,039,327.

The following table shows the number of cases on which death compensation was being paid on June 30 of the year named by the veterans' bureau, and the approximate amount of the disbursements:

| Year | Number | Amount |
|---|---|---|
| 1919 | 222 | $ 43,226 |
| 1920 | 389 | 191,203 |
| 1921 | 431 | 159,289 |
| 1922 | 465 | 150,055 |
| 1923 | 501 | 167,985 |
| 1924 | 532 | 177,656 |
| 1925 | 645 | 249,041 |
| 1926 | 782 | 309,977 |
| 1927 | 823 | 291,474 |
| 1928 | 841 | 299,421 |
| 1929 | 877 | 307,560 |
| 1930 | 914 | 352,847 |
| 1931 | 963 | 339,593 |
| Total | | $3,039,327 |

The following table shows the number of cases on which disability compensation was being paid on June 30 of the year named, and the amount:

| Year | Number | Amount |
|---|---|---|
| 1919 | 635 | $ 117,037 |
| 1920 | 3,420 | 2,016,193 |
| 1921 | 3,943 | 2,570,875 |
| 1922 | 4,428 | 2,648,697 |
| 1923 | 4,764 | 2,777,173 |
| 1924 | 4,659 | 2,498,529 |
| 1925 | 4,977 | 2,445,848 |
| 1926 | 5,326 | 3,132,061 |
| 1927 | 5,452 | 3,225,785 |
| 1928 | 5,571 | 3,265,999 |
| 1929 | 5,319 | 4,072,096 |
| 1930 | 5,237 | 3,984,491 |
| 1931 | 5,386 | 4,455,648 |
| Total | | $37,210,432 |

Recapitulation of amounts paid out in Colorado from 1918 to 1931, inclusive, as shown by the above tables is as follows:

| | |
|---|---|
| Pensions | $33,118,368 |
| Death compensation | 3,039,327 |
| Disability compensation | 37,210,432 |
| Disability allowance | 350,048 |
| Retired emergency officers | 331,778 |
| Total | $74,049,953 |

In addition to the number receiving pensions and disability compensation on June 30, 1930, there were 115 persons in the state who had retired from government service and were receiving annuities, an increase of 24 during the fiscal year.

## FEDERAL LAND AND JOINT STOCK BANKS

Two agencies for making loans to farmers under the supervision of the federal farm loan board, a bureau of the United States treasury department, operate in Colorado. One of these is The Federal Land Bank of Wichita, Kansas, and the other is the Denver Joint Stock Land Bank of Denver, District No. 9, served by The Federal Land Bank, includes the states of Colorado, Kansas, Oklahoma and New Mexico, and the Denver Joint Stock Land Bank's territory embraces Colorado and Wyoming. While under the supervision of a bureau of the treasury department, these banks do not make "government loans," but are financed independently by the sale of bonds secured by farm mortgages and approved by the farm loan board, and by sale of stock as hereinafter stated.

The Federal Land Bank operates in connection with National Farm Loan associations, organizations composed of borrowers, the loans to individual members of the associations being limited to a maximum of $25,000 and borrowers must have aggregate loans of not less than $20,000 to form an association. Each borrower must be the owner-operator of the farm offered as security and must subscribe for association stock to the amount of five per cent of his loan, which the association invests in stock of The Federal Land Bank. He shares proportionately in the profits of the association during the period of his loan, and upon the payment of his loan his stock is retired at its value, not to exceed par. All the mortgages and notes of members of an association must be indorsed by the association. Loans are made at rates not over one per cent higher than the interest rate on the last issue of bonds made by the bank prior to executing the loan. The bank sets aside 25 per cent of its profit each year for a reserve fund, and has been declaring four per cent dividends semi-annually. No dividends were declared June 30 and December 31, 1931.

While the capital stock of federal land banks is sold only to associations of borrowers, the joint stock land banks are financed much in the same way as any other bank or industrial corporation. The contact between the farmer and the banks may be made either by applying to the nearest farm loan association, or direct to the joint stock bank for the district in which he resides.

There was in Colorado on December 31, 1931, a total of 118 national farm loan associations. From the beginning in April, 1917, to December 31, 1931, a total of 11,266 loans, aggregating $35,678,600, had been made by the federal land bank in Colorado. Of these, 2,217, aggregating $6,412,400, had been paid in full and cancelled, and 9,049 were in force at the close of 1931.

The federal land bank has disposed of 337 farms acquired through foreclosure of loans in Colorado, of which 124 were sold for a gain of $47,476.26 and 211 were sold for a loss of $214,-771.33, and two were sold for investment, the net loss being $167,295.07. It owns 42 judgments for $148,253.45, and 123 farms valued at $487,630.31.

Joint stock land bank loans in Colorado up to January 31, 1932, aggregated $13,066,489.91.

## FEDERAL EXPENDITURES AND RECEIPTS IN COLORADO

The secretary of the interior, whose department is responsible for the administration of the public lands, compiled a statement showing the principal expenditures made by the federal government during the fiscal year ending June 30, 1926, in the 20 public land states. The statement also shows payments to the federal government from these states for services rendered.

The statement shows that the federal government spent $509,209,985 in these 20 public land states during the year for direct services performed within the respective states, while ♦197,734,690 was collected in the states. The difference between expenditures and receipts was $311,475,-293, or a ratio of about one dollar contributed by the states for every $2.50 expended therein by the federal government.

Expenditures in Colorado, as shown by this statement, amounted to $21,-545,903, and the receipts were $8,-523,523, the difference being $13,022,-379. Colorado ranked ninth among the 20 states both in expenditures and receipts. Such fiscal items as income-tax and customs receipts, which were collected for general governmental purposes, are excluded. Statistics of income-tax receipts, for example, the statement says, show collections according to the residence of taxpayers and not according to localities responsible for the income going to individuals who make the payments.

However, since income-tax receipts of foreign corporations and individuals paid in other states, but operating in Colorado, probably will offset the condition mentioned, these items are included in the following table for the purpose of bringing together as nearly as possible all expenditures and receipts of the federal government in the state:

| | |
|---|---:|
| Receipts | $ 8,523,523.67 |
| Internal reVenue | 14,830,350.29 |
| Customs receipts | 211,639.57 |
| Total receipts | $23,565,513.53 |
| Expenditures | 21,545,903.31 |
| Excess receipts over expenditures | $ 2,019,610.22 |

A table showing the expenditures and receipts for Colorado, by departments, compiled from the secretary of the interior's statement, has appeared in previous editions of this work.

## U. S. INTERNAL REVENUE

United States internal revenue taxes in Colorado are collected through the commissioner of internal revenue of the treasury department. The Colorado district comprises the state of Colorado, and the collector's office for the district is at Denver. Tax receipts are credited to the districts in which the collections are made. Receipts in the various districts do not indicate the tax burden of the respective districts, since the taxes may be eventually borne by persons in other districts. Repeal of laws imposing taxes on various classes of business and changes in rates account largely for variations in the amounts.

Total revenue receipts from all sources for the Colorado district by fiscal years ending June 30 are as follows:

| Year | Amount |
|---|---:|
| 1921 | $34,214,956 |
| 1922 | 19,956,650 |
| 1923 | 15,988,678 |
| 1924 | 15,228,016 |
| 1925 | 14,215,162 |
| 1926 | 14,830,350 |
| 1927 | 13,473,226 |
| 1928 | 11,879,300 |
| 1929 | 11,539,236 |
| 1930 | 12,468,450 |
| 1931 | 15,667,230 |

A table is published herewith showing the sources of internal revenue from Colorado for 1928 to 1931, inclusive, and for 1921. Most of the internal revenue comes from individual and corporation income taxes. These sources supplied 97.5 per cent of the total revenues in 1930.

Income-tax receipts for the Colorado district, by fiscal years, are as follows:

| Year | Corporation | Individual | Total |
|---|---:|---:|---:|
| 1921 | .... | ....... | $25,085.243 |
| 1922 | .... | ....... | 14,545,633 |
| 1923 | .... | ....... | 10,920,851 |
| 1924 | .... | ....... | 11,543,616 |
| 1925 | $7,595,438 | $4,145,230 | 11,740,668 |
| 1926 | 7,740,854 | 4,234,848 | 11,975,702 |
| 1927 | 8,969,799 | 3,686,845 | 12,656,644 |
| 1928 | 7,923,577 | 3,528,993 | 11,452,570 |
| 1929 | 6,831,459 | 4,206,231 | 11,037,690 |
| 1930 | 7,835,966 | 4,212,450 | 12,048,416 |
| 1931 | 11,935,132 | 3,337,149 | 15,272,281 |

There were 7,317 corporation returns filed in the Colorado district in 1929, of which 3,311 reported net income, 2,474 reported no net income and 1,532 were inactive, reporting no income data. The 3,311 returns reporting net income showed a gross income of $738,303,447 and a net income of $52,-349,386. The 2,474 returns reporting no net income showed a gross income of $200,275,469 and a deficit of $21,-166,262. Transportation and other public utilities showed the largest net income of any in the major groups, 114 corporations reporting a gross income of $116,935,244 and a net income of $13,619,189. There were 95 in this group that reported a gross income of $3,386,308 and a deficit of $958,439. The trade group showed the largest gross income, 1,087 in this group reporting a gross income of $250,040,709 and a net income of $7,641,572. In this group 679 reported a gross income of $78,972,306 and a deficit of $5,043,723.

An accompanying table shows the gross and net income and gross income and deficit of all corporations by major groups in 1929. Another table shows the same data by years from 1916 to 1929, inclusive.

There were 31,268 individual income-tax returns filed in the Colorado district in 1929, reporting a net income of $158,751,528, upon which the tax amounted to $3,534,404. This tax total does not agree with receipts reported above, as the receipts are for the fiscal year and the income and tax are for the calendar year, the last two payments overlapping. The average net income per return in 1929 was $5,-077.12 and the average tax was $113.04 per return. Personal exemption and credit for dependents amounted to $96,731,299.

The distribution of the individual income returns in 1929 was as follows:

| | No. of Returns | Net Income |
|---|---|---|
| Joint returns of husbands and wives... | 17,656 | $105,447,250 |
| Single men—heads of families .......... | 2,253 | 8,755,738 |
| Single Women—heads of families......... | 814 | 3,744,157 |
| Single men—not heads of families........ | 6,892 | 21,528,213 |
| Single Women — not heads of families.. | 2,925 | 11,896,278 |
| Wives filing separate returns from husbands ............. | 728 | 7,379,892 |
| Totals .............. | 31,268 | $158,751,528 |

The total income of the 31,268 persons making the above returns in 1929 was $191,304,294. Deductions amounted to $32,552,766, leaving a net income of $158,751,528. The sources of income were as follows:

| | |
|---|---|
| Wages and salaries.....,....$ | 68,499,794 |
| Business ................... | 34,136,489 |
| Partnership ................ | 10,173,444 |
| Profit from sale of real estate, stocks, bonds, etc.. | 15,221,025 |
| Capital net gain from sale of assets held more than two years .................... | 3,466,098 |
| Rents and royalties........ | 9,275,488 |
| Interest on government obligations not wholly exempt | 379,105 |
| Dividends on stocks of domestic corporations ...... | 31,178,737 |
| Fiduciary ................. | 1,925,385 |
| Interest and other income... | 17,048,729 |
| Total income.............$ | 191,304,294 |

**General Deductions**

| | |
|---|---|
| Net loss from sale of real estate, stocks, bonds, etc..$ | 4,282,108 |
| Contributions .............. | 2,876,721 |
| All others................. | 25,393,937 |
| Total deductions...........$ | 32,552,766 |
| Net income..............$ | 158,751,528 |

A table published herewith gives the number of individual income returns, the net income, the average income, the total tax and the average tax for the Colorado district by years.

Three persons in the Colorado district had aggregate incomes of $2,-256,688 in 1929, or an average of $752,229 each. On the commonly accepted basis that net income is five per cent of principal, these three persons were worth $45,133,760, or an average of $15,044,588 each. On the same basis there were 181 persons in Colorado in 1929 who might be classed as millionaires. These 181 persons reported an aggregate net income of $18,993,049, their incomes ranging from $50,000 to $500,000, or more.

The distribution of 1929 income, according to numbers and amounts, is as follows:

| Income in Thousands | No. of Returns | Net Income |
|---|---|---|
| Under 5.............23,595 | | $ 63,216,228 |
| 5 under 10....... 5,123 | | 34,788,933 |
| 10 under 25....... 1,990 | | 28,885,355 |
| 25 under 50....... 379 | | 12,867,963 |
| 50 under 100....... 129 | | 8,573,461 |
| 100 under 150....... 30 | | 3,543,260 |
| 150 under 250....... 10 | | 1,790,590 |
| 250 under 500....... 9 | | 2,829,050 |
| 500 under 1,000....... 3 | | 2,256,688 |
| Total ............31,268 | | $158,751,528 |

| | | |
|---|---|---|
| Non-taxable returns..14,257 | | $ 37,398,408 |
| Taxable returns......17,011 | | 121,353,120 |

In 1929 there were 52 returns of estates of resident decedents, the aggregate gross estate amounting to $23,487,394. Of these, 43, with a gross estate of $22,065,382, were subject to $750,134 tax, and nine, with a gross estate of $1,422,012, were not subject to a tax.

**INDIVIDUAL FEDERAL INCOME TAX RETURNS FOR COLORADO DISTRICT BY YEARS**
(From Reports of the U. S. Bureau of Internal Revenue)

| YEAR | Number Returns | Net Income | | Tax | |
|---|---|---|---|---|---|
| | | Total | Average | Total | Average |
| 1916 | 4,435 | $ 53,854,130 | $12,143 | $ 1,055,758 | $238 |
| 1917 | 40,627 | 137,853,875 | 3,393 | 5,184,948 | 128 |
| 1918 | 54,160 | 159,487,951 | 2,945 | 5,844,925 | 108 |
| 1919 | 57,256 | 191,001,999 | 3,320 | 7,196,593 | 125 |
| 1920 | 74,198 | 219,277,184 | 2,955 | 6,766,900 | 91 |
| 1921 | 69,676 | 174,490,980 | 2,504 | 3,862,862 | 55 |
| 1922 | 67,463 | 184,572,407 | 2,736 | 4,869,555 | 72 |
| 1923 | 72,366 | 200,572,724 | 2,772 | 3,267,732 | 45 |
| 1924 | 73,350 | 205,087,973 | 2,796 | 3,162,736 | 43 |
| 1925 | 35,808 | 150,363,411 | 4,199 | 2,840,926 | 79 |
| 1926 | 35,110 | 154,804,655 | 4,409 | 2,959,248 | 84 |
| 1927 | 31,727 | 148,473,486 | 4,680 | 3,307,180 | 104 |
| 1928 | 31,091 | 158,931,875 | 5,112 | 4,459,057 | 143 |
| 1929 | 31,268 | 158,751,528 | 5,077 | 3,534,404 | 113 |

Note.—Changes in the revenue acts affect the comparability of the above figures.

**CORPORATION INCOME RETURNS IN COLORADO BY MAJOR GROUPS IN 1929**
(Compiled from Reports of the Bureau of Internal Revenue, U. S. Treasury Department)

| | Corporations Reporting Net Income | | | Corporations Reporting No Net Income | | |
|---|---|---|---|---|---|---|
| | No. Returns | Gross Income* | Net Income | No. Returns | Gross Income* | Deficit |
| Agriculture and related industries | 174 | $ 6,261,058 | $ 804,239 | 156 | $ 10,551,645 | $ 1,541,702 |
| Mining and quarrying | 169 | 80,839,879 | 6,997,848 | 368 | 11,689,032 | 5,881,677 |
| Manufacturing: | | | | | | |
| Food products, beverages and tobacco | 126 | 153,385,452 | 8,276,270 | 62 | 15,618,958 | 947,210 |
| Textiles and textile products | 18 | 2,945,080 | 125,449 | 20 | 2,862,338 | 113,938 |
| Leather and leather products | 5 | 1,505,183 | 15,736 | 7 | 457,109 | 23,333 |
| Rubber and related products | 3 | 6,776,341 | 557,299 | 2 | 2,061 | 915 |
| Lumber and wood products | 14 | 1,067,012 | 30,606 | 15 | 4,446,433 | 287,306 |
| Paper, pulp and products | 3 | 736,149 | 32,797 | 3 | 330,294 | 11,299 |
| Printing and publishing | 65 | 11,454,649 | 2,556,434 | 36 | 1,524,432 | 91,784 |
| Chemicals and allied substances | 32 | 4,328,781 | 394,057 | 27 | 422,715 | 77,069 |
| Stone, clay and glass products | 26 | 13,132,614 | 2,237,391 | 21 | 681,607 | 96,980 |
| Metal and metal products | 66 | 13,954,990 | 897,069 | 51 | 2,264,225 | 317,660 |
| Manufacturing not elsewhere classified | 37 | 2,977,755 | 106,740 | 29 | 899,273 | 171,636 |
| Construction | 56 | 5,250,864 | 253,743 | 49 | 3,853,132 | 429,123 |
| Transportation and other public utilities | 114 | 116,935,244 | 13,619,189 | 95 | 3,386,308 | 958,439 |
| Trade | 1,087 | 250,040,709 | 7,641,572 | 679 | 78,972,306 | 5,043,723 |
| Service: | | | | | | |
| Professional, amusements, hotels, etc. | 285 | 14,687,075 | 1,245,857 | 193 | 8,776,472 | 1,012,437 |
| Finance: | | | | | | |
| Banking, insurance, real estate and holding companies, stock and bond brokers, etc. | 1,008 | 51,893,996 | 6,537,387 | 639 | 53,326,998 | 4,094,722 |
| Nature of business not given | 23 | 130,616 | 19,703 | 22 | 206,118 | 65,309 |
| Total | 3,311 | $738,303,447 | $ 52,349,386 | 2,474 | $200,271,456 | $ 21,166,262 |

Note.—Total number of returns for 1929 was 7,317, of which 3,311 were corporations reporting net incomes, 2,474 were corporations reporting no net income, and 1,532 were inactive corporations reporting no income data.
*Gross income corresponds to total income as reported on the face of the returns, plus cost of goods sold.

## CORPORATION INCOME RETURNS FOR THE COLORADO DISTRICT BY YEARS
(Compiled from U. S. Internal Revenue Reports)

| YEAR | Corporations Reporting Net Income | | | Corporations Reporting No Net Income | | |
|---|---|---|---|---|---|---|
| | No. of Returns | Gross Income | Net Income | No. of Returns | Gross Income | Deficit |
| 1916 | 2,986 | $238,993,105 | $ 57,043,218 | 4,493 | $ 42,771,522 | $ 13,040,522 |
| 1917 | 3,539 | 673,894,965 | 96,761,318 | 4,079 | 48,956,851 | 12,506,521 |
| 1918 | 3,273 | 654,000,372 | 74,209,860 | 3,897 | 79,061,007 | 11,030,270 |
| 1919 | 3,107 | 807,999,998 | 79,287,797 | 3,597 | 165,788,176 | 16,828,247 |
| 1920 | 2,976 | 870,395,990 | 66,034,834 | 3,836 | 173,583,367 | 18,021,558 |
| 1921 | 2,340 | 486,204,976 | 34,041,045 | 4,219 | 318,578,783 | 134,544,456 |
| 1922 | 2,720 | 664,017,735 | 55,835,080 | 4,135 | 178,570,909 | 29,747,821 |
| 1923 | 2,636 | 686,561,409 | 60,490,802 | 3,708 | 175,895,200 | 25,414,654 |
| 1924 | 2,891 | 707,149,477 | 60,846,149 | 3,603 | 180,972,193 | 26,209,210 |
| 1925 | 2,983 | 821,001,998 | 60,448,005 | 3,416 | 161,788,373 | 26,159,041 |
| 1926 | 3,071 | 853,411,805 | 62,872,037 | 3,509 | 182,200,330 | 21,333,038 |
| 1927 | 3,144 | 745,766,162 | 47,758,479 | 2,291 | 292,356,251 | 27,717,330 |
| 1928 | 3,342 | 941,131,878 | 59,932,477 | 2,313 | 147,987,789 | 17,102,817 |
| 1929 | 3,311 | 738,303,447 | 52,349,386 | 2,474 | 200,275,469 | 21,166,262 |

Note.—Changes in the revenue acts affect the comparability of statistical data from income tax returns of corporations. Gross income in 1916 represents gross profit and does not include the cost of goods, as in later years. For 1916-1924, inclusive, gross income is incomplete, due to gross operating revenue of railroads and other public utilities not being completely tabulated. In all years excepting 1918, dividends received from stock of domestic corporations are included in gross income.

## UNITED STATES INTERNAL REVENUE FROM COLORADO
(For fiscal years ending June 30)

| Sources | 1931 | 1930 | 1929 | 1928 | 1921 |
|---|---|---|---|---|---|
| Income, individuals, partnerships and corporations | $15,272,280 | $12,048,415 | $11,037,690 | $11,452,570 | $25,085,242 |
| Estates, transfers of, gifts | 193,975 | 153,801 | 150,095 | 65,364 | 2,210,595 |
| Distilled spirits and alcohol beverages | 17,238 | 20,690 | 25,457 | 29,189 | 20,974 |
| Tobacco and tobacco manufacturers | 14,544 | 19,812 | 25,284 | 25,540 | 271,071 |
| Oleomargarine and adulterated butter | 19,216 | 24,777 | 24,449 | 24,519 | 26,091 |
| Documentary Stamp taxes: | | | | | |
| Revenue stamps sold by postmasters | -------- | -------- | -------- | -------- | 254,102 |
| Bonds, capital stock, conveyances, etc. | 55,851 | 88,196 | 99,918 | 81,256 | 250,681 |
| Capital stock transfers | 5,987 | 14,318 | 15,126 | 9,515 | 35,611 |
| Miscellaneous | 652 | 1,031 | 1,040 | 1,091 | 15,075 |
| Transportation | -------- | -------- | -------- | -------- | 2,001,702 |
| Telegraph and telephone | -------- | -------- | -------- | -------- | 599,927 |
| Insurance | -------- | -------- | -------- | -------- | 47,553 |
| Manufacturers' excise tax: | | | | | |
| Autos, trucks, tires, accessories, etc. | -------- | -------- | -------- | 94 | 184,198 |
| Candy | -------- | -------- | -------- | -------- | 188,786 |
| Miscellaneous | -------- | -------- | -------- | 2,098 | 30,309 |
| Consumers' and dealers' excise tax: | | | | | |
| Sculpture, paintings, etc. | -------- | -------- | -------- | -------- | 5,197 |
| Carpets, trunks, wearing apparel, etc. | -------- | -------- | -------- | -------- | 221,902 |
| Watches, clocks, jewelry, etc. | -------- | -------- | -------- | -------- | 201,998 |
| Perfumes, cosmetics, medicinal, etc. | -------- | -------- | -------- | -------- | 80,370 |
| Non-alcoholic beverages | -------- | -------- | -------- | -------- | 428,892 |
| Narcotics | 6,069 | 5,259 | 5,578 | 14,281 | 15,267 |
| Corporation capital stock tax | -------- | -------- | -------- | -------- | 804,134 |
| Stock and produce brokers | -------- | -------- | -------- | -------- | 19,554 |
| Theatres, museums, circuses, bowling alleys, etc. | -------- | -------- | -------- | 65,747 | 90,619 |
| Admissions to theatres and club dues | 78,300 | 84,142 | 80,627 | 70,421 | 1,106,057 |
| Miscellaneous | 3,118 | 8,009 | 73,972 | 37,615 | 19,049 |
| Total, all sources | $15,667,230 | $12,468,450 | $11,539,236 | $11,879,300 | $34,214,956 |

## NUMBER OF EACH CLASS OF SPECIAL TAX PAYERS IN COLORADO
(For fiscal years ending June 30)

| Class | 1931 | 1930 | 1929 | 1928 | 1927 | 1926 |
|---|---|---|---|---|---|---|
| Distilled Spirits: | | | | | | |
|   Retail dealers .............. | 36 | 31 | 28 | 30 | 20 | 31 |
|   Wholesale dealers ......... | 6 | 4 | 4 | 4 | 2 | 5 |
| Oleomargarine: | | | | | | |
|   Manufacturers ............. | 2 | 2 | 2 | 1 | 1 | 1 |
|   Wholesale dealers.......... | 24 | 24 | 25 | 23 | 21 | 23 |
|   Retail dealers ............. | 2,087 | 2,502 | 2,461 | 2,363 | 2,611 | 2,228 |
| Mixed flour manufacturers...... | 1 | 1 | 1 | 1 | 1 | 1 |
| Tobacco manufacturers ........ | .. | .. | .. | .. | .. | 69 |
| Corporations paying capital stock tax ...................... | .. | .. | .. | .. | .. | 3,721 |
| Brokers ...................... | .. | .. | .. | .. | .. | 104 |
| Proprietors billiard and pool tables and bowling alleys... | .. | .. | .. | .. | .. | 875 |
| Proprietors shooting galleries... | .. | .. | .. | .. | .. | 6 |
| Proprietors automobiles for hire | .. | .. | .. | .. | .. | 357 |
| Opium, Cocoa, Etc.: | | | | | | |
|   Wholesale dealers ......... | 30 | 43 | 37 | 38 | 64 | 41 |
|   Retail dealers.............. | 539 | 494 | 525 | 510 | 905 | 521 |
|   Practitioners, hospitals, etc.. | 1,818 | 1,965 | 1,811 | 1,706 | 3,146 | 1,748 |
|   Dealers in untaxed narcotics | 67 | 92 | 96 | 105 | 150 | 91 |
|     Totals................. | 4,610 | 5,158 | 4,990 | 4,781 | 6,921 | 9,822 |

## UNITED STATES MINT

One of the three mints owned and operated by the United States government is located at Denver. The other two are at Philadelphia and San Francisco. The Denver mint was completed in 1905 and the treasury department took possession and occupied it in September of that year. The coinage of money began in 1906. Total investment, including equipment, machinery, etc., is approximately $4,000,-000, of which $60,000 was for the site and $812,679 was for the building.

Electrolytic refineries for refining gold and silver are operated at the Denver and San Francisco mints and at the New York assay office. The Denver mint had 79 employes on June 30, 1931. The gross income of the mint for the fiscal year was $192,524 and gross expenses were $198,482.

Paper money is not produced at the Denver mint, its output consisting entirely of coin. Bullion is received not only from the principal mining states in this country but from several foreign countries. Gold and silver for minting also are obtained from redeposits, jewelry, and United States and foreign coin. Domestic coin manufactured at the mint from the opening of the institution in 1906 up to and including December, 1931, aggregated 939,579,000 pieces, of a total value of $451,746,755.

Denominations, value and number of pieces manufactured during this period were as follows:

| | Value | Pieces |
|---|---|---|
| Double eagles .. | $262,160,000 | 13,108,000 |
| Eagles ........ | 59,092,800 | 5,909,280 |
| Half eagles .... | 26,463,300 | 5,292,660 |
| Quarter eagles. | 2,704,200 | 540,840 |
| Dollars ........ | 45,836,600 | 45,836,600 |
| Half dollars.... | 13,681,160 | 27,362,320 |
| Quarter dollars. | 15,816,300 | 63,265,200 |
| Dimes ......... | 15,150,380 | 151,503,800 |
| Nickels ........ | 5,718,015 | 114,360,300 |
| Cents ......... | 5,124,000 | 512,400,000 |
| Totals ...... | $451,746,755 | 939,579,000 |

The mints of the United States have produced since the first mint was established in Philadelphia in 1793 down to the end of 1930 a total of 11,-584,710,801 pieces of money valued at $5,952,149,866.26.

United States money, including gold coin and bullion, gold certificates, standard silver dollars, silver certificates, treasury notes, federal reserve notes and subsidiary coins, amounted to $11,274,487,113 on June 30, 1931, of which $2,226,058,715 was held by the federal reserve banks, $4,821,933,298 was in circulation and $4,226,495,100 was money held in the treasury. The money in circulation was equal to $38.86 per capita, which compares with $36.71 per capita on June 30, 1930, and $53.21 per capita on October 31, 1920.

The value and number of pieces manufactured in the Denver mint vary from year to year in accordance with demand. In 1930 there was a continued demand for one-cent bronze pieces and that was the only type of coin minted in that year, the number being 40,100,000. In 1931 there were 106,500 double eagles, 1,260,000 dimes and 4,480,000 one-cent pieces coined.

Coinage for the calendar years of 1927 to 1931, inclusive, was as follows:

### 1927

| | Value | Pieces |
|---|---|---|
| Double eagles..... | $3,600,000 | 180,000 |
| Standard silver dollars ......... | 1,268,900 | 1,268,900 |
| Quarter dollars.... | 244,100 | 976,400 |
| Dimes ............ | 481,200 | 4,812,000 |
| Nickels .......... | 286,500 | 5,730,000 |
| Cents .......... | 271,700 | 27,170,000 |
| Totals.......... | $6,152,400 | 40,137,300 |

### 1928

| | | |
|---|---|---|
| Quarter dollars....$ | 406,900 | 1,627,600 |
| Dimes ............ | 416,100 | 4,161,000 |
| Nickels .......... | 321,800 | 6,436,000 |
| Cents ............ | 311,700 | 31,170,000 |
| Totals.......... | $1,456,500 | 43,394,600 |

### 1929

| | | |
|---|---|---|
| Half dollars.......$ | 500,600 | 1,001,200 |
| Quarter dollars.... | 339,500 | 1,358,000 |
| Dimes ............ | 503,400 | 5,034,000 |
| Nickels .......... | 418,500 | 8,370,000 |
| Cents ............ | 417,300 | 4,173,000 |
| Totals.......... | $2,179,300 | 19,936,200 |

### 1930

| | | |
|---|---|---|
| Cents ............$ | -401,000 | 40,100,000 |

### 1931

| | | |
|---|---|---|
| Double eagles .....$ | 2,130,000 | 106,500 |
| Dimes ............ | 126,000 | 1,260,000 |
| Cents ............ | 44,800 | 4,480,000 |
| Totals.......... | $2,300,800 | 5,846,500 |

## FEDERAL COURTS IN COLORADO

The state comprises a federal judicial district known as the District of Colorado. Headquarters are in the Postoffice building, Denver. J. Foster Symes, of Denver, appointed in 1922, is district judge. His salary is $10,000 per year. The clerk of the court is Charles W. Bishop. Ralph L. Carr is district attorney and C. A. Patton is marshal.

The court has sittings in Denver, Pueblo, Montrose, Grand Junction, Durango and Sterling. Dates for the beginning of terms of the court are as follows:

Denver, first Tuesday in May and first Tuesday in November.

Pueblo, first Tuesday in April.

Montrose, third Tuesday in September.

Grand Junction, second Tuesday in September.

Durango, fourth Tuesday in September.

Sterling, second Monday in June.

Terms of court at Denver, Pueblo and Montrose are fixed by statute.

Sessions at Grand Junction, Durango, and Sterling are not necessary unless there is sufficient business upon the docket to justify them.

Denver is headquarters for the United States circuit court of appeals for the tenth circuit, which embraces Colorado, Wyoming, Kansas, Oklahoma, Utah and New Mexico. This circuit was created by congress in 1929 out of the eighth circuit, in which Colorado formerly was included. Four judges for the court are Robert E. Lewis, of Denver, presiding judge; Orie L. Phillips, of Denver; John H. Cotteral, Guthrie, Okla.; and George T. McDermott, of Topeka, Kans. Albert Trego is clerk of the court and H. A. McIntyre, deputy.

The circuit court of appeals consists of the district and circuit judges in the respective circuits, together with a justice of the supreme court assigned to that circuit. Justice Willis Van Devanter, of Wyoming, is the justice assigned to the tenth circuit.

The sittings of the court are as follows: Second Monday in January at Oklahoma City, second Monday in April at Wichita, and second Monday in September at Denver.

## REPRESENTATIVES OF FOREIGN GOVERNMENTS

Belgium—Jean Mignolet, consul general, 2549 Birch St., Denver.

Bulgaria—See Greece.

Denmark—W. C. Hansen, 526 Sixteenth St., Denver.

France — Jean Mignolet, consular agent, 2549 Birch St., Denver.

Germany—William Godel, consul, American National bank, Denver.

Great Britain—Temporary vacancy.

Greece—Nikias C. Calogeras, vice consul, 525 University Bldg., Denver. Represents Bulgaria and Macedonia.

Hungary—Coleman Jonas, vice consul, 1037 Broadway, Denver.

Italy—Pietro Gerbore, consul, 801 Midland Savings Bldg., Denver.

Japan—Representative, Japanese Society, 417 Barclay Bldg., 18th and Larimer Sts., Denver.

Macedonia—See Greece.

Mexico—Y. M. Vasquez, consul, 402 Mercantile Bldg., Denver.

Netherland—G. J. Rollandet, consul, 919 Security Bldg., Denver.

Switzerland—Paul Weiss, consul, 307 American National Bank Bldg., Denver.

## NARCOTIC LAW OPERATIONS

All persons in the United States handling habit-forming drugs are required by the provisions of the Harrison narcotic law to obtain licenses. This gives the bureau of narcotics, in the United States treasury department, which now is in charge of narcotic activities, a close check on all operations in that business.

The enforcement of the law in Colorado is under the supervision of division headquarters at Denver, the division comprising Colorado, Utah, Wyoming, Arizona and New Mexico.

Registrations in Colorado under the act during the fiscal years ending on June 30 were as follows:

| | |
|---|---|
| 1924 | 2,513 |
| 1925 | 4,423 |
| 1926 | 4,832 |
| 1927 | 4,199 |
| 1928 | 3,595 |
| 1929 | 4,557 |
| 1930 | 4,680 |
| 1931 | 4,419 |

Distribution of permits in 1929 to 1931, inclusive, is as follows:

| Dealers: | 1931 | 1930 | 1929 |
|---|---|---|---|
| Wholesale | 32 | 24 | 38 |
| Retail | 499 | 513 | 515 |
| Class 4* | 1,665 | 1,797 | 1,755 |
| Class 5 (a) | 2,223 | 2,346 | 2,249 |
| Totals | 4,419 | 4,680 | 4,557 |

*Physicians, dentists, veterinary surgeons, and other practitioners and hospitals, sanatoria, etc. (a) Dealers in and manufacturers of untaxed narcotic preparations.

Narcotic drugs and preparations, including opium, morphine, heroin, cocain, etc., seized in the enforcement of the laws in Colorado by fiscal years ending June 30, were as follows:

| | Ounces | Grains |
|---|---|---|
| 1924 | 128 | ... |
| 1925 | 61 | 19 |
| 1926 | 19 | 293 |
| 1927 | 36 | 146 |
| 1928 | 133 | 213 |
| 1929 | 45 | 191 |
| 1930 | 26 | 417 |
| 1931 | 13 | 371 |

Convictions, aggregate sentences and fines imposed for violations of the narcotic laws by fiscal years are as follows:

| | Number Convictions | Aggregate Sentences, Years | Fines Imposed |
|---|---|---|---|
| 1924 | 51 | 27 | $ 2,215 |
| 1925 | 104 | 78 | 17,875 |
| 1926 | 56 | 27 | 9,400 |
| 1927 | 49 | 22 | 1,385 |
| 1928 | 46 | 58 | 275 |
| 1929 | 43 | 53 | .... |
| 1931 | 36 | 81 | 100 |

## FITZSIMONS GENERAL HOSPITAL

One of the seven general hospitals of the United States army is located at Aurora, near the eastern city limits of Denver, known as the Fitzsimons General hospital. The plant is located upon a tract of 600 acres and comprises 160 buildings, with a total bed capacity of 1,832. When constructed in 1918 it was intended primarily for the treatment of tuberculosis, but of late years the need for such specialization has gradually decreased and at present 40 per cent of the patients are of a general medical and surgical nature. The daily average number of patients is approximately 1,200. The average personnel employed is as follows: Medical officers, 48; dental officers, 4; quartermaster officers, 3; finance officers, 1; medical administrative officers, 6; chaplains, 2; internes with the grade of first lieutenant, medical corps reserve, 10; army nurse corps, 128; warrant officers, 3; enlisted men of the medical department, quartermaster corps, finance department and signal corps, 345; and civilian employes, 510. The average cost per year for operation and maintenance is $2,250,000. Total investment is in excess of $10,000,000.

## VETERANS' HOSPITAL

Veterans' Administration Hospital No. 80 is located seven miles northeast of Las Animas, in Bent County, at Fort Lyon, Colorado.

The hospital formerly was owned by the United States navy department and was operated as a naval hospital for tuberculosis. At the close of the world war it was transferred to the United States Veterans' bureau and is now operated by the Veterans' Administration, Washington, D. C., in connection with the hospitalization of male veterans of any war, occupation or expedition.

The site comprises a square mile of ground and the numerous buildings cover 60 acres. The grounds are attractive, with paved streets and modern improvements. The entire plant represents an investment of approximately $3,000,000. The hospital has a medical officer in charge, 18 medical officers and 405 employes, with a bed capacity of 600 patients. On February 9, 1931, a building of modern construction, costing approximately $300,000, was opened for the treatment of neuropsychiatric diseases. A new clinical building, to accommodate 200 patients, is contemplated during 1932, together with additional mess facilities.

## FORT LOGAN MILITARY POST

The only army post in Colorado is Fort Logan, located near Denver. The post comprises a military reservation of 1,000 acres, upon which are 136 buildings, including officers' quarters, barracks and other structures. The total appraised value of the property is $1,300,000. The Second Regiment of Engineers, totaling 440 men, and 75 men of auxiliary branches (Quartermaster, Medical, etc.) are at present stationed at the post.

The land upon which the fort is located was donated to the government by citizens of Denver. Major General Phil Sheridan selected the site and on February 28, 1887, congress authorized the secretary of war to establish the post and appropriated $100,000 for construction work. Construction of permanent headquarters was started in November, 1887. The post was named Fort Sheridan in honor of the civil war veteran, but General Sheridan later changed it to Fort Logan, in honor of Major General John A. Logan.

The post has played an important part in the military life of Colorado. The Citizens' Military Training corps, the Reserve Officers Training corps, and other units like the Engineers and Chemical Warfare Reserve officers train at the fort each year, usually for 30 days in July. The headquarters of the 103rd Reserve division are located in Denver. This reserve includes 2,870 men, mostly officers, residing principally in Colorado, Arizona and New Mexico.

## COLORADO NATIONAL GUARD

The maximum authorized strength of the Colorado national guard is 1,927 men, consisting of 156 officers, 1,770 enlisted men and one warrant officer. The actual strength as of April 1, 1930, was 132 officers, 1,651 enlisted men and one warrant officer. These belong to the 157th infantry regiment; the 1st battalion, 168th field artillery; 1st squadron, 117th cavalry; the 45th division tank company; the 45th division aviation; the 45th division headquarters staff; and the 89th infantry brigade headquarters.

The guard is a part of the military arm of the federal government, which pays the expenses of equipment and caretakers and the maintenance and

expenses of all summer camps. The cost to the federal government is approximately $106,000 a year. The state's portion of the cost is provided by a mill levy of .07 of a mill, from which is derived approximately $106,-000 a year.

The property used for military purposes is appraised at $3,160,000, of which $1,860,000 is for the federal government's part and $1,300,000 for that belonging to the state. Included in this property are 18 armories located at Greeley, Craig, Fruita, Delta, Montrose, Lamar, Boulder, Manzanola, Fort Collins, Brighton, Brush, Fort Morgan, Loveland, Burlington, Canon City, Monte Vista, Pueblo and Golden. The guard also has a military station in close proximity to Denver and on the Golden highway, known as the state rifle range, where warehouses and shops are maintained and where a state encampment is held in June of each year.

The air service is located at the Lowry aviation field in Denver, where an instructor from the United States army is stationed. Lowry field has nine planes in service.

## INDUSTRIAL ALCOHOL

There were two plants engaged in the production of alcohol for industrial purposes in operation in Colorado during the fiscal year ending June 30, 1931, under permits from the federal commissioner of industrial alcohol. Two bonded warehouses in which the product is stored under government supervision and two denaturing plants to make the alcohol unfit for human consumption also operated under permits. During the year there was produced and deposited in the warehouses 55,967 proof gallons of alcohol. This compares with 28,586 gallons in 1930 and 44,246 gallons in 1929.

A summary of alcohol deposited in, withdrawn from and remaining in the bonded warehouses in the state for years ending June 30, as reported by the commissioner, in proof gallons, is as follows:

|  | 1931 | 1930 | 1929 |
|---|---|---|---|
| On hand | 1,767 | 17,777 | 21,274 |
| Produced and deposited in warehouses | 55,967 | 28,586 | 44,246 |
| Withdrawn, tax paid | 14,666 | 17,746 | 22,220 |
| Losses in warehouse | 175 | 537 | 23 |
| Withdrawn for hospital, scientific and educational uses | 13,241 | 14,183 | 14,320 |
| Transfers to denaturing warehouses | 25,950 | 12,129 | 11,173 |
| On hand end of year | 3,702 | 1,767 | 17,778 |

Materials used in producing the alcohol deposited in the warehouses in 1931 included the following:

(in pounds)

| | |
|---|---|
| Corn | 96,000 |
| Malt and malt sprouts | 63,505 |
| Potatoes | 59,876 |
| Pumpkin seed | 62 |

(in gallons)

| | |
|---|---|
| Molasses | 60,752 |
| Liquids containing one-half of 1 per cent of alcohol | 228,935 |
| | |
| Total pounds | 219,443 |
| Total gallons | 289,687 |

There were 33 manufacturers in the state in the year ending June 30, 1931, using specially denatured alcohol for manufacturing purposes, which used 8,560 gallons, compared with 33 manufacturers, using 8,983 gallons, in 1930, and 31 manufacturers, using 8,940 gallons, in 1929.

Tax-paid alcohol and other liquor received by physicians, hospitals, etc., during the fiscal year ending June 30, 1931, included the following:

Alcohol used in first-aid treatment, 14 gallons.

Hospitals engaged in treatment of recognized diseases received 26 gallons of alcohol and six gallons of whiskey.

Physicians received 1,251 gallons of alcohol.

Physicians of the homeopathic school received 49 gallons of alcohol.

Dentists received 735 gallons of alcohol.

Veterinarians received 29 gallons of alcohol.

Chiropractors and osteopaths each received one gallon of alcohol.

There were 1,546 permits in force in Colorado on June 30, 1931, which compares with 1,527 on the same date in 1930. Of those in effect in 1931, seven were to wholesale druggists, four were permits to transfer, 431 were permits to use intoxicating liquors in the manufacture of preparations unfit for use for beverage purposes and for experimental purposes, 36 were permits to use and sell, 1,003 were permits to physicians, five were permits to manufacture vinegar, three were permits to use syrups in manufacturing soft drinks, 39 were permits to hospitals, and 18 were permits to dentists, veterinarians, etc.

A new regulation went into effect permitting physicians to use prescription books. There were 1,898 physicians in the state on June 30, 1931, of whom 524, or 27.6 per cent, were using prescription books, and to these 296 prescription books had been issued.

Wine, in wine gallons, shipped or delivered in Colorado for sacramental purposes, by fiscal years ending June 30, are as follows:

| | |
|---|---|
| 1929 | 3,473 |
| 1930 | 3,599 |
| 1931 | 3,290 |

# Federal Lands and Reserves

WHILE exact figures are impossible of compilation because of the numerous federal laws and the conflict of reserves, withdrawals and classifications, it is certain that the United States government is by far the largest landholder in Colorado. The government's ownership and control of surface titles alone aggregates approximately 37 per cent of the entire area of the state, and its control of subsurface deposits covers a much larger area. A rounded estimate of the distribution of title in the surface areas of the state is approximately as follows:

| | Acres | Per Cent of Total Area |
|---|---|---|
| Federal, including Indian | 24,647,687 | 37.15 |
| State lands | 3,076,570 | 4.64 |
| Privately owned (assessed) | 37,174,876 | 56.04 |
| Unaccounted for, survey errors, etc. | 1,441,987 | 2.17 |
| Totals | 66,341,120 | 100.00 |

The state immigration bureau has made as complete a compilation of separate government titles and other varieties of surface control as is possible in the light of inaccuracies of surveys and conflicting and overlapping titles, and has found, in round numbers, the following acreages as of June 30, 1931:

| | Acres |
|---|---|
| Public domain, unappropriated and unreserved | 7,657,140 |
| Unperfected entries; public lands entered but not yet patented | 2,131,471 |
| National forests, excluding privately owned lands within their limits | 13,323,566 |
| Ute Indian lands; 39,461 privately owned and 356,682 tribal; not taxed | 396,000 |
| National parks and monuments, excluding those within national forests and included in forest areas above | 355,596 |
| Carey Act withdrawals, including 23,000 relinquished by Colorado but not restored to entry on federal records | 54,634 |
| Power reserves of all classes | 439,780 |
| Reservoir sites | 1,727 |
| Reclamation, including only public lands in reclamation projects | 5,000 |
| Public water reserves | 8,013 |
| Naval oil reserves | 64,560 |
| Stock driveways | 210,200 |
| Total | 24,647,687 |

## WITHDRAWALS AND CLASSIFICATIONS

In addition to the control and ownership of surface titles, the federal government controls the mineral deposits on vast areas of land long since in private ownership, through reservations included at the time of patent. Millions of acres, for instance have passed into private ownership through patent under the stock-grazing or 640-acre homestead law, in all of which the mineral deposits were forever reserved to the federal government, and the same is true of non-metallic minerals in most of the public domain which has passed into private ownership since passage of the oil and gas leasing acts of 1914 and 1920.

It is impossible to compile, with anything approaching accuracy, a complete statement of both surface and sub-surface control of lands in Colorado by the federal government. The withdrawals and classifications listed below include all reported by the various federal agencies and constitute in many instances duplications of the federal surface title areas shown in the preceding table. Areas on which surface titles are available but in which minerals are reserved to the federal government are included in the public domain area, and lands upon which surface titles are not available but on which mineral rights may be secured under the leasing laws are shown under stock driveways, water reserves, etc.

Federal withdrawals and classifications frequently overlap or are superimposed upon each other, and areas withdrawn or classified are reported by the federal government on the basis of all acreage included within the outer boundaries, regardless of privately owned lands or other excluded lands, so no accurate tabulation is possible. The following table, including all known withdrawals and classifications, reported in round numbers and harmonized as nearly as possible, is chiefly valuable as showing the wide variety of federal control exercised over Colorado lands under various statutes, and cannot be taken as influencing the total of surface control shown in the preceding table. The report as of June 30, 1931, since when there have been no important changes, showed the following:

**Withdrawn Lands** **Acres**

| | |
|---|---|
| Coal | 4,142,200 |
| Oil | 215,300 |
| Administrative sites | 320 |
| In aid of legislation | 16,500 |
| For classification | 573,200 |
| For national monument | 60 |
| For proposed monument | 320 |
| Pending re-survey | 567,000 |
| Public waters | 9,300 |
| Power sites | 225,500 |
| Miscellaneous power | 56,000 |
| Stock driveways | 210,200 |
| Reservoir sites | 102,500 |
| Carey act | 55,000 |
| Reclamation | 5,000 |

**Classifications**

| | |
|---|---|
| Coal | 3,082,300 |
| Oil shale | 952,200 |
| Naval oil shale | 64,600 |
| Power sites | 194,000 |

## LIMITATIONS UPON MINING

There are practically no limitations upon metal mining on the federal lands in Colorado, the outstanding exception being that no metal mining is permitted within the limits of the two national parks, aggregating 293,120 acres. The federal government exacts no royalties on the production of metal mines, and no prospecting permits are required. The mineral deposits under stock-grazing homesteads and inside the limits of withdrawn stock driveways and water reserves are open to search and development, and in the case of metallic deposits may be explored and developed without royalty or other limitation except the protection of surface property rights.

Deposits of coal, oil, gas, phosphate and other non-metallic minerals are subject to more rigid limitations and to royalty obligations to the federal government. Such deposits within the national parks and national forests are subject to the provisions of the general leasing acts of 1914 and 1920, as are lands within the limits of stock driveways, water reserves, patented stock-grazing homesteads and all other public lands coming under the provisions of the general leasing acts referred to.

Development of the minerals on public lands under the various leasing acts from the date of passage to June 30, 1931, show the following totals:

### Coal

There were outstanding June 30, 1931, 81 leases aggregating 12,609 acres, 42 permits aggregating 22,952 acres and three licenses covering 120 acres. Production, in tons, since passage of the coal leasing act, and royalties and bonuses accruing to the federal government were as follows:

| Year | Production | Royalty |
|---|---|---|
| 1912-1925 | 2,028,940 | $ 93,014 |
| 1926 | 353,434 | 60,431 |
| 1927 | 448,552 | 60,117 |
| 1928 | 439,650 | 51,076 |
| 1929 | 490,446 | 59,550 |
| 1930 | 434,871 | 55,624 |
| 1931 | 396,389 | 53,540 |
| Totals | 4,592,282 | $433,352 |

At the close of the fiscal year of 1931 there were 79 producing leases, of which 16 were classified as shipping and 63 as wagon mines.

### Oil and Gas

On June 30, 1931, there were 21 oil and gas leases in effect on public lands in Colorado, all being classed as producing, and 414 permits to prospect. Production, in barrels, since passage of the oil and gas leasing act, and royalties accruing to the federal government were as follows:

| Year | Production | Royalties |
|---|---|---|
| 1922 | 30 | $ 10 |
| 1923 | 270 | 60 |
| 1924 | 17,730 | 2,970 |
| 1925 | 409,060 | 36,750 |
| 1926 | 825,180 | 64,300 |
| 1927 | 723,190 | 55,460 |
| 1928 | 921,640 | 51,600 |
| 1929 | 962,170* | 47,300 |
| 1930 | 725,040* | 43,016 |
| 1931 | 665,320* | 33,155 |
| Totals | 5,249,630 | $334,621 |

*Also 64,360 M cu. ft. of natural gas and 73,522 gallons of gasoline in 1929; 877,430 M cu. ft. of gas and 14,642 gallons of gasoline in 1930, and 1,709,179 M cu. ft. of natural gas and 17,916 gallons of gasoline in 1931.

### Sodium

On June 30, 1931, there were two sodium prospecting permits outstanding on 2,160 acres, but no production was reported.

### Royalties Accruing to United States

| Year | Coal | Oil and Gas | Total |
|---|---|---|---|
| To 6-30-1925 | $ 93,014 | $ 39,790 | *$216,853 |
| 1926 | 60,430 | 64,300 | 124,730 |
| 1927 | 60,117 | 55,460 | 115,577 |
| 1928 | 51,076 | 51,600 | 102,676 |
| 1929 | 59,550 | 47,300 | 106,850 |
| 1930 | 55,624 | 43,016 | 98,640 |
| 1931 | †53,540 | 33,155 | 86,695 |
| Totals | $433,351 | $334,621 | *$852,021 |

*Includes $84,049 in miscellaneous royalty receipts.
†Includes $1,000 in bonuses.

### DISTRIBUTION OF PUBLIC LAND RECEIPTS

Under various public land laws the earnings from such lands within the state are distributed as follows:

From the sale of public lands and tees and commissions in connection therewith Colorado receives nothing except a 5 per cent allotment from the net proceeds of the sales of agricultural lands lying within its borders. Public land states receive no part of the fees and commissions in connection with the disposition of such lands. Under that provision, including totals for the year ending June 30, 1929, the federal government had collected from sales, fees and commissions in Colorado, $11,800,000, of which amount $521,726 was paid to the state and $10,051,927 was paid into the United States reclamation fund.

Receipts from all operations of the United States forests are divided between the federal government and the states within which the forests lie, 25 per cent of the total collections being remitted to the counties in proportion to their national forest acreages. In addition, 10 per cent of the total collections is devoted to road and trail construction within the forest where the earnings are made.

Receipts of the federal government from royalties and bonuses under the mineral leasing act are divided as follows: Ten per cent to the general treasury of the United States, 37½ per cent to the state where the royalties or bonuses are earned, for road and school purposes, and 52½ per cent to the United States reclamation fund. Actual receipts by the federal government and payments to the state of Colorado under that provision, from passage of the leasing act to June 30, 1930, were as follows:

| Year | Receipts from Colorado | Payments to Colorado |
|---|---|---|
| To 6-30-1923 | $ 26,405 | $ 9,851 |
| 1924 | 33,513 | 12,562 |
| 1925 | 71,285 | 26,647 |
| 1926 | 94,418 | 31,532 |
| 1927 | 109,047 | 40,867 |
| 1928 | 96,839 | 34,919 |
| 1929 | 101,903 | 36,816 |
| 1930 | 97,858 | 36,687 |
| 1931 | 83,581 | 31,292 |
| Totals | $714,849 | $261,173 |

The foregoing statements and tabulations showing amounts collected from operations in Colorado and amounts or proportions returned to the state do not take into consideration administrative expenditures within the state or a variety of other avenues through which a portion of the money collected in Colorado is returned to it, directly or indirectly. They include only cash returns to the state provided by law.

## DUAL USE OF PUBLIC LANDS

Most of the government's land is available for the use of the public in some form. The unappropriated and unreserved land is open for homestead and other entries. Also, the surface of coal and other mineral land withdrawn is open for entry for homesteads, the government retaining the mineral or sub-surface rights only. Most of the mineral land is subject to leasing for prospecting and development, except that on March 12, 1929, the president withdrew the privilege of filing prospecting permits for oil and gas on the public domain. Information concerning these matters may be obtained from the registers of the local land offices listed under a description of homestead land. Lands in the national forests are available for grazing and other purposes, and with the national parks, monuments and power sites, are described in more detail in articles elsewhere in this publication.

The homestead lands of the state, more fully discussed in the chapter under that title in this volume, are now administered through two local district offices, located at Denver and Pueblo, the number of local land districts having been reduced materially in recent years, owing to the fact that much of the most desirable land is now privately owned.

# Federal and State Prohibition Operations in Colorado

THE enforcement of federal prohibition laws in Colorado is under the direction of the prohibition administrator for the tenth district, comprising Colorado, Wyoming, Utah, Arizona and New Mexico, with headquarters in Denver. Carl Jackson is administrator for the district. Up to June 30, 1930, Colorado was in the eighteenth district, comprising Colorado, Wyoming and New Mexico. The division is under the supervision of the bureau of prohibition in the department of justice. The division for the issuance of permits, maintained as a separate unit since 1930, is under the bureau of industrial alcohol in the treasury department, and Colorado is in the tenth district, which is under the supervision of G. E. Ellsworth, with headquarters in Denver. Information as to the issuance of permits for alcohol, whiskey, wines, etc., quantities used, etc., and wine used for sacramental purposes will be found under the sub-heading "Industrial Alcohol."

The prohibition department omitted for reasons of economy the detailed annual report for the fiscal year ending June 30, 1931, but a summary of operations in Colorado for that period is as follows:

**Criminal Cases:**

Cases on the docket June 30, 1930 ..................... 181
Cases in which arrests were made ..................... 309
Held by commissioner........ 300
Cases placed on docket........ 192

**Terminations:**

By convictions:
Verdicts of guilty.......... 16
Pleas of guilty............. 134
By acquittals, nolle prossed, etc. ..................... 115

Unfinished cases on docket June 30, 1931..................... 108
Average jail sentence (days).... 171.4
Average fine.................... $336.04

**Equity:**
Permanent injunctions granted 18

**Law:**
Judgments of forfeiture....... 2

**Seizures:**
Autos ........................ 126
Stills ....................... 46
Beer fermenters .............. 54
Beer (gallons)................ 1,280
Spirits (gallons) ............ 2,934
Wine (gallons) ............... 1,320

Operations in Colorado in fiscal years ending June 30, 1930, and 1929, were reported as follows:

| | 1930 | 1929 |
|---|---|---|
| Illicit apparatus seized: | | |
| Distilleries .......... | 118 | 90 |
| Stills ................ | 24 | 3 |
| Still worms .......... | 74 | 2 |
| Fermenters .......... | 2,219 | 1,968 |
| Liquors seized, gallons: | | |
| Spirits .............. | 6,715 | 5,351 |
| Malt liquor........... | 3,077 | 1,338 |
| Wine ................ | 3,918 | 2,381 |
| Mash ............... | 95,708 | 73,711 |
| Autos seized .......... | 150 | 72 |
| Value autos seized..... | $59,583 | $35,385 |
| Appraised value property seized and destroyed.$ | 1,420 | $ 1,976 |
| Appraised value property seized and not destroyed ..............$ | 60,012 | $35,603 |
| Persons arrested: | | |
| By federal officers.... | 562 | 353 |
| By state officers, assisted by federal officers .............. | 790 | 510 |
| Prosecutions: | | |
| Dismissals .......... | 107 | 42 |
| Nolle prossed......... | 26 | 65 |
| Acquittals ........... | 31 | 25 |
| Convictions ......... | 267 | 231 |
| Sentences, aggregate years .............. | 81 | 84 |
| Amount of fines......$ | 48,825 | $43,517 |

The following table shows the number of stills and gallons of liquor seized, value of property (cars) seized and not destroyed, and number of persons arrested by fiscal years ending on June 30:

| Year | Stills and Apparatus Seized | Gals. Spirits, Wines, Malt, Etc., Seized | Value Property Seized and Not Destroyed | Persons Arrested |
|------|------|------|------|------|
| 1921 | 263 | 25,470 | $ 8,475 | 409 |
| 1922 | 407 | 76,769 | 21,762 | 633 |
| 1923 | 148 | 66,604 | 6,442 | 498 |
| 1924 | 189 | 57,205 | 15,907 | 502 |
| 1925 | 942 | 72,030 | 16,644 | 1,066 |
| 1926 | 236 | 201,194 | 20,216 | 745 |
| 1927 | 135 | 10,322 | 24,127 | 726 |
| 1928 | 117 | 8,148 | 31,374 | 787 |
| 1929 | 2,063 | 82,782 | 35,603 | 863 |
| 1930 | 2,435 | 109,418 | 60,012 | 1,352 |

## PROHIBITION IN COLORADO

The sixteenth general assembly of Colorado passed a local option law in the spring of 1907 which permitted the people in any individual subdivision of the commonwealth to determine by vote whether that subdivision should become anti-saloon territory.

An amendment to the state constitution prohibiting the manufacture and sale of intoxicating liquors was submitted to the people of the state at a general election on November 5, 1912. It was defeated.

A similar amendment, known as "Article XXII—Intoxicating Liquors," was submitted at a general election on November 3, 1914, and was adopted. The amendment provided that the law should become effective at midnight on December 31, 1915.

An amendment to the constitution legalizing the manufacture of beer and its sale direct to the consumer was submitted at a general election on November 16, 1916. It was defeated.

An initiated measure known as the "bone dry" act was submitted at a general election on November 5, 1918, and was adopted.

A proposal to amend Article XXII of the state constitution, permitting the manufacture and sale of light wines and beer, was submitted at a general election in 1926 and was defeated.

In 1932 a proposal to amend the constitution by a measure repealing all existing legislation and constitutional provisions governing the question of intoxicating liquors, and providing that the traffic shall be governed by legislative regulation, was submitted to popular vote. The measure, which becomes effective June 30, 1933, was carried by a majority of 50,540.

The vote on the above named measures was as follows:

| Year | For | Against |
|------|------|------|
| 1912 | 75,877 | 116,774 |
| 1914 | 129,589 | 118,017 |
| 1916 | 77,345 | 163,134 |
| 1918 | 113,636 | 64,740 |
| 1926 | 107,749 | 154,672 |
| 1932 | 233,311 | 182,771 |

Article 18, known as the liquor prohibition amendment to the federal constitution, was proposed to the legislatures of the several states by the 65th congress on December 18, 1917, and on January 29, 1919, the secretary of state of the United States proclaimed its adoption by 36 states and declared it in effect at midnight on January 16, 1920.

The Volstead act (national prohibition act) to enforce the 18th amendment was passed by congress in October, 1919. It was vetoed by President Wilson and was passed over his veto on October 28, 1919, and became effective on January 17, 1920.

The Willis-Campbell act, strengthening the prohibition act, became a law on November 23, 1921, and the Jones law, an amendment making more drastic the national prohibition act, was approved by President Coolidge on March 2, 1929.

Ten counties in Colorado had become anti-saloon territory between the enactment of the local option law in 1907 and January 1, 1916, when the statewide prohibition act went into effect. These were Delta, Larimer, Logan, Montrose, Morgan, Mesa, Phillips, Sedgwick, Washington and Yuma counties. In addition to the counties, there were a number of incorporated places which had voted for the abolition of the saloon. Approximately 54 per cent of the state's population was residing in anti-saloon territory when the state amendment went into effect.

The quantity of liquor consumed in Colorado prior to prohibition is not definitely known. In 1913, when the consumption in the country was near, or at the peak, the per capita consumption for the United States, based on the federal government's figures, was 22.68 gallons. This figure included light wines and beer. This per capita consumption applied to the 46 per cent of Colorado's population not in anti-saloon territory prior to January 1, 1916, which included the larger cities where consumption normally was heavier than in rural communities, gave an indicated annual consumption of around 10,000,000 gallons.

## VOTE ON PROHIBITION MEASURES

NOTE.—Measures voted upon were: 1912, constitutional amendment prohibiting manufacture and sale of intoxicating liquors; 1914, constitutional amendment (Art. XXII) prohibiting manufacture and sale of intoxicating liquors; 1916, amendment legalizing manufacture and sale of beer; 1918, initiated measure known as the "bone dry" act; 1926, amendment permitting manufacture and sale of light wines and beer.

| COUNTY | 1926 | | 1918 | | 1916 | | 1914 | | 1912 | |
|---|---|---|---|---|---|---|---|---|---|---|
| | For | Against | For | Against | For | Against | For | Against | For | Against |
| Adams | 1,920 | 2,197 | 1,893 | 914 | 1,095 | 1,600 | 1,180 | 1,299 | 713 | 1,397 |
| Alamosa | 970 | 987 | 517 | 374 | 329 | 1,001 | 792 | 626 | ---- | ---- |
| Arapahoe | 2,201 | 3,061 | 1,856 | 971 | 1,061 | 2,300 | 1,737 | 1,734 | 898 | 1,720 |
| Archuleta | 408 | 297 | 333 | 158 | 238 | 573 | 387 | 453 | 279 | 364 |
| Baca | 338 | 1,449 | 1,001 | 219 | 470 | 1,356 | 629 | 304 | 487 | 210 |
| Bent | 528 | 1,838 | 850 | 214 | 332 | 1,761 | 1,223 | 543 | 814 | 664 |
| Boulder | 3,189 | 7,241 | 4,047 | 2,204 | 2,828 | 7,069 | 5,852 | 3,671 | 3,637 | 3,931 |
| Chaffee | 1,238 | 1,074 | 955 | 804 | 831 | 2,099 | 1,427 | 1,380 | 966 | 1,453 |
| Cheyenne | 433 | 831 | 824 | 230 | 311 | 971 | 560 | 282 | 415 | 378 |
| Clear Creek | 545 | 435 | 539 | 515 | 558 | 927 | 723 | 890 | 349 | 1,004 |
| Conejos | 1,251 | 847 | 531 | 383 | 264 | 1,402 | 1,029 | 670 | 1,620 | 1,365 |
| Costilla | 658 | 248 | 358 | 171 | 341 | 562 | 382 | 254 | 297 | 248 |
| Crowley | 414 | 1,186 | 916 | 262 | 403 | 1,303 | 976 | 577 | 609 | 571 |
| Custer | 472 | 271 | 221 | 307 | 334 | 435 | 263 | 496 | 131 | 444 |
| Delta | 1,233 | 3,207 | 1,988 | 560 | 697 | 3,280 | 2,969 | 1,254 | 2,097 | 1,526 |
| Denver | 36,644 | 32,845 | 26,524 | 19,724 | 23,112 | 34,195 | 29,553 | 38,139 | 11,824 | 34,241 |
| Dolores | 197 | 159 | 169 | 89 | 102 | 136 | 52 | 132 | 20 | 108 |
| Douglas | 631 | 798 | 604 | 416 | 390 | 782 | 535 | 646 | 217 | 634 |
| Eagle | 659 | 492 | 383 | 372 | 438 | 781 | 539 | 722 | 280 | 694 |
| Elbert | 609 | 1,388 | 1,057 | 410 | 592 | 1,159 | 853 | 814 | 523 | 781 |
| El Paso | 4,440 | 10,353 | 6,663 | 2,877 | 3,334 | 10,551 | 9,171 | 5,144 | 4,749 | 7,206 |
| Fremont | 1,903 | 5,203 | 2,714 | 1,324 | 1,331 | 3,799 | 3,277 | 2,197 | 2,713 | 2,429 |
| Garfield | 1,356 | 1,519 | 1,316 | 711 | 854 | 2,261 | 1,887 | 1,447 | 1,241 | 1,675 |
| Gilpin | 384 | 168 | 157 | 393 | 433 | 495 | 432 | 715 | 163 | 681 |
| Grand | 531 | 400 | 303 | 266 | 340 | 374 | 277 | 564 | 182 | 427 |
| Gunnison | 1,025 | 872 | 647 | 646 | 753 | 1,265 | 793 | 1,261 | 492 | 1,110 |
| Hinsdale | 94 | 84 | 99 | 76 | 66 | 157 | 111 | 100 | 49 | 161 |
| Huerfano | 1,037 | 1,273 | 1,399 | 1,637 | 1,331 | 1,958 | 1,871 | 2,031 | 942 | 1,930 |
| Jackson | 174 | 185 | 209 | 100 | 115 | 261 | 170 | 224 | 124 | 172 |
| Jefferson | 2,831 | 3,416 | 2,439 | 1,461 | 1,802 | 2,881 | 2,328 | 2,721 | 1,105 | 2,761 |
| Kiowa | 241 | 1,015 | 918 | 261 | 356 | 1,099 | 812 | 378 | 673 | 336 |
| Kit Carson | 654 | 2,331 | 1,456 | 472 | 587 | 1,585 | 1,005 | 664 | 755 | 607 |
| Lake | 1,510 | 486 | 588 | 1,327 | 1,680 | 1,492 | 1,149 | 2,420 | 638 | 2,134 |
| La Plata | 1,652 | 1,716 | 840 | 656 | 685 | 2,265 | 1,528 | 1,438 | 1,055 | 1,552 |
| Larimer | 2,007 | 6,344 | 3,757 | 1,207 | 1,316 | 5,435 | 4,106 | 2,333 | 3,026 | 2,642 |
| Las Animas | 3,978 | 3,164 | 2,825 | 2,303 | 3,327 | 3,105 | 2,596 | 5,416 | 1,340 | 5,430 |
| Lincoln | 760 | 1,543 | 1,316 | 458 | 632 | 1,783 | 1,123 | 743 | 699 | 700 |
| Logan | 1,405 | 3,052 | 2,350 | 818 | 867 | 2,766 | 1,956 | 1,031 | 1,327 | 866 |
| Mesa | 2,063 | 4,800 | 3,176 | 1,204 | 1,447 | 4,951 | 3,883 | 2,349 | 3,546 | 2,310 |
| Mineral | 149 | 64 | 101 | 135 | 106 | 249 | 215 | 184 | 145 | 311 |
| Moffat | 440 | 737 | 606 | 168 | 247 | 865 | 350 | 375 | 310 | 309 |
| Montezuma | 610 | 865 | 615 | 240 | 280 | 1,292 | 1,015 | 498 | 560 | 588 |
| Montrose | 824 | 2,767 | 1,861 | 746 | 768 | 2,725 | 2,420 | 1,208 | 1,506 | 1,106 |
| Morgan | 1,010 | 2,714 | 2,184 | 672 | 885 | 2,558 | 1,900 | 1,021 | 1,327 | 930 |
| Otero | 1,356 | 4,425 | 3,115 | 1,010 | 1,335 | 4,776 | 4,286 | 1,695 | 2,701 | 1,621 |
| Ouray | 386 | 318 | 420 | 289 | 286 | 828 | 703 | 655 | 388 | 735 |
| Park | 440 | 296 | 412 | 248 | 349 | 440 | 291 | 550 | 101 | 434 |
| Phillips | 495 | 1,322 | 702 | 270 | 292 | 862 | 555 | 376 | 497 | 330 |
| Pitkin | 515 | 260 | 403 | 358 | 406 | 624 | 412 | 644 | 234 | 738 |
| Prowers | 769 | 2,777 | 1,693 | 573 | 690 | 2,819 | 1,818 | 934 | 1,376 | 986 |
| Pueblo | 7,090 | 9,376 | 6,730 | 4,721 | 5,949 | 9,777 | 1,739 | 8,273 | 4,941 | 8,619 |
| Rio Blanco | 462 | 427 | 416 | 272 | 316 | 606 | 321 | 500 | 166 | 488 |
| Rio Grande | 770 | 1,482 | 988 | 405 | 442 | 1,742 | 1,458 | 560 | 1,106 | 770 |
| Routt | 985 | 1,342 | 1,105 | 481 | 766 | 1,703 | 1,158 | 1,080 | 722 | 953 |
| Saguache | 740 | 669 | 612 | 324 | 310 | 1,080 | 871 | 689 | 444 | 688 |
| San Juan | 342 | 127 | 156 | 135 | 322 | 406 | 216 | 636 | 157 | 552 |
| San Miguel | 606 | 371 | 574 | 440 | 555 | 955 | 688 | 1,098 | 474 | 970 |
| Sedgwick | 425 | 842 | 605 | 356 | 261 | 649 | 500 | 378 | 453 | 242 |
| Summit | 345 | 234 | 247 | 289 | 284 | 477 | 315 | 511 | 201 | 535 |
| Teller | 1,319 | 667 | 1,082 | 932 | 1,844 | 2,772 | 2,558 | 2,480 | 1,267 | 2,694 |
| Washington | 539 | 1,931 | 1,574 | 661 | 721 | 1,452 | 893 | 767 | 591 | 567 |
| Weld | 3,727 | 9,114 | 6,863 | 2,731 | 2,951 | 8,779 | 7,471 | 3,830 | 4,182 | 3,699 |
| Yuma | 822 | 2,770 | 1,834 | 789 | 998 | 2,523 | 1,800 | 1,008 | 1,063 | 1,047 |
| Total | 107,749 | 154,672 | 113,636 | *64,740 | 77,345 | 163,134 | *129,589 | *118,017 | *75,877 | 116,774 |

*The totals used are those taken from the published official abstract of votes, although they do not agree with the totals of the county figures. It is impossible at this time to locate and correct the errors. See preceding page for result of 1932 election on prohibition repeal.

# Persons in Governmental Service

A SURVEY undertaken in 1927 for the purpose of ascertaining as nearly as possible the number of salaried officials and employes engaged in all branches of governmental service in Colorado shows a total of 25,292. This total does not include seasonal employes paid on a daily wage basis, such as laborers on road construction, in the national forests and on reclamation projects, or officials of a number of small incorporated towns who receive no compensation for their services, but does include a considerable number of officials and employes of small towns who receive only nominal salaries, and members of the national guard and other persons who devote only a part of their time to governmental service.

The survey was the first of the kind undertaken by this department and yielded some unexpected results. The questionnaires sought information on the number of salaried officials and employes only, and while the total appears large, it was found that a considerable per cent of the number do not depend upon compensation for governmental services for a livelihood.

The public school system of the state accounted for the largest number of salaried officials and employes, there being 9,514 teachers and 650 administrative officials and employes, including janitors, the last-named figure being partially estimated, as complete data are not available.

The federal government occupies second place, with 6,922 salaried officials and employes in the state. This number includes those employed in the national forests, in the reclamation service, the postoffice department, railway mail service, inspection bureans and government hospitals. It also includes the national guard of the state, members of which receive one day's salary per week for services in attending drill. Postmasters and postoffice employes throughout the state make up a considerable part of the total. The figure does not include approximately 1,000 seasonal employes engaged in work in the national forests, on reclamation work, and similar enterprises who are not on a salary basis and whose work is confined mostly to the summer months. While the number of federal officials and employes is comparatively large, many of these have jurisdiction over areas greater in extent than that of the state, being identified with regional offices.

The cities and towns of the state occupy third place, with a total of 4,237 reported for 213 incorporated places. Denver ranked first, with a total of 2,250; Colorado Springs second with 346 and Pueblo third with 220. The Colorado Springs figures include salaried employes of the light and power and water system, which are municipally owned. Denver's figures are not included in the total for counties, since the city and county of Denver are coextensive. Twenty-two incorporated towns reported that they had no salaried officials or employes. Nine towns failed to reply to questionnaires and no estimates were made for these. The largest town not reporting was Trinidad. One town reported that its officials received salaries of one dollar each per year. Another reported eight officials receiving salaries of one dollar per month each, while several reported only nominal salaries paid.

The state government reported a total of 2,315 salaried officials and employes. This number includes all executive and administrative departments, the supreme and district courts, members of the legislature and legislative employes, the penal and eleemosynary institutions and state colleges and universities. The state educational institutions rank first in number, there being a total of 660, of whom 555 are professors and instructors. This figure, however, does not include the faculties of summer schools, many of which embrace members of the faculty for the regular terms. The Colorado State hospital comes next, with a total of 287. There are 100 members and 94 employes of the legislature included in the number. The highway department comes next with 120, the penitentiary next with 80, and the fish and game department next with 62. The military department reported 26, the remainder of that branch being paid by the federal government.

The counties of the state reported the lowest number of employes of any of the political subdivisions, the total being 1,654. Fifty-seven counties reported a total of 1,564, and five counties, from which no reports were received, are estimated at 90.

# Government and Political Record

THE accompanying list gives the names of all senators, representatives and governors of Colorado since the creation of Colorado territory in 1861. The lists of other state officials include only the names of those elected to the various offices since the admission of Colorado into the Union as a state, in 1876, and the time each served. A star (*) indicates that the incumbent died in office.

## ELECTED STATE OFFICIALS

### Delegates and Representatives to Congress

Hiram J. Graham (Delegate for people of Pike's Peak). 1858-1859
Beverly D. Williams (Delegate from "Jefferson Territory") 1859-1860

### Territorial Representatives

| | |
|---|---|
| Hiram P. Bennett | 1861-1865 |
| Allen A. Bradford | 1865-1867 |
| George M. Chilcott | 1867-1869 |
| Allen A. Bradford | 1869-1871 |
| Jerome B. Chaffee | 1871-1875 |
| Thomas M. Patterson | 1875-1876 |

### State Representatives in Congress

| | |
|---|---|
| James B. Belford (R) | 1876-1877 |
| Thomas M. Patterson (D) | 1877-1879 |
| James B. Belford (R) | 1879-1885 |
| George G. Symes (R) | 1885-1889 |
| Hosea Townsend (R) | 1889-1893 |
| John C. Bell (R) | 1893-1903 |
| Lafe Pence (P) | 1893-1895 |
| John F. Shafroth (R) | 1895-1903 |
| Robert W. Bonynge (R) | 1903-1909 |
| Herschel M. Hogg (R) | 1903-1907 |
| Franklin E. Brooks (R) | 1903-1907 |
| George W. Cook (R) | 1907-1909 |
| Warren A. Haggot (R) | 1907-1909 |
| Atterson W. Rucker (D) | 1909-1913 |
| John A. Martin (D) | 1909-1913 |
| Edward Keating (D) | 1913-1919 |
| George J. Kindel (D) | 1913-1915 |
| H. H. Seldomridge (D) | 1913-1915 |
| B. C. Hilliard (D) | 1915-1919 |
| William N. Vaile (R) | *1919-1927 |
| S. Harrison White (D) | 1927-1928 |
| Charles B. Timberlake (R) | 1915-1933 |
| Guy U. Hardy (R) | 1919-1933 |
| William R. Eaton (R) | 1928-1933 |
| Edward T. Taylor (D) | 1909—— |
| Lawrence Lewis (D) | 1933—— |
| Fred Cummings (D) | 1933—— |
| John A. Martin (D) | 1933—— |

### United States Senators

| | |
|---|---|
| Henry M. Teller (R) | 1876-1882 |
| Jerome B. Chaffee (R) | 1876-1879 |
| Nathaniel P. Hill (R) | 1879-1885 |
| George M. Chilcott (R) | 1882 |
| Horace A. W. Tabor (R.) | 1883 |
| Thomas M. Bowen (R) | 1883-1889 |
| Henry M. Teller (R) and (D) | 1885-1909 |
| Edward O. Wolcott (R) | 1889-1901 |
| Thomas M. Patterson (D) | 1901-1907 |
| Simon Guggenheim (R) | 1907-1913 |
| Charles J. Hughes, Jr. (D) | 1909-1911 |
| Charles S. Thomas (D) | 1913-1921 |
| John F. Shafroth (D) | 1913-1919 |
| Lawrence C. Phipps (R) | 1919-1931 |

| | |
|---|---|
| S. D. Nicholson (R) | 1921-1923 |
| Alva B. Adams (D) | 1923-1925 |
| Rice W. Means (R) | 1925-1927 |
| Charles W. Waterman (R) | *1927-1932 |
| Edward P. Costigan (D) | 1931—— |
| Walter Walker (D) | 1932 |
| Karl C. Schuyler (R) | 1932-1933 |
| Alva B. Adams (D) | 1933—— |

### Justices of the Supreme Court

| | |
|---|---|
| Benjamin F. Hall | 1861-1865 |
| Charles Lee Armour | 1861-1865 |
| Allen A. Bradford | 1862-1865 |
| Stephen S. Harding | 1863-1865 |
| Charles F. Holly | 1865-1866 |
| William H. Gale | 1865-1866 |
| Moses Hallett | 1866-1876 |
| Wm. R. Gorsline | 1866-1870 |
| Christian S. Eyster | 1866-1871 |
| James B. Belford | 1870-1875 |
| Ebenezer T. Wells | 1871-1875, 1877 |
| Andrew W. Brazee | 1875-1876 |
| Amherst W. Stone | 1875-1876 |
| Henry C. Thatcher | 1877-1879 |
| Samuel H. Elbert | 1877-1888 |
| Wilbur F. Stone | 1877-1886 |
| William E. Beck | 1879-1889 |
| Joseph C. Helm | 1879-1892, 1907-1909 |
| Melville B. Gerry | 1888-1889 |
| Victor A. Elliott | 1889-1895 |
| Charles D. Hayt | 1889-1898 |
| Luther M. Goddard | 1891-1901, 1905-1909 |
| William H. Gabbert | 1897-1917 |
| Robert W. Steele | 1901-1911 |
| Julius C. Gunter | 1905-1907 |
| John M. Maxwell | 1905-1909 |
| George W. Bailey | 1905-1909 |
| Charles F. Caswell | *1907-1907 |
| Morton S. Bailey | 1909-1917 |
| William A. Hill | 1909-1919 |
| George W. Musser | 1909-1915 |
| S. Harrison White | 1909-1919 |
| James E. Garrigues | 1909-1919 |
| Tully Scott | 1913-1923 |
| James T. Teller | 1915-1925 |
| George W. Allen | 1917-1927 |
| John H. Denison | 1919-1929 |
| John W. Sheafor | *1923-1928 |
| R. Hickman Walker | 1928 |
| Greeley W. Whitford | 1921-1931 |
| Wilbur M. Alter | 1928-1933 |
| Haslett P. Burke | 1919—— |
| John Campbell | 1895-1913, 1923—— |
| John T. Adams | 1925—— |
| Charles C. Butler | 1927—— |
| Julian H. Moore | 1929—— |
| Benjamin C. Hilliard | 1931—— |
| Francis E. Bouck | 1933—— |

### Justices of Court of Appeals

| | |
|---|---|
| George Q. Richmond | 1891-1893 |
| Julius B. Bissell | 1891-1893 |
| Gilbert B. Reed | 1891-1893 |
| Charles I. Thompson | 1893-1899 |
| Adair Wilson | 1896-1905 |
| Julius C. Gunter | 1901-1905 |
| John M. Maxwell | 1903-1905 |
| Tully Scott | 1912-1913 |
| Edwin W. Hurlbut | 1912-1915 |
| Stuart W. Walling | 1912-1915 |
| Louis W. Cunningham | 1912-1915 |
| Alfred R. King | 1912-1915 |
| John C. Bell | 1913-1915 |
| William B. Morgan | 1913-1915 |

## Territorial Governor

| | |
|---|---|
| William Gilpin | 1861-1862 |
| John Evans | 1862-1865 |
| Alexander Cummings | 1865-1867 |
| A. C. Hunt | 1867-1869 |
| Edward McCook | 1869-1873 |
| Samuel H. Elbert | 1873-1874 |
| Edward McCook | 1874-1875 |
| John L. Routt | 1875-1876 |

## State Governor

| | |
|---|---|
| John L. Routt | 1876-1879 |
| Frederick R. Pitkin | 1879-1883 |
| James B. Grant | 1883-1885 |
| Benjamin H. Eaton | 1885-1887 |
| Alva Adams | 1887-1889 |
| Job A. Cooper | 1889-1891 |
| John L. Routt | 1891-1893 |
| Davis H. Waite | 1893-1895 |
| Albert W. McIntire | 1895-1897 |
| Alva Adams | 1897-1899 |
| Charles S. Thomas | 1899-1901 |
| James B. Orman | 1901-1903 |
| James H. Peabody | 1903-1905 |
| Alva Adams | 1905 |
| James H. Peabody | 1905 |
| Jesse F. McDonald | 1905-1907 |
| Henry A. Buchtel | 1907-1909 |
| John F. Shafroth | 1909-1913 |
| Elias M. Ammons | 1913-1915 |
| George A. Carlson | 1915-1917 |
| Julius C. Gunter | 1917-1919 |
| Oliver H. Shoup | 1919-1923 |
| William E. Sweet | 1923-1925 |
| Clarence J. Morley | 1925-1927 |
| William H. Adams | 1927-1933 |
| Edwin C. Johnson | 1933—— |

## Lieutenant Governor

| | |
|---|---|
| Lafayette Head | 1877-1879 |
| Horace A. W. Tabor | 1879-1883 |
| William H. Meyers | 1883-1885 |
| Peter W. Breene | 1885-1887 |
| Norman H. Meldrum | 1887-1889 |
| William G. Smith | 1889-1891 |
| William Story | 1891-1893 |
| David H. Nichols | 1893-1895 |
| Jared L. Brush | 1895-1899 |
| Francis Carney | 1899-1901 |
| David C. Coates | 1901-1903 |
| Warren H. Haggott | 1903-1905 |
| Arthur Cornforth | 1905-1907 |
| E. R. Harper | 1907-1909 |
| Stephen R. Fitzgarrald | 1909-1915 |
| Moses E. Lewis | 1915-1917 |
| James E. Pulliam | 1917-1919 |
| George Stephan | 1919-1921 |
| Earl Cooley | 1921-1923 |
| Robert F. Rockwell | 1923-1925 |
| Sterling B. Lacy | 1925-1927 |
| George M. Corlett | 1927-1931 |
| Edwin C. Johnson | 1931-1933 |
| Ray H. Talbot | 1933—— |

## Secretary of State

| | |
|---|---|
| William M. Clark | 1877-1879 |
| Norman H. Meldrum | 1879-1883 |
| Melvin Edwards | 1883-1887 |
| James Rice | 1887-1891 |
| Edwin J. Eaton | 1891-1893 |
| Nelson O. McClees | 1893-1895 |
| Albert B. McGaffey | 1895-1897 |
| Charles H. S. Whipple | 1897-1899 |
| Elmer F. Beckwith | 1899-1901 |
| David F. Mills | 1901-1903 |
| James Cowie | 1903-1907 |
| Timothy O'Connor | 1907-1909 |
| James B. Pearce | 1909-1915 |
| John E. Ramer | 1915-1917 |
| James R. Noland | 1917-1921 |
| Carl S. Milliken | 1921-1927 |
| Charles M. Armstrong | 1927—— |

## State Treasurer

| | |
|---|---|
| George C. Corning | 1877-1879 |
| Nathan S. Culver | 1879-1881 |
| W. S. Sanders | 1881-1883 |
| Fred Walson | 1883-1885 |
| George R. Swallow | 1885-1887 |
| Peter W. Breene | 1887-1889 |
| W. H. Bisbane | 1889-1891 |
| James N. Carlile | 1891-1893 |
| Albert Nance | 1893-1895 |
| Harry E. Mulnix | 1895-1897 |
| George W. Kephart | 1897-1899 |
| John H. Fesler | 1899-1901 |
| James N. Chipley | 1901-1903 |
| Witney Newton | 1903-1905 |
| John A. Holmberg | 1905-1907 |
| Alfred E. Bent | 1907-1909 |
| William J. Galligan | 1909-1911 |
| Roady Keneban | 1911-1913 |
| Michael A. Leddy | 1913-1915 |
| Allison E. Stocker | 1915-1917 |
| Robert H. Higgins | 1917-1919 |
| Harry E. Mulnix | 1919-1921 |
| Arthur M. Stong | 1921-1923 |
| Harry E. Mulnix | 1923-1925 |
| William D. MacGinnis | 1925-1927 |
| Harry E. Mulnix | *1927 |
| Herbert Fairall | 1927-1929 |
| William D. MacGinnis | 1929-1931 |
| John M. Jackson | 1931-1933 |
| Homer F. Bedford | 1933—— |

## Auditor of State

| | |
|---|---|
| David C. Crawford | 1877-1879 |
| Eugene K. Stimson | 1879-1881 |
| Joseph A. Davis | 1881-1883 |
| J. C. Abbott | 1883-1885 |
| Hiram A. Spurance | 1885-1887 |
| Darwin P. Kingsley | 1887-1889 |
| L. B. Schwanbeck | 1889-1891 |
| John M. Henderson | 1891-1893 |
| F. M. Goodykoontz | 1893-1895 |
| Clifford C. Parks | 1895-1897 |
| John W. Lowell | 1897-1899 |
| George W. Temple | 1899-1901 |
| Charles W. Crowter | 1901-1903 |
| John A. Holmberg | 1903-1905 |
| Alfred E. Bent | 1905-1907 |
| George D. Statler | 1907-1909 |
| Roady Kenehan | 1909-1911 |
| Michael A. Leddy | 1911-1913 |
| Roady Kenehan | 1913-1915 |
| Harry E. Mulnix | 1915-1917 |
| Charles H. Leckenby | 1917-1919 |
| Arthur M. Stong | 1919-1921 |
| Harry E. Mulnix | 1921-1923 |
| Arthur M. Stong | 1923-1925 |
| Charles Davis | 1925-1927 |
| W. D. MacGinnis | 1927-1929 |
| John M. Jackson | 1929-1931 |
| William D. MacGinnis | 1931-1933 |
| Benj. F. Stapleton | 1933—— |

## Attorney General

| | |
|---|---|
| A. J. Sampson | 1877-1879 |
| Charles W. Wright | 1879-1881 |
| Charles Toll | 1881-1883 |
| D. C. Urmy | 1883-1885 |
| Theodore H. Thomas | 1885-1887 |
| Alvin Marsh | 1887-1889 |
| Samuel W. Jones | 1889-1891 |
| Joseph H. Maupin | 1891-1893 |
| Eugene Engley | 1893-1895 |
| Byron L. Carr | 1895-1899 |

| | |
|---|---|
| David M. Campbell | 1899-1901 |
| Charles C. Post | 1901-1903 |
| Nathan C. Miller | 1903-1907 |
| William H. Dickson | 1907-1909 |
| John T. Barnett | 1909-1911 |
| Benjamin J. Griffith | 1911-1913 |
| Fred Farrar | 1913-1917 |
| Leslie E. Hubbard | 1917-1919 |
| Victor E. Keyes | 1919-1923 |
| Russell W. Fleming | *1923 |
| Wayne C. Williams | 1924-1925 |
| William L. Boatright | 1925-1929 |
| Robert E. Winbourn | *1929 |
| John S. Underwood | *1930 |
| Clarence L. Ireland | 1931-1933 |
| Paul P. Prosser | 1933—— |

**Superintendent of Public Instruction**

| | |
|---|---|
| Joseph C. Shattuck | 1877-1881 |
| Leonidas S. Cornell | 1881-1883 |
| Joseph C. Shattuck | 1883-1885 |
| Leonidas S. Cornell | 1885-1889 |
| Fred Dick | 1889-1891 |
| Nathan Coy | 1891-1893 |
| John F. Murray | 1893-1895 |
| Angenette J. Peavey | 1895-1897 |
| Grace Espey Patton | 1897-1899 |
| Helen L. Grenfell | 1899-1905 |
| Katherine L. Craig | 1905-1909 |
| Katherine Cook | 1909-1911 |
| Helen M. Wixon | 1911-1913 |
| Mary C. C. Bradford | 1913-1921 |
| Katherine L. Craig | 1921-1923 |
| Mary C. C. Bradford | 1923-1927 |
| Katherine L. Craig | 1927-1931 |
| Inez Johnson Lewis | 1931—— |

## DISTRICT JUDGES AND DISTRICT ATTORNEYS

Note—Terms of District Judges and District Attorneys expire January 12, 1937. Salary of District Judges is $4,000 per annum.

| District | Judge | Party | District Attorney | Party | Address |
|---|---|---|---|---|---|
| First—Gilpin, Clear Creek, Arapahoe, Jefferson, Adams | Johnson, Samuel W. | D | Behm, Harry | D | Brighton |
| Second—Denver | McDonough, Frank, Sr. | R | Wettengel, Earl | R | Denver |
| | Calvert, H. A. | R | | | |
| | Dunklee, George F. | D | | | |
| | Holland, E. V. | D | | | |
| | Sackmann, Charles C. | R | | | |
| | Starkweather, Jas. C. | R | | | |
| | Steele, Robert W. | D | | | |
| Third—Baca, Bent, Huerfano, Las Animas, Prowers | Hollenbeck, A. F. | D | East, John L. | D | Walsenburg |
| | McChesney, A. C. | D | | | |
| Fourth—Cheyenne, Douglas, Elbert, El Paso, Kit Carson, Lincoln, Teller | Cornforth, Arthur | R | Starrett, Clyde L. | D | Colorado Springs |
| | Young, John C. | D | | | |
| Fifth—Eagle, Lake, Summit | *Bouck, Francis E. | D | Meehan, Wm. J. | D | Eagle |
| Sixth—Archuleta, Dolores, La Plata, Montezuma, San Juan | O'Rourke, John B. | D | Noland, James M. | D | Durango |
| Seventh—Delta, Gunnison, Hinsdale, Mesa, Montrose, Ouray, San Miguel | Bruce, George W. | D | Haywood, Wm. F. | D | Grand Junction |
| | Logan, Straud M. | R | | | |
| Eighth—Boulder, Jackson, Larimer, Weld | Coffin, Claude C. | R | Baker, Herbert M. | D | Longmont |
| | Graham, Neil F. | D | | | |
| Ninth—Pitkin, Garfield, Rio Blanco | Shumate, John T. | D | Delaney, Frank | D | Glenwood Springs |
| Tenth—Crowley, Kiowa, Otero, Pueblo | Trimble, Samuel D. | D | Taylor, French L. | D | Pueblo |
| | Voorhees, John H. | D | | | |
| Eleventh—Chaffee, Custer, Fremont, Park | Cooper, James L. | R | Locke, James T. | D | Canon City |
| Twelfth—Alamosa, Conejos, Costilla, Mineral, Rio Grande, Saguache | Palmer, John I. | R | Haynie, L. M. | D | Manassa |
| Thirteenth—Logan, Morgan, Phillips, Sedgwick, Washington, Yuma | Munson, Halley E. | R | Johnson, Roy T. | R | Sterling |
| | Taylor, Arlington | R | | | |
| Fourteenth—Grand, Moffat, Routt | Herrick, C. H. | D | Monson, C. R. | D | Steamboat Spgs. |

*Elected to Colorado Supreme Court. Vacancy to be filled by appointment.

## COLORADO STATE OFFICIALS FOR 1933-1934.

(Note—This list includes officers holding over or elected at the November, 1932, election. Officers retiring after that election, except for one vacancy appointment, appear in the Year Book for 1931.

### United States Senators

Edward P. Costigan..Dem.... ............Term: March 4, 1931, to March 4, 1937
Walter Walker......Dem................Appointed to fill Vacancy due to the death of Charles W. Waterman, serving to Dec. 7, 1932.
Karl C. Schuyler.....Rep.................Elected to fill Vacancy. Term Dec. 7, 1932, to March 4, 1933.
Alva B. Adams......Dem................Term: March 4, 1933, to March 4, 1939.

The salary of a United States senator is $9,000 per annum.

### Congressmen

Lawrence Lewis...........Dem..............First District..............Denver
Fred Cummings...........Dem...............Second District.......Fort Collins
John A. Martin...........Dem..............Third District.............Pueblo
Edward T. Taylor........Dem...............Fourth District..Glenwood Springs

Terms of all congressmen expire March 4, 1935. The salary is $9,000 per annum.

### Executive State Officers

Governor ................Edwin C. Johnson............Dem..............Craig
Lieutenant-Governor ......Ray H. Talbot.................Dem...........Pueblo
Secretary of State.........Charles M. Armstrong......... Rep...........Denver
Treasurer ...............Homer F. Bedford.............Dem..........Greeley
Auditor ..................Benjamin F. Stapleton..........Dem...........Denver
Attorney General.........Paul P. Prosser................Dem...........Denver
Supt. Public Instruction....Inez Johnson Lewis............Dem..Colorado Springs

Terms of state executive officials expire in January, 1935. Salaries per annum are as follows: Governor, $5,000; lieutenant-governor, $1,000; treasurer, $6,000; secretary of state, $4,000; auditor, $4,000; attorney general, $5,000; superintendent of public instruction, $3,000.

### Justices of the Supreme Court

John T. Adams, Rep., Chief Justice, Alamosa

Charles C. Butler, Rep., Denver
Haslett P. Burke, Rep., Sterling
Benjamin C. Hilliard, Dem., Denver

John Campbell, Rep., Colorado Springs
Julian H. Moore, Rep., Denver
Francis E. Bouck, Dem., Leadville

The justices of the supreme court receive salaries of $5,000 and are elected for terms of ten years.

## OFFICIAL AND OTHER BIRDS

The twenty-eighth general assembly of the Colorado legislature passed an act in 1931 declaring the Lark Bunting, scientifically known as Calamospiza Melanocorys Stejneger, to be the official state bird. The act was approved by Governor William H. Adams on April 29, 1931. The Lark Bunting is six to seven inches long, with a stout, conical bill and long, pointed wings. The male has black feathers with white edgings on the tail and wings and the female is brown with white edgings. It is an inhabitant of the prairie country, does not frequent the mountains and is to be found mostly in the eastern part of the state. It is seldom seen on the western slope of the mountains. The bird migrates to the south, usually about the 10th of September, and returns about the same date in May. It usually arrives in large flocks. It builds its nest on the ground. One of its peculiar characteristics is the method of its flight. It rises almost perpendicularly from the ground and invariably sings as it mounts upward. It is noted as a singer.

Between 405 and 420 species of birds are to be found in Colorado, the number including migratory birds that remain only for a season. All known species are on exhibition at the Colorado museum of natural history in Denver, either mounted individually or in groups or in study collections.

## STATE SENATORS
### (29th General Assembly)

Key: R. Republican; D. Democrat; H-O. Holdover; E. Elected in 1932; term, November, 1932-November, 1936. The term of Holdover Senators expires November, 1934.

| Dist. | Name | Party | Address | Counties in District |
|---|---|---|---|---|
| 1st | Gilliam, Edward R. | D.E. | 1330 High St., Denver | Denver |
| | Healey, John F., Jr. | D.E. | 1601 Adams St., Denver | Denver |
| | Hill, Vern S. | D.E. | 715 E. 10th Ave., Denver | Denver |
| | Ammons, Teller | D.H-O. | 2062 Eudora St., Denver | Denver |
| | Kettering, Chas. E. | D.H-O. | 1361 Bellaire St., Denver | Denver |
| | Manley, George C. | R.H-O. | 755 Lafayette St., Denver | Denver |
| | Quiat, Ira L. | D.H-O. | 2388 Ash St., Denver | Denver |
| 2nd | Horn, Chas. F. | D.H-O. | 111 W. 12th St., Pueblo | Pueblo |
| | Ritchie, Curtis P. | D.E. | 1101 E. 8th St., Pueblo | Pueblo |
| 3rd | Brady, Emory J. | R.H-O. | Colorado Springs | El Paso |
| | Elliot, David | R.E. | Colorado Springs | El Paso |
| 4th | Madrid, J. M. | R.E. | Trinidad | Las Animas |
| 5th | Affolter, Edward | D.E. | Boulder | Boulder |
| 6th | Ehrhart, Thos. J. | D.H-O. | Centerville | Chaffee, Lake |
| 7th | Wheeler, Chas. F. | D.E. | Greeley | Weld |
| 8th | Broad, Richard, Jr. | R.E. | Golden | Jefferson |
| 9th | Smith, Lynn | D.E. | Florence | Fremont |
| 10th | Warren, Nate C. | R.H-O. | Fort Collins | Larimer |
| 11th | Hotchkiss, Clair | D.E. | Hotchkiss | Gunnison, Delta |
| 12th | King, John H. | D.H-O. | Sterling | Logan, Sedgwick, Phillips, Washington, Yuma |
| 13th | Walbridge, L. B. | D.E. | Meeker | Jackson, Routt, Rio Blanco, Moffat |
| 14th | Unfug, Adolph | R.H-O. | Walsenburg | Costilla, Huerfano, Custer |
| 15th | Headlee, A. Elmer | D.H-O. | Monte Vista | Rio Grande, Saguache, Mineral |
| 16th | Bannister, Ollie E. | D.H-O. | Grand Junction | Mesa |
| 17th | Knous, Lee | D.H-O. | Montrose | Dolores, Montrose, San Miguel |
| 18th | Rumbaugh, Chas. F. | D.H-O. | Pagosa Springs | Archuleta, Hinsdale, Ouray, San Juan |
| 19th | Sanders, Grant | D.E. | Durango | La Plata, Montezuma |
| 20th | Peiffer, Vernon | D.H-O. | Cripple Creek | Teller, Park |
| 21st | Gaylord, Fred | D.E. | Rifle | Eagle, Garfield, Pitkin |
| 22nd | Houston, Harvey H. | D.E. | Aurora | Adams, Arapahoe, Morgan |
| 23rd | Hunter, D. E. | D.E. | Manzanola | Crowley, Otero |
| 24th | Christensen, Fred T. | D.E. | Sanford | Conejos, Alamosa |
| 25th | Tempel, Fred A. | R.H-O. | Wiley | Baca, Bent, Kiowa, Prowers |
| 26th | Herrin, V. C. | D.E. | Idaho Springs | Clear Creek, Gilpin, Grand, Summit |
| 27th | Nelson, Henry C. | R.H-O. | Cheyenne Wells | Kit Carson, Cheyenne, Douglas, Elbert, Lincoln |

Note.—The senate is composed of 26 Democrats and 9 Republicans.

## STATE REPRESENTATIVES
(29th General Assembly)

Note.—Terms of Representatives expire November, 1934.

| District | Name | Party | Address |
|---|---|---|---|
| Adams | Preston, Willard B. | R | Adena |
| Alamosa | Woodard, Dave S. | D | 212 Poncha Ave., Alamosa |
| Arapahoe-Elbert | Prather, A. G. | D | 3361 So. Logan St., Englewood |
| Boulder | Burke, Robert F. | D | R. F. D. No. 1, Boulder |
| Boulder | Bixler, Frank | R | R. F. D., Lafayette |
| Chaffee | Burnett, J. A. | D | Poncha Springs |
| Clear Creek | Barrick, Wm. H. | D | Dumont |
| Conejos | *Atencio, H. J. | R | La Jara |
| Crowley-Otero | Trainor, J. J. | D | Ordway |
| Crowley-Otero | Bishop, N. D. | D | La Junta |
| Delta | Tinsley, A. C. | D | Paonia |
| Denver | Morris, David H. | D | 2968 Birch St., Denver |
| Denver | Constantine, Joseph P. | D | 1649 St. Paul St., Denver |
| Denver | Brownlow, James A. | D | 637 So. Corona St., Denver |
| Denver | Newman, Joseph Evans | D | 548 Logan St., Denver |
| Denver | Hirschfeld, A. B. | D | 1474 Bellaire St., Denver |
| Denver | Vincent, Craig S. | D | 801 E. 8th Ave., Denver |
| Denver | Keating, Bert | D | 4336 Zuni St., Denver |
| Denver | Cullen, William E. | D | 3208 Curtis St., Denver |
| Denver | Palmer, Robert S. | D | 1312 Lafayette St., Denver |
| Denver | Moynahan, James S. | D | 1520 Glenarm St., Denver |
| Denver | Burns, T. Mitchell, Jr. | D | 360 Clermont St., Denver |
| Denver | Kavanagh, Wm. P. | R | 1474 Clayton St., Denver |
| Douglas | Seidensticker, Edward G. | D | Castle Rock |
| Eagle | Johns, Harry C. | D | Gypsum |
| El Paso | Hillman, Charles A. | D | Calhan |
| El Paso | Hinkley, William Charles | D | 1122 N. Cascade, Colorado Springs |
| El Paso | Higby, W. E. | R | Monument |
| Fremont | McCandless, Charles G. | R | 711 W. 8th St., Florence |
| Garfield-Rio Blanco | Oldland, R. | D | Meeker |
| Gilpin | Parfet, Wilbur S. | R | Central City |
| Gunnison | Fogg, H. H. | D | Gunnison |
| Hinsdale-Archuleta-Mineral | Fisher, Royal I. | D | Creede |
| Huerfano-Costilla | Barron, Joseph A. | D | Walsenburg |
| Jefferson | Johnston, David C. | D | Golden |
| Kiowa-Bent | Rogers, Byron G. | D | 752 Grand Ave., Las Animas |
| Lake | Hoefnagels, Edward J. | D | 301 W. 7th St., Leadville |
| La Plata | Childress, T. E. | D | 1015 Fifth Ave., Durango |
| Larimer | Irwin, George Beverly | D | 308 E. Magnolia St., Fort Collins |
| Las Animas | Day, William H. | D | 126 Cedar St., Trinidad |
| Las Animas | McDonald, Andy | R | El Moro |
| Lincoln-Kit Carson-Cheyenne | Dunn, Duncan | D | Kit Carson |
| Logan-Sedgwick | Jankovsky, Joe C. | D | Ovid |
| Mesa | Aspinall, Wayne N. | D | Palisade |
| Montezuma-Dolores | Calkins, Royal W. | R | Cortez |
| Montrose | Wilson, J. Carl | D | Olathe |
| Morgan-Washington | White, Glenn S. | D | 403 Walnut St., Fort Morgan |
| Ouray | Mowatt, Thomas | D | Ouray |
| Phillips-Yuma | Weeks, H. E. | D | Eckley |
| Pitkin | Twining, Warren H. | D | Aspen |
| Pueblo | England, W. J. | D | 123 W. Evans Ave., Pueblo |
| Pueblo | Dameron, Thomas H. | D | 1709 Berkley Ave., Pueblo |
| Pueblo | Hoag, Walter | D | 1901 Court St., Pueblo |
| Pueblo | Cawfield, Sterling | D | Avondale |
| Prowers-Baca | Hudson, Guy | D | Wiley |
| Rio Grande | Harney, R. E. | D | |
| Routt-Moffat | Poppen, A. H. | D | Steamboat Springs |
| Saguache-Custer | Sutley, M. M. | D | Center |
| San Juan | McNaughton, D. C. | D | 1434 Reese St., Silverton |
| San Miguel | Wood, A. T. | D | Placerville |
| Summit-Grand-Jackson | Galloway, James D. | R | Breckenridge |
| Teller-Park | Hallen, George | D | Garo |
| Teller-Park | Miller, George A. | D | Como |
| Weld | LaFollette, Albert A. | D | 1002 5th St., Greeley |
| Weld | Smith, Moses E. | D | Ault |

*Contest pending.

Note.—The House of Representatives is composed of 54 Democrats and 11 Republicans.

## REPRESENTATION OF COUNTIES IN THE STATE SENATE BY AREA, POPULATION AND ASSESSED VALUATION
### (Based on United States Census for 1930 and State Tax Commission Reports for 1930)

### Under Present Apportionment

| District | No. of Senators | Counties | Area in Sq. Miles | Total Population | Total Assessed Valuation |
|---|---|---|---|---|---|
| 1st | 7 | Denver | 58 | 287,861 | $459,992,853 |
| 2nd | 2 | Pueblo | 2,433 | 66,038 | 83,025,130 |
| 3rd | 2 | El Paso | 2,121 | 49,570 | 75,322,405 |
| 4th | 1 | Las Animas | 4,809 | 36,008 | 41,974,002 |
| 5th | 1 | Boulder | 764 | 32,456 | 47,414,950 |
| 6th | 1 | Chaffee and Lake | 1,454 | 3,125 | 17,345,985 |
| 7th | 1 | Weld | 4,022 | 65,097 | 102,130,907 |
| 8th | 1 | Jefferson | 808 | 21,810 | 28,644,700 |
| 9th | 1 | Fremont | 1,557 | 18,896 | 22,871,813 |
| 10th | 1 | Larimer | 2,629 | 33,137 | 52,357,595 |
| 11th | 1 | Gunnison and Delta | 4,380 | 9,731 | 30,348,200 |
| 12th | 1 | Logan, Phillips, Sedgwick, Washington and Yuma | 7,929 | 54,527 | 105,660,018 |
| 13th | 1 | Jackson, Moffat, Rio Blanco and Routt | 11,822 | 18,579 | 33,531,329 |
| 14th | 1 | Costilla, Custer and Huerfano | 3,432 | 24,965 | 24,437,936 |
| 15th | 1 | Mineral, Rio Grande and Saguache | 4,897 | 16,843 | 23,388,009 |
| 16th | 1 | Mesa | 3,163 | 25,908 | 30,755,510 |
| 17th | 1 | Dolores, Montrose and San Miguel | 4,595 | 15,338 | 18,752,949 |
| 18th | 1 | Archuleta, Hinsdale, Ouray and San Juan | 3,163 | 7,372 | 13,704,793 |
| 19th | 1 | La Plata and Montezuma | 3,902 | 20,773 | 21,592,450 |
| 20th | 1 | Teller and Park | 2,789 | 6,193 | 13,734,720 |
| 21st | 1 | Eagle, Garfield and Pitkin | 5,746 | 15,669 | 30,087,021 |
| 22nd | 1 | Adams, Arapahoe and Morgan | 3,390 | 61,176 | 83,861,291 |
| 23rd | 1 | Bailey and Otero | 2,067 | 30,324 | 41,862,338 |
| 24th | 1 | Conejos and Alamosa | 1,979 | 18,405 | 19,300,640 |
| 25th | 1 | Baca, Bent, Kiowa and Prowers | 7,504 | 38,252 | 62,647,450 |
| 26th | 1 | Clear Creek, Gilpin, Grand and Summit | 3,037 | 6,462 | 20,009,703 |
| 27th | 1 | Cheyenne, Douglas, Elbert, Kit Carson and Lincoln | 9,208 | 31,376 | 81,708,206 |
| Total | 35 | | 103,658 | 1,035,791 | $1,586,462,903 |

### Under New Apportionment

| District | No. of Senators | Counties | Area in Sq. Miles | Total Population | Total Assessed Valuation |
|---|---|---|---|---|---|
| 1st | 8 | Denver | 58 | 287,861 | $459,992,853 |
| 2nd | 2 | Pueblo | 2,433 | 66,038 | 83,026,130 |
| 3rd | 2 | El Paso | 2,121 | 49,570 | 75,322,405 |
| 4th | 1 | Las Animas | 4,809 | 36,008 | 41,974,002 |
| 5th | 1 | Boulder | 764 | 32,456 | 47,414,950 |
| 6th | 1 | Chaffee, Park, Gilpin and Clear Creek | 4,394 | 17,686 | 32,233,327 |
| 7th | 2 | Weld | 4,022 | 65,097 | 102,130,907 |
| 8th | 1 | Jefferson and Douglas | 1,653 | 25,308 | 40,482,405 |
| 9th | 1 | Fremont and Custer | 2,304 | 21,620 | 25,947,248 |
| 10th | 1 | Larimer | 2,629 | 33,137 | 52,357,595 |
| 11th | 1 | Delta, Gunnison and Hinsdale | 5,351 | 20,180 | 31,527,183 |
| 12th | 1 | Logan, Sedgwick and Phillips | 3,041 | 31,323 | 64,941,184 |
| 13th | 1 | Rio Blanco, Moffat, Routt, Jackson and Grand | 13,688 | 20,687 | 40,420,009 |
| 14th | 1 | Huerfano, Costilla and Alamosa | 3,412 | 31,443 | 31,457,571 |
| 15th | 1 | Saguache, Mineral, Rio Grande and Conejos | 6,149 | 26,646 | 32,593,579 |
| 16th | 1 | Mesa | 3,163 | 25,908 | 30,755,510 |
| 17th | 1 | Montrose, Ouray, San Miguel and Dolores | 5,114 | 17,122 | 22,845,402 |
| 18th | 1 | Kit Carson, Lincoln and Kiowa | 8,304 | 25,084 | 66,396,508 |
| 19th | 1 | San Juan, Montezuma, La Plata and Archuleta | 5,575 | 25,912 | 30,025,807 |
| 20th | 1 | Washington and Yuma | 4,888 | 23,204 | 40,718,834 |
| 21st | 1 | Garfield, Summit, Eagle, Lake and Pitkin | 6,766 | 21,555 | 42,055,422 |
| 22nd | 1 | Arapahoe and Elbert | 2,699 | 29,227 | 40,431,992 |
| 23rd | 1 | Otero and Crowley | 2,067 | 30,324 | 41,862,338 |
| 24th | 1 | Adams and Morgan | 2,548 | 38,529 | 59,905,062 |
| 25th | 1 | Bent, Prowers and Baca | 5,706 | 31,466 | 49,612,680 |
| Total | 35 | | 103,658 | 1,035,791 | $1,586,462,903 |

Note—At the election in November, 1932, a measure providing for a new legislative apportionment was submitted to popular vote and carried. It will become effective at the election in November, 1934.

# REPRESENTATION IN THE STATE HOUSE OF REPRESENTATIVES

(Based on United States Census for 1930 and State Tax Commission Reports for 1930)

## Under Present Apportionment

| Counties in Representative District | No. of Representatives | Area in Sq. Miles | Total Population | Total Assessed Valuation |
|---|---|---|---|---|
| Denver | 12 | 58 | 287,861 | $459,992,853 |
| Pueblo | 4 | 2,433 | 66,038 | 83,025,130 |
| El Paso | 3 | 2,121 | 49,570 | 75,322,405 |
| Weld | 2 | 4,622 | 65,097 | 102,130,907 |
| Larimer | 1 | 2,629 | 33,137 | 52,357,595 |
| Boulder | 2 | 764 | 32,456 | 47,414,959 |
| Mesa | 2 | 3,163 | 25,908 | 30,755,510 |
| Las Animas | 2 | 4,809 | 36,008 | 41,974,002 |
| Teller and Park | 1 | 2,789 | 6,193 | 13,734,720 |
| Fremont | 1 | 1,557 | 18,896 | 22,871,813 |
| Crowley and Otero | 2 | 2,067 | 30,324 | 41,862,333 |
| Jefferson | 1 | 809 | 21,810 | 28,644,700 |
| Arapahoe and Elbert | 1 | 2,699 | 29,227 | 40,434,992 |
| Garfield and Rio Blanco | 1 | 6,330 | 12,955 | 24,008,570 |
| Delta | 1 | 1,201 | 14,204 | 14,688,795 |
| Montrose | 1 | 2,264 | 11,742 | 12,050,922 |
| Conejos | 1 | 1,252 | 9,803 | 9,205,570 |
| Alamosa | 1 | 727 | 8,602 | 10,005,070 |
| Adams | 1 | 1,262 | 20,245 | 32,186,300 |
| Pitkin | 1 | 1,019 | 1,770 | 3,816,490 |
| La Plata | 1 | 1,851 | 12,975 | 15,351,155 |
| Lake | 1 | 371 | 4,899 | 7,487,065 |
| Rio Grande | 1 | 898 | 9,953 | 11,137,246 |
| Chaffee | 1 | 1,083 | 8,126 | 9,858,980 |
| Morgan and Washington | 1 | 3,807 | 27,875 | 43,640,236 |
| Clear Creek | 1 | 390 | 2,155 | 5,434,895 |
| Gilpin | 1 | 132 | 1,212 | 3,204,732 |
| Ouray | 1 | 519 | 1,784 | 4,092,453 |
| San Juan | 1 | 453 | 1,935 | 3,796,488 |
| Logan and Sedgwick | 1 | 2,353 | 25,526 | 49,526,549 |
| Phillips and Yuma | 1 | 3,055 | 19,410 | 40,211,995 |
| Gunnison | 1 | 3,179 | 5,527 | 15,669,405 |
| Saguache and Custer | 1 | 3,880 | 8,374 | 15,837,705 |
| Douglas | 1 | 845 | 3,498 | 11,837,705 |
| Lincoln, Kit Carson and Cheyenne | 1 | 6,506 | 21,298 | 53,391,738 |
| Kiowa and Bent | 1 | 3,322 | 12,920 | 26,764,640 |
| Prowers and Baca | 1 | 4,382 | 25,332 | 35,882,810 |
| San Miguel | 1 | 1,288 | 2,184 | 4,635,150 |
| Archuleta, Hinsdale and Mineral | 1 | 3,057 | 4,293 | 7,483,151 |
| Moffat and Routt | 1 | 6,967 | 14,213 | 24,064,494 |
| Grand, Jackson and Summit | 1 | 4,147 | 4,481 | 15,040,816 |
| Eagle | 1 | 1,620 | 3,924 | 8,058,056 |
| Costilla and Huerfano | 1 | 2,685 | 22,841 | 21,362,501 |
| Dolores and Montezuma | 1 | 3,094 | 9,210 | 8,308,172 |
| **Total** | **65** | **103,658** | **1,035,791** | **$1,586,462,903** |

## Under New Apportionment

| Counties in Representative District | No. of Representatives | Area in Sq. Miles | Total Population | Total Assessed Valuation |
|---|---|---|---|---|
| Denver | 15 | 58 | 287,861 | $459,992,853 |
| Pueblo | 4 | 2,433 | 66,038 | 83,025,130 |
| El Paso | 3 | 2,121 | 49,570 | 75,322,405 |
| Weld | 4 | 4,022 | 65,097 | 102,130,907 |
| Larimer and Jackson | 2 | 4,261 | 34,523 | 56,028,335 |
| Boulder | 2 | 764 | 32,456 | 47,414,950 |
| Mesa | 2 | 3,163 | 25,908 | 30,755,510 |
| Las Animas | 2 | 4,809 | 36,008 | 41,974,002 |
| Park, Teller and Douglas | 1 | 3,634 | 9,691 | 25,572,425 |
| Fremont and Custer | 2 | 2,304 | 21,020 | 25,947,248 |
| Crowley and Otero | 2 | 2,067 | 30,324 | 41,862,338 |
| Jefferson | 1 | 808 | 21,810 | 28,644,700 |
| Arapahoe and Elbert | 1 | 2,699 | 29,227 | 40,434,992 |
| Rio Blanco and Garfield | 1 | 6,330 | 12,955 | 24,008,570 |
| Delta | 1 | 1,201 | 14,204 | 14,688,795 |
| Montrose and Ouray | 1 | 2,783 | 13,526 | 16,343,375 |
| Conejos and Archuleta | 1 | 2,472 | 13,007 | 13,842,439 |
| Alamosa and Costilla | 1 | 1,912 | 14,381 | 15,388,480 |
| Adams | 1 | 1,262 | 20,245 | 32,186,300 |
| Eagle, Pitkin, Summit, Clear Creek and Gilpin | 1 | 3,810 | 10,048 | 24,995,669 |
| La Plata and San Juan | 1 | 2,304 | 14,910 | 19,147,643 |
| Lake and Chaffee | 1 | 1,454 | 13,025 | 17,345,985 |
| Rio Grande and Mineral | 1 | 1,764 | 10,593 | 12,804,545 |
| Morgan | 1 | 1,286 | 18,284 | 27,718,762 |
| Washington | 1 | 2,521 | 9,591 | 15,921,474 |
| Routt, Moffat and Grand | 1 | 8,833 | 16,321 | 30,953,174 |
| San Miguel, Dolores and Montezuma | 1 | 4,382 | 11,394 | 12,943,322 |
| Baca | 1 | 2,552 | 10,570 | 14,318,800 |
| Sedgwick and Phillips | 1 | 1,219 | 11,377 | 28,385,323 |
| Logan | 1 | 1,822 | 19,946 | 36,555,861 |
| Yuma | 1 | 2,367 | 13,613 | 24,797,360 |
| Hinsdale, Gunnison and Saguache | 1 | 7,283 | 12,226 | 27,421,852 |
| Huerfano | 1 | 1,500 | 17,062 | 16,069,091 |
| Kit Carson | 1 | 2,159 | 9,725 | 21,154,833 |
| Lincoln and Cheyenne | 1 | 4,347 | 11,573 | 32,236,905 |
| Kiowa and Bent | 1 | 3,322 | 12,920 | 26,764,640 |
| Prowers | 1 | 1,630 | 14,762 | 21,564,010 |
| **Total** | **65** | **103,658** | **1,035,791** | **$1,586,462,903** |

## AREA, POPULATION AND VALUATION FOR EACH SENATOR AND REPRESENTATIVE IN DISTRICTS HAVING MORE THAN ONE SENATOR OR REPRESENTATIVE

(Based on United States Census for 1930 and State Tax Commission Reports for 1930)

### Under Present Apportionment

| District | Representation | For Each Senator | | | For Each Representative | | |
|---|---|---|---|---|---|---|---|
| | | Sq. Mi. | Pop. | Valuation | Sq. Mi. | Pop. | Valuation |
| Denver | 7 Sen. 12 Rep. | 8.3 | 41,123 | $65,713,265 | 4.8 | 23,988 | $38,332,737 |
| Pueblo | 2 Sen. 4 Rep. | 1,216 | 33,019 | 41,512,565 | 608 | 16,510 | 20,756,283 |
| El Paso | 2 Sen. 3 Rep. | 1,060 | 24,785 | 37,661,203 | 707 | 16,523 | 25,107,469 |
| Boulder | 2 Rep. | | | | 382 | 16,228 | 23,707,475 |
| Las Animas | 2 Rep. | | | | 2,405 | 18,004 | 20,987,001 |
| Crowley and Otero | 2 Rep. | | | | 1,034 | 15,162 | 20,931,169 |
| Teller and Park | 2 Rep. | | | | 1,394 | 3,096 | 6,867,360 |
| Weld | 2 Rep. | | | | 2,011 | 32,549 | 51,065,454 |

### Under New Apportionment

| District | Representation | For Each Senator | | | For Each Representative | | |
|---|---|---|---|---|---|---|---|
| | | Sq. Mi. | Pop. | Valuation | Sq. Mi. | Pop. | Valuation |
| Denver | 8 Sen. 15 Rep. | 7.25 | 35,983 | $57,499,107 | 3.9 | 19,191 | $30,666,190 |
| Pueblo | 2 Sen. 4 Rep. | 1,216 | 33,019 | 41,512,565 | 608 | 16,510 | 20,756,283 |
| El Paso | 2 Sen. 3 Rep. | 1,060 | 24,785 | 37,661,203 | 707 | 16,523 | 25,107,469 |
| Boulder | 2 Rep. | | | | 382 | 16,228 | 23,707,475 |
| Las Animas | 2 Rep. | | | | 2,405 | 18,004 | 20,987,001 |
| Crowley and Otero | 2 Rep. | | | | 1,034 | 15,162 | 20,931,169 |
| Arapahoe and Elbert | 2 Rep. | | | | 1,350 | 14,614 | 20,217,496 |
| Weld | 2 Sen. 4 Rep. | 2,011 | 32,549 | 51,065,454 | 1,006 | 16,274 | 25,532,727 |
| Mesa | 2 Rep. | | | | 1,582 | 12,954 | 15,377,765 |
| Larimer and Jackson | 2 Rep. | | | | 2,131 | 17,262 | 28,014,168 |

ELECTED COUNTY OFFICIALS, 1933

| COUNTY | CLERK | TREASURER | ASSESSOR | SHERIFF |
|---|---|---|---|---|
| Adams | Earle J. Tripp | Ben Shearston | J. W. Tarlton | Lee Templeton |
| Alamosa | Chas. M. VanFleet | A. C. Kline | Olof Bergman | Maurice Smith |
| Arapahoe | E. E. Anderson | Claude Cartwright | H. C. Ohlman | Edward E. Monzingo |
| Archuleta | Philip R. Johnson | Fred Catchpole | Kenneth D. Hill | John H. Lattin |
| Baca | Walter P. Powell | Jason L. Beatty | V. L. Finch | D. T. Potter |
| Bent | Bernice Limbach | Arthur S. Dean | C. N. Troup | Casto Dunavin |
| Boulder | Fred W. Burger | Herman A. Lenartz | Aylwin A. Smith | George A. Richart |
| Chaffee | A. W. Samson | Chas. C. White | Theo. M. Jacobs | H. J. Swain |
| Cheyenne | Thos. H. McKown | Jennie E. Ross | R. A. Martinson | Phil Hollander |
| Clear Creek | C. S. Work | W. E. Walthers | Edmund Rowse | Edward J. Burns |
| Conejos | Kit Carson | Benj. Espinoza | J. C. Salazar | J. Parley Haynie |
| Costilla | J. J. Jaramillo | W. Dryden Smith | Anastacio Sanchez | Adolfo Rodriguez |
| Crowley | R. R. Franklin | J. J. O'Connell | A. W. Drescher | Wiley J. Woodruff |
| Custer | Williard A. Walker | L. H. Schoolfield | Fred W. Stewart | Mel H. Manning |
| Delta | Paul K. Osborne | Clement A. Bowle | T. C. Wand | Ray Lockhart |
| Denver* | | | | |
| Dolores | Earl Eyre | H. G. Keown | E. E. Ballenger | Emil Baer |
| Douglas | Arch Curtis | Wm. T. Jones | Hugh L. Shellabarger | C. H. Lowell |
| Eagle | Nettie M. Cave | Harry S. Dickerson | N. E. Bucholz | W. M. Wilson |
| Elbert | Loyd L. Moreland | J. W. Worrall | Jas. F. Mauldin | G. R. Brown |
| El Paso | C. R. Furrow | Albert H. Horton | A. W. Sparkman | Robert M. Jackson |
| Fremont | Katherine Komfala | Thos. M. Warner | Blake Rogers | D. P. VanBuskirk |
| Garfield | Walter J. Frost | Charles H. Durant | Erle E. Hubbard | George L. Winters |
| Gilpin | Clifford I. Parsons | Hugh L. Lawry | William O. Ziege | Oscar William |
| Grand | R. O. Throckmorton | W. S. Kennedy | Simon Olson | Mark E. Fletcher |
| Gunnison | Sam C. Hartman | B. H. Snyder | Chas. F. Whinnery | Ed. T. Lindsley |
| Hinsdale | Mabel B. Rawson | Wm. F. Green | Walter E. Vernon | Hugh A. Coburn |
| Huerfano | Damacio Vigil | F. H. Danford | Felix B. Maestes | Harry J. Capps |
| Jackson | L. F. Mitchell | Florence A. Wilkins | Wm. H. Winscom | John D. Bulis |
| Jefferson | M. C. Everitt | S. A. Koenig | Paul V. Pattridge | James G. Biggins, Jr. |
| Kiowa | Mark Clay | C. W. Coughenour | A. A. Hall | W. P. Mayne |
| Kit Carson | Orville Swaim | Claus Rose, Jr. | Leonard I. Dawson | C. C. Gates |
| Lake | John Gregory | Frank E. Kendrick | John J. Bohen | Morgan Walsh |
| La Plata | Edith C. Kiel | E. A. Chubb | Chas. H. Conroy | H. T. Ayres |
| Larimer | Hervey D. Hubbell | C. S. Ikes | H. K. Mitton | George Saunders |
| Las Animas | Edward G. Hower | F. Elmer Dunlavy | A. Tom McCarty | Elijah A. Duling |
| Lincoln | John Abell | A. C. Moschel | Guy Hicks | John Johnson |
| Logan | Samuel J. Neely | Wm. F. Alexander | Robert H. Swinney | Ray R. Powell |
| Mesa | E. W. Jordan | W. S. Meek | Jas. F. Shults | Chas. S. Lumley |
| Mineral | H. D. Barnhart | Wm. T. Jackson | John J. Weaver | William Orthen |
| Moffat | M. E. McMahan | L. W. Failing | W. O. Miner | Tom G. Blevins |
| Montezuma | Mabel C. Waldron | Claude H. Wilson | John G. Dunning | W. W. Dunlap |
| Montrose | Ira C. Foster | F. E. Spencer | C. I. Moore | A. M. McAnally |
| Morgan | Loyal O. Baker | Edw. H. Madison | Robert Glassey | Rufus A. Johnston |
| Otero | C. M. Wilson | W. Lucas Woodall | Mac. V. Danford | Ralph J. Whitton |
| Ouray | Harold F. Kiesel | Harry E. Stark | Patricio Stealey | Jess M. Wood |
| Park | Harry L. Moyer | Glen A. Young | James T. Witcher | Neal W. Brown |
| Phillips | Emma S. Kramer | Ray Crosby | Roy E. Owens | Frank A. Berger |
| Pitkin | Melbern M. Neihardt | Robert S. Killey | Paul Caley | J. Hod Nicholson |
| Prowers | Vera Rosebrough | Fred Clark | Jesse E. Wright | Elton L. Leighton |
| Pueblo | A. G. Kochenberger | Jewel E. Creel | Thos. A. Christian | Lewis Worker |
| Rio Blanco | C. J. Wilson | George E. Aicher | F. W. Hossack | J. Sam Gourley |
| Rio Grande | E. J. Short | Edna L. McGuire | Ed Goodding | A. H. Webster |
| Routt | John R. Crawford | William Curtis | Clarence E. Horton | Fred Foster |
| Saguache | Jno. T. Seyfried | Wm. L. Hammond | Jos. M. Sheesley | Ed Pau |
| San Juan | Edna G. Gibbs | Raymond H. Doud | A. M. Kimball | M. H. Dou |
| San Miguel | Harold T. Hogan | Chas. L. Spillman | M. E. Ballard | L. G. Warriel |
| Sedgwick | Ferne Sheaffer | Mark Gyger | Leslie I. Bennett | R. L. Ireland |
| Summit | E. C. Peabody | George Robinson | Edward T. Stuard | J. G. Detwile |
| Teller | L. S. Cox | Walter D. Tatum | Blanche A. Cassidy | Ed Vinar |
| Washington | Verl R. Carpenter | Chester Kinchelae | Brandt Wenig | Wm. Meredit |
| Weld | Walter F. Morrison | Harvey E. Witwer | Charles M. Whiteside | W. W. Wyat |
| Yuma | Ray F. Morgan | Robert Sheverbush | Bell H. Yount | Raymond VanHor |

*Denver's officers are municipal, rather than county. See Gazeteer of cities and towns in cover pocke

ELECTED COUNTY OFFICIALS, 1933—Continued

| COUNTY | COUNTY JUDGE | CORONER | SURVEYOR ' | SUPERINTENDENT OF SCHOOLS |
|---|---|---|---|---|
| Adams | Homer G. Preston | Dr. J. Wm. Wells | P. O'Brian, Sr. | Bertha L. Baker |
| Alamosa | James Hyndman | Glen Miracle | Mark U. Watrous | Mabel M. O'Laughlin |
| Arapahoe | Henry Bruce Teller | Elizabeth A. Mackin | S. L. Stewart | Minnie O. Davis |
| Archuleta | F. A. Byrne | L. C. Jackisch | Robert A. Howe | Rachel Bunch |
| Baca | Fred E. Bear | Dr. D. D. Hamilton | Vacancy | Paul M. Mitchell |
| Bent | Herman A. Bailey | George W. Powell | Sydney Flinn | Loren D. Root |
| Boulder | E. J. Ingram | A. E. Howe | Fred A. Fair | Isabella D. Mayhoffer |
| Chaffee | Joseph Newitt | L. B. Stewart | Howard Sneddon | Bessie M. Shewalter |
| Cheyenne | Carl L. Law | A. H. Brentlinger | D. H. Zuck | Olive E. McComish |
| Clear Creek | George D. Criley | Richard H. Pearce | Chas. L. Harrington | Elia N. Conwell |
| Conejos | C. A. Green | H. H. Haynie | J. F. Thomas | Mrs. Estella Sowards |
| Costilla | Amos P. Rodriguez | Levi R. Wilhelm | A. H. Martin | Eleuto Medina |
| Crowley | I. H. Stanley | J. E. Jeffery | J. Logan Tucker | Nona Broadbent |
| Custer | Edward L. Mott | Charles A. Menzel | Frank Wagner | Lou C. Beaman |
| Delta | W. Guy Merritt | E. A. Martin | Homer D. Graham | Hazel Leavitt |
| Denver* | | | | |
| Dolores | V. H. Lee | Dr. R. S. Lipscomb | George N. Herron, Jr. | Mary E. Livingston |
| Douglas | John L. Briscoe | Samuel E. Livingston | Henry H. Curtis | Elizabeth E. Bennet |
| Eagle | Albert K. Ethel | W. L. Conway | Carl I. Dismant | Georgia H. Clark |
| Elbert | F. D. Hart | Dale O. Groves | D. M. Sultz | Pauline V. Weiss |
| El Paso | J. F. Sanford | J. Thomas Coghlan | R. M. Cannon | Lucile Dee Horton |
| Fremont | Kent L. Eldred | C. H. Graves | L. D. Miller | Grace E. Edwards |
| Garfield | Carl W. Fulghum | Dr. G. A. Hopkins | W. H. Trumbor | Alma M. Harris |
| Gilpin | Louis J. Carter | G. L. Hamliik | Harry L. Barr | Amanda Wagner |
| Grand | J. N. Pettingell | A. C. Esmiol | Roy F. Polhamus | Dorothy L. Traber |
| Gunnison | R. G. Montgomery | Alex Campbell | J. H. Robinson | Bertha N. McLain |
| Hinsdale | James T. Palmer | Elt. T. Beam | Charles H. Harkness | Anna Ewart |
| Huerfano | W. W. Hammond | Herbert Furphy | A. S. Willburn | Amanda Simpson |
| Jackson | John A. McNamara | Dr. M. A. Durham | A. B. McKenzie | Ethlyn F. Riddle |
| Jefferson | George H. Lerg | O. A. Saunders | Harold W. Gardner | Naomi K. Olson |
| Kiowa | W. M. Ramsdale | James G. Hopkins | Vacancy | Alma Vrooman |
| Kit Carson | Clarence L. Magee | Dr. E. J. Remington | Ira B. Rowbotham | Ora J. Cruickshank |
| Lake | Thomas Evans | James J. Corbett | Fred J. McNair | Annie M. Holden |
| La Plata | Thomas E. Higgins | O. B. Rensch | A. L. Kroeger | Celia F. Marshall |
| Larimer | Albert P. Fischer | Charles Day | James Andrews | Una S. Andrews |
| Las Animas | Bertram B. Beshoar | Roy Campbell | Earl T. Lindsay | W. F. Templin |
| Lincoln | Charles M. Somerville | W. M. Deits | Vacancy | Burton Rice |
| Logan | H. Lawrence Hinkley | Arthur D. Jackson | John E. Youngquist | Kate Lester |
| Mesa | Adair J. Hotchkiss | T. F. Voorhees | Frank C. Merriell | F. N. Nisley |
| Mineral | Clarence Y. Butler | Wm. H. Warren | Don C. LaFont | Mrs. E. E. Vanaken |
| Moffat | Frank M. Smay | I. J. Robacker | L. G. Dolan | Mrs. E. C. McWilliams |
| Montezuma | J. M. Brumley | Dr. E. E. Johnson | H. L. Owens | Mrs. Myrtle E. Jordan |
| Montrose | Earl Herman | C. G. Addington | J. E. McDaniel | Lucile Anfreae |
| Morgan | A. W. Dulweber | L. H. Parker | A. W. Hill | Rose B. Glassey |
| Otero | A. B. Wallis | Dr. A. S. Hansen | V. R. Guthrie | R. H. McNeal |
| Ouray | D. N. McDonald | C. V. Bates | Geo. R. Hurlburt | Jennie L. Brownlee |
| Park | Ed. N. Barlow | Frank Dunkle | Gerald F. Galloway | Mayme R. O'Mailia |
| Phillips | Avery T. Searle | H. B. Radford | C. A. Guernsey | Charles R. Peter |
| Pitkin | Wm. R. Shaw | Frank Hamilton | Frank Willoughby | Hattie B. Burch |
| Prowers | Edw. O. Russell | C. T. Knuckey | Geo. H. Russell | Bernice W. Wilmoth |
| Pueblo | Hubert Glover | Dr. C. N. Caldwell | H. C. Wetmore | Nettie S. Freed |
| Rio Blanco | John E. Wix | A. J. Cole | Maurice Ruckman | Esta Gentry |
| Rio Grande | M. T. Hancock | Geo. Nicoll | Glenn Cochran | Nina M. Weiss |
| Routt | John M. Childress | A. W. Heyer | Stanley Dismuke | Mrs. Pearl A. Funk |
| Saguache | Birt Clare | S. W. Truitt | Raymond Johnson | Mrs. Ora Carson |
| San Juan | Wm. Palmquist | Wm. E. Maguire | A. W. Harrison | Anna C. Bell |
| San Miguel | H. E. Dill | C. S. Mollohan | B. W. Purdy | Eloise W. Morgan |
| Sedgwick | B. D. Parker, Jr. | G. H. Austin | C. M. Slusser | Elizabeth K. Zorn |
| Summit | Martin J. Waltz | Lester C. Owens | Ralph C. Black | Mary H. Williams |
| Teller | R. A. Weisgerber | Florence M. Craven | T. H. Evans Jones | Loretta S. Davis |
| Washington | L. F. Crawford | Walter T. Gough | E. G. Beechler | Josie D. Jones |
| Weld | Robert G. Strong | Richard F. Armstrong | L. L. Stimson | Jerre F. Moreland |
| Yuma | I. L. Barker | W. H. Hitchcock | Grant Woodward | A. E. Stevenson |

*Denver's officers are municipal, rather than county. See Gazeteer of cities and towns in cover pocket.

## COUNTY COMMISSIONERS, 1933

Adams—R. S. McIntosh, George S. Kemp, George A. Welsh.

Alamosa—Frank Guartney, R. E. Sellers, Thos. W. Taylor.

Arapahoe—W. W. Hanson, Charles O. SeVier, C. D. Courtright.

Archuleta—Louis Montroy, Harry C. Macht, Vic Johnson.

Baca—F. H. Schnaufer, W. A. Greathouse, Claude L. Bosley.

Bent—O. H. Lubers, Alva C. Bart, Prowers Hudnall.

Boulder—William Mitchell, M. G. Gelwicks, Matt McCaslin.

Chaffee—H. Lovel Johnson, Frank Fehling, S. L. Taber.

Cheyenne—Chas. E. Collins, F. H. Hadley, W. A. Baber.

Clear Creek—George H. Curnow, Wm. F. Buckley, H. W. Kirby.

Conejos—J. E. Braiden, Benj. F. Espinoza, Max Duran.

Costilla—Jerry L. Morris, Tranquilino Manchego, J. M. Pacheco.

Crowley—J. G. Boget, Chas. Roth, F. D. Taylor.

Custer—A. H. Johnston, Chas. J. Donahoe, Ernest H. Georges.

Delta—George S. Roller, Montford Gallup, Ed. H. Crawford.

DenVer—Walter B. Lowry, Harry P. Risley, Wm. E. McGlone.

Dolores—R. W. Prout, Percy R. Krautz, Ed. Baird.

Douglas—L. R. Higby, Albert E. Failing, Xavier J. Baldauf.

Eagle—Alfred M. Sloss, Geo. Watson, H. A. Nottingham.

Elbert—Tom Burnside, Perry DaVis, I. W. Northrup.

El Paso—D. B. Campbell, Eugene M. Portner, Chas. N. Wheeler.

Fremont—John B. Bald, Chas. Sell, Finis L. Parks.

Garfield—John L. Heuschkel, Otto Hahnewald, C. G. Kendall.

Gilpin—A. M. Fairchild, Neil McKay, W. T. Sterling.

Grand—Frank Stafford, Jas. E. Quinn, Arthur Wold.

Gunnison—E. R. Williams, Ralph A. Little, W. H. Whalen.

Hinsdale—John R. Liska, V. E. Osgerby, Paul C. Ramsey.

Huerfano—J. G. Archuleta, W. E. Smith, Geo. S. Niebuhr.

Jackson—T. John Payne, John Petersen, Wm. Simpson.

Jefferson—W. G. DuVall, John R. BroWne, Gus A. Johnson.

Kiowa—P. O. Meyer, A. F. Wenger, J. O. Walker.

Kit Carson—John F. Lueken, R. A. Bowers, G. M. Baxter.

Lake—Charles E. SlaVin, Adolph T. Schaefer, William G. Frank.

La Plata—W. I. Gifford, Ross E. Nixon, John Perino.

Larimer—Henri McClelland, A. L. Johnson, Wm. J. Rausler.

Las Animas—W. W. Taylor, Frank Patterson, Mauro CordoVa.

Lincoln—R. E. Bucklen, Henry Hoepner, John Freel.

Logan—Alvah L. Litel, Dewey J. Harman, Ray E. Rieke.

Mesa—M. G. Hinshaw, Chas. S. Jones, H. O. Lambeth.

Mineral—John G. Dabney, C. O. Withrow, Samuel McKibbin.

Moffat—P. L. Templeton, Thos. W. Rogers, H. T. Deakins.

Montezuma—Frank Philley, Geo. W. Menefee, E. S. Porter.

Montrose—H. P. Steel, Verdie L. Hotchkiss, D. Lewis Williams.

Morgan—Geo. Glenn, E. Rosener, Soren Bach.

Otero—I. F. Haines, J. R. Cole, D. P. McClaren.

Ouray—E. C. Fisher, Harry GaVin, J. W. Donald.

Park—Arch W. Head, Harry C. Bishop, Hollis R. Mills.

Phillips—S. J. Meakins, John Sandquist, R. Claymon.

Pitkin—Geo. B. Brown, Louis Vagneur, John R. Williams.

Prowers—L. M. Appel, Ray McGrath, Geo. A. H. Baxter.

Pueblo—J. Will Goss, Robert Rapalje, Geo. Herrington.

Rio Blanco—Fred A. Nichols, Thos. J. Cassidy, Dennis Murray.

Rio Grande—H. J. Gilbreath, O. A. Lindstrum, W. C. Lewis.

Routt—Henry J. Summer, Joseph F. Long, Stanley Larson.

Saguache—Joseph W. Alexander, Wm. E. Gardner, Jacob Barsch.

San Juan—Norman F. BaWden, James Cole, C. W. Fleming.

San Miguel—Charles H. McKeever, Geo. G. Wagner, Edgar C. Haskill.

Sedgwick—R. L. Franklin, W. T. Johnson, Henry Anderson.

Summit—Andrew Lindstrom, B. F. Rich, C. W. Bradley.

Teller—Alf. Coulson, H. L. Potts, Silas M. Pinion.

Washington—A. Mitchell, R. S. Stanley, R. L. Sergeant.

Weld—Wm. A. Carlson, James S. Ogilvie, S. K. Clark.

Yuma—Harry M. McKinney, Joseph H. Rogers, J. H. Dickson.

**COLORADO'S VOTE BY YEARS FOR PRESIDENT AND GOVERNOR**

| Year | President | | Governor | |
|------|-----------|-----------|------------|-----------|
| | Republican | Democrat | Republican | Democrat |
| 1876 | ...... | ...... | 13,316 | 14,154 |
| 1878 | ...... | ...... | 14,396 | 11,573 |
| 1880 | 27,450 | 24,647 | ...... | ...... |
| 1882 | ...... | ...... | 27,552 | 29,897 |
| 1884 | 36,290 | 27,723 | 30,471 | 27,420 |
| 1886 | ...... | ...... | 26,533 | 28,129 |
| 1888 | 50,774 | 37,567 | ...... | ...... |
| 1890 | ...... | ...... | ...... | ...... |
| 1892 | 38,620 | *53,584 | 38,806 | 8,944 |
| 1894 | ...... | ...... | 93,502 | 8,337 |
| 1896 | 26,279 | 161,269 | 71,816 | 87,387 |
| 1898 | ...... | ...... | 50,880 | 92,274 |
| 1900 | 93,039 | 122,733 | 93,245 | 121,995 |
| 1902 | ...... | ...... | 87,512 | 80,217 |
| 1904 | 134,687 | 100,105 | 113,499 | 124,617 |
| 1906 | ...... | ...... | 92,646 | 74,512 |
| 1908 | 123,700 | 126,644 | 118,953 | 130,141 |
| 1910 | ...... | ...... | 97,648 | 115,627 |
| 1912† | 58,386 | 114,232 | 63,061 | 114,044 |
| 1914‡ | ...... | ...... | 129,096 | 95,640 |
| 1916§ | 102,308 | 178,816 | 117,723 | 151,962 |
| 1918 | ...... | ...... | 112,693 | 102,397 |
| 1920 | 173,298 | 104,936 | 174,488 | 108,738 |
| 1922 | ...... | ...... | 134,353 | 138,098 |
| 1924¶ | 193,956 | 75,238 | 177,298 | 150,229 |
| 1926 | ...... | ...... | 116,756 | 183,342 |
| 1928 | 253,872 | 133,131 | 144,167 | 240,160 |
| 1930 | ...... | ...... | 124,157 | 197,067 |
| 1932 | 189,617 | 250,877 | 174,540 | 243,950 |

Note—The vote for governor in 1932 is unofficial, as the official canvass is not made until the January following election.

* People's party.
† Progressive party vote was 72,306 for president and 66,132 for governor. Socialist vote, 16 418 for president and 16,194 for governor.
‡ Progressive vote for governor was 33,320; Socialist, 10,516.
§ Socialist vote, 10,049 for president and 12,495 for governor.
¶ La Follette Progressive vote for president, 57,368.
In 1892 Populist vote for governor was 44,242.
In 1894 Populist vote for governor was 74,894.
Vote for governor in 1880, 1888 and 1890 is not available.

**COLORADO CONGRESSIONAL DISTRICTS**

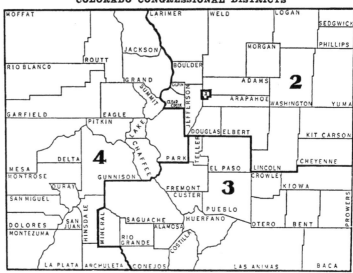

**ELECTION RETURNS BY COUNTIES FOR PRESIDENT**

| COUNTY | 1932 | | 1928 | | 1924 | | |
|---|---|---|---|---|---|---|---|
| | Roose-velt Dem. | Hoover Rep. | Hoover Rep. | Smith Dem. | Coolidge Rep. | Davis Dem. | La Follette Prog. |
| Adams .......... | 4,554 | 2,812 | 4,031 | 2,265 | 2,955 | 1,209 | 893 |
| Alamosa ........ | 2,141 | 1,306 | 1,759 | 1,239 | 1,012 | 625 | 812 |
| Arapahoe ....... | 5,796 | 4,287 | 6,086 | 2,463 | 4,222 | 1,209 | 997 |
| Archuleta ....... | 928 | 462 | 610 | 447 | 453 | 269 | 291 |
| Baca ........... | 2,247 | 1,349 | 2,108 | 524 | 1,125 | 653 | 559 |
| Bent ........... | 1,948 | 1,327 | 1,957 | 741 | 1,475 | 804 | 417 |
| Boulder ........ | 8,412 | 7,487 | 9,457 | 4,363 | 7,614 | 3,273 | 1,839 |
| Chaffee ........ | 2,393 | 1,061 | 1,880 | 1,230 | 1,322 | 612 | 1,017 |
| Cheyenne ....... | 1,042 | 746 | 945 | 500 | 837 | 236 | 399 |
| Clear Creek...... | 939 | 597 | 790 | 481 | 726 | 284 | 80 |
| Conejos ........ | 2,641 | 1,190 | 1,463 | 1,692 | 1,463 | 995 | 137 |
| Costilla ........ | 1,475 | 707 | 657 | 1,079 | 744 | 665 | 92 |
| Crowley ........ | 1,266 | 811 | 1,243 | 635 | 1,079 | 667 | 324 |
| Custer .......... | 729 | 413 | 600 | 389 | 415 | 281 | 221 |
| Delta .......... | 3,467 | 2,311 | 3,731 | 1,672 | 2,689 | 1,345 | 781 |
| Denver ......... | 72,867 | 59,372 | 73,543 | 41,238 | 59,047 | 15,764 | 13,054 |
| Dolores ........ | 464 | 183 | 387 | 278 | 100 | 157 | 169 |
| Douglas ........ | 1,061 | 836 | 1,107 | 603 | 869 | 383 | 248 |
| Eagle .......... | 1,348 | 712 | 1,014 | 570 | 680 | 431 | 414 |
| Elbert ......... | 1,649 | 1,277 | 1,933 | 738 | 1,396 | 506 | 539 |
| El Paso......... | 11,353 | 12,017 | 16,243 | 5,063 | 9,965 | 4,140 | 3,636 |
| Fremont ........ | 4,295 | 3,294 | 5,365 | 2,352 | 4,422 | 1,550 | 1,135 |
| Garfield ....... | 2,916 | 1,734 | 2,435 | 1,562 | 1,927 | 917 | 808 |
| Gilpin ......... | 539 | 271 | 299 | 236 | 361 | 161 | 124 |
| Grand .......... | 771 | 598 | 770 | 451 | 658 | 308 | 239 |
| Gunnison ....... | 1,807 | 985 | 1,456 | 1,135 | 1,125 | 598 | 744 |
| Hinsdale ........ | 138 | 94 | 128 | 106 | 133 | 79 | 53 |
| Huerfano ....... | 4,159 | 2,490 | 3,260 | 3,343 | 2,802 | 1,219 | 1,570 |
| Jackson ........ | 115 | 390 | 401 | 249 | 385 | 111 | 72 |
| Jefferson ....... | 6,023 | 5,522 | 6,754 | 2,880 | 4,861 | 1,271 | 1,312 |
| Kiowa .......... | 1,113 | 769 | 1,024 | 458 | 781 | 431 | 430 |
| Kit Carson...... | 2,289 | 1,835 | 2,486 | 1,137 | 2,030 | 720 | 574 |
| Lake .......... | 1,436 | 801 | 990 | 1,449 | 1,024 | 613 | 510 |
| La Plata........ | 3,156 | 2,121 | 2,837 | 1,872 | 1,474 | 1,516 | 930 |
| Larimer ........ | 6,494 | 7,040 | 8,213 | 3,203 | 6,486 | 1,970 | 533 |
| Las Animas..... | 8,964 | 3,651 | 5,367 | 6,459 | 5,721 | 2,758 | 2,936 |
| Lincoln ........ | 1,979 | 1,452 | 2,110 | 888 | 1,647 | 634 | 384 |
| Logan .......... | 3,641 | 3,157 | 4,377 | 1,620 | 2,898 | 946 | 1,315 |
| Mesa .......... | 6,682 | 4,388 | 6,446 | 3,223 | 4,053 | 2,388 | 2,291 |
| Mineral ........ | 210 | 112 | 144 | 187 | 150 | 101 | 70 |
| Moffat ......... | 1,388 | 880 | 1,346 | 710 | 1,012 | 647 | 151 |
| Montezuma ..... | 1,779 | 887 | 1,341 | 772 | 686 | 721 | 557 |
| Montrose ....... | 2,516 | 1,992 | 2,873 | 1,297 | 2,071 | 1,239 | 1,106 |
| Morgan ......... | 3,181 | 3,370 | 4,197 | 1,242 | 3,267 | 757 | 370 |
| Otero .......... | 5,107 | 3,974 | 5,788 | 1,876 | 4,624 | 1,938 | 1,106 |
| Ouray .......... | 706 | 398 | 535 | 479 | 496 | 256 | 307 |
| Park .......... | 1,057 | 577 | 740 | 419 | 645 | 316 | 158 |
| Phillips ........ | 1,453 | 903 | 1,440 | 705 | 1,058 | 397 | 635 |
| Pitkin ......... | 727 | 239 | 485 | 454 | 437 | 204 | 121 |
| Prowers ........ | 3,020 | 2,568 | 3,228 | 1,216 | 2,566 | 1,042 | 505 |
| Pueblo .......... | 15,325 | 10,414 | 15,541 | 7,881 | 10,609 | 4,917 | 3,460 |
| Rio Blanco...... | 826 | 687 | 860 | 429 | 741 | 407 | 64 |
| Rio Grande...... | 2,539 | 1,557 | 2,254 | 1,226 | 1,588 | 922 | 391 |
| Routt .......... | 2,643 | 1,568 | 2,304 | 1,645 | 1,824 | 1,116 | 229 |
| Saguache ....... | 1,427 | 931 | 1,491 | 854 | 1,211 | 591 | 234 |
| San Juan........ | 544 | 160 | 277 | 436 | 215 | 206 | 55 |
| San Miguel...... | 862 | 383 | 721 | 554 | 673 | 567 | 251 |
| Sedgwick ....... | 1,288 | 884 | 1,247 | 580 | 799 | 372 | 297 |
| Summit ........ | 397 | 224 | 362 | 306 | 343 | 241 | 124 |
| Teller .......... | 1,534 | 752 | 1,184 | 1,037 | 1,262 | 592 | 616 |
| Washington .... | 2,378 | 1,385 | 2,132 | 851 | 1,771 | 720 | 681 |
| Weld .......... | 11,182 | 10,754 | 13,719 | 5,762 | 10,211 | 3,406 | 2,169 |
| Yuma .......... | 3,220 | 2,129 | 3,401 | 1,383 | 2,721 | 865 | 832 |
| Total........ | 250,877 | 189,617 | 253,872 | 133,131 | 193,956 | 75,238 | 57,368 |

# Bank Statistics

THERE were 221 active banks located in Colorado on December 31, 1931. These included all institutions operating under federal and state charters. The combined assets of these banks at the close of 1931 amounted to $319,289,223 and their deposits aggregated $259,134,580. A table published herewith shows the number of banks, loans and discounts, deposits and assets at the close of each calendar year beginning with 1916. The figures indicate the expansion of business during the war period, the postwar adjustment and the recovery in more recent years. Another accompanying table shows loans and discounts, deposits and total assets of banks by counties as of December 31, 1931, with comparative figures for 1930. A third table gives the bank clearings in the principal cities by years and a fourth contains a list of all banks in the state by counties and the cities and towns in which they are located.

## COLORADO BANK STATISTICS
(As of December 31 of the Year Named)

| YEAR | No. of Banks | Loans and Discounts | Total Deposits | Total Assets |
|---|---|---|---|---|
| 1916 ................... | * | $128,371,147 | $228,154,528 | * |
| 1917 ................... | * | 155,557,002 | 257,115,214 | $299,885,059 |
| 1918 ................... | 373 | 164,633,522 | 255,887,031 | 305,782,264 |
| 1919 ................... | 403 | 211,091,565 | 319,594,259 | 381,780,464 |
| 1920 ................... | 402 | 219,304,440 | 296,208,939 | 368,644,393 |
| 1921 ................... | 387 | 189,272,334 | 270,207,824 | 327,655,318 |
| 1922 ................... | 311 | 193,293,542 | 304,585,906 | 367,510,948 |
| 1923 ................... | 357 | 188,994,720 | 299,786,014 | 355,960,695 |
| 1924 ................... | 338 | 181,523,399 | 329,909,726 | 380,811,824 |
| 1925 ................... | 317 | 169,220,508 | 321,062,937 | 364,966,320 |
| 1926 ................... | 306 | 165,407,957 | 321,696,881 | 366,082,565 |
| 1927 ................... | 284 | 162,723,310 | 321,739,131 | * |
| 1928 ................... | 284 | 172,236,431 | 327,598,487 | 371,722,374 |
| 1929 ................... | 275 | 172,871,041 | 311,040,485 | 357,265,628 |
| 1930 ................... | 257 | 147,521,449 | 309,991,117 | 379,998,686 |
| 1931 ................... | 221 | 117,196,645 | 259,134,580 | 319,289,223 |

*Data not available.

## BANK CLEARINGS OF PRINCIPAL CITIES

| Year | Denver | Pueblo | Colorado Springs |
|---|---|---|---|
| 1920 | $1,968,274,696 | $52,079,068 | $62,282,893 |
| 1921 | 1,527,547,229 | 41,480,801 | 50,096,140 |
| 1922 | 1,551,636,800 | 40,394,514 | 53,841,091 |
| 1923 | 1,655,870,320 | 44,549,719 | 61,091,662 |
| 1924 | 1,611,163,932 | 50,384,169 | 56,755,109 |
| 1925 | 1,732,799,082 | 59,266,536 | 63,681,224 |
| 1926 | 1,688,644,834 | 63,275,607 | 61,751,001 |
| 1927 | 1,732,674,525 | 69,302,494 | 64,167,039 |
| 1928 | 1,863,582,872 | 76,582,861 | 70,177,442 |
| 1929 | 2,027,274,024 | 90,395,740 | 71,753,636 |
| 1930 | 1,694,207,214 | 79,301,192 | 61,740,665 |
| 1931 | 1,342,832,980 | 62,042,177 | 51,016,097 |

### COLORADO BANK STATISTICS

| COUNTY | December 31, 1931 | | | December 31, 1930 | |
|---|---|---|---|---|---|
| | Loans and Discounts | Deposits | Total Assets | Loans and Discounts | Deposits |
| Adams............... | $      458,937 | $      831,034 | $   1,150,387 | $      828,894 | $   1,289,601 |
| Alamosa............. | 877,723 | 1,325,222 | 1,701,507 | 1,028,186 | 1,868,373 |
| Arapahoe............ | 705,664 | 1,509,970 | 1,965,973 | 1,010,962 | 2,059,392 |
| Archuleta........... | 113,497 | 149,121 | 262,619 | 145,050 | 201,952 |
| Baca................ | 445,270 | 577,249 | 874,606 | 574,696 | 731,827 |
| Bent................ | 674,863 | 782,774 | 1,345,005 | 837,265 | 1,059,934 |
| Boulder............. | 3,284,173 | 6,421,413 | 8,306,311 | 4,136,114 | 7,464,121 |
| Chaffee............. | 430,100 | 1,388,033 | 1,620,574 | 587,097 | 1,858,309 |
| Cheyenne............ | 209,918 | 167,593 | 377,511 | 302,954 | 267,744 |
| Clear Creek......... | 115,453 | 211,314 | 326,767 | 288,724 | 447,961 |
| Conejos............. | 317,860 | 441,429 | 658,998 | 378,175 | 660,669 |
| Costilla............ | 48,612 | 92,809 | 141,421 | 137,293 | 199,705 |
| Crowley............. | 309,242 | 445,066 | 728,396 | 364,202 | 649,849 |
| Custer.............. | 118,419 | 174,454 | 292,873 | 147,423 | 233,794 |
| Delta............... | 1,147,477 | 1,558,885 | 2,618,188 | 1,338,202 | 1,906,945 |
| Denver.............. | 55,871,323 | 142,097,217 | 164,427,834 | 70,664,014 | 168,315,061 |
| Dolores............. | ........ | ........ | ........ | ........ | ........ |
| Douglas............. | 347,885 | 449,324 | 618,736 | 421,575 | 540,829 |
| Eagle............... | 230,131 | 345,226 | 411,310 | 240,162 | 458,621 |
| Elbert.............. | 516,043 | 639,489 | 1,155,532 | 639,384 | 923,832 |
| El Paso............. | 10,352,825 | 18,060,319 | 22,945,927 | 11,739,505 | 19,724,721 |
| Fremont............. | 1,368,152 | 3,530,260 | 4,057,234 | 1,567,702 | 4,258,467 |
| Garfield............ | 1,628,713 | 2,492,160 | 3,068,802 | 1,749,993 | 2,726,973 |
| Gilpin.............. | 24,576 | 248,218 | 308,538 | 20,441 | 253,217 |
| Grand............... | 165,034 | 335,413 | 500,447 | 209,260 | 440,783 |
| Gunnison............ | 627,056 | 1,211,205 | 1,692,215 | 739,791 | 1,648,599 |
| Hinsdale............ | ........ | ........ | ........ | ........ | ........ |
| Huerfano............ | 957,142 | 2,194,805 | 2,607,786 | 1,068,697 | 2,553,099 |
| Jackson............. | ........ | ........ | ........ | ........ | ........ |
| Jefferson........... | 535,372 | 1,287,083 | 1,495,294 | 545,510 | 1,372,288 |
| Kiowa............... | 264,352 | 302,496 | 507,286 | 317,638 | 378,770 |
| Kit Carson.......... | 301,228 | 432,229 | 597,110 | 747,429 | 910,899 |
| Lake................ | 87,197 | 1,063,725 | 1,195,050 | 130,838 | 1,173,796 |
| La Plata............ | 1,171,878 | 2,235,057 | 2,897,348 | 1,214,207 | 2,586,251 |
| Larimer............. | 3,342,508 | 5,317,701 | 7,251,340 | 4,300,810 | 6,215,512 |
| Las Animas.......... | 1,877,924 | 6,295,993 | 7,362,865 | 3,077,978 | 7,633,795 |
| Lincoln............. | 498,222 | 631,027 | 806,509 | 723,983 | 800,869 |
| Logan............... | 1,321,047 | 1,944,423 | 3,233,795 | 1,907,490 | 2,323,649 |
| Mesa................ | 2,211,022 | 3,111,286 | 4,494,949 | 2,544,742 | 4,110,442 |
| Mineral............. | ........ | ........ | ........ | ........ | ........ |
| Moffat.............. | 243,788 | 458,241 | 592,407 | 343,612 | 625,091 |
| Montezuma........... | 917,287 | 855,873 | 1,467,923 | 994,452 | 1,261,998 |
| Montrose............ | 1,333,351 | 1,768,401 | 2,269,208 | 1,412,476 | 2,121,952 |
| Morgan.............. | 2,138,684 | 2,373,127 | 4,076,349 | 2,707,032 | 2,994,667 |
| Otero............... | 1,432,671 | 2,181,211 | 3,290,611 | 1,893,862 | 2,757,673 |
| Ouray............... | 183,926 | 271,043 | 454,969 | 203,584 | 305,788 |
| Park................ | 95,729 | 163,000 | 258,729 | 124,682 | 225,103 |
| Phillips............ | 749,401 | 973,917 | 1,476,763 | 900,778 | 1,251,084 |
| Pitkin.............. | 116,919 | 359,610 | 476,529 | 115,758 | 372,722 |
| Prowers............. | 912,917 | 1,475,853 | 2,085,971 | 1,270,661 | 1,781,697 |
| Pueblo.............. | 7,780,372 | 23,069,640 | 28,549,186 | 9,356,612 | 26,285,440 |
| Rio Blanco.......... | 508,829 | 339,419 | 608,518 | 595,190 | 712,473 |
| Rio Grande.......... | 835,404 | 1,123,886 | 1,959,759 | 1,357,045 | 1,885,801 |
| Routt............... | 258,965 | 323,966 | 582,931 | 817,867 | 990,043 |
| Saguache............ | 526,761 | 604,594 | 972,390 | 551,552 | 807,794 |
| San Juan............ | 107,478 | 455,874 | 570,659 | 101,042 | 515,143 |
| San Miguel.......... | ........ | ........ | ........ | ........ | ........ |
| Sedgwick............ | 394,997 | 402,967 | 687,412 | 526,189 | 645,949 |
| Summit.............. | 42,447 | 104,439 | 146,885 | 51,525 | 113,689 |
| Teller.............. | 147,575 | 1,542,531 | 1,610,229 | 201,635 | 1,860,632 |
| Washington.......... | 274,445 | 474,963 | 594,136 | 354,270 | 539,605 |
| Weld................ | 4,422,835 | 8,347,629 | 10,760,776 | 5,668,460 | 9,842,397 |
| Yuma................ | 815,026 | 1,163,374 | 1,789,840 | 1,296,779 | 1,843,727 |
| State............... | $117,196,645 | $259,134,580 | $319,289,223 | $147,521,449 | $309,991,117 |

# Colorado Banks

(As of November 1, 1932)

### Adams County

First National Bank_____Aurora
Bennett State Bank_____Bennett
Brighton State Bank_____Brighton

### Alamosa County

Alamosa National Bank_____Alamosa
American National Bank_____Alamosa
First State Bank of Alamosa_____Alamosa
Hooper State Bank_____Hooper

### Arapahoe County

Byers State Bank_____Byers
First National Bank_____Englewood
Englewood State Bank_____Englewood
First National Bank_____Littleton
Littleton National Bank_____Littleton
First National Bank_____Strasburg

### Archuleta County

Citizens Bank of Pagosa Springs_____
_____Pagosa Springs

### Baca County

First State Bank_____Pritchett
First National Bank_____Springfield
Bank of Baca County_____Two Buttes
Colorado State Bank_____Walsh

### Bent County

Bent County Bank_____Las Animas
First National Bank_____Las Animas
McClave State Bank_____McClave

### Boulder County

Boulder National Bank_____Boulder
First National Bank_____Boulder
Mercantile Bank & Trust Co._____Boulder
National State Bank_____Boulder
First National Bank_____Longmont
Longmont National Bank_____Longmont
First State Bank of Louisville_____Louisville
State Bank of Lyons_____Lyons

### Chaffee County

First National Bank_____Salida

### Cheyenne County

Cheyenne County State Bank__Cheyenne Wells
Kit Carson State Bank_____Kit Carson

### Clear Creek County

Bank of Idaho Springs_____Idaho Springs

### Conejos County

Commercial State Bank_____Antonito
First National Bank_____La Jara
Colonial State Bank_____Manassa

### Costilla County

San Luis State Bank_____San Luis

### Crowley County

Crowley State Bank_____Crowley
First National Bank_____Ordway
Ordway State Bank_____Ordway
State Bank of Sugar City_____Sugar City

### Custer County

Westcliffe State Bank_____Westcliffe

### Delta County

First National Bank_____Cedaredge
Crawford State Bank_____Crawford
Colorado Bank & Trust Co._____Delta
First State Bank_____Hotchkiss
First National Bank_____Paonia

### Denver County

American National Bank_____Denver
Colorado State Bank of Denver_____Denver
Central Savings Bank & Trust Co._____Denver
Colorado National Bank_____Denver
Denver National Bank_____Denver
First National Bank_____Denver
Guardian Trust Co._____Denver
International Trust Co._____Denver
Motor Bank _____Denver
National City Bank_____Denver
Stockyards National Bank_____Denver
United States National Bank_____Denver

### Dolores County

No Banks.

### Douglas County

First National Bank_____Castle Rock
Douglas County Bank_____Parker

### Eagle County

First National Bank_____Eagle

### Elbert County

Elbert County State Bank_____Elbert
Elizabeth State Bank_____Elizabeth
Kiowa State Bank_____Kiowa
Stockgrowers State Bank_____Kiowa
Simla State Bank_____Simla

### El Paso County

Colorado Savings Bank_____Colorado Springs
Colorado Springs National Bank_____
_____Colorado Springs
Colorado Title & Trust Co.___Colorado Springs
Exchange National Bank_____Colorado Springs
First National Bank_____Colorado Springs
Bank of Manitou_____Manitou
Farmers State Bank_____Peyton
State Bank of Ramah_____Ramah

### Fremont County

Colorado State Bank_____Canon City
First National Bank_____Canon City
Fremont County National Bank____Canon City
First National Bank_____Florence

### Garfield County

First National Bank_____Carbondale
Citizens National Bank_____Glenwood Springs
First National Bank_____Glenwood Springs
Garfield County State Bank____Grand Valley
New Castle State Bank_____New Castle
First State Bank_____Silt

### Gilpin County

First National Bank_____Central City

### Grand County

First State Bank of Sulphur Springs____
_____Hot Sulphur Springs
Bank of Kremmling_____Kremmling

### Gunnison County

First National Bank_____Gunnison
Gunnison Bank & Trust Co._____Gunnison

### Hinsdale County

No Banks.

### Huerfano County

First National Bank_____La Veta
First National Bank_____Walsenburg
Guaranty State Bank_____Walsenburg

### Jackson County

No banks.

### Jefferson County

First National Bank_____Arvada
Ruhey National Bank_____Golden

### Kiowa County

First National Bank_____Eads
Peoples State Bank of Towner_____Towner

### Kit Carson County

Bank of Burlington_____Burlington
First National Bank_____Flagler
Seibert State Bank_____Seibert
First National Bank_____Stratton

### Lake County

Carbonate American Nat'l Bank_____Leadville

### La Plata County

Burns National Bank_____Durango
Durango Trust Company_____Durango
First National Bank_____Durango
Ignacio State Bank_____Ignacio

### Larimer County

Berthoud National Bank_____Berthoud
Estes Park Bank_____Estes Park
First National Bank_____Ft. Collins
Fort Collins National Bank_____Ft. Collins
Poudre Valley National Bank_____Ft. Collins
Larimer Co. Bank & Trust Co._____Loveland
First National Bank_____Loveland
First National Bank_____Wellington

### Las Animas County

Commercial Savings Bank_____Trinidad
First National Bank_____Trinidad
Trinidad National Bank_____Trinidad

### Lincoln County

First National Bank_____Hugo
First National Bank_____Limon
Limon National Bank_____Limon

### Logan County

First National Bank_____Fleming
Iliff State Bank_____Iliff
Merino State Bank_____Merino
First National Bank_____Peetz
Commercial Savings Bank_____Sterling
Security State Bank_____Sterling

### Mesa County

Stockman's Bank_____Collbran
Bank of DeBeque_____DeBeque
First National Bank_____Fruita
Grand Valley National Bank___Grand Junction
United States Bank_____Grand Junction
Palisades National Bank_____Palisades

### Mineral County

No Banks.

### Moffat County

No Banks.

### Montezuma County

Montezuma Valley National Bank_____Cortez
J. J. Harris & Company, Bankers_____Dolores
First National Bank_____Mancos

### Montrose County

First National Bank_____Montrose
Montrose National Bank_____Montrose
First National Bank_____Olathe

### Morgan County

Farmers State Bank_____Brush
First National Bank_____Brush
Farmers State Bank_____Ft. Morgan
First National Bank_____Ft. Morgan
Peoples State Bank_____Ft. Morgan
First State Bank of Hillrose_____Hillrose
Weldon Valley State Bank_____Weldona

### Otero County

Fowler State Bank_____Fowler
First National Bank_____Fowler
Colorado Savings & Trust Co._____La Junta
First National Bank_____La Junta
La Junta State Bank_____La Junta
J. N. Beatty & Company, Bankers_Manzanola
Rocky Ford National Bank_____Rocky Ford
First State Bank of Swink_____Swink

### Ouray County

Citizens State Bank_____Ouray

### Park County

Bank of Alma_____Alma
Bank of Fairplay_____Fairplay

### Phillips County

Farmers State Bank_____Haxtun
Haxtun State Bank_____Haxtun
Citizens State Bank_____Holyoke
First National Bank_____Holyoke
Paoli State Bank_____Paoli

### Pitkin County

Aspen State Bank_____Aspen

### Prowers County

American State Bank_____Granada
Hartman State Bank_____Hartman
First National Bank_____Holly
First National Bank_____Lamar
Lamar National Bank_____Lamar
Valley State Bank_____Lamar
Bank of Wiley_____Wiley

### Pueblo County

First National Bank_____Pueblo
Minnequa Bank of Pueblo_____Pueblo
Pueblo Savings Bank & Trust Co._____Pueblo
Southern Colorado Bank_____Pueblo
Western National Bank_____Pueblo
Bank of Rye_____Rye

### Rio Blanco County

First National Bank_____Meeker
First State Bank_____Meeker

### Rio Grande County

Rio Grande State Bank_____Del Norte
Monte Vista Bank & Trust Co.___Monte Vista
The Wallace State Bank_____Monte Vista

### Routt County

Oak Creek State Bank_____Oak Creek
Bank of Steamboat Springs_Steamboat Springs

### Saguache County

First National Bank_____Center
Saguache County National Bank____Saguache

### San Juan County

First National Bank_____Silverton

### San Miguel County

No banks.

### Sedgwick County

First National Bank_____Julesburg
State Bank of Ovid_____Ovid
First National Bank_____Sedgwick

### Summit County

Engle Brothers Exchange Bank_Breckenridge

### Teller County

First National Bank_____Cripple Creek

### Washington County

Citizens National Bank_____Akron
Farmers State Bank_____Cope
First National Bank_____Otis

### Weld County

| | |
|---|---|
| Farmers National Bank | Ault |
| Briggsdale State Bank | Briggsdale |
| First National Bank | Eaton |
| Erie Bank | Erie |
| Fort Lupton State Bank | Fort Lupton |
| First National Bank | Greeley |
| Greeley Union National Bank | Greeley |
| Weld County Savings Bank | Greeley |
| Hereford State Bank | Hereford |
| First State Bank of Hudson | Hudson |
| First National Bank | Johnstown |
| First State Bank | Keenesburg |
| First State Bank | Nunn |
| Platteville National Bank | Platteville |
| Roggen State Bank | Roggen |
| Farmers Bank of Severance | Severance |
| First National Bank | Windsor |

### Yuma County

| | |
|---|---|
| Eckley State Bank | Eckley |
| First State Bank | Idalia |
| First State Bank | Kirk |
| Laird State Bank | Laird |
| Vernon State Bank | Vernon |
| First National Bank | Wray |
| National Bank | Wray |
| Farmers State Bank | Yuma |

## STATE FLAG

The eighteenth general assembly of the Colorado legislature enacted a measure creating a state flag for the state of Colorado. This act was filed with the secretary of state on June 5, 1911, and became a law without being signed by the governor. The specifications of the flag as provided by the act are as follows:

The width of the flag shall be two-thirds of its length.

It shall consist of three alternate stripes to be of equal width and at right angles to the staff.

The white stripe shall be the center stripe. (The original law did not specify the color of the other two stripes, but blue was the color universally used.)

At a distance from the staff end of the flag of one thirty-sixth of the total length of the flag there shall be a circular red C, of the same color as the red in the United States flag.

The diameter of the letter C shall be one-sixth of the width of the flag.

The inner line of the opening of the letter C shall be three-fourths of the width of its body or bar and the outer line of the opening shall be double the length of the inner line thereof.

Completely filling the open space inside the letter C shall be a golden disk.

Attached to the flag shall be a cord of gold and silver, intertwined, with tassels, one of gold and the other of silver.

The flag was designed by A. C. Carson, at one time manager of a Denver theater. The colors are typical of Colorado; the blue for the skies, the gold for the sunshine, the white for the snow-capped mountains and the red in the letter C standing for the Spanish interpretation of the name of the state. The gold and silver cord and tassels signify the principal metals mined in the state.

## STATE SEAL AND MOTTO

The seal of the state of Colorado, as determined by statutory enactment, is described as follows:

It shall be two and one-half inches in diameter with the following device inscribed thereon: An heraldic shield bearing in chief, or upon the upper portion of same upon a red ground, three snow-capped mountains; above, surrounding clouds; upon the lower part thereof, upon a golden ground, a miner's badge as prescribed by the rules of heraldry; as a crest above the shield, the eye of God, being golden rays proceeding from the lines of a triangle; below the crest and above the shield as a scroll, the Roman fasces, bearing upon a band of red, white and blue the words "Union and Constitution"; below the whole the motto "Nil Sine Numine," the whole to be surrounded by the words "State of Colorado" and the figures "1876."

The meaning of the Latin motto "Nil Sine Numine" is "Nothing without Providence."

The secretary of state alone is authorized to use or affix the seal to any document whatever, and he only in pursuance of the law. He is the custodian of the seal. Severe penalties are provided for counterfeiting or illegally using the seal.

## GEOGRAPHICAL CENTER OF COLORADO

The geographical center of Colorado, as computed by the United States geological survey, is approximately 30 miles northwest of Pikes peak, in the central eastern part of Park county between Tarryall and Lost Park creeks and to the west of Lake Cheesman. The exact position cannot be determined from the data available, but the approximate position given is sufficiently exact for ordinary purposes. The geographical center of an area may be defined as that point on which the surface of the area would be balanced if it were a plane of uniform thickness, or in other words, the center of gravity of the surface.

# Colorado Commercial Organizations

ACTIVE commercial organizations in all parts of the state are doing excellent work toward building up their respective communities and developing the rich resources of the entire state. Almost every county in the state now has one or more of these organizations which are prepared to furnish direct and detailed information concerning resources, opportunities and attractions in the communities which they serve.

The following list includes those organizations which are members of the State Association of Commercial Organizations of Colorado, of which Elmore Petersen of the State university at Boulder is secretary. In addition to those organizations of a local nature it includes several of regional or state-wide scope, and there are many luncheon clubs and similar groups which are doing splendid community and sectional work, but which cannot be included in a condensed tabulation.

## STATE AND REGIONAL ORGANIZATIONS

State Association of Commercial Organizations of Colorado—J. F. Greenawalt, Denver, president; Elmore Petersen, Boulder, secretary.

Colorado Association of Real Estate Boards—W. R. Williams, Pueblo, president; Wesley J. Towne, 217 Chamber of Commerce building, Denver, secretary.

Colorado Association — F. H. Reid, president; B. M. Rastall, executive vice-president; Dudley R. Griggs, secretary; 514 Sixteenth Street, Denver.

Colorado Manufacturers and Merchants Association—E. J. Yetter, Denver, president; E. C. Dawson, Denver, executive secretary; office, City Auditorium, Denver.

Moffat Tunnel League—E. H. Godfrey, Oak Creek, president; J. R. Burroughs, Steamboat Springs, secretary.

The following table of commercial organizations by counties is revised to April 14, 1932.

## COLORADO COMMERCIAL ORGANIZATIONS

### Adams County
Aurora—Commercial Club; Frank M. Shedd, president; John F. Burke, secretary.

### Alamosa County
Alamosa—Chamber of Commerce; L. B. Olsen, president; Charles L. Dynes, secretary.

### Arapahoe County
Byers—Commercial Association; W. L. Best, president; Hal Parmeter, secretary.
*Englewood—Chamber of Commerce; C M. Hall, president; E. B. Cartwright, secretary.
*Littleton—Civic and Commercial Association; F. M. Moore, president; H. S. Ramsey, secretary.

### Baca County
Springfield—Chamber of Commerce; Ralph Williams, president; Ben Wofford, secretary.

### Bent County
*Las Animas—Chamber of Commerce; Dr. W. H. Fickel, president; G. G. Caldwell, secretary.

### Boulder County
Allens Park—Chamber of Commerce; George Pheefee, president; Wm. Morgan, secretary.
*Boulder — Chamber of Commerce; Loren H. Hays, president; Eben G. Fine, secretary.
*Longmont—Chamber of Commerce; C. S. Wees, president; R. B. Miller, secretary.
Lyons—Commercial Association; J. G. Parks, president; Mrs. C. L. Niner, secretary.

### Chaffee County
Buena Vista—Chamber of Commerce; C. R. Sindlinger, president; L. P. Perschbacher, secretary.
Salida—Chamber of Commerce; H. G. Frantz, president; W. E. Patterson, secretary.

### Cheyenne County
Cheyenne Wells—Chamber of Commerce; J. C. Milne, president; R. A. Pfost, secretary.
Kit Carson—Chamber of Commerce; Elden Platner, president; Duncan Dunn, secretary.

### Clear Creek County
Empire—Commercial Association; G. H. Anderson, president; E. E. Koch, secretary.

### Conejos County
Antonito—Chamber of Commerce; G. A. Jenkins, president; J. D. Frazey, secretary.

### Crowley County
Ordway—Lions Club; George Wunderlick, president; C. E. Barker, secretary.
*Sugar City—Service Club; L. A. Richards, president; T. W. Butler, secretary.

*Members of State Association of Commercial Executives.

### Delta County

Cedaredge—Chamber of Commerce; F. T. Clark, president; P. K. Yonge, secretary.

Crawford — Chamber of Commerce; Henry E. Welborn, president; Chas. M. Hillman, secretary.

*Delta—Delta Chamber of Commerce; A. E. Penley, president; James F. Weeland, secretary.

Hotchkiss—North Fork Chamber of Commerce; C. F. Myers, president; H. D. Shiles, secretary.

*Paonia—Chamber of Commerce; C. L. Oliver, president; O. J. Stone, secretary.

### Denver County

*Denver — Chamber of Commerce; Adolph F. Zang, president; G. E. Collison, secretary.

*Denver—Colorado Association; F. H. Reid, president; Dudley R. Griggs, secretary.

Denver—Rocky Mountain Motorists, Inc.; John Huntington, president; Clarence Werthan, secretary.

### Dolores County

*Rico—Dolores County Chamber of Commerce; Dennis Mullins, president; F. J. Koenig, secretary.

### Eagle County

*Eagle—Chamber of Commerce; Forrest W. Cave, president; Leo F. Fessenden, secretary.

### El Paso County

*Colorado Springs—Chamber of Commerce; O. E. Hemenway, president; E. E. Jackson, secretary.

### Fremont County

*Canon City—Chamber of Commerce; D. E. Nichelson, president; Mary Jo Shores, secretary.

*Florence — Chamber of Commerce; Sidney R. Hahn, president; Lynn Smith, secretary.

*Penrose—Beaver Park Farm and Commercial Club; E .A. Stowe, president; W. G. Keiry, secretary .

### Garfield County

*Glenwood Springs—Chamber of Commerce; C. L. Hubbard, president; C. W. Filghum, secretary.

Grand Valley—Chamber of Commerce; Henry Alber, president; G. E. Richardson, secretary.

Rifle—Chamber of Commerce; F. A. Dunham, president; E. P. Brown, secretary.

### Grand County

*Hot Sulphur Springs—Commercial Club; H. O. Gray, president; N. C. Huffaker, secretary.

### Gunnison County

Gunnison—Gunnison County Chamber of Commerce; R. E. Porter, president; S. C. Hartman, secretary.

### Huerfano County

*La Veta—Commercial Club; C. C. Webster, president; O. B. Lauth, secretary.

### Jefferson County

*Arvada — Chamber of Commerce; Newt Olson, president; John E. Meier, secretary.

Edgewater — East Jefferson County Commercial Club, 5223 West Colfax Avenue; Captain J. L. Dixon, president; Charles Fitch, secretary.

### Kiowa County

Eads—Business Men's Club; W. M. Ramsdale, president; J. R. Wood, secretary.

### Kit Carson County

Burlington—Chamber of Commerce; H. W. Gleason, president; P. L. Bruner, secretary.

Flagler—Community Club; G. M. Baxter, president; Gust Westman, secretary.

### La Plata County

*Durango—Chamber of Commerce; J. A. Clay, president; Richard T. Nelson, secretary.

### Larimer County

*Berthoud—Chamber of Commerce; Walter G. Albrecht, president; P. R. Stranahan, secretary.

*Estes Park—Chamber of Commerce; R. L. Reed, president; Louis Bessemer, secretary.

*Fort Collins—Chamber of Commerce; F. W. Humphrey, president; D. L. Anderson, secretary.

*Loveland—Chamber of Commerce; Hatfield Chilson, president; William Hammond, secretary.

*Wellington—Chamber of Commerce; E. T. Puleston, president; A. L. Carlson, secretary.

### Las Animas County

*Trinidad — Trinidad - Las Animas County Chamber of Commerce; Leo R. Gottlieb, president; J. C. Caldwell, secretary.

### Lincoln County

Arriba—Arriba Commercial Club; John Freel, president; W. E. Kliewer, secretary.

Hugo—Commercial Club; G. D. Randolph, president; J. J. Missemer, secretary.

Limon—Chamber of Commerce; F. E. Ainsworth, president; D. W. Wills, secretary.

### Logan County

*Merino—Merino Progress Club; W. E. Outcalt, president; K. C. Brown, secretary.

*Sterling—Chamber of Commerce; H. B. Swedlund, president; Mervin Brown, secretary.

### Mesa County

*Collbran—Plateau Valley Chamber of Commerce; Dr. Wm. Zinke, president; J. C. Mardis, secretary.

Fruita—Chamber of Commerce; F. W. Bocking, president; G. L. Miller, secretary.

*Grand Junction—Chamber of Commerce; L. W. Burgess, president; W. M. Wood, secretary.

*Palisade — Chamber of Commerce; Grant Crissy, president; Wayne N. Aspinall, secretary.

### Moffat County

*Craig—Lions Club; C. A. Stoddard, president; John H. McGinnis, secretary.

### Montezuma County

*Cortez—Chamber of Commerce; Dr. R. W. Calkins, president; F. L. Miller, secretary.

*Dolores—Chamber of Commerce; S. H. Phlegar, president; C. H. Webb, secretary.

*Mancos—Chamber of Commerce; E. C. Mallett, president; R. L. Rider, secretary.

### Montrose County

Montrose—Montrose County Chamber of Commerce; L. A. Pinkstaff, president; Mrs. N. M. Fleming, secretary.

### Morgan County

Brush—Civic Club; C. W. Emerson, president; C. E. Baker, secretary.
*Fort Morgan — Chamber of Commerce; C. H. Mayborn, president; C. E. Wagner, secretary.
*Orchard—Commercial Club; H. J. Gearhart, president; Joseph Korsoski, secretary.
*Weldona—Chamber of Commerce; J. L. Markley, president; M. O. York, secretary.

### Otero County

La Junta—Chamber of Commerce; V. N. Lagerquist, president; F. R. Brown, secretary.
Manzanola—Commerce Club; E. L. Stephens, president; A. W. Warner, secretary.
*Rocky Ford—Chamber of Commerce; F. S. Johnson, president; J. L. Miller, secretary.

### Ouray County

Ouray—Chamber of Commerce; John Schwend, president; M. W. Driscoll, secretary.

### Prowers County

*Granada—Granada Promotion Club; C. D. Baldwin, president; A. L. McDonald, secretary.
Holly—Commercial Club; H. D. Steel, president; E. J. Thayer, secretary.
*Lamar—Chamber of Commerce; J. C. Johnston, president; L. M. Markham, secretary.
*Wiley — Commercial Club; Charles Lennox, president; R. H. Horner, secretary.

### Pueblo County

*Pueblo—Chamber of Commerce; J. M. Holmes, president; P. A. Gray, secretary.
Rye—Chamber of Commerce; J. W. Stewart, president; C. W. Miller, secretary.

### Rio Blanco County

Meeker—Rio Blanco Commercial Club; F. A. Carstens, president; J. E. Sexson, secretary.

### Rio Grande County

*Del Norte—Chamber of Commerce; Charles R. Ewing, president; Charles W. Donnen, secretary.
*Monte Vista—Commercial Club; H. E. Lague, president; Esther Godfrey, secretary.

### Routt County

Hayden—Lions Club; H. B. Pleasant, president; M. F. Hofstetter, secretary.
Oak Creek—Chamber of Commerce; R. T. Gwillim, president; Louis Bell, secretary.
*Steamboat Springs—Moffat Tunnel League; E. H. Godfrey, president; J. R. Burroughs, secretary.
Steamboat Springs—Commercial Club; J. A. Brobeck, president; J. R. Burroughs, secretary.

### San Juan County

Silverton—Commercial Club; E. W. Walter, president; James Pilling, secretary.

### San Miguel County

Norwood—Chamber of Commerce; C. H. McKeever, president; Dr. J. H. Cheney, secretary.
Telluride—Lions Club; F. B. Wilson, president; L. G. Denison, secretary.

### Summit County

*Dillon—Chamber of Commerce; E. C. Peabody, president; I. W. Blundell, secretary.

### Teller County

Cripple Creek—Cripple Creek Motor and Commercial Club; Paul H. House, president; F. W. Bruington, secretary.
Victor—Commercial Club; Eric Johnson, president; Dan Harrington, secretary.

### Washington County

*Otis—Commercial Club; Albert M. Williss, president; Usher Kelsey, secretary.

### Weld County

*Ault—Community Club; Jens Jeremiassen, president; E. Wedmaier, secretary.
Eaton—Eaton Rotary Club; Chas. N. Beckner, president; E. K. McMillen, secretary.
Erie—Consolidated Commercial Association; Wm. Nicholson, president; C. R. Hunt, secretary.
*Greeley — Chamber of Commerce; Chas. Hansen, president; E. H. Folbrecht, secretary.
Hudson—Commercial Club; Alfred Olson, president; S. R. Smith, secretary.
*Johnstown—Commercial Club; C. H. Criswell, president; C. M. Keller, secretary.
Milliken—Community Club; Charles Stroh, president; O. L. AltVater, secretary.
*Windsor—Community Club; Chas. E. Petersen, president; G. I. Richards, secretary.

### Yuma County

Wray—Commercial Club; V. V. Vining, president; Joe C. Graham, secretary.
Yuma—Chamber of Commerce; C. E. Fritts, president; G. S. Thompson, secretary.

---

*Members of State Association of Commercial Executives.

## STATE SONG

The twentieth general assembly of the Colorado legislature enacted a measure approved on May 8, 1915, by Gov. George A. Carlson, by which a song entitled "Where the Columbines Grow" was adopted as the official state song of Colorado to be used on all appropriate occasions. The words and music were written and composed by Dr. Arthur J. Fynn, a prominent educator identified for many years with the Denver public schools. Following the death of Dr. Fynn in 1931, Mrs. Rose C. Fynn, his widow, presented the copyright to the Daughters of Colorado, an organization of native-born Colorado women, which will use the proceeds of sales to erect markers on historic spots throughout the state. On July 10, 1931, the Columbine Day association dedicated a blue spruce tree on the state capitol ground in honor of Dr. Fynn.

## Colorado Postoffices

COLORADO had on January 1, 1932, a total of 713 postoffices, of which 56 belonged to the first and second classes and 657 were designated as third and fourth class postoffices. The number on January 1 of the years named was as follows:

| Year | Class 1 & 2 | Class 3 & 4 | Total |
|------|-----|-----|------|
| 1927 ............ | 55 | 726 | 781 |
| 1929 ............ | 59 | 704 | 763 |
| 1930 ............ | 60 | 673 | 733 |
| 1931 ............ | 59 | 671 | 730 |
| 1932 ............ | 56 | 657 | 713 |

All postmasters are appointed by the president and confirmed by the senate. Postmasters of the first and second classes receive stipulated salaries for their services, while salaries of postmasters of third and fourth-class offices are based on stamp sales.

The stamp sales of first and second class postoffices, by years, were as follows:

| Year | Amount |
|------|--------|
| 1925 ........................ | $4,837,745 |
| 1926 ........................ | 5,301,024 |
| 1927 ........................ | 5,608,286 |
| 1928 ........................ | 5,700,006 |
| 1929 ........................ | 6,060,555 |
| 1930 ........................ | 5,920,741 |
| 1931 ........................ | 5,334,234 |

Stamp sales by third and fourth class postoffices, by years, follow:

| Year | Amount |
|------|--------|
| 1925 ........................ | $764,235 |
| 1926 ........................ | 729,681 |
| 1927 ........................ | 709,200 |
| 1928 ........................ | 684,508 |
| 1929 ........................ | 714,966 |
| 1930 ........................ | 641,278 |
| 1931 ........................ | 601,802 |

Total sales by all offices in the state, by years, were as follows:

| Year | Amount |
|------|--------|
| 1925 ........................ | $5,601,980 |
| 1926 ........................ | 6,030,705 |
| 1927 ........................ | 6,317,486 |
| 1928 ........................ | 6,384,510 |
| 1929 ........................ | 6,775,521 |
| 1930 ........................ | 6,562,019 |
| 1931 ........................ | 5,936,036 |

The postoffice department, according to a survey made in 1927, has in Colorado a total of 2,393 salaried officials and employes, of whom 2,196 are postoffice employes and 197 are in other branches of the service, such as railway mail service and inspection departments. The number of persons employed is almost equally divided between the first and second class postoffices, which reported 762, and the third and fourth class postoffices, with approximately 750 persons. These figures do not include assistants in the third and fourth class postoffices and seasonal employes in offices that operate only a part of the time.

There is published herewith a table showing location, cost of sites and cost of buildings of postoffice property in Colorado under the jurisdiction of the treasury department, exclusive of equipment. These figures are for cost only and not present value, some sites being donated, and most of the properties appreciating in value since completion.

### GOVERNMENT-OWNED PROPERTIES IN COLORADO
(Includes only those under the control of the U. S. Treasury Department)

| LOCATION | Character | Cost of Site | Cost of Building |
|----------|-----------|-------------:|-----------------:|
| Boulder ..................... | Postoffice ............ | $ 24,540.98 | $ 59,951.85 |
| Canon City................. | Postoffice (old)....... | 11,000.00 | (No Bldg.) |
| Canon City................. | Postoffice (new)....... | 14,000.00 | (*) |
| Colorado Springs........... | P. O. and Court House | 65,066.89 | 241,582.98 |
| Denver ..................... | Mint ................. | 60,261.71 | 770,625.04 |
| Denver ..................... | P. O. and Court House | 486,879.62 | 1,999,869.31 |
| Denver ..................... | Custom House........ | 65,825.17 | 570,410.52 |
| Denver ..................... | Custom House (new).. | 300,000.00 | 921,747.73 |
| Durango ................... | Postoffice ............ | 10,000.00 | 127,850.00 |
| Fort Collins............... | Postoffice ............ | 12,000.00 | 87,893.74 |
| Fort Morgan............... | Postoffice ............ | 9,785.00 | 47,412.99 |
| GlenWood Springs........... | Postoffice ............ | 9,500.00 | 83,951.96 |
| Grand Junction........... | Postoffice ............ | 9,800.00 | 173,899.17 |
| Greeley ................... | Postoffice ............ | 15,000.00 | 102,011.21 |
| Greeley ................... | Postoffice (new)...... | 9,737.36 | (No Bldg.) |
| La Junta.................. | Postoffice ............ | 1.00 | 84,934.84 |
| Leadville ................. | Postoffice ............ | 12,084.34 | 71,469.97 |
| Monte Vista............... | Postoffice ............ | 3,900.00 | (**) |
| Montrose ................. | P. O. and Court House | 15,000.00 | (***) |
| Pueblo ................... | Postoffice ............ | 28,008.07 | 298,990.93 |
| Sterling .................. | Postoffice ............ | 15,000.00 | 196,494.84 |
| Trinidad ................. | Postoffice ............ | 68.65 | 74,931.35 |
| Total................. | | $1,177,458.79 | $5,914,028.43 |

*Contract awarded ($78,300). Building in progress.
**Contract awarded ($98,000).
***Contract awarded ($128,000).

FIRST AND SECOND CLASS POSTOFFICES AND STAMP SALES

| Postoffice | County | Stamp Sales | | | | |
|---|---|---|---|---|---|---|
| | | 1931 | 1930 | 1929 | 1928 | 1927 |
| Akron | Washington | $ 8,711 | $ 8,833 | $ 9,103 | $ 9,135 | $ 9,264 |
| Alamosa | Alamosa | 33,082 | 35,735 | 35,755 | 33,500 | 31,534 |
| Arvada | Jefferson | 8,823 | 7,078 | 8,140 | 8,616 | * |
| Boulder | Boulder | 92,286 | 101,780 | 105,425 | 103,390 | 109,884 |
| Brighton | Adams | 16,625 | 17,401 | 17,318 | 16,526 | 16,336 |
| Brush | Morgan | 12,658 | 13,707 | 14,603 | 13,878 | 13,969 |
| Burlington | Kit Carson | 13,645 | 15,796 | 13,339 | 13,128 | 12,186 |
| Canon City | Fremont | 37,077 | 37,749 | 40,422 | 40,262 | 41,339 |
| Cheyenne Wells | Cheyenne | 10,649 | 13,067 | 13,599 | * | * |
| Colorado Springs | El Paso | 272,107 | 302,486 | 313,517 | 293,355 | 254,574 |
| Craig | Moffat | 11,150 | 14,848 | 14,965 | 13,403 | 12,629 |
| Cripple Creek | Teller | 7,666 | 8,088 | 7,812 | 9,261 | 8,643 |
| Delta | Delta | 20,494 | 21,072 | 22,335 | 22,004 | 22,117 |
| Del Norte | Rio Grande | 8,097 | 8,901 | 8,808 | 8,307 | * |
| Denver | Denver | 3,616,415 | 3,978,946 | 4,059,830 | 3,730,058 | 3,688,955 |
| Durango | La Plata | 33,231 | 40,142 | 42,353 | 41,460 | 42,710 |
| Eaton | Weld | ‡ | 8,089 | 8,614 | 8,697 | 9,210 |
| Estes Park | Larimer | 12,109 | 11,808 | 12,404 | 11,687 | 12,893 |
| Florence | Fremont | 11,074 | 12,969 | 13,672 | 15,178 | 15,183 |
| Fort Collins | Larimer | 65,156 | 73,945 | 75,902 | 75,617 | 76,112 |
| Fort Lupton | Weld | 8,266 | 9,413 | 8,307 | 8,603 | 8,951 |
| Fort Morgan | Morgan | 25,263 | 25,245 | 27,388 | 27,835 | 28,085 |
| Glenwood Springs | Garfield | 18,096 | 19,155 | 19,066 | 19,299 | 19,871 |
| Golden | Jefferson | 17,414 | 17,727 | 18,380 | 17,429 | 16,770 |
| Grand Junction | Mesa | 95,349 | 103,985 | 117,001 | 118,471 | 120,269 |
| Greeley | Weld | 84,822 | 92,033 | 87,784 | 91,036 | 90,793 |
| Gunnison | Gunnison | 13,313 | 13,916 | 15,289 | 13,811 | 14,117 |
| Haxtun | Phillips | ‡ | 8,012 | 8,108 | 8,072 | * |
| Holly | Prowers | 8,102 | 8,468 | 8,708 | 7,562 | 8,155 |
| Holyoke | Phillips | 8,435 | 9,846 | 10,199 | 9,564 | 9,729 |
| Idaho Springs | Clear Creek | 7,333 | 8,014 | 7,824 | 7,633 | 8,372 |
| Julesburg | Sedgwick | 7,574 | 11,335 | 10,317 | 9,896 | 11,661 |
| La Junta | Otero | 32,871 | 36,345 | 36,967 | 34,653 | 34,181 |
| Lamar | Prowers | 30,610 | 35,005 | 32,698 | 29,955 | 29,867 |
| Las Animas | Bent | 16,169 | 16,664 | 17,346 | 15,099 | 15,327 |
| Leadville | Lake | 15,994 | 16,853 | 18,860 | 18,557 | 20,035 |
| Limon | Lincoln | 7,223 | 7,485 | 7,535 | 7,477 | 7,475 |
| Littleton | Arapahoe | 15,324 | 21,025 | 25,378 | 20,386 | 17,754 |
| Longmont | Boulder | 29,489 | 31,544 | 27,755 | 30,731 | 26,468 |
| Loveland | Larimer | 22,006 | 23,849 | 23,247 | 23,456 | 23,318 |
| Manitou | El Paso | 2,637 | 13,997 | 15,114 | 12,963 | 13,974 |
| Meeker | Rio Blanco | 7,525 | 9,362 | 9,791 | 9,569 | 9,709 |
| Monte Vista | Rio Grande | 16,829 | 23,365 | 20,584 | 18,253 | 20,488 |
| Montrose | Montrose | 24,646 | 27,145 | 27,479 | 27,004 | 26,425 |
| Oak Creek | Routt | 5,832 | 8,227 | 7,159 | 7,388 | 7,174 |
| Palisades | Mesa | 8,057 | 7,530 | 8,677 | 7,225 | 8,759 |
| Paonia | Delta | 7,135 | 8,519 | 10,702 | 11,731 | 11,127 |
| Pueblo | Pueblo | 275,710 | 307,492 | 319,216 | 347,538 | 366,544 |
| Rifle | Garfield | 9,029 | 10,974 | 11,626 | 11,056 | 10,504 |
| Rocky Ford | Otero | 27,035 | 28,563 | 28,021 | 27,239 | 30,318 |
| Salida | Chaffee | 22,448 | 24,959 | 25,506 | 25,399 | 24,898 |
| Springfield | Baca | 10,860 | 12,206 | 10,759 | 8,963 | * |
| Steamboat Springs | Routt | 12,265 | 13,404 | 14,257 | 14,097 | 13,602 |
| Sterling | Logan | 42,806 | 45,661 | 44,885 | 44,327 | 39,360 |
| Telluride | San Miguel | † | † | 4,957 | 6,142 | 7,949 |
| Trinidad | Las Animas | 66,424 | 80,846 | 82,436 | 81,817 | 76,691 |
| Victor | Teller | ‡ | 6,500 | 8,151 | 8,146 | 8,050 |
| Walsenburg | Huerfano | 19,456 | 21,685 | 23,476 | 24,831 | 24,244 |
| Wray | Yuma | 10,715 | 11,492 | 11,741 | 10,242 | 10,667 |
| Yuma | Yuma | 10,112 | 10,454 | 9,438 | 9,090 | 9,066 |
| Total | | $5,334,234 | $5,920,741 | $6,060,555 | $5,700,007 | $5,608,285 |

* Included in aggregate for third and fourth class offices, in which classification these offices were carried until recently.
†Changed to third class July 1, 1930.
‡Changed to third class July 1, 1931.

# Third and Fourth Class Postoffices

(Corrected to July 1, 1932)

| Post Office | County | Post Office | County | Post Office | County |
|---|---|---|---|---|---|
| Abarr | Yuma | Burns | Eagle | Drake | Larimer |
| Ackmen | Montezuma | 'Byers² | Arapahoe | Dumont | Clear Creek |
| Adams City | Adams | Caddoa² | Bent | Dunkley | Routt |
| Adena | Morgan | Cahone | Dolores | Dunton | Dolores |
| Agate² | Elbert | Caisson | Moffat | Dupont | Adams |
| Aguilar² | Las Animas | Calhan² | El Paso | Dyke | Archuleta |
| Alamo | Huerfano | Cameo | Mesa | | |
| Alcreek | Las Animas | Campo² | Baca | Eads² | Kiowa |
| Allenspark | Boulder | Capulin | Conejos | 'Eagle² | Eagle |
| Allison | La Plata | 'Carbondale² | Garfield | East Lake | Adams |
| Alma | Park | Carlton | Prowers | Eaton | Weld |
| Almont³ | Gunnison | Carr | Weld | Eckert² | Delta |
| Amherst | Phillips | Cascade | El Paso | Eckley² | Yuma |
| Amity² | Prowers | Castle Rock² | Douglas | 'Edgewater² | Jefferson |
| Amy | Lincoln | Cebolla² | Gunnison | Edler | Baca |
| Andrix | Las Animas | Cedar | San Miguel | Edwards | Eagle |
| Antlers | Garfield | 'Cedaredge² | Delta | Eggers³ | Larimer |
| Antonito² | Conejos | Cedarwood | Pueblo | Egnar | San Miguel |
| Arapahoe² | Cheyenne | Center² | Saguache | Elba | Washington |
| Arboles | Archuleta | Central City | Gilpin | Elbert² | Elbert |
| Arickaree | Washington | Chama¹ | Costilla | Eldora³ | Boulder |
| Arlington | Kiowa | Chandler | Fremont | Eldorado Springs | Boulder |
| Armel | Yuma | Cheneycenter | Prowers | Elizabeth² | Elbert |
| Aroya | Cheyenne | Cheraw | Otero | Elk Springs | Moffat |
| Arriba² | Lincoln | 'Cherokee Park³ | Larimer | Emma | Pitkin |
| Arriola | Montezuma | Chivington | Kiowa | El Moro | Las Animas |
| 'Aspen² | Pitkin | Chromo | Archuleta | Empire² | Clear Creek |
| Association Camp³ | Larimer | Cimarron | Montrose | ⁶Englewood² (Branch of | |
| Atchee | Garfield | Clark | Routt | Denver) | Arapahoe |
| Atwood | Logan | ³Cliffdale¹ | Jefferson | Erie² | Weld |
| 'Ault² | Weld | 'Clifton² | Mesa | Escalante Forks | Mesa |
| Aurora² | Arapahoe | Climax² | Lake | Eskdale | Adams |
| Austin² | Delta | Coal Creek² | Fremont | Espinoza | Conejos |
| Avalo | Weld | Coaldale | Fremont | Estabrook | Park |
| Avon | Eagle | Coalmont | Jackson | ³Eureka² | San Juan |
| Avondale | Pueblo | Cokedale | Las Animas | Evans | Weld |
| Axial | Moffat | 'Collbran² | Mesa | Evergreen² | Jefferson |
| Ayer | Otero | Colona | Ouray | | |
| | | Columbine | Routt | Fairplay² | Park |
| Bailey | Park | Como² | Park | Falcon | El Paso |
| Baldwin | Gunnison | Conejos | Conejos | Falfa | La Plata |
| Barnesville | Weld | Cope² | Washington | Farisita | Huerfano |
| Bartlett | Baca | Copper Spur | Eagle | Farr | Huerfano |
| Barr Lake | Adams | Cornish | Weld | Firestone | Weld |
| 'Basalt² | Eagle | Cortez² | Montezuma | Firstview | Cheyenne |
| Battle Creek | Routt | Cory | Delta | Fitzsimons² | Adams |
| 'Bayfield² | La Plata | Cotopaxi | Fremont | Flagler² | Kit Carson |
| Bear River | Routt | Cowdrey | Jackson | Fleming² | Logan |
| Bedrock | Montrose | Cragmor² | El Paso | Florissant | Teller |
| Beecher Island | Yuma | Crawford² | Delta | Floyd Hill | Clear Creek |
| Bellvue | Larimer | 'Creede² | Mineral | Flues | Las Animas |
| Bennett² | Adams | 'Crested Butte³ | Gunnison | Fondis | Elbert |
| Berthoud² | Larimer | Crestone | Saguache | Forder | Lincoln |
| Bethune | Kit Carson | Critchell | Jefferson | Fort Garland | Costilla |
| Beulah | Pueblo | Crook² | Logan | Fort Logan² | Arapahoe |
| Blackhawk² | Gilpin | Cross Mountain | Moffat | Fort Lyon² | Bent |
| Blaine | Baca | Crowley² | Crowley | Fosson | Weld |
| Blanca² | Costilla | Cuchara Camps | Huerfano | Fountain² | El Paso |
| Bloom | Otero | Cumbres | Conejos | 'Fowler² | Otero |
| Bonanza² | Saguache | | | Foxton | Jefferson |
| Boncarbo¹ | Las Animas | Dacona | Weld | Franktown | Douglas |
| Boone² | Pueblo | Dailey | Logan | Fraser³ | Grand |
| Bovina | Lincoln | Dalerose | Las Animas | Frederick² | Weld |
| Bowie¹ | Delta | 'De Beque² | Mesa | Frisco | Summit |
| Boyero | Lincoln | ³Deckers | Douglas | 'Fruita² | Mesa |
| Brandon | Kiowa | Deepcreek | Routt | | |
| Branson² | Las Animas | 'Deertrail² | Arapahoe | Galatea | Kiowa |
| 'Breckenridge² | Summit | Delagua² | Las Animas | Galeton | Weld |
| Breen | La Plata | Delcarbon | Huerfano | Garcia | Costilla |
| Briggsdale² | Weld | Delhi | Las Animas | Gardner | Huerfano |
| 'Bristol² | Prowers | De Nova | Washington | Garfield | Chaffee |
| Brodhead | Las Animas | Deora | Baca | Garo | Park |
| Brook Forest | Jefferson | Derby | Adams | Gary | Morgan |
| Brookvale | Clear Creek | Dicks | Las Animas | Gateway | Mesa |
| Broomfield | Boulder | Dillon | Summit | Genoa² | Lincoln |
| Buckingham² | Weld | Divide | Teller | 'Georgetown² | Clear Creek |
| 'Buena Vista² | Chaffee | Dolores² | Montezuma | Gilcrest | Weld |
| Buffalo Creek | Jefferson | Dove Creek | Dolores | Gill | Weld |
| Buford | Rio Blanco | Doyleville | Gunnison | Gilman² | Eagle |
| Burdett | Washington | | | Glade Park | Mesa |
| | | | | Glendevey | Larimer |

| Post Office | County | Post Office | County | Post Office | County |
|---|---|---|---|---|---|
| Ramah[2] | El Paso | [5]Silverton[2] | San Juan | Twin Lakes | Lake |
| Rand | Jackson | Simla | Elbert | Two Buttes | Baca |
| Rangely | Rio Blanco | Simpson | Adams | Tyrone | Las Animas |
| Rapson | Las Animas | Sinbad | Montrose | | |
| Rattlesnake Butte | Huerfano | Skull Creek | Moffat | Ute | Montrose |
| Raven | Garfield | [3]Skyway | Mesa | Utleyville | Baca |
| Ravenwood | Huerfano | Slater | Moffat | | |
| Read | Delta | Sligo | Weld | Valdez | Las Animas |
| Redcliff[2] | Eagle | Snowmass | Pitkin | Valleroso | Las Animas |
| Red Lion | Logan | Snyder | Morgan | Vanadium | San Miguel |
| Redmesa | La Plata | Somerset[2] | Gunnison | Vernon | Yuma |
| Redstone | Pitkin | Sopris[2] | Las Animas | Veta Pass | Costilla |
| Redvale | Montrose | South Fork | Rio Grande | Villagrove | Saguache |
| Redwing | Huerfano | South Platte | Jefferson | Villagreen | Las Animas |
| Richards | Baca | [5]Spicer | Jackson | Vim | Weld |
| Rico[2] | Dolores | [5]Spivak[2] | Jefferson | Virginia Dale | Larimer |
| Ridge | Jefferson | Starkville[2] | Las Animas | Vona[2] | Kit Carson |
| [5]Ridgway[2] | Ouray | Stone City | Pueblo | Vroman | Otero |
| Riland | Garfield | Stoneham[2] | Weld | | |
| Rio Blanco | Rio Blanco | Stoner | Montezuma | Wages | Yuma |
| River Bend | Elbert | Stonington[2] | Baca | Wagon Wheel Gap[3] | Mineral |
| Roach | Larimer | Strasburg[2] | Arapahoe | Waitley[1] | Washington |
| Rockvale[2] | Fremont | [5]Stratton[2] | Kit Carson | Walden[2] | Jackson |
| Rockwood | La Plata | Sugar City[2] | Crowley | Walsen[2] | Huerfano |
| Rodley | Baca | Sugar Loaf | Boulder | Walsh[2] | Baca |
| Roggen | Weld | Sunbeam | Moffat | Ward[2] | Boulder |
| Rollinsville | Gilpin | Superior | Boulder | Watkins | Adams |
| Romeo | Conejos | Swallows | Pueblo | Waunita Hot Springs[1] | |
| Rosita | Custer | Swink[2] | Otero | | Gunnison |
| Routt | Routt | | | Weldona[2] | Morgan |
| Ruedi | Eagle | Tabernash[2] | Grand | Wellington[2] | Larimer |
| Rugby | Las Animas | Tacoma | La Plata | [5]Westcliffe[2] | Custer |
| Rush | El Paso | Tacony | El Paso | Westminster | Adams |
| Russell Gulch[2] | Gilpin | Tarryall | Park | Weston[2] | Las Animas |
| Rye[4] | Pueblo | Telluride | San Miguel | West Plains | Logan |
| | | Tennessee Pass | Lake | West Portal[3] | Grand |
| Saguache[2] | Saguache | Tercio | Las Animas | Wetmore | Custer |
| Saint Elmo[1] | Chaffee | Texas Creek | Fremont | Wheatridge[2] | Jefferson |
| Sams | San Miguel | Thatcher | Las Animas | Whitewater | Mesa |
| San Acacio[2] | Costilla | Thornburg | Rio Blanco | [5]Wiggins[3] | Morgan |
| Sanford[2] | Conejos | Thurman | Washington | Wild Horse[2] | Cheyenne |
| San Luis[2] | Costilla | Tiffany | La Plata | Wilds | Larimer |
| San Pablo | Costilla | Tigiwon[3] | Eagle | Wiley[2] | Prowers |
| Sapinero | Gunnison | Tiger | Summit | Willard | Logan |
| Sargents | Saguache | Timnath | Larimer | [4]Windsor[2] | Weld |
| Sedalia | Douglas | Timpas | Otero | Wolcott | Eagle |
| Sedgwick[2] | Sedgwick | Tioga | Huerfano | Woodland Park | Teller |
| Segundo | Las Animas | Tobe | Las Animas | Woodman[2] | El Paso |
| [5]Seibert[2] | Kit Carson | Tolland | Gilpin | Woodrow | Washington |
| Serene | Weld | Tollerberg | Las Animas | Woody | Pitkin |
| Severence | Weld | Toltec | Huerfano | Wormington | Las Animas |
| Sharpsdale | Huerfano | Toponas | Routt | | |
| Shaw | Lincoln | Towoac | Montezuma | Yampa[2] | Routt |
| Shawnee | Park | Towner[2] | Kiowa | Yellow Jacket | Montezuma |
| Sheephorn | Eagle | [3]Trappers Lake | Garfield | Yoder | El Paso |
| Sheridan Lake | Kiowa | Trinchera | Las Animas | Youghal[1] | Moffat |
| Sidney | Routt | Troublesome | Grand | | |
| Sigman | Adams | Trout Creek[1] | Routt | | |
| Siloam | Pueblo | Troutville[3] | Eagle | | |
| Silt[2] | Garfield | Troy | Las Animas | | |
| Silver Cliff | Custer | Tungsten[2] | Boulder | | |
| Silver Plume[2] | Clear Creek | Turret | Chaffee | | |

[1] Do not issue money orders.
[2] International money order offices.
[3] Summer offices.
[4] Postal Savings depositories.
[5] Winter offices.

# Cost of Living in Colorado

A STUDY of available figures on the cost of living clearly establishes the fact that it is no more expensive for the individual or family to live in Colorado than in other parts of the country. On the contrary, the cost is shown to be less in typical communities than the average for the country as a whole.

Conditions governing the cost of living vary to such an extent in different localities as to make it next to impossible to prepare tables composed of arbitrary figures disclosing actual conditions in each. The United States department of labor, however, has an elaborate organization for gathering statistics on the average retail prices of food and other commodities throughout the country. It uses the Denver prices as an index for the state, this data being comparable with other cities of the country in which similar information is obtained and with the country as a whole.

The department of labor compiles

monthly data on the average retail prices of 42 articles of food in the principal cities of the United States. The combined cost of one unit (pound, dozen or can) of each of these articles for the United States on October 15, 1931, based on the average retail price, was $8.48. On the same date the aggregate cost of the same units at the average retail prices in Denver was $7.86, or 62 cents less than the average price for the United States. In other words, the average retail prices of the 42 articles of food on that date was 7.3 per cent less in Denver than the average for the country as a whole.

The aggregate cost of the 42 articles of food at average retail prices in Denver and the United States (one unit of each) on October 15 for the years named is as follows:

|  | Denver | U. S. |
|---|---|---|
| 1926 | $ 9.82 | $10.98 |
| 1927 | 9.64 | 10.77 |
| 1928 | 10.11 | 11.10 |
| 1929 | 9.86 | 10.90 |
| 1930 | 9.30 | 10.21 |
| 1931 | 7.86 | 8.48 |

There is published herewith a table showing the combined cost of one unit of each of the 42 articles of food at the average retail prices in Denver and 17 typical cities on October 15, 1931, with comparisons for the same date in 1930, 1929, 1928 and 1927. This comparison shows that the aggregate cost in Denver was lower than in any of the other cities with which comparisons are made. Denver held relatively the same position with these cities in preceding years, thereby showing that the relatively low cost of living in Denver is a normal condition. The same table shows the percentages of increase in the retail cost of food in October, 1931, compared with the same data in 1913. These figures reveal that food cost 9.5 per cent more on October 15, 1931, than on the same date in 1913 in Denver, while in the United States the increase between the two dates was 19.1 per cent. In this table Los Angeles, Portland, Oregon, and Salt Lake City showed smaller increases than Denver. Of 38 cities compared, 34 showed a larger per cent increase and four a smaller per cent than Denver.

The cost of living in Denver, including food, clothing, rent, fuel and light, housefurnishing goods and miscellaneous, was practically the same in December, 1931, as in the same month in 1917, the difference on all items being less than one per cent. Food was 30.6 per cent lower in December, 1931, than in the same month in 1917; clothing was 6.5 per cent lower; rents were

37.1 per cent higher; fuel and light were 7.1 per cent higher; housefurnishing goods were 0.2 per cent lower; and miscellaneous items were 36.5 per cent higher. An accompanying table gives the changes in the cost of living in 13 cities, in percentages, between December, 1931, and the same month in 1917.

The average retail prices of bituminous coal, prepared sizes, per ton of 2,000 pounds for household use on October 15, 1931, with comparisons on the same date in 1930 and 1929, in typical cities in which the classification of grades are comparable, were as follows:

|  | 1931 | 1930 | 1929 |
|---|---|---|---|
| Denver | $ 8.13 | $10.29 | $10.31 |
| Atlanta | 6.78 | 7.47 | 7.78 |
| Birmingham | 6.46 | 7.51 | 7.61 |
| Dallas | 10.83 | 12.58 | 12.83 |
| Kansas City | 6.12 | 6.93 | 7.28 |
| Los Angeles | 16.25 | 16.50 | 16.50 |
| Omaha | 9.00 | 9.79 | 9.67 |
| Pittsburgh | 4.86 | 4.91 | 5.30 |
| Portland, Ore. | 12.51 | 13.27 | 13.38 |
| St. Louis | 5.70 | 6.29 | 6.77 |
| Salt Lake City | 7.63 | 8.41 | 7.93 |
| Seattle | 10.62 | 10.68 | 10.68 |

Natural gas is used extensively for household purposes in a number of cities and towns of the state. The rates mostly are based on sliding scales and prices depend upon the quantity used. Pueblo and other cities generally have the same rate as Denver. The department of labor computes the net price per 1,000 cubic feet on the basis of a family consumption of 5,000 cubic feet per month. The net price per 1,000 cubic feet on that basis in Denver on December 15, 1930, was 99 cents. This compares with $1.00 in Atlanta, 75 cents in Cincinnati, 60 cents in Cleveland, 48 cents in Columbus, 79 cents in Dallas, 95 cents in Kansas City, 84 cents in Los Angeles, 45 cents in Louisville, 60 cents in Pittsburgh, 99 cents in Salt Lake City and 97 cents in San Francisco.

The Colorado industrial commission made a detailed study of changes in the cost of living in Denver covering the period of 1914 to 1926, inclusive. The purpose of this study was to determine the "minimum or comfort-level budget necessary for the theoretical family of five, consisting of the so-called 'wage-earner,' the mother and three children of school age." The estimates were based on the current retail prices of the individual items composing the budget, which were gathered at weekly or monthly intervals. No similar data has been compiled by the commission since 1926. The figures are of value at this time principally as an index of costs of living. The commission reported that the peak in prices was reached in June-July, 1920, in the period from 1914 to 1926, inclusive. Its data covers monthly reports for the period named, from which the following yearly averages have been computed:

| Item | 1914 | 1920 | 1926 |
|------|------|------|------|
| Housing ...... | $108.00 | $ 154.24 | $ 173.40 |
| Car fare....... | 30.30 | 36.36 | 45.45 |
| Food ......... | 360.49 | 597.32 | 510.35 |
| Clothing ..... | 104.20 | 278.34 | 286.20 |
| Fuel and light. | 33.55 | 56.35 | 54.50 |
| Health ....... | 20.00 | 22.09 | 25.00 |
| Insurance .... | 22.88 | 22.88 | 22.88 |
| Sundries ..... | 60.00 | 77.58 | 80.00 |
| Totals....... | $739.42 | $1,245.16 | $1,197.78 |

An accompanying table shows the average retail price 'of 42 articles of food in the United States and Denver on October 15, 1931, with comparisons with 1913, 1926, 1929, and 1930.

## OFFICIAL STATE FLOWER

The twelfth general assembly of the Colorado legislature enacted a measure declaring the white and lavender columbine to be the state flower of the state of Colorado. It was approved April 4, 1899, by Gov. Charles S. Thomas.

### CHANGES IN COST OF LIVING IN 13 CITIES, DECEMBER, 1917, TO DECEMBER, 1931
(Department of Labor)

| City | Per Cent of Increase Over December, 1917, in Expenditures for | | | | | | |
|------|------|------|------|------|------|------|------|
| | Food | Cloth-ing | Rent | Fuel and Light | House Furnish-ing Goods | Miscel-laneous | All Items |
| Denver ............ | *30.6 | *6.5 | 37.1 | 7.1 | *0.2 | 36.5 | 0.3 |
| Atlanta ........... | *29.2 | *16.7 | 19.6 | 4.8 | *5.7 | 28.7 | *6.2 |
| Birmingham ....... | *33.2 | *20.1 | 1.5 | 24.9 | *11.0 | 24.1 | *9.6 |
| Cincinnati ........ | *24.2 | *22.4 | 43.9 | 64.6 | *5.1 | 50.3 | 5.8 |
| Indianapolis ...... | *29.1 | *19.4 | 11.3 | 23.7 | *12.4 | 49.2 | *0.8 |
| Kansas City ....... | *28.9 | *9.9 | 16.3 | 14.3 | *11.5 | 42.3 | *1.1 |
| Memphis ......... | *34.2 | *10.4 | 18.4 | 48.3 | *0.9 | 35.2 | *0.5 |
| Minneapolis ...... | *25.5 | *16.2 | 19.8 | 44.3 | *2.7 | 36.1 | 2.1 |
| New Orleans....... | *30.3 | *9.7 | 38.7 | 4.1 | *0.5 | 45.2 | 0.3 |
| Pittsburgh ........ | *29.2 | *13.3 | 52.3 | 83.8 | *6.4 | 45.6 | 4.5 |
| Richmond ......... | *29.2 | *8.6 | 21.8 | 37.6 | 15.5 | 40.3 | 0.3 |
| St. Louis......... | *29.8 | *19.2 | 44.0 | 20.7 | *0.6 | 39.2 | 1.4 |
| Scranton ......... | *22.8 | *7.1 | 51.8 | 69.5 | 7.3 | 55.2 | 8.4 |

*Denotes decrease.

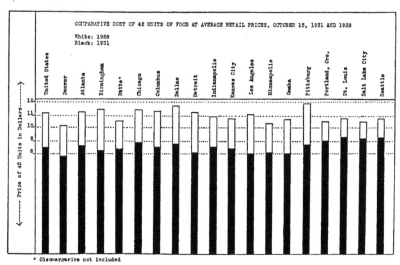

COMPARATIVE COST OF 42 UNITS OF FOOD AT AVERAGE RETAIL PRICES, OCTOBER 15, 1931 AND 1928

White: 1928
Black: 1931

* Oleomargarine not included

## COST OF LIVING IN DENVER
### Average Retail Price of Food Products (U. S. Department of Labor)

| Article | Unit | Average for U. S. on October 15 | | | | | Average for Denver on October 15 | | | | |
|---|---|---|---|---|---|---|---|---|---|---|---|
| | | 1931 | 1930 | 1929 | 1926 | 1913 | 1931 | 1930 | 1929 | 1926 | 1913 |
| | lb. | Cts. | Cts. | Cts. | Cts. | Cts. | Cts. | Cts. | Cts. | Cts. | Cts. |
| Sirloin steak | " | 38.6 | 44.5 | 50.3 | 41.5 | 25.7 | 30.1 | 36.4 | 42.1 | 33.6 | 23.9 |
| Round steak | " | 33.6 | 39.3 | 44.5 | 36.0 | 23.1 | 27.4 | 33.1 | 37.4 | 30.2 | 21.4 |
| Rib roast | " | 28.0 | 32.5 | 37.0 | 30.5 | 20.0 | 24.0 | 28.3 | 30.1 | 24.0 | 17.8 |
| Chuck roast | " | 20.7 | 25.4 | 30.0 | 22.8 | 16.4 | 18.4 | 22.8 | 26.1 | 12.5 | 15.8 |
| Plate beef | " | 13.5 | 17.2 | 21.0 | 14.6 | 12.3 | 10.9 | 14.2 | 17.1 | 11.1 | 10.0 |
| Pork chops | " | 29.3 | 37.9 | 38.9 | 42.6 | 22.6 | 28.2 | 36.9 | 38.4 | 40.6 | 20.8 |
| Bacon | " | 34.3 | 42.6 | 43.7 | 51.7 | 27.8 | 33.9 | 41.3 | 42.2 | 53.3 | 28.0 |
| Ham (sliced) | " | 44.2 | 53.1 | 55.1 | 59.8 | 27.6 | 43.3 | 52.6 | 53.3 | 60.8 | 31.7 |
| Lamb | " | 27.5 | 32.8 | 38.5 | 38.3 | 18.4 | 25.0 | 28.9 | 36.1 | 35.8 | 14.6 |
| Hens | " | 29.9 | 33.8 | 38.4 | 37.6 | 21.2 | 24.8 | 26.2 | 31.3 | 29.8 | 19.4 |
| Salmon, canned* | " | 30.3 | 34.0 | 31.9 | 35.6 | --- | 31.3 | 33.8 | 33.2 | 34.5 | --- |
| Milk, fresh | qt. | 12.0 | 14.0 | 14.4 | 14.0 | 9.0 | 10.3 | 11.3 | 12.0 | 12.0 | 8.4 |
| Milk, evaporated | † | 8.8 | 9.9 | 10.6 | 11.4 | --- | 9.0 | 9.9 | 9.9 | 10.7 | --- |
| Butter | lb. | 39.9 | 47.8 | 55.7 | 54.3 | 38.2 | 38.5 | 42.9 | 49.3 | 49.0 | 39.0 |
| Oleomargarine | " | 18.8 | 25.0 | 27.0 | 30.2 | --- | 18.9 | 23.2 | 24.5 | 29.0 | --- |
| Cheese | " | 27.1 | 34.2 | 37.9 | 36.7 | 22.4 | 27.7 | 36.1 | 39.0 | 37.4 | 26.1 |
| Lard | " | 12.4 | 17.7 | 18.3 | 21.9 | 16.0 | 12.2 | 17.5 | 18.4 | 22.6 | 16.1 |
| Vegetable lard substitute | " | 22.7 | 24.1 | 24.7 | 25.7 | --- | 19.7 | 20.3 | 20.9 | 24.3 | --- |
| Eggs, strictly fresh | doz. | 37.9 | 44.8 | 58.0 | 58.1 | 41.6 | 31.0 | 40.0 | 53.3 | 55.6 | 37.1 |
| Bread | lb. | 7.3 | 8.6 | 8.9 | 9.4 | 5.6 | 6.4 | 7.2 | 7.6 | 8.3 | 5.5 |
| Flour | " | 3.3 | 4.3 | 5.2 | 5.7 | 3.3 | 2.4 | 3.2 | 3.9 | 4.5 | 2.6 |
| Corn meal | " | 4.4 | 5.3 | 5.3 | 5.1 | 3.1 | 3.9 | 4.7 | 4.6 | 4.0 | 2.6 |
| Rolled oats | " | 7.9 | 8.6 | 8.8 | 9.1 | --- | 7.0 | 7.5 | 7.6 | 8.3 | --- |
| Corn flakes | ‡ | 8.9 | 9.3 | 9.5 | 10.9 | --- | 9.1 | 9.7 | 9.5 | 11.1 | --- |
| Wheat cereal | § | 23.3 | 25.4 | 25.5 | 25.4 | --- | 23.3 | 24.7 | 24.6 | 24.9 | --- |
| Macaroni | lb. | 16.3 | 19.1 | 19.7 | 20.2 | --- | 18.1 | 19.7 | 19.4 | 19.7 | --- |
| Rice | " | 7.8 | 9.5 | 9.7 | 11.6 | 8.1 | 7.0 | 9.0 | 8.9 | 10.6 | 8.6 |
| Beans, navy | " | 6.7 | 11.3 | 14.2 | 9.1 | --- | 6.4 | 9.9 | 13.1 | 9.6 | --- |
| Potatoes | | 1.8 | 3.1 | 3.8 | 3.8 | 1.8 | 1.7 | 2.6 | 3.0 | 3.3 | 1.4 |
| Onions | " | 4.3 | 4.2 | 5.3 | 5.0 | --- | 4.2 | 3.8 | 4.4 | 3.7 | --- |
| Cabbage | " | 3.2 | 3.6 | 4.5 | 4.0 | --- | 2.2 | 2.3 | 3.5 | 2.4 | --- |
| Beans, baked | ‖ | 10.3 | 10.8 | 11.7 | 11.7 | --- | 10.6 | 10.7 | 11.6 | 11.4 | --- |
| Corn, canned | " | 12.6 | 15.2 | 15.8 | 16.3 | --- | 12.7 | 14.4 | 14.1 | 14.8 | --- |
| Peas, canned | " | 13.7 | 16.0 | 16.7 | 17.4 | --- | 13.9 | 15.3 | 15.3 | 15.8 | --- |
| Tomatoes, canned | " | 9.8 | 12.1 | 12.6 | 12.1 | --- | 10.6 | 12.8 | 12.9 | 12.1 | --- |
| Sugar, granulated | lb. | 5.6 | 5.8 | 6.7 | 7.2 | 5.5 | 6.3 | 6.4 | 7.4 | 7.6 | 5.4 |
| Tea | " | 75.6 | 77.1 | 77.6 | 77.3 | 54.5 | 73.0 | 71.9 | 68.7 | 69.3 | 52.8 |
| Coffee | " | 32.1 | 39.1 | 49.1 | 50.9 | 29.7 | 39.2 | 41.6 | 50.1 | 51.0 | 29.4 |
| Prunes | " | 11.1 | 14.5 | 17.1 | 16.9 | --- | 12.6 | 15.3 | 19.6 | 18.3 | --- |
| Raisins | " | 11.4 | 11.7 | 12.2 | 14.8 | --- | 11.6 | 11.5 | 12.1 | 14.5 | --- |
| Oranges | doz. | 37.3 | 66.8 | 44.9 | 56.0 | --- | 31.1 | 61.5 | 37.2 | 50.3 | --- |
| Bananas | " | 24.0 | 29.4 | 32.4 | 34.9 | --- | ‡8.0 | ‡8.4 | ‡11.1 | --- | --- |

*Both pink and red.     ‡8-ounce package.     ‖No. 2 can.
†15-16-ounce can.     §28-ounce package.     ‡Per lb.

## AGGREGATE COST OF 42 UNITS OF FOOD AT AVERAGE RETAIL PRICES IN THE UNITED STATES AND 18 TYPICAL CITIES ON OCTOBER 15, 1930, WITH COMPARISONS

(Compiled from U. S. Department of Labor Statistics)

| | Percentage Increase Oct., 1931 Compared with 1913 | Aggregate Cost on October 15 | | | | |
|---|---|---|---|---|---|---|
| | | 1931 | 1930 | 1929 | 1928 | 1927 |
| United States... | 19.1 | $ 8.48 | $10.21 | $10.90 | $11.10 | $10.77 |
| Denver ....... | 9.5 | 7.86 | 9.30 | 9.86 | 10.11 | 9.64 |
| Atlanta ....... | 15.3 | 8.61 | 10.31 | 11.32 | 11.26 | 11.18 |
| Birmingham ... | 14.6 | 8.26 | 10.38 | 11.21 | 11.36 | 10.35 |
| Butte* ....... | ... | 8.31 | 9.57 | 10.39 | 10.46 | 10.10 |
| Chicago ...... | 31.3 | 8.83 | 10.60 | 11.12 | 11.43 | 11.10 |
| Columbus ..... | ... | 8.53 | 10.46 | 11.10 | 11.35 | 10.91 |
| Dallas ........ | 11.8 | 8.77 | 10.70 | 11.58 | 11.69 | 11.34 |
| Detroit ....... | 18.1 | 8.10 | 10.06 | 10.93 | 11.24 | 11.05 |
| Indianapolis ... | 13.8 | 8.53 | 10.35 | 11.11 | 10.97 | 10.64 |
| Kansas City .... | 17.4 | 8.34 | 9.86 | 10.59 | 10.69 | 10.35 |
| Los Angeles.... | 8.6 | 8.00 | 9.79 | 10.87 | 11.06 | 10.62 |
| Minneapolis .... | 19.7 | 8.09 | 9.72 | 10.21 | 10.33 | 9.83 |
| Omaha ....... | 11.7 | 8.02 | 9.67 | 10.41 | 10.66 | 10.14 |
| Pittsburgh ..... | 17.6 | 8.71 | 10.75 | 11.60 | 11.85 | 11.48 |
| Portland, Ore.... | 7.5 | 8.99 | 9.41 | 10.38 | 10.51 | 10.23 |
| St. Louis....... | 19.8 | 8.30 | 9.75 | 10.52 | 10.63 | 10.36 |
| Salt Lake City. | 4.7 | 8.22 | 9.71 | 10.35 | 10.47 | 10.08 |
| Seattle ....... | 15.5 | 8.29 | 9.93 | 10.65 | 10.78 | 10.35 |

*Oleomargarine is not included in Montana. Average retail price of that commodity should be added for comparative purposes.

## NUMBER OF TELEPHONES

According to data collected at the quinquennial census of electrical industries taken in 1928 by the department of commerce, there were 183,250 telephones in use in Colorado in 1927. This compares with 150,652 in 1922, an increase of 32,598, or 21.6 per cent. Of this total number, 168,442 were for the Bell system and 14,808 for all other systems or lines. The number of telephones operated by the Bell system increased 24.2 per cent between 1922 and 1927, and for other systems and lines there was a decrease of 1.4 per cent. There were 24 states reporting a larger number and 24 states (including the District of Columbia) a smaller number of telephones than Colorado. The number of telephones in the United States increased 29.1 per cent in the period named.

The number of originating telephone calls in the state in 1927 was 312,926,-084, of which 229,101,860 calls were for systems with incomes of $10,000 or more per year. That was equal to five calls per telephone per day and 258 calls per inhabitant for the year.

## POET LAUREATE

The office of state poet laureate is an honorary one created by gubernatorial action and without legislative enactment. It has been held by only two persons. Alice Polk Hill, a Colorado pioneer, was appointed to the office on September 10, 1919, by Gov. Oliver H. Shoup. On January 24, 1923, the present incumbent, Nellie Burget Miller, of Colorado Springs, was appointed to the office by Gov. William E. Sweet to fill a vacancy caused by the death of Mrs. Hill.

## LYNCHING RECORD

Colorado is one of the few states of the Union in which no lynchings have occurred in the 11 years ending with 1930, according to the annual summaries of the Tuskogee institute. Of 4,308 lynchings reported in the United States since 1885, only 29 were in Colorado, of which 24 were white and five were negroes. Colorado's proportion of the total is less than seven-tenths of one per cent.

# Insurance

THE development of insurance of all kinds in Colorado can be traced with accuracy through the reports of the state insurance commissioner. Owing to the varying reports filed by the companies operating in the state, it is impossible to give the gross amount of insurance in force at any particular time, but the reports of annual premiums and losses paid present a fair view of the situation. The growth of ordinary life insurance is shown by a comparison of the number of policies in force and the aggregate risk. There were 2,237 such policies in force in 1882, covering an aggregate risk of $7,120,297. At the end of 1930 there were 682,492 policies in force, and the aggregate risks amounted to $875,-969,130.

There were 592 companies, associations, exchanges and societies operating in Colorado on December 31, 1931, compared with 524 on the same date in 1927, classified as follows:

|  | 1931 | 1927 |
|---|---|---|
| Fire and marine (stock) | 251 | 237 |
| Fire and marine (mutual) | 33 | 26 |
| Life—legal reserve | 98 | 89 |
| Casualty and miscellaneous | 136 | 91 |
| County mutual fire and hail | 5 | 5 |
| Assessment life | .. | 1 |
| Assessment health and accident | 4 | 3 |
| Reciprocal exchanges | 18 | 22 |
| Fraternal societies | 47 | 50 |
| Totals | 592 | 524 |

Premiums received by these companies from Colorado business in 1931 amounted to $41,925,896, which compares with $33,529,413 in 1930, $48,-089,054 in 1929 and $38,176,452 in 1927. Losses paid in 1931 amounted to $15,188,697, which compares with $16,-319,541 in 1930, $15,485,623 in 1929 and $11,538,749 in 1927.

Losses paid by all companies from 1882 to 1931, inclusive, aggregated $268,062,865 as follows:

| Class | Period | Amount |
|---|---|---|
| Fire and marine | 1882-1931 | $ 69,218,701 |
| Life—legal reserve | 1882-1931 | 115,816,978 |
| Casualty, etc. | 1882-1931 | 42,940,629 |
| County mutual | 1910-1931 | 654,830 |
| Assessment—life, etc. | 1893-1931 | 3,800,964 |
| Reciprocal | 1916-1931 | 1,191,257 |
| Colorado assessment hail | 1921-1927 | 483,033 |
| Foreign assessment hail | 1910-1925 | 1,143,333 |
| Fraternal | 1916-1931 | 32,813,140 |
| Total | | $268,062,865 |

The following table shows premium receipts and loss payments by all of the companies operating in the state, as shown by their reports for various dates filed with the state insurance commissioner:

| Nature of Insurance | Year | Premiums | Losses |
|---|---|---|---|
| Fire and Marine | 1882 | $ 600,919 | $ 300,680 |
| | 1900 | 2,000,451 | 750,828 |
| | 1924 | 6,573,031 | 3,062,025 |
| | 1925 | 7,005,632 | 3,225,868 |
| | 1926 | 7,439,471 | 2,858,858 |
| | 1927 | 7,237,788 | 3,129,880 |
| | 1928 | 6,919,719 | 2,622,770 |
| | 1929 | 6,850,251 | 2,404,199 |
| | 1930 | 6,423,428 | 2,789,064 |
| | 1931 | 5,928,817 | 2,258,434 |
| Legal Reserve Life | 1882 | 115,160 | 75,193 |
| | 1900 | 2,298,432 | 790,922 |
| | 1924 | 16,583,309 | 4,640,777 |
| | 1925 | 18,525,284 | 4,968,856 |
| | 1926 | 20,237,140 | 5,506,278 |
| | 1927 | 21,680,094 | 6,702,442 |
| | 1928 | 23,333,505 | 7,564,028 |
| | 1929 | 25,345,538 | 7,547,786 |
| | 1930 | 26,517,099 | 8,302,497 |
| | 1931 | 26,819,302 | 7,899,487 |
| Casualty, Fidelity and Surety | 1882 | 41,656 | 21,073 |
| | 1900 | 509,970 | 291,517 |
| | 1924 | 4,998,581 | 2,398,773 |
| | 1925 | 5,393,390 | 2,662,455 |
| | 1926 | 5,508,630 | 2,743,259 |
| | 1927 | 5,960,900 | 2,404,142 |
| | 1928 | 5,968,870 | 2,622,985 |
| | 1929 | 6,593,712 | 2,842,462 |
| | 1930 | 6,462,038 | 2,965,108 |
| | 1931 | 6,018,609 | 3,119,182 |
| Assessment Life Health and Accident | 1893 | 215,076 | 220,647 |
| | 1900 | 145,782 | 64,008 |
| | 1924 | 147,616 | 81,688 |
| | 1925 | 185,991 | 115,343 |
| | 1926 | 170,318 | 101,120 |
| | 1927 | 190,064 | 100,086 |
| | 1928 | 198,811 | 110,559 |
| | 1929 | 127,686 | 80,548 |
| | 1930 | 121,960 | 64,377 |
| | 1931 | 124,570 | 68,144 |
| Reciprocal Fire and Casualty | 1916 | 24,649 | 1,626 |
| | 1924 | 381,927 | 57,353 |
| | 1925 | 433,158 | 77,470 |
| | 1926 | 437,501 | 90,668 |
| | 1927 | 439,173 | 90,590 |
| | 1928 | 437,753 | 116,348 |
| | 1929 | 249,377 | 103,612 |
| | 1930 | 997,721 | 96,637 |
| | 1931 | 188,987 | 71,674 |
| Fraternal | 1916 | 1,828,389 | 1,511,741 |
| | 1924 | 2,512,753 | 2,007,089 |
| | 1925 | 2,598,537 | 2,015,467 |
| | 1926 | 2,610,670 | 2,039,578 |
| | 1927 | 2,617,822 | 2,294,747 |
| | 1928 | 2,636,708 | 2,765,132 |
| | 1929 | 2,884,545 | 2,483,308 |
| | 1930 | 2,946,660 | 2,034,418 |
| | 1931 | 2,791,247 | 1,729,152 |
| County Mutual Fire | 1910 | 3,070 | 261 |
| | 1924 | 38,213 | 59,792 |
| | 1925 | *72,040 | *62,373 |
| | 1926 | *52,979 | *58,864 |
| | 1927 | *49,338 | 48,272 |
| | 1928 | 53,164 | 33,724 |
| | 1929 | 37,941 | 23,713 |
| | 1930 | 60,457 | 67,490 |
| | 1931 | 54,364 | 42,624 |

*Includes foreign Assessment Hail for these years.

| Nature of Insurance | Year | Premiums | Losses |
|---|---|---|---|
| Assessment Hail | | | |
| (Colorado) | 1921 | $ 136,739 | $ 85,263 |
| | 1924 | 3,297 | 7,121 |
| | 1925 | 27,208 | 20,127 |
| | 1926 | 26,528 | 22,020 |
| | 1927 | 1,273 | 1,949 |
| Assessment Hail | | | |
| (Foreign) | 1910 | 2,516 | 3,525 |
| | 1920 | 293,512 | 232,181 |
| | 1924 | 17,115 | 71,403 |

## STATE HAIL INSURANCE

The state of Colorado, through a legislative enactment, put into effect in 1929 a law creating a state hail insurance department, which insures farmers against losses by hail. The department is in charge of a commissioner and under the supervision of a board of three members appointed by the governor. Insurance on crops is written by county assessors, their deputies and local representatives. The farmer pays no fee for the writing of the insurance and the only fee connected with the service is the payment of one dollar by the department for each policy written. Insurance rates are based on the class of crops insured and the location of the land.

The time limit of insurance is from May 15 to August 15 for fall wheat, rye, barley and canning peas; from June 1 to September 1 on spring small grain other than barley; from June 15 to September 15 on beans, corn, potatoes, alfalfa, sugar beets, broom corn, cabbage, tomatoes, onions and cucumbers, and from June 20 to September 20 for all crops grown in altitudes above 6,000 feet.

Crops which may be insured are divided into two classes. Class A, which takes the lower rate, includes wheat, oats, emmer, speltz, corn, alfalfa, potatoes, broom corn, sorghums, flax and millet. Class B, which takes the higher rate, includes barley, rye, peas and beans, tomatoes, cabbage, onions and cucumbers.

The maximum amount of insurance permitted under the policy is $7 per acre on non-irrigated land and $15 per acre on irrigated land, except that garden or canning peas and beans, cabbages, tomatoes and cucumbers may be insured up to $25 per acre. The maximum amount of insurance which may be carried by any one person in any one section is $2,000. The rates vary from 10 per cent on Class A crops and 15 per cent on Class B crops down to three and five per cent, depending upon the location of the counties in which the crops are insured.

Net insurance written by years is as follows:

| Year | Amount |
|---|---|
| 1929 | $ 545,181.88 |
| 1930 | 1,426,041.06 |
| 1931 | 780,671.53 |

The farmer may pay the premium on his insurance in cash or it may be levied as a tax on his land, payable on January 1 of the year following. The net hail tax collected, by years, was as follows:

| Year | Amount |
|---|---|
| 1929 | $ 57,495.47 |
| 1930 | 146,429.44 |
| 1931 | 77,691.88 |

Net losses paid, by years, were as follows:

| Year | Amount |
|---|---|
| 1929 | $ 26,045.03 |
| 1930 | 65,335.68 |
| 1931 | 51,907.18 |

Net assets of the department on January 1, 1932, amounted to $104,825.72.

# Colorado Mortality Statistics

THERE were 13,207 deaths in Colorado in the calendar year of 1930 as reported by the division of vital statistics of the bureau of the census. This compares with 12,874 in 1929, an increase of 333. The death rate per 100,000 population in 1930 was 1,272.4, which compares with 1,251.4 in 1929. Pneumonia (all forms) was responsible primarily for the increase in the mortality for the state. The number of deaths from pneumonia increased from 1,054 in 1929 to 1,226 in 1930, and the rate per 100,000 population from 102.5 in 1929 to 118.1 in 1930. Diseases of the heart increased from 1,775 deaths to 1,887 and the rate from 172.5 to 180.8. Although the general mortality rate for the state increased, there was a great decrease in the mortality from influenza, the number of deaths having reduced from 639 to 563 in 1930, and the rate from 62.1 in 1929 to 55 in 1930.

The following table shows the number of deaths from all causes in Colorado by years and the rate per 1,000 population for Colorado and the registration area:

| Year | Number | Rate Colo. | Area |
|------|--------|------------|------|
| 1920 | .... | 14.4 | 13.1 |
| 1922 | 13,216 | 13.3 | 11.8 |
| 1923 | 12,259 | 12.5 | 12.3 |
| 1924 | 12,522 | 12.6 | 11.8 |
| 1925 | 12,549 | 12.0 | 11.8 |
| 1926 | 12,260 | 11.6 | 12.2 |
| 1927 | 13,082 | 12.2 | 11.4 |
| 1928 | 14,077 | 12.9 | ... |
| 1929 | 12,874 | 12.5 | ... |
| 1930 | 13,207 | 12.7 | ... |

The largest number of deaths from any single cause is from diseases of the heart. The number in 1930 was 1,877, or at the rate of 180.8 per 100,000 population. Heart diseases accounted for 14.2 per cent of all deaths in the state in 1930. The number of deaths from this cause by years is as follows:

| | |
|---|---|
| 1925 | 1,385 |
| 1927 | 1,612 |
| 1928 | 1,861 |
| 1929 | 1,775 |
| 1930 | 1,877 |

Tuberculosis (all forms) came second, with 1,283 deaths from that cause in 1930, or at the rate of 125.6 per 100,000 population. This disease accounted for 9.7 per cent of all deaths in that year. Deaths from tuberculosis in all forms, by years, is as follows:

| | |
|---|---|
| 1925 | 1,495 |
| 1927 | 1,492 |
| 1928 | 1,415 |
| 1929 | 1,282 |
| 1930 | 1,283 |

Race stock, occupations of the inhabitants, the sex and age distribution of the populatioon, and the relative number of deaths of non-residents are factors that must be considered before it can be determined that one state is more healthful than another. It is apparent that Colorado, being a state that attracts thousands of tourists and healthseekers, is affected by a large percentage of non-resident deaths, and this undoubtedly is the cause of the state's comparatively high rate for certain classes of diseases, such as tuberculosis and pneumonia. The refined rate for Colorado in 1925, a rate based on the death of residents only, whether they died in Colorado or some other state, was 11.9 per 1,000 population, or only one-tenth of one per cent higher than for the entire registration area.

The number of deaths, distribution and rate per 1,000 population in 1925 and 1927 for Colorado were as follows:

| | 1925 Number | Rate | 1927 Number | Rate |
|---|---|---|---|---|
| White | 12,176 | 11.9 | 12,739 | 12.0 |
| Colored | 373 | 24.2 | 343 | 22.6 |
| Total | 12,549 | 12.1 | 13,082 | 12.2 |
| Urban | 5,908 | 15.2 | 5,969 | 14.9 |
| Rural | 6,641 | 10.2 | 7,113 | 10.6 |
| Total | 12,549 | 12.1 | 13,082 | 12.2 |

The months in which the largest number of deaths in the state occurred in 1927 were January, 1,240; December, 1,178, and March, 1,175. The months in which the smallest number occurred were July, 952, and October, 998. The ages at which the deaths occurred were as follows:

| | |
|---|---|
| Under 1 year | 1,710 |
| 65 to 69 years | 1,050 |
| 70 to 74 years | 1,010 |
| 75 to 79 years | 923 |
| 60 to 64 years | 883 |
| 55 to 59 years | 757 |
| 50 to 54 years | 640 |
| 1 to 4 years | 636 |
| 80 to 84 years | 633 |
| 35 to 39 years | 612 |
| 30 to 34 years | 598 |
| 45 to 49 years | 589 |
| 40 to 44 years | 587 |
| 25 to 29 years | 553 |
| 20 to 24 years | 493 |
| 15 to 19 years | 363 |
| 85 to 89 years | 337 |
| 5 to 9 years | 307 |
| 10 to 14 years | 243 |
| 90 to 94 years | 109 |
| 95 to 99 years | 27 |
| 100 years and over | 6 |
| Age unknown | 16 |
| Total deaths | 13,082 |

An accompanying table shows the death rate per 100,000 population in Colorado for the years 1921 to 1930, inclusive.

The number of deaths from various causes and the totals for 1929 and 1930 were as follows:

| Cause | 1930 | 1929 |
|-------|------|------|
| Typhoid and paratyphoid fever | 56 | 66 |
| Smallpox | 1 | 5 |
| Measles | 91 | 7 |
| Scarlet fever | 25 | 15 |
| Whooping-cough | 130 | 49 |
| Diphtheria | 41 | 39 |
| Influenza | 363 | 639 |
| Dysentery | 30 | 23 |
| Erysipelas | 27 | 39 |
| Acute poliomyelitis and acute polioencephalitis | 17 | 6 |
| Lethargic or epidemic encephalitis | 10 | 14 |
| Epidemic cerebrospinal meningitis | 50 | 128 |
| Tuberculosis (all forms) | 1,283 | 1,282 |
| Of the respiratory system | 1,192 | 1,202 |
| Of the meninges, central nervous system | 31 | 25 |
| Other forms | 60 | 55 |
| Syphilis† | 126 | 113 |
| Malaria | 2 | 2 |
| Cancer and other malignant tumors | 1,035 | 1,028 |
| Rheumatism and gout | 38 | 40 |
| Diabetes mellitus | 151 | 137 |
| Pellagra | 5 | 4 |
| Pernicious anemia | 44 | 44 |
| Alcoholism (acute or chronic) | 37 | 29 |
| Meningitis (nonepidemic) | 40 | 45 |
| Cerebral hemorrhage, embolism, thrombosis and softening | 901 | 832 |
| Hemiplegia, other paralysis, cause not specified | 22 | 29 |
| Diseases of the heart | 1,877 | 1,775 |

| Cause | 1930 | 1929 |
|---|---|---|
| Diseases of the arteries, atheroma, aneurysm, etc. | 287 | ‡ |
| Bronchitis | 40 | 32 |
| Pneumonia (all forms) | 1,226 | 1,054 |
| Respiratory diseases other than bronchitis and pneumonia (all forms) | 131 | ‡ |
| Ulcer of the stomach and duodenum | 99 | 73 |
| Diarrhea and enteritis | 506 | 425 |
| Diarrhea and enteritis (under 2 years) | 416 | 357 |
| Diarrhea and enteritis (2 years and over) | 90 | 68 |
| Appendicitis | 258 | 252 |
| Hernia, intestinal obstruction | 136 | 151 |
| Cirrhosis of the liver | 59 | 58 |
| Nephritis | 824 | 817 |
| Puerperal septicemia | 72 | 71 |
| Puerperal causes other than puerperal septicemia | 68 | 84 |
| Congenital malformations and diseases of early infancy | 757 | 719 |
| Suicide | 203 | 168 |
| Homicide | 88 | 90 |
| Accidental and unspecified external causes | 973 | 980 |
| Burns (conflagration excepted)§ | 53 | 57 |
| Accidental drowning§ | 61 | 72 |
| Accidental shooting | 33 | 41 |
| Accidental falls§ | 205 | 169 |
| Excessive heat (burns excepted) | 1 | 3 |
| Other external causes | 620 | ‡ |

| Cause | 1930 | 1929 |
|---|---|---|
| All other defined causes | 1,001 | ‡ |
| Unknown or ill-defined causes | 77 | 73 |
| **Supplemental** | | |
| Mine and quarry accidents | 54 | 79 |
| Machinery accidents | 31 | 17 |
| Railroad accidents: | | |
| Collision with automobile | 9 | 22 |
| Other railroad accidents | 43 | 50 |
| Street car accidents: | | |
| Collision with automobile | 1 | 7 |
| Other street car accidents | 5 | 7 |
| Automobile accidents (excluding collision with railroad trains and street cars) | 271 | 258 |
| Other transportation accidents£ | 32 | ‡ |
| *Total deaths all causes | 13,207 | 12,874 |

*Exclusive of stillbirths.

†Includes tabes dorsalis (locomotor ataxia) and general paralysis of the insane.

‡Not comparable.

§Includes deaths from this cause where the accident occurred in a mine or quarry, by machinery, or in connection with transportation.

£Includes air, motorcycle and water transportation accidents.

## DEATH RATE PER 100,000 POPULATION
(Compiled from Census Reports)

| Cause of Death | Colorado | | | | | | | | | |
|---|---|---|---|---|---|---|---|---|---|---|
| | 1930 | 1929 | 1928 | 1927 | 1926 | 1925 | 1924 | 1923 | 1922 | 1921 |
| Typhoid and paratyphoid fever | 5.4 | 6.4 | 3.9 | 7.2 | 5.9 | 8.8 | 6.7 | 10.5 | 11.4 | 10.1 |
| Malaria | 0.2 | 0.2 | 0.2 | 0.3 | 0.3 | 0.2 | ---- | ---- | 0.2 | ---- |
| Smallpox | .01 | 0.5 | 0.1 | 0.3 | 0.1 | ---- | ---- | 1.6 | 27.8 | 4.7 |
| Measles | 8.8 | 0.7 | 5.0 | 12.7 | 1.2 | 0.8 | 21.5 | 9.8 | 0.7 | 8.4 |
| Scarlet fever | 2.4 | 1.5 | 4.4 | 5.9 | 2.1 | 2.9 | 4.4 | 4.2 | 5.4 | 5.9 |
| Whooping cough | 12.5 | 4.8 | 11.1 | 5.3 | 17.2 | 9.9 | 6.5 | 10.5 | 6.0 | 10.2 |
| Diphtheria | 3.9 | 3.8 | 3.8 | 9.1 | 9.2 | 14.3 | 15.6 | 23.9 | 27.4 | 24.8 |
| Influenza and pneumonia (all forms) | ---- | ---- | 220.2 | 139.6 | 154.5 | 157.3 | 156.7 | 166.2 | 191.0 | 130.4 |
| Tuberculosis (all forms) | 123.6 | 124.6 | 129.8 | 139.2 | 144.2 | 152.4 | 163.1 | 168.5 | 183.3 | 184.6 |
| Cancer and other malignant tumors | 99.7 | 99.9 | 93.3 | 93.5 | 82.1 | 86.7 | 83.3 | 85.9 | 73.8 | 74.7 |
| Diabetes mellitus | 14.5 | 13.3 | 17.1 | 12.3 | 13.4 | 10.2 | 9.9 | 13.1 | 14.6 | 14.3 |
| Alcoholism | 3.6 | 2.8 | ---- | 2.4 | 2.3 | 1.7 | 2.9 | 3.7 | 4.2 | 3.2 |
| Cirrhosis of the liver | 5.6 | 5.7 | 4.6 | 6.3 | 4.8 | 4.7 | 6.2 | 5.4 | 6.4 | 5.6 |
| Diseases of the heart | 180.8 | 172.5 | 170.7 | 150.1 | 142.7 | 133.3 | 126.5 | 126.0 | 133.5 | 122.6 |
| Pneumonia (all forms) | 118.1 | 102.5 | 116.4 | 99.4 | 98.5 | 101.2 | 122.5 | 122.2 | 131.7 | 110.5 |
| Diarrhea and enteritis | 48.7 | 41.3 | 31.5 | 34.1 | 29.5 | 46.3 | 38.4 | 41.1 | 43.6 | 41.5 |
| Acute and chronic nephritis | 79.4 | 79.4 | 80.3 | 73.5 | 72.1 | 71.6 | 76.3 | 70.7 | 78.4 | 68.8 |
| Old age | ---- | ---- | ---- | 13.5 | 13.0 | 11.5 | 10.6 | 10.6 | 14.1 | 14.4 |
| Suicide | 19.6 | 16.3 | 16.9 | 15.5 | 14.7 | 17.4 | 16.3 | 14.2 | 18.0 | 14.8 |
| Homicide | 8.5 | 8.7 | 5.6 | 5.5 | 6.6 | 8.1 | 10.0 | 9.2 | 11.7 | 11.8 |
| Automobile accidents | 26.1 | 25.1 | 20.3 | 21.8 | 16.5 | 14.0 | 15.7 | 15.9 | 16.3 | 12.6 |
| Unknown or ill-defined diseases | 7.4 | 7.1 | 4.8 | 4.7 | 2.4 | 0.3 | 4.6 | 2.9 | 4.5 | 2.6 |

## DEATHS FROM AUTOMOBILE ACCIDENTS

Deaths from automobile accidents in Colorado, exclusive of collisions with railroad trains and street cars, were 271 in 1930, the largest in any year on record. Deaths where automobiles come into collision with railroad trains and street cars are listed under railroad accidents. There were 10 deaths from such collisions in 1930; 29 in 1929, 15 in 1928 and 22 in 1927.

The number of deaths and rates per 100,000 population in Colorado and the registration area by years, from automobile accidents as described above, are as follows:

| Year | No. | Rate Colo. | Area |
|---|---|---|---|
| 1918 | 120 | 13.1 | 9.3 |
| 1919 | 118 | 12.7 | 9.4 |
| 1920 | 117 | 12.4 | 10.4 |
| 1921 | 121 | 12.6 | 11.5 |
| 1922 | 159 | 16.3 | 12.5 |
| 1923 | 157 | 15.9 | 14.9 |
| 1924 | 158 | 15.7 | 15.7 |
| 1925 | 146 | 14.0 | 17.0 |
| 1926 | 175 | 16.5 | 17.9 |
| 1927 | 234 | 21.8 | 19.5 |
| 1928 | 221 | 20.3 | ... |
| 1929 | 258 | 25.1 | ... |
| 1930 | 271 | 26.1 | ... |

## DEATHS BY SUICIDE

There were 203 deaths by suicide in Colorado in 1930, an increase of 35 compared with 1929. These occurred at the rate of 19.6 for every 100,000 persons in the state, the highest rate reported in 18 years.

The following table gives the number of suicides and the rate per 100,000 population for Colorado and the registration area by years as reported by the state board of health and the bureau of the census:

| Year | No. | Rate Colo. | Area |
|---|---|---|---|
| 1913 | ... | 22.1 | 15.8 |
| 1914 | ... | 19.2 | 16.6 |
| 1915 | ... | 18.8 | 16.7 |
| 1916 | ... | 13.3 | 14.2 |
| 1917 | ... | 13.7 | 13.4 |
| 1918 | ... | 14.6 | 12.2 |
| 1919 | ... | 14.2 | 11.4 |
| 1920 | ... | 15.7 | 10.2 |
| 1921 | ... | 14.8 | 12.6 |
| 1922 | 176 | 18.0 | 11.9 |
| 1923 | 137 | 14.2 | 11.6 |
| 1924 | 164 | 16.3 | 12.2 |
| 1925 | 181 | 17.4 | 12.1 |
| 1926 | 148 | 14.7 | 12.8 |
| 1927 | 166 | 15.5 | 13.2 |
| 1928 | 184 | 16.9 | ... |
| 1929 | 168 | 16.3 | ... |
| 1930 | 203 | 19.6 | ... |

The largest number of deaths in 1925 and 1927 by suicide were of persons between the ages of 35 and 44 years. The number in 1925 was 41 out of the total of 181, and in 1927 was 36 out of a total of 166. The next largest number were of ages between 45 and 54 years, there being 29 of those ages in 1925 and 35 in 1927. Principal methods of committing suicide were as follows:

| | 1925 | 1927 |
|---|---|---|
| By poison | 22 | 13 |
| By corrosive substances | 12 | 21 |
| By poisonous gas | 19 | 19 |
| By hanging or strangulation | 17 | 12 |
| By drowning | 7 | 4 |
| By firearms | 88 | 85 |
| By cutting or piercing instruments | 9 | 8 |
| By jumping from high places | 2 | .. |
| By crushing | 2 | 2 |
| By other causes | 3 | 2 |
| | 181 | 166 |

Detailed statistics for years subsequent to 1927 have not as yet been released.

## HOMICIDE DEATHS

There were 88 deaths from homicide in Colorado reported in 1930, which compares with 90 in 1929. The maximum number of deaths from homicide in the past nine years was in 1922, when the total was 114.

The figures are those reported by the state health department and the United States census bureau. The term "homicide" as here used includes murder, manslaughter, justifiable homicide and incendiarism, but not legal executions. In connection with preventive measures it is noted that 66 out of the 84 homicides in 1925 were by firearms. This is equal to 78.5 per cent of the total. Four were by cutting or piercing instruments and 14 by other means.

In 1927, 46 out of the 59 homicides, or 93.8 per cent, were by firearms, five were by cutting or piercing instruments and eight by other means. Detailed figures for years later than 1927 have not as yet been released.

The number of deaths, as far as records are available, and the rate per 100,000 population for Colorado and for the registration area of the United States, by years, are as follows:

| Year | No. | Rate Colo. | Area |
|---|---|---|---|
| 1915 | ... | 10.6 | 7.0 |
| 1916 | ... | 8.2 | 7.1 |
| 1917 | ... | 8.9 | 7.7 |
| 1918 | ... | 7.5 | 6.8 |
| 1919 | ... | 10.6 | 7.5 |
| 1920 | ... | 9.2 | 7.1 |
| 1921 | ... | 11.8 | 8.5 |
| 1922 | 114 | 11.7 | 8.4 |
| 1923 | 90 | 9.2 | 8.1 |
| 1924 | 100 | 10.0 | 8.5 |
| 1925 | 84 | 8.1 | 8.6 |
| 1926 | 69 | 6.6 | 8.8 |
| 1927 | 59 | 5.5 | 8.7 |
| 1928 | 59 | 5.6 | ... |
| 1929 | 90 | 8.7 | ... |
| 1930 | 88 | 8.5 | ... |

## DEATHS FROM ALCOHOLISM

Colorado became a prohibition state on January 1, 1916, when laws prohibiting the manufacture, sale and possession of intoxicating liquors became effective. The federal constitutional amendment prohibiting the sale of liquors became effective on January 16, 1920. Colorado was, therefore, a "dry" state four years before prohibition became a national law.

Data from the census bureau show that in the year Colorado prohibited the sale of liquors deaths from alcoholism decreased 58 per cent under the preceding year and continued to decrease until 1920, when the total decrease amounted to 90 per cent. The next two years showed substantial increases.

The following table shows the death rate per 100,000 population in Colorado from alcoholism by years, with comparative rate for the registration area of the United States.

| Year | Colorado | Reg. Area |
|---|---|---|
| 1914 | 8.3 | 4.9 |
| 1915 | 7.2 | 4.4 |
| 1916 | 3.0 | 5.8 |
| 1917 | 2.3 | 5.2 |
| 1918 | 1.4 | 2.7 |
| 1919 | 0.8 | 1.6 |
| 1920 | 0.7 | 1.0 |
| 1921 | 3.2 | 1.8 |
| 1922 | 4.2 | 2.6 |
| 1923 | 3.7 | 3.2 |
| 1924 | 2.9 | 3.2 |
| 1925 | 1.7 | 3.6 |
| 1926 | 2.3 | 3.9 |
| 1927 | 2.4 | 4.0 |
| 1929 | 2.8 | .. |
| 1930 | 3.6 | .. |

## PRISONERS AND CRIME CONDITIONS

The absence of any uniform system for compiling statistics on crime conditions makes it almost impossible to prepare data of any practical value. This is due to several causes. Crime detection and punishment is handled by a variety of agencies, including federal, state, county and municipal authorities, and the lack of any central agency to eliminate duplications, report upon disposition of prisoners and to classify the crimes imposes a problem that has not been solved satisfactorily. A single prisoner may be charged with several offenses and may be tried in courts of different jurisdictions. One agency may compile records principally of offenses reported, another of convictions secured and a third upon an entirely different basis, and these cannot be harmonized for comparative purposes. The survey presented here is confined principally to prisoners received in the county jails of the state. Some additional information is given in another chapter on the state penitentiary and reform institutions.

There were received in the county jails of the state during the year ending November 30, 1931, a total of 13,271 prisoners, exclusive of Kit Carson county, for which data are not available. Of that number 12,277 were males and 994 were females. This was an increase of 2,337 over the number of prisoners received in 1930, and the largest gain in seven years. The number of prisoners in the county jails of the state on November 30, 1931, was 619, which compares with 913 on the same date in 1930, 496 in 1929 and 660 on the same date in 1928.

Twenty counties received no female prisoners in 1931, which compares with 17 counties in 1930, 16 in 1929, 21 in 1928 and 18 counties in 1927.

The numbers received by years, and by sex, were as follows:

| Year | Male | Female | Total |
|---|---|---|---|
| 1925 | 11,071 | 729 | 11,800 |
| 1926 | 9,132 | 574 | 9,706 |
| 1927 | 9,956 | 505 | 10,461 |
| 1928 | 10,193 | 474 | 10,667 |
| 1929 | 9,904 | 682 | 10,586 |
| 1930 | 10,115 | 819 | 10,934 |
| 1931 | 12,277 | 994 | 13,271 |

The percentages of males and females received by years were as follows:

| Year | Per Cent Male | Per Cent Female |
|---|---|---|
| 1925 | 93.82 | 6.18 |
| 1926 | 94.09 | 5.91 |
| 1927 | 95.17 | 4.83 |
| 1928 | 95.56 | 4.44 |
| 1929 | 93.57 | 6.43 |
| 1930 | 92.50 | 7.50 |
| 1931 | 92.55 | 7.45 |

A table published on page 338 in this volume shows the number of prisoners received in jails by counties and years, and number of prisoners confined at the end of the fiscal years.

The number of prisoners in the county jails of the state on November 30, of the years named, as reported by the sheriffs, were as follows:

| Year | Male | Female | Total |
|---|---|---|---|
| 1924 | .. | .. | 847 |
| 1925 | 518 | 41 | 559 |
| 1926 | 492 | 29 | 521 |
| 1927 | 676 | 43 | 719 |
| 1928 | 604 | 43 | 647 |
| 1929 | 471 | 25 | 496 |
| 1930 | 849 | 64 | 913 |
| 1931 | 571 | 48 | 619 |

## PRISONERS IN COUNTY JAILS, YEARS ENDING NOVEMBER 30
### (From Records of County Sheriffs)

| COUNTY | Prisoners Received | | | | | | No. Prisoners at End of Year | | |
|---|---|---|---|---|---|---|---|---|---|
| | 1931 | | | 1930 | 1929 | 1928 | 1931 | 1930 | 1929 |
| | Male | Female | Total | | | | | | |
| Adams.......... | 579 | 16 | 595 | 339 | 368 | 308 | 8 | 11 | 15 |
| Alamosa....... | 66 | 5 | 71 | 42 | 44 | 28 | 3 | 1 | 4 |
| Arapahoe...... | 96 | 3 | 99 | 67 | 130 | 68 | 5 | 7 | 3 |
| Archuleta...... | 2 | ... | 2 | 3 | 4 | ... | ... | ... | 1 |
| Baca.......... | 86 | ... | 86 | 91 | 32 | 75 | 4 | 6 | ... |
| Bent.......... | 152 | 1 | 153 | 114 | 77 | 64 | 6 | 3 | 4 |
| Boulder........ | 547 | 39 | 586 | 533 | 530 | 562 | 12 | 15 | 8 |
| Chaffee........ | 62 | 3 | 65 | 31 | 42 | 29 | 5 | 5 | 8 |
| Cheyenne...... | 53 | ... | 53 | 20 | 25 | 12 | 1 | 2 | 1 |
| Clear Creek.... | 33 | 4 | 37 | 26 | 15 | 32 | 1 | 2 | 3 |
| Conejos........ | 50 | ... | 50 | 10 | 27 | 7 | 11 | 8 | 1 |
| Costilla........ | 35 | ... | 35 | 23 | 11 | 5 | 5 | 3 | ... |
| Crowley....... | 82 | 11 | 93 | 111 | 77 | 94 | 7 | 3 | ... |
| Custer......... | 4 | ... | 4 | 6 | 2 | 2 | 1 | 2 | 1 |
| Delta.......... | 79 | 2 | 81 | 54 | 65 | 68 | 1 | 3 | 5 |
| Denver........ | 4,792 | 508 | 5,300 | 4,422 | 4,369 | 4,756 | 284 | 290 | 243 |
| Dolores........ | 8 | ... | 8 | 6 | * | 22 | ... | ... | * |
| Douglas....... | 25 | ... | 25 | 70 | 54 | 35 | ... | ... | ... |
| Eagle.......... | 48 | 3 | 51 | 33 | 23 | 41 | 5 | 10 | ... |
| Elbert......... | 18 | ... | 18 | 8 | 21 | * | ... | 1 | ... |
| El Paso........ | 474 | 77 | 551 | 506 | 442 | 385 | 22 | 16 | 16 |
| Fremont....... | 86 | 5 | 91 | 104 | 107 | 91 | 4 | 8 | 5 |
| Garfield........ | 102 | 5 | 107 | 71 | 108 | 105 | 8 | 10 | 8 |
| Gilpin......... | 16 | ... | 16 | 32 | 12 | 10 | ... | ... | ... |
| Grand......... | 36 | 2 | 38 | 25 | 29 | 26 | ... | ... | ... |
| Gunnison...... | 64 | 4 | 68 | 59 | 42 | 47 | 2 | 3 | 1 |
| Hinsdale...... | 3 | ... | 3 | ... | * | ... | ... | ... | ... |
| Huerfano...... | 137 | 12 | 149 | 146 | 136 | 143 | 6 | 7 | 5 |
| Jackson....... | 3 | ... | 3 | 2 | 2 | 1 | ... | ... | ... |
| Jefferson...... | 515 | 25 | 540 | 302 | 327 | 278 | 9 | 11 | 11 |
| Kiowa......... | 10 | ... | 10 | 20 | 13 | 6 | ... | ... | ... |
| Kit Carson..... | * | * | * | * | 72 | 41 | * | * | 5 |
| Lake.......... | 59 | 4 | 63 | 134 | 175 | 395 | 1 | 4 | ... |
| La Plata....... | 164 | 15 | 179 | 165 | 185 | 167 | 7 | 7 | 7 |
| Larimer....... | 257 | 10 | 267 | 266 | 230 | 237 | 11 | 9 | 8 |
| Las Animas.... | 299 | 25 | 324 | 319 | 328 | 477 | 5 | 7 | 7 |
| Lincoln........ | 79 | ... | 79 | 50 | 22 | ... | 8 | 11 | ... |
| Logan......... | 154 | 11 | 165 | 172 | 134 | 157 | 2 | 16 | 3 |
| Mesa.......... | 154 | 19 | 173 | 160 | 194 | * | 7 | 8 | 12 |
| Mineral........ | 5 | 2 | 7 | 1 | 3 | 1 | ... | ... | 2 |
| Moffat......... | 87 | 2 | 89 | 64 | 44 | 35 | 4 | 5 | 2 |
| Montezuma.... | 57 | 4 | 61 | 55 | 36 | 39 | 4 | 1 | 1 |
| Montrose...... | 140 | 3 | 143 | 86 | 85 | 87 | 13 | 7 | ... |
| Morgan........ | 237 | 21 | 258 | 262 | 194 | 202 | 5 | 5 | 7 |
| Otero.......... | 279 | 14 | 293 | 293 | 218 | 233 | 12 | 273 | 11 |
| Ouray......... | 18 | ... | 18 | 28 | 25 | 6 | 1 | ... | ... |
| Park.......... | 24 | 1 | 25 | 10 | 11 | 14 | 1 | ... | ... |
| Phillips........ | 54 | 2 | 56 | 49 | 18 | 2 | 4 | 5 | 4 |
| Pitkin......... | 11 | ... | 11 | 1 | 6 | 1 | ... | ... | ... |
| Prowers....... | 347 | 26 | 373 | 271 | 223 | 155 | 16 | 13 | 12 |
| Pueblo........ | 534 | 72 | 606 | 543 | 486 | 356 | 61 | 74 | 35 |
| Rio Blanco..... | 12 | 1 | 13 | 9 | 8 | 15 | ... | 2 | 2 |
| Rio Grande.... | 82 | 1 | 83 | 67 | 71 | 85 | ... | 5 | ... |
| Routt......... | 87 | 11 | 98 | 90 | 54 | * | 5 | 7 | 3 |
| Saguache...... | 68 | 6 | 74 | 10 | 48 | 74 | 7 | 4 | 6 |
| San Juan...... | 7 | ... | 7 | 2 | 6 | 12 | ... | ... | ... |
| San Miguel..... | 10 | ... | 10 | 2 | 6 | 7 | ... | ... | ... |
| Sedgwick...... | 28 | ... | 28 | * | * | 43 | 2 | * | * |
| Summit........ | 11 | ... | 11 | 8 | 7 | 8 | ... | ... | 4 |
| Teller......... | 74 | 1 | 75 | 82 | 50 | 57 | 3 | ... | ... |
| Washington.... | 79 | 2 | 81 | 22 | 40 | 21 | 6 | ... | 1 |
| Weld.......... | 519 | 14 | 533 | 437 | 378 | 361 | 24 | 23 | 19 |
| Yuma.......... | 78 | 2 | 80 | * | 95 | 79 | ... | * | 2 |
| State........ | 12,277 | 994 | 13,271 | 10,934 | 10,586 | 10,667 | 619 | 913 | 496 |

*Data not available.

## LIBRARIES IN COLORADO

Colorado has extensive library facilities available to the public, many of which are maintained in whole or in part by public funds. These include libraries owned by the state, public libraries in the cities and towns, and libraries owned by educational institutions and private organizations, most of which are available to the public. The Colorado state library is located in the capitol building at Denver and a constitutional provision makes the state superintendent of public instruction the librarian. This library is used as a depository for the preservation of state records and reports and is also a depository for United States government reports and documents. There are more than 125,000 volumes in this library. A state law library, which is under the supervision of the supreme court, is located in the capitol and contains 35,000 volumes. An historical library, which is under the supervision of the State Historical society, is located in the state museum building.

The Colorado Library commission was created by the twenty-seventh general assembly. It is given power to do all things necessary to create and keep in operation free traveling libraries for the state of Colorado. It is also the duty of the commission to further library development throughout the state, to give assistance to free libraries and to committees which propose to establish them, and to aid in the selection of books, cataloging and other details of administration. The traveling library, which is under the commission's administration, endeavors to keep in circulation books in rural communities where public libraries are not available. The circulation of this library in 1930 was 31,794 volumes.

Available records cover 64 state, public and institutional libraries which contain an aggregate of 1,339,686 volumes. This list does not, however, include 49 public libraries in small towns which failed to report to the state library commission, and numerous community libraries maintained by local clubs and other organizations. A summary of libraries and number of volumes is as follows:

| | **Volumes** |
|---|---|
| State libraries | 163,500 |
| Publicly controlled universities and colleges | 263,975 |
| Privately controlled universities and colleges | 200,750 |
| Public libraries | 711,461 |

The number of volumes in the libraries of privately controlled colleges and universities in Colorado are reported as follows:

| | **No. Vols.** |
|---|---|
| Colorado college | 110,000 |
| Colorado Woman's college | 3,750 |
| Iliff School of Theology | 13,000 |
| Regis college | 27,000 |
| University of Denver | 32,000 |
| Westminster Law school | 5,000 |
| Loretta Heights college | 10,000 |
| Total | 200,750 |

The number of volumes in the libraries of publicly controlled colleges and universities are reported as follows:

| | **No. Vols.** |
|---|---|
| University of Colorado | 185,000 |
| Agricultural college | 57,625 |
| School of Mines | 21,350 |
| Total | 263,975 |

An accompanying table shows the locations of public libraries reporting to the state library commission, the number of volumes, circulation, appropriations for their maintenance, the number of borrowers and the number of hours in which they are open each week.

In addition to libraries, or in connection therewith, 34 cities and towns maintain reading rooms where files of newspapers and magazines are available. The location of these reading rooms, the number of publications and number of readers, is as follows:

| Town | No. Publications | No. Readers |
|---|---|---|
| Alamosa | 47 | 15,000 |
| Boulder | 66 | No Record |
| Brighton | 32 | No Record |
| Brush | 42 | 26,284 |
| Burlington | 16 | 356 |
| Canon City | 45 | 14,742 |
| Colorado Springs— Branch | 41 | 17,551 |
| Delta | 36 | No Record |
| Denver | 775 | ..... |
| Durango | 61 | 14,779 |
| Eaton | 12 | No Record |
| Estes Park | 8 | 1,870 |
| Evergreen | 23 | No Record |
| Florence | 30 | 15,827 |
| Fort Collins | 122 | 26,083 |
| Fort Morgan | 50 | 23,083 |
| Glenwood Springs | 17 | 500 |
| Golden | 7 | 309 |
| Greeley | 100 | No Record |
| Idaho Springs | 30 | No Record |
| Lamar | 72 | 8,823 |
| Las Animas | 31 | 3,220 |
| Littleton | 25 | 5,024 |
| Longmont | 89 | No Record |
| Loveland | 90 | 22,974 |
| Mancos | 20 | No Record |
| Monte Vista | 32 | 24,241 |
| Montrose | 26 | No Record |
| Pueblo | 90 | No Record |
| Rocky Ford | 70 | 17,052 |
| Salida | 75 | No Record |
| Sterling | 63 | 7,198 |
| Swink | 9 | 100 |
| Victor | 12 | 500 |

## PUBLIC LIBRARIES IN COLORADO
(From Reports of the Colorado Library Commission)

| CITY OR TOWN | No. of Volumes | Circu- lation | Appro- priation | No. of Borrow- ers | Hours Per Week |
|---|---|---|---|---|---|
| Alamosa .................. | 5,343 | 25,753 | $  2,962 | 1,162 | 45 |
| Ault ...................... | 1,525 | 60 | 60 | .... | 4 |
| Aurora ................... | 3,500 | 7,000 | 780 | .... | .. |
| Boulder .................. | 17,082 | 65,693 | 5,131 | 6,000 | 75½ |
| Brighton ................ | 7,185 | 36,193 | 2,327 | 2,879 | 30 |
| Brush .................... | 6,713 | 22,184 | 1,590 | 1,507 | 25½ |
| Buena Vista.............. | 2,600 | 3,000 | 120 | 66 | 12 |
| Burlington ............... | 3,400 | 8,000 | 700 | 750 | 18 |
| Canon City ............... | 9,066 | 19,031 | 2,400 | .... | 66 |
| Colorado Springs ......... | 44,300 | 146,327 | 19,221 | .... | .. |
| Colorado Springs—Branch... | 7,340 | 23,558 | 3,640 | .... | 42 |
| Delta .................... | 8,073 | 28,118 | 2,400 | 2,328 | 45 |
| Denver .................. | 329,303 | 1,963,984 | 240,000 | .... | 79 |
| Durango ................. | 14,780 | 37,988 | 5,000 | 3,692 | 76 |
| Eaton ................... | 5,025 | 7,860 | 700 | 245 | 12 |
| Estes Park ............... | 4,400 | 7,321 | 1,000 | .... | 4 |
| Evergreen ............... | 7,792 | 5,847 | None | 562 | 42 |
| Flagler .................. | 2,500 | 2,000 | 100 | .... | 10 |
| Fort Collins ............. | 19,356 | 94,214 | 6,985 | 4,500 | 75½ |
| Fort Lupton.............. | 2,816 | 8,839 | 1,196 | .... | 9 |
| Fort Morgan............. | 10,000 | 17,712 | 3,163 | 6.559 | 36 |
| Glenwood Springs.......... | 4,700 | 10,000 | 400 | 505 | 20 |
| Golden .................. | 6,000 | 4,140 | 500 | 497 | 42 |
| Greeley ................. | 25,679 | 136,307 | 14,000 | 7,000 | 76 |
| Hayden .................. | 2,000 | 400 | 300 | 400 | 10 |
| Holyoke ................. | 5,000 | 4,000 | None | 300 | 20 |
| Hugo .................... | .... | 7,284 | .... | .... | .. |
| Idaho Springs............. | 6,947 | 10,824 | 1,000 | 547 | 36 |
| Lamar ................... | 6,591 | 11,628 | 1,200 | 600 | 38 |
| Las Animas .............. | 6,500 | 15,528 | 1,600 | 2,928 | 28 |
| Littleton ................ | 4,200 | 19,461 | 1,400 | 880 | 33 |
| Longmont ............... | 12,000 | 44,098 | 4,500 | .... | 75 |
| Louisville ............... | 980 | 2,000 | 200 | .... | 4 |
| Loveland ................ | 8,701 | 43,466 | 4,000 | 3,500 | 48 |
| Mancos ................. | 3,000 | 2,500 | .... | .... | 54 |
| Manzanola ............... | 2,468 | .... | 60 | 124 | 6 |
| Merino .................. | 1,452 | 4,985 | .... | 210 | 6 |
| Monte Vista.............. | 5,230 | 23,610 | 1,736 | 1,727 | 45 |
| Montrose ............... | 7,399 | 26,351 | 2,950 | 4,000 | 39 |
| Platteville .............. | 1,915 | 1,360 | 100 | .... | 6 . |
| Pueblo .................. | 38,590 | 158,288 | 12,000 | 12,248 | 78 |
| Rifle .................... | 3,000 | 12,000 | 550 | .... | 13½ |
| Rocky Ford.............. | 8,200 | 40,506 | 3,000 | 1,740 | 54 |
| Salida .................. | 9,300 | 12,000 | 2,700 | 1,000 | 42 |
| Sterling ................. | 11,329 | 59,136 | 6,185 | 3,873 | 59 |
| Swink .................. | 2,250 | 1,050 | 120 | 200 | 6 |
| Victor .................. | 9,500 | 9,600 | .... | 800 | 14 |
| Virginia Dale............. | 230 | .... | 10 | .... | .. |
| Wellington ............... | 1,700 | 2,860 | 60 | .... | 4 |
| Windsor ................. | 2,501 | 7,500 | 600 | 1,173 | 15 |
| Wray ................... | 2,000 | 5,400 | 700 | 175 | 9 |
| Totals............... | 711,461 | 3,206,994 | $359,346 | 74,677 | |

Public libraries in the following cities and towns did not report to the State Library Commission: Akron, Alma, Breckenridge, Briggsdale, Center, Central City, Cheraw, Collbran, Craig, Cripple Creek, Del Norte, EastonVille, Englewood, Evans, Fairplay, Forbes, Fowler, Georgetown, Grand Junction, Gunnison, Haswell, Hillrose, Hotchkiss, Johnstown, Julesburg, La Junta, Lazear, Leadville, Manitou, Maybelle, Meeker, Milliken, Morrison, New Raymer, Oak Creek, Olathe, Otis, Ouray, Ovid, Pagosa Springs, Penrose, San Acacio, Silverton, Steamboat Springs. Sugar City, Telluride, Trinidad, Walsenburg.

## NOTABLE TUNNELS IN COLORADO

The propensity of man to battle and overcome natural barriers in his path of progress is illustrated in Colorado by the many miles of tunnels which have been constructed to level railroad grades through the mountains, convey water from the rivers to the valleys for irrigation purposes, recover the minerals in the earth and to generate hydro-electric power for industrial and domestic uses. Some of the mining districts in the state, such as Cripple Creek and Leadville, are literally honeycombed with underground tunnels, shafts, entries and drifts, while in some of the older coal mining areas the sub-surface workings extend for miles in all directions like the radiating streets of a city. Rivers have been diverted through mountain ranges in order that their waters might be harnessed for the use of tillers of the soil, or to supply the domestic needs of a city or town, and mighty streams have been conquered and controlled so that their power might be used in the mines and the mills. Mountains that were barriers to transportation routes have been penetrated and trains that could not go over them now go through them.

The Denver & Salt Lake (Moffat) railroad, which runs westward from Denver directly through the main range of the Rockies, is a notable example of the use of tunnels to reduce grades for economical transportation purposes. In a distance of 232 miles between Denver and Craig it goes through 52 tunnels with an aggregate length of 56,618 feet, or 10.7 miles, including the Moffat tunnel. The Denver & Rio Grande Western has 16 tunnels with an aggregate length of 11,030 feet, exclusive of tunnels on the Rio Grande Southern railroad.

It is next to impossible to compile a record of all the tunnels that have been driven in Colorado, even if such a list would be of any great value, but there are many that stand out as among the notable borings of the world. The more important of these are described as follows:

The Moffat tunnel was cut under a shoulder of James peak, 50 miles west of Denver, for the purpose of eliminating heavy railroad grades over the Continental Divide and shortening railroad distances. It is a public improvement constructed by the Moffat Tunnel Improvement district, created by the state legislature on April 29, 1922. It

was named in honor of David H. Moffat, a pioneer banker and railroad builder, to whom is given the credit for having originated the undertaking.

The Moffat Tunnel Commission is composed of the following members: George P. Schumacker and Rodney J. Bardwell, Jr., both of Denver; William J. Bennett of Arvada, Charles H. Leckenby of Steamboat Springs, and Thomas H. Iles of Axial. The members, under a recent statute, are elected by the taxpayers of the district.

The district includes Denver, Grand, Moffat and Routt counties and portions of Gilpin, Jefferson, Eagle, Adams and Boulder counties. The cost of the tunnel was approximately $18,000,000, of which the major part was defrayed by the proceeds of four bond issues totalling $15,470,000, and the remainder from profits from concessions.

The tunnel is 6.4 miles long, 24 feet in height and 18 feet in width. A pioneer tunnel bored parallel with the main tunnel to facilitate the work is eight feet high and eight feet wide.

The pioneer tunnel was officially "holed" through on February 18, 1927, the blast of dynamite being set off by President Coolidge upon pressing a key in Washington, and the program being broadcasted to the country by radio from the heart of the mountain. This tunnel is under lease for a nominal rental to the city of Denver, which is maintaining it with a view of using it for water transportation purposes. The railroad tunnel was "holed" through on July 7, 1927, and formally turned over completed to the lessee on February 26, 1928. The railway tunnel has been leased to the Denver & Salt Lake Railway company for 50 years. Projected railroad connections through the tunnel will shorten the distance between Denver and the Pacific coast by 176 miles.

The project involved the excavation of 750,000 cubic yards, or 3,000,000,000 pounds of rock, equal to 1,600 freight trains of 40 cars each; 2,500,000 pounds of dynamite discharged; 700 miles of drill holes; 800,000 pounds of drill steel; 11,000,000 F. B. M. timber, equivalent to more than 2,000 miles of 1 by 12-inch plank; and the use of 28,000,000 K. W. H. electric power.

The Gunnison tunnel is located in Montrose county, near the town of that name, in western Colorado, and was constructed by the United States reclamation service as a part of the Uncompahgre reclamation project, at a cost of $2,905,317. It is 30,645 feet, or 5.8 miles long and is the shape of a horseshoe, being 10 feet wide at the base and 12.4 feet high at the center of the arch. The elevation is 6,433 feet above sea level at the upper end and it is 2,157 feet under ground at the apex. It diverts water from the Gunnison river into the Uncompahgre river basin. F. C. Lauzon, who for a number of years had been a miner, is credited with the conception of the idea out of which the project grew. Mr. Lauzon claimed that the idea came to him in a dream. At the time of its completion it was rated as the longest irrigation tunnel in the world. Work started on the project in January, 1905, and its completion was celebrated on September 23, 1909, when President Taft, accompanied by a party of distinguished people, touched a golden plate attached to a silver bell that was electrically equipped to open the headgate and release the waters of the river into the tunnel. Its construction was attended with a number of dramatic and difficult events. A year after work started it encountered a seam carrying warm water surcharged with carbonic acid gas, which caused a suspension of operations for six months until a shaft for ventilation purposes could be constructed. At 2,000 feet it went through a geological fault and work went ahead in a highly saturated atmosphere at a temperature of 90 degrees Fahrenheit. Cloudbursts and water streams hindered the work at several intervals.

The Frederick mine, near Valdez, in Las Animas county, owned and operated by the Colorado Fuel & Iron company, has 154,000 feet, or 29.15 miles, of underground tunnels, or entries as they are known in the industry, the workings having two entries, one for the intake and the other for the return. It is one of the largest, if not the largest, coal mine in the state.

The Busk-Ivanhoe tunnel is located across the boundary between Lake and Pitkin counties, west of Leadville. It penetrates the Sawatch mountain range and connects the Atlantic and Pacific slopes of the continental divide, a distance of 9,394 feet. The elevation is 10,810 feet above sea level at Busk and 10,944 feet at Ivanhoe, and at the time of its construction it was the second highest tunnel in the world. It was driven almost entirely through granite and cost $1,250,000. Thirty men were killed in

the progress of the work. It was started on August 1, 1890, as a private enterprise, the promoters expecting to lease or sell it to the Colorado Midland railway which had been completed in 1889 from Colorado Springs by way of Ute Pass and Leadville to New Castle. The tunnel saved 530 feet in elevation and seven miles in distance for the railroad. The project was a financial failure, the promoters having undertaken its construction without a contract for its use by the railroad and the latter subsequently bought it at a fractional part of its original cost. The railroad, in turn, was unprofitable and passed into the hands of a private owner, who junked most of it during the world war. On May 13, 1922, he quit-claimed the right-of-way for that portion of the railroad abandoned to the state highway department for highway purposes, title in the tunnel itself not being transferred. State highway No. 104 now runs thrugh the tunnel.

The Yak tunnel, in the Leadville mining district in Lake county, was constructed for drainage, transportation and development purposes in connection with deep mining. It goes from California Gulch eastward below Iron and Breece hill and emerges near the London mine in Park county. The elevation is 10,333 feet and its length is four miles. The venture was started by A. A. Blow and at first was known as the Blow tunnel. Construction started in 1886 and it was completed in 1910. It is seven feet wide and seven feet high.

The Newhouse, or Argo tunnel as it is now known, is located at Idaho Springs, in Clear Creek county, and was constructed for mining development purposes. It is eight feet wide by eight feet high and 4.16 miles long. Hand work started on it in September, 1893, and machines were installed the following January. It was completed on November 17, 1910.

The Shoshone tunnel is located near Glenwood Springs, in Garfield county, the intake being 12 miles above Glenwood Springs on the Colorado river. It was constructed in 1906-1910 by the Central Colorado Power company to generate electricity by water power and now belongs to the Public Service company of Colorado. Tunnelling was through granite for the entire distance. It is 12 feet wide and 16.8 feet high. The total length is 12,453 feet and the cost, exclusive of the concrete lining, was $927,653.

The Laramie-Poudre tunnel, which was constructed for the purpose of diverting water from the Laramie river to be used in irrigating 125,000 acres of land in Larimer and Weld counties, is located near Home, in Larimer county, the intake being on the east bank of the Laramie river near the mouth of West Fork. It is seven and one-half feet wide and nine and one-half feet high and 11,306 feet long. It cost approximately $500,000, including an open cut 1,100 feet long on the western end. It has a capacity of 1,000 cubic feet of water per second. The water taken from the Laramie river and diverted through the tunnel empties into the Cache la Poudre river. Construction began on August 25, 1902, and was completed on July 20, 1911. It is sometimes called the Greeley-Poudre tunnel.

The Lucania tunnel, at Idaho Springs, in Clear Creek county, was constructed for mine development and transportation purposes. It was started in the fall of 1901 and up to January 1, 1911, had been driven 6,385 feet. The projected length is 12,000 feet. The size of the tunnel is eight feet square.

The Big Five, or Central tunnel, at Idaho Springs, Clear Creek county, constructed for mine drainage and transportation purposes, is 9,000 feet long. It is 12 feet wide by eight feet high for a distance of 2,500 feet and the remainder is five feet wide by seven feet high.

The Rowley tunnel at Bonanza, Saguache county, was started on May 27, 1911, and completed in October, 1912. It is eight feet wide, seven feet high and 6,600 feet long. It was constructed for mine drainage and development purposes.

The Marshall-Russell tunnel, which was constructed for mine drainage, transportation and development purposes, is located at Empire, in Clear Creek county. Construction work started in October, 1901, and it was completed in 1912. It is eight feet wide, nine feet high and 6,700 feet long.

The Roosevelt tunnel is located in the Cripple Creek district in Teller county and was constructed to drain gold mines in the district. It is 10 feet wide, six feet high and 14,167 feet long. It cost $386,421. Work started on it in June, 1907, and it was finished to the extent that the first drainage had begun in 1910.

Among the tunnels listed in Bulletin 57 of the United States Bureau of Mines, by David W. Brunton and John A. Davis, but not included in the above are:

| Name | Location | Length |
|---|---|---|
| Burleigh | Silver Plume | 3,000 |
| Carter | Ohio City | 7,600 |
| Gold Links | Ohio City | 3,900 |
| Raymond | Ohio City | 3,200 |
| Sawatch | Leadville | 5,000 |
| Stillwell | Telluride | 2,500 |

## RETAIL DISTRIBUTION IN COLORADO

There are 14,063 retail stores in Colorado, which had net sales in 1929 amounting to $497,852,191, according to reports of the bureau of the census on the 1930 census of retail distribution. This is equal to 13.6 stores per 1,000 population, which compares with 12.6 stores per 1,000 population for the 48 states and the District of Columbia. The per capita sales of these stores in 1929 amounted to $480.65 as against $407.53 per capita for the United States. There are eight states, including the District of Columbia, in which the per capita sales are larger than in Colorado, and 40 states in which they are less. Five of the eight states with larger per capita sales than Colorado also have a larger number of stores per 1,000 population.

The summary of retail distribution divides the business into 10 groups which, in turn, are subdivided. The automotive group led all others with net sales of $116,028,283, or 23.3 per cent of total net sales for all groups. The food group came second with net sales of $115,857,617, or 23.28 per cent of the total. A table published herewith gives the number of stores, net sales and per cent of the total for the various groups. The detailed tables showing the subdivisions of the various groups are omitted for lack of space, but these are available in the printed reports of the census bureau.

There are 15 kinds of business in the automotive group with 3,000 stores and other retail establishments and total sales of $116,028,283. The sales at retail of motor vehicles, both new and used, aggregated more than $79,-200,000, accessories more than $6,-700,000, sales through 1,368 filling stations exceeded $21,700,000 and various other automotive establishments accounted for the balance.

The general merchandise group with 608 stores consists of 60 department stores selling more than $48,600,000 annually; 271 dry gooas stores exceeding $7,600,000 in sales; 115 variety, 5-and-10, and to-a-dollar stores with sales of $5,693,679; and 162 general stores with more than $9,800,000 of aggregate sales.

In the apparel group the report shows 16 kinds of stores, the more important of which are men's stores, women's ready-to-wear specialty stores and shoe stores. The 806 apparel stores sell $29,083,161 of goods annually.

The furniture and household group of 408 stores report sales of $19,989,254, or 4 per cent of the state total. The principal kinds of stores in this group are furniture stores and electrical household appliances stores. There are nine other kinds of stores shown in detail within this group.

There are 28 cafeterias, 425 restaurants with full table service, 508 lunch rooms, 170 lunch counters, refreshment stands, and box lunches, and 105 fountains and soft drink stands. The group of 1,236 eating places does an aggregate business of $17,752,008, or 4 per cent of the total retail business of the state.

The lumber and building group, with 776 yards and stores, shows total sales of $30,711,272, or 6 per cent of the state total of all retail business. More than half of this amount is reported by 267 lumber and building materials yards; 169 hardware stores show sales of $4,524,454. There are 36 electrical shops, 63 lumber and hardware, 126 plumbing, heating and ventilating shops, 30 roofing establishments, 13 heating appliance retailers (including installers of domestic oil burners), 68 paint and glass stores, and 4 glass and mirror shops.

Among the other retail stores shown in detail in this census report are 210 coal and wood yards, 80 feed stores, 93 dealers in farm implements, 93 florists, 116 radio dealers, and 645 country general stores. There are 253 cigar stands, 14 cigar stores with fountains, and 126 cigar stores without fountains, 482 drug stores with fountains and 171 drug stores without fountains, and 216 jewelry stores, 12 of which are installment credit jewelers. There are 40 other kinds of businesses, each as precisely described as the above. In all, there are 3,464 stores in the group described as "Other retail stores." In addition, there are 272 secondhand stores, shown in 11 classifications in this comprehensive census report.

Another table presented herewith shows that of the 14,063 retail stores in the state, 12,141 are single-store independents, 418 are national chain stores and 339 are sectional chain stores. The net sales of the single-store independents was $359,799,554, or 72.27 per cent of the total, the national chain stores $31,926,026, or 6.41 per cent, and the sectional chain stores $29,685,495, or 5.96 per cent, an aggregate for the national and sectional chain stores of $61,611,527, or 12.37 per cent.

There are also given in connection with this chapter tables giving summaries of retail distribution in the principal cities of the state.

## TYPES OF OPERATION IN COLORADO

| | Number of Stores | Net Sales (1929) | Per Cent of Total Net Sales |
|---|---|---|---|
| Single-store independents | 12,141 | $359,799,554 | 72.27 |
| Two-store independents | 458 | 30,148,948 | 6.06 |
| Three-store independents | 168 | 10,415,591 | 2.09 |
| Local chains of four stores and over | 411 | 18,534,422 | 3.72 |
| Sectional chains | 339 | 29,685,495 | 5.96 |
| National chains | 418 | 31,926,026 | 6.41 |
| Mail-order business | 10 | 10,787,396 | 2.17 |
| Direct selling (house-to-house) | 5 | 92,142 | .02 |
| Industrial stores | 7 | 99,301 | .02 |
| Leased department chains | 8 | 331,852 | .07 |
| Utility-operated retail stores | 52 | 3,036,950 | .61 |
| Manufacturer-controlled chains (sales branches) | 22 | 1,619,487 | .33 |
| Co-operative stores | 12 | 514,736 | .10 |
| Branch systems of four stores and over | 2 ⎫ | 546,434 | .11 |
| Rolling stores | 2 ⎬ | | |
| Unclassified types | 8 | 313,857 | .06 |
| Totals | 14,063 | $497,852,191 | 100.00 |

## SUMMARY OF PRINCIPAL RETAIL GROUPS IN DENVER

| | Num-ber of Stores | Employes (full time) | Net Sales (1929) | Per Cent of Total | Stocks on Hand End of Year (at cost) | Salaries and Wages (total) |
|---|---|---|---|---|---|---|
| Food group | 1,335 | 2,223 | $ 57,658,296 | 25.70 | $ 1,880,373 | $ 2,996,425 |
| Automotive group | 769 | 2,827 | 41,333,103 | 18.42 | 3,136,153 | 4,257,500 |
| General merchandise group | 127 | 4,848 | 40,940,532 | 18.25 | 8,471,527 | 5,329,344 |
| Apparel group | 324 | 1,620 | 17,145,436 | 7.64 | 3,712,712 | 2,526,885 |
| Furniture and household group | 125 | 1,422 | 11,546,727 | 5.15 | 2,615,750 | 2,019,640 |
| Restaurants and eating places | 425 | 2,217 | 9,551,980 | 4.26 | 115,219 | 2,009,539 |
| Lumber and building group | 179 | 684 | 7,727,789 | 3.44 | 1,739,002 | 1,255,363 |
| All other stores | 1,194 | 3,838 | 38,466,458 | 17.14 | 7,136,588 | 5,922,931 |
| Totals | 4,478 | 19,679 | $224,370,321 | 100.00 | $28,807,324 | $26,317,627 |

## SUMMARY OF PRINCIPAL RETAIL GROUPS IN PUEBLO

| | Num-ber of Stores | Employes (full time) | Net Sales (1929) | Per Cent of Total | Inventory (at cost) | Salaries and Wages (total) |
|---|---|---|---|---|---|---|
| Automotive group | 121 | 483 | $ 6,574,293 | 23.68 | $ 558,692 | $ 704,396 |
| Food group | 234 | 330 | 6,062,752 | 21.83 | 315,159 | 393,905 |
| General merchandise group | 20 | 492 | 4,622,027 | 16.64 | 985,730 | 595,859 |
| Apparel group | 54 | 168 | 2,129,729 | 7.67 | 665,879 | 231,022 |
| Eating places | 64 | 245 | 800,656 | 2.88 | 21,558 | 163,790 |
| Furniture and household group | 19 | 116 | 1,408,414 | 5.07 | 352,525 | 166,085 |
| Lumber and building group | 30 | 183 | 1,667,448 | 6.00 | 439,716 | 266,998 |
| All other stores | 164 | 457 | 4,507,070 | 16.23 | 1,005,531 | 664,521 |
| Totals | 706 | 2,474 | $27,772,389 | 100.00 | $4,344,790 | $3,186,576 |

## SUMMARY OF PRINCIPAL RETAIL GROUPS IN COLORADO SPRINGS

| | Num-ber of Stores | Employes (full time) | Net Sales (1929) | Per Cent of Total | Inventory (at cost) | Salaries and Wages (total) |
|---|---|---|---|---|---|---|
| Automotive group | 98 | 549 | $ 6,526,067 | 25.83 | $ 643,572 | $ 777,923 |
| Food group | 168 | 302 | 5,289,040 | 20.94 | 303,681 | 380,352 |
| General merchandise group | 14 | 376 | 2,807,290 | 11.11 | 644,835 | 410,540 |
| Lumber and building group | 40 | 264 | 2,419,301 | 9.58 | 612,081 | 439,758 |
| Apparel group | 60 | 168 | 2,163,124 | 8.56 | 807,536 | 254,873 |
| Furniture and household group | 19 | 78 | 825,768 | 3.27 | 195,760 | 109,127 |
| Restaurants and eating places | 38 | 181 | 687,386 | 2.72 | 15,291 | 143,363 |
| All other stores | 142 | 460 | 4,546,077 | 17.99 | 977,186 | 629,914 |
| Totals | 579 | 2,378 | $25,264,053 | 100.00 | $4,199,942 | $3,145,850 |

## SUMMARY OF PRINCIPAL RETAIL GROUPS IN FORT COLLINS

| | Num-ber of Stores | Employes (full time) | Net Sales (1929) | Per Cent of Total | Stocks on Hand End of Year (at cost) | Salaries and Wages (total) |
|---|---|---|---|---|---|---|
| Automotive group | 55 | 147 | $ 2,061,243 | 26.82 | $ 231,931 | $ 236,385 |
| Food group | 44 | 89 | 1,890,622 | 24.60 | 145,825 | 113,273 |
| General merchandise group | 8 | 110 | 876,624 | 11.41 | 245,361 | 91,992 |
| Lumber and building group | 20 | 56 | 672,574 | 8.75 | 253,461 | 101,773 |
| Apparel group | 16 | 24 | 405,141 | 5.27 | 122,898 | 36,696 |
| Furniture and household group | 8 | 35 | 396,094 | 5.15 | 137,977 | 53,316 |
| Restaurants and eating places | 16 | 45 | 223,993 | 2.91 | 8,869 | 35,265 |
| All other stores | 44 | 103 | 1,158,687 | 15.09 | 224,580 | 165,625 |
| Totals | 211 | 609 | $ 7,684,978 | 100.00 | $1,370,902 | $ 834,325 |

## SUMMARY OF PRINCIPAL RETAIL GROUPS IN GREELEY

|  | Number of Stores | Employes (full time) | Net Sales (1929) | Per Cent of Total | Inventory (at cost) | Salaries and Wages (total) |
|---|---|---|---|---|---|---|
| Automotive group | 54 | 214 | $ 3,935,346 | 33.44 | $ 331,317 | $ 350,260 |
| Food group | 46 | 96 | 2,126,916 | 18.08 | 133,599 | 139,154 |
| General merchandise group | 11 | 139 | 1,445,501 | 12.29 | 316,497 | 149,743 |
| Lumber and building group | 26 | 89 | 1,083,661 | 9.20 | 283,575 | 147,884 |
| Apparel group | 20 | 38 | 583,488 | 4.96 | 146,929 | 61,868 |
| Restaurants and eating places | 23 | 76 | 414,543 | 3.52 | 8,184 | 71,088 |
| Furniture and household group | 6 | 71 | 378,229 | 3.22 | 117,822 | 129,097 |
| Other retail stores | 60 | 119 | 1,799,458 | 15.29 | 296,384 | 200,147 |
| Totals | 246 | 842 | $11,767,142 | 100.00 | $1,634,307 | $1,249,241 |

## SUMMARY OF PRINCIPAL RETAIL GROUPS IN BOULDER

|  | Number of Stores | Employes (full time) | Net Sales (1929) | Per Cent of Total | Inventory (at cost) | Salaries and Wages (total) |
|---|---|---|---|---|---|---|
| Food group | 68 | 86 | $ 1,991,642 | 26.44 | $ 118,235 | $ 116,835 |
| Automotive group | 67 | 129 | 1,702,084 | 22.60 | 143,006 | 175,664 |
| Apparel group | 24 | 69 | 826,648 | 10.97 | 268,828 | 92,286 |
| Lumber and building group | 11 | 45 | 500,274 | 6.64 | 184,029 | 79,940 |
| General merchandise group | 5 | 66 | 465,575 | 6.18 | 84,444 | 46,385 |
| Restaurants and eating places | 23 | 103 | 396,562 | 5.26 | 3,679 | 74,707 |
| Furniture and household group | 6 | 25 | 297,619 | 3.95 | 120,706 | 41,175 |
| All other stores | 68 | 125 | 1,352,674 | 17.96 | 346,431 | 167,815 |
| Totals | 272 | 648 | $ 7,533,078 | 100.00 | $1,269,358 | $ 794,807 |

## SUMMARY OF PRINCIPAL RETAIL GROUPS IN GRAND JUNCTION

|  | Number of Stores | Employes (full time) | Net Sales (1929) | Per Cent of Total | Inventory (at cost) | Salaries and Wages (total) |
|---|---|---|---|---|---|---|
| Food group | 34 | 124 | $ 3,068,593 | 33.12 | $ 243,504 | $ 246,258 |
| Automotive group | 41 | 143 | 1,979,585 | 21.36 | 208,319 | 201,096 |
| General merchandise group | 9 | 136 | 1,185,192 | 12.80 | 313,586 | 137,234 |
| Lumber and building group | 17 | 50 | 581,134 | 6.27 | 188,305 | 99,417 |
| Apparel group | 12 | 34 | 579,946 | 6.25 | 263,070 | 55,075 |
| Furniture and household group | 10 | 36 | 398,908 | 4.31 | 117,457 | 55,082 |
| Restaurants and eating places | 15 | 90 | 340,523 | 3.67 | 11,902 | 66,937 |
| All other stores | 58 | 125 | 1,132,081 | 12.22 | 273,518 | 168,509 |
| Totals | 196 | 738 | $ 9,265,962 | 100.00 | $1,619,661 | $1,029,608 |

## SUMMARY OF PRINCIPAL RETAIL GROUPS IN TRINIDAD

| | Num-ber of Stores | Employes (full time) | Net Sales (1929) | Per Cent of Total | Inventory (at cost) | Salaries and Wages (total) |
|---|---|---|---|---|---|---|
| Automotive group_____ | 48 | 169 | $ 2,693,589 | 31.21 | $ 174,023 | $ 258,210 |
| Food group_____ | 58 | 83 | 1,943,212 | 22.52 | 118,747 | 101,384 |
| General merchandise group_____ | 18 | 195 | 1,612,522 | 18.69 | 405,975 | 176,948 |
| Lumber and building group_____ | 13 | 41 | 497,674 | 5.77 | 146,016 | 96,133 |
| Restaurants and eating places___ | 19 | 105 | 328,297 | 3.80 | 7,083 | 65,871 |
| Apparel group_____ | 16 | 34 | 327,327 | 3.79 | 109,710 | 46,930 |
| Furniture and household group__ | 5 | 79 | 222,522 | 2.58 | 44,866 | 153,522 |
| All other stores_____ | 42 | 99 | 1,004,452 | 11.64 | 258,700 | 139,064 |
| Totals _____ | 219 | 805 | $ 8,629,595 | 100.00 | $1,265,120 | $ 1,038,062 |

Note.—Attention is called to the fact that in reports on retail distribution in the cities and towns no service businesses, such as laundries and barber shops, are included. The total number of employes does not include those working part time, but the total payroll includes the salaries of both full-time and part-time employes. Later reports will show the number of part-time employes and their wages. They will show the number of proprietors who are wholly or primarily engaged in the operation of their stores but who are not classified as employes. The abridged figures above do not provide the basis for correctly computing average wages, average sales per employe nor rate of stock turn.

## SUMMARY OF THE PRINCIPAL RETAIL GROUPS IN COLORADO
(1930 Population, 1,035,791; Per Capita Sales, $480.65)

| | Number of Stores | Net Sales (1929) | Per Cent of Total Net Sales |
|---|---|---|---|
| Automotive group........................ | 3,000 | $116,028,283 | 23.30 |
| Food group ............................. | 3,493 | 115,857,617 | 23.28 |
| General merchandise group.............. | 608 | 71,899,357 | 14.44 |
| Lumber and building group.............. | 776 | 30,711,272 | 6.17 |
| Apparel group ......................... | 806 | 29,083,161 | 5.83 |
| Furniture and household group.......... | 408 | 19,989,254 | 4.01 |
| Restaurants and eating places........... | 1,236 | 17,752,008 | 3.56 |
| Country general stores................... | 645 | 17,111,753 | 3.43 |
| All other stores........................ | 2,819 | 76,812,818 | 15.44 |
| Secondhand stores ..................... | 272 | 2,606,668 | .54 |
| Total, retail stores.................. | 14,063 | $497,852,191 | 100.00 |

## WHOLESALE BUSINESS

The bureau of the census of the United States department of commerce collected statistics in 1930 for the first time showing wholesale distribution. The data cover wholesale operations in 1929. The census for Colorado showed that there were 2,075 wholesale establishments in the state in 1929, employing 14,628 persons, exclusive of proprietors, paying $48,352,641 in expenses, including salaries and wages, and having net sales during the year amounting to $539,625,526.

In addition to wholesalers of the conventional type, the census covers wholesalers rendering limited services, such as desk jobbers and cash-and-carry wholesalers, and the whole range of organizations engaged in wholesale trade or operating on a wholesale basis, including brokers, commission merchants, chain-store warehouses, manufacturers' sales branches, selling agents, assemblers of agricultural products, etc. The statistics have been condensed into 24 groups. These groups comprise 88 major classifications and 351 minor or detailed classifications. For the purpose of conserving space, a summary for Colorado published herewith comprises all establishments engaged in the wholesale business, reduced to 24 major classifications. Persons desiring more detailed information will find it available in the complete census reports.

The wholesale trade in farm products (including only those not specified under other classifications) ranked first in 1929, with 357 establishments having net sales of $142,459,705. Livestock, other than horses and mules, accounted for $85,982,512 of the total, and grain for $50,629,104. Food products not elsewhere specified were second, with 392 establishments doing a wholesale business of $80,948,860. Under this classification fruits and vegetables accounted for $46,407,787 and meats and meat products for $20,228,265. Groceries and food specialties ranked third, with 164 wholesale establishments having net sales of $78,470,500, of which the general line of groceries accounted for $41,914,439 and food and grocery specialties for $36,556,061. Metals and minerals, except petroleum and scrap, ranked fourth, with 34 establishments having net sales of $42,091,974. Petroleum and petroleum products came fifth, with 445 establishments having net sales of $31,471,903 and machinery, equipment and supplies, exclusive of electrical, came sixth, with 149 establishments and net sales of $26,423,030. The automotive group came seventh, with 68 establishments and net sales of $25,815,127. Under this classification, automobiles and other motor vehicles accounted for $13,158,207, auto equipment for $5,691,980; parts, $1,262,949, and tires and tubes, $4,701,982.

The principal commodity sales, by kind, in the order of their rank, per cent of total sales, and volume, are as follows:

| Commodity | Per cent | Net sales |
|---|---|---|
| Livestock | 18.1 | $80,607,000 |
| Fruits and Vegetables.. | 7.6 | 33,941,000 |
| Iron and steel products | 7.4 | 32,999,000 |
| Groceries | 5.3 | 23,427,000 |
| Petroleum and petroleum products | 4.8 | 21,507,000 |
| Grain | 4.3 | 19,231,000 |
| Meats and meat products | 4.0 | 17,729,000 |
| Dairy products and eggs | 3.1 | 13,761,000 |
| Automobiles | 3.0 | 13,377,000 |
| Auto equipment | 3.0 | 13,131,000 |
| Machinery, equipment and supplies | 2.9 | 12,853,000 |
| Electrical appliances... | 2.7 | 11,927,000 |
| Coal and coke | 2.5 | 11,166,000 |
| Cigars, cigarets and tobacco | 2.2 | 9,851,000 |
| Canned goods | 1.9 | 8,466,000 |

Another table published herewith shows wholesale trade by cities in 1929.

**WHOLESALE TRADE IN COLORADO. SUMMARY BY PRINCIPAL CLASSIFICATIONS, 1929**
(Compiled from Census Reports)

| KIND OF BUSINESS | No. of Establishments | No. of Employes, (Proprietors Not Included) | Salaries and Wages | Total Expenses, Including Salaries and Wages | Stocks on Hand, End of Year, at Cost | Net Sales |
|---|---|---|---|---|---|---|
| Amusements and sporting goods_ | 33 | 421 | $ 644,563 | $ 1,318,751 | $ 552,989 | $ 5,456,250 |
| Automotive | 68 | 1,088 | 2,203,924 | 4,102,603 | 2,997,370 | 25,815,127 |
| Chemicals, drugs and allied products | 41 | 506 | 914,247 | 1,665,418 | 2,265,529 | 13,426,150 |
| Dry goods and apparel | 62 | 356 | 540,685 | 1,122,314 | 945,153 | 7,591,374 |
| Electrical | 56 | 746 | 1,217,017 | 2,461,506 | 1,862,335 | 20,964,324 |
| Farm products (not elsewhere specified) | 357 | 1,018 | 1,688,575 | 3,655,588 | 4,787,764 | 142,459,705 |
| Farm supplies (except machinery and equipment) | 18 | 256 | 253,835 | 532,444 | 391,186 | 6,386,130 |
| Food products (not elsewhere specified) | 392 | 3,090 | 3,600,870 | 6,880,403 | 3,919,657 | 80,948,860 |
| Forest products (except lumber)_ | 4 | 75 | 112,658 | 124,896 | 108,810 | 341,437 |
| Furniture and house-furnishings_ | 28 | 270 | 477,798 | 311,189 | 966,444 | 6,492,598 |
| Groceries and food specialties___ | 164 | 1,712 | 3,132,026 | 7,328,437 | 6,077,687 | 78,470,500 |
| Hardware | 20 | 306 | 526,050 | 1,207,217 | 1,560,340 | 5,286,498 |
| Iron and steel scrap and other waste metals | 22 | 99 | 95,195 | 181,600 | 160,432 | 2,282,092 |
| Jewelry and optical goods | 16 | 106 | 187,429 | 331,511 | 425,761 | 1,177,068 |
| Leather and leather goods (except gloves and shoes) | 9 | 79 | 149,293 | 290,369 | 472,973 | 1,190,699 |
| Lumber and building materials (other than metal) | 44 | 484 | 921,653 | 1,824,125 | 618,111 | 13,765,210 |
| Machinery, equipment and supplies (except electrical) | 149 | 1,229 | 2,325,750 | 4,269,398 | 3,634,023 | 26,423,030 |
| Metals and minerals (except petroleum and scrap) | 34 | 243 | 598,904 | 1,390,736 | 374,841 | 42,091,974 |
| Paper and paper products | 20 | 415 | 656,492 | 1,130,438 | 1,175,851 | 5,380,023 |
| Petroleum and petroleum products | 445 | 1,190 | 2,221,939 | 4,616,983 | 1,859,625 | 31,471,903 |
| Plumbing and heating equipment and supplies | 34 | 373 | 634,848 | 1,337,899 | 1,121,517 | 6,996,368 |
| Tobacco and tobacco products (except leaf) | 23 | 179 | 333,186 | 742,736 | 419,633 | 10,481,085 |
| All others | 36 | 387 | 510,299 | 1,026,080 | 750,566 | 4,777,171 |
| Total, state | 2,075 | 14,628 | $23,947,236 | $48,352,641 | $37,448,597 | $539,625,526 |

Note.—This table includes wholesalers only, bulk and tank stations, district and general sales offices, manufacturers' sales branches, agents and brokers, assemblers and country buyers and wholesale manufacturers, and is inclusive of 351 minor or detailed classifications which are omitted for lack of space, but which are available in detail in the census reports.

## WHOLESALE TRADE IN COLORADO, BY CITIES, 1929
(Compiled from Census Reports)

| CITY | No. of Establishments | No. of Employes (Proprietors not included) | Salaries and Wages | Total Expenses, Including Salaries and Wages | Stocks on Hand, End of Year, at Cost | Net Sales |
|---|---|---|---|---|---|---|
| Alamosa (Pop. 5,107) | 12 | 44 | $ 100,087 | $ 181,050 | $ 112,438 | $ 1,796,229 |
| Boulder (Pop. 11,223) | 12 | 38 | 58,612 | 106,252 | 109,348 | 733,152 |
| Canon City (Pop. 5,938) | 12 | 52 | 54,553 | 115,193 | 53,369 | 798,170 |
| Colorado Springs (Pop. 33,237) | 43 | 318 | 491,118 | 997,097 | 493,407 | 8,359,227 |
| Denver (Pop. 287,861) | 934 | 10,564 | 18,343,311 | 37,109,154 | 25,720,052 | 395,958,075 |
| Fort Collins (Pop. 11,489) | 12 | 63 | 101,551 | 207,146 | 252,341 | 2,901,759 |
| Grand Junction (Pop. 10,247) | 29 | 218 | 382,669 | 682,539 | 905,529 | 7,579,111 |
| Greeley (Pop. 12,203) | 23 | 186 | 203,194 | 426,926 | 276,899 | 4,911,267 |
| La Junta (Pop. 7,193) | 10 | 27 | 46,597 | 89,047 | 55,861 | 676,681 |
| Longmont (Pop. 6,029) | 16 | 28 | 57,231 | 119,365 | 129,006 | 1,045,361 |
| Loveland (Pop. 5,506) | 7 | 14 | 28,724 | 65,726 | 66,226 | 642,783 |
| Pueblo (Pop. 50,096) | 65 | 711 | 1,018,672 | 2,074,289 | 2,144,148 | 18,965,425 |
| Salida (Pop. 5,065) | 7 | 42 | 36,560 | 79,293 | 47,995 | 459,870 |
| Sterling (Pop. 7,195) | 19 | 88 | 164,023 | 286,231 | 302,782 | 4,887,011 |
| Trinidad (Pop. 11,732) | 25 | 189 | 397,706 | 788,552 | 619,178 | 12,712,997 |
| Walsenburg (Pop. 5,503) | 11 | 34 | 62,812 | 150,986 | 142,999 | 1,372,639 |

## LATITUDE AND LONGITUDE

Colorado lies between the 37th and 41st parallels north of the equator and the 102nd and 109th meridians west of Greenwich. Parallels are imaginary lines encircling the earth, each parallel being an equal distance at all points from the equator. A meridian is a great circle on the surface of the earth passing through the poles and any given place. Latitude is the distance north or south from the equator measured on the meridians. Longitude is the distance east or west of Greenwich measured on the parallels. The distance between parallels and between meridians is measured by degrees. A degree of latitude (distance between two parallels) is 68.704 miles at the equator and 69.407 at the poles. The average in Colorado is approximately 69 miles. Thus, Colorado lies from 2,553 to 2,829 miles north of the equator. A degree is equal to 60 minutes and a minute is equal to 60 seconds.

The latitude and longitude of designated points in Colorado are as follows:

| | Latitude | Longitude |
|---|---|---|
| | ° ′ ″ | ° ′ ″ |
| Denver | 39 40 36N | 104 56 56W |
| Mt. Elbert | 39 07 04N | 106 26 41W |
| Mt. Ouray | 38 25 22N | 106 13 27W |
| Pike's Peak | 38 50 26N | 105 02 37W |

°Degree.  ′Minutes.  ″Seconds.

The following table gives the distance in miles north and south of Denver, reckoned on latitude, of important cities of the world. It is based on an average of 69 miles to the degree. The distance given is not from Denver to the city named, but from an imaginary line encircling the earth at Denver's latitude to the city due north or south of that line:

— Miles —

| City | South of Denver | North of Denver |
|---|---|---|
| Algiers, Algeria | 131 | ... |
| Archangel, Russia | ... | 1,716 |
| Berkeley, California | 55 | ... |
| Berlin, Germany | ... | 885 |
| Bismarck, North Dakota | ... | 493 |
| Bogota, Columbia | 2,351 | ... |
| Boston, Massachusetts | ... | 185 |
| Calcutta, India | 1,112 | ... |
| Carson City, Nevada | 36 | ... |
| Chicago, Illinois | ... | 150 |
| Cincinnati, Ohio | 37 | ... |
| Colon, Panama | 2,022 | ... |
| Constantinople, Turkey | ... | 92 |
| Dry Tortugas, Florida | 968 | ... |
| Dublin, Ireland | ... | 946 |
| Fairbanks, Alaska | ... | 1,736 |
| Gibraltar | 177 | ... |
| Hongkong, China | 1,126 | ... |
| Honolulu, H. I. | 1,199 | ... |
| Indianapolis, Indiana | ... | 7 |
| Leningrad, Russia | ... | 1,398 |
| London, England | ... | 814 |
| Los Angeles, Calif. | 343 | ... |
| Manila, P. I. | 1,663 | ... |
| Melbourne, Victoria | 5,346 | ... |
| Montreal, Canada | ... | 403 |
| Moscow, Russia | ... | 1,110 |
| Nashville, Tennessee | 174 | ... |
| New Orleans, Louisiana | 603 | ... |
| New York, New York | ... | 78 |
| Omaha, Nebraska | ... | 109 |
| Paris, France | ... | 632 |
| Portland, Maine | ... | 275 |
| Portland, Oregon | ... | 404 |
| Rio de Janeiro, Brazil | 4,455 | ... |
| Rome, Italy | ... | 153 |
| St. Louis, Missouri | 71 | ... |
| San Francisco, Calif. | 100 | ... |
| Sidney, N. S. W. | 5,024 | ... |
| Washington, D. C. | 52 | ... |

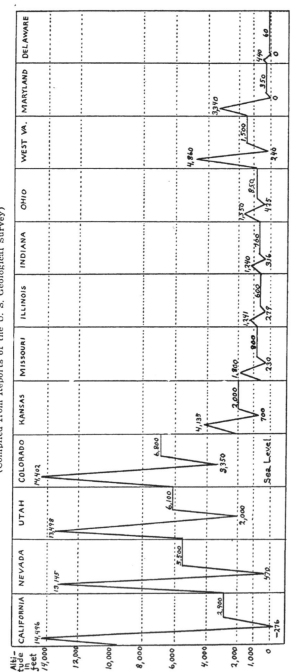

**HIGHEST AND LOWEST POINTS AND APPROXIMATE MEAN ALTITUDE OF STATES THROUGH WHICH PASSES THE THIRTY-NINTH PARALLEL**

(Compiled from Reports of the U. S. Geological Survey)

## TOTAL OF 1932 CROP PRODUCTION LOANS MADE IN COLORADO FROM UNITED STATES GOVERNMENT FUNDS

| County | No. of Loans | Approved Amount of Loans |
|---|---|---|
| Adams | 170 | $ 37,857.00 |
| Alamosa | 108 | 28,205.97 |
| Arapahoe | 82 | 12,513.00 |
| Archuleta | 24 | 1,378.90 |
| Baca | 120 | 21,031.00 |
| Bent | 58 | 9,869.00 |
| Boulder | 6 | 821.00 |
| Chaffee | 15 | 2,226.00 |
| Cheyenne | 115 | 21,200.00 |
| Clear Creek | ... | ........ |
| Conejos | 355 | 71,367.11 |
| Costilla | 174 | 20,953.76 |
| Crowley | 98 | 22,710.00 |
| Custer | 72 | 9,012.00 |
| Delta | 98 | 14,455.83 |
| Denver | 2 | 470.00 |
| Dolores | 54 | 6,183.30 |
| Douglas | 14 | 2,551.00 |
| Eagle | 21 | 2,863.30 |
| Elbert | 100 | 14,661.00 |
| El Paso | 126 | 18,656.00 |
| Fremont | 9 | 1,046.00 |
| Garfield | 44 | 7,028.00 |
| Gilpin | 1 | 150.00 |
| Grand | 4 | 556.00 |
| Gunnison | 5 | 938.50 |
| Hinsdale | ... | |
| Huerfano | 43 | 5,443.00 |
| Jackson | 1 | 208.50 |
| Jefferson | 32 | 6,304.00 |
| Kiowa | 137 | 25,872.00 |
| Kit Carson | 215 | 36,849.00 |
| Lake | ... | ........ |
| La Plata | 108 | 11,762.64 |
| Larimer | 38 | 8,590.00 |
| Las Animas | 81 | 14,421.00 |
| Lincoln | 242 | 42,560.00 |
| Logan | 179 | 31,157.00 |
| Mesa | 170 | 19,700.80 |
| Mineral | ... | ........ |
| Moffat | 47 | 4,498.85 |
| Montezuma | 173 | 22,146.35 |
| Montrose | 66 | 11,693.69 |
| Morgan | 128 | 25,475.00 |
| Otero | 34 | 6,557.00 |
| Ouray | 7 | 1,614.50 |
| Park | 3 | 250.00 |
| Phillips | 138 | 32,460.00 |
| Pitkin | 3 | 222.00 |
| Prowers | 173 | 30,917.00 |
| Pueblo | 164 | 36,438.00 |
| Rio Blanco | 21 | 2,431.00 |
| Rio Grande | 170 | 48,364.18 |
| Routt | 72 | 9,508.55 |
| Saguache | 111 | 28,371.50 |
| San Juan | ... | ........ |
| San Miguel | 18 | 2,583.50 |
| Sedgwick | 212 | 51,866.00 |
| Summit | ... | ........ |
| Teller | 11 | 1,230.00 |
| Washington | 179 | 34,072.00 |
| Weld | 341 | 72,389.00 |
| Yuma | 219 | 41,582.00 |
| Total | 5,411 | $996,241.73 |

## RADIO DEVELOPMENT

Colorado had 12 radio broadcasting stations operating on May 1, 1932, under licenses issued by the federal radio commission, a decrease of one compared with the number on March 1, 1931, station KFUP, operated at the Fitzsimons hospital near Denver, having been transferred to the United States army intercommunication system. A table giving a list of these stations, their locations, call signals, owners, power and frequency and time is published herewith.

In addition to the broadcasting stations there were in the state on May 1, 1932, 237 amateur stations operated under permits and nine radio stations other than broadcast and amateur. The latter includes an experimental broadcast station operated by the National Broadcasting company in connection with plans to construct a 5u,000-watt transmitter station for which a permit has been granted; two aeronautical stations; two stations operated in connection with the Denver municipal water supply system for emergency purposes; a municipal police system in Denver, through which communication with cruising police automobiles is maintained; one United States army intercommunications station; a station operated at the state school of mines in connection with geophysical work; and one United States department of commerce airways station. A list of these stations, call signals, power, frequency and service is given in a separate table.

Preliminary figures of the bureau of the census shows that there were 69 radio and electrical retail shops doing business in the state in 1929, with net sales of $967,903, and 47 radio and musical instruments retail establishments, which had net sales of $3,109,264 in 1929, a total of $4,077,167. These retail distribution figures do not include department stores and other establishments which handled radios and equipment as a part of numerous lines.

Wholesale distribution figures of the bureau of the census give 12 wholesale radio and radio equipment establishments in the state in 1929, these establishments having net sales in that year of $4,138,213. These establishments had 137 employes, exclusive of proprietors, and salaries and wages paid amounted to $268,467. Total expenses, including salaries and wages, were $640,011. Stocks on hand at the end of 1929, at cost, amounted to $428,761.

There were 267,324 families in Colorado in 1930 as reported by the census. Preliminary figures on the number of families having radio sets in that year showed a total of 101,376, or 37.8 per cent. These figures, which are subject to revision, on the basis of estimates of the number of listeners, indicate a possible state audience for a broadcasting program of 495,366 persons if all radios were tuned in at the same time and all members of the family were listening. The distribution of radio sets varies considerably in different areas of the state and follows no set rule. Jefferson county ranked first with 54.1 per cent of all families having radios, while Jackson county, which is remote from the larger cities, ranked second with 52.2 per cent. One out of every two families in Denver, or 50.7 per cent of the total, reported sets in 1930. Conejos county was the lowest in the state, with only 4.5 per cent.

The following table, which is taken from the United States census report for 1930, being preliminary figures and subject to change, gives the number of families by counties having radio sets, and the per cent of the total number of families in the county:

|  | Families Having Radio Sets | Per Cent of County Total |
|---|---|---|
| Adams | 1,936 | 41.7 |
| Alamosa | 472 | 22.4 |
| Arapahoe | 2,915 | 48.3 |
| Archuleta | 91 | 11.7 |
| Baca | 495 | 20.1 |
| Bent | 533 | 25.7 |
| Boulder | 3,827 | 42.4 |
| Chaffee | 616 | 29.9 |
| Cheyenne | 278 | 29.9 |
| Clear Creek | 307 | 41.0 |
| Conejos | 288 | 14.0 |
| Costilla | 57 | 4.5 |
| Crowley | 377 | 26.3 |
| Custer | 181 | 29.0 |
| Delta | 820 | 22.7 |
| Denver | 40,526 | 50.7 |
| Dolores | 50 | 12.8 |
| Douglas | 443 | 45.8 |
| Eagle | 306 | 29.8 |
| Elbert | 636 | 37.9 |
| El Paso | 5,934 | 41.8 |
| Fremont | 1,431 | 30.0 |
| Garfield | 752 | 28.7 |
| Gilpin | 128 | 30.7 |
| Grand | 211 | 33.8 |
| Gunnison | 352 | 23.1 |
| Hinsdale | 48 | 31.8 |
| Huerfano | 663 | 16.7 |
| Jackson | 206 | 52.2 |
| Jefferson | 3,163 | 54.1 |
| Kiowa | 234 | 24.7 |
| Kit Carson | 788 | 34.2 |
| Lake | 336 | 23.8 |
| La Plata | 647 | 19.9 |
| Larimer | 3,473 | 40.2 |
| Las Animas | 1,585 | 18.5 |
| Lincoln | 778 | 39.6 |
| Logan | 1,525 | 33.8 |
| Mesa | 1,822 | 27.5 |
| Mineral | 61 | 28.0 |
| Moffat | 361 | 25.8 |
| Montezuma | 297 | 15.6 |
| Montrose | 612 | 21.5 |
| Morgan | 1,435 | 33.6 |
| Otero | 1,661 | 27.5 |
| Ouray | 126 | 22.0 |
| Park | 245 | 38.5 |
| Phillips | 691 | 47.5 |
| Pitkin | 164 | 30.3 |
| Prowers | 910 | 25.8 |
| Pueblo | 4,885 | 30.4 |
| Rio Blanco | 185 | 23.9 |

|  | Families Having Radio Sets | Per Cent of County Total |
|---|---|---|
| Rio Grande | 638 | 26.7 |
| Routt | 809 | 31.9 |
| Saguache | 394 | 25.5 |
| San Juan | 122 | 27.2 |
| San Miguel | 111 | 17.8 |
| Sedgwick | 477 | 36.5 |
| Summit | 122 | 36.9 |
| Teller | 370 | 27.1 |
| Washington | 801 | 35.1 |
| Weld | 5,586 | 36.0 |
| Yuma | 1,083 | 32.3 |
| Total, state | 101,376 | 37.8 |

The following table shows the number of families in cities of 10,000 or more population having radio sets in 1930 and the per cent of the total. The figures are preliminary and subject to correction.

| Cities | Families Having Radio Sets | Per Cent of Total |
|---|---|---|
| Boulder | 1,589 | 46.2 |
| Colorado Springs | 4,257 | 42.4 |
| Denver | 40,526 | 50.7 |
| Fort Collins | 1,426 | 45.0 |
| Grand Junction | 903 | 30.5 |
| Greeley | 1,595 | 46.3 |
| Pueblo | 3,975 | 32.2 |
| Trinidad | 906 | 29.3 |

Colorado has the distinction of being the first state west of the Mississippi river and one of the first in the country in which were established stations conducting daily broadcasts on regular schedules as broadcasting is now known. The Westinghouse Electric & Manufacturing company's station KDKA, in Pittsburgh, is generally credited with being the first station in the country to begin the commercial transmission of programs. This service, under a broadcasting license issued by the department of commerce, was inaugurated on November 2, 1920, and consisted of the announcement of election returns and the election of President Harding. Prior to this date, however, in 1919, Dr. W. D. Reynolds, who then resided in Colorado Springs, was operating under a special amateur's license, No. 9 ZAF, this being the only license of the kind granted to Colorado parties at the time. In 1920 Dr. Reynolds moved to Denver and began broadcasting market reports, daily weather reports, etc., and each Sunday broadcasted sermons by a Denver pastor. The first commercial license issued to KLZ, as the station has since been known, was dated March 10, 1922.

The first law, covering in a general way the regulation of wave lengths used and interference produced by the radio stations, was enacted by congress in 1912 and empowered the secretary of commérce to issue licenses. This act failed to solve the problems arising and congress enacted what is known as the "Radio Act of 1927," which called for the establishment of the federal radio commission. The commission was given broad powers over all classes of radio transmission and was authorized to specify the frequency, power, location and other conditions of the operations of stations. The act was amended in 1928, authorizing the commission to apportion broadcasting assignments equally to the five zones into which the country was divided in proportion to population. The commission put into effect on November 11, 1928, a reallocation of broadcasting stations of the country. Colorado is in the fifth of the five zones, the other states included in the zone being Montana, Wyoming, New Mexico, Idaho, Utah, Arizona, Nevada, Washington, Oregon and California.

### LICENSED BROADCASTING STATIONS IN COLORADO MAY 1, 1932

| Location | Call Signal | Owner | Power (Watts) | Frequency in Kilocycles | Time |
|---|---|---|---|---|---|
| Colorado Springs | KVOR | Reynolds Radio Co. | 1,000 | 1,270 | Unlimited |
| Denver (Edgewater)* | KFEL | Eugene P. O'Fallon, Inc. | 500 | 920 | Shares with KFXF |
| Denver | KFXF | Colorado Radio Corp. | 500 | 920 | Shares with KFEL |
| Denver | KLZ | Reynolds Radio Co. | 1,000 | 560 | Unlimited |
| Denver | KOA | National Broadcasting Co. | †12,500 | 830 | Unlimited |
| Denver (Westminster)* | KPOF | Pillar of Fire, Inc. | 500 | 880 | Shares with KFKA |
| Fort Morgan | KGEW | City of Fort Morgan | 100 | 1,200 | Shares with KGEK |
| Grand Junction | KFXJ | Western Slope Broadcasting Co. | 100 | 1,310 | Half time |
| Greeley | KFKA | Midwestern Radio Corp. | ‡1,000 | 880 | Shares with KPOF |
| Pueblo | KGHF | Curtis P. Ritchie, et al. | §500 | 1,320 | Unlimited |
| Trinidad | KGIW | Leonard E. Wilson | 100 | 1,420 | Unlimited |
| Yuma | KGEK | Beeler Electrical Equipment Co. | 100 | 1,200 | Shares with KGEW |

*Transmitter location.
†Permit granted to construct a 50,000-watt station.
‡1,000 for day, 500 for night.
§500 for day, 250 for night.
Note.—Applications pending for 100-watt stations at Alamosa (Antonito) and Lamar.

### RADIO STATIONS IN COLORADO OTHER THAN BROADCAST OR AMATEUR MAY 1, 1932

| Location | Call Signal | Power (Watts) | Frequency in Kilocycles | Service |
|---|---|---|---|---|
| Denver | W9XA | 12,500 | 830 | Experimental broadcast |
| Denver | KGSP | 150 | 278; 2,720; 3,072.5; 5,692.5; 6,530; 8,015 | Aeronautical |
| Denver | KGPX | 150 | 2,442 | Police |
| Denver | KICX | 50 | 3,190 | Water emergency |
| Eleven Mile Canon | KICL | 50 | 3,190 | Water emergency |
| Fitzsimons Hospital | WTS | 250 | 4,090; 8,180 | U. S. Army |
| Golden | W9XE | 5 | 1,604; 2,398 | Geophysical portable (School of Mines) |
| Pueblo | KGSR | 150 | 278; 2,720; 3,072.5; 5,692.5; 6,530; 8,015 | Aeronautical |
| Pueblo | KCAR | 2,000 | 302; 3,410; 5,955 | U. S. Dept. of Commerce, Airways |

## AIRPORTS, AIRCRAFT, PILOTS AND ROUTES

There were 38 airports and landing fields in Colorado on January 1, 1932, as reported by the aeronautics branch of the United States department of commerce. This is an increase of 11 as compared with April 1, 1930. These include 17 municipal airports, eight commercial fields, five department of commerce intermediate landing fields, seven auxiliary fields which are not used regularly for aircraft operations, and one army field. The location and classification of the fields as of September 1, 1931, is as follows:

Akron, American Legion airport, auxiliary.
Alamosa, municipal.
Buena Vista, municipal.
*Castle Rock, intermediate.
Center, Center Legion airport, municipal.
Cheyenne Wells, Cheyenne Wells landing field, auxiliary.
Colorado Springs, Alexander airport, commercial.
†Colorado Springs, Colorado Springs airport, municipal.
Craig, Craig airport, municipal.
Delta, Delta airport, municipal.
Denver, Curtiss field, commercial.
†Denver, Denver airport, municipal. (Rating A1A.)
†Denver, Lowry field, National Guard, army.
Dolores, Dolores field, auxiliary.
*Dover, intermediate.
Durango, Durango airport, municipal.
Florence, Florence Flying field, commercial.
Fort Collins, Fort Collins airport, municipal.
*Fort Lupton, intermediate.
Grand Junction, Grand Junction airport, municipal.
†Greeley, Greeley airport, municipal.
Gunnison, Meeker ranch field, auxiliary.
Holly, Holly airport, municipal.
Holyoke, Holyoke airport, municipal.
La Junta, American Legion airport, auxiliary.
Las Animas, Las Animas airport, municipal.
Longmont, Blackwell airport, auxiliary.
Monte Vista, Monte Vista airport, municipal.
Montrose, Montrose airport, municipal.
*Monument, intermediate.
Otis, Otis airport, municipal.
†Pueblo, Pueblo airport, municipal.
Saguache, auxiliary.
Salida, American Legion airport, commercial.
Sterling, municipal.
Trinidad, Holloway field.
*Wigwam, intermediate.

---

*Department of commerce intermediate landing field, marked and lighted by the department.
†Airports equipped with partial or complete lighting equipment.

A survey made in 1930 by the aeronautics branch of the department of commerce covered 20 airports, of which 15 were municipal and five were commercial and private airports. As the purpose was to determine the status of airports available to civil aeronautics for regular flying operations, military and miscellaneous government airports and auxiliary and intermediate landing fields were not included. This survey showed that the average investment per airport for municipal airports was $35,000, or a total of $525,000, and the average for commercial and private airports was $53,400, or a total of $367,000, a grand total of $892,000 for both municipal and commercial and private.

The status of aircraft, gliders, pilots, glider pilots and mechanics, as of dates given, as reported by the air commerce bulletin, is as follows:

| | Jan. 1, 1932 | Mar. 30, 1931 | 1930 |
|---|---|---|---|
| Aircraft: | | | |
| Licensed | 44 | 50 | 52 |
| Unlicensed | 43 | 24 | 39 |
| Total | 87 | 74 | 91 |
| Gliders | 94 | 97 | .. |
| Pilots: | | | |
| Transport | 62 | 56 | 52 |
| Limited commercial | 18 | 32 | 12 |
| Private | 63 | 59 | 47 |
| Total | 143 | 147 | 111 |
| Mechanics | 80 | 76 | 72 |

The Denver municipal airport is one of four in the United States which has received a high rating of A-1-A by the department of commerce, being the second so designated. The other three are the Rickenbacker airport at Sioux City, Iowa, and the municipal airports at Pontiac, Michigan, and Brownsville, Texas.

United States air transport routes in Colorado include the following:

**Pueblo to Cheyenne, Wyoming,** inaugurated May 31, 1926, carries mail, passengers and express. It operates a daily service over a 200-airway-miles route with a daily plane-miles schedule of 400.

**Kansas City to Denver,** inaugurated July 29, 1929, carries passengers and mail. It operates on a daily schedule over a 577-airway-miles route and has a daily plane-mile schedule of 1,154.

**Denver to Cheyenne,** inaugurated August 1, 1931, carries mail, passengers and express. It operates on a daily schedule over a 96-airway-miles route and has a daily plane-mile schedule of 192.

**Albuquerque to Pueblo,** inaugurated

August 1, 1931, carries mail, passengers and express. It operates on a daily schedule over a 248-airway-miles route and has a daily plane-mile schedule of 496.

**Amarillo to Pueblo,** inaugurated August 1, 1931, carries mail, passengers and express. It operates on a daily schedule over a 261-airway-miles route

and has a daily plane-mile schedule of 522.

**Denver to Billings,** inaugurated April 16, 1931, carries passengers. It operates on a daily schedule over a 476-airway-miles route and has a daily plane-mile schedule of 952.

All the routes named make connections at terminals with other routes.

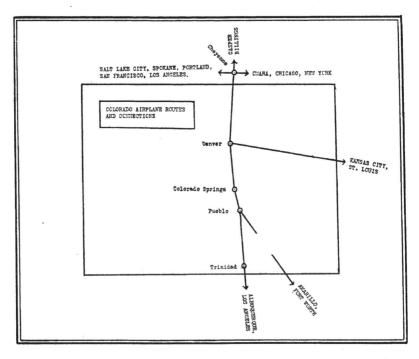

## INDUSTRIAL ACCIDENTS IN COLORADO

Colorado has efficient industrial laws providing for the payment of compensation to workmen for disability due to accidents or to dependents in the event of death. The law is administered by the state industrial commission, to which reports of accidents in all industrial lines except farm and ranch labor, domestic service and railway employment are made. The amount of compensation is fixed by law, but the commission conducts hearings and decides controversies arising out of the liability of the employer and the application of the compensation.

The members of the industrial commission, three in number, are appointed by the governor for terms of

six years, one appointment expiring every two years. The appointments must be confirmed by the senate. One member represents the employers, another the employes and the third the public. The plan is considered to have been effective in forestalling labor troubles in many instances, although the power of the commission to prevent strikes is limited.

The commission began to function on August 1, 1915, and from that date to November 30, 1931, a total of 276,-892 accidents was reported, of which the largest number, 25,846, was reported in 1929, and the smallest, 11,358, was reported in 1919. Arising out of these accidents there were 73,203 claims, or 26.4 per cent, filed between August 15, 1915, and November 30, 1931. Of claims filed up to the end of 1930 66,484 of the injured were males and 2,217 were females. Fatal claims (deaths) aggregated 2,662. Of these 991, or 37.2 per cent, were in the coal industries; 496, or 18.6 per cent, in the metal industries; and 1,175, or 44.1 per cent, in miscellaneous industries. Of the 66,039 non-fatal claims filed, 14,665, or 22.2 per cent, were from accidents in the coal industry; 7,878, or 11.9 per cent, in the metal industries; and 43,396, or 65.9 per cent, were in miscellaneous industries. The average weekly wage for the entire period was $24.14. This average is obtained under the law by taking the amount of the compensation received by the claimant in the year preceding the accident and dividing it by 52 weeks. The average weekly rate of compensation for the entire period was $9.94.

An accompanying table shows the number of accidents, number of claims, average weekly wage and average weekly compensation by years.

Employers of labor are required under the law to carry insurance for the protection of employes coming under the compensation act. The state has its own compensation insurance fund for the protection of its employes and those of counties and school districts. Other employers may come under this fund, provide their own insurance, or take out insurance with private agencies. In 1915 to 1931, inclusive, premiums paid by the employers to the various agencies aggregated $27,730,077, and losses paid aggregated $13,376,266. An accompanying table shows premium income and losses paid in Colorado by years.

### WORKMEN'S COMPENSATION INSURANCE PREMIUMS AND LOSSES
(Reports of Industrial Commission)

| Year | Stock Companies | Mutual Companies | State Fund | Yearly Totals |
|---|---|---|---|---|
| **Net Premium Income:** | | | | |
| *1915 | $ 32,602.56 | $ 163,526.58 | $ 46,710.00 | $ 242,839.14 |
| 1916 | 475,402.36 | 254,351.63 | 134,371.41 | 864,125.40 |
| 1917 | 664,049.89 | 303,466.36 | 192,323.45 | 1,159,844.70 |
| 1918 | 854,239.28 | 382,528.75 | 370,593.75 | 1,607,361.78 |
| 1919 | 818,782.86 | 313,432.55 | 267,612.12 | 1,399,827.53 |
| 1920 | 906,639.75 | 502,262.10 | 460,116.11 | 1,869,017.96 |
| 1921 | 931,622.93 | 416,087.25 | 364,009.52 | 1,711,719.70 |
| 1922 | 590,611.51 | 330,407.73 | 339,537.41 | 1,260,556.65 |
| 1923 | 665,509.93 | 402,663.69 | 404,562.16 | 1,472,735.78 |
| 1924 | 806,751.61 | 398,077.73 | 412,733.56 | 1,617,562.90 |
| 1925 | 1,033,794.56 | 351,428.79 | 554,868.86 | 1,940,092.21 |
| 1926 | 1,031,537.78 | 348,613.55 | 605,630.54 | 1,985,781.87 |
| 1927 | 1,001,375.17 | 357,852.64 | 880,400.39 | 2,239,628.20 |
| 1928 | 965,159.08 | 420,823.09 | 676,327.54 | 2,062,309.71 |
| 1929 | 1,092,230.06 | 434,515.26 | 720,568.78 | 2,247,314.10 |
| 1930 | 1,050,513.00 | 373,002.00 | 747,652.00 | 2,171,167.00 |
| 1931 | 877,422.00 | 302,816.00 | 697,955.00 | 1,878,193.00 |
| Total | $13,798,244.33 | $6,055,855.70 | $7,875,977.60 | $27,730,077.63 |
| **Net Losses Paid:** | | | | |
| *1915 | $ 1,738.02 | $ 2,637.46 | $ 2,563.65 | $ 6,939.13 |
| 1916 | 128,719.80 | 23,188.98 | 28,535.76 | 180,444.54 |
| 1917 | 191,556.57 | 58,546.16 | 42,497.24 | 292,599.97 |
| 1918 | 243,915.88 | 74,008.02 | 51,391.68 | 369,315.58 |
| 1919 | 294,156.65 | 98,135.51 | 86,546.79 | 478,838.95 |
| 1920 | 356,059.22 | 111,893.71 | 128,333.71 | 596,286.64 |
| 1921 | 389,800.87 | 130,440.08 | 168,340.20 | 688,581.15 |
| 1922 | 385,124.75 | 141,611.72 | 178,710.00 | 705,446.47 |
| 1923 | 499,806.15 | 134,095.21 | 201,169.98 | 835,071.34 |
| 1924 | 528,407.02 | 134,713.11 | 246,969.03 | 910,089.16 |
| 1925 | 567,364.78 | 139,083.34 | 279,972.80 | 986,420.92 |
| 1926 | 596,449.24 | 139,019.76 | 310,296.34 | 1,045,765.34 |
| 1927 | 596,618.80 | 149,883.31 | 372,349.08 | 1,118,851.19 |
| 1928 | 610,412.52 | 156,431.50 | 413,826.79 | 1,180,670.81 |
| 1929 | 618,767.28 | 180,333.88 | 484,386.67 | 1,282,487.83 |
| 1930 | 646,477.00 | 183,490.00 | 510,018.00 | 1,339,985.00 |
| 1931 | 620,509.00 | 187,744.00 | 549,219.00 | 1,357,472.00 |
| Total | $7,275,883.55 | $2,045,255.75 | $4,055,126.72 | $13,375,266.02 |

*August 1, 1915, to December 31, 1915.

## ACCIDENTS AND CLAIMS, WORKMEN'S COMPENSATION

|  | 1931 | 1930 | 1929 | 1928 | 1927 | 1926 | 1925 | 1924 |
|---|---|---|---|---|---|---|---|---|
| Number of accidents------------ | 21,132 | 22,973 | 25,846 | 19,773 | 19,571 | 19,797 | 18,143 | 17,513 |
| Number of all claims----------- | 4,502 | 5,150 | 5,467 | 5,312 | 5,751 | 5,584 | 5,807 | 5,660 |
| Death claims---------------- | 108 | 151 | 177 | 147 | 180 | 155 | 152 | 140 |
| Non-fatal ----------------- | 4,394 | 4,999 | 5,290 | 5,165 | 5,571 | 5,429 | 5,655 | 5,520 |
| Average weekly wage---------- | $24.66 | $26.10 | $25.12 | $24.93 | $25.49 | $23.63 | $25.02 | $25.32 |
| Average weekly compensation--- | $11.00 | $11.56 | $11.08 | $10.79 | $10.77 | $10.63 | $10.74 | $10.83 |

## MUSEUMS AND ZOOLOGICAL EXHIBITS

Colorado has a number of museums housing works of art, relics of ancient races, historical documents, specimens of prehistoric beasts and reptiles and present fauna and flora. The exhibits in some of these museums are among the finest in the country and afford excellent opportunities for study by scientists, archaeologists, geologists and ethnologists, as well as being of interest to the general public. The collections are being continually augmented by specimens gathered by expeditions sent out not only to explore ruins in Colorado and other states but to gather specimens in foreign countries.

One of the largest museums in the state is the Colorado Museum of Natural History, owned by the city of Denver and located in one of its parks.

The buildings were constructed at a cost of $270,917, part of which was provided by the municipality and part by private donations. The cost of exhibits, cases, library and furniture was $471,533, but this figure by no means represents the value of the exhibits, many of which are rare and which would be difficult, if not impossible, to replace. The nucleus for the museum was a collection of Colorado mammals and birds made by Edwin Carter, who came to the state in 1870 for his health and lived at Breckenridge. Contracts for part of the building were made on November 8, 1901. The east extension was completed in June, 1903, the main building was finished in July, 1908, and the south, or James wing, was completed in 1929.

There were 218,910 visitors to the museum in 1931, 222,525 in 1930, 199,-255 in 1929 and 246,698 in 1928. The record from 1912 to 1931, inclusive, shows an admission of 3,967,388 during that period.

The state museum is located just south of the capitol in Denver and is housed in a building constructed by the state of Colorado at a cost of $500,000. It is conducted by the State Historical and Natural History society and comprises two departments, the department of history and the department of archaeology and ethnology. The museum contains many relics of early life in Colorado, specimens from the ruins of cliffdwellers and other ancient races that once inhabited this territory, and many valuable documents and records of great historical value. Membership in the society is confined to citizens of Colorado. Additions to its ethnological exhibits are made at frequent intervals by expeditions sent out to explore ruins of the earlier inhabitants. Further information concerning this exploration work is given elsewhere in this volume under the heading, "Archaeological."

The Denver Art museum is located in the new Denver municipal building and, as its name indicates, is devoted to the furthering of the arts. It is supported in part by the city and in part by private subscriptions through its membership. It has on exhibition the largest and most valuable art collection in the state and is open to the public. Chappell house, which sends out travelling exhibits and supplements the work of the museum, is conducted as a part of the organization. The last named maintains an excellent exhibit of Indian art.

The Cody Memorial Museum is located on Lookout mountain near Golden, in Denver's mountain park system, and contains relics of Col. W. F. ("Buffalo Bill") Cody, a noted scout, whose grave adjoins the site of the museum.

The Mesa Verde Park museum is located in the Mesa Verde national park, in Montezuma county, in the southwestern part of the state, and houses relics of the cliffdwellers, being entirely an archaeological collection gathered in the ruins in the park. It is owned by the government and conducted by the park officials. This collection was made possible by the contributions of friends of the park. The museum now contains the largest and most comprehensive exhibit of the archaeology of the park that is available for public inspection anywhere. A noteworthy addition to the museum was made in 1930. Through the co-operation of Charles L. Bernheimer, of New York City, Dr. Clark Wissler, of the American museum of natural history, and Earl H. Morris, of the Carnegie institute of Washington, the American museum of natural history made a permanent loan of the basket maker material collected during the field season of 1929 in southeastern Utah by the seventh Bernheimer expedition.

The Canon City museum, located in Canon City, is owned by the city and contains natural history exhibits.

There are also museums connected with the State Teachers college at Greeley, the University of Colorado at Boulder, Colorado college at Colorado Springs, and the State Agricultural college at Fort Collins. The University of Colorado museum has a very large collection of prehistoric pottery, etc., from southwestern United States; about 300,000 fossils representing all geological periods from Cambrian to Pleistocene; more than 300,000 mollusks, of thousands of species; 3,200 birds and mammals; thousands of fishes, reptiles, amphibians, starfishes, sea-urchins, sponges, brachiopods, insects, etc., a mineral collection, and an extensive herbarium.

The city and county of Denver owns and maintains in its City park the largest and most important zoo in the state, or in the Rocky Mountain region. It was established in 1896 when a cub bear named "Billy Bryan" was presented to the mayor. A den was built for the bear in the park and from this beginning there grew a zoological garden which at the end of 1930 contained 1,285 specimens of animals and birds. These included 40 species of mammals, one of reptiles and 148 of birds.

## MOTION PICTURE THEATERS

There were 298 motion picture theaters in Colorado on January 1, 1931, of which 138 were wired for sound, according to the Film Daily Year Book. These theaters, which include all types, are located in 214 cities and towns and their seating capacity is 119,213, exclusive of a few small theaters in the little towns. Denver leads the list, with 44 theaters with a seating capacity of 39,994; Colorado Springs is second, with 10 theaters with a seating capacity of 6,329; and Pueblo is third, with eight theaters with a seating capacity of 5,787. Seven of the Denver theaters are silent houses (not wired for sound). Colorado Springs has two silent houses and Pueblo has none. Five theaters in Denver have an aggregate seating capacity of 10,895, an average of 2,447 per theater.

Denver is a distributing center for motion picture films and equipment over a large territory and 15 branches of national distributors and independent exchanges are located in the city. There is only one establishment engaged commercially in producing films in the state.

## PREDATORY ANIMAL AND RODENT CONTROL

For the protection of crops, livestock and game the bureau of biological survey of the United States department of agriculture co-operates with the state board of stock inspection commissioners in predatory animal control, and with the state board of agriculture through the agricultural extension service in rodent control. Livestock associations, counties, individuals, and the forest service also co-operate in these control activities.

During the fiscal year 1931 co-operative predatory animal control accounted for 3,113 coyotes, 162 bobcats, seven lynx, six mountain lions and 48 stock-killing bears.

In co-operative rodent control campaigns a total of 220,073 pounds of poisoned bait has been distributed. The poisoned baits were used in treating 609,000 acres for the control of prairie dogs, and 125,446 acres for the control of ground squirrels. More than 3,200 pounds of poisoned bait was placed for the control of rats, pocket gophers and jackrabbits.

## COLORADO'S TOTAL WEALTH

The bureau of the census of the department of commerce undertakes at certain periods to estimate the wealth of the nation and of the states. The term "wealth" used in making these estimates applies to tangible property, regardless of whether it is in the physical possession or control of its owner. A farm, for instance, and not the mortgage upon it; a railroad, and not the bonds issued against it, or a factory and its equipment, not the capital stock outstanding, constitute wealth. Mortgages, bonds, stocks, notes and money merely are the evi-· dences of ownership. Wheat, for example, may represent a part of the wealth of a Colorado farm, although the owner of the farm may reside in another state. It is possible for one to have wealth and own no property. A burglar, having stolen goods in his possession, may be in possession of wealth, but from a legal standpoint he has no property. The difficulties of wealth measurement are recognized by the census bureau in preparing its estimates.

The last estimate of the nation's total wealth made by the census bureau was for the year 1922. The next estimate will be made for 1932. The estimated value of all property in Colorado in 1922, as reported by the bureau of the census, was $3,229,412,-000. This estimate was distributed as follows:

| | |
|---|---|
| Realty .................. | $1,758,446,000 |
| Livestock ............... | 100,664,000 |
| Manufacturers' machinery, tools and implements.... | 86,808,000 |
| Railroads and equipment... | 364,963,000 |
| Motor Vehicles............ | 59,893,000 |
| Farm implements and machinery ................. | 35,059,000 |
| Street railways, water works, etc............... | 143,485,000 |
| Agricultural products...... | 51,829,000 |
| Manufactured products.... | 125,060,000 |
| Imported merchandise..... | 6,207,000 |
| Mining products.......... | 11,885,000 |
| Clothing, jewelry, furniture, etc............... | 485,113,000 |
| Total ................. | $3,229,412,000 |

The above item of $1,758,446,000 value for realty in 1922 includes $1,388,819,000 for taxed property and $369,628,000 for property exempt from taxation. Taxable and non-taxable property are discussed elsewhere in this volume under that title. The figures on taxed property used therein are based on the valuation established for taxation purposes and are not comparable with estimates of total wealth, since the latter are on tangible property adjusted to actual value.

The National Industrial Conference Board, Inc., which is affiliated with numerous industrial organizations and which co-operates with the bureau of the census, compiles estimates of total wealth for years in which no census is taken. The total wealth of Colorado, by years, as estimated by these agencies, is as follows:

| | |
|---|---|
| 1890 (Census)............. | $1,145,712,000 |
| 1900 (Census)............. | 938,171,000 |
| 1904 (Census)............. | 1,207,542,000 |
| 1912 (Census)............. | 2,315,310,000 |
| 1920 (N. I. C. ) | 5,182,000,000 |
| 1921 (N. I. C. B.)......... | 3,269,000,000 |
| 1922 (Census)............. | 3,229,412,000 |
| 1925 (N. I. C. B.).......... | 3,521,000,000 |
| 1926 (N. I. C. B.)....·..... | 3,478,000,000 |
| 1927 (N. I. C. B ) | 3,405,000,000 |
| 1928 (N. I. C. B.).......... | 3,505,000,000 |
| 1929 (N. I. C. B.).......... | 3,516,000,000 |
| 1930 (N. I. C. B.).......... | 3,286,000,000 |

The per capita wealth of Colorado, for the years named, is estimated as follows:

| | |
|---|---|
| 1890 (Census) .................. | $2,780 |
| 1900 (Census) .................. | 1,738 |
| 1904 (Census) .................. | 2,046 |
| 1912 (Census) .................. | 2,702 |
| 1922 (Census) .................. | 3,285 |
| 1928 (N. I. C. B.) ............... | 3,216 |
| 1929 (N. I. C. B.) ............... | 3,418 |
| 1930 (N. I. C. B.) ............... | 3,165 |

Colorado ranked 29th among the states of the Union in 1922, according to the census bureau's figures, and the state had a fraction more than one per cent of the country's total wealth.

A table is published herewith showing the estimated value of all property in Colorado in 1922, 1912, 1904 and 1900, as reported by the census.

## ESTIMATED VALUE OF ALL PROPERTY IN COLORADO, BY YEARS
(Compiled from Census Reports)

| | 1922 | 1912 | 1904 | 1900 |
|---|---|---|---|---|
| Taxed real property.. | $1,388,818,000 | $1,123,067,000 | $ 530,893,000 | $ 402,784,000 |
| Exempt property ... | 369,628,000 | 100,445,000 | 106,770,000 | 102,909,000 |
| Livestock .......... | 100,664,000 | 88,059,000 | 57,363,000 | 52,019,000 |
| Farm implements and machinery ........ | 35,059,000 | 14,401,000 | 5,353,000 | 4,747,000 |
| Manufacturing machinery, tools and implements ....... | 86,808,000 | 91,354,000 | 44,521,000 | 21,495,000 |
| Railroads and their equipment ........ | 364,963,000 | 297,625,000 | 198,261,000 | 146,784,000 |
| All other*.......... | 883,472,000 | 600,359,000 | 264,381,000 | 207,433,000 |
| Total, all weath. ... | $3,229,412,000 | $2,315,310,000 | $1,207,542,000 | $ 938,171,000 |

*All other includes motor Vehicles, street railways, water works, agricultural products, manufactured products, imported merchandise, mining products, clothing, personal adornments, furniture, etc.

## ARCHAEOLOGICAL

Certain areas of Colorado, principally the southwestern part of the state, are known to contain many ruins of ancient races, rich in relics showing the customs and manners of people who lived from one to three thousand years ago. The most important and best known of these areas is the Mesa Verde national park in Montezuma county, where many hundreds of ruins of cliff dwellings, temples and other structures have been uncovered and many others are known to exist. It is estimated that the Mesa Verde area once had a population of at least 70,000 people.

The Colorado state historical society, of which George Woodbury is curator, did considerable exploration work in 1928 under a permit from the government on an area in Montezuma county, 32 miles northwest of Cortez, for the purpose of obtaining specimens for the state museum. In this area have been found ruins of a city of a very early type, one of the distinguishing features of which is the remains of many secret underground passages connecting numerous towers and ceremonial chambers. This city, unlike the cliff dwellings, is on an open mesa.

In 1931 the society made an archaeological survey of the Paradox valley in Montrose county and found ruins of Pueblos similar to those further to the south, but no discoveries of outstanding importance resulted. Excavations made in 1925 by the society on Chimney Rock mesa, 22 miles west of Pagosa Springs, revealed some valuable discoveries. The area is one by one and one-fourth miles in size. Numerous ruins were discovered, including one chamber 209.7 feet long and more than 80 feet wide. They were inhabited in the period of the post-basket makers culture, dating back approximately 3,000 years. Among the discoveries were two human skulls, one of the roundhead and the other the longhead type. The society has a permit to make explorations in a new area in western Colorado in 1931.

The University of Colorado was engaged in 1925 in excavating and removing specimens from ruins in the region south of the Mesa Verde national park for its museum, under a government permit. A permit was granted the same university in 1929 to conduct a reconnaissance in parts of La Plata county during that year. There are several operations of like nature on patented land owned by private parties, where specimens are being obtained for museums. Congress passed a law in 1906 for the preservation of American antiquities, which provides that permits must be obtained before excavations can be made on government land. The government also retained title to all ruins on government land which has gone to patent since that date. Specimens can be obtained only for reputable museums, universities, colleges and scientific societies under these permits.

Additional information concerning the Mesa Verde and other ruins may be found in the chapters on "National Parks and Monuments" and "Museums in Colorado" in this volume.

## ROYAL GORGE BRIDGE

The highest suspension bridge in the world spans the canon of the Arkansas river, known as the Royal Gorge, six miles west of Canon City in Fremont county. Construction work started on June 4, 1929, and the structure was dedicated on December 8, 1929. The floor of the bridge is 1,053 feet above the bed of the river. The bridge across the Grand Canon of the Colorado river at Lee's Ferry, Arizona, is 467 feet high and the bridge at Twin Falls, Idaho, across the Snake river, is 500 feet high. There is a bridge in southern France 435 feet high.

The main span of the Royal Gorge bridge is 880 feet long and the total length, exclusive of approaches, is 1,260 feet. The roadway, which provides for two-way motor vehicle and pedestrian traffic, is 18 feet wide and is protected with guard rails four and one-half feet high. The two cables upon which the bridge is suspended rest upon twin towers at both ends, 150 feet high. The cables, which were fabricated in place, contain 2,100 strands of wire of 120,000 pounds per square inch tensile strength each, comprising an aggregate of 1,300 miles of wire. The cables are anchored at each end in solid granite. Trenches four feet square and 100 feet long were cut in the stone. At the bottom of each trench 100 two-inch pipes were set three feet into the rock and fastened by a sulphur process. Twenty-one wires of the cable were placed in each pipe and forced tight with rods. Concrete was then poured into the trenches until they were level with the surrounding stone. The floor rests on 15-inch steel "I" beams, on nine lines of eight-inch steel "I" beams used for joists. The bridge floor is cambered and is six feet higher in the center than at the ends.

The bridge was built as a private enterprise. A state highway runs to the north end of the bridge. The Denver & Rio Grande Western railroad runs through the gorge just above the level of the river. The canon itself is a noted tourist attraction. The railroad crosses the river in the canon on a "hanging" bridge. The canon was discovered by Zebulon Pike in 1806, and was the scene of a notable struggle between two railroad companies in the late 70s for its possession.

## EARTHQUAKES

One of the two seismic stations in the Jesuit Seismological association for the observance of earthquakes and gathering data for seismic research is located at Regis college in Denver. It was established in 1909, and since then the instrument has never ceased recording the vibrations of the earth. A. W. Forstall, S. J., a member of the Seismological Society of America, which has its seat at Leland Stanford university, is director of the Regis college station. The instrument belongs to the class of medium period for general observations and was invented by the well-known seismologist Dr. Wiechert, of Gottingen, Germany, and was constructed by the firm of Spindler and Hoyer, of the same town.

The seismograph and the clocks by which it is regulated are located in a room on the ground floor of the administration building, which is remarkably free from changes in temperature, a condition very important for the maintenance of a perfect adjustment. It is mounted on a masonry pier that rests upon the solid earth to eliminate all disturbances originating in the building, for the slightest vibration of the floor would be recorded by the pens. It is protected from drafts by a large glass case and means have been provided for making certain adjustments without opening this case. The earthquake vibrations are registered by two delicate pens writing on smoked paper. The minutes of time as well as the hours are automatically marked off on the blank by electric connections with the clocks. The United States weather bureau and the United States coast and geodetic survey co-operate with the association

through the publication of its reports. The stations of the association also exchange telegrams immediately after large quakes have been registered in order to locate their epicenters as early as possible for the benefit of the other stations, the people and the press. This is done through the aid of "Science Service," at Washington.

The three-fold program of the association for the past 22 years has been: To collect data of seismic value by securing daily blanks; each station to analyze and interpret its observations and publish them, as well as to keep them at the disposal of all the stations of the world; and by means of these data collected from its own and other observatories, to endeavor to solve the intricate problems relating to the nature of seismic waves, their speed, their reflection, their refraction, and by means of this knowledge to arrive at a true concept of the interior conditions of the earth and its geology.

## COLORADO TROOPS IN WORLD WAR

Official figures place the number of troops furnished by Colorado for the World war, including commissioned and enlisted men, at 42,898. The number includes enlistments in the army, navy and marine corps. The total number for the country was 4,727,988, of which Colorado furnished approximately 1 per cent.

During the fiscal year ending June 30, 1926, the war department completed the task of rechecking all authorization and credits for wounds incurred by members of the American Expeditionary Forces. The final figures on battle casualties for Colorado are as follows:

|  | Officers | Enlisted Men | Total |
|---|---|---|---|
| Killed in action..... | 18 | 224 | 242 |
| Died of wounds..... | 9 | 75 | 84 |
| Wounds* .......... | 82 | 1,091 | 1,173 |
| Individuals wounded* ........ | 76 | 1,042 | 1,118 |
| Wounds not mortal. .. |  | ... | 1,089 |
| Grand total casualties........ |  |  | 1,415 |

*"Wounds" and "Individuals wounded" include mortal wounds received by individuals enumerated under "Died of wounds."

## COLORADO HOSPITALS

Colorado is well supplied with hospitals and sanitariums which rank among the best in the country in equipment and quality of service rendered the public. The American College of Surgeons, an international organization covering North and South America, conducts an annual survey of hospitals in Colorado in its standardization movement. This movement provides for the establishment of minimum requirements for the proper conduct of hospitals as to the competency and character of physicians and surgeons upon hospital staffs, adequate equipment, maintenance of proper records, prohibition of fee-splitting, etc., before a hospital is given full approval. The survey for 1931 lists 35 hospitals in the state, of which 32 are fully approved and three are conditionally approved. The conditionally approved are those which have accepted the minimum standards required but which for lack of ample time or other acceptable reasons have not completed the adoption of these requirements in detail.

The 35 hospitals approved in 1931 had a capacity of 7,318, including cribs and bassinettes for the new-born. This compares with 7,025 beds in 1930,

6,781 beds in 1929 and 6,624 beds in 1928. The organization's staff reported upon 40 hospitals in the state in 1929, of which 32 were approved as of October 1, 1929. Eighty per cent of the hospitals reported upon were approved, which compares with 68.6 per cent for the United States, including the Canal Zone, Hawaii and Porto Rico. Eleven states only showed a larger per cent of approved hospitals than Colorado. The largest hospital in the country operated by the United States army, navy or public health service is located near Denver and is known as the Fitzsimons general hospital.

In addition to these hospitals, there are a number of private sanitariums and smaller hospitals in the various cities and towns in the state, where satisfactory accommodations may be secured.

An accompanying table gives the location, names, capacity and management of hospitals in the state approved by the college of surgeons.

### HOSPITALS APPROVED BY THE AMERICAN COLLEGE OF SURGEONS, 1931

| Location | Name | Capacity | Governed by |
|---|---|---|---|
| Boulder | Boulder-Colorado sanitarium | 120 | Seventh Day Adventists. |
| Boulder | Community | 60 | Board of Directors. |
| Colorado Springs | Beth-El General | 100 | Methodist Episcopal Church. |
| Colorado Springs | Cragmor Sanatorium | 150 | Private Owners. |
| Colorado Springs | Glockner Sanatorium and hospital | 225 | Sisters of Charity. |
| Colorado Springs | National Methodist Episcopal Sanatorium for Tuberculosis | 70 | Methodist Episcopal Church. |
| Colorado Springs | St. Francis hospital | 125 | Sisters of St. Francis. |
| Denver | Agnes Memorial sanatorium | 154 | Board of Trustees. |
| Denver | Beth Israel | 67 | Board of Directors. |
| Denver | Children's | 175 | Board of Directors. |
| Denver | *Colorado General | 238 | University—Board of Regents. |
| Denver | Denver General | 515 | City and county—health department. |
| Denver | Fitzsimons General | 1,832 | U. S. Army. |
| Denver | Mercy | 190 | Sisters of Mercy. |
| Denver | National Jewish | 270 | Board of Managers. |
| Denver | Porter Sanitarium and hospital | 62 | Seventh Day Adventists. |
| Denver | Presbyterian | 175 | Presbyterian Church. |
| Denver | St. Anthony's | 200 | Sisters of St. Francis. |
| Denver | St. Joseph's | 249 | Sisters of Charity. |
| Denver | St. Luke's | 249 | Board of Managers. |
| Denver | Sanatorium of the Jewish Consumptives' Relief Society | 300 | Jewish Relief Society. |
| Durango | Mercy | 42 | Sisters of Mercy |
| Fort Lyon | United States Veterans | 638 | Government—Veterans' Bureau. |
| Grand Junction | St. Mary's | 74 | Sisters of Charity. |
| Greeley | Greeley hospital | 130 | County Commissioners. |
| La Junta | Atchison, Topeka & Santa Fe Railroad | 36 | Railway Hospital Association. |
| La Junta | Mennonite Hospital and Sanitarium | 80 | Board of Missions and Charities. |
| Longmont | Longmont | 40 | Board of Trustees. |
| Pueblo | Corwin | 234 | Industrial corporation. |
| Pueblo | Parkview | 80 | Board of Directors. |
| Pueblo | St. Mary's | 162 | Sisters of Charity. |
| Salida | Denver & Rio Grande Western Railroad | 85 | Railway Employes' Association. |
| Salida | Red Cross | 42 | Private—Board of Directors. |
| Sterling | St. Benedict | 36 | Sisters of St. Benedict. |
| Trinidad | Mt. San Rafael | 80 | Sisters of Charity. |

*Includes Colorado General and Colorado Psychopathic hospitals of the University of Colorado.

## NATIONAL AND STATE COMMITTEES

The Colorado members of the Democratic national committee are Raymond Miller of Denver and Mrs. B. C. Hilliard, Jr., of Denver. The chairman of the Democratic state committee is James A. Marsh of Denver, and Walter F. Scherer, Denver, is secretary.

The Colorado members of the Republican national committee are Lawrence C. Phipps, Denver, and Mrs. John E. Hillman, Delta. The chairman of the Republican state committee is Jesse F. McDonald of Leadville. E. C. Abbey, Grover, is secretary.

## BUILDING PERMITS

The value of buildings constructed, or remodelled, in 20 cities and towns of the state in 1930 for which permits were issued was $11,707,791. The following table shows the amounts by years and the number of towns and cities reporting:

| Year | No. Reporting | Value |
|---|---|---|
| 1924 | 20 | $33,157,975 |
| 1925 | 20 | 32,618,354 |
| 1926 | 17 | 19,325,549 |
| 1927 | 19 | 20,624,702 |
| 1928 | 19 | 21,234,508 |
| 1929 | 20 | 21,575,638 |
| 1930 | 20 | 11,707,791 |
| 1931 | 19 | 9,127,502 |

An accompanying table shows the value of permits by cities and towns and by years.

## VALUE OF BUILDING PERMITS IN PRINCIPAL CITIES AND TOWNS

| TOWN | 1931 | 1930 | 1929 | 1928 | 1927 |
|---|---|---|---|---|---|
| Boulder | $ 136,135 | $ 271,684 | $ 216,510 | $ 326,475 | $ 416,930 |
| Colorado Springs. | 387,963 | 926,322 | 1,030,026 | 812,495 | 577,398 |
| Denver | 7,127,400 | 8,007,100 | 16,633,300 | 15,958,400 | 15,902,650 |
| Durango | 72,756 | 139,718 | 162,352 | 282,249 | 205,305 |
| Eads | ...... | 14,600 | 15,000 | 2,000 | 3,000 |
| Eaton | 1,450 | 3,050 | 12,900 | 121,530 | 90,000 |
| Englewood | 70,640 | 189,670 | 148,097 | 169,428 | 200,000 |
| Fort Collins | 182,810 | 256,297 | 276,578 | 333,866 | 223,292 |
| Fort Morgan | 82,315 | 102,973 | 199,965 | ...... | ...... |
| Grand Junction | 146,928 | 127,575 | 316,938 | 236,145 | 204,950 |
| Greeley | 164,155 | 295,360 | 453,527 | 624,919 | 644,395 |
| Lafayette | 16,170 | 8,800 | 1,500 | 2,750 | 1,500 |
| La Junta | 8,000 | 60,000 | 1,040 | 60,000 | 200,000 |
| Littleton | 26,000 | 21,710 | 30,000 | 35,000 | 10,000 |
| Longmont | 48,610 | 104,730 | 127,515 | 115,000 | 105,000 |
| Manitou | 37,291 | 28,052 | 25,295 | 21,225 | 23,700 |
| Platteville | 7,500 | 1,050 | 23,869 | 7,000 | 3,000 |
| Pueblo | 453,423 | 537,205 | 1,572,521 | 1,468,012 | 1,625,382 |
| Sterling | 56,956 | 439,645 | 123,705 | 402,180 | 146,200 |
| Trinidad | 101,000 | 172,250 | 205,000 | 255,834 | 42,000 |
| Totals | $9,127,502 | $11,707,791 | $21,575,638 | $21,234,508 | $20,624,702 |

## COLORADO PRODUCTION OF ELECTRICITY FOR PUBLIC USE
(Compiled by Division of Power Resources, U. S. Geological Survey)

|  | 1931 | 1930 | 1929 |
|---|---|---|---|
| Production (kilowatt-hours): |  |  |  |
|     Water power | 189,706,000 | 235,843,000 | 230,423,000 |
|     Fuel power | 339,111,000 | 337,498,000 | 333,390,000 |
|     Total power | 528,817,000 | 573,341,000 | 563,813,000 |
| Consumption of fuel: |  |  |  |
|     Coal (short tons) | 399,602 | 419,295 | 420,093 |
|     Oil (barrels) | 16,076 | 8,574 | 6,328 |
|     Natural gas (cu. ft.) | 149,759,000 | ........ | ........ |
| Number companies operating January 1 | 29 | 31 | 29 |
| Number plants operated January 1 | 67 | 64 | 61 |
| Generator capacity (kilowatt-hours) | 228,643 | 224,516 | 222,127 |

Note—Additional information on this subject will be found in chapter "Water Power Resources."

## EXPORTS FROM COLORADO

Exports from Colorado, merchandise shipped from this state to foreign countries, amounted to $2,841,000 in the calendar year of 1931, according to a special survey made by the Denver office of the bureau of foreign and domestic commerce in co-operation with local exporters. This figure is preliminary and compares with $5,140,-046 in 1930 and $4,600,984 in 1929.

There are two sources of statistics indicating the volume of products exported from Colorado. The first set of statistics is based upon original figures given by shippers in the United States official export declaration. This source takes care of only those shipments which are forwarded on through export bills of lading and does not provide a completely accurate index of the exact volume of export shipments from the state. Firms located in the interior states such as Colorado often sell their products to or through export commission houses, export sales agents and foreign purchasing agents, usually located at seaboard points. These business houses located on the coast file their own shippers' export declaration, failing to note the actual point of origin of the merchandise. This procedure makes it necessary for customs officials to credit customs districts where such shipments leave the country, therefore direct shipments from Colorado on through bills of lading are practically the only ones credited to the state.

The value of exports shipped from Colorado on through bills of lading for which the state is given credit in this manner are, by years, as follows:

| | |
|---|---|
| 1927 | $3,394,095 |
| 1928 | 3,419,934 |
| 1929 | 4,001,887 |
| 1930 | 3,238,588 |
| 1931 | 2,012,659 |

The second source of statistics, those compiled by the Denver office of the bureau of domestic and foreign commerce in co-operation with local exporters, which comprise exports made from Colorado regardless of whether they are shipped on through bills of lading or in connection with agencies located at the seaboard, are more representative of export activities of Colorado firms. This co-operative survey has been made each year, beginning with 1929, and reveals the following statistics for the state for calendar years:

| | |
|---|---|
| 1929 | $4,600,984 |
| 1930 | 5,140,046 |
| 1931 | *2,841,000 |

*1931 figures are preliminary.

The bulk of the Colorado exports consists of mining equipment. The depression has especially affected the world's mineral industry and this has accounted for the temporary falling off of the volume of exports from this state. However, it is expected that with the revival of world business and especially renewed activity in the mineral industry, the exports from Colorado will again resume their upward march.

The world must look to Denver for some years to come as a source of machinery for the mining of complex ores. It was in Colorado that the mining engineers first successfully met the many problems in the extraction of metals from these difficult ores.

In order to do this special mining and metallurgical machinery was developed. The manufacturing of this equipment has largely remained in Denver due to the fact that over a period of years trained engineers, designers and workmen have been developed and for these reasons it is expected that the exports of mining machinery from Colorado will account for the bulk of all exports from this state for some years to come.

There is a wide variety of other products exported from Colorado, which include automobile tires and accessories, signs, dance floor wax, canvas water bags, beans, potatoes, medicines, incubators, paint, glass, explosives, mountain seeds, radio parts, school supplies, rock drills, fire bricks, steel wire, nails, and innumerable other articles.

Canada and Mexico for a number of years have been the best customers of Colorado exporters. However, Colorado exports go to practically every country of the world; one firm ships to 102 political divisions.

## LUMBER, TIMBER AND PLANING MILL INDUSTRIES

Colorado has immense quantities of merchantable timber, from which there is produced in the state annually $4,000,000 worth of lumber and timber and planing mill products. There were 147 mills active in the state in 1930, including logging camps, saw mills and planing mills, as reported by the bureau of the census in co-operation with the forest service and the department of agriculture. The output of sawed lumber for that year was 54,688,000 board feet, a decrease from several preceding years, due to some of the larger mills being inactive part of the time. The maximum output was established in 1926, with a production of 75,278,000 board feet, and the minimum output since 1922 was 38,233,000 board feet in 1923. These mills produce rough lumber, lath, shingles, railroad ties and other unfinished products. The following table shows the number of active mills and quantity of lumber sawed by years:

| Year | No. of Active Mills | Quantity Lumber Sawed (board ft.) |
|---|---|---|
| 1922 | 128 | 38.917,000 |
| 1923 | 113 | 38,233,000 |
| 1924 | 122 | 42,014,000 |
| 1925 | 145 | 71.069,000 |
| 1926 | 128 | 75,278,000 |
| 1927 | 116 | 67,321,000 |
| 1928 | 140 | 72,257,000 |
| 1929 | 134 | 71,535,000 |
| 1930 | 147 | 54,688,000 |

Most of the lumber produced in the state is softwood, the only hardwood being cottonwood. Of the 54,688,000 board feet sawed in 1930 only 124,000 board feet was hardwood. The kind of wood and the quantity of each produced in 1930, 1928 and 1926 are given in the following table:

| Kind | Quantity M Ft. B. M. | | |
|---|---|---|---|
| | 1930 | 1928 | 1926 |
| Cedar | .... | .... | 1 |
| Douglas fir | 6,878 | 4,157 | 2,895 |
| Lodgepole pine | 15,426 | 9,875 | 9,740 |
| Spruce | 11,210 | 9,814 | 10,529 |
| Western yellow pine | 20,070 | 47,038 | 51,022 |
| White fir | 980 | 1,316 | 767 |
| Cottonwood | 124 | 57 | 324 |
| Total | 54,688 | 72,257 | 75,278 |

Colorado ranked first among the states of the Union in 1930 in the production of lodgepole pine, its output being 15,426,000 feet, or 50.7 per cent of the output of 30,411,000 feet for the entire country. This timber is used extensively in the construction of telephone and telegraph lines and other industries where tall, strong and uniformly shaped timber is required. The state ranked eighth in 1930 among the states in the production of spruce.

A considerable part of the timber cut in Colorado comes from the national forests, the annual output being 50,000,000 to 70,000,000 board feet. The national forest service estimates standing timber of all species in these reserves at 31,918,969,000 board feet. Additional information on this subject will be found in the chapter on "National Forests."

Of the 147 mills active in 1930 nine were in class 3, those sawing between 1,000,000 and 4,000,000 board feet; 35 in class 2, sawing between 500,000 and 999,000 board feet; and 103 were in class 1, those sawing between 50,000 and 499,000 board feet.

Most of the rough lumber sawed is used for remanufacture purposes. In the summary of the lumber and timber industry as reported in the census on manufactures, logging mills are not included in the number of establishments. This summary for 1929 and 1919, which includes saw mills and planing mills operated in conjunction with them, but not independent planing mills, is as follows:

| | 1929 | 1919 |
|---|---|---|
| Number of establishments | 61 | 136 |
| Salaried officers and employes | 77 | 84 |
| Aver. number wage earners | 1,219 | 823 |
| Salaries | $136,615 | $117,845 |
| Wages | $1,455,939 | $1,053,332 |
| Value of products | $2,278,660 | $2,450,731 |
| Value added by manufacture | $1,932,497 | $1,772,173 |

The independent planing mills are those which are not operated in conjunction with saw mills and which produce dressed lumber, doors, sash, blinds, interior woodwork and molding. A summary of same for the census years 1929 and 1919 for Colorado is as follows:

| | 1929 | 1919 |
|---|---|---|
| Number of establishments | 29 | 41 |
| Salaried officers and employes | 62 | 54 |
| Aver. number Wage earners | 312 | 411 |
| Salaries | $146,692 | $81,827 |
| Wages | $479,135 | $512,061 |
| Value of products | $1,507,322 | $1,572,132 |
| Value added by manufacture | $939,218 | $819,035 |

Included in the industry were four establishments in 1929 engaged in the manufacture of wooden boxes, etc., which employed 103 officials and wage earners, paid $100,654 in salaries and wages, and produced products valued at $439,578.

## DENVER'S MOUNTAIN PARKS

Located in Jefferson, Clear Creek, Arapahoe, Douglas, Gilpin and Boulder counties, to the northwest, west and south of Denver, is a series of mountain parks, all of which are connected by highways, which comprise what is known as the Denver mountain park system. These parks are owned by the municipality of Denver and were acquired, improved and opened to the public for the purpose of making the mountains available for the people. In undertaking the project, there were no precedents to follow. The idea was unique, never before considered by any municipality and no other American city has since undertaken a project that is similar.

The system comprises a chain or series of parks in the mountains forming somewhat of a semi-circle and extending as far west as Echo lake and the summit of Mt. Evans, the latter at an altitude of 14,262 feet above sea level, and including Lookout mountain, Bergen park, Genesee park, the Garden of the Red Rocks and other areas offering unique and attractive scenic advantages. All of the parks are connected with well-built highways and these highways tie into others radiating from Denver to the west and south. In the mountain parks are several lakes. Mountain lodges have been built at most attractive locations, shelter houses erected, water systems installed, fireplaces for outdoor cooking constructed and many other improvements made for the comfort and convenience of the people. The federal government, especially the forest service, the state government and the city of Denver participated in the construction of the highway to the summit of Mount Evans. Counties in which the parks and highways are located also have contributed to the construction and maintenance of the roads.

While the establishment of this park system had been discussed as early as about 1901, the actual movement towards that end began in 1911, when committees of the civic and commercial organizations of Denver engaged in developing the idea were combined into a single general committee. In May, 1912, at a municipal election, the charter of Denver was amended so as to permit the city to acquire, own and operate properties outside of the municipality's corporate limits. The following year the legislature passed an act granting Denver eminent domain and police powers in respect to the mountain parks. The land for the park was acquired by purchase, by donations from the federal government and as gifts from individuals. A project so unique and so extensive aroused considerable opposition and the right of the municipality to levy taxes for undertakings outside of the city was taken into court, with the result that not only did the supreme court uphold this right, but held the amendment to the city charter to be constitutional and valid. The first work undertaken was the construction of a highway from Golden to the summit of Lookout mountain, which was begun in 1913. Improvements in the parks and the acquisition of additional holdings have

since continued progressively as they were needed.

The area owned by the city on June 1, 1927, was 10,295 acres, of which 4,419 acres was acquired prior to 1923. Between that year and 1927, 1,311 acres was secured through patents to parks, 4,352 acres by patents to tracts and 214 acres by deeds to parks. From 1912 to 1929, inclusive, total expenditures on the mountain parks aggregated $1,895,153. These expenditures by years are as follows:

| | |
|---|---:|
| 1912 | $ 3,864.67 |
| 1913 | 59,443.97 |
| 1914 | 87,465.15 |
| 1915 | 129,282.57 |
| 1916 | 48,093.90 |
| 1917 | 73,757.19 |
| 1918 | 72,103.05 |
| 1919 | 51,128.37 |
| 1920 | 96,623.70 |
| 1921 | 99,633.26 |
| 1922 | 151,748.26 |
| 1923 | 74,424.74 |
| 1924 | 135,711.90 |
| 1925 | 112,176.95 |
| 1926 | 98,972.24 |
| 1927 | 259,132.96 |
| 1928 | 174,712.02 |
| 1929 | 166,878.46 |
| 1930 | 165,332.21 |
| 1931 | 168,337.67 |
| Total | $2,228,823.24 |

## MEXICAN LAND GRANTS

Maps of Colorado generally show large areas of land along the southern boundary which are designated as land grants. These are referred to popularly as "Spanish land grants," but more correctly they are known as Mexican land grants, since they were made subsequent to the proclaiming in 1810 of Mexico's independence of Spain. Most of these grants, in which the titles originate in the government of Mexico, were bestowed in the early 40s, but successful occupation of the tracts was not accomplished for a number of years. Following the signing of the Treaty of Guadalupe Hildalgo in 1848, which guaranteed to the Mexicans their private property rights, the United States set up the machinery necessary to ascertain the origin, nature and extent of the claims to the land under the laws, usages and customs of Spain and Mexico, and such claims as were found to be valid were confirmed by congress. In the years following the confirmation of titles down to the present the land embraced in the grants has been extensively developed and within the areas are cities and towns, agricultural communities, valuable coal and mineral properties and other evidences of substantial growth.

One of the largest of the grants in Colorado and New Mexico is known as the Beaubien and Miranda, or Maxwell land grant, which embraces more than one million acres of land, of which approximately 380,000 acres is in Colorado. The Colorado part of the grant is in the southern and southwestern parts of Las Animas county. The grant was confirmed by congress in 1860.

The Sangre de Cristo grant, the largest of the group and including more than a million acres, embraces the greater part of the valleys of the Costilla, Culebra and Trinchera rivers in the San Luis valley and extends from the Rio Grande river to the summit of the Sangre de Cristo range. It is principally in Costilla county.

The Nolan grant, located along the St. Charles river, in Pueblo county, to the south and southwest of Pueblo, was confirmed in 1870 as to 48,695 acres.

The Vigil and St. Vrain grant is in the valleys of the Huerfano, Apishapa and Cucharas rivers, lies to the north of the Maxwell grant and southeast of the Nolan grant and originally embraced more than 4,000,000 acres, but was reduced by congress to 97,390 acres.

The Conejos grant, involving a large tract in Conejos county, was never confirmed and most of the land was taken up under the United States homestead laws, in many instances by original grantees.

The Tierra Amarilla grant is mostly in New Mexico, with only a small part of it extending up into Archuleta county.

### MARRIAGES AND DIVORCES IN COLORADO BY YEARS
(From the Bureau of Census Reports)

|  | Marriages | | Divorces | |
|---|---|---|---|---|
|  | United States | Colorado | United States | Colorado |
| **Number reported:** | | | | |
| 1916 | 1,040,684 | 9,071 | 112,036 | 1,061 |
| 1922 | 1,134,151 | 11,456 | 148,815 | 2,075 |
| 1923 | 1,229,784 | 12,077 | 165,096 | 2,278 |
| 1924 | 1,184,574 | 11,972 | 170,952 | 2,118 |
| 1925 | 1,188,334 | 11,602 | 175,449 | 2,243 |
| 1926 | 1,202,574 | 11,957 | 180,853 | 2,288 |
| 1927 | 1,201,053 | 11,969 | 192,037 | 2,370 |
| 1928 | 1,182,497 | 12,065 | 195,939 | 2,362 |
| 1929 | 1,232,559 | 13,047 | 201,468 | 2,392 |
| 1930 | 1,128,280 | 11,733 | 191,591 | 2,245 |
| **Increase (number):** | | | | |
| 1922 over 1916 | 52,789 | 2,287 | 34,980 | 1,005 |
| 1923 over 1922 | 95,633 | 621 | 16,281 | 203 |
| 1924 over 1923 | −45,210 | −105 | 5,856 | −160 |
| 1925 over 1924 | 3,760 | −370 | 4,497 | 125 |
| 1926 over 1925 | 14,240 | 355 | 5,404 | 45 |
| 1927 over 1926 | −1,521 | 12 | 11,184 | 92 |
| 1928 over 1927 | −18,556 | 96 | 3,902 | −8 |
| 1929 over 1928 | 50,062 | 982 | 5,529 | 30 |
| 1930 over 1929 | −104,279 | −1,314 | −9,877 | −147 |
| **Per cent increase:** | | | | |
| 1922 over 1916 | 5.1 | 25.2 | 31.2 | 94.7 |
| 1923 over 1922 | 8.4 | 5.4 | 10.9 | 12.2 |
| 1924 over 1923 | −3.7 | −0.9 | 3.6 | −7.0 |
| 1925 over 1924 | 0.3 | −3.1 | 2.6 | 5.9 |
| 1926 over 1925 | 1.2 | 3.1 | 3.1 | 2.0 |
| 1927 over 1926 | −0.1 | 0.1 | 6.2 | 3.6 |
| 1928 over 1927 | −1.5 | 0.8 | 2.0 | −0.3 |
| 1929 over 1928 | 4.2 | 8.1 | 2.8 | 1.3 |
| 1930 over 1929 | −8.5 | −10.1 | −4.9 | −6.1 |
| **Number per 1,000 population:** | | | | |
| 1916 | 10.68 | .... | 1.13 | 1.22 |
| 1922 | 10.32 | 11.65 | 1.35 | 2.11 |
| 1923 | 11.03 | 12.06 | 1.48 | 2.28 |
| 1924 | 10.46 | 11.70 | 1.51 | 2.07 |
| 1925 | 10.35 | 11.70 | 1.53 | 2.26 |
| 1926 | 10.32 | 11.95 | 1.55 | 2.29 |
| 1927 | 10.16 | 11.85 | 1.62 | 2.35 |
| 1928 | 9.87 | 11.84 | 1.63 | 2.32 |
| 1929 | 10.14 | 12.68 | 1.66 | 2.33 |
| 1930 | 9.16 | 11.30 | 1.56 | 2.16 |

Minus sign denotes decrease.
Note—Rates of marriages and divorces for recent years have been revised to conform to the 1930 census.

## STATE CAPITOL BUILDING

The Colorado state capitol building is located on an elevated site bounded by Lincoln and Grant streets and Colfax and East Fourteenth avenues in the city of Denver, with the main entrance facing due west. It stands at an altitude of exactly one mile above sea level. The structure, from the standpoint of its location, its architectural beauty and imposing appearance, is one of the outstanding state capitol buildings of the country. The grounds in front of the building include the entire block between Lincoln street and Broadway and face the Denver civic center. The main range of the Rocky mountains for a distance of 150 miles north and south is visible from the capitol entrance.

The building is of the Corinthian order of architecture, and E. E. Myers was the architect. The cornerstone was laid on July 4, 1890, by the Masonic lodge and the building was first occupied in 1895 and was completed in 1896. The site, consisting of 10 acres, was donated to the state by Henry C. Brown and the block fronting on Broadway was purchased for $100,000. The cost of the building was $2,800,000 and replacement value at this time is estimated at $8,000,000. It is constructed of gray granite, cut on straight lines except for the massive pillars above the entrances. The interior is finished principally in onyx with lacquered brass cappings and corner trimmings. The dome is plated with pure leaf gold which cost $14,680, and seven and one-half tons of lead was used in placing same. The struc-

ture is shaped similar to a Greek cross, with entrances on Colfax avenue, Grant street and East Fourteenth avenue, with the main entrance on the Lincoln street side. In its construction 230,000 cubic feet of granite was used.

The dimensions of the building are as follows:

```
Length ..............383 feet 11 inches
Width ................313 feet
Height of dome........272 feet  2 inches
Length of corridors
    east and west.......199 feet
Diameter of circular
    corridor beneath dome 42 feet
Number of rooms......160
```

The cornerstone contains a copy of the Bible, an American flag, constitutions of Colorado and the United States, the Declaration of Independence, census reports, numerous documents and public addresses of officials, a number of souvenirs, copies of the newspapers of that day and gold and silver coins of all denominations.

In 1915 a quarter-block south of the capitol and across East Fourteenth avenue was purchased and the state museum building was constructed upon it at a cost of $480,000. The structure was built of granite and marble, and houses a museum of archaeological and mineral exhibits and relics of wars.

In 1919 a quarter-block north of the capitol and across Colfax avenue was purchased, and upon the site was constructed the state office building, four stories high and built of granite and marble at a cost of $1,475,000. It was occupied in 1921. In it are located numerous boards and departments of the state government.

## Colorado Boards, Bureaus and Commissions

IN the following tabulation is presented a list of all state boards, bureaus and commissions, as well as departments headed by individual executives but representing distinct governmental activities. Agencies which are sub-departments of other regular departments, such as the motor vehicle bureau under the secretary of state, and the factory and labor inspectors under the same official, are not reported, nor are inspectors working out of the market director's office and similar employes under other departments. To include all such officials and employes would extend the list materially. The purpose here is to list all independent and distinct agencies

of the state government. Elected state and county officials are shown under the heading "Government and Political Record," as are district judges and district attorneys, and those names are not repeated here.

For brevity the following symbols have been adopted:

1. Appointed by the governor.
2. Appointed by the governor, subject to confirmation by the senate.
3. No compensation except expenses incurred in the discharge of official duties.
4. No compensation of any kind provided by law.
5. Compensation or expenses, or both, payable only from collections of the department.
6. Officer or employe is under civil service.

## BOARDS GOVERNING STATE INSTITUTIONS

**Regents, Colorado University, Boulder** (3)—Martin D. Currigan, E. R. Campbell and Clifford W. Mills, Denver; Frank H. Means, Saguache; Mrs. Jos. D. Grigsby, Pueblo; Charles D. Bromley, Fort Morgan. Dr. George Norlin*, president†. Elected for six-year terms.

**Trustees, School for Deaf and Blind, Colorado Springs** (2-3)—R. H. Malone and Earl R. Hoage, Denver; G. E. West, Durango; J. A. Ritter and Asa T. Jones, Colorado Springs.

**Trustees, School of Mines, Golden** (2-3)—Fred Steinhauer and W. H. Smiley, Denver; W. A. Way, Silverton; B. F. Hill, Cripple Creek; Robert Sayer, Central City. Dr. M. F. Coolbaugh*, president.

**Trustees, Teachers College, Greeley, and Normal Schools, Gunnison and Alamosa** (2-3)—Mrs. Inez Johnson Lewis†; C. P. Rex, Alamosa; E. M. Hedrick, Wray; T. W. Monell, Montrose; H. V. Kepner, Denver; C. N. Jackson, Greeley; C. H. Stewart, Delta. Dr. G. W. Frasier*, president.

**Board of Agriculture, Agricultural College, Fort Collins, and Fort Lewis School** (2-3) — The Governor†; Dr. Charles A. Lory*, president†; J. C. Bell, Montrose; W. I. Gifford, Hesperus; J. P. McKelvey, La Jara; H. B. Dye, Manzanola; T. J. Warren, Fort Collins; Dr. O. E. Webb, Milliken; Mrs. Mary H. Isham, Brighton; J. W. Goss, Pueblo.

**Board of Corrections: Penitentiary, Canon City; Reformatory, Buena Vista; Insane Hospital, Pueblo** (2-3)—T. A. Duke, Pueblo; Rt. Rev. Irving P. Johnson, Denver; R. J. Wann, Canon City. Roy Best (*-6), acting warden penitentiary; R. L. Shaw (*-6), warden reformatory; F. H. Zimmerman (*-6), superintendent insane hospital.

**Trustees, Junior College, Trinidad** (1-4)—J. C. Caldwell, F. C. Nicholls, R. E. McClung, Trinidad.

**Trustees, Junior College, Grand Junction** (1-4)—R. E. Tope, E. W. DinWiddie, Henry Tupper, Grand Junction.

**Board of Control, Industrial School for Boys, Golden** (2-3)—Sterling B. Lacy, Denver; Miss Lila O'Boyle and Oscar L. Chapman, Denver. B. T. Poxson (*-6), superintendent.

**Board of Control, Industrial School for Girls, Morrison** (2-3)—Margaret P. Taussig, E. C. Stimson, E. S. Kassler, Leila C. Eaton, Mrs. Lelia B. Chamberlin, Denver. Miss Anna L. Cooley (*-6), superintendent.

**Commissioners, Soldiers' and Sailors' Home, Monte Vista** (2-3)—W. C. Danks, Steamboat Springs; H. O. Neville, Denver; Susie Carr McGuire, Longmont; Donald Shakespear, Monte Vista; Alba J. Rawson, Denver. John T. Greene (*-6), commandant.

**Board of Control, Home for Dependent and Neglected Children, Denver** (1-3)—Mrs. P. C. Porter, Mrs. S. P. Thomas, Mrs. A. M. Whitaker, Mrs. Anna R. Morse, Denver. John L. McMenamin (*-6), superintendent.

**Commissioners, Home for Mental Defectives, Ridge and Grand Junction** (2-3)—J. H. Lee and Sterling B. Lacy, Grand Junction; Rev. Val H. Higgins, Denver. Superintendents: Dr. C. L. Pershing (*-6), Ridge; Dr. B. L. Jefferson (*-6), Grand Junction.

## EXECUTIVE BOARDS AND COMMISSIONS

**Public Utilities Commission** (*-2)—Worth Allen, Greeley; Dan S. Jones, Center; E. E. Wheeler, Ouray.

**Industrial Commission** (*-2)—Thomas Annear, Denver; Wm. H. Young, Pueblo; W. E. Renshaw, Idaho Springs.

**Land Commissioners** (*-2)—Raymond Miller, Galatea; A. H. King, Sterling: W. R. Murphy, Las Animas.

**Civil Service Commission** (*-1)—John M. Jones, Boulder; Mrs. Clara Wilkins, Alamosa; W. T. Lambert, Sedalia.

**Board of Capitol Managers** (1-3)—The Governor of Colorado†; F. L. Birney, Geo. T. Bradley, W. H. Gates, Denver; C. B. Noxon, Englewood. James Merrick (*-6), superintendent of buildings.

**Military Board** (†-4)—The Governor of Colorado; L. deR. Mowry, judge advocate; A. P. Ardourel, quartermaster; R. A. Johnston, senior line officer; Col. W. C. Danks, adjutant general.

**Tax Commission** (*-6)—E. D. Morgan and S. E. Tucker, Denver; J. R. Seaman, Fort Collins.

**Board of Health** (2-3)—Dr. Sherman Williams, Dr. Paul J. Connor, Dr. G. W. Bumpus, Denver; Dr. W. P. Gasser, Loveland; Dr. U. O. Mussick, Colorado Springs; Dr. C. A. Davlin, Alamosa; Dr. B. B. Beshoar, Trinidad; Dr. N. M. Burnett, Lamar; Dr. S. R. McKelvey (*-6), secretary, Denver.

**Stock Inspection Commissioners** (1-3)—E. R. Mourning, Kiowa; John Welch, Eagle; J. W. Birkle, Platteville; M. M. Stimpson, McClave; C. T. Stevens, Gunnison; Frank Parsons, Weston; A. H. Tetsell, Sterling; William Hansen, Alamosa; Bruce Roup, Yampa. R. F. Lobdell (*-6), secretary; Dr. C. G. Lamb (*-6), veterinarian.

**Board of Immigration** (2-3)—The Governor of Colorado†; Neil W. Kimball, Golden; Thomas Lytle, Montrose; Fred M. Betz, Lamar. Edward D. Foster (*-6), commissioner.

**Racing Commission** (1-4)—A. P. Drew, Grand Junction; J. T. Allen, Denver; Henry Leonard, Colorado Springs; C. F. Cusack, Denver; Robert Russell, Littleton.

**Commission for the Blind** (1-3)—E. W. Pfeiffer, Mrs. H. K. Dunklee and Dr. Edward Jackson, Denver; Ray Jewel, Pueblo; H. H. Brooks, Ordway. Mrs. Kathryn Barkhausen (*-6), executive secretary.

**Boxing Commission** (1-3) — Norton Montgomery, Edgewater; T. J. Morrissey and G. E. Hartung, Denver. W. L. Morrissey (*-6), secretary.

**Directors, Metal Mining Fund** (1-3)—R. M. Henderson, Breckenridge; W. A. Kyner, Cripple Creek; John Harvey and J. M. Kleff, Leadville; H. A. Brown, Aspen; Alex McLellan, Boulder; J. C. Bailey, Colorado Springs; T. B. Crawford, Ouray; S. D. Collins, Creede. C. L. Collbran (*-6), secretary.

**State Fair Commission** (1-3)—John J. Tobin, Montrose; Ray H. Talbot, Pueblo; T. P. Detamore, Denver. J. J. Clark (*-6), secretary, Pueblo.

**Library Commission** (1-3)—Mrs. L. I. Harrington, M. G. Wyer, Denver; Mrs. J. S. Brown, Littleton; Mrs. Geo. Lerg, Lakewood; Mrs. Lucy F. Hall, Denver.

**Gas Conservation Commission** (1-4)—S. H. Keoughan, H. C. Bretschneider, the state oil inspector†; one vacancy.

**Highway Advisory Board** (1-3)—The Governor of Colorado†; Peter Seerie, Denver; L. C. Moore, Fort Collins; J. H. Davis, Colorado Springs; F. H. Blair, Sterling; William Weiser, Grand Junction; E. G. Middlekamp, Pueblo; I. Floyd Beauchamp, Trinidad; C. D. Vail†, highway engineer (*-6).

**Uniform Laws Commission** (2-3)—Allen Moore, E. L. Brock and H. W. Toll, Denver.

**Geological Survey** (3)—An ex-officio board created by statute, consisting of the governor, the metal mining commissioner and the presidents of the state university, agricultural college, school of mines and Metal Mining Association.

## EXAMINING BOARDS

**Architects** (1-5)—W. N. Bowman, George H. Williamson, G. M. Musick and F. W. Frewen, Jr., Denver; C. E. Thomas, Colorado Springs. Per diem of $5 and actual expenses for attendance upon examinations.

**Teachers** (3)—Inez Johnson Lewis†; I. E. Stutsman, Greeley; H. M. Corning, Colorado Springs; J. F. Keating, Pueblo; S. M. Andrews, Walsenburg; Allie V. Richmond, Las Animas; E. N. Freeman, Wheatridge; Estelle Bogess and W. H. Smiley, Denver. Appointed by the state board of education.

**Coal Mine Inspection** (5)—F. W. Whiteside, Denver; R. N. Moore, Coalmont; Thomas Llewellyn, Silt; Harold Williams, Grand Junction; James Dalrymple†, chief inspector (*-6). Three members appointed by district judges and the fourth by the governor. Board members receive no stated salary but are allowed variable per diem and expenses for attending meetings.

**Barbers** (1-5)—J. T. Brooks, Denver; C. R. Hamilton, Pueblo; Wm. Timbel, Denver. Per diem of $8, with necessary traveling expenses.

**Nurses** (1-5)—Freida Off, Dorothy Conrad, Ruth Colestock and Irene Murchison*, Denver; Sadie L. Heckert, Colorado Springs.

**Medical** (1-5)—Dr. H. R. McGraw, Dr. W. W. Williams, Dr. J. G. Locke, Dr. E. B. Swerdfeger, Dr. D. L. Clark, Denver; Dr. Rodney Wren, Pueblo; Dr. F. R. Spencer, Boulder; Dr. V. A. Hutton, Florence. Per diem and travel expenses as fixed by the board.

**Pharmacy** (1-5)—Arthur D. Baker, Denver; J. E. Stauffer, Rifle; J. P. Murray, Colorado Springs. Per diem of $5 and necessary travel expenses.

**Dentists** (1-3-5)—Dr. R. L. Gray, Dr. Z. T. Roberts, Dr. J. J. O'Neill, Denver; Dr. W. W. Cogswell, Pueblo; Dr. W. C. Davis, Alamosa.

**Optometry** (1-5)—J. C. Bloom, W. E. McLain, L. A. Moore, Denver; L. C. Larsen, La Junta; E. J. Haefeli, Greeley. Per diem of $10 and necessary traveling expenses.

**Accountancy** (1-5)—G. W. Maynard, A. L. Baldwin, Julius von Tobel, Denver. Per diem of $10 and necessary traveling expenses.

**Veterinarians** (1-3-5)—L. L. Glynn, Monte Vista; E. E. Tobin, Greeley; A. N. Carroll, Pueblo.

**Embalmers** (1-5)—Carl Meyer, Denver; G. L. Hamlik, Central City; F. J. Allnut, Greeley; John Scavarda, Canon City; Dr. S. R. McKelvey†.

**Engineers and Land Surveyors** (1-3-5)—M. C. Hinderlider†; James Underhill, Idaho Springs; J. A. Hunter, Boulder; H. I. Reld, Colorado Springs; H. S. Sands, Denver.

**Shorthand Reporters** (1-3-5)—E. J. Braund, Montrose; Ralph Ellithorpe, Del Norte; Fuller Spruill, Denver.

**Real Estate Brokers** (1-3-5)—A. V. Dworak, Longmont; Wardner Williams, Pueblo; B. B. Harding, Denver. A. J. Morley (*-6), chief clerk.

**Abstracters** (1-3-5)—Roger M. Chandler, Hugo; E. H. Zimmerman, Steamboat Springs; C. L. Hubbard, Glenwood Springs.

**Aeronautics** (1-4)—Eddie Brooks, Dr. John Chase, Denver; P. H. Philbin, Jr., Pueblo.

**Cosmetologists** (1-5)—Mrs. L. P. Williams, Mrs. Elizabeth Powell, Denver; Mrs. G. E. Cook, Las Animas. Per diem of $10 and necessary traveling expenses.

**Lawyers** (4)—Law Committee: W. F. Denious, Fred Farrar, I. C. Rothgerber, S. T. Wallbank, D. C. McCreery, Denver; T. E. Monson, Sterling; Fred W. Stover, Fort Collins; J. A. Phelps, Pueblo; S. H. Kinsley, Colorado Springs. Bar Committee: W. R. Kelly, Greeley; A. L. Doud, R. W. Steele, E. H. Ellis, W. E. Hutton, Denver. Appointed by the supreme court.

## INDIVIDUAL DEPARTMENTS

**Bank Commissioner** (6)—Grant McFerson*, Boulder.

**Insurance Commissioner** (6)—Jackson Cochrane*, Denver.

**Game and Fish Commissioner** (6)—Roland G. Parvin*, Denver.

**Printing Commissioner** (6)—Alfred T. May*, Denver.

**Metal Mines Commissioner** (6)—John T. Joyce*, Durango.

**Interstate Water Compact Commissioner** (1)—D. E. Carpenter, Greeley. Compensation fixed by the governor and the attorney general.

**Budget and Efficiency Commissioner** James P. McInroy, Denver.

**Inspector of Building and Loan Associations** (6)—Eli M. Gross*, Denver.

**Oil Inspector** (6)—James Duce*, Boulder.

**Boiler Inspector** (6)—W. M. Crowley*, Denver.

**State Engineer** (6)—M. C. Hinderlider*, Denver. (For division engineers and water commissioners see Pages X-XI, Session Laws 1931.)

**State Librarian**—Inez Johnson Lewis†; Mrs. Annie P. Hyder (*-6), assistant.

**Director of Markets** (6)—John J. Tobin*, Montrose.

## MISCELLANEOUS

**Bureau of Child and Animal Protection** (4)—The Governor†, the Superintendent of Public Instruction† and the Attorney General†; E. A. Colburn, Frank S. Byers, W. W. Watson, Denver. E. K. Whitehead (*-6), secretary. All except ex-officio members appointed by the Colorado Humane Society.

**Board of Education** (†-4)—The Superintendent of Public Instruction, the Secretary of State and the Attorney General.

**Board of Equalization and Auditing Board** (†-4)—Composed of the governor, secretary of state, auditor, treasurer and attorney general. John E. Davidson (*-6), secretary.

**State Historical Society of Colorado** (4)—The Governor†, Ernest Morris, Theron R. Field, Dr. J. N. Hall, Lawrence Lewis, Henry Swan, Henry A. Dubbs, Frank E. Gove, Caldwell Martin, Edward B. Morgan, Denver. Members elected by the society.

**Child Welfare Bureau**—R. J. Walters, Miss Emily Griffith, Denver; J. D. Heilman, Greeley; Mrs. Charles A. Lory, Fort Collins; Mrs. Frederick Haver, Boone. Miss Marie Wickert (*-6), executive secretary. Three members appointed by the governor and two by the superintendent of public instruction.

**Board of Hail Insurance**—A. O. Johnson, La Jara; P. O. Wells, Colorado Springs; C. W. Swayze, Denver. T. P. Detamore (*-6), commissioner. Members appointed by the state board of agriculture. Per diem of $7 and necessary traveling expenses for meetings.

**Public Trustees** (*-2-5)—C. L. Starrett, Colorado Springs; J. F. Redman, Greeley; R. A. Nicholas, Fort Collins; F. F. Dolan, Boulder; Bertram Beshoar, Trinidad; W. S. Peck, Denver; M. J. Kochevar, Pueblo; Walter Johnson, Golden. Fee office, maximum salary depending upon classification of the county.

**Poet Laureate** (1-4)—Nellie Burget Miller, Colorado Springs.

———

\* Indicates salaried executive of department.
† Indicates member ex-officio.

## HOTELS IN COLORADO

There were 354 hotels operating in Colorado in 1929 as reported by the bureau of the census. Of these 37 were owned by corporations and 317 by individuals and partnerships. The distribution as to plan of operation is as follows:

| | |
|---|---|
| European plan | 313 |
| American plan | 20 |
| Mixed plan | 21 |
| Total | 354 |

The total number of guest rooms reported by the 354 establishments was 20,651, distributed as follows:

| | |
|---|---|
| European plan | 17,769 |
| American plan | 1,242 |
| Mixed plan | 1,640 |
| Total | 20,651 |

The 354 establishments had a seating capacity at one time in their dining rooms for 7,867 persons, distributed as follows:

| | |
|---|---|
| European plan | 3,352 |
| American plan | 2,119 |
| Mixed plan | 2,396 |
| Total | 7,867 |

The average number of employes was 3,389, of whom 1,827 were male and 1,562 were female. Salaries and wages aggregated $2,555,000. Total receipts from all sources were $10,689,000, distributed as follows:

| | |
|---|---|
| Rooms | $5,619,000 |
| Meals | 1,655,000 |
| Rooms and meals | 2,478,000 |
| Other sources | 937,000 |
| Total | $10,689,000 |

There were 437 proprietors and firm members engaged in the business, of whom 237 were males and 200 females.

# INDEX